Psychopathology

BPS Textbooks in Psychology

BPS Wiley presents a comprehensive and authoritative series covering everything a student needs in order to complete an undergraduate degree in psychology. Refreshingly written to consider more than North American research, this series is the first to give a truly international perspective. Written by the very best names in the field, the series offers an extensive range of titles from introductory level through to final year optional modules, and every text fully complies with the BPS syllabus in the topic. No other series bears the BPS seal of approval!

Many of the books are supported by a companion website, featuring additional resource materials for both instructors and students, designed to encourage critical thinking, and providing for all your course lecturing and testing needs.

For other titles in this series, please go to **http://psychsource.bps.org.uk**

Psychopathology

Research, Assessment and Treatment in Clinical Psychology

SECOND EDITION

GRAHAM DAVEY

The British
Psychological Society

Brief Contents

Contents

Chapter 14   Dissociative Experiences   469

Acknowledgements

This second edition could not have been produced without a lot of hard work on the part of the Wiley commissioning and production team, including Andrew McAleer, Georgia King, Ellie Wilson, Juliet Booker, Claire Jardine and Deborah Egleton, and to them I am particularly grateful. I'd also like to continue to thank those people who advised me on the first edition, much of which is still relevant to the second edition. These include Alison Brown, Kate Cavanagh, Roger Cocks, Rudi Dallos, Andy Field, Daniel Freeman, Theresa Gannon, David Green, Richard Hastings, Marko Jelicic, Jo Johnson, Fergal Jones, Ruth Mann, Charlie Martin, Lance McCracken, Michael Morgan, Peter Muris, Ben Smith, Helen Startup, Emma Veitch, Brendan Weekes, and Leonora Wilkinson. More recently, people who have provided help and advice on the second edition include Chris Brewin, Kate Cavanagh, Suzanne Dash, Thomas Ehring, Fergal Jones, Nick Lake, Fran Meeten, Michael Morgan and Filip Raes, as well as a number of nameless reviewers of the first edition who have all helped to shape this revised text.

Writing a book is usually easiest when you start with a blank sheet of paper and a pen; reshaping a first edition of a book into its second edition feels much harder – rather like trying to prepare quail consommé from the leftovers of a bacon sandwich! So, a big thank you to all those people who have actively endured my 'culinary' frustrations over the past 18 months – especially Benie, my daughters Kate and Lizzie, and Emily, Doon, Lucy, Simon, Cathy, my mother Betty, Owl and Mogg (both of whom periodically attempted to motivate me with gifts of rodent body parts), and finally Megan the banana-eating dog.

If you have time on your hands, you can follow my ramblings on mental health and psychology on Twitter at http://twitter.com/GrahamCLDavey, visit my website at http://www.papersfromsidcup.com, or read my blogs at http://www.papersfromsidcup.com/graham-daveys-blog.html, and http://www.psychologytoday.com/blog/why-we-worry.

As soon as this book is with the printers, it's my intention to revisit the cold beers and stunning sunsets offered by La Trata and Paradise bars on Naxos in the Greek Islands, where I wrote the acknowledgements to the first edition. I hope you enjoy the second edition as much as I'm intending to enjoy those cold beers and magnificent sunsets.

Graham C. L. Davey
Brighton, July 2014

Preface to Second Edition

Clinical psychology is a topic that fascinates a majority of undergraduate psychology students. This is hardly surprising given that a substantial proportion of students entering degree programmes in psychology do so with a career in applied psychology firmly in mind. For these students, clinical psychology offers an understanding of people and their mental health problems, as well as a means to research and treat those problems. The first edition of this text was designed specifically to provide those students with a comprehensive coverage of both psychopathology and clinical practice, and we have attempted to improve significantly on that coverage in this second edition.

The main emphases of the second edition are still to provide students at undergraduate level with a comprehensive and accessible introduction to psychopathology, and, in addition, to provide a source book for more in-depth study for postgraduate students, researchers and clinical psychologists. Conveying the research basis for clinical psychology is a main theme of this book, as is the desire to describe how treatments and interventions work in practice – and many of the latter are described in the book's *Treatment in Practice* features. This second edition has specifically focused on updating the research on which an understanding of mental health problems is based, and rounds off an understanding of research and treatment in clinical psychology by introducing a new chapter on clinical provision that describes how mental health services implement the research and development that occurs in psychopathology. Perhaps most significantly, this second edition brings to the reader the new diagnostic criteria published in DSM-5 in May 2013 and we mix a description of these revised diagnostic criteria with a critical discussion of how these changes were developed and what their significance might be. There are also three important changes in the early chapters. Chapter 1 now provides (1) a fuller history of psychopathology, including the development from asylums to community care; (2) a significantly expanded section on explanatory approaches to psychopathology that provides the reader with a foundation knowledge of the psychological and biological substrates that are used to explain psychopathology, and this includes new material on neuroscience, genetics and epigenetics; and (3) an expanded section devoted to stigma and mental health – in particular what stigma is, who holds stigmatizing beliefs, why stigma matters, and

methods developed to try and eliminate stigma. In addition we have continued to provide multiple perspectives on mental health problems from a range of psychological, biological and genetic approaches, and to emphasize the important significance of experimental psychopathology to good clinical psychology research. We have also expanded our coverage of cross-cultural issues and included an expanded *Focus Point* in Chapter 1 devoted to sociocultural factors and psychopathology that draws together some of the cross-cultural, gender and ethnicity issues discussed throughout the book.

Finally, student readers often fail to appreciate the wealth of additional material and resources that are provided on the websites that accompany books such as this. In this second edition these online resources have been significantly expanded. For students we still have our large bank of self-test questions, online glossary and chapter learning objectives, but to this we've added a significant range of instructional and supplementary videos covering such topics as descriptions of symptoms and aetiologies, examples of diagnosis and diagnostic interviews, recounted personal experiences of people with mental health problems and discussions and examples of treatment. There are also student learning activities, discussion topics, lists of relevant journal articles (many of which provide free links to relevant articles published in Wiley-Blackwell journals), and topics for discussion related to clinical research and clinical practice. Instructor resources include essay questions, access to all figures and plates for inclusion on class handouts or PowerPoint presentations, template PowerPoint presentations for each chapter, and a separate instructor-only bank of multiple-choice questions for student assessments.

Just like the first edition, the second edition is supplemented by a range of features designed to facilitate effective teaching and learning. These include:

- **Focus Points**   These provide more in-depth discussion of particular topics that are conceptually important, controversial or simply of contemporary interest. Whenever possible these are linked to everyday examples – such as high-profile news items – that allow the reader to consider the issues in a contemporary, everyday context.
- **Research Methods Boxes**   These features contain detailed descriptions of methods utilized in

psychopathology research, and describe the pros and cons of individual methods, their potential uses, and these examples act to supplement the general material provided on research methods in Chapter 3. Like most researchers, those involved in clinical psychology research are often imaginative in their use of research methods and many of the examples provided in research methods boxes attempt to convey how methods from other areas of psychology and science generally can be adapted to study issues relevant to psychopathology.

- **Case Histories**   Most chapters contain example case histories describing the symptoms, experiences and life circumstances encountered by individuals experiencing particular psychopathologies. Each of these examples concludes with a *clinical commentary* that is designed to link the detail of that specific case history to the general facts to be learnt in the text.

- **The Client's Perspective**   Many chapters also contain examples of an individual's own descriptions of the experience of psychopathology. These are designed to provide the reader with an insight into the phenomenology of different psychopathologies, and the way that symptoms affect moods, experiences, and affect everyday living – including social, occupational and educational functioning. These descriptions are also supplemented by the *personal accounts* of psychopathologies that begin each chapter. As with case histories, client's perspective features usually conclude with a *clinical commentary* that links the personal experiences of the psychopathology to the academic content of the text.

- **Treatment in Practice Boxes**   These boxes attempt to provide the reader with a more detailed insight into how individual treatments are conducted in practice. It is often difficult for a student to understand, for example, how a therapy is conducted in practice from descriptions given in academic texts. These boxes will provide some specific examples of how a practitioner might implement the principles of a treatment in a specific case.

- **Self-Test Questions**   Throughout each chapter the reader will encounter *self-test questions*. These are designed to test the reader's absorption of basic factual and conceptual knowledge. Instructors and teachers can also use these questions as a basis for discussing key material in class or in small group discussions.

- **Key Terms and Definitions**   When each term first appears in the text, it is highlighted in bold

and is either described or defined at that point. Highlighting these terms makes them easy to locate, and the list of key terms online can serve as a revision check-list – especially for students due to take multiple-choice questionnaire assessments.

Finally, I hope you find this second edition readable, accessible and enlightening, and a worthwhile addition to your teaching and learning activities. It's been a monster project for me, and I've learnt a lot in the process. I hope you do, too – good luck!

Graham Davey
Brighton, July 2014

NEW TO THE SECOND EDITION

Chapter 1 – An Introduction to Psychopathology: Concepts, Paradigms and Stigma

- Begins with a new section covering the history of psychopathology, including demonic possession, the medical and disease models, and developments from asylums to community care.

- Contains a new section dedicated to 'Mental health and stigma', and includes discussion of who holds stigmatizing beliefs, what causes stigma, why stigma matters, and how we might eliminate it.

- Expanded sections on explanatory approaches to psychopathology, with new basic material on biological approaches, including genetics, epigenetics and neuroscience.

- Revised with newly featured material, including sociocultural factors and psychopathology, and a new, updated mental health quiz.

Chapter 2 – Classification and Assessment in Clinical Psychology

- This chapter has been expanded to include both classification and assessment.

- The newly revised classification system DSM-5 is fully described, including the main changes from DSM-IV-TR, the controversies and criticisms of the new system, and a discussion of issues involved in the development of classification systems.

- All sections of the chapter have been updated with the most recent research and with developments in assessment techniques, including neuroimaging techniques and the WAIS-IV.

Chapter 3 – Research Methods in Clinical Psychology

- Information on research designs has been updated with examples.
- The section on meta-analyses is expanded to include systematic reviews, with examples of how meta-analyses and systematic reviews should be reported.
- Updated information on ethical issues has been added, including informed consent, together with examples of contemporary consent forms.
- There are new Focus Points on scientific methods as a model for clinical psychology research.
- Recent developments in the reporting of research findings are discussed, including the shift in importance from statistical significance to effect sizes.

Chapter 4 – Treating Psychopathology

- The section on cognitive therapies has been expanded to include description and examples of new 'waves' of CBT, including mindfulness-based cognitive therapy (MCBT) and acceptance and commitment therapy (ACT).
- Sections on drug treatments have been updated with the most recent research.
- Gestalt therapy is now briefly described in a Focus Point.
- Modes of Treatment Delivery have been expanded to now include 'telepsychiatry' and a discussion of the 'Improving Access to Psychological Therapies' (IAPT) programme and the role of psychological well-being practitioners.
- The section on evaluating treatment now includes a fuller discussion of the types of ways in which treatments can be measured and evaluated, and what RCTs tell us about the efficacy of a treatment.
- A full discussion of the 'Dodo Bird Verdict' is included, examining the ways in which different types of interventions might be more or less effective as each other, and the factors that contribute to effective psychological treatment generally.

Chapter 5 – Clinical Practice

- This is an entirely new chapter covering aspects of clinical practice and service provision.
- The chapter begins by looking at the scale of mental health problems and what might be required to help people deal with these problems.

- There is a full discussion of the range of mental health professionals involved in service provision for mental health and their roles in that delivery.
- The range and structure of mental health services is described.
- The latter part of the chapter focuses on the role of clinical psychologists, their key capabilities and competences, and how they are trained.
- The chapter also contains examples of how clinical psychologists work and what their weekly routines might be like.

Chapter 6 – Anxiety and Stressor-Related Problems

- This chapter now includes all the new DSM-5 diagnostic criteria and covers the distinctions between anxiety disorders, the inclusion of OCD as a separate diagnostic category, and the development of a stressor-related category.
- All aetiology discussions have been updated with the most recent research.
- The section on specific phobias now includes a discussion of the contribution of neuroimaging studies to understanding phobias.
- Genetic factors are included in the coverage of social anxiety disorder, including the role of behavioural inhibition.
- The section on panic disorder includes fuller discussion of agoraphobia as a separate disorder category and includes a discussion of the role of safety behaviours.
- Generalized anxiety disorder includes discussion of some newer theories of GAD and worrying, including a revamped discussion of information processing biases and the role of meta-beliefs in pathological worrying.
- A new Focus Point describes the development of attention bias modification (ABM) techniques for the treatment of anxiety.
- Included in the section on OCD are some newly defined OCD-related disorders, including hoarding disorder and hair-pulling disorder (trichotillomania).
- The OCD-related disorder body dysmorphic disorder is now included in this chapter as a new Focus Point.
- The aetiology of OCD now includes new discussion on mental contamination and a discussion of the role of clinical constructs in the explanation of OCD.

- Finally a new overarching section entitled 'Trauma and stress-related disorders' discusses the definitions of PTSD and acute stress disorder. The chapter provides a description of the new diagnostic criteria for these disorders and updates research relevant to the understanding and explanation of stress-related disorders.

Chapter 7 – Depression and Mood Disorders

- This chapter has been restructured to include separate main sections on major depression and bipolar disorder.
- All mood disorders have been updated with the latest diagnostic criteria from DSM-5 as well as more recent prevalence data.
- The sections on the aetiology and explanation of bipolar disorder have been expanded to include recent research, a fuller description of genetic factors, and a discussion of the triggers for depression and mania in bipolar disorder.
- There is a new Research Methods section discussing the role of experimental psychopathology methodologies in depression research.
- The section on deliberate self-harm has been updated with recent DSM-5 diagnostic criteria.
- New Focus Points discuss a range of depression-related problems as well as new research linking depression with inflammation.
- The section on suicide has been expanded to include discussion of the role of contemporary living problems, such as the effect of the economic recession on mood disorders.
- The research on media contagion and suicide among young people is also a new discussion feature.

Chapter 8 – Experiencing Psychosis: Schizophrenia Spectrum Problems

- Updated with the most recent DSM-5 diagnostic criteria, including new disorder categories delusional disorder and brief psychotic disorder.
- Updated data on prevalence rates.
- Discussion of attenuated psychotic symptoms syndrome.
- Updated with the latest research on the genetics of schizophrenia.
- Sections on brain neurotransmitters and the neuroscience of schizophrenia include most recent research.

- Significantly expanded section on cognitive theories of psychosis, including sections on cognitive biases, 'jumping to conclusions' and cognitive factors involved in 'hearing voices'.
- Updated discussion of the latest trials data on antipsychotic drugs as treatment for psychotic symptoms.
- A new separate section discussing cognitive behaviour therapy for psychosis (CBTp).
- Section devoted to cognitive remediation training (CRT).
- New Focus Point on the role of early intervention strategies for dealing with psychosis.
- Discussion of the relationship between schizophrenia and violence, including recent data and psychological models.
- Focus Points on (1) schizophrenia and influenza, and (2) cannabis use and psychotic symptoms, updated with most recent research.

Chapter 9 – Substance Use Disorders

- Includes updated statistics on prevalence rates and drug usage rates – both worldwide and in the UK.
- Updated with the latest diagnostic criteria for substance use disorders in DSM-5.
- New detailed sections on (1) Reward pathways in the brain, and (2) The nature and role of drug 'craving'.
- Discussion of new and controversial treatment programmes for substance use disorder, including supervised drug injections and monetary rewards for abstinence.
- Detailed descriptions of the characteristics of drugs of abuse on the book's website.
- Newly structured sections dedicated to alcohol use disorder, tobacco use disorder and cannabis use disorder.
- Discussion of the aetiology of substance use disorders updated with the most recent research findings.

Chapter 10 – Eating Disorders

- Fuller discussion of CBT and transdiagnostic approaches to eating disorders and their treatment.
- Inclusion of the tripartite model and how peer, media and parental influences may lead to eating disorders.

- Updated with the latest diagnostic criteria for eating disorders in DSM-5, plus description of other feeding and eating disorders.
- Focus Point on historical examples of eating disorders.
- Describes and discusses each of the main eating disorders in separate sections – namely, anorexia nervosa, bulimia nervosa and binge eating disorder.
- Updated with all the latest statistics on eating disorders and obesity from both the UK and WHO.
- All aetiology sections updated with the most recent research on the causes of eating disorders – especially genetic and neurobiological explanations.

Chapter 11 – Sexual and Gender Problems

- Updated with the latest DSM-5 diagnostic criteria for sexual dysfunctions, paraphilic disorders and gender dysphoria.
- All aetiology and treatment sections updated with the latest research.

Chapter 12 – Personality Disorders

- Extensive discussion of the issues raised by DSM-5 around the diagnosis of personality disorders.
- Description of DSM-5 diagnostic criteria and the alternative model for diagnosis proposed for research in DSM-5.
- Sections on aetiology of personality disorders updated with the most recent research.
- New discussion on the problems associated with estimating the prevalence rates of personality disorders.
- New Focus Point discussing the possible relationships between ADHD and antisocial personality disorder.
- New section on schema therapy for personality disorders.

Chapter 13 – Somatic Symptom Disorders

- Fully updated to take account of changes to this category of disorders published in DSM-5.
- Disorders covered include somatic symptom disorder, illness anxiety disorder (formerly hypochondriasis), conversion disorder and factitious disorder.
- All sections updated with the latest research on somatic symptom disorders and their aetiology.

Chapter 14 – Dissociative Experiences

- All diagnostic criteria updated to be DSM-5 compliant.
- New section on the relationship between dissociative experiences and PTSD, including a description of complex PTSD.
- Updated with new research on memory processes in dissociative disorders.

Chapter 15 – Neurocognitive Disorders

- Categorization of neurocognitive disorders updated according to the new diagnostic categories in DSM-5.
- Information on all neurocognitive disorders updated with the new DSM-5 diagnostic criteria.
- New section describing frontotemporal neurocognitive disorder.
- All prevalence rates updated with more recently available data.
- All aetiology sections updated with recent research published up to and including 2013.
- New Focus Point discussing the pros and cons of genetic testing for degenerative neurocognitive disorders.
- Treatment and rehabilitation section updated with the most recent efficacy and RCT outcome studies.

Chapter 16 – Childhood and Adolescent Psychological Problems

- All diagnostic criteria updated to be DSM-5 compliant.
- Greater emphasis on developmental psychopathology approaches.
- All aetiology sections updated with recent findings from genetic and epigenetic studies.
- All prevalence figures for mental health problems in children and adolescents updated with the most recently available figures.
- Section on drug treatments for childhood and adolescent psychological problems includes the most recent evidence on the regulation of drugs for childhood conditions and the risks vs. benefits of certain types of medication.
- Extended section on CBT as applied to childhood and adolescent problems.

Chapter 17 – Neurodevelopmental Disorders

- All diagnostic criteria updated to be DSM-5 compliant, along with changes in the structure of individual sections as dictated by changes in DSM-5.
- Updated research on the genetics of intellectual disorders and autistic spectrum disorders.

- New section and Focus Point on the empathizing–systematizing theory of autistic spectrum disorder.
- Discussion of the implications of changes to autistic spectrum disorder diagnostic criteria in DSM-5 on prevalence rates.

Accompanying Online Resources for Instructors and Students

RESORCES FOR STUDENTS

An *all new* student website is available at **www.wiley-psychopathology.com**.

> The website houses all the student resources including video, reading and activities as well as a live feed into the author blog.

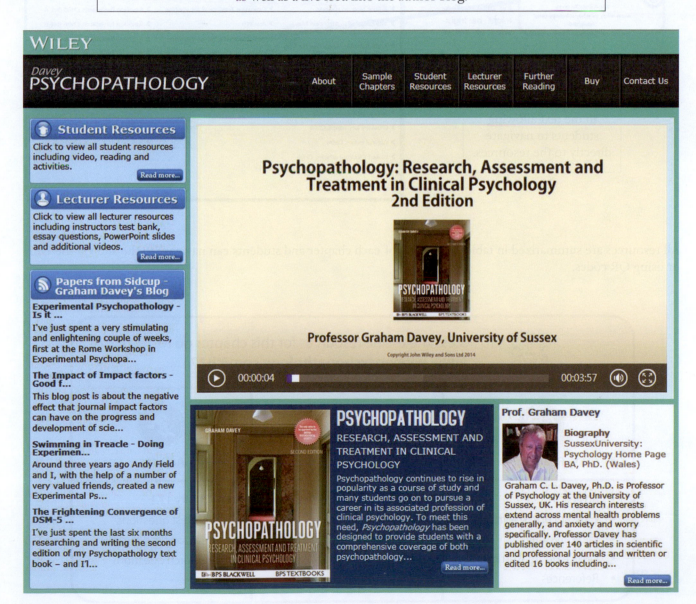

The website has been developed in parallel with the textbook and all the online materials relate directly to features and content from the book.

CLIENT'S PERSPECTIVE 6.2:
POST-TRAUMATIC STRESS DISORDER

'I thought I was over it. Just when I think I'm getting better and don't have to worry about it anymore, something will trigger a memory and I'll be right back there again. Sometimes it's just a feeling I have, and other times I'll see something that reminds me of what happened and it feels like it's happening all over again. It's been almost a year now and I'm seeing a therapist three times a week as well as taking antidepressants. I can have good days – maybe two or three in a row – then my mood will get worse and the blackness will come back. It feels as if my thoughts aren't my own and my mind is somewhere else while my body is just going through the motions. Every time the black moods come it feels harder and harder to get back from them. It makes me so angry when I feel like this and my mind becomes full of violent thoughts; this rage takes over and I can't control it. I'm scared of what I might do when I'm feeling this angry. I don't want to tell my friends or family about what I'm thinking because they might be frightened of me or

what I'll do, and I know they just want me to move on. I wish I could but I just can't see a way out.'

Clinical Commentary

This description is typical of many PTSD sufferers and highlights feelings of depression, lack of control and anger. Some theories of PTSD (such as 'mental defeat') emphasise that those who develop PTSD after a severe trauma tend to view themselves as a victim, process all information about the trauma negatively, and view them-

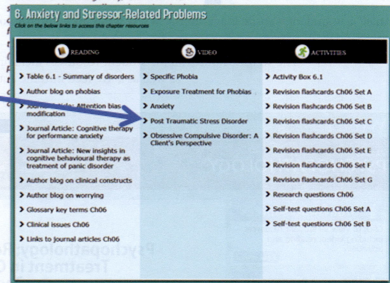

For a video on post-traumatic stress disorder go to
www.wiley-psychopathology.com/video/ch6

> Links are embedded in the text allowing students to navigate directly to the resources.

All resources are summarized in tables at the end of each chapter and students can navigate to the site via the URL or using QR codes.

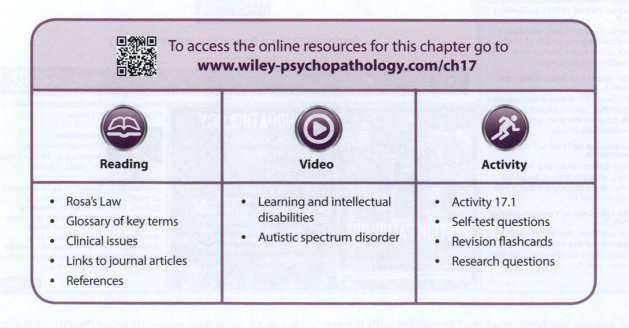

To access the online resources for this chapter go to
www.wiley-psychopathology.com/ch17

Reading	Video	Activity
• Rosa's Law • Glossary of key terms • Clinical issues • Links to journal articles • References	• Learning and intellectual disabilities • Autistic spectrum disorder	• Activity 17.1 • Self-test questions • Revision flashcards • Research questions

The student website houses a huge variety of new digital material curated especially for the new edition, including more than **50 instructional and supplementary videos** covering descriptions of symptoms and aetiologies, examples of diagnosis and diagnostic interviews, recounted personal experiences of people with mental health problems, and discussions and examples of treatment.

The site also contains **hundreds of new student quizzes**, as well as revision flashcards, student **learning activities**, discussion topics, lists of relevant **journal articles** (many of which provide free links to relevant articles published in Wiley Blackwell journals), and topics for discussion related to clinical research and clinical practice.

 Visit **www.wiley-psychopathology.com** to view all student resources.

RESOURCES FOR LECTURERS

The online resources for lecturers have all been fully updated for the new edition and an additional suite of 15 bespoke **videos of diagnostic interviews** is now available for lecturers to use in the classroom.

A fully updated **lecturer test bank** has been developed for the new edition, including over 1,000 unique questions. Additional essay questions, exam questions and additional discussion topics are also available along with a full set of PowerPoint presentation slides.

All of these resources can be accessed by instructors on our lecturer book companion site at **www.wiley.com/college/davey**.

Part I
Introducing Psychopathology: Concepts, Procedures and Practices

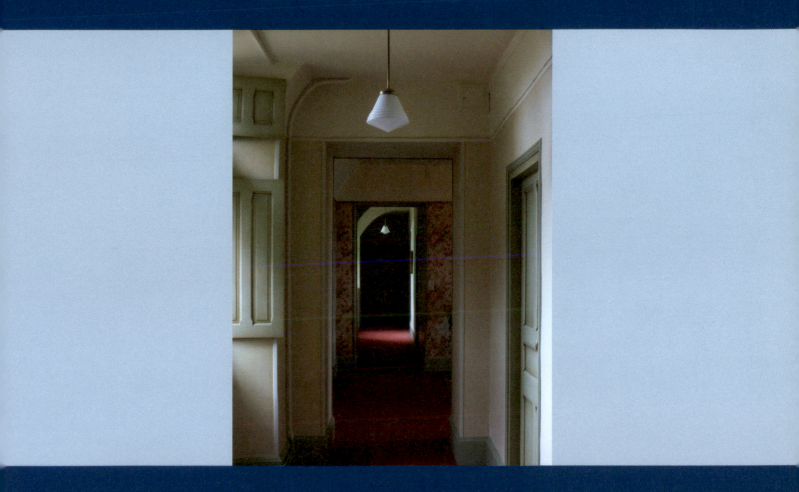

1 An Introduction to Psychopathology: Concepts, Paradigms and Stigma

 To access the online resources for this chapter go to
www.wiley-psychopathology.com/ch1

ROUTE MAP OF THE CHAPTER

This first chapter introduces the reader to a number of basic issues concerned with the definition and explanation of psychopathology – including the issue of 'stigma' that is often an outcome of how psychopathology is conceptualized and portrayed. The first section describes a brief history of how mental health problems have been conceived and treated. This is followed, in the second section, by a discussion of how psychopathology can be defined, and how we identify behaviour that is in need of support and treatment. The third section describes some of the most common explanatory approaches that have been developed to help us understand psychopathology, and these approaches are ones that the reader will encounter frequently throughout this book. Finally, the fourth section takes a close look at mental health stigma, how it is manifested, why it is important, and how stigma can be dealt with.

CHAPTER OUTLINE

LEARNING OUTCOMES

When you have completed this chapter, you should be able to:

1. Discuss the pros and cons of a number of different approaches to defining psychopathology.

2. Describe important developments in the history of our understanding and response to mental health problems.

3. Describe and evaluate the nature and causes of mental health stigma.

4. Compare and contrast approaches to the explanation of psychopathology, including historical approaches, the medical model and psychological models.

Am I Crazy? I don't know what is wrong with me. I did have depression in the past and what I am going through doesn't feel a lot like what I had before. My moods change every 30 minutes at times. I have been like this for a while. I started out about once a week I would have a day where I was going from one extreme to the next. In the past few weeks it has gotten worse. It seems like my moods change for no reason at all. There are times that I will just lay down and cry for what appears to be no reason at all and then 2 hours later I will be happy. I find myself yelling at my son for stupid reasons and then shortly after I am fine again. I truly feel that I am going crazy and the more I think about it the worse I get. I am not sleeping or eating much and when I do eat I feel like I will be sick.

Joan's Story

For the past 10 months serving in Iraq I've told myself not to think about all that's going on around me. I've forced myself to go about my daily activities in some sort of normal manner. I knew that if I thought too much about the fact that mortars could hit me at any time, or if I laid in bed every night knowing that a mortar could drop through the ceiling while I slept, or if I focused too much on the randomness of death here, I'd go crazy.

And for the past 10 months, I've managed to put these things out of my head for the most part. I've managed to try to live a normal life here while people die around me. But for some reason, since I got back from leave, I can't seem to shake the jitters, the nervousness, the just plain uneasiness I feel walking around or driving through the city streets.

 For a video on post-traumatic stress disorder go to **www.wiley-psychopathology.com/video/ch1**

Everywhere I walk I'm constantly thinking about where I'm going to go if a mortar lands. I'm always looking for the next bunker. When I leave the relative safety of the base, I'm constantly running scenarios through my head of the worst case situations. There comes a point where living in fear is not living at all.

Greg's Story

When I was a child I regularly experienced dreams in which there was an awful buzzing noise; at the same time I could see what I can only describe as the needle from a machine such as a lie detector test drawing lines. I had a dream where an older alien cloaked in orange took me on a ship and told me things that I can't remember yet. He took me over an island (I think it was Australia) everything was dead and there was a mushroom cloud over it. Then there were five or six aliens, and one was holding a clear ball. I knew that inside there was an embryo. They put it inside me. About one and a half weeks later I was confirmed pregnant. Then, when we were driving on the motorway, I seem to have lost 2 hours before seeing a brilliant flash above the car. I got pains in my left temple, behind my left eye and in my left cheekbone. There is a scar on my right leg which I can't explain. Some people think I'm crazy, but I know it happened.

Betty's Story

I started using cocaine at 13. Before, I was using marijuana and alcohol and it didn't really work for me, so I wanted to step it up a level. I started using heroin when I was 15. I began using it to come down from cocaine and get some sleep. But I started liking the heroin high and started using it straight. Every day, after a while. Along with cocaine, I also began taking prescription drugs when I was 13. They were so easy to get. I never had to buy them or get them from a doctor. I would just get them from friends who had gone through their parents' medicine cabinet. I also thought that prescription drugs were 'safer' than other drugs. I figured that it was okay for people to take them, and if they were legal, I was fine. Like I said, prescription drugs were incredibly easy to get from friends, and it always seemed to be a last-minute thing. Heroin was also easy to get – all I had to do was go into town and buy it. My heroin use started spiralling out of control. I stopped going to school. I was leaving home for days at a time. My whole life revolved around getting and using drugs – I felt like I was going crazy.

Erica's Story

Introduction

We begin this book with personal accounts from four very different individuals. Possibly the only common link between these four accounts is that they each use the word 'crazy' in relating their story. *Joan* questions whether she is going crazy, *Greg* tells us how he tries to prevent himself from going crazy, other people think *Betty* is crazy, and *Erica*'s life gets so out of control that she too felt like she was 'going crazy'. We tend to use words like 'crazy', 'madness' and 'insanity' regularly – as if we knew what we meant by those terms. However, we do tend to use these terms in a number of different circumstances – for example, (1) when someone's behaviour deviates from expected norms, (2) when we are unclear about the reasons for someone's actions, (3) when a behaviour seems to be irrational, or (4) when a behaviour or action appears to be maladaptive or harmful to the individual or others. You can try seeing whether these different uses of the term 'crazy' or 'mad' apply to each of our personal accounts, but they probably still won't capture the full meaning of why they each used the word 'crazy' in their vignettes. Trying to define our use of everyday words like 'crazy', 'madness' and 'insanity' leads us on to thinking about those areas of thinking and behaving that seem to deviate from normal or everyday modes of functioning. For psychologists the study of these deviations from normal or everyday functioning are known as **psychopathology**, and the branch of psychology responsible for understanding and treating psychopathology is known as **clinical psychology**.

> **psychopathology** The study of deviations from normal or everyday psychological or behavioural functioning.

> **clinical psychology** The branch of psychology responsible for understanding and treating psychopathology.

Let's examine our four personal accounts a little closer. *Joan* is distressed because she appears to have no control over her moods. She feels depressed; she shouts at her son; she feels sick when she eats. *Greg* feels anxious about the dangers of his daily life serving in Iraq. He feels nervous and jittery. *Betty* doesn't think she's crazy – but other people do. They think that her story about being abducted by aliens is a sign of psychosis or disordered thinking – she thinks it seems perfectly logical. Finally, *Erica*'s behaviour has become controlled by her need for drugs. She feels out of control and all other activities in her life – such as her education – are suffering severely because of this.

These four cases are all ones that are likely to be encountered by clinical psychologists and although very different in their detail, they do all possess some commonalities that might help us to define what represents psychopathology. For example, (1) both *Joan* and *Greg* experience debilitating distress, (2) both *Joan* and *Erica* feel that important aspects of their life (such as their moods or cravings) are out of their control and they cannot cope, (3) both *Joan* and *Erica* find that their conditions have resulted in them failing to function properly in certain spheres of their life (e.g. as a mother or as a student), and (4) *Betty*'s life appears to be controlled by thoughts and memories which are delusional and are probably not real. As we shall see later, these are all important aspects of psychopathology, and define to some extent what will be the subject matter of clinical practice. However, deciding what are proper and appropriate examples of psychopathology is not easy. Just because someone's behaviour deviates from accepted norms or patterns does not mean they are suffering from a mental or psychiatric illness, and just because we might use the term 'crazy' to describe someone's behaviour does not mean that it is the product of disordered thinking. Similarly, we cannot attempt to define psychopathology on the basis that some 'normal' functioning (psychological, neurological or biological) has gone wrong. This is because (1) we are still some way from understanding the various processes that contribute to psychopathology, and (2) many forms of behaviour that require treatment by clinical psychologists are merely extreme forms of what we would call 'normal' or 'adaptive' behaviour. For example, we all worry and we all get depressed at some times, but these activities do not significantly interfere with our everyday living. However, for some other people, their experience of these activities may be so extreme as to cause them significant distress and to prevent them from undertaking normal daily living. Before we continue to discuss individual psychopathologies in detail, it is important to discuss how the way we define psychopathology has evolved over time, and ways in which we can define and classify psychopathology and mental health problems generally.

1.1   A BRIEF HISTORY OF PSYCHOPATHOLOGY

Throughout history, we have been willing to label behaviour as 'mad', 'crazy' or 'insane' if it appears unpredictable, irrational, harmful, or if it simply deviates from accepted contemporary social norms. Characters from history who have been labelled in such a way include the Roman Emperor Caligula, King George III, Vincent Van Gogh, King Saul of Israel, and Virginia Woolf, to name just a few. But the term 'madness' does not imply a cause – it simply redescribes the behaviour as something that is odd. Views about what *causes* 'mad' behaviour have changed significantly over the course of history, and it is instructive to understand how the way we attribute the causes of mental health problems have developed over time. An historical perspective on psychopathology and 'madness' is important because it helps us to understand how our views of the causes of mental health problems have changed and developed over time, and it also helps us to understand how approaches to treating and dealing with mental health problems have changed. We will begin by looking at an historical perspective on explaining psychopathology, which is known as **demonic possession**. We will then describe how the **medical model** of psychopathology developed, and finish with a discussion of the transition from asylums to community care.

demonic possession Historical explanations of psychopathology such as 'demonic possession' often alluded to the fact that the individual had been 'possessed' in some way.

medical model An explanation of psychopathology in terms of underlying biological or medical causes.

1.1.1   Demonic Possession

Many forms of psychopathology are accompanied by what appear to be changes in the individual's personality, and these changes in personality or behaviour are some of the first symptoms that are noticed. The reserved person may become manic and outgoing, and the gregarious person withdrawn and sombre. They may start behaving in ways that mean they neglect important daily activities (such as parenting or going to work), or may be harmful to themselves or others. The fact that an individual's personality seems to have changed (and may do so very suddenly) has historically tended people towards describing those exhibiting symptoms of psychopathology as being 'possessed' in some way. That is, their behaviour has changed in such a way that their personality appears to have been taken over and replaced by the persona of someone or something else.

Explanations of psychopathology in terms of 'possession' have taken many forms over the course of history, and it is a form of explanation that has meant that many who have been suffering debilitating and distressing psychological problems have been persecuted and physically abused rather than offered the support and treatment they need. Many ancient civilizations, such as those in Egypt, China, Babylon and Greece, believed that those exhibiting symptoms of psychopathology were possessed by bad spirits (this is known as **demonology**), and the only way to exorcise these bad spirits was with elaborate ritualized ceremonies that frequently involved direct physical attacks on the sufferer's body in an attempt to force out the demons (e.g. through torture, flogging or starvation). Not surprisingly, such actions usually had the effect of increasing the distress and suffering of the victim.

demonology Many ancient civilizations, such as those in Egypt, China, Babylon and Greece, believed that those exhibiting symptoms of psychopathology were possessed by bad spirits – known as demonology.

In Western societies, demonology survived as an explanation of mental health problems right up until the 18th century, when witchcraft and demonic possession were common explanations for psychopathology. This contrasts with the Middle Ages in England when individuals were often treated in a relatively civilized fashion. When someone exhibited symptoms typical of psychopathology a 'lunacy trial' was held to determine the individual's sanity, and if the person was found to be insane, they were given the protection of the law (Neugebauer, 1979). Nevertheless, demonic possession is still a common explanation of psychopathology in some less developed areas of the world – especially where witchcraft and voodoo are still important features of the local culture such as Haiti and some areas of Western Africa (Desrosiers & Fleurose, 2002). The continued adoption of demonic possession as an explanation of mental health problems (especially in relation to psychotic symptoms) is often linked to local religious beliefs (Ng, 2007; Hanwella, de Silva, Yoosuf, Karunaratne & de Silva, 2012), and may often be accompanied by exorcism as an attempted treatment – even in individuals with a known history of diagnosed psychotic symptoms (e.g. Tajima-Pozo, Zambrano-Enriquez, de Anta, Moron, Carrasco, Lopez-Ibor *et al.*, 2011).

FOCUS POINT 1.1

SPIRIT POSSESSION AS A TRAUMA-RELATED PHENOMENON IN UGANDAN CHILD SOLDIERS

DOMINIQUE AUBERT/Getty Images

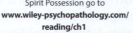

To read the article by Neuner *et al.* on Spirit Possession go to **www.wiley-psychopathology.com/ reading/ch1**

Even today, many cultures still believe that unusual behaviour that may be symptomatic of psychopathology is caused by spirit possession – especially in some less developed areas of the world where such beliefs are still important features of the local culture. Interestingly, beliefs about spirit possession are not simply used to try and explain the effects of psychopathology-related experiences, but are also regularly used to control and coerce individuals.

Neuner, Pfeiffer, Schauer-Kaiser, Odenwald *et al.* (2012) carried out a study investigating the prevalence of *cen*, a local variant of spirit possession, in youths aged between 12 and 25 years in war-affected regions of northern Uganda. They compared youths who had been abducted and forced to fight as child soldiers in the so-called *Lord's Resistance Army* – a group that has waged a long and brutal campaign to overthrow the government of Uganda – with youths who had never been abducted.

Cen is a form of spirit possession where the 'ghost of a deceased person visits the affected individual and replaces his or her identity'. The table below shows that reporting of spirit possession is significantly higher in former abducted child soldiers than in non-abductees. They also found that reports of spirit possession were related to trauma exposure (such as sexual assault and being forced to kill), to psychological distress, and to higher rates of suicide and post-traumatic stress disorder.

Neuner, Pfeiffer, Schauer-Kaiser, Odenwald *et al.* (2012) conclude that in many of the areas of the world where beliefs about spirit possession are widely held, such beliefs are a standard consequence of psychological trauma and may be a way of explaining the dissociative symptoms that often accompany intense traumatic experiences (see Chapter 14). These beliefs about spirit possession can then be used by various local agencies to manipulate the behaviour of individuals – even to the extent of coercing them into acts of extreme brutality.

Frequencies of characteristics of spirit possession in total and divided by abduction status

Characteristics of spirit possession (%)	Total	Abductees	Non-abductees	p
Within the past 4 weeks, were you haunted by ghosts of a deceased person?	14.4	21.3	9.2	<.001
Within the past 4 weeks, did these spirits enter your body and replace your inner self?	10.3	17.3	5.2	<.001
Within the past 4 weeks, during the time the spirit possessed you, did you show behaviour or make movements that were not under your control, but controlled by the spirit?	9.0	15.4	3.9	<.001
Within the past 4 weeks, did it occur that you had lack of memory for parts of the time or the whole time the spirit possessed you?	15.1	23.6	8.8	<.001
Did you ever seek help because ghosts haunted you?	15.1	23.6	8.8	<.001
Four or more characteristics (high spirit possession)	8.2	14.3	3.7	<.001

Source: Neuner, F., Pfeiffer, A., Schauer-Kaiser, E., Odenwald, Elbert T. & Ertl, V. (2012) Haunted by ghosts: Prevalence, predictors and outcomes of spirit possession experiences among former child soldiers and war-affected civilians in Northern Uganda. *Social Science & Medicine, 75,* 548–554, Table 1. Reproduced with permission.

1.1.2   *The Medical or Disease Model*

As cultures develop, then so too do the types of causes that they attribute behaviour to. In particular, as we began to understand some of the biological causes of physical disease and illness, then our conception of 'madness' moved very slowly towards treating it as a disease (hence the term 'mental illness'). The impetus for this change in conception came in the 19th century when it became apparent that many forms of behaviour typical of psychopathology were the result of physical illnesses, such as strokes or viral infections. For example, without proper treatment, the later stages of the sexually transmitted disease syphilis are characterized by the inability to coordinate muscle movements, paralysis, numbness, gradual blindness and dementia – and many of these symptoms cause radical changes in the individual's personality. The discovery that syphilis had a biological cause, and was also an important contributor to the mental disorder known as **general paresis**, implied that many other examples of mental or psychological illness might also have medical or biological explanations. This became known as the **somatogenic hypothesis**, which advocated that the causes or explanations of psychological problems could be found in physical or biological impairments.

general paresis A brain disease occurring as a late consequence of syphilis, characterized by dementia, progressive muscular weakness and paralysis.

somatogenic hypothesis The hypothesis that the causes or explanations of psychological problems can be found in physical or biological impairments.

The medical model of psychopathology that was fostered by the somatogenic hypothesis was an important development because it introduced scientific thinking into our attempts to understand psychopathology, and shifted explanations away from those associated with cultural and religious beliefs. The medical model has given rise to a large body of scientific knowledge about psychopathology that is based on medicine, and this profession is known as **psychiatry**. The primary approach of the medical model is to identify the biological causes of psychopathology and treat them with medication or surgery. As we shall see in later chapters, there are many explanations of psychopathology that allude to biological causes, and these attempt to explain symptoms in terms of such factors as brain abnormalities (e.g. in dementia, autism), biochemical imbalances (especially imbalances of brain neurotransmitters) (e.g. major depression, bipolar disorder, schizophrenia), genetic factors (e.g. learning disabilities, autism, schizophrenia), chromosome disorders (e.g. intellectual disabilities),

psychiatry A scientific method of treatment that is based on medicine, the primary approach of which is to identify the biological causes of psychopathology and treat them with medication or surgery.

congenital risk factors (such as maternal infections during pregnancy) (e.g. intellectual disorders, ADHD), abnormal physical development (e.g. autism), and the physical effects of pathological activities (e.g. the effect of hyperventilation in panic disorder) amongst others. However, while such biological factors may play a role in the aetiology of some psychopathologies, biological explanations are not the only way in which psychopathology can be explained, and nor is biological dysfunction necessarily a factor underlying all psychopathology. As we shall see later, it is often a person's experiences that are dysfunctional, not their biological substrates.

However, despite its obvious importance in developing a scientific view of psychopathology and providing some influential treatments, the medical model of psychopathology has some important implications for the way we conceive mental health problems. Firstly, an obvious implication is that it implies that medical or biological causes underlie psychopathology. This is by no means always the case, and bizarre behaviour can be developed by perfectly normal learning processes. For example, in Chapter 8 we describe the example of the schizophrenia sufferer who learnt through perfectly normal learning processes to carry a broom around with them for 24 hours a day (see Focus Point 8.5). Similarly, children with autism or intellectual disabilities often learn disruptive, challenging or self-harming behaviours through normal learning processes that have nothing to do with their intellectual deficits (see Treatment in Practice Box 17.1). Furthermore, in contrast to the medical model, both psychodynamic and contemporary cognitive accounts of psychopathology argue that many psychological problems are the result of the individual acquiring dysfunctional ways of thinking and acting, and acquiring these characteristics through normal, functional learning processes. In this sense, it is not the individual or any part of their biology that is dysfunctional, it is the *experiences* they have had that are dysfunctional and have led to them thinking and acting in the way they do.

Secondly, the medical model adopts what is basically a reductionist approach by attempting to reduce the complex psychological and emotional features of psychopathology to simple biology. If you look at the personal accounts provided at the beginning of this chapter, it is arguable whether the phenomenology (i.e. the personal experience of psychopathology) or the complex cognitive factors involved in many psychological problems can be reduced to simple biological descriptions. Biological reductionism cannot easily encapsulate the distress felt by sufferers; nor can it easily explain the dysfunctional beliefs and forms of thinking that are characteristic of many psychopathologies. In addition, complex mental health problems are often not just biological or even simply reducible to psychological problems and processes, they are influenced by the socio-economic situation in which the individual lives, their potential for employment and education, and the support they are given that will provide hope for recovery and support for social inclusion (this broad ranging approach to understanding and treating mental health problems is known as the recovery model, and is discussed in more detail in section 5.3.3). All of these factors arguably contribute to a full understanding and explanation of psychopathology.

Finally, as we have mentioned already, there is an implicit assumption in the medical model that psychopathology is caused by 'something not working properly'. For example, this type of explanation may allude to brain processes not functioning normally, brain or body biochemistry being imbalanced, or normal physical development being impaired. This 'something is broken and needs to be fixed' view of psychopathology is problematic for a couple of reasons. First, rather than reflecting a dysfunction, psychopathology might just represent a more extreme form of normal behaviour. We all get anxious, we all worry, and we all get depressed. Yet anxiety, worry and depression in their extreme form provide the basis of many of the mental health problems we will cover in this book. If we take the example of worry, we can all testify to the fact that we worry about something at some time. However, for some of us it may become such a prevalent and regular activity that it becomes disabling, and may lead to a diagnosis of generalized anxiety disorder (GAD; see Chapter 6). Nevertheless, there is no reason to suppose that the cognitive mechanisms that generate the occasional bout of worrying in all of us are not the same ones that generate chronic worry in others (Davey, 2003). In this sense, psychopathology can be viewed as being on a dimension rather than being a discrete phenomenon that is separate from normal experience. There is accumulating evidence that important psychopathology symptoms are on a dimension from normal to distressing, rather than being qualitatively distinct (e.g. Haslam, Williams, Kyrios, McKay & Taylor, 2005; Olatunji, Williams, Haslam, Abramowitz & Tolin, 2008). A second reason this view is problematic is that, by implying that psychopathology is caused by a normal process that is broken, imperfect or dysfunctional, the medical model may have an important influence on how we view people suffering from mental health problems and, indeed, how they might view themselves. At the very least it can be stigmatising to be labelled as someone who is biologically or psychologically imperfect, and people with mental health problems are often viewed as second-class citizens – even when their symptoms are really only more prominent and persistent versions of characteristics that we all possess.

1.1.3 From Asylums to Community Care

Prior to the 18th century, hospitals and asylums were few and far between, and those that were established were often devoted to very specific and often highly infectious illnesses (such as leprosy). 'Madness' was considered to be a local or domestic problem, and individuals suffering mental health problems would either be cared for by their families or by their local parish authorities. However, as many traditional infectious diseases became less common, many hospices for these diseases were converted into **asylums** for the confinement of individuals with mental health problems.

> **asylums** In previous centuries asylums were hospices converted for the confinement of individuals with mental health problems.

Because there was no coordinated government response to mental health issues until the 19th century, individual privately funded hospitals or 'madhouses' began to appear prior to this time, and the most famous of these was the Bethlem Hospital in Moorfields, London, which in 1676 had a capacity for 100 inmates (Porter, 2006). Life in these asylums was often cruel and inhumane, and because 'madhouses' were essentially businesses established for financial profit, many expanded to take more and more sufferers in conditions that were not subject to inspection under the relevant legislation of the time (MacKenzie, 1992). Any medical treatments provided were usually crude and often painful (e.g. drawing copious quantities of blood from the brain, hot and cold baths, mercury pills, or administration of the opiate laudanum to pacify inmates), and the nature of the inmates often expanded to include not just those with mental health problems, but paupers and individuals from poor backgrounds – especially young pregnant women, who were considered to be 'wayward' or 'morally degenerate'. This growing hotchpotch of inmates in 18th- and 19th-century asylums gave rise to ad hoc approaches to mental health care that were based around combating moral degeneration and 'social weakness', and such approaches probably represent the roots of the modern-day stigma that is associated with mental health problems. Indeed, in Victorian times, the public could buy tickets to view the inmates of asylums, a process that will have increased the conception that individuals with mental health problems were objects of curiosity excluded from everyday society.

However, in the 19th century there was a gradual movement towards more humane treatments for individuals in asylums, and these developments were led by a number of important reforming pioneers. Philippe Pinel (1745–1826) is often considered to be the first to introduce more humane treatments during his time as the superintendent of the Bicêtre Hospital in Paris. He began by removing the chains and restraints that had previously been standard ways of shackling inmates, and started to treat these inmates as sick human beings rather than animals. Further enlightened approaches to the treatment of asylum inmates were pioneered in the USA by Benjamin Rush of Philadelphia, and by the Quaker movement in the UK. The latter developed an approach known as **moral treatment**, which abandoned contemporary medical approaches in favour of understanding, hope, moral responsibility, and occupational therapy (Digby, 1985).

moral treatment Approach to the treatment of asylum inmates, developed by the Quaker movement in the UK, which abandoned contemporary medical approaches in favour of understanding, hope, moral responsibility, and occupational therapy.

Even into the 20th century and up until the 1970s in both the UK and the USA, hospitalization was usually the norm for individuals with severe mental health problems, and lifelong hospitalization was not uncommon for individuals with chronic symptoms. However, it became clear that custodial care of this kind was neither economically viable nor was it providing an environment in which patients had an opportunity to improve. Because of the growing numbers of in-patients diagnosed with mental health problems, the burden of care came to rest more and more on nurses and attendants who, because of lack of training and experience, would resort simply to restraint as the main form of intervention. This would often lead to deterioration in symptoms, with patients developing what was called *social breakdown syndrome*, consisting of confrontational and challenging behaviour, physical aggressiveness, and a lack of interest in personal welfare and hygiene (Gruenberg, 1980).

Between 1950 and 1970, these limitations of hospitalization were being recognized and there was some attempt to structure the hospital environment for

PHOTO 1.1 *This photograph shows a ward in Cardiff City Mental Hospital, Whitchurch, UK, in the early 20th century. Beds are crowded close together allowing little personal space for patients, who were often hospitalized for much of their lives.*

patients. The first attempts were known as **milieu therapies**, which were the first attempts to create a therapeutic community on the ward which would develop productivity, independence, responsibility and feelings of self-respect. This included mutual respect between staff and patients, and the opportunity for patients to become involved in vocational and recreational activities. Patients exposed to milieu therapy were more likely to be discharged from hospital sooner and less likely to relapse than patients who had undergone traditional custodial care (Paul & Lentz, 1977; Cumming & Cumming, 1962). A further therapeutic refinement of the hospital environment came with the development of **token economy** programmes (Ayllon & Azrin, 1968). These were programmes based on operant reinforcement, where patients would receive tokens (rewards) for exhibiting desired behaviours. These desired behaviours would usually include social and self-help behaviours (e.g. communicating coherently to a nurse or other patient, or washing or combing hair), and tokens could subsequently be exchanged for a variety of rewards such as chocolate, cigarettes and hospital privileges. A number of studies have demonstrated that token economies can have significant therapeutic gains. For example, Gripp & Magaro (1971) showed that patients in a token economy ward improved significantly more than patients in a traditional ward, and Gershone, Errickson, Mitchell & Paulson (1977) found that patients in a token economy scheme were better groomed, spent more time in activities and less time in bed, and made fewer disturbing comments than patients on a traditional ward. Patients on token economy schemes also earn discharge significantly sooner than patients who are not on such a scheme or have been involved in a milieu therapy programme (Hofmeister, Schneckenbach & Clayton, 1979; Paul & Lentz, 1977). However, despite the apparent success of token economies, their use in the hospital setting has been in serious decline since the early 1980s (Dickerson, Tenhula & Green-Paden, 2005). There are a number of reasons for this decline, and they are discussed in Focus Point 1.2.

Since the 1970s treatment and care of individuals diagnosed with severe mental health problems has moved away from long-term hospitalization to various forms of community care. However, the psychiatric hospital is still an important part of the treatment picture for those displaying severe and distressing symptoms – especially since it will often be the environment in which treatment takes place for an individual's first acute experience (e.g. a first psychotic episode). However, length of stay in hospital for individuals has been significantly reduced as a

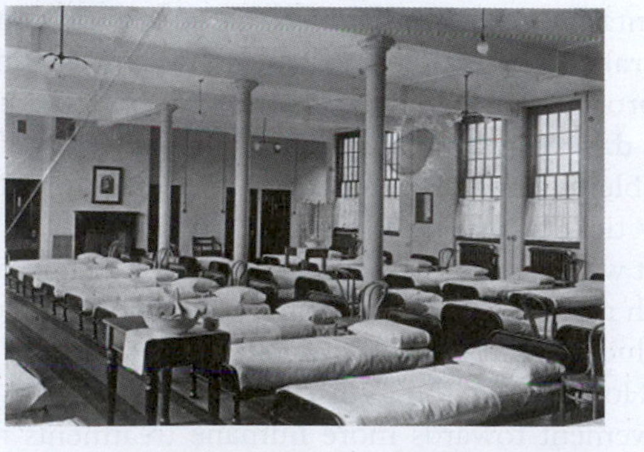

milieu therapies The first attempts to structure the hospital environment for patients, which attempted to create a therapeutic community on the ward in order to develop productivity, independence, responsibility and feelings of self-respect.

token economy A reward system which involves participants receiving tokens for engaging in certain behaviours, which at a later time can be exchanged for a variety of reinforcing or desired items.

FOCUS POINT 1.2

THE DECLINE OF THE TOKEN ECONOMY

Despite its apparent therapeutic advantages, recent surveys indicate that the use of 'token economies' in clinical settings is in serious decline (Corrigan, 1995; Hall & Baker, 1973; Boudewyns, Fry & Nightengale, 1986; Dickerson, Tenhula & Green-Paden, 2005). A number of reasons have been put forward for this decline.

- There are legal and ethical issues that need to be considered. This is especially so when decisions have to be made about who will participate in token economies, for how long, and what will be made available as positive reinforcers. Legislation over the past 25 years has sought to protect patients' rights, and treatment staff are severely constrained with regard to the use of more basic items as reinforcers (Glynn, 1990) – especially when patients now have a legal right to their own personal property and humane treatment, including comfortable bed, chair, bedside table, nutritious meals, cheerful furnishings, and suchlike.

- One of the major challenges for token economies has been maintenance and generalization of therapeutic effects. To the extent that patients can obtain reinforcers outside the programme and avoid punishment by exiting from the programme, the therapeutic benefit of token economies becomes less useful (Glynn, 1990). It is true that some studies have shown that behaviours targeted for improvement in a token economy

scheme return to low baseline levels outside of the program (e.g. Ayllon & Azrin, 1968; Walker & Buckley, 1968). However, there are other studies that have shown positive effects of maintenance and generalization (Banzett, Liberman & Moore, 1984). Nevertheless, it should be pointed out that generalization is not a passive process, and clinicians must actively build into the programme strategies that transfer positive effects to settings outside the treatment scheme (Stokes & Baer, 1977; Stokes & Osnes, 1988).

- Some other proponents of the token economy have argued that its decline has been the result of unfounded misconceptions about the nature and efficacy of such programmes (e.g. Corrigan, 1995). These include such misconceptions as token economies not being therapeutically effective, their benefits do not generalize, they do not provide individualized treatment, they are abusive and coercive, and they are not practical to implement in the context of present-day attempts to treat patients in the community. Corrigan (1995) argues that these are all unfounded, and that the token economy remains an important and valuable tool for the management of patients and staff in treatment settings.

Source: From Davey G.C.L. (1998). Learning theory. In C.E. Walker (Ed.) *Comprehensive clinical psychology: Foundations of clinical psychology, Vol. 1.* Elsevier. Reproduced with permission.

---

result of the development of more effective early intervention treatments and supportive community care and outreach programmes. With the development of more effective pharmacological and psychological treatments in the 1950s and 1960s, it became clear that most people diagnosed with severe mental health symptoms could be treated to a point where they were capable of living at least some kind of life back in the community. This helped relieve the economic burden of lifelong hospitalization and custodial care. However, even when living back in their communities, it was clear that many individuals diagnosed with mental health problems would often need support and supervision. They would need help maintaining their necessary medication regime, finding and keeping a job or applying for and securing welfare benefits. They may also have needed help with many aspects of normal daily living that others would take for granted, such as personal hygiene, shopping,

feeding themselves, managing their money, and coping with social interactions and life stressors.

In 1963, the US Congress passed a Community Mental Health Act that specified that, rather than be detained and treated in hospitals, people with mental health problems had the right to receive a broad range of services in their communities. These services included outpatient therapy, emergency care, preventative care, and aftercare. Growing concerns about the rights of mental health patients and a change in social attitudes away from the stigma associated with mental health problems meant that other countries around the world swiftly followed suit in making mental health treatment and aftercare available in the community (Hafner & van der Heiden, 1988). These events led to the development of a combination of services usually termed assertive community treatment or assertive outreach, and, in the US alone, this has led to around a

THE CLIENT'S PERSPECTIVE 1.1:
THE EXPERIENCE OF HOSPITALIZATION

Janey describes her first experience of a psychiatric ward after exhibiting psychotic symptoms in 1985. She then describes her experiences on being readmitted to the same ward after relapse in 2000.

1985

'The ward was supposed to be for 24 people but it was my bad luck that they were decorating one of the other wards and we had four extra beds squashed into various corners. The whole area smelled of smoke, floor cleaner and urine – in that order. I was given a bed – one of five in a four-person room – and introduced to my two neighbours. A nurse went through my things, listing my valuables and in the end confiscating my birth control pills. I argued about that too because I didn't see how oestrogen and progesterone could be seen as dangerous.

The other patients terrified me; some seemed to have strange glassy-eyed expressions or shambling walks. There were people pacing the ward in silence, someone smashed a guitar against the wall, another person wet the floor. One of my room-mates, an oldish, sleepy-looking woman called Amy, told me that she had entered 'The Brain of Britain' programme in the past but frankly, I didn't believe her. And there was a young man in a wheelchair, who, I was informed, had jumped off a building. Most people were smoking heavily.

I ate someone else's dinner (they were on leave) because food was ordered two days ahead and I had yet to fill in menus. Then I retreated onto my bed to hide and to try to read – desperately attempting to act normal so I could go home as soon as possible. Fortunately, my husband came to visit me and I felt happier for a while.

I heard a weird conversation between two women in my room who were to have a treatment in the morning. Both were scared because they didn't know what to expect and I couldn't imagine what was going to happen to them.

That night I had to queue at the drug trolley for my birth control pill. The quantity of medication some of the patients were getting surprised and shocked me. The only drug whose name I recognized was chlorpromazine because I had been given it when I was 15. Some people received a bright orange sticky liquid that had to be measured out carefully, others a large amount of a brown liquid.

Afterwards there was hot milk to make a bedtime drink of chocolate or Ovaltine but I was not quick enough so I didn't get any. I spent the night getting up to switch the night light off because it was too bright to sleep, only to have the staff switch it back on again. The bed was not very comfortable and creaked with every breath. It took a long time for morning to come.

I spent the next few days feeling bored and frustrated because I was not allowed off the ward on my own and there was not a lot to do. The two women went for their treatment. One came back with a headache and one felt sick and was told to go and lay on her bed. There was intense drama for a while when a man abruptly kicked at one of the doors and tore it off its hinges. Someone seeing it set an alarm off and suddenly there were nurses everywhere. The man (who never spoke the whole time I was there) was given some medication and order was resumed. The Christmas decorations were put up – paper chains and plastic baubles only. Later another man in black leather silently and inexplicably held my hand while we were watching TV.'

2000

'Of course the building hasn't changed and, although there have obviously been several facelifts within the ward, it still has that lived-in look, with splodges of something-or-other on the floor and walls. The internal structure of the place has changed a little, so the nurses have a big room, as compared with a little one (6 years ago) and a nursing station (15 years ago). I didn't walk into a sea of smoke this time, all smoking has been confined to one room. We have carpet in the corridor and there are more single rooms too. But other than that, the basic cubicle with bed, wardrobe and locker are the same. Drug times, ward rounds and that sort of thing seem immutable, set in stone. Unfortunately, even some of the patients have stayed the same – though I suppose they can say that of me.

The rules of the ward are stricter, with notices pinned up to remind us of them. 'No visitors until four o'clock', 'no mobile phones', 'no smoking except in the smoking room', 'drug and alcohol use will result in the police being called', and so on. And good behaviour is enforced with a 'sin bin', the seclusion room (I was threatened with seclusion for kicking the door in a moment's temper.) Surprisingly, all of this makes for a more relaxed, less dog-eat-dog atmosphere.

There is a mission statement on the wall by the new and bigger nurses' room now. It contains lots of long words like 'integrity', 'confidentiality' and 'valuing individuals' – the shortest is 'caring'. I guess this is a response to hospital trusts and The Patients' Charter, though I'm not sure that practically it makes any difference at all. Observation levels are more relaxed: the hell of having a nurse with you all the time – even in the loo – seems to have disappeared. The food is still bad, with little green vegetables.

The queue for medication still takes time to get through, and ECT is still done on Tuesday and Friday. Sadly, the suicide of those with a mental health problem has not changed at all. During my three weeks in the ward, one of my fellow patients found a way to kill himself.

Once more I'm back out in the community, trying to sort my life and planning not to have to go into hospital again.'

Source: Adapted from http://www.schizophrenia.co.uk/treatment/treatment_articles/treatment.

tenfold decrease in the number of people being treated in hospital for mental health problems (Torrey, 2001). Assertive community treatment programmes help people recovering from psychotic episodes with their medication regimes, psychotherapy, assistance in dealing with everyday life and its stressors, guidance on making decisions, residential supervision and vocational training (Bebbington, Johnson & Thornicroft, 2002). In the UK, assertive outreach is a way of working with groups of individuals with severe mental health problems who do not effectively engage with mental health services. Assertive outreach staff would expect to meet their clients in their own environments, whether that is a home, café, park or street, and the aim is to build a long-term relationship between the client and mental health services.

SELF-TEST QUESTIONS

- Why was demonic possession such a popular way of explaining psychopathology in historical times?
- What are the pros and cons of the medical model of psychopathology?
- How has care for people with mental health problems developed from the times of asylums to the present day?

SECTION SUMMARY

1.1 A BRIEF HISTORY OF PSYCHOPATHOLOGY

This section has provided an historical perspective on the way in which people have attempted to understand and explain mental health problems, and also describes how people with mental health problems have been treated over the centuries. Today, most models of mental health provision espouse compassion, support, understanding, and empowerment for individuals suffering mental health problems (Repper & Perkins, 2006), but it has been a long journey to get to this point. It has required us to understand that individuals with mental health problems are not 'possessed', they do not need to have 'demons' exorcised or driven from their bodies by physical force, they do not need to be incarcerated in asylums, and nor do they need life-long custodial care in psychiatric institutions. However, while most of the physical constraints and impositions imposed on individuals with mental health problems have been lifted, attitudes to mental health problems have been slower to evolve, and the stigma and discrimination associated with mental health problems remain a significant issue in need of resolution (see section 1.4).

The key points are:

- Historical explanations of psychopathology such as 'demonic possession' often alluded to the fact that the individual had been 'possessed' in some way.
- The *medical model* attempts to explain psychopathology in terms of underlying biological or medical causes.
- Historically individuals with mental health problems were often locked away in *asylums* or given lifelong custodial care in psychiatric hospitals.
- Current models of mental health care espouse compassion, support, understanding, and empowerment.

1.2 DEFINING PSYCHOPATHOLOGY

The personal accounts at the beginning of this chapter have been chosen to represent rather different and contrasting examples of mental health problems. However, it is not hard to believe that the experiences reported by *Joan*, *Greg* and even *Erica* are ones for which they would be happy to receive some structured help and support. Interestingly, even though her behaviour may seem the most bizarre of each of these introductory accounts, *Betty* is the one who doesn't believe she has a problem. So how do we define what is a problem that should be considered suitable for support and treatment, and what is not? Unlike medicine, we can't simply base our definitions on the existence of a pathological cause. This is because we have already argued that psychological problems often do not have underlying physical or biological causes; and, secondly, knowledge of the aetiology of many psychopathologies is still very much in its infancy, so we are not yet in a position to provide a classification of psychopathologies that is based on causal factors. This leads us to try to define psychopathology in ways that are independent of the possible causes of such problems – and, as we shall see, many attempts to do this have important ethical and practical implications.

The problems of defining psychopathology not only revolve around what criteria we use to define psychopathology, but also what terminology we use. For example, there are still numerous psychopathology courses and text books that use the title **abnormal psychology**. Merely using this title implies that people suffering from mental health problems are in some way 'abnormal' either in the statistical or the functional

> **abnormal psychology** An alternative definition of psychopathology, albeit with stigmatising connotations relating to not being 'normal'.

sense. But the term 'abnormal' also has more important ramifications because it implies that those people suffering psychopathology are in some way 'not normal' or are inferior members of society. In this sense, the 'abnormal' label may affect our willingness to fully include such individuals in everyday activities and may lead to us treating such individuals with suspicion rather than respect (see section 1.4 for a fuller account of mental health stigma and how this affects people suffering with mental health problems). Individuals with mental health problems have become increasingly vocal about how psychopathology and those who suffer from it are labelled and perceived by others, and examples of groups set up to communicate these views include

service user groups (groups of individuals who are end users of the mental health services provided by, for example, government agencies such as the NHS), charitable organizations that champion the rights of mental health service users, such as Rethink (www.rethink.org), and 'Time to Change', a national UK programme aiming to promote awareness of mental health problems and to combat stigma and discrimination (www .time-to-change.org.uk).

> **service user groups** Groups of individuals who are end users of the mental health services provided by, for example, government agencies such as the NHS.

So, when considering how to define psychopathology we must consider not only whether a definition is useful in the scientific and professional sense, but also whether it provides a definition that will minimize the stigma experienced by sufferers, and facilitate the support they need to function as inclusive members of society. Let us bear this in mind as we look at some potential ways of identifying and defining psychopathology.

1.2.1 Deviation from the Statistical Norm

We can use statistical definitions to decide whether an activity or a psychological attribute deviates substantially from the **statistical norm**, and in some areas of clinical psychology this has been used as a means of deciding whether a particular

> **statistical norm** The mean, average or modal example of a behaviour.

disorder meets diagnostic criteria. For example, in the area of intellectual disability, if an IQ score is significantly below the norm of 100 this has been used in the past as one criterion for diagnosing intellectual disability (see Table 17.3). Figure 1.1 shows the distribution of IQ scores in a standard population, and this indicates that the percentage of individuals with IQ scores below 70 would be relatively rare (i.e. around 2–3 per cent of the population). However, there are at least two important problems with using deviations from statistical norms as indications of psychopathology. Firstly, in the intellectual disability case, an IQ of less than 70 may be statistically rare, but rather than simply forcing the individual into a diagnostic category, a better approach would be to evaluate the specific needs of individuals with intellectual disabilities in a way that allows us to suggest strategies, services and supports that will optimize individual functioning. Secondly, as we can see from Figure 1.1, substantial deviation from the norm does not necessarily imply psychopathology because individuals with exceptionally high IQs are also statistically rare – yet we would not necessarily be willing to consider this group of individuals as candidates for psychological intervention. We might feel that adopting a definition of psychopathology that is statistically based

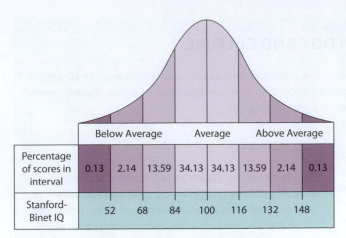

	Below Average			Average		Above Average	
Percentage of scores in interval	0.13	2.14	13.59	34.13	34.13	13.59	2.14	0.13
Stanford-Binet IQ		52	68	84	100	116	132	148

FIGURE 1.1 *This figure represents a normal distribution curve for IQ scores. From this distribution it can be seen that 68 per cent of people score between 84 and 116 points, while only 2.27 per cent of people have an IQ score below 68 points. This graph suggests that around 2–3 per cent of the population will have IQs lower than the 70 points that is the diagnostic criterion for intellectual development disorder. However, the problem for basing a definition of psychopathology on scores that deviate substantially from the norm is that high IQ also is very rare. Only 2.27 per cent of the population have an IQ score greater than 132 points.*

lends some objectivity and measurability to our definition. However, where we draw our cut-off points between normality and abnormality will still be a subjective judgment. Finally, emotions such as anxiety and depression that underlie the most common mental health problems are not statistically rare emotions. They are experienced almost daily by most people, and this represents another reason why deviation from the statistical norm does not make a good basis on which to define psychopathology.

1.2.2   Deviation from Social and Political Norms

There is often a tendency within individual societies for the members of that society to label a behaviour or activity as indicative of psychopathology if it is far removed from what they consider to be the social norms for that culture. We assume (perhaps quite wrongly) that socially normal and acceptable behaviours have evolved to represent adaptive ways of behaving, and that anyone who deviates from these norms is exhibiting psychopathology. However, it is very difficult to use deviation from social norms, or even violations of social norms, as a way of defining psychopathology.

First, different cultures often differ significantly in what they consider to be socially normal and acceptable. For example, in the Soviet Union during the 1970s and 1980s,

political dissidents who were active against the communist regime were regularly diagnosed with schizophrenia and incarcerated in psychiatric hospitals. At first, we might think that this is a cynical method of political repression used to control dissent, but amongst many in the Soviet Union at the time it represented a genuine belief that anti-Soviet activity was indeed a manifestation of psychopathology (surely, anyone who wanted to protest against the perfect social system must be suffering from mental health problems!). Soviet psychiatrists even added to the official symptoms of schizophrenia by including '*reformist delusions*: a belief that an improvement in social conditions can be achieved only through the revision of people's attitudes, in accordance with the individual's own ideas for the transformation of reality' and '*litigation mania*: a conviction, which does not have any basis in fact, that the individual's own rights as a human being are being violated and flouted' (Goldacre, 2002). However, since the collapse of the Soviet system, few would suspect that these kinds of beliefs and activities are representative of psychopathology.

Second, it is difficult to use cultural norms to define psychopathology because cultural factors seem to significantly affect how psychopathology manifests itself. For example: (1) social and cultural factors will affect the vulnerability of an individual to causal factors (e.g. poor mental health is more prevalent in low-income countries) (Desjarlais, Eisenberg, Good & Kleinman, 1996); (2) culture can produce 'culture-bound' symptoms of psychopathology which seem confined to specific cultures and can influence how stress, anxiety and depression manifest themselves (two examples of such 'culture-bound' effects are described in Focus Point 1.3, and these are known as **Ataque de Nervios**, a form of panic disorder found in Latinos from the Caribbean (Salman, Liebowitz, Guarnaccia, Jusino, Garfinkel *et al.*, 1998), and **Seizisman**, a state of psychological paralysis found in the Haitian community (Nicolas, De Silva, Grey & Gonzalez-Eastep, 2006)), and (3) society or culture can influence the course of psychopathology – for example, schizophrenia in developing countries has a more favourable course and outcome than in developed countries (Weisman, 1997).

Ataque de Nervios A form of panic disorder found in Latinos from the Caribbean.

Seizisman A state of psychological paralysis found in the Haitian community.

1.2.3   Maladaptive Behaviour and Harmful Dysfunction

It is often tempting to define psychopathology in terms of whether it renders the individual incapable of adapting to what most of us would consider normal daily living. That is, whether a person can undertake and hold

PSYCHOPATHOLOGY AND CULTURE

Psychopathology can manifest itself in different forms in different cultures, and this can lead to some disorders that are culture specific (i.e. have a set of symptoms which are found only in that particular culture). Two such examples are *Ataque de Nervios*, which is an anxiety-based disorder found almost exclusively amongst Latinos from the Caribbean (Salman *et al.*, 1998), and *Seizisman*, a state of psychological paralysis found in the Haitian community (Nicolas, DeSilva, Grey & Gonzalez-Eastep, 2006).

ATAQUE DE NERVIOS

Its literal translation is 'attack of nerves', and symptoms include trembling, attacks of crying, screaming uncontrollably, and becoming verbally or physically aggressive. In some cases, these primary symptoms are accompanied by fainting bouts, dissociative experiences and suicide attempts.

Research on *Ataque de Nervios* has begun to show that it is found predominantly in women, those over 45 years of age, and those from low socio-economic backgrounds and disrupted marriages (Guarnaccia *et al.*, 1989). The symptoms appear to resemble many of those found in panic disorder, but with a coexisting affective disorder characterized by emotional lability and anger (Salman *et al.*, 1998).

From this research, it appears that *Ataque de Nervios* may be a form of panic disorder brought on by stressful life events (such as economic or marital difficulties), but whose expression is determined by the social and cultural norms within that cultural group. In particular, Latino cultures place less emphasis on self-control and emotional restraint than other Western cultures, and so the distress of panic disorder in Latinos tends to be externalized in the form of screaming, uncontrolled behaviour and aggression. In contrast, in Western cultures the distress of panic disorder is usually coped with

by adopting avoidance and withdrawal strategies – hence the common diagnosis of panic disorder with agoraphobia.

SEIZISMAN

The name literally means 'seized-up-ness' and refers to a state of paralysis usually brought on by rage, anger, or sadness, and in rare cases happiness. Events that can cause *Seizisman* include a traumatic event (such as receiving bad news), a family crisis, and verbal insults from others. Individuals affected by the syndrome become completely dysfunctional, disorganized and confused, and unresponsive to their surroundings (Laguerre, 1981). The following quote illustrates how viewing traumatic events while working within a Haitian community that is attuned to the symptoms of this syndrome can actually give rise to these culture-bound symptoms:

> I remember over and over, when I was a UN Human Rights Monitor and I was down there in Port-au-Prince viewing cadaver after cadaver left by the Haitian army, people would say, 'Now go home and lie down or you will have Seizisman'. And I never really had a problem, you know? I never threw up or fainted no matter what I saw, but I started to feel 'stressed', which is an American illness defined in an American way. After viewing one particularly vile massacre scene, I went home and followed the cultural model I had been shown. I lay down, curled up, and went incommunicado. 'Ah-hah! Seizisman!' said the people of my household.

Source: Nicholas, G., De Silva, A.M., Grey, K.S. & Gonzalez-Eastep, D. (2006), Using a multicultural lens to understand illness among Haitians living in America. *Professional Psychology: Research and Practice, 37,* 702–707. American Psychological Society. Reprinted with permission.

---

down a job, can cope with the demands of being a parent, develop loving relationships, and function socially. In its extreme form, maladaptive behaviour might involve behaving in a way that is a threat to the health and well-being of the individual and to others. It is certainly the case that current diagnostic criteria, such as DSM-5, do use deficits in social, occupational and educational functioning as one criterion for defining many psychological disorders, but it is by no means the only criterion by which

those disorders are defined. The problem with defining psychopathology solely in terms of maladaptive behaviour is also apparent when we discuss forms of behaviour that we might call maladaptive, but we would not necessarily want to label as psychopathology. The behaviour of many people convicted of murder or terrorist acts, for example, is maladaptive in the sense that it is harmful to others, but it is by no means the case that all murderers or terrorists commit their crimes because they have mental health problems. On the other side of the coin, it can be argued that many forms of psychopathology may not be

To read more about DSM-5 go to
http://tinyurl.com/yzsclmj

representative of maladaptive behaviour but instead serve a protective or adaptive function. For example, a case can be made for suggesting that specific phobias such as height phobia, water phobia, snake and spider phobia are adaptive responses which protect us from exposure to potentially life-threatening situations (e.g. Seligman, 1971; see Chapter 6).

A similar approach is to assume that mental health problems can be defined as **harmful dysfunction** (Wakefield, 1997). This view assumes that psychopathology is defined by the 'dysfunction' of a normal process that has the consequence of being in some way harmful. For example, 'hearing voices' during episodes of psychosis may be caused by the brain's inability to turn off unwanted thoughts, and these may give rise to potentially harmful consequences such as extreme paranoia. The problem with this type of definition is that we still know very little about the brain mechanisms that generate psychopathology symptoms, so it is very difficult to know what 'normal' process might be dysfunctioning. In addition, there are now a number of taxometric studies suggesting that many common mental health problems are best considered as dimensional rather than categorical (e.g. Haslam, Williams, Kyrios, McKay & Taylor, 2005; Olatunji, Williams, Haslam, Abramowitz & Tolin, 2008). That is, distressing mental health symptoms are just more extreme versions of normal emotions and behaviours, and are not in any way as qualitatively different from normal behaviour as the harmful dysfunction model would imply.

> **harmful dysfunction** Assumption that psychopathology is defined by the 'dysfunction' of a normal process that has the consequence of being in some way harmful.

1.2.4   Distress and Disability

Later in this chapter we will look at some of the ways in which psychologists and psychiatrists have attempted to classify psychopathology, and in order to be diagnosed as a psychological disorder one of the most common requirements is that the symptoms must cause 'clinically significant distress or impairment in social, academic, or occupational functioning'. It is clearly the case that many individuals with severe symptoms of psychopathology do suffer considerable personal distress – often to the point of wanting to take their own lives. Defining psychopathology in terms of the degree of distress and impairment expressed by the sufferer is useful in a number of ways. Firstly, it allows people to judge their own 'normality' rather than subjecting them to judgments about their 'normality' made by others in society, such as psychologists or psychiatrists. Many people who are diagnosed with psychological disorders originally present themselves for treatment because of the distress and impairment caused by their symptoms, and to some degree this makes them judges of their own needs. Secondly, defining psychopathology in terms of the degree of distress and impairment experienced can be independent of the type of lifestyle chosen by the individual. This means we do not judge whether someone has a psychopathology purely on the basis of whether they are perceived as productively contributing to society or not, or whether they actively violate social norms, but on the basis of how they are able to cope with their lifestyle.

As attractive as this definition for defining psychopathology seems, it does have a number of difficulties. Firstly, this approach does not provide any standards by which we should judge behaviour itself. For example, in our introductory personal accounts, *Betty's* behaviour and thoughts do not entirely seem to be based in reality, and they could be manifestations of the thought-disordered behaviour that is sometimes characteristic of those experiencing psychotic episodes (see Chapter 8). But *Betty* does not express any feelings of distress or impairment. Similarly, in *Erica's* story she does admit that her substance dependency is beginning to cause her some distress, but should we consider that a teenager's drug addiction is in need of treatment only if they express unhappiness about their situation? Finally, psychopathology classification schemes do include so-called 'disorders' in which diagnosis does not require that the sufferer necessarily reports any personal distress or impairment. A good example of this is that group of disorders known as *personality disorders* (see Chapter 12). For example, individuals diagnosed with borderline personality disorder or antisocial personality disorder frequently exhibit behaviour that is impulsive, emotional, threatening, and harmful to themselves and others. Yet they are often unwilling to admit that their behaviour is unusual or problematic.

SELF-TEST QUESTIONS

- What are the problems with using the normal curve to define psychopathology?
- How do cultural factors make it difficult to define psychopathology in terms of deviations from social norms?
- What are the pros and cons of using maladaptive behaviour or distress and impairment as means of defining psychopathology?

SECTION SUMMARY

1.2   DEFINING PSYCHOPATHOLOGY

None of these individual ways of defining psychopathology is ideal. They may fail to include examples of behaviour that we intuitively believe are representative of mental health problems (the distress and impairment approach), they may include examples we intuitively feel are *not* examples of psychopathology (e.g. the statistical approach, the deviation from social norms approach), or they may represent forms of categorisation that would lead us simply to imposing stigmatising labels on people rather than considering their individual needs (e.g. the statistical approach). In practice, classification schemes tend to use an amalgamation of all these approaches with emphasis being placed on individual approaches depending on the nature of the symptoms and disorder being classified.

To sum up:

* Potential ways of defining psychopathology include deviation from the statistical norm, deviation from social norms, exhibiting maladaptive behaviour, and experiencing distress and impairment.

1.3   EXPLANATORY APPROACHES TO PSYCHOPATHOLOGY

Despite the fact that symptoms of mental health problems seemed baffling to many people, there was still a strong desire to understand psychopathology, to describe its causes, and, as a consequence, to develop effective interventions. Section 1.1 described some of the important milestones in the history of psychopathology, and how an understanding of mental health problems has evolved from the level of primitive beliefs, through an application of medical knowledge, to current models of care. This section will now introduce you to the main contemporary explanatory approaches to psychopathology, and these are ones that you will encounter regularly in the following chapters.

At this point it is important to understand what an explanatory paradigm is, and why we can explain mental health problems in many different ways within a number of different paradigms. Firstly, human beings are multifaceted organisms; they consist of a genetically propagated biological substrate which serves as a basis for behaviour and a whole range of psychological processes, such as thinking, learning, remembering, perceiving, and so on. These genetic, biological, behavioural and psychological processes are interdependent and together make up our conception of the complete thinking and behaving human being. But genetic, biological, behavioural and psychological processes can also be studied independently; they have their own language of description, and researchers may be skilled in studying people only within one of these basic *paradigms*.

Secondly, this view also applies to psychopathology. For example, symptoms of psychosis might be explained genetically (in terms of the inheritance of genes that give rise to a predisposition for these symptoms), biologically (in terms of abnormalities in brain function that generate symptoms), behaviourally (in terms of how symptomatic behaviours are learnt through experience), and psychologically (in terms of how symptoms might be generated by dysfunctional ways of thinking). In many cases, a specific psychopathology can be explained at all these different levels. Furthermore, these explanations within different paradigms are not mutually exclusive – they supplement each other and provide a fuller, richer understanding of that psychopathology.

The following sections introduce you to some examples of these different paradigms and how they each contribute to our broad understanding of psychopathology.

1.3.1   *Biological Models*

Genetics and neuroscience are two of the most important biological paradigms through which researchers attempt to understand psychopathology. The discipline of genetics provides us with a variety of techniques that allow an assessment of whether psychopathology symptoms are inherited or not, and neuroscience techniques allow us to determine whether psychopathology symptoms are associated with abnormalities or differences in brain or central nervous system functioning.

Genetics

Genetics is a fast growing and important branch of science, and collaborations such as the Human

genetics The study of heredity and the variation of inherited characteristics.

Genome Project are attempting to identify those genes that may be responsible for human characteristics, disorders and diseases (Collins & McKusick, 2001). People are biological organisms who come into the world with a biological substructure that will be significantly determined by the genes they have inherited from their ancestors. It is therefore almost a truism to say that behaviour – and mental health problems too – will therefore have at least some genetic component. In some cases the genetic component may be extremely influential (e.g. in Huntington's disease – see Focus Box 1.4); in others it may be a necessary component but may not always be sufficient to trigger a mental health problem; in still other cases the genetic component may be relatively nonspecific and less important to the development of a mental health problem than the experiences that an individual may have during their lifetime.

The way in which genetics might influence psychopathology can be studied in a variety of ways:

1. By studying psychopathology symptoms across different family members who may differ in the extent to which they are genetically related to each other. These studies are known as **concordance studies**, where the probability of symptoms occurring can be related to the degree to which different family members share genes in common.

> **concordance studies** Studies designed to investigate the probability with which family members or relatives will develop a psychological disorder depending on how closely they are related – or, more specifically, how much genetic material they have in common.

2. **Twin studies** compare the probability with which monozygotic (MZ) and dizygotic (DZ) twins both develop psychopathology symptoms. MZ twins share 100 per cent of their genetic material, whereas DZ twins share only 50 per cent of their genes, so a genetic explanation of psychopathology would predict that there would be greater concordance

> **twin studies** Studies in which researchers have compared the probability with which monozygotic (MZ) and dizygotic (DZ) twins both develop symptoms indicative of a psychopathology in order to assess genetic contributions to that psychopathology.

FOCUS POINT 1.4

THE GENETICS OF INHERITING MENTAL HEALTH PROBLEMS

Huntington's disease is a degenerative neurological condition that can often give rise to dementia, and it is caused by a dominant mutation in a gene on the fourth chromosome. Each person has two copies of this gene (each one called an allele), one inherited from each parent. In the case of Huntington's disease an individual only needs one copy of the mutant allele to develop the disease. Parents randomly give one of their two alleles to their offspring, so a child of a parent who has Huntington's disease has a 50 per cent chance of inheriting the mutant version of the gene from their parent. A grandchild of a person with Huntington's disease has a 25 per cent chance of inheriting the mutant gene and so developing the disease.

The gene for Huntington's disease is dominant, and so the disease can be inherited even if only one parent has the mutant gene. In this case, inheriting the mutant gene is the primary factor in the affected individual developing the disease. In other mental health problems where genetic factors have been found to be important (e.g. schizophrenia), inheritance is only one of a number of factors that has been found to contribute to the development of symptoms, and this has led researchers to advocate a diathesis–stress model in which inherited factors provide a vulnerability to develop symptoms, but these symptoms do not appear unless the individual encounters stressful life experiences.

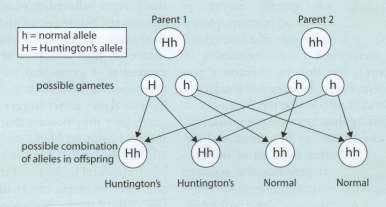

in the diagnosis of a mental health problem in MZ than in DZ twins (see Chapter 8 for some examples of this approach).

3. Because both families and twins are likely to share similar environments as well as genes, interpretation of family and twin studies can be difficult. However, many of these difficulties of interpretation can be overcome by studying the *offspring* of MZ and DZ twins rather than the twins themselves (Gottesman & Bertelsen, 1989). If one MZ twin develops psychopathology symptoms and the other does not, any genetic element in symptoms should still show up in the children of *either* of the two MZ twins. That is, the children of the MZ twins should still exhibit similar rates of risk for the psychopathology (because they have inherited the same predisposition) – even though one of their parents developed the symptoms and the other did not.

However, in the vast majority of psychopathologies we will describe in this book, people do not solely inherit a mental health problem through their genes, a mental health problem develops because of an interaction between a genetic predisposition and our interactions with the environment (Shenk, 2010). This is basically what is known as a **diathesis–stress model** of psychopathology, where 'diathesis' refers to an inherited predisposition and 'stress' refers to a variety of experiences that may trigger the inherited predisposition (this is a model that is particularly important in the understanding of psychosis: see Chapter 8). This interaction between genes and experiences gives rise to the notion of heritability. **Heritability** is a measure of the degree to which symptoms can be accounted for by genetic factors, and this ranges from 0 to 1; the nearer this figure is to 1, the more important are genetic factors in explaining the symptoms. In the case of Huntington's disease described in Focus Point 1.4, the heritability of Huntington's symptoms is very close to 1 because if you inherit the dominant gene for this disorder, that is sufficient to ensure that the individual will develop the disease.

Not only do genetic approaches to psychopathology attempt to estimate the heritability of individual disorders, the area of **molecular genetics** also seeks to identify individual genes that may be involved in

> **diathesis–stress model** Model that suggests a mental health problem develops because of an interaction between a genetic predisposition and our interactions with the environment.

> **heritability** A measure of the degree to which symptoms can be accounted for by genetic factors. It ranges from 0 to 1, and the nearer this figure is to 1, the more important are genetic factors in explaining the symptoms.

> **molecular genetics** Genetic approach that seeks to identify individual genes that may be involved in transmitting psychopathology symptoms.

transmitting psychopathology symptoms. One method of identifying individual genes that has been particularly applied to psychopathology is **genetic linkage analysis**. Linkage analysis works by comparing the inheritance of characteristics for which gene location is known (e.g. eye colour) with the inheritance of psychopathology symptoms. For example, if the inheritance of eye colour follows the same pattern within a family as particular psychopathology symptoms, then it can reasonably be concluded that the gene controlling the psychopathology symptoms can probably be found on the same chromosome as the gene controlling eye colour. While such methods are extremely valuable, it should be pointed out that it is very rare that psychopathology symptoms can be traced to an individual gene, and very often symptoms are associated with multiple genes, which testifies to the complex and often heterogeneous nature of mental health problems (e.g. Badner & Gershon, 2002; Levinson, Lewis & Wise, 2002; Faraone, Doyle, Lasky-Su, Sklar, D'Angelo et al., 2007). In addition, an alternative means of identifying psychopathology-relevant genes is to use non-human animals. For example, researchers can manipulate specific genes in animals with some accuracy, and in mice studies can even delete individual genes. This then enables the researcher to determine whether that gene is linked to any changes in the animal's behaviour that might be indicative of psychopathology (e.g. by observing more anxious behaviour) (Gross, Zhuang, Stark, Ramboz et al., 2002).

Finally, one new area of genetics highly relevant to psychopathology is **epigenetics**. We know that aspects of psychopathology and mental health can be influenced by genetics and hereditary factors, and we also know that personal experiences can also influence psychopathology. However, recent research in the developing area of epigenetics suggests that the way that parents behaved or what they ate can also affect the subsequent behaviour of their offspring by influencing their offspring's genetic heritage, either by changing the nature of their DNA or triggering or inhibiting the expression of genes that may represent risk factors for psychopathology. Similarly, the early experiences of an individual may either trigger or inhibit the expression of genes they may possess that make them vulnerable to mental health problems such as anxiety or depression, and in this way there can be a direct interaction between environmental factors and inherited factors. For example, early life stress can enable the expression of genes that control the neuroendocrinology of post-traumatic

> **genetic linkage analysis** A method of identifying individual genes by comparing the inheritance of characteristics for which gene location is known (e.g. eye colour) with the inheritance of psychopathology symptoms.

> **epigenetics** The study of changes in organisms caused by modification of gene expression rather than alteration of the genetic code.

stress disorder (PTSD), which then puts such individuals at higher risk of developing PTSD after highly traumatic life experiences (Yehuda, Flory, Pratchett, Buxbaum *et al.*, 2010). This has important implications for our understanding of how mental health problems develop and the aetiology of those disorders (Kofink, Boks, Timmers & Kas, 2013).

Neuroscience

The neuroscience paradigm seeks an understanding of psychopathology by identifying aspects of the individual's biology that may contribute to symptoms. The main focus of this paradigm is on brain structure and function, although the broader activity of the neuroendocrine system has also been implicated in some psychopathology symptoms, especially mood disorders (the neuroendocrine system involves interactions between the brain and the endocrine system that produces hormone secretions in the body).

Brain structure and function

The brain is the organ that controls and organizes most of a person's behaviour – including their actions and their thoughts, so it is not surprising that the brain has been a focus for attempting to understand psychopathology. The brain is divided into two mirror-image hemispheres that are connected by a set of nerve fibres called the **corpus callosum**. The outer convoluted area of the brain is known as the **cerebral cortex**, and the large troughs in the convolutions are called fissures (see Figure 1.2a). The lateral and central fissures divide the cerebral cortex into four lobes: the frontal, occipital, temporal and parietal lobes, and these areas serve various specific functions. The **occipital lobe** is the area for visual perception, the **temporal lobe** is considered to be a focus for memory processes, and the **parietal lobe** is associated with visuomotor coordination (Kolb & Whishaw, 2009). However, the **frontal lobes** are especially important, and are the areas of the brain that are considered to make us uniquely human. The frontal lobes are known to be important

in executive functions such as planning and decision making, error correction and troubleshooting, novel situations, and inhibiting habitual and impulsive responses (Norman & Shallice, 1980). Given the important functions of the frontal lobes, it is an area of the brain where deficits or abnormalities have been implicated in many types of psychopathology, including attention disorders, perseveration and stereotyped behaviour patterns, lack of drive and motivation, inability to plan ahead, and apathy and emotional blunting. Alternatively, because the frontal lobes also control response inhibition, deficits in this area can also be associated with impulsivity, euphoria, and aggressive behaviour – especially in relation to personality disorders (Brower & Price, 2001; Meyers, Berman, Scheibel & Hayman, 1992).

A further set of brain areas that are often implicated in psychopathology are collectively known as the **limbic system**. The limbic system comprises the hippocampus, mammillary body, amygdala, hypothalamus, fornix and thalamus. It is situated beneath the cerebral cortex (see Figure 1.2b) and is thought to be critically involved in emotion and learning. For example, the **hippocampus** is involved in spatial learning and the amygdala is an important region coordinating attention to emotionally relevant stimuli (e.g. threatening or fear-relevant stimuli). Because of its function in regulating emotional responses, the **amygdala** is an important brain structure in understanding many aspects of psychopathology. It is involved in the formation and storage of emotion-relevant stimuli and provides feedback to the thalamus that results in appropriate motor action (Del Casale, Ferracuti, Rapinesi, Serata *et al.*, 2012). Because of this role, the amygdala is important in activating phobic fear (Ahs, Pissiota, Michelgard, Frans, Furmark *et al.*, 2009), and depressed individuals show more activity in the amygdala when viewing emotional stimuli than non-depressed individuals (Sheline, Barch, Donnelly, Ollinger *et al.*, 2001).

Brain neurotransmitters

These are the chemicals that help neurones to communicate with each other and thus are essential components of the mechanisms that regulate efficient and effective brain functioning. During synaptic transmission, neurones release a neurotransmitter that crosses the synapse and interacts with receptors on neighbouring neurones, and most neurotransmitters relay, amplify and modify

---

corpus callosum A set of nerve fibres which connects the two mirror-image hemispheres of the brain.

cerebral cortex The outer, convoluted area of the brain.

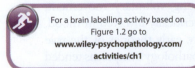
For a brain labelling activity based on Figure 1.2 go to
www.wiley-psychopathology.com/activities/ch1

occipital lobe Brain area associated with visual perception.

temporal lobe The areas of the brain that lie at the side of the head behind the temples and which are involved in hearing, memory, emotion, language, illusions, tastes and smells.

parietal lobe Brain region associated with visuo-motor coordination.

frontal lobe One of four parts of the cerebrum that control voluntary movement, verbal expressions, problem solving, will power and planning.

limbic system A brain system comprising the hippocampus, mammillary body, amygdala, hypothalamus, fornix and thalamus. It is situated beneath the cerebral cortex and is thought to be critically involved in emotion and learning.

hippocampus A part of the brain which is involved in spacial learning.

amygdala The region of the brain responsible for coordinating and initiating responses to fear.

For a brain labelling activity based on Figure 1.3 go to
www.wiley-psychopathology.com/activities/ch1

(a) The Cerebral Cortex

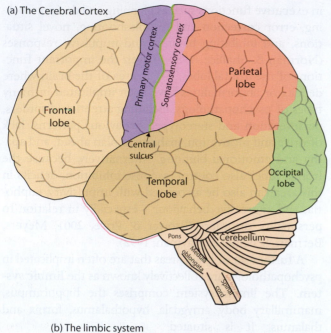

(b) The limbic system

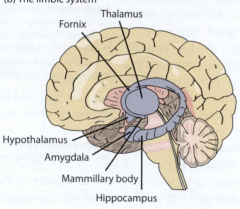

FIGURE 1.2 *The neuroanatomy of the brain.*
(a) The cerebral cortex
(b) The limbic system

brain neurotransmitters Brain neurotransmitters are chemicals that help neurones to communicate with each other and are essential components of the mechanisms that regulate efficient and effective brain functioning.

dopamine A compound that exists in the body as a neurotransmitter and as a precursor of other substances including adrenalin.

serotonin An important brain neurotransmitter where low levels are associated with depression.

norepinephrine A neurotransmitter thought to play a role in anxiety symptoms.

gamma-aminobutyric acid (GABA) A neurotransmitter thought to play a role in anxiety symptoms.

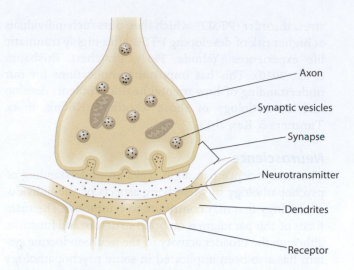

FIGURE 1.3 *Neurons, neurotransmitters and nerve impulses.*
The cells in the brain are called neurons and consist of (1) the cell body, (2) dendrites, and (3) one or more axons of varying length. When a neuron sends a signal to another neuron, a nerve impulse travels down the axon to the synapse between the two neurons. The end of the axon contains synaptic vesicles which are small structures filled with neurotransmitters. When the neurotransmitter is released into the synapse, some of the molecules reach the receptor and a message is sent to the post-synaptic cell. Once a pre-synaptic neuron has sent its signal, the synapse then has to return to its normal state by either breaking down any remaining neurotransmitter in the synapse or taking it back into the axon through a process called re-uptake.

signals between neurones (see Figure 1.3). There are many different types of **brain neurotransmitters** that can be grouped according to either their chemical structure or to their function, and a number of different neurotransmitters have been implicated in psychopathology, including **dopamine**, **serotonin**, **norepinephrine**, and **gamma-aminobutyric acid (GABA)**. Abnormalities in levels of serotonin and norepinephrine have been implicated in the symptoms

of mood disorders (see Chapter 7); dopamine is central to important theories of schizophrenia and psychotic symptoms (see section 8.5.1); and norepinephrine and GABA may play a role in anxiety symptoms. Even so, the functions of neurotransmitters are often not simple or easy to define. For example, dopamine has many functions in the brain, including important roles in regulating voluntary movement, motivation and reward, and is critically involved in mood, attention and learning. Similarly, early theories of the role of neurotransmitters in psychopathology symptoms tended to assume that symptoms were caused by either too little or too much of a particular neurotransmitter. This picture, however, is much too simple, and more recent theories suggest that symptoms may be associated with much more complex interactions between different neurotransmitters (e.g. Carlsson, Waters, Holm-Waters, Tedroff *et al.*, 2001).

Summary

Most chapters of this book will have a section on biological explanations of psychopathology where explanations of the causes of symptoms will be discussed in terms of genetics, brain structure and function, and brain neurotransmitters. Because behaviour and thought cannot occur in the absence of a biological substrate, it is clear that biological explanations of psychopathology will be highly relevant. They will tell us whether all or some of the symptoms of a mental health problem are inherited or not; they will also provide us with information about whether abnormalities in brain function or neurotransmitter activity are associated with psychopathology. There are some clear advantages to the biological approach – especially in terms of treatments. One prominent example is that if we can identify associations between psychopathology and imbalances in neurotransmitters, then we can develop pharmaceutical products that might resolve this imbalance – and this has been particularly the case with mood disorders and psychotic symptoms. However, mental health problems cannot always be reduced simply to biological descriptions, and a full understanding of the causes and experience of mental health problems will require description and explanation at other levels (e.g. how a person's experiences influence their thoughts and behaviour, how their interpretation of events affects their emotions, and how distress is experienced and manifested). We will discuss some of these alternative – but complimentary – paradigms below.

1.3.2 Psychological Models

Moving away from the biological model of psychopathology, some approaches to understanding and explaining mental health problems still see mental health problems as symptoms produced by an underlying cause (what is known as the pathology model), but hold that the causes are psychological rather than biological or medical. These approaches often view the cause as a perfectly normal and adaptive reaction to difficult or stressful life conditions (such as the psychoanalytic view that psychopathology is a consequence of perfectly normal psychodynamic processes that are attempting to deal with conflict). As such, psychological models of psychopathology tend to view mental health symptoms as normal reactions mediated by intact psychological or cognitive mechanisms, and not the result of processes that are abnormal, 'broken' or malfunctioning.

The following sections describe in brief some of the main psychological approaches to understanding and explaining psychopathology.

The psychoanalytical or psychodynamic model

This approach was first formulated and pioneered by the Viennese neurologist **Sigmund Freud** (1856–1939). He collaborated with the physician Josef Breuer in an attempt to understand the causes of mysterious physical symptoms such as hysteria and spontaneous paralysis – symptoms which appeared to have no obvious medical causes. Freud and Breuer first tried to use hypnosis as a means of understanding and treating these conditions,

Sigmund Freud An Austrian neurologist and psychiatrist who founded the psychoanalytic school of psychology.

but during these cases clients often began talking about earlier traumatic experiences and highly stressful emotions. In many cases, simply talking about these repressed experiences and emotions under hypnosis led to an easing of symptoms. Freud built on these cases to develop his influential theory of **psychoanalysis**, which was an attempt to explain both normal and abnormal psychological functioning in terms of how various psychological mechanisms help to defend against anxiety and depression by repressing memories and thoughts that may cause conflict and stress. Freud argued that three psychological forces shape an individual's personality and may also generate psychopathology. These are the id (instinctual needs), the ego (rational thinking), and the superego (moral standards).

psychoanalysis An influential psychological model of psychopathology based on the theoretical works of Sigmund Freud.

The concept of the **id** was used to describe innate instinctual needs – especially sexual needs. He noted that from a very early age, children obtained pleasure from nursing, defecating, masturbating, and other 'sexually' related activities and that many forms of behaviour were driven by the need to satisfy the needs of the id.

id In psychoanalysis, the concept used to describe innate instinctual needs – especially sexual needs.

As we grow up, Freud argued that it becomes apparent to us that the environment itself will not satisfy all our instinctual needs, and we develop a separate part of our psychology known as the **ego**. This is a rational part of the psyche that attempts to control the impulses of the id, and **ego defence mechanisms** develop by which the ego attempts to control unacceptable id impulses and reduce the anxiety that id impulses may arouse.

ego In psychoanalysis, a rational part of the psyche that attempts to control the impulses of the id.

ego defence mechanisms Means by which the ego attempts to control unacceptable id impulses and reduce the anxiety that id impulses may arouse.

The **superego** develops out of both the id and ego, and represents our attempts to integrate 'values' that we learn from our parents or society. Freud argued that we will often judge ourselves by these values that we assimilate and if we think our behaviour does not meet the standards implicit in these values we will feel guilty and stressed.

superego Key concept in Sigmund Freud's psychoanalytic theory. The superego develops out of both the id (innate instinctual needs) and ego (a rational part of the psyche that attempts to control the impulses of the id), and represents our attempts to integrate 'values' that we learn from our parents or society.

According to Freud, the id, ego and superego are often in conflict, and psychological health is maintained only when they are in balance. However, if these three factors are in conflict then behaviour may begin to exhibit signs of psychopathology. Individuals attempt to control conflict between these factors and also reduce stress and conflict from external events by developing **defence mechanisms**. Table 1.1 describes some of these defence

defence mechanisms In psychoanalysis, the means by which individuals attempt to control conflict between the id, ego and superego and also reduce stress and conflict from external events.

mechanisms together with some examples of how they are presumed to prevent the experience of stress and anxiety.

A further factor that Freud believed could cause psychopathology was how children negotiated various **stages of development** from infancy to maturity.

stages of development Progressive periods of development from infancy to maturity.

He defined a number of important stages through which childhood development progressed, and each

of these stages was named after a body area or erogenous zone. If the child successfully negotiated each stage then this led to personal growth and a psychologically healthy person. If, however, adjustment to a particular stage was not successful, then the individual would become fixated

oral stage According to Freud, the first 18 months of life are based on the child's need for food from the mother. If the mother fails to satisfy these oral needs, the child may become fixated at this stage and in later life display 'oral stage characteristics' such as extreme dependence on others.

on that early stage of development. For example, Freud labelled the first 18 months of life as the **oral stage** because of the child's need for food from the mother. If the mother fails to satisfy these oral needs,

the child may become fixated at this stage and in later life display 'oral stage characteristics' such as extreme dependence on others. Other stages of development include the anal stage (18 months to 3 years), the phallic stage (3 to 5 years), the latency stage (5 to 12 years), and the genital stage (12 years to adulthood).

There is no doubt that the psychoanalytical model has been extremely influential, both in its attempts to provide explanations for psychopathology and in the treatments it has helped to develop. Psychoanalysis was arguably the first of the 'talking therapies' and as many as 20 per cent of modern practising clinical psychologists identify themselves at least in part with a psychoanalytical or psychodynamic approach to psychopathology (Prochaska & Norcross, 2003). Psychoanalysis was also the first approach to introduce a number of perspectives on psychopathology that are still important today, including (1) the view that psychopathology can have its origins in early experiences rather than being a manifestation of biological dysfunction, and (2) the possibility that psychopathology may often represent the operation of 'defence mechanisms' that reflect attempts by the individual to suppress stressful thoughts and memories (see, for example, cognitive theories of chronic worrying in Chapter 6 and theories of dissociative disorders in Chapter 14). Theorists in the psychoanalytic tradition have elaborated on Freud's original theory, and we will see many examples of psychodynamic explanations applied to specific psychopathologies presented later in this book. However, psychoanalytic theory does have many shortcomings, and it is arguably no longer the explanation or treatment of choice for most psychological problems; nor is it a paradigm in which modern day evidence-based researchers attempt to understand psychopathology. This is largely because the central concepts in psychoanalytic theory are hard to objectively define and measure. Because concepts such as the id, ego and superego are difficult to observe and measure, it is therefore difficult to conduct objective research on them to see if they are actually related to

TABLE 1.1 *Defence mechanisms in psychoanalytic theory*

Denial	The individual denies the source of the anxiety exists (e.g. I didn't fail my exam, it must be a mistake).
Repression	Suppressing bad memories, or even current thoughts that cause anxiety (e.g. repressing thoughts about liking someone because you are frightened that you may be rejected if you approach them).
Regression	Moving back to an earlier developmental stage (e.g. when highly stressed you abandon normal coping strategies and return to an early developmental stage – for instance, by smoking if you are fixated at the oral stage).
Reaction formation	Doing or thinking the opposite to how you feel (e.g. the person who is angry with their boss may go out of their way to be kind and courteous to them).
Projection	Ascribing unwanted impulses to someone else (e.g. the unfaithful husband who is extremely jealous of his wife might always suspect that she is being unfaithful).
Rationalization	Finding a rational explanation for something you've done wrong. (e.g. you didn't fail the exam because you didn't study hard enough but because the questions were unfair).
Displacement	Moving an impulse from one object (target) to another (e.g. if you've been told off by your boss at work, you go home and shout at your partner or kick the dog).
Sublimation	Transforming impulses into something constructive (e.g. redecorating the bedroom when you're feeling angry about something).

Each of the Freudian defence mechanisms described above function to reduce the amount of stress or conflict that might be caused by specific experiences.

symptoms of psychopathology in the way that Freud and his associates describe (Erdelyi, 1992).

The behavioural model

Most psychological models have in common the view that psychopathology is caused by how we assimilate our experiences and how this is reflected in thinking and behaviour. The behavioural model adopts the broad view that many examples of psychopathology reflect our learnt reactions to life experiences. That is, psychopathology can be explained as learnt reactions to environmental experiences, and this approach was promoted primarily by the behaviourist school of psychology.

During the 1950s and 1960s, many clinical psychologists became disillusioned by psychoanalytic approaches to psychopathology and sought an approach that was more scientific and objective. They turned to that area of psychology known as **learning theory** and argued that just as

> **learning theory** The body of knowledge encompassing principles of classical and operant conditioning (and which is frequently applied to explaining and treating psychopathology).

adaptive behaviour can be acquired through learning, then so can many forms of dysfunctional behaviour. The two important principles of learning on which this approach was based are classical conditioning and operant conditioning. **Classical conditioning** represents the learning of an association between two stimuli, the first of which (the conditioned stimulus, CS) predicts the occurrence of the second (the unconditioned stimulus, UCS). The prototypical example of this form of learning is Pavlov's experiment in which a hungry dog learns to salivate to a bell (the CS) that predicts subsequent delivery of food (the UCS), and this is represented schematically in Figure 1.4. In contrast, **operant conditioning** represents the learning of a specific behaviour or response because that behaviour has

> **classical conditioning** The learning of an association between two stimuli, the first of which (the conditioned stimulus, CS) predicts the occurrence of the second (the unconditioned stimulus, UCS).

> **operant conditioning** The modification of behaviour as a result of its consequences. Rewarding consequences increase the frequency of the behaviour, punishing consequences reduce its frequency.

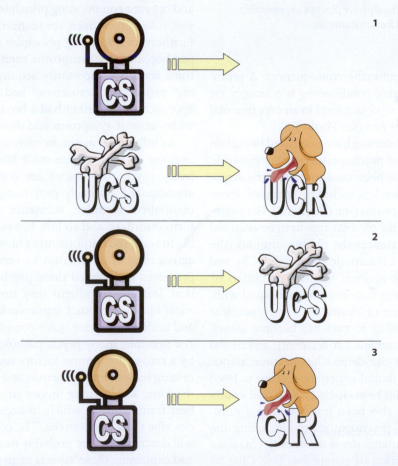

FIGURE 1.4 *Classical conditioning.*
(1) Before conditioning takes place, Pavlov's dog salivates only to the presentation of food and not to the presentation of the bell; (2) pairing the bell with food then enables the dog to learn to predict food whenever it hears the bell; and (3) this results in the dog subsequently salivating whenever it hears the bell. This type of learning has frequently been used to explain psychopathology, and one such example is the acquisition of specific phobias where the phobic stimulus (the CS) elicits fear because it has been paired with some kind of trauma (the UCS) (see Figure 6.2).

PHOTO RESEARCHERS/SCIENCE PHOTO LIBRARY

PHOTO 1.2 *Operant conditioning.*

In operant conditioning, the rat learns to press the lever in this Skinner Box because it delivers food, and food acts to reinforce that behaviour so that it occurs more frequently in the future (known as operant reinforcement). Operant reinforcement has been used to explain how many behaviours that are typical of psychopathology are acquired and maintained. That is, many bizarre and disruptive behaviours may be acquired because they actually have positive or rewarding outcomes (see Focus Point 8.5 as an example).

certain rewarding or reinforcing consequences. A prototypical example of operant conditioning is a hungry rat learning to press a lever to obtain food in an experimental chamber called a Skinner Box (see Photo 1.2).

These two forms of learning have been used to explain a number of examples of psychopathology. For instance, classical conditioning has been used to explain the acquisition of emotional disorders including many of those with anxiety-based symptoms (see Chapter 6). For example, some forms of specific phobias appear to be acquired when the sufferer experiences the phobic stimulus (the CS) in association with a traumatic event (the UCS), and such experiences might account for the acquisition of dog phobia (in which dogs have become associated with, for example, being bitten or chased by a dog), accident phobia (in which travelling in cars has become associated with being in a traumatic car accident), and dental phobia (when being at the dentist has become associated with a traumatic dental experience) (Davey, 1989; Kuch, 1997; Doogan & Thomas, 1992). Classical conditioning processes have also been implicated in a number of other forms of psychopathology, including the acquisition of post-traumatic stress disorder (PTSD) (see Chapter 6), the acquisition of paraphilias (see Chapter 11), and substance dependency (see Chapter 9). Operant conditioning has been used extensively to explain why a range of psychopathology-relevant behaviours may have been acquired and maintained. Examples you will find

in this book include learning approaches to understanding the acquisition of bizarre behaviours in schizophrenia (Ullman & Krasner, 1975), how the stress-reducing or stimulant effects of nicotine, alcohol and many illegal drugs may lead to substance dependency (e.g. Schachter, 1982), how hypochondriacal tendencies and somatoform disorders may be acquired when a child's illness symptoms are reinforced by attention from parents (Latimer, 1981), and how the disruptive, self-harming or challenging behaviour exhibited by individuals with intellectual or developmental disabilities may be maintained by attention from family and carers (Mazaleski *et al.*, 1993).

The behavioural approach led to the development of important behavioural treatment methods, including behaviour therapy and behaviour modification. For example, if psychopathology is learned through normal learning processes, then it should be possible to use those same learning processes to help the individual 'unlearn' any maladaptive behaviours or emotions. This view enabled the development of treatment methods based on classical conditioning principles (such as flooding, systematic desensitisation, aversion therapy: see Chapter 4) and operant conditioning principles (e.g. functional analysis, token economies: see section 1.1.3 and Chapter 17). Furthermore, learning principles could be used to alter psychopathology symptoms even if the original symptoms were not necessarily acquired through conditioning processes themselves, and so the behavioural approach to treatment had a broad appeal across a very wide range of symptoms and disorders.

As influential as the behavioural approach has been over the years, it too has some limitations. For example, many psychopathologies are complex and symptoms are acquired gradually over many years (e.g. obsessive compulsive disorder, substance dependence, somatoform disorders, and so on). It would be almost impossible to trace the reinforcement history of such symptoms across time in an attempt to verify that reinforcement processes had shaped these psychopathologies. In addition, learning paradigms may simply not represent the most ideal conceptual framework in which to describe and understand some quite complex psychopathologies. For example, many psychopathologies are characterized by a range of cognitive factors such as information processing biases, belief schemas and dysfunctional ways of thinking, and learning theory jargon is probably not the best framework in which to accurately and inclusively describe these phenomena. The cognitive approaches we will describe next are probably more suited to describing and explaining these aspects of psychopathology.

The cognitive model

Perhaps the most widely adopted current psychological model of psychopathology is the cognitive model, and one in four of all present-day clinical psychologists would describe their approach as cognitive (Prochaska & Norcross, 2003). Primarily, this approach considers psychopathology to be the result of individuals acquiring irrational beliefs, developing dysfunctional ways of thinking, and processing information in biased ways. It was an approach first pioneered by Albert Ellis (1962) and Aaron Beck (1967). Albert Ellis argued that emotional distress (such as anxiety or depression) is caused primarily because people develop a set of irrational beliefs by which they need to judge their behaviour. Some people become anxious, for example, because they make unrealistic demands on themselves. The anxious individual may have developed unrealistic beliefs such as 'I must be loved by everyone', and the depressed individual may believe 'I am incapable of doing anything worthwhile'. Judging their behaviour against such 'dysfunctional' beliefs causes distress. Aaron Beck developed a highly successful cognitive therapy for depression based on the view that depressed individuals have developed unrealistic distortions in the way they perceive themselves, the world, and their future (see Chapter 7). For example, the cognitive approach argues that depression results from the depressed individual having developed negative beliefs about themselves (e.g. 'I am worthless'), the world (e.g. 'bad things always happen'), and their future (e.g. 'I am never going to achieve anything'), and these beliefs act to maintain depressive thinking.

The view that dysfunctional ways of thinking generate and maintain symptoms of psychopathology has been applied across a broad range of psychological problems, including both anxiety disorders and mood disorders, and has also been applied to the explanation of specific symptoms, such as paranoid thinking in schizophrenia (Morrison, 2001), antisocial and impulsive behaviour in personality disorders (Young, Klosko & Weishaar, 2003), dysfunctional sexual behaviour in sex offenders and paedophiles (Ward, Hudson, Johnston & Marshall, 1997), and illness reporting in hypochondriasis and somatoform disorders (Warwick, 1995) to name but a few.

The cognitive approach has also been highly successful in generating an influential approach to treatment. If dysfunctional thoughts and beliefs maintain the symptoms of psychopathology, then these dysfunctional thoughts and beliefs can be identified, challenged and replaced by more functional cognitions. This has given rise to a broad-ranging therapeutic approach known as **cognitive behaviour therapy (CBT)**, and many examples of the use of this approach will be encountered in this book.

As successful as the cognitive approach seems to have been in recent years, it too also has some

cognitive behaviour therapy (CBT) An intervention for changing both thoughts and behaviour. CBT represents an umbrella term for many different therapies that share the common aim of changing both cognitions and behaviour.

limitations. For example, rather than being a cause of psychopathology, it has to be considered that dysfunctional thoughts and beliefs may themselves simply be just another symptom of psychopathology. For example, we have very little knowledge at present about how dysfunctional thoughts and beliefs develop. Are they the product of childhood experiences? Do they develop from the behavioural and emotional symptoms of psychopathology (i.e. do depressed people think they are worthless because of their feelings of depression)? Or are they merely post hoc constructions that function to help the individual rationalize the way they feel? These are all potentially fruitful areas for future research.

The humanist–existential approach

Some approaches to psychopathology believe that insights into emotional and behavioural problems cannot be achieved unless the individual is able to gain insight into their lives from a broad range of perspectives. People not only acquire psychological conflicts and experience emotional distress, they also have the ability to acquire self-awareness, develop important values and a sense of meaning in life, and pursue freedom of choice. If these latter abilities are positively developed and encouraged, then conflict, emotional distress and psychopathology can often be resolved. This is the general approach adopted by humanistic and existential models of psychopathology, and the aim is to resolve psychological problems through insight, personal development, and self-actualisation.

Because such approaches are interested primarily in insight and personal growth when dealing with psychopathology, they are relatively uninterested in aetiology and the origins of psychopathology, but more interested in ameliorating symptoms of psychopathology through encouraging personal development. An influential example of the is **humanistic-existentialist approach** is **client-centred therapy** developed by Carl Rogers (1951, 1987). This approach stresses the goodness of human nature and assumes that if individuals are unrestricted by fears and conflicts, they will develop into well-adjusted, happy individuals. The client-centred therapist will try to create a supportive climate in which the client is helped to acquire positive self-worth. The therapist will use *empathy* to help them understand the client's feelings and *unconditional positive regard*, by which the therapist expresses their willingness to totally accept the client for who he or she is.

humanist-existentialist approach A model of psychopathology which aims to resolve psychological problems through insight, personal development, and self-actualization.

client-centred therapy An approach to psychopathology stressing the goodness of human nature, assuming that if individuals are unrestricted by fears and conflicts, they will develop into well-adjusted, happy individuals.

As we said earlier, this type of approach to psychopathology does not put too much emphasis on how psychopathology was acquired, but does try to eradicate psychopathology by moving the individual from one phenomenological perspective (e.g. one that contains fears and conflicts) to another (e.g. one that enables the client to view themself as a worthy, respected and achieving individual). Approaches such as humanistic and existentialist ones are difficult to evaluate. For example, most controlled studies have indicated that clients undergoing client-centred therapy tend to fair no better than those undergoing non-therapeutic control treatments (Patterson, 2000; Greenberg, Watson & Lietaer, 1998). Similarly, exponents of existential therapies believe that experimental methodologies are inappropriate for estimating the effectiveness of such therapies, because such methods either dehumanize the individuals involved or are incapable of measuring the kinds of existential benefits that such approaches claim to bestow (Walsh & McElwain, 2002; May & Yalom, 1995). Nevertheless, such approaches to treatment are still accepted as having some value and are still used at least in part by clinical psychologists, counselling psychologists and psychotherapists.

SELF-TEST QUESTIONS

- What are the main approaches to understanding psychopathology that are advocated by the biological approach?
- Can you describe the basic concepts underlying psychoanalytic and psychodynamic approaches to psychopathology?
- What are the learning principles on which the behavioural approach to psychopathology is based?
- Who were the main founders of the cognitive approach to psychopathology, and what were their main contributions?
- How do humanistic–existential approaches to psychopathology differ from most of the others?

SECTION SUMMARY

1.3   EXPLANATORY APPROACHES TO PSYCHOPATHOLOGY

The four psychological paradigms we have discussed in this section have tended to evolve historically from explanatory paradigms that have represented different 'schools' of psychology generally, but all have a relevant place in explaining psychopathology – either at different levels of explanation (e.g. cognitive vs. behavioural), or using different philosophical approaches to explaining human behaviour and psychopathology (e.g. the hypothetical constructs developed by the psychoanalytical approach vs. the learning paradigm developed by behaviourist approaches). In addition to pure psychological paradigms, clinical psychologists are continually developing new ways of conceptualising and studying the factors that influence the development of mental health problems, and one approach of growing importance is to consider how sociocultural factors might affect the acquisition of psychopathology. Some examples of this latter approach are discussed in Focus Point 1.5.

The key points are:

- *Psychological models* view psychopathology as caused primarily by psychological rather than biological processes.
- Influential psychological models of psychopathology include *biological models*, the *psychoanalytical model*, the *behavioural model*, the *cognitive model*, and the *humanist–existential model*.
- *Biological models* attempt to explain psychopathology in terms of processes such as *genetics* and *brain structure and function*.
- *Psychoanalytical models* attempt to discuss psychopathology in terms of the psychological mechanisms that help to defend against anxiety and depression.
- *Behavioural models* use processes of learning such as *classical conditioning* and *operant conditioning* to understand how psychopathology might be acquired.
- *The cognitive model* considers psychopathology to be the result of individuals acquiring irrational beliefs, developing dysfunctional ways of thinking, and processing information in biased ways.
- *The humanist–existential approach* attempts to help the individual to gain insight into their lives from a broad range of perspectives and develop a sense of meaning in life.

SOCIOCULTURAL FACTORS AND PSYCHOPATHOLOGY

There is a growing realization that sociocultural factors can influence both the acquisition of mental health problems and the way that psychopathology is expressed. These factors include gender, culture, ethnicity and socioeconomic factors such as poverty and deprivation, and we will discuss some examples of these here.

GENDER

Your gender is likely to be a significant factor in whether you are likely to develop a particular mental health problem. For example, the prevalence of major depression is twice as high in women as it is in men, women are significantly more likely to develop anxiety-based problems such as social anxiety disorder, panic disorder or generalized anxiety disorder (see Chapter 6), and women are also significantly more likely to develop eating disorders such as anorexia nervosa or bulimia nervosa (see Chapter 10). Alternatively, males are more likely to develop conduct disorders, attention deficit hyperactivity disorder (ADHD) (see Chapter 16), and antisocial personality disorder (Chapter 12). How gender differentially affects the acquisition of these various disorders is far from clear, and could be linked to gender-based biological differences (e.g. men appear to possess a gene that imparts risk for alcohol abuse and dependency, and this can be passed on to their sons; Chapter 9), to factors associated with the gender roles that males and females adopt in different societies (e.g. women's roles in society may be more stressful than men's and so increase the risk of mental health problems), or differences in gender-based coping practices (e.g. women ruminate more than men, while men frequently react to stress by distracting themselves; Just & Alloy, 1997). An interesting discussion of the role of gender in risk for major depression is provided in Activity 7.1.

CULTURE

The culture in which you live can also be a factor that will determine whether you develop a particular mental health problem and also how that problem will manifest itself. For example, prevalence rates for many common mental health problems differ significantly across the world. In the case of major depression, prevalence rates can vary between 1.5 per cent and 19 per cent (Weissman, Bland, Canino, Faravelli et al., 1996), and may be affected by the stigma associated with reporting symptoms, cultural differences in diagnosing symptoms, and depression being expressed in more physical terms in some societies (called somatisation) (Patten, 2003; Compton et al., 1991). Eating disorders are

another example where prevalence rates are higher in most Western cultures, but may only be rarely reported in less socio-economically developed societies (Keel & Klump, 2003). Finally, some combinations of mental health problems may be found only in certain specific cultures, and be examples of the culturally specific ways in which stress and trauma are manifested. Two specific examples of this are provided in Focus Point 1.3.

ETHNICITY

The frequency of diagnosis of many mental health problems also differs across different ethnicities. For example, schizophrenia is more frequently diagnosed in individuals of African descent than white European origin. Conversely, specific types of eating disorders – such as anorexia nervosa – are found more commonly in white women than black women (Lovejoy, 2001). In some of these cases, there may be a genetic component (e.g. individuals of Asian descent inherit a gene which makes drinking large amounts of alcohol aversive, and so makes them less likely to develop alcohol dependency and abuse problems; Wall et al., 2001), but equally it may be the case that diagnostic criteria are either wittingly or unwittingly applied differently to people from different ethnic backgrounds (e.g. it is caused by a cultural bias in assessment – see section 2.2.6). For example, black Americans have a higher rate of diagnosis of disorders such as schizophrenia and alcoholism, whereas white Americans are more likely to be given the less stigmatizing diagnosis of major depression (Garb, 1997), and such differential effects may reflect differential diagnoses driven by implicit racial and ethnic stereotyping.

POVERTY

Finally, the socio-economic conditions in which an individual is either raised or lives in is an important contributor to the development of psychopathology. Obvious examples include the development of conduct disorders, some personality disorders such as antisocial personality disorder, and substance abuse and dependency problems. However, poverty is also a risk factor for the development of many common mental health problems such as anxiety and depression, possibly because of the additional stressors and traumas that accompany poverty, unemployment, substandard accommodation, and neglect (Evans & Kim, 2012). Indeed, so specific are many of the stressors that afflict people living in poverty that it may be necessary to develop interventions that are tailored to the specific sociocultural experiences of low-income families (Goodman et al., 2013).

1.4 MENTAL HEALTH AND STIGMA

There are still attitudes within most societies that view symptoms of psychopathology as threatening and uncomfortable, and these attitudes frequently foster stigma and discrimination towards people with mental health problems. Reactions to people often change when they suffer a mental health problem, and this leads to loss of respect and consideration. Such reactions are common when people are brave enough to admit they have a mental health problem, and they can often lead on to various forms of exclusion or discrimination – either within social circles or within the workplace. In the following sections we will look at five key questions: (1) what is mental health stigma?; (2) who holds stigmatising beliefs and attitudes?; (3) what factors cause stigma?; (4) why does stigma matter?; and (5) how can we eliminate stigma?

1.4.1 What Is Mental Health Stigma?

Mental health stigma can be divided into two distinct types. The first, **social stigma**, is characterized by prejudicial attitudes and discriminating behaviour directed towards individuals with mental health problems as a result of the psychiatric label they have been given. In contrast, **perceived stigma** or **self-stigma** is the internalising by the mental health sufferer of their perceptions of discrimination (Link, Cullen, Struening & Shrout, 1989), and perceived stigma can significantly affect feelings of shame and lead to poorer treatment outcomes (Perlick, Rosenheck, Clarkin, Sirey 2001).

In relation to social stigma, studies have suggested that stigmatising attitudes towards people with mental health problems are widespread and commonly held (Crisp, Gelder, Rix, Meltzer & Rowlands, 2000; Bryne, 1997; Heginbotham, 1998). In a survey of over 1700 adults in the UK, Crisp *et al.* (2000) found that (1) the most commonly held belief was that people with mental health problems were dangerous – especially those with schizophrenia, alcoholism and drug dependence, (2) people believed that some mental health problems such as eating disorders and substance abuse were self-inflicted, and (3) respondents believed that people with mental health problems were generally hard to talk to. People tended to hold these negative beliefs regardless of their age, regardless of what knowledge they had of mental health problems, and regardless of whether they knew someone who had a mental health problem. More recent studies of attitudes to individuals with a diagnosis of schizophrenia or major depression convey similar findings. In both cases, a significant proportion of members of the public considered that people with mental health problems such as depression or schizophrenia were unpredictable and dangerous, and they would be less likely to employ someone with a mental health problem (Wang & Lai, 2008; Reavley & Jorm, 2011).

mental health stigma Mental health stigma can be divided into two distinct types: social stigma is characterized by prejudicial attitudes and discriminating behaviour directed towards individuals with mental health problems. Perceived stigma or self-stigma is the internalizing by the mental health sufferer of their perceptions of discrimination. This can significantly affect feelings of shame and lead to poorer treatment outcomes.

social stigma Stigma characterized by prejudicial attitudes and discriminating behaviour directed towards individuals with mental health problems as a result of the psychiatric label they have been given.

perceived stigma/self-stigma The internalising by the mental health sufferer of their perceptions of discrimination. This can significantly affect feelings of shame and lead to poorer treatment outcomes. See also *Mental health stigma*.

1.4.2 Who Holds Stigmatizing Beliefs about Mental Health Problems?

Perhaps surprisingly, stigmatising beliefs about individuals with mental health problems are held by a broad range of individuals within society, regardless of whether they know someone with a mental health problem, have a family member with a mental health problem, or have a good knowledge and experience of mental health problems (Crisp *et al.*, 2000; Moses, 2010; Wallace, 2010). For example, Moses (2010) found that stigma directed at adolescents with mental health problems came from family members, peers and teachers. Forty-six per cent of these adolescents described experiencing stigmatisation by family members in the form of unwarranted assumptions (e.g. the sufferer was being manipulative), distrust, avoidance, pity and gossip; 62 per cent experienced stigma from peers, which often led to friendship losses and social rejection (Connolly, Geller, Marton & Kutcher, 1992); and 35 per cent reported stigma perpetrated by teachers and school staff, who expressed fear, dislike, avoidance, and underestimation of abilities. Mental health stigma is even widespread in the medical profession, at least in part because it is given a low priority during the training of physicians and GPs (Wallace, 2010).

1.4.3 What Factors Cause Stigma?

The social stigma associated with mental health problems almost certainly has multiple causes. We've seen in the section on historical perspectives that throughout history people with mental health problems have been treated differently, excluded and even brutalized. This treatment may come from the misguided views that people with mental health problems may be more violent or unpredictable than people without such problems, or somehow just 'different', but none of these beliefs has any basis in fact (see e.g. Swanson, Holzer, Ganju & Jono,

1990). Similarly, early beliefs about the causes of mental health problems, such as demonic or spirit possession, were 'explanations' that would almost certainly give rise to reactions of caution, fear and discrimination. Even the medical model of mental health problems is itself an unwitting source of stigmatising beliefs. Firstly, the medical model implies that mental health problems are on a par with physical illnesses and may result from medical or physical dysfunction in some way (when many may not be simply reducible to biological or medical causes). This itself implies that people with mental health problems are in some way 'different' from 'normally' functioning individuals. Secondly, the medical model implies diagnosis, and diagnosis implies a label that is applied to a 'patient'. That label may well be associated with undesirable attributes (e.g. 'mad' people cannot function properly in society, or can sometimes be violent), and this again will perpetuate the view that people with mental health problems are different and should be treated with caution.

'CREATING' MENTAL HEALTH PROBLEMS THROUGH THE MEDICALISATION OF EVERYDAY PROBLEMS OF LIVING

It is worth considering when an everyday 'problem in living' becomes something that should be categorized as a mental health problem. It is a fact of life that we all have to deal with difficult life situations. Sometimes these may make us anxious or depressed, sometimes we might feel as though we are 'unable to cope' with these difficulties. But they are still problems that almost everyone encounters. Many people have their own strategies for coping with these problems: some get help and support from friends and family and in more severe cases perhaps seek help from their doctor or GP. However, at what point do problems of living cease to be everyday problems and become mental health problems? In particular, we must be wary about 'medicalising' problems in daily living so that they become viewed as 'abnormal', symptoms of illness or disease, or even as characteristics of individuals who are 'ill' or in some way 'second class'.

Below are two useful examples of how everyday problems in living might become medicalized to the point where they are viewed as representing illness or disease rather than normal events of everyday living.

First, experiencing *depression* is the third most common reason for consulting a doctor or GP in the UK (Singleton *et al.*, 2001), and in order for GPs to be able to provide treatment for such individuals, there is a tendency for them to over diagnose mild or moderate depression (Middleton *et al.*, 2005). This may have contributed to the common view expressed by lay people that depression is a 'disease' rather than a normal consequence of everyday life stress (Lauber *et al.*, 2003). If lay people already view depression as a 'disease' or biological illness, and GPs are more than willing to diagnose it, then we run the risk of the 'medicalisation' of normal everyday negative emotions such as mild distress or even unhappiness (Shaw & Woodward, 2004).

Second, some clinical researchers have argued that the medical pharmaceutical industry in particular has attempted to manipulate women's beliefs about their sexuality in order to sell their products (Moynihan, 2006). Some drug companies claim that *sexual desire problems* affect up to 43 per cent of American women (Moynihan, 2003), and can be successfully treated with, for example, hormone patches. However, others claim that this figure is highly improbable and includes women who are quite happy with their reduced level of sexual interest (Bancroft, Loftus & Long, 2003). Tiefer (2006) lists a number of processes that have been used either wittingly or unwittingly in the past to 'medicalize' what many see as normal sexual functioning – especially the normal lowering of sexual desire found in women during the menopause. These include (1) taking a normal function and implying that there is something wrong with it and it should be treated (e.g. implying that there is something abnormal about the female menopause, when it is a perfectly normal biological process), (2) imputing suffering that is not necessarily there (i.e. implying that individuals who lack sexual desire are 'suffering' as a result), (3) defining as large a proportion of the population as possible as suffering from the 'disease', (4) defining a condition as a 'deficiency', disease or disease of hormonal imbalance (e.g. implying that women experiencing the menopause have a 'deficiency' of sexual hormones), and (5) taking a common symptom that could mean anything and making it sound as if it is a sign of a serious disease (e.g. implying that lack of sexual desire is a symptom of underlying dysfunction). While sexual dysfunctions are sometimes caused by medical conditions, lack of sexual desire and interest is itself often portrayed as a medical condition in need of treatment. Yet a reduction in sexual interest and desire can be a healthy and adaptive response to normal changes in body chemistry or as a normal reaction to adverse life stressors or relationship changes. 'Medicalising' symptoms in this way leads to us viewing what are normal everyday symptoms and experiences as examples of dysfunction or psychopathology.

We will discuss ways in which stigma can be addressed below, but it must also be acknowledged here that the media regularly play a role in perpetuating stigmatising stereotypes of people with mental health problems. The popular press is a branch of the media that is frequently criticized for perpetuating these stereotypes, and a particular example of this is provided in Focus Point 1.7. Blame can also be levelled at the entertainment media. For example, cinematic depictions of schizophrenia are often stereotypic and characterized by misinformation about symptoms, causes and treatment. In an analysis of English-language movies released between 1990 and 2010 that depicted at least one character with schizophrenia, Owen (2012) found that most schizophrenic characters displayed violent behaviour, one-third of these violent characters engaged in homicidal behaviour, and a quarter committed suicide. This suggests that negative portrayals of schizophrenia in contemporary movies are common and are sure to reinforce biased beliefs and stigmatising attitudes towards people with mental health problems. While the media may be getting better at increasing their portrayal of anti-stigmatising material over recent years, studies suggest that there has been no proportional decrease in the news media's publication of stigmatising articles, suggesting that the media are still a significant source of stigma-relevant misinformation (Thornicroft, Goulden, Shefer, Rhydderch *et al.*, 2013).

1.4.4   Why Does Stigma Matter?

Stigma embraces both prejudicial attitudes and discriminating behaviour towards individuals with mental health problems, and the social effects of this include exclusion, poor social support, poorer subjective quality of life, and low self-esteem (Livingston & Boyd, 2010). As well as its affect on the quality of daily living, stigma also has a detrimental effect on treatment outcomes, and so hinders efficient and effective recovery from mental health problems (Perlick, Rosenheck, Clarkin, Sirey *et al.*, 2001). In particular, self-stigma is correlated with poorer vocational outcomes (employment success) and increased

social isolation (Yanos, Roe & Lysaker, 2010). These factors alone represent significant reasons for attempting to eradicate mental health stigma and ensure that social inclusion is facilitated and recovery can be efficiently achieved.

1.4.5   How Can We Eliminate Stigma?

We now have a good knowledge of what mental health stigma is and how it affects sufferers, both in terms of their role in society and their route to recovery. It is not surprising, then, that attention has most recently turned to developing ways in which stigma and discrimination can be reduced. As we have already described, people tend to hold these negative beliefs about mental health problems regardless of their age, regardless of what knowledge they have of mental health problems, and regardless of whether they know someone who has a mental health problem. The fact that such negative attitudes appear to be so entrenched suggests that campaigns to change these beliefs will have to be multifaceted, will have to do more than just impart knowledge about mental health problems, and will need to challenge existing negative stereotypes especially as they are portrayed in the general media (Pinfold, Toulmin, Thornicroft, Huxley *et al.*, 2003). In the UK, the **Time to Change** campaign is one of the biggest programmes attempting to address mental health stigma and is supported both by charities and mental health service providers (www.time-to-change.org .uk). This programme provides blogs, videos, TV advertisements, and promotional events to help raise awareness of mental health stigma and the detrimental effect this has on mental health sufferers. However, raising awareness of mental health problems simply by providing information about these problems may not be a simple solution – especially since individuals who are most knowledgeable about mental health problems (e.g. psychiatrists, mental health nurses) regularly hold strong

> **Time to Change**   A national UK programme aiming to promote awareness of mental health problems and to combat stigma and discrimination.

FOCUS POINT 1.7

The popular press can often present mental illness in a way which propagates the stigmas attached to mental illness. In September 2003, the ex-heavyweight champion boxer, Frank Bruno was treated for depression at a psychiatric hospital, and the mental health charity Sane (http://www.sane.org.uk) subsequently criticized unsympathetic coverage of his illness in the media.

The BBC News website reported that an early edition of the *Sun* newspaper had the front page headline 'Bonkers Bruno Locked Up', which was later changed to 'Sad Bruno in Mental Home'.

Sane chief executive Marjorie Wallace said: 'It is both an insult to Mr Bruno and damaging to many thousands of people who endure mental illness to label him as "bonkers" or "a nutter" and having to be "put in a mental home".'

Source: http://news.bbc.co.uk/1/hi/uk/3130376.stm.

stigmatising beliefs about mental health themselves! (Schlosberg, 1993; Caldwell & Jorm, 2001). As a consequence, attention has turned towards some methods identified in the social psychology literature for improving intergroup relations and reducing prejudice (Brown, 2010). These methods aim at promoting events to encourage mass participation social contact between individuals with and without mental health problems and to facilitate positive intergroup contact and disclosure of mental health problems (one example is the Time to Change *Roadshow*, which sets up events in prominent town centre locations with high footfall). Analysis of these kinds of intergroup events suggests that they (1) improve attitudes towards people with mental health problems, (2) increase future willingness to disclose mental health problems, and (3) promote behaviours associated with anti-stigma engagement (Evans-Lacko, London, Japhet, Rusch *et al*., 2012; Thornicroft, Brohan, Kassam & Lewis-Holmes, 2008). A fuller evidence-based evaluation of the Time to Change initiative can be found in a special issue dedicated to this topic in the *British Journal of Psychiatry* (vol. 202, issue s55, April 2013).

To read more about facts and myths of mental health statistics go to **http://tinyurl.com/qeoenzd**

SELF-TEST QUESTIONS

- Describe the main characteristics of mental health stigma.
- What kinds of interventions have been developed to try to reduce mental health stigma?

SECTION SUMMARY

1.4 MENTAL HEALTH AND STIGMA

Hopefully, this section has introduced you to the complex nature of mental health stigma and the effects it has on both the daily lives and recovery of individuals suffering from mental health problems. We have discussed how mental health stigma manifests itself, the effect it has on social inclusion, self-esteem, quality of life and recovery. We ended by describing the development of multifaceted programmes to combat mental health stigma and discrimination.

The key points are:

- *Social stigma* is characterized by prejudicial attitudes and discriminating behaviour directed towards individuals with mental health problems.
- Stigmatising beliefs about people with mental health are held by a broad range of individuals within society, including family members, peers, teachers, and members of the medical profession.
- The popular media often play a role in perpetuating stigmatising stereotypes of people with mental health problems.
- Stigma has a detrimental effect on treatment outcome for people with mental health problems.
- Stigma can be addressed by adopting methods described in the social psychology literature for improving intergroup relations.

1.5 CONCEPTS, PARADIGMS AND STIGMA REVISITED

This chapter has introduced the reader to the important concepts and paradigms that surround psychopathology. We have set the scene with a brief history of psychopathology, looking at traditional ways in which people have tried to understand and explain mental health problems and how people with mental health problems have been treated. This has given us a backdrop by which to discuss the many contemporary ways in which psychopathology can be defined and the explanatory paradigms that are used in modern day scientific study of psychopathology. Defining exactly what kinds of symptoms or behaviour should be considered as examples of psychopathology is also problematic. The four types of definition that we discussed (deviation from the statistical norm, deviation from social norms, maladaptive behaviour, and distress and impairment) all have limitations. Some fail to cover examples of behaviour that we would intuitively believe to be representative of mental health problems, others may cover examples that we intuitively feel are not examples of psychopathology, or they may represent forms of categorisation that would lead us to imposing stigmatising labels on people suffering from psychopathology. In practice, classification schemes end up using an amalgamation of these different approaches to definition, and we will discuss some of these issues in Chapter 2. Finally, this chapter has introduced the notion of mental health stigma, described what it is and how it affects individuals with mental health problems. Stigma and discrimination are currently important targets for change, and programmes designed to challenge stigma are a significant part of most mental health services.

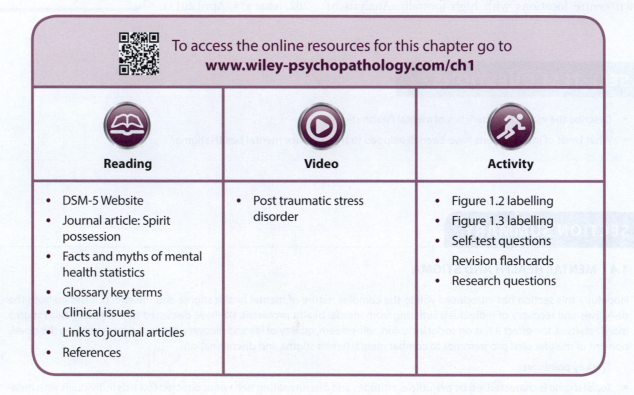

To access the online resources for this chapter go to
www.wiley-psychopathology.com/ch1

Reading

- DSM-5 Website
- Journal article: Spirit possession
- Facts and myths of mental health statistics
- Glossary key terms
- Clinical issues
- Links to journal articles
- References

Video

- Post traumatic stress disorder

Activity

- Figure 1.2 labelling
- Figure 1.3 labelling
- Self-test questions
- Revision flashcards
- Research questions

2 Classification and Assessment in Clinical Psychology

To access the online resources for this chapter go to
www.wiley-psychopathology.com/ch2

ROUTE MAP OF THE CHAPTER

This chapter describes the various ways in which clinicians gather information about a client's problems. This information can then be used to help them classify the person's problems, understand the causes of those problems, and to treat their problems. The chapter begins by discussing classification of mental health problems and in particular the most recent developments found in the classification system DSM-5. We then continue by discussing the benefits and limitations of clinical interviews, psychological tests, biologically based assessments and clinical observation, and introduce the reader to the concepts of reliability and validity. The chapter ends by discussing cultural biases in clinical assessments and the popular use of case formulations as a means of understanding the client's problems and developing a strategy for treatment.

CHAPTER OUTLINE

LEARNING OUTCOMES

When you have completed this chapter, you should be able to:

1. Compare and contrast the pros and cons of DSM as a means of classifying and diagnosing psychopathology.

2. Describe a range of clinical assessment methods and evaluate the benefits and limitations of each.

3. Describe the concepts of reliability and validity as applied to clinical assessment methods.

4. Critically analyse some of the sources of cultural bias that may influence the process of clinical assessment.

5. Explain what a case formulation is, and provide some examples from different psychological approaches.

I saw Mrs Ann Smith, aged 39, in my clinic today. She met criteria for depression, with a 5 month history of low mood. This was triggered by an argument with her husband during the Christmas period. Despite receiving a lot of support from her husband, Ann continues to experience 'black spells', which can go on for 5 days per episode. In March she expressed some suicidal thoughts, which precipitated her referral to psychiatric services.

At interview Ann was well presented, clear and articulate. However, both her eye contact and concentration were poor, and she reported having lost 10lbs in weight. This is the first time she has been referred to psychiatric services, but has been prescribed anti-depressant medication on three previous occasions by her GP. She states that she has experienced low times throughout her life.

She is the middle child of three and stated that she missed a lot of schooling due to the combination of having chronic asthma and an overprotective mother. She left school without qualifications, feeling she has not realized her potential in any area. She

 For a video on depression go to www.wiley-psychopathology.com/video/ch2

married Michael 14 years ago. Owing to his job as a vicar, they entertain frequently. She finds the entertaining difficult. I would welcome your assessment of this case, with a view of taking her on for therapy.

Ann's Story (as told by Blackburn, James & Flitcroft, 2006)

Introduction

Ann has low mood. She has been prescribed antidepressant medication by her GP, who subsequently referred her to a psychiatrist. Following an interview with the psychiatrist, the latter sent the above referral letter on to a clinical psychologist. The referral letter immediately raises a number of questions, the main one being: 'Can we help this person?' But this question itself raises a number of other questions that will need answering. These questions include: (1) Are Ann's symptoms typical of a specific psychological problem (e.g. depression)? (2) Do they meet the criteria for formal diagnosis of a mental health problem? (3) What has led this person to have these problems? (4) Are there specific events that trigger her symptoms? (5) How can we help this person? (6) By what criteria will we judge that we have successfully helped this person? These are all questions that the clinical psychologist must answer by gathering a variety of information about the client, and this information is often gathered using a range of different clinical tools and techniques. Clinical assessment procedures are formal ways of finding answers to these questions, especially: 'Precisely what problems does this person have?' 'What has caused their problems?' 'What is the best way to treat their problems?' 'Did our treatment work?'

Clinicians use a wide range of assessment procedures to gather this information. In many cases, the types of techniques they use will depend on their theoretical orientation to psychopathology. For example, the cognitive-behavioural clinician may want to find out quite different information to a psychodynamic clinician – largely because their conceptions of the causes of psychopathology are different, and because the kinds of therapeutic techniques they employ are different. The cognitive therapist will want to know what kinds of cognitions may trigger symptoms so that these cognitions can be addressed in therapy, whereas a psychodynamic therapist may want to explore the client's history of conflicts and defence mechanisms in order to assess their suitability for psychodynamic therapy (Marzillier & Marzillier, 2008).

In this chapter we will describe the range of assessment techniques available to clinicians that enables them to answer the basic questions about a case that we have just raised. These techniques are an aid to diagnosis, an aid to determining the best intervention for a client, and a help in establishing whether treatment has successfully dealt with the client's symptoms. We will discuss these assessment types individually, but to gain a complete picture of the client's condition, the clinician will usually use a range of different assessments (Meyer, Finn, Eyde, Kay *et al.*, 2001). The chapter begins by discussing the ways in which we currently classify and diagnose mental health problems, since many forms of assessment are structured in ways that enable classification. We then move on to discussing different types of assessment, including the interview, psychological tests, biologically based tests, and observation. Finally we discuss some issues relating to diagnosis and how diagnosis can be associated with the development of a treatment plan (known as formulation).

2.1   CLASSIFYING PSYCHOPATHOLOGY

In Chapter 1 we discussed the difficulties associated with defining what is and is not a mental health problem. Given the inherent difficulties surrounding this question you may be saying to yourself 'why try to define and classify psychopathology at all?' Nevertheless, there are some good reasons for wanting to do this. Firstly, as a social and biological science, psychology will want to try to understand the causes of mental health problems. This is important so that we can develop effective treatments that address the root causes of psychopathology and also develop prevention strategies designed to reduce the risk of individuals developing symptoms of psychopathology. Most sciences use classification to group phenomena into categories according to their similarities. Categorisation and classification is thus an important first stage in the pursuit of knowledge about causes and aetiology, and it would be difficult to discuss aetiology in this book if there were not some form of classification that enabled us to understand how different causes relate to different symptoms. Secondly, classification is necessary if we are to effectively organize services and support for sufferers. For example, the needs of individuals with intellectual disabilities, major depression, an anxiety-based

disorder or substance dependency are all very different and require different approaches and different means of support and intervention. We need to have some basis for differentiating between these different kinds of problems and determining the different kinds of support that each might need, and classification systems provide a common language for reporting and monitoring mental health problems which allows the world to share and compare data in a consistent way. Thirdly, how do we decide if our interventions and support for sufferers have been effective unless we have some objective way of defining what constitutes the symptoms of psychopathology? One important and objective way of determining whether an individual is responding to treatment is to see if there has been any improvement in objectively defined and measurable symptoms. Classification systems based on clusters of symptoms may help us to do this. Finally, whether we like it or not, modern day society requires that we assess and classify people for a number of reasons, and this is also the case with psychopathology. For example, we might want to know whether a person is psychologically fit to stand trial for a criminal offence, whether a child has disabilities that will require special educational needs, or whether financial compensation or damages should be awarded to an individual because of psychological symptoms caused by the actions of others. All of these requirements of modern society necessitate a form of assessment and classification that can adequately and objectively deal with these kinds of issues.

2.1.1   *The Development of Classification Systems*

Arguably the first person to develop a comprehensive classification system for psychopathology was the German psychiatrist Emil Kraepelin (1883–1923). He suggested that psychopathology, like physical illness, could be classified into different and separate pathologies, each of which had a different cause and could be described by a distinct set of symptoms that he called a **syndrome**. Kraepelin's work provided some hope that mental illness could be described and successfully treated in much the same way as other medical illnesses.

> **syndrome** A distinct set of symptoms.

Following on from Kraepelin's scheme, the first extensive system for classifying psychopathology was developed by the World Health Organisation (WHO), which added psychological disorders to the **International List of Causes of Death (ICD)** in 1939.

> **International List of Causes of Death (ICD)** The international standard diagnostic classification developed by the World Health Organisation (WHO).

Despite this development, the mental disorders section in the ICD was not widely accepted, and in 1952 the **American Psychiatric Association (APA)** published its first **Diagnostic and Statistical Manual (DSM)**. In 1968 the APA produced a second version of its diagnostic manual (DSM-II) and in 1969 the WHO published a new classification system, which was more widely accepted, while in the UK a glossary of definitions was produced to accompany the WHO system (General Register Office, 1968). However, the WHO system was simply a listing of diagnostic categories, and while DSM-II and the British *Glossary of mental disorders* provided more information on which to base diagnoses, the actual practice of diagnosing psychopathology varied widely. However, in 1980, the APA produced a substantially revised and expanded DSM-III which has come to be accepted as the most influential diagnostic system. The most recent version that is used in this book is DSM-5, which was published in 2013. The ICD system is currently in its tenth edition (ICD-10), with ICD-11 under development and due to be published in 2015. Most revisions of the DSM have been coordinated with the ICD to ensure some consistency of diagnosis across systems. For convenience and consistency, we will be using only the DSM diagnostic system in this book (see Cooper, 1994, for a guide to the ICD-10 classification system, and http://www.who.int/classifications/icd/revision/en/index.html for details of the most recent ICD revision).

> **Diagnostic and Statistical Manual (DSM)** First published in 1952 by the American Psychiatric Association (APA), the DSM extended the World Health Organisation's (WHO) *International List of Causes of Death* (ICD) classification system to include a more widely accepted section on mental disorders.

2.1.2   DSM-5

Defining and diagnosing psychopathology

Before attempting to classify psychopathology it was necessary for DSM to define what it considers to be a mental disorder. As we have already seen in Chapter 1 this is not a simple matter. However, DSM does make some attempt to rule out behaviours that are simply socially deviant as examples of psychopathology and puts the emphasis on distress and disability as important defining characteristics. Distress relates to the chronic experience of pain or distressing emotions, and disability refers to the fact that distress can lead to impairment in one or more important areas of functioning, such as education, employment, and dealing with family and social responsibilities. It is also important to try to define at this point what exactly the DSM system is designed to do. Wakefield (1997) argues that DSM has

four basic objectives: (1) it must provide necessary and sufficient criteria for correct differential diagnosis, (2) it should provide a means of distinguishing 'true' psychopathology (in the medical or dysfunctional sense) from non-disordered human conditions that are often labelled as everyday 'problems in living', (3) it should provide diagnostic criteria in a way that allows them to be applied systematically by different clinicians in different settings, and (4) the diagnostic criteria it provides should be theoretically neutral, in the sense that they do not favour one theoretical approach to psychopathology over another. Whether DSM can achieve these four objectives will be to some extent the measure of its success. The breakdown of the chapters in DSM-5 is shown in Table 2.1.

TABLE 2.1 *Chapters in DSM-5*

Neurodevelopmental Disorders
Schizophrenia Spectrum and Other Psychotic Disorders
Bipolar & Related Disorders
Depressive Disorders
Anxiety Disorders
Obsessive-Compulsive and Related Disorders
Trauma- and Stressor-Related Disorders
Dissociative Disorders
Somatic Symptom Disorders
Feeding and Eating Disorders
Elimination Disorders
Sleep–Wake Disorders
Sexual Dysfunctions
Gender Dysphoria
Disruptive, Impulse Control and Conduct Disorders
Substance-Related and Addictive Disorders
Neurocognitive Disorders
Personality Disorders
Paraphilic Disorders
Other Disorders

The number of total disorders in DSM-5 has not increased significantly, but some disorders have now had their importance recognized by being allocated separate chapter headings (e.g. obsessive compulsive disorder). The chapter on neurodevelopmental disorders is a new heading containing autism spectrum disorders, intellectual development disorder, and attention/hyperactivity disorder (ADHD). The chapter on substance use and addictive behaviours now includes gambling disorder. The importance of both bipolar disorder and depressive disorders is recognized by them being allocated to separate chapters.

DSM classification systems also provide the following information: (1) *essential features* of the disorder (those that 'define' the disorder and allow for consistent diagnosis across clinicians), (2) *associated features* (i.e. those that are usually, but not always, present), (3) *diagnostic criteria* (a list of symptoms that must be present for the patient to be given this diagnostic label), and (4) information on *differential diagnosis* (i.e. information on how to differentiate this disorder from other, similar disorders). Finally, as we mentioned earlier, an important feature of DSM is that it avoids any suggestion about the cause of a disorder unless the cause has been definitely established. This means that diagnosis is made almost entirely on the basis of observable behavioural symptoms rather than any supposition about the underlying cause of the symptoms.

General problems with classification

While classification systems such as DSM attempt to provide an objective and reliable set of criteria by which psychopathology symptoms can be diagnosed, they are in many senses imperfect.

Firstly, we have already mentioned that DSM does not classify psychopathology according to its causes, but does so merely on the basis of symptoms. This can be problematic in a number of different ways. For example, psychopathologies that look the same on the surface may have different causes, and as a consequence require different forms of treatment. Also, diagnosis on the basis of symptoms gives the illusion of explanation, when it is nothing more than a re-description of the symptoms (Carson, 1996). So, to say that 'she hears voices because she has schizophrenia' sounds like an explanation, but, within DSM, schizophrenia is merely a collective term for the defining symptoms.

Secondly, simply using DSM criteria to label people with a disorder can be stigmatising and harmful. We saw in Chapter 1 that individuals with a mental health diagnosis tend to be viewed and treated differently within society. In addition, diagnostic labels actually encourage individuals to adopt a 'sick' role and can result in people adopting a long-term role as an individual with what they perceive as a debilitating illness (Scheff, 1975).

Thirdly, DSM diagnostic classification tends to define disorders as *discrete entities* (i.e. after being assessed, you will either be diagnosed with a disorder or you will not). However, much recent evidence has begun to suggest that psychopathology may be *dimensional* rather than discrete (Krueger & Piasecki, 2002). That is, symptoms diagnosed as a disorder may just be more extreme versions of everyday behaviour. For example, at times we all worry about our own life problems – some more than others. In extreme cases worry can become so regular and persistent that it will interfere with our daily living and may meet DSM criteria for diagnosis as a disorder (e.g. generalized anxiety disorder, GAD; see Chapter 6). However, chronic worrying and GAD symptoms appear to be dimensional, and range in frequency and intensity across the general population (Niles, Lebeau, Liao, Glenn & Craske, 2012). In such circumstances, the cut off point for defining an activity such as worrying as a disorder becomes relatively arbitrary. DSM had traditionally attempted to deal with this problem by adding a clinical significance criterion to many diagnostic categories which required that symptoms cause 'significant distress or impairment in social, occupational, or other important areas of functioning' (Spitzer & Wakefield, 1999), and the purpose of this was to try and differentiate symptoms that reflect normal reactions to stress that the individual may be able to cope with from those that may require intervention and treatment to restore functioning. However, with growing evidence that psychopathology symptoms are on a dimension, DSM-5 has included simple dimensional measures of disorder severity to accompany more specific diagnostic criteria. For example, in the case of GAD, dimensional measures such as per cent of the day spent worrying can provide an indication of symptom severity on a dimensional scale.

Fourthly, DSM conceptualizes psychopathology as a collection of hundreds of distinct categories of disorders, but what happens in practice provides quite a different picture. For example, the discrete, differentially defined disorders listed in DSM regularly co-occur. This is known as **comorbidity**, where an individual client will often be diagnosed with two or more distinct disorders (e.g. an anxiety disorder such as obsessive compulsive disorder and major depression). What is interesting is that comorbidity is so common that it is the norm rather than the exception. For example, surveys suggest that up to 79 per cent of individuals diagnosed with a disorder at some point during their lifetime will have a history of more than one disorder (Kessler, McGonagle, Zhao, Nelson *et al.*, 1994). The frequency of comorbidity suggests that most disorders as defined by DSM may indeed not be independent discrete disorders, but may represent symptoms of either **hybrid disorders** (e.g. a disorder that contains elements of a number of different disorders) or a more

comorbidity The co-occurrence of two or more distinct psychological disorders.

hybrid disorders Disorders that contain elements of a number of different disorders.

disorder spectrum The frequency of comorbidity suggests that most disorders as defined by DSM may indeed not be independent discrete disorders, but may represent symptoms of a disorder spectrum that represents a higher-order categorical class of symptoms.

mixed anxiety-depressive disorder An example of a hybrid disorder whereby people exhibit symptoms of both anxiety and depression, yet do not meet the threshold for either an anxiety or a depression diagnosis.

broad ranging **syndrome** or **disorder spectrum** that represents a higher order categorical class of symptoms (Krueger, Watson & Barlow, 2005; Widiger & Samuel, 2005). An example of a hybrid disorder is **mixed anxiety-depressive disorder**, and many people exhibit symptoms of both anxiety and depression, yet do not meet the threshold for either an anxiety or a depression diagnosis (Barlow & Campbell, 2000). Examples such as this suggest that because DSM defines disorders as numerous individual discrete entities, it fails to recognize when combinations of discrete symptoms may each not reach a level significant enough for diagnosis, but may collectively be causing significant distress. There is also a broader theoretical implication to the fact that comorbidity is so common, and this is that psychopathology may occur in a spectrum that has a hierarchical structure rather than consisting merely of numerous discrete disorders. For example, Watson (2005) argues that anxiety and depression (which are both diagnosed as separate disorders in DSM-5) may both be members of a larger spectrum of emotional disorders. This is based on the facts that (1) 58 per cent of individuals with major depression also meet DSM criteria for a comorbid anxiety

disorder (Kessler, Nelson, McGonagle, Liu, Schwartz *et al.*, 1996), (2) various anxiety disorders are highly comorbid with each other (Brown, Campbell, Lehman, Grisham & Mancill, 2001), and (3) depression and anxiety are together both highly comorbid with other psychopathologies, such as substance abuse, eating disorders, somatoform disorders and personality disorders (Mineka, Watson & Clark, 1998; Widiger & Clark, 2000). Figure 2.1 provides a schematic representation of this proposed spectrum of emotional disorders, indicating its hierarchical structure and showing how individual disorders defined in DSM may only represent the bottom level of this hierarchy. Defining psychopathology in such hierarchical structures rather than defining them as discrete independent entities has the benefit of explaining and predicting comorbidity and it begins to provide some theoretical insight into how different symptoms may be related.

One final problem with DSM is that it can be conceived as a 'hodgepodge' collection of disorders, that have been developed and refined in a piecemeal way across a number of revisions (see Focus Point 2.1) – and this makes it almost impossible to frame a definition of what a mental health problem actually is. Frances & Widiger (2012) characterize this 'hodgepodge' view in the following quote:

The current list of mental disorders certainly constitutes a hodgepodge collection. Some describe short-term states, others life-long personality. Some reflect

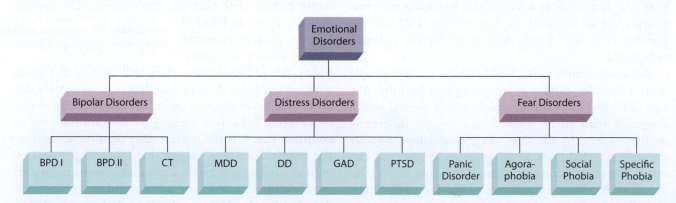

FIGURE 2.1 *More detailed research on anxiety and depressive disorders can help reveal the way in which individual disorders are related and why many diagnosable disorders are frequently comorbid. This figure shows a proposed spectrum of emotional disorders which indicates how anxiety and depression may be related. For example, the fact that MDD and GAD are both classified as 'distress disorders' provides some indication of why these two apparent different DSM disorders are frequently comorbid. Only the bottom line of the figure represents the individual disorders defined in DSM-5 (after Watson, 2005). BPD I = bipolar I disorder; BPD II = bipolar II disorder; CT = cyclothymia; MDD = major depressive disorder; DD = dysthymic disorder; GAD = generalized anxiety disorder; PTSD = post-traumatic stress disorder.*

Source: Watson, D. (2005). Rethinking the mood and anxiety disorders: A quantitative hierarchical model for DSM-V. *Journal of Abnormal Psychology*, 114, 522–536. American Psychological Association. Reprinted with permission

inner misery, others bad behaviour. Some represent problems rarely or never seen in normals, others are just slight accentuations of the everyday. Some reflect too little self-control, others too much. Some are quite intrinsic to the individual; others are defined against varying and changing cultural mores and stressors. Some begin in infancy, others in old age. Some affect primarily thought; others emotions, behaviors, or interpersonal relations; and there are complex combinations of all these. Some seem more biological, others more psychological.

—(*Frances & Widiger, 2012, p. 111*)

While DSM is not ideal, it is the most comprehensive classification system we have available, and while we have just listed a number of criticisms of DSM we must also remember that classification in and of itself does also have some advantages (see p. 37).

Changes in DSM-5

Published in 2013, DSM-5 arguably represents the most comprehensive revision of the DSM so far, and it has involved many years of deliberation and field trials to determine what changes to mental health classification and diagnosis are essential and empirically justifiable. The main changes between DSM-5 and its predecessor (DSM-IV-TR) are listed in Table 2.2. Firstly, previous versions of DSM placed mental health problems on a number of different axes representing clinical disorders (Axis I), developmental and personality disorders (Axis II), or general medical conditions (Axis III). This multiaxial system has been scrapped – largely because there was not enough evidence to justify the differences between them. Instead, in DSM-5, clinicians will be encouraged to rate severity of symptoms along continuums developed for each disorder. Secondly, the importance of some disorder categories has been recognized either by allocating them to their own chapter or by recognising them as new individual diagnostic categories. For example, obsessive compulsive disorder (OCD) is recognized as a significant mental health problem by being allocated its own chapter in DSM-5, and

To read more about DSM-5 go to
http://tinyurl.com/yzsclmj

CRITICISMS OF THE DSM DEVELOPMENT PROCESS

DSM regularly undergoes an intensive revision process to take account of new research on mental health problems and to refine the diagnostic categories from earlier versions of the system. One would assume that this would be a deliberate and objective process that could only further our understanding of psychopathology, and that is certainly the intention of the majority of those involved. However, at least some people argue that the process of developing a classification system such as DSM can never be entirely objective, free from bias, or free from corporate or political interests. Allen Frances and Thomas Widiger were two individuals who were prominent in the development of the fourth edition of the DSM, and they have written a fascinating account of the lessons they believe should be learned from previous attempts to revise and develop mental health classification systems (Frances & Widiger, 2012). They make the following points:

1. Just as the number of mental health clinicians grows, so too will the number of life conditions that work their way into becoming disorders. This is because the proliferation of diagnostic categories tends to follow practice rather than guide it.

2. Because we know very little about the true causes of mental health problems, it is easier and simpler to proliferate multiple categories of disorder based on relatively small differences in descriptions of symptoms.

3. Most experts involved in developing DSM are primarily worried about false negatives (i.e. the missed diagnosis or patient who doesn't fit neatly into the existing categorisations), and this leads to either more inclusive diagnostic criteria or even more diagnostic categories. Unfortunately, experts are relatively indifferent to false positives (patients who receive unnecessary diagnosis, treatment, and stigma) and so are less likely to be concerned about over-diagnosis.

4. Political and economic factors have also shaped the 'medical model' view of psychopathology on which DSM is based, and also contributed to the establishment and proliferation of diagnostic categories. For example, the pharmaceutical industry benefits significantly from the sale of medications for mental health problems, and its profits will be dependent on both (1) conceptions of mental health based on a medical model that implies a medical solution, and (2) a diagnostic system that will err towards over-diagnosis rather than under-diagnosis (see Pilecki, Clegg & McKay, 2011).

TABLE 2.2 *Summary of changes in DSM-5*

Axes I, II and II will be combined
– Disorders no longer categorized as acute or life-long.

New chapters for OCD and Trauma and Stress-Related Disorders
– Confirms the growing importance of these types of disorder as possibly independent of other anxiety-based problems.

Autism Spectrum Disorder will incorporate many previously separate labels (e.g. Asperger's disorder).

New Disruptive Mood Dysregulation Disorder
– Diagnoses children with persistent irritability.

Binge Eating Disorder, Hoarding Disorder and Skin-Picking Disorder included
– All recognized as new independent disorder categories.

Personality Disorders retained with added dimensional scales.

PTSD included in new chapter on stress
– Emphasizes the importance of trauma-related disorders.

Removal of bereavement exclusion in Major Depression
– Allows bereavement to be included as a contributor to Major Depression.

Substance use disorder combines substance abuse and substance dependence.

See text for further elaboration.

new diagnostic categories within this chapter include 'Hoarding disorder' (see Chapter 6) and 'Excoriation disorder' (skin-picking disorder). Similarly, DSM-5 has a new chapter, 'Trauma and stress-related disorders', that now includes post-traumatic stress disorder (PTSD). DSM-5 focuses more on the behavioural symptoms that accompany PTSD and proposes four distinct diagnostic clusters instead of the previous three. Thirdly, major changes have been made to the criteria for diagnosing autistic spectrum disorder (ASD), specific learning disorders, and substance use disorders. Autistic spectrum disorder has become a diagnostic label that will incorporate many previous separate labels (e.g. Asperger's syndrome, childhood disintegrative disorder, pervasive developmental disorder) in an attempt to provide more consistent and accurate diagnosis for children with autism (see Chapter 17). DSM-5 will retain the categorical model for personality disorders outlined in DSM-IV-TR, but rating scales are provided to assess how well an individual's symptoms fit within these different types (Chapter 12). The new specific learning disorder category is broadened to represent distinct disorders which interfere with the acquisition and use of one or

more of a number of academic skills, including oral language, reading, written language or mathematics (Chapter 17), and the new substance use disorder category will combine the previous DSM-IV-TR categories of substance abuse and substance dependence into one overarching disorder. Some other important changes include (1) the elevation of binge-eating disorder from an appendix to a recognized diagnostic category, (2) disruptive mood regulation disorder as a new category for diagnosing children who exhibit persistent irritability and behavioural outbursts, and (3) the removal of the 'bereavement exclusion' from the diagnosis of major depression (which means that depressive symptoms lasting less than 2 months following the death of a loved one can be included amongst the criteria for diagnosing major depression, and reflects the recognition that bereavement is a severe psychological stressor that can precipitate major depression).

Criticisms of changes in DSM-5

While these most recent changes to the DSM have been extensively discussed and researched, many of the revisions have been received critically, and it is worth discussing some of these criticisms because they provide an insight into the difficulties of developing a mental disorders classification system that is fair and objective.

For a video on criticism of the changes to DSM-5 go to **www.wiley-psychopathology.com/video/ch2**

Firstly, many of the diagnostic changes will reduce the number of criteria necessary to establish a diagnosis. This is the case with attenuated psychosis syndrome, major depression, and generalized anxiety disorder, and this runs the risk of increasing the number of people that are likely to be diagnosed with common mental health problems such as anxiety and depression. It is a debatable point whether increases in the number of diagnosed cases is a good or a bad thing, but it is likely to have the effects of 'medicalising' many everyday emotional experiences (such as 'grief' following a bereavement, or worry following a stressful life event), and creating 'false-positive' epidemics (Frances, 2010; Wakefield, 2013).

Secondly, DSM-5 has introduced disorder categories that are designed to identify populations that are at risk for future mental health problems, and these include mild neurocognitive disorder (which would diagnose cognitive decline in the elderly) and **attenuated psychosis syndrome**

attenuated psychosis syndrome DSM-5 has introduced disorder categories that are designed to identify populations that are at risk for future mental health problems. Attenuated Psychosis Syndrome is seen as a potential precursor to psychotic episodes.

(seen as a potential precursor to psychotic episodes). Once again, these initiatives run the risk of medicalising states that are not yet full-blown disorders, and could facilitate the diagnosis of normal developmental processes as psychological disorders.

Thirdly, there are concerns that changes in diagnostic criteria will result in lowered rates of diagnosis for some particularly vulnerable populations. For example, applying the DSM-5 criteria for autistic spectrum disorder to samples of children with DSM-IV-TR diagnoses that would no longer be available in DSM-5 suggested that 9 per cent of this latter group would lose their autism diagnosis with the introduction of the new DSM-5 criteria (Huerta, Bishop, Duncan, Hus & Lord, 2012). Similar concerns have been voiced about changes to **specific learning disabilities** diagnostic criteria in DSM-5, and the possibility that deletion of the term **dyslexia** as a diagnostic label will disadvantage individuals with specific phonologically based, developmental reading disabilities.

> **specific learning disabilities** Disorders such as dyslexia and communication disabilities.

> **dyslexia** A persistent, chronic learning disability in which there are developmental deficits in spelling, reading and writing abilities.

Finally, two enduring criticisms of DSM generally that have continued to be fired specifically at DSM-5 have been that (1) DSM-5 has continued the process of attempting to align its diagnostic criteria with developments and knowledge from neuroscience (Regier, Narrow, Kuhl & Kupfer, 2011) when there is in fact very little new evidence from neuroscience that helps define specific mental health problems, and (2) most mental health problems (and psychological distress generally) are now viewed as dimensional, so

> To read about the proposed DSM-5 changes, which continue to spark controversy, go to
> **http://tinyurl.com/pf4od43**

any criteria defining a diagnostic cut-off point will be entirely arbitrary. DSM-5 has attempted to recognize the importance of the dimensionality of symptoms by introducing dimensional severity rating scales for individual disorders. But as we have seen from the discussion above, each iteration change in DSM diagnostic criteria changes the number and range of people who will receive a diagnosis, and this makes it increasingly hard to accept diagnostic categories as valid constructs (see e.g. Kendler, Kupfer, Narrow, Phillips & Fawcett, 2009).

2.1.3   Conclusions

Despite its conceptual difficulties and its many critics, DSM is still the most widely adopted classification and diagnostic system for mental health problems. Such a system is needed for a number of reasons, including determining the allocation of resources and support for mental health problems, for circumstances that require a legal definition of mental health problems, and to provide a common language that allows the world to share and compare data on mental health problems. Having said this, there are still many significant problems associated with DSM, and diagnosing and labelling people with specific psychological disorders raises other issues to do with stigma and discrimination. Indeed, we should be clear that diagnostic systems are not a necessary requirement for helping people with mental health problems to recover, and many clinical psychologists prefer not to use diagnostic systems such as DSM-5, but instead prefer to treat each client as someone with a unique mental health problem that can best be described and treated using other means such as case formulation (see section 2.3 for a fuller description and examples of case formulation).

SELF-TEST QUESTIONS

- Can you briefly describe the history of the development of psychopathology classification systems?
- What is the DSM classification system primarily designed to do?
- DSM is not an ideal classification system. Can you describe at least four problems associated with this method of classification?
- What are the main changes that were implemented in DSM-5?

SECTION SUMMARY

2.1 CLASSIFYING PSYCHOPATHOLOGY

- The two most influential classification systems are the American Psychiatric Association (APA) *Diagnostic and Statistical Manual* and the World Health Organisation (WHO) *International List of Causes of Death* (ICD).

- Currently, the most widely adopted classification system is DSM-5.

2.2 METHODS OF ASSESSMENT

This section describes in some detail a range of assessment tools that clinical psychologists can use to aid diagnosis, determine the best forms of intervention for an individual's problems, and assess their progress towards recovery. But first, it is important to be sure that a method of assessment is both reliable and valid.

2.2.1   The Reliability and Validity of Assessment Methods

In order for assessment methods to provide objective information about clients we need to be sure about two things. First, we need to be sure that the method has high **reliability**; that is, that the method will provide the same result when used by different clinicians on different occasions. Second, we also need to be sure that the assessment has **validity**; that is, that it actually does measure what it claims to measure (e.g. if it is a test measuring anxiety, then scores on the test should correlate well with other ways of measuring anxiety).

> **reliability** The extent that an assessment method will still provide the same result when used by different clinicians on different occasions.

> **validity** The extent that an assessment method actually does measure what it claims to be measuring.

Reliability
Reliability refers to how consistently an assessment method will produce the same results, and reliability can be affected by a number of different factors. First, **test–retest reliability** refers to the extent

> **test–retest reliability** The extent that a test will produce roughly similar results when the test is given to the same person several weeks or even months apart (as long as no treatments or interventions have occurred in between).

to which the test will produce roughly similar results when the test is given to the same person several weeks or even months apart (as long as no treatments or interventions have occurred in between). Most psychological tests are based on the assumption that most traits and personal characteristics are relatively stable and can be reliably measured (see p. 47). If the test has high test–retest reliability, then when an individual is given the test on two separate occasions, the two scores should be highly correlated.

Second, **inter-rater reliability** refers to the degree to which two independent clinicians will actually agree when interpreting or scoring a particular test. Most highly structured tests, such as personality inventories, will have high inter-rater reliability because the scoring system is clearly defined and there is little room for individual clinician judgements when interpreting the test. However, some other tests have much lower inter-rater reliability, especially where scoring schemes are not rigidly defined, and projective tests are one example of this (see pp. 50–53).

> **inter-rater reliability** The degree to which two independent clinicians or researchers actually agree when interpreting or scoring a particular test.

Third, many assessment tests have multiple items (e.g. personality and trait inventories) and internal consistency within such tests is important. **Internal consistency** refers to the extent to which all the items in the test consistently relate to each other. For example, if there are 20 items in a test, then we would expect scores on each of those 20 items to correlate highly with each other. If one item doesn't correlate highly with the others, then it may lower the internal consistency of the test. The internal consistency of a questionnaire or inventory can usually be assessed by using a statistical test called **Cronbach's α**, and this test will also indicate whether any individual item in the test is significantly reducing the internal consistency of the test (Field, 2013a, pp. 708–710).

> **internal consistency** The extent to which all the items in a test consistently relate to one another.

> **Cronbach's α** Statistical test used to assess the internal consistency of a questionnaire or inventory.

Validity

It is important to be sure that an assessment method actually measures what it claims to be measuring, and this is covered by the concept of test validity. However, validity is a complex concept, and we will begin by discussing some of the more obvious issues surrounding this problem.

To determine whether a test actually measures what it claims to measure, we need to establish the **concurrent validity** of the test. That is, we need to see if scores on that test correlate highly with scores from other types of assessment that we know also measure that attribute. For example, the Spider Phobia Questionnaire (SPQ) purports to be a measure of the spider phobic's anxious reaction to spiders (Watts & Sharrock, 1984), but in order to establish the concurrent validity of this questionnaire, we might need to be sure that scores actually correlate highly with other measures of spider fear such as the magnitude of physiological anxiety measures taken while the individual is viewing a spider.

A particular assessment method may appear to be valid simply because it has questions which intuitively seem relevant to the trait or characteristic being measured. This is known as **face validity**, but just because a test has items that seem intuitively sensible does not mean that the test is a valid measure of what it claims to be. For example, a questionnaire measuring health anxiety may ask about how frequently the respondent visits a doctor. Although this would be a characteristic of health anxiety, it is also a characteristic of individuals who are genuinely ill or have chronic health problems.

For an assessment method to have high **predictive validity** it must be able to help the clinician to predict future behaviour and future symptoms, and so be valuable enough to help with the planning of care, support or treatment for that individual. For example, a good measure of depression would predict that certain types of antidepressant medication will help to alleviate the symptoms. Some assessment measures are predictive in the sense that they help us to understand the kinds of factors that might pose as risk factors for subsequent psychopathology. For example, assessments that allow us to gather

> **concurrent validity** A measure of how highly correlated scores of one test are with scores from other types of assessment that we know also measure that attribute.

> **face validity** The idea that a particular assessment method may appear to be valid simply because it has questions which intuitively seem relevant to the trait or characteristic being measured.

> **predictive validity** The degree to which an assessment method is able to help the clinician predict future behaviour and future symptoms.

reliable information about childhood abuse and neglect will indicate that such individuals are likely to suffer a range of possible psychopathologies in later life (see Table 16.1).

Finally, **construct validity** is also an important concept in clinical assessment. A construct is a hypothetical or inferred attribute that may not be directly observable or directly measurable. Hypothetical constructs are used frequently in the study of psychopathology to help understand some of the cognitive factors that may cause or maintain mental health problems, and so being able to measure them is a useful tool in diagnosis and subsequent treatment. For example, individuals with obsessive compulsive disorder (OCD) tend to have inflated conceptions of their own responsibility for preventing harm, and this inflated responsibility appears to be an important vulnerability factor in developing OCD (Salkovskis, 1985; Rachman, 1998; see Chapter 4). However, inflated responsibility is not directly observable, but has to be inferred from indirect measures of the individual's behaviour, and so questionnaires such as the Obsessive Beliefs Questionnaire (OBQ) have been developed to measure beliefs about inflated responsibility (see p. 49). The more independent evidence that can be gathered to show that a measure of a construct like inflated responsibility is related to other similar measures (e.g. compulsive perseveration at checking tasks, or higher scores in groups diagnosed with OCD than non-clinical control participants), the greater the construct validity of the measure.

> **construct validity** Independent evidence showing that a measure of a construct is related to other similar measures.

2.2.2 Clinical Interviews

The nature of clinical interviews

We have all probably been interviewed at some point in our lives. This may be for a job, a place at university, or by a doctor enquiring about symptoms of an illness. An interview usually represents an informal, relatively unstructured conversation between two or more people, the purpose of which is to gather some information about one or more of those people in the interview. The clinical interview is probably the first form of contact that a client will have with a clinician, and the clinical psychologist will usually be trying to gain a broad insight into the client and their problems. Questions may relate to the nature of

For a video on anxiety go to www.wiley-psychopathology.com/video/ch2

the symptoms the client experiences, their past history, and their current living and working circumstances. The type of questions that will be asked in a clinical interview will depend very much on the theoretical orientation of the clinician. For example, psychodynamic clinicians are likely to want to ask questions about the client's childhood history, their memories of past events, and to take note of any strong emotional responses that may indicate unconscious processes (see Chapter 1). In contrast, the behavioural interviewer will want to explore any relationships between the client's symptoms and environmental events, such as the consequences of symptoms that may reinforce them. Finally, the cognitive clinician will want to try to discover whether the client holds any assumptions or beliefs that may maintain or influence their problems.

In general, those conducting clinical interviews must be skilful in guiding the client towards revealing the kinds of information they are looking for. They must be able to establish a good rapport with the client, they must gain their trust, they must be able to convince the client of the value of the theoretical approach they are taking, and in most cases they must be able to empathize with their clients in order to encourage them to elaborate on their concerns and to provide information that they may otherwise be reluctant to give. The clinical interviewer can encounter a number of difficulties when conducting an interview and these will often require all their experience and skill to overcome. For example, (1) many clients will want to withhold information about themselves, especially if it involves painful or embarrassing memories, or if the information concerns illegal or unsocial activities (such as illegal drug use or illegal sexual activities), and (2) clients may well have poor self-knowledge, and so be unable to answer questions accurately or with any real insight into why they behave or feel the way they do. It is the skilled interviewer's job to find ways to deal with these problems and to reveal the reliable information that they need to form a diagnosis, to understand the causes of the client's problems, and to formulate a treatment programme.

Structured interviews

The clinician can also use the interview method to acquire the kinds of standardized information they need to make a diagnosis or to construct a case formulation (see section 2.3), but this requires that they conduct the interview in a structured way. The normal clinical interview would probably contain many open questions such as 'Tell me something about yourself and what you do', and the direction of the interview will be to some extent determined by the client's responses to these open questions. However, structured interviews can be used to enable the clinician to make decisions about diagnosis and functioning. One

such **structured interview** technique is known as the **Structured Clinical Interview for DSM-IV-TR (SCID)** (Spitzer, Gibbon & Williams, 1986), which can be used for determining diagnoses. The SCID is a branching, structured interview in which the client's response to one question will determine the next question to be asked. This enables the clinician to establish the main symptoms exhibited by a client, their severity (on a scale of 1 to 3), and whether a combination of these symptoms and severity meet DSM criteria for a particular disorder. The SCID has been shown to provide highly reliable diagnoses for many disorders (Segal, Herson & Van Hasselt, 1994; Lobbestael, Leurgans & Arntz, 2011), with one study indicating 85.7 per cent agreement on diagnosis between different clinicians using the SCID (Miller, Dasher, Collins, Griffiths & Brown, 2001).

> **structured interview** An interview in which questions to be asked, their sequence and detailed information to be gathered are all predetermined.

> **Structured Clinical Interview for DSM-IV-TR (SCID)** A branching, structured interview in which the client's response to one question will determine the next question to be asked.

Structured interviews can also be used to determine overall levels of psychological and intellectual functioning, especially in older people who may be suffering from degenerative disorders such as dementia. One such structured interview is the Mini Mental State Examination (MMSE), which is a structured test that takes 10 minutes to administer and can provide reliable information on the client's overall levels of cognitive and mental functioning. A fuller description of this structured interview is given in Chapter 15 (see Focus Point 15.2).

Limitations of the clinical interview

The clinical interview is usually a good way of beginning the process of assessment, and it can provide a range of useful information for the clinician. However, there are limitations to this method. First, the reliability of clinical interviews is probably quite low. That is, no matter how skilled they may be, two different clinicians are quite likely to end up with rather different information from an **unstructured interview**. For example, clients are likely to give different information to an interviewer who is 'cold' and unresponsive than to one who is 'warm' and supportive (Eisenthal, Koopman & Lazare, 1983), and a teenage client is likely to respond differently to a young interviewer who is dressed casually than to an older interviewer who is dressed formally. There is also significant evidence that an interviewer's race and sex will influence a client's responses (Paurohit, Dowd & Cottingham, 1982). As we have already mentioned, many clients may have quite poor self-awareness, so only

> **unstructured interview** A free-flowing interview in which questions to be asked, their sequence and detailed information to be gathered are not predetermined.

a skilled interviewer will be able to glean the information they require by inferring information from the client's responses. Interviewers are also prone to biases that may affect the conclusions they draw from an interview. For example, they may rely too heavily on first impressions (the primacy effect), or give priority only to negative information (Meehl, 1996), and may be influenced by irrelevant details such as the client's biological sex, race, skin colour or sexual orientation. Finally, there are some psychological disorders in which sufferers may intentionally mislead the interviewer or lie to them, and this can mean that the client can manipulate the interview or deliberately provide misleading information. This can often occur with personality disorders, such as borderline personality disorder or antisocial personality disorder, or in the case of sexual disorders such as paedophilia (see Chapters 11 and 12).

2.2.3 Psychological Tests

Psychological tests represent highly structured ways of gathering information about an individual. They usually take the form of a written questionnaire in which the client has to respond to a series of questions or stimuli. However, they can be given verbally by the clinician or completed on a computer. The psychological test is one of the most common forms of assessment in clinical psychology and it is considerably more structured than the interview method. Psychological tests have a number of advantages as methods of assessment: (1) they usually assess the client on one or more specific characteristics or traits (e.g. levels of anxiety, depression, IQ, cognitive functioning, or individual psychopathology traits such as hypochondriasis, paranoia, conversion hysteria, and suchlike); (2) they will usually (but not always) have very rigid response requirements so that the questions can be scored according to a pre-conceived scoring system. Table 2.3 provides an example of the question format for a measure of trait anxiety – the State-Trait Anxiety Inventory (STAI) (Spielberger, Gorsuch, Lushene, Vagg & Jacobs, 1983) – and this is a test format common to many psychometric tests; (3) once data from these tests have been collected from large numbers of participants, statistical norms for the tests can be established. This is known as **standardisation**, and allows the clinician to see where an individual client's score on the test falls in relation to the normal distribution of scores for that test (e.g. see Figure 1.1). It also means that the clinician may be able to use the score on a particular test to estimate whether a client might meet the diagnostic criteria

> **standardisation** The establishment of statistical norms for clinical tests, which allows the clinician to see where an individual client's score on the test falls in relation to the normal distribution of scores for that test.

for a psychological disorder. For example, scores on a test such as the Clark–Beck Obsessive-Compulsive Inventory (CBOCI) (Clark & Beck, 2003) can be used to estimate the probability with which a client might meet diagnostic criteria for OCD; and (4) unlike the ad hoc quizzes and questionnaires you might find in popular magazines, most structured psychological tests are rigorously tested to ensure that they are both valid and reliable (see section 2.2.1). That is, they are tested to ensure that they are a valid measure of what they claim to be measuring (e.g. that scores on a written psychological test claiming to measure anxiety actually correlate with behavioural measures of anxiety) and that the test is reliable in the sense that it yields consistent scores when it is given to the same person on different occasions.

Most psychological tests are based on the **psychometric approach**. That is, the test assumes that there are stable underlying characteristics or traits (e.g. anxiety, depression, compulsiveness, worry, and so on) that exist at different levels in everyone. The psychological tests we will discuss below can take a number of different forms and serve a number of different functions. For example, some tests stick rather rigidly to the structured question, response and scoring format similar to that shown in Table 2.3 (personality inventories, specific symptom inventories), while others (such as projective tests) may closely define the questions or stimuli to be presented to the client, but allow a much wider range of potential responses. The clinical psychologist will use psychological tests for a variety of different purposes, including the assessment of psychopathology symptoms, intelligence, and neurological or cognitive deficits.

> **psychometric approach** The idea that a psychological test assumes that there are stable underlying characteristics or traits (e.g. anxiety, depression, compulsiveness, worry) that exist at different levels in everyone.

Personality inventories

The most well-known of the personality inventories used by clinical psychologists and psychiatrists is the **Minnesota Multiphasic Personality Inventory (MMPI)**. This was originally developed in the 1940s by Hathaway and McKinley (1943), and has been updated by Butcher, Dahlstrom, Graham, Tellegen & Kraemer (1989) (now known as the MMPI-2). The MMPI-2 consists of 567 self-statements to which the client has to respond on a three-point scale by replying either 'true', 'false' or 'cannot say'. The questions cover topics such as mood, physical concerns, social attitudes, psychological symptoms and feelings of well-being. The

> **Minnesota Multiphasic Personality Inventory (MMPI)** A well-known personality inventory used by clinical psychologists and psychiatrists.

> To read more about The Minnesota Multiphasic Personality Inventory go to **http://tinyurl.com/pws65k4**

TABLE 2.3 *Measuring state and trait anxiety using a questionnaire*

The STAI is a well-known psychometric test for measuring levels of state and trait anxiety. Its questions take the following format, and this format is one that is regularly used in psychological tests of this kind (after Spielberger, Gorsuch, Lushene, Vagg, & Jacobs, 1983).

A number of statements which people have used to describe themselves are given below. Read each statement and then circle the appropriate number to the right of the statement to indicate how you *generally* feel. There are no right or wrong answers. Do not spend too much time on any one statement but give the answer which seems to describe how you generally feel.

1 = Almost never
2 = Sometimes
3 = Often
4 = Almost always

1.	I feel pleasant	1	2	3	4
2.	I feel nervous and restless	1	2	3	4
3.	I feel satisfied with myself	1	2	3	4
4.	I wish I could be as happy as others seem to be	1	2	3	4
5.	I feel like a failure	1	2	3	4

The scale of 1 to 4 is known as a '*Likert scale*' where the client has to specify their level of agreement with each statement. Some items will be reversed so that the respondent cannot simply endorse each item in the same way (e.g. Q3 is a reversed item in which the anxious individual would endorse a low number rather than a high number). The clinician can then create a total score for a client by adding together the individual scores that the client has circled (but remembering to reverse score any reversed items – e.g. on Q3 4 would be scored as 1, 3 as 2, and so on). When data have been collected from a large number of participants from differing age groups and demographic backgrounds statistical norms for the test can be established, and this is known as '*standardisation*'. This allows the clinician to compare the score of their client with the normal distribution of scores that occur in the population in general.

original authors asked around 800 psychiatric patients to indicate whether the questions were true for them, and compared their responses with those from 800 non-psychiatric patients. They then included in the inventory only those questions that differentiated between the two groups. The test now has four validity scales and ten clinical scales, and examples of these are shown in Table 2.4. The test provides scores for each scale between 0 and 120, and scores above 70 on a scale are considered to be indicative of psychopathology. The scores from the various scales can be displayed on a graph to give a distinctive profile indicating the client's general personality features, potential psychopathology, and emotional needs. The validity scales are particularly useful, because they allow the clinician to estimate whether a client has been providing false information on the test. Clients might provide false information for a number of reasons: (1) because they want to 'look good', and so respond in a socially acceptable way (measured by the lie scale), (2) because they may want to fake psychopathology symptoms in order to receive attention and treatment (measured by the F scale) (Rogers, Sewell, Martin & Vitacco, 2003), (3) because they are being evasive or simply having difficulty reading or interpreting the questions (measured by the ?

scale), or (4) because they are defensive and want to avoid appearing incompetent (measured by the K scale).

Clinical research has indicated that the MMPI has good internal reliability, and scores on the MMPI appear to have excellent clinical validity by corresponding accurately with clinical diagnoses and ratings of symptoms made by both clinicians and members of the client's own family (Ganellan, 1996; Graham, 1990; Vacha-Hasse, Kogan, Tani & Woodall, 2001). One limitation of the MMPI is the time that it takes to administer, and answering 567 questions requires some stamina on the part of both the client and the overworked clinician. However, shortened versions of the MMPI-2 are available, and these show both good reliability and validity (Dahlstrom & Archer, 2000).

Specific trait inventories

While personality inventories such as the MMPI assess characteristics of the client across a range of different traits and domains, other inventories have been developed simply to measure functioning in one specific area or one specific psychopathology. Such tests may measure emotional functioning, such as levels

TABLE 2.4 *Subscales and sample items from the MMPI*

Subscale	What the scale measures	Sample item
?	Evasiveness or difficulty interpreting the question	(Number of items left unanswered)
L (lie scale)	Tendency of respondent to respond in a socially acceptable way	"I approve of every person I meet"
F	Respondent is trying to fake psychopathology symptoms	"Everything tastes sweet"
K	Respondent is defensive and trying not to look incompetent	"Things couldn't be going any better for me"
Hypochondriasis (HS)	Abnormal concern with bodily sensations	"I am often aware of tingling feelings in my body"
Depression (D)	Pessimism and hopelessness	"Life never feels worthwhile to me"
Conversion Hysteria (Hy)	Uses physical symptoms to avoid conflicts and responsibilities	"My muscles often twitch for no apparent reason"
Psychopathy (Pd)	Emotional shallowness and disregard for social norms	"I don't care about what people think of me"
Masculinity–femininity (Mf)	Identifies respondents with non-traditional gender characteristics	"I like to arrange flowers"
Paranoia (Pa)	Pathological suspiciousness or delusions of grandeur or persecution	"There are evil people trying to influence my mind"
Psychasthenia (Pt)	Identifies respondents with obsessions, compulsions, guilt, and irrational fears	"I save everything I buy, even after I have no use for it"
Schizophrenia (Sc)	Identifies bizarre sensory experiences and beliefs	"Things around me do not seem real"
Hypomania (Ma)	Identifies emotional excitement, hyperactivity and impatience	"Sometimes I have a strong impulse to do something that others will find appalling"
Social Introversion (Si)	Identifies someone who is shy, modest and prefers solitary activities	"I am easily embarrassed"

of anxiety, depression or anger, or they may measure aspects of behaviour such as social skills. More recently, other tests have been developed in an attempt to measure cognitive functioning or cognitive constructs that are relevant to psychopathology. One such example is the Obsessive Belief Questionnaire (OBQ) (Steketee, Frost, Bhar, Bouvard *et al.*, 2005) which was designed to assess beliefs and appraisals considered critical to the acquisition and maintenance of obsessions. This measures six cognitive constructs thought to play a role in OCD, including: (1) intolerance of uncertainty, (2) overestimation of threat, (3) control of thoughts, (4) importance of thoughts, (5) beliefs about inflated responsibility, and (6) perfectionism. (You may want to look at section 6.5 to understand how these cognitive constructs are relevant to the aetiology of OCD.) Specific tests such as these can be used to measure variables that are directly observable and measurable, such as characteristics found in observable behaviour. But they are becoming increasingly used to measure

hypothetical constructs that are not necessarily directly observable but have to be inferred from the answers given to a range of questions. For example, the degree to which an individual cannot tolerate uncertainty (a factor that has been implicated in the acquisition and maintenance of a number of anxiety disorders) is assessed on the OBQ by asking respondents to endorse statements such as 'If I am uncertain there is something wrong with me' or 'I should be 100 per cent certain that everything around me is safe'. Taken together, such questions provide an estimate of how much the individual is able to 'tolerate' uncertainty.

Because of their potential diagnostic and theoretical value (such inventories can also be used as research tools to help us understand the causes of psychopathology), the number of specific trait inventories available to clinicians and researchers has burgeoned in the past

> **hypothetical constructs** Constructs that are not necessarily directly observable but have to be inferred from other data.

10–15 years. While some are very valuable and have good face validity, many others are relatively underdeveloped. For example, unlike the MMPI, a majority of specific trait inventories fail to include any questions to indicate whether respondents are faking responses or are merely being careless with their answers, and many are not subjected to stringent standardisation, validation and reliability tests. There is even a view that researchers may simply create a specific trait inventory to serve their own theoretical purposes and to give their theoretical perspective a façade of objective credibility (i.e. they may create an inventory simply to 'measure' a construct that they themselves have invented) (Davey, 2003).

Projective tests

This group of tests usually consists of a standard fixed set of stimuli that are presented to the client, but are ambiguous enough for the client to put their own interpretation on what the stimuli represent. This often allows for considerable variation in responses between clients, and also considerable variation between clinicians in how the responses should be interpreted. The most widely used of the **projective tests** are the Rorschach Inkblot Test, the Thematic Apperception Test (TAT), and the Sentence Completion Test. Projective tests were originally based on the psychodynamic view that people's intentions and desires are largely unconscious, and must be inferred indirectly (Dosajh, 1996). Most projective tests were designed during the mid-20th century and were extremely popular for assessment purposes right up to the turn of the century. However, as we shall see below, because they are open-ended tests that allow significant variation in client responding, they are significantly less reliable and valid than more structured tests. Nevertheless, even though their popularity has declined in recent years (Piotrowski, Belter & Keller, 1998), many clinicians still use these types of tests to give them some first impressions of a client's symptoms or as part of a larger battery of assessment procedures.

The **Rorschach Inkblot Test** was originally developed by the Swiss psychiatrist Hermann Rorschach. He created numerous inkblots by dropping ink onto paper and then folding the paper in half to create a symmetrical image. He discovered that everyone he showed them to saw designs and shapes in the blots, and he assumed that their responses revealed information about the individual's psychological condition. Most versions of the Rorschach Inkblot Test now use around 10 official inkblots of which five are black ink on white, two are black and red ink on white, and three are multicoloured. An example of a black-and-white and multicoloured inkblot are given in Figure 2.2. The clinician will have available to them a highly structured scoring system (e.g. Exner & Weiner, 1995) that allows them to compare the scores the client provides with a set of standardized personality norms, that may provide indications of underlying psychopathology. However, if the test is used as a formal assessment procedure, it is still heavily dependent on the clinician's interpretation of the client's responses. For example, if certain themes keep appearing in the client's responses they may provide evidence of underlying conflicts, such as the repeated perception of 'eyes' on the inkblots perhaps providing evidence of paranoia the clinician may want to explore further. Nevertheless, the Rorschach test can be a valid and reliable test for the detection of thought disorders that may be indicative of schizophrenia or people at risk of developing schizophrenia (Lilienfeld, Wood & Garb, 2000; Viglione, 1999).

The **Thematic Apperception Test (TAT)** is a projective personality test consisting of 30 black-and-white pictures of people in vague or ambiguous situations (Morgan & Murray, 1935). The client is asked to create a dramatic story around the picture, describing what they think is happening in the picture, what events preceded it , what the individuals in the picture are saying, thinking or feeling, and what the outcome of the situation is likely to be. Many clinicians claim that this test is particularly useful for eliciting information about whether the client is depressed, has suicidal thoughts, or strong aggressive impulses (Rapaport, Gill & Shaefer, 1968). Clients usually identify with one of the characters in the pictures (known as the 'hero') and the picture then serves as a vehicle for the client to describe their own feelings and emotions as if they were involved in the ambiguous scene. The TAT may also allow the clinician to determine the client's expectations about relationships with peers, parents, other authority figures, and romantic partners. It can also be a useful tool after a client has been formally diagnosed in order to match them with a suitable form of psychotherapy, and the TAT has also been used to evaluate the motivations and attitudes of individuals who have been accused of violent crimes (Kim, Cogan, Carter & Porcerelli., 2005).

Finally, the **Sentence Completion Test** is a useful open-ended assessment

---

projective tests A group of tests usually consisting of a standard fixed set of stimuli that are presented to clients, but which are ambiguous enough for clients to put their own interpretation on what the stimuli represent.

Rorschach Inkblot Test A projective personality test using inkblots created by dropping ink onto paper and then folding the paper in half to create a symmetrical image.

Thematic Apperception Test (TAT) A projective personality test consisting of 30 black-and-white pictures of people in vague or ambiguous situations.

Sentence Completion Test An open-ended projective personality test that provides clients with the first part of an uncompleted sentence which they complete with words of their own.

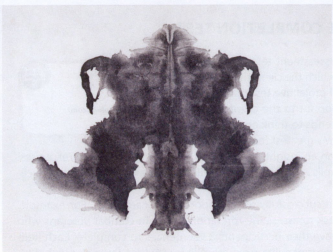
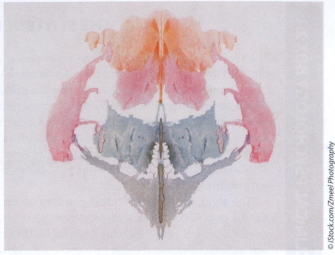

FIGURE 2.2 *The Rorschach Inkblot Test.*

The Rorschach Inkblot Test usually consists of ten official inkblots. Five inkblots are black ink on white. Two are black and red ink on white. Three are multicoloured, and the pictures above give examples of a black-and-white inkblot and a multicoloured one. The clinician shows the inkblots in a particular order and asks the client: 'What might this be?' (a free association phase). After the patient has seen and responded to all the inkblots, the clinician then presents them again one by one to study (the inquiry phase). The client is asked to list everything they see in each blot, where they see it, and what there is in the blot that makes it look like that. The blot can also be rotated. The clinician also times the patient, which then factors into the overall assessment.

Methods of interpretation differ. The most widely used method in the United States is based on the work of John E. Exner (Exner & Weiner, 1995). In this system, responses are scored systematically with reference to their level of vagueness or synthesis of multiple images in the blot, the location of the response, which of a variety of determinants is used to produce the response (e.g. whether the shape of the inkblot, its colour, or its texture is primary in making it look like what it is said to resemble), the form quality of the response (to what extent a response is faithful to how the actual inkblot looks), the contents of the response (what the respondent actually sees in the blot), the degree of mental organising activity that is involved in producing the response, and any illogical, incongruous, or incoherent aspects of responses.

test that was first developed in the 1920s, and provides clients with the first part of an uncompleted sentence, such as 'I like . . .', 'I think of myself as . . .', 'I feel guilty when . . .', which the client then completes with words of their own. This test allows the clinician to identify topics that can be further explored with the client, and can also help to identify ways in which an individual's psychopathology might bias their thinking and the way they process information. Research Methods in Clinical Psychology Box 2.1 shows how the sentence completion task has been used to identify trauma-relevant thinking biases in combat veterans with PTSD (Kimble, Kaufman, Leonard, Nestor *et al.*, 2002). Such thinking biases help to maintain emotional problems, and using the sentence completion task can help the clinician to identify ways of thinking that can be targeted during treatment.

As we mentioned earlier, the popularity of projective tests has declined steadily over the years. There are a number of reasons for this: (1) such tests are mainly

FIGURE 2.3 *The Thematic Apperception Test (TAT).*

The Thematic Apperception Test consists of 30 black-and-white pictures similar to the one above. The client is asked to create a dramatic story around the picture. Clients will usually identify with one of the characters in the pictures, which enables them to express their own feelings and emotions as if they were involved in the scene.

RESEARCH METHODS IN CLINICAL PSYCHOLOGY BOX 2.1

THE SENTENCE COMPLETION TEST

The sentence completion task is an open-ended assessment test that provides the client with the first part of a sentence which the client then has to complete in their own words. This is a useful projective test that allows the clinician to identify topics that are important to the client, and to identify any biases in the way that a client tends to think about things. For example, incomplete sentences such as 'My greatest fear . . .', 'I feel . . .', 'I need . . .' and so on can give the clinician an insight into some of the client's emotional responses. Similarly, questions such as 'My father . . .', 'Other pupils . . .', 'Most girls . . .' will provide some insight into the client's feelings about others.

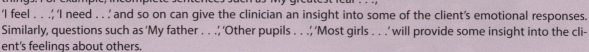
To read the article by Kimble *et al.* (2002), which reports on sentence completion tests, go to **www.wiley-psychopathology.com/reading/ch2**

The sentence completion task can also be used successfully as an important research tool. For example, Kimble *et al.* (2002) used a sentence completion task to assess interpretation biases in combat veterans who were diagnosed with PTSD (see Chapter 6). They gave their participants 33 sentences to complete. Each item was generated so that it could be completed with words of military or non-military content. Examples included:

'He was almost hit by a . . .'
'The night sky was full of . . .'
'The air was heavy with the smell of . . .'
'The silence was broken by the . . .'

For instance, 'He was almost hit by a . . .' could be completed with the word 'rock' or the word 'bullet'. The figure below shows that veterans with PTSD completed sentences with significantly more 'war' or trauma-relevant words than veterans without PTSD. These findings suggest that individuals diagnosed with PTSD have biases in the accessibility, encoding and retrieval of trauma-relevant information, and that sentence completion tasks of this kind might help to differentiate individuals with a diagnosable mental health condition from those without.

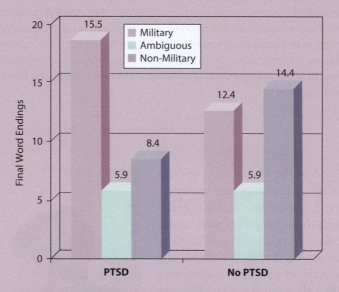

Source: Kimble, M.O., Kaufman, M.L., Leonard, L.L., Nestor, P.G. *et al.* (2002). Sentence completion test in combat veterans with and without PTSD: Preliminary findings. *Psychiatry Research, 113,* 303–307. Reproduced with permission.

based on revealing information that is relevant to psychodynamic approaches to psychopathology, and the role of psychodynamic approaches in the assessment and treatment of psychopathology has itself declined over the past 30 years; (2) even though standardized procedures for scoring projective tests have developed over recent years, the reliability of such tests is still disappointingly low (Lilienfeld, Wood & Garb, 2000), and different clinicians will often interpret the same responses in quite different ways; (3) even with highly standardized scoring methods, some projective tests such as the Rorschach Test often result in psychopathology being inferred when other evidence for such a conclusion is sparse. For instance, Hamel, Shaffer & Erdberg (2000) administered the Rorschach Test to 100 school children and, although none of them had any history of mental health problems, the results of the test were interpreted in almost all cases as evidence of faulty reasoning that might be indicative of schizophrenia or mood disorder; (4) projective tests such as the TAT have intrinsic cultural biases. For instance, in the traditional set of TAT pictures there are no ethnic minority characters even though the client is expected to identify with one of the characters in the picture. In some cases, this has been overcome by developing more contemporary TAT pictures that contain figures from ethnic minorities (Costantino, Flanagan & Malgady, 2001); and (5) most projective tests are labour intensive for the limited amount of objective information they provide. Clinicians need extensive training in order to administer tests such as the Rorschach and TAT, and they are time-consuming to administer, interpret and score. Given the development of more objective and easily scored inventories, this has inevitably led to a decline in the popularity of projective tests.

Intelligence tests

Intelligence tests are regularly used by clinicians in a variety of settings and for a variety of reasons. **IQ (intelligence quotient) tests**, as they are now generally known,

> **IQ (intelligence quotient) tests** Tests used as a means of estimating a person's intellectual ability.

were first devised in the early part of the 20th century as a means of comparing intellectual ability in specific groups of people (e.g. army recruits). Arguably the first IQ test was that produced by the French psychologist Alfred Binet in 1905, and this was a test that purported to measure intelligence across a number of verbal and nonverbal skills. From early tests such as this there are now over 100 tests of intelligence available, most of which are standardized to have a score of 100 as the mean and a score of 15 or 16 as the standard deviation (see Figure 1.1). As you can see from Figure 1.1, 68 per cent of the population will score between 84 and 116 (one standard deviation from the mean) on IQ tests, and around 2 to 3 per cent of the population will have IQ scores less than two standard deviations from the mean (e.g. less than 70). Because of their continued development over the previous 100 years, IQ tests have *high internal consistency* (i.e. a client will score roughly the same on different items that measure the same ability), *high test–retest reliability* (i.e. a client who takes the same test twice but some months or years apart will achieve roughly the same score both times), and *good validity* (i.e. the tests are good at predicting intellectual ability or future educational performance) (Sparrow & Davies, 2000).

To read Sparrow & Davies's article on assessment of intelligence go to www.wiley-psychopathology.com/reading/ch2

Intelligence tests are used by clinicians in a number of contexts. For example, (1) they are used with other measures of ability to diagnose intellectual and learning disabilities, and the cardinal DSM-IV-TR diagnostic criterion for 'mental retardation' was based primarily on an IQ score two standard deviations below the mean (e.g. an IQ score of less than 70; see Chapter 17); (2) IQ tests are also used to try to assess the needs of individuals with learning, developmental or intellectual disabilities so that support can be provided in any specific areas of need. Tests that provide scores on a range of different ability scales are best suited for this purpose, and one such example is the **Wechsler Adult Intelligence Scale**, now in its fourth edition (WAIS-IV) (Wechsler, 2008). This contains scales that measure vocabulary, arithmetic ability, digit span, information comprehension, letter–number sequencing, picture completion ability, reasoning ability, symbol search and object assembly ability. Tests such as the WAIS-IV can also be used as part of a

> **WAIS (Wechsler Adult Intelligence Scale)** A test designed to measure intelligence in adults and older adolescents. It contains scales that measure vocabulary, arithmetic ability, digit span, information comprehension, letter–number sequencing, picture completion ability, reasoning ability, symbol search and object assembly ability.

battery of tests to assess whether an individual is eligible for special educational needs, and it will provide information that will suggest strategies, services and support that will optimize the individual's functioning within society; and (3) intelligence tests are frequently used as part of a battery of assessments used in neurological evaluations (see section 15.1), and can help to detect when a client has brain damage caused by traumatic injury or cerebral infection, or has a degenerative brain disorder such as Alzheimer's disease.

However, despite their practical benefits across a range of clinical contexts, intelligence tests still have a number of limitations. Firstly, intelligence is an inferred construct. That is, it does not objectively exist in the same way that physical attributes such as heart rate or blood pressure exist, but is a hypothetical construct that has been developed by psychologists to help us try to understand how well individuals can adapt to various problems. This has led some sceptical psychologists to suggest that there is no clear definition of intelligence but that 'intelligence is merely what IQ tests measure'! Secondly, if that latter statement is true, then our conception of whether someone is intelligent or not will depend on the reliability and validity of the individual IQ test we use to measure their intelligence, and this can raise some difficulties. For example, many IQ tests are culturally biased, and appear to be based on middle-class, majority ethnic background views of what is adaptive (Gopaul-McNichol & Armour-Thomas, 2002), and so will disadvantage those from lower socio-economic backgrounds, from ethnic minorities, or from poorer quality educational backgrounds (Walker, Batchelor & Shores, 2009). While attempts have been made over the years to eradicate cultural bias of this kind, it is difficult to eliminate it entirely. For instance, a test question may ask whether a cup goes with a bowl, a spoon or a saucer, but a child from a low socio-economic background may never have drunk from a cup with a saucer, and may be more likely to associate a cup or mug with a spoon. Even so, because it is widely known that some ethnic minorities perform relatively poorly on IQ tests, this knowledge alone can interfere with test performance in that group (Spencer, Steele & Quinn, 1999). Thirdly, intelligence tests mainly tend to be rather 'static' tests of intellectual ability and provide a snapshot of ability at any point in time. What they do not usually appear to measure is the individual's capacity to learn or their potential to acquire new cognitive abilities (Grigorenko & Sternberg, 1998). Fourthly, many researchers argue that our current conception of intelligence as measured by IQ tests is too narrow. There are many other skills that are not usually included in our conceptions of, and measures of intelligence, and these include music ability, physical skill, the ability to perceive, understand and express emotion (known as 'emotional intelligence'), and the ability to implement solutions to real-world problems (Gardner, 1998; Mayer, Salovey & Caruso, 2000). For example, are Lionel Messi's footballing skills as much an intelligent skill as arithmetic or verbal ability (Bishop, Wright, Jackson & Abernethy, 2013)?

Neurological impairment tests

Many psychological and cognitive problems are not caused by problematic life experiences or by dysfunctional ways of thinking, but are caused by damage to the structure and functioning of the brain and the central nervous system. Such damage can be caused by traumatic injury (such as might be received in a car accident), cardiovascular problems (such as a stroke), cerebral infection (such as meningitis), a brain tumour, or be the result of a degenerative brain disorder (such as Alzheimer's disease). In such cases damage to the brain can cause both changes in personality (e.g. change someone from a passive into an aggressive individual) and cause deficits in cognitive functioning depending on the areas of the brain that are affected. These issues are discussed more thoroughly in Chapter 15, but at this point we will mention the value of neurological assessment tests in enabling the clinician to determine the nature of any cognitive deficits (e.g. memory deficits, deficits in language skills, and so on), to identify whether such deficits are the result of brain damage, and in many cases to identify the area of the brain that has been affected. Clinicians will usually employ a battery of tests when assessing for possible neurological deficits, and these may include EEG analyses, brain scans such as

PET scans and fMRI scans (see next section), blood tests (to assess potential inherited or genetic components to a disorder), and chemical analyses of cerebrospinal fluids. But of equal importance in this overall assessment is the use of neurological tests that measure cognitive, perceptual and motor performance as indicators of underlying brain dysfunction (Rao, 2000). The rationale behind the use of such neurological tests is that different psychological functions (such as motor skills, memory, language, planning and executive functioning) are localized in different areas of the brain (see Table 15.1), so discovering a specific cognitive deficit can help to identify the area of the brain where any damage may be localized. In addition, collecting such information is also crucial for identifying the focus of rehabilitation strategies and in patient care and planning for the client (Veitch, 2008). Tests that are commonly used by clinical neuropsychologists in this respect are the **Adult Memory and Information Processing Battery (AMIPB)** (Coughlan & Hollows, 1985), the **Halstead–Reitan Neuropsychological Test Battery** (Broshek & Barth, 2000), and the previously mentioned Mini Mental State Examination (MMSE). Each of these tests is described in more detail in Chapter 15, and their administration and scoring is an important part of the day-to-day tasks undertaken by clinical neuropsychologists (Veitch, 2008; see 'A week in the life of a clinical psychologist', Chapter 15).

> **Adult Memory and Information Processing Battery (AMIPB)** A neuropsychological test in wide use in the UK, comprising two tests of speed of information processing, verbal memory tests (list learning and story recall) and visual memory tests (design learning and figure recall).

> **Halstead–Reitan Neuropsychological Test Battery** A common neuropsychological test used in the USA, compiled to evaluate brain and nervous system functioning across a fixed set of eight tests. The tests evaluate function across visual, auditory and tactile input, verbal communication, spatial and sequential perception, the ability to analyse information, and the ability to form mental concepts, make judgements, control motor output and to attend to and memorize stimuli.

2.2.4 Biologically Based Assessments

In many cases, information about biological structures and biological functioning can help to inform the assessment and diagnosis of psychological problems. There are two main types of biologically based assessment that we will describe here: psychophysiological tests and brain imaging.

Psychophysiological tests

There are a number of psychophysiological tests that can be used to provide information about potential psychological problems. For example, anxiety causes increased activity in the sympathetic nervous system and is regularly accompanied by changes in physiological measures such as heart rate, blood pressure, body temperature and electrodermal responding. Similarly, anger is usually associated with physiological changes in blood pressure and heart rate. So, psychophysiological tests can provide useful information related to emotionally based psychological problems.

One important measure of physiological activity is **electrodermal responding**, sometimes known as the galvanic skin response (GSR) or skin conductance response (SCR). Emotional responses such as anxiety, fear or anger increase sweat-gland activity, and changes in this activity can be recorded with the use of electrodes that would normally be attached to the fingers of the participant. Changes in skin conductance caused by sweat-gland activity can then be measured as changes on a polygraph – a pen that records changes in skin conductance on a continually moving roll of graph paper (see Photo 2.1). Skin conductance measures have been used in a variety of contexts: (1) to assess the kinds of stimuli or events that elicit anxiety in a client (Cuthbert, Lang, Strauss, Drobes *et al.*, 2003; Alpers, Wilhelm & Roth, 2005); (2) to assess autonomic or physiological reactivity in certain diagnostic groups (e.g. individuals diagnosed with antisocial personality disorder tend to have less reactive autonomic nervous systems than non-clinical samples) (Lykken, 1995); (3) to assess the ability of clients to cope following treatment interventions (Bobadilla & Taylor, 2007; Grillon, Cordova, Morgan, Charney & Davis, 2004); and (4) whether autonomic indices of anxiety or arousal correspond with appropriate changes in behaviour (e.g. in panic disorder, avoidance responses may be triggered by physiological changes indicative of anxiety) (Karekla, Forsyth & Kelly, 2004). Other useful examples of psychophysiological measurement techniques include the **electromyogram (EMG)**, which measures the electrical activity in muscles, and the **electrocardiogram (ECG)** for measuring heart rate. Although measures such as electrodermal responding can indicate emotional changes indicative of anxiety, fear or anger, it is not always foolproof. Rather than specifically indicating the presence of these discrete emotions, skin conductance is more properly an indicator of general physiological arousal, and this can be caused by a variety of factors, including simply orienting towards or attending to an event (Siddle, 1983). This issue is nowhere better illustrated than in the history of

> **electrodermal responding** A psychophysiological measure which uses electrodes attached to the fingers of participants to test emotional responses such as anxiety, fear or anger by measuring changes in sweat-gland activity.

> **electromyogram (EMG)** A psychophysiological measurement technique that measures the electrical activity in muscles.

> **electrocardiogram (ECG)** A psychophysiological measurement technique used for measuring heart rate.

the use of lie detectors. **Lie detectors** use changes in autonomic responding in an attempt to identify whether an individual is lying in response to specific preset questions, and this technique has often been used in criminal prosecutions and employment screening – especially in the USA (Krapohi, 2002). However, while a polygraph may detect anxiety or arousal caused by the participant lying, it is also likely to detect changes in arousal caused by factors other than lying (e.g. the question simply being a stressful or unusual one), and so may represent an anxious – but innocent – participant as one who may appear to be guilty (Raskin & Honts, 2002). As a result, findings from lie detector tests in the USA are now used significantly less as evidence of criminal guilt (Daniels, 2002).

Finally, another important psychophysiological assessment measure is the **electroencephalogram (EEG)**. This involves electrodes being attached to the scalp that record underlying electrical activity and can help to localize unusual brain patterns in different areas of the brain. Abnormal electrical patterns detected by EEG can indicate a number of problems, including epilepsy, brain tumours or brain injury (Cuthill & Espie, 2005).

> **lie detectors** The measurement of changes in autonomic responding used to identify whether an individual is lying in response to specific preset questions. This is a controversial technique that has often been used in criminal prosecutions and employment screening.

> **electroencephalogram (EEG)** A psychophysiological assessment measure which involves electrodes being attached to the scalp that record underlying electrical activity and can help to localize unusual brain patterns in different areas of the brain.

RIA NOVOSTI/SCIENCE PHOTO LIBRARY

PHOTO 2.1 *The polygraph is a device used to measure changes in physiological responding that may indicate emotional changes such as anxiety, fear or anger. The polygraph works by recording physiological measures (such as skin conductance or heart rate) on a continually moving roll of graph paper. In more recent times, these measures can be analysed directly by computer and the output displayed on the computer screen.*

OBSERVATIONAL CODING FORMS

Shown here are four different types of observational coding forms. Which one a clinician would use would depend on the type of data they want to collect. Figure 1 is a simple coding scheme in which the observer merely describes the behaviours they observe plus the antecedents and consequences of these behaviours. Because the observer is describing the behaviours in their own words, there is likely to be poor inter-rater reliability using this scheme. Figure 2 provides a coding system that simply measures the frequency of selected behaviours. Figure 3 extends this by providing the frequency of selected behaviours over a period of time. This will allow the clinician to see if there is anything interesting in the sequence or order that behaviours are emitted. Finally, Figure 4 provides a coding scheme that allows the recording of quite complex information, including the behaviour of the client in relation to others in the situation, such as teacher and peers.

FIGURE 1 *Sample descriptive coding form.*

Situation	Behaviour	Antecedents	Consequences
Sitting in circle time			
9.00 AM	Slapped peer sitting immediately to his left with open hand	None observed	Peer and teacher both ignored
9.03 AM	Yelled "NO!" at teacher and remained seated	Teacher gave specific command for all students to return to their seats	Teacher ignored, students laughed
9.05 AM	Got up and sat in seat	Peer came over to him and whispered in his ear	Teacher gave specific, labeled praise to target child

FIGURE 2 *Sample checklist for coding child behaviour.*

Behaviour	Frequency
Fidgeting in seat	IIIII
Getting out of seat	III
Running around classroom	I
Interrupting others	IIII
Physical aggression toward peers	I
Physical aggression toward teachers	
Verbal threats of aggression toward peers	II
Verbal threat of aggression toward teachers	I

FIGURE 3 *Sample interval coding form.*

Behaviours	30"	1'	30"	2'	30"	3'	30"	4'	30"	5'	30"	6'	30"	7'	30"	8'	30"	9'	30"	10'
Inappropriate Movement	√				√															
Inattention		√	√						√	√						√	√	√	√	√
Physical Aggression	√	√																		
Self-Injurious Behaviour						√	√							√						
(continued)																				

FIGURE 4 *Sample interval coding form with antecedents, behaviours, and consequences.*

Target Behaviour	Antecedents	Consequences						Comments
		Teacher +	Teacher –	Teacher 0	Peer +	Peer –	Peer 0	
Physical Aggression	Teacher left room Child took his toy		I	IIIIII	IIIIII I			
	None observed			I	I			
Positive Social Interaction	Teacher specific prompt			IIIII			IIIII	
	None observed			III			III	
(continued)								

Source: Nock, M.K. & Kurtz, S.M.S. (2005). Direct behavioural observation in school settings: Bringing science to practice. *Cognitive & Behavioral Practice, 12,* 359–370. Reproduced with permission.

Focus Point 2.2 provides some examples of how behaviours and events can be coded when undertaking a clinical observation (Nock & Kurtz, 2005), and which type of coding method you use will depend largely on what you want to find out (e.g. do you want to just find out how frequently a behaviour occurs, or do you want to know more about the context in which a behaviour is emitted?).

There are a number of advantages to using observational techniques. First, if the observer is appropriately trained, observation can provide important objective measures of the frequency of behaviours and those events that precede and follow them, and the latter information will often provide an insight into the purpose the problematic behaviour serves (e.g. in Treatment in Practice Box 17.1, systematic observation reveals that the purpose of Andy's self-injurious behaviour is to enable him to be removed from noisy and crowded situations) (Kazdin, 2001; Miltenberger, 1997). Second, observational data has greater external or **ecological validity** than self-reports or other forms of testing because such data provide a measurement of the behaviour as it is actually occurring in a context. Third, observation of behaviour in a context can often suggest workable answers to problem behaviour as can clearly be seen in Treatment in Practice Box 17.1. Once it was established that Andy's self-injurious behaviour was functioning to get him removed from a stressful environment, staff could look out for signs that he was becoming overstimulated and remove him from the room before he began to injure himself.

Having listed these advantages of clinical observation, it also has a number of drawbacks. Firstly, it is one of the more time-consuming forms of assessment, not just in terms of the amount of time required to simply observe behaviour, but also in terms of the amount of time needed to properly train observers in the use of the various coding systems (see e.g. Abikoff, Gittelman & Klein, 1980; see also Focus Point 2.2). This is especially so if members of the client's family need to be trained to make systematic observations in the home setting. Secondly, observation will usually take place in a specific setting (e.g. the school classroom or the home), and behaviour in this specific context may not be typical of behaviour in other contexts (Nock & Kurtz, 2005). Thirdly, the presence of an observer may lead those involved in the observation setting to behave differently to how they would normally behave (Kazdin, 1978; Skinner, Dittmer & Howell, 2000), and this may often be the case with children, who will show dramatic improvements in behaviour when they are aware they are being observed. This problem can often be overcome by video-recording behaviour without an observer present and then analysing the recording at a later time. Similarly, the clinician may want to undertake **analogue observations** in a controlled environment that allows surreptitious observation of the client. For example, children can be observed interacting in a playroom while the observer is situated behind a two-way mirror. Fourthly, unless observers are properly trained in the coding methods used, there may be poor inter-observer reliability (Kamphaus & Frick, 2002). That is, two different observers assessing the same participant may focus on quite different aspects of behaviour and context, and arrive at quite different conclusions about the frequency and causes of behaviour. Fifthly, as in

ecological validity The extent to which conditions simulated in the laboratory reflect real-life conditions.

analogue observations Clinical observations carried out in a controlled environment that allows surreptitious observation of the client.

all observational procedures, the data can be influenced by the observer's expectations. Observer expectations can cause biases in the way that information is viewed and recorded and this can be caused by the theoretical orientation of the observer and what they already know about the person being observed.

One final form of clinical observation that is frequently used is known as **self-observation** or **self-monitoring**. This involves asking the client to observe and record their own behaviour, perhaps by using a diary or a smart phone (see Focus Point 2.3) to note when certain behaviours or thoughts occur and in what contexts they occur. This has the benefit of collecting data in real time and overcomes problems associated with poor and biased recall of behaviour and events when using retrospective recall methods (Strongman & Russell, 1986). The increasing use of electronic diaries for self-observation has come to be known as **ecological momentary assessment (EMA)** (Stone & Shiffman, 1994), and such methods have been used to gather information about clients' day-to-day experiences, to aid diagnosis, to plan treatment, and to evaluate the effectiveness of treatment (Piasecki, Hufford, Solhan & Trull, 2007). In addition, self-monitoring itself can have beneficial effects on behaviour even prior to any attempts at intervention. For example, many problematic behaviours (e.g. smoking, illicit drug use, excessive eating) can occur without the individual being aware of how frequently they happen and in what circumstances they happen, and self-monitoring can begin to provide some self-knowledge that can be acted on by the individual (see Figure 2.7). As a result, self-monitoring often has the effect of increasing the frequency of desirable behaviours and decreasing the frequency of undesirable behaviours (McFall & Hammen, 1971). This is known as *reactivity*, and clinicians can often take advantage of this process to facilitate behaviour change.

> **self-observation** A form of clinical observation that involves asking clients to observe and record their own behaviour, perhaps by using a diary or a smartphone to note when certain behaviours or thoughts occur and in what contexts they occur.

> **self-monitoring** A form of clinical observation which involves asking clients to observe and record their own behaviour, to note when certain behaviours or thoughts occur, and in what contexts they occur.

> **ecological momentary assessment (EMA)** The use of diaries for self-observation or self-monitoring, perhaps by using an electronic diary or a smartphone.

2.2.6   *Cultural Bias in Assessment*

A majority of the most widely used assessment methods have been developed on populations consisting largely of people from a single cultural background and with a limited ethnic profile – that is, most tests have been developed on white European or white American populations. Because of this fact, many tests and assessment methods may be culturally biased and provide a less than

---

FOCUS POINT 2.3

APPS FOR SELF-MONITORING

Smartphone apps are increasingly used by clinical psychologists and researchers to facilitate patient and participant self-monitoring of behaviours, symptoms and moods. They are convenient to carry and easy to use, and provide information that can be sent electronically from the smartphone to the relevant data collection point at any time. A commercial example of an app for self-monitoring is *MoodPanda*, an app that allows the individual to record their mood wherever they are, post the data to a central collection point, and – if needs be – collate data into a graphical format to view progress. However, even with sophisticated apps, self-reporting of mood can still be very unreliable, and apps are now being developed that can record mood changes throughout the day by detecting tell-tale changes in a person's voice that indicate the emotional state they are in. Miller (2012) provides a detailed review of previous psychological research using mobile electronic devices, and outlines what smartphones can do now and will be able to do in the future.

Reproduced by permission of MoodPanda.

Source: http://www.newscientist.com/article/mg21729056.600-moodsensing-smartphone-tells-your-shrink-how-you-feel.html

> For further reading on mood-sensing smartphone tells your shrink how you feel go to
> **www.wiley-psychopathology.com/ch02**

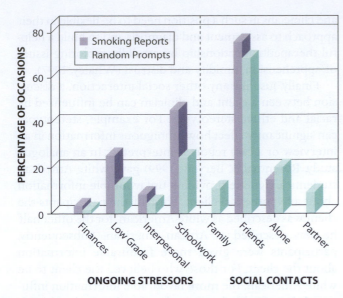

FIGURE 2.7 *Self-monitoring of smoking behaviour.*

This figure shows the results of a smoking self-monitoring task undertaken by a college student. The student was asked to record what they were doing each time a cigarette was smoked and each time they were given random prompts by a palm-top computer. Comparing the base rates (random prompts) with smoking rates when in various situations allows the clinician to see whether certain situations are triggers for smoking. In this case comparisons suggest that low grades and doing school work represent triggers for smoking, whereas being with family or partner usually elicits no cigarette smoking.

Source: Piasecki, T.M., Hufford, M.R., Solhan, M. & Trull, T.J. (2007). Assessing clients in their natural environments with electronic diaries: rationale, benefits, limitations, and barriers. *Psychological Assessment*, 19, 25–43. American Psychological Association. Reproduced with permission.

accurate picture of the mental health of individuals from different cultural backgrounds. As we shall see below, these biases can manifest in many different ways, and clinicians must be aware that such biases may affect both their judgements and their diagnoses.

Examples of cultural anomalies in assessment and diagnosis

Cultural anomalies can be identified in a number of different ways. First, some ethnic groups score differently on assessment tests than others. For example, American Asians tend to score significantly higher on most scales of the MMPI than white Americans (McNulty, Graham, Ben-Porath & Stein, 1997). Second, black Americans have a higher rate of diagnosis of disorders such as alcoholism or schizophrenia whereas white Americans are more likely to be given the less stigmatising diagnosis of major depression (Garb, 1998). Similarly, it was clear during the 1970s that West Indian immigrants to the UK

were significantly more likely to be hospitalized with a diagnosis of schizophrenia than non-immigrants or immigrants from other areas of the world (Cochrane, 1977). While this might be considered as an ethnic difference in susceptibility to some psychiatric disorders, subsequent studies suggested that many West Indian immigrants who had been hospitalized with a diagnosis of schizophrenia lacked the symptoms commonly regarded as primary indicators of the disorder (Littlewood, 1992). Similar studies suggested that alcoholism was preferentially diagnosed in Irish immigrants to the UK – often independently of a proper assessment of symptoms – and this suggested that popular ethnic stereotypes were often carried over into medical and psychiatric practice (Bagley & Binitie, 1970). As well as the apparent bias in assessment and diagnosis in ethnic minorities, individuals from low socio-economic groups may also experience bias. For example, many clinicians tend to view clients from lower socio-economic backgrounds as more disturbed than those from higher socio-economic groups (Bentacourt & Lopez, 1993; Robins & Regier, 1991), and this may result from the clinicians' stereotypes of different socio-economic groups being able to influence judgements made during unstructured interviews (Garb, 1997).

Causes of cultural anomalies in assessment and diagnosis

The reasons for cultural differences in assessment and diagnosis are multifaceted and not simply due to the fact that most structured assessment tools were developed without regard to cultural diversity. We will discuss some of the factors below, and these include (1) the fact that mental health symptoms may manifest differently in different cultures, (2) language differences between client and clinician, (3) the effect of cultural differences in religion and spiritual beliefs on the expression and perception of psychopathology, (4) the way that cultural differences affect client–clinician relationships, and (5) the role of cultural stereotypes in the perception of 'normality' and 'abnormality' in ethnic groups.

First, we saw in Chapter 1 that stress and mental health problems can actually manifest quite differently in different cultures and Focus Point 1.3 provides two examples of this. Since the diagnosis of psychopathology is based almost entirely on the presence of observable symptoms (especially in DSM) then this will complicate and confuse the process of diagnosis when assessing clients from different cultural backgrounds.

Second, language differences and difficulties can also create biases in assessment and diagnosis. For example, a number of studies have suggested that the diagnosis that a client receives may depend critically on whether they are assessed in their first or second language. Interestingly, when a client is interviewed in their second language their symptoms are often assessed as significantly *less* severe than if they are interviewed in their first language (Malgady & Costantino, 1998), and this appears to be because undertaking an interview in a second language requires the client to organize their thoughts better and therefore appear more coherent. However, this is not the only distortion that can affect assessment and diagnosis. Some other studies have suggested that undertaking a diagnostic interview in the client's second language can also result in symptoms being assessed as significantly *more* severe than if it was in their first language, and this distortion seems to be caused by the client's misuse of words, hesitations and misunderstanding of questions suggesting a lack of coherent thought (Cuellar, 1998). Even the misunderstanding of colloquialisms when client and clinician are both using their first language can affect assessment. For example, Turner, Hersen & Heiser (2003) point to the use by African-Americans of the phrase 'That's all right' when asked about their motives for engaging in certain behaviours. A white American clinician might see this response as the individual condoning what might be seen as pathological behaviour, but in African-American speech this phrase is used to mean 'Although I know exactly how to answer you, I have no intention of doing so'.

Third, differences in spiritual or religious beliefs between cultures can affect assessment and diagnosis. For example, behaviour that may be considered as a symptom of psychopathology in one culture may be seen as relatively normal or to have non-psychological causes in other cultures. We saw in Chapter 1 that some cultural beliefs view unusual behaviour as evidence that the individual is possessed by evil spirits rather than suffering mental health problems. Similarly, in some other cultures visual or auditory hallucinations with a religious content may be considered to be a normal part of religious experience rather than a sign of psychopathology, and the clinician may be faced with a client who is not necessarily exhibiting the early symptoms of schizophrenia but is merely indulging in religious experiences common to their culture.

Fourth, when facing a clinician who is a member of an ethnic majority, the client who is from an ethnic minority is quite likely to experience apprehension and timidity, and this can affect the way that the client presents themselves at interview and can also affect the clinician's view of their symptoms (Terrell & Terrell, 1984; Whaley, 1998). For example, apprehension and timidity can often make the client seem incoherent or withdrawn, and this would need to be disentangled from any similar symptoms that were a true manifestation of psychopathology. In more extreme examples, the client from an ethnic minority may be distrustful of a clinician from an ethnic majority,

and clinicians in such a position need to be flexible in their approach to assessment and diagnosis and to build a helpful therapeutic relationship by candidly exploring issues of apprehension, timidity and distrust (Whaley, 1997).

Finally, just like any other social interaction, a discussion between a client and clinician can be influenced by racial and ethnic stereotypes. For example, stereotypes can significantly affect how ambiguous information in an interview or a case report is interpreted. In an analogue study, Rosenthal & Berven (1999) gave white American students a vignette providing unfavourable information about a hypothetical client. For half the participants the client was described as white American, for the other half he was described as African-American. Subsequently, participants were given more favourable information about the client. For those who believed the client to be white American, the more favourable information influenced their final judgement, but for those who though he was a black American, the positive information failed to change their original negative view. Common stereotypes held about African-American and Hispanic clients by clinicians are that they are violent, hostile and unmotivated for treatment (Pavkov, Lewis & Lyons, 1989; Whaley, 1998), and these perceptions undoubtedly affect their clinical judgments. Garb (1997) called this a **confirmatory bias**, whereby clinicians ignore information that does not support their initial hypotheses or stereotypes, and they interpret ambiguous information as supporting their hypotheses.

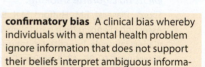

To read Garb's article on bias go to **www.wiley-psychopathology.com/ reading/ch2**

> **confirmatory bias** A clinical bias whereby individuals with a mental health problem ignore information that does not support their beliefs interpret ambiguous information as supporting their beliefs.

In some cases these biased judgements are the result of direct racism, but more often they are probably manifestations of indirect racism in which the clinicians are unaware of their stereotype biases. Whether direct or indirect racism is involved, clinicians have a responsibility to learn about and eradicate their own stereotypes and prejudices, and to provide an honest and unbiased assessment process for clients from ethnic minorities (Hollar, 2001; Adebimpe, 1994).

Addressing cultural anomalies in assessment and diagnosis

Clinicians need to work hard to eliminate cultural bias from their assessment and diagnostic processes, and this needs to be addressed at a number of levels, including eradicating bias from existing assessment tools, developing new culture-free assessments, adopting assessment procedures that minimize cultural bias, and training clinicians to identify cultural and racial bias in their own thinking and in the assessment processes that they use.

DSM has made some attempt to identify potential cultural anomalies in diagnosis by including a specific section on 'Culture, age and gender' factors within most diagnostic categories. For example, we note in Chapter 16 that when diagnosing conduct disorder the clinician is asked to take account of the social background of the client. In certain deprived inner-city areas, behaviours characteristic of conduct disorder may be seen as being protective and may represent the norm for that environment. They may also serve an adaptive function in dealing with poverty and the threatening behaviour of others rather than being symptoms of an underlying pathology.

In addition to this, clinicians need proper education and training when required to assess and diagnose minority persons (Hall, 1997; Aklin & Turner, 2006). They would need to understand minorities' construction of self, their understanding of illness, and their attitudes to mental health provision and medicine in general (Littlewood, 1992). Sadly, clinicians from minority groups are often as ill-equipped to deal with the diagnosis of clients from minority groups as their non-minority colleagues, largely because they have been trained in the same programmes (Turner, Herson & Heiser, 2003).

Finally, we can attempt to aspire to culture-free assessment methods by making tests and assessments more valid and reliable. Aklin & Turner (2006) advocate the development of structured interviews to replace the current unstructured interview that is frequently the main vehicle for diagnosis, and support for this view comes from studies indicating there are fewer problems with the assessment of ethnic minorities when structured rather than unstructured methods of interviewing are used (Widiger, 1997).

SELF-TEST QUESTIONS

- Can you define what is meant by test–retest reliability, inter-rater reliability and internal reliability?
- Can you define what is meant by concurrent validity, face validity, predictive validity and construct validity?
- What are the main benefits and limitations of the clinical interview?
- What is a structured interview? Can you provide an example of one?
- What are the advantages of psychological tests as methods of assessment?
- Can you describe a detailed example of a personality inventory?
- How do projective tests differ from other types of psychological test?
- Can you describe the features of at least one projective test?
- What are the benefits and limitations of intelligence tests?
- Can you name and describe at least two psychophysiological tests that might be used for clinical assessment?
- Can you name and describe three different neuroimaging techniques?
- What are the benefits and limitations of clinical observation techniques?
- What is ecological momentary assessment (EMA)?
- Can you provide at least three examples of cultural bias in assessment and diagnosis?
- Can you describe at least two studies that have identified some of the causes of cultural bias in assessment and diagnosis?

SECTION SUMMARY

2.2   METHODS OF ASSESSMENT

You can see from the preceding sections that cultural bias in assessment and diagnosis is a complex and pervasive phenomenon. The clinician needs to be aware of the sources of any cultural bias in these processes, and should be reflective about their own potential stereotypes of ethnic minorities and the effect this might have on their clinical judgments. A special issue of the journal *Professional Psychology: Research & Practice* (2012, vol. 43, issue 3) is dedicated to discussing multicultural practice in professional psychology, and provides a valuable summary of contemporary issues and solutions.

The key points introduced in this section are:

- *Test reliability* measures whether the test will provide the same result when used by different clinicians on different occasions.

- *Test validity* measures whether an assessment method actually measures what it claims to measure.

- An *unstructured clinical interview* is probably the first contact a client will have with a clinician.

- *Structured interviews* can be used to help make decisions about diagnosis and functioning. One such example is the *Structured Clinical Interview for DSM (SCID)*.

- *Psychological tests* are a highly structured way of gathering information about the client.

- The most well-known personality inventory is the *Minnesota Multiphasic Personality Inventory (MMPI)*.

- *Specific trait inventories* are used to measure functioning in one specific area (e.g. depression).

- *Projective tests* include the *Rorschach Inkblot Test*, the *Thematic Apperception Test (TAT)*, and the *Sentence Completion Test*.

- Both *IQ tests* and tests of general ability, such as the *Wechsler Adult Intelligence Scale (WAIS)*, are regularly used by clinicians.

- *Neurological impairment tests* are used to measure deficits in cognitive functioning that may be caused by abnormalities in brain functioning.

- *Psychophysiological tests* can be used to measure emotional responding.

- *Neuroimaging techniques* generate images of the brain that provide information on any abnormalities in brain functioning.

- Important neuroimaging techniques include *computerized axial tomography (CAT)*, *positron emission tomography (PET)*, *magnetic resonance imaging (MRI)*, and *functional magnetic resonance imaging (fMRI)*.

- *Clinical observation* techniques can be used to gather objective information about the frequency of behaviours or the contexts in which behaviours occur.

- Because assessment methods have usually been developed on populations from a single cultural background, they often result in biased assessments when applied to individuals from a different cultural background.

2.3   CASE FORMULATION

The various forms of assessment we have described in the previous section are all used by clinicians to gather useful information about the client and their problems. Some clinicians use this information to establish a psychiatric diagnosis (e.g. to determine whether the client's symptoms meet DSM-5 criteria for a specific disorder), whereas others use this information to draw up a psychological explanation of the client's problems and to develop a plan for therapy. This latter approach is known as **case formulation**, and is an approach that has been increasingly adopted over the past 20 years by clinicians who consider that each client's problems are uniquely different, and so require an individualized approach (Persons, 1989). It is an approach also championed by those who view the psychiatric diagnostic model of psychopathology as unhelpful in practice and stigmatising to clients (e.g. Boyle, 2007; May, 2007).

> **case formulation** The use of clinical information to draw up a psychological explanation of the client's problems and to develop a plan for therapy.

Most practising clinical psychologists will usually develop a case formulation when dealing with a client, and this is an attempt to work towards explaining the client's problems in established theoretical terms. In most cases, the explanation developed will also suggest interventions that may be successful in resolving those problems, and it will be a precise account of the patient's problems developed in collaboration with the client, not imposed on the client (as psychiatric diagnosis might be). Persons (1989) has described case formulation as having six components: (1) creating a list of the client's problems, (2) identifying and describing the underlying psychological mechanisms that might be mediating these problems (and the nature of the mechanisms described will depend on the theoretical orientation of the clinical psychologist – see below), (3) understanding the way in which the psychological mechanisms generate the client's problems, (4) identifying the kinds of events that may have precipitated the client's problems, (5) identifying how these precipitating events may have caused the current problems through the proposed psychological mechanisms, and (6) developing a scheme of treatment based on these explanations and predicting any obstacles to treatment.

How a case formulation is constructed will depend on the theoretical orientation of the clinical psychologist and, within an individual formulation, explanation of the client's problems will be couched in terms of the psychologist's own preferred theoretical approach. For example, those who work within a cognitive or behavioural model of psychopathology (see section 1.3.2) will attempt to find explanations for the client's problems based on cognitive and behavioural causes – sometimes known as an ABC approach. That is, they will attempt to identify the antecedents (A) to the problems, describe the beliefs (B) or cognitive factors that are triggered by these antecedents, and the consequences (C) of these events. For example, if a client suffers from panic attacks, the case formulation may discover that (1) these occur in situations where there are crowds of people (antecedents), (2) that the client believes that feeling hot, sweaty and faint are signals for an impending heart attack (beliefs), and (3) the client indulges in certain 'safety' behaviours designed to keep her 'safe' – such as avoiding going out of the house – but which reinforce the symptoms and beliefs (consequences) (Marzillier & Marzillier, 2008). Based on this knowledge, the clinical psychologist can begin to understand the factors that are causing and maintaining these problems (e.g. the faulty beliefs and the 'safety' behaviours) and develop therapeutic interventions to try to deal with these.

In contrast, psychologists who hold a psychodynamic perspective use formulations to address the way that current problems reflect underlying unconscious conflicts and early developmental experiences, and will couch their formulations in these kinds of ways. For those psychologists who believe that a holistic or systemic view of a person's problems is important (e.g. their problems can only be fully understood within a family or social context), the formulation will be developed in terms of the important relationships between the client and important other people in their life. For example, within the context of the family, someone with a psychological problem may be seen as a weak and dependent person, and this may influence how other members of the family treat the client, and determine what demands the client may make on their family. Thus, the client's problems can be formulated as interactions between various 'actors' (the family members) which may maintain the client's problems (Marzillier & Marzillier, 2008; Dallos & Draper, 2005). Figure 2.8 provides a simple example of a systemic formulation which attempts to explain how a client's problems are maintained by the relationships between him and other members of his family.

In many cases clinicians prefer to represent their formulations in a diagrammatic form that permits easy identification of factors that may be causing the client's problems, and it also enables the clinician to clearly explain the formulation to the client. Activity 2.1 provides a detailed and structured example of how a formulation based on a cognitive-behavioural approach could be attempted, and provides an example of a formulation interview that the reader can attempt to interpret in terms of the theoretical model provided. This example shows how the case formulation for a client suffering panic disorder would be interpreted by a cognitive-behavioural psychologist in terms of existing cognitive models of panic disorder (see Chapter 6). Once the diagram is completed this should suggest some possible targets for interventions (e.g. using CBT to change misinterpretations of bodily sensations and to prevent the use of safety behaviours – see section 6.3).

> To complete Activity 2.1 – a case formulation for panic disorder – go to **www.wiley-psychopathology.com/ activities/ch2**

Tarrier (2006) lists the various advantages of the case formulation approach: (1) it allows a flexible and idiosyncratic understanding of each client's individual problems irrespective of individual diagnoses they may have been given (i.e. in clinical practice, a client's problems do not usually fall into simple diagnostic categories, but may reflect a range of problems unique to that individual), (2) it is collaborative and treats the client with regard, (3) it

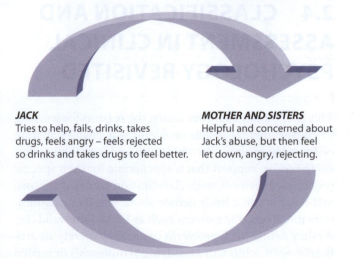

JACK
Tries to help, fails, drinks, takes drugs, feels angry – feels rejected so drinks and takes drugs to feel better.

MOTHER AND SISTERS
Helpful and concerned about Jack's abuse, but then feel let down, angry, rejecting.

FIGURE 2.8 *A systemic case formulation.*
   Jack has problems with both drugs and drink. He later became involved in petty crime, and was diagnosed as depressed. He also began to exhibit paranoia and delusional ideation. This simple formulation shows how the reactions of Jack and his mother and sisters reinforce Jack's feelings of rejection and his abuse of drink and drugs.
Source: Dallos, R. & Stedmon, J. (2006). Mapping the family dance. In L. Johnstone & R. Dallos (Eds.) *Formulation in psychology and psychotherapy.* London: Routledge. Reproduced with permission.

is firmly based on a theoretical understanding of psycho-pathology (unlike diagnosis which is based entirely on a description of symptoms), (4) it can include information about a client's past history (e.g. their exposure to risk factors) and the client's personal, social and family history, and (5) it allows the development of treatment strategies that can be moulded to the specific needs of that individual client, which is especially advantageous in treating complex cases that do not easily conform to standard diagnostic categories.

SELF-TEST QUESTIONS

- What are the main components of a case formulation?
- Can you describe how a cognitive-behavioural clinician and a psychodynamic clinician might approach case formulation differently?

SECTION SUMMARY

2.3   CASE FORMULATION

- A case formulation is used by clinicians to draw up a psychological explanation of a client's problems and to develop a plan for therapy.
- The clinician's theoretical approach will determine how they explain the client's problems and what information they require during the case formulation process.

2.4   CLASSIFICATION AND ASSESSMENT IN CLINICAL PSYCHOLOGY REVISITED

This chapter began by discussing the reasons for wanting to classify mental health problems – it enables sharing of knowledge about mental health and it enables sufferers to receive support that is appropriate for their specific problems. However, with classification comes diagnosis, and there is still a lively debate about whether classification and diagnostic systems such as DSM-5 are valid (i.e. do they define 'real' problems or are they merely an artificial way of arbitrarily classifying symptoms?) or indeed useful (does labelling someone with a psychiatric diagnosis help or hinder their recovery?)

This chapter has also reviewed the diverse and varied ways in which clinicians gather information by which they can classify, understand and treat the mental health problems brought to them by their clients. This information is used to address a number of questions, including: 'Precisely what problems does this person have?' 'What has caused their problems?' 'What is the best way to treat their problems?' 'Did our treatment work?' By far the most common assessment method is the clinical interview, and this may be entirely unstructured or may have a very rigid structure depending on the nature of the information the clinician wants to gather (Activity 2.1 provides a good example of a structured interview designed to gather very specific information about a client). However, as well as benefits, the clinical interview also has many limitations. Its reliability is quite low, depends on the client's willingness to provide valid information about themselves and their problems, and is prone to cultural bias when clinician and client are from differing ethnic backgrounds. More structured ways of gathering information include psychological tests, and under this heading we have reviewed personality inventories, specific trait inventories, projective tests, and intelligence tests. Biologically based assessments such as psychophysiological tests and brain neuroimaging techniques can be valuable for confirming the validity of interview or pencil-and-paper tests, and can often identify whether any impairments in brain functioning may be underlying the client's problems. Finally, we have discussed the use of case formulations, which have become a popular tool for clinicians of most theoretical persuasions. The case formulation allows the clinician to draw up a psychological explanation of the client's problems and to develop a plan for therapy, and this allows a flexible and personal understanding of each client's individual problems.

To access the online resources for this chapter go to
www.wiley-psychopathology.com/ch2

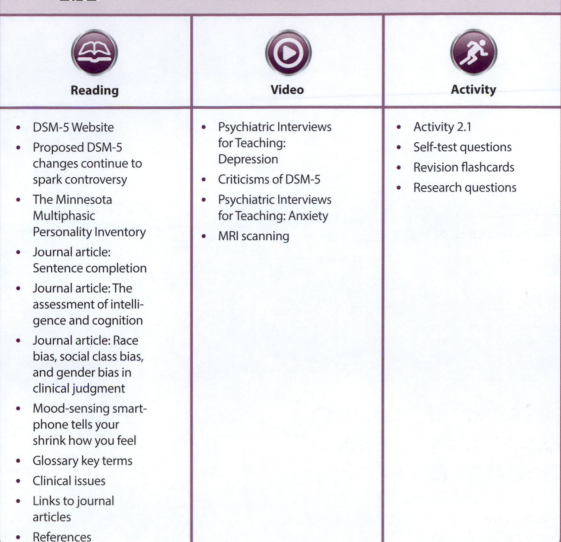

Reading	Video	Activity
• DSM-5 Website • Proposed DSM-5 changes continue to spark controversy • The Minnesota Multiphasic Personality Inventory • Journal article: Sentence completion • Journal article: The assessment of intelligence and cognition • Journal article: Race bias, social class bias, and gender bias in clinical judgment • Mood-sensing smartphone tells your shrink how you feel • Glossary key terms • Clinical issues • Links to journal articles • References	• Psychiatric Interviews for Teaching: Depression • Criticisms of DSM-5 • Psychiatric Interviews for Teaching: Anxiety • MRI scanning	• Activity 2.1 • Self-test questions • Revision flashcards • Research questions

3 Research Methods in Clinical Psychology

 To access the online resources for this chapter go to
www.wiley-psychopathology.com/ch3

ROUTE MAP OF THE CHAPTER

This chapter begins by describing what research is, and then discusses a number of ways in which research can be conducted, with special attention being paid to the role of scientific method in clinical psychology research. The chapter then describes why clinical psychologists might want training in research, and what kinds of questions they are interested in addressing. The bulk of the chapter is concerned with describing and evaluating a range of research designs used by clinical psychology researchers. Finally, a chapter on research would not be complete without a full discussion of the ethical issues that clinical psychologists are likely to encounter while undertaking research.

CHAPTER OUTLINE

LEARNING OUTCOMES

When you have completed this chapter, you should be able to:

1. Describe and evaluate a range of research methods that can be used in clinical psychology research.

2. Describe the types of research questions that are central to clinical psychology research.

3. Critically evaluate the ethical issues relevant to clinical psychology research.

I am a clinical psychologist. Among the healthcare professions, clinical psychology is one of the few to provide extensive research training, and a clinical psychologist can be involved in both basic and applied research. Because of the breadth of their training in research methods, clinical psychologists are well suited to design, implement, and evaluate research, and to conduct evaluations of the services provided by mental health care agencies. When you are a practicing clinical psychologist, finding time to conduct research of any kind is difficult. But when I am involved it helps me to satisfy my curiosity, to generate new knowledge on which more effective treatments may be based, and to evaluate whether the current services we offer are effective.

Sarah's Story

Introduction

Why might a profession whose main aim is arguably to alleviate mental health problems want to do research or be involved in research? Why are clinical psychologists given such a rigorous training in research methods anyway – shouldn't they simply be taught how to help people recover from their mental health problems? The personal account above goes some way to answering these questions. Even if they are simply offering a treatment-based service, clinical psychologists should be able to evaluate whether their services are effective and successful, and to do this with any degree of objectivity requires a knowledge of scientific method. *Sarah's story* reflects a widely held view that the clinical psychologist should be thought of as a **scientist-practitioner** or an **applied scientist** – someone who is competent as both a researcher and a practitioner. This view arose in the early 20th century when psychology was thought of as an experimental science. However, as the discipline of psychology developed from being a pure research subject to an applied profession, clinical psychology still maintained its links with universities and the academic world. Indeed, in the UK, almost all clinical psychology training courses are based in university psychology departments, and have substantial research training components to them. The current view of the link between research and practice that is held in the UK tends to be one in which scientific method is systematically integrated into clinical work (Barker, Pistrang & Elliott, 2002). Shapiro (1985) defines this applied scientist view of clinical psychologists as (1) applying the findings of general psychology to the area of mental health, (2) using only methods of assessment that have been scientifically validated, and (3) doing clinical work within the framework of scientific method. However, this view of clinical psychologists, their approach to research, and how they use research is not as clear cut as it sounds, and in order to understand how research is used by clinicians and integrated into their role as mental health professionals we need to spend a little time understanding what is meant by (1) research and (2) scientific method, and also we need to look at what value research might have within the broader scope of psychopathology. For example, some researchers simply want to understand what causes psychopathology, others want to know whether there is empirical evidence supporting the efficacy of specific treatments, and others simply want a systematic way of understanding and interpreting the symptoms of their clients.

scientist-practitioner Someone who is competent as both a researcher and a practitioner.

applied scientist Someone who is competent as both a researcher and a practitioner.

3.1   RESEARCH AND SCIENCE

3.1.1   *What Is Research?*

If you are a psychology student, you have probably already encountered a course designed to teach you about research. You will probably have undertaken some practical classes designed to teach you about research methods, and you will also have learnt about the role that statistics plays in interpreting research data. But did anyone actually tell you what research is in the first place? In general, psychology considers itself to be either a biological or a social science, so the emphasis is on using scientific method to understand human behaviour. But research can mean much more than this. In its broadest sense, research is a form of investigation aimed at discovering some facts about a topic or about furthering understanding of that topic through careful consideration or study. In this respect, research does not necessarily have to adhere to scientific principles, and understanding of a topic may be enhanced in many other ways. For example, we can learn a lot about human behaviour and human nature from literature and the way that many classical authors describe everyday experiences and their consequences. Many clinicians and psychotherapists claim that they gain understanding and knowledge from their own clinical experiences which they can use systematically and successfully when treating their clients (Morrow-Bradley & Elliott, 1986). Even historical research can be used to further understanding of psychopathology. In a systematic search of the historical literature on spiders and how humans have perceived them over the centuries, Davey (1994) found that spiders had been traditionally linked with the spread of disease and illness – a finding which may help us to understand why fear of spiders is so prevalent in Western societies today. What is common to these different approaches is that they are attempts to understand an issue through systematic and careful consideration of the relevant facts. However, how we collect the facts that are relevant to our considerations can vary considerably. Literature collects facts usually through the author's observations of life and everyday living which are then presented within an unfolding story; historical research collects facts by accumulating evidence from historical documents or artefacts; and the practicing clinician gathers facts from their everyday experiences with clients. In each case, these facts can then be considered systematically in an attempt to enhance our understanding.

In contrast, scientific method advocates that facts are collected in rather specific ways. Usually this means that we should collect our facts for consideration in a systematic way defined by objectivity and precise measurement (usually so that our collecting of facts can be replicated by others and our conclusions verified by them). Because the scientific method is used predominantly in psychological research and clinical psychology research, we will discuss this approach in detail below.

3.1.2   *Scientific Method*

Scientific method espouses the pursuit of knowledge through systematic and thorough observation. It also requires that research findings are replicable and testable.

By *replicable*, we mean that the results of the research have been collected under controlled conditions that will allow any other researcher to reproduce those exact same findings. Researchers using the scientific method attempt to achieve this by precise measurement of stimuli and behaviour and accurate and complete description of the methods by which the data were collected. Replicability is essential to the progress of scientific knowledge because it means that different researchers can be sure that a research finding is a legitimate fact that can be relied upon when developing explanations of a phenomenon. This is especially true in the case of human behaviour, where the subject matter is often complex and may differ significantly from situation to situation. Activity 3.1 provides a discussion of one of the seminal research papers in human psychopathology – the attempt by Watson & Rayner (1920) to condition a phobia in an 11-month-old infant (see section 6.1.1). You will see from this discussion that although this paper is often considered to be one of the founding pieces of scientific research in psychopathology, the ability of other contemporary researchers to replicate it was limited – largely because Watson & Rayner were less than systematic in the way they collected their data and reported it.

To read Watson & Rayner's article on conditioned emotional reactions go to **www.wiley-psychopathology.com/ reading/ch3**

By *testable*, we mean that a scientific explanation is couched in such a way that it clearly suggests ways in which it can be tested and potentially falsified. Scientific method often relies on the construction of theories to explain phenomena, and a **theory** is a set of propositions that usually attempt to explain a phenomenon by describing the cause–effect relationships that contribute to that phenomenon. Theories are expected to be able to take into account all relevant research findings on a phenomenon,

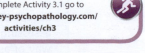

To complete Activity 3.1 go to **www.wiley-psychopathology.com/ activities/ch3**

theory A set of propositions that usually attempt to explain a phenomenon by describing the cause–effect relationships that contribute to that phenomenon.

and be articulated in such a way that they will also have predictive value. That is, they should be able to predict what might happen in as yet untested situations. Thus, a good theory will allow the researcher to generate **hypotheses** about what might happen, and to test these hypotheses in other research studies. If the hypotheses are confirmed in these other studies the theory is upheld, but if the hypotheses are disconfirmed then the theory is either wrong or needs to be changed in detail to explain the new facts. This process illustrates one of the important distinctions between science and so-called non-science. Karl Popper (1959) proposed that science must be able to formulate hypotheses that are capable of refutation or

hypotheses Tentative explanations for a phenomenon used as a basis for further investigation or predicting the outcome of a scientific study.

falsification, and if it is not possible to falsify a theory by generating testable hypotheses, then that theory is not scientific, and, in Popper's view, is of little explanatory value. Activity 3.2 provides an example of a psychological theory that attempts to explain why some people develop panic disorder (see section 6.3). This is a theory that can be represented schematically as a series of cause–effect relationships, and the sequence of cause–effect relationships described in this theory are assumed to precipitate regular panic attacks in those diagnosed with panic disorder. This relatively simple theory is constructed in such a way that we can generate a number of testable hypotheses from it, and so we could potentially falsify the theory according to Popper's criteria.

To complete Activity 3.2 go to www.wiley-psychopathology.com/activities/ch3

FOCUS POINT 3.1

SCIENTIFIC METHOD AS A MODEL FOR CLINICAL PSYCHOLOGY RESEARCH: THE PROS AND CONS

We have described what the scientific method is, but is it the best model by which to conduct clinical psychology research? In many countries of the world, clinical psychology has either explicitly or implicitly adopted the scientist-practitioner model described in section 3.1.2, with the implication that practising clinical psychologists are willing to at least call themselves scientists by training even if they do not regularly practice as scientists. Nevertheless, in many countries there is a growing pressure for mental health services to provide scientific evidence that treatments and therapies are effective and economical. In the UK, one such agency that attempts to assess and recommend effective forms of treatment for mental health problems is the National Institute for Health and Care Excellence (known as NICE, www.nice.org.uk). It does this primarily by recommending treatments whose efficacy can be labelled as '**evidence-based**': that is, whose efficacy has been proven through research using the scientific method. There is thus some pressure from these agencies for clinical psychologists to accept the scientific method – at least as a way of assessing the effectiveness of therapies – and as a way of assessing the cost effectiveness of individual interventions, which is an important consideration for agencies providing psychological services (e.g. Crow, Agras, Halmi, Fairburn *et al.*, 2013; Radhakrishnan,

evidence-based Treatments whose efficacy has been proven through research using the scientific method.

Hammond, Jones, Watson *et al.*, 2013). However, as we shall see on numerous occasions throughout this book, many forms of therapy are not couched in ways that make them amenable to assessment through a traditional scientific approach (e.g. psychoanalysis). As a result, at least some clinicians view processes designed to scientifically assess treatments (such as those reported by NICE) as being ways in which those clinicians who support therapies derived from traditional scientific approaches can impose their own view of what treatments are effective (Elliott, 1998; Roth & Fonagy, 1996). Let us look at some of the benefits and costs of clinical psychology adopting the scientific method in its research.

There are several apparent benefits to clinical psychology using the scientific method as a model for research. Firstly, there is probably no doubt that clinical psychology has used its scientific credentials as a means of acquiring prestige and establishing its status as an independent discipline within the field of mental health (Lavender, 1996). There was no greater proponent of this approach than one of the founders of British clinical psychology, H.J. Eysenck, who was a vigorous supporter of science and scientific method in clinical psychology research. Secondly, some writers have argued that clinical psychologists often consistently fail to use research evidence to inform their treatments and instead rely on anecdotal clinical experience (Dawes, 1994). If this is so, then there becomes a thin line between clinicians who base their interventions on unvalidated experience and a bogus psychotherapist who invents a so-called therapy whose basic tenets are not amenable to objective assessment. Keeping abreast of recent developments in evidence-based research is therefore an important component of good practice for clinical psychologists, and scientific method provides the theoretical and empirical developments by which the clinician can achieve this (Singer, 1980). Thirdly, Belar & Perry (1992) have argued that scientific method provides a useful framework for theory building that allows clinicians to test out their clinical observations and assess their efficacy. Otherwise, they argue, clinical experiences are in danger of becoming simply a set of random observations that the clinician is unable to categorize into effective and ineffective interventions.

In contrast, at least some clinicians have argued that the scientific method in its strictest form may not be suitable for clinical psychology research or practice. Firstly, some writers claim that to base clinical psychology research on strict scientific method aligns it too closely to the medical model of psychopathology and invites many of the problems associated with a strict medical model of psychopathology (see Chapter 1) (Corrie & Callahan, 2000). Secondly, while the scientist-practitioner model is often seen as the model for clinical psychology, it is seldom an ideal that is fulfilled in practice (Barlow, Hayes & Nelson, 1984). For the clinical psychologist, the need to alleviate a client's psychological problems is often more pressing than the need to be scientifically rigorous. Similarly, the demands placed on overworked clinicians in under-resourced mental health services means that they are rarely likely to engage in any meaningful research independently of their clinical practice (Head & Harmon, 1990) and will certainly rank research as a priority significantly lower than their service commitment (Allen, 1985; Corrie & Callahan, 2000). The pressures of their work mean that they will often view the research literature (whether based

on scientific method or not) as irrelevant to their professional practice (Barlow, Hayes & Nelson, 1984). Thirdly, in contrast to scientific method, an alternative approach to research in clinical psychology is one based on social constructionism (Burr, 1995). This approach emphasizes that reality is a social construction, and so there are no basic 'truths' of the kind that we seek to discover using the scientific method. Instead, knowledge consists of multiple realities that are constructed by people and may be historically and culturally specific. It is claimed this approach has particular relevance in clinical psychology because psychopathology frequently involves individuals creating their own realities (e.g. the paranoid individual creates a reality in which everyone is against them, and the depressed individual creates a reality in which they view themselves as worthless). These various realities can be accessed through analysing language and social interactions, and so those who advocate a social constructionist approach argue that the study of language and discourse is the only means of understanding human experience and, as a consequence, human psychopathology.

Despite the fact that at least some clinicians have adopted alternative frameworks (e.g. the social constructionist approach), scientific method is still the most favoured model for research in most areas of clinical psychology, including research on the causes of psychopathology (aetiology), research pursuing the development of new forms of treatment, and research assessing the efficacy and cost-effectiveness of treatments. Even though each person may develop their own individual psychological reality, the fact that human beings are evolved biological organisms means that there are almost certain to be general 'truths' or processes common to all humans that can be discovered using scientific method. As a consequence, there are also likely to be a set of general 'truths' or processes common to psychopathology across all individuals.

SELF-TEST QUESTIONS

- Can you describe the main principles of the scientific method?
- What is the difference between a theory and a hypothesis?
- What do we mean when we say that decisions about the effectiveness of an intervention should be evidence-based?
- What are the benefits and drawbacks with clinical psychology using the scientific method as a model for research?
- What is social constructionism and how does it offer a different research approach to the scientific method?

CHAPTER 3 RESEARCH METHODS IN C

SECTION SUMMARY

3.1   RESEARCH AND SCIENCE

- *Research* is about furthering understanding of a topic through careful consideration or study.

- *Scientific method* espouses the pursuit of knowledge through systematic observation, and requires that research findings are *replicable* and *testable*.

- A *theory* is a set of propositions that attempt to explain a phenomenon.

- There is growing pressure for mental health services to recommend treatments whose efficacy is *evidence-based*.

- *Social constructionism* is one research approach in clinical psychology that is an alternative to the scientific method.

3.2   CLINICAL PSYCHOLOGY RESEARCH – WHAT DO WE WANT TO FIND OUT?

3.2.1   How Does Clinical Psychology Research Help Us to Understand Psychopathology?

Clinical psychology researchers use research methods in a variety of different ways to answer a number of different questions. We will describe the range of research methods available to clinical psychologists in the next section, but first let's briefly look at how research can help us understand psychopathology.

Research can have a number of immediate goals. These goals include description, prediction, control and understanding (explanation), and a clinical psychology researcher may be using research methods to achieve any one or more of these goals.

For example, **description** involves the defining and categorising of events and relationships, and a researcher may simply want to find suitable ways of describing and categorising psychopathology. To some extent this is what is represented in DSM-5 (the categorising of psychopathology), but other researchers have used research methods to discover whether different symptoms are related or co-occur (e.g. Watson, 2005). For example, Figure 2.1 provides an example of how research methods have been used to understand how symptoms of anxiety and depression are related, and such categorisation of symptoms is a first step towards defining the biological or psychological mechanisms that link anxiety and depression.

description The defining and categorising of events and relationships relevant to psychopathology.

Once we have been able to describe and categorize psychopathology then we are one step away from **prediction**. A logical next stage is to use these descriptions and categorisations to help us predict psychopathology. For example, we may know that certain childhood or developmental experiences may increase the risk of developing psychopathology later in life, and one such list of these risk factors is provided in Table 16.1. This table indicates how various forms of childhood abuse or neglect can raise the risk of developing a range of psychopathologies (as one example, childhood physical and sexual abuse increases the risk of developing adolescent eating disorders). However, while research may have identified such experiences as **risk factors**, this does not imply a direct causal relationship between the risk factor and the psychopathology – it merely indicates that the early experience in some as yet unknown way increases the possibility that a psychopathology will occur.

prediction A statement (usually quantitative) about what will happen under specific conditions as a logical consequence of scientific theories.

risk factors Factors that may increase the risk of developing psychopathology later in life.

The next aim of research would move beyond describing and categorising events to actually trying to **control** them in a way that (1) provides us with a clear picture of the causal relationships involved, and (2) allows us to develop methods of changing events for the better. In the case of psychopathology, this latter aim would include using our knowledge of the causal relationships between events to control behaviour so that we could change it – the basic tenet of many forms of treatment and psychotherapy. One of the main tools for discovering causal relationships between events is the experimental method, which we will describe in more detail in section 3.3. For example, numerous studies have indicated that experimentally inducing a bias to interpret

control Using our knowledge of the causal relationships between events to manipulate behaviour or cognitions.

ambiguous events as threatening causes an increase in experienced anxiety (Wilson, MacLeod, Mathews & Rutherford, 2006). As a consequence this research suggests that if we can decrease this interpretation bias in anxious individuals, it should significantly reduce the anxiety they experience (e.g. see Treatment in Practice Box 6.4).

The final aim of research is **understanding**. That is, once we have described and categorized psychopathology, and once we have begun to identify some of the causal factors affecting psychopathology, we are probably at a point where we want to describe how all these factors interact, and this will provide us with a theory (or **model**) of the phenomenon we are trying to explain. Activity 3.2 provides a useful example of how researchers believe the various causal factors involved in panic disorder interact, and it is the development of models such as this (describing the interrelationships between events) that can add significantly to our understanding of psychopathology and suggest practical ways of alleviating and treating symptoms.

understanding A full description of how the causal factors affecting psychopathology interact.

model A hypothetical description of a process or mechanism (such as a process or psychological mechanism involved in psychopathology).

3.2.2   What Questions Do Clinical Psychologists Use Research to Try to Answer?

Potentially we can use research methods to try to understand any aspect of psychopathology that might interest us. Arguably, the primary aim of clinical psychology research is to further our knowledge and understanding of psychopathology and its treatment, and one important aspect of this is an understanding of the causes of psychopathology, and especially an understanding of the aetiology of psychological problems and disorders. Although the term **aetiology** is mainly used in medical settings to refer to the causes of diseases or pathologies, it is also a term widely used in psychopathology to describe the causes or origins of psychological symptoms. We will discuss in detail research that has led to an understanding of aetiology in sections specifically set aside for this in later chapters. One practical implication of research into the aetiology of mental health problems is that understanding the causes of psychopathology will inevitably suggest methods of intervention that might be used to alleviate those problems. Once again, Activity 3.2 provides a useful example that illustrates this. The model of panic disorder displayed in this Activity describes the causal factors that generate a panic

aetiology A term widely used in psychopathology to describe the causes or origins of psychological symptoms.

attack that have been identified using controlled research methods (Clark, 1986). Clearly, in this model, panic attacks are precipitated by the individual catastrophically misinterpreting ambiguous bodily sensations. This implies that attempting to control and change this tendency to catastrophically misinterpret bodily sensations should help to reduce the frequency and intensity of panic attacks in panic disorder, and, over the years, interventions of this kind have been refined to a point where they offer successful treatment for many suffering panic disorder (Wells, 2006; Fisher, 2008).

To be useful in helping to understand psychopathology, research does not necessarily have to be carried out on those who have mental health problems or who display symptoms of psychopathology. In Chapter 1 we discussed the possibility that much of what is labelled as psychopathology is often just an extreme form of common and accepted behaviours. That is, symptoms diagnosed as a psychological disorder may just be more extreme versions of everyday behaviour. One good example is worrying. Worrying is usually viewed as a perfectly normal reaction to the challenges and stressors encountered in daily life and the activity of worrying may often help us to cope with these problems by enabling us to think them through. However, once uncontrollable worrying becomes a chronic reaction to even minor stressors it then begins to cause distress and interfere with normal daily living. Because symptoms diagnosed as a disorder may just be more extreme versions of everyday behaviour, then what we find out about activities such as worrying in non-clinical populations will probably provide some insights into the aetiology of pathological worrying when it is a significant indicator of a psychological disorder such as generalized anxiety disorder (GAD). Undertaking research on healthy, non-clinical populations in order to shed light on the aetiology of psychopathology is known as **analogue research**, and such research makes an important contribution to the understanding of psychopathology (Davey, 2003; Vredenburg, Flett & Krames, 1993).

analogue research Research on healthy, non-clinical populations in order to shed light on the aetiology of psychopathology.

Another important function of clinical psychology research is to determine the efficacy of treatments and interventions. This includes testing the effectiveness of newly developed drug, surgical or psychological treatments. Research may even try to compare the effectiveness of two different types of treatment for a psychological disorder (e.g. comparing a drug treatment for depression with a psychological treatment for depression). Such studies are not quite as simple as they may initially seem because the researcher will have to compare those who undergo the treatment with those who do not, and they will also have to control for extraneous factors that might influence improvement that are not directly due to the therapy being tested (e.g. how attentive the therapist is, or the degree to which the client participating in the study 'expects' to get better). We will discuss therapy outcome research of this kind in more detail in Chapter 4, but the interested reader may want to have a look at Sloane, Staples, Cristol, Yorkston & Whipple (1975), Shapiro, Barkham, Rees, Hardy, Reynolds *et al.* (1994) or Clark, Ehlers, Hackmann, McManus *et al.* (2006) as examples of how intervention outcome research is conducted.

Finally, practising clinical psychologists often have pressing questions that, for various reasons, they need to answer. Very often these are questions of a practical nature related to their employment as mental health professionals working in organisations that provide mental health services. For example, in the UK, most NHS service providers will want to ensure that the service they are offering is effective, and this is known as **evaluation research** or **clinical audit**. Clinical audit uses research methods to determine whether existing clinical knowledge, skills and resources are effective and are being properly used, and the kind of questions addressed will include 'what is the service trying to achieve?' and

> **evaluation research** See *clinical audit.*

'how will we know if the service has achieved what it is trying to achieve?' (Barker, Pistrang & Elliott, 2002). In this sense, clinical audit does not add to the body of knowledge about psychopathology, but is an attempt to ensure that current knowledge is being effectively used. In particular, clinical audit is intended to influence the activities of a local team of clinicians, rather than influencing clinical practice generally (Cooper, Turpin, Bucks & Kent, 2005), and clinical audit uses research methods to assess how much end users value the services on offer, their satisfaction with these services, and what is perceived as good and bad about the services offered (for an example, see Tulett, Jones & Lavender, 2006).

> **clinical audit** The use of research methods to determine whether existing clinical knowledge, skills and resources are effective and are being properly used. Also known as evaluation research.

These, then, are some of the reasons why clinical psychologists do research. They include attempts to answer pressing practical problems (e.g. what treatments are effective?) and attempts to add to the body of knowledge about psychopathology (e.g. what causes specific psychopathologies?). The next section introduces you to some of the research methods that can be used to answer these questions.

SELF-TEST QUESTIONS

- Can you name four main goals of research?
- What does the term aetiology mean?
- What is analogue research?
- What is clinical audit?

SECTION SUMMARY

3.2 CLINICAL PSYCHOLOGY RESEARCH – WHAT DO WE WANT TO FIND OUT?

- The main goals of research are *description*, *prediction*, *control*, and *understanding*.
- Clinical psychology research is often aimed at understanding the *aetiology*, or causes of psychopathology.
- *Analogue research* involves using healthy non-clinical participants or non-human animal studies to understand psychopathology.

3.3 RESEARCH DESIGNS IN CLINICAL PSYCHOLOGY

There is a whole range of research designs that are relevant to clinical psychology research and the type of method you choose will be determined by a number of

factors, including (1) the nature of the question you are asking (e.g. do you want to find out whether one event causes another or whether these events are merely correlated?), (2) the nature of the population you are studying (e.g. is the psychopathology you are studying rare, and so you only have access to a few participants?), and (3) whether your research is at an early or advanced stage (e.g. you may simply want to be able to describe some of the phenomena associated with a psychopathology rather than to explain its causes in detail). The following represent examples of the main research designs used in clinical psychology research, and other more specific examples can be found in the specialized Research Methods Boxes found in individual chapters.

3.3.1 Correlational Designs

Correlational designs are among those most commonly used in clinical psychology research. The aim of this methodology is to try to determine whether there is a relationship between two or more variables. For example, is trait anxiety associated with worrying? Is body dissatisfaction associated with excessive dieting in eating disorders? Is the availability of drugs associated with substance abuse in adolescents? As long as we have valid and reliable ways of measuring the variables we want to study (see section 2.2.1), then we can undertake a correlational analysis. Basically a correlational analysis will tell you whether two variables co-vary. That is, if you increase the value of one measure then does the value of the other also increase? In the examples we have just given, a positive correlation between trait anxiety and worrying would indicate that as trait anxiety increased, worry would also increase, and a positive correlation between body dissatisfaction and dieting would indicate that as body dissatisfaction increased so too would dieting behaviour. Note that this does not imply a causal relationship between the two variables and it does not explain why they are related; it only indicates that scores on one variable co-vary with scores on the other variable. So, for example, a positive correlation between trait anxiety and worrying could mean any of the following: (1) that increases in worrying cause an increase in trait anxiety, (2) that increases in trait anxiety cause an increase in worrying, or (3) that some other variable causes similar changes in both worry and trait anxiety (e.g. increases in depression could cause both increases in worrying *and* increases in trait anxiety). So a correlational analysis is often a method that is used at the very beginning of a research programme to simply try to map out how the relevant variables involved in a particular phenomenon interrelate.

To undertake a correlational analysis the researcher needs to obtain pairs of scores on the variables being studied. For example, if you are interested in whether there is a relationship between trait anxiety and worrying, you can ask participants to complete questionnaires measuring worry and trait anxiety. You will then have two scores for each participant, and these scores can be entered into a spreadsheet for a computer statistical

correlational designs Research designs which enable a researcher to determine if there is a relationship or association between two or more variables.

package such as **Statistical Package for the Social Sciences (SPSS)** (Field, 2013a). This will compute a correlation coefficient (denoted by the symbol r) which measures the degree of relationship between the two variables. The correlation coefficient can range from +1.00 through 0.00 to −1.00, with 1.00 denoting a perfect **positive correlation** between the two variables (i.e. as scores on one variable increase, then scores on the other variable will increase) and −1.00 denoting a perfect **negative correlation** between the two variables (i.e. as scores on one variable increase, then scores on the other variables will decrease). A correlation coefficient of 0.00 indicates that the two variables are completely unrelated. The relationship between two variables can also be represented graphically in what is known as a **scattergram**, and Figure 3.1 provides three examples of scattergrams representing three different types of relationships between variables. These scattergrams show how the **line of best fit** differs with the nature of the relationship between the two variables concerned. The statistical package that calculates the correlation coefficient and prints out the scattergram for you will also provide you with an indication of the **statistical significance** of your results. A researcher will want to know the degree to which their results occurred by chance, and if the probability of their results occurring by chance is low then they can be relatively assured that the finding is a reliable one. Traditionally, a correlation is considered statistically significant if the probability of it occurring by chance is less than 5 in 100, and this is written as $p < .05$ (p stands for probability). From the examples given in Figure 3.1 you can see that the correlations in both Figures 3.1a and 3.1b are statistically significant (because the p values are less than .05). However, the correlation in Figure 3.1c is not significant (because the p value is higher than .05), meaning there is probably no important relationship between the two variables. (see also Focus Point 3.3 later in the chapter for a discussion of probability levels and effect sizes).

Correlational designs are valuable for clinical psychology researchers in a variety of ways. First, they allow the researcher to begin to understand what variables may be interrelated and this provides a useful first

Statistical Package for the Social Sciences (SPSS) A computer program specifically developed for statistical analysis for the social sciences.

positive correlation A relationship between two variables in which a high score on one measure is accompanied by a high score on the other.

negative correlation A relationship between two variables in which a high score on one measure is accompanied by a low score on the other.

scattergram A graphical representation showing the relationship between two variables.

line of best fit A straight line used as a best approximation of a summary of all the points in a scattergram.

statistical significance The degree to which the outcome of a study is greater or smaller than would be expected by chance.

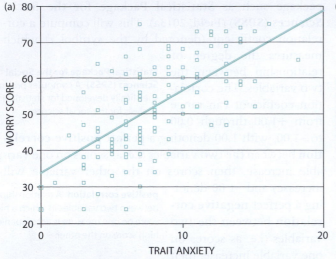

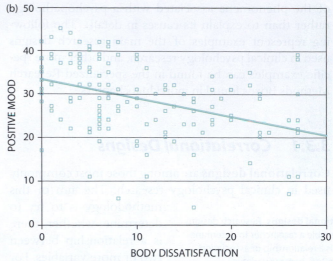

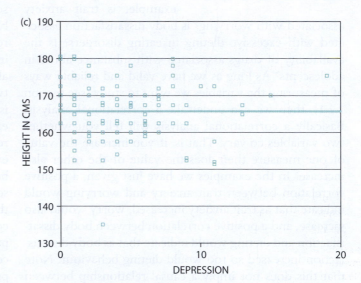

FIGURE 3.1 *Correlation scattergrams.*

In a questionnaire study, 132 female college student participants were asked to fill in valid and reliable questionnaires measuring (1) the extent to which they worried, (2) their level of trait anxiety, (3) the degree of positive mood they exhibited over the past 6 months, (4) their level of dissatisfaction with their body shape, (5) their current level of depression, and (6) their height.

(a) This scattergram shows the relationship between worry scores and trait anxiety scores for the 132 participants. This exhibits a positive correlation, and the line of best fit (the straight line) indicates this by showing an increasing trend. The correlation coefficient calculated by SPSS was r = .66, and this was significant at p < .001.

(b) This scattergram shows the relationship between measures of positive mood and body dissatisfaction for the 132 participants. This exhibits a negative correlation, and the line of best fit (the straight line) indicates this by showing a decreasing trend. The correlation coefficient calculated by SPSS was r = −.40, and this was significant at p < .001.

(c) This scattergram shows the relationship between measures of height and depression for the 132 participants. This indicates that these variables are unrelated with the line of best fit (the straight line) showing neither an increasing nor decreasing trend. The correlation coefficient calculated by SPSS was r = .01, with p > .80, and this was non-significant.

step towards understanding a particular phenomenon. Second, correlational designs are useful for researching how individual differences and personality factors may relate to psychopathology. For example, they would allow us to determine whether a personality factor, such as perfectionism, was related to a psychopathology, such as obsessive-compulsive disorder (e.g. Tolin, Woods & Abramowitz, 2003). Third, they would also allow us to determine whether certain experiences were associated with specific psychopathologies, such as whether the

experience of stressful events is associated with depression (e.g. Brown & Harris, 1978).

However, as we indicated earlier, correlational designs are limited. They certainly do not allow us to draw any conclusions about causality, and they usually provide very little insight into the mechanism or process that might mediate the relationship between the two variables that are correlated. We need to use other designs (such as the experimental design) to help us answer the question of *how* the two variables are related.

3.3.2 Longitudinal Studies and Prospective Designs

An alternative form of correlational design is known as the **longitudinal study** or prospective design. In the traditional correlational

> **longitudinal study** Research that takes measures from the same participants at two or more different times in order to specify the time relationships between variables. This may extend over many years or over a participant's whole lifetime.

CORRELATION AND CAUSATION

© iStock.com/muldoon

A significant positive correlation between two variables does not imply causation, nor does it provide any real insight into why or how the two variables are related. Take the following example.

There is a significant positive correlation between body piercings and measures of negative mood (Skegg, Nada-Raja, Paul & Skegg, 2007). Does this mean that body piercing causes negative mood, or that negative mood causes a person to have body piercings? We certainly can't tell from the correlation alone. However, the significant relationship between these two variables may not even represent a causal relationship between them at all, but that they may both be caused by some other **third variable** that was not measured in the correlational study. In this case, both having body piercings and negative mood may be caused by some other variable, such as (1) *being young*, and so being more likely to indulge in body piercing and experience adolescent depression (Caliendo, Armstrong & Roberts, 2005), (2) *having a tendency to indulge in risk-taking behaviours*, and so being more likely to be less socially conformist but negatively affected by unusual experiences (Carroll, Riffenburgh, Roberts & Myhre, 2002), or (3) *being a substance abuser*, and so more likely to be drawn to socially nonconformist cultures that might include body piercing as a fashion statement as well as experiencing the negative emotions that are associated with substance abuse (Forbes, 2001).

> **third variable** A factor that may mediate the relationship between two other measures that are significantly correlated.

---

design, all measures are taken at the same point in time (known as a **cross-sectional design**, because the study simply takes a sample of measures as a 'cross-section' of ongoing behaviour). However, in longitudinal or prospective designs, measures are taken at two or more different times. In a longitudinal study, measures are taken from the same participants on different occasions usually over extended periods of time. This may extend over many years, or, in more long-term studies, over a participant's whole lifetime. Prospective studies take measures of the relevant variables at a particular point in time (usually called time 1), and then go back to the same participants at some future time and take the same or similar measures again (usually called time 2). Both longitudinal and **prospective designs** enable the researcher to specify more precisely the time-order relationships between variables that are correlated. That is, because measures are taken from the same participant at both times 1 and 2, the researcher can not only see whether there are correlations between variables *X* and *Y*, but also whether variable *X* measured at time 1 predicts *changes* in measures of variable *Y* that occurred between times 1 and 2. A detailed example of a prospective design is given in Research Methods in Clinical Psychology Box 7.2 where a

> **cross-sectional design** A research design that involves the collection of data from a sample at just one point in time.

> **prospective designs** Research that takes measures from the same participants at two or more different times in order to specify the time relationships between variables.

measure of negative attributional style at time 1 was shown to predict increases in depression scores between times 1 and 2. This type of design enables the researcher to understand the time course of relationships between two variables, and to determine whether one variable predicts changes in a second variable. In the case given in Research Methods Box 7.2, a negative attributional style predicts future increases in depression, and can therefore be identified as a risk factor for depression.

One example of a longitudinal study is the Dunedin Multidisciplinary Health and Development Study – a longitudinal investigation of health and behaviour in a complete birth cohort (http://dunedinstudy.otago.ac.nz). Participants in the study were born in Dunedin, New Zealand, between April 1972 and March 1973, and over 1000 of these individuals then participated in follow-up assessments at age 3, 5, 7, 9, 11, 13, 15, 18, 21, 26, 32 and 38 years. The study has enabled researchers to understand the time-order relationships between variables associated with health and psychopathology, and to understand how some variables can be identified as predictors or risk factors for later behaviour. For example, using prospective data from the Dunedin study, Reichenberg, Caspi, Harrington, Houts, Keefe *et al*. (2010) found that children who grow up to develop adult schizophrenia enter primary school struggling with verbal reasoning and lag further behind peers in working memory, attention, and processing speed as they grow older.

increasingly controversial because of changing views on the ethical implications of using non-human animals in scientific experiments (Rollin, 2006; Rowan, 1997).

Another important use of the experimental design in psychopathology research is in studies testing the effectiveness of treatments for mental health problems. These types of studies are often known as **clinical trials** and attempt to test whether (1) a treatment is more effective than no treatment, (2) whether treatment A is more effective than treatment B, or (3) whether a newly developed treatment is more effective than existing treatments. In a standard treatment efficacy experiment, researchers will allocate clients or patients with a specific psychopathology (e.g. depression) to different experimental conditions. The experimental group will receive the treatment manipulation whose efficacy is being tested (e.g. a form of psychotherapy), and control groups will undergo other manipulations depending on what comparisons need to be made. For example, if the researchers want to discover if the psychotherapy treatment is more effective than a drug treatment, then a control group will receive the drug instead of psychotherapy. The researchers will then measure symptoms at various points in time after the two treatments to assess which is more effective (e.g. Ward, King, Lloyd, Bower *et al.*, 2000; Leff, Vearnals, Brewin, Wolff *et al.*, 2000). Sometimes, researchers may want to assess whether a particular intervention is more effective than simply doing nothing. However, this is not as simple a comparison as it sounds. Logically you would imagine that a researcher would subject half the participants to the intervention, and allocate the other half to a control condition in which they receive no treatment. Suppose the researcher wants to assess the effectiveness of a drug treatment for depression. Just giving the experimental group a pill containing the drug and giving the control group nothing has a number of problems. First, the experimental group may get better simply because they are being giving a pill and this leads them to *expect* to get better. This is known as a **placebo effect**, where a participant may improve simply because the procedure they are undergoing leads them to believe they should or might get better. To control for this possibility, a control group should be included in which the participants are given a pill that contains an inactive substance (such as a sugar pill). This is known as a **placebo control condition** that controls for the possibility that participants may improve simply because they are being

clinical trials Experimental research studies used to test the effectiveness of treatments for mental health problems.

placebo effect The effect when participants in a clinical trial show improvement even though they are not being given a theoretically structured treatment.

placebo control condition A control group that is included in a clinical trial to assess the effects of participant expectations.

given a pill regardless of what is in the pill. Nevertheless, suffice it to say here that the experimental method does provide a useful paradigm for assessing the effectiveness of different interventions, but we will discuss the complexities and limitations of this approach when we discuss treatment methods more thoroughly in the next chapter.

Summary

The experiment is arguably the most powerful research tool that we have because it allows us to draw conclusions about the direction of causality between variables, and this is the first step towards putting together theories and models of how psychopathology is caused. However, in order to provide valid results, experiments must be carefully designed and well controlled. Experiments are more than just data collection exercises, and the experimenter needs to *manipulate* important variables in order to discover causal relationships between events and behaviour. This means that in some cases the experiment can be too intrusive for use with clients suffering psychopathology, and this means that many of our studies investigating psychopathology need to be conducted on analogue populations such as healthy volunteers and non-human animals.

3.3.5   Mixed Designs

One of the basic principles of experimental design is that participants must be assigned to different groups on a random basis. However, this principle can be set aside if the research question being tackled requires a **mixed design**. For example, suppose we wanted to see whether negative mood caused anxious individuals to worry more than depressed individuals. In an experiment of this kind, we would still be experimentally inducing negative mood (the experimental manipulation), but we would not be assigning participants randomly to the experimental groups; we would want to ensure that in one experimental group we only had anxious individuals and in a second experimental group we only had depressed individuals. We would select the participants pre-experimentally on the basis of these attributes and assign them non-randomly to each group. This is known as a mixed design because (1) we are adopting elements from the experimental approach (i.e. we are manipulating an independent variable), but (2) we are assigning our participants non-randomly to the experimental groups. This is a design that is used quite frequently in psychopathology research because the clinical psychology researcher may often want to know if a particular variable will affect individuals with different psychopathologies in similar or different ways.

mixed design Research which uses the non-random assignment of participants to groups in an experiment.

An example of a mixed design is a study by Sanderson, Rapee & Barlow (1989) investigating the effects of expectations on panic disorder. They pre-selected two groups of participants: one group consisted of individuals diagnosed with panic disorder and the other group consisted of individuals with no psychiatric diagnosis. They then subjected both groups to an experimental manipulation. In this case, they asked all participants to inhale compressed air and but told them they were inhaling CO_2, which could induce a panic attack. Even though the compressed air itself could not have induced a panic attack, participants diagnosed with panic disorder were significantly more likely to have a panic attack after the manipulation, suggesting that in such individuals the mere expectation of a panic attack is likely to induce one.

Mixed designs are frequently used in treatment outcome studies, where the effectiveness of a particular intervention is being assessed on individuals with different psychiatric diagnoses or with different severity of symptoms. Figure 3.2 shows the results of a mixed design study carried out by Huppert, Schultz, Foa & Barlow (2004) designed to assess the effects of administering a placebo pill to three different groups of participants, each diagnosed with a different psychiatric disorder. In this study they found that their experimental manipulation (the administration of a placebo pill) significantly reduced the severity of reported symptoms in individuals diagnosed with social phobia and panic disorder, but not in individuals diagnosed with OCD.

This example illustrates how useful the mixed design can be when attempting to assess how individuals with different diagnoses or groups of symptoms will react to an experimental manipulation (such as a treatment intervention). However, we must always be aware of the fact that one of the variables in a mixed design (in this case the diagnostic groups) is not manipulated, and so we cannot infer a direct *causal* relationship between the diagnostic category and the effects of the manipulation. For example, in Figure 3.2 we cannot infer that the failure of the OCD group to improve after being given a placebo is caused by the specific fact that they are suffering from OCD because we have not explicitly manipulated that variable. It could be that some other variable related to OCD is causing the failure to respond, such as having less faith in drug treatments generally, or individuals with OCD may be more resistant to any treatment than those in the other groups.

3.3.6 *Natural Experiments*

Most experiments are the result of a deliberate manipulation carried out under controlled conditions by an experimenter. However, in the case of clinical psychology research, nature may sometimes provide us with the opportunity to observe the effects on behaviour of a natural manipulation. **Natural experiments** usually allow us to collect data on the effects of events that we would not usually be able to manipulate in the laboratory, and such events

> **natural experiments** Research which allows researchers to observe the effects on behaviour of a naturally occurring 'manipulation' (such as an earthquake).

include natural disasters such as earthquakes and floods, traumatic disasters or accidents such as the Kings Cross tube station fire, or terrorist attacks such as those on the World Trade Center in New York on 11 September 2001. For example, van Griensven, Chakkraband, Thienkrua, Pengjuntr *et al.* (2006) studied survivors of the 2004 tsunami in southern Thailand, and found that the event had caused elevated rates of symptoms of PTSD, anxiety and depression in survivors of this event. Other studies have used naturally occurring disasters as a tool to assess whether such events increase psychopathology only in individuals with particular characteristics. For instance, Weems, Pina, Costa, Watts *et al.* (2007) found that PTSD symptoms in children following the devastation caused by Hurricane Katrina in the southern USA in 2005 was highest in those children who had high levels of trait anxiety prior to the disaster.

Other variables that may play a part in the development of psychopathology include poverty and social

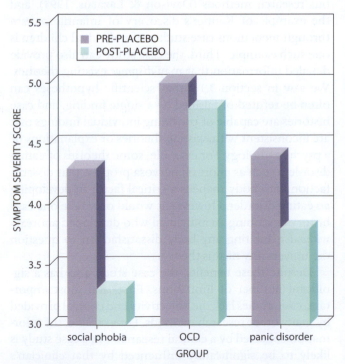

FIGURE 3.2 *Example of a mixed design.*
Source: Huppert, J.D., Schultz, L.T., Foa, E.B. & Barlow, D.H. (2004). Differential response to placebo among patients with social phobia, panic disorder, and obsessive-compulsive disorder. *American Journal of Psychiatry, 161,* 1485–1487.

deprivation, and these are clearly factors that we could not easily manipulate in a controlled experiment. However, Costello, Compton, Keeler & Angold (2003) took advantage of the opening of a casino in an American Indian reservation to study how poverty and conduct disorder in children might be linked (see section 16.2.2). The introduction of the casino provided income that moved many of the local families out of poverty, and Costello *et al.* found that this resulted in a significant decrease in the symptoms of conduct disorder in local children – but only in those children whose families had benefited financially from the introduction of the casino, suggesting either a direct or indirect link between poverty and symptoms of childhood conduct disorder.

3.3.7 Single-Case Studies

For a variety of reasons, clinical psychology researchers may study just one individual, and gather the information and knowledge they require from detailed description and analysis of a single case. This may take the form of a comprehensive **case study** in which the clinician gathers detailed information about the individual, including details of symptoms, family history, medical history, details of personal experiences, educational background and suchlike, and then attempts to ascertain what light these details may cast on an understanding of the individual's psychopathology. In some respects, the case formulation that clinical practitioners undertake when conducting therapy is a form of case study in which they attempt to understand the causes of an individual client's symptoms in terms of that person's cognitions, experiential history or personal relationships (see section 2.3). An alternative form of the single-case study is the **single-case experiment**, in which a participant's behaviour is observed and measured both before and after an experimental manipulation. The researcher can then make some assumptions about what is happening by comparing the participant's behaviour before the manipulation with their behaviour after the manipulation, and that individual then acts as both experimental participant and control participant.

> **case study** An in-depth investigation of an individual participant.

> **single-case experiment** A single case study in which a participant's behaviour is observed and measured both before and after an experimental manipulation.

Case studies

Before the development of sophisticated research designs, the case study was one of the most widely used methods of collecting information about psychopathology, and knowledge collected in this way often served as the basis for the development of early theories of psychopathology. One famous exponent of the case study was Freud himself, and many important features of psychoanalytic theory were based on Freud's detailed observation and analysis of individual cases. One such example is the famous case of Little Hans, a 5-year-old boy who had a fear of horses. Focus Point 6.1 describes how Freud studied this single case in detail, and how it enabled him to develop his view that many childhood fears were caused by a subconscious Oedipus complex. In a different example in the 1940s, case studies of disturbed children provided the Austrian psychiatrist Leo Kanner with a set of observations indicating a consistent set of symptoms that he called *infantile autism*, and which gave rise to the symptom classification that we currently know as autistic spectrum disorder (see Chapter 17).

Case studies are valuable in a number of different circumstances. First, they are useful when there are only a few instances of a particular psychopathology available for study. This was the case when dissociative identity disorder (DID) (multiple personalities) was first reported as a specific disorder in the 1950s and 1960s, and an example of the use of case histories in the first descriptions of this disorder is provided in Case History 14.1. Second, case studies are also valuable for providing new insights into existing psychopathologies, and the detailed information that a case study can offer often provides new ways of looking at a particular problem and new facts that can subsequently be subjected to more rigorous research methods (Davison & Lazarus, 1995), and the example of Kanner's discovery of infantile autism through meticulous case studies of individual children is one such example. Third, the case study can also provide detailed information that may *disprove* existing theories. We saw in section 3.1.2 that scientific hypotheses can often be refuted or falsified by a single finding, and case histories are capable of providing individual findings that are inconsistent with existing theories or explanations of a psychopathology. For example, some theories of eating disorders such as anorexia nervosa propose that dissatisfaction with body shape is a critical factor in developing an eating disorder. However, it would only take one case history describing an individual who developed anorexia *without* exhibiting any body dissatisfaction to question the universality of this theory.

Despite these benefits, the case study also has a significant number of limitations. First, and most important, case studies lack the objectivity and control provided by many other research methods. For example, the information collected by a clinical researcher in a case study is likely to be significantly influenced by that clinician's theoretical orientation. Arguably, the detailed information on Little Hans collected by Freud was significantly influenced by Freud's own theoretical views on psychopathology, and it was quite likely that he collected and used only that information that was consistent with his existing views. Freud clearly spent much time finding out about Little Hans's childhood whereas more cognitively or behaviourally oriented psychologists would focus on current cognitions or those current environmental factors that might be maintaining Little Hans's behaviour (see section 1.3.2). Second, case studies are usually low on **external validity**. That is, the findings from one case are rarely generalisable to other cases. For instance, because of the subjective nature of the information collected by a clinician in a case study, how can we be sure the supposed causes of psychopathology in that case study will also be true for other individuals with similar psychopathologies? Finally, we have just argued that the case study can be valuable in providing evidence that could disprove a theory, but because of the uncontrolled way in which case studies are collected it is not particularly useful for providing evidence to support theories. For example, a case study may indicate that a young woman with an eating disorder is dissatisfied with her body shape. This is information that is *consistent* with theories of eating disorders that assume a role for body dissatisfaction, but it is not evidence that differentially favours that theory because the case study does not (1) rule out other explanations, or (2) indicate that body dissatisfaction plays a critical role in causing the eating disorder.

external validity The extent to which the results of a study can be extrapolated to other situations.

Single-case experiments

The single-case experiment has a particular value in psychopathology research and is used relatively frequently. The main value of this method is that it enables the researcher (1) to undertake an experimental manipulation (and so potentially make some inferences about causal relationships between variables), and (2) to use one individual as both experimental and control participant. There is a particular advantage to using a single participant and subjecting that individual to both experimental and control conditions. First, in many psychopathology studies the use of a control group may mean denying individual participants a treatment that they need. For example, if a researcher is attempting to assess the efficacy of a particular treatment, they would have to compare the treatment with a control group who did not receive that treatment. This obviously raises ethical issues about withholding treatment from clients who may benefit from it. Second, some psychopathologies are quite rare, and it can be quite difficult to gather enough participants to form groups of experimental and control participants, and conducting an experiment on a single participant may be a necessity.

The single-case experiment allows the experimenter to take some baseline measures of behaviour (the control condition) before introducing the experimental manipulation (the experimental condition), and behaviour during baseline can then be compared with behaviour following the manipulation. Most single-case experiments use variations of what are known as the ABA or ABAB design. In the **ABA design**, an initial baseline stage involves the observation and measurement of behaviour without any intervention (A); this is then followed by a treatment or manipulation stage where the experimental manipulation is introduced and its effect on behaviour observed and measured (B); subsequently a final return-to-baseline stage is then introduced (A), in which behaviour is once more observed in the absence of the treatment or manipulation. The second baseline stage is included to ensure that any behaviour change that occurs in stage B is caused by the manipulation and not any confounding factor such as a natural drift in behaviour over time. In the **ABAB design** (sometimes known as a *reversal design*), a second treatment or manipulation stage is introduced and provides extra power in demonstrating that any changes in behaviour are explicitly due to the manipulation or treatment. Figure 3.3 provides an example of the use of an ABAB design. This demonstrates the effectiveness of providing a social story conveying information about appropriate mealtime behaviour for an individual with Asperger's syndrome (Bledisoe, Smith Myles & Simpson, 2007). In this example, the effectiveness of the manipulation was demonstrated by the fact that behaviours returned to baseline levels following the withdrawal of the manipulation (the second A stage), and across all four stages the frequency of the measured behaviour fluctuated in accordance with whether the experimental manipulation was present (B) or not (A).

One disadvantage to the ABAB design is that it alternates periods of treatment with non-treatment, and this may be problematic if the study is assessing the effectiveness of a treatment that has important benefits for the participant (e.g. it prevents self-injurious behaviour or alleviates distress). This can be overcome by using a **multiple-baseline design**. There are two variations to this procedure: (1) using a single participant, the researcher can select two or more

ABA design A single-case experiment which involves an initial baseline stage of observation and measurement of behaviour without any intervention (A), followed by a treatment or manipulation stage where the experimental manipulation is introduced and its effect on behaviour observed and measured (B). A final return-to-baseline stage is then introduced (A) in which behaviour is once more observed in the absence of the treatment or manipulation.

ABAB design A single-case experiment, similar to the ABA design, with the addition of a second treatment or manipulation stage, providing extra power in demonstrating that any changes in behaviour are explicitly due to the manipulation or treatment.

multiple-baseline design An experimental design in which the researcher studies several behaviours at a time.

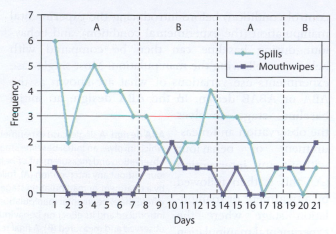

FIGURE 3.3 *Example of a single-case experimental ABAB design. The participant in this study was a 13-year-old male with Asperger's syndrome and attention deficit hyperactivity disorder (ADHD) (see Chapter 17) who exhibited a number of eating-related problems (e.g. talking with mouth full, spilling food, talking in a loud voice.). Days 1–7 show the baseline levels of spills (a 'bad' response) and mouthwipes (a 'good' response) (the first A phase). The intervention used (phase B) was a social story provided to the participant to help him improve his eating habits. The figure shows how good eating behaviours tended to increase and bad behaviours tended to decrease in frequency during the intervention phases, but return to normal during baseline phases.*
Source: Bledisoe, R., Smith Myles, B. & Simpson, R.L. (2007). Use of a social story intervention to improve mealtime skills of an adolescent with Asperger syndrome. *Autism* 7(3), 289–295. © 2007 by SAGE. Reprinted by permission of SAGE.

behaviours to measure and can target the treatment or manipulation on one behaviour but allow the other behaviours to act as control comparisons, or (2) the researcher can use multiple participants by first taking baseline measures from each (stage A), and then introducing the treatment or manipulation (B) successively across the participants. The multiple baseline design means that each individual within the study can receive the treatment for a maximum amount of time without compromising the experimental balance of the study (e.g. Thompson, Kearns & Edmonds, 2006).

While the single-case experiment has a number of significant benefits, it too also has some limitations. Most importantly, it is still a single-case study, so it may be difficult to generalize the results to other individuals with similar psychopathologies – just because a treatment works for one person does not necessarily mean it will work for another. Group designs overcome this problem by using statistical inference across a number of participants to determine the probability that the findings from the study will be generalisable to a larger population. However, the problem of generalisability

can be overcome to some extent by using more than one participant. If the treatment or manipulation is effective across more than one participant then this increases the chances that it will be generalisable to other individuals.

3.3.8   Meta-Analyses and Systematic Reviews

Many different researchers frequently conduct studies investigating the same or similar phenomena, so it is usually the case that we end up with many studies providing information on the same issue. For example, we may want to know whether cognitive behaviour therapy (CBT) is a successful treatment for depression, and many different researchers may end up conducting studies and experiments to this end. Some of these studies may convincingly demonstrate that CBT is effective, some others may suggest that its effectiveness is marginal, and still others may fail to provide any evidence for its effectiveness. So how do we decide which studies to believe, and how do we try to make an informed decision about the effectiveness of CBT in treating depression? Traditionally, this task would have been undertaken in review articles in which the reviewer would collect together all the relevant studies, and try to make an informed judgement across the whole range of studies and their results (e.g. Brewin, 1996; Marcotte, 1997; Laidlaw, 2001). However, this approach is likely to be highly subjective, and one reviewer may significantly disagree with another about the importance of individual studies. In addition, some researchers with vested interests in particular types of treatment may consciously or unconsciously bias the way they interpret findings (e.g. those favouring drug treatments for depression are likely to be less convinced by studies demonstrating the effectiveness of CBT than others) (Field, 2013b).

These problems with subjective reviews have led to attempts to develop more objective reviews using standardized review procedures and statistical methods. Meta-analyses and systematic reviews are the outcome of this process, and are now becoming accepted ways of objectively assessing the strength of findings across different studies. A **systematic review** is a review of a clearly formulated question that uses systematic and explicit methods to identify, select, and critically appraise relevant research, and to collect and analyse data from the studies that are included in the review. Guidelines for collecting and reporting clinically relevant systematic reviews are provided by groups such as PRISMA (Preferred Reporting Items for Systematic

> **systematic review** A review of a clearly formulated question that uses systematic and explicit methods to identify, select, and critically appraise relevant research, and to collect and analyse data from the studies that are included in the review.

Reviews & Meta-Analyses: http://www.prisma-statement .org/index.htm), QUORUM (Quality of Reporting Meta-Analyses: Moher, Liberati, Tetzlaff, Altman & The PRISMA Group, 2009), and the American Psychological Association (MARS, Meta-Analysis Reporting Standards: Cooper, Maxwell, Stone, Sher & Board, 2008). Figure 3.4 provides an example of a flow-chart provided by PRISMA for recording and reporting how studies for a systematic review were sourced and collated.

In addition to a systematic review, a **meta-analysis** attempts to detect trends across studies found through

> **meta-analysis** A statistically accepted way of assessing the strength of a particular finding across a number of different studies.

systematic review that may have used different procedures, different numbers of participants, different types of control procedures, and different forms of measurement, and it does this by comparing effect sizes across studies. An **effect size** is an objective and stand-

ardised measure of the magnitude of the effect observed in a study (i.e.

> **effect size** An objective and standardized measure of the magnitude of the effect observed in a research study.

the difference in measured outcome between participants in a treatment or experimental group and those in appropriate control conditions), and the fact that it is standardized means that we can use this measure to compare the outcomes of studies that may have used different forms of measurement. Meta-analyses are now an almost accepted way of overviewing an area of studies that address the same or a similar research issue, and are particularly popular as a statistical tool for assessing the effectiveness of interventions for psychopathology (for examples, see Cuijpers, van Straten & Warmerdam, 2007; Hanrahan, Field, Jones & Davey, 2013; De Maat, Dekker, Schoevers & De Jonghe, 2006).

While many meta-analyses have been carried out specifically on the effectiveness of individual treatments and

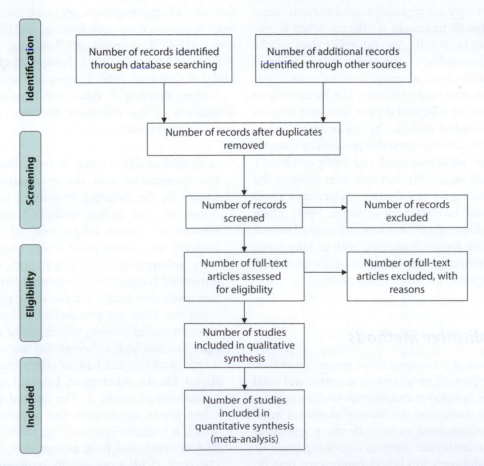

PRISMA 2009 Flow Diagram

FIGURE 3.4 PRISMA flow diagram.

An example of a flow chart for recording and reporting how studies for a systematic review are sourced and selected.

Source: Moher, D., Liberati, A., Tetzlaff, J., Altman, D.G. & The PRISMA Group (2009). Preferred reporting items for systematic reviews and meta-analyses: The PRISMA statement. *PLoS Med*, 6(6), e1000097. DOI: 10.1371/journal.pmed1000097 (for more information, visit www.prisma-statement.org).

interventions, the basis of comparison can be other factors such as type of psychopathology being treated or the comparison of drug treatments generally versus psychotherapy interventions. One of the earliest meta-analyses was a large-scale study carried out by Smith, Glass & Miller (1980) assessing whether psychotherapies were more effective than no treatment at all. From the results of their meta-analyses they concluded that (1) a very wide range of psychotherapies were more effective at reducing symptoms of psychopathology than no treatment at all, and (2), perhaps more controversially, that effect sizes did not differ significantly across different types of psychotherapies – implying that all psychotherapies were equally effective! (See Focus Point 4.4.)

Nevertheless, while a meta-analysis may seem like an objective solution to the problem of reviewing the findings from groups of studies, this method too has its limitations. First, meta-analyses frequently rely almost entirely on analysing the results of published studies, and published studies are much more likely to have significant results than non-significant results (Dickersin, Min & Meinert, 1992). This means that meta-analyses are likely to overestimate mean effect sizes because they are unlikely to include unpublished studies that are probably non-significant. The result is that they are probably biased towards claiming that a variable or treatment is effective when it may not be (Field, 2013a, 2013b). Second, effect sizes will be influenced by the quality of the research (e.g. whether the control conditions are adequate or whether outcome measures are accurate and sensitive), but meta-analyses include all studies equally, and do not take into account the quality of individual studies. The researcher undertaking a meta-analysis can overcome this problem by comparing effect sizes in 'well-conducted' and 'badly conducted' studies (Field, 2013a, 2013b), but this then involves the researcher in making some subjective judgements about what is 'good' and 'bad' research (Eysenck, 1994). There is even the possibility that meta-analyses might become a self-perpetuating form of analysis, with at least some studies now attempting meta-analyses of meta-analyses (e.g. Butler, Chapman, Forman & Beck, 2006)!

3.3.9   Qualitative Methods

So far we have mainly discussed those research methods that place an important emphasis on accurate and valid measurement of behaviour and attempt to draw conclusions from their studies on the basis of statistical inference. These methods tend to be collectively known as **quantitative methods**, but there is a growing body of research methodologies in clinical psychology that do place less emphasis on exact measurement and statistical analysis, and these are known as **qualitative methods**. Instead of emphasising mathematical analyses of data,

the raw material for qualitative research is ordinary language, and any analysis is verbal rather than statistical. The raw data in qualitative studies are usually the participant's own descriptions of themselves, their experiences, their feelings and thoughts, their ways of communicating with others, and their ways of understanding the world. Study samples are often small, and data are collected using unstructured or semi-structured interview techniques that can be analysed in a variety of non-statistical ways. Qualitative methods are particularly suited to clinical psychology research because they enable the researcher to gain an insight into the full experience of psychopathology, including the sufferer's feelings, ways of coping, and the specific ramifications that the psychopathology has on everyday life (see Research Methods in Clinical Psychology Box 3.1). In recent years, qualitative methods have provided information relevant to scale development, informed theories of psychopathology, and provided explanations for unusual research findings and unusual case histories (Hill, Thompson & Williams, 1997; Rennie, Watson & Monteiro, 2002; Nelson & Quintana, 2005; Miller & Crabtree, 2000; Harper & Thompson, 2011).

Barker, Pistrang & Elliot (2002) provide a succinct illustration of the difference between qualitative and quantitative research:

A simplified illustration of the difference between the quantitative and the qualitative approach is shown in the differing responses to the question 'How are you feeling today?' A quantitative orientated researcher might ask the participant to respond on a seven-point scale, ranging from 1 = 'very unhappy' to 7 = 'very happy', and receive an answer of 5, signifying 'somewhat happy'. A qualitative researcher might ask the same person the same question, 'How are you feeling today?', but request an open-ended answer, which could run something like 'Not too bad, although my knee is hurting me a little, and I've just had an argument with my boyfriend. On the other hand, I think I might be up for promotion at work, so I'm excited about that.' In other words, the quantitative approach yields data which are relatively simple to process, but are limited in depth and hide ambiguities; the qualitative approach yields a potentially large quantity of rich, complex data which may be difficult and time consuming to analyse. (Barker, Pistrang & Elliot, 2002, p.73; reproduced with permission)

quantitative methods Research methods that place an important emphasis on accurate and valid measurement of behaviour and attempt to draw conclusions from their studies on the basis of statistical inference.

qualitative methods Research methods that rely on the analysis of verbal reports rather than on statistical analyses of quantifiable data.

A QUALITATIVE STUDY OF DENTAL PHOBIA

This example is based on a paper by Abrahamsson *et al.* (2002) and gives you an insight into how qualitative methods might be used in clinical psychology research. The following sections describe the aims of the study, how it was conducted, and how the results were analysed to provide a theoretical perspective on the experience of dental phobia.

AIMS

To explore the situation of dental phobic patients and to investigate (1) how their dental phobia interferes with their normal routines, their daily functioning and their social activities and relationships, (2) what factors contribute to the maintenance of their phobia, and (3) how they cope with their fear.

STUDY SAMPLE

Eighteen patients applying for treatment at a specialized dental fear clinic in Göteborg, Sweden. All patients were currently refusing dental treatment because of their phobia.

IN-DEPTH INTERVIEWS

Audio-taped, open-ended interviews were conducted with each participant. The purpose of using open-ended interviews was to explore the situation of dental phobics as expressed by the participants themselves. An interview guide was used as a basic checklist to make sure that relevant topics were covered. These included onset of dental fear, family, experiences in dental care, health and effects on everyday life, coping strategies. Interviews were introduced with questions such as 'Does your dental fear have an impact on your daily life?' 'In what way?', 'What do you do/feel?' and so on.

ETHICAL ISSUES

It was stressed that participation was voluntary, all data collected would be confidential, and the participant had the right to end participation at any time. All participants completed and signed an informed consent form.

ANALYSIS OF DATA

Interview transcripts were analysed using grounded theory (see section 3.3). The aim of this method is to focus on different qualities of phenomena in order to generate a model or a theory. Different qualities of phenomena might include psychosocial processes, existing problems caused by dental phobia, how participants coped with their problems, and so on. This process should be conducted with the original aims of the study clearly in mind. The interviews were analysed line-by-line and broken down into segments reflecting their content. Segments with similar contents were then grouped together to form more abstract categories.

EXAMPLES OF FORMING ABSTRACT CATEGORIES

One participant expressed the following: 'What I'm most afraid of is that infections will spread. . . I've had a lot of colds in the last year. . . I don't know if it has anything to do with my teeth. I only know that I've waited much too long.' Another participant said: 'The idea of having false teeth at 45, then I'd be at rock bottom. . . I don't know if I could handle it psychologically.' Similar comments made by a number of participants led the researchers to create the abstract category 'Threat to own health' to describe this group of responses.

Similarly, participants also provided responses of the following kind: 'My worries about going to the dentist are a matter for me and me alone . . . maybe I could tell someone but they probably wouldn't care at all' and 'A friend said he had booked an appointment for me [at the dentist] and I went completely cold. When the time got nearer [for the appointment], I saw the date couldn't be right and understood that it was a joke.' These and similar responses were grouped into the abstract category of 'Lack of social support and understanding'.

CONCLUSIONS

This analysis allowed the researchers to construct a model or theory of the experience of dental phobia, which is represented schematically below. Four main categories of experience were developed: threat to self-respect and well-being, avoidance, readiness to act, and ambivalence in coping. This provides a rich description of how dental fear affects the daily lives of these individuals and how social and psychological factors interact to determine how they cope with this fear.

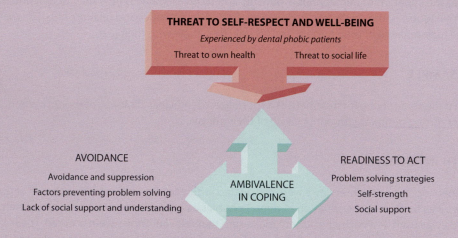

Source: Abrahamsson, K.H., Berggren, U., Hallberg, L.R. & Carlsson, S.G. (2002). Ambivalence in coping with dental fear: A qualitative study. *Journal of Health Psychology, 7,* 653–664. © 2003 by SAGE. Reprinted by permission of SAGE.

This example shows how qualitative methods are non-quantitative, usually open-ended (in the sense that the researcher does not know before the study exactly what data they may collect), and enable the researcher to begin to understand an individual's lived experiences, the feelings they have about their experiences, and the perceptions and meaning they give to their experiences (Nelson & Poulin, 1997; Polkinghorne, 1983). Given these characteristics, a typical qualitative study will involve detailed interviewing of participants to identify themes involving feelings and the meaning that those participants give to their feelings.

The advantages of using qualitative methods are: (1) some aspects of psychopathology are difficult to express numerically, and a qualitative approach allows data to be collected about more complex aspects of experience, (2) they permit intensive and in-depth study of individuals or small groups of individuals, (3) because interviewing techniques are usually open-ended, the researcher may discover interesting things about a psychopathology that they were not originally looking for, and (4) they can be an extremely valuable source of information at the outset of a research programme, and provide the researcher with a rich source of information

which may lead them to construct hypotheses suitable for study using quantitative methods.

Conducting and analysing qualitative studies

Qualitative studies are not entirely unstructured, and qualitative techniques specify ways in which data should be collected and analysed. First, unlike quantitative methods that tend to emphasize the random selection of participants and allocation to experimental groups, qualitative methods tend to deliberately specify groups of participants for sampling depending on the phenomenon or psychopathology the researcher is interested in. For example, these may include individuals who have suffered childhood abuse, families with a member who is suffering a mental health problem, parents of autistic children, and suchlike (Cresswell, 1998). Once selected, participants will then usually take part in a semi-structured, open-ended interview in a relaxed and comfortable interaction (Kvale, 1996). All interview questions would normally be related back to the original research question(s) posed prior to the study. For instance, a research question might be 'How do individuals with panic disorder cope with day-to-day living?' In this example, the interviewer can ask very general questions or more specific questions that are derived from the original research question. A general question might be 'What problems do you encounter each day because of your panic attacks, and how do you cope with them?' A more specific question might be 'How do you feel about not being able to leave the house because of the possibility you might have a panic attack?' In this kind of structure, the participant has the opportunity to respond to both general and specific questions. The general questions allow the participant to create their own picture of their experiences, and the specific questions allow the researcher to obtain detailed information that is relevant to the original research question.

Once detailed responses from the interview have been collected, the researcher has the task of making sense of the data, picking out consistent themes that emerge in the participant's responding, and deciding how these themes might relate to the original research question that was posed. The first step is to break up the interview transcript into manageable and meaningful units. There are a number of ways to do this (Giorgi, 1985; Merleau-Ponty, 1962), but for simplicity we will describe a commonly used approach known as grounded theory.

grounded theory An approach to qualitative analysis which involves identifying consistent categories or themes within the data, then building on these to provide more abstract theoretical insights into the phenomenon being studied.

Grounded theory is an approach to qualitative analysis that was developed by Glaser and Strauss (1967). It involves identifying consistent categories or themes within the data, and then building on these to provide more abstract theoretical insights into the phenomenon being studied. Research Methods Box 3.1 provides a detailed specific example of how grounded theory has been used to understand how dental phobics cope with their psychopathology, and how it affects their day-to-day living. As we can see, this study was able to identify a number of consistent themes that emerged from the interview data, and provided a rich insight into the everyday experiences and feelings of individuals with dental phobia. The study also provided some higher level theoretical insights by suggesting how several psychological and social factors interact to determine how dental phobics cope with their fear (Abrahamsson, Berggren, Hallberg & Carlsson, 2002). Grounded theory can be used with data collected in a number of forms, including interviews, focus groups, observation of participants, and diary material. It is also an approach that allows a constant dynamic interaction between research and theory. For example, the study reported in Research Methods Box 3.1 provided some theoretical insights into how dental phobics coped with their fear, and this theoretical insight can then provide the basis of a refined research question and a subsequent qualitative study pursuing this issue in further detail.

To read the article by Abrahamsson *et al.* on 'Ambivalence in coping with dental fear' go to **www.wiley-psychopathology.com/ reading/ch3**

In summary, qualitative methods lend themselves particularly well to understanding and describing many aspects of psychopathology, and are becoming increasingly used in clinical psychology research (Barker, Pistrang & Elliot, 2002). They are useful for collecting data on everyday feelings and experiences associated with psychopathology, and data collected in this way can make a significant contribution to theory. In this section of the chapter it has not been possible to convey the full range of qualitative methods available to the researcher, nor to convey the important philosophical and epistemological underpinnings of many of these techniques (see Willig, 2001; Henwood & Pidgeon, 1992). However, qualitative methods are not just an alternative to quantitative methods; the two can be combined in a useful and productive way in clinical psychology research. Examples include using qualitative data to clarify quantitative findings, beginning research in a new area with qualitative research but moving this on using quantitative methods, or using qualitative data to develop quantitative measures (Barker, Pistrang & Elliot, 2002).

SELF-TEST QUESTIONS

- What are the main aims of correlational designs?
- What is the difference between a positive and negative correlation?
- Can you identify how a scattergram can tell us how two variables are related (see Figure 3.1)?
- How do longitudinal and prospective studies differ from correlational studies?
- Can you describe the different ways in which prevalence rates can be measured?
- Which research design is the most effective for identifying causal relationships between variables?
- Can you describe what an independent variable (IV) and a dependent variable (DV) are?
- Experimental designs use control groups. What are they and how would you design one?

- What are the demand characteristics of an experiment?
- What are clinical trials?
- What is a placebo control condition?
- Can you describe what a mixed design is?
- What are the advantages and drawbacks of using case studies in research?
- What is an ABAB design?
- How do multiple-baseline designs differ from ABAB designs?
- How is effect size used to overview studies in a meta-analysis?
- What are the main differences between quantitative and qualitative research methods?
- What is grounded theory?

SECTION SUMMARY

3.3 RESEARCH DESIGNS IN CLINICAL PSYCHOLOGY

This section of the book has reviewed the various research methodologies that are available to the clinical psychology researcher. All of these methodologies include ways of collecting information and, in many cases, ways of interpreting that information. As we indicated at the outset of this section, the type of research method you adopt will depend very much on (1) the nature of the research question you are asking (do I want to discover whether there are causal relationships between variables, or do I just want to know if two variables are related in some way?), (2) the nature of the population you are studying (e.g. do you have lots of participants available or just a few?), and (3) whether your research is at an early or advanced stage (if it is the former you may want to use qualitative methods; if the latter, then quantitative methods may be more appropriate).

The key points are:

- *Correlational designs* enable the researcher to determine if there is a relationship between two or more variables.

- A correlation coefficient can range from +1.00 through 0.00 to −1.00, with +1.00 referring to a perfect *positive correlation* between two variables and −1.00 denoting a perfect *negative correlation*.

- Both *longitudinal* and *prospective studies* take measures from the same participants at two or more different times in order to specify the time-relationships between variables.

- *Epidemiological studies* provide details about the *prevalence* of psychological disorders.

- *Experiments* involve the researcher manipulating one of the variables (the *independent variable*) and then measuring the effect of this on behaviour (the *dependent variable*).

- To be valid, experimental studies need to use appropriately designed *control conditions*.

- *Clinical trials* are types of experiments that are used to test the effectiveness of treatments.

- A *placebo effect* is when a participant in a clinical trial shows improvement even though they are not being given an effective treatment.

- *Mixed designs* use the non-random assignment of participants to groups in an experiment.

- *Natural experiments* allow researchers to observe the effects on behaviour of a naturally occurring 'manipulation' (such as an earthquake).

- *Single-case studies* allow researchers to collect data from just one individual.

- The single-case experiment uses *ABA*, *ABAB* or *multiple-baseline designs* to carry out controlled experiments on individual participants.

- *Meta-analyses* are statistically accepted ways of assessing the strength of a particular finding across a number of different studies.

- *Systematic reviews* are reviews that use systematic and explicit methods to identify, select, and critically appraise relevant research.

- *Qualitative methods* use ordinary language as their raw material, and adopt verbal rather than statistical analyses.

- *Grounded theory* is one particular example of a qualitative method that is used extensively in clinical psychology research.

3.4   ETHICAL ISSUES IN CLINICAL PSYCHOLOGY RESEARCH

It would be almost impossible to do psychological research in general, and clinical psychology research in particular, without the individuals who are needed to act as participants. However, the people that we recruit as participants have rights that need to be protected, they have a dignity that needs to be preserved, and their well-being needs to be maintained. These all form part of the ethical deliberations that need to be fully considered before we begin a particular piece of research. Examples of ethical issues that might be encountered in clinical psychology research include: 'Is it harmful to induce panic attacks in an experiment?' 'What will be the effect of inducing a negative mood in my participants, and how can I ensure this doesn't affect them after the experiment?' 'Is giving a participant a placebo pill instead of an active drug tantamount to withholding treatment?' 'Does my experiment involve deceiving the participants in any way?' 'How can I be sure that my participants' involvement in the study is truly voluntary?' Most organisations that host clinical psychology research (such as universities or hospitals) now have ethical committees that are required to vet all research proposals to check that they meet basic ethical standards and protect the participants in the research. Ethical issues in clinical psychology research fall under three main headings: (1) **Informed consent**, (2) Causing distress or withholding benefits, and (3) Privacy and confidentiality.

> **informed consent** Detailed information about an experiment is given to potential participants to enable them to make an informed decision to participate.

3.4.1   Informed Consent

Researchers should always properly inform participants about what it is they will be participating in, what they will be asked to do, and what experiences they might have while taking part in the study. This information needs to be detailed enough for the researcher to be sure that the potential participant can make a rational and informed decision about whether to participate or not. This means that the information provided about the study should be as detailed as possible, and – importantly – it should be couched in a language that the participant will understand and not include technical jargon that is only likely to be comprehensible to the researcher. This information should include (1) details of the purpose of the experiment, (2) a description of the procedures the participant will encounter, (3) the duration of the study,

(4) who will know about the participant's involvement in the study and whether confidentiality will be maintained, (5) whether participation is voluntary or a payment is being offered, and (6) a clear indication to the participant that they can withdraw from the study at any time and without prejudice if they so wish. Participants should also be given the opportunity to ask questions about the study in order to enable them to make an informed decision about participation, and they should also be given sufficient time to reflect on this information.

All of this information is usually provided in a written **informed consent form** that the participant must then sign to acknowledge that they understand what the study involves and that they formally consent to take part in the study. A simple example of an informed consent form is provided in Figure 3.5. Consent forms may be more or less detailed depending on the complexity of the study and the nature of the participants required for the study. For example, if the study is one that requires the participation of individuals already undergoing treatment for mental health problems, then the participant may need to know how their involvement in the study might affect their treatment and whether it might have an adverse effect on their existing mental health condition. In such circumstances, informed consent forms might also want to include further details such as (1) the identity of the researchers and their contact details, (2) a clear description of any complex procedures (e.g. any procedures that may be invasive), (3) the identity of others who might be directly or indirectly associated with the research (e.g. organisations that might be funding the research, such as drug companies or mental health charities), (4) reasons why the participant has been selected (in case the participant may feel stigmatized by being approached to participate), (5) the possible harms and benefits of the procedure (especially if the participant has an existing mental health problem), and (6) details of any future use of the data that is collected from the study.

> **informed consent form**   See *Informed consent.*

The issue of informed consent becomes problematic when an individual's understanding of the information provided in a consent form is limited. This is particularly so with children and certain categories of adults – for example those who have learning disabilities or exhibit psychotic symptoms (Bersoff & Bersoff, 1999; Fisher, Cea, Davidson & Fried, 2006). In the case of children and adolescents below the age of 17 years, the written consent of the parent or guardian is required as well as either the verbal or written agreement of the child.

Obtaining full informed consent of a participant also becomes somewhat problematic if informing the participant of all the details of the study is likely to significantly affect the results. For example, participants in many drug

experimenter may be able to provide the location and phone number of the university counselling service). Clearly, making people distressed in a research study is not an acceptable end in itself, and the researcher must always weigh up whether the potential benefits of their research (in terms of its contribution to knowledge) outweighs the potential distress that may be caused to some participants.

On the other side of the coin, a study may not cause distress but may involve the active withholding of benefits for the participant. This is especially the case with studies attempting to assess the effectiveness of treatments for psychopathology. For example, let us assume a researcher is attempting to find out if a new psychotherapy is effective for treating depression. The study would involve participants diagnosed with depression and some would be allocated to the experimental condition and receive the new psychotherapy while for comparison purposes others would need to be allocated to control conditions that did *not* receive the new psychotherapy. This raises a significant ethical issue. Should we withhold effective treatment for someone suffering depression simply because we need to allocate them to a **no treatment control condition**? A similar issue is that such studies also have very narrow inclusion criteria. That is, to be able to interpret their results clearly, the researcher would want to ensure that the study only included participants who had a simple diagnosis of depression. Interpreting the data would be complicated if the study also included participants who were diagnosed with other disorders that were comorbid with depression. This means that those with more complex psychopathologies are likely to be excluded from treatment outcome studies and so denied access to the treatment programme associated with the study. Researchers tend to try to overcome the ethical issues involved in allocating a patient to a no treatment condition by adopting what are called *waiting-list controls*. That is, they use patients who are on a waiting list for treatment as their no treatment control condition. Such individuals would not be receiving treatment anyway during the time that they are on the waiting list. This may be a suitable way out of this particular ethical dilemma, but as the reader is probably aware, it is a solution that paradoxically is available only as long as service providers are unable to offer immediate treatment!

3.4.3   Privacy and Confidentiality

All participants in psychological research have a right to privacy and confidentiality. **Privacy** means that participants can decide not to provide some forms of information to the researcher if they so wish (e.g. their age or sexual orientation), and **confidentiality** means participants in psychological research have a right to expect that information they provide will be treated confidentially. For example, if a piece of research is eventually published in a scientific journal, participants who contributed to the study should not be identifiable. In the event that confidentiality and/or anonymity cannot be guaranteed, the participant must be warned of this in advance of agreeing to participate. Indeed, according to legislation in many countries (such as the Data Protection Act in the UK) information obtained about a participant during a study is confidential unless otherwise agreed in advance. In many cases, such as questionnaire studies, researchers will ensure that all data collected are anonymous, and participants will usually only have to provide basic demographic information (e.g. sex, age, and so on) that will not usually allow them to be identified. In some other circumstances (such as longitudinal studies, where participants may have to be contacted to provide data on more than one occasion) it may be necessary to retain some information that will identify the participant over the course of the study, but this can be erased once all the data are collected. In studies where personal or sensitive information is being collected (such as studies involving participants with mental health problems), the informed consent form should clearly state who will have access to the data and the findings of the study. If interviews with participants are audiotaped or videotaped, it should be clear to the participant who will hold those tapes and how long they will be retained before being destroyed.

However, issues of confidentiality and anonymity become problematic when the participant discloses information about illegal activities or events or circumstances that may be detrimental to an individual's psychological or physical health. For example, what should a researcher do if a participant tells them about suicidal intentions, serious drug abuse, criminal activities, physical or sexual abuse and the like? Certainly, a researcher has a legal and moral obligation to consider appropriate action if they believe a crime has been committed or is intended, and in some countries it is mandatory by law, for example, to report information about criminal activities such as child abuse (Becker-Blease & Freyd, 2006). Perhaps it is important to be clear that confidentiality is not the same as secrecy, and is therefore not absolute. If the researcher believes that a study might reveal information about illegal or immoral activities, then they

> **no treatment control condition** The allocation of participants to a control condition, in which they do not receive the treatment under investigation.

> **privacy** The right of participants to decide not to provide some forms of information to the researcher if they so wish (e.g. their age or sexual orientation).

> **confidentiality** The right of participants in psychological research to expect that information they provide will be treated in confidence.

might inform participants at the outset of the study that (1) confidentiality is not absolute, and (2) the researcher will inform the participant if confidentiality is broken. However, providing such information at the outset of a study is likely to mean that participants will be significantly less willing to provide sensitive information (Bersoff & Bersoff, 1999).

Finally, what should a researcher do when a participant provides information that they are likely to harm themselves or others or are seriously distressed? This obviously requires a judgement on the part of the researcher, and no one can morally turn a blind eye knowing that others may be harmed or an individual is in a state of life-threatening distress. Because of their knowledge of psychopathology and the provision of treatments, most clinical psychology researchers are usually in the privileged position of being able to offer at least some kind of support and guidance to those disclosing information indicating serious distress. As a consequence, a researcher may be able to suggest treatment or referral to an appropriate support service immediately after the study.

SELF-TEST QUESTIONS

- What is informed consent?
- What ethical issues need to be considered when a research study may cause distress to a participant or lead to the withholding of benefits?
- What issues of privacy and confidentiality should be considered when designing and conducting a research study?

SECTION SUMMARY

3.4   ETHICAL ISSUES IN CLINICAL PSYCHOLOGY RESEARCH

No description of research using human participants is complete without a thorough discussion of ethical issues. Proper ethical procedures are designed to protect the rights, dignity and well-being of participants in research, and are a necessary part of any clinical psychology research project. Ethical issues can be grouped under three broader headings, namely: (1) informed consent (e.g. 'are the participants fully informed about the study and can they freely and voluntarily give their informed consent to participate?'); (2) causing distress or withholding benefits (e.g. 'what is the risk that a research procedure will cause a participant harm or distress, and how can we avoid this?'); and (3) privacy and confidentiality (e.g. 'are the participants' rights to privacy and confidentially being properly respected?').

The key points are:

- Participants in clinical psychology research have *rights* that need to be protected, a *dignity* that needs to be preserved, and a *well-being* that needs to be maintained.
- The *informed consent* of participants should always be obtained before they take part in a study.
- Participation in any research study should be *voluntary*.
- Researchers have an obligation to be vigilant throughout a study for any indication that the participant might be experiencing *distress*.
- All participants in psychological research have a right to *privacy* and *confidentiality*.

3.5   RESEARCH METHODS IN CLINICAL PSYCHOLOGY REVISITED

Research is an important and central feature of clinical psychology. Research techniques allow us to (1) describe the symptoms of psychopathologies and the feelings and experiences of those who suffer with mental health problems, (2) understand the causes of psychopathologies, (3) assess the efficacy of interventions developed to treat psychopathology, and (4) assess the effectiveness of services provided to treat and support those with mental health problems (known as evaluation research or clinical audit). Different research methods may be based on different theories of knowledge, and a theory of knowledge represents a way of trying to understand the world. Many of the research methods we have described in this chapter are based on the scientific method espoused by Karl Popper, and require that research results should be replicable and that theories should be experimentally testable. However, even within the realm of clinical psychology there are many who feel that the scientific method is not well suited to exploring many of the important aspects of psychopathology such as the phenomenology of psychopathology.

We have then described in detail a range of research methods that are available to the clinical psychology researcher, and the type of method adopted will usually depend very much on the nature of the research question being asked. For example, correlational and longitudinal methods are useful for determining if there is a relationship between two or more variables, the experimental method is useful for identifying causal relationships between variables, case studies provide important ways of studying a phenomenon when the number of available participants is restricted, and qualitative methods are useful for gaining an insight into the full experience of psychopathology or beginning new research in an area. The final and essential part of a description of research methods in clinical psychology is a discussion of ethical issues, and these are vital in the protection of the rights, dignity and well-being of those who participate in clinical psychology research.

To access the online resources for this chapter go to
www.wiley-psychopathology.com/ch3

Reading	Video	Activity
• Journal article: Conditioned emotional reactions • Author blog: An effect is not an effect until it is replicated (pre-cognition or experimenter demand effects) • Journal article: Ambivilence in coping with dental fear • Glossary key terms • Clinical issues • Links to journal articles • References	• Conducting experiments in psychopathology	• Activity 3.1 • Activity 3.2 • Activity 3.3 • Self-test questions • Revision flashcards • Research questions

4 Treating Psychopathology

To access the online resources for this chapter go to
www.wiley-psychopathology.com/ch4

LEARNING OUTCOMES

When you have completed this chapter, you should be able to:

1. Describe some of the reasons for wanting to treat psychopathology.

2. Describe and compare and contrast the basic theoretical principles on which at least four different types of psychotherapy are based.

3. Describe and evaluate at least three to four different modes of delivery for treatments of psychopathology.

4. Critically assess methods for determining the effectiveness of treatments for psychopathology.

I was a 22-year-old trainee working for a publishing company in London, and I was obsessed with food. I made a pact with myself to limit myself to less than 700 calories a day. This worked well for a while, but then I started binge eating, and my fear of gaining weight led me to make myself sick. Sometimes up to five or six times a day. This left me totally drained – both emotionally and physically, and my relationship with my partner began to go downhill rapidly. I really hated myself, and I felt fat and disgusting most days. If only I felt thinner I would feel better about myself. My GP eventually referred me to a clinical psychologist, who helped me to understand how my thinking was just plain wrong. He explained to me how I evaluated my self-worth purely on the basis of my weight and body shape. My thinking was also 'black and white' – I believed that foods were either 'good' or, if not, they were 'bad'. During therapy I learnt to identify and challenge my irrational thoughts about food and eating, this helped me to begin to eat relatively normally again, and I began to feel less anxious and worthless. What amazed me most was that eating normally didn't mean I put on weight, and I felt in control again – the first time for years. All this was so wonderful that I became anxious about the possibility of therapy ending and that I'd simply go back to starving and bingeing. But I was encouraged to practise a number of coping strategies and learnt what I should do in circumstances where I felt I might relapse back into my old ways.

Elly's Story

Introduction

Psychopathology can take many forms and involve anxiety, depression, worthlessness, guilt, and feelings of lack of control, amongst others. For many people these feelings become so intense that they cause personal distress and significantly impair normal daily functioning. Some people are able to deploy adaptive coping strategies that allow them to successfully negotiate such periods in their life (e.g. by seeking help and support from friends and family, or using problem-solving strategies to deal with life problems that may be causing their symptoms). Others may be less able to cope constructively, and choose less adaptive means of dealing with their symptoms, such as resorting to substance abuse and dependency or deliberate self-harm. Whatever route an individual may take, the distress and disruption that symptoms of psychopathology cause will often lead an individual to seek professional help and support for their problems. The first port of call is usually the individual's doctor or GP, and the GP may be able to offer sufficient help to deal with acute bouts of psychopathology such as those involving depression, stress and anxiety-based problems. In most cases, this support will usually be in the form of suitable medication, but it may also take the form of providing access to stress-management courses, short-term counselling or psychotherapy, access to self-help information or even computerized CBT (e.g. van Boeijen, van Oppen, van Balkom, Visser *et al.*, 2005). In other cases, it may be necessary for the individual to be referred for more specific and specialized treatment, and the nature of this treatment may often depend on the nature and severity of that person's symptoms. This is a fairly standardized route by which individuals suffering psychopathology come into contact with the treatment methods required to alleviate their symptoms and their distress. Others may simply decide to by-pass the health services available in their community and directly approach an accredited counsellor or psychotherapist who can privately supply the treatment services they require. Whichever route is followed, the aim is to find a suitable specialist who can successfully alleviate the symptoms of psychopathology and ease the distress that is experienced.

4.1 THE NATURE AND FUNCTION OF TREATMENTS FOR PSYCHOPATHOLOGY

Elly's story provides her personal account of how therapy helped to alleviate her eating problems, provided her with insight into the thought patterns that gave rise to her psychopathology, and how she learnt to cope with situations that might give rise to relapse. Based on the example in *Elly's story*, treatments for psychopathology will usually possess some, if not all, of the following characteristics: (1) they can provide relief from the distress caused by symptoms, (2) they can provide the client with self-awareness and insight into their problems, (3) they enable the client to acquire coping and problem-solving skills that will prevent similar problems occurring in the future, and (4) they attempt to identify and resolve the causes of the psychopathology, whether those causes are recognized as problematic ways of behaving, problematic ways of thinking, or problematic ways of dealing with or assimilating life experiences. Many treatments only possess some of these characteristics. For example, many drug treatments for psychopathology will have a **palliative effect** (i.e. reduce the severity of symptoms and so alleviate distress), but they may only rarely provide the client with insight into their problems. Some other therapies may serve the primary purpose of helping the client to achieve insight into their problems (e.g. psychodynamic psychotherapies), but it does not always follow that this insight will bring about behaviour change or provide suitable coping skills (Prochaska & Norcross, 2001). Still other therapies may provide effective ways of changing behaviour (such as many behaviour therapies), but do not necessarily provide the client with insight into the causes of their problems.

The treatment that is provided for a psychopathology will depend on at least two factors: (1) the theoretical orientation and training of the therapist, and (2) the nature of the psychopathology. Firstly, a therapist will tend to adopt those treatment practices that they have most experience with and were originally trained to use. This will often involve therapies with a specific theoretical approach (e.g. a psychodynamic approach, a client-centred approach, a cognitive approach or a behavioural approach – see section 1.3.2), and these theoretical approaches will not just advocate different treatment procedures, but will also advocate quite different approaches to understanding and explaining psychopathology. Most

> **palliative effect** The reduction of the severity of symptoms and alleviation of distress.

accredited therapists will now also have to demonstrate that they have periodically engaged in *continuing professional development* (CPD). That is, they must demonstrate that they regularly update their knowledge of recent developments in treatment techniques. If a therapist is unable to demonstrate that they are actively engaged in CPD, then they may be in danger of losing their status as a legally registered practitioner. This has meant that practitioners have become much more eclectic in the types of treatment they will offer as they learn new treatment methods through the need to demonstrate their continuing professional development. While some practising therapists may also use the research literature as a way of updating their therapeutic skills, most rely on information from less formal sources, such as colleagues, professional newsletters, workshops and conferences (Goldfried & Wolfe, 1996).

Secondly, treatments may be chosen largely on the basis that they are effective at treating a certain type of psychopathology. In the UK, the **National Institute for Health and Care Excellence** (**NICE**) recommends treatments for specific psychopathologies on the basis that their effectiveness is evidence-based and empirically supported by scientifically rigorous research (see also Focus Point 3.1),

> **National Institute for Health and Care Excellence (NICE)** An independent UK organisation responsible for providing national evidence-based guidance on promoting good health and preventing and treating ill health.

and we will discuss some of these recommendations in later chapters when we discuss treatment programmes for specific psychopathologies. Nowadays, most types of theoretical approach have been adapted to treat most psychopathologies, or at least some aspect of most psychopathologies and these will be discussed in detail in the treatment sections of each ensuing chapter.

4.1.1 Theoretical Approaches to Treatment

Traditionally, popular therapies have been developed around a relatively small number of important theoretical approaches. We discussed these theoretical approaches in some detail in section 1.3 and you may want to return to this section in order to refresh your memory about how these different theoretical models conceptualize and explain psychopathology. This section continues with a summary of how these theoretical approaches are adapted to treat psychopathology.

Psychodynamic approaches

The aim of most psychodynamic therapies is to reveal unconscious conflicts that may be causing symptoms of psychopathology. Most **psychodynamic approaches** assume that unconscious conflicts develop early in life, and part of the therapy is designed to identify life events that may have caused these unconscious conflicts. Once these important developmental life events and unconscious conflicts have been identified, the therapist will help the client to acknowledge the existence of these conflicts, bring them into conscious awareness, and work with the client to develop strategies for change. One important form of psychodynamic therapy is psychoanalysis, and this is a type of therapy based on the theoretical works of Sigmund Freud (1856–1939). The aim of psychoanalysis is to bring any unconscious conflicts into awareness, to help the individual understand the source of these conflicts (perhaps by identifying past experiences or discussing the nature of important relationships), and to help the individual towards a sense of control over behaviour, feelings and attitudes. There are several basic techniques used by psychoanalysts to achieve these goals. For example:

> **psychodynamic approaches** Forms of therapy which attempt to reveal unconscious conflicts that may be causing psychopathology.

1. **Free association**: here the client is encouraged to verbalize all thoughts, feelings and images that come to mind while the analyst is normally seated behind them, and this process functions to bring into awareness any unconscious conflicts or associations between thoughts and feelings.

> **free association** A technique used in psychoanalysis where the client is encouraged to verbalize all thoughts, feelings and images that come to mind.

2. **Transference**: Here the analyst is used as a target for emotional responses, and the client behaves or feels towards the analyst as they would have behaved towards an important person in their lives. This allows the client to achieve understanding of their feelings by acting out any feelings or neuroses that they have towards that person.

> **transference** A technique used in psychoanalysis where the analyst is used as a target for emotional responses: clients behave towards the analyst as they would have behaved towards an important person in their lives.

3. **Dream analysis**: Freud believed that unconscious conflicts often revealed themselves in symbolic forms in dreams, and this made the analysis of dream content an important means of accessing unconscious beliefs and conflicts.

> **dream analysis** The analysis of dream content as a means of accessing unconscious beliefs and conflicts.

4. **Interpretation**: Finally, the skilled psychoanalyst has to interpret information from all of the above sources and help the client to identify important underlying conflicts and help the client develop ways of dealing with these conflicts.

> **interpretation** In psychoanalysis, helping the client to identify important underlying conflicts.

Frosh (2012, p.100) summarizes Freud's conception of psychoanalysis as a therapeutic process in the following way:

- Psychoanalysis is a way of exploring the unconscious that might have therapeutic effects, but it is not solely or necessarily therapeutic in its aims.

- The assumption that psychological conflict arises from unconscious complexes suggests that if psychoanalysis brings unconscious material into consciousness, it will have the effect of lessening psychological disturbance.

- Freud was cautious about the power of psychoanalysis to make a significant difference but nevertheless believed that the movement from 'unconscious to conscious' was an important step in advancing individual well-being as well as social life.

- Psychological disturbance is caused by a complex array of phenomena, but at its core is the relationship between anxiety and repression, which produces a variety of strategies aimed at keeping troubling unconscious material out of awareness.

- The different strategies (defences) adopted by different people and in different circumstances (see *Table 1.1*) characterize the various forms of psychological disturbance – neurosis, psychosis and so on.

- Psychoanalysis as a mode of therapy aims at producing insight. It's main methods of therapeutic activity are focused on interpretation and transference.

As a form of treatment, psychoanalysis may take up to three to five sessions a week and change is expected to take place at a normal maturational rate, and so may require anything between 3 and 7 years for the full therapeutic benefits of the therapy to be recognized. Other forms of psychodynamic therapy may be briefer and less intensive than psychoanalysis, and may draw on techniques from other sources, such as family therapy (see the section below). Primarily, psychoanalysis represents a quest for self-knowledge, where an individual's problems are viewed in the context of the whole person, and in particular, any conflicts they may have repressed. It can be a helpful treatment for many people with moderate to severe anxiety or depression-based problems – especially when other, more conventional, therapies have failed. In studies where the effects of long-term psychoanalytic therapy have been measurable, it has been shown to only be more effective than control treatments that do not possess a specialized psychotherapy component, suggesting that the evidence for the effectiveness of long-term psychoanalytic therapy for psychopathology is still limited and at best conflicting (Smit, Huibers, Ioannidis, van Dyck *et al.*, 2012).

Behaviour therapy

In the 1940s and 1950s there was a growing dissatisfaction with the medical or disease model of psychopathology, and also with the unscientific approaches to psychopathology being generated by many psychodynamic theories. These dissatisfactions led psychologists to look towards the developing area of experimental psychology for objective knowledge that might be used to inform treatment and therapy. The body of knowledge that psychologists turned to was that of **conditioning** (see section 1.3.2), and this gave rise to the development of what came to be known as **behaviour therapy**. Firstly, such therapies stressed the need to treat symptoms of psychopathology as *bona fide* behavioural problems rather than the mere symptoms of some other, hidden underlying cause. Secondly, at the time, many psychologists believed that numerous psychological disorders were the result of what was called **faulty learning**, and that symptoms were acquired through simple conditioning processes. For example, it was believed that anxiety symptoms could be acquired through classical conditioning (see Figure 6.2), and behavioural problems might be acquired through processes of operant conditioning – e.g. bizarre and inappropriate behaviours might be acquired because they have been reinforced or rewarded in the past (see Focus Point 8.5). The reasoning here was that, if psychological problems were acquired through learning, then conditioning principles could be used to develop therapies that effectively helped the individual to 'unlearn' those problematic associations. Two distinctive strands of behaviour therapy developed from these assumptions. The first was a set of therapies based on the principles of classical conditioning, and the second based on principles of operant conditioning. While the former group of therapies continues to be known as behaviour therapy, the latter group has also come to be known as **behaviour modification** or

conditioning A form of associative learning on which behaviour therapies are based.

behaviour therapy A term currently used for all interventions that attempt to change the client's behaviour (and have largely been based on principles from learning theory).

faulty learning A view that the symptoms of psychological disorders are acquired through the learning of pathological responses.

behaviour modification Behavioural treatment methods based on operant conditioning principles, which assume that learnt psychopathology can be 'unlearnt' using normal learning processes.

behaviour analysis. The term behaviour therapy is often used even more eclectically nowadays to refer to any treatment that attempts to directly change behaviour (rather than, say, cognitions), whether the underlying principles are based on conditioning or not.

behaviour analysis An approach to psychopathology based on the principles of operant conditioning (also known as behaviour modification).

Therapies based on classical conditioning principles
Behaviour therapy effectively originates from the writings of Wolpe (1958), who argued that many forms of emotional disorder could be treated using the classical conditioning principle of **extinction**. The assumption was that if emotional problems such as anxiety disorders were learnt through classical conditioning, they could be 'unlearnt' by disrupting the association between the anxiety-provoking cues or situations and the threat or traumatic outcomes that they have become associated with. In practice, this means ensuring that the anxiety-provoking stimulus, event or situation is experienced in the absence of accompanying trauma so that the former no longer comes to evoke the latter. The most famous behaviour therapy techniques to apply extinction principles are **flooding**, **counterconditioning** and **systematic desensitisation**, and they have collectively come to be known as **exposure therapies** (Richard & Lauterbach, 2007; Craske, Liao, Brown & Vervliet, 2012) because they are all based on the need to expose the client to the events and situations that evoke their distress and anxiety – so that they can learn that they are no longer threatening (see Davey, 1998). Wolpe (1958) also introduced the principle of **reciprocal inhibition**, in which an emotional response is eliminated not just by

extinction The classical conditioning principle which assumes emotional problems can be 'unlearnt' by disrupting the association between the anxiety-provoking cues or situations and the threat or traumatic outcomes with which they have become associated.

flooding A form of exposure therapy for the treatment of phobias and related disorders in which the patient is repeatedly exposed to highly distressing stimuli.

counterconditioning A behaviour therapy technique designed to use conditioning techniques to establish a response that is antagonistic to the psychopathology.

systematic desensitisation A behaviour therapy based on classical conditioning used in the treatment of phobias and anxiety disorders, during which the client overcomes their fears through gradual and systematic exposure.

exposure therapy Treatment in which sufferers are helped by the therapist to confront and experience events and stimuli relevant to their trauma and their symptoms.

reciprocal inhibition A principle of behaviour therapy in which anxiety is eliminated not just by extinguishing the relationship between the anxiety-inducing cue and the threatening consequence, but also by attaching a response to the anxiety-inducing cue which is incompatible with anxiety.

extinguishing the relationship between the emotion-inducing cue and the threatening consequence, but also by attaching a response to the emotion-inducing cue which is incompatible with anxiety (e.g. relaxation). It has often been assumed that these techniques can only be applied to the treatment of emotional problems such as anxiety disorders, but they have in fact been applied to a range of disorders including addictive disorders (O'Leary & Wilson, 1975), marital conflict (Jacobson & Weiss, 1978), and sexual dysfunction (Mathews, Bancroft, Whitehead, Hackmann et al., 1976).

Aversion therapy is another treatment based on classical conditioning, but is rather different to the proceeding therapies because it attempts to condition an aversion to a stimulus or event to which the individual is inappropriately attracted. For example, aversion therapy is most widely used in the treatment of addictive behaviours such as alcoholism, and in these procedures the taste of alcohol is paired with aversive outcomes (e.g. sickness-inducing drugs) in order to condition an aversive reaction to alcohol (e.g. Voegtlin & Lemere, 1942; Lemere & Voegtlin, 1950) (see Chapters 9 and 11 for discussion of the use of aversion therapy in the treatment of substance abuse and paraphilias). Since the 1950s and 1960s, this type of procedure has been used to treat a wide variety of problems, including inappropriate or distressing sexual activities (e.g. Feldman & MacCulloch, 1965), drug and alcohol addiction (McRae, Budney & Brady, 2003), and even obsessions and compulsions associated with anxiety (Lam & Steketee, 2001). Aversion therapy was popularized in the 1971 cult film *A Clockwork Orange* where the lead character's excessive violence was treated by 'conditioning' him to vomit whenever he saw a violent act. However, while aversion therapy for some problems (e.g. alcoholism, sexual offending) has been shown to have some therapeutic gains when used in conjunction with broader community support programmes (Azrin, 1976) or social skills training (Maletzky, 1993), substance abuse or sexual offending responses are often very resistant to this form of treatment, and there is very little evidence that aversion therapy alone has anything other than short-lived effects (e.g. Wilson, 1978), and does not significantly reduce reoffending in sexual offenders (Marques, Wiederanders, Day et al., 2005).

aversion therapy A treatment based on classical conditioning which attempts to condition an aversion to a stimulus or event to which the individual is inappropriately attracted.

Therapies based on operant conditioning principles

The principles of operant conditioning offer some rather different approaches to treatment and therapy than do those of classical conditioning. Operant conditioning is concerned with influencing the frequency of a behaviour by manipulating the consequences of that behaviour. For example, if a behaviour is followed by rewarding or reinforcing consequences, it will *increase* in frequency. If it is followed by punishing or negative consequences, it will *decrease* in frequency (Davey, 1989). Operant conditioning principles have mainly been used in therapy in three specific ways: (1) to try to understand what rewarding or reinforcing factors might be maintaining an inappropriate or maladaptive behaviour – this is known as functional analysis (e.g. trying to understand what factors might be maintaining challenging or aggressive behaviours in individuals with intellectual disabilities); (2) to use reinforcers and rewards to try to establish new or appropriate behaviours (e.g. to establish self-help or social behaviours in individuals who have become withdrawn because of their psychopathology); and (3) to use negative or punishing consequences to try to suppress or eliminate problematic behaviours in need of urgent attention (e.g. to eliminate or suppress self-injurious behaviours in individuals with intellectual disabilities or severe autistic symptoms) (see section 17.3.5.2).

A **functional analysis** is where the therapist attempts to identify consistencies between problematic behaviours and their consequences – especially to try to discover whether there might be a consistent event or consequence that appears to be maintaining the behaviour by rewarding it. For example, self-injurious or challenging behaviours may be maintained by a range of reinforcing consequences, such as the attention the behaviour may attract or the sensory stimulation it provides (see Treatment in Practice Box 17.1). Identifying the nature of the consequence allows the therapist to disrupt the reinforcement contingency and, if necessary, reduce the frequency of that behaviour through extinction (Wacker, Steege, Northrup, Sasso et al., 1990). Functional analysis has been adopted across a range of clinical settings, and has been successfully applied to controlling aggressive/challenging behaviour (O'Reilly, 1995), tantrums (Darby, Wacker, Sasso, Steege et al., 1992), ADHD (Northrup et al., 1995), depression (Ferster, 1985), eating problems (Slade, 1982), and self-injurious behaviour (Iwata, Dorsey, Slifer et al., 1985).

functional analysis An observational method for identifying the consistencies between problematic behaviours and the consequences that may be reinforcing them.

Other influential interventions based on operant conditioning principles include the token economy, response shaping, and behavioural self-control. In the psychiatric setting, a token economy involves participants receiving tokens (a generalized reinforcer) for engaging in behaviours defined by the programme, and at a later time these tokens can then be exchanged for a variety of reinforcing or desired items (e.g. access to the hospital grounds, a visit to the cinema, and so on). In psychiatric care, the token economy was first used to foster prosocial or self-help behaviours (e.g. combing hair, bathing, brushing teeth, and suchlike) in previously withdrawn patients, although its use and popularity has declined significantly over the past 20 years (for a fuller discussion of this decline, see Focus Point 1.2). **Response shaping** is a procedure that can be used to encourage new behaviours that are not already

response shaping A reinforcement procedure that is used to develop new behaviours.

occurring at a reasonable frequency. This may be especially a problem with

withdrawn individuals or individuals with restricted behavioural repertoires (such as those with severe intellectual disabilities). However, the technique of response shaping by successive approximations is a way around this problem. Here, the therapist will first reinforce a behaviour that does occur quite frequently and is an approximation to the specific target response. Once this general response is established, reinforcement is given only for closer and closer approximations to the target response. An example of the use of response shaping is provided in Treatment in Practice Box 4.1. Finally, the use of operant conditioning principles for behaviour change purposes does not have to be overseen or administered by a therapist. The principles are quite clear and can be used by any individual to control and manage their own behaviour. This personal use of operant conditioning principles has come to be known as **behavioural self-control** (e.g. Thoresen & Mahoney, 1974), and has since

behavioural self-control The personal use of operant conditioning principles to change or control one's own behaviour.

been developed into multi-faceted behavioural programmes to deal with a variety of personal prob-

lems, including addiction, habits, obsessions, and other behavioural problems (Lutzker & Martin, 1981; Stuart & Davis, 1972). A programme developed by Stuart (1967) provides a good example of a multifaceted behavioural self-control scheme designed to address obesity by controlling behaviours contributing to overeating. The main elements of this programme were: (1) recording the time and quantity of food consumption (self-observation), (2) weighing in before each meal and before bedtime (helping the individual to discriminate how eating might have contributed to weight gain), (3) removal of food from all places in the house except the kitchen (so that only the kitchen comes to act as a cue for eating), (4) pairing eating with no other activity that might make eating enjoyable, and so reinforce it (e.g. eating should *not* occur while watching an enjoyable TV programme), (5) setting a weight loss goal of 1–2 pounds/week (setting clearly attainable goals), (6) slowing down the pace of eating

(defining appropriate responses), and (7) substituting other activities for between-meal eating (programming acceptable competing responses). These principles are relatively easy to apply to your own behaviour, and Activity 4.1 provides some suggestions as to how you might develop your own behavioural self-control programme to promote an activity such as studying.

To complete Activity 4.1 go to **www.wiley-psychopathology.com/ activities/ch4**

Cognitive therapies

The origins of cognitive therapy
In the past 40 years, one of the most impressive developments in our understanding of psychopathology has been our evolving insight into the cognitive factors that play important roles in causing and maintaining psychopathology. For example, some psychopathologies are caused by dysfunctional 'ways of thinking' – either about the self or the world (e.g. in major depression). In other cases, psychopathologies are characterized by dysfunctional ways of processing and interpreting incoming information. For example, many anxiety disorders are characterized by a bias towards processing threatening or anxiety-relevant information (e.g. generalized anxiety disorder, see Treatment in Practice Box 6.4) or to interpreting ambiguous information negatively (e.g. panic disorder, see Figure 6.5). In both cases these biases act to develop and maintain anxiety. If such cognitive factors are maintaining psychopathology, then developing treatments that try to address and change these dysfunctional cognitive features is important. Two early forms of cognitive therapy based on these assumptions were rational emotive therapy (RET) and Beck's cognitive therapy.

How people construe themselves, their life and the world is likely to be a major determinant of their feelings, and **rational emotive therapy (RET)** developed by Albert Ellis (1962) was one of the first cognitive therapies to address these factors. In particular, Ellis believed that people carry around with them a set of

rational emotive therapy (RET) A cognitive therapy technique developed by Albert Ellis (1962) which addresses how people construe themselves, their life and the world.

implicit assumptions which determines how they judge themselves and others, and that many of these implicit assumptions may be irrational and cause emotional distress. For example, two irrational beliefs include (1) demanding perfection from oneself and from others, and (2) expecting approval from others for everything one does. Clearly, there will be many occasions when these goals are not met, and this will cause anxiety, depression and emotional discomfort. Rational emotive therapy attempts to challenge these irrational beliefs and to persuade the individual to set more attainable life goals. As such, RET is a good example of a

CLINICAL PERSPECTIVE – TREATMENT IN PRACTICE BOX 4.1: AN EXAMPLE OF RESPONSE SHAPING

Response shaping is a useful procedure for strengthening rarely occurring behaviours or building up complex response repertoires, and this method is utilized regularly in behaviour modification programmes. An early study by Isaacs, Thomas & Goldiamond (1960) serves to illustrate this method. They attempted to reinstate verbal behaviour in a psychiatric in-patient who had been mute for over 19 years. In this example, the target behaviour occurs relatively infrequently, and thus has to be approached via the reinforcement of successive approximations to the behaviour. They discovered that although the patient was withdrawn, he did appear to respond to chewing gum, which they considered would act as an effective reinforcer. They then broke down the target behaviour so that it could be reached by reinforcing a series of approximations to verbal behaviour. The first responses to be reinforced were fairly simple, discrete responses whose baseline levels were high enough for them to occur spontaneously within a training session. The shaping programme went as follows:

1. when the patient moved his eyes towards the chewing gum, he was reinforced by being given the gum – after 2 weeks the probability of this response was relatively high;

2. the experimenters then only gave the patient gum when he moved his mouth and lips – by the end of week 3, these behaviours were relatively frequent;

3. the experimenters then withheld gum until the patient made vocalisations of some sort – by the end of the fourth week the patient was moving his eyes and lips and making audible 'croaking' noises;

4. during weeks 4 and 5, the experimenter asked the patient to 'say gum', repeating this each time the patient vocalized – at the end of week 6, the patient spontaneously said 'gum please';

5. in later sessions the patient verbally responded to questions from the experimenters, but only in the therapeutic situation;

6. to enable verbal behaviour to generalize beyond the experimental setting, the patient was placed back on the ward and the nursing staff were asked to attend to his needs, but only if he verbalized them.

This example demonstrates a number of features of the response-shaping procedure in clinical settings. First, it provides an example of how response shaping can be a powerful and effective means of establishing complex response repertoires relatively quickly. Second, it also illustrates the distinction between 'arbitrary' and 'natural' reinforcers in behaviour modification. In this case, chewing gum was an effective reinforcer for the behaviours being shaped; but it is an 'arbitrary' one in that it is not a normal reinforcer for verbal behaviour. Thus, while chewing gum may have acted as an effective reinforcer during the shaping process, in order to be maintained in any way, verbalisations need to be transferred to a more 'natural' reinforcer for those behaviours. This was the aim of stage 6 in the study, where the patient's needs were met only if he verbalized them.

Finally, there was no apparent follow-up analysis of the gains achieved in this study, and one suspects that, once back in the unstructured setting of the ward, the patient in the Isaacs, Thomas & Goldiamond study would have reverted to his previous mute state. However, this study does still emphasize two things. Firstly, behaviour change has to be subsequently supported by stable and structured changes to the individual's environment which will maintain the therapeutic gains achieved in the behaviour modification programme. Secondly, whether the patient in this study did revert to a mute state still does not deny the usefulness of response-shaping procedures in swiftly developing relatively complex behaviour repertoires – the problem of response maintenance, however, usually requires other considerations (cf. Glynn, 1990; Stokes & Baer, 1977; Stokes & Osnes, 1988).

> To read Issacs, Thomas & Goldimond's article on reinstating verbal behaviour in psychotics go to
> **www.wiley-psychopathology.com/ reading/ch4**

Source: From Davey G.C.L. (1998). Learning theory. In C. E. Walker (Ed.) *Comprehensive clinical psychology: Foundations of clinical psychology. Vol 1.* Elsevier. Reproduced by permission.

group of therapies that attempt to change a set of core beliefs about the world that may be dysfunctional (i.e. either fallacious, or a source of conflict and emotional distress). However, make no mistake about it, changing an individual's core beliefs – which have been developed and refined over a period of many years – is no easy thing. This is why highly structured **cognitive therapy** is required for successful treatment, and this therapy will normally go through a process of challenging existing dysfunctional beliefs, replacing these with more rational beliefs, and then getting the

cognitive therapy A form of psychotherapy based on the belief that psychological problems are the products of faulty ways of thinking about the world.

individual to test out this new set of beliefs in structured behavioural exercises.

Aaron Beck's cognitive theory of depression is outlined in more detail in Chapter 7, and from this theory he developed a cognitive therapy for depression. Beck argues that depression results when the individual develops a set of cognitive schemas (or beliefs) which bias the individual towards negative interpretations of the self, the world and the future, and any therapy for depression must therefore address these schemas, deconstruct them and replace them with more rational schemas that do not always lead to negative interpretations. **Beck's cognitive therapy** does this by engaging the depressed individual in an objective assessment of their beliefs, and requires them to provide evidence for their biased views of the world. This enables the individual to perceive their existing schemas as biased, irrational and overgeneralized (see section 7.3.2).

> **Beck's cognitive therapy** An intervention derived from Beck's view that depression is maintained by a 'negative schema' that leads depressed individuals to hold negative views about themselves, their future and the world (the 'negative triad').

Out of these early pioneering cognitive therapies developed what is now known as **cognitive behaviour therapy (CBT)**, which is an intervention for changing both thoughts and behaviour, and represents an umbrella term for many different therapies that share the common aim of changing both cognitions and behaviour. A CBT intervention usually possesses most of the following characteristics:

> **cognitive behaviour therapy (CBT)** An intervention for changing both thoughts and behaviour. CBT represents an umbrella term for many different therapies that share the common aim of changing both cognitions and behaviour.

1. the client is encouraged to keep a diary noting the occurrence of significant events and associated feelings, moods, and thoughts in order to demonstrate how events, moods and thoughts might be interlinked;

2. with the help of the therapist, the client is urged to identify and challenge irrational, dysfunctional or biased thoughts or assumptions;

3. clients are given homework in the form of 'behavioural experiments' to test whether their thoughts and assumptions are accurate and rational; and

4. clients are trained in new ways of thinking, behaving and reacting in situations that may evoke their psychopathology.

As an example, Treatment in Practice Box 6.3 demonstrates how a cognitive behaviour therapist would conduct an interview designed to identify and challenge irrational and dysfunctional beliefs in an individual diagnosed with panic disorder.

'Waves' of CBT   CBT has not been a static treatment innovation, and just like any other knowledge-based development, new forms of CBT have evolved out of earlier ones. These progressive developments have come to be known as 'waves', and at the present time we are experiencing what is called the 'third wave' of CBT techniques. The 'first wave' occurred during the 1950s and 1960s and was represented largely by behaviour therapy techniques based on learning theory and conditioning principles. The 'second wave' developed in the 1970s and 1980s when it became clear that what we do is not just influenced by our learning and conditioning experiences, but also by what and how we think (cognitions), and how the way we think affects our emotions. This gave rise to the traditional forms of CBT initially developed by therapists such as Aaron Beck and described in the previous section. However, a 'third wave' or 'third generation' of CBT methods has developed which emphasizes mindfulness and acceptance.

Mindfulness-based cognitive therapy (MBCT) is a direct extension of traditional CBT in which treatments emphasize achieving a mental state characterized by present-moment focus and non-judgemental awareness (Bishop, Lau, Shapiro, Carlson *et al.*, 2004; Kabat-Zinn, 2003). The purpose of this is to improve emotional well-being by increasing awareness of how automatic cognitive and behavioural reactions to thoughts, sensations and emotions can cause distress. Clients are encouraged to acknowledge and accept their thoughts and feelings, and by focusing on the present rather than the past or future, the individual can learn to deal more effectively with life stressors and challenges that generate anxiety or depression. Mindfulness interventions are considered to reduce symptoms of common mental health problems such as anxiety and depression by countering avoidance strategies, helping the individual to respond reflectively rather than reflexively to stressors, and reducing physical symptoms by advocating the use of meditation and yoga exercises (Kabat-Zinn, 1982). Since its early development, mindfulness has now been successfully applied to a wide range of mental health problems, including anxiety, depression, pain relief, post-traumatic stress disorder, and psychosis (Williams & Kuyken, 2012; Kocovski, Segal & Battista, 2009; Vujanovic, Niles, Pietrefesa *et al.*, 2011; Chadwick, Hughes, Russell *et al.*, 2009).

> **mindfulness-based cognitive therapy (MBCT)** A direct extension of traditional CBT in which treatments emphasize achieving a mental state characterized by present-moment focus and non-judgemental awareness.

Acceptance and commitment therapy (ACT) is another third wave CBT intervention that has grown in popularity over recent years. It is an approach that adopts some aspects

> **acceptance and commitment therapy (ACT)** A 'third wave' CBT intervention that adopts some aspects of mindfulness, but has developed more from the Skinnerian approach to understanding behaviour.

of mindfulness, but has developed more from the behaviour analysis or Skinnerian approach to understanding behaviour (see section 1.3.2). ACT differs from traditional CBT in that, rather than getting individuals to manage and change their thoughts and the way they think, it teaches them to 'just notice', accept, and embrace private events such as thoughts (especially thoughts that may be intrusive, distressing, or unwanted). As such, it aims to help the individual clarify their personal values, to take action on them, and to increase their psychological flexibility (Zettle, 2005; Hayes, Luoma, Bond, Masuda & Lillis, 2006). Activity 4.2 provides you with an example of how ACT attempts to help you distance yourself from negative or distressing thoughts.

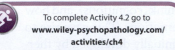

To complete Activity 4.2 go to
www.wiley-psychopathology.com/
activities/ch4

While 'new wave' developments bring new and exciting ways of delivering CBT across a range of disorders, these new approaches are still being evaluated. Studies suggest that third wave therapies such as MBCT and ACT should not be considered as separate from the growing body of CBT approaches (Hofman, Sawyer & Fang, 2010), may have their successful therapeutic effects through similar mechanisms to CBT (Hofman, Asmundson & Beck, 2013), and are generally equally effective as each other (Öst, 2008; Gaudiano, 2009). CBT in general is perceived as an evidence-based and cost-effective form of treatment that can be successfully applied to a very broad range of psychopathologies (Butler, Chapman, Forman & Beck, 2006), is equally as effective as other forms of psychotherapy, and superior to many other forms of psychotherapy when treating anxiety and depressive disorders (Tolin, 2010).

Humanistic therapies

Throughout the 20th century, many psychotherapists felt that psychological therapy was becoming too focused on psychological and behavioural mechanisms, or on psychological structures (such as personality), and was losing sight of both the feelings of the individual and the individual themselves. As a consequence, a number of what are called 'humanistic' therapies developed, including Gestalt therapy (Perls, 1969), existential therapies (Cooper, 2003), primal therapy (Janov, 1973), narrative therapy (Freedman & Combs, 1996), and transpersonal therapy (Wellings, Wilde & McCormick, 2000) and, arguably the most successful among these, client-centred therapy (Rogers, 1961). These **humanistic therapies** had a number of factors in common: (1) they espoused the need for the therapist to develop a more personal relationship with the client in order to help their clients reach a state of realisation that they can help themselves; (2) they were **holistic therapies** in that they emphasized the need to consider the 'whole' person and not just those 'bits' of the person that manifest psychopathology; (3) therapy should be seen as a way of enabling individuals to make their own decisions and to solve their own problems rather than imposing structured treatments or ways of thinking on them; (4) humanistic therapies espouse the need for the therapist–client relationship to be a genuine reciprocal and empathetic one, rather than the limited skilled professional–referred client

> **humanistic therapies** Therapies that attempt to consider the 'whole' person and not just the individual symptoms of psychopathology.

> **holistic therapies** Therapies which emphasize the need to consider the 'whole' person, not just those 'bits' of the person that manifest psychopathology.

FOCUS POINT 4.1

GESTALT THERAPY

Gestalt therapy is a popular existential humanistic therapy that was originally developed by Fritz Perls and colleagues in the 1940s and 1950s (Perls, 1947; Perls, Hefferline & Goodman, 1951). It focuses on an individual's experiences in the present moment, the therapist–client relationship, and the contexts in which the individual lives their life. It emphasizes that the most helpful focus of psychotherapy is on what a person is doing, thinking, and feeling at the present moment, rather than on what was, might be, or could be. It is also a method of awareness practice very similar to mindfulness, discussed above, in which current perceiving, feeling and acting are helpful to interpreting, explaining, and conceptualising experience. Much of the Gestalt approach is about the client exploring their relationship with themselves, and one method of

achieving this is by using the role-playing *empty-chair technique*, which involves the client addressing the empty chair as if another person was in it and acting out the two sides of a discussion.

Gestalt therapy is often considered a good method for managing tension, depression and anxiety, and uncontrolled outcome studies suggest that Gestalt therapy provides participants with better emotional well-being and a heightened sense of hope (Leung, Leung & Ng, 2013). At least some psychotherapists believe that the methods deployed by Gestalt therapy might be productively integrated with more conventional interventions such as cognitive therapy (Tonnesvang, Sommer, Hammink & Sonne, 2010), and might make a useful contribution to modern psychiatric practice (Clegg, 2010).

relationship that exists in many forms of psychological therapy; and (5) increasing emotional awareness is a critical factor in alleviating psychological distress, and is necessary before the client can begin to resolve life problems.

Client-centred therapy focuses on the individual's immediate conscious experience, and critical to this form of humanistic therapy is the creation of a therapeutic climate that allows the client to progress from a state of rigid self-perception to one which encourages the client to become independent, self-directed, and to pursue self-growth. For Carl Rogers (1902–1987), **empathy** ('putting yourself in someone else's shoes') was the central important feature of any therapist–client relationship, and it is this ability that is essential in guiding the client towards resolving their own life problems. Empathy has at least two main components in this context: (1) an ability to understand and experience the client's own feelings and personal meanings, and (2) a willingness to demonstrate **unconditional positive regard** for the client. This latter feature involves valuing the client for who they are and refraining from judging them. Another important feature of client-centred therapy is that it is not directive. The therapist acts primarily as an understanding listener who assists the client by offering advice only when asked. The overriding goal is to develop the client through empathy, congruence and unconditional positive regard to a point where they are successful in experiencing and accepting themselves, and are able to resolve their own conflicts and difficulties.

> **empathy** An ability to understand and experience a client's own feelings and personal meanings, and a willingness to demonstrate unconditional positive regard for the client.

> **unconditional positive regard** Valuing clients for who they are without judging them.

In much the same way that psychoanalysis has evolved, client-centred therapy has developed not just as a therapy, but also as a process for fostering personal self-growth. The general approach places relatively little emphasis on how the psychopathology was acquired, but attempts to eliminate symptoms by moving the client from one phenomenological state (e.g. a state of anxiety, depression, and suchlike) to another (e.g. one that enables the client to view themselves as worthy and respected individuals).

Family and systemic therapies

Family therapy is a form of intervention that is becoming increasingly helpful as a means of dealing with psychopathology that may result from the relationship dynamics within the family (Dallos & Draper, 2005). Family therapy has a number of purposes: (1) it helps to improve communications between

> **family therapy** A form of intervention involving family members that is helpful as a means of dealing with psychopathology that may result from the relationship dynamics within the family.

members of the family – especially where communication between individuals might be the cause of psychopathology in one or more family members; (2) it can resolve specific conflicts – for example, between adolescents and their parents; and (3) it may apply **systems theory** (attempting to understand the family as a social system) to treatment by trying to understand the complex relationships and alliances that exist between family members, and then attempting to remould these relationships into those expected in a well-functioning family (the latter may usually involve ensuring that the primary relationship in the family – between the two parents – is strong and functional) (Minuchin, 1985).

> **systems theory** Approach that attempts to understand the family as a social system.

In family therapy, the therapist or family therapy team meets with those members of the family willing to participate in discussion about a topic or problem raised by one or more members of the family. In the case of an adolescent eating disorder, the parents may have raised the issue of how their child's eating disorder affects family functioning, and this may be explored with the family over a series of meetings. Family therapists are usually quite eclectic in the range of approaches they may bring to family therapy, and these may include cognitive-behavioural methods, psychodynamic approaches, and systemic analyses depending on the nature of the problem and its underlying causes. In many cases, family therapists may focus on how patterns of interaction within the family maintain the problem (e.g. an eating disorder) rather than trying to identify the cause (the latter may be seen as trying to allocate blame for the problem within the family). Over a period of between 5 and 20 sessions, the family therapist will attempt to identify family interaction patterns that the family may not be aware of, and to suggest to family members different ways of responding to each other. A case example of the use of family therapy with an adolescent with an eating disorder is provided in Treatment in Practice Box 10.1.

Drug treatments

Pharmacological or drug treatments are regularly used to alleviate some of the symptoms of psychopathologies. They are often the first line of treatment provided by GPs and doctors to tackle anxiety and mood-based problems, and may be sufficient to enable an individual to see through an acute bout of anxiety or depression. Some of the most commonly used drug treatments include **antidepressant drugs** to deal with symptoms of depression and mood disorder, **anxiolytic drugs** to treat symptoms of anxiety

> **antidepressant drugs** Drug treatments intended to treat symptoms of depression and mood disorder.

> **anxiolytic drugs** Drug treatments intended to treat symptoms of anxiety and stress.

antipsychotic drugs Drug treatments intended to treat symptoms of psychosis and schizophrenia spectrum disorders.

and stress, and **antipsychotic drugs** prescribed for symptoms of psychosis and schizophrenia.

Drug treatments for depression

Drug treatments for depression were first successfully developed in the 1960s and the drugs that were first developed were called **tricyclic antidepressants** (because of their chemical structure). These drugs have their effect by increasing the amount of norepinephrine and serotonin available for synaptic transmission. Other antidepressants introduced during this period were **monoamine oxidase inhibitors (MAOIs)** (such as phenelzine and tranylcypromine). MAOIs are effective for some people with major depression who do not respond to other antidepressants. They are also effective for the treatment of panic disorder and bipolar depression. Most recently, we have seen the development of the first 'designer drugs' for depression, and these include fluoxetine (Prozac), sertraline (Zoloft), paroxetine (Paxil), and citalopram (Celexa). These newer drugs are collectively called **selective serotonin reuptake inhibitors (SSRIs)** because they selectively affect the uptake of only one neurotransmitter – usually serotonin. SSRIs can reduce the symptoms of depression as rapidly as tricyclic antidepressants, and have far fewer side effects. SSRIs – especially Prozac – have often been viewed as the miracle drug for depression. However, it can also cause some side effects (such as a loss of sexual desire in up to 30 per cent of users – Montgomery, 1995) and is possibly at the point where it is becoming overprescribed by GPs who are perhaps failing to look further for more structured psychological treatment for their patients (Olfson & Klerman, 1993). In relation to this latter point, recent studies suggest that antidepressants are more effective than placebos for people with severe depression, but not for those with mild depression (Fournier, DeRubeis, Hollon *et al.*, 2010), yet GPs and physicians are often more than ready to prescribe these drugs for people with mild, first-episode depression. This issue is compounded by the fact that almost 40 per cent of those who are prescribed with antidepressants stop taking the drug within the first month – often because of the side effects (Olfson, Blanco, Liu *et al.*, 2006). Finally, although antidepressants

tricyclic antidepressants Antidepressant drugs developed in the 1960s which have their effect by increasing the amount of norepinephrine and serotonin available for synaptic transmission.

monoamine oxidase inhibitors (MAOIs) Antidepressants which are effective for some people with major depression who do not respond to other antidepressants.

selective serotonin reuptake inhibitors (SSRIs) A recent group of antidepressant drugs that selectively affect the uptake of only one neurotransmitter – usually serotonin.

do appear to hasten recovery from an episode of depression, relapse is extremely common after the drug is discontinued (Reimherr, Strong, Marchant *et al.*, 2001).

Drug treatments for anxiety

There are numerous psychological disorders that are characterized by chronic, high levels of anxiety. The more prevalent of these include clinically diagnosable specific phobias, panic disorder, generalized anxiety disorder (GAD), obsessive compulsive disorder (OCD), and post-traumatic stress disorder (PTSD) (see Chapter 6). The symptoms of these disorders can usually be treated with anxiolytics (tranquillizers) such as the **benzodiazepines** (which include the well-known tranquillizer Valium), and they have their effect by increasing the level of the neurotransmitter GABA at synapses in the brain. Benzodiazepines are usually prescribed only for short periods because they can encourage dependence if taken over a longer period, and can also be abused if available in large doses. However, it is important to be aware that anxiolytics will usually offer only symptom relief, and do not address the psychological and cognitive factors that may be maintaining the anxiety. **Serotonin–norepinephrine reuptake inhibitors (SNRIs)** are a more recently developed class of drugs for anxiety-based symptoms (Hoffman & Mathews, 2008). SNRIs selectively inhibit norepinephrine and serotonin reuptake and have been shown to be effective and well tolerated treatments in individuals with anxiety disorders (Dell'Osso, Buoli, Baldwin & Altamura, 2010), making them superior to benzodiazepines in terms of reduced side effects and less likelihood of withdrawal symptoms following discontinuation (Schweizer, Rickels, Case & Greenblatt, 1990).

benzodiazepines A group of anxiolytics which have their effect by increasing the level of the neurotransmitter GABA at synapses in the brain.

serotonin–norepinephrine reuptake inhibitors (SNRIs) A recent group of drugs for anxiety-based symptoms which selectively inhibit norepinephrine and serotonin reuptake and have been shown to be effective and well tolerated in individuals with anxiety disorders.

Drug treatments for psychosis

Drug treatments for psychosis and schizophrenia have radically revolutionized the way that schizophrenia sufferers are treated and cared for. The use of effective antipsychotic drugs became common in the 1960s and 1970s, and this had the effect of drastically reducing the number of individuals with psychotic symptoms who needed long-term institutionalized care, and has enabled many experiencing such symptoms to achieve a level of functioning that permits relatively normal day-to-day functioning. Prior to the 1980s, it was estimated that two out of three schizophrenia sufferers would spend most of their lives in a psychiatric institution; beyond the 1980s, the average length of stay has come down to as little as 2 months (Lamb, 1984).

Antipsychotics (such as chlorpromazine and halop-eridol) have their effects by blocking dopamine receptors and help to reduce the high levels of dopamine in the brain (see Chapter 8). This not only reduces the major positive symptoms (such as thought disorder and hallucinations), but can also reduce the major negative symptoms (such as social withdrawal). However, while these drugs have had a remarkable effect on reducing the symptoms of psychosis, and, as a consequence, reducing the burden of institutionalized care for sufferers, there are some negative factors to consider. For example, most antipsychotics do have some undesirable side effects for some people (such as blurred vision, muscle spasms, blood disorders, cardiac problems, and so on), and these side effects can cause relapse, or make sufferers unwilling to take their medication on a regular basis (which needs constant monitoring if the individual is being cared for in the community).

Problems with drug treatments   Despite the fact that appropriate medication can often provide relief from the symptoms of psychopathology, there is a view that interventions using drugs alone may be problematic for a number of reasons. Firstly, prescribing drugs for some mild psychopathology symptoms may effectively 'medicalize' what are merely everyday problems of living, and lead people to believe that acute bouts of anxiety or depression are 'diseases' that will not be alleviated until medical treatment has been sought (Shaw & Woodward, 2004; see Focus Point 1.6). Similarly, many drugs are tested for their effectiveness on individuals with severe symptoms, and some recent studies suggest that they may be ineffective for people with only mild symptoms (Fournier, DeRubeis, Hollon *et al.*, 2010; Kirsch, Deacon, Huedo-Medina *et al.*, 2008). Secondly, long-term prescription of drugs for a psychopathology may lead sufferers to believe that their symptoms are unchangeable and that their psychological and social functioning will depend on them continuing to take their medication. This can often prevent such individuals from trying to understand their symptoms and from gaining insight into symptoms that may be primarily psychological rather than medical in nature (Bentall, 2003; see Activity 8.2 for an example related to drug interventions for psychotic symptoms). Finally, there is some evidence that while drug treatment of psychopathology may alleviate the immediate symptoms, it may worsen the long-term course of a disorder. For example, while antidepressant drugs may alleviate the immediate symptoms of depression, there is evidence that they may also increase vulnerability to relapse over the longer-term (Fava, 2003). This may be a result of drug tolerance effects as a result of continued drug use plus the fact that drug treatment alone may not facilitate the

kinds of beneficial insights into the psychopathology that psychological therapies may provide. This account is consistent with the fact that when drug treatments are successful over the longer term, this is more likely to be the case if drug treatment is combined with psychological treatment (e.g. CBT) (Hollon & Beck, 1994; Thase, Greenhouse, Frank, Reynolds *et al.*, 1997).

Summary of theoretical approaches

Each of the theoretical approaches to treatment we have discussed in this section can be used to treat a range of different psychopathologies, and we will look more closely at how to evaluate their success later in this chapter. Each of these approaches differs not only in the basic intervention procedures they use, but also in the way they attempt to explain psychopathology (see Chapter 1). Contemporary practitioners may well be skilled in using more than one of these approaches, and, indeed, a combination of approaches may be used to address specific psychopathologies (e.g. the use of both drug treatment and CBT to treat depression).

4.1.2   Modes of Treatment Delivery

The standard and traditional mode of psychotherapy delivery is in one-to-one, face-to-face meetings or sessions between a therapist and a client, and this is still the most prevalent mode of delivery today. However, with the pressing need to treat ever increasing numbers of individuals referred with symptoms of psychopathology, overstretched clinicians and service providers often look to find more cost-effective and efficient ways to deliver treatment interventions. The following section looks briefly at some of the modes of delivery that have been developed to supplement the traditional one-to-one therapist–client model.

Group therapy

Therapy can also be undertaken in a group and not just on a one-to-one therapist–client basis. **Group therapy** can be useful (1) when a group of individuals share similar problems or psychopathologies (e.g. self-help groups), or (2) when there is a need to treat an individual in the presence of others who might have a role in influencing the psychopathology (e.g. family therapy). Group therapies can have a number of advantages, especially when individuals (1) may need to work out their problems in the presence of others (e.g. in the case of emotional problems relating to relationships, feelings of isolation, loneliness and rejection), (2) may need comfort and support from others, and (3) may

> **group therapy** Therapy taken in the form of a group, usually when individuals share similar problems or psychopathologies.

acquire therapeutic benefit from observing and watching others. There are now many different types of group therapy (Bloch & Crouch, 1987), and these include experiential groups and **encounter groups** (which encourage therapy and self-growth through disclosure and interaction) and **self-help groups** (which bring together people who share a common problem in an attempt to share information and help and support each other: e.g. Alcoholics Anonymous, http://www.alcoholics-anonymous.org.uk/; see Focus Point 9.1). However, interventions that have traditionally been used only in one-to-one client–therapist situations are now being adapted to group settings, and two of these include CBT and mindfulness (Arch, Ayers, Baker, Almklov *et al*., 2013). Adapting interventions for groups is likely to be a cost-effective solution for service providers as well as an effective way of helping clients to manage symptoms of psychopathology.

> **encounter groups** Group therapy which encourages therapy and self-growth through disclosure and interaction.

> **self-help groups** Group therapy which brings together people who share a common problem in an attempt to share information and help and support one another.

Counselling

Counselling is still a developing and evolving profession that has burgeoned in the past 20–30 years, and its expansion has partly resulted from the increasing demand for trained specialists able to provide immediate support and treatment across a broad range of problems and client groups. Counsellors receive specialized training in a range of support, guidance and intervention techniques, and their levels of training are monitored and accredited by professional bodies such as the British Association for Counselling and Psychotherapy (BACP) in the UK, or Division 17 (Counselling Psychology) of the American Psychological Association. Arguably, the primary task for counselling is to give the client an opportunity to explore, discover and clarify ways of living more satisfyingly and resourcefully (British Association for Counselling, 1984), and to 'help clients to understand and clarify their views of their lifespace, and to learn to reach their self-determined goals through meaningful, well-informed choices and through resolution of problems of an emotional or interpersonal nature' (Burks & Stefflre, 1979, p.14). These definitions indicate that counselling is a profession that aims at both promoting personal growth and productivity and alleviating any personal problems that may reflect underlying psychopathology. In order to achieve these aims,

> For a video on the benefits of talking therapy go to **www.wiley-psychopathology.com/activities/ch4**

> **counselling** A profession that aims both to promote personal growth and productivity and to alleviate any personal problems that may reflect underlying psychopathology.

counsellors tend to adopt a range of theoretical approaches, with the main ones being psychodynamic, cognitive behavioural, and humanistic (MacLeod, 2003). Counsellors with different theoretical orientations may often focus on different outcomes. Humanistic counsellors tend to promote self-acceptance and personal freedom; psychodynamic counsellors focus primarily on insight; and cognitive behavioural counsellors are mainly concerned with the management and control of behaviour and symptoms of psychopathology (MacLeod, 2003). Some counsellors specialize in areas such as marital breakdown, rape, bereavement or addictions, and their specialized roles may be recognized by the use of titles such as **mental health counsellor**, **marriage counsellor** or **student counsellor**. Counselling agencies have been established in a range of organisations to supplement community mental health services and provide more direct and immediate access to support for vulnerable or needy individuals. Counselling services may be directed towards people with particular medical conditions such as AIDS and cancer, and also to the carers of individuals suffering these illnesses, and these services are often provided by voluntary and charitable organisations set up specifically for these purposes. Even individual companies and organisations may have set up their own in-house counselling services to help people through difficulties and anxieties associated with their work.

> **mental health counsellor** A counsellor who specializes in mental health problems.

> **marriage counsellor** A counsellor who specializes in marriage problems.

> **student counsellor** A counsellor who specializes in students' problems.

Computerized CBT (CCBT)

Because a treatment such as CBT has a highly organized structure, it lends itself well to delivery by other modes and as a package that might be used independently by the client. In recent years, **computerized CBT (CCBT)** has been developed as an alternative to therapist delivered CBT, and consists of highly developed software packages that can be delivered via an interactive computer interface on a personal computer, over the internet or via the telephone using interactive voice response (IVR) systems (Moritz, Schilling, Hauschildt, Schröder & Treszl, 2012). Two CCBT packages that have been recommended by the UK Department of Health are 'Beating the Blues' and 'Fear Fighter': (1) **Beating the Blues**® as an

> **computerized CBT (CCBT)** Developed as an alternative to therapist delivered CBT, CCBT consists of highly developed software packages that can be delivered via an interactive computer interface on a personal computer, over the internet or via the telephone using interactive voice response (IVR) systems.

> **Beating the Blues**® A computer-based CBT programme used in the management of mild and moderate depression.

option for delivering computer-based CBT in the management of mild and moderate depression, and (2) **Fear Fighter**™ as an option for delivering computer-based CBT in the management of panic and phobia (NICE,

> **Fear Fighter™** A computer-based CBT programme used in the management of panic and phobia.

2008). Beating the Blues consists of a 15 minute introductory video and eight 1 hour interactive sessions, including homework to be completed between sessions. The programme helps the client identify thinking errors, challenge negative thoughts, and identify core negative beliefs, and provides help and advice on more adaptive thinking styles (http://www.ultrasis; see also Treatment in Practice Box 7.1). Fear Fighter is a CBT-based package for phobic, panic and anxiety disorders and is divided into nine steps with support available from trained helpers via telephone calls or emails throughout treatment. The package helps clients identify specific problems, develop realistic treatment goals, and monitor achievement through self-exposure (http://www.fearfighter.com).

CCBT is recommended by the UK National Institute for Health and Care Excellence as a suitable intervention for individuals with persistent sub-threshold depressive symptoms or mild to moderate depression (NICE, 2008). Studies comparing CCBT with other forms of support and intervention are still in their infancy, but those available are relatively supportive and suggest that CCBT along with other guided self-help programmes can be a valuable and effective way of treating individuals with common mental health problems (Cuijpers, Marks, van Straten, Cavanagh *et al.*, 2009; Kaltenthaler, Parry, Beverley & Ferriter, 2008). For example, Proudfoot, Ryden, Everitt, Shapiro *et al.* (2004) found that Beating the Blues provided a more effective treatment for depression and anxiety than GP treatment as usual, and in a review of 16 studies exploring the efficacy of CCBT, Kaltenthaler, Parry & Beverley (2004) found that five studies showed CCBT to have equivalent outcomes to therapist led CBT, and four studies found CCBT to be more effective than GP treatment as usual. CCBT offers a number of advantages to both clients and service providers, including increased flexible access to evidence-based treatments, reduction of waiting lists, and savings in therapist time (Learmonth, Trosh, Rai, Sewell & Cavanagh, 2008; Titov, 2007). However, there are still issues surrounding client engagement with CCBT. Clearly, clients need to have a minimum knowledge of computers, and may often view CCBT as both mechanical and impersonal (Beattie, Shaw, Kaur & Kessler, 2009). CCBT may also lack many of the ingredients to successful therapy that are a function of the therapeutic relationship between therapist and client (Dogg-Helgadottir, Menzies, Onslow, Packman & O'Brian, 2009), but there are recent indications that it is possible to incorporate these important 'alliance' ingredients into self-help programmes such

as CCBT (Ormrod, Kennedy, Scott & Cavanagh, 2010; Barazzone, Cavanagh & Richards, 2012).

E-therapy

The rapid growth of the internet over the past 15–20 years has meant people now have almost immediate access to information about mental health problems and email provides another potential form of communication between therapists and clients. As a result more and more therapists and practitioners are using email as

> **e-therapy** A treatment method which involves the use of email and internet technology.

an integral part of the treatment they provide and this is often known as **e-therapy** (Hsiung, 2002). Email is a useful adjunct to face-to-face sessions in a number of ways:

1. it may be used to enhance weekly sessions, monitor treatment from a distance, monitor behaviour daily, communicate with the client's family members, or intervene in a crisis (Yellowlees, 2002; Yager, 2002);

2. it allows clients to initiate contact with the therapist more easily and, because the communication is online, this may make the client feel more secure (Ainsworth, 2002);

3. it allows clients who may be withdrawn or shy in personal face-to-face interviews (such as adolescents with eating disorders) to be more open and compliant (Yager, 2002), and

4. it enables clients to contact therapists more regularly in areas where resources are more difficult to access in person, or when clients are living in remote and inaccessible areas (Gibson, Morley & Romeo-Wolff, 2002).

However, at present there is very little research on the effectiveness of online services or the potential beneficial effects of email communication between therapists and clients. There are also some limitations to email communication, including miscommunication because neither party to the communication is able to see the nonverbal cues being given by the other, it is very difficult to ensure the confidentiality of online communications, and online communication makes it very difficult to intervene effectively in severe emergencies, such as when, for example, a client may have suicidal intentions.

'Telepsychiatry': Therapy by telephone and videoconferencing

Most clients telephone their therapists, if only to schedule an appointment, but the telephone can also provide a means of facilitating and conducting treatment (which is known as **telepsychiatry**).

> **telepsychiatry** Therapy facilitated by telephone or videoconference.

For example, Ludman, Simon, Tutty & Von Korff (2007) report an evaluation of a telephone-based CBT programme for depression in which clients were given eight core sessions using standard CBT procedures adapted for use over the telephone. This was supplemented by homework exercises for clients, and regular assessments also conducted over the phone. Figure 4.1 shows that CBT conducted over the phone was more successful in reducing depression scores than usual care (clients receiving antidepressants) up to 12–18 months post-treatment, and these supplement results of other outcome studies suggesting that telephone therapy is both acceptable and effective (Leach & Christensen, 2006; Lynch, Tamburrino & Nagel, 1997; Mohr, Hart, Julian, Catledge et al., 2005).

Telephone therapy may prove to be an effective form of intervention when clients live in remote or inaccessible areas, and it is a mode of delivery that can save time and reduce travel costs. Furthermore, with continued developments in computer technology, real-time video conferencing is also a means by which psychotherapy can be delivered to clients who are physically disabled or live remotely, and comparative studies of face-to-face, real-time video conferencing, and two-way audio therapy suggest that differences in outcomes among the three modes of treatment delivery are surprisingly small (Day & Schneider, 2002; Shore, 2013).

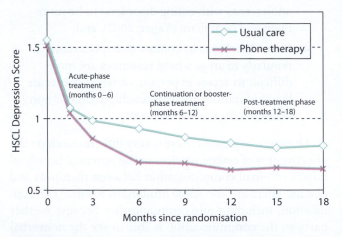

FIGURE 4.1 *Improvement in depression scores as a function of therapy by telephone (CBT) or care as usual (pharmacotherapy). CBT by telephone results in a marked improvement in depression scores over pharmacotherapy in the first 6 months of treatment and gains are maintained up to 18 months after the start of treatment. (HSCL = Hopkins Symptom Checklist, a measure of the remission of depression).*
Source: After Ludman, E.J., Simon, G.E., Tutty, S. & Von Korff, M. (2007). A randomized trial of telephone psychotherapy and pharmacotherapy for depression: Continuation and durability of effects. *Journal of Consulting and Clinical Psychology*, 75, 257–266. American Psychological Association. Adapted with permission.

Improving Access to Psychological Therapies (IAPT)

It is now clear that mental health problems are far from uncommon. One in four people will suffer a diagnosable mental health problem in their lifetime (Bebbington, Brugha, Coid, Crawford *et al.*, 2007), and one in six people in the UK will be diagnosed with either chronic anxiety or depression. These statistics have implications for the well-being of those who suffer these disabilities, their families, the agencies that are attempting to provide services for those with mental health problems, and also the contribution that sufferers can make to the economic prosperity of the countries in which they live. Mental health is the largest single cause of disability in the UK, with the total loss of economic output due to depression and anxiety in the UK estimated to be in excess of £12 billion a year (London School of Economics & Political Science, 2006; Department of Health, 2012). It therefore not only makes good therapeutic sense to improve access to mental health treatments, it also makes good economic sense to help people recover from their problems. Given the evidence-based success of therapies such as CBT for common mental health problems, many countries are now trying to find ways to increase and improve access to these therapies. This has given rise to large-scale initiatives, commonly known as **Improving Access to Psychological Therapies (IAPT)**, which aim at increasing significantly the availability of evidence-based interventions – such as CBT. To meet these goals involves: (1) training significant numbers of practitioners in psychological therapies such as CBT – known as **psychological well-being practitioners (PWPs)** (Focus Point 4.2 provides a personal account of someone who was trained to deliver low-intensity CBT under the IAPT scheme); (2) improving access and reducing waiting times for treatment; and (3) increasing client choice and satisfaction. A consequence of this will be improved social and economic participation as those previously suffering common mental health problems return to work and normal social and family functioning. As a result, the costs of the IAPT programme are considered to be offset by the increased economic contribution of those who have recovered from their mental health problems (e.g. Radhakrishnan, Hammond, Jones, Watson *et al.*, 2013). Key successes of the programme in the UK in the first 3 years include (1) treating more than 1 million people in

> **Improving Access to Psychological Therapies (IAPT)** NHS programme providing services across England for treating people with depression and anxiety disorders.

> **psychological well-being practitioners (PWPs)** People trained under the IAPT initiative to deliver psychological therapies such as CBT.

IAPT services, (2) recovery rates in excess of 45 per cent (see section 4.2.2 for a discussion of recovery rates for psychological therapies), and (3) over 45,000 people moving off benefits into paid employment (Department of Health, 2012). Schemes for improving access to psychological therapies are now being rolled out in many countries, including developing countries such as India, Pakistan and Uganda (Patel, Chowdhary, Rahman & Verdeli, 2011), where lay and community health workers are being trained in evidenced-based practices. However, the challenges of providing access to psychological therapies for those who need them are still immense, with the 'treatment gap' (a term used to describe the shortfall in mental health provision for sufferers) exceeding 75 per cent in most parts of the world (Kohn, Saxena, Levav & Saraceno, 2004).

FOCUS POINT 4.2

TRAINING PRACTITIONERS UNDER THE IAPT INITIATIVE

ASHLEY SNOWDON'S EXPERIENCE

Psychological Well-being Practitioner, Teeside IAPT Service

Working as a psychological wellbeing practitioner (PWP) in Teesside IAPT has been challenging and rewarding over the past few years. Since completing my training, I have seen over 200 people, some with relatively complex problems who have never accessed mental health treatment before, for whom brief interventions have had a huge impact on their functioning. The range of problems clients have presented with has been surprisingly broad, and has given me excellent development opportunities as well as developing my confidence as a clinician.

Teaching people CBT-based skills has meant that they have been able to take control of their own problems and are more able to manage them in future. I have often found that people integrate CBT skills into their lives and then come back and report that they have been teaching them to their friends and family! I have also been closely involved in a pilot scheme working with drug and alcohol users, who have responded really well to the short-term, time-limited work, because they can see quicker results and seem to feel empowered by the guided self-help approach.

Source: IAPT three-year report: The first million patients, November 2012. http://www.hsj.co.uk/Journals/2012/12/04/w/g/m/9265-2900428-TSO-IAPT-3-year-report-pdf.pdf. Reproduced with permission.

SELF-TEST QUESTIONS

- What are the main principles of psychodynamic therapy?
- Can you describe some of the basic techniques used by psychoanalysts?
- Can you describe the behaviour therapy techniques that are based on classical conditioning?
- Can you describe some of the treatment techniques that have been developed based on principles of operant reinforcement?
- Can you describe at least two types of cognitive therapy?
- What are 'third wave' CBT methods – can you describe at least one of these?
- What are the main theoretical principles on which humanistic therapies are based?
- What are the main principles used in client-centred therapy?
- What is family therapy and how is it conducted?
- Can you name the main types of drug treatments for psychopathology?
- Can you describe two to three types of group therapy?
- What are the main characteristics of counselling?
- Can you describe the main features of computerized CBT (CCBT), e-therapy, and therapy by telephone?
- What does IAPT stand for, and what is it trying to achieve?

4.1 THE NATURE AND FUNCTION OF TREATMENTS FOR PSYCHOPATHOLOGY

With the average waiting-time for conventional treatments provided by community mental health services in many parts of the world often longer than 1–2 years – especially for popular and specialized treatments such as CBT – practitioners and service providers are under pressure to provide more cost-effective and immediate forms of interventions for people with mental health problems (Layard, 2007). We have reviewed some of the modes of delivery that may prove to be more immediate and cost effective, although most of these modes of delivery represent relatively new innovations that have yet to be fully and properly evaluated.

- The treatment provided for a psychopathology will depend on the theoretical orientation of the therapist and the nature of the psychopathology.

- *Psychodynamic approaches* to therapy attempt to reveal unconscious conflicts that may be causing psychopathology.

- *Behaviour therapies* are mainly based on the principles of *classical* and *operant conditioning*.

- Behaviour therapies based on classical conditioning include *flooding, counterconditioning, systematic desensitisation*, and *aversion therapy*.

- Therapies based on operant conditioning include *functional analysis, token economy, response shaping*, and *behavioural self-control*.

- Important *cognitive therapies* include *rational emotive therapy (RET), Beck's cognitive therapy*, and *cognitive behaviour therapy (CBT)*.

- 'Third wave' cognitive therapies include *mindfulness-based cognitive therapy (MBCT)* and *acceptance and commitment therapy (ACT)*.

- *Humanistic therapies* attempt to consider the 'whole' person and not just the symptoms of psychopathology.

- *Family therapy* attempts to deal with psychopathology by addressing relationship dynamics within the family.

- *Drug treatments* have been developed to alleviate some of the symptoms of psychopathology, particularly in disorders associated with depression, anxiety and psychosis.

- Important drug treatments include *antidepressant drugs, anxiolytic drugs*, and *antipsychotic drugs*.

- Recently developed modes of treatment delivery include *group therapy, counselling, computerized CBT (CCBT), e-therapy, 'telepsychiatry'*, and the *Improving Access to Psychological Therapies (IAPT)* programme.

4.2 EVALUATING TREATMENT

All of the therapies and treatments we have discussed in previous sections of this chapter have at least some degree of intuitive plausibility as treatments for psychological problems. Nevertheless, how do we assess how effective a treatment is? This is not as simple as it sounds. Firstly, we often have to try to compare the efficacy of therapies that have quite different assumptions about what 'successful therapy' is (e.g. cognitive therapies would expect to see some significant improvement after a few weeks or months, whereas psychoanalytic and humanistic therapies are seen as developmental, life-long processes promoting self-growth). And secondly, we have to decide on what constitutes a therapeutic gain (i.e. on what particular measures are we expecting to see improvement?). For example, Erwin (2000) describes how different

theoretical approaches to treatment use radically different criteria for judging outcomes. Therapists using CBT typically use elimination of psychopathology symptoms as the main criterion of success; behaviour therapists view the modification of maladaptive behaviours as important; psychodynamic therapists view the elimination of unconscious conflicts as critical to therapeutic success; and humanistic psychotherapists see enhancement of personal autonomy as their main therapeutic objective. Erwin concludes that, at the end of the day, what constitutes a successful therapeutic intervention is often a subjective judgement and may boil down to little more that the outcome was beneficial in some way to the client – or at least to someone!

Despite these difficulties in deciding on a common set of criteria for gauging success across different treatment types, there are some good reasons for wanting to try to objectively assess how successful therapies are: (1) psychological disorders are distressing to the individual, and we have a moral and professional obligation to seek ways of alleviating this distress rapidly and effectively; (2) some treatments may have short-term gains but be significantly less effective over the longer term – leaving the individual open to relapse – so we need to be sure that therapies have lasting therapeutic effects; and (3) individuals with psychological problems are a very vulnerable group of people, and we need to ensure that they are not exploited financially and psychologically by what is a growing industry of essentially bogus therapies with shallow – but often beguiling – rationales, and little or no medium-term therapeutic benefit.

4.2.1 Factors Affecting the Evaluation of Treatments

On what basis do therapists decide whether their treatments are successful? Focus Point 4.3 provides an interesting example of this (described by Davey, 2002). The therapist in this example assumed that her treatment was being effective because no one ever returned to complain about it! But there could be many reasons why individuals may not complain, and the client in this example is quite happy to return for more therapy even though her first session was not as successful as she was led to believe it should be. The moral of this story is that a client simply saying they are satisfied with the outcome of the therapy does not mean either (1) that any objective therapeutic gain has been achieved, or (2), if some therapeutic gain was achieved, that it was due explicitly to the type of therapy that was used. Therapeutic interventions are generally very complex things, and they will often contain many factors that might help (or hinder) recovery. Some obvious factors that might help recovery include a sympathetic therapist, a rationale for recovery that the client understands and believes will help them, a therapeutic intervention with well thought-out principles that have been tried and successfully tested before. Factors that might hinder recovery include an unsympathetic therapist, an unsupportive home environment, or the use of an intervention that is poorly structured and not soundly based on proven psychotherapy principles. These are all factors that need to be considered when evaluating the effectiveness of a therapy, and we will discuss these in turn below. However, one of the central issues in evaluative research is determining whether an intervention is effective primarily because of the therapeutic principles in the intervention (e.g. psychoanalytic principles, cognitive-behavioural principles, and so on), and determining whether a treatment works because of the principles it contains is known as assessing its **internal validity**.

> **internal validity** Determining whether a treatment works because of the principles it contains.

Because therapeutic interventions are usually a conglomeration of many different factors, assessing the reasons for the efficacy of therapies is difficult, and the sections below describe some of the factors that can confound the assessment of therapeutic effectiveness.

Spontaneous remission

Just because someone exhibits objective improvement in symptoms after treatment does not necessarily mean that the treatment was the cause of the improvement.

STOP SMOKING IN ONE SESSION!

As I was passing a local 'holistic' health clinic, I noticed a sign outside which – in large letters – implored "STOP SMOKING IN ONE SESSION!" (Which session? Surely not the first one?!) Having interests in both clinical and health psychology areas, I was intrigued to find out more. As it turns out, a friend of mine had just recently visited the clinic and had received a single 1 hour session of hypnotherapy in an attempt to stop smoking – cost £50. Knowing the literature on psychological treatments for smoking and how difficult it is to achieve abstinence, I decided to find out a little more about these treatment claims. I emailed the hypnotherapists offering services at the clinic and asked if stopping smoking in one session of hypnotherapy was achievable, and what their success rates were like. I did get a reply from one of the practitioners, who had worked as a hypnotherapist for 7 years. She replied:

'I did not do follow-up calls as I thought this would be intrusive so, therefore, I do not have stats on my success rates. However, I know I have had a high success rate because people referred others to me and came back to me for help on other issues.' Interestingly, my friend who had attended the clinic was smoking regularly again within 3 days of the hypnotherapy session, and – despite having long discussions with me about the validity of the treatment and its lack of success – said she was thinking of attending again (this time in relation to other aspects of her life) because the hypnotherapist had been so caring, understanding and interested in her problems!

Source: From Davey G.C.L. (2002). Smoking them out. First published in *The Psychologist, 15*(10). Published by The British Psychological Society (www.thepsychologist.org.uk).

The famous British psychologist Hans Eysenck argued that many people who have mental health problems will simply get better anyway over a period of time – even without therapy (Eysenck, 1961), and this can often be the result of an individual's changing life experiences (e.g. positive life changes) (Neeleman, Oldehinkel & Ormel, 2003). This is known as **spontaneous remission**, and the current estimate is that around 30 per cent of those diagnosed with anxiety and depression-based disorders will get better without structured treatment (Jacobson & Christenson, 1996). So, if we are assessing the effectiveness of a therapy we would expect to see improvement rates *significantly greater* than 30 per cent in order to take into account the fact that many of those undertaking the therapy would show a spontaneous improvement in symptoms anyway.

> **spontaneous remission** The fact that many people who have psychological disorders will simply get better anyway over a period of time, even without therapy.

Placebo effects

If someone suffering with anxiety symptoms is given a sugar pill but they are told that it is an anxiolytic medication, they often report significant improvements in those symptoms. This suggests that individuals will often get better because they *expect* to get better – even though the actual treatment that they have been given is effectively useless (Paul, 1966). This is known as the *placebo effect* (Paul, 1966; see also section 3.3.4). Thus, it may be the case that many psychological treatments have beneficial effects because the client *expects* them to work – and *not* because they are treatments that are effective in tackling the factors maintaining the psychopathology. Unfortunately, the positive gains produced by placebo effects are short-lived, and comparative studies of placebo effects with actual structured psychotherapies strongly suggest that structured psychotherapies lead to greater improvement than placebo control conditions (Robinson, Berman & Neimeyer, 1990; Andrews & Harvey, 1981).

Unstructured attention, understanding and caring

In addition, we know that people with psychological problems also show some improvement in symptoms when they can simply talk about their problems in an unstructured way with either a professional therapist or a friend or relative (Lambert, Shapiro & Bergin, 1986). This suggests that many forms of social support may have a therapeutic effect in and of themselves (Borkovec & Costello, 1993), and this factor must be taken into account when judging how effective a structured therapy is. One of the important things that we want to find out about therapies is not just whether they are effective

in making people better, but whether they make people better specifically because of the principles they contain (see above).

Consequently, studies that attempt to evaluate the effectiveness of a therapy's principles also need to control for other factors such as the amount of attention or empathy that the client is receiving from the therapist. One recently developed form of control condition for attention, understanding and caring is known as **befriending**. This is a control condition designed to provide participants with approximately the same amount of therapist contact as the treatment conditions being tested, with sessions spaced at similar intervals. In the befriending condition the therapist aims to be empathetic and nondirective and does not attempt to directly tackle symptoms, and the session is normally focused on discussion of neutral topics such as hobbies, sport, and current affairs (Sensky, Turkington, Kingdon, Scott *et al.*, 2000; Bendall, Jackson, Killackey, Allott *et al.*, 2006).

> **befriending** A form of control condition for attention, understanding and caring used in treatment outcome studies.

4.2.2 Methods of Assessing the Effectiveness of Treatments

We have to begin this section by acknowledging that the advocates of some therapeutic approaches do not believe that the success or otherwise of their therapeutic approaches can be assessed using objective or quantitative methods (e.g. Marzillier, 2004). This is because those therapists view their treatments not as attempts to eliminate symptoms of psychopathology, but as attempts to reconstruct a client's meaning of the world (e.g. Rosen, 1996), or to move the client from one phenomenological state to another (e.g. humanistic approaches). In each case, these are not changes that are easy to objectively measure, and nor are there particularly well-defined criteria for when these goals have been reached.

Nevertheless, there are still many compelling reasons for wanting to assess in some formal way whether a treatment is effective and successful, and we have aired some of the moral and compassionate reasons for wanting to do this at the beginning of section 4.2. In addition to these reasons, mental health service providers have a duty to ensure that the services they are offering are effective, and they will need some benchmark by which to measure whether the treatments they offer are either successful or at least provide satisfaction for the end-users they are providing for.

Two popular methodologies for assessing the effectiveness of treatments are: (1) randomized controlled trials, and (2) meta-analyses and systematic reviews.

Randomized controlled trials (RCTs)

What are RCTs? The current methodology of choice for assessing the effectiveness of therapies is **randomized controlled trials** (**RCTs**) (e.g. Barker, Pistrang & Elliott, 2002, pp.153–159; Jadad & Enkin, 2007). This procedure compares the effectiveness of the treatment being assessed (across a range of objective measures) with a variety of control conditions, and with other forms of therapy and treatment (if necessary). Participants in the study are assigned *randomly* to each of these conditions. Apart from the treatment being assessed, the control conditions used in RCTs are those that will control for the kinds of effects described in section 4.2.1. These will include: (1) a no treatment or a **waiting list control** group of participants who will receive no treatment (to control for the effects of spontaneous remission), a condition that is often difficult to achieve because of the ethical issues involved in withholding treatment from clinically distressed individuals (see section 3.4.2); (2) an expectancy and relationship control group, to control for placebo effects and for the beneficial effects of contact with a therapist (e.g. 'befriending' – see section 4.2.1); and (3) a comparative treatment group, in which the original therapy can be compared with a plausible alternative therapy that is known to have beneficial effects. For the original therapy to be deemed effective and possess internal validity, participants receiving that therapy must show greater improvement than those in both the no treatment and the expectancy and relationship control conditions, and improvement that is at least equivalent to that exhibited by the comparative treatment group. Figure 4.2 provides a schematic example of one RCT study comparing the efficacy of cognitive therapy and exposure plus applied relaxation treatments for social phobia. This shows how the original 116 participants in the study were assessed, the reasons why 54 were excluded from the study, how they were randomly allocated to one of three treatment conditions, how many dropped out of the study before completion, and when the outcome assessments were taken. The graph below the flow chart shows that the cognitive therapy condition was significantly more effective at reducing symptoms of social phobia than both exposure and applied relaxation and those in a waiting list control condition.

> **randomized controlled trials (RCTs)** Comparison of the effectiveness of a treatment being assessed with a variety of control conditions, and with other forms of therapy and treatment (if necessary).

> **waiting list control** Participants in a randomized controlled trial who will receive no treatment; often difficult to achieve because of the ethical issues involved in withholding treatment from clinically distressed individuals.

Problems with RCTs While RCTs do provide an objective way of assessing the effectiveness of therapies, they do have a number of practical limitations: (1) participants do drop out of these studies, and may do so more from some conditions – e.g. the no treatment conditions – than others, (2) RCTs are costly and time consuming to undertake, and (3) because participants are assigned randomly to conditions, it does not take account of the fact that some participants may prefer some types of therapy to others (Brewin & Bradley, 1989).

Furthermore, to be genuinely objective, RCTs need to be free of any form of explicit or implicit bias that might influence the results of a basic comparison between the intervention being assessed and the control conditions. Unfortunately, this is often not the case. Firstly, those who carry out the RCT often have an allegiance to the psychotherapy being tested, and this may be a source of experimenter bias that favours the effectiveness of that intervention. Meta-analytic reviews suggest that researcher allegiance to a particular intervention does indeed substantially bias the results of an RCT (Munder, Brütsch, Leonhart, Gerger & Barth, 2013). Secondly, there is a significant bias in scientific publication to publishing findings when there is a significant difference between experimental interventions and control conditions, but not when this difference is non-significant (the latter are known as 'null findings') (Dwan, Altman, Arnaiz, Bloom *et al.*, 2008). Thus, there may well be a large number of RCTs that have shown no effect of a treatment compared with control conditions, but have never been published. This has the effect of biasing RCTs towards providing published evidence that a treatment 'works' rather than 'doesn't work'. In addition, commercial interests may be associated with whether an RCT is published that reports a positive finding or a negative finding. For example, Yaphe, Edman, Knishkowy & Hermand (2001) found that RCTs assessing the effectiveness of drug treatments were significantly more likely to report a positive or significant effect if the study had been funded by the pharmaceutical industry than if funds came from non-industry sources!

Finally, we must remember that RCTs have traditionally only told us whether a particular intervention is significantly better than a control condition or significantly better than an alternative intervention (in terms of effect sizes; see section 4.2.3). What they often do *not* tell us is what percentage of the participants in the study exhibited recovery or clinically significant change to the point where they no longer meet the criteria for a clinical diagnosis (Jacobson & Truax, 1991; Wise, 2004). The latter is known as **clinical significance** and the former reflects

> **clinical significance** The percentage of participants in a study who exhibited recovery or clinically significant change to the point where they no longer meet the criteria for a clinical diagnosis.

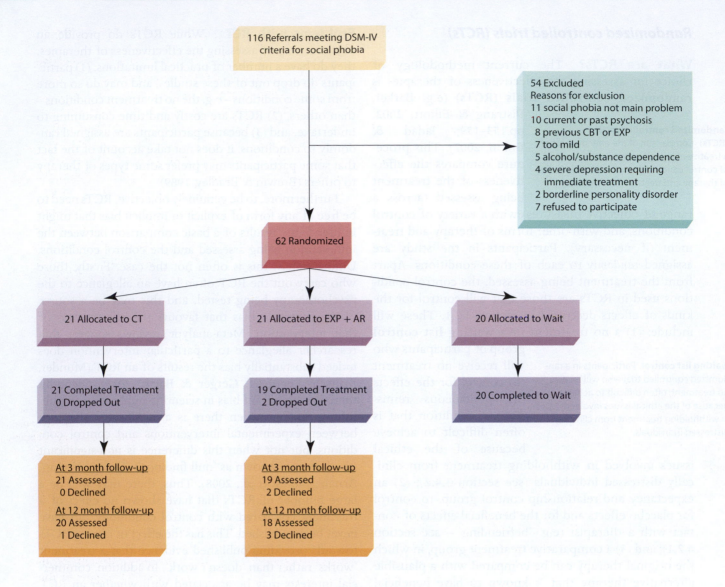

116 Referrals meeting DSM-IV criteria for social phobia

54 Excluded
Reasons for exclusion
11 social phobia not main problem
10 current or past psychosis
 8 previous CBT or EXP
 7 too mild
 5 alcohol/substance dependence
 4 severe depression requiring immediate treatment
 2 borderline personality disorder
 7 refused to participate

62 Randomized

21 Allocated to CT

21 Allocated to EXP + AR

20 Allocated to Wait

21 Completed Treatment
0 Dropped Out

19 Completed Treatment
2 Dropped Out

20 Completed to Wait

At 3 month follow-up
21 Assessed
0 Declined
At 12 month follow-up
20 Assessed
1 Declined

At 3 month follow-up
19 Assessed
2 Declined
At 12 month follow-up
18 Assessed
3 Declined

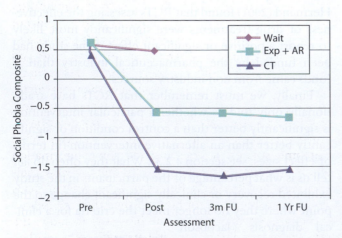

FIGURE 4.2 *A random controlled trial comparing the effectiveness of CBT and applied relaxation for social phobia.*

The flow chart shows how the 116 participants in the study were allocated to experimental conditions and assessed. The graph below the flow chart shows that the CBT condition (CT) was more effective at reducing the symptoms of social phobia than exposure and applied relaxation (Exp + AR) and a 'waiting list' control (Wait).

Source: Clark, D.M., Ehlers, A., Hackmann, A., McManus, F. *et al.* (2006). Cognitive therapy versus exposure and applied relaxation in social phobia: A randomized controlled trial. *Journal of Consulting and Clinical Psychology,* 74, 568–578. American Psychological Association. Reproduced with permission.

recovery rates The percentage of people who are no longer diagnosable once they have finished treatment.

recovery rates. Jacobson & Truax (1991) pointed out that statistical significance and clinical significance do not convey the same kinds of information about an intervention, and that it is important to determine whether the intervention 'moves the client from the dysfunctional to the functional range during the course of therapy' (Jacobson, Follette, Revenstorf, Baucom *et al.*, 1984, p.340). While most structured interventions are more effective than no treatment control conditions, a look at recovery rates often suggests a less than perfect picture. Even for well-established psychological and pharmaceutical interventions, recovery rates for common mental health problems (the percentage of people that are no longer diagnosable once they have finished treatment) is normally between 50 and 70 per cent (e.g. Hanrahan, Field, Jones & Davey, 2013; Baldwin, Woods, Lawson & Taylor, 2011; Craske, Liao, Brown & Vervliet, 2012), suggesting that such interventions fail to 'cure' between 30 and 50 per cent of those being treated. This probably testifies more to the complexity of many mental health problems and the factors that maintain psychopathology than the relative ineffectiveness of our current interventions. But clearly more needs to be done to develop interventions that will help larger proportions of sufferers to fully recover.

 To read the author's blog on 'The lost 40%' go to **http://tinyurl.com/px4znd5**

Nevertheless, despite some of these limitations, RCTs have remained a popular method for assessing the relative effectiveness of treatments and are still considered to be the main standard by which the effectiveness of an intervention is experimentally tested.

Meta-analyses and systematic reviews

We have already discussed meta-analyses and systematic reviews as a research method in section 3.3.8, and the reader is referred back to this in the first instance. The benefit of meta-analyses is that they can be used to compare the effectiveness of studies that may have used different procedures, different numbers of participants, different types of control procedures, and different forms of measurement, and they do this by comparing effect sizes across studies. One important use of meta-analyses has been to try to answer an enduring question in psychotherapy: are psychotherapies more effective than no treatment at all? An early large-scale meta-analysis carried out by Smith, Glass & Miller (1980) concluded that psychotherapies were more effective than no treatment, but that effect sizes did not differ across different psychotherapies, suggesting that all different psychotherapies were equally effective.

4.2.3 What Treatments Are Effective?

Although we have identified a couple of objective ways of assessing whether therapies are effective, what do studies using these methods tell us? Comparative studies tend to suggest that most of the accepted therapies are more effective than no treatment or expectancy control conditions, but that the therapies themselves do not differ in their relative effectiveness. For example, in a study of depressed individuals, Gibbons, Hedeker, Elkin, Waternaux *et al.* (1993) found that cognitive therapy, interpersonal therapy, and antidepressant medication were all as effective as each other, but all more effective than a placebo control condition (after 16 weeks of treatment). Similarly, the meta-analysis conducted by Smith, Glass & Miller (1980) also indicated that psychotherapies were all more effective than no treatment, but none was significantly more effective than another. This has come to be known as the **Dodo Bird Verdict**, which is a phrase taken from Lewis Carroll's *Alice's Adventures in Wonderland*, implying that all psychotherapies are winners and produce equivalent benefits for clients. This debate is considered in more detail in Focus Point 4.4.

Dodo Bird Verdict An expression from Lewis Carroll's *Alice's Adventures in Wonderland*, implying that all psychotherapies are more effective than no treatment, but produce equivalent benefits.

Rather than conducting objective and well-controlled outcome studies, some others have approached the issue of the effectiveness of treatments by viewing the client as a consumer and canvassing their views on how satisfied they have been with the treatment 'product' that they received. Seligman (1995) reported the results of a large-scale survey of individuals in the USA who had undergone psychotherapy and concluded that: (1) respondents claimed they benefited significantly from psychotherapy, (2) psychotherapy alone did not differ in effectiveness from medication plus psychotherapy, (3) psychologists, psychiatrists, social workers and counsellors did not differ in their effectiveness as therapists, and (4) the longer the duration of their treatment, the larger the positive gains respondents reported. While the empirical rigour of this consumer-based study falls far short of that expected in well-controlled outcome studies, it does provide some information about how the recipients of psychotherapy view their treatment and its effects. But, as we have noted in Focus Point 4.3, asking a client how satisfied they are following treatment may not be the best way to judge the effectiveness of a treatment and may reflect the involvement of psychological factors that extend beyond the original purpose of the treatment.

methods for assessing treatments. Most large-scale studies indicate that psychotherapies generally are more effective than no treatment, but there is little convincing evidence that one psychotherapy method is necessarily more effective than another (known as the 'Dodo Bird Verdict'). Nevertheless, the past 20 years have seen a significant increase in the number of treatment outcome studies published, and many of these indicate that certain types of treatments may be more effective than others at treating individual specific psychopathologies (see also the treatment sections in the following chapters covering individual psychopathologies).

To access the online resources for this chapter go to
www.wiley-psychopathology.com/ch4

Reading

- Author blog - The Lost 40%
- The therapist effect
- Journal article: Application of operant conditioning to reinstate verbal behavior in psychotics
- Glossary key terms
- Clinical issues
- Links to journal articles
- References

Video

- The benefits of talking therapy

Activity

- Activity 4.1
- Activity 4.2
- Self-test questions
- Revision flashcards
- Research questions

5 Clinical Practice

 To access the online resources for this chapter go to
www.wiley-psychopathology.com/ch5

ROUTE MAP OF THE CHAPTER

This chapter starts by taking a broad perspective of clinical practice by describing the scale of mental health problems that service providers face. We then discuss the types of mental health professionals that work in this sector, how individuals with mental health problems access services, and the facilities that are available across mental health services. We end the chapter by focusing on clinical psychologists and discussing their key capabilities and competences, how they are regulated, and how they are trained.

CHAPTER OUTLINE

CHAPTER

SECTION SUMMARY

5.1   THE ECONOMIC COST OF MENTAL HEALTH PROBLEMS

- At least one in four people in the UK will experience a mental health problem in any single year.

- The economic cost of mental health problems in the UK has been estimated at £105.2 billion each year.

5.2   WHO ARE MENTAL HEALTH PROFESSIONALS?

Mental health problems are often complex and, as a result, need to be treated in many different ways by a range of people with a variety of skills. Chapters 6 to 17 in this book will demonstrate how different the various psychiatric disorders are – in the way that symptoms manifest, how sufferers are affected, and what is required to aid recovery – and highlight why mental healthcare professionals therefore have many different roles to play in the recovery process.

The local general practitioner or physician will usually be an individual's first point of contact with mental healthcare services, and it is estimated that around one-quarter to one-third of the people that GPs see on a daily basis have either emotional or psychological problems. GPs can often make an initial assessment, prescribe medication (such as antidepressants), and make referrals to other more specialized services, such as counselling or child and adolescent services. Interestingly, although they are usually the first port of call for people with mental health problems, GPs often do not undergo full continuing professional development in mental health issues as often as might be required given the percentage of their patient base that present with mental health problems (Lester, 2005). Consequently, 91 per cent of people with a mental health problem will be treated within the primary care system, with only a small percentage referred on to specialist mental health services (Airey, Boreham, Erens & Tobin, 2003).

Once an individual has been referred onwards to more specialized services, they are likely to come into contact with one or more professional mental healthcare workers, depending on their individual needs and requirements. **Community mental health nurses** (CMHNs) or community psychiatric nurses (CPNs) are registered nurses with specialist training in mental health They have a range of skills, from offering counselling and psychotherapy (e.g. CBT for common mental

> **community mental health nurses** Registered nurses with specialist training in mental health.

health problems such as anxiety and depression) to administering medication. They may specialize in treating certain types of patient groups, such as children or people with substance dependency problems, and may be attached to GP surgeries or operate from community mental health centres.

Once referred for a more detailed assessment of their mental health problems, an individual is likely to then be seen either by a psychiatrist or a clinical psychologist. **Psychiatrists** are qualified medical doctors who have received further training in mental health problems. Psychiatrists can make initial assessments of a person's condition and needs, and can also prescribe medications. **Clinical psychologists** are normally psychology graduates who have completed up to 3 years of intensive postgraduate training to learn the skills required for clinical practice, and they will specialize in the assessment and treatment of mental health problems. Clinical psychologists will often specialize in working with only one or maybe two client groups, often within a preferred psychological approach (e.g. cognitive, behavioural, systemic, psychodynamic or humanistic: see Chapter 4). Some may work exclusively within child and adolescent services, known in the UK as Children and Adolescent Mental Health Services (CAMHS) (see Treatment in Practice Box 5.1); others may be involved in learning disability, with older people, or with substance dependency. Clinical psychologists will often work within multidisciplinary teams and are closely involved in providing care and interventions for mental health problems, but – unlike psychiatrists – are not able to prescribe medications.

> **psychiatrists** Medical practitioners specialising in the diagnosis and treatment of mental illness.

> **clinical psychologists** Psychology graduates who have completed up to 3 years of intensive postgraduate training to learn the skills required for clinical practice, and who specialize in the assessment and treatment of mental health problems.

Others involved in the provision of mental health services include counsellors, psychotherapists, occupational therapists, social workers, and approved mental health workers. **Counsellors** are trained to offer *talking therapies*

> **counsellors** People who are trained to offer talking therapies that will support people with mental health problems and help them to cope better with their lives and their symptoms.

TREATMENT IN PRACTICE BOX 5.1: CHILDREN AND ADOLESCENT MENTAL HEALTH SERVICES (CAMHS)

In the 1990s, the UK NHS Health Advisory Service published a wide-ranging review of children and adolescent mental health services in the UK. This proposed a four-tier model for planning and delivering mental health services for children. This four-tier scheme has come to be known as Child and Adolescent Mental Health Services or CAMHS for short (see www.camhscares.nhs.uk). The scheme acknowledges that supporting children and young people with mental health problems is not the responsibility of individual specialist services, but requires the cooperation and coordination of all services working with children, whether they are health, education, social services or other agencies.

Details of the four tiers of provision are given below. Most children and adolescents with mental health problems will be seen at Tiers 1 and 2. The following table provides a rough guide to the services available and the problems treated at each tier although it is not always the case that individual services or individual mental health problems will fall into one particular tier.

Tier	Services and agencies involved	Types of problems addressed and services
TIER 1	Mainly practitioners who are not mental health specialists: *GPs, health visitors, school nurses, teachers, social workers, youth justice workers, speech and language therapists, voluntary agencies*	• Mental health problems in the initial stages or in mild forms • Offer general advice • Contribute towards mental health promotion • Refer cases to more specialist services if necessary
TIER 2	Practitioners providing services with some mental health focus: *school and GP counsellors, school nurses, paediatricians, family support services, family mediation services, educational psychologists, voluntary sector mental health organisations (specialising in bereavement, domestic violence, and so on)*	• Problems such as anxiety, sleep disorders, toileting disorders, behavioural difficulties, low mood, adjustment to adverse life events (e.g. bullying, divorce, illness) • More complex cases referred to Tier 3 when necessary
TIER 3	Multidisciplinary teams working in community mental health clinics or child psychiatry outpatient services, providing specialist services for children and adolescents with more severe and persistent disorders	• Severe and persistent cases referred up from Tier 2 • Some cases might come straight to Tier 3, such as psychosis, bipolar disorder, OCD, anorexia, significant self-harm/suicidal ideation, and suchlike
TIER 4	Inpatient services, day units, and highly specialized outpatient teams and inpatient units (e.g. *forensic adolescent units, eating disorder units, specialist neuropsychiatric teams, and other specialist teams*)	• Similar mental health problems seen at Tier 3, but at the most severe end of the spectrum

that will support people with mental health problems and help them to cope better with their lives and their symptoms (see section 4.1.2). **Psychotherapists** have a similar role to counsellors by providing a range of psychotherapy support to individuals with mental health problems. Psychotherapists will often specialize in a particular therapeutic approach and provide support for longer-term mental health problems. **Occupational therapists** are available to help people with mental health problems adjust to the demands of normal day-to-day living, including developing personal independence and achieving levels of functioning required for employment. **Social workers** are trained to provide a valuable link between mental health services and broader social service provision, and they can provide advice and support on issues such as welfare benefits, housing, day care, and occupational training. Finally,

psychotherapists Individuals who are involved in the treatment of mental health problems by psychological rather than medical means.

occupational therapists Clinicians who specialize in assessing and training (or re-training) occupational and daily living skills.

social workers Professionals whose main focus is clients' social care needs (e.g. housing). Approved Social Workers are also involved in Mental Health Act assessments.

approved mental health workers
Professionals who are trained to offer treatments that will support people with mental health problems and help them to cope better with their lives and their symptoms. They will not normally have the kinds of professional clinical qualifications possessed by other mental health professionals, but will have received special training.

approved mental health workers will not normally have the kinds of professional clinical qualifications possessed by other mental health professionals, but will also have received special training in assessing and helping people who may need to be compulsorily detained because of their mental health problems.

In many cases, mental health provision is characterized by professionals working in **multidisciplinary teams (MDTs)**, and

multidisciplinary teams (MDTs) MDTs include workers from a range of disciplines that specialize in different aspects of health and social care, e.g. psychiatrists, clinical psychologists, social workers and occupational therapists.

this enables professionals to bring a range of skills from health and social care that will provide the basis for support and recovery for individuals with mental health problems. MDTs will provide individual clients with more holistic care and are especially helpful for dealing with complex and challenging cases. Within this team, the clinical psychologist's role will be to offer a perspective on each case based on their own professional skills, and this may involve providing assessments for diagnosis or the evaluation of a client's needs, considering aetiology or causes, or suggesting support and conducting suitable interventions for the client's specific problems. Table 5.1 provides the descriptions of members of a typical MDT offering community mental health services (Jones, 2008).

TABLE 5.1

Clinical psychologists frequently work as members of multidisciplinary teams (MDTs). Part of the rationale for MDTs is that they can provide clients with more holistic care, since they include workers from a range of disciplines that specialize in different aspects of health and social care. In community mental health teams (CMHTs), the team members can include:

Team manager	Usually a social worker or nurse by background, who is responsible for organising and managing the team
Psychiatrists	Medical doctors specialising in mental health, whose role includes making diagnoses, prescribing medication and being involved in assessments under the Mental Health Act, which can result in clients being involuntarily detained in hospital for assessment or treatment
Psychotherapists, counsellors, clinical psychologists and counselling psychologists	Professionals who can offer psychological assessments and interventions (some of the distinctions between these groups are discussed later)
Mental health nurses	Nurses specialising in mental health, whose role includes monitoring clients' mental health, administrating medication and providing other support
Social workers	Professionals whose main focus is clients' social care needs (e.g. housing). Approved social workers are also involved in Mental Health Act assessments
Occupational therapists	Clinicians who specialize in assessing and training (or re-training) occupational and daily living skills
Community support workers	An individual with experience in helping people with mental health problems to build relationships within the community
Secretarial staff	Responsible for administering the team (e.g. organising appointments and documentation)

Source: From Jones, F. (2008). What is clinical psychology? Training and practice. In G.C.L. Davey (Ed.) *Clinical psychology.* Hodder.

SELF-TEST QUESTIONS

- How do people with mental health problems access mental health services?
- Can you name at least five different types of mental health professionals in the UK?

SECTION SUMMARY

5.2 WHO ARE MENTAL HEALTH PROFESSIONALS?

- The local general practitioner or physician will usually be an individual's first point of contact with mental healthcare services.

- Professional mental healthcare workers include community mental health nurses (CMHNs), psychiatrists, clinical psychologists, counsellors, psychotherapists, occupational therapists, social workers, and approved mental health workers.

- In many cases, mental health provision is characterized by professionals working in multidisciplinary teams (MDTs).

5.3 PROVIDING MENTAL HEALTH SERVICES

5.3.1 What Facilities are Available?

Mental health problems are both diverse and experienced by many members of society and so will require services that are flexible and geared towards managing symptoms that are varied in type and severity. Some people will need specialized short-term help in order to recover; others will need long-term support and care.

As a result, mental health services provide a range of facilities geared to helping with a multiplicity of problems. Most people with a mental health problem can be treated on an **outpatient basis** and treatment can take

> **outpatient basis** Most people with a mental health problem can live in the community and be treated at a dedicated community mental health centre, a day clinic, or some larger GP or physician surgeries.

> **inpatient hospital care** Treatment provided to a client who has voluntarily admitted himself or herself to hospital. Some people can be compulsorily detained in a hospital under the Mental Health Act if their mental health problems are severe enough.

place at a dedicated community mental health centre, a day clinic, or some larger GP or physician surgeries. Some people may need voluntary **inpatient hospital care** – especially if that is agreed between the patient and their psychiatrist, psychologist or care plan team. Some people can even be detained in a hospital under the Mental Health Act if their mental health problems are severe enough, and they can be compulsorily detained (1) in the interests of their own health or safety, or (2) for the protection of other people. In England in 2011–2012, 48,000 people were detained under the Mental Health Act (Health & Social Care Information Centre, 2012), and this number has been steadily growing over recent years. However, the number of people that are compulsorily detained under the Mental Health Act is still a small percentage of the people with diagnosable mental health problems each year (around 0.3 to 0.5 per cent). The organisation Rethink Mental Illness has a factsheet providing information about detention under the Mental

Health Act. It can be found at http://www.rethink.org/how_we_can_help/our_advice_information/fact sheets_az.html.

In addition to psychiatric hospitals, **regional secure units** and secure hospitals are available to treat individuals who have been admitted by the courts under the Mental Health Act, transferred from prison under the Mental Health Act, or have been transferred from an ordinary hospital ward because they may need treatment in a more secure setting.

> **regional secure units** Facilities available to treat individuals who have been admitted by the courts under the Mental Health Act, transferred from prison under the Mental Health Act, or have been transferred from an ordinary hospital ward because they may need treatment in a more secure setting.

Finally in this section, it should be emphasized once again that while the range and type of facilities available for treating mental health problems is quite varied, the vast majority of people with a mental health problem are treated voluntarily on an outpatient basis, usually by a care team of professionals with a range of skills. Compulsory detention or treatment is extremely rare, and the overwhelming majority of people with mental health problems are neither violent nor a danger to themselves or others.

5.3.2 How are Mental Health Services Structured?

Apart from the facilities that are available for treatment, services need to be structured so that the different skills of healthcare professionals can be focused on the different sets of problems that make up mental health problems generally. Within the UK National Health Service, this is currently achieved by organising services around different client groups. Very broadly, these client groups are likely to include (1) children and young people services (commonly known as CAMHS – Children and Adolescent Mental Health Services – see Treatment in Practice Box 5.1) for children and adolescents with mental health and physical health problems, (2) working age adults who may experience a range of mental health problems,

(3) older adults who often have mental health problems combined with physical health problems, (4) children and adults with a learning disability, (5) individuals with substance misuse problems, and (6) people with brain injuries or neurological deficits.

Most services are also likely to have a secure and forensic team to deal with mental health problems related to criminal behaviour, and an access team devoted to ensuring that individuals seeking help with mental health problems receive rapid access to appropriate services. Figure 5.1 provides an example of how the services for one particular mental health trust are structured, but this may differ from area to area depending on the locality of the trust and the nature of the mental health problems found in that area.

5.3.3   The Recovery Model

As well as the physical structure of mental health services, it is also important to consider the 'philosophy' or approach to treatment that underpins these services. When someone has a physical illness, it is relatively easy to talk about a 'cure' and to define criteria by which a treatment will have been successful or not. If someone has a broken leg, an X-ray will show that it has mended successfully after treatment. If someone has a viral disease, drugs can be shown to have dealt with this when the virus is no longer detected in the body. This is not so easy to do within mental health because mental health problems will largely be defined by the degree of distress and disability caused by the symptoms and the individual's ability to cope with them – and distress and disability tend to be relative rather than absolute concepts (see Chapter 2).

Instead, within the mental health sphere a number of countries have adopted the **recovery model** as a basis for their provision of services. The National Institute for Mental Health in England (NIMHE) endorsed a recovery model as a guiding principle of mental health provision in 2005, and many NHS Trusts have now actively implemented this approach. In this model, recovery is viewed as a personal journey rather than a set outcome, and this involves not just individual development but also how the individual relates to their community and their society (Repper & Perkins, 2006).

Repper & Perkins (2006) note the following as important features of recovery:

> **recovery model** Broad-ranging treatment approach which acknowledges the influence and importance of socio-economic status, employment and education and social inclusion in helping to achieve recovery from mental health problems.

- *Hope:* Developing an ability to persevere through uncertainty and setbacks and developing a sustainable belief in oneself.
- *A secure base:* Ensuring appropriate housing, income, health care and security.
- *Self:* Developing a durable sense of self, a sense of social belonging and a set of interests.
- *Supportive relationships:* The development of supportive relationships not just with mental health professionals, but with friends, family and the community.
- *Empowerment and inclusion:* Developing the confidence for independent decision making and help-seeking, and challenging stigma and prejudice about mental health problems.

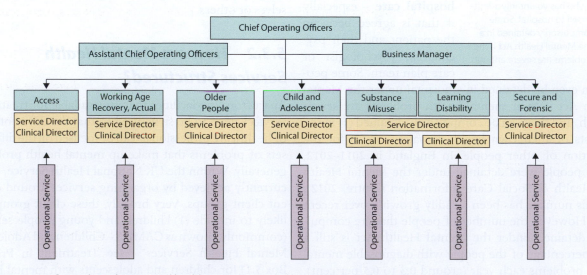

FIGURE 5.1   *This figure shows how mental health services provided by an NHS Foundation Trust are structured and managed around themes that reflect the underlying mental health needs of the local community served by the Trust.*

- *Coping strategies:* The development of a range of coping strategies and problem-solving skills that will enable the individual to identify and deal with stressors and crisis points.

- *Meaning:* Developing a sense of purpose that may be related to a social or work role.

For an activity on the features of recovery go to www.wiley-psychopathology.com/activities/ch5

The recovery model represents a holistic approach to mental health provision, and embraces the view that good mental health requires more than the treatment of individual symptoms but requires the development of the person within society. For example, what is the benefit of treating an individual's mental health problems if they are then being sent back to

the original social and economic conditions that might have given rise to those problems in the first place? The recovery model attempts to empower people and to provide them with the hope and skills they might need to cope with and rise above these background conditions. However, in many ways the recovery model is at odds with the diagnostic model of mental health problems as enshrined in DSM-5 (see Chapter 2). DSM-5 rarely takes account of the causes of mental problems; it infers that the removal of cardinal diagnostic symptoms alone will imply recovery; and it does not recognize the need for others to change as well as those singled out for the diagnosis (e.g. family and friends involved in supporting the sufferer) (Compton, 2007). This is an ongoing tension between those who support a more eclectic recovery model of mental health and the more traditional medical model of psychiatric symptoms.

SELF-TEST QUESTIONS

- What different types of mental health facilities are available in the UK?
- How are mental health services structured?
- What is the recovery model, and what are its main features?

SECTION SUMMARY

5.3   PROVIDING MENTAL HEALTH SERVICES

- Mental health services provide facilities on an *outpatient basis, voluntary hospital care,* and *regional secure units* for people who have been admitted to psychiatric hospitals by the courts.

- Mental health services are structured so that the skills of different healthcare professionals can be focused on the different sets of problems that make up mental health problems generally.

- The *recovery model* represents a holistic approach to mental health provision and embraces the view that recovery requires the development of the person within society.

5.4   THE ROLE OF THE CLINICAL PSYCHOLOGIST

We have briefly described who clinical psychologists are and offered a sketch of what they do in section 5.2. In this section we will take a more in-depth look at the role of clinical psychologists and the skills they deploy as mental health professionals. Before you begin to read this section take a look at Focus Point 5.1 in which a clinical psychologist describes a typical week for her working with people with psychosis. This gives a flavour of the range of roles that a clinical psychologist undertakes on almost a daily

basis, including working in teams and with families, conducting assessments, and providing treatment and support to people with distressing mental health problems.

5.4.1   Key Capabilities and Competencies

Clinical psychologists receive training in a range of different approaches, including cognitive-behavioural, psychodynamic and systemic (see section 4.1.1). However, these skills are deployed in a wider framework that would normally consist of four stages: assessment, formulation, intervention and evaluation.

has been the impact of the intervention? Is the intervention having the desired effects? **Evaluation** can be done in

a number of ways, including discussion with the client and with the use of validated questionnaires. Therapeutic change can often be very gradual so the client might not have good insight into the changes that may have begun to occur, and validated questionnaires can often provide a more objective measure of change. Indeed, the use of validated means of measuring the effectiveness of interventions is a central feature of evaluation nowadays – largely because of the need to ensure that interventions can be identified as effective using evidence-based criteria that will allow services to use objective criteria by which to decide what types of interventions are effective and which are not.

In summary, a clinical psychologist needs to have the competencies to assess, formulate, intervene and evaluate, and to be able to do this in collaboration with other mental health professionals. In addition to these core competencies, clinical psychologists will also need to be able to communicate effectively with their clients – both verbally and in writing (Hall & Llewellyn, 2006, pp.22–25), and these are all skills that will be taught during the clinical psychologist's extensive period of training (see Davey, 2011, chapter 6).

5.4.2 The Reflective Practitioner Model

In Chapter 3 we discussed the widely held view that clinical psychologists should be thought of as scientist-practitioners who are competent as both researchers and practitioners. Many clinical psychologists are happy with this label – especially given the shift towards mental health professionals being seen to provide evidence-based interventions. However, not all clinical psychologists readily accept this conception of themselves. For example, some prefer to adopt alternative philosophical approaches that place less emphasis on traditional science (such as social constructionist approaches that are described in Focus Point 3.1). Nevertheless, despite differences in agreement about the importance of science in professional clinical psychology practice (e.g. Lilienfeld, Ritschel, Lynn, Cautin & Latzman, 2013), clinical psychologists are generally expected to

adopt a **reflective practitioner model** in their work (Schön, 1983). This is considered to be an important key competency in which

clinical psychologists reflect on their own experience when working with clients, and reflect on the process of interaction with their client (Hall & Llewelyn, 2006, p.17). This reflection is considered to have a number of benefits: (1) it facilitates the process of developing the clinical psychologist as an autonomous, qualified and self-directed professional, (2) it enables clinical psychologists to develop their practice by overcoming habitualized approaches to treatment and intervention, and to consider the needs of each individual client, and (3) it encourages self-motivation and self-directed learning. Most importantly it is one method by which clinical psychologists can learn from their own experiences, and practitioners may also attend regular reflective practice groups through which individuals share experiences, or work with a supervisor who may facilitate reflective practice. A more structured way of facilitating reflective practice is for the clinical psychologist to receive his or her own psychotherapy. This is often the norm in many forms of psychotherapy practice, but it is an issue of disagreement within clinical psychology practice (Macran & Shapiro, 1998).

Finally, it must be pointed out that the reflective practitioner and scientist-practitioner approaches are not entirely mutually exclusive, and no matter which philosophical approach you take to your clinical practice, it will almost certainly be beneficial to regularly reflect on that practice.

5.4.3 Regulation and Continuing Professional Development

Because clinical psychologists provide services to vulnerable groups of people their practice needs to be properly regulated to protect the public from malpractice and exploitation from untrained individuals. Since 2009, clinical psychologists in the UK have been regulated by an agency known as the **Health and Care Professions Council (HCPC)** (www.hpc-uk.org), and its role is to protect the public by ensuring that clinical psychologists (amongst other groups of practicing healthcare professionals) meet specified standards of training, professional skills, behaviour

and health. The HCPC maintains a register of clinical psychologists who meet these required standards, and it has also specified that 'clinical psychologist' is a **protected title** that can only be used if the individual has received appropriate training and is registered with the HCPC. The HCPC has the authority to take out criminal prosecutions against anyone who uses this protected title and is not trained or registered to do so. In addition, the HCPC can take action against any clinical psychologist who does not meet their standards of conduct, performance and ethics. In such circumstances, further actions taken by the HCPC may include recommendations for further training and supervision, preventing a clinical psychologist from practising for a specific period of time, or striking that person off the register for life (see Davey, 2011, ch. 1 for further details of HCPC and standards of conduct, performance and ethics).

The way that clinical psychologists are regulated differs from country to country. In the USA and Canada a licence is required to practise as a clinical psychologist, and the terms of this licence often differ between states. But, in general terms, all states require: (1) graduation from an accredited training institution with an appropriate degree, (2) completion of supervised clinical experience, and (3) passing a written exam and, in some cases, an oral exam.

Once they have qualified, clinical psychologists are expected to undertake **continuing professional development (CPD)** throughout their career in order to develop their professional competencies. This can include reading about the latest research, attending conferences and training workshops, carrying out new activities (e.g. supervising trainee clinical psychologists or applying for a research grant) and undertaking further qualifications (e.g. specialist training in a particular type of psychological therapy).

continuing professional development (CPD) The demonstration by accredited therapists that they regularly update their knowledge of recent developments in treatment techniques.

5.4.4 Training to be a Clinical Psychologist

Training to become a clinical psychologist requires skill and dedication. This section describes some of the pre-training qualifications and attributes required to become a clinical psychologist followed by a brief overview of clinical psychology training.

Pre-training qualifications and experiences

Training to become a clinical psychologist is a challenging and competitive experience. Once a student has decided that clinical psychology is the career for them, they need to obtain the necessary qualifications and experience to become eligible for a place on a clinical psychology training course. In the UK, students will need a first degree in psychology or an equivalent (e.g. a conversion course) that will make them eligible for graduate basis for chartered membership (GBC) of the British Psychological Society

(BPS). Once they have this qualification they can apply for a place on a clinical training course, and these courses will be looking for evidence of experience and capability in three areas: academic, clinical and research. In terms of the academic experience, most training courses will require either a first or a good upper-second class degree, with some additional weight given to postgraduate degrees such as relevant taught master's degree courses or a PhD. Candidates are also expected to have some clinical experience in mental health areas by working as interns or volunteers in mental health settings, or alternatively working as an assistant psychologist – the latter usually within the NHS mental health services. Possessing good research skills is also an important quality preferred by many clinical training courses. One of the features of clinical psychologists that differentiates them from many other types of mental health professionals is their research skills. These research skills are important for a number of reasons. They provide clinical psychologists with the abilities necessary for understanding, critically appraising and evaluating the clinical literature. Clinical psychologists can also use their research skills to evaluate existing services and interventions and conduct research that might lead to the development of new psychological theories and interventions. Since much of the time during clinical training is taken up learning clinical skills, many clinical course admissions tutors prefer to take applicants with an existing good knowledge of research methodology, and so some courses are taking an increasing number of candidates who have successfully completed a research PhD.

Applications for clinical training courses in the UK are all managed through the **Clearing House for Postgraduate Courses in Clinical Psychology (CHPCCP)** (http://www.leeds.ac.uk/chpccp/). However, applications are assessed, interviews conducted, and final decisions on acceptance made by members of faculty at each of the relevant training institutions that a student has applied to. Apart from evidence of academic and research ability and clinical experience, courses are usually also looking for a good interpersonal manner, strong communication skills, and self-awareness. Competition for places on clinical training courses in the UK is intense, with applications increasing significantly between 2009 and 2012 (see Figure 5.2), and in 2012 there were 3857 applicants for 586 places – an applications-to-places ratio of 6.5:1!

Clearing House for Postgraduate Courses in Clinical Psychology (CHPCCP) The CHPCCP manages all applications for clinical training courses in the UK (see http://www.leeds.ac.uk/chpccp/).

Clinical training

Clinical training courses in the UK are usually 3 year programmes that lead to a doctorate in clinical psychology. This doctorate confers eligibility to register as a

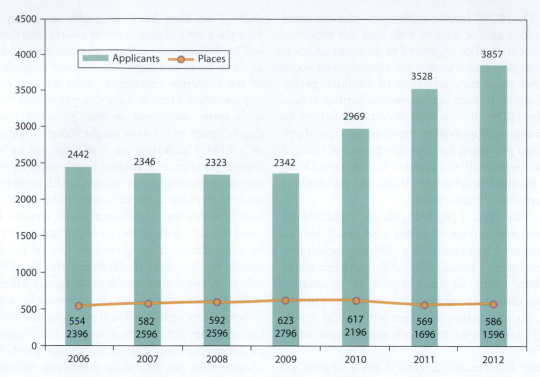

FIGURE 5.2 *Applications vs. places for UK clinical training.*
This chart shows the number of applications and actual places for UK clinical training courses between 2006 and 2012. Note that in 2012 the applications: places ratio was 6.5:1
© *Clearing House for Postgraduate Courses in Clinical Psychology. Reproduced with permission.*

chartered psychologist with the BPS and as a practitioner psychologist with the HCPC. Training usually takes place in service with the NHS, with the latter covering the trainee's training fees. Training can be divided into three components:

1. *An academic component* that takes place in a university setting and consists of conventional teaching and learning practices covering such topics as human development and interaction, psychological problems and mental well-being, and some skills learning associated with different psychological approaches to mental health problems. Students will learn about the main approaches to alleviating mental health problems, including cognitive-behavioural, psychodynamic and systemic, and a key part of training is concerned with integrating concepts and interventions from different models to develop interventions that best suit an individual's needs.

2. *A clinical placement component*, in which the trainee learns how to apply these different approaches to different client groups, usually within the NHS. These placements take up 3 days

a week for as long as 6 months, and a trainee will gain experience by taking placements across a range of settings and client groups, the latter of which will normally include working-age adults with mental health problems, people with learning disabilities, children with mental health problems, and older adults. During their placements, trainees receive support and guidance from at least one supervisor who will be a practising clinical psychologist.

3. *A research component*, in which research skills are developed through both teaching and the trainee conducting their own research projects. The research projects usually consist of small-scale service-based research such as an evaluation of an intervention, and the most substantial of these projects will form the trainee's doctoral dissertation.

Table 5.2 provides some examples of what a clinical psychology trainee will experience during their training and covers the nature of the placements they encounter, the types of psychological models they will learn about, and some of the key competencies they will acquire.

TABLE 5.2 *Some examples to illustrate the range of client groups, models and competencies typically covered in clinical psychology training*

Core clinical placements

Working age adults with mental health problems
Children with mental health problems and their families
People with learning disabilities
Older people with mental health problems

Possible supplementary placements

Further experience in one of the 'core' areas
Adults with brain injury
Children with physical health problems
Adults with physical health problems

Classes of models

Cognitive-behavioural
Psychodynamic
Systemic
Developmental
Neuropsychological

Key competencies

The ability to communicate effectively with a range of different clients.
The ability to build and maintain effective relationships with others.
The ability to conduct assessments appropriate to different settings.
The ability to develop 'formulations', by forming theory–practice links.
The ability to facilitate interventions appropriate to particular clients and problems.
The ability to evaluate clinical work.
Sufficient self-awareness to be able to reflect on and learn from clinical work.
The ability to understand, conduct and apply the findings of psychological research.

Source: Jones, F. (2011). Clinical Psychology: Training & Development. In Davey, G. (Ed.), *Applied Psychology*. BPS Blackwell. Reproduced with permission.

SELF-TEST QUESTIONS

- What are the four key capabilities and competencies of clinical psychologists?

- What is the reflective practitioner approach to clinical practice?

- Can you describe how clinical psychologists in the UK are regulated?

- What pre-training qualifications and experiences would someone need before applying for a clinical training place in the UK?

- What are the three main components of a clinical training programme in the UK?

SECTION SUMMARY

5.4   THE ROLE OF THE CLINICAL PSYCHOLOGIST

- Key capabilities and competences of clinical psychologists include their ability to conduct *assessments*, create *formulations* of an individual's problems, prescribe and conduct *interventions*, and carry out *evaluations* of services.

- Clinical psychologists tend to adopt a *reflective practitioner* approach to their work, reflecting on their own experience when working with clients.

- Clinical psychologists in the UK are regulated by the Health and Care Professions Council (HCPC).

- Training to become a clinical psychologist usually consists of three components: an *academic component*, a *clinical component*, and a *research component*.

5.5 CLINICAL PRACTICE REVIEWED

This chapter has covered a number of important aspects of clinical practice and service provision. We began by looking at the scale of mental health problems in terms of both personal suffering and economic cost, and it is clearly an immense task faced by service providers to deal with the high prevalence rates of mental health problems – especially when mental health services are relatively underfunded compared with funding for other health problems (In 2012, *The Guardian* reported that mental health problems account for 40 per cent of all illness but only 13 per cent of NHS funds are devoted to their treatment.)

Because of their complexity, mental health problems require a range of mental health professionals with a variety of skills, and we have discussed who these professionals are, what skills they possess, how they work, and where they work. Finally, we focused on the role of the clinical psychologist and covered their role in the treatment and recovery of people with mental health problems, their key skills and competencies, and how they are trained.

> To read 'It is inexcusable that mental health treatments are still underfunded' go to
> **http://tinyurl.com/cbaz2w9**

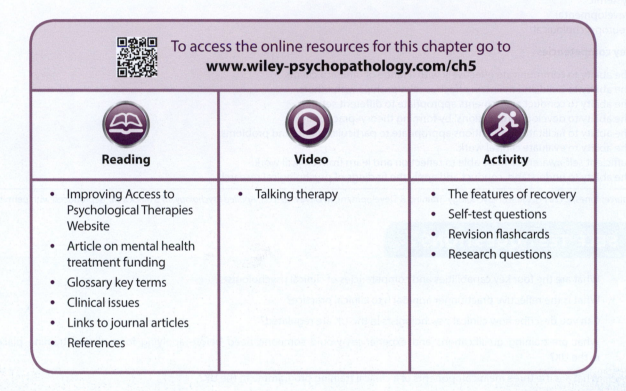

To access the online resources for this chapter go to
www.wiley-psychopathology.com/ch5

Reading	**Video**	**Activity**
• Improving Access to Psychological Therapies Website • Article on mental health treatment funding • Glossary key terms • Clinical issues • Links to journal articles • References	• Talking therapy	• The features of recovery • Self-test questions • Revision flashcards • Research questions

Part II
Psychopathology and Psychological Disorders

6 Anxiety and Stressor-Related Problems

To access the online resources for this chapter go to
www.wiley-psychopathology.com/ch6

ROUTE MAP OF THE CHAPTER

This chapter describes some of the main anxiety-based problems. It discusses contemporary accounts of their causes (aetiology) and describes a range of relevant and effective treatments for each. It is divided into six main sections covering specific phobias, social anxiety disorder, panic disorder, generalized anxiety disorder, obsessive compulsive disorder, and trauma and stress-related disorders such as post-traumatic stress disorder. These topics are chosen because they represent some of the most prevalent anxiety and stress-based problems (e.g. panic disorder, generalized anxiety disorder), and they consist of some of the most thoroughly researched disorders where our understanding of their causes has become relatively well developed.

CHAPTER OUTLINE

LEARNING OUTCOMES

When you have completed this chapter, you should be able to:

1. Describe the kinds of presenting symptoms that are associated with individual anxiety and stressor-based problems.

2. Describe the characteristics and diagnostic criteria of six of the important anxiety and stressor disorders.

3. Describe, compare and contrast at least two contemporary theories of the aetiology of each disorder.

4. Distinguish between biological and psychological explanations of anxiety-based problems.

5. Describe the relevance of research methodologies that have contributed to the understanding of the acquisition of anxiety and stress-related disorders.

6. Describe, compare and contrast at least two therapeutic procedures used for each individual anxiety disorder or stress-related disorder.

I'm 26 years old and experience severe anxiety. I've had on and off panic attacks since I was 17. I've really worked hard to manage it using breathing, daily exercise and diet. I thought I'd beaten it . . . two years pretty symptom free. But shortly after becoming engaged, the panic attacks started and anxiety came back with a vengeance. I can barely manage my days at work, I have little appetite and I'm terrified of negative thoughts I've been having. My scariest thought in the past was having a heart attack. But knowing I'm in such good physical shape I know this isn't a possibility. My scary thought for the past few weeks has been what if I kill myself . . . so scary I try not to be alone. My doctor has given me some medication, but I don't know if it's working. My friends who know about psychology say I'm fine and those thoughts are my anxiety.

Michelle's Story

Introduction

Anxiety and stress are common features of everyday living, and will be experienced by us all in one form or another. As an adaptive emotion anxiety can help us prepare to deal effectively with anticipated threats and challenges by increasing our arousal and reactivity, focusing our attention, and helping us to problem solve. However, we can often find there will be times in our lives when we have difficulty managing our anxiety, and it starts to feel uncontrollable and distressing. *Michelle's story* provides an example of how anxiety can come to feel distressing and her commentary gives us a real insight into some of the more debilitating symptoms of an anxiety problem. These include panic attacks, lack of appetite, scary, uncontrollable thoughts, thoughts about physical illness, even suicidal ideation. Anxiety generally has both physical and cognitive attributes. First, there are the physical symptoms of anxiety – such as muscle tension, dry mouth, perspiring, trembling and difficulty swallowing. In its more chronic form, anxiety can also be accompanied by dizziness, chronic fatigue, sleeping difficulties, rapid or irregular heartbeat, diarrhoea or a persistent need to urinate, sexual problems, and nightmares. In contrast, the cognitive features of anxiety include a feeling of apprehension or fear, usually resulting from the anticipation of a threatening event or situation. Usually accompanying anxiety are intrusive thoughts about the threat, catastrophic bouts of worrying about the possible negative outcomes associated with the threat, and – in some specific types of problems – uncontrollable flashbacks about past traumas and anxiety-provoking experiences. Overly anxious people also find it hard to stop thinking negative and threatening thoughts, and this is in part due to the cognitive biases that have developed with the experience of anxiety.

We all experience feelings of anxiety quite naturally in many situations – such as just before an important exam, while making a presentation at college or work, at an interview, or on a first date. Most anxiety reactions are perfectly natural, and they have evolved as adaptive responses that are essential for us to perform effectively in challenging circumstances. However, anxiety can often become so intense or attached to inappropriate events or situations, that it becomes maladaptive and problematic for the individual (Lepine, 2002). This is

anxiety disorder A psychological disorder characterized by an excessive or aroused state and feelings of apprehension, uncertainty and fear.

when an **anxiety disorder** may develop. In a sufferer of an anxiety disorder, the anxiety response may:

1. be out of proportion to the threat posed by the situation or event (e.g. in specific phobias);

2. be a state that the individual constantly finds themselves in and may not be easily attributable to any specific threat (e.g. in generalized anxiety disorder, or some forms of panic disorder);

3. persist chronically and be so disabling that it causes constant emotional distress to the individual, who is unable to plan and conduct their normal day-to-day living. This can result in an inability to hold down a regular job, maintain long-term relationships with friends, partners and family, and so forth.

Anxiety-based problems are relatively common, and around 30–40 per cent of individuals in Western societies will develop a problem that is anxiety related at some point in their lives (Shepherd, Cooper, Brown *et al.*, 1996; NIMH, 2005) (see Figure 6.1). As a result, pathological anxiety imposes a high individual and social burden, tends to be more chronic than many other psychological problems, and can be as disabling as physical illness. In both Europe and the US, the cost of treating anxiety-based problems runs into many billions of pounds annually, making them more economically

expensive than any other psychological problem (Rovner, 1993; Greenberg, Sisitsky, Kessler, Finkelstein *et al.*, 1999). These economic costs include psychiatric, psychological, and emergency care, hospitalization, prescription drugs, reduced productivity, absenteeism from work, and suicide (Lepine, 2002).

In this chapter we will discuss in detail six of the main anxiety and stress-related disorders. The details of these disorders can be reviewed online in the table 'Anxiety Disorders – Summary', which is available on the website at www.wiley-psychopathology.com/ch6. Readers may want to refer back to this table when they have read and digested the information on each separate disorder. Throughout this book we have summarized the DSM-5 diagnostic criteria for the disorders discussed to give the student reader a briefer overview, and therefore they cannot be read as full diagnostic criteria. Please refer to your library's copy of DSM-5 for full criteria and aetiology.

> To read the anxiety disorders summary table go to
> **www.wiley-psychopathology.com/ch6**

The six main anxiety and stress-related disorders are:

1. specific phobias
2. social anxiety disorder
3. panic disorder
4. generalized anxiety disorder (GAD)
5. obsessive compulsive disorder (OCD)
6. post-traumatic stress disorder (PTSD).

Anxiety as a comorbid condition

Anxiety disorders are diagnosed when subjectively experienced anxiety is present and recurs on such a regular and chronic basis that it is distressing and disrupts normal daily living. However, many of the symptoms of anxiety are common to a number of different anxiety disorders, and so it is relatively common for an individual to suffer from more than one anxiety disorder (Hofmeijer-Sevink, Batelaan, Harold, van Megen *et al.*, 2012). When anxiety disorders are comorbid with each other in this way they have an earlier age of onset, a higher rate of chronicity, and are also likely to be associated with depression, and with greater social disability. Anxiety symptoms may be particularly prone to comorbidity because many of the physiological and cognitive components of anxiety can be found across different disorders, and so these vulnerability factors may trigger the development of multiple anxiety problems. Some common cross-disorder phenomena that may lead to anxiety–anxiety comorbidity include:

1. Physiological symptoms of panic are found not only in panic disorder, but also in the reactions to phobic stimuli in specific phobias.

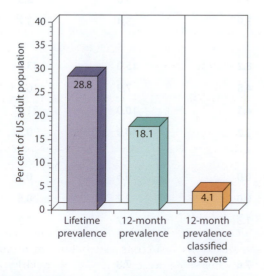

FIGURE 6.1 *Prevalence rates for diagnosed anxiety disorders in the US population.*

Lifetime prevalence rates shows that 28.8 per cent of adults will be diagnosable with an anxiety disorder in their lifetime (NIMH, 2005). The study also showed that the average age of onset is 11 years.

Source: National Institute of Mental Health

2. Cognitive biases – such as information processing biases that tend to cause anxious people to selectively attend to threatening stimuli (Mathews & MacLeod, 2005) – are common to almost all anxiety disorders.

3. A number of prominent psychopathologies are characterized by the dysfunctional and uncontrollable perseveration of certain thoughts, behaviours or activities (e.g. pathological worrying in generalized anxiety disorder, perseverative compulsions in obsessive compulsive disorder, and rumination during periods of depression), and the psychological mechanism that underlies dysfunctional perseveration may be similar across all these disorders (Davey, 2006).

4. Certain specific early experiences can be found in the aetiology of a number of different anxiety disorders (e.g. physical or sexual abuse during childhood), and experiences such as these may increase an individual's risk of developing several anxiety-based problems.

Anxiety disorders are also commonly comorbid with other psychological disorders (Rodriguez, Weisberg, Pagano, Machan *et al.*, 2004; McLean, Asnaani, Litz & Hofmann, 2011), which means that a range of symptoms associated with psychological problems can also co-occur with anxiety (e.g. depression, substance abuse and eating disorders are commonly experienced with anxiety). Table 6.1 shows prevalence rates and comorbidity figures for a number of anxiety and stress-related disorders from a survey by McLean *et al.* (2011). In this recent survey, lifetime prevalence rates for developing an anxiety disorder that was comorbid with another psychological disorder was 44 per cent for women and 34 per cent for men. In particular, anxiety disorders were highly comorbid with mood disorders and with substance use disorders.

Let's look at each of the anxiety diagnostic categories in turn, starting with a closer look at specific phobias.

TABLE 6.1 *Lifetime and 12-month prevalence rates of comorbid disorders among individuals diagnosed with an anxiety disorder*

Disorder	12-Month		Lifetime	
	Women (%)	Men (%)	Women (%)	Men (%)
Mood disorders				
Major depressive disorder	23.7	19.1	38.3	30.0
Dysfunctional beliefs	11.2	8.9	12.9	10.6
Bipolar 1	2.4	3.3	3.0	3.3
Bipolar 2	3.3	3.9	3.4	3.2
Substance use disorders				
Alcohol abuse	4.3	8.2	15.0	33.2
Alcohol dependency	2.9	4.8	7.9	16.7
Drug abuse	1.4	4.5	10.0	21.8
Drug dependency	1.0	2.2	4.9	9.3
Eating disorders				
Anorexia nervosa	0.0	0.0	0.6	0.2
Bulimia nervosa	1.0	0.0	2.2	0.5
Binge-eating disorder	2.0	1.3	2.7	2.3
Other				
Attention deficit/hyperactivity disorder	6.9	7.6	7.8	11.1
Intermittent explosive disorder	9.4	12.5	11.6	19.3
Anxiety disorder				
Any additional	37.3	27.9	44.8	34.2

Source: McLean, C.P., Asnaani, A., Litz, B.T. & Hofmann, S.G. (2011). Gender differences in anxiety disorders: Prevalence, course of illness, comorbidity and burden of illness. *Journal of Psychiatric Research*, 45, 1027–1035.

6.1   SPECIFIC PHOBIAS

For a video on specific phobias go to **www.wiley-psychopathology.com/ video/ch6**

specific phobias An excessive, unreasonable, persistent fear triggered by a specific object or situation.

Specific phobias are defined as a 'marked fear or anxiety about a specific object or situation (e.g. flying, heights, animals, receiving an injection, seeing blood)', and the DSM criteria for specific phobia are presented in DSM-5 Summary Table 6.1. The phobic trigger usually elicits extreme fear and often panic, which usually means that the phobic individual develops avoidance strategies designed to minimize the possibility of contact with that phobic trigger. Phobics are normally aware that their fear of the phobic situation or event is excessive or unreasonable (in comparison either with the actual threat it represents or with the less fearful responses of other people), but they do acquire a strong set of **phobic beliefs** that appear to control their

phobic beliefs Beliefs about phobic stimuli that maintain the phobic's fear and avoidance of that stimulus or situation.

fear (Thorpe & Salkovskis, 1997). These beliefs normally contain information about why they think the

phobia is threatening and how to react when they are in the phobic situation (e.g. avoid contact, and so on) (see Table 6.2). Many contemporary psychological treatments for specific phobias are designed to challenge these dysfunctional phobic beliefs and replace them with more functional beliefs that foster approach and contact with the phobic stimulus instead of avoidance.

Prevalence

Specific phobias are extraordinarily common, with surveys suggesting that a clear majority of the general population (60.2 per cent) experience 'unreasonable fears' (Chapman, 1997) – although in most cases these fears are rarely severe enough to result in impairment or distress. Recent surveys suggest that as many as 20 per cent of adults will be

DSM-5 SUMMARY TABLE 6.1   *Criteria for specific phobia*

- Disproportionate and immediate fear relating to a specific object or situation
- Objects or situations are avoided, or are tolerated with intense fear or anxiety
- Symptoms cannot be explained by other mental disorders and persist for at least six months
- Phobia causes significant distress and difficulty in performing social or occupational activities

TABLE 6.2   *The phobic beliefs of spider phobics*

Phobics develop a set of dysfunctional beliefs about their phobic stimulus or event. These beliefs are very rarely challenged because the phobic avoids all circumstances where such beliefs might be disconfirmed. These beliefs maintain phobic fear and serve to motivate responses designed to avoid contact with the phobic stimulus. Below are some examples of phobic beliefs held by spider phobics. Such beliefs are the kinds that are challenged in both exposure therapy and cognitive therapy procedures.

Harm beliefs:
When a spider is in my vicinity I believe that the spider will:
- (a) bite me
- (b) crawl towards my private parts
- (c) do things on purpose to tease me
- (d) get on to parts of me that I cannot reach.

Chaser and prey beliefs:
When I encounter a spider it will:
- (a) run towards me
- (b) stare at me
- (c) settle on my face
- (d) not be shaken off once it is on me.

Unpredictability and speed beliefs:
When I encounter a spider:
- (a) its behaviour will be very unpredictable
- (b) it will be very quick
- (c) it will run in an elusive way.

Invasiveness beliefs:
When I encounter a spider it will:
- (a) crawl into my clothes
- (b) walk over me during the night
- (c) hide in places I do not want, such as my bed.

Response beliefs:
When I encounter a spider I will:
- (a) feel faint
- (b) lose control of myself
- (c) go hysterical
- (d) scream.

Source: Adapted from Arntz , Lavy, van den Berg & van Rijsoort (1993) and Thorpe & Salkovskis (1997).

diagnosable with a specific phobia in their lifetime (Kessler, Avenevoli, Costello, Green *et al.*, 2012), which suggests that severe and disruptive phobic symptoms can be quite common. Table 6.3 shows the prevalence rates for some of the more common forms of specific phobia. There is also a clear gender difference in the prevalence of specific phobias, with women being twice as likely as men to be diagnosed with a specific phobia (Kessler, McGonagle, Zhao, Nelson, Hughes, *et al.*, 1994).

Common phobias

Interestingly, common phobias tend to focus on a relatively small group of objects and situations, and the main ones are animal phobias (including fear of snakes,

TABLE 6.3 *Lifetime prevalence rates for common specific phobias*

	Lifetime prevalence rates
Social phobia	3.2%[1]
Blood–injury–injection phobia	3.5%[3]
Animal phobias generally	1.1%[1]
Dental phobia	3–5%[2]
Water phobia	3.3%[1]
Height phobia	4.7%[1]
Claustrophobia/enclosed spaces	2.4%[1]

[1]Taken from the Epidemiologic Catchment Area (ECA) study (see Chapman, 1997).
[2]Kent (1997).
[3]Bienvenu & Eaton (1998).

spiders, rats, mice, creepy-crawlies such as cockroaches, invertebrates, such as maggots and slugs), social phobia, dental phobia, water phobia, height phobia, claustrophobia, and a cluster of blood, injury and inoculation fears (known as BII). Most other types of phobias are less common and can be thought of as quite unusual given the degree of threat they might realistically pose – such phobias include fear of cotton wool, buttons, chocolate, dolls and vegetables (McNally, 1997) (see Photo 6.1)! DSM-5 specifies five subgroups of specific phobias which are (1) animal phobias (e.g. spiders, insects, dogs), (2) natural environment phobias (e.g. heights, storms, water), (3) blood–injection–injury phobias (BII) (e.g. needles, invasive medical procedures), (4) situational phobias (e.g. airplanes, elevators, enclosed spaces), and other phobias (e.g. situations that may lead to choking or vomiting; in children, loud sounds or costumed characters!). There is some evidence that if you suffer from a specific phobia in one of these categories, you are more likely to suffer a phobia of one or more of the other phobias in that category (e.g. Davey, 1992b; Fredrikson, Annas, Fischer & Wik, 1996) and, thus, phobias within each category can have a higher incidence of comorbidity (Kendler, Myers, Prescott & Neale, 2001). There are also important cultural differences in the kinds of stimuli and events that can become the focus of clinical phobias. For example, Taijin-kyofusho (TKS) is a common Japanese syndrome characterized by a fear of embarrassing or offending other people (Prince & Tcheng-Laroche, 1987). This is different to the Western syndrome of social phobia, where the fear is based on the public embarrassment experienced by the phobic individual himself or herself. Davey *et al.* (1998) also found a number of important cross-cultural differences in animal fears. For example, while fear of spiders is a common phobic reaction in most Western cultures, spiders were significantly less feared in the Indian sample

PHOTO 6.1 *Small animal phobias are very common and consist of creepy-crawlies, insects, mollusks, rodents, spiders, snakes and lizards, etc. Interestingly, if you are fearful of one of these types of animals you are more likely to be fearful of others in this group. Fear of such animals may be related more to the emotion of disgust rather than anxiety.*
All images used under license from Shutterstock.com.

used in the study. This kind of cross-cultural variability suggests that 'fear-relevance' may at least in part be determined and developed by factors that are specific to individual cultures, and this should be contrasted with more biologically oriented views which argue that fear-responses have been universally pre-wired by evolutionary selection pressures (Davey, 1995; see the section on 'The role of evolution' below).

6.1.1 The Aetiology of Specific Phobias

Attempts to explain specific phobias have a long history and date back to the early days of the psychoanalytic approaches pioneered by Freud and the conditioning views developed by the behaviorist J.B. Watson. Originally, there was a tendency to try to explain all types of phobias with just one explanatory theory (e.g. classical conditioning), but this approach has now given way to the view that different types of phobias might be acquired in quite different ways (a multifaceted approach). Over the years, an intriguing debate has taken place about whether phobias are biologically determined through evolutionary processes or whether they are responses learnt during the lifetime of the individual. This debate will be an important feature of what follows.

Psychoanalytic accounts

Phobias have intrigued psychologists for more than a century. This may be because they manifest as irrational fears of things that usually pose little if any realistic threat, and their acquisition more often than not cannot be explained by recourse to simple learning experiences such as a specific traumatic event. This has led at least some approaches to psychopathology to view phobias as symbolic of other, more deep-rooted psychological difficulties. For example, psychoanalytic theory as developed by Freud saw phobias as a defence against the anxiety produced by repressed id impulses, and this fear became associated with external events or situations that had a symbolic relevance to that repressed id impulse. Focus Point 6.1 describes the classic case of 'Little Hans', a 5-year-old boy who developed a severe phobia of horses. Within Freud's psychoanalytic theory, the function of phobias was to avoid confrontation with the real, underlying issues (in this case, a repressed childhood conflict). However, because of the nature of psychoanalytical theorising, there is little in the way of objective evidence to support such accounts of phobias. Nevertheless, there is often an element of insight that can be drawn from the symbolic interpretations of case histories provided by psychoanalysis, and many anxiety disorders may indeed function for the sufferer as a way of avoiding confrontation with more challenging life issues and difficulties.

Classical conditioning and phobias

Attempts to explain phobias in terms of classical conditioning (see section 1.3) date back to the famous 'Little Albert' study reported by Watson & Rayner in 1920. Albert was an 11-month-old infant, and Watson & Rayner

---

FOCUS POINT 6.1

LITTLE HANS: THE PSYCHOANALYTIC INTERPRETATION OF A SPECIFIC PHOBIA

One of the most famous cases in the history of psychoanalysis is that of 'Little Hans', a 5-year-old who revealed many of his perceptions, fantasies, and fears to his physician father, who, in turn, reported them to Sigmund Freud. Hans began to have a fear of horses, which eventually grew to the point that he refused to leave the house. The immediate event that precipitated this phobia was seeing a big, heavy horse fall down. Freud interpreted this to mean that Hans at that moment perceived his own wish that his father would fall down. Then Hans, a little Oedipus, could take his father's place with his beautiful mother. Another part of the fear derived from the large size of horses, which Hans unconsciously identified with the great power of his father. He expressed the fear that a horse would come into his room. He also became afraid not only of horses biting him, but of carts, furniture vans, and buses. This revealed, to the

psychoanalyst, still another aspect of Hans' unconscious fantasies, namely that the falling-down horse stood not only for his father, but also for his mother in childbirth, the box-like carts and vehicles representing the womb. All these complicated, repressed feelings and perception were thus incorporated in a single phobia.

It is important to note that Little Hans was basically a straightforward, cheerful child who experienced normal psychosexual development marred only by the episode of the phobia, from which he recovered rather promptly. Fourteen years later, 19-year-old Hans went to see Freud. He had continued to develop well and had survived without unusual difficulty the divorce and remarriage of both parents. The problems of his childhood were used by Freud to illustrate the normal process of psychosexual development – the complex, intense, erotic drama of early childhood.

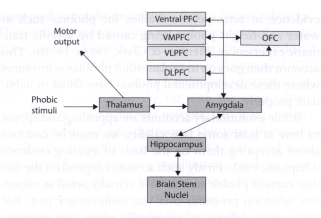

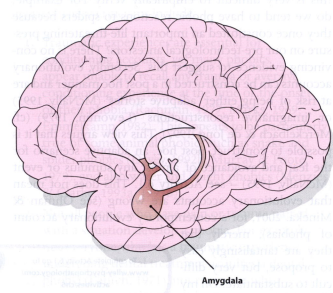

Amygdala

FIGURE 6.3 *The amygdala at the crossroads of fear-related information processing.*

Phobic stimuli enter the amygdala through the thalamus and are then processed by the amygdala, which provides connections to both higher brain function-related cortical areas (light grey) and subcortical nuclei (darker grey). On receiving their output, the amygdala integrates messages, thus providing feedback to the thalamus to generate a motor output. (DLPFC = dorsolateral prefrontal cortex; OFC = orbitofrontal cortex; ventral PFC = ventral frontopolar prefrontal cortex; VLPFC = ventrolateral prefrontal cortex; VMPFC = ventromedial prefrontal cortex).
Source: After Del Casale A., Ferracuti S., Rapinesi C., Serata D. *et al.* (2012). Functional neuroimaging in specific phobia. *Psychiatry Research: Neuroimaging*, 202, 181–197.

by the fact that there is a linear relationship between subjective experience of fear and amygdala activation (Goossens, Schruers, Peeters, Griez *et al.*, 2007; Ahs, Pissiota, Michelgard, Frans *et al.*, 2009).

Functional neuroimaging studies have also demonstrated that blood–injury–injection phobia and dental phobia are functionally different to other phobias, in that they can lead to a biphasic response that begins with an

increase in heart rate and blood pressure but then can result in decreased parasympathetic responding that causes fainting. Accounts of specific phobias in terms of brain neurocircuitry are not in conflict with other types of explanations of phobias (e.g. conditioning, evolutionary accounts), but help to specify how the conditions through which specific phobias are acquired are stored and activated in the brain.

Multiple pathways to phobias

There is no reason why the acquisition of all phobias should be explained by just a single process – and evidence is now accumulating to suggest that different types of phobias are acquired in quite different ways (Merckelbach, de Jong, Muris & van den Hout, 1996). We have already suggested that some phobias, such as dog phobia, dental phobia, choking phobia and accident phobia, are caused by traumatic conditioning experiences. In contrast, many other common phobias do not appear to be characterized by a traumatic experience at their outset – in fact, sufferers often cannot recall the exact onset of their phobia, which suggests that the onset may be gradual and precipitated by factors that are not immediately obvious to the individual. Phobias that fit this description include most animal phobias (including snake and spider phobia) (Murray & Foote, 1979; Merckelbach, Muris & Schouten, 1996), and water and height phobia (Menzies & Clarke, 1993a, 1993b).

Recent evidence suggests that at least some phobias are closely associated with the emotion of **disgust**. High levels of disgust sensitivity have been found to be associated with small animal phobias in general (Ware, Jain, Burgess & Davey, 1994; Davey, 1994a), spider phobia specifically (Mulkens, de Jong & Merckelbach, 1996), and has been hypothesized to play a role in mediating blood–injury–injection phobia and contamination fears (Page, 1994; Olatunji, Sawchuk, Lohr & de Jong, 2004). Disgust is a food-rejection emotion whose purpose is to prevent the transmission of illness and disease through the oral incorporation of contaminated items (Davey, 1994b; Rozin & Fallon, 1987), and elevated disgust sensitivity implies increased avoidance of disgust-relevant objects (such as faeces or mucus). In the case of animal phobias, Davey (1994a) has argued that many animals that become the focus for phobic responding do so because they have disgust relevance. Specifically, they may have acquired a disgust relevance (1) by directly spreading disease and being a source of contamination (e.g. rats, cockroaches), (2) by possessing features which mimic primary disgust relevant stimuli (by resembling, for instance, faeces or mucus; e.g. slugs or animals that are

> **disgust** A food-rejection emotion whose purpose is to prevent the transmission of illness and disease through the oral incorporation of contaminated items.

perceived as slimy such as snakes, snails or lizards), or (3) by having contemporary or historical significance as stimuli that signalled disease, illness or contamination (e.g. maggots, spiders; cf. Davey, 1994a). This **disease-avoidance model** of animal phobias (Matchett & Davey, 1991) is supported by the findings that having a high level of disgust sensitivity is a vulnerability factor for animal phobias (such as spider phobia), and can mitigate against successful therapy if it is not directly addressed in treatment (de Jong, Andrea & Muris, 1997; Mulkens, de Jong & Merckelbach, 1996).

> **disease-avoidance model** The view that some animal phobias are related to attempts to avoid disease or illness that might be transmitted by these animals.

Alternatively, there is evidence that factors closely associated with panic and panic disorder (see section 6.3) are also linked to a number of specific phobias. First, there is a fairly high comorbidity rate between panic disorder and some specific phobias. Studies have identified comorbidity rates of between 40 per cent and 65 per cent (de Ruiter, Rijken, Garssen, van Schaik & Kraaimaat, 1989; Starcevic, Uhlenhuth, Kellner, & Pathak, 1992), suggesting that panic is common in people suffering from many different types of specific phobia. Second, some categories of specific phobia – especially situational phobias – share important characteristics in common with panic disorder. For example, situational phobias appear to have a preponderance of spontaneous onsets typical of panic disorder (Himle, Crystal, Curtis & Fluent, 1991), have a significantly higher rate of comorbidity with panic disorder than do other types of phobias, such as animal phobias (Starcevic & Bogojevic, 1997), and frequently have uncontrollable panic attacks as one of the symptoms of phobic responding (e.g. height phobia, Antony, Brown & Barlow, 1997; flying phobia, McNally & Louro, 1992; claustrophobia, McIsaac, 1995). Similarly, both claustrophobia and height phobia share aetiological factors in common with panic disorder. For instance, subjective fear in claustrophobia is focused not just on external dangers but on anxiety expectancies and bodily sensations (Craske, Mohlman, Yi, Glover & Valeri, 1995), and spontaneous panic attacks are found significantly more often in claustrophobics than in other types of phobias (Rachman & Levitt, 1985; Craske & Sipsas, 1992). Height phobia is associated not only with heightened discrimination of bodily sensations, but also with a bias towards interpreting ambiguous bodily sensations as threatening – a characteristic which is central to the aetiology of panic disorder (Davey, Menzies & Gallardo, 1997) (see section 6.3.1).

These examples suggest that specific phobias may have a number of different causes – depending on the nature of the phobic stimulus or event – and the aetiologies appear to involve quite different vulnerability factors and psychological processes. This being so, specific phobias are a coherent category only on the basis of their defining symptoms, and therapists may need to look more closely at the different aetiologies to construct successful treatments.

6.1.2 The Treatment of Specific Phobias

Traditionally, successful treatment for specific phobias has tended to revolve around some form of exposure to the phobic stimulus or situation, and, in the past, behavioural treatments of choice for specific phobias have tended to include systematic desensitisation, flooding and counterconditioning (see section 4.1.1). One important issue in therapy for specific phobias is to address the phobic beliefs that sufferers hold about their phobic event or situation (see Table 6.2 above). These beliefs are often dysfunctional in that they do not match with the reality of the threat (or lack of it) posed by the phobic stimulus, and they also maintain fear and avoidance responses. Because of their strong avoidance of any contact with their phobic situation, sufferers rarely find themselves in a situation where they encounter evidence that disconfirms their phobic beliefs (e.g. continually avoiding spiders never helps the spider phobic to disconfirm their belief that, for example, 'I would come to physical harm in the presence of a spider') (Thorpe & Salkovskis, 1995, 1997). One important feature of exposure therapy is that it does put the phobic in situations where they can experience evidence that is contrary to their dysfunctional

Courtesy Dr. Hunter Hoffman

PHOTO 6.2 *Exposure therapy is one of the most successful treatments for specific phobias. For many sufferers, however, the thought of having to encounter a real spider is severely distressing. Instead, therapists have developed virtual reality exposure treatments, in which the client can first encounter spiders in a controlled virtual environment. This and various other forms of treatment for specific phobias are discussed in Choy, Fyer & Lipsitz (2007).*

beliefs. More recently, specific behavioural treatments have been combined with cognitive therapy techniques to produce integrated short-term therapies that involve cognitive restructuring, intensive exposure to the phobic event or stimulus, and modelling, and these can be effective in as little as one 3 hour session (Öst, 1997).

In conclusion, it must be remembered that many people can live with their phobias – either because they are sub-clinical in intensity or their fears are so specific that they do not interfere substantially with their daily lives. So, only those with the most distressing or disabling phobias are the ones who seek treatment. In general, recently developed therapies for specific phobias have been shown to be extremely effective and successful (Öst, 1997). These therapies are usually multifaceted and combine aspects of exposure therapy with cognitive restructuring.

THE CLINICAL PERSPECTIVE – TREATMENT IN PRACTICE BOX 6.1: ONE SESSION RAPID TREATMENT OF SPIDER PHOBIA

One-session treatments for specific phobias were developed during the 1990s and are remarkably successful as effective and long-lasting treatments for many specific phobias (Öst, 1997; Koch, Spates & Himle, 2004; Öst, Alm, Brandberg & Breitholtz, 2001). One-session treatments usually include a combination of graduated *in vivo* exposure and modelling. Below is an example of a one-session treatment procedure for spider phobia.

STEP 1: CATCHING A SMALL SPIDER IN A PLASTIC BOWL

The therapist first models how the client should pick up the spider by putting a bowl over it and then sliding a card underneath to trap the spider and then picking the bowl up using the card as a lid. This is repeated three or four times and on the last occasion the client is instructed to hold the bowl in the palm of his or her hand. At this point a brief role-play can be carried out by having the therapist play the part of a person born blind, and the client has to describe what is happening (thus forcing the client to look at the spider in the bowl).

STEP 2: TOUCHING THE SPIDER

The therapist asks the client what they think will happen if they touch the spider. Most spider phobics say the spider will climb up their arm. This is a prediction that can be tested by the therapist who then touches the spider. This is repeated up to 10 times to show the client that the spider's reaction is almost always to run away. This is followed by the client touching the spider – usually with some physical guidance from the therapist.

STEP 3: HOLDING THE SPIDER IN THE HAND

The therapist takes the spider on his or her hand, letting it walk from one hand to another. The client is then encouraged to put their index finger on the therapist's hand so that the spider can walk across the finger and back to the therapist's hand. This is repeated a number of times until the spider walks across all the client's fingers. Gradually, the therapist withdraws physical support and the client allows the spider to walk from one hand to another.

These three steps are then repeated with spiders of increasingly larger size. Throughout the session, the client is taught that he/she can acquire control over the spider by gradually being able to predict what the spider will do. The goal of the therapy is to ensure that at the end of the session the client can handle two spiders with low or no anxiety and no longer believe his/her catastrophic cognitions about spiders.

Source: Öst, L.G. (1997). Rapid treatment of specific phobias. In G.C.L. Davey (Ed.) *Phobias: A handbook of theory, research and treatment.* Chichester. John Wiley & Sons. Reproduced with permission.

SELF-TEST QUESTIONS

- What are the main diagnostic criteria for specific phobias?
- What are the most common phobias, and what are the kinds of *phobic beliefs* that accompany them?
- How do classical conditioning and evolutionary theories attempt to explain the acquisition of phobias? What are their similarities and differences?
- What is the role of brain areas such as the amygdala in the formation of specific phobias?
- Why is exposure such an important feature of treatment for specific phobias?

SECTION SUMMARY

SECTION SUMMARY

6.1 SPECIFIC PHOBIAS

- Specific phobias are defined as an excessive, unreasonable, persistent fear triggered by a specific object or situation.

- Around 10 per cent of people will meet DSM-5 criteria for a specific phobia within their lifetime.

- Common phobias include small animal phobias (insects, rodents, spiders, snakes), social phobia, dental phobia, water phobia, height phobia, claustrophobia, and blood–injury–inoculation (BII) phobia.

- The famous 'Little Albert' study by Watson and Rayner (1920) is an example of how phobias can be acquired through classical conditioning.

- Evolutionary accounts of phobias suggest that we have an inbuilt biological predisposition to fear certain stimuli and events (e.g. heights, water, snakes), because these stimuli were life-threatening to our pre-technological ancestors. Evolutionary accounts of phobias include biological preparedness theory and the non-associative fear acquisition model.

- The amygdala is a brain area that plays a significant role in the formation and storage of memories associated with specific fears and phobias.

- There is now strong evidence that different phobias may be caused by quite different processes: some involve classical conditioning, some are caused by high disgust sensitivity, while others appear to be caused by processes similar to those that cause panic disorder.

- Successful treatment for phobias tends to depend on some kind of exposure to the phobic stimulus or situation, and exposure therapies that are combined with cognitive behaviour therapy can be effective in as little as one 3 hour session.

6.2 SOCIAL ANXIETY DISORDER

Social anxiety disorder is distinguished by a severe and persistent fear of social or performance situations. The social phobic tries to avoid any kind of social situation in which they believe they may behave in an embarrassing way or in which they believe they may be negatively evaluated, and these types of situation can range from something as simple as having a conversation, eating or drinking in front others, or performing in front of others (e.g. giving a speech). So pervasive is anxiety of these socially based situations that it is also a predictor of several other debilitating problems such as depression and substance abuse (Rapee & Spence, 2004).

DSM-5 describes some of the defining features of social anxiety disorder, which include situations in which the sufferer believes he or she will show anxiety symptoms that will be negatively evaluated (e.g. they will be humiliated, embarrassed, or rejected) or will offend others. They may fear public speaking because of concern that others will notice their trembling hands or voice. Or they may experience extreme anxiety when conversing with others because of fear they will appear inarticulate. They may avoid eating, drinking, or writing in public because of fear of being embarrassed by having others see

their hands shake. Individuals with **social anxiety disorder** almost always experience symptoms of anxiety (e.g. palpitations, tremors, sweating, gastrointestinal discomfort, diarrhoea, muscle tension, blushing, confusion) in the feared social situations, and, in severe cases, these symptoms may turn into a full-blown panic attack. As a result of their reluctance to engage with social situations, sufferers of social anxiety disorder also tend to underperform in education and in the workplace, have impaired social and romantic relationships, and reduced productivity (Moitra, Beard, Weisberg & Keller, 2011; Kessler, 2003). Social anxiety disorder is as common in adolescence as it is in adulthood (Chavira, Stein, Bailey & Stein, 2005), is a common reason for school refusal in young children, and is the only mood or anxiety disorder that has consistently been associated with dropping out of school early (Stein & Kean, 2000). DSM-5 Summary Table 6.2 lists the DSM criteria for the diagnosis of social anxiety disorder.

social anxiety disorder A severe and persistent fear of social or performance situations.

Prevalence

Social anxiety disorder has a lifetime prevalence rate of between 4 and 13 per cent in Western societies and, with a gender prevalence of 3:2 females to males, afflicts females significantly more often than males (Wittchen & Fehm,

DSM-5 SUMMARY TABLE 6.2 *Criteria for social anxiety disorder*

- Distinct fear of social interactions, typified by anxiety around receiving negative judgment or of giving offense to others
- Social interactions are avoided, or are experienced with intense fear or anxiety
- The avoidance, fear or anxiety often lasts for 6 or more months and causes significant distress and difficulty in performing social or occupational activities
- Anxiety cannot be explained by the effects of other mental or medical disorders, drug abuse or medication

2003; Xu, Schneier, Heimberg, Princisvalle *et al.*, 2012; Memik, Yildiz, Tural & Agaoglu, 2011). Age of onset is considerably earlier than for many of the other anxiety disorders, with a typical age of onset in the early to middle teens, and usually prior to 18 years of age (Rapee, 1995; Otto, Pollack, Maki, Gould *et al.*, 2001). It is also a particularly persistent disorder, and has the lowest overall remission rate of the main anxiety disorders (Massion, Dyke, Shea, Phillips *et al.*, 2002; Hirshfeld-Becker, Micco. Simoes & Henin, 2008). Cross-cultural studies have shown that prevalence rates are significantly lower in South-East Asian countries (e.g. Korea and Taiwan), than in Western societies (Furmark, 2002), but this may be due at least in part to the fact that the expression of social anxiety differs across cultures. For example, in Japan, Taijin-kyofusho (TKS) is a form of social phobia in which the main fear is of offending others (see section 6.1). In Western cultures, social anxiety manifests itself primarily as fear of embarrassing oneself.

6.2.1 The Aetiology of Social Anxiety Disorder

Although it is a phobia in its own right, social anxiety disorder is considered separately from specific phobias in DSM-5. There are several reasons for this. Firstly, it is a highly prevalent disorder, and compares with generalized anxiety disorder (GAD) as one of the most common of the anxiety disorders. Secondly, as we will see below, theories of social anxiety disorder suggest that factors specific to social anxiety are important in the aetiology of social anxiety disorder. In particular, social phobics possess a range of information processing and interpretation biases that cause them to make excessively negative predictions about future social events, and we discuss these various types of bias in the following sections after we have first discussed genetic and developmental factors.

Genetic factors

There is evidence accruing that there is an underlying genetic component to social anxiety disorder, although it is not clear how specific this genetic component might be. For example, children with social anxiety disorder are more likely to have parents with the disorder than non-phobic children (Lieb, Wittchen, Hoefler, Fuetsch, *et al.*, 2000; Mancini, Van Ameringen, Szatmari, Fugere *et al.*, 1996), and twin studies also suggest that there is a significant but moderate genetic influence on the development of social anxiety disorder (Beatty, Heisel, Hall, Levine & La France, 2002; Ollendick & Hirshfeld-Becker, 2002). While indicating the importance of genetic influences, such studies do beg the question of what aspect of social anxiety disorder is inherited. Some studies have been able to identify specific constructs related to social anxiety disorder that appear to have a genetic component, and these include submissiveness, anxiousness, social avoidance and **behavioural inhibition** (Warren, Schmitz & Emde, 1999; Robinson, Kagan, Reznick & Corley, 1992). Other studies indicate that social anxiety disorder contains an inherited component that is shared with other anxiety disorders – and this suggests that what might be inherited is a vulnerability to anxiety disorders generally rather than social phobia specifically (Kendler, Walters, Neale, Kessler *et al.*, 1995; Nelson, Grant, Bucholz, Glowinski *et al.*, 2000). Several genes have been associated with socially anxious traits such as shyness and introversion, although these studies have been far from consistent in their findings (Gelernter, Page, Stein & Woods, 2004; Stein & Stein, 2008; Arbelle, Benjamin, Golin, Kremer *et al.*, 2003). Nevertheless, there may still be a modest inherited element that is specific to social anxiety disorder, and this has been estimated to account for as much as 13 per cent of the variance in social fears generally (Kendler, Myers, Prescott & Neale, 2001). Inherited components that are not specific to social anxiety, but related more to the inheritance of anxiety characteristics generally, may be as high as 30–50 per cent (Kendler, Karkowski & Prescott, 1999; Kendler, Neale, Kessler, *et al.*, 1992).

> **behavioural inhibition** A construct used to define the characteristic in some children of seeming quiet, isolated and anxious when confronted either with social situations or with novelty.

Familial and developmental factors

Family studies have indicated that offspring with social anxiety disorder are also more likely to have parents (and particularly mothers) with social anxiety disorder (Merikangas, Lieb, Wittchen & Avenevoli, 2003; Lieb, Wittchen, Hofler, Fuetsch *et al.*, 2000), and offspring of parents with an anxiety disorder are marginally more likely to have social anxiety disorder than offspring of parents with depression (Hirshfeld-Becker, Micco, Simoes & Henin, 2008), suggesting there is a specific familial link between anxiety generally and an offspring developing social anxiety disorder. Because social anxiety appears at

CLIENT'S PERSPECTIVE 6.1:
SOCIAL ANXIETY DISORDER

'Fear and anxiety have plagued me for as long as I can remember. If you don't suffer from SAD you can't begin to imagine what it's like to wake up every day feeling an intense dread of just getting out of bed and going to school or getting on a bus full of people. It's as if I'm living in a nightmare where everyday things become terrifying and confusing.

'My SAD started when I was about 10 and I had to perform in our school play. The teacher wanted everybody to join in and, because she knew I was shy, I was given a minor role along with some other kids. I woke up every morning in tears, terrified of going to school and dreading the moment when I would have to line up in front of everyone. The idea that all the children and teachers would be looking at me made me so scared I would shake all over and my hands trembled so much I couldn't even get into my costume. When I was in the rehearsals I would turn bright red and I'd stutter so much I couldn't speak. I could feel everyone looking at me and I was so self-conscious I would try and hide behind the other kids, thinking if nobody could see me I would be safe. When it came to the day of the performance I hid in the toilets and cried the whole way through.

'When I moved into secondary school my SAD got so bad. I couldn't talk aloud in class and when the teachers asked me questions I would stammer and blush. I knew everybody noticed how embarrassed I was and I felt that they were laughing at how red my face would go. I became really self-conscious about my blushing and I couldn't stop thinking about how much I would sweat when I was scared in class. I was convinced that people could smell how sweaty I was and that they thought I was disgusting. I became obsessed with putting on deodorant, I'd go into the toilets at least five times each day to put more on. At lunchtime I would hide in an empty classroom and eat on my own. Thinking about getting on the school bus scared me so much I had panic attacks at the end of each

day, and I'd walk home on my own instead: it was a 4 mile walk and took me almost 2 hours.

For a video on social anxiety disorder go to **www.wiley-psychopathology.com/ video/ch6**

'Eventually I dropped out of school altogether and I spend most days now at home by myself or out walking on my own. I'm too scared to get a job or to try and go to college, as I know my SAD will make it so hard, and I don't want to fail again. Since being diagnosed with SAD I have started to understand my behaviour and my fears more and I'm hoping to begin a distance learning course next year.'

Clinical Commentary

This client's perspective highlights the extreme fear experienced by many social phobics in a range of social and performance situations, and the impact it can have on social functioning specifically and life planning more generally. This description highlights a number of important features of social anxiety disorder, including (1) the biased interpretations that social phobics have of the reactions of others to them (e.g. 'I knew everybody noticed how embarrassed I was and I felt that they were laughing at how red my face would go'), (2) the belief that there are obvious physical signs of their nervousness which observers interpret judgmentally (e.g. 'I was convinced that people could smell how sweaty I was and that they thought I was disgusting'), and (3) the tendency of social phobics to focus their attention on themselves and their own reactions to the possible detriment of their own performance (e.g. 'Eventually I dropped out of school altogether and I spend most days now at home by myself').

a relatively early age compared with other anxiety disorders, it has been argued that various developmental factors and early experiences may precipitate the disorder (Neal & Edelmann, 2003). For example, there is considerable evidence that children who exhibit a behaviourally inhibited (BI) temperament style are at increased risk for subsequent social anxiety disorder (Neal, Edelmann & Glachan, 2002; Kagan, Reznick, Clark, *et al.*, 1984). However, it is also the case that a significant proportion of children who are highly behaviourally inhibited in early life do *not* subsequently develop social anxiety

disorder – so childhood behavioural inhibition is not a sufficient condition for social anxiety disorder (Schwartz, Snidman & Kagan, 1999) (see Focus Point 6.2). Early parent–child interaction styles may also play a role in the development of social anxiety. Studies of parent–child interactions suggest that the parents of children with social anxiety disorder exert greater control over their children, show less warmth, are less sociable than the parents of individuals without social anxiety disorder, and also use shame as a method of discipline (Rapee & Melville, 1997; Siqueland, Kendall & Steinberg, 1996;

BEHAVIOURAL INHIBITION (BI) AND SOCIAL ANXIETY DISORDER

Many children seem quiet, isolated and anxious when confronted either with social situations or with novelty, and this characteristic has come to be defined by the construct called behavioural inhibition (BI) (Kagan Reznick, Clark, Snidman *et al.*, 1984). BI represents 'a consistent tendency to display extreme fearfulness, withdrawal, reticence, and restraint in the face of novelty' (Hirschfeld-Becker, 2010), and toddlers exhibiting BI will show overt distress and cling to their mothers in unfamiliar or novel situations. They are also reluctant to approach novel objects, peers, and adults. Preschoolers with BI seem quiet and are reticent to speak or play spontaneously, and by age 7 the reluctance to socialize is found mainly in group contexts. BI is estimated to have quite a high level of inheritability – between 50 and 70 per cent (Smoller & Tsuang, 1998) – and BI is considered to be a specific risk factor for social anxiety disorder (Hirschfeld-Becker, 2010).

Bruch & Heimberg, 1994). While these factors seem to be important predictors of subsequent social anxiety disorder, it is impossible to determine at present whether they represent actual causal factors.

Cognitive factors

There appear to be a number of cognitive processes that are characteristic of social anxiety disorder and which may all act in some way to maintain fear of social situations (Stravynski, Bond & Amado, 2004). Firstly, individuals diagnosed with social anxiety disorder possess an information processing and interpretation bias in which they make excessively negative predictions about future social events (Heinrichs & Hofmann, 2001; Hirsch & Clark, 2004). For example, individuals with social anxiety disorder rate the probability of negative social events occurring as higher than either non-clinical controls or individuals with other anxiety disorders (Foa, Franklin, Perry & Herbert, 1996; Gilboa-Schechtman, Franklin & Foa, 2000), and this negative evaluation is likely to maintain their avoidance of social situations. Secondly, individuals with social anxiety disorder interpret their performance in social situations significantly more critically than non-sufferers and independent assessors who have observed their behaviour (Stopa & Clark, 1993; Rapee & Lim, 1992) and also underestimate their own social skills (Dodd, Hudson, Lyneham, Wuthrich *et al.*, 2011). Social phobics also find it very difficult to process positive social feedback (see Figure 6.4) (Alden, Mellings & Laposa, 2004). This focus on negative aspects of the social situation, and the relative inability to take anything 'good' from a social performance are likely to maintain the social phobic's dysfunctional beliefs that social situations are threatening and that their own performance is likely to be flawed. Thirdly, some theories of social anxiety disorder argue that sufferers show a strong tendency to shift their attention inwards onto themselves and their own anxiety responses during social performance – especially when they fear they will be negatively evaluated (Clark & Wells, 1995; Rapee & Heimberg, 1997) This is

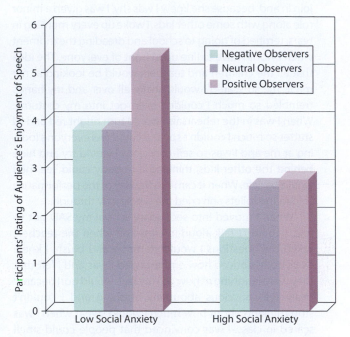

FIGURE 6.4 *High and low socially anxious participants were asked to give a speech to a group of observers. After giving the speech, the high socially anxious participants rated the observers' enjoyment of their speech significantly lower than low socially anxious participants. The high socially anxious participants even do this when the observers have been instructed to provide positive feedback, suggesting that socially phobic individuals do not attend to positive feedback cues given by an audience.*
Source: After Perowne S. & Mansell W. (2002). Social anxiety, self-focused attention and the discrimination of negative, neutral and positive audience members by their non-verbal behaviours. *Behavioural and cognitive psychotherapy*, 30, 11–23.

known as **self-focused attention** (Spurr & Stopa, 2002; Bogels & Mansell, 2004), and has the effect of leading socially anxious individuals to believe they may look as anxious as they feel inside. This prevents

> **self-focused attention** A theory of social anxiety disorder arguing that sufferers show a strong tendency to shift their attention inwards onto themselves and their own anxiety responses during social performance – especially when they fear they will be negatively evaluated.

objective processing of the social situation, leads them to engage in critical self-evaluation, and may well adversely affect their actual performance in the social situation (e.g. see Kley, Tuschen-Caffier & Heinrichs, 2011). Studies have shown that social phobics do indeed display higher levels of self-reported self-focused attention than nonclinical populations (Bogels & Lamers, 2002), and that they recall social memories more often from an observer perspective than a personal perspective (suggesting that they do indeed 'observe' themselves while performing socially) (Wells, Clark & Ahmad, 1998). Self-focused attention therefore appears to have the effect of reinforcing the individual's perception of their own anxiety in the social situation, can distract the individual from focusing on the social task at hand and lead to unskilled performance, and result in avoidance of future social situations (Alden, Teschuk & Tee, 1992). Finally, individuals with social anxiety disorder also indulge in excessive post-event processing of social events that includes critical self-appraisal of performance and assessment of symptom severity. Such post-event rumination has the effect of maintaining negative appraisals of performance over time and maintaining social anxiety (Abbott & Rapee, 2004; Rachman, Gruter-Andrew & Shafran, 2000).

6.2.2 The Treatment of Social Anxiety Disorder

Both pharmacological treatments and cognitive behaviour therapy (CBT) have been shown to be effective in alleviating the symptoms of social anxiety disorder (Rodebaugh, Holaway & Heimberg, 2004; Davidson, 2003), and both are used widely to treat the disorder.

Successful CBT treatments include elements of the following:

- Exposure therapy (where the client remains in a feared social situation despite distress) – either *in vivo*, or through the therapist taking on the role of a stranger in a social situation (Heimberg & Becker, 2002).

- Social skills training (consisting of modelling, behavioural rehearsal, corrective feedback and positive reinforcement) – this training addresses the social skills deficits usually characteristic of social phobics.

- Cognitive restructuring (designed to challenge and replace the negative biases in information processing and the dysfunctional negative self-evaluations of social performance, and to reduce self-focused attention) (Rodebaugh & Chambless, 2004).

THE CLINICAL PERSPECTIVE – TREATMENT IN PRACTICE BOX 6.2: COGNITIVE THERAPY FOR SOCIAL ANXIETY DISORDER

The following provides a step-by-step account of the cognitive therapy for social anxiety disorder devised by Clark & Wells (1995). The aims of this procedure are (1) to decrease self-focused attention, (2) to reduce the level of negative interpretations of internal information (e.g. sweating as a sign of poor performance), (3) eliminate the use of safety behaviours, which maintain negative beliefs (e.g. if the phobic believes they are trembling and this may be visible, they may grip objects tightly in order to conceal it, and this response merely maintains the phobic's belief that they are anxious and trembling), and (4) reduce negative post-event processing (see section 6.2).

STEP 1 The initial phase is designed to inform the client about those factors that are maintaining their social phobia (see above), and that these are the factors that the therapy is specifically designed to target.

STEP 2 The second phase attempts to manipulate safety behaviours. Here the client has to role-play a social situation and observe his or her own responses and identify key safety behaviours. The client will then attempt to drop these safety behaviours during subsequent role-playing.

STEP 3 Clients are trained to shift their attention externally and away from their own internal responses and cognitions.

STEP 4 Video feedback of performance can be used to modify distorted self-imagery.

STEP 5 The client is provided with some behavioural experiments in which they specify their fears of particular social situations and then test out whether they occurred during role-play sessions.

STEP 6 Problematic post-event processing is identified and modified using focused cognitive restructuring techniques.

Source: Stangier, U., Heidenreich, T., Peitz, M., Lauterbach, W. & Clark, D.M. (2003). Cognitive therapy for social phobia: Individual versus group treatment. *Behaviour Research and Therapy, 41*(9), 991–1007. Reproduced with permission.

Each of these elements used alone do show therapeutic gains, but an integrated CBT programme appears to result in maintenance of gains over 6–12 month follow-up periods (Feske & Chambless, 1995). Recent reviews of treatments for social anxiety disorder in youth suggest that CBT might be more efficacious if integrated with specific social skills training (Scharfstein & Beidel, 2011).

Drugs such as monoamine-oxidase inhibitors (MAOIs), and more recently selective serotonin reuptake inhibitors (SSRIs) (see section 4.1.1), have been shown to cause improvement in measures of social anxiety (Blanco,

Schneier, Schmidt, Blanco-Jerez *et al.*, 2003; Van der Linden, Stein & van Balkom, 2000), as have benzodiazepines and beta-adrenergic blockers (Schneier, 2011). Comparative outcome studies have suggested that both pharmacological and CBT treatments are more effective than non-treatment controls (Gould, Buckminster, Pollock, Otto & Yap, 1997), but that the two types of therapy may offer complementary benefits – drug therapy offering a more immediate benefit than CBT, but CBT helping patients to maintain their therapeutic gains over time (Liebowitz, Heimberg, Schneier, Hope *et al.*, 1999).

SELF-TEST QUESTIONS

- What are the main diagnostic criteria for social anxiety disorder and how does this disorder manifest itself?
- Can you describe the various cognitive factors that appear to play an important role in maintaining social anxiety disorder?
- How do cognitive behaviour therapies and drug treatments complement each other in the treatment of social anxiety disorder?

SECTION SUMMARY

6.2   SOCIAL ANXIETY DISORDER

- Social anxiety disorder is distinguished by a severe and persistent fear of social or performance situations.
- Social anxiety disorder has a lifetime prevalence rate of between 4 and 13 per cent in Western societies.
- There is evidence for a genetic component to social anxiety disorder, but this may be a predisposition to develop anxiety disorders generally rather than social anxiety disorder specifically.
- There are a number of cognitive factors that are characteristic of social anxiety disorder, and these include a tendency (1) to make excessively negative predictions about future social events, (2) to over-critically evaluate their own social performance, (3) to shift their attention inwards on to themselves, and (4) to indulge in post-event critical appraisal of their own performance.
- Both monoamine-oxidase inhibitors and selective serotonin reuptake inhibitors have been shown to be successful pharmacological treatments for social anxiety disorder, as well as cognitive behaviour therapy.

6.3   PANIC DISORDER AND AGORAPHOBIA

Panic disorder and agoraphobia are related – but separable – anxiety-based problems. Panic disorder is the more prevalent of the two, but around one-third of those suffering panic disorder also suffer agoraphobia. In those with agoraphobic symptoms, around half will experience regular panic attacks but the remainder will not (Andrews, Charney, Sirovatka *et al.*, 2009). Furthermore, for a majority of those people who develop agoraphobic symptoms, these symptoms will begin within a year of an initial panic attack, and are usually the result of

fearing the consequences of having a panic attack in public. However, there is still a substantial number of people who suffer agoraphobia symptoms without panic attacks, and who appear to fear what might happen if other anxiety symptoms develop.

Panic disorder

As the name suggests, **panic disorder** is characterized by repeated **panic** or anxiety attacks. These attacks are associated with a variety of physical symptoms, including heart palpitations, perspiring, dizziness, hyperventilating, nausea and

panic disorder An anxiety disorder characterized by repeated panic or anxiety attacks.

panic A sudden uncontrollable fear or anxiety.

PANIC DISORDER

Marilyn is a 33-year-old single woman who works at a local telephone company and lives alone in her apartment. She has panic disorder with agoraphobia and her first panic attack occurred 3 years ago when driving over a bridge on a very rainy day. She experienced dizziness, pounding heart, trembling and difficulty breathing. She was terrified her symptoms meant she was about to pass out and lose control of her car. Since that time she has experienced eight unexpected panic attacks during which she feared she was about to pass out and lose control of herself. She frequently experiences limited symptom attacks (e.g., feels dizzy and fears she may pass out). As a result of her intense fear of having another panic attack she is avoiding the following situations: waiting in line, drinking alcohol, elevators, movie theatres, driving over bridges, driving on the freeway, flying by plane, and heights (e.g., will not go out on her tenth-floor balcony). She is often late for work because of taking a route that doesn't require her to take the freeway. She is also finding herself avoiding more and more activities. She frequently feels tearful and on guard. Sometimes she gets very angry at herself as she does not understand why she has become so fearful and avoidant.

Sharon is a 38-year-old single mother of two teenage daughters who works as a fitness instructor at a local gym. She experienced her first panic attack during her teens when watching a horror movie with friends at a local movie theatre. Since that time she has experienced one to two full panic attacks per year that come out of the blue in a variety of situations (e.g., while waiting in line at the bank, at a shopping mall, walking alone at the park). The panic attacks reoccurred out of the blue when she was 29 while eating a hot and spicy meal at a local restaurant. Her panic attacks always include dizziness, feeling of choking, dry mouth, unreality, feeling detached from her body, and feeling as if she may lose bowel control. Her main fear is that she is dying due to a stroke although medical problems have been ruled out. Sharon does not avoid anything to prevent the panic attacks and there has not been a huge negative impact of the panic attacks upon her work, family or social functioning.

Source: http://www.anxietybc.com/disorders/PANIC.html.

Clinical Commentary

Both Marilyn and Sharon exhibit a number of physical symptoms typical of panic attacks, although these examples show that not everyone experiences similar symptoms. Panic attacks often come 'out of the blue' and are unpredictable, and this adds to their frightening nature. In both examples, the individual believes that the symptoms are signs of impending physical illness or loss of control (catastrophic misinterpretation). The pervasive fear of further attacks means that Marilyn has developed avoidance responses in an attempt to minimize future attacks. These avoidance responses interfere with her normal daily life (causing further stress), and inadvertently help to maintain dysfunctional catastrophic beliefs.

trembling. In addition, the individual may experience real feelings of terror or severe apprehension, and depersonalization (a feeling of not being connected to your own body or in real contact with what is happening around you). Most people will experience at least one panic attack in their lifetime, but panic disorder is diagnosed when recurrent, unexpected panic attacks keep occurring, and are followed by at least 1 month of persistent concerns about having a further attack. For some individuals panic attacks are unpredictable, but for others they may become associated (perhaps through classical conditioning; see section 1.3.2) to specific situations or events (e.g. riding on public transport).

DSM-5 defines a panic attack as an abrupt surge of intense fear or discomfort in which four or more of a list of symptoms develops suddenly (see DSM-5 Summary Table 6.3). The criteria for panic disorder state that the

individual must experience recurrent panic attacks, and in addition they must develop a persistent concern that future panic attacks will occur (see DSM-5 Summary Table 6.4). The frequency of panic attacks in panic disorder

DSM-5 SUMMARY TABLE 6.3 *Criteria for a panic attack*

A sudden feeling of extreme fear or distress, which can originate from either a calm or an anxious state. Symptoms intensify in a short space of time and will include a range of sensations such as:

- fluctuations in heart rate
- shortness of breath or chest pain
- nausea
- dizziness
- shaking

The person may fear they are dying or 'going crazy'

in producing panic attacks (Bailey, Argyropoulos, Lightman & Nutt, 2003), and that norepinephrine is implicated in the symptomatology of panic disorder (Sand, Mori, Godau, Stober et al., 2002). One particular view related to putative overactivity in the noradrenergic system is that patients with panic disorder are deficient in the gamma-aminobutryic (GABA) neurons that inhibit noradrenergic activity, and PET scan studies have tended to support this view (Malizia, Cunningham, Bell, Liddle et al., 1998). Nevertheless, it is still unclear whether the role of the noradrenergic system is to mediate the symptoms of panic attacks when they occur, or whether noradrenergic overactivity represents a vulnerability factor in the aetiology of panic disorder.

Psychological theories of panic disorder

Classical conditioning Goldstein & Chambless (1978) were the first to suggest that an important feature of panic disorder was the sufferer's 'fear of fear'. That is, when they detected what they thought were any internal signs of a panic attack (e.g. mild dizziness), they would immediately become fearful of the possible consequences. This would then precipitate a full-blown attack. Goldstein & Chambless (1978) interpreted this as a form of interoceptive classical conditioning, in which the internal cue (such as dizziness) had become established as an internal conditioned stimulus (CS) predicting a panic attack (the unconditioned stimulus, UCS). However, while this account has intuitive appeal, it is not clear in conditioning terms what is the CS and what is the UCS. For example, is a skipped heartbeat a CS that precipitates a panic attack, or is it a symptom of the panic attack itself (the UCS) (McNally, 1990)? Bouton, Mineka & Barlow (2001) have attempted to address these conceptual difficulties by suggesting that anxiety and panic are separable aspects of panic disorder. They suggest that anxiety is anticipatory and prepares the system for a trauma, whereas panic deals with a trauma that is already in progress. In this conditioning account, anxiety is the learned reaction, called conditioned response (CR) to the detection of cues conditioned stimulus (CS) that might predict a panic attack, and once conditioned anxiety develops it will exacerbate subsequent panic attacks and lead to the development of panic disorder. As predicted by this model, studies confirm that panic attacks are regularly preceded by anxiety in individuals with panic disorder (Barlow, 1988; Kenardy & Taylor, 1999).

Anxiety sensitivity What is clear about the phenomenology of panic disorder is that sufferers become extremely anxious when they detect any cues (internal or external) that may be indicative of a panic attack. So any theory of panic disorder needs to explain why sufferers are made anxious by the detection of these cues, and how

this subsequently leads to a full-blown panic attack. Individuals who do *not* suffer panic disorder report a number of interoceptive and affective responses in biological challenge tests, but they are only rarely made anxious by these symptoms and hardly ever panic (Bass & Gardner, 1985; Starkman, Zelnik, Nesse & Cameron, 1985). So, what determines whether someone will panic in response to unusual bodily sensations? Reiss & McNally (1985) proposed that some individuals have pre-existing beliefs that bodily sensations may predict harmful consequences. They developed the construct of **anxiety sensitivity**, which refers to fears of anxiety symptoms that are based on beliefs that such symptoms have harmful consequences (e.g. that a rapid heart beat predicts an impending heart attack). In order to measure this construct, Reiss, Peterson, Gursky & McNally (1986) developed the **Anxiety Sensitivity Index** (ASI) (e.g. Table 6.4) (see also the Revised Anxiety Sensitivity Index, ASI-R, Taylor & Cox, 1998), and this contains items such as 'Unusual body sensations scare me' and 'It scares me when I feel faint'. Studies have shown that individuals with panic disorder score significantly higher on the ASI than either non-clinical controls or individuals diagnosed with other anxiety disorders (Taylor & Cox, 1998; Rapee, Ancis & Barlow, 1988). Furthermore, in a prospective study, high ASI scores predicted the occurrence of subsequent panic attacks in army recruits undergoing a stressful period of training (Schmidt, Lerew & Jackson, 1997), and this suggests that elevated anxiety sensitivity may be a risk factor for panic and perhaps panic disorder (McNally, 2002).

anxiety sensitivity Fears of anxiety symptoms based on beliefs that such symptoms have harmful consequences (e.g. that a rapid heartbeat predicts an impending heart attack).

Anxiety Sensitivity Index A measure, developed by Reiss, Peterson, Gursky & McNally (1986), to measure anxiety sensitivity.

Catastrophic misinterpretation of bodily sensations

Based on the fact that panic disorder sufferers are clearly anxious about the possible consequences of bodily symptoms, Clark (1986, 1988) developed an influential model of panic disorder in which he hypothesized that panic attacks are precipitated by the individual catastrophically misinterpreting their bodily sensations as threatening. Many body sensations are ambiguous: for instance, the heart skipping a beat could mean either an imminent heart attack (negative interpretation) or that someone you like has just walked into the room (positive interpretation). However, individuals who tend to develop panic disorder appear to exhibit **catastrophic misinterpretation of bodily sensations**; that is, they have a cognitive bias towards accepting the more threatening interpretation of their sensations

catastrophic misinterpretation of bodily sensations A feature of panic disorder where there is a cognitive bias towards accepting the more threatening interpretation of an individual's own sensations.

TABLE 6.4 *Example items from the anxiety sensitivity index (ASI-R)*

The ASI-R measures anxiety sensitivity, and this is a measure of an individual's fear of anxiety. Anxiety sensitivity is one of the best predictors of future panic attacks and may be a risk factor for panic disorder.

1. When I feel like I'm not getting enough air, I get scared that I might suffocate
2. When my chest feels tight, I get scared I won't be able to breathe properly
3. It scares me when I feel faint
4. When my throat feels tight, I worry that I could choke to death
5. It scares me when my heart beats rapidly
6. It scares me when I feel shaky (trembly)
7. When I have trouble swallowing, I worry that I could choke
8. It scares me when my body feels strange or different in some way
9. I think it would be horrible for me to faint in public
10. When I tremble in the presence of others I fear what people might think of me
11. When I feel a strong pain in my stomach, I worry it could be cancer
12. When my heart is beating rapidly, I worry that I might be having a stroke
13. When I feel dizzy, I worry there is something wrong with my brain
14. When my stomach is upset, I worry that I might be seriously ill
15. It scares me when I feel tingling or prickling sensations in my hands
16. When I feel 'spacey' or spaced out I worry that I may be mentally ill

Source: Taylor, S. & Cox, B.J. (1998). Anxiety sensitivity: Multiple dimensions and hierarchic structure. *Behaviour Research and Therapy*, *36*(1), 37–51. Reproduced with permission.

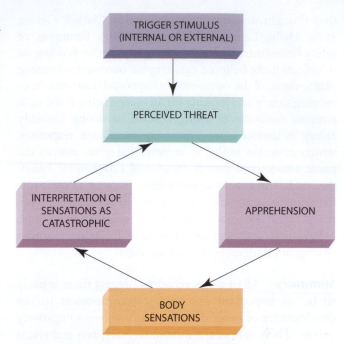

FIGURE 6.5 *Clark's (1986) model of panic disorder.*
Perception of a threat triggers apprehension and then bodily sensations associated with that apprehension are interpreted catastrophically. This causes further anxiety which feeds into a vicious cycle that triggers a full-blown panic attack.
Source: Clark, D.M. (1986). A cognitive approach to panic. *Behaviour Research and Therapy, 24* (4), 461–470. Reproduced with permission.

(Clark, Salkovskis, Ost, Breitholz *et al.*, 1997; see Austin & Richards, 2001, for a review). Clark argues that this leads to a vicious cycle where any apprehension is interpreted threateningly and increases the perceived threat, which leads to an escalation of anxiety symptoms that then precipitate a panic attack, and this is represented schematically in Figure 6.5. There is a good deal of evidence to support this psychological account. Individuals with panic disorder have been shown to attend to and discriminate their bodily sensations more closely than individuals without panic disorder (Ehlers & Breuer, 1992), and panic disorder sufferers report that thoughts of imminent danger typically accompany their attacks (Hibbert, 1984;

Ottaviani & Beck, 1987). In addition, individuals with panic disorder will experience a panic attack when they have been told they will receive a CO_2 challenge, but in fact are given only *compressed air* (Sanderson, Rapee & Barlow, 1989), suggesting that just the *expectancy* of an attack is enough to trigger one.

The role of safety behaviours   What is intriguing about panic disorder is that, while some sufferers may have experienced hundreds of panic attacks over a period of years, they still misinterpret the physical symptoms in a catastrophic way – even though nothing catastrophic has happened to them following a panic attack. So the person who believes that a slight sensation in the chest signals an imminent heart attack still interprets this sensation in this catastrophic way, even though they have never had a heart attack following many previously similar panic attacks. The reason for this is that individuals suffering panic disorder tend to develop **safety behaviours**. Safety behaviours are activities that the sufferer will deploy as soon as they think they are having a panic attack, and they develop the belief that this activity has saved them from the catastrophic outcome

safety behaviours Activities deployed by sufferers of panic disorder as soon as they think they are having a panic attack, developed in the belief that this activity has saved them from a catastrophic outcome.

they thought would happen (Salkovskis, Clark & Gelder, 1996; Helbig-Lang & Petermann, 2010). Examples of safety behaviours include: seeking support by holding on to objects if the believed catastrophic outcome is fainting; sitting down if the outcome is a supposed heart attack; or moving slowly and looking for an escape route if the catastrophic outcome is losing control or acting foolishly. Safety behaviours are effectively avoidance responses, which maintain both the anxiety that gives rise to the panic attacks and the dysfunctional catastrophic beliefs that make the attacks so distressing. Because of their role in maintaining panic disorder, safety behaviours are a primary target for manipulation and elimination in both behavioural and cognitive therapies for panic disorder (Rachman, Radomsky & Shafran, 2008).

Summary All of these accounts suggest there is likely to be an important psychological component to the development of panic disorder that involves a negatively valenced bias in how the individual interprets and reacts to their own bodily sensations. This interpretation bias

appears to trigger anxiety, which in turn triggers a panic attack. The issues that remain to be resolved in these accounts are (1) exactly how the anxiety elicited by catastrophic misinterpretation of bodily sensations leads to panic, and (2) why some individuals have acquired high levels of anxiety sensitivity and catastrophic beliefs in the first place.

6.3.2 *The Treatment of Panic Disorder*

Because of the distressing physical symptoms experienced in panic disorder, psychoactive medication is usually the first line of treatment provided for sufferers, and both tricyclic antidepressants and benzodiazepines may be effective in controlling symptoms (Roy-Byrne & Cowley, 1998) (see section 4.1.1).

However, there is good evidence that structured exposure therapy or cognitive behaviour therapy (CBT) is as effective, if not superior, to drug treatments over the longer term (e.g. Craske, Brown & Barlow, 1991).

THE CLINICAL PERSPECTIVE – TREATMENT IN PRACTICE BOX 6.3: COGNITIVE THERAPY FOR PANIC DISORDER

The following transcript gives an example of how a cognitive therapist (T) would try to challenge the catastrophic beliefs of a panic disorder sufferer (P) who believes that signs of an impending panic attack are signals for an imminent heart attack.

P: When I'm panicking, it's terrible. I can feel my heart pounding; it's so bad I think it could burst through my chest.

T: What thoughts go through your mind when your heart is pounding like that?

P: Well, I'll tell you what I think: it's so bad that I think I'm going to have a heart attack. It can't be good for your heart to be beating like that.

T: So, are you concerned that anxiety can damage your heart or cause a heart attack?

P: Yes, it must do you some damage. You hear of people dropping down dead from heart attacks caused by stress.

T: Do you think more people have stress in their lives than die of heart attacks?

P: Yes, I suppose so.

T: How can that be if stress causes heart attacks?

P: Well, I suppose it doesn't always cause problems. Maybe it does only in some people.

T: Yes, that's right: stress can cause some problems in some people. It tends to be people who have something wrong with their hearts in the first place. But stress is not necessarily the same as sudden anxiety or panic. When you panic your body releases adrenalin which causes the heart to speed up and your body to work faster. It's a way of preparing you to deal better with danger. If adrenalin damaged the heart or body, how would people have evolved from dangerous primitive times? Wouldn't we all have been wiped out?

P: Yes, I suppose so.

T: So maybe panic itself doesn't cause heart attacks; there has to be something physically wrong for that to happen. When people have had heart attacks they are often given an injection of adrenalin directly into the heart in order to help start it again. Do you think they would do that if it damaged the heart even more?

P: No I'm sure they wouldn't.

T: So, how much do you now believe that anxiety and panic will damage your heart?

Source: Wells, A. (1997). *Cognitive therapy of anxiety disorders: A practical manual and conceptual guide.* Chichester: John Wiley & Sons, pp. 123–124. Reproduced with permission.

In exposure-based treatments, the client is persuaded to experience the conditions that precipitate a panic attack in the controlled environment of the therapy situation (Barlow & Craske, 1994; Craske & Barlow, 2001). For example, someone whose attacks are preceded by bouts of dizziness may be asked to spin around in a chair, or if hyperventilation is a trigger, the individual will be asked to breathe rapidly for a period of time. At the first bodily signs of the symptoms associated with panic, the client is then asked to apply cognitive and physical techniques designed to manage the attack (such as applying relaxation techniques). This enables the client to manage the attack under relatively 'safe' conditions, and to learn to exercise control over the cues that would normally predict panic (Craske, Maidenberg & Bystritsky, 1995).

Clearly, an important distinguishing feature of individuals with panic disorder is their fear of bodily sensations, their catastrophic misinterpretation of these sensations, and the effect these cognitions have in triggering a panic attack. The development of CBT for panic disorder has therefore focused specifically on providing clients with challenges to these beliefs in the form of both corrective information and experiences designed to eliminate faulty emotional responding (e.g. Clark, Salkovskis, Hackmann, Middleton, Anastasiades & Gelder, 1994;

Telch, Lucas, Schmidt, Hanna, Jaimez & Lucas, 1993; Luermans, De Cort, Scruers & Griez, 2004). A typical treatment programme would include:

1. Education about the nature and physiology of panic attacks,
2. Breathing training designed to control hyperventilation,
3. Cognitive restructuring therapy to identify and challenge faulty threat perceptions,
4. Interoceptive exposure to reduce fear of harmless bodily sensations, and
5. Prevention of safety behaviours that may maintain attacks and avoid disconfirmation of maladaptive threat beliefs.

Such programmes have been shown to produce a durable reduction in symptoms and a significant increase in quality of life for panic disorder sufferers (Barlow, Gorman, Shear & Woods, 2000; Telch, Schmidt, Jaimez, Jacquin & Harrington, 1995). More recent studies have also suggested that CBT programmes may be effective specifically because they significantly reduce the tendency to react fearfully to benign bodily sensations (Smits, Powers, Cho & Telch, 2004).

SELF-TEST QUESTIONS

- Can you describe the main symptoms of a panic attack, and the diagnostic criteria for panic disorder?
- What is the relationship between symptoms of panic disorder and agoraphobia?
- How does hyperventilation cause a panic attack?
- What role does the catastrophic misinterpretation of bodily sensations play in the acquisition and maintenance of panic disorder?
- Can psychological explanations of panic disorder explain more of the facts of panic disorder than biological explanations?
- What is the role of safety behaviours in maintaining panic disorder?
- What are the important features of cognitive behaviour therapy for panic disorder?

SECTION SUMMARY

6.3 PANIC DISORDER AND AGORAPHOBIA

- Panic disorder is characterized by repeated panic or anxiety attacks associated with a variety of physical symptoms, including heart palpitations, dizziness, perspiring, hyperventilation, nausea, trembling, and depersonalization.
- Agoraphobia is a fear or anxiety of any place where the sufferer does not feel safe or feels trapped, and is accompanied by a strong urge to escape to a safe place (e.g. home).
- The lifetime prevalence rate for panic disorder is between 1.5 and 3 per cent, although prevalence rates do differ between different cultures.

- Hyperventilation is a common feature of panic disorder, and some theorists have argued that the effect of hyperventilation on body CO_2 levels is a causal factor in the development of a panic attack.

- Individuals with panic disorder have high levels of anxiety sensitivity, which is a fear of anxiety symptoms.

- Individuals who develop panic disorder tend to catastrophically misinterpret bodily sensations, and interpret them as signs of an imminent physical threat (e.g. an imminent heart attack signalled by a missed heartbeat). This cognitive bias leads to a vicious cycle which increases the anxiety symptoms that precipitate a panic attack.

- Safety behaviours are activities that a panic disorder sufferer will deploy during a panic attack and will maintain the belief that panic attacks might have catastrophic consequences.

- Tricyclic antidepressants and benzodiazepines are an effective first-line treatment for panic disorder, but structured exposure therapy or cognitive behaviour therapy (CBT) is as effective, if not superior, to drug treatments over the longer term.

6.4 GENERALIZED ANXIETY DISORDER (GAD)

Generalized anxiety disorder (GAD) is a pervasive condition in which the sufferer experiences continual apprehension and anxiety about future events, and this leads to chronic and pathological worrying about those events. We all worry about things to some degree – and, indeed, many people find it beneficial to think about how they might deal with challenging future events. However, worrying for the individual with GAD has a number of features that make it disabling and a source of extreme emotional discomfort. For example, for the individual suffering GAD:

generalized anxiety disorder A pervasive condition in which the sufferer experiences continual apprehension and anxiety about future events, and this leads to chronic and pathological worrying about those events.

1. Worrying is a chronic and pathological activity that is not only directed at major life issues (e.g. health, finances, relationships, work-related matters), but also to many minor day-to-day issues and hassles that others would not perceive as threatening (Craske, Rapee, Jackel & Barlow, 1989; Tallis, Davey & Capuzzo, 1994);

2. Worrying is perceived as uncontrollable – the individual with GAD feels they cannot control either the onset or termination of a bout of worrying;

3. Worrying is closely associated with the **catastrophising** of worries – that is, worry bouts persist for longer in GAD, they are associated with increasing levels of anxiety and distress as the bout continues, and worrying seems to make the problem *worse* rather than better (see Table 6.5). While pathological and chronic worrying is

catastrophising An example of magnification in which the individual takes a single fact to its extreme, one example being catastrophic worrying.

the cardinal diagnostic feature of GAD it may also be accompanied by physical symptoms such as fatigue, trembling, muscle tension, headache, and nausea.

Diagnosis and prevalence

The DSM-5 criteria for diagnosis of GAD are shown in DSM-5 Summary Table 6.6 and include:

- Excessive anxiety and worry about two or more domains of activities or events on more days than not for 3 months or more,

- Anxiety and worry are associated with physical symptoms such as restlessness or muscle tension,

- Anxiety and worry are accompanied by one or more of: avoidance of events with possible negative outcomes; excessive time and effort spent preparing for events with negative outcomes; procrastination; or repeated reassurance-seeking about worries

- Finally, a consequence of these symptoms will be clinically significant distress or impairment in social, occupational, or other important areas of functioning.

GAD is twice as common in women as in men, and can often persist from adolescence to old age (Barlow, Blanchard, Vermilyea, Vermilyea & DiNardo, 1986). Over 5 per cent of the population will be diagnosed with GAD at some point in their lifetime (Wittchen & Hoyer, 2001), and over 12 per cent of those who attend anxiety disorder clinics will present with symptoms typical of GAD (Kessler, Keller & Wittchen, 2001). Comorbidity is also highly prevalent in sufferers of GAD, with rates ranging from 45 per cent to 98 per cent (Goisman, Goldenberg, Vasile & Keller, 1995), and individuals diagnosed with GAD are also likely to suffer other mental health problems, such as depression and eating disorders (Brown, O'Leary & Barlow, 2001). In addition, GAD is

TABLE 6.5 *Catastrophising in worriers and non-worriers*

These catastrophising sequences generated by a chronic worrier (top) and a non-worrier (bottom) were generated using the catastrophic interview procedure in which the individual is first asked 'What is your main worry at the moment?' In this case both participants replied, 'Getting good grades in school'. The interviewer then passes this response back to the participant by saying 'What is it that worries you about getting good grades in school?'. Each time the participant responds, the interviewer passes that response back by asking what it is about the response that worries them. The interview continues until the participant can no longer think of any reasons.

By looking at the catastrophising sequences above, we can deduce a number of things about chronic worriers: (1) they produce significantly more catastrophising steps than non-worriers, (2) they experience increasing emotional distress as catastrophising continues, as evidenced by their 'discomfort' scores, and (3) the content of their catastrophising steps becomes more and more threatening and catastrophic, as evidenced by their increasing 'likelihood' scores as catastrophising progresses.

	Discomfort	Likelihood
Chronic worrier topic: Getting good grades in school		
Catastrophising step		
I won't live up to my expectations	50	30
I'd be disappointed in myself	60	100
I'd lose my self-confidence	70	50
My loss of self-confidence would spread to other areas of my life	70	50
I wouldn't have as much control as I'd like	75	80
I'd be afraid of facing the unknown	75	100
I'd become very anxious	75	100
Anxiety would lead to further loss of self-confidence	75	80
I wouldn't get my confidence back	75	50
I'd feel like I wouldn't have any control over my life	75	80
I'd be susceptible to things that normally wouldn't bother me	75	80
I'd become more and more anxious	80	80
I'd have no control at all and I'd become mentally ill	85	30
I'd become dependent on drugs and therapy	50	30
I'd always remain dependent on drugs	85	50
They'd deteriorate my body	85	100
I'd be in pain	85	100
I'd die	90	80
I'd end up in hell	95	80
Non-worrier topic: Getting good grades in school		
Catastrophising step		
I might do poorly on a test	3	20
I'd get a bad grade in the class	3	100
That would lower my grade-point average	2	100
I'd have less of a chance of getting a good job	2	60

TABLE 6.5 *(Cont'd)*

	Discomfort	Likelihood
Non-worrier topic: Getting good grades in school		
Catastrophising step		
I'd end up in a bad job	2	80
I'd get a low salary	2	100
I'd have less money to spend on what I want	2	100
I'd be unhappy	2	35
It would be a strain on me	2	10
I'd worry more	2	5

Source: Vasey, M.D. & Borkovec, T.D. (1992). A catastrophizing assessment of worrisome thoughts. *Cognitive Therapy and Research*, 16(5), 505–520. Reproduced with permission.

DSM-5 SUMMARY TABLE 6.6 *Criteria for diagnosing generalized anxiety disorder*

- Disproportionate fear or anxiety relating to areas of activity such as finances, health, family, or work/school life
- The individual experiences fear relating to at least two different areas of activity and symptoms of intense anxiety or worry will last for 3 months or more, and will be present for the majority of the time during this period
- Feelings of anxiety or worry will be accompanied by symptoms of restlessness, agitation or muscle tension
- Anxiety or worry are also associated with behaviours such as frequently seeking reassurance, avoidance of areas of activity that cause anxiety, or excessive procrastination or effort in preparing for activities
- Symptoms cannot be explained by other mental disorders such as panic disorder

associated with significant impairments in psychosocial functioning, role functioning, work productivity and health-related quality of life (Revicki, Travers, Wyrwich, Svedsater *et al.*, 2012)

6.4.1 The Aetiology of Generalized Anxiety Disorder

The challenge in explaining GAD is to understand why some individuals worry chronically and pathologically, while many other individuals – often with more stressful lifestyles – worry significantly less. Theories will therefore have to explain why GAD sufferers persist with their worrying even when it causes them significant distress.

Biological theories

There is some evidence for a genetic component in both anxiety generally and GAD specifically (Noyes, Woodman, Garvey, Cook, Suezer *et al.*, 1992), which suggests that GAD has an inherited component. Twins studies estimate the heritable component at around 30 per cent (Dellava, Kendler & Neale, 2011; Hettema, Neale & Kendler, 2001), but what appears to be inherited more than anything else is a vulnerability to anxiety disorders generally, and less an inherited vulnerability to a specific disorder such as GAD (Tambs, Czajkowsky, Roysamb, Neale *et al.*, 2009). Neuropsychological perspectives on GAD are still in their infancy, with neuroimaging studies of worry implicating prefrontal brain regions in this activity (Hoehn-Saric, Schlund & Wong, 2004; Paulesu, Sambugaro, Torti, Danelli *et al.*, 2010), but such studies have not yet provided any convincing reasons why worrying in GAD sufferers should be so extreme and distressing. Other neuroimaging studies have focused on possible abnormalities in emotional regulation in GAD sufferers (Mennin, Holaway, Fresco, Moore & Heimberg, 2007). Etkin, Prater, Hoeft, Menon & Schatzberg (2010) found reduced regulatory activity in pregenual anterior cingulate and parietal cortices in patients with GAD, suggesting a reduced capacity for emotional regulation that might be a risk factor for GAD.

Psychological theories

Information processing biases in GAD   A good deal of research has now indicated that anxious individuals, and especially those suffering GAD, have a series of **information processing biases** which appear to maintain their hypervigilance for threat, create further sources for worry, and maintain anxiety. For example, experimental evidence has demonstrated that individuals with GAD preferentially allocate attention to threatening stimuli and threatening information (Mogg & Bradley, 1998; Mathews & MacLeod, 2005). Highly anxious individuals also exhibit a threat-interpretation bias. That is, they resolve ambiguity by selecting the more negative or threatening interpretation of ambiguous information (Blanchette & Richards, 2010). Anxious individuals also have a bias towards expecting negative outcomes following predictive cues in classical conditioning studies (Davey, 1992), and they also exhibit reasoning biases that maintain threatening interpretations of events (de Jong, Weertman, Horselenberg & van den Hout, 1997; de Jong, Haenen, Schmidt & Mayer, 1998). Many of these threat-related information processing biases co-occur in individuals with anxiety and increase the anxious individual's vulnerability to interpreting daily events as threatening and challenging. It is easy to conceive of ways in which this interpretational bias might maintain anxiety by maintaining the range of potential threats perceived by

> **information processing biases**   Biases in interpreting, attending to, storing or recalling information which may give rise to dysfunctional thinking and behaving.

THE CLINICAL PERSPECTIVE – TREATMENT IN PRACTICE BOX 6.4: ATTENTION BIAS MODIFICATION (ABM)

Because highly anxious individuals have attentional and interpretational biases towards threat that are known to cause anxiety, a practical way of reversing these biases is to use experimental procedures that will neutralize them. This training procedure is known as *attention bias modification* (ABM) and has been used successfully to modify both attentional and interpretation biases in anxious individuals, and to reduce anxiety vulnerability and levels of dysfunctional anxiety (MacLeod & Mathews, 2012; Hakamata, Lissek, Bar-Haim, Britton *et al.*, 2010).

The procedure uses the classic dot probe task that has traditionally been used to measure attentional biases. Stimuli are presented on a computer screen. First, the participant sees a focus point (+), and this is followed by two words presented simultaneously for a very short duration (usually 500 milliseconds). One will be threatening, (e.g. 'Humiliated') and the other with be non-threatening (e.g. 'Dishwasher'). In the ABM procedure, immediately after the words have appeared a 'probe' appears (e.g. a colon) and the participant has to respond as quickly as possible by indicating where the probe appeared. However, in the ABM task, the probe always appears in the position where the non-threatening word had been presented. This process trains the individual to attend more rapidly to the non-threatening than the threatening word, and so ameliorates any attentional bias to threat that the participant possessed.

To read a journal article on attention bias modification go to **www.wiley-psychopathology.com/reading/ch6**

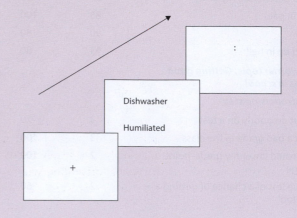

the individual (Davey, 2006). Indeed, recent studies have shown that these biases causally contribute to worrying in anxious individuals typically diagnosed with GAD (Hirsch, MacLeod, Mathews, Sandher *et al.*, 2011). Furthermore, there appears to be an important reciprocal relationship between experienced anxiety and threat-interpretation biases. Early research indicated that anxiety gave rise to threat-interpretation biases (Mathews & MacLeod, 1994; Mogg & Bradley, 1998; Butler & Mathews, 1983), but more recent research has indicated that forced learning of threat-interpretation biases also increases the individual's reported experience of anxiety (Mathews & MacLeod, 2002; Hertel, Mathews, Peterson & Kintner, 2003; Mathews & Mackintosh, 2000; Wilson, MacLeod, Mathews & Rutherford, 2006). This has given rise to interventions for anxiety and GAD that attempt to correct the attentional bias to threat found in anxious individuals (MacLeod & Mathews, 2012). This is known as **attention bias modification (ABM)** and is described in Treatment in Practice Box 6.4.

> **attention bias modification (ABM)** Highly anxious individuals have attentional and interpretational biases towards threat that are known to cause anxiety. ABM is a practical way of reversing these biases and uses experimental procedures that will neutralize them.

Beliefs, meta-beliefs and the function of worrying
We mentioned earlier that individuals with GAD persist chronically with their worrying even though it causes them considerable distress and generates symptoms that disrupt normal day-to-day living. This suggests that worrying may serve a particular *function* for such individuals, and this functionality may outweigh the negative effects of their worrying. Some theories of GAD emphasize this functional aspect of worrying. Firstly, both pathological worriers and individuals diagnosed with GAD hold strong beliefs that worrying is a necessary process that must be undertaken fully and properly in order to avoid future catastrophes (Davey, Tallis & Capuzzo, 1996; Wells, 1995; Borkovec, Hazlett-Stevens & Diaz, 1999), and these dysfunctional beliefs about the utility of worrying appear to motivate the worrier to persist with their worrying. A similar view is taken by metacognitive theories of GAD (e.g. Wells, 1995, 2010). Metacognitions are overarching cognitive processes that are responsible for appraising, monitoring and controlling thinking, and so have an important influence on what we think about and how long we will persist in thinking about something. Metacognitive theories of worry argue that the individual with GAD engages in worrying in response to negative thoughts (e.g. 'What if I lose my job?') as a means of trying to anticipate problems, avoid them or find a solution. However, individuals with GAD have developed metacognitive beliefs about worry that drive their worrying and also make that worry process distressing. These include positive metacognitive beliefs that worrying will help them solve or avoid problems, as well as negative metacognitive beliefs that worrying will be uncontrollable or harmful. It is the apparent contradiction between these two sets of beliefs that causes the worry-related distress in GAD according to this model, and metacognitive therapy is a specific form of intervention developed to deal with these GAD-causing beliefs (Wells, 2010).

Secondly, there is growing evidence that worrying may indeed be reinforced because it distracts the worrier from experiencing other negative emotions and processing even more stressful phobic images. That is, worry is an internal narrative process that prevents the individual from processing other – often more stressful – information (Borkovec, 1994; Borkovec & Lyonfields, 1993). Evidence to support this view comes from the fact that worry produces very little physiological or emotional arousal (Hoehn-Saric & McLeod, 1988) and appears to block the processing of emotional images (Borkovec, Lyonfields, Wiser & Diehl, 1993).

Dispositional characteristics of worriers
While there is still some way to go in understanding the psychological and developmental processes that lead to individuals becoming pathological worriers, there is a good deal of knowledge available about what kinds of psychological features they possess. For example, worriers are intolerant of uncertainty (Ladoucer, Talbot & Dugas, 1997; Birrell, Meares, Wilkinson & Freeston, 2011), are high on perfectionism (Pratt, Tallis & Eysenck, 1997), and have feelings of responsibility for negative outcomes (Startup & Davey, 2003; Wells & Papageorgiou, 1998), which suggests they possess characteristics that will drive them to attempt to think about resolving problematic issues. However, worriers also have poor problem-solving confidence (Davey, 1994d), and couch their worries in ways that reflect personal inadequacies and insecurities (Davey & Levy, 1998). This contrasting combination of characteristics appears to drive the individual to try to resolve problems, but the process is thwarted by their personal doubt about their own ability to solve them successfully (Davey, 1994c).

6.4.2 The Treatment of Generalized Anxiety Disorder

As with most of the anxiety disorders, GAD can be treated either with drugs or with structured psychological therapy such as CBT, or with a combination of both. However, deciding what type of treatment to use is often the most important decision for service providers and therapists – especially for a disorder that is as prevalent as GAD. Medication might be a suitable first step if immediate management of the problem is important (for instance, if the patient is experiencing extreme distress or has suicidal ideation). Otherwise, longer term structured psychological therapy (such as CBT) or self-help programmes should be offered. Some self-help options are outlined in my blog

 To read more about why we worry go to
http://tinyurl.com/clclwfd

on '10 tips to manage your worrying' and in Chapter 6 of our CBT self-help guide for managing anxiety (Davey, Cavanagh, Jones, Turner & Whittington, 2012).

Pharmacological treatments

Because GAD involves chronic daily anxiety and emotional discomfort, we might expect that anxiolytics – such as the benzodiazepines – would be the first line of treatment for sufferers. However, at least 50 per cent of GAD sufferers receive initial treatment with antidepressants such as selective serotonin reuptake inhibitors (SSRIs) or serotonin–norepinephrine reuptake inhibitors (SNRIs) on the basis of their proven effectiveness in treating the symptoms of GAD in clinical trials, while only around 35 per cent are treated with benzodiazepines (Berger, Edelsberg, Bollu, Alvir et al., 2011). Treatment with antidepressants is justified in many cases because GAD is regularly comorbid with depression and SSRIs tend to be better tolerated than benzodiazepines. Nevertheless, the long-term effectiveness of pharmacological treatments for GAD is questionable given the relative lack of longitudinal outcome studies and poor identification of patient groups who are likely to respond positively to medication-based interventions (Baldwin, Ajel & Garner, 2010).

Psychological treatments

stimulus control treatment An early behavioural intervention for worry in GAD which adopted the principle of stimulus control, based on the conditioning principle that the environments in which behaviours are enacted come to control their future occurrence and can act to elicit those behaviours.

Psychological treatments for GAD have developed using both behavioural and cognitive methodologies. For example, **stimulus control treatment** was originally developed out of behaviour therapy principles for dealing with worry behaviours, while a number of effective variants of CBT are now available for dealing with the pathological worrying found in GAD (e.g. cognitive restructuring and metacognitive therapy).

Stimulus control treatment One of the earliest behavioural interventions for worry in GAD adopted the principle of stimulus control. This is based on the conditioning principle that the environments in which behaviours are enacted come to control their future occurrence, and can act to elicit those behaviours (the principle of stimulus control). Because worrying can occur almost anywhere, and so come under the control of a vast range of contexts, the first aim of stimulus control treatment is to limit the contexts in which worrying occurs. This is achieved by telling clients that they can worry – but only for a specific period in a particular location each day (Borkovec, Wilkinson, Folensbee & Lerman, 1983). For example, as outlined in Treatment in Practice Box 6.5, they are instructed to worry at a specific time (e.g. between waking and the end of breakfast) or in a particular location (the living room).

Cognitive behaviour therapy In the previous section we have reviewed a number of psychological theories of GAD which suggest that cognitive biases and dysfunctional beliefs about the function of worrying may be central to the development and maintenance of the disorder. This being so, integrated cognitive behavioural therapy seems a suitable method to tackle GAD. CBT for GAD normally consists of a number of elements, the main ones being:

- self-monitoring
- relaxation training
- cognitive restructuring
- behavioural rehearsal.

THE CLINICAL PERSPECTIVE – TREATMENT IN PRACTICE BOX 6.5: STIMULUS CONTROL TREATMENT FOR GENERALIZED ANXIETY DISORDER

Stimulus control treatment for GAD is an effective treatment for reducing the frequency of worry by controlling the range of contexts in which the activity occurs (see section 6.4.2).

There are four basic instructions underpinning this procedure:

1. Learn to identify worrisome thoughts and other thoughts that are unnecessary or unpleasant. Distinguish these from necessary or pleasant thoughts related to the present moment.

2. Establish a half-hour worry period to take place at the same time and in the same location each day.

3. When you catch yourself worrying, postpone the worry to the worry period and replace it with attending to present-moment experience.

4. Make use of the half-hour worry period to worry about your concerns and to engage in problem solving to eliminate those concerns.

Source: From Borkovec (2005); Borkovec, Wilkinson, Folensbee & Lerman (1983).

Self-monitoring involves making the client aware of their fixed patterns of behaviour and the triggers that may precipitate worry. These triggers are often thoughts about future events that have very low probabilities of happening (e.g. the accidental death of a loved one while driving to work), and the client's attention is drawn to the fact that these are cognitively constructed rather than real events. **Relaxation training** is an obvious way of dealing with the chronic stress experienced by GAD sufferers. The specific technique of progressive muscular relaxation is often used (Bernstein, Borkovec & Hazlett-Stevens, 2000), and relaxation is found to be as effective as some forms of cognitive therapy (Arntz, 2003). **Cognitive restructuring** methods are used to challenge the biases that GAD sufferers hold about how frequently bad events might happen (Beck, Emery & Greenberg, 1985), and to generate thoughts that are more accurate (Borkovec, 2005). One way of doing this is by using an outcome diary in which the client writes down on a daily basis their worries and how likely they think the focus of their worries will actually happen. Clients can then compare their own inflated estimate of the likelihood

of the event with subsequent reality (Borkovec, Hazlett-Stevens & Diaz, 1999). Other types of cognitive restructuring involve the challenging and replacement of dysfunctional metacognitive beliefs about worrying – known as *metacognitive therapy* (Wells, 1999, 2010) – or the belief held by pathological worriers that uncertainty has to be resolved by thinking through every possible scenario (Dugas, Ladouceur, Leger, Freeston *et al.*, 2003). Finally, **behavioural rehearsal** involves either the actual or imagined rehearsal of adaptive coping responses that need to be deployed when a worry trigger is encountered. These coping strategies may involve the deployment of relaxation exercises or pleasant distracting activities designed to avoid worry (Butler, Fennell, Robson & Gelder, 1991). CBT for GAD has been shown to be effective with or without the use of pharmacological treatments (Lang, 2004), and has long-term effectiveness for a significant proportion of clients (Durham, Chambers, MacDonald, Power & Major, 2003). However, recent meta-analyses suggest that while CBT treatments for GAD have improved over the past 10–15 years, there is still a significant percentage of sufferers who fail to recover fully following cognitive treatments for GAD (Hanrahan, Jones, Field & Davey, 2013).

relaxation training A method of dealing with the chronic stress experienced by psychopathology sufferers. A specific technique of progressive muscular relaxation is often used, and relaxation is found to be as effective as some forms of cognitive therapy.

cognitive restructuring Methods used to challenge the biases that a client might hold about how frequently bad events might happen and to generate thoughts that are more accurate.

behavioural rehearsal A coping strategy that involves either the actual or imagined rehearsal of adaptive coping responses that need to be deployed when a worry trigger is encountered.

SELF-TEST QUESTIONS

- What is the cardinal diagnostic feature of GAD?
- What are the features of worry in GAD that make it a distressing experience for the sufferer?
- How do information processing biases and cognitive factors contribute to the acquisition, maintenance and experience of anxiety in GAD?
- How do psychological treatments of GAD attempt to bring the activity of worrying under control?

SECTION SUMMARY

6.4   GENERALIZED ANXIETY DISORDER (GAD)

- The cardinal diagnostic characteristic of GAD is chronic uncontrollable worrying, which is accompanied by physical symptoms such as irritability, muscle tension, fatigue, poor concentration, restlessness, and disturbed sleep.

- Over 5 per cent of the population will be diagnosed with GAD in their lifetime, and 12 per cent of those who attend anxiety disorder clinics will present with GAD.

- Individuals with GAD possess an information processing bias which appears to maintain their hypervigilance for threat and create the opportunity to catastrophically worry about events. There is evidence that these information processing biases may actually cause anxiety generally, and can be manipulated therapeutically using attention bias modification techniques.

- Worrying in GAD appears to be maintained by dysfunctional beliefs about the utility of worrying, which appear to motivate the individual with GAD to persist with their worrying.

- Anxiolytics are useful for dealing with the anxiety symptoms exhibited by individuals with GAD, but treatments based on controlling the process of worrying and challenging dysfunctional beliefs about worrying appear to have a more long-term benefit.

6.5 OBSESSIVE COMPULSIVE DISORDER (OCD)

We have all occasionally gone back to check whether we locked a door, and we have all experienced a sudden, intrusive thought that we find disturbing and out of place (e.g. harming our own child). However, for the person with **obsessive compulsive disorder (OCD)** such thoughts and actions are repeated often and result in a distressing and disabling way of life. OCD has two important and sometimes independent characteristics. **Obsessions** are intrusive and recurring thoughts that the individual finds disturbing and uncontrollable. These obsessive thoughts frequently take the form of causing some harm or distress to oneself or to some important other person (such as a partner or offspring). Common obsessions also take the form of fear of contamination (i.e. contaminating oneself or important others), and thoughts about harm, accidents, and unacceptable sex (Rowa & Purdon, 2005; Berry & Laskey, 2012). Obsessive thoughts can also take the form of pathological doubting and indecision, and this may lead to sufferers developing repetitive behaviour patterns such as compulsive checking or washing. Very often, obsessive thoughts can be 'autogenous' – that is, they seem uncontrollable and 'come out of the blue' – and it is this autogenous characteristic that helps to make obsessive thoughts distressing. **Compulsions** represent repetitive or ritualized behaviour patterns that the individual feels driven to perform in order to prevent some negative outcome happening. This can take the form of ritualized and persistent checking of doors and windows (to ensure that the house is safe), or ritualized washing activities designed to prevent infection and contamination. Ritualized compulsions such as these also act to reduce the stress and anxiety caused by the sufferer's obsessive

obsessive compulsive disorder (OCD) A disorder characterized either by obsessions (intrusive and recurring thoughts that the individual finds disturbing and uncontrollable) or by compulsions (ritualized behaviour patterns that the individual feels driven to perform in order to prevent some negative outcome happening).

obsessions Intrusive and recurring thoughts that an individual finds disturbing and uncontrollable.

compulsions Repetitive or ritualized behaviour patterns that an individual feels driven to perform in order to prevent some negative outcome happening.

fears. While the main compulsions are usually related to checking or washing, compulsions can also manifest less regularly as compulsive hoarding (Steketee, Frost & Kyrios, 2003), compulsive hair-pulling or skin picking, superstitious ritualized movements, or the systematic arranging of objects (Radomsky & Rachman, 2004). In most cases, compulsions are clearly excessive, and are usually recognized as so by the sufferer. Rituals can become rigid, stereotyped sequences of behaviours that the individual is driven to perform as a result of cognitive triggers such as intrusive thoughts related to the individual's specific fears. For example, individuals distressed by unwanted immoral or blasphemous thoughts can attempt to suppress the thought and reduce anxiety by indulging in compulsive acts such as counting backwards from a number until the thought has gone.

Diagnosis and prevalence

In DSM-5, the importance of OCD was recognized by including OCD and its related disorders as a separate chapter independent of anxiety disorders generally, and this acknowledges some of the special features that OCD and related disorders possess. DSM-5 Summary Table 6.7 shows the main diagnostic criteria for OCD. Diagnosis is dependent on the obsessions or compulsions causing marked distress, being time consuming, or significantly interfering with the person's normal daily living. This latter diagnostic criterion delineates OCD compulsions

DSM-5 SUMMARY TABLE 6.7 *Criteria for obsessive compulsive disorder*

- Presence of obsessions such as repeated and unwanted thoughts, urges or images that the individual tries to ignore or suppress, and/or

- Presence of compulsions where the individual feels compelled to repeat certain behaviours or mental activities

- The individual believes that the behaviours will prevent a catastrophic event but these beliefs have no realistic connections to the imagined event, or are markedly excessive

- Obsessions and compulsions consume at least 1 hour per day and cause difficulty in performing other functions

- Symptoms cannot be explained by the effects of other mental or medical disorders, drug abuse or medication

OBSESSIVE COMPULSIVE DISORDER

Luke was 21 years old and attending university, living a considerable distance from his family with whom he had always been close. It was 2 months before his final year exams and his alarm went off at 8.30 a.m. Turning to switch off his alarm, Luke was immediately overwhelmed by the feeling of dread that had been with him constantly since the beginning of term.

He quickly got out of bed and went to the bathroom. Luke washed his hands and brushed his teeth before washing his hands twice more. Stepping into the shower Luke scrubbed himself all over with shower gel, and washed his hands several more times in between cleaning the rest of his body. After rinsing his hair through Luke washed his hands again and got out of the shower; by now it was 9.30.

Luke began to dry his hair but he felt that his hands were still dirty, though by now they were red raw. He washed them again, rapidly rubbing the backs of his hands and cleaning repeatedly under his nails. They still felt dirty. Telling himself not to be stupid, Luke moved to the door of the bathroom but felt a strong urge to go back and clean his hands once more. The feeling was too strong to resist so he quickly rinsed his hands again, dousing them in sanitizer gel and rushed out of the bathroom, knowing he would be late for his lecture.

Before he could leave the house, Luke checked that the back door was locked and all his housemates' windows were securely closed, then he went back to the bathroom to wash his hands twice more. Grabbing a clean towel from the wash, Luke carefully wrapped up his hand so he could open the front door without touching the dirty handle. Once the door was open, Luke ran back inside to check that he had remembered to secure the windows in all his friends' rooms and to close all the doors.

Pulling the front door shut with his foot, Luke tested it was firmly shut and then ran towards the bus stop. It was now 10.15 and he was already 15 minutes late. A bus was arriving just as he reached the stop, hot and out of breath. Sitting on the bus, Luke felt the sweat on the palms of his hands and wiped them clean on a tissue, repeatedly cleansing them with the sanitizer gel he always carried with him.

Halfway through the journey, Luke began to panic that he hadn't locked up the house and imagined coming home to find he had been burgled and all his housemates' belongings had been ransacked. Luke got off at the next stop and took another bus back home, only to find that the doors and windows were locked. Cursing himself for his irrationality, Luke turned to leave the house once more but, looking at his watch, saw it was now 11.30 and his lecture was almost over.

Later on, when Luke was diagnosed with obsessive compulsive disorder, 6 months after failing his exams, he felt a huge sense of relief and was pleased that he could now give his friends and family a logical explanation for his behaviour. Luke is now receiving treatment for his OCD and, when he explained his condition to the university, they agreed he could return and re-sit his exams.

Clinical Commentary

This example shows how obsessions and compulsions in OCD are often compelling and difficult for the sufferer to resist – even when the individual is aware that these thoughts and actions are 'stupid' or irrational. Luke's compulsions are fueled by the 'feelings of dread' that he experiences most mornings when he wakes up, and this provides the highly anxious state under which compulsions (such as compulsive washing) are performed. 'Doubting' is also a common feature of OCD, and Luke experiences this on his way to university in the form of doubting whether the doors and windows are locked. The high levels of inflated responsibility usually possessed by OCD sufferers mean that Luke is driven to continually check that his doubts are unfounded.

from other urges, such as the uncontrollable desire to eat, drink or gamble, because these are often engaged in with pleasure (see Chapters 9 and 10 for discussions of these alternative types of compulsions).

OCD onset is usually gradual and frequently begins to manifest itself in early adolescence or early adulthood following a stressful event such as pregnancy, childbirth, relationship or work problems (Kringlen, 1970). OCD

symptoms are also a common way for anxiety to manifest itself in childhood, and this is discussed further in Chapter 16. Lifetime prevalence is around 2.5 per cent with a 1-year prevalence rate of between 0.7 and 2.1 per cent, and affects women marginally more frequently than men (Stein, Forde, Anderson & Walker, 1997; Adam, Meinlschmidt, Gloster & Lieb, 2012). Few studies have investigated the effect of cultural factors on the prevalence and manifestation of OCD symptoms. However, a cross-cultural study reported by Fontenelle, Mendlowicz, Marques & Versiani (2004) concluded that universal characteristics of sufferers regardless of cultural background included a predominance of females, a relatively early age of onset, and a preponderance of mixed obsessions and compulsions. The exception to this was the apparent content of obsessions, which in Brazilian and Middle Eastern samples exhibited a predominance of aggressive or religious obsessions (compared with North America, Europe and Africa).

OCD-related disorders

DSM-5 has divided OCD-type problems into a number of separate diagnostic categories. The main OCD diagnostic category is described in DSM-5 Summary Table 6.7, but other OCD-related diagnostic categories include:

1. *Body dysmorphic disorder*: This is a pre-occupation with perceived defects or flaws in physical appearance that are not usually perceived by others. This gives rise to compulsive grooming,

mirror checking, and reassurance seeking (see Focus Point 6.3).

2. *Hoarding disorder:* **Hoarding disorder** centres around a difficulty discarding or parting with possessions to the point where the individual's living area is severely congested by clutter (see Focus Point 6.4).

> **hoarding disorder** Difficulty discarding or parting with possessions to the point where the individual's living area is severely congested by clutter.

3. *Hair-pulling disorder* (**trichotillomania**): the individual compulsively pulls out their own hair resulting in significant hair loss.

> **trichotillomania** Hair-pulling disorder in which the individual compulsively pulls out their own hair resulting in significant hair loss.

4. *Skin-picking disorder:* **Skin-picking disorder** is the recurrent picking of the skin that results in skin lesions.

> **skin-picking disorder** Recurrent picking of the skin that results in skin lesions.

See Davey, Dash & Meeten (2014) for a fuller description of OCD-related disorders.

FOCUS POINT 6.3

BODY DYSMORPHIC DISORDER

One OCD-related disorder described in DSM-5 is body dysmorphic disorder (BDD). This is a preoccupation with assumed defects in appearance that are often imaginary, but if there is a physical anomaly, those suffering from BDD will greatly exaggerate its importance. Common complaints include flaws in facial features or facial asymmetry, hair thinning, acne, wrinkles, scars, vascular markings, irregular complexions, or excessive facial hair. Other common preoccupations include body shape generally (e.g. preoccupations with being obese or overweight), and dissatisfaction with specific body parts, such as breasts, genitals, buttocks. Sufferers will often be so embarrassed about their supposed appearance defects that they will often only talk about them in general terms, and may simply refer to themselves as being 'ugly'. The way in which BDD overlaps with OCD is in the obsessive thoughts that sufferers have about their appearance, and sufferers can also develop ritualistic compulsions around their defects, spending many hours a day viewing themselves in mirrors or attempting to deal with their problems with excessive grooming behaviour (e.g. skin picking, hair combing, applying cosmetics, dieting, and suchlike), with such behaviours usually adding to the distress that is experienced. Concerns about appearance in BDD are frequently accompanied by a host of repetitive and time-consuming behaviours, aimed at verifying, camouflaging, or enhancing the person's appearance, and

© RioPatuca. Used under license from Shutterstock.com.

one particular repetitive behaviour is known as 'mirror gazing' (Windheim, Veale & Anson, 2011). Studies have shown that about 80 per cent of individuals with BDD will repetitively check their appearance in mirrors – often for considerable periods of time. Interestingly, the remaining 20 per cent tend to avoid mirrors altogether (Veale & Riley, 2001). Mirror gazing can be construed as a 'safety seeking behaviour' which briefly acts to reduce distress. However, for individuals with low body-image satisfaction mirror gazing for more than 3.5 minutes results in a more negative opinion about their attractiveness (Mulken & Jansen, 2009), and mirror gazing behaviour in the longer term increases distress, maintains negative beliefs about appearance, and reinforces repetitive appearance-checking behaviours (Veale & Riley, 2001).

Individuals with body dysmorphic disorder also develop dysfunctional beliefs about their appearance, and are quite convinced that their own perceptions are correct and undistorted. As a result they may regularly seek cosmetic surgery in order to correct their 'defects'. In a study of individuals seeking cosmetic surgery, Aouizerate, Pujol, Grabot, Faytout et al. (2003) found that 9.1 per cent of applicants were diagnosable with body dysmorphic disorder. In fact, in those applicants who had no defects or only a slight physical defect, 40 per cent were diagnosable with body dysmorphic disorder.

A preoccupation with apparent physical defects often leads to the catastrophising of these characteristics, and sufferers will frequently comment on their appearance to others in negative ways (e.g. 'I am ugly', 'I am fat'). Nevertheless, regular reassurance from others fails to change these views, and the sufferer can slip into a negative decline that incurs further psychopathology such as major depression, anxiety, social anxiety disorder,

deliberate self-harm and suicide attempts (Phillips, 2001). In addition, adolescents with body dysmorphic disorder experience high levels of impairment in school and work functioning, with studies reporting attempted suicide rates of around 45 per cent (Phillips, Didie, Menard, Pagano et al., 2006).

The exact prevalence rates of BDD disorder are unclear, although a nationwide German study suggested that the point prevalence of BDD was 1.8 per cent (Buhlmann, Glaesmer, Mewes, Fama et al., 2010). This study also indicated that those diagnosable with BDD had high rates of previous cosmetic surgery (15.6%), and higher rates of suicidal ideation (31%). BDD is also relatively common in individuals who already have a diagnosis of OCD, with a lifetime prevalence rate for BDD of 12.1 per cent in individuals with OCD (Costa, Assuncao, Ferrao, Conrado et al., 2012), reinforcing the view that OCD and BDD may be related disorders.

FOCUS POINT 6.4

HOARDING DISORDER

© Barcroft Media via Getty Images

safety risks. Initial epidemiology studies suggest that hoarding disorder afflicts around 5.8 per cent of the current population, and affects men and women equally (Timpano, Exner, Glaesmer, Rief et al., 2011).

Individuals with hoarding disorder may often try to organize their possessions, but their lack of organisational skills simple makes the chaos worse. The disorder is particularly associated with an inability to throw away even normally disposable items such as food and sweet wrappings. If the individual has other, more classic, OCD symptoms this can compound the problem. For example, fear of contamination and superstitious thoughts (e.g. 'throwing something away will result in a catastrophe of some kind') may prevent the sufferer from touching or throwing away items. However, the accumulation of clutter in hoarding disorder is not simply something that is tolerated by the individual, the hoarding causes clinically significant distress and has a significant impact on social and occupational functioning.

Hoarding Disorder is a new diagnostic category included in DSM-5 (Frost, Steketee & Tolin, 2012; Pertusa, Frost, Fullana, Samuels et al., 2010). It is a complex problem made up of three specific attributes: (1) collecting too many items (some sufferers will actually actively collect or steal more items to hoard), (2) difficulty parting with or getting rid of hoarded items, and (3) general problems with organising their possessions, probably as a result of problems with more fundamental cognitive processes such as information processing, attention, categorisation, and decision making (e.g. Tolin & Villavicencio, 2011). The result of this hoarding is large piles of clutter that make living spaces impassable, home utilities (such as a toilet) unusable, and this can pose both health and

Hoarding appears to begin in childhood or adolescence, with a chronic and progressive course throughout the lifespan. This means that many sufferers of hoarding disorder are elderly, and it is often comorbid with dementia and other psychiatric diagnoses such as major depression, social anxiety disorder and inattentive ADHD (Frost, Steketee & Tolin, 2011). Hoarding disorder can also be restricted to collecting and hoarding individual types of items. *Animal hoarding* is one recently identified example that can lead to considerable animal suffering and neglect (Patronek, 1999; Frost, Patronek & Rosenfield, 2011).

6.5.1 The Aetiology of Obsessive Compulsive Disorder

When considering the aetiology of OCD, the reader should be aware that it represents a psychological problem that possesses a number of quite different, and often independent, features. For example, obsessions do not always occur with compulsions, and the two main types of compulsions (i.e. washing and checking) rarely occur together in the same individual. This means that many theories of the aetiology of OCD have been developed to address only some of its features (e.g. thought suppression accounts are relevant to explaining only obsessive thoughts), and they are not meant to be universal explanations of OCD. Bear this in mind when reading through the following sections.

Biological factors

As with other anxiety disorders, there is evidence of an inherited component to OCD. Twin studies have found high concordance for OCD in monozygotic twins (80–87 per cent) compared with dizygotic twins (47–50 per cent) (Carey & Gottesman, 1981). Furthermore, family relatives of individuals with OCD are also more likely to have a diagnosis of OCD than non-family controls (Lenane, Swedo, Leonard, Pauls *et al.*, 1990; Hanna, Veenstra-VanderWeele, Cox, Boehnke *et al.*, 2002), with some studies concluding that familial transmission of OCD is a result of genetic rather than environmental factors (Nestadt, Samuels, Riddle, Bienvenu *et al.*, 2000). More recent genetic linkage studies have also begun to identify some of the candidate genes for the transmission of the inherited component to OCD (e.g. see Wang, Samuels, Chang, Grados *et al.*, 2008).

Onset of OCD can also be associated with traumatic brain injury or encephalitis (Jenike, 1986), which suggests that there may be a neuropsychological deficit in some forms of OCD. This neuropsychological deficit may give rise to the 'doubting' that things have been done properly, which is a central feature of many forms of OCD. Areas of the brain that have been identified as important in this respect include the frontal lobes and the basal ganglia. When sufferers are shown stimuli representative of their obsession or compulsion (e.g. an unlocked door) blood flow increases in both the frontal lobes and the basal ganglia, suggesting that these areas may have at least some role in OCD (Rauch, Jenike, Alpert, Baer *et al.*, 1994). In other neuropsychological studies, OCD sufferers appear to demonstrate a variety of basic information processing and executive functioning deficits (the latter referring to processes that are involved in planning and attentional control), and these include deficits in spatial working memory, spatial recognition, visual attention, visual memory, and motor response

initiation (Greisberg & McKay, 2003; Rao, Reddy, Kumar, Kandavel & Chandrashekar, 2008). An alternative view of brain dysfunction and OCD is based on findings from neuroimaging studies. For example, Rapoport (1989) has argued that obsessions and compulsions are genetically stored and learnt behaviours that are involuntarily triggered by the brain. Baxter, Ackermann, Swerdlow, Brody *et al.* (2000) have developed this approach by suggesting that uncontrollable compulsions in OCD result from the brain being unable to inhibit these genetically stored behaviours. In particular, they use evidence from neuroimaging studies to argue that OCD compulsions result from the failure of inhibitory pathways projecting via the basal ganglia to inhibit innate behaviour patterns (Saxena, Brody, Schwartz & Baxter, 1998). While this hypothesis can account for the rather restricted set of behaviours that manifest as compulsions (i.e. it is argued that only certain behaviours have been genetically stored) it still represents an oversimplification of how brain structures such as the basal ganglia might be involved in OCD (Frampton, 2003).

Psychological factors

Memory deficits 'Doubting' is a central feature of OCD, and especially the compulsions associated with the disorder. As a result, it has been suggested that OCD may be characterized by memory deficits that give rise to the doubting that, for example, doors have been locked or hands have been washed properly. Memory deficit models take a number of different forms. It has been suggested that OCD sufferers may have:

- a general memory deficit (Sher, Mann & Frost, 1984);
- less confidence in the validity of their memories (Watts, 1993); or
- a deficit in the ability to distinguish between the memory of real and imagined actions (Brown, Kosslyn, Breiter, Baer & Jenike, 1994).

However, evidence supporting the role of these memory deficits in OCD is equivocal (Hermans, Engelen, Grouwels, Joos *et al.*, 2008), and recent theoretical views suggest that the deficits that give rise to OCD 'doubting' may not be problems with memory or working memory per se, but are the result of a deficit in executive functioning in general (Harkin & Kessler, 2011). For example, if OCD sufferers spend a lot of time checking both relevant and irrelevant things on a daily basis, this will overload executive processes and result in poor encoding of information and poor attention to relevant information, which in turn will cause memory deficits. This is consistent with another body of evidence which suggests that lack of confidence in recall may be a *consequence* of compulsive checking or washing rather than a cause of it (van den Hout & Kindt, 2003; Harkin & Kessler, 2009; Radomsky & Alcolado, 2010). In effect, the more someone checks, the less confident they will be about what they have checked.

Clinical constructs and OCD   Clinical psychology researchers regularly use their clinical experience as a starting point for understanding the causes of a disorder; from this experience they develop what are known as **clinical constructs**, and the purpose of these constructs is to link thoughts, beliefs and cognitive processes to sub-

> **clinical constructs** Clinical psychology researchers develop constructs in order to describe the combination of thoughts, beliefs, cognitive processes and symptoms observed in individual psychopathologies.

sequent symptoms. These constructs can be developed in such a way that they can be objectively measured (e.g. with questionnaires) and in many cases manipulated experimentally. This then provides an insight into how symptoms are affected by the cognitive factors that clinicians observe in

> To read the author's blog about clinical constructs go to **http://tinyurl.com/k9xx9g2**

their everyday practice. In this section we will briefly look at the role of three clinical constructs that have helped us to understand OCD. These are *inflated responsibility*, *thought–action fusion*, and *mental contamination*. A critical view of clinical constructs can be found in my blog.

Inflated responsibility   Everyone experiences uncontrollable intrusive thoughts on almost a daily basis (Rachman & DeSilva, 1978). However, what differentiates these normal intrusive thoughts from the distressing and obsessive thoughts experienced in OCD is the meaning attached to them by OCD sufferers. Individuals diagnosed with OCD appear to have developed a series of dysfunctional beliefs about their obsessional thoughts. For example:

1. Because they had the thought, they feel responsible for its content – so, if a sufferer thinks of murdering their child, they believe they may be going crazy and *will* murder their child (Salkovskis, 1985).

2. Sufferers appraise obsessional thoughts as having potentially harmful consequences and this causes intense anxiety and triggers compulsive actions designed to eradicate the thought or to make sure the perceived harm does not occur (e.g. compulsive thought suppression strategies such as counting backwards or checking and re-checking locks and windows to ensure that the home is safe).

3. Individuals with OCD tend to have inflated conceptions of their own responsibility for

preventing harm, and this **inflated responsibility** appears to be an important vulnerability factor in developing OCD (Salkovkis, 1985; Rachman, 1998).

Salkovskis, Rachman, Ladouceur, Freeston, *et al.* (1996) have defined inflated responsibility as 'the belief that one has power which is pivotal to bring about or prevent subjectively cru-

> **inflated responsibility** The belief that one has power to bring about or prevent subjectively crucial negative outcomes. These outcomes are perceived as essential to prevent. They may be actual: that is, having consequences in the real world, and/or at a moral level.

cial negative outcomes. These outcomes are perceived as essential to prevent. They may be actual, that is having consequences in the real world, and/or at a moral level.' There is considerable evidence that inflated responsibility is a characteristic that is a central causal feature of obsessive compulsive disorder generally (Salkovskis, Shafran, Rachman & Freeston, 1999; Salkovskis, Wroes, Gledhill, Morrison, Forrester *et al.*, 2000) and compulsive checking specifically (Rachman, 2002; Bouchard, Rheaume & Ladouceur, 1999). Experimental studies that have manipulated inflated responsibility have shown that it *causes* increases in perseverative activities such as compulsive checking (Lopatka & Rachman, 1995; Bouchard, Rheaume & Ladouceur, 1999).

Thought–action fusion   It is a common clinical experience that many individuals with OCD believe that their unpleasant, unacceptable thoughts can influence events in the world. For example, if they have an intrusive thought about an airplane crashing, they believe this may cause an airplane to crash. If they have a thought about becoming ill, they believe this makes it more likely that they will become ill. This is known as **thought–action fusion** (TAF) (Shafran & Rachman, 2004), and it is a belief that simply having thoughts can in some way directly affect what happens in the world. If the

> **thought–action fusion** A dysfunctional assumption held by OCD sufferers that having a thought about an action is like performing it.

supposed consequences of thoughts are aversive or negative, then this will cause the sufferer to try and suppress these thoughts (see section below on thought suppression), and it will generate considerable distress and anxiety. Interestingly, TAF will be related to the degree to which an individual assigns importance to thoughts, and this is something that in many cases has been shown to be closely related to religiosity. For example, the degree to which individuals assign importance to thoughts is also related to Christian religiosity (Abramowitz, Deacon, Woods & Tolin, 2004), and Christian groups have been shown to score higher on measures of TAF than other religious groups (Siev & Cohen, 2007). However, the relationship between religiosity, TAF and OCD symptoms is less straightforward, and recent studies suggest

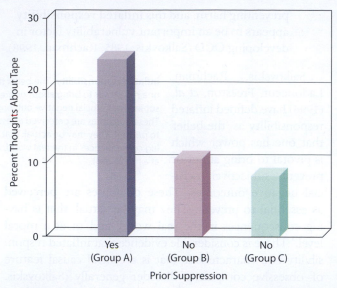

FIGURE 6.6 *After listening to a tape of a recorded story, participants were then asked to verbalize their stream of conscious thoughts. However, participants in one group (Group A) were asked to suppress their thoughts of the tape during this period, while other participants were not (Groups B and C). In the final period, all participants were asked to think about anything. The figure shows that participants in the suppression condition subsequently reported more thoughts about the tape than participants in the other groups (a 'rebound' effect).*
Source: After Clark, D.M., Ball, S. & Pape, D. (1991). An experimental investigation of thought suppression. *Behaviour Research and Therapy*, 29(3), 253–257.

that moral TAF translates into OCD symptoms only in religious groups for whom the importance of thoughts is not the norm (Siev, Chambless & Huppert, 2010).

Mental contamination

While there are a significant number of OCD sufferers who fear actual contamination (e.g. by contact with dirt, germs, and suchlike), there is also another group for whom comparable feelings of dirtiness can be provoked without any physical contact with a contaminant, and this has come to be called **mental contamination** (Rachman, 2004, 2006). Mental contamination can be caused by images, thoughts, and memories, and tends to be caused by a violation of some kind by another person, such as degradation, betrayal, emotional abuse, physical abuse or humiliation, which gives rise to feelings of dirtiness or pollution, and in many cases may be associated with compulsive washing or cleansing (Rachman, 2010; Zhong & Liljenquist, 2006). In addition to these feelings of contamination, individuals also experience anxiety, disgust, shame, anger, guilt, and sadness (Rachman, Radomsky, Elliot & Zysk, 2012). While mental contamination seems to represent a very specific form

> **mental contamination** Feelings of dirtiness can be provoked without any physical contact with a contaminant. Mental contamination can be caused by images, thoughts, and memories and may be associated with compulsive washing and even betrayal experiences.

of OCD contamination fear that is caused by quite specific experiences, it is possible to ameliorate the symptoms using adaptations of standard CBT interventions (Warnock-Parkes, Salkovskis & Rachman, 2012).

Thought suppression Because individuals with obsessive thoughts find these intrusions aversive and distressing, they may try to actively suppress them (using either **thought suppression** or distraction techniques). However, there is good evidence that actively suppressing an unwanted thought will actually cause it to occur more frequently

> **thought suppression** A defence mechanism used by individuals with obsessive thoughts to actively suppress them (using either thought suppression or distraction techniques).

once the period of suppression or inhibition is over (known as a 'rebound' effect), and this may account to some degree for the fact that OCD sufferers experience significantly more intrusions than non-clinical populations (Wenzlaff & Wegner, 2000). Wenzlaff, Klein & Wegner (1991) have also argued that suppressing an unpleasant thought induces a strong negative emotional state that results in the suppressed thought becoming associated with that negative mood state. Whenever that negative mood state occurs in the future, it is therefore more likely to elicit the unwanted and aversive thought, and this may also contribute to the OCD sufferer experiencing regular, uncontrollable intrusions.

Perseveration and the role of mood OCD is one example of a number of perseverative psychopathologies, each of which is characterized by the dysfunctional perseveration of certain thoughts, behaviours or activities (others include pathological worrying and chronic rumination in depression). In almost all examples of these psychopathologies the perseveration (e.g. compulsive checking, washing) is viewed as excessive, out of proportion to the functional purpose that it serves, and a source of emotional discomfort for the individual concerned. In this context, some theories have attempted to explain why OCD sufferers *persevere* at an activity for significantly longer than non-sufferers. One such account is the **mood-as-input hypothesis** (Meeten & Davey, 2011; Davey, 2006; MacDonald & Davey, 2005a). This model states that OCD sufferers persevere with their compulsive activities because (1) they use an implicit 'stop rule' for the compulsive activity which says they must only stop when they are sure they have completed the task fully and properly (known as an 'as many as can' stop rule); and (2) they undertake the task in a strong negative mood (usually an anxious mood). The mood-as-input account claims that OCD sufferers use their concurrent mood as 'information' to assess whether they have met their strict stop rule criteria. However, their endemic

> **mood-as-input hypothesis** A hypothesis claiming that people use their concurrent mood as information about whether they have successfully completed a task or not.

negative mood is interpreted as providing information that they have *not* completed the task properly – so they persevere (i.e. a negative mood implies all is not well and the criteria have not been met). This model is supported by the fact that the inflated responsibility that OCD sufferers possess is likely to give rise to deployed 'as many as can' stop rules (to ensure that, for example, checking or washing is done properly so that no harm will ensue). Interestingly, and consistent with the mood-as-input account, inflated responsibility is not a *sufficient* condition for an individual to persevere at a compulsive activity – it has to be accompanied by negative mood (MacDonald & Davey, 2005b). This is because a negative mood is continually being interpreted as providing feedback that the important goals of the compulsive activity have not been met, so the activity needs to be continued.

Summary   As we mentioned at the outset of this section on aetiology, many of these theories are designed to address only specific features of OCD rather than represent universal explanations of the disorder. For example, some theories try to explain why 'doubting' is a central feature of OCD (these include both neurophysiological and memory deficit models), others address why intrusive thoughts become so aversive and uncontrollable (e.g. inflated responsibility and thought suppression accounts), and yet others try to explain why individuals with OCD show dysfunctional perseveration at activities such as checking or washing (e.g. the mood-as-input model). Undoubtedly, a full account of OCD will contain at least some, if not all, of these different elements of explanation.

6.5.2 The Treatment of Obsessive Compulsive Disorder

Exposure and ritual prevention (ERP) treatments

The most common, and arguably the most successful, therapy for OCD is **exposure and ritual prevention treatment** (also known as exposure and response prevention treatment) (Meyer, 1966; Kyrios, 2003). This therapy consists of two components. The first is graded exposure to the situations and thoughts that trigger distress – e.g. for someone with compulsive washing this may involve touching a dirty dish or imagining touching a dirty dish (the latter is called *imaginal exposure*) (see Treatment in Practice Box 6.6). Clients will encounter their triggers in a graded and planned way until distress levels have significantly decreased. The second component is ritual or response

> **exposure and ritual prevention treatment** A means of treatment for obsessive compulsive disorder (OCD) which involves graded exposure to the thoughts that trigger distress, followed by the development of behaviours designed to prevent the individual's compulsive rituals.

prevention, which involves strategies such as practising competing behaviours, habit reversal, or modification of compulsive rituals (again, see Treatment in Practice Box 6.6). Preventing the client from engaging in their rituals:

1. Allows anxiety to extinguish by habituating the links between obsessions and their associated distress;

2. Eliminates ritualistic behaviours that may negatively reinforce anxiety (Steketee, 1993);

3. Contributes to the disconfirmation of dysfunctional beliefs (e.g. 'I will catch an infectious disease if I touch a dirty cup') by forcing the client to encounter feared situations and experience the reality of the outcomes associated with that action.

ERP is a highly flexible therapy that can be adapted to group, self-help, inpatient, outpatient, family therapy, and computer-guided interventions (Fischer, Himle & Hanna, 1998; Grayson, 1999; Wetzel, Bents & Florin, 1999; Hand, 1998; Grunes, 1999; Nakagawa, Marks, Park Bachofen *et al.*, 2000). Controlled outcome studies suggest that ERP is a long-term effective treatment for around 75 per cent of clients treated with ERP (Franklin & Foa, 1998; Kyrios, 2003).

For a video on exposure treatment for phobias go to www.wiley-psychopathology.com/video/ch6

For a video on obsessive compulsive disorder go to www.wiley-psychopathology.com/video/ch6

Cognitive behaviour therapy (CBT)

Although ERP has been the treatment of choice for OCD for over 20 years, it is often a difficult treatment for many sufferers to enter. This is because sufferers may feel unable to expose themselves to their fear triggers and find it impossible to prevent themselves acting out their rituals. As many as 30 per cent of clients drop out of ERP before completing treatment (Wilhelm, 2000). An alternative form of therapy for such individuals is cognitive behaviour therapy (CBT) based on targeting and modifying the dysfunctional beliefs that OCD sufferers hold about their fears, thoughts, and the significance of their rituals (Abramowitz, Brigidi & Roche, 2001; Salkovskis, 1999; Wilhelm, 2000; Marks, 2003; see the section 'Inflated responsibility' above). Dysfunctional beliefs that are usually challenged in cognitive therapy for OCD include:

- *responsibility appraisals*, where the sufferer believes they are solely responsible for preventing any harmful outcomes;

- the *over-importance of thoughts*, where sufferers believe that having a thought about an action

THE CLINICAL PERSPECTIVE – TREATMENT IN PRACTICE BOX 6.6: EXPOSURE HIERARCHIES AND RESPONSE PREVENTION IN ERP TREATMENTS OF OCD

Arguably the most effective therapies for OCD are exposure and ritual prevention treatments (ERP) (see section 6.5.2). Table 1 gives examples of a graded exposure regime for fear of contamination from germs, and distressing thoughts about sexual abuse. Table 2 provides some examples of response prevention techniques.

Table 1

Example 1: Fear of contamination (*distress level/100*)	Example 2: Teacher's distressing intrusive thoughts about sexually abusing students (*distress level/100*)
1. Touch rim of own unwashed coffee cup (30)	1. Watch video or listen to audio tape of expert discussing sexual abuse of children (40)
2. Touch rim of partner's unwashed coffee cup (40)	2. Listen to tape of expert while looking at class photo (50)
3. Eat snack from dish in cupboard after touching partner's unwashed coffee cup (45)	3. Listen to loop tape of own distressing thoughts about sexually abusing students in general (60)
4. Drink water from partner's glass (55)	4. Listen to loop tape about students in general looking at class photo (65)
5. Eat snack straight from unwashed table top (65)	5. Listen to loop tape of distressing thought about sexually abusing specific student (70)
6. Have coffee at a café (70)	6. Listen to loop tape about specific student looking at class photo (75)
7. Have meal at a restaurant (80)	7. Listen to loop tape holding specific student's homework (80)
8. Touch toilet seat at home without washing hands for 15 minutes (85)	8. Stand in front of class repeating statement on loop tape to self (90)
9. Touch toilet seat at home without washing hands for 30 minutes (90)	9. Stand close to specific student repeating statement on loop tape to self (95)
10. Using public toilet (100)	10. Stand next to specific student repeating statement on loop tape to self (100)

Table 2

OCD Symptom	Response Prevention Strategy
Hand-washing or cleaning rituals	Response delay (i.e. extending period between 'contamination' and cleaning or washing); use of ritual restrictions (e.g. decreasing cleaning or washing time); clenching fists; extension strategies to undermine avoidance (e.g. touch self, clothes, and suchlike)
Checking lights, switches, oven, appliances, and so on	Response delay; use of ritual restrictions (e.g. restrict number of checks); turning and walking away; extension strategies (whistle a happy tune)
Counting (e.g. bricks, words)	Refocusing techniques; singing a song; going 'blank'; meditation

Source: Kyrios, M. (2003). Exposure and response prevention for OCD. In R.G. Menzies & P. de Silva (Eds.) *Obsessive-compulsive disorder: Theory, research and treatment*. Chichester: John Wiley & Sons. Reproduced with permission.

is like performing the action (thought–action fusion) (see Treatment in Practice 6.6);

- *exaggerated perception of threat*, where the sufferer has highly inflated estimates of the likelihood of harmful outcomes (Van Oppen & Arntz, 1994).

An integrated cognitive therapy for OCD would thus consist of:

- educating clients that intrusive thoughts are quite normal, and that having a thought about an action is not the same as performing it (Salkovskis, 1999);

- focusing on changing the client's abnormal risk assessment – perhaps by working through the probabilities associated with feared outcomes (Van Oppen & Arntz, 1994);

- providing the client with behavioural exercises that will disconfirm their dysfunctional beliefs (e.g. a client who fears shouting out blasphemous thoughts in church would be asked to go to church and see if this happens) (Salkovskis, 1999).

Pharmacological and neurosurgical treatments

Pharmacological treatments have proved to be a short-term, effective and cheap way of treating OCD, although relapse tends to be common on discontinuation of the drug treatment (McDonough, 2003; Pato, Zohar-Kadouch, Zohar & Murphy, 1988). Serotonin and selective serotonin reuptake inhibitors (SSRIs) are the most commonly prescribed drug and have the effect of increasing brain serotonin levels (see section 4.1.1). However, there is still no consensus view on a model of serotonin dysfunction in OCD (Delgado & Moreno, 1998), and it has been suggested that the beneficial effects of SSRIs may be restricted simply to its nonspecific ameliorative effect on dysfunctional brain circuits. Tricyclic antidepressants can have beneficial effects across some specific symptoms of OCD (such as reducing the persistence and frequency of compulsive rituals), but seem to have their effect only when OCD is comorbid with depression (Hohagen, Winkelmann, Rasche-Ruchle, Hand *et al.*, 1998). Comparative studies have suggested that both SSRIs and tricyclic drugs are less effective than standard psychological therapies such as exposure and ritual prevention (ERP) (Rauch & Jenike, 1998; Greist, 1998). In general, ERP is equally as effective as drug treatments in the short term, free from physical and psychological side effects, and associated with greater long-term gains (Greist, 1998; Marks, 1997). When pharmacological and psychological treatments have failed, neurosurgery has become an intervention of last resort in OCD. The most common procedure is **cingulotomy**, which involves destroying cells in the cingulum, close to the corpus callosum. These treatments do report some improvement in OCD symptoms (Dougherty, Baer, Cosgrove, Cassem *et al.*, 2002), but there is a lack of evidence on the longer term gains of neurosurgical treatments and their possible side-effects (McDonough, 2003).

> **cingulotomy** A neurosurgical treatment of OCD involving destroying cells in the cingulum, close to the corpus callosum.

SELF-TEST QUESTIONS

- Can you describe what *obsessions* and *compulsions* are, and provide some examples of each?

- How have biological theories attempted to explain the obsessions and compulsions found in OCD?

- How does the construct of *inflated responsibility* help to explain how OCD is acquired and maintained?

- What are the similarities and differences between exposure and ritual prevention treatment (ERP) and cognitive behaviour therapy (CBT) for OCD?

SECTION SUMMARY

6.5 OBSESSIVE COMPULSIVE DISORDER (OCD)

- OCD is characterized by either obsessions, which are intrusive and recurring thoughts that the individual finds disturbing and uncontrollable, or compulsions, which are ritualized behaviour patterns that the individual feels driven to perform in order to prevent some negative outcome happening.

- Common compulsions include washing, checking, and the systematic arrangement of objects. Related compulsions include hoarding, hair-pulling (trichotillomania) and skin-picking.

- OCD onset is usually gradual and has a lifetime prevalence rate of around 2.5 per cent.

- Biological theories of OCD argue that there may be neurological deficits underlying OCD which either give rise to the typical 'doubting' behaviour common in the disorder, or result in an inability to inhibit certain behaviour patterns (such as checking).

- OCD tends to be associated with a number of dysfunctional beliefs, and the most prominent is the sufferer's inflated conception of their own responsibility for preventing harm, and this 'inflated responsibility' appears to be an important vulnerability factor in developing OCD.

- Exposure and ritual prevention (ERP) treatments are the most common, and arguably the most successful, means of treatment for OCD. These involve graded exposure to the thoughts that trigger distress, followed by the development of behaviours designed to prevent the individual's compulsive ritual.

- Pharmacological treatments for OCD can also be effective (e.g. serotonin and selective serotonin reuptake inhibitors), and psychosurgery is sometimes a treatment of last resort (e.g. cingulotomy).

6.6 TRAUMA AND STRESS-RELATED DISORDERS

In this section we will explore trauma and stress-related disorders. In DSM-5 these forms of disorder are now listed separately from anxiety disorders, but the major diagnostic category in this section remains **post-traumatic stress disorder (PTSD)**. There is still considerable debate about whether PTSD should be considered an anxiety disorder, a stress-induced fear response, a dissociative disorder (see Chapter 14), or a trauma and stressor-related disorder, but acknowledgement that its primary precipitating cause is a traumatic experience has led to PTSD being placed in its own broader diagnostic category (Friedman, Resick, Bryant, Strain et al., 2011).

post-traumatic stress disorder (PTSD)
A set of persistent anxiety-based symptoms that occurs after experiencing or witnessing an extremely fear-evoking or life-threatening traumatic event.

Diagnosis and prevalence of trauma and stress-related disorders

The DSM diagnostics criteria for PTSD and acute stress disorder are provided in DSM-5 Summary Table 6.8 and 6.9. PTSD is one of the few disorders in DSM-5 in which the cause of the disorder is a defining factor. In this case, *diagnosis of PTSD* is considered only if the individual has experienced an extreme trauma prior to symptoms. They may have (1) directly experienced the trauma (e.g. been involved in a natural disaster such as an earthquake or fire, or been subjected to life-threatening physical abuse such as rape), (2) witnessed a

CLIENT'S PERSPECTIVE 6.2: POST-TRAUMATIC STRESS DISORDER

'I thought I was over it. Just when I think I'm getting better and don't have to worry about it anymore, something will trigger a memory and I'll be right back there again. Sometimes it's just a feeling I have, and other times I'll see something that reminds me of what happened and it feels like it's happening all over again. It's been almost a year now and I'm seeing a therapist three times a week as well as taking antidepressants. I can have good days – maybe two or three in a row – then my mood will get worse and the blackness will come back. It feels as if my thoughts aren't my own and my mind is somewhere else while my body is just going through the motions. Every time the black moods come it feels harder and harder to get back from them. It makes me so angry when I feel like this and my mind becomes full of violent thoughts; this rage takes over and I can't control it. I'm scared of what I might do when I'm feeling this angry. I don't want to tell my friends or family about what I'm thinking because they might be frightened of me or what I'll do, and I know they just want me to move on. I wish I could but I just can't see a way out.'

For a video on post-traumatic stress disorder go to www.wiley-psychopathology.com/video/ch6

Clinical Commentary

This description is typical of many PTSD sufferers and highlights feelings of depression, lack of control and anger. Some theories of PTSD (such as 'mental defeat') emphasize that those who develop PTSD after a severe trauma tend to view themselves as a victim, process all information about the trauma negatively, and view themselves as unable to act effectively. Such individuals believe they are unable to influence their own fate and do not have the necessary skills to protect themselves from future trauma. Ehlers & Clark (2000) suggest that such individuals only partially process their memory of the trauma because of their perceived lack of control over it, and so they do not integrate that event fully into their own autobiographical knowledge.

DSM-5 SUMMARY TABLE 6.8 *Criteria for diagnosing post-traumatic stress disorder*

- The individual has been exposed to or threatened with death, serious injury or sexual violation: by direct experience or by witnessing a traumatic event; upon learning about a violent or accidental death of a close friend or family member; or by extreme or repeated exposure to the effects of a traumatic event, such as emergency workers encountering human remains

- Intrusive symptoms associated with the traumatic event will be experienced, such as: disturbing dreams or feeling that the event is recurring while awake; uncontrolled memories of the event; extreme physical reactions or mental distress upon being reminded of the trauma

- Individuals will avoid internal and/or external reminders of the trauma

- At least two changes to mood or thought processes will occur, such as: feelings of disconnection; continual negative emotions and ongoing difficulty in experiencing positive emotions; extreme and disproportionate negative expectations; reduced interest in activities; being unable to remember certain aspects of the traumatic event

- Changes to reactive behaviour will occur, and individuals will display two or more of the following symptoms: recklessness, aggression, hypervigilance, inability to concentrate, difficulty sleeping, an exaggerated startle response

- Symptoms began or worsened after the traumatic event(s) and continued for at least 1 month, causing significant difficulty in functioning

- Symptoms cannot be explained by the effects of other mental or medical disorders, drug abuse or medication

DSM-5 SUMMARY TABLE 6.9 *Criteria for the diagnosis of acute stress disorder*

The individual has been exposed to or threatened with death, serious injury or sexual violation: by direct experience or by witnessing a traumatic event; upon learning about a violent or accidental death of a close friend or family member; or by extreme or repeated exposure to the effects of a traumatic event. At least nine of the following symptoms will be displayed:

- Recurrent, intrusive and involuntary memories of the traumatic event

- Repeated distressing dreams related to the traumatic event, or feeling that the event is recurring while awake

- Extreme physical reactions or mental distress upon being reminded of the trauma

- Numbness or detachment from others

- Changes in the individual's sense of reality and an altered perspective of oneself or one's surroundings

- Difficulty in remembering aspects of the traumatic event

- Avoidance of internal and/or external reminders of the trauma

- Difficulties in sleeping

- Hypervigilance

- Irritability or aggression

- Difficulty in concentrating

- Exaggerated startle response

Symptoms may begin within 3 days to 1 month of the trauma taking place and will persist for at least 3 days or up to 1 month

Symptoms cannot be explained by the effects of other mental or medical disorders, drug abuse or medication

Symptoms cause difficulties in performing important functions and cause clinically significant distress

traumatic event in which others may have suffered (e.g. witnessing the 9/11 terrorist attacks on New York), (3) learnt that a severe traumatic event has happened to a close family member or friend, or (4) been subjected repeatedly to distressing details of trauma (e.g. the kind of regular exposure to details of trauma that might be experienced by police officers or emergency workers).

The symptoms typical of PTSD are grouped into four categories. These are (1) *intrusive symptoms* such as flashbacks, intrusive thoughts, or physiological reactions, (2) *avoidance responding* such as active avoidance of thoughts, memories or reminders of the trauma, (3) *negative changes in cognition and mood* such as persistent fear, horror, anger, guilt or shame, persistent negative beliefs about themselves, others or the world (e.g. 'no one can be trusted', 'I've lost my soul for ever'), or dissociative feelings of detachment or estrangement from others, and (4) *increased arousal and reactivity* such as hypervigilance and exaggerated startle responses. Once symptoms develop, PTSD is often a chronic condition that can last for years (Perkonigg, Pfister, Stein, Hofler *et al.*, 2005). It is also associated with depression, guilt, shame, anger, marital problems, physical illness, sexual dysfunction,

substance abuse, suicidal thoughts, and stress-related violence (Jacobsen, Southwick & Kosten, 2001; Zatzick, Marmer, Weiss, Browner *et al.*, 1997; Hobfoll, Spielberger, Breznitz, Figley *et al.*, 1991), as well as suicidal thoughts (Bernal, Haro, Bernert, Brugha *et al.*, 2007) and self-harm (Weierich & Nock, 2008). The kinds of traumatic events that precipitate PTSD are often life-threatening in their severity. Studies suggest that PTSD symptoms are developed by up to 90 per cent of rape victims (Rothbaum, Foa, Riggs, Murdock *et al.*, 1992), between 70 and 90 per cent of torture victims (Moisander & Edston, 2003), over 50 per cent of prisoners of war (Engdahl, Dikel, Eberly & Blank, 1997), between 20 and 25 per cent of earthquake and flood survivors (Basoglu, Kilic, Salcioglu & Livanou, 2004; North, Kawasaki, Spitznagel & Hong, 2004), and around 15 per cent of motor vehicle accident victims (Bryant & Harvey, 1998). DSM-5 also emphasizes that PTSD symptoms can be acquired in cases where the stressor has not been life-threatening to the sufferer (e.g. suffering PTSD after the loss of a loved one), or has involved simply viewing stressful images of life-threatening traumas (e.g. watching images of the 9/11 terrorist attacks on TV – Piotrowski & Brannen, 2002), and this extension of the diagnostic criteria for PTSD has generated controversy, either because it makes the symptoms of PTSD easier to fake in those who might benefit financially from a diagnosis (Rosen, 2004), or because it confuses PTSD with merely experiencing stress (McNally, 2003a).

The lifetime prevalence rate for PTSD is between 1 and 3 per cent (Helzer, Robins & McEvoy, 1987). However, prevalence rates are significantly higher for groups who are at risk of experiencing severe trauma. These include a 12–33 per cent prevalence rate for civilians living in war zones (Farhood & Dimassi, 2012; Charlson, Steel, Degenhardt, Chey *et al.*, 2012), 10 per cent for rescue workers (Berger, Coutinho, Figueira, Marques-Portella *et al.*, 2012), and 13.2 per cent for members of operational infantry in the recent Iraq and Afghanistan conflicts (Kok, Herrell, Thomas & Hoge, 2012). Around 50 per cent of adults experience at least one event in their lifetime that might qualify as a PTSD-causing trauma (Ozer & Weiss, 2004). Following such events, women are significantly more likely than men to develop PTSD (by a factor of 2.4:1), and this is not explained simply by differences in the perceived threat to life from the experience (Holbrook, Hoyt, Stein & Sieber, 2002). Apart from gender differences in prevalence rates, there is also some emerging evidence on the role that cultural variables play in PTSD. Ethnic groups can differ quite significantly in the prevalence of PTSD – Caucasian disaster victims show lower prevalence rates than Latinos or African Americans – and these differences cannot be entirely explained simply by differences in the frequency of exposure to traumatic experiences (Perilla, Norris & Lavizzo, 2002; Norris, Perilla, Ibanez & Murphy, 2001). The fact that around 50 per cent of the population will experience at least one event in their life that could be classified as a PTSD-relevant trauma means that many people experience trauma but do *not* develop PTSD. It is understanding these individual differences in susceptibility to PTSD that will give us some insight into the mechanisms that give rise to PTSD.

The symptoms of **acute stress disorder (ASD)** are very similar to those of PTSD, but the duration is much shorter (3 days to 1 month after trauma exposure). DSM-5 criteria have been explicitly modified to make ASD symptoms much more compatible with PTSD, and so ASD may well be a diagnostic category that predicts subsequent PTSD – but that remains to be determined. There has been some prior debate about whether ASD actually represents a psychological disorder as such, or whether it is a normal short-term psychological and physical reaction to severe trauma (Harvey & Bryant, 2002). However, with the diagnostic criteria for ASD in DSM-5

acute stress disorder (ASD) A short-term psychological and physical reaction to severe trauma. Symptoms are very similar to those of PTSD, but the duration is much shorter (3 days to 1 month after trauma exposure).

shifting significantly towards that of PTSD, it remains to be seen whether fewer post-trauma survivors are diagnosed with ASD as were with DSM-IV-TR criteria.

6.6.1   The Aetiology of Post-Traumatic Stress Disorder (PTSD)

The diagnostic criteria for PTSD specify either a life-threatening trauma or severe stress as a causal factor in the disorder. However, not everyone who has these kinds of experiences develops PTSD. This is the main challenge for any theory of the aetiology of PTSD – why do some people develop PTSD symptoms after these experiences, but not others? The answer must lie either in psychological or biological vulnerability factors, or in the psychological strategies that individuals have developed to deal with events like trauma and stress (e.g. differences in learnt coping strategies). Also, because PTSD has many different symptom features, some theories address specific features of the symptomatology (e.g. the flashbacks), and others address the time course of the disorder and how it is emotionally experienced (Brewin & Holmes, 2003). We will explore these various possibilities below when we look at some of the main models of the aetiology of PTSD.

Biological factors

Studies carried out on war veterans have suggested that PTSD has a genetic element to it, and a heritability component of 30 per cent has been estimated (True, Rice, Eisen, Heath *et al.*, 1993). This has led some to suggest that PTSD develops as a result of gene x environment vulnerability factors interacting, and the combination of an extreme trauma experience and a genetic predisposition to PTSD are required to generate PTSD symptoms (Mehta & Binder, 2012). What the biologically conferred vulnerability factor might be is still as yet unclear. Some possibilities are:

1. A relatively small or under-developed hippocampus. The hippocampus is that region of the brain that plays a critical role in memories related to emotion, and studies have indicated that this region is significantly smaller in individuals who develop PTSD (Bremner, Vythilingam, Vermetten, Southwick *et al.*, 2003) and a smaller hippocampus represents a real risk factor for the development of PTSD following a traumatic experience (Gilbertson, Shenton, Ciszewski, Kasal *et al.*, 2002).

2. Failure of brain centres such as the ventromedial frontal cortex to dampen activation of the brain's fear coordinating centre, the amygdala (Koenigs & Grafman, 2009), which means that the individual is unable to control the activation of fear following trauma.

3. Genetically endowed heightened startle responses and fear-relevant endocrine secretion (Broekman, Olff & Boer, 2007; Segman & Shalev, 2003).

Vulnerability factors

As not everyone who experiences a life-threatening trauma develops PTSD, there must be factors that make some people more vulnerable than others. A number of factors have been identified that characterize those individuals likely to develop PTSD after trauma, which include:

- A tendency to take personal responsibility for the traumatic event and the misfortunes of others involved in the event (Mikhliner & Solomon, 1988);

- Developmental factors such as early separation from parents or an unstable family life during early childhood (King, King, Foy & Gudanowski, 1996);

- A family history of PTSD (Foy, Resnick, Sipperelle & Carroll, 1987);

- Existing high levels of anxiety or a pre-existing psychological disorder (Breslau, Davis, Andreski *et al.*, 1997).

Interestingly, low intelligence is also a vulnerability factor (Vasterling, Duke, Brailey *et al.*, 2002), and high IQ is the best predictor of resistance to the development of PTSD (Silva, Alpert, Munoz *et al.*, 2000). This may be because there is a link between IQ level and the development of coping strategies to deal with experienced trauma or stress. Other important predictors of PTSD development are the experiences reported by trauma victims at the time of the trauma. These include the reporting of dissociative symptoms at the time of the trauma (see below), and a belief that one is about to die (McNally, 2003b). These types of experiences may be important in that they may relate to how the individual processes and stores information about the trauma at the time, and this is important in some specific theories of PTSD symptoms.

Avoidance and dissociation

After any distressing and traumatic experience, how the individual copes with that experience will be critical to the subsequent psychological health. One coping style that is not conducive to a beneficial outcome is avoidance coping, and individuals who avoid thinking about their trauma are more likely to develop PTSD following a traumatic experience (Sharkansky, King, King, Wolfe *et al.*, 2000). One psychological process that seems to be used to enable individuals to detach and distance themselves from trauma is dissociation (see Chapter 14). Dissociation is the feeling that one is detached from both mind and body, and is associated with an inability to recall important personal information of a stressful nature. In the context of PTSD, dissociation may represent an avoidant strategy

for coping or confronting painful or stressful memories. In particular, dissociation seems to be an important risk factor for PTSD. Individuals who experience dissociation either just before or during the trauma are more likely to develop PTSD (Ehlers, Mayou & Bryant, 1998); using dissociation as a coping strategy after the trauma, they are at risk of chronic long-term PTSD symptoms (Briere, Scott & Weathers, 2005). Dissociative symptoms immediately after rape also predict the development of PTSD (Brewin & Holmes, 2003). (See section 14.1.2 for a discussion of the relationship between PTSD and dissociative experiences.)

Conditioning theory

Because there is always an identifiable traumatic experience in the history of PTSD, it is quite reasonable to suppose that many of the symptoms of PTSD may be due to classical conditioning (see section 1.3). That is, trauma (the unconditioned stimulus, UCS) becomes associated at the time of the trauma with situational cues associated with the place and time of the trauma (the conditioned stimulus, CS) (Keane, Zimering & Caddell, 1985). When these cues (or similar cues) are encountered in the future, they elicit the arousal and fear that was experienced during the trauma. For example, seeing a pile of bricks on the ground may elicit strong arousal, fear and startle responses for an earthquake survivor, because such cues had become associated with the fear experienced during the traumatic earthquake experience. The conditioning model would further argue that such conditioned fear responses do not extinguish because the sufferer develops both cognitive and physical avoidance responses which distract them from fully processing such cues and therefore does not allow the associations between cues and trauma to extinguish. The reduction in fear resulting from these avoidance responses reinforces those responses and maintains PTSD symptoms. There is probably an element of classical conditioning in the development of PTSD, largely because formally neutral cues do come to elicit PTSD symptoms. There is also evidence that individuals suffering PTSD will more readily develop conditioned responses in laboratory-based experiments than non-sufferers (Orr, Metzger, Lasko, Macklin *et al.*, 2000). However, classical conditioning does not provide a full explanation of PTSD. It does not explain why some individuals who experience trauma develop PTSD and others do not, and it cannot easily explain the range of symptoms peculiar to PTSD but rarely found in other anxiety disorders, such as re-experiencing symptoms, dissociative experiences, and so on.

Emotional processing theory

Foa, Steketee & Rothbaum (1989) have suggested that the intense nature of the trauma in PTSD creates a representation of the trauma in memory that becomes strongly associated with other contextual details of the event (e.g. if a person has been badly injured in a serious traffic accident, cues to do with roads, cars, hospitals, and even travelling generally will come to selectively activate the fear network in memory). The avoidance of any contexts that might activate this fear network means that there is little opportunity for the PTSD sufferer to weaken these associations between fear and the everyday cues that will activate that fear. This account has elements in common with classical conditioning models of PTSD, but it differs in some significant ways. Firstly, **emotional processing theory** claims that severe traumatic experiences are of such major significance to the individual that they lead to the formation of representations and associations in memory that are quite different from those formed as a result of everyday experience. For example, if severe trauma has become associated with certain cues (e.g. after being assaulted in an alleyway), this experience will now override any other positive associations formed as a result of previous experience with that cue (the alleyway). Secondly, severe trauma not only results in cues eliciting very strong fear responses, it also changes the individual's previous assumptions about how safe the world is, so many more cues than previously will come to elicit responses related to fear, startle and hypervigilance (Foa & Rothbaum, 1998).

> **emotional processing theory** Theory that claims that severe traumatic experiences are of such major significance to an individual that they lead to the formation of representations and associations in memory that are quite different to those formed as a result of everyday experience.

The emotional processing theory is an example of those theories of PTSD that have attempted to include explanations about how fear responses are learnt, stored and triggered, and about how the traumatic event changes the individuals assumptions and beliefs about themselves and the world. These types of theories have come to be known as information-processing models because they specify how fear memories are laid down and activated in fear networks. They have also given rise to some successful therapeutic procedures for PTSD which address how the fear network resulting from traumatic experience can be modified (Foa & Rothbaum, 1998). In addition, this account of PTSD has been elaborated more recently to take account of the fact that individuals who prior to the trauma have relatively fixed views about themselves and the world are actually more vulnerable to PTSD (Foa & Riggs, 1993).

Mental defeat

Ehlers and Clark (2000) have suggested that there is a specific psychological factor that is important in making an individual vulnerable to PTSD. This is a specific frame of mind called **mental defeat**, in which the individual sees themselves as a victim: they process all information about the trauma negatively, and view themselves as unable to act effectively.

> **mental defeat** A specific frame of mind in which the individual sees themselves as a victim. This is a psychological factor that is important in making an individual vulnerable to PTSD.

This negative approach to the traumatic event and its consequences simply adds to the distress, influences the way the individual recalls the trauma, and may give rise to maladaptive behavioural and cognitive strategies that maintain the disorder. In effect, these individuals believe they are unable to influence their own fate and do not have the necessary skills to protect themselves from future trauma. Ehlers & Clark (2000) suggest that such individuals only partially process their memory of the trauma because of their perceived lack of control over it, and so they do not integrate that event fully into their own autobiographical knowledge. This leads to symptoms such as re-experiencing the trauma in the present (outside of a temporal context), difficulty in recalling events from the trauma, and dissociation between the experience of fear responses and their meaning. The 'mental defeat' model is supported by evidence suggesting that PTSD sufferers do indeed have negative views of the self and the world, including negative interpretations of the trauma (Dunmore, Clark & Ehlers, 1999), negative interpretations of PTSD symptoms (Clohessy & Ehlers, 1999; Mayou, Bryant & Ehlers, 2001), negative interpretations of the responses of others (Dunmore, Clark & Ehlers, 1999), and a belief that the trauma has permanently changed their life (Dunmore, Clark & Ehlers, 1999; Ehlers, Maercker & Boos, 2000).

Dual representation theory

A rather different approach to explaining PTSD, called **dual representation theory**, is that it may be a hybrid disorder consisting of the involvement of two separate memory systems (Brewin, 2001; Brewin, Dalgleish & Joseph, 1996). The *verbally accessible memory* (VAM) system registers memories of the trauma that are consciously processed at the time. These memories are narrative in nature and contain information about the event, its context, and personal evaluations of the experience. They are integrated with other autobiographical memories and can be readily retrieved. The *situationally accessible memory* (SAM) system, however, records information from the trauma that may have been too brief to apprehend or take in consciously, and this includes information about sights and sounds, and extreme bodily reactions to trauma. The SAM system is thus responsible for the vivid, uncontrollable flashbacks experienced by PTSD sufferers which are difficult to communicate to others (because these memories are not stored in a narrative form). There is good neuropsychological evidence for the existence of these two separate memory systems and their links with the brain centre associated with fear (the amygdala) (Brewin, 2001). There is also evidence that is consistent with predictions from the dual representation theory.

> **dual representation theory** An approach to explaining post-traumatic stress disorder (PTSD) suggesting that it may be a hybrid disorder involving two separate memory systems.

For example, Hellawell & Brewin (2004) found that, when describing their memories, PTSD sufferers characterized flashback periods with greater use of detail, particularly perceptual detail, by more mentions of death, more use of the present tense, and more mention of fear, helplessness, and horror. In contrast, ordinary memories were characterized by more mention of secondary emotions such as guilt and anger. These findings are consistent with the view that flashbacks are the result of sensory and response information stored in the SAM system.

Summary

Once again, it is clear that PTSD has a number of different features, each of which requires explanation. Some theories have tried to explain some of the specific features of PTSD (such as dual representation theory's attempt to explain specific features such as flashbacks), while others have tried to identify the dispositional features that make some individuals vulnerable to developing PTSD while others do not (e.g. mental defeat). Others attempt to describe why severe trauma causes the symptoms that it does, and why these anxiety-based symptoms persist for such long periods (e.g. conditioning theory and emotional processing theory).

6.6.2 The Treatment of Post-Traumatic Stress Disorder

The treatment of PTSD has two main aims. The first is to try to prevent the development of PTSD after an individual has experienced a severe trauma. The second is to treat the symptoms of PTSD once these symptoms have developed. Rapid psychological debriefing has usually been the accepted way of trying to intervene immediately after trauma in order to try to prevent the development of PTSD, although there is now some doubt about whether this kind of rapid intervention provides any therapeutic gains. Once symptoms have developed, most psychological therapies either rely on some form of exposure therapy (usually involving the client imagining events during their traumatic experience) in an attempt to extinguish fear symptoms, or adopt other treatments that focus on the patient's trauma memories or their meanings, and international treatment guidelines recommend trauma-focused psychological treatments as the first-line treatment for PTSD (Ehlers, Bisson, Clark, Creamer et al., 2010). Therapies that possess this exposure element include imaginal flooding, eye movement desensitisation and reprocessing (EMDR), and cognitive restructuring, but there is an ever-expanding set of emerging treatments for PTSD (see Cukor, Spitalnick, Difede, Rizzo et al., 2009), which meta-analyses suggest may all be equally effective in treating PTSD symptoms (Benish, Imel & Wampold, 2008).

Psychological debriefing

Over the past 20 years or so there has been a growing belief amongst mental health professionals that PTSD can be prevented by immediate and rapid debriefing of trauma victims within 24–72 hours after the traumatic event (Caplan, 1964; Bisson, 2003). The exact form of the intervention can vary, with the most widely used techniques referred to as crisis intervention or critical incident stress management (CISM) (Everly, Flannery & Mitchell, 2000). The purpose of these interventions is to reassure the participants that they are normal people who have experienced an abnormal event, to encourage them to review what has happened to them, to express their feelings about the event, and to discuss and review support and coping strategies in the immediate post-trauma period. **Psychological debriefing** has been used with survivors, victims, relatives, emergency care workers, and providers of mental health care (Bisson, 2003). The scale of this type of intervention can be gauged by reactions to the terrorist attacks on the World Trade Center on September 11, 2001, when more than 9000 counsellors went to New York to offer immediate aid to victims and families of the attack (McNally, Bryant & Ehlers, 2003). Critical incident stress debriefing includes a number of components, including:

> **psychological debriefing** A structured way of trying to intervene immediately after trauma in order to try to prevent the development of PTSD.

- explanation of the purpose of the intervention
- asking participants to describe their experiences
- discussion of the participant's feelings about the event
- discussion of any trauma-related symptoms the participant may be experiencing
- encouraging the participant to view their symptoms as normal reactions to trauma
- discussing the participant's needs for the future (Mitchell & Everly, 1993).

As laudable as immediate professional help may seem in these circumstances, there is much criticism of psychological debriefing and its value as an intervention for PTSD. Firstly, it is not clear whether victims will gain any benefit from being counselled by strangers and possibly 'coerced' into revealing thoughts and memories that in the immediate wake of the trauma may be difficult to reveal. Secondly, many of the survivors of severe trauma do not display symptoms of psychological disorders, nor will they develop PTSD. Psychological debriefing techniques make little attempt to differentiate these survivors from those who may genuinely need longer term guidance and treatment. Thirdly, controlled comparative studies that have attempted to evaluate the effects of psychological debriefing techniques suggest there is little convincing evidence that debriefing reduces the incidence of PTSD – and indeed it may in some cases *impede* natural recovery following trauma (Bisson, 2003; McNally, Bryant & Ehlers, 2003). Most recent reviews of early psychological interventions for the prevention of PTSD suggest that no psychological intervention can be recommended for routine use following traumatic events, and early psychological intervention may even have an adverse effect on some people (Roberts, Kitchiner, Kenardy & Bisson, 2009).

Exposure therapies

Arguably the most effective form of treatment for PTSD is exposure therapy, in which the sufferer is helped by the therapist to confront and experience events and stimuli relevant to their trauma and their symptoms. The rationale behind exposure therapy is that (1) it will help to extinguish associations between trauma cues and fear responses (Foa & Rothbaum, 1998), and (2) it will help the individual to disconfirm any symptom-maintaining dysfunctional beliefs that have developed as a result of the trauma (e.g. 'I can't handle any stress') (Foa & Rauch, 2004). For the individual suffering PTSD, exposure to their fear triggers is often a difficult step to take, and exposure may even make symptoms worse in the early stages of treatment (Keane, Gerardi, Quinn & Litz, 1992). This being the case, exposure can be tackled in a number of different forms – especially in various imaginal forms. This can be achieved (1) by asking the client to provide a detailed written narrative of their traumatic experiences (Resick & Schnicke, 1992), (2) with the assistance of virtual reality technology using computer-generated imagery (Rothbaum, Hodges, Ready, Graap & Alarcon, 2001), or (3) by simply asking the client to visualize feared, trauma-related scenes for extended periods of time (known as **imaginal flooding**) (Keane, Fairbank, Caddell & Zimering, 1989). Such imaginal treatments are usually then supplemented with subsequent *in vivo* exposure that would require graded exposure to real trauma-related cues. Comparative studies generally indicate that exposure-based therapies provide therapeutic gains that are superior to medication and social support (Foa & Meadows, 1997; Marks, Lovell, Noshirvani, Livanou *et al.*, 1998).

A recently developed, and somewhat controversial form of exposure therapy for PTSD is known as **eye movement desensitisation and reprocessing (EMDR)** (Shapiro, 1989, 1995). In this form of treatment, the client is required to focus their attention on a traumatic image or memory while simultaneously visually following the therapist's finger that is moving backwards and forwards in front of their eyes. This continues until the client reports a significant decrease in anxiety to the image or memory. The therapist then encourages the client to restructure the memory positively, by thinking positive thoughts in relation to that image (e.g. 'I can deal with this'). The rationale for this procedure is that combining eye movements with attention to fearful images encourages rapid deconditioning and restructuring of the feared image (Shapiro, 1995, 1999). There is evidence that EMDR is more effective than no treatment, supportive listening and relaxation (McNally, 1999), but some studies have shown that it has a higher relapse rate than cognitive behaviour therapy (Devilly & Spence, 1999). Nevertheless, recent reviews suggest that EMDR is one of the most effective treatments for PTSD, despite its controversial status (Bradley, Greene, Russ et al., 2005). Critics of EMDR argue that, although it does have some success in treating the symptoms of PTSD, it is little more than just another form of exposure therapy. However, experimental studies have demonstrated that the eye movement component of EMDR is essential for successful treatment no matter how this might be achieved (e.g. up and down eye movements are as effective as side to side movements) (Lee & Cuijpers, 2013). What does appear to be important is that the eye movement task – however achieved – should tax working memory and so weaken traumatic memories (van den Hout & Engelhard, 2012).

Cognitive restructuring

There are various forms of cognitive restructuring therapy for PTSD, but most attempt to help clients do two things: evaluate and replace intrusive or negative automatic thoughts; and evaluate and change dysfunctional beliefs about the world, themselves and their future that have developed as a result of the trauma (Marks, Lovell, Noshirvani & Livanou, 1998; Foa & Rothbaum, 1998). For example, Foa & Rothbaum (1998) suggested that two basic dysfunctional beliefs mediate the development and maintenance of PTSD. These are (1) 'the world is a dangerous place', and (2) 'I am totally incompetent'. Foa & Cahill (2001) argued that immediately after a severe trauma, all victims develop a negative view of the world and themselves, but for most individuals these beliefs become disconfirmed through daily experience. However, those who avoid trauma-related thoughts will also avoid disconfirming these extreme views and this will foster the development of chronic PTSD. While exposure therapy alone may encourage

> **eye movement desensitisation and reprocessing (EMDR)** A form of exposure therapy for PTSD in which clients are required to focus their attention on a traumatic image or memory while simultaneously visually following the therapist's finger moving backwards and forwards before their eyes.

> **imaginal flooding** A technique whereby a client is asked to visualize feared, trauma-related scenes for extended periods of time.

experiences that disconfirm these dysfunctional beliefs, cognitive therapists have proposed that procedures that directly attempt to alter PTSD-related cognitions should also be included in the treatment (Resick & Schnicke, 1992; Steil & Ehlers, 2000). However, studies that have analysed treatments that contain both exposure and cognitive restructuring components suggest that cognitive restructuring does not significantly augment exposure therapy in producing changes in dysfunctional cognitions (Foa & Rauch, 2004).

SELF-TEST QUESTIONS

- Can you describe the main symptoms of PTSD and how they may differ from the symptoms found in other anxiety disorders?
- What are the diagnostic differences between PTSD and acute stress disorder?
- Can you list some of the important risk factors for PTSD, and describe how they might contribute to the development of PTSD?
- We discussed the main theories of the aetiology of PTSD (conditioning theory, emotional processing theory, 'mental defeat', and dual representation theory). Can you describe the main features of at least two of these and discuss their similarities and differences?
- What are the main treatments for PTSD, and how have these been derived from theories of the aetiology of PTSD?

SECTION SUMMARY

6.6 TRAUMA AND STRESS-RELATED DISORDERS

- The diagnosis of PTSD is based on identifying exposure to a specific fear-evoking, and usually life-threatening, event (e.g. being involved in a natural disaster, serious physical assault and suchlike).
- Acute stress disorder is a short-term psychological and physical reaction to severe trauma.
- The main symptoms of PTSD include increased arousal, numbing of emotions, flashbacks and the re-experiencing of the trauma.
- The lifetime prevalence rate for PTSD is between 1 and 3 per cent (even though around 50 per cent of adults experience at least one event in their lifetime that might qualify as a PTSD-causing event).
- Vulnerability factors for PTSD include a tendency to take personal responsibility for the event, developmental factors such as an unstable early family life, a family history of PTSD, and existing high levels of anxiety or a pre-existing psychological disorder.
- There is no consensus on a specific psychological model of PTSD, and current explanations include: (1) classical conditioning, (2) emotional processing theory, (3) 'mental defeat', and (4) dual representation theory.
- Attempting to prevent the development of PTSD through the rapid and immediate debriefing of trauma victims (critical incident stress debriefing) is now generally acknowledged to be ineffective and even counterproductive.
- The most effective forms of treatment for PTSD are exposure therapies, where the sufferer is helped by the therapist to confront and experience events and stimuli relevant to their trauma. These may include imaginal flooding or eye movement desensitisation and reprocessing (EMDR); and graduated exposure treatment can be supplemented with cognitive restructuring designed to evaluate and change dysfunctional beliefs about the world.

6.7 ANXIETY AND STRESSOR-RELATED PROBLEMS REVIEWED

In this chapter we have reviewed six of the main anxiety-based problems – specific phobia, social anxiety disorder, panic disorder, generalized anxiety disorder (GAD), obsessive compulsive disorder (OCD), and trauma and stressor-related problems such as post-traumatic stress disorder (PTSD). Common to all of these disorders is the intense experience of anxiety that the individual finds distressing and which causes significant impairment in social, occupational, or other important areas of functioning. At this point it is worth referring back to the table given on the website in which we began by summarising some of the important features of these problems. This table shows that anxiety manifests itself in many different ways in these different disorders – as pathological worrying in GAD, as compulsive ritualized thoughts and actions in OCD, as physical panic attacks in panic disorder, and the re-experiencing of trauma in PTSD. Many of these anxiety problems are precipitated by periods of stress in a person's life (e.g. panic disorder, GAD, OCD), yet we do not yet know why an individual who has experienced a period of life stress will develop one particular disorder (e.g. OCD) rather than another (e.g. panic disorder). This will be an important issue for future clinical research.

Just as the symptoms of these anxiety-based problems are often quite different, so are the theories that try to explain them, and there is certainly no single, unified theory that can convincingly explain the development of anxiety-based problems generally. However, there are some features that are common to these different problems and these may provide some insight into how different anxiety-based problems develop. These features include the information-processing and interpretational biases that accompany most anxiety disorders, and also the dysfunctional beliefs that anxiety sufferers seem to form and which maintain their symptoms (e.g. the spider phobic's beliefs that spiders are threatening and harmful, and the GAD sufferer's belief that worrying is an important and necessary activity to engage in). These phenomena may eventually form the basis of a unified theory of anxiety-based problems.

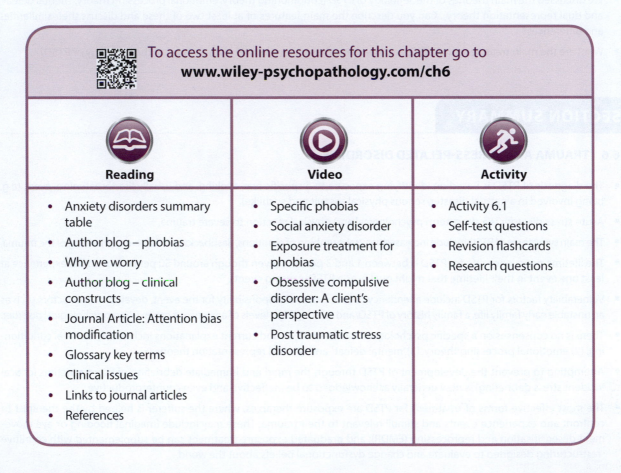

To access the online resources for this chapter go to

www.wiley-psychopathology.com/ch6

Reading	Video	Activity
• Anxiety disorders summary table • Author blog – phobias • Why we worry • Author blog – clinical constructs • Journal Article: Attention bias modification • Glossary key terms • Clinical issues • Links to journal articles • References	• Specific phobias • Social anxiety disorder • Exposure treatment for phobias • Obsessive compulsive disorder: A client's perspective • Post traumatic stress disorder	• Activity 6.1 • Self-test questions • Revision flashcards • Research questions

7 Depression and Mood Disorders

 To access the online resources for this chapter go to
www.wiley-psychopathology.com/ch7

ROUTE MAP OF THE CHAPTER

This chapter describes depression and mood disorders, their symptoms, theories of their aetiology, and the main forms of treatment for these problems. The two main mood disorders covered are major depression (sometimes known as unipolar depression), and bipolar disorder (characterized by periods of mania alternating with periods of depression). The chapter covers a range of theories of depression and mood disorders including biological theories and psychological theories. The section on treatment looks at the way in which antidepressant drugs help to alleviate the symptoms of depression, and how a number of psychological therapies have been developed to address the cognitive biases that characterize major depression. The chapter ends by discussing two phenomena associated with mood disorders and depression in particular, namely deliberate self-harm and suicide.

their own future (Beck, 1987; Gable & Shean, 2000), and this generates *pessimistic* thinking where sufferers believe nothing can improve their own lot. This in turn leads to a lack of initiative, with individuals reporting impaired ability to think, concentrate or make decisions. This inability to affect the future also generates other problematic beliefs, such as a sense of worthlessness, shame and guilt. Because of this, many depressed individuals develop the dysfunctional belief that others would be better off if they were dead, and this can often lead to transient but recurrent suicidal thoughts (see section 7.5).

> **major depression** A psychological problem characterized by relatively extended periods of clinical depression which cause significant distress to the individual and impairment in social or occupational functioning. See also *unipolar depression*.

> **bipolar disorder** A psychological disorder characterized by periods of mania that alternate with periods of depression.

> **unipolar depression** A psychological disorder characterized by relatively extended periods of clinical depression that cause significant distress to the individual and impairment in social or occupational functioning. See also *major depression*.

There are two main types of clinical depression. The first, and most common, is **major depression**, and the second is **bipolar disorder**. The main features of these two types of mood disorder can be reviewed online in the depression and mood disorders summary table, which is available on the website at **www .wiley-psychopathology. com/ch7**. Readers may want to refer back to this table when they have read and digested the information in this chapter. Major depression (sometimes known as **unipolar depression**) is one of the most common of all the psychological problems, and is characterized by relatively extended periods of clinical depression that cause significant distress to the individual and impairment in social or occupational functioning. Bipolar disorder is characterized by periods of mania that alternate with periods of depression, and this leads individuals with bipolar disorder to describe their lives as an 'emotional roller-coaster'. Sufferers experience the extremes of these emotions in ways that cause emotional discomfort and distress.

This chapter now continues by discussing the diagnosis, prevalence and aetiology of major depression, and then – in section 7.2 – the diagnosis, prevalence and aetiology of bipolar disorder.

7.1 MAJOR DEPRESSION

7.1.1 The Diagnosis and Prevalence of Major Depression

DSM-5 has introduced a number of changes to the way in which major depression is categorized and diagnosed.

It specifies the criteria for a **major depressive episode** (which is not a codable disorder), which can be found in DSM-5 Summary Table 7.1. Major depressive disorder is defined by the presence of five or more depressive symptoms during the same 2-week period (DSM-5 Summary Table 7.1). However, depression is often a normal reaction to a number of life events (such as bereavement, financial problems, natural disasters, and suchlike), and for depression to become clinically problematic a diagnosis of major depressive disorder requires the presence of dysfunctional symptoms such as feelings of worthlessness, suicidal ideation, and impairment of daily functioning. In addition, there has been much discussion about whether depression in response to bereavement should be included as one of the criteria

> **major depressive episode** Episode of major depression, defined by the presence of five or more depressive symptoms during the same 2-week period, as stated by the DSM-5.

DSM-5 SUMMARY TABLE 7.1 *Criteria for a major depressive episode*

- At least five of the following are present, including either depressed mood or loss of interest:
  - Depressed mood most of the time
  - Less interest or enjoyment of most activities
  - Significant weight change not associated with dieting
  - Insomnia or excessive sleep
  - Excessive increase or reduction in physical movement
  - Substantial fatigue or lack of energy
  - Feelings of worthlessness or excessive or inappropriate guilt
  - Lack of concentration or ability to think or make decisions
  - Recurrent thoughts of death and suicide or suicide attempt
- The symptoms are not better accounted for by schizoaffective disorder or other mental disorder or due to the effects of a substance or other medical condition

DSM-5 SUMMARY TABLE 7.2 *Criteria for major depressive disorder*

Major depressive disorder
- Presence of a single major depressive episode (not attributable to normal and expected reactions to bereavement, etc.) without previous manic or hypomanic episode where symptoms are not better accounted for by other disorders
- The symptoms must cause clinically significant distress or impairment in social, occupational or other forms of functioning.

contributing to a diagnosis of major depressive disorder and bereavement symptoms had been excluded prior to DSM-5. However, recent research has indicated that bereavement-related depression is not significantly different from major depressive disorder that presents in other contexts; it is most likely to occur in individuals with past histories of major depressive disorder; and is also likely to be chronic and recurrent (Zisook, Corruble, Duan, Iglewicz *et al.*, 2012). For these reasons, bereavement-related symptoms are now no longer excluded from the diagnostic criteria.

Chronic mood disturbances primarily characterized by depressive symptoms can also be diagnosed, although these conditions must have been apparent for at least 2 years, and would normally not be severe enough to disrupt normal social and occupational functioning and warrant a diagnosis of major depression. The most significant of these is **dysthymic disorder**, in which the sufferer has experienced at least 2 years of depressed mood for more days than not (see DSM-5 Summary Table 7.3). Individuals diagnosed with this disorder experience many of the behavioural and cognitive characteristics of major depression, but these are less severe (meeting only two or more of the symptom criteria for major depression).

> **dysthymic disorder** A form of depression in which the sufferer has experienced at least 2 years of depressed mood for more days than not.

However, diagnosing depression is a controversial issue for a number of reasons. Firstly, DSM-5 requires the identification of five symptoms for a period of 2 weeks for a diagnosis of major depression. But are such people any different in their experiences and their functioning from someone who exhibits only three symptoms? Studies have suggested that individuals with three symptoms exhibit similar levels of distress and problems with day-to-day living as individuals with five symptoms (Gotlib, Lewinsohn & Seeley, 1995).

DSM-5 SUMMARY TABLE 7.3 *Criteria for dysthymic disorder*

- Depressed mood most of the time for at least 2 years
- Presence of at least two of the following:
  - Poor appetite or overeating
  - Lack of or excessive sleeping
  - Low levels of energy or fatigue
  - Low self-esteem
  - Poor concentration or decision-making abilities
  - Feelings of hopelessness
- The symptoms are not due to the effects of a substance or other medical condition

Secondly, depression is one of the most prevalent of all psychological problems and is experienced in some form or other by almost everyone at some time in their life. Indeed, experiencing depression is the third most common reason for consulting a doctor or GP in the UK (Singleton, Bumpstead, O'Brien, Lee *et al.*, 2001). In order for GPs to be able to provide treatment for such individuals, there is a tendency for them to over-diagnose mild or moderate depression (Middleton, Shaw, Hull & Feder, 2005). This raises a number of issues, including the possible stigmatisation that such a label might incur for the patient. In addition, lay beliefs about depression suggest that many people already view depression as a 'disease' that is a consequence of everyday life stress (Lauber, Falcato, Nordt & Rossler, 2003). If lay people already view depression as a 'disease' or biological illness, and GPs are more than willing to diagnose it, then we run the risk of the 'medicalisation' of normal everyday negative emotions such as mild distress or even unhappiness (Shaw & Woodward, 2004).

Thirdly, depression occurs in a variety of different guises within psychopathology and is commonly comorbid with other important disorders (Kessler, Nelson, McGonagle, Liu *et al.*, 1996; Table 7.1). This has given rise to a range of different diagnosable disorders that have depression as a central feature within them. As a result, major depressive disorder is a relatively 'pure' diagnosis where the cause of depression cannot be attributed either to some other disorder (such as the consequences of substance abuse) or to specific biological, environmental factors or other life events (such as post-natal depression). Prominent examples of diagnosable problems which have depression as a significant core element include **premenstrual dysphoric disorder**, **seasonal affective disorder (SAD)** and **chronic fatigue syndrome (CFS)** (or myalgic encephalomyelitis, ME), and these are discussed briefly in Focus Point 7.2.

Finally, depression is highly comorbid with anxiety problems and around 60 per cent of people with depression will also experience an anxiety disorder (Moffit, Caspi, Harrington, Milne *et al.*, 2007). This has given rise to a diagnostic category called *mixed anxiety/ depressive disorder* that is used to describe a significant

> **premenstrual dysphoric disorder**
> A condition in which some women experience severe depression symptoms between 5 and 11 days prior to the start of the menstrual cycle. Symptoms then improve significantly within a few days after the onset of menses.

> **seasonal affective disorder (SAD)**
> A condition of regularly occurring depressions in winter with a remission the following spring or summer.

> **chronic fatigue syndrome (CFS)**
> A disorder characterized by depression and mood fluctuations together with physical symptoms such as extreme fatigue, muscle pain, chest pain, headaches and noise and light sensitivity.

TABLE 7.1 *Comorbidity of major depressive disorder with other DSM disorders*

	Lifetime comorbidity (%)	12-month comorbidity (%)
Anxiety disorders		
Generalized anxiety disorder (GAD)	17.2	15.4
Agoraphobia	16.3	12.6
Specific phobia	24.3	23.7
Social phobia	27.1	20.0
Panic disorder	9.9	8.6
Post-traumatic stress disorder (PTSD)	19.5	15.2
Any anxiety disorder	58.0	51.2
Substance use disorders		
Alcohol dependence	23.5	13.0
Drug dependence	13.3	7.5
Alcohol abuse w/o dependence	4.1	1.4
Drug abuse w/o dependence	6.5	1.1
Any substance use disorder	38.6	18.5
Other disorders		
Dysthymia	6.7	4.0
Conduct Disorder	16.2	–
Aggregate number of disorders		
One	24.7	58.9
>One	74.0	26.9
Two	17.4	15.4
>Three	31.9	16.5

Note that the lifetime comorbidity rate of major depression with another anxiety disorder is 58 per cent and with more than one other DSM disorder is 74 per cent, suggesting that individuals with depression tend to experience a range of negative emotions and comorbid disorders.

Source: After Kessler, R.C., Nelson, C.B., McGonagle, K.A., Liu, J., Swartz, M. & Blazer, D.G. (1996). Comorbidity of DSMIII-R major depressive disorder in the general population: Results from the US national comorbidity survey. *British Journal of Psychiatry,* 168(1), 17–30. Reproduced by permission of the Royal College of Psychiatrists.

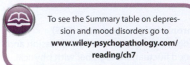
To see the Summary table on depression and mood disorders go to **www.wiley-psychopathology.com/reading/ch7**

number of people who experience a mix of anxiety and depression (around 8 per cent of people with either depression or anxiety symptoms meet the criteria for mixed/anxiety depressive disorder

(Zinbarg, Barlow, Liebowitz *et al.*, 1994). This has led some researchers to suggest that depression and anxiety are not truly independent disorders but represent subcategories of a larger group of emotional disorders with symptoms that can often intermix (e.g. Watson, 2005).

Depression is arguably the most prevalent of the psychopathologies that are covered in this book. Estimates of lifetime prevalence rates for major depression in American community samples range from 5.2 per cent to 17.1 per cent (Kessler, McConagle, Zhao, Nelson *et al.*, 1994; Weissman, Bland, Canino, Favarelli *et al.*, 1996), and depression is now so commonly recognized that it contributes 12 per cent to the total burden of nonfatal global disease (Ustun, Ayuso-Mateos, Chatterji, Mathers *et al.*, 2004). The lifetime risk for major depression may be as high as 20 per cent for men and 30 per cent for women (Kruijshaar, Barendregt, Vos, de Graaf *et al.*, 2005), and the World Health Organisation estimates that 350 million people worldwide of all ages suffer from depression (WHO, 2012). However, gauging the prevalence of depressive symptoms has been difficult because (1) prevalence rates appear to differ significantly across different cultures, (2) the incidence of the diagnosis of depression has increased steadily over the past 90 years, and (3) different studies have tended to use different diagnostic tools when assessing prevalence. For example, studies conducted by the Crossnational Collaborative Group reported very large cultural variations in the prevalence of major depression. These ranged from 1.5 per cent in Taiwan to 19.0 per cent in Lebanon. Lifetime prevalence rates for Puerto Rico and Korea were relatively low at 4.3 per cent and 2.9 per cent respectively, compared with 10.2 per cent for the US (Weissman, Bland, Canino, Favarelli *et al.*, 1996). There appear to be a number of reasons for these large international variations in lifetime prevalence rates. These include (1) the stigmatising of psychopathology in many non-Western societies such as Taiwan, indicating that many individuals in those societies will be unwilling to report symptoms of major depression (Compton, Helzer, Hwu, Yeh *et al.*, 1991), (2) higher levels of somatisation (the expression of psychological distress in physical terms) in non-Western countries (Simon, VonKorff, Piccinelli, Fullerton *et al.*, 1999), (3) the fact that – unlike many other conditions (such as obesity and hypertension) – depression cannot be observed or measured directly, so there will always be an element of subjectivity in the way the symptoms are measured and recorded (Patten, 2003a), and (4) lifetime prevalence rates will always be affected by recall problems, and recall failure with age appears to account for the fact that lifetime prevalence rates decrease with increasing age cohorts (Patten, 2003b).

DEPRESSION-RELATED PROBLEMS

SEASONAL AFFECTIVE DISORDER (SAD)

Seasonal affective disorder (SAD) is a condition of regularly occurring depressions in winter with a remission the following spring or summer, and is a relatively common condition affecting 1–3 per cent of adults in temperate climates (Westrin & Lam, 2007). The main symptoms include depressed mood, lack of energy, hypersomnia, craving for carbohydrates, overeating, and weight gain (Blehar & Rosenthal, 1989). There is some evidence that individuals who develop SAD do so because the longer periods of darkness in winter increase their secretion of the hormone **melatonin**, which acts to slow organisms down, making them sleepy and less energetic (Wetterberg, 1999). The answer to this is to provide individuals suffering from SAD with light therapy or photo therapy in which they are exposed to periods of artificial sunlight during the darker winter months (Magnusson & Boivin, 2003; Reeves, Nijjar, Langenberg, Johnson et al., 2012).

melatonin A hormone that acts to slow organisms down, making them sleepy and less energetic.

CHRONIC FATIGUE SYNDROME (CFS)

Chronic fatigue syndrome (CFS) is characterized by depression and mood fluctuations together with physical symptoms such as extreme fatigue, muscle pain, chest pain, headaches, and noise and light sensitivity (Yancey & Thomas, 2012). Its causes are unclear at present, and this may be the reason why it is given a variety of names, including 'yuppie flu' because of its tendency to afflict predominantly successful young people – especially women – struggling with stressful work and family responsibilities (Ho-Yen, 1990). About 75 per cent of reported cases are adult white females (Showalter, 1997), but this may simply reflect the reluctance of males to report such symptoms. The causes of CFS have not been clearly identified, although theories have argued for the involvement of viral or immunological factors (Behan, More & Behan, 1991) and environmental stressors such as pollution or organophosphates (Jason, Wagner, Taylor, Ropacki et al., 1995). Other researchers have pointed out that depression can be identified as a risk factor in CFS, with a predisposition among CFS sufferers to develop depression and to exhibit frequency of depression prior to CFS onset at twice the level of controls (Straus, Dale, Tobi, Lawley et al., 1988). Interestingly, studies that have provided cognitive behaviour therapy for adolescents with CFS have resulted in significant decreases in fatigue severity and functional impairment, suggesting that addressing psychological factors in CFS may play a significant role in successfully treating the syndrome (Stulemeijer, de Jong, Fiselier, Hoogveld & Bleijenberg, 2005).

PREMENSTRUAL DYSPHORIC DISORDER (PMDD)

PMDD is a condition in which some women will experience severe depression symptoms between 5 and 11 days prior to the start of the menstrual cycle, but these symptoms then improve significantly within a few days after the onset of menses. DSM-5 notes that such symptoms can cause significant distress and disruption to normal daily living and include symptoms such as mood swings, irritability or anger, feelings of hopelessness, decreased interest in usual activities, disruption of normal sleep patterns, lethargy, and food cravings. PMDD affects between 2 and 5 per cent of women during the years they experience menstrual periods (Epperson, Steiner, Hartlage, Eriksson et al., 2012), but can be successfully treated using healthy lifestyle management (e.g. adopting a balanced diet and taking regular exercise), antidepressant medication, or CBT (Kleinstauber, Witthoft & Hiller, 2011).

The incidence of major depression has steadily increased since 1915 and median age of onset has decreased to around 27 years in the US (Kessler, 2002). Women are almost twice as vulnerable to periods of major depression as men (Nolen-Hoeksema, 2002), and this is independent of cultural background.

To complete Activity 7.1 go to www.wiley-psychopathology.com/activities/ch7

7.1.2 The Aetiology of Major Depression

Biological theories

Genetic factors There is good evidence that depressive symptoms run in families, and this suggests the possible existence of an inherited or genetic component to major depression, and first-degree relatives of major depression sufferers are around two to three times more likely to develop depressive symptoms than are individuals who are not first-degree relatives of sufferers (Gershon, Hamovit, Guroff, Dibble *et al.*, 1982; Maier, Lichtermann, Minges, Heun *et al.*, 1992). In addition, heritability based on twin studies is moderate and estimated to be between 30 and 40 per cent (Kendler, Gardner, Neale & Prescott, 2001; Sullivan, Neale & Kendler, 2000; Agrawal, Jacobson, Gardner, Prescott & Kendler, 2004), with adoption studies suggesting that this is a genuine inherited effect rather than a familial one (Wender, Kety, Rosenthal, Schulsinger *et al.*, 1986; Cadoret, 1978). However, after two decades of genetic research the specific genes contributing to this inherited component are still largely unknown. Candidate genes include the serotonin transporter gene (SLC6A4) that can enhance or terminate the action of the brain neurotransmitter serotonin (see next section on Neurochemical factors) (Clarke, Flint, Attwood & Munafò, 2010; Levinson, 2006), although recent reviews have cast some doubt on the critical role of this gene in mediating the inherited component of major depression (Munafò, 2012).

Neurochemical factors Depression and mood disorders have been shown to be reliably associated with abnormalities in the levels of certain brain neurotransmitters, and three neurotransmitters are particularly significant – namely, serotonin, norepinephrine and dopamine (Delgardo & Moreno, 2000), and major depression is often associated with low levels of these neurotransmitters. A number of factors led to findings about the importance of serotonin and norepinephrine levels in particular. First, in the 1950s it was noticed that many medications for high blood pressure also caused depression (Ayd, 1956), and this effect was found to be the result of such medications decreasing brain serotonin levels. The 1950s also saw the development of drugs that significantly alleviated the symptoms of depression. The main ones were **tricyclic drugs** (such as imipramine) and monoamine oxidase (MAO) inhibitors (such as tranylcypromine). Both of these drugs have their effects by increasing levels of both serotonin and norepinephrine in the brain. These findings led to the development of neurochemical theories of depression that argued that depression was caused by either low norepinephrine activity (Bunney & Davis, 1965) or low serotonin activity (Golden & Gilmore, 1990). Because these neurotransmitters are necessary for the successful transmission of impulses between

> **tricyclic drugs** Drugs which block the reuptake of both serotonin and norepinephrine.

neurones, their abnormally low levels in depressed individuals may account for the cognitive, behavioural and motivational deficits found in major depression. In addition to abnormalities in serotonin and norepinephrine levels, it is also believed that low levels of the neurotransmitter dopamine might be involved in major depression (Naranjo, Tremblay & Busto, 2001). Dopamine is significantly involved in the reward systems in the brain, and so depleted dopamine levels may be responsible for deficits in this system in depression giving rise to a lack of motivation, initiative, and pleasure (Treadway & Zald, 2011).

The tricyclic drugs that are often prescribed for people suffering major depression have their beneficial effects by preventing the reuptake by the presynaptic neurone of neurotransmitters serotonin and norepinephrine. This results in higher levels of these neurotransmitters in the synapse, and this facilitates the transmission of impulses to the postsynaptic neurone – thus facilitating brain activity (see Figure 7.1). More recently, the development

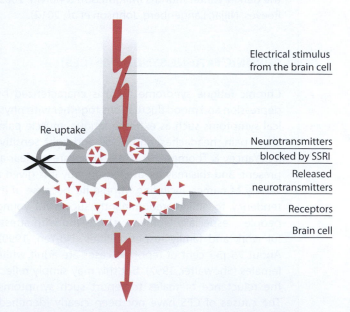

Electrical stimulus from the brain cell

Re-uptake

Neurotransmitters blocked by SSRI

Released neurotransmitters

Receptors

Brain cell

FIGURE 7.1 *Neurones release the neurotransmitters serotonin and norepinephrine from their endings when they fire and these help transmission between brain cells. Some of the neurotransmitter molecules are recaptured by the neurone using a reuptake mechanism, and this can occur before they are received by the receptor neurone, thus weakening the transmission between neurones. Both tricyclic drugs and SSRIs have their effect by blocking the reuptake of these neurotransmitters and so ensure that neural transmission is more effective. Tricyclic drugs block the reuptake of both serotonin and norepinephrine, while SSRIs selectively block the reuptake only of serotonin.*

of selective serotonin reuptake inhibitors (SSRIs) (such as Prozac) has allowed researchers to assess the specific role of serotonin in depression, and researchers now believe that serotonin levels play a central role in major depression. However, this picture is relatively simplistic, and the most recent neurochemical theories of mood disorders suggest that interactions between different neurotransmitters may be important. Some researchers suggest that depression is associated more with an *imbalance* in neurotransmitters than with deficits in specific neurotransmitters (Rampello, Nicoletti & Nicoletti, 2000; Ressler & Nemeroff, 1999). Other theorists have suggested that low levels of serotonin interact with levels of norepinephrine in rather complex ways, such that combinations of low levels of both serotonin and norepinephrine produce depression, but low levels of serotonin and high levels of norepinephrine result in mania (Mandell & Knapp, 1979).

Brain abnormalities and depression

Recent developments in cognitive neuroscience together with the evolution of new technologies for scanning and photographing the brain (e.g. magnetic resonance imaging (MRI); see section 2.2.4) have led to a greater understanding of the brain areas involved in depression and mood disorders (Davidson, Pizzagalli, Nitschke & Putnam, 2002). Studies have identified dysfunction or abnormalities in a number of brain areas that appear to be associated with depression. These areas are the prefrontal cortex, the anterior cingulate cortex, the hippocampus, and the amygdala, and these areas are illustrated in Figure 7.2. This raises the question of the role that such areas may play in relation to depression, and Davidson *et al.* (2002) have attempted to address these issues. First, depression is associated with significantly lower levels of activation in the prefrontal cortex (Drevets, 1998), and this area is important in maintaining representations of goals and the means to achieve them. Decreased activation in this area may result in the failure to anticipate incentives, which is a common feature of depression. Second, decreased **anterior cingulate cortex** (**ACC**) activation is also reported in major depression (Beauregard, Leroux, Bergman, Arzoumanian *et al.*, 1998). Evidence suggests that ACC activation is present when effortful emotional regulation is required in situations where behaviour is failing to achieve a desired outcome (Ochsner & Barrett, 2001), and Davidson *et al.* (2002) suggest that this may reflect a

anterior cingulate cortex (ACC) The frontal part of the cingulate cortex resembling a 'collar' form around the corpus callosum, used for the relay of neural signals between the right and left hemispheres of the brain.

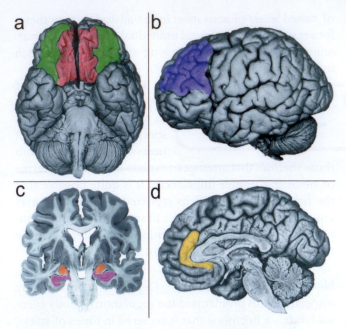

FIGURE 7.2 *Key brain regions involved in affect and mood disorders: (a) orbital prefrontal cortex (green) and the ventromedial prefrontal cortex (red), (b) dorsolateral prefrontal cortex (blue), (c) hippocampus (purple) and amygdale (orange), (d) anterior cingulated cortex (yellow).*
Source: After Davidson, R.J., Pizzagalli, D., Nitschke, J.B. & Putnam, K. (2002). Depression: Perspectives from affective neuroscience. *Annual Review of Psychology, 53*, 545–574. *Annual Review of Psychology* by Stone, Calvin Perry. Reproduced with permission of ANNUAL REVIEWS in the format Republish in a book via Copyright Clearance Center.

deficit in the 'will-to-change' that is also characteristic of depressed individuals. Third, individuals with depression and mood disorders also show signs of dysfunction in the hippocampus (Mervaala, Fohr, Kononen, Valkonen-Korhonen *et al.*, 2000). The hippocampus is important in adrenocorticotropic hormone secretion and is also critical in learning about the *context* of affective reactions (Fanselow, 2000). Thus, deficits in hippocampus function in depression may result in the individual dissociating affective responses from their relevant contexts. In depression, this may manifest itself as feelings of sadness occurring independently of contexts in which we would normally expect such emotions (i.e. sadness is experienced in all contexts, not just following relevant life events such as a bereavement). Finally, major depression has also been found to be associated with structural and functional abnormalities in the amygdala, and especially with increased amygdala activation (Abercrombie, Schaefer, Larson, Oakes *et al.*, 1998). A role of the amygdala is in directing attention to affectively salient stimuli and prioritising the processing of such stimuli. The effect of raised levels of activation in the amygdala may therefore result in the depressed individual prioritising threatening information for processing and interpreting such information negatively.

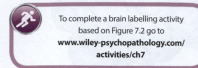

To complete a brain labelling activity based on Figure 7.2 go to www.wiley-psychopathology.com/activities/ch7

These explanations of depressive symptomatology in terms of dysfunction in specific brain areas are not necessarily inconsistent with those theories that attempt to explain depression in terms of neurotransmitter imbalances. It is quite possible that the functional brain deficits reported in depression may indeed result from imbalances in specific neurotransmitters such as serotonin, dopamine and norepinephrine (e.g. Kupfer, Frank & Phillips, 2012).

Neuroendocrine factors
Depression is regularly associated with problems in the regulation of body cortisol levels – a hormone that is secreted in times of stress. We mentioned earlier that the hippocampus is important in adrenocorticotropic hormone secretion, and that depressed individuals frequently exhibit hippocampal abnormalities (Mervaala, Fohr, Kononen, Valkonen-Korhonen *et al.*, 2000). These hippocampal abnormalities are regularly linked with high levels of **cortisol** (an adrenocortical hormone),

cortisol An adrenocortical hormone.

and patients receiving chronic corticosteroid therapy for endocrine problems have smaller hippocampal volumes and higher depression ratings than nonpatient controls (Brown, Woolston, Frol, Bobadilla *et al.*, 2004). In addition, the hypothalamic–pituitary–adrenocortical (HPA) network is the biological system that manages and reacts to stress, and triggers the secretion of cortisol in response to stress. It is the lack of inhibitory control over cortisol secretion that is linked with depression, and around 80 per cent of individuals who are hospitalized because of their depressive symptoms show poor regulation of the HPA network (Heuser, Yassourides & Holsboer, 1994) and are more likely to be prone to future bouts of depression (Aubry, Gervasoni, Osiek, Perret *et al.*, 2007).

Cortisol may influence depressive symptoms by causing enlargement of the adrenal glands and in turn lowering the frequency of serotonin transmitters in the brain (Roy, Virkkunen & Linnoila, 1987). We saw earlier that low levels of the neurotransmitter serotonin in the brain have been established as an important factor in depression. As noted above, cortisol is also a hormone that is released by the body during times of stress (Holsboer, 2001), and it is no coincidence that periods of depression are often preceded by stressful life events. So, according to this account, life stressors raise levels of the adrenocortical hormone cortisol that in turn lowers levels of the brain neurotransmitter serotonin, which results in

the cognitive, behavioural and motivational symptoms of depression (see also Focus Point 7.3 describing how inflammation might affect the experience of depression through its affect on neurotransmitters).

Summary of biological theories
The preceding evidence suggests that biological factors may play an important role in the development and maintenance of mood disorders such as major depression. There is clearly an inherited component (which accounts for about one-third of the variance in measures of depression), and imbalances in specific brain neurotransmitters such as serotonin, norepinephrine and dopamine have been clearly linked to symptoms of depression. Recent developments in brain scanning technology have also allowed researchers to identify abnormalities in specific areas of the human brain that are associated with depression. These are all impressive and important findings, but we must remember that depression and mood disorders almost certainly do not stem solely from biological dysfunction. As we shall see in the next section, psychological and cognitive factors are equally important in the aetiology and maintenance of mood disorders, and supplement our knowledge of biological factors. Biological and psychological explanations are not mutually exclusive and they attempt to explain phenomena at different levels of description. Indeed, it is still not clear whether many of the biological factors we have described in this section are truly *causal* factors in depression, or whether they simply represent biological changes that reflect the *experience* of depression. That is, biological factors may give rise to many of the symptoms of depression, but psychological processes may in turn trigger these biological factors.

Psychological theories

Psychodynamic explanations
There are numerous different psychodynamic views of depression (see Blatt & Homann, 1992), but the most well-established is the psychoanalytic account pioneered by Freud (1917/1963) and Abraham (1916/1960). This view argues that depression is a response to loss, and, in particular, a response to the loss of a loved one such as a parent. The first stage of response to this loss is called **introjection**, where the individual regresses to the oral stage of development, and this allows them to integrate the identity of the person they have lost with their own. Introjection also

introjection A response to a loss where individuals regress to the oral stage of development, which allows them to integrate the identity of the person they have lost with their own.

allows them to direct all of the feelings they would have for the loved one onto themselves. These include anger if they feel that the loved one has 'deserted them' and

FOCUS POINT 7.3

DEPRESSION AND INFLAMMATION

As we mentioned at the beginning of this chapter, depression is a widely experienced mental health problem. It has significantly high prevalence rates; it is highly comorbid with other psychopathologies; it is also commonly experienced during many physical illnesses (such as cardiac illnesses, cancer, diabetes, rheumatoid arthritis, and multiple sclerosis); and it is also experienced during degenerative brain disorders such as Parkinson's disease and Alzheimer's disease (see Chapter 15). However, depression is not just a consequence of physical illness, it is also in many cases a predictor of future illness. For example, depression is known to be a risk factor for coronary artery disease (Stewart, Rand, Muldoon & Kamarck, 2009; Suls & Bunde, 2005) and for strokes (May, McCarron, Stansfield, Ben-Shlomo *et al.*, 2002).

This link between depression and physical illnesses has led to the development of theories arguing that inflammation may contribute to the experience of depression. Central to this view are *cytokines* – proteins made by immune cells that control responses to foreign antigens and germs, generating inflammation and fever. Consistent with this is the fact that depression also seems in be associated with changes in the immune system, especially those changes that involve cytokines. Studies have also shown that both medically ill and medically healthy individuals with major depression exhibit all the cardinal features of inflammation, including elevations in inflammatory cytokines and symptoms such as fatigue, cognitive dysfunction, and impaired sleep (Miller, Maletic & Raison, 2009; Meyers, Albitar & Estey, 2005).

So, how might inflammation and symptoms of depression be causally linked? Animal studies suggest administration of cytokines can profoundly affect the metabolism of the neurotransmitters implicated in depression, including serotonin, norepinephrine and dopamine (Anisman, Merali & Hayley, 2008; Felger, Alagbe, Hu, Mook *et al.*, 2007). Cytokines also generate behaviours strikingly similar to symptoms found in depression, such as listlessness, loss of appetite, lack of interest in socialising and sex, and increased sensitivity to pain. From an adaptive viewpoint, it makes sense for an organism that is fighting disease and infection to restrict activity generally and eat less to allow available resources to be focused on the area that is under physical attack from illness.

There is still much more research required before we can be confident that inflammation is a process that contributes significantly to the experience of depression, but the current arguments seem compelling and logical. It remains to be seen whether inflammation is an explanation for all depression experience, or whether some other causes of depression and depression experience are independent of inflammation. However, if inflammation and depression are inseparably bound together, then one implication of this is that treatment for depression will also need to take account of those medical processes that can alleviate inflammation and relieve physical illness.

---

guilt if they experience any positive emotions in the wake of the loss. The individual begins to experience self-hatred that develops very rapidly into low self-esteem, and this adds to feelings of depression and hopelessness. Because such losses return the individual to the oral stage of development, psychoanalysis argues that depression has a functional role to play, in that it returns the person to a period in their life when they were dependent on others (their parents). During their depressed state, this regression to the oral stage allows the individual to become dependent on their relationships with others in order to utilize the support that this will offer. One problem with this psychoanalytic interpretation is that not everyone who experiences depression has lost a loved one, and this led Freud to propose the concept of **symbolic loss** in which other kinds of losses within one's life (e.g. losing a job)

are viewed as equivalent to losing a loved one. These losses then cause the individual to regress to the oral stage of development and may trigger memories of inadequate parental support during childhood. In addition, parental loss is no longer seen as a necessary condition for the development of depression, and poor parenting is a more significant risk factor (Lara & Klein, 1999). Support for this view comes from studies that have shown a relationship between risk for depression in adulthood and having experienced a particular kind of parenting style known as **affectionless control** (Garber & Flynn, 2001). This type of parenting is characterized by high levels of overprotection combined with a lack of warmth and care.

There is some empirical support for this psychoanalytic view of depression. For example, individuals who report that their childhood needs were not adequately

symbolic loss A Freudian concept whereby other kinds of losses within one's life (e.g. losing a job) are viewed as equivalent to losing a loved one.

affectionless control A type of parenting characterized by high levels of overprotection combined with a lack of warmth and care.

met by their parents are more likely to become depressed after experiencing a loss (Goodman, 2002). Also, there is evidence for a link between parental loss and depression. Women whose mothers either died or abandoned them during their childhood are more likely to develop depression than women who have not had these kinds of experiences (Harris, Brown & Bifulco, 1990). Nevertheless, there are difficulties with the psychoanalytic view. Firstly, much of the empirical evidence that is consistent with this view is also consistent with many other theories of depression, so the evidence does not help to differentiate between theoretical approaches. Secondly, many individuals who do experience parental loss or poor parenting do not go on to develop depression. Psychoanalytic approaches do not clearly explain why this is the case. Finally, because of the way that psychodynamic theories are formulated, many of the key aspects of the theory are difficult to test. Concepts such as introjection, fixation at the oral stage of development and symbolic loss are all difficult to operationalize and measure, and so verify empirically. This difficulty is compounded by the Freudian belief that such processes are thought to operate at the unconscious level.

Behavioural theories

The most obvious characteristics of depressed individuals include their lack of motivation and initiative, a considerably diminished behavioural repertoire, and a view of the future that lacks positive and fulfilling experiences. Some theorists have suggested that these characteristics provide evidence that depression results from a lack of appropriate reinforcement for positive and constructive behaviours (Lewinsohn, 1974). This leads to the extinction of existing behaviours, and to a 'behavioural vacuum' in which the person becomes inactive and withdrawn. It is certainly the case that periods of depression follow life 'losses' such as bereavement, retirement, or redundancy, and each of these events represent the loss of important sources of reward and reinforcement for social and occupational behaviours (see also Figure 7.5 showing how suicide rates increase during a financial recession). In support of this account, it has been shown that depressed individuals report fewer rewards in their life than non-depressed individuals, and introducing rewards into the lives of depressed individuals helps to elevate their mood (Lewinsohn, Youngren & Grosscup, 1979; Jacobson, Martell & Dimidjian, 2001). The fact that life 'losses' are likely to result in the reduction of reinforcing events for the depressed individual also leads to a vicious cycle that can establish depression as a chronic condition. For example, once the individual becomes depressed, then their lack of initiative and withdrawal is unlikely to lead to the development of other alternative sources of reinforcement. Indeed, the demeanour of the depressed individual is likely to

be an active contributor to their lack of reinforcement – especially social reinforcement. For example, depressed individuals are significantly more likely than non-depressed individuals to elicit negative reactions in others (Joiner, 2002) – perhaps because they do not enter into the reciprocal reinforcing activities that social interaction requires. Depressed individuals are also less skilled at interacting with others than non-depressed individuals (Joiner, 2002; Segrin, 2000). In particular, they will usually communicate negative attitudes, appear withdrawn and unresponsive, and tend to demand reassurance. Indeed, when interacting with depressed individuals, non-depressed control participants exhibit less positive social behaviour, are less verbal, and are less positive than when interacting with a non-depressed individual (Gotlib & Robinson, 1982).

The frequent failure of depressed individuals to elicit reinforcing reactions from individuals with whom they are communicating has led to **interpersonal theories** of depression. These theories argue that depression is maintained by a cycle of excessive reassurance seeking from depressed individuals that is subsequently rejected by family and friends because of the negative and repetitive way in which the depressed individual talks about their problems (Joiner, 1995). Excessive reassurance seeking is defined as 'the relatively stable tendency to excessively and persistently seek reassurances from others that one is lovable and worthy, regardless of whether such assurance has already been provided' (Joiner, Metalsky, Katz & Beach, 1999), and the negative beliefs about themselves, their world and their future leads depressed individuals to doubt any reassurances they are given by friends and family, and this continual doubting may come to annoy friends and family who try to provide reassurance (Joiner & Metalsky, 1995). Interestingly, excessive reassurance seeking in depressed individuals predicts future depressive symptoms (Joiner, Metalsky, Katz et al., 1999; Haeffel, Voelz & Joiner, 2007), and roommates of depressed college students report greater hostility to them than to non-depressed roommates (Joiner, Alfano & Metalsky, 1992). Excessive reassurance seeking by depressed individuals is also associated with motivation to obtain self-confirming negative feedback, which is another risk factor for depressive symptoms and interpersonal rejection that creates a vicious cycle of rejection and depression (Davila, Stroud & Starr et al., 2009). Evidence such as this appears to support the view that the behaviour and attitudes displayed by depressed individuals elicits negative responses in others, and this in turn can exacerbate the symptoms of depression (Evraire & Dozois, 2011).

> **interpersonal theories** Theories that argue that depression is maintained by a cycle of reassurance-seeking by depressed individuals that is subsequently rejected by family and friends because of the negative way in which depressed individuals talk about their problems.

However, we must be cautious about how we interpret this evidence as a causal factor in depression. Firstly, much of the research on the link between lack of reinforcement and depression has been retrospective in nature, and it is quite reasonable to suppose that depressed individuals may underestimate the extent of the actual rewards in their life. Secondly, we need to understand whether excessive reassurance seeking and seeking negative feedback are dispositional factors that create a risk for depressive symptoms or whether depressive symptoms themselves elicit these characteristics (Evraire & Dozois, 2011).

Negative cognitions and self-schema

One of the most influential of all the theories of depression is Beck's cognitive theory (Beck, 1967, 1987). This theory introduced the idea that depression could be caused by biases in ways of thinking and processing information. We know that depressed individuals indulge in a good deal of 'negative thinking', and that they experience more negative intrusive thoughts than non-depressed individuals (Reynolds & Salkovskis, 1992). Facts such as this have led Beck (1987) to claim that depressed individuals have developed a broad-ranging **negative schema** that tends them towards viewing the world and themselves in a negative way (see Figure 7.3). In turn, these negative schema influence the selection, encoding, categorisation, and evaluation of stimuli and events in the world in a way

negative schema A set of beliefs that tends individuals towards viewing the world and themselves in a negative way.

that leads to a vicious cycle of depressive affect and symptomatology. Beck argued that these negative schema are a relatively stable characteristic of the depressed individual's personality, and develop as a result of early adverse childhood experiences – especially concerning loss (such as the loss of a parent figure). In later life, a stressful experience will reactivate this negative schema and give rise to the biased thinking that generates depressive symptoms such as deficits in motivational, affective, cognitive and behavioural functioning.

Beck argued that the depressed individual's negative schema maintained some interrelated aspects of negative thinking that Beck called the **negative triad**. In particular, depressed people hold negative views of *themselves* (e.g. 'I am unattractive'), negative views of their *future* (e.g. 'I will never achieve anything'), and of the *world* (e.g. 'the world is a dangerous and unsupportive place'). This set of negative beliefs eventually generates self-fulfilling prophecies. That is, the depressed individual interprets events negatively, fails to take the initiative, and then inevitably experiences failure. The negative triad of beliefs leads to a number of systematic biases in thinking, including arbitrary inference, selective abstraction, overgeneralization, magnification and minimization, personalization, and all-or-none thinking (see Table 7.2).

negative triad A theory of depression in which depressed people hold negative views of themselves (e.g. 'I am unattractive'), of their future (e.g. 'I will never achieve anything') and of the world (e.g. 'The world is a dangerous and unsupportive place').

There is considerable evidence that depressed individuals do show the negative cognitive biases that Beck's theory predicts. First, some studies have shown attentional biases to negative information in depressed individuals that results in them prioritising that negative information. In the emotional Stroop procedure, depressed individuals are slower at naming the colour of negative words than positive words, suggesting that their attention is drawn towards the meaning of such words (Gotlib & Cane, 1987; Epp, Dobson, Dozois & Frewen, 2012). Also, in a dichotic listening procedure, depressed individuals have greater difficulty ignoring negative words that are presented as distractors than do non-depressed participants (Ingram, Bernet & McLaughlin, 1994). The exact nature of this attentional bias is unclear, and some studies have failed to replicate these experimental effects (e.g. Mogg, Bradley, Williams & Mathews, 1993). Nevertheless, there is sufficient evidence to suggest that there is a bias towards processing negative information in depression – especially if it is information that is specifically relevant to depression (rather than general negative words) (Gotlib, Gilboa & Sommerfeld, 2000). Second, memory biases are also apparent in depression, with depressed individuals able to recall more negative words than positive words in explicit memory tests

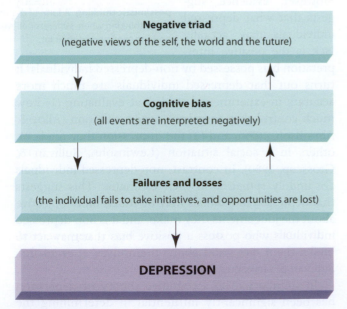

FIGURE 7.3 *Beck's negative schema in depression.*
This figure shows how the negative biases in the thinking of depressed individuals leads to a vicious cycle in which depression becomes a self-fulfilling prophecy.

TABLE 7.2 *Thinking biases in Beck's model of depression*

Arbitrary inference	Jumping to a conclusion when evidence is lacking or is actually contrary to the conclusion
Selective abstraction	Abstracting a detail out of context and missing the significance of the total situation
Overgeneralization	Unjustified generalization on the basis of a single incident (e.g. making a single mistake and concluding 'I never do anything right')
Magnification and minimization	Perceiving events as either totally bad or neutral or irrelevant. Catastrophising is an example of magnification, in which the individual takes a single fact to its extreme (e.g. a scratch on a new car means the car is wrecked and needs replacing)
Personalization	The propensity to interpret events in terms of their personal meaning to the individual rather than their objective characteristics (e.g. believing that a frown on another person's face means they are annoyed specifically with you)
All-or-none thinking	Events are labelled as black or white, good or bad, wonderful or horrible (e.g. assuming that everyone will either accept you or reject you)

(Mathews & MacLeod, 1994), but this again seems to apply predominantly to depression-relevant material rather than threat-relevant material generally (Watkins, Mathews, Williamson & Fuller, 1992). Furthermore, recent studies have indicated that depressed individuals will remember more negative than positive information about themselves (Alloy, Abramson, Murray, Whitehouse & Hogan, 1997), and of particular interest is the biased recall of autobiographical memories by depressed individuals. Not only do they recall fewer positive autobiographical experiences than non-depressed individuals, but those positive memories that are retrieved are more general and less detailed (Williams & Scott, 1988; Raes, Hermans, Williams & Eelen, 2006). Subsequent studies have suggested that there may be an association between experiencing early life trauma (such as childhood abuse) and reduced autobiographical memory specificity (Raes, Hermans, Williams & Eelen, 2005), and that poorly detailed autobiographical memories may be linked to the deficits in problem-solving ability that are characteristic of depressed individuals (Pollock & Williams, 2001). Third, there is experimental evidence that depressed individuals exhibit the interpretational bias that would lead them to

interpreting ambiguous events negatively or to judge events more negatively. There is considerable evidence, for example, that depressed affect is associated with more critical self-judgement and a raising of personal performance standards (Forgas, Bower & Krantz, 1984; Scott & Cervone, 2002). More recent theories suggest that the combination of biases in attention, interpretation, memory and cognitive control and their interaction may be a better predictor of depressive symptoms than any of these biases alone (Hirsch, Clark & Mathews, 2006; Everaert, Koster & Derakshan, 2012), and this is a potentially fruitful direction for future research in this area.

In addition to the evidence supporting the existence of negative information processing biases in depression, there is also evidence that supports specific predictions from Beck's theory. For example, studies using the Dysfunctional Attitude Scale (DAS) – which measures dysfunctional negative beliefs – have shown that negative thinking in combination with a recent negative life event can trigger depression (Lewinsohn, Rohde, Seeley & Baldwin, 2001). Further research has suggested that depressed individuals may have two different types of negative schema – one related to dependency and the other related to criticism (Nietzel & Harris, 1990). In the case of a dependency self-schema, losses would trigger depression (e.g. bereavement), but in the case of the criticism self-schema, depression would be triggered by failures (e.g. failing an interview) (Coyne & Whiffen, 1995).

Finally, we tend to associate depression, and Beck's cognitive theory of depression in particular, with **pessimistic thinking** caused by negative self-schemas. However, evidence suggests that what depressed individuals may actually lack is the positive interpretation bias possessed by non-depressed individuals. It turns out that depressed individuals are much more accurate in experimental studies at evaluating (1) how much control they may have over a situation (Alloy & Abramson, 1979), and (2) the impression they made on others in a social situation (Lewinsohn, Sullivan & Grosscup, 1980). In contrast, non-depressed individuals are unduly *optimistic* in their estimates. This suggests that depressed individuals may be much more objective about the judgements they make, and it is non-depressed individuals who possess a positive bias that may act to 'make them feel good about themselves' (Lewinsohn, Sullivan & Grosscup, 1980).

In summary, Beck's cognitive theory of depression has been significantly influential in determining the way we conceptualize, research and treat depression. It has generated a range of research on cognitive biases in depression and has contributed substantially to cognitive-based treatments of depression (see section 7.3.1). However, it is still unclear whether the negative cognitive

> **pessimistic thinking** A form of dysfunctional thinking where sufferers believe nothing can improve their lot.

USING EXPERIMENTAL PSYCHOPATHOLOGY METHODS TO UNDERSTAND DEPRESSION

Theories of depression that allude to biases in thinking and dysfunctional beliefs (such as Beck's cognitive theory of depression) need to be empirically tested to find out whether such biases do mediate depression. One important way of doing this is to use **experimental psychopathology** to study the psychological processes that underlie basic mental health problems such as depression (Vervliet & Raes, 2012).

One aim of experimental psychopathology is to mimic in healthy individuals those processes thought to underlie the cognitive or neurological mechanisms that give rise to psychopathology, and so either increase our understanding of those mechanisms, or to confirm that such mechanisms do indeed lead to increases in symptoms. There are many ways in which this can be achieved. One is by re-creating in the experimental lab the conditions thought to give rise to symptoms, and testing these out on healthy individuals (e.g. by using negative mood inductions to generate sad mood in healthy participants, and see if this affects attentional and memory biases in ways predicted by Beck's theory – see section 7.1.2); an alternative is to create animal models of individual psychopathologies that can be tested in experimental studies on animals such as rats or mice (e.g. testing the inflammation model of depression on laboratory rats by experimentally investigating the effects of administered cytokines on the metabolism of neurotransmitters implicated in depression; see Focus Point 7.3).

> **experimental psychopathology**
> Experimental field of psychological science aimed at understanding the processes underlying psychopathology.

Vervliet & Raes (2012) point out that when conducting experimental psychopathology methods on healthy participants, we need to be sure that such methods have *external validity* and are able to bridge what is called the 'translational gap' from healthy individuals to clinical cases. Up to four criteria need to be met for external validity: (1) *face validity* – where there is at least a degree of phenomenological similarity between the behaviour of the model and the symptoms in the disorder, (2) *predictive validity* – where performance in the model predicts performance in the disorder, (3) *construct validity* – where the experimental psychopathology procedure accurately recreates the aetiological processes or mechanisms known to operate in the disorder, and (4) *diagnostic validity* – where the procedure shows that any experimental manipulations produce behavioural or cognitive outcomes that can be properly extrapolated to those found in diagnosed patients (e.g. in intensity or frequency).

One example of the use of experimental psychopathology methods in the study of depression is a study by Hepburn, Barnhofer & Williams (2006). They studied the effect of experimentally induced positive and negative mood in healthy participants on the cognitive processes underlying future thinking. They found that participants induced into a negative mood (equivalent to depression) rated positive future events as more negative than those in a positive mood and became less fluent at generating future positive events. They conclude that increased negative or depressed mood may significantly reduce the accessibility of positive future events, and also lead to the assessment of those events when retrieved as less positive than when in a neutral or positive mood. This may have significant relevance to the processes underlying hopelessness (see section 7.1.2) and may be a risk factor for suicidality.

biases defined by Beck's theory actually cause depression, or whether these biases are simply a consequence of experienced depression. Further research will be needed to clarify issues such as this.

Learned helplessness and attribution
During a person's lifetime they may experience a number of unavoidable and uncontrollable negative life events. These may include the sudden death of a close friend or relative, or being made redundant from a job. Seligman (1975) proposed that depression could be linked specifically to these kinds of experiences, and that they give rise to a 'cognitive set' that makes the individual learn to become 'helpless', lethargic and depressed. It is the perceived uncontrollability of these negative life events that is important, and leads the individual to the pessimistic

belief that negative life events will happen whatever they do. Seligman (1974) first derived this hypothesis from animal learning experiments in which dogs were first given unavoidable electric shocks, and then subsequently taught to learn a simple avoidance response that would avoid the shocks. He found that dogs that were given prior unavoidable electric shocks were subsequently unable to learn the avoidance response and simply lay down in the apparatus and 'quietly whined'. One example of how **learned helplessness** theory has been applied to depression is in the case of battered women. Walker (2000) has suggested that a pattern of repeated partner abuse leads battered

> **learned helplessness** A theory of depression that argues that people become depressed following unavoidable negative life events because these events give rise to a cognitive set that makes individuals learn to become 'helpless', lethargic and depressed.

women to believe that they are powerless to change their situation. As a result, such women come to exhibit all the symptoms of depression and display the 'passivity' found in **battered woman syndrome**.

battered woman syndrome The view that a pattern of repeated partner abuse leads battered women to believe that they are powerless to change their situation.

However, while animal experiments on learned helplessness do appear to have a formalistic similarity to human depression, there are a number of reasons for believing that it is not a full or comprehensive account of depression. Firstly, some studies with humans have suggested that prior experience with uncontrollable negative events may actually facilitate subsequent performance (Wortman & Brehm, 1975). Secondly, many depressed individuals see themselves as being responsible for their failures and losses – yet someone who perceives himself or herself as helpless should not blame themselves for these events. Thirdly, in the specific case of battered woman syndrome, passivity may not be the result of the woman learning that she is helpless, but it may be a learned adaptive response to abuse. This may take the form of the woman thinking, 'If I do not make requests and acquiesce to his demands, he is less likely to hit me' (Peterson, Maier & Seligman, 1993).

These difficulties and inconsistencies in the original learned helplessness theory led to the development of a revised theory that included the important concept of attribution (Abramson, Seligman & Teasdale, 1978). **Attribution theories** of depression argue that people learn to become helpless, or more specifically 'hopeless', because they possess certain attributional styles that generate pessimistic thinking. Attributions are the explanations that individuals have for their behaviour and the events that happen to them. In particular, Abramson, Seligman & Teasdale (1978) argue that people become depressed when they attribute negative life events primarily to factors that either cannot easily

attribution theories Theories of depression which suggest that people who are likely to become depressed attribute negative life events to internal, stable and global factors.

be manipulated or are unlikely to change. In particular, people who are likely to become depressed attribute negative life events to (1) *internal* rather than external factors (e.g. to personal traits rather than outside events), (2) *stable* rather than unstable factors (e.g. things that are unlikely to change in the near future), and (3) *global* rather than specific factors (e.g. causes that have an effect over many areas of their life rather than being specific to one area of functioning). Table 7.3 provides an example of the range of attributions that someone might make in relation to failing a maths exam. In this case, the global, stable, and internal attribution is 'I lack intelligence', and this attribution is likely to have a number of negative consequences. First, it is the kind of cause that is not easily changed so that future failures might be avoided. Second, it reflects negatively on the individual's self-concept, and so is likely to reduce self-esteem. Third, it is a global attribution, and so the individual is likely to believe that they will fail at many other things, and not just a maths exam, and this is likely to lead to the kinds of pessimistic thinking typical of depression. In contrast, if the student had attributed their failure to specific, unstable factors, such as 'I am fed up with maths' or 'my maths test was numbered 13', they would have been less likely to experience helplessness (because these are factors that could change quite easily or reduced self-esteem).

In order to test the attributional account of depression, Peterson, Semmel, von Baeyer, Abramson *et al.* (1982) developed the Attributional Style Questionnaire (ASQ) which measures tendencies to make the particular kinds of causal inference that are hypothesized to play a causal role in depression (see Table 7.4). Several studies have subsequently found that use of the global/stable attributional style is a vulnerability factor for future depression (Butters, McClure, Siegert & Ward, 1997; Chaney, Mullins, Wagner, Hommel *et al.*, 2004) – especially following negative life events (Hankin & Abramson, 2002). A study by Metalsky, Joiner, Hardin & Abramson (1993) gave students the ASQ prior to a midterm exam and then measured depressive symptoms over the subsequent

TABLE 7.3 *Why I failed my GCSE maths exam*

Degree	Internal (personal)		External (environmental)	
	Stable	**Unstable**	**Stable**	**Unstable**
Global	I lack intelligence	I am exhausted	These tests are unfair	It's an unlucky day
Specific	I lack mathematical ability	I am fed up with maths	The test is unfair	My maths test was numbered 13

People who become depressed tend to attribute negative life events to internal, stable global causes (in this example 'I lack intelligence' is an example of this). In contrast, had the individual attributed their failure to specific, unstable factors (such as 'I am fed up with maths' or 'My maths test was numbered 13'), they would have been less likely to experience helplessness.

TABLE 7.4 *The Attributional Style Questionnaire (ASQ)*

The ASQ contains a number of hypothetical situations designed to measure the individual's bias towards making certain kinds of attributions for both positive and negative events. Abramson, Seligman & Teasdale (1978) argued that people who attribute negative events to internal, stable and global events are most likely to develop helplessness and depression.

Sample situation and items:

You have been looking for a job unsuccessfully for some time.

1. Write down the *one* major cause.

2. Is the unsuccessful job search due to something about you or to something about other people in the circumstances?

| TOTALLY DUE TO OTHER PEOPLE OR CIRCUMSTANCES | 1 | 2 | 3 | 4 | 5 | 6 | TOTALLY DUE TO ME |

3. In the future when looking for a job, will this cause be present?

| WILL NEVER AGAIN BE PRESENT | 1 | 2 | 3 | 4 | 5 | 6 | WILL ALWAYS BE PRESENT |

4. Is the cause something that just influences looking for a job or does it also influence other areas of your life?

| INFLUENCES JUST THIS PARTICULAR SITUATION | 1 | 2 | 3 | 4 | 5 | 6 | INFLUENCES ALL SITUATIONS IN MY LIFE |

5. How important would this situation be if it happened to you?

| NOT AT ALL IMPORTANT | 1 | 2 | 3 | 4 | 5 | 6 | EXTREMELY IMPORTANT |

Item 2 measures internality, item 3 measures stability, and item 4 measures globality

---

5 days. They found that the students' enduring depressive reactions during this period were predicted by a global/stable attributional style together with low self-esteem and exam failure. This suggests that the global/stable attributional style in the context of a negative life event (e.g. exam failure) is a good predictor of subsequent depression. Finally, a computer-based cognitive bias modification task (see Treatment in Practice Box 6.4) can be used to create either negative or positive attributional styles, and individuals in which the positive attributional style is induced subsequently report less depressed mood in response to a stressor than individuals in which a negative attributional style is induced (Peters, Constans & Mathews, 2011). Experimental studies such as this suggest a direct causal link between attributional style and depressed mood.

Hopelessness theory The attributional/helplessness account of depression has been further refined to account for the fact that attributional style appears to interact with a number of other factors to cause depression.

Abramson, Metalsky & Alloy (1989) suggested that the tendency to attribute negative events to global/stable causes represents a diathesis which, in the presence of negative life events, increases vulnerability to a group of depressive symptoms, including retarded initiation of voluntary responses, apathy, lack of energy and psychomotor retardation. This cluster of symptoms is known as hopelessness, which is an expectation that positive outcomes will not occur, negative outcomes will occur, and that the individual has no responses available that will change this state of affairs. **Hopelessness theory** is very similar to attributional/helplessness accounts in that negative life events are viewed as interacting with a global/stable attributional style to generate depressed symptomatology. However, hopelessness theory also predicts that other factors, such as low self-esteem, may also be involved as vulnerability factors (Metalsky, Joiner, Hardin & Abramson, 1993). Many

hopelessness theory A theory of depression in which individuals exhibit an expectation that positive outcomes will not occur, negative outcomes will occur, and that the individual has no responses available that will change this state of affairs.

- Can you describe how behavioural theories and interpersonal theories explain the development of depression?
- What is Beck's 'negative triad'?
- What is the evidence that depressed individuals hold negative beliefs about themselves and the world?
- What are the benefits and the limitations of learned helplessness as an explanation of depression?
- What kinds of attributions are likely to lead to depressed thinking?
- What are the important features of hopelessness theory of depression?

SECTION SUMMARY

7.1   MAJOR DEPRESSION

- Major depression (or unipolar depression) and bipolar depression are the two main types of clinical depression.
- Depression is the third most common reason for consulting a doctor or GP in the UK.
- The lifetime comorbidity rate of major depression with another anxiety disorder is 58 per cent and with more than one other DSM disorder is 74 per cent suggesting that individuals with depression experience a range of negative emotions.
- Premenstrual dysphoric disorder, seasonal affective disorder (SAD), and chronic fatigue syndrome (CFS) are three prominent disorders with depression as a significant element.
- Estimates of lifetime prevalence rates for major depressive disorder range from 5.2 to 17.1 per cent.
- Major depression is almost twice as common in women as in men.
- The incidence of major depression has increased since 1915 with a median onset age of around 27 years.
- There is good evidence for a genetic component to major depression.
- Abnormalities in the levels of the brain neurotransmitters serotonin, dopamine and norepinephrine are associated with depressed mood.
- Depressed mood has been shown to be associated with abnormal activity in a number of brain areas, including the prefrontal cortex, the anterior cingulate cortex, the hippocampus, and the amygdala.
- High levels of cortisol may lead to depression by causing enlargement of the adrenal glands and in turn lowering the frequency of serotonin transmitters in the brain.
- Psychoanalytic theory argues that depression is a response to loss, and the loss of a loved one such as a parent.
- Behavioural theories claim that depression results from a lack of appropriate reinforcement for positive and constructive behaviours, and this is especially the case following a 'loss' such as bereavement or losing a job.
- Interpersonal theories of depression claim that depressed individuals alienate family and friends because of their perpetual negative thinking, and this alienation in turn exacerbates the symptoms of depression.
- Beck's cognitive theory of depression argues that depression is maintained by a 'negative schema' that leads depressed individuals to hold negative views about themselves, their future and the world (the 'negative triad').
- Learned helplessness theory argues that people become depressed following unavoidable negative life events because these events give rise to a cognitive set that makes individuals learn to become 'helpless', lethargic and depressed.
- Attributional accounts of depression suggest that people who are likely to become depressed attribute negative life events to internal, stable, and global factors.
- Hopelessness is a cluster of depression symptoms that are characterized by an expectation that positive outcomes will not occur, negative outcomes will occur, and the individual has no responses available that will change this state of affairs.
- Depressive rumination can increase the risk of depression or increase the risk of relapse.

7.2 BIPOLAR DISORDER

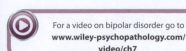

For a video on bipolar disorder go to **www.wiley-psychopathology.com/video/ch7**

Bipolar disorder is a mood disorder characterized by alternating periods of depression and mania. Often the swings between these two states can be very rapid, taking the individual from an extreme 'high' to an extreme 'low' very quickly. The personal accounts of experiences of bipolar disorder described in Client's Perspective 7.1 provide some insight into the desperation generated by periods of depression and the frightening confusion that can be experienced during periods of sustained mania. Someone who suffers bipolar disorder and is in a manic phase can be recognized by many characteristics, including the expression of a constant, sometimes unconnected, stream of thoughts and ideas; attention span may be limited and the person shifts rapidly from topic to topic. They will be loud and often interrupt ongoing conversations to talk about something that has just caught their attention. Individuals in a manic phase may spontaneously start conversations with strangers, and indulge in inappropriate or imprudent sexual interactions. These behaviours are usually recognized as excessive by those who know the sufferer, but any attempt to quell these excesses is usually met with anger and annoyance. As a result, irritability and lability of mood is often one of the significant features of the manic individual. Periods of mania can last for days or even weeks, and onset can occur rapidly over the course of a single day. DSM-5 Summary Table 7.4 provides the criteria for a manic episode (although this is not a codable disorder). Because of these symptoms, bipolar disorder is a severely debilitating condition that can limit functioning and workplace productivity; it is associated with increased mortality and relatively high rates of relapse (Newberg, Catapano, Zarate & Manji, 2008).

For a video on mania go to **www.wiley-psychopathology.com/video/ch7**

CLIENT'S PERSPECTIVE 7.1
THE EXPERIENCE OF BIPOLAR DISORDER

Descriptions offered by people with bipolar disorder give valuable insights into the various mood states associated with the disorder:

DEPRESSION

'I doubt completely my ability to do anything well. It seems as though my mind has slowed down and burned out to the point of being virtually useless . . . [I am] haunt[ed] . . . with the total, the desperate hopelessness of it all . . . Others say, "It's only temporary, it will pass, you can get over it", but of course they haven't any idea of how I feel, although they are certain they do. If I can't feel, move, think or care, then what on earth is the point?'

HYPOMANIA

'At first when I'm high, it's tremendous . . . ideas are fast . . . like shooting stars you follow until brighter ones appear . . . All shyness disappears, the right words and gestures are suddenly there . . . uninteresting people, things become intensely interesting. Sensuality is pervasive; the desire to seduce and be seduced is irresistible. Your marrow is infused with unbelievable feelings of ease, power, well-being, omnipotence, euphoria . . . you can do anything . . . but, somewhere, this changes.'

MANIA

'The fast ideas become too fast and there are far too many . . . overwhelming confusion replaces clarity . . . you stop keeping up with it – memory goes. Infectious humour ceases to amuse. Your friends become frightened . . . everything is now against the grain . . . you are irritable, angry, frightened, uncontrollable, and trapped.'

Clinical Commentary

*This provides an insight into how the different mood states in bipolar disorder are experienced, and how the transition from a depressive episode moves through the mild manic episode called **hypomania** to full blown mania. Typical of the transition from depression to full-blown mania are (1) the overwhelming flow of thoughts and ideas that lead to the sufferer seeming incoherent and interrupting ongoing conversations, (2) the temptation to indulge in inappropriate sexual interactions as everyone around becomes a focus of interest and shyness is lost, and (3) the inevitable drift by the sufferer into irritability, frustration and anger as friends and acquaintances try to quell the excesses of thought and behaviour.*

DSM-5 SUMMARY TABLE 7.4 *Criteria for a manic episode*

- Unusual and continual elevated, unreserved or irritable mood and unusual and continual increase in energy levels lasting at least a week
- Presence of at least three of the following:
  - Inflated self-esteem or grandiosity
  - Less need for sleep
  - Increased talkativeness
  - Racing thoughts
  - Easily distractible
  - Increase in goal-directed activity or unintentional and purposeless motions
  - Unnecessary participation in activities with a high potential for painful consequences

7.2.1   The Diagnosis and Prevalence of Bipolar Disorder

DSM-5 defines two main types of bipolar disorder, namely 'bipolar disorder I' and 'bipolar disorder II'. DSM-5 Summary Table 7.5 illustrates the main diagnostic features of these two definitions. The most common of these two diagnoses is bipolar disorder I, where individuals exhibit full manic and major depressive episodes in alternating sequences. In bipolar disorder II, major depressive episodes alternate with periods of **hypomania** (mild manic episodes – see DSM-5 Summary Table 7.6 for a definition of hypomania). While the symptoms of bipolar disorder II must be sufficiently severe to cause distress or impairment, individuals with this disorder can

> **hypomania**   Mild episodes of mania.

FOCUS POINT 7.4

MOOD DISORDERS AND CREATIVITY

Brian Wilson, T.S. Eliot, Mark Twain and Vincent Van Gogh. These artists are a few of many that have all suffered from symptoms of bipolar disorder, and there is an enduring belief that creativity in the arts is associated with psychological disturbance and even 'madness'. Is this just a myth or is there some truth in this belief? Kay Jamison (1992), a psychiatrist, spent some years studying the lives of famous contributors to the arts, including poets, artists and musicians. She concluded that there did seem to be a link between mood disorders such as bipolar disorder and creativity and artistic achievement. She found that British poets during the 18th century were significantly more likely than members of the general population to have suffered symptoms of bipolar disorder, have been committed to a lunatic asylum, or have committed suicide. This view has been reinforced by a recent large-scale study showing that bipolar disorder is more prevalent in groups of people with artistic or scientific professions, such as dancers, researchers, photographers and authors (Kyaga, Landén, Boman, Hultman *et al.*, 2013). But what exactly might this link between bipolar disorder and creativity be?

The first question to ask is 'what comes first – the creativity or the psychological disturbance?' There is some evidence that creative individuals do have a family history of psychological problems, suggesting that their psychological difficulties may precede their creativity. For example, creative individuals often had parents who suffered from psychological disorders, and may have suffered the kind of childhood abuse that might give rise to psychological problems later in life. For instance, the author Virginia Woolf was known to have suffered childhood sexual abuse. In addition to this evidence that psychological problems may precede creativity, some studies have found that individuals with bipolar disorder score higher on measures of creativity than do non-clinical control participants (Richards, Kinney, Lunde *et al.*, 1988).

In contrast to this evidence, it could be argued that artistic communities, where emotional expression is a valued commodity, are welcoming places for individuals with psychological or mood disorders (Ludwig, 1995). We must also remember that psychological disorder is not a prerequisite for creative achievement, and (1) many people make significant artistic and creative contributions without exhibiting any signs of mental health problems, and (2) those artists suffering psychological problems often continue to make impressive contributions to their art even after successful treatment of their disorders (Jamison, 1995; Ludwig, 1995).

Even so, it is worth considering how psychological problems such as bipolar disorder might contribute to creativity. First, *mania* gives individuals the energy and sharpened thinking that may be required for creative achievement, and it also gives the individual confidence and feelings of inspiration that may not otherwise be experienced. Second, there is evidence that *depressed mood* can also make a contribution to creativity by raising performance standards. For example, Martin & Stoner (1996) found that negative moods lead to lower confidence in the adequacy of creative effort, and this spurs individuals in negative moods on to greater efforts.

> To read more on bipolar disorder and creativity go to
> **http://tinyurl.com/9jg2q7m**

DSM-5 SUMMARY TABLE 7.5 *Criteria for bipolar disorder I and bipolar disorder II*

Bipolar disorder I
- Presence or history of at least one manic episode(s)
- The manic episode may have been preceded by and may be followed by hypomanic or major depressive episodes.
- Symptoms are not better accounted for by schizoaffective disorder or other disorders

Bipolar disorder II
- Presence or history of at least one major depressive episode(s)
- Presence or history of at least one hypomanic episode(s)
- No history of manic episode(s)
- Symptoms are not better accounted for by schizoaffective disorder or other disorders

DSM-5 SUMMARY TABLE 7.6 *Definition of hypomania*

- Unusual and continual elevated, unreserved or irritable mood and unusual and continual increase in energy levels lasting at least a week
- Presence of at least three of the following:
  - Inflated self-esteem or grandiosity
  - Less need for sleep
  - Increased talkativeness
  - Racing thoughts
  - Easily distractible
  - Increase in goal-directed activity or unintentional and purposeless motions
  - Unnecessary participation in activities with a high potential for painful consequences
- A noted change in functionality which is not usually seen in the individual and changes in functionality and mood are noticeable by others
- The episode is not due to the use of medication, drug abuse or other treatment

DSM-5 SUMMARY TABLE 7.7 *Criteria for cyclothymic disorder*

- For at least 2 years there have been many periods with hypomanic symptoms that do not meet the criteria for a hypomanic episode and many periods with depressive symptoms that do not meet the criteria for a major depressive episode. These symptoms have not been absent for more than 2 months at a time
- No major depressive episode, manic episode or hypomanic episode has been present during the first 2 years of the disorder
- The episode is not due to the use of medication, drug abuse or other treatment

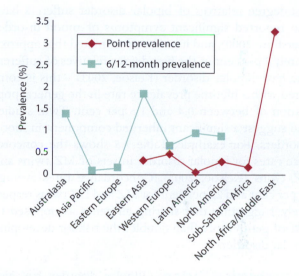

FIGURE 7.4 *Prevalence of bipolar disorder across various regions of the world.*
Source: Ferrari, A.J., Baxter, A.J. & Whiteford, H.A. (2011). A systematic review of the global distribution and availability of prevalence data for bipolar disorder. *Journal of Affective Disorders, 134*(1), 1–13, Figure 2. Reproduced with permission.

often be relatively productive during their periods of hypomania (Jamison, 1995).

Cyclothymic disorder is a mild form of bipolar disorder in which the sufferer has mood swings over a period of years that range from mild depression to euphoria and excitement. It is characterized by at least 2 years of hypomania symptoms that do not meet the criteria for a manic episode, and the sufferer will experience alternating periods of withdrawal then exuberance, inadequacy and then high self-esteem, and so on (see DSM-5 Summary Table 7.7).

Bipolar disorder is much less common than major depressive disorder, and epidemiological studies

cyclothymic disorder A form of depression characterized by at least 2 years of hypomania symptoms that do not meet the criteria for a manic episode and in which the sufferer experiences alternating periods of withdrawal then exuberance, inadequacy and then high self-esteem.

suggest a lifetime prevalence rate of around 1 per cent (Merikangas, Akiskal, Angst, Greenberg *et al.*, 2007). This appears to be supported by a systematic review of global prevalence data showing a 12-month prevalence rate of 0.8 per cent when data are compared across 20 geographic regions of the world (see Figure 7.4) (Ferrari, Baxter & Whiteford, 2011).

7.2.2   The Aetiology of Bipolar Disorder

Biological theories

Genetic factors   There is good evidence that bipolar disorder has an inherited component. For example, family studies have indicated that 10–25 per cent of

TABLE 7.5 *Concordance rates in selected twin studies of bipolar disorder*

Study	Monozygotic twins (MZ) (%)	Dizygotic twins (DZ) (%)
Rosanoff *et al.* (1935)	69.6	16.4
Kallman (1954)	92.6	23.6
Bertelsen (1979)	58.3	17.3
Kendler *et al.* (1993)	60.7	34.9
TOTAL	**69.6**	**29.3**

Source: Kelsoe, J.R. (2003). Arguments for the genetic basis of the bipolar spectrum. *Journal of Affective Disorders, 73,* 183–197. Reproduced with permission.

first-degree relatives of bipolar disorder sufferers have also reported significant symptoms of mood disorder (Gershon, 2000), and it has been estimated that approximately 7 per cent of the first-degree relatives of sufferers also have bipolar disorder (Kelsoe, 2003) – this is compared with a lifetime prevalence rate in the general population of between 0.4 and 1.6 per cent. Twin studies also suggest a significant inherited component in mood disorders. For example, Table 7.5 shows the concordance rates for bipolar disorder in sets of MZ twins and DZ twins (Kelsoe, 2003). Concordance rates average 69 per cent and 29 per cent for MZ and DZ twins respectively, suggesting that sharing all genes as opposed to half of genes more than doubles the risk for developing bipolar disorder.

Neurochemical factors Bipolar disorder has also been shown to be reliably associated with abnormalities in levels of brain neurotransmitters. Like major depression, bipolar disorder seems to be associated with dopamine and norepinephrine irregularities, but serotonin does not appear to play such a central role in bipolar symptoms, and this is evidenced by the fact that serotonin reuptake is not a sufficient condition for antidepressant efficacy in bipolar depression (Fountoulakis, Kelsoe & Akiskal, 2012). In addition, the mania found in bipolar disorder is found to be associated specifically with high levels of norepinephrine (Bunney, Goodwin & Murphy, 1972; Altshuler, Curran, Hauser, Mintz *et al.*, 1995). A common popular form of treatment for bipolar disorder is a combination of the antipsychotic drug **olanzapine** and the antidepressant SSRI drug **fluoxetine (Prozac)**. This

olanzapine An antipsychotic drug commonly prescribed in combination with the antidepressant SSRI drug fluoxetine as a treatment for bipolar disorder.

fluoxetine (Prozac) A selective serotonin reuptake inhibitor (SSRI) which reduces the uptake of serotonin in the brain and is taken to treat depression.

can have a significant effect on both mania and depression symptoms within a 7–8 week period compared with placebo controls, but it is still unclear how the beneficial effects of this drug combination might act through their effects on specific brain neurotransmitters (Deeks & Keating, 2008).

Triggers for depression and mania in bipolar disorder

Bipolar disorder consists of two quite different symptom types in depression and mania, and what interests clinical researchers is the triggers for these two different types of symptoms. The triggers for a depressive episode in bipolar disorder appear to be very similar to the factors that instigate depression generally, namely experiences such as losses, failures, and negative life events generally (Johnson, Cuellar & Miller, 2010). The triggers for bouts of mania also appear to be varied and include an increased responsiveness to rewards (e.g. mania can be a reaction to a positive life event such as passing an exam) (Meyer, Johnson & Winters, 2001), reactions to antidepressant medication, disrupted sleep patterns and circadian rhythms, seasonality (bouts of mania increase in either spring or summer), stressful life events generally, and exposure to high emotional expression in family members or caregivers (Proudfoot, Doran, Manicavasagar & Parker, 2011).

Study of some of these triggers has resulted in a number of models of mania. Firstly, the study of how mania is triggered by goal attainment (e.g. passing an exam) suggests that mania may be associated with dysregulation in the behavioural activation system (BAS) that regulates sensitivity to rewards, and the goal-directed behaviours that are facilitated by the BAS are very similar to those behaviours exhibited by bipolar sufferers during a manic phase (e.g. physiological arousal, increased sociability and incentive-reward motivation) (Depue & Iacono, 1989). Secondly, the fact that mania is associated with disruption to sleep and circadian rhythms suggests that this may be an important cause of mania. Not only does sleep duration predict hypomanic symptoms the following morning (Leibenluft, Albert, Rosenthal & Wehr, 1996), but disruption to normal circadian rhythms (e.g. driving through the night, long airplane journeys, working night shifts) also results in a shift to hypomania within 24 hours. The close relationship between sleep/circadian rhythm disruption and manic episodes has led some theorists to suggest that sleep deprivation may be the final common pathway through which a variety of other factors precipitate episodes of bipolar mania (Wehr, Sack & Rosenthal, 1987).

SELF-TEST QUESTIONS

- What are dysthymic disorder and cyclothymic disorder?
- What is the distinction between bipolar disorder I and bipolar disorder II?
- Describe the evidence that suggests there is a genetic component to bipolar disorder.
- What are the main types of pharmacological treatment for bipolar disorder?
- What factors trigger either periods of depression or periods of mania in bipolar disorder?

SECTION SUMMARY

7.2 BIPOLAR DISORDER

- Bipolar disorder is characterized by periods of mania that alternate with periods of depression.
- Hypomania are defined as mild manic episodes.
- Cyclothymic disorder is a mild form of bipolar disorder which ranges from mild depression to mania.
- The lifetime risk for bipolar disorder is 0.4 to 1.6 per cent.
- There is good evidence for a genetic component to bipolar disorder. Generally, 10 to 25 per cent of first-degree relatives of bipolar disorder sufferers also report symptoms of mood disorder, as do 5–10 per cent of first-degree relatives of major depression sufferers.
- Two significant triggers for mania in bipolar disorder include goal attainment and sleep disruption.

7.3 THE TREATMENT OF DEPRESSION AND MOOD DISORDERS

The previous sections illustrate the broad range of theories addressing the aetiology of mood disorders, and these theories have each given rise to a variety of different treatments for these disorders. These include a number of biological-based treatments such as drug therapy and **electroconvulsive therapy (ECT)** which address the known neurochemical imbalances in depression, and a wide range of psychological therapies including psychodynamic, behavioural and cognitive behavioural therapies. **Stepped-care models** for the treatment of depression are often adopted, and these models advise that the type of treatment provided for depression should be tailored to the severity of the symptoms and the personal and social circumstances of the sufferer. An example of a stepped-care model would be one where (1) GPs and physicians – who are normally the first port of call for many people experiencing depression – are advised to ensure that proper assessment is made of individuals who might present with symptoms of depression, and they should not simply respond by providing medication, (2) medication would not normally be recommended for the initial treatment of depression but should be reserved for the treatment of moderate to severe depression where there is more evidence for its effectiveness, and (3) mild depression should be treated primarily with brief behavioural and cognitive interventions, and these include structured exercise (e.g. three sessions per week, of moderate duration, for 10–12 weeks), guided self-help and computerized CBT programmes (an example of which is 'Beating the Blues™' – see Treatment in Practice Box 7.1 and section 4.1.2) (Scogin, Hanson & Welsh, 2003; NICE, 2008).

electroconvulsive therapy (ECT) A method of treatment for depression or psychosis, first devised in the 1930s, which involves passing an electric current of around 70–130 volts through the head of the patient for around half a second.

stepped-care models Treatments for psychopathology that emphasize that the type of treatment provided for those individuals should be tailored to the severity of their symptoms and their personal and social circumstances.

To read more about 'Beating the Blues' go to **www.beatingtheblues.co.uk**

TREATMENT IN PRACTICE 7.1
BEATING THE BLUES USING COMPUTERIZED CBT

The UK National Institute for Health & Care Excellence (NICE) guidelines for treating depression recommend that computerized CBT (CCBT) is considered for persistent sub-threshold depressive symptoms or mild to moderate depression (NICE, 2008).

One particular programme that has been developed for this purpose is 'Beating the Blues'™. The programme uses interactive multimedia techniques to maximize user-friendliness and patient engagement. It provides role-models in the form of case study videos that guide the patient's progress at each stage of therapy. Patients follow a unique pathway through the programme driven by their current needs, including homework projects to complete between sessions, and clinical outcomes are monitored on a session-by-session basis.

The programme helps the user to identify thinking errors, challenging negative automatic thoughts, modifying attributional style, and identifying core negative beliefs. It also provides guidance on behavioural techniques (including graded exposure, sleep management, problem solving, task breakdown, activity scheduling and so forth) that are designed to promote more helpful thinking styles and behavioural repertoires.

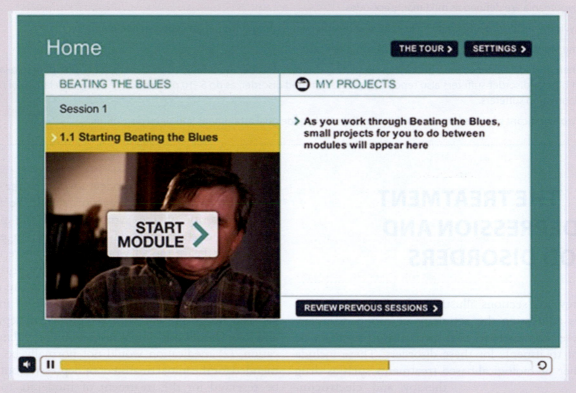

A sample page from the CCBT programme 'Beating the Blues'™
Source: Reproduced by permission of Ultrasis Plc.

7.3.1 Biological Treatments

Drug therapy

We saw earlier that depression is commonly associated with deficits or imbalances in the neurotransmitters serotonin, norepinephrine and dopamine and over the past 50 years various drugs have been developed that attempt to address these imbalances and deal with the symptoms of depression. The three main types of medication for depression are (1) trycyclic drugs (such as imipramine), (2) monoamine oxidase (MAO) inhibitors (such as tranylcypromine), and (3) selective serotonin reuptake inhibitors (SSRIs such as Prozac). The first two types of drug have their effect by increasing levels of both

TABLE 7.6 *Side effects of drugs used to treat major depression and bipolar disorder*

Category	Side effects
Tricyclic drugs	Blurred vision, anxiety, fatigue, dry mouth, increased risk of heart attack and stroke, constipation, gastric disorders, hypotension, sexual dysfunction, weight gain
Monoamine oxidase inhibitors (MAOIs)	Hypertension, dry mouth, dizziness, headaches and nausea
Selective serotonin reuptake inhibitors (SSRIs)	Anxiety, fatigue, gastric disorders, headaches, dizziness, sleeping difficulties
Lithium	Cardiac arrhythmia, fatigue, blurred vision, tremors, on overdose can cause delirium, convulsions and fatalities

serotonin and norepinephrine in the brain, while SSRIs act selectively on serotonin and prevent its reuptake by the presynaptic neurone (see Figure 7.1). All of these drugs act by facilitating the transmission of impulses between neurones. Treatment outcome studies have generally indicated that depressed individuals given these forms of medication benefit when compared with individuals taking placebos. Around 60–65 per cent of individuals taking trycyclic drugs show improvement (Gitlin, 2002) along with around 50 per cent taking monoamine oxidase inhibitors (Thase, Trivedi & Rush, 1995). Although these forms of drug treatment are relatively effective, they often have significant physical and psychological side effects and these are listed in Table 7.6. The most recently developed of these drugs, SSRIs, do have some benefits over trycyclic drugs and MAO inhibitors in that they produce fewer side effects (Enserink, 1999) and it is harder to overdose on them (Isbister, Bowe, Dawson & Whyte, 2004). However, SSRIs such as fluoxetine (Prozac) take around 2 weeks to begin to have an effect on symptoms (which is roughly the same as trycyclics), and also have their own side effects such as headache, gastric disorders and sexual dysfunction (Rosen, Lane & Menza, 1999). There is also controversy about whether SSRIs such as Prozac increase the risk of suicide. Recent meta-analyses suggest that increased risk of suicide with the use of SSRIs cannot be ruled out, but these risks should be balanced against the effectiveness of SSRIs in treating depression (Gunnell, Saperia & Ashby, 2005). Nevertheless, despite these cautions, the drugs that have been developed to treat depression do help to alleviate symptoms in a significant number of cases, they provide relatively

rapid relief from symptoms in around half of those treated, and are effective not only with bouts of major depression, but also with chronic depressive disorders such as dysthymic disorder (Hellerstein, Kocsis, Chapman, Stewart & Harrison, 2000). Meta-analyses suggest that both tricyclic drugs and SSRIs are more effective than placebo controls, and generate significant improvement in around 55–60 per cent of those treated, with both tricyclic drugs and SSRIs being equally effective (Arroll, Macgillivray, Ogston, Reid *et al.*, 2005). However, relapse is a common occurrence after drug treatment for depression has been withdrawn (Reimherr, Strong, Marchant, Hedges & Wender, 2001), and a more effective treatment may be to combine drug therapy with psychological therapies such as CBT (Kupfer & Frank, 2001).

In contrast to those drugs prescribed for major depression, the drug therapies of choice for bipolar disorder are rather different. The traditional treatment for bipolar disorder has been **lithium carbonate**. Around 80 per cent of bipolar disorder sufferers who take lithium benefit from it, and the drug can provide relief from symptoms of both manic and depressive episodes (Prien & Potter, 1993). There is some debate about how lithium actually moderates the symptoms of bipolar disorder. Early views suggested that lithium stabilizes the activity of sodium and potassium ions in the membranes of neurones, and it is the instability of these ions that give rise to the symptoms of bipolar disorder (Swonger & Constantine, 1983). Other accounts argue that it changes synaptic activity in neurons in such a way as to help neurotransmitters to bind to a receiving neuron, thus helping to facilitate and stabilize neuronal transmission (Ghaemi, Boiman & Goodwin, 1999). More recently, it has been suggested that lithium modulates neuronal transmission by affecting the expression of genes that govern these activities (Lenox & Hahn, 2000). However, treatment of bipolar symptoms with lithium carbonate does have some disadvantages. Firstly, discontinuation often increases the risk of relapse (Suppes, Baldessarini, Faedda & Tohen, 1991), and, secondly, an added disadvantage of lithium treatment is the difficulty in prescribing a suitable dosage on an individual basis. Lithium is a toxic substance and the effective dose for alleviating symptoms is often close to the toxic level. As a consequence, an overdose can cause delirium, convulsions and, in rare cases, can be fatal. More recently, combinations of antipsychotic drugs and SSRIs have been used successfully to address symptoms of bipolar disorder. (e.g. a combination of the antipsychotic drug olanzapine and the antidepressant SSRI drug fluoxetine), and this combination has been shown to have significant effects on both mania and depression symptoms (Deeks & Keating, 2008).

lithium carbonate A drug used in the treatment of bipolar disorder.

Electroconvulsive therapy (ECT)

This method of treatment was first discovered in the 1930s (Bini, 1938) and involves passing an electric current of around 70–130 volts through the head of the patient for around half a second. It was first used as an experimental means of inducing brain seizures, but was subsequently found to have beneficial effects on symptoms of severe depression. Today, ECT is used primarily with individuals suffering severe depression who have not responded well to other forms of treatment (Cohen, Taieb, Flament, Benoit et al., 2000). While it can provide effective short-term relief from symptoms of severe depression, it also has a number of controversial features. Firstly, it has a number of side effects, the most common of which is memory loss that affects the ability to learn new material (anterograde amnesia) and the ability to recall material learnt before the treatment (retrograde amnesia). These effects can last for up to 7 months following ECT (Lisanby, Maddox, Prudic, Devanand & Sackeim, 2000; Sackeim, Prudic, Fuller, Keilp, Lavori et al., 2007). Secondly, many people find the idea of having a strong electric current passed through their brain frightening, and will be resistant to the use of this kind of therapy. Indeed, many view the physical nature of ECT as a form of 'assault' on the patient, and a means of managing unruly inpatients rather than a form of therapy. This was a view that was strikingly portrayed in the 1975 film *One Flew Over The Cuckoo's Nest* starring Jack Nicholson. Thirdly, no one is clear how ECT does work in alleviating the symptoms of severe depression, but it has been suggested that shock affects the levels of serotonin and norepinephrine in the brain (Mann & Kapur, 1994). However, this beneficial effect may be short-term and limited to as little as 4 weeks (Breggin, 1997), and the relapse rate is high (Royal College of Psychiatrists, 2002). Other researchers have argued that the short-term beneficial effects of ECT are nothing more than would be expected following *any* trauma to the brain – with immediate symptoms being confusion, headache and nausea followed by a period of emotional shallowness, denial and artificial euphoria that may last for a few weeks (Breggin, 1997).

Nevertheless, despite these criticisms, ECT may still have a role to play in the treatment of severe depression in both Major and bipolar depression when symptoms are resistant to pharmacological treatment (Medda, Perugi, Zanello, Cuiffa & Cassano, 2009), and the almost immediate beneficial effects of ECT may be helpful in alleviating depression when suicide is a real possibility.

7.3.2 Psychological Treatments

Psychoanalysis

In section 7.1.2 we discussed some of the psychodynamic explanations of depression. Central to these accounts is the view that depression is a response to loss (perhaps of a loved one) and may manifest as *symbolic loss*, in which other kinds of losses (such as losing a job) are seen as equivalent to losing a loved one. Psychodynamic theories (such as those developed by Freud and Abraham) argue that the individual's response to loss is to turn their anger at the loss inwards, and this in turn can develop into self-hate resulting in low self-esteem (Frosh, 2012, ch.13). The aim of psychodynamic therapy, therefore, is to help the depressed individual achieve insight into this repressed conflict and to help release the inwardly directed anger. Psychodynamic therapy will do this by using various techniques to help people explore the long-term sources of their depression (see section 4.1.1), and this will involve exploring conflicts and problematic relationships with attachment figures – such as parents – and discussing long-standing defensive patterns. For example, the psychodynamic therapist may use free association or **dream interpretation** to help the individual recall early experiences of loss that may have contributed to repressed conflicts and symptoms of depression. In this way, psychodynamic therapies attempt to bring meaning to the symptoms of depression, and help the individual understand how early experiences may have contributed to their symptoms and affected their current interpersonal relationships.

> **dream interpretation** The process of assigning meaning to dreams.

Evidence for the therapeutic efficacy of psychodynamic therapies in the treatment of depression is meagre. This is in part because processes within psychodynamic therapies are difficult to objectify and study in a controlled way. Psychodynamic therapists also differ significantly in the way they interpret psychodynamic principles in practice. A controlled study by the American Psychiatric Association (APA, 1993) reported that there was no evidence for the long-term efficacy of psychodynamic treatment of depression, although some more recent studies have indicated that short-term psychodynamic interventions may be as effective as CBT in significantly reducing symptoms of depression (Leichsenring, 2001; Lemma, Target & Fonagy, 2011).

Social skills training

It was Lewinsohn and his colleagues (e.g. Lewinsohn & Shaw, 1969) who first drew attention to the fact that depressed individuals (1) have deficits in the general social skills that are required for efficient and effective interactions, and (2) possess a demeanour that others (e.g. other family members) find aversive. These two features of the depressed individual will act to accentuate depression by reducing the frequency of social interactions and reducing the rewards that the individual might obtain from these interactions. The kinds of interpersonal social skills deficits possessed by depressed individuals range from negative self-evaluation of their own skills to deficits in behavioural indicators of social skills such as eye contact, relevant facial expressions, and speed of response in conversations (Segrin, 2000).

In response to these deficits, social skills training therapy for depression was developed (Becker, Heimberg & Bellack, 1987). **Social skills training** assumes that depression in part results from the individual's inability to communicate and socialize appropriately, and that addressing these skill deficits should help to alleviate many of the symptoms of depression. This may involve training assertion skills, conversational interaction skills, dating skills, and job interview skills, and can involve procedures such as modelling, rehearsal, role-playing, and homework assignments out of the therapeutic setting (Jackson, Moss & Solinski, 1985; Becker, Heimberg & Bellack, 1987).

> **social skills training** A therapy for depression that assumes that depression in part results from an individual's inability to communicate and socialize appropriately, and that addressing these skill deficits should help to alleviate many of the symptoms of depression.

An example of one particular social skills training programme for depression is that designed by Herson, Bellack and colleagues (Hersen, Bellack & Himmelhoch, 1980; Thase, 2012). This involved 1-hour sessions for 12 weeks and began by focusing on skills appropriate for interactions with family, friends, work colleagues, and strangers respectively. Particular features of this programme included (1) role-playing tasks, feedback, modelling and positive reinforcement for appropriate behaviours, and (2) attention to the specific details of social interactions such as smiles, gestures, use of eye contact and so on. Clients were subsequently given homework tasks requiring them to practise their skills outside of the therapy situation. As a result of this programme, clients showed not only improvements in their social skills but also a decrease in symptoms of depression that were still apparent 6 months after the end of the programme. Studies evaluating the efficacy of social skills training for depression have shown that such programmes result in an improvement in a range of social skills and a decrease in reported symptoms of depression (Zeiss, Lewinsohn & Munoz, 1979). They also suggest that social skills training is equally as effective as other psychological therapies commonly employed for depression (Fine, Forth, Gilbert & Haley, 1991; Miller, Norman, Keitner, Bishop & Dow, 1989).

Behavioural activation therapy

Behavioural theories of depression emphasize that depression may be triggered by a life-event loss (such as a bereavement), and this event may represent the loss of important sources of reward and reinforcement for the individual. This leads the depressed individual into a vicious cycle where this lack of reward generates depressive symptoms, and in turn, the individual's depressive behaviour may ultimately lead to aversive social consequences in the form of negative social reactions from friends and family (Coyne, 1976). This view has led to the development of **behavioural activation therapy** for depression that attempts to increase the client's access to pleasant events and rewards and decrease their experience of aversive events and consequences (Lewinsohn, Sullivan & Grosscup, 1982; Turner & Leach, 2012). Early behavioural activation programmes attempted to achieve these goals through daily monitoring of pleasant/unpleasant events and the use of behavioural interventions that developed activity scheduling (e.g. scheduling reinforcing activities so that they will reinforce less attractive activities). They also include social skills and time management training (Lewinsohn & Shaffer, 1971; Zeiss, Lewinsohn & Munoz, 1979). The use of behavioural activation therapy was given a further boost by the fact that a number of studies demonstrated that cognitive change is just as likely to occur following purely behavioural interventions as after cognitive interventions (Jacobson & Gortner, 2000; Simons, Garfield & Murphy, 1984). That is, reductions in negative thinking and negative self-statements in depression can be decreased by behavioural interventions that contain no explicit cognitive change components. Recent developments of behavioural activation therapy include the self-monitoring of pleasant/unpleasant experiences and the identification of behavioural goals within major life areas (e.g. relationships, education) that can be targeted for development and reinforcement, and behavioural activation therapy has also been shown to be beneficial for individuals suffering chronic depression (Erickson & Hellerstein, 2011). Treatment in Practice Box 7.2 gives an example of how a brief behavioural activation therapy programme is structured and executed (Lejuez, Hopko, LePage, Hopko & McNeil, 2001).

> **behavioural activation therapy** A therapy for depression that attempts to increase clients' access to pleasant events and rewards and decrease their experience of aversive events and consequences.

Outcome studies suggest that behavioural activation therapies are at least as effective as supportive psychotherapy in reducing the symptoms of depression (Hopko, Lejuez, LePage, McNeil & Hopko, 2003), and equally as effective as CBT in preventing relapse after 24 months (Gortner, Gollan, Dobson & Jacobson, 1998).

Cognitive therapy

As we saw in section 7.1.2, dysfunctional cognitions appear to play an important part in the maintenance of depressive symptoms. Beck's cognitive theory of depression (Beck, 1967, 1987) argues that depression is maintained by a systematic set of dysfunctional negative

TREATMENT IN PRACTICE 7.2
BRIEF BEHAVIOURAL ACTIVATION TREATMENT FOR DEPRESSION (BATD)

BATD is conducted over 8 to 15 sessions, and sessions progress through the following stages:

1. Assessing the function of depressed behaviour; weakening access to positive reinforcement (e.g. sympathy) and negative reinforcement (e.g. escape from responsibilities); establishing rapport with the client and introducing the treatment rationale.

2. Increasing the frequency and subsequent reinforcement of healthy behaviour; clients begin a weekly self-monitoring exercise that serves as a baseline assessment of daily activities and orientates clients to the quantity and quality of their activities, and generates ideas about activities to target during treatment.

3. Emphasis is shifted to identifying behavioural goals within major life areas, such as relationships, education, employment, hobbies and recreational activities, physical/health issues, spirituality.

4. Following goal setting, an activity hierarchy is constructed in which 15 activities are rated ranging from 'easiest' to 'most difficult' to accomplish. With progress being monitored by the therapist, over a period of weeks the client progressively moves through the hierarchy from easiest to most difficult. Patients are urged to identify weekly rewards that can be administered if activity goals are met.

Source: Hopko, D.R., Lejuez, C.W., Ruggiero, K.J. & Eifert, G.H. (2003). Contemporary behavioural activation treatments for depression: Procedures, principles, and progress. *Clinical Psychology Review, 23*, 699–717. Reproduced with permission.

beliefs that form a negative schema though which the depressed individual views themselves, their world, and their future. From this theory Beck developed one of the most successful and widely adopted therapeutic approaches for depression, and this has come to be known by various names including cognitive therapy, **cognitive retraining** or cognitive restructuring. The thrust of this approach is (1) to help the depressed individual identify their negative beliefs and negative thoughts, (2) to challenge these thoughts as dysfunctional and irrational, and (3) to replace these negative beliefs with more adaptive or rational beliefs. For example, depressed individuals tend to hold beliefs and attributional styles that are *overgeneralized*. They will respond to a specific failure (such as failing their driving test) with statements such as 'Everything I do ends in failure' or 'The world is against me'. The cognitive therapist will attempt to identify these overgeneralized beliefs and challenge them as irrational – using, if at all possible, relevant examples from the client's own experiences. In addition to this, the client will be asked to monitor the **negative automatic thoughts** that give rise to negative beliefs and depressive symptoms, often using a form which allows them to link the automatic thoughts to particular situations and outcomes, and to think through possible rational alternatives to the negative automatic thought (see Table 7.7). The overall philosophy of cognitive therapy for depression is to correct the negative thinking bias possessed by depressed individuals, and in some cases this aim can be supplemented with the use of **reattribution training** (Beck, Rush, Shaw & Emery, 1979). Reattribution training attempts to get the client to interpret their difficulties in more hopeful and constructive ways rather than in the negative, global, stable ways typical of depressed individuals (see Tables 7.3 and 7.4).

Outcome studies have shown that cognitive therapy is usually at least as effective as drug therapy in treating the symptoms of depression (Rush, Beck, Kovacs & Hollon, 1977), and some have shown that it is superior to drug therapy at 1-year follow-up (Blackburn & Moorhead, 2000; Hollon, Shelton & Davis, 1993). DeRubeis, Hollon, Amsterdam, Shelton *et al.* (2005) compared cognitive therapy with drug therapy (paroxetine) and a placebo-control condition. After 8 weeks they found improvement in 43 per cent of the cognitive therapy group, 50 per cent of the drug treatment group, against

cognitive retraining An approach to treating depression developed by Aaron Beck. Also known as cognitive therapy or cognitive restructuring.

negative automatic thoughts Negatively valenced thoughts that the individual finds difficult to control or dismiss.

reattribution training A technique used in the treatment of depression which attempts to get clients to interpret their difficulties in more hopeful and constructive ways rather than in the negative, global, stable ways typical of depressed individuals.

TABLE 7.7

Below is an example of a *thought record* form used to record the negative automatic thoughts ('hot thoughts') experienced by depressed individuals. This form relates these thoughts to possible situational triggers and attempts to get the depressed individual to think up evidence that might be contrary to that 'hot thought'

1. Situation	2. Moods	3. Automatic thoughts (images)	4. Evidence that supports the hot thought	5. Evidence that does not support the hot thought	6. Alternative/ balanced thoughts	7. Rate moods now
Who? What? When? Where?	What do you feel? Rate each mood (0–100%)	What was going through your mind just before you started to feel this way? Any other thoughts? Images?			Write an alternative or balanced thought. Rate how much you believe in each alternative or balanced thought (0–100%)	Re-rate moods listed in column 2 as well as any new moods (0–100%)
In hotel room – alone – Sunday 10pm	Depressed 100% Lonely 100% Empty 100% Confused 100% Unmotivated 100% Stressed	I need something to make me feel numb and take away the pain Nothing is going right for me I'm worthless – I can never achieve anything At the moment I simply feel like ending it all What is there to look forward to in life? I feel like an empty shell	The hurt inside is unbearable Killing myself will solve all this People have tried to help me and I've been given many drugs, none of which work	When I'm with other people, talking about myself, things begin to feel better I've felt like this before and have managed to get myself through it Some mornings I wake up feeling and thinking differently, so there may be hope My friends tell me that I have something to offer I do laugh when I'm with others		

Source: After Greenberger, D. & Padesky, C. (1995). Clinician's guide to mind over mood. New York: Guilford Press.

only 25 per cent in the placebo group, and these levels of improvement were maintained at 16 weeks. Cognitive therapy also appears to have longer term beneficial effects by preventing relapse compared with medication (Hensley, Nadiga & Uhlenhuth, 2004; Dobson, Hollon, Dimidjian, Schmaling *et al.*, 2008), but a combination of cognitive therapy with drug treatment appears to be superior to either treatment alone (Kupfer & Frank, 2001). Cognitive therapy has also been successfully adapted to treat individuals with bipolar disorder in conjunction with appropriate medication (Newman, Leahy, Beck *et al.*, 2002) in both individual (da Costa, Range, Malagris, Sardinha *et al.* (2010) and group (Gomes, Abreu, Brietzke, Caetano *et al.*, 2011) settings. These interventions help the sufferer with medication compliance, mood monitoring, anticipating stressors, interpersonal functioning and problem solving (Scott, Garland & Moorhead, 2001; Danielson, Feeny, Findling & Youngstrom, 2004).

While there is no doubt that cognitive therapy is successful in helping to treat depression, there is still some debate about *how* it achieves these effects. We have seen earlier that cognitive change is just as likely to occur following purely behavioural treatments as they are after cognitive treatments. Cognitive therapy contains both elements of cognitive restructuring, which aims at changing cognitions directly, and behavioural exercises designed to establish new cognitions – so, is the cognitive restructuring element entirely necessary? In addition, there is evidence that cognitive therapy not only changes negative cognitions, but also results in improvements in abnormal biological processes (Blackburn & Moorhead, 2000). This raises the question of whether cognitive therapy has its effects by changing cognitions or biological processes. Nevertheless, regardless of *how* it works, cognitive therapy certainly *does* work, and recent evidence suggests that it not only reduces the occurrence of negative cognitions in depression, but it also helps to dissociate negative cognitions from the symptoms of depression better than other treatments (Beevers & Miller, 2005).

Mindfulness-based cognitive therapy (MBCT)

A critical issue in the treatment of depression is how to predict and eliminate possible relapse after remission or successful treatment. In the case of major depression, it appears that the risk of relapse increases with every consecutive bout of depression, and this increased risk also means that depression can reoccur with less and less external provocation (such as a stressful life event) (Kendler, Thornton & Gardner, 2000). This increased risk of relapse in recovered depressed individuals appears to be caused by periods of negative mood (dysphoria) activating patterns of negative or depressogenic thinking, such as self-devaluation and hopelessness (Ingram, Miranda & Segal, 1998; Segal, Gemar & Williams, 1999). That is, as soon as the recovered depressed individual begins to feel depressed again, this reactivates negative thinking that leads to a downward spiral to relapse. MBCT was developed to try to combat this linkage between periods of dysphoria and the onset of negative thinking, and it aims at getting individuals to take a 'decentred' perspective by being aware of negative thinking patterns and viewing them purely as mental events rather than accurate reflections of reality (Teasdale, 1988; Teasdale, Segal & Williams, 1995). MBCT is based on an integration of aspects of CBT and components of the mindfulness-based stress reduction programme that contains elements of meditation and provides training in the deployment of attention (Kabat-Zinn, 1990). Clients are taught to become more aware of, and relate differently to, their thoughts, feelings and bodily sensations, and treat thoughts and feelings as passing events in the mind rather than identifying with them. It also teaches skills that allow individuals to disengage from habitual dysfunctional cognitive routines and depression-related patterns of ruminative thought. Studies suggest that MBCT can: (1) significantly reduce the probability of future relapse (Ma & Teasdale (2004) found that MBCT reduced relapse from 78 per cent to 36 per cent, and in participants who had experienced four or more bouts of depression only 38 per cent of those receiving MBCT relapsed compared with 100 per cent in the treatment-as-usual control group); and (2) significantly reduce symptoms of mood disorders (Hofman, Sawyer, Witt & Oh, 2010). These findings suggest that teaching previously depressed individuals to adopt a detached, decentred relationship to their depression-related thoughts and feelings can have significant therapeutic gains. Included in the online resources is a Science Oxford Live lecture on the science of mindfulness by Professor Mark Williams.

For a video on the science of mindfulness go to **www.wiley-psychopathology.com/video/ch7**

SELF-TEST QUESTIONS

- What is a stepped-care model for the treatment of depression?
- What drugs are important in controlling brain neurotransmitter levels, and how do they have their effect?
- What are the important components of social skills training for depression?
- What is the rationale behind behavioural activation therapy for depression?
- How does cognitive therapy attempt to eradicate negative thinking?
- What is reattribution training?
- What is mindfulness-based cognitive therapy and what role does it play in the management of depression?
- What are the main types of pharmacological treatment for bipolar disorder?

7.3 THE TREATMENT OF DEPRESSION AND MOOD DISORDERS

- Drug treatments have been developed that attempt to address the imbalance in neurotransmitters such as serotonin, dopamine and norepinephrine.

- Three main types of medication for depression are trycyclic drugs, monoamine oxidase (MAO) inhibitors, and selective serotonin reuptake inhibitors (SSRIs).

- Lithium carbonate is the main drug prescribed for bipolar disorder.

- Symptoms of bipolar disorder have also been treated successfully with a combination of antidepressant and antipsychotic drugs (e.g. olanzapine and fluoxetine).

- Electroconvulsive therapy (ECT) is sometimes used with individuals suffering severe depression who have not responded well to other forms of treatment.

- Psychodynamic therapy uses a range of techniques (e.g. free association, dream analysis) to help the individual to explore the long-term sources of their depression.

- Social skills training assumes that depression results from the depressed individual's inability to communicate and socialize appropriately, and addresses this deficit using social skills training programmes.

- Behavioural activation therapies attempt to increase the individual's access to pleasant events and rewards and decrease their experience of aversive events.

- Cognitive therapy for depression attempts to help the depressed individual identify negative beliefs and thoughts, challenge these beliefs as irrational, and replace them with positive rational beliefs.

- Outcome studies suggest that cognitive therapy is at least as effective as drug therapy.

- Mindfulness-based cognitive therapy (MBCT) has been developed to prevent relapse in recovered depressed individuals by making them aware of negative thinking patterns that may be triggered by subsequent bouts of depression.

- Computerized CBT is also an effective treatment for milder forms of depression.

7.4 DELIBERATE SELF-HARM

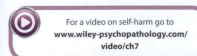

For a video on self-harm go to
www.wiley-psychopathology.com/
video/ch7

deliberate self-harm A parasuicidal phenomenon that commonly includes cutting or burning oneself, taking overdoses, hitting oneself, pulling hair or picking skin, or self-strangulation.

Deliberate self-harm is defined as direct and deliberate bodily harm in the absence of suicidal intent (Nock, 2010), and most frequently takes the form of cutting and carving the skin with a knife or similar sharp instrument (usually on arms, legs and stomach), burning, taking overdoses, pulling hair or picking skin. Deliberate self-harm is included under a new DSM-5 diagnostic category called **non-suicidal self-injury** that covers 'intentional self-inflicted damage

non-suicidal self-injury The act of deliberately causing injury to one's body without conscious suicidal intent.

to the surface of the body that is likely to induce bleeding or bruising' (see DSM-5 Summary Table 7.8). This phenomenon has previously been labelled in many ways, including 'self-mutilation', 'self-harm', 'cutting', and parasuicide, but it is important to distinguish deliberate self-harm from both suicide and parasuicide. The large majority of people who indulge in deliberate self-harm do not have suicidal intentions and nor are they at risk for suicide (Greydanus & Shek, 2009).

As noted in Client's Perspective 7.2, deliberate self-harm is predominantly an adolescent activity, with surveys suggesting that between 13 and 45 per cent of adolescents may have deliberately self-harmed at some time (e.g. Plener, Libal, Keller, Fegert & Muehlenkamp, 2009) but only 4–5 per cent of adults (Briere & Gil, 1998; Klonsky, 2011). People typically engage in self-harm when they are alone and experiencing negative thoughts and feelings (e.g. having a bad memory, feeling angry, experiencing self-hatred or numbness) (Nock, Prinstein & Sterba, 2009). This suggests that self-injury is performed as either a means of self-soothing or of

DSM-5 SUMMARY TABLE 7.8 *Criteria for non-suicidal injury*

- Over the previous year on at least five occasions the individual has intentionally self-inflicted damage to the surface of their body to induce bleeding, bruising or pain with the anticipation that the injury will lead to only minor or moderate physical injury

- Presence of at least two of the following:

  - Negative feelings or thoughts such as depression, anxiety, and suchlike immediately prior to the self-injury

  - Prior to the self-injury a period of fixation with the intended self-injury which is hard to resist

  - Preoccupation with self-injury occurs frequently even when not acted upon

  - The self-injury is carried out with the expectation that it will relieve a negative feeling or induce a positive feeling during or directly after the self-injury

- The self-injury does not occur only during states of psychosis, delirium or intoxication

- There is no suicidal intent

help-seeking (e.g. with the end goal of enlisting others to help the individual cope with their negative feelings or negative self-image) (Muehlenkamp, Engel, Wadeson, Crosby *et al.*, 2009). Many adolescents who self-harm do not usually suffer any long-term psychological effects from doing so, but there are groups of individuals who are more at risk of developing self-harm activities, and these include depressed adolescents (Hawton & James, 2005) – especially those going through interpersonal crises, or individuals with existing mental health problems such as eating disorders (Wedig & Nock, 2010), excessive alcohol intake (Hussong, 2003), substance abuse (Koob & Kreek, 2007; Greydanus & Shek, 2009), and psychosis (Gerard, de Moore, Nielssen & Large, 2012). In particular, adolescents at risk of deliberate self-harm show intrapersonal vulnerabilities such as higher physiological arousal in response to frustrating tasks and stressful events (Nock & Mendes, 2008; Nock, Wedig, Holmberg & Hooley, 2008), and poor verbal communication and social problem-solving skills (Nock & Mendes, 2008; Nock & Photos, 2006).

Preventing self-harm can be difficult because acts of self-harm are often impulsive, carried out in secret, and denial is a common feature of those who self-harm – especially when the self-harm may have a positive effect by providing temporary relief from their difficulties. Similarly, most self-injurers also report feeling little or no pain during self-harming, and this also makes the activity difficult to detect (Favazza, 1996; Nock & Prinstein, 2004). However, it may be possible to target vulnerable groups and to ensure that they have access to mental health services and support services. As we have noted above, vulnerable groups that have been identified include (1) depressed adolescents, (2) those

CLIENT'S PERSPECTIVE 7.2
DELIBERATE SELF-HARM

Comments from an adolescent self-harmer posted on an internet message board:

'Hello. . . Um where to start. The thing is self-harm is the only way I can deal with things. Ive tried everything in the book and yeah, none of it even comes close to cutting. I tried the rubber-band thing and ended up with huge welts that actually bruised and thats just anouther form of self-harm. I tryied writing, doing other things. . . None of it helps. My scars are another thing about self-harm that I cant draw myself away from. I like them in some odd way. . . I know. Your probably thinking im insane or an attention-getter or somthing. . . But is there ANYONE who feels the same? I mean likes the way it feels and honestly doesnt want to stop even though its bad and all. . .?'

Deliberate self-harm is primarily an adolescent phenomenon, and estimates suggest that between 13 and 45 per cent of adolescents have deliberately self-harmed at some time (e.g. Plener, Libal, Keller, Fegert & Muehlenkamp, 2009). Self-harm usually occurs when the person is alone and experiencing negative thoughts or feelings, and appears to serve a self-soothing or help-seeking function (Nock, 2010). The most common forms of deliberate self-harm are cutting or carving the skin with a sharp instrument, usually on the arms, legs and stomach, but can also include burning, taking overdoses, pulling hair and picking skin. Many adolescents who self-harm do not suffer any long-lasting psychological effects from doing so, but there are vulnerable groups of adolescents for whom self-harm may be a more enduring problem. These include depressed adolescents, those with interpersonal crises, or individuals with some existing mental health problems such as psychosis, substance abuse problems, or eating disorders (Hawton & James, 2005; Greydanus & Shek, 2009).

with interpersonal crises, such as those who have lost a partner or have run away from home, and (3) those who have previously self-harmed (especially in conjunction with substance misuse and conduct disorder) (Hawton & James, 2005).

There are at present no evidence-based psychological or pharmacological treatments for deliberate self-harm (Nock, 2010). However, one of the more effective forms of treatment for deliberate self-harm appears to be problem-solving therapy. This is often used with adolescents and enables them to bring new coping strategies to the difficulties in their lives, and, when extended to the individual's family, this can facilitate the sharing and expression of feelings. CBT for depression can also be used if depression and low self-esteem are major underlying factors in an individual's self-harm.

SELF-TEST QUESTIONS

- How is deliberate self-harm defined and what kinds of problems lead adolescents in particular to self-harm?
- What are the most common forms of deliberate self-harm?
- What psychological functions is deliberate self-harm thought to serve?

SECTION SUMMARY

7.4 DELIBERATE SELF-HARM

- Deliberate self-harm is common in adolescence, and commonly includes cutting and carving the skin, burning, taking overdoses, pulling hair or picking skin.
- Deliberate self-harm can be performed as a form of self-soothing or as help-seeking.
- One of the more effective treatments for deliberate self-harm includes problem-solving therapy.

7.5 SUICIDE

The World Health Organisation estimates that 1 million people commit suicide each year (WHO, 2012), but the number of people who attempt suicide is 20 times higher. The WHO report also described other sobering facts about suicide. **Suicide** is the second highest cause of death worldwide amongst 15- to 19-year-olds, and suicide rates continue to be a serious problem in high-income countries, but are increasing significantly in middle- and low-income countries.

suicide The action of killing oneself intentionally.

Suicide attempts often occur in the context of mental health problems (especially depression), and it has been estimated that 90 per cent of suicide victims may have a diagnosable psychiatric disorder at the time of their death (Isometsa, Henriksson, Marttunen *et al.*, 1995). Over half of those that successfully commit suicide are usually significantly depressed before the fatal attempt (Isacsson & Rich, 1997), and the cognitive construct of 'hopelessness' is probably one of the best single predictors of suicide (Beck, Steer, Kovacs & Garrison, 1985) (see section 7.1.2). Recent estimates of suicide rates indicate that the 12-month prevalence rate for suicide attempts for developed countries is 0.4 per cent and for suicidal ideation is 2 per cent (Borges, Nock, Kessler, Haro Abad, Hwang *et al.*, 2010). Studies that have investigated the lifetime prevalence rates for suicide suggest that 13.5 per cent of people report lifetime suicidal ideation, 3.9 per cent have planned a suicide, and 4.6 per cent have attempted suicide in their lifetime (Kessler, Borges & Walters, 1999). The likelihood of an individual committing suicide tends to increase with age, although there has been an alarming increase in the number of younger people attempting suicide in recent years, with a rise in the US of 200 per cent since 1960 reported by the US National Center for Health Statistics. Women are around three times more likely to *attempt* suicide than men, but the rate for *successful* suicide is around four times higher in men than women (Peters & Murphy, 1998), and this

TABLE 7.8 *Characteristics that define suicide attempters and completers*

Characteristics	Attempters	Completers
Gender	Mainly female	Mainly male
Age	Mainly young	Increased risk with age
Method	Pills, cutting	More violent (guns, jumping)
Common diagnoses	Mild depression, borderline personality disorder, schizophrenia	Major depression, alcoholism
Dominant affect	Depression with anger	Depression with hopelessness
Motivation	Change in situation, cry for help	Death, self-annihilation

Source: Fremouw, W., Callahan, T. & Kasden, J. (1993). Adolescent suicide risk: Psychological, problem-solving and environmental factors. *Suicide and Life-Threatening Behaviour, 23*(1), 46–54. Reproduced with permission.

is because men will tend to adopt more lethal methods than women (such as guns and jumping, see Table 7.8). Suicidal phenomena have become more common in teenagers and adolescents, and suicide is reported to be the second or third most frequent cause of death among 15- to 24-year-olds in many countries (Commonwealth Department of Health and Family Services, Australia, 1997). Up to 15 per cent of American high-school students have been reported as attempting suicide at least once (King, 1997), and suicidal phenomena in adolescents include suicide attempts, deliberate self-harm, and suicidal plans, threats and thoughts (Hawton, Rodham, Evans & Weatherall, 2002). The reasons for the increase in adolescent suicide rates is unclear, but a number of factors may be relevant: (1) modern teenagers are probably exposed to many of the life stressors experienced by adults, yet may lack the coping resources to deal with them effectively (Reynolds & Mazza, 1994); (2) suicide is also a sociological as well as a psychological phenomenon, and media reports of suicide often trigger a significant increase in suicides (Gould, Jamieson & Romer, 2003), which is especially true in the case of adolescents and teenagers, where news of celebrity suicides are often associated with increases in the rate of teenage suicide attempts (see Focus Point 7.5); and (3) there is a strong relationship between depression, substance abuse and suicide, and the increasing use of drugs and alcohol in young teenagers may well provide one of the reasons for increased rates of suicide and deliberate self-harm in this group (Gould & Kramer, 2001).

FOCUS POINT 7.5

MEDIA CONTAGION AND SUICIDE AMONG THE YOUNG

When Nirvana lead singer Kurt Cobain committed suicide in April 1994 It had a significant impact on young people, who saw Cobain as the spokesman for their troubled generation. The sudden deaths of celebrities in this way have given prominence to social factors that may influence suicide – especially amongst the young. That is, reporting of suicide in the media may trigger 'contagion' effects in which young people imitate their idols. However, the evidence for media contagion effects on suicide rates is equivocal. Some studies have found evidence for increased rates of adolescent suicide after high-profile media stories about suicide (Motto, 1970; Phillips & Carstensen, 1986; Littman, 1985), while others have failed to find any effect. In particular, Martin & Koo (1997) investigated the effect of the suicide of Kurt Cobain on Australian adolescent suicide rates for the 30-day period after his suicide. They found no evidence for a 'suicide contagion' effect, with suicide rates for the 30-day period after Cobain's death being lower than rates for the same period in some previous years. Nevertheless, a recent systematic review of the effects of media reporting on suicide rates concludes that media reporting and suicidality are probably related, suggesting that the media need to be responsible about the way they report celebrity suicides in order to minimize imitation by vulnerable groups (Sisask & Varnik, 2012).

7.5.1   Risk Factors for Suicide

One of the best predictors of future suicide attempts is a history of at least one previous suicide attempt (Leon, Friedman, Sweeney *et al.*, 1990). However, since only 20–30 per cent of those who attempt suicide have made a previous attempt, it is important to look at other risk factors. Suicide is a complex phenomenon, and risk factors encompass a broad range of domains such as psychiatric, psychological, physical, personal, familial and social factors (Evans, Hawton & Rodham, 2004). For example: (1) suicide is related to diagnoses of depression, schizophrenia, borderline personality disorder, panic disorder, alcoholism, and substance abuse (e.g. Isometsa, Henriksson, Marttunen *et al.*, 1995). Nordentoft, Mortensen & Pedersen (2011) found that absolute risk of suicide was highest for those with a diagnosis of bipolar disorder (6–10 per cent) and major depression (5–7 per cent), but all psychiatric disorders studied resulted in an increase in suicide risk of between 2 and 8 per cent compared with the rate of less than 1 per cent found in the control group of individuals without a psychiatric diagnosis; (2) psychological predictors of suicide include the cognitive construct of 'hopelessness' (Alloy, Abramson, Hogan, Whitehouse *et al.*, 2000), and also low self-esteem (Fergusson & Lynskey, 1995); (3) both poor physical health and physical disability are also predictors of suicide (Dubow, Kausch, Blum, Reed & Bush, 1989; Wagman Borowsky, Resnick, Ireland & Blum, 1999); and (4) low socio-economic status is also a significant risk factor (Li, Page, Martin & Taylor, 2011), and the impact of the recent worldwide economic recession has resulted in a significant 3.8 per cent increase in the suicide rate since its onset (Reeves, Stuckler, McKee, Gunnell *et al.*, 2012) (see Figure 7.5). In a large-scale study of risk factors carried out for the World Health Organisation, Borges, Nock, Kessler, Haro *et al.* (2010) found that risk factors for suicidal behaviours in both developed and developing countries included being female, being young, lower education and income, unmarried status, unemployment, parent psychopathology, childhood adversities, and a current DSM psychiatric diagnosis. A combination of these risk factors was able to predict suicide attempts with some accuracy. Perhaps not surprisingly, life stress is one of the most significant predictors of suicide, and suicide attempts are often preceded by a significant negative life event. The types of life events that may trigger suicide can differ across age groups. For adolescents and teenagers these are more likely to be relationship issues, separations and interpersonal conflicts; in middle age they are more likely to be financial issues; and in later life they tend to be related to disability and physical health (Rich, Warsadt, Nemiroff *et al.*, 1991).

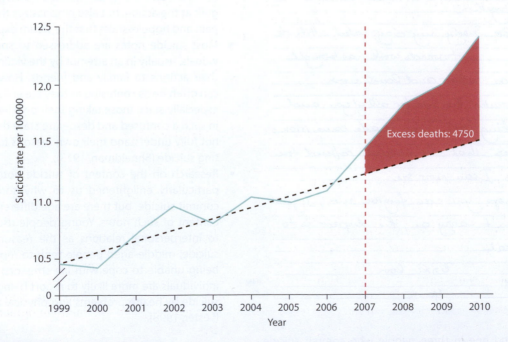

FIGURE 7.5 *Suicide and the economic recession.*
Time trend analysis of suicide rates in 50 US states between 1999 and 2010. Vertical line shows onset of the economic recession.
Source: After Reeves, A., Stuckler, D., McKee, M., Gunnell, D., Chang, S. & Basu, S. (2012). Increase in state suicide rates in the USA during economic recession. *Lancet, 380*(9856),1813–1814. Reproduced with permission.

Finally, there is also a genetic element to suicidal behaviour. Both twin studies and adoption studies support the view that suicidality has an inherited component that may be as high as 48 per cent (Joiner, Brown & Wingate, 2005) and which is independent of the heritability of other psychiatric disorders (Rujescu, Zill, Rietschel & Maier, 2009). This may be related to factors controlling low levels of serotonin metabolites in the brain which have been found to be associated with suicidal behaviour in individuals suffering major depression (Van Praag, Plutchik & Apter, 1990; Winchel, Stanley & Stanley, 1990).

This diversity of risk factors has led researchers to argue that suicide probably results from a complex interplay between sociocultural factors, traumatic events, psychiatric history, personality traits and genetic vulnerability (e.g. Rujescu, Zill, Rietschel & Maier, 2009; Balazic & Marusic, 2005), all of which will need to be included in a comprehensive model of suicide aetiology.

7.5.2 Identifying and Preventing Suicide

It is notoriously difficult to pick up the signs that an individual is seriously contemplating a suicide attempt. Prior to an attempt, suicidal individuals will often seem calm, rational, and even show signs of improvement in their psychological condition. This calm and rationality may simply reflect the period of thought and planning that many who decide to attempt suicide go through. Individuals planning suicide will often meticulously dispose of their possessions, plan how their family will be cared for, and take time to plan the act itself – often choosing a time and place where they cannot be disturbed. According to Kessler, Borges & Walters (1999), a national survey of suicide in the USA suggested that about 39 per cent of those who attempt suicide are determined to die, while 47 per cent do not wish to die but are communicating a 'cry for

---

CLIENT'S PERSPECTIVE 7.3
SUICIDE NOTES

> I have looked at our 18 years
> mainly as happy years and
> had hoped to spent old age
> together
> So Surely my exaggerated attitude
> towards work has brought
> you sorrow and loneliness.
> I wanted the best for all of you and
> looking back I too made some sacri-
> fices. That the children suffered from
> this I can now see.
> I hope you can forgive me, I just
> can't carry on, the despair is to
> great.
> With love
> Your

individuals who are no longer around to explain why they took their own life.

- This suicide note was written by an individual who committed suicide by jumping under a moving train in the UK, and it is typical in that it is short, expresses guilt at the action, but also emphasizes the extreme pain and hopelessness that the victim experiences.

- Most suicide notes are addressed to specific individuals, usually in an attempt by the victim to justify their actions to family and friends. However, they can often be as confusing as they are enlightening – especially since those taking their own lives may be in such a confused and desperate state that they do not fully understand their own reasons for committing suicide (Shneidman, 1973).

- Research on the content of suicide notes has not particularly enlightened us to why some people commit suicide, but there are age differences in the content of such notes. Young people usually point to interpersonal relations as the reason for their suicide; middle-aged people tend to report simply being unable to cope with life stressors; and older individuals are more likely to report being driven to suicide by health problems and physical disabilities (Lester, 1998).

- Around one in three people who commit suicide leave a suicide note, and analysis of such notes can provide an insight into the feelings and motives of

help' to friends and relatives in an attempt to convey their pain and hopelessness. Their survey also suggested that around 72 per cent of those who had constructed a suicide plan went on to make a suicide attempt, and they suggest that prevention is best focused on those who plan suicide attempts and identifying those factors that indicate that a suicidal individual is drawing up a plan.

The fact that around half of those attempting suicide do not want to die, but need to convey their pain and despair, means that intercepting these individuals before they make a successful suicide attempt is important. The main forms of intervention include 24-hour helplines and telephone support lines such as those provided by the Samaritans in the UK (http://www.samaritans.org.uk/). School-based educational programmes are also being developed, and these are aimed at warning teenagers about the early signs of suicidal tendencies in their peers and providing them with appropriate support information. However, while these prevention schemes have some success with some groups of users (e.g. young females), they are less effective in preventing suicide in other groups (e.g. adolescent boys) (Gould & Kramer, 2001). Multilevel interventions for suicide preventions are also being developed, and best practices that have been identified as effective are (1) training general practitioners (GPs) or family physicians to recognize and treat depression and suicidality, (2) improving accessibility of care for at-risk individuals, and (3) restricting access to means of suicide (van der Feltz-Cornelis, Sarchiapone, Postuvan, Volker et al., 2011). Related to this last point, awareness of methods used to commit suicide and attempts to reduce the lethality of those methods is also important in reducing the number of successful suicides. For example, an Australian study found that lethality rates for suicide attempts involving motor vehicle exhaust fumes and hanging had decreased sharply over the previous 10 years (Spittal, Pirkis, Miller & Studdert, 2012). This appeared to be a consequence of the introduction of catalytic converters on car engines that significantly reduced lethal carbon monoxide emissions, and systematic removal of ligature points from institutional settings in which those at risk of suicide might be living.

Finally, both psychological and pharmacological treatments can be helpful for individuals who are at high risk for repeated suicide attempts. Medications for mood disorders (see section 7.3.1) can reduce the risk of suicide significantly, and these may include antidepressants (Bruce, Ten Have, Reynolds, Katz et al., 2004) and antipsychotics (Meltzer, Gatwood, Goodman & Ford, 2003). CBT can also be used successfully to reduce suicide risk and suicide behaviours in particular client groups, such as adolescents (Stanley, Brown, Brent, Wells et al., 2009) and individuals suffering psychosis (Tarrier, Haddock, Lewis, Drake & Gregg, 2006).

SELF-TEST QUESTIONS

- Can you name the main risk factors for suicide?
- What are the best ways of identifying and preventing suicide?

SECTION SUMMARY

7.5   SUICIDE

- Over half of those that successfully commit suicide are significantly depressed before the fatal attempt.
- Suicidal ideation is reported by 13.5 per cent of people during their lifetime.
- Women are three times more likely to attempt suicide than men, but the rate for successful suicide is four times higher in men than women.
- Risk factors for suicide include an existing psychiatric diagnosis, low self-esteem, poor physical health and physical disability, and experiencing a significant negative life event.
- There is an inherited component to suicide which may be as high as 48 per cent.
- The main forms of intervening to prevent suicide include 24-hour helplines and telephone support lines (e.g. the Samaritans), and school-based educational programmes warning about the early signs of suicidal tendencies.
- Both medications for mood disorders and CBT can be helpful in reducing suicide risk in vulnerable people.

7.6 DEPRESSION AND MOOD DISORDERS REVIEWED

Depression is arguably the most prevalent of all the main psychopathology symptoms we will cover in this text (lifetime prevalence rates between 5.2 and 17.1 per cent), it afflicts women twice as frequently as men, and it is estimated that it contributes 12 per cent to the total burden of non-fatal global disease (Ustun, Ayuso-Mateos, Chatterji, Mathers & Murray, 2000). It is an emotion that all of us experience at some point – especially in relation to losses and failures in our lives. However, for some it is a sustained, crippling and distressing problem (see the personal description given at the beginning of this chapter), and may even lead to suicidal ideation, and suicide attempts (section 7.5). Bipolar disorder is the other main mood disorder covered in this chapter, and this is characterized by alternating periods of depression and mania (see Client's Perspective 7.1). This is a significantly less prevalent disorder (lifetime prevalence rate between 0.4 and 1.6 per cent) that appears to have a basis in neurotransmitter imbalances in the brain (section 7.2.2). A look back at the online 'Summary' table reminds us of the various theories that have been developed to try to explain all or parts of the symptoms of depression. These theories range from biological theories covering inherited factors, brain neurochemical imbalances and brain abnormalities, to a full spectrum of psychological theories attempting to explain both the behavioural and cognitive features of depression. Drug treatments, such as trycyclic drugs, monamine oxidase inhibitors, and, more recently, selective serotonin reuptake inhibitors (SSRIs), have been shown to alleviate many of the symptoms of severe depression (section 7.3.1). However, both behavioural and cognitive therapies appear to have promise as long-term effective treatments for depression, and these therapies help the sufferer by enabling them to identify and challenge ingrained negative views of themselves and the world. Finally, two important clinical phenomena related to mood disorders and depression are deliberate self-harm and suicide. Deliberate self-harm is an increasingly recognized problem that mainly afflicts adolescents, while mental health problems generally – and mood disorders specifically – are a significant risk factor for suicide.

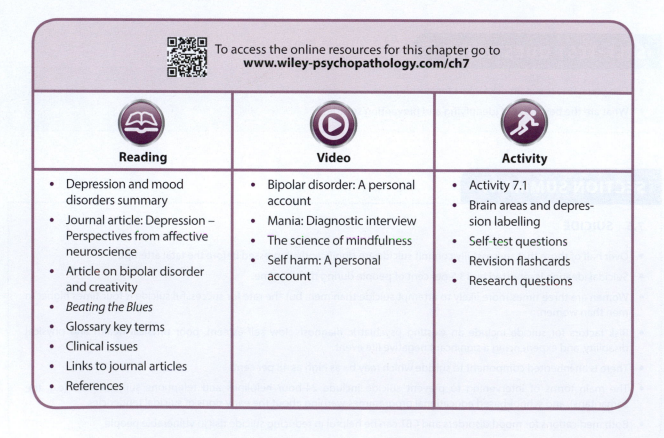

To access the online resources for this chapter go to
www.wiley-psychopathology.com/ch7

Reading	**Video**	**Activity**
• Depression and mood disorders summary	• Bipolar disorder: A personal account	• Activity 7.1
• Journal article: Depression – Perspectives from affective neuroscience	• Mania: Diagnostic interview	• Brain areas and depression labelling
• Article on bipolar disorder and creativity	• The science of mindfulness	• Self-test questions
• *Beating the Blues*	• Self harm: A personal account	• Revision flashcards
• Glossary key terms		• Research questions
• Clinical issues		
• Links to journal articles		
• References		

8 Experiencing Psychosis: Schizophrenia Spectrum Problems

 To access the online resources for this chapter go to
www.wiley-psychopathology.com/ch8

ROUTE MAP OF THE CHAPTER

This chapter describes the symptoms of psychosis and examines the heterogeneous diagnostic categories within DSM-5. We begin by describing the main symptoms of psychosis and then cover the main diagnostic categories within schizophrenia spectrum disorder. We also consider the stages through which psychotic symptoms develop. We then describe and evaluate a range of explanations of psychosis, and these theories often attempt to explain symptoms at a number of different levels, such as biological, psychological and social levels. We finish by describing a variety of biological and psychological treatments for psychotic symptoms, and end by discussing the role of community care as a means of long-term supervision and management for those suffering from psychosis.

CHAPTER OUTLINE

LEARNING OUTCOMES

When you have completed this chapter, you should be able to:

1. Describe the main clinical symptoms of psychosis, and the key features of the main diagnostic categories defining schizophrenia spectrum disorders in DSM-5.

2. Describe and evaluate the main biological theories of the aetiology of psychosis – especially the role of brain neurotransmitters and brain abnormalities.

3. Describe, evaluate and compare the main psychological and sociocultural theories of the aetiology of psychosis.

4. Describe and evaluate the role of familial and psychological factors in relapse following remission.

5. Describe a range of treatments for psychotic symptoms, including biological, psychological, familial, and community care interventions.

Trying to look at the lead up to an illness is difficult. Before I had any symptoms, I was generally feeling like I couldn't cope, but I didn't know how to go about getting any help. I was in a bad relationship and it ended, but I dearly wanted something to take its place.

I moved to Birmingham, to do a post-graduate diploma in housing. I recognized that I wasn't really feeling together, but I just hoped that things would improve. I lived on my own in a bedsit and generally became antagonistic towards others.

I had passed my first-year exams and was working as a student placement for Warwick District Council. By about October of 1992, I believed that DJs on the radio were talking directly to me. When I told other people this they just laughed. But these DJs started to become very important to me, so I continued to believe it was happening, despite what other people were saying. I just kept it as my secret, until eventually when I was not at work I would listen to the radio 24 hours a day.

I believed that a radio DJ wanted a relationship with me, and throughout the course of our courtship – over the airwaves – the DJ and myself would actually discover the meaning of life. Everything had a meaning and eventually I had a sort of vision: God, he spoke to me and said 'No matter what happens, I will always love you'. I felt special and chosen and at the same time I thought that other people were telepathic and could read my mind.

I was still working and started a 2-week placement at Newtown neighbourhood office. By now the world looked very different, with people being able to read my mind. Whenever names were said, such as Lorraine or Pat, it had something to do with the state of my relationship with the radio DJ. Lorraine meant sorrow or floods of tears like rain; Pat meant that someone was patronising me, or I them, depending on the context; Jackie meant that I was being chucked or that I was chucking him. I used to ring up the radio station under different names, all of which had a hidden meaning, such as Dawn – meaning that something had just dawned on me. Maureen meant that I was marooned.

Whilst on this placement – I was only there for 2 days – I began to get physical or tactile hallucinations. I thought that I had been shot in the head to remove a blood clot. Then, as I was working with one of my colleagues, I actually felt my brain crack open, then masses of blood came out of one of my ears, then a small trickle from the other. This for me meant that I was dead or dying in spirit, which I believed in more than the mortal body. At this point I started crying. My colleague went to put his hands on my arm, which he quickly removed as my arms were red hot. I asked to go home early, which was allowed.

That night, I thought that the devil was after me: I saw him come through one of the speakers of my stereo system. I was also probably hearing voices, but they were mixed in with the talk of the radio DJs. Suddenly, I became frustrated and ran out of the house into the middle of the road and started screaming. My neighbour came out and told me to come inside. He told me he had called the police and I started thumping him thinking he was the devil.

The experiences of the illness left me socially inept, mainly because I couldn't think to speak and engage in interpersonal relationships. I tried very hard to overcome the symptoms of the illness, including lack of motivation, but I was also conscious not to do too much. I did voluntary work and finished off my course. But, I was generally feeling different and less capable than everyone else. I tended to sleep an awful lot, but always tried to keep going, although many times I felt like giving up. But, this time I had come so far away from my delusions that there seemed like no going back. Eventually, I found employment and I am currently working part-time.

Sophie's Story

Introduction

Psychotic symptoms can be crippling and are often characterized by disturbances in thought and language, sensory perception, emotion regulation, and behaviour. Sufferers may experience sensory hallucinations and also develop thinking biases that may lead to pervasive false beliefs or delusions about themselves and the world around them. Individuals with psychotic symptoms may often withdraw from normal social interaction because of these disturbances of perception and thought, and this can result in poor educational performance, increasing lack of productivity, difficulties in interpersonal relationships, neglect of day-to-day activities and a preoccupation with a personal world to the exclusion of others. As a result, many individuals exhibiting psychotic symptoms fall to the bottom of the social ladder or even become homeless because they cannot hold down a job or sustain a relationship – a phenomenon known as *downward drift* (Hollingshead & Redlich, 1958) (see section 8.5.3).

Sophie's story is a particularly severe example of how psychotic symptoms can manifest themselves. Her story starts with a stressful life – exemplified by being in a difficult relationship – and an overwhelming feeling of inability to cope. Whilst living alone she finds maintaining relationships with others difficult. The developing symptoms of psychosis include delusions (that the DJ is talking directly to her and that others were developing telepathic powers that enabled them to read her mind) and she begins to feel that she possesses special powers. Eventually Sophie begins to experience sensory hallucinations in which she felt that she had been shot in the head and her brain had cracked open. Sophie's story ends with her experiences leaving her feeling socially inept and affecting her longer term ability to be productive and motivated.

Psychosis is a collective name given to an extensive range of disparate symptoms that can often leave an individual feeling frightened and confused, and the presence of different combinations of these symptoms may lead to a diagnosis of any one of a number of **schizophrenia spectrum disorders**. DSM-5 has moved away from a single overriding diagnostic category (schizophrenia) split into a series of subtypes (paranoid, disorganized, catatonic, undifferentiated), and now lists a number of separate psychotic disorders that range across a spectrum depending on severity, duration and complexity of symptoms. The main diagnostic categories in DSM-5 are schizophrenia, schizotypal personality disorder, delusional disorder, brief psychotic disorder, and schizoaffective disorder, and we will discuss these individually later in this chapter. But first we will discuss the key cognitive and behavioural features that define psychosis – combinations of which give rise to the different diagnoses. These key features include delusions, hallucinations, disorganized thinking, abnormal motor behaviour, and negative symptoms (indicative of diminished emotional expression).

For a video on psychosis go to **www.wiley-psychopathology.com/video/ch8**

schizophrenia spectrum disorders The name for separate psychotic disorders that range across a spectrum depending on severity, duration and complexity of symptoms.

FOCUS POINT 8.1

HISTORY OF SCHIZOPHRENIA AS A DIAGNOSTIC CATEGORY

The symptoms of psychosis have been reported throughout history, but because the symptoms can be so varied and wide ranging, 'schizophrenia' has only gradually been isolated as a single diagnostic category to cover these heterogeneous characteristics.

The European psychiatrist, Emil Kraepelin (1896), was the first to distinguish schizophrenia from a range of other psychiatric symptoms (such as manic depressive illness). He did this by bringing together a number of contemporary diagnostic concepts including paranoia, catatonia and hebephrenia (symptoms indicative of incoherence and fragmentation of personality) under the general term **dementia praecox**. He assumed that dementia praecox was a single disease that manifested itself in late adolescence or early adulthood and had a deteriorating prognosis from which there was no recovery. In contrast to Kraepelin, the Swiss psychiatrist Eugen Bleuler (1908) believed that the onset of dementia praecox was not simply restricted to adolescence and early adulthood and also believed that it did not inevitably lead to dementia. He preferred to use the term schizophrenia (from the Greek *schiz*, to spilt, and *phren*, the mind), because he felt that it properly described the splitting of different psychological functions within a single personality. Unfortunately, this term has also had its problems, with the popular belief that the term schizophrenia refers to a split- or double-personality. In order to try to unify the various symptoms under a single diagnostic category, Bleuler used the concept of the 'breaking of associative threads' as being central to all of the symptoms of schizophrenia. That is, effective thinking, communication and action were not possible if the ability to associate things together was disrupted. In this

dementia praecox An early, general term for a number of diagnostic concepts including paranoia, catatonia and hebephrenia (symptoms indicative of incoherence and fragmentation of personality).

respect, it is interesting to note that in later sections in this chapter we will see that there is evidence that at least some of the clinical symptoms of schizophrenia may be determined by dysfunctions in associative and attentional processes (see section 8.5.2).

Recent diagnostic criteria recognize the complexity of schizophrenia as a diagnostic category, and up until the publication of DSM-5, diagnosis was not dependent on one essential symptom, but on the basis of the presence of at least two or three of five basic symptoms. This inevitably meant that people could receive a diagnosis of schizophrenia but exhibit quite different symptoms. The latest diagnostic manual, DSM-5, has moved away from defining a single overriding diagnostic category with a series of subtypes towards considering schizophrenia as a spectrum disorder. The important diagnostic categories in this spectrum are *schizophrenia*, *schizotypal personality disorder*, *delusional disorder*, *brief psychotic disorder*, and *schizoaffective disorder*, and these will be discussed later in this chapter.

8.1   THE NATURE OF PSYCHOTIC SYMPTOMS

DSM-5 lists five important characteristics for diagnosing schizophrenia spectrum disorders. The first four of these characteristics are traditionally known as **positive symptoms**, because they tend to reflect an excess or distortion of normal functions (e.g. developing inappropriate beliefs or perceiving things that are not there), and the final category represents what are known as **negative symptoms**, and these reflect symptoms characteristic of a diminution or loss of normal functions.

> **positive symptoms** Characteristics of psychotic symptoms which tend to reflect an excess or distortion of normal functions.

> **negative symptoms** Symptoms characteristic of a diminution or loss of normal functions.

8.1.1   Delusions

Delusions are firmly held but erroneous beliefs that (1) usually involve a misinterpretation of perceptions or experiences, and (2) become fixed beliefs that are not amenable to change in light of conflicting or contradictory evidence. Such delusions are commonly experienced by around 75 per cent of those individuals hospitalized because of their psychotic symptoms (Maher, 2001), and while some delusions may be clearly bizarre (e.g. the individual may believe that their entire internal organs have been taken out and replaced by those of someone else), others may not (e.g. a paranoid belief that the individual is constantly under surveillance by the police). Regardless of how bizarre a delusion is, the sufferer is often able to bring reason and logic to support their delusion – even though the underlying belief itself is clearly absurd (Maher, 2001). This ability to support absurd beliefs with logical thought has led some clinicians to suggest that delusions may be the result of an inability to integrate perceptual input with prior knowledge even though rational thought processes are still intact (Frith, 1996; Frith & Dolan, 2000). For other clinicians it is suggestive of the development of biased information processing and the development of dysfunctional beliefs about the world (e.g. Freeman, Garety, Kuipers, Fowler & Bebbington, 2002; Morrison, 2001), or decision-making processes that lead the individual to 'jump to conclusions' on the basis of minimal evidence (e.g. Moritz & Woodward, 2005; Garety & Freeman, 1999).

The main types of delusion found in those experiencing psychosis are: (1) **Persecutory delusions** (paranoia), in which the individual believes they are being persecuted, spied upon, or are in danger (usually as the result of a conspiracy of some kind); (2) **Grandiose delusions**, in which the individual believes they are someone with fame or power or have exceptional abilities, wealth or fame (e.g. Jesus Christ, or a famous music star); (3) **Delusions of control**, where the person believes that their thoughts, feelings or their actions are being controlled by external forces (e.g. extraterrestrial or supernatural beings), and this is often associated with the belief that control is being exerted through devices (such as the radio) which are sending messages directly to the person's brain; (4) **Delusions of reference**, where the individual believes that independent external events are making specific reference to them (e.g. in *Sophie's Story*, she believes

> **delusions** Firmly held but erroneous beliefs that usually involve a misinterpretation of perceptions or experiences.

> **persecutory delusions** Delusions in which the individual believes they are being persecuted, spied upon, or are in danger (usually as the result of a conspiracy of some kind).

> **grandiose delusions** Delusions in which the individual believes they are someone with fame or power or have exceptional abilities, wealth or fame.

> **delusions of control** Delusions where the person believes that his or her thoughts, feelings or actions are being controlled by external forces (e.g. extraterrestrial or supernatural beings).

> **delusions of reference** Delusions where the individual believes that independent external events are making specific reference to him or her.

nihilistic delusions Delusions where individuals believe that some aspect of either the world or themselves has ceased to exist (e.g. the person may believe that they are in fact dead).

erotomanic delusions Relatively rare psychotic delusions, where an individual has a delusional belief that a person of higher social status falls in love and makes amorous advances towards them.

For an activity on types of delusions go to
**www.wiley-psychopathology.com/
activities/ch8**

that the DJ on the radio is talking directly to her); (5) **Nihilistic delusions**, where the individual believes that some aspect of either the world or themselves has ceased to exist (e.g. the person may believe that they are in fact dead) or a major catastrophe will occur; and (6) **Erotomanic delusions**, when an individual falsely believes that another person is in love with him or her (see Focus Point 8.2).

One common feature of psychotic thought is that sufferers frequently believe that their thoughts are being interfered with or controlled in some way, either by being openly broadcast to others or by having thoughts planted into their mind by external forces. This type of delusion is so common that it may offer some insight into the cognitive deficits underlying a majority of psychotic thought. For example, in an experimental study, Blakemore, Oakley & Firth (2003) used hypnosis to generate beliefs in non-clinical participants that their

self-generated actions could be attributed to an external source. They found that such erroneous beliefs generated higher than normal levels of activation in the parietal cortex and cerebellum and they suggest that these areas of the brain may be altered during psychotic episodes so that self-produced actions and thoughts are experienced as external.

8.1.2   Hallucinations

People suffering psychotic symptoms regularly report sensory abnormalities across a broad range of sensory modalities, and this is usually manifested as perceiving things that are not there. **Hallucinations** can occur in any modality (e.g. auditory, olfactory, gustatory and tactile), but the most common are auditory hallucinations that are reported by around 70 per cent of sufferers (Cleghorn, Franco, Szechtman, Kaplan *et al.*, 1992). Auditory hallucinations are usually manifested as voices, and these can be experienced as external voices commanding the individual to act in certain ways, two or more voices conversing with each other,

hallucinations A sensory experience in which a person can see, hear, smell, taste or feel something that isn't there.

FOCUS POINT 8.2

EROTOMANIA AND STALKING

One form of psychotic delusion is called erotomania. This is a relatively rare disorder where an individual has a delusional belief that a person of higher social status falls in love and makes amorous advances towards them. As a result of these delusions, the individual suffering erotomanic delusions may often end up stalking their target by regularly visiting their home in an attempt to meet and talk with them or by following them as they go about their daily business. There are two types of erotomanic delusion. The first is where the individual believes their victim loves them. In this case the individual believes they are having a relationship with their victim, and they will make regular attempts to try to contact and meet their victim in order to substantiate the relationship. The American actress Rebecca Schaeffer was tragically shot in 1989 by a stalker who was rebuffed by her when attempting to talk to her about their 'relationship'. The second form of erotomanic delusion is when the individual believes that they are destined to be with their victim, even though they are aware they may never have met them. So, if they pursue them long enough, they will

eventually come to have a relationship with their victim. An example of this is the case of Agnetha from the Swedish pop group ABBA, who was stalked for some years by a Dutch man who believed he was destined to be with her.

Stalking appears to be on the increase in many Western countries (Pathe, 2002), causes substantial distress to its victims, and can be caused by a range of psychopathologies (e.g. erotomanic delusions, severe personality disorder, obsessive compulsive disorders). Studies of individuals with erotomanic delusions indicate that they are usually isolated loners without a partner or full-time occupation and around half have a first-degree relative with a delusional disorder (Kennedy, McDonough, Kelly & Berrios, 2002). Many also develop fantasies in which they are driven to protect, help or even harm their victims (Menzies, Federoff, Green & Isaacson, 1995). One example is the German stalker who was obsessed with tennis star Steffi Graf, and this drove him to attack and stab her tennis rival, Monica Seles, during a tournament in Hamburg in 1993 in a deluded attempt to try to further Graf's career.

or a voice commentating on the individual's own thoughts. In all cases these voices are perceived as being distinct from the individual's own thoughts. Research into brain areas involved in speech generation and the perception of sounds suggests that when sufferers claim to hear 'voices' this is associated with neural activation in these areas of the brain (Keefe, Arnold, Bayen, McEvoy & Wilson, 2002; McGuire, Silbersweig, Wright, Murray *et al.*, 1996), and the sufferer attributes them to external sources. Visual hallucinations are the second most common type of hallucination and can take either a diffuse form as in the perception of colours and shapes that are not present, or they can be very specific such as perceiving that a particular person (e.g. a partner or parent) is present when they are not. Other hallucinations can be tactile and somatic (e.g. feeling that one's skin is tingling or burning) or olfactory and gustatory (e.g. experiencing smells that are not present or foods that taste unusual).

For those who believe that their hallucinations are real, such experiences can be extremely frightening. However, while some individuals suffering psychosis are convinced their hallucinations are real, many others are aware that their hallucinations may *not* be real. This suggests that psychotic episodes may be associated with a reality-monitoring deficit. That is, individuals suffering psychotic symptoms may have difficulty identifying the source of a perception and difficulty distinguishing whether it is real or imagined. In support of this possibility, Brebion, Amador, David, Malaspina *et al.* (2000) found that when individuals diagnosed with schizophrenia and non-clinical controls were asked to remember words that had either been generated by themselves or been generated by the experimenter, schizophrenic individuals differed in three important ways from non-clinical controls. Firstly, they were more likely to identify items as having been in the generated list of words when they were not (false positives); secondly, they were more likely to report that words they had generated themselves were generated by the experimenter; and thirdly, they were more likely to report that spoken items had been presented as pictures. These results suggest that individuals diagnosed with schizophrenia have a **reality-monitoring deficit** (i.e. a problem distinguishing between what actually occurred and what did not occur), and a **self-monitoring deficit** (i.e. they cannot distinguish between thoughts and ideas they generated themselves and thoughts or ideas that other people generated).

reality-monitoring deficit Where an individual has a problem distinguishing between what actually occurred and what did not occur.

self-monitoring deficit Where individuals cannot distinguish between thoughts and ideas they generated themselves and thoughts or ideas that other people generated.

8.1.3 Disorganized Thinking (Speech)

Disorganized thinking will normally be inferred from the individual's speech, and there are a number of common features displayed by individuals experiencing psychotic symptoms. The most common are **derailment** or **loose associations**, where the individual may drift quickly from one topic to another during a conversation. Their answers to questions may be tangential rather than relevant ('**tangentiality**'), and in some cases their speech may be so disorganized that it is neither structured nor comprehensible. Instances of the latter are '**clanging**', the use of **neologisms**, and '**word salads**': Focus Point 8.3 provides examples of the confused speech generated by some individuals exhibiting psychotic symptoms. These loose associations that appear to govern psychotic speech suggest that sufferers (1) have difficulty inhibiting associations between thoughts (Titone, Holzman & Levy, 2002) and so tend to follow the track of the first association that comes to mind, and (2) have difficulties understanding the full context of a conversation (Cohen, Barch, Carter & Servan-Schreiber, 1999), and so cannot distinguish the full meaning of a conversation or sentence from its detail. The result of these loose associations is that psychotic speech can be very detailed in terms of number of words, breadth of ideas, and grammatical correctness, but it will usually convey very little (**poverty of content**).

derailment A disorder of speech where the individual may drift quickly from one topic to another during a conversation.

loose associations Disorganized thinking in which the individual may drift quickly from one topic to another during a conversation.

tangentiality A disorder of speech in which answers to questions may be tangential rather than relevant.

clanging A form of speech pattern in schizophrenia where thinking is driven by word sounds. For example, rhyming or alliteration may lead to the appearance of logical connections where none in fact exists.

neologisms Made up words, frequently constructed by condensing or combining several words.

word salads When the language of the person experiencing a psychotic episode appears so disorganized that there seems to be no link between one phrase and the next.

poverty of content A characteristic of the conversation of individuals suffering psychosis in which their conversation has very little substantive content.

8.1.4 Grossly Disorganized or Abnormal Motor Behaviour

Grossly disorganized or abnormal motor behaviour may manifest itself in a variety of ways. Behaviour may be child-like and silly (and inappropriate for the person's chronological age), or inappropriate to the context (e.g. masturbating in public). It may be unpredictable and agitated (e.g. shouting and swearing in the street) and the individual may have

FOCUS POINT 8.3

DISORGANIZED SPEECH INDICTATIVE OF DISORGANIZED THINKING

Psychotic symptoms frequently exhibit a range of attributes that indicate disordered thinking. Below are examples of some of the more common of these disorganized speech symptoms.

WORD SALAD

In many cases, the language of the person experiencing a psychotic episode appears so disorganized that there seems to be no link between one phrase and the next, and this is known as a 'word salad'. Some word salads simply do not seem to be attempts to communicate anything structured and appear to drift without substance from one unconnected sentence to the next:

> 'Everything is going around in slow motion. The boxes are clanging and chattering to be let out. Behind my forehead the past is surfacing, mixing a bottle of acid solution. A stake jams a door that leads to a mirage of broken appearances. Inside a box, pounding fists try to pull down my imagination. The ground work is split into hundreds of pieces; each fragment is separate as if it had some kind of individual purpose. The truth is locked up in a unit.'

In other cases, word salads appear to be sets of phrases or words linked by association to the previous phrase. For example, in answer to the question 'What colour is your dress?', a sufferer answered 'red . . . Santa Claus . . . flying through the sky . . . God'. This is known as *loose association* or *derailment* and makes it very difficult to follow the conversation of an individual when a single, often unimportant word from the previous sentence becomes the focus of the next sentence.

NEOLOGISMS

To try and communicate, many individuals suffering psychotic symptoms often make up words and use them in their attempts to communicate. These are called neologisms, and are frequently constructed by condensing or combining several words. Some examples given by individual sufferers are the following:

SPECTROAUTOROTATION	Circling in everywhere, as with checkers or a bat in baseball
SNIGGERATION	A giggle or sniggering. I do it sometimes
RELAUDATION	Praising over and over
CIRCLINGOLOGY	Study of a rolling circle; a fruit can in the form of a cylinder rolling

CLANGING

People exhibiting psychotic symptoms often try to communicate using words that rhyme, and this is known as 'clanging'. If you go back to look at *Sophie's story* at the beginning of this chapter, you will see that she used a series of names to denote the state of her mind or how she was feeling. These names rhymed with words that described her feelings (e.g. Lorraine – Tears like rain; Pat – Patronising; Jackie – Being Chucked; Maureen – Marooned). In other cases, sufferers only appear able to construct sentences if the words in them rhyme – and this communication may begin with a sensible response but then degenerate into nonsense because of the urge to 'clang' as the following transcript shows:

Therapist:	'What colour is your dress?'
Client:	'Red. . . . Like a bed.'
Therapist:	'Why is it like a bed?'
Client:	'Because it's dead.'
Therapist:	'Why is a bed like being dead?'
Client:	'I dunno . . . maybe it's a med.'
Therapist:	'What's a med?'
Client:	'A bled.'

difficulty completing any goal-directed activity (e.g. an inability to focus on or complete basic day-to-day tasks such as cooking or maintaining personal hygiene). The person's appearance may be dishevelled and they may well dress in an inappropriate manner (e.g. wearing heavy, thick clothing in hot weather or walking around in public in only their underwear). **Catatonic motor behaviours** are characterized by a significant decrease in reactivity to the environment (catatonic stupor), maintaining rigid, immobile postures (catatonic rigidity), resisting attempts to be moved (catatonic negativism), or purposeless and excessive motor activity that often consists of simple, stereotyped movements (catatonic excitement or stereotypy) (see Photo 8.1).

catatonic motor behaviours
Characterized by a decrease in reactivity and maintaining rigid, immobile postures.

Grunnitus Studio/Science Photo Library. Reproduced with permission.

PHOTO 8.1 *In some very severe cases of psychosis, the individual may lapse into a* catatonic stupor. *Those who lapse into this state become withdrawn and inactive for long periods. In extreme cases this may take the form of catatonic rigidity, in which the individual will adopt a rigid, often awkward posture for many hours. Others exhibit what is known as* waxy flexibility, *and will maintain a posture into which they have been placed by someone else.*

8.1.5 Negative Symptoms

Negative symptoms are common within a diagnosis of schizophrenia, but less so in the other schizophrenia spectrum disorders. Negative symptoms include diminished emotional expression, avolition, alogia, anhedonia, and asociality. **Diminished emotional expression** (also described as **affective flattening**) includes reductions in facial expressions of emotion, lack of eye contact, poor voice intonation, and lack of head and hand movements that would normally give rise to emotional expression. **Avolition** represents an inability to carry out or complete normal day-to-day goal-oriented activities, and this results in the individual showing little interest in social or work activities. **Alogia** is characterized by a lack of verbal fluency in which the individual gives very brief, empty replies to questions. **Anhedonia** is the decreased ability to experience pleasure from positive stimuli or an inability to recall pleasurable events (Kring & Neale, 1996). Finally, **asociality** refers to a lack of interest in social interactions, perhaps brought about by a gradual withdrawal from social interactions generally.

diminished emotional expression A reduction in facial expressions of emotion, lack of eye contact, poor voice intonation, and lack of head and hand movements that would normally give rise to emotional expression.

affective flattening Limited range and intensity of emotional expression; a 'negative' symptom of schizophrenia.

avolition An inability to carry out or complete normal day-to-day goal-oriented activities, and this results in the individual showing little interest in social or work activities.

alogia A lack of verbal fluency in which the individual gives very brief, empty replies to questions.

anhedonia Inability to react to enjoyable or pleasurable events.

asociality A lack of interest in social interactions, perhaps brought about by a gradual withdrawal from social interactions generally.

SELF-TEST QUESTIONS

- What is the difference between the positive and negative symptoms of schizophrenia?
- Can you name some of the different types of delusional states found in delusional disorder?
- What are the most common forms of hallucination experienced in schizophrenia and approximately what percentage of sufferers report hallucinations?
- Can you name the different forms of disordered speech and communication exhibited by individuals diagnosed with schizophrenia and provide some examples of each?
- What are the characteristics of catatonic motor behaviours?
- Can you describe some of the specific symptoms that are collectively known as negative symptoms?

SECTION SUMMARY

8.1 THE NATURE OF PSYCHOTIC SYMPTOMS

- The first four characteristics are known as *positive symptoms*, and the fifth category represents *negative symptoms*.

- Roughly 75 per cent of people hospitalized with a diagnosis of schizophrenia experience delusions.

- The main types of delusions are (1) persecutory delusions, (2) grandiose delusions, (3) delusions of control, (4) delusions of reference, and (5) nihilistic delusions.

- Around 70 per cent of individuals diagnosed with schizophrenia report auditory hallucinations.

- Individuals suffering hallucinations may have a reality-monitoring deficit (distinguishing between what actually occurs and what does not).

- The most common forms of disorganized speech are *derailment*, *loose associations*, *clanging*, *neologisms* and *word salads*.

- Grossly disorganized or abnormal motor behaviour is usually behaviour inappropriate to a context (e.g. masturbating in public). Catatonic motor behaviours are characterized by a decrease in reactivity and maintaining rigid, immobile postures.

- Negative symptoms are characterized by flat affect, lack of interest in social or work activities, poverty of speech (alogia) and apathy (avolition).

8.2 THE DIAGNOSIS OF SCHIZOPHRENIA SPECTRUM DISORDERS

DSM-5 has organized schizophrenia spectrum disorders along a gradient of psychopathology and impairment – from less severe to more severe and disabling. Clinicians are asked to consider diagnosis along this continuum, taking into account the number of diagnosable symptoms, the severity of those symptoms, and the time period over which symptoms have been manifested. We will describe the diagnostic criteria for four of these spectrum disorders, namely delusional disorder, brief psychotic disorder, schizophrenia, and schizoaffective disorder. Although DSM-5 considers schizotypal personality disorder to be within the schizophrenia spectrum, it is normally considered as a personality disorder, and so its diagnostic criteria and description can be found in Chapter 12, Personality Disorders.

8.2.1 Delusional Disorder

The diagnostic criteria for delusional disorder are given in DSM-5 Summary Table 8.1. Subtypes of delusional disorder include the most common which is the *persecutory* type, where the individual believes they are being

DSM-5 SUMMARY TABLE 8.1 *Criteria for delusional disorder*

- One or more delusions lasting at least 1 month
- Apart from the impact of the delusions, normal functioning is not markedly impaired and behaviour is not bizarre
- Any manic or major depressive episodes which have occurred have been brief in relation to the delusional episode
- The disorder is not directly attributable to the use of a substance or medication and is not better explained by other mental disorder

conspired against, cheated, spied on, followed, poisoned, maliciously maligned, harassed, or obstructed in the pursuit of long-term goals. Other common subtypes are *erotomanic* type (see Focus Point 8.2) and the *grandiose* type (where the individual has a strong conviction that they have some great talent or insight). Grandiose delusions may often have a religious content or consist of beliefs that the individual has a special relationship with a prominent person. Apart from the direct impact of the delusions, psychosocial functioning in such individuals may seem quite normal. However, depending on the type of delusional belief held by the individual, this may often give rise to social, marital or work problems. Many also exhibit mood problems associated with their delusional beliefs, especially anger outbursts or antagonistic behaviour when their beliefs are not taken seriously.

8.2.2 Brief Psychotic Disorder

The core feature of **brief psychotic disorder** is the sudden onset of at least one of the main psychotic symptoms – namely, delusions, hallucinations, disorganized speech, or grossly abnormal psychomotor behaviour (see section 8.1.4), with this change from a non-psychotic state to the appearance of symptoms occurring within 2 weeks and being associated with emotional turmoil or overwhelming confusion. The diagnostic criteria are provided in DSM-5 Summary Table 8.2.

brief psychotic disorder The sudden onset of at least one of the main psychotic symptoms, with this change from a non-psychotic state to the appearance of symptoms occurring within 2 weeks and being associated with emotional turmoil or overwhelming confusion.

8.2.3 Schizophrenia

A diagnosis of **schizophrenia** is given when there is range of symptoms covering cognitive, behavioural and emotional dysfunction and also impaired occupational or social functioning – but no single symptom is characteristic of this diagnosis. DSM-5 Summary Table 8.3 shows the diagnostic criteria for schizophrenia and two or more of the five symptoms in the first point must be present for a significant proportion of time during a 1-month period or longer. The following point is also important as it recognizes that symptoms must be associated with impaired functioning across areas such as work, interpersonal relations, or self-care. Prodromal symptoms often precede the active phase, and residual symptoms may follow it (see below). Similarly, negative symptoms or social isolation are common during the prodromal

schizophrenia The main diagnostic category for psychotic symptoms. The five central characteristics are delusions, hallucinations, disorganized speech, grossly disorganized or catatonic behaviour and flattened affect, poverty of speech and apathy.

phase and can be a significant indicator of later full-blown symptoms of psychosis (Lencz, Smith, Auther, Correll & Cornblatt, 2004). Additional symptoms displayed by individuals with a diagnosis of schizophrenia may include inappropriate affect (e.g. laughing inappropriately), depressed mood, anxiety or anger, disturbed sleep patterns and lack of interest in eating. Individuals with a diagnosis of schizophrenia may often show a lack of insight into their symptoms, and may be hostile and aggressive. However, aggression is more common in younger males and for individuals with a past history of violence, non-adherence to treatment, substance abuse and impulsivity (DSM-5, p.101). It must, however, be emphasized that the vast majority of people with a diagnosis of schizophrenia are not aggressive and are more likely to be the victims of violence and aggression than be the perpetrators.

DSM-5 SUMMARY TABLE 8.3 *Criteria for schizophrenia*

- At least two of the following must be present for a significant period of time during a one month period:
  - Delusions
  - Hallucinations
  - Disorganized speech
  - Highly disorganized or catatonic behaviour
  - Negative symptoms such as diminished emotional expression
- The ability to function in one or more major areas such as work, self-care or interpersonal relationships is markedly diminished
- Continuous signs of the disturbance last for at least 6 months
- The disorder is not directly attributable to the use of a substance or medication and is not better explained by other mental disorder

DSM-5 SUMMARY TABLE 8.2 *Criteria for brief psychotic disorder*

- Presence of at least one of the following:
  - Delusions
  - Hallucinations
  - Disorganized speech
  - Highly disorganized or catatonic behaviour
- The disturbance lasts between 1 day and 1 month with eventual return to normal behaviour
- The disorder is not directly attributable to the use of a substance or medication and is not better explained by other mental disorder

DSM-5 SUMMARY TABLE 8.4 *Criteria for schizoaffective disorder*

- A continuous period of illness during which there is a major mood episode (major depressive or manic)
- Delusions or hallucinations for 2 or more weeks without the occurrence of a major mood episode
- Symptoms for a major mood episode are present for the majority of the duration of the illness
- The disorder is not directly attributable to the use of a substance or medication and is not better explained by other mental disorder

8.2.4   Schizoaffective Disorder

Schizoaffective disorder is diagnosed when an individual displays symptoms that meet the criteria for schizophrenia (see above), but where there is also a significant mood

> **schizoaffective disorder** Characterized by schizophrenia symptoms plus a period reflecting either depression or mania.

episode reflecting either depression or mania that are present for the majority of the duration of the illness (DSM-5 Summary Table 8.4). Schizoaffective disorder will frequently impair occupational functioning and may be associated with restricted social functioning, difficulties with self-care, and an increased risk for suicide.

SELF-TEST QUESTION

- What are the four main schizophrenia spectrum disorder diagnostic categories in DSM-5?

SECTION SUMMARY

8.2   THE DIAGNOSIS OF SCHIZOPHRENIA SPECTRUM DISORDERS

- DSM-5 has organized schizophrenia spectrum disorders along a gradient of psychopathology and impairment – from less severe to more severe and disabling.

- The most common forms of delusional disorder are *persecutory* type and *grandiose* type.

- *Brief psychotic disorder* is typified by the sudden onset of one of the main psychotic symptoms.

- *Schizophrenia* is the main diagnostic category in schizophrenia spectrum disorders, and occurs when there is range of symptoms covering cognitive, behavioural and emotional dysfunction and also impaired occupational or social functioning.

- *Schizoaffective disorder* is characterized by schizophrenia symptoms plus a period reflecting either depression or mania.

8.3   THE PREVALENCE OF SCHIZOPHRENIA SPECTRUM DISORDERS

When precise methods for its diagnosis are applied, the lifetime prevalence rate for a diagnosis of schizophrenia is between 0.3 and 0.7 per cent – around 24 million people worldwide (van Os & Kapur, 2009), and mostly in the age group 15–35 years. The World Health Organisation has recognized that schizophrenia is one of the top 10 medical disorders causing disability (WHO, 1990), and the mortality rate among people with a diagnosis of schizophrenia is around 50 per cent higher than normal. In addition, sufferers tend to die around 10 years earlier than individuals who have never been diagnosed with schizophrenia (Jeste, Gladsjo, Lindamer et al., 1996). Around 10 per cent die by suicide (NICE, 2010). While treatments and interventions for psychosis are continually improving, a significant number of people with a diagnosis of schizophrenia continue to suffer lifelong impairment,

with over 80 per cent continuing to have problems with social functioning and 79 per cent undertaking no work of any kind (Thornicroft, Tansella, Becker, Knapp et al., 2004). The World Health Organisation found the prevalence of schizophrenia roughly similar across the world. However, interestingly, the course of schizophrenia tends to be less severe in developing countries than in developed nations (Thara, Henrietta, Joseph, Rajkumar & Eaton, 1994). The reasons for this difference in prognosis are unclear, although the central support role of the family and differences in beliefs about the origins of psychological disorders in developing countries may be important (Lin & Kleinman, 1988).

Some studies have identified some consistent cultural differences in the prevalence of schizophrenia within individual countries. For example, in a UK-based study, King, Nazroo, Weich, McKenzie et al (2005) found that the reporting of psychotic symptoms was higher in ethnic minority groups than in ethnic white individuals. This increase in the reporting of symptoms was twice as high in people of African-Caribbean origin as in whites. There have been a number of hypotheses that have attempted to explain this apparent cultural difference, and there is at least some evidence that the higher symptom levels in black American men than white American men may be the result of racial disparities in mental health treatment between blacks and whites in the USA (Whaley, 2004). In other within-country studies, immigrants have been shown to have significantly higher rates of schizophrenia diagnosis than members of the indigenous population. A personal or family history of migration is an important risk factor, and immigrants from developing countries are at greater risk than those from developed countries (Cantor-Graae & Selten, 2005). At least part of the explanation for the higher incidence in immigrants can be traced to the stress caused by many of the initial consequences of immigration, such as language difficulties,

unemployment, poor housing, and low socio-economic status (Hjern, Wicks & Dalman, 2004). Finally, the incidence of schizophrenia is similar for males and females, although females tend to have a later age of onset and fewer hospital admissions, and this may be the result of females attaining higher levels of social role functioning before illness, which confers a better outcome (Hafner, 2000; Murray & van Os, 1998; Angermeyer, Kuhn & Goldstein, 1990).

Finally, delusional disorder and brief psychotic disorder are new diagnostic categories within schizophrenia spectrum disorders, but DSM-5 estimates that the lifetime prevalence rate for delusional disorder is around 0.2 per cent, and that brief psychotic disorder may account for 9 per cent of cases of first-onset psychosis.

SELF-TEST QUESTIONS

- What is the estimated lifetime prevalence rate for a diagnosis of schizophrenia?
- Some ethnic and cultural differences in the prevalence rates of schizophrenia have been found within individual countries. Can you describe some of these differences?

SECTION SUMMARY

8.3   THE PREVALENCE OF SCHIZOPHRENIA SPECTRUM DISORDERS

- The lifetime prevalence rate for a diagnosis of schizophrenia is between 0.5 and 0.7 per cent, and is similar across different countries and cultures.
- Rates of diagnosis of schizophrenia do tend to be higher in some ethnic groups (e.g. people of African-Caribbean origin in the UK), and in immigrant populations generally.
- Estimates for the lifetime prevalence rate for delusional disorder is around 0.2 per cent.

8.4   THE COURSE OF PSYCHOTIC SYMPTOMS

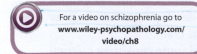

For a video on schizophrenia go to
**www.wiley-psychopathology.com/
video/ch8**

Psychotic symptoms usually develop through a well-defined succession of stages. The three predominant phases are (1) the prodromal stage, (2) the active stage, and (3) the residual stage.

8.4.1   *The Prodromal Stage*

The large majority of those who develop psychotic symptoms show the first signs of these symptoms during

late adolescence or early adulthood. A study of nine countries by the World Health Organisation found that 51 per cent of individuals diagnosed with schizophrenia were between 15 and 25 years of age (Sartorius, Jablensky, Korten, Ernberg *et al.*, 1986), and over 80 per cent are between 15 and 35 years of age. For some individuals, the onset of psychotic symptoms can be rapid and dramatic, but for most it represents a slow deterioration from normal functioning over an average period of around 5 years (Hafner, Maurer, Loffler, van der Heiden *et al.*, 2003). This slow deterioration is known as the **prodromal stage**, and is first exhibited as slow withdrawal from normal life and social interaction, shallow and inappropriate

prodromal stage The slow deterioration from normal functioning to the delusional and dysfunctional thinking characteristic of many forms of schizophrenia, normally taking place over an average of 5 years.

emotions, and deterioration in personal care and work or school performance, with some evidence that grey matter loss may occur in those brain areas mediating social cognition (Bhojraj, Sweeney, Prasad, Eack *et al.*, 2011). That psychosis initially develops during late adolescence is one of the basic facts of this psychopathology, but why should onset occur during this rather specific point in an individual's lifespan? The course of psychosis is best understood in terms of a stress-diathesis model, in which psychotic symptoms are caused by an underlying inherited biological vulnerability, but this vulnerability frequently manifests as specific symptoms if the individual has certain critical and stressful life experiences. There is a good deal of evidence that over 70 per cent of individuals who first show symptoms of psychosis have experienced stressful life events in the previous 3 weeks (Brown & Birley, 1968), and the transition from adolescence to adulthood is arguably one of the most stressful periods of an individual's life. In addition, Harrop & Trower (2001) argue that prodromal-like signs in normal adolescents appear to be linked to normal development, and that psychotic symptoms may emerge from a troubled teenage state that has failed to cope with normal maturation. This leaves the adolescent unable to cope with a majority of the life challenges that they will have to deal with at this stage of development, and the resulting response is a withdrawal from social interaction and a fall in educational performance. Eventually such tendencies will become noted by family and friends, and the development of disordered thoughts, delusions and erratic and bizarre behaviour mark the onset of the active stage.

During the development of DSM-5, a case was made for including what was to be called *attenuated psychotic symptoms syndrome* (also known as 'psychosis risk syndrome') (Woods, Walsh, Saksa & McGlashan, 2010). This would have been characterized by mild psychotic symptoms that don't meet the diagnostic criteria for full-blown schizophrenia, but would enable clinicians to identify at least some individuals who were in the

---

CASE HISTORY 8.1

THE PRODROMAL STAGE – IDENTIFYING THE EARLY SIGNS

'Fifteen-year-old Caitlin was an excellent student with many friends when she entered the ninth grade. One year later, she suddenly became restless in school, stopped paying attention to her teachers, and eventually failed all of her subjects. At home she appeared increasingly withdrawn and isolated, spending hours sleeping or watching television. The previously even-tempered adolescent became angry, anxious, and suspicious of those around her, and was occasionally seen talking to herself while making repetitive, odd hand motions. Several years later, hearing voices and insisting that the CIA was hatching an elaborate plot to murder her and her family, she was diagnosed with schizophrenia.'

Source: Can we prevent or delay schizophrenia? Retrieved from http://www.med.nyu.edu/content?ChunkIID=14245

Clinical Commentary

This description of the development of Caitlin's symptoms is typical of the prodromal stage of schizophrenia. She became withdrawn, ill-tempered, anxious and suspicious, and showed a marked decline in academic performance. Unfortunately, these signs are often difficult to differentiate from many of the behavioural changes exhibited by normal individuals as they progress through adolescence, so diagnosis at an early stage is often difficult. These difficulties with early diagnosis are unfortunate because evidence suggests that the earlier treatment begins after the development of actual psychosis, the more rapid the immediate recovery and the better the overall outcome (see Focus Point 8.9 on Early Intervention Services).

Some more specific prodromal features associated with schizophrenia include:

- *Peculiar behaviours*
- *Impairment in personal hygiene and grooming*
- *Inappropriate affect (e.g. laughing when talking about something sad)*
- *Vague, overly elaborate, or circumstantial speech*
- *Poverty of speech*
- *Odd beliefs or magical thinking*
- *Unusual perceptual experiences.*

prodromal state for subsequent schizophrenia spectrum disorders. However, the final decision was to omit this category from DSM-5 because of the poor diagnostic reliability revealed in an earlier clinical trial (Carpenter & van Os, 2011).

8.4.2   The Active Stage

In the **active stage**, the individual begins to show unambiguous symptoms of psychosis, which may manifest as delusions, hallucinations, disordered speech and communication, and a range of full-blown symptoms that are outlined in section 8.1.

> **active stage** The stage in which an individual begins to show unambiguous symptoms of psychosis, including delusions, hallucinations, disordered speech and communication, and a range of full-blown symptoms.

8.4.3   The Residual Stage

Recovery from the symptoms of psychosis is usually gradual, but many sufferers may still retain some symptomatology over the longer term. The **residual stage** is reached when the individual ceases to show prominent signs of positive symptoms (such as delusions, hallucinations,

> **residual stage** The stage of psychosis when the individual ceases to show prominent signs of positive symptoms (such as delusions, hallucinations or disordered speech).

disordered speech). However, during the residual stage they may well still exhibit negative symptoms, such as blunted affect, withdrawal from social interaction, and find it difficult to cope with normal day-to-day activities such as holding down a job. Long-term studies have suggested that around 28 per cent of sufferers will remit after one or more active stage, 22 per cent will continue to show positive symptoms over the longer term, and around 50 per cent will alternate between active and residual stages (Wiersma, Nienhuis, Slooff & Giel, 1998). These statistics indicate that relapse is relatively common, and relapse can often be traced to either (1) stressful life events or return to a stressful family environment after a period of hospitalization or care (see section 8.5.3), or (2) non-adherence to medication. It is estimated that around 40–50 per cent of those diagnosed with schizophrenia fail at some point to adhere to their course of medication (Lacro, Dunn, Dolder, Leckband & Jeste, 2002), and partial compliance is likely to result in significantly higher levels of relapse and re-hospitalization (Eaddy, Grogg & Locklear, 2005). The factors most associated with non-adherence or non-compliance with medication include poor insight, negative attitudes to medication, a history of non-adherence, substance abuse, inadequate discharge or aftercare planning, and poorer therapeutic relationships between patient and service providers (Lacro et al., 2002).

SELF-TEST QUESTIONS

- What are the main stages through which psychotic symptoms normally develop?
- What are the factors that may contribute to relapse following recovery from an acute psychotic episode?

SECTION SUMMARY

8.4   THE COURSE OF PSYCHOTIC SYMPTOMS

- The large majority of those who develop psychotic symptoms show the first signs of symptoms during late adolescence or early adulthood. This is known as the *prodromal stage*.

- Around 70 per cent of those who show first signs of psychotic symptoms have experienced stressful life events in the previous 3 weeks.

- Around 28 per cent of those diagnosed with schizophrenia will remit after 1 or more active stages, 22 per cent will continue to show positive symptoms over the long term, and 50 per cent will alternate between active and residual stages.

8.5 THE AETIOLOGY OF PSYCHOTIC SYMPTOMS

The evidence we have reviewed so far portrays psychosis as a broad range of loosely associated symptoms. It can manifest as disordered thinking and communication, disordered perceptions, hallucinations and delusions, and as behavioural deficits. In addition, no one single clinical symptom is the cardinal feature by which the main DSM-5 diagnostic category of schizophrenia is characterized. This being the case, theories of the aetiology of psychosis are also diverse and include biological, psychological and sociological approaches to understanding this psychopathology. The overarching approach to understanding psychosis is a **diathesis-stress** perspective. That is, psychosis is thought to be caused by a combination of a genetically inherited biological diathesis (a biological predisposition to schizophrenia) and environmental stress. This means that even if you have a genetically pre-programmed disposition to psychosis, you may well not develop any symptoms unless you experience certain forms of life stressors. Such stressors might involve early rearing factors (Schiffman, Abrahamson, Cannon, LaBrie *et al.*, 2001), dysfunctional relationships within the family (Bateson, 1978), an inability to cope with the stresses of normal adolescent development (Harrop & Trower, 2001), or with educational or work demands. In addition, recent research on the diathesis-stress approach to schizophrenia suggests that stress may worsen symptoms in those with a genetic vulnerability to psychosis through its effect on cortisol production in the body (Jones & Fernyhough, 2007).

> **diathesis-stress** The perspective that psychopathology is caused by a combination of a genetically inherited biological diathesis (a biological predisposition) and environmental stress.

Because of the heterogeneous nature of schizophrenia as a diagnostic category and the range of diverse symptoms that accompany psychosis, the study of the causes of these symptoms has focused on explaining specific features of psychosis rather than attempting to elaborate an all-inclusive explanation. This is sometimes known as a 'complaint-oriented approach' (Bentall, 2006), which not only argues that there is a need to study individual symptoms, but also that individual symptoms may have their origin in psychological mechanisms that underlie normal experience (Bentall, 2004). For example, some theories have attempted to identify the inherited component of individual symptoms; others the abnormalities in brain biochemistry or brain functions that accompany psychotic symptoms. Still others have tried to understand the cognitive processes that underlie

delusions, and disordered thought and communication – many of which do have their origins in normal psychological processes. Others have attempted to identify the nature of the stressors that might trigger psychotic symptoms in vulnerable individuals. Finally, sociocultural views of psychosis take an entirely different perspective and argue that the course of psychotic symptoms may be determined by the simple act of diagnosing someone with schizophrenia or by the fact that they are born into a disadvantaged socio-economic group, and factors such as these may be enough to promote the development of psychotic symptoms. We will explore all of these different approaches in the following sections.

8.5.1 Biological Theories

Genetic factors

It has always been known that psychotic symptoms appear to run in families, and this suggests that there may well be some form of inherited predisposition. That psychosis has an inherited component has been supported by the results of *concordance studies*. If an individual is diagnosed with schizophrenia, Table 8.1 shows the probability with which a family member or relative will also develop the disorder. This shows that the probability with which the family member or relative will develop schizophrenia is dependent on how closely they are related – or, more specifically, how much genetic material the two share in common (Gottesman, McGuffin & Farmer, 1987; Cardno, Marshall, Coid, Macdonald *et al.*, 1999). Recent studies have suggested that an individual who has a first-degree relative diagnosed with schizophrenia is 10 times more likely to develop psychotic symptoms than

TABLE 8.1 *Concordance rates for individuals with a diagnosis of schizophrenia*

Relation to proband	% diagnosed with schizophrenia
Spouse	1.00
Grandchildren	2.84
Nieces/nephews	2.65
Children	9.35
Siblings	7.30
Dizygotic (fraternal) twins	12.08
Monozygotic (identical) twins	44.30

Source: Gottesman, I.I, McGuffin, P. & Farmer, A.E. (1987). Clinical genetics as clues to the real genetics of schinzophrenia (a decade of modest gains while playing for time). *Schizophrenia Bulletin, 13*(1), 23–47. By permission of Oxford University Press.

someone who has no first-degree relatives diagnosed with schizophrenia (Schneider & Deldin, 2001).

However, simply because psychotic symptoms tend to run in families does not establish a genetic basis for this psychopathology. For example, some family environments may have dysfunctional elements (e.g. difficulties in communication between family members) that may give rise to the development of psychosis. In order to examine the genetic basis more carefully, many researchers have undertaken *twin studies*, in which they have compared the probability with which monozygotic (MZ) and dizygotic (DZ) twins both develop symptoms indicative of schizophrenia. MZ twins share 100 per cent of their genetic material, whereas DZ twins share only 50 per cent of their genes, so a genetic explanation of psychotic symptoms would predict that there would be greater concordance in the diagnosis of schizophrenia in MZ than in DZ twins. This can clearly be seen in Table 8.1 where the concordance rate for MZ twins is 44 per cent, but falls to only 12 per cent in DZ twins. Twin studies have indicated that the heritability estimate for schizophrenia is approximately 80 per cent (Cardno & Gottesman, 2000; Sullivan, Kendler & Neale, 2003), which makes schizophrenia one of the most heritable of psychiatric disorders (Gejman, Sanders & Kendler, 2011). As convincing as these data may seem, there are still problems in interpreting twin studies. For example, (1) MZ twins will always be the same sex whereas DZ twins may not be, (2) MZ twins are usually physically identical, unlike DZ twins, and this may lead to family and friends treating MZ twins more similarly than they would DZ twins (i.e. MZ twins could experience more similar environmental factors than DZ twins), and (3) MZ twins are likely to have shared the same placenta prior to birth whereas DZ twins do not, and this would mean that any interuterine abnormalities would be more likely to affect both MZ twins through the shared placenta (Davis & Phelps, 1995). However, many of these difficulties of interpretation can be overcome by studying the *offspring* of MZ and DZ twins rather than the twins themselves (Gottesman & Bertelsen, 1989). If one MZ twin develops psychotic symptoms and the other does not, any genetic element in psychosis should still show up in the children of *either* of the two MZ twins. That is, the children of the MZ twins should still exhibit similar rates of risk for schizophrenia (because they have inherited the same predisposition) – even though one of their parents developed schizophrenia and the other did not. This is exactly what Gottesman & Bertelsen (1989) found: 16.8 per cent of the offspring of the MZ twins that were diagnosed with schizophrenia were likely to develop psychotic symptoms themselves, and 17.4 per cent of the offspring of the MZ twins that were *not* diagnosed with schizophrenia were also likely to develop

psychotic symptoms. This suggests that a genetic risk factor has been passed on to offspring, even though one set of parents did not develop schizophrenia themselves.

Another way of tackling the problems of separating out the influence of genetic inheritance and environmental experience is to look at the incidence of schizophrenia in children who are biologically similar but have been reared apart (**adoptions studies**). If there is an important genetic element to psychosis, then we would expect the children of a mother diagnosed with schizophrenia to have similar probabilities of developing schizophrenia regardless of whether they had been reared with their mother or not. A seminal study by Heston (1966) compared 47 adopted children who were reared apart from their schizophrenic biological mothers with 50 control adopted children whose mothers were not diagnosed with schizophrenia. He found symptoms of psychosis in 16.6 per cent of the adopted children of the schizophrenic mothers, and no symptoms in the adopted children of mothers without schizophrenia. Studies of adopted children conducted in Denmark have shown similar results. Kety (1988) and Kety, Wender, Jacobsen, Ingraham *et al.* (1994) found that adopted children who develop psychotic symptoms are significantly more likely to have had biological relatives with a diagnosis of schizophrenia (21.4 per cent) than adoptive relatives with a diagnosis of schizophrenia (5.4 per cent). These types of studies provide strong evidence for a genetic component to schizophrenia and psychosis. However, some more recent adoption studies suggest that genetic liability still interacts with environmental factors to predict the development of psychotic symptoms. Wahlberg, Wynne, Hakko, Laksy *et al.* (2004) found that in adopted children, inherited genetic factors were an important predictor of a diagnosis of schizophrenia but only in combination with certain environmental factors found in the adopted home environment. In this particular study, an adopted child was more likely to be diagnosed with schizophrenia if they had a biologically inherited predisposition *and* they were also brought up in an adopted home environment where there were dysfunctional communication patterns (see section 8.5.3). While genetic inheritance is an important predictor of psychotic symptoms, this is further evidence that genetic factors interact with environmental factors in a way predicted by diathesis-stress models.

Not only are these kinds of genetic studies important in determining whether a diagnosis of schizophrenia has a significant inherited component, they are also beginning to show that individual symptoms associated with a diagnosis of schizophrenia may also have an important inherited component, and these include factors such as experiencing hallucinations (Hur, Cherny & Sham,

adoption studies Research conducted on children who have been reared by individuals other than their biological parents.

2012), volume of grey matter in specific brain regions (van Haren, Rijsdijk, Schnack & Picchioni, 2012), and catatonia (Beckmann & Franzek, 2000). However, for some other psychotic symptoms there is less evidence for overriding genetic determination, and these include some negative symptoms such as anhedonia (Craver & Pogue-Geile, 1999) and delusions (Cardno & McGuffin, 2006; Varghese, Wray, Scott & Williams, 2013). Finally, recent genetic studies of schizophrenia and its related disorders have begun to show that there are genetic overlaps between schizophrenia and some other psychiatric disorders, such as bipolar disorder and autism, suggesting that variation in a specific gene or set of genes may simultaneously affect the development of these different diagnoses (Gejman, Sanders & Kendler, 2011).

To read the article on 'The heritability of delusional-like experiences' by Varghese *et al.* go to www.wiley-psychopathology.com/reading/ch8

Molecular genetics

If, as seems likely, there is a genetic component to psychosis, how is it transmitted between related individuals, and how does this inherited component influence the development of psychotic symptoms? In recent years, much effort has been directed at attempting to identify the specific genes through which the risk for psychosis may be transmitted (Harrison & Owen, 2003), the chromosomes on which these genes are located (Kendler, Myers, O'Neill, Martin *et al.*, 2000), and how these genes and their possible defects may give rise to psychotic symptoms (Andreasen, 2001). These endeavours have primarily involved *genetic linkage analyses*, in which blood samples are collected in order to study the inheritance patterns within families that have members diagnosed with schizophrenia. Linkage analyses work by comparing the inheritance of characteristics for which gene location is well known (e.g. eye colour) with the inheritance of psychotic symptoms. If the inheritance of, for example, eye colour follows the same pattern within the family as psychotic symptoms, then it can reasonably be concluded that the gene controlling psychotic symptoms is probably found on the same chromosome as the gene controlling eye colour, and is probably genetically linked to that 'marker' characteristic in some way. Research Methods Box 8.1 illustrates an example of how a particular trait of those diagnosed with schizophrenia, in this case poor eye-tracking of a moving object, can be used as a genetic marker to track other psychotic symptoms that may be linked genetically to this characteristic.

RESEARCH METHODS 8.1

SMOOTH-PURSUIT EYE-TRACKING AS A MARKER FOR THE INHERITANCE OF PSYCHOSIS

Smooth-pursuit eye-tracking is the ability to follow a moving object in a smooth continuous movement with your eyes while keeping your head still. However, many individuals with a diagnosis of schizophrenia are unable to do this, and can only follow a moving object with jerky movements of the eyes (known as saccadic movements) (Schneider & Deldin, 2001). This may seem like a relatively innocuous symptom, but it has importance because it is a characteristic that can be used as a *genetic marker* for schizophrenia. That is, unlike the broader symptoms of schizophrenia (such as thought disorder, delusions, and hallucinations), abnormalities in smooth-pursuit eye-tracking are probably related to a rather specific neurological abnormality which may be directly linked to abnormalities in individual genes. If this is so, then the gene responsible for specific eye-tracking deficits may also be associated with many of the more disabling symptoms of schizophrenia. So, by tracing the gene responsible for eye-tracking deficits we may also locate the gene or genes responsible for other psychotic symptoms.

There is now a large body of evidence indicating that around 30–45 per cent of first-degree relatives of individuals diagnosed with schizophrenia exhibit poor performance in smooth pursuit eye-tracking tasks – even when those first degree relatives have not been diagnosed with schizophrenia (Karoumi, Saoud, d'Amato, Rosenfeld *et al.*, 2001; Louchart-de la Chapelle, Nkam, Houy, Belmont *et al.*, 2005), and this suggests that deficits in eye-tracking performance are likely to be an indicator of an inherited predisposition to schizophrenia. In addition, studies of twins in which only one of the pair has developed psychotic symptoms (discordant twins) show that concordance of eye-tracking abnormalities are twice as high in monozygotic twins (MZ) than dizygotic (DZ) twins (Levy & Holzman, 1997) (see section 8.5.1 for an explanation of concordance studies in twins), providing more evidence for the involvement of inherited genetic factors. Studies have still been unable to track down the specific gene associated with this eye-tracking abnormality, although there is some evidence that it may be linked with a number of genes that are also responsible for interfering with dopamine metabolism (Trillenberg, Lencer & Heide, 2004), and this may be the important connection between eye-tracking deficits and the broader symptoms of schizophrenia.

Using analyses such as these, genes associated with the development of psychotic symptoms have been identified on a number of chromosomes including 8 and 22 (Kendler, Myers, O'Neill, Martin *et al.*, 2000), 2, 3, 5, 6, 11, 13 and 20 (Badner & Gershon, 2002; Levinson, Lewis & Wise, 2002), and 1 and 15 (Gejman, Sanders & Kendler, 2011). Also, other techniques, such as **genome-wide association studies (GWAS)** allow researchers to identify rare mutations in genes that might give rise to

> **genome-wide association studies (GWAS)** Technique which allows researchers to identify rare mutations in genes that might give rise to psychopathology symptoms.

psychotic symptoms – especially those mutations that give rise to 'copy number variations' (CNVs), a term that refers to an abnormal copy of DNA in a gene (either a deletion or a duplication). Mutations resulting in DNA deletions (International Schizophrenia Consortium, 2008) as well as mutations causing DNA duplications (Levinson, Duan, Oh, Wang *et al.*, 2011; Kirov, Grozeva, Norton, Ivanov *et al.*, 2009) have been found to be associated with schizophrenia. However, while many studies have shown associations between individual genes and schizophrenia symptoms, there have also often been failures to replicate these findings (Kim, Zerwas, Trace & Sullivan, 2011). This probably testifies to the heterogeneity of schizophrenia as a diagnostic category, and that different people with a diagnosis of schizophrenia may not have the same underlying genetic factors contributing to their symptoms. For example, many of the mutations causing the CNVs mentioned above are very rare, and so schizophrenia symptoms may be caused by many different and very rare gene mutations. Secondly, some of the gene factors associated with schizophrenia may have their impact on quite specific aspects of psychological functioning. For example, deficits in executive functioning (planning, working memory, problem solving) are known to be characteristic of schizophrenia, and some genes have been identified which are associated specifically with executive functioning deficits in schizophrenia (Harrison & Weinberger, 2004; Owen, Williams & O'Donovan, 2004). But executive functioning deficits are also associated with many other psychiatric disorders, such as autistic spectrum disorder and intellectual disabilities, and so this particular gene mutation may not be purely a risk factor for schizophrenia and we might predict it to be present without an individual necessarily developing psychotic symptoms.

Brain neurotransmitters

Cognition and behaviour are very much dependent on the efficient working of brain neurotransmitters, which enables effective communication between brain cells and functionally different parts of the brain itself. It is not surprising, therefore, that many researchers have suspected that the thought disorders, hallucinations and behaviour problems characteristic in the diagnosis of schizophrenia may be caused by malfunctions in these brain neurotransmitters. The biochemical theory of schizophrenia that has been most prominent over the past 50 years is known as the **dopamine hypothesis**, and this account argues that the symptoms of schizophrenia are importantly related to excess activity of the neurotransmitter dopamine. There are a number of factors that have led to the implication of excess dopamine activity.

> **dopamine hypothesis** A theory which argues that the symptoms of schizophrenia are related to excess activity of the neurotransmitter dopamine.

First, the discovery of antipsychotic drugs that helped to alleviate the symptoms of psychosis (such as the **phenothiazines**) led to the discovery that such drugs acted by blocking the brain's dopamine receptor sites and so reduced dopamine activity (Schneider & Deldin, 2001). Interestingly, while the administration of anti-

> **phenothiazines** A group of antipsychotic drugs that help to alleviate the symptoms of psychosis by blocking the brain's dopamine receptor sites and so reduce dopamine activity.

psychotic drugs alleviated many of the positive symptoms of schizophrenia, such as thought disorder and social withdrawal, they also had the side effect of producing muscle tremors very similar to those seen in Parkinson's disease, and it was already known that Parkinson's disease was caused by low levels of dopamine. In contrast, when people suffering Parkinson's disease were given the drug L-dopa to raise brain dopamine levels, they often began to exhibit psychotic symptoms (Grilly, 2002). This evidence strongly suggests that either high levels of brain dopamine or excess dopamine activity is responsible for many of the symptoms of psychosis. Subsequent research has suggested that many antipsychotic drugs have their effect by binding specifically to dopamine receptors and reducing brain dopamine activity (Burt, Creese & Snyder, 1977).

Second, during the 1970s it was noticed that there was a strong link between excessive use of amphetamines and a syndrome known as **amphetamine psychosis**. When taken in high doses for long periods of time, amphetamines produce behavioural symptoms in humans and animals that closely resemble symptoms of psychosis. These include paranoia and repetitive, stereotyped behaviour patterns (Angrist,

> **amphetamine psychosis** A syndrome in which high doses of amphetamines taken for long periods of time produce behavioural symptoms in humans and animals that closely resemble symptoms of psychosis.

Lee & Gershon, 1974). Subsequently we have learnt that amphetamines produce these disturbed behaviour patterns by increasing brain dopamine activity, and giving amphetamines to those diagnosed with schizophrenia actually increases the severity of their symptoms (Faustman, 1995).

Third, brain imaging studies have indicated that individuals diagnosed with schizophrenia show excessive levels of dopamine released from areas of the brain such as the basal ganglia – especially when biochemical precursors to dopamine, such as dopa, are administered to the individual (Carlsson, 2001; Goldsmith, Shapiro & Joyce, 1997).

Finally, post-mortem studies have found increased levels of dopamine and significantly more dopamine receptors in the brains of deceased schizophrenia sufferers – especially in the limbic area of the brain (Seeman & Kapur, 2001).

So, how might dopamine activity be involved in the production of psychotic symptoms? Figure 8.1 illustrates two important dopamine pathways in the brain, the **mesolimbic pathway** and the **mesocortical pathway**.

mesolimbic pathway One of two important dopamine pathways in the brain, which may be impaired during schizophrenia. The other pathway is the mesocortical pathway.

mesocortical pathway One of two important dopamine pathways in the brain, which may be impaired during schizophrenia. The other pathway is the mesolimbic pathway.

These two pathways begin in the ventral tegmental area of the brain, but may have quite different effects on the appearance of psychotic symptoms. First, an excess of dopamine receptors only seems to be related to the positive symptoms associated with schizophrenia (hallucinations, delusions, disordered speech). This is consistent with the fact that antipsychotic drugs only appear to attenuate positive symptoms and have little or no effect on negative symptoms (the behavioural symptoms associated with flattened affect), and this effect of excess dopamine appears to be localized in the mesolimbic dopamine pathway (Davis, Kahn, Ko & Davidson, 1991). However, the mesocortical pathway begins in the ventral tegmental area but projects to the prefrontal cortex, and the dopamine neurons in the prefrontal cortex may be underactive. This has important implications for cognitive activity because the prefrontal cortex is the substrate for important cognitive processes such as working memory, and these cognitive processes contribute to motivated and planned behaviour (Winterer & Weinberger, 2004). In this way, dopamine activity might account for both the positive and the negative symptoms observed in schizophrenia, but because antipsychotic drugs block dopamine receptors only in the mesolimbic pathway, this accounts for why such drugs only affect positive symptoms.

While the dopamine hypothesis has been an influential biochemical theory of schizophrenia for more than 30 years, there is still some evidence that does not fit comfortably within this hypothesis. First, while antipsychotic drugs are usually effective in dealing with many of the symptoms of schizophrenia, they do not start having an effect

For a brain labelling activity based on Figure 8.1 go to **www.wiley-psychopathology.com/ activities/ch8**

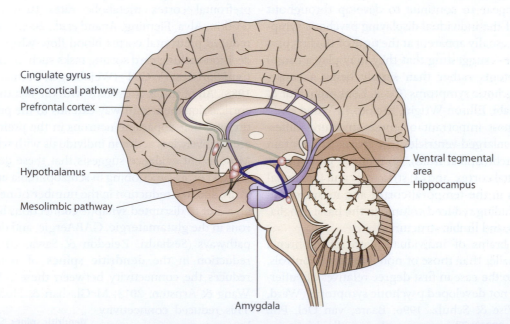

FIGURE 8.1 *Abnormalities in dopamine activity may be linked to the brain's mesocortical pathway and the mesolimbic pathway. Both begin in the ventral tegmental area, but the former projects to the prefrontal cortex and the latter to the hypothalamus, amygdala, hippocampus and nuclear accumbens. The dopamine neurons in the prefrontal cortex may be underactive (leading to the negative symptoms of schizophrenia), and this underactivity may then fail to inhibit dopamine neurons in the mesolimbic pathway causing an excess of dopamine activity in this pathway (resulting in positive symptoms) (see e.g. Davis, Kahn, Ko & Davidson, 1991).*

on symptoms until about 6 weeks after treatment has commenced. This is unusual, because antipsychotic drugs are known to start blocking dopamine receptors in the brain within hours of administration, so we would expect improvement to be immediate (Sanislow & Carson, 2001; Davis, 1978). Second, many new antipsychotic drugs are effective despite having only a minimal effect on brain dopamine levels (e.g. clozapine) or appear to be effective because they not only block dopamine receptors, but also block other neurotransmitters (Nordstrom, Farde, Nyberg, Karlsson et al., 1995). Other neurotransmitters that have been implicated in psychotic symptoms include serotonin, glutamate and GABA neurons (Stone, Morrison & Pilowsky, 2007), and this is perhaps not so surprising given that serotonin neurons regulate dopamine neurons in the mesolimbic pathway, and glutamate and dopamine dysregulation may interact with each other. A full understanding of the role of neurotransmitters in psychotic symptomatology will only result from a full understanding of how these brain neurotransmitters affect each other, and how this interaction influences brain processes that give rise to both positive and negative symptoms.

The neuroscience of schizophrenia

The brains of individuals with a diagnosis of schizophrenia show a number of structural differences to those of non-sufferers, and these differences can often be linked to the nature of the symptoms displayed by sufferers. These differences appear to continue to develop throughout the lifetime of the individual displaying psychotic symptoms, and are usually apparent at the time of the first psychotic episode – suggesting that they may play a causal role in symptoms rather than simply being a consequence of psychotic symptoms (Cecil, Lenkinski, Gur & Gur, 1999; Olabi, Ellison-Wright, McIntosh, Wood et al., 2011). The most important of these structural differences are (1) enlarged ventricles (the spaces in the brain filled with cerebrospinal fluid), (2) reduced grey matter in the prefrontal cortex, and (3) structural and functional abnormalities in the temporal cortex and its surrounding areas, including reduced volume in the basal ganglia, hippocampus, and limbic structures.

First, the brains of individuals with schizophrenia tend to be smaller than those of non-diagnosed controls, and this is also the case in first-degree relatives of sufferers who have not developed psychotic symptoms (Ward, Friedman, Wise & Schulz, 1996; Baare, van Oel, Pol, Schnack et al., 2001). This suggests that smaller brain size may be determined by genetic rather than environmental factors. This is consistent with the most frequently confirmed finding that schizophrenia is associated with **enlarged ventricles**

enlarged ventricles Enlargement of the areas in the brain containing cerebrospinal fluid, associated with schizophrenia.

(the areas in the brain containing cerebrospinal fluid) and this is associated with overall reduction in cortical grey matter (Andreasen, Flashman, Flaum, Arndt et al., 1994). In cases of chronic schizophrenia, the enlargement of the ventricles is a continuous on-going process (Mathalon, Sullivan, Lim & Pfefferbaum, 2001), and this may suggest that enlarged ventricles are a consequence of schizophrenic symptoms rather than a cause of it. However, enlarged ventricles are found even in individuals who have just experienced their first psychotic episode, implying it may be a feature that is present prior to the first symptoms developing (Cecil, Lenkinski, Gur & Gur, 1999).

Second, schizophrenia is associated with reduced volume of grey matter in the prefrontal cortex (Buchanan, Vladar, Barta & Pearlson, 1998). This area plays an important role in a number of cognitive processes, the most important being executive functioning, which enables planning, goal-directed behaviour, and decision making; it also mediates speech and coordinates working memory. Deficits in executive functioning would encompass poor performance on cognitive tasks associated with speed and accuracy, abstraction/categorisation, memory and sustained attention, and they are also associated with negative symptoms of schizophrenia such as blunted affect and social withdrawal (Antonova, Sharma, Morris & Kumari, 2004; Artiges, Martinot, Verdys, Attar-Levy et al., 2000; Pinkham, Penn, Perkins & Lieberman, 2003). In particular, individuals with a diagnosis of schizophrenia who exhibit negative symptoms show significantly lower prefrontal cortex metabolic rates than non-sufferers (Potkin, Alva, Fleming, Anand et al., 2002), and they have reduced prefrontal cortex blood flow when undertaking decision-making card sorting tasks such as the Wisconsin Card Sort Test (WCST) (Weinberger, Berman & Illowsky, 1988). All of this is consistent with the fact that the mesocortical dopamine pathway extends to the prefrontal cortex, and that dopamine neurons in the prefrontal cortex are relatively less active in individuals with schizophrenia. Most recent evidence suggests that these deficits in prefrontal cortex functioning in schizophrenia are not necessarily due to a reduction in the number of neurons in this area, but to disrupted synaptic connections between neurons in the glutamatergic, GABAergic, and dopaminergic pathways (Seshadri, Zeledon & Sawa, 2013) and to a reduction in the **dendritic spines** of neurons which reduces the connectivity between these cells (Paspalas, Wang & Arnsten, 2013; McGlashan & Hoffman, 2000). This reduced connectivity between neurons in an area of the brain responsible for executive functioning may

dendritic spines Small protrusion from a neuron's dendrite that receives input from a single synapse of an axon.

well give rise to the disordered speech and behavioural disorganisation often found in schizophrenia. Figure 8.2 shows how a PET scan reveals decreased frontal lobe

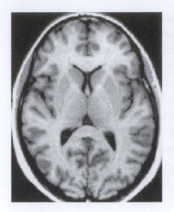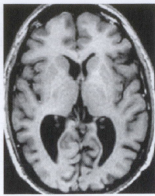

FIGURE 8.2 *These pictures show ventricular enlargement in the brains of an individual diagnosed with schizophrenia (right) and a healthy control (left). Ventricular enlargement is a common feature of the brains of individuals diagnosed with schizophrenia, and is indicated by differences in the dark areas shown in these MRI scans.*
Source: Reig, S., Penedo, M., Gispert, J.D., Pascau, J., Sánchez-González, J., García-Barreno, P. and Desco, M. (2007). Impact of ventricular enlargement on the measurement of metabolic activity in spatially normalized PET. *NeuroImage 35,* 742–758, Figure 5. Reproduced with permission of Elsevier.

activity in a schizophrenia sufferer compared with a healthy control participant, as well as the enlarged ventricles in the brain of the schizophrenia sufferer.

Third, brain imaging studies have also shown abnormalities in the **temporal cortex**, including limbic structures, the **basal ganglia** and the **cerebellum** (Shenton, Dickey, Frumin & McCarley, 2001; Gur, Cowell, Latshaw, Turetsky *et al.*, 2000; Gur, Turetsky, Cowell, Finkelman *et al.*, 2000). Abnormalities in neural activity in the temporal lobe–limbic system are more associated with the positive symptoms of schizophrenia, such as hallucinations and symptoms of thought disorder (McCarley, Salisbury, Hirayasu, Yurgelun-Todd *et al.*, 2002), and auditory hallucinations have been shown to be associated with neural activation in the temporal lobes–limbic system (Shergill, Brammer, Williams, Murray & McGuire, 2000). These deficits are also associated with reduced volume in the temporal cortex and hippocampus in individuals with a diagnosis of schizophrenia (Steen, Mull, McClure *et al.*, 2006; Fischer, Keller, Arango, Pearlson, *et al.*, 2012). Furthermore, impaired hippocampal function in schizophrenia could underlie a range of symptoms because of the role of the hippocampus in memory for events and facts and in pattern completion, all of

temporal cortex Abnormalities in this brain area are associated with symptoms of schizophrenia.

basal ganglia A series of structures located deep in the brain responsible for motor movements.

cerebellum The part of the brain at the back of the skull that coordinates muscular activity.

which are disrupted in schizophrenia and could give rise to spurious associations, chaotic speech, and hallucinations (Tamminga, Stan & Wagner, 2010).

These findings tend to suggest that abnormalities in different areas of the brain may each be associated with different symptoms of psychosis. Some individuals with a diagnosis of schizophrenia show abnormalities in some of these brain areas, but many others show abnormalities in all of them – which explains why many exhibit both positive and negative symptoms (Kubicki, Westin, Maier, Frumin *et al.*, 2002).

One final issue, of course, it what causes these structural and functional differences in the brains of individuals with a diagnosis of schizophrenia? One factor we have already mentioned is genetic mutation in genes that control the development of the brain and its associated cognitive processes. Many of the neurological defects found in schizophrenia research are ones that could only have occurred during early brain development when the complex structure of the brain is developing, and this suggests that prenatal factors may be important in causing subsequent brain abnormalities (Allin & Murray, 2002). In particular, individuals diagnosed with schizophrenia do not show the normal hemispheric asymmetry in brain development that occurs during the second trimester of pregnancy (4–6 months), and this may give rise to deficits in those areas of the brain concerned with language and associative learning (Sommer, Aleman, Ramsey, Bouma & Kahn, 2001). In addition, brain damage or abnormalities that occur after the third trimester of pregnancy are normally self-repairing through a process known as glial reactions. That such repair is not found in post-mortem studies of the brains of individuals diagnosed with schizophrenia suggests that brain areas must have been damaged or suffered abnormal development prior to the third trimester (Brennan & Walker, 2001).

Another important consideration is that environmental factors may influence the early development of the brain either during gestation or at birth. Two particular risk factors that have been postulated include birth complications and maternal infections. *Birth complications –* such as reduced supply of oxygen to the brain – appear to occur at a higher rate in individuals who eventually display symptoms of psychosis (Brown, 2011; Walker, Kestler, Bollini & Hochman, 2004), but, of course, not everyone who suffers birth complications then develops psychosis, so other factors must be involved. The probability of an offspring developing schizophrenia is also significantly higher in mothers who have suffered an *infection* during pregnancy (Brown & Derkits, 2010), and one particular infection that has been widely studied in this respect is influenza. For example, one recent study suggested that a mother's exposure to influenza during the first trimester of pregnancy resulted in a sevenfold increase in the probability of their offspring developing psychotic symptoms (Brown, Begg, Gravenstein *et al.*, 2004). However, the effect sizes in studies such as these are small, and there have been many failed attempts to demonstrate that maternal influenza is a risk factor for offspring psychosis, so the jury is still out on this issue. Some of the evidence for a role of maternal influenza on offspring psychosis is discussed in Focus Point 8.4.

Finally, if the causes of schizophrenia can be traced to early brain development, then why don't at-risk individuals develop psychotic symptoms until they are usually well into adolescence? There may be at least two reasons for this. First, we have argued that many of the symptoms of schizophrenia – and especially the negative symptoms – can be traced to abnormalities in the prefrontal cortex, the area that controls many complex cognitive activities. However, the prefrontal cortex is a brain structure that only fully matures in adolescence and early adulthood, so any developing deficits in that brain region are only likely to manifest in an obvious way at maturation (Giedd, 2004), and this is consistent with adolescents at risk for psychosis showing prodromal symptoms such as social withdrawal, shallow emotion, and deterioration

FOCUS POINT 8.4

VIRAL INFECTIONS AND PSYCHOTIC SYMPTOMS

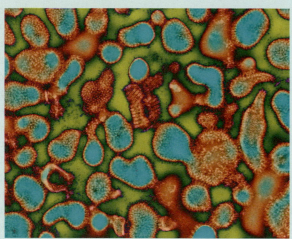

Source: Dr R. Dourmashkin/Science Photo Library. Reproduced with permission.

One interesting hypothesis is that psychotic symptoms may be triggered by viral infections experienced either prenatally or postnatally (Torrey, 1991; Mednick, Machon, Huttunen & Bonnett, 1988). There is a range of converging, but largely circumstantial, evidence for the involvement of viral infections in the aetiology of psychosis. First, epidemiological studies have shown that people diagnosed with schizophrenia are significantly more likely than others to have been born in the winter, and so were more likely to have been exposed to viruses prenatally or during the first 6 months of their lives (Torrey, Miller, Rawlings & Yolken, 1997). Second, there also appears to be a relationship between the outbreak of epidemics, such as influenza epidemics, and the development of psychotic symptoms. Individuals who were exposed prenatally to influenza are significantly more likely to develop psychotic symptoms in later life (Mednick, Machon, Huttenen & Bonett, 1988). Third, mothers of individuals diagnosed with schizophrenia are more likely to have been exposed to influenza during pregnancy than the mothers of individuals who are not diagnosed with schizophrenia, and recent systematic reviews strongly suggest that prenatal exposure to a number of infections and inflammatory responses may be associated with increased risk of adult schizophrenia (Khandaker, Zimbron, Lewis & Jones, 2013). In particular, exposure to the influenza virus appears to be important during the first trimester (Brown, Begg, Gravenstein, Schaefer *et al.*, 2004) and the third trimester (de Messias, Cordeiro, Sampaio, Bartko & Kirkpatrick, 2001) – and the latter is a prenatal period which is known to be connected to the possible development of brain abnormalities associated with schizophrenia.

Most viral infections have their effects relatively immediately, so how might viral infections prenatally or in early childhood lead to the development of psychotic symptoms in later adolescence? One possibility is that viral infections – especially prenatally – might disrupt brain development and lead to the kinds of brain abnormalities that are typical in individuals diagnosed with schizophrenia. To this extent, animal research is currently providing some useful information suggesting that rats or mice prenatally infected with viruses such as influenza experience developmental abnormalities that result in permanent changes in brain structure and function (Pearce, 2001; Fatemi, Pearce, Brooks & Sidwell, 2005; Kneeland & Fatemi, 2013). However, we must remember that not everyone who is exposed to viruses at a critical age develops psychotic symptoms and we need to be able to explain this fact. For example, it may be that if viruses do cause developmental abnormalities leading to psychotic symptoms, this may only happen in those who already have an inherited vulnerability to these symptoms.

in school work during their early teens. Second, late adolescence is also a period associated with increased stress, and especially exposure to stressors that the individual will not have experienced before (e.g. sexual relationships, and social and educational responsibilities). Stress increases cortisol levels which in turn activates brain dopamine activity, and any factor that stimulates brain dopamine activity in at-risk individuals is likely to trigger the onset of psychotic symptoms (Walker, Mittal & Tessner, 2008).

In summary, there is now good evidence that psychotic symptoms are associated with deficits in important brain areas. These deficits manifest as lower brain volume, neurotransmitter imbalances – especially in dopamine, glutamate and GABA pathways – and poorer performance on cognitive neuropsychological tasks. Particularly important brain areas exhibiting deficits are the prefrontal cortex, the temporal cortex and the hippocampus, and deficits in functioning in the prefrontal cortex and temporal cortex can be clearly associated with both negative and positive symptoms respectively. The causes of these structural and functional brain deficits in schizophrenia are unclear, although gene mutations, environmental factors influencing prenatal development, and maternal infections are all possibilities that are being currently researched.

8.5.2   Psychological Theories

Over the past 30 years or so, most research has been focused on genetic and biological theories of schizophrenia, and psychological models have generally received less attention. However, there has recently been a resurgence of interest in psychological models of psychosis – especially cognitive models that view psychotic symptoms as the result of cognitive biases in attention, reasoning and interpretation (Savulich, Shergill & Yiend, 2012). We will begin this section by discussing some traditional psychological interpretations of psychosis – especially psychodynamic and behavioural accounts. We will then move on to consider cognitive accounts of psychosis, including both cognitive deficits (impairments in cognitive functioning) and cognitive biases (the tendency to attend to a certain type of stimulus or interpret ambiguity in just one particular direction).

Psychodynamic theories

Freud (1915, 1924) hypothesized that psychosis is caused by regression to a previous ego state which gives rise to a preoccupation with the self – this is known in psychoanalytic terminology as regression to a state of **primary narcissism** characteristic

primary narcissism Regression to a previous ego state which gives rise to a preoccupation with the self.

of the oral stage of development. This regression is thought to be caused by cold and unnurturing parents, and the regression to a state of primary narcissism gives rise to a loss of contact with reality. Freud described the symptoms of thought disorder, communication disorder and withdrawal typical of psychosis as evidence of a self-centred focus, and he argued that any attempts to re-establish contact with reality give rise to the hallucinations and delusions characteristic of psychosis.

In the 1950s and 1960s, many psychodynamic explanations of psychosis were related to dysfunctional family dynamics, and championed by such contemporary psychodynamic theorists as Gregory Bateson and R.D. Laing. Prior to this, Fromm-Reichmann (1948) had developed the concept of the '**schizophrenogenic mother**' – literally a mother who causes schizophrenia! According to Fromm-Reichmann, schizophrenogenic mothers were cold, rejecting, distant and dominating. Such mothers demanded dependency and emotional expressions from

schizophrenogenic mother A cold, rejecting, distant and dominating mother who causes schizophrenia according to Fromm-Reichmann.

their children, but simultaneously rejected displays of affection and even criticized the dependency that they implicitly attempted to foster in their children. This account suggests that when subjected to such conflicting messages and demands from a dominant close relative, the child withdraws and begins to lose touch with reality – at least in part as a way of avoiding the stresses and conflicts created by the mother.

The empirical evidence supporting these psychodynamic theories of psychosis is meagre. First, genetic accounts of psychosis are now largely accepted as important contributors to psychosis – even by psychodynamic theorists, and have been incorporated in some way into psychodynamic theories. In some cases it is argued that inherited biological predispositions may facilitate regression to earlier psychological states (Willick, Milrod & Karush, 1998), while others suggest biological predispositions may prevent the individual from developing an 'integrated self', and this gives rise to the disrupted behaviour patterns exhibited in individuals diagnosed with schizophrenia (Pollack, 1989). Second, there is very little evidence that mothers of individuals displaying psychotic symptoms actually possess the characteristics of the schizophrenogenic mother described by Fromm-Reichmann (Waring & Ricks, 1965).

Behavioural theories

There are a number of views that suggest a role for learning and conditioning in the development of psychotic symptoms – if not as a full theory of psychosis, then as an explanation of why unusual behaviour patterns are typical of many forms of psychosis. Ullman &

Krasner (1975) argued that the bizarre behaviours of individuals diagnosed with schizophrenia developed because they are rewarded by a process of operant reinforcement. That is, because of the disturbed family life often experienced by individuals diagnosed with schizophrenia and the attentional difficulties that are a central feature of the psychopathology, such individuals tend to find it difficult to attend to normal social cues and involve themselves in normal social interactions. Instead, their attention becomes attracted to irrelevant cues, such as an insect on the floor, an unimportant word in a conversation, a background noise, and so forth. Attention to irrelevant cues such as these makes their behaviour look increasingly bizarre, and as a result it gets more and more attention, which acts as a reinforcer to strengthen such behaviours.

There is some limited evidence to support the view that inappropriate reinforcement may generate some bizarre behaviours, and it may account for the *frequency* of inappropriate behaviour emitted by an individual diagnosed with schizophrenia. For example, Focus Point 8.5 describes a study conducted some years ago by Ayllon, Haughton & Hughes (1965). They reinforced a female resident in a psychiatric hospital for carrying a broom. Whenever she was observed holding the broom nurses were asked to approach her, offer her a cigarette or give her a token which could be exchanged for a cigarette. Eventually, when this behaviour was established, it was transferred from a continuous to an intermittent reinforcement schedule until the patient was carrying the broom around for a considerable part of the day. This study suggests that what look like quite bizarre and inappropriate behaviours can be developed by simple contingencies of reinforcement. Further support for a learning view comes from evidence that extinction procedures can be used to eliminate or to significantly reduce the frequency of inappropriate behaviours simply by withdrawing attention or withholding rewards when these inappropriate behaviours are emitted. Allyon (1963) describes the behaviour of a 47-year-old female diagnosed with schizophrenia who insisted on wearing around 25 pounds of excess clothing, even in hot weather. This individual's bizarre clothing habits were, however, soon returned to normal when a weight limit was set each time she tried to enter the hospital dining room. On each day she was allowed into the dining room only if she weighed 2 pounds less than the previous day. This could only be achieved by discarding some of the excess clothing and within 14 weeks she was down to wearing quite normal clothing. The fact that inappropriate behaviours can be eliminated and acceptable social and self-care behaviours developed using operant reinforcement procedures does suggest that at least some of the unusual behaviours emitted by individuals diagnosed with schizophrenia may be under the control of contingencies of reinforcement.

FOCUS POINT 8.5

CAN PERFECTLY NORMAL PROCESSES CAUSE BIZARRE BEHAVIOUR?

A revealing study by Ayllon, Haughton & Hughes in 1965 provides insight into some of the processes that might generate the kinds of bizarre and apparently irrational behaviour that make up some forms of psychopathology.

They used operant reinforcement methods (see section 1.3.2) to reward a female patient diagnosed with schizophrenia for carrying a broom.

Whenever she was observed holding the broom a nurse would approach her, offer her a cigarette, or give her a token which could be exchanged for a cigarette. After a period of this reinforcement, the patient was carrying the broom around for most of the day, and even taking it to bed with her when she slept.

At this point, the researchers called in two psychiatrists (who were unaware of the reinforcement schedule) to give their opinions on the nature of the behaviour. One of them gave the following reply:

'Her constant and compulsive pacing, holding a broom in the manner she does, could be seen as a ritualistic procedure, a magical action. . . Her broom would be then: (1) a child that gives her love and she gives him in return her devotion, (2) a phallic symbol, (3) the scepter of an omnipotent queen . . . this is a magical procedure in which the patient carries out her wishes, expressed in a way that is far beyond our solid, rational and conventional way of thinking and acting.'

(Ayllon, Haughton & Hughes, 1965, p.3)

First, this psychodynamic explanation given by one of the psychiatrists is a good example of how easy it is to overspeculate about the causes and meaning of a behaviour when the real causes are unknown. Second, it shows how behaviour that is viewed as representative of psychopathology can be acquired through a perfectly normal learning mechanism (in this case operant reinforcement).

Cognitive theories

Cognitive deficits   One of the most obvious characteristics of psychosis is the individual's seeming inability on some occasions to make simple associations between relevant events (e.g. sticking to the theme of a conversation), but on other occasions to make associations that are irrelevant (e.g. being unable to prevent themselves from 'clanging' or emitting words that rhyme). These opposing tendencies seem to reflect deficits in attentional processes, where the individual seems unable to focus attention on relevant aspects of the environment (underattention), or overattends to irrelevant aspects of the environment (overattention). One characteristic of normal attentional processes is the **orienting response**, which is a physiological reaction consisting of changes in skin conductance, brain activity, heart rate and blood pressure. These responses naturally occur when the individual is presented with a novel or prominent stimulus, and they indicate that the stimulus is being attended to and processed. However, around 50 per cent of individuals diagnosed with schizophrenia show abnormalities in their orienting reactions, suggesting that they are not attending to or processing important environmental stimuli (Olbrich, Kirsch, Pfeiffer & Mussgay, 2001). While we might expect such difficulties in attentional processing to give rise to disordered thinking and responding to environmental stimuli, deficits in orienting responses have also been found to be correlated with the negative symptoms of schizophrenia such as withdrawal and blunted affect (Slaghuis & Curran, 1999). In contrast, overattention is when an individual attends to all aspects of their environment and is unable to filter out irrelevant stimuli. Studies have shown that individuals with a diagnosis of schizophrenia are highly distractable, and perform poorly at cognitive tasks when they are also presented with irrelevant, distracting stimuli or information (Wielgus & Harvey, 1988). Interestingly, such individuals actually perform *better* than non-diagnosed control participants at tasks where attending to distracting stimuli can improve performance. For example, the *negative priming effect* is when a non-clinical participant shows an increased reaction time when asked to name a target word they have previously been asked to ignore. However, participants diagnosed with schizophrenia fail to exhibit this negative priming effect, and perform just as well whether they have been asked to ignore the relevant prime or not (Peters, Pickering, Kent, Glasper *et al.*, 2000). This inability to screen out irrelevant stimuli or to ignore distractions correlates highly with many of the positive symptoms of schizophrenia (Cornblatt, Lenzenweger, Dworkin & Kimling, 1985)

orienting response A physiological reaction to a stimulus consisting of changes in skin conductance, brain activity, heart rate and blood pressure.

and may well be a contributing factor to the disordered thought and communication exhibited by individuals diagnosed with schizophrenia. These attentional deficits and high distractibility appear to be related to the fact that individuals with a diagnosis of schizophrenia typically demonstrate impairments in working memory and executive functioning (Reichenberg, 2005; Verdoux, Liraud, Assens, Albalan & van Os, 2002; Gopal & Variend, 2005), and these deficits are likely to be a consequence of impaired neurological functioning in the prefrontal cortex (see section 8.5.1).

Cognitive biases   Of specific interest to cognitive theorists are the delusional beliefs that are regularly developed during psychotic episodes, and over 50 per cent of individuals diagnosed with schizophrenia are diagnosed with **paranoid schizophrenia** (Guggenheim & Babigian, 1974). This raises the issue of why so many sufferers should develop these particular kinds of delusions. Amongst individuals diagnosed with schizophrenia who are living in the community, Harris (1987) found that they were 20 times more likely than non-sufferers to report intrusive or confrontational experiences, such as threats from landlords, police enquiries, burglaries and unwanted sexual propositions, so there may be some basis in experience to the development of persecutory beliefs. However, researchers have pointed out that paranoid delusions may also be the result of *cognitive biases* that have been developed by the sufferer (in much the same way that cognitive biases may underlie the experience of anxiety and its related disorders, see section 6.4.1). In the following section, we will consider the evidence for four types of biased cognition: attentional biases, attributional biases, reasoning biases, interpretational biases, and then consider theory of mind impairments. In particular, these types of accounts have led to a greater understanding of how individuals develop paranoid ideation in delusional disorder, and why 'hearing voices' is such a prominent feature of psychotic delusions.

paranoid schizophrenia A sub-type of schizophrenia characterized by the presence of delusions of persecution.

Attentional biases   Anxiety disorders are typically associated with attentional biases towards threatening stimuli (see Section 6.4.1) and individuals suffering psychotic symptoms also show some similar attentional biases. There is preliminary evidence that individuals with delusional disorder selectively attend to pathology congruent information. For example, individuals with persecutory delusions exhibit attentional biases towards stimuli that have emotional meaning or are paranoia relevant (Fear, Sharp & Healy, 1996; Bentall & Kaney, 1989). Interestingly, individuals prone to persecutory delusions

FOCUS POINT 8.6

CANNABIS USE AND PSYCHOTIC SYMPTOMS

There has long been a view that regular psychotropic drug use may be related to the development of psychotic symptoms, and this has recently focused on the relationship between cannabis use and subsequent diagnosis of schizophrenia (Arsencault, Cannon, Witton & Murray, 2004). Apart from legal substances such as alcohol and tobacco, cannabis is the most widely used illicit drug used by schizophrenia sufferers, and substance use disorder generally is estimated to be 4.6 times higher in schizophrenia sufferers than the general population (Regier, Farmer, Rae, Locke *et al.*, 1990).

Cross-sectional studies have shown that individuals diagnosed with schizophrenia use cannabis significantly more often than other individuals in the general population (Degenhardt & Hall, 2001). Some have argued that this relationship between cannabis use and schizophrenia reflects a form of 'self medication', in which individuals may start using cannabis because of a predisposition for schizophrenia (Khantzian, 1985). However, others have argued for a direct causal link between cannabis use and schizophrenia, and case history studies frequently describe psychotic episodes being preceded by the heavy use of cannabis (Wylie, Scott & Burnett, 1995), and cannabis use being associated with earlier onset of symptoms (Bühler, Hambrecht, Löffler, an der Heiden & Häfner, 2002).

Prospective studies that have monitored cannabis use and psychotic symptoms in individuals over a lengthy period of time appear to indicate that there is indeed a causal link between cannabis and the development of psychotic symptoms. First, Andreasson, Allebeck, Engstrom & Rydberg (1987) found a dose–response relationship between cannabis use at 18 years and later increased risk of psychotic symptoms. Subsequent prospective studies have found that 18-year-olds meeting the criteria for cannabis dependence had rates of subsequent psychotic symptoms that were twice the rate of young people not meeting these criteria (Fergusson, Horwood & Swain-Campbell, 2003). Also, this relationship could not be explained by high cannabis use being associated with any pre-existing psychiatric symptoms (Fergusson, Horwood & Ridder, 2005). Statistical modelling of these longitudinal data show that the direction of causality appears to be from cannabis use to psychotic symptoms and not vice versa (Fergusson *et al.*, 2005).

In addition, further studies have demonstrated that cannabis use increases the risk of psychotic symptoms, but has a greater impact on those that already have a vulnerability to schizophrenia (Verdoux, Gindre, Sorbara, Tournier, Swendsen, 2003; Henquet, Krabbendam, Spauwen, Kaplan *et al.*, 2005). Finally, meta-analyses suggest that the mean age of onset of psychotic symptoms among cannabis users is almost 3 years earlier than that of non-cannabis users – even when other factors such as tobacco use are controlled for (Myles, Newall, Nielssen & Large, 2012), and patients with schizophrenia using cannabis are more regularly hospitalized than non-cannabis users (van Dijk, Koeter, Hijman, Kahn & van den Brink, 2012).

For a video on cannabis and psychosis go to www.wiley-psychopathology.com/video/ch8

To read the article on 'Causal linkages between cannabis use and psychotic symptoms' by Fergusson *et al.* go to www.wiley-psychopathology.com/reading/ch8

So if there is a causal link between cannabis use and schizophrenia, what is the mechanism that mediates this link? First, there may be a neurological explanation. Research suggests that cannabis has an important effect on brain chemistry, and the compound tetrahydrocannabinol (THC) that is found in cannabis can release the neurotransmitter dopamine (Tanda, Pontieri & DiChiara, 1997; Arnold, Boucher & Karl, 2012). Excess dopamine activity has been identified in the aetiology of schizophrenia, and heavy cannabis use may therefore raise brain dopamine activity to levels triggering psychotic episodes. In addition, regular cannabis use may also affect the course of brain maturational processes associated with schizophrenia, and has been shown to result in smaller cerebellar white-matter volume in schizophrenia patients who use cannabis regularly (Solowij, Yücel, Respondek, Whittle, Lindsay *et al.*, 2011). Alternatively, Freeman, Garety, Kuipers, Fowler & Bebbington (2002) have argued that anomalous experiences (that do not have a simple and obvious explanation) are one of the fundamental factors contributing to the development of delusional thinking, and psychoactive street drugs such as cannabis are likely to increase the frequency of such anomalous experiences. If the individual is in an anxious state and already feeling isolated, then these anomalous experiences are likely to be interpreted threateningly and give rise to the persecutory and paranoid ideation often found in schizophrenia.

are slower to locate angry faces than control participants (Green, Williams & Davidson, 2001), and make fewer fixations and show reduced attention to the salient information of facial features than controls (Loughland, Williams & Gordon, 2002; Phillips & David, 1998). This is particularly interesting given that potentially angry facial expressions would have added significance for someone with a persecutory delusion, and suggests that although they may be initially attentive to threat, they then adopt an avoidance strategy that involves avoiding fixating on threatening stimuli (Green, Williams & Davidson, 2003).

Attributional biases

A good deal of research has indicated that individuals with delusional beliefs (particularly persecutory beliefs) have a bias towards attributing negative life events to external causes (Bentall, 1994; Bentall & Kinderman, 1998, 1999; Bentall, Corcoran, Howard, Blackwood & Kinderman, 2001). For example, using the Attributional Style Questionnaire (see Table 7.4), Kaney & Bentall (1989) found that patients with paranoid delusions made excessively stable and global attributions for negative events (just like depressed individuals), but also attributed positive events to internal causes and negative events to external causes. A subsequent study by Bentall, Kaney & Dewey (1991) found that this tendency of individuals with paranoid delusions to attribute negative events to external causes was only evidenced when there was a perceived threat to the self – they did not necessarily attribute negative events to external sources when describing the experiences of others. These studies all suggest that individuals exhibiting paranoid delusions have had significantly more negative, threatening life events than control individuals without a diagnosis, and have also developed a bias towards attributing negative events to external causes. At the very least, this attributional bias will almost certainly act to maintain paranoid beliefs, and maintain their delusions that someone or something external is threatening them.

Reasoning biases

Over the past 15 years or so, considerable evidence has accrued to suggest that individuals with delusional disorders have a reasoning bias in the form of **jumping to conclusions**. That is, such individuals make a decision about the meaning or importance of an event on the basis of significantly less evidence than someone without a delusional disorder. This has been demonstrated using the classic 'jumping to conclusions' task (Huq, Garety & Hemsley, 1988; Westermann, Salzmann, Fuchs & Lincoln, 2012). In this task, participants view two jars each containing 100 beads: Jar A with 85 red beads and 15 yellow beads, and Jar B with 85 yellow beads and 15 red beads. The

> **jumping to conclusions** The process of making a decision about the meaning or importance of an event on the basis of insufficient evidence.

experimenter hides the jars from view and then, one by one, draws a series of beads from one of the jars and asks the participant to say which jar the beads are being drawn from. The fewer the number of beads drawn before the participant reaches a decision indicates a greater jumping to conclusions bias. Typically, individuals with a delusional disorder witness the drawing of three beads or fewer before making a decision (Fine, Gardner, Craigie & Gold, 2007; Peters & Garety, 2006), and this jumping to conclusions bias has been shown in individuals that are delusion-prone (Colbert & Peters, 2002), are at high risk for psychosis (Broome, Johns, Valli, Woolley et al., 2007), and are suffering a first episode of psychosis (Falcone, Wiffen, O'Connor, Kolliakou et al., 2010). These studies collectively suggest that jumping to conclusions may create a biased reasoning process that leads to the formation and acceptance of delusional beliefs and eventually to delusional symptoms (Savulich, Shergill & Yiend, 2012). However, it's not clear whether jumping to conclusions is symptomatic of all delusional beliefs (e.g. delusions of grandeur or reference), or whether it is restricted to persecutory delusions (Startup, Freeman & Garety, 2008).

One final issue with reasoning biases in psychosis is what causes these reasoning biases – especially jumping to conclusions – and how might these biases interact with the experiences of psychosis-prone individuals to cause persecutory symptoms? One particular model that attempts to deal with these issues is the *threat-anticipation model* of persecutory delusions (Freeman, Garety, Kuipers, Fowler & Bebbington, 2002). This model argues that four factors are important in contributing to the development of cognitive biases involved in persecutory ideation. These are: (1) anomalous experiences (such as hallucinations) that do not appear to have a simple and obvious explanation (and are therefore open to biased interpretations); (2) anxiety, depression and worry that would normally cause a bias towards negative thinking and threatening interpretations of events (see section 6.4.1); (3) reasoning biases on the part of the individual which lead them to seek confirmatory evidence for their persecutory interpretations rather than question them (e.g. jumping to conclusions); and (4) social factors, such as isolation and trauma, which add to feelings of threat, anxiety and suspicion. Of particular importance is the relationship between anxiety and jumping to conclusions, where anxiety is known to increase the tendency to jump to conclusions even in a healthy population, and so to generate and reinforce paranoid ideation (Lincoln, Peters, Schafer & Moritz, 2009). In addition, there is now a growing body of evidence showing that there is a significant association between state anxiety and jumping to conclusions in individuals with a diagnosis of schizophrenia (Ellett, Freeman & Garety, 2008; Lincoln, Lange, Burau, Exner & Moritz, 2009) (Photo 8.2).

PHOTO 8.2 *People vulnerable to paranoid thinking try to make sense of unusual internal experiences by using those feelings as a source of evidence that there is a threat, and they then incorporate other evidence around them to substantiate that belief (e.g. interpreting the facial expressions of strangers in the street as additional evidence that they are threatened). Freeman (2007) argues that these paranoid interpretations often occur in the context of emotional distress, are often preceded by stressful events (e.g. difficult interpersonal relationships, bullying, isolation), and happen against a background of previous experiences that have led the person to have beliefs about the self as vulnerable, others as potentially dangerous, and the world as bad. In addition, living in difficult urban areas is likely to increase the accessibility of such negative views about others.*

FOCUS POINT 8.7

ABDUCTION BY ALIENS – A RECIPE FOR CREATING UNUSUAL BELIEFS?

Many people worldwide have claimed to have been abducted by aliens, been taken against their will to an alien spacecraft or enclosed place, questioned or physically examined, and they remember these experiences either consciously or through methods such as hypnosis. Indeed, many of those people who claim to be alien abductees are seemingly sincere, psychologically healthy, nonpsychotic people. So, are their experiences real or have they developed a rather unusual set of beliefs to try and give meaning to their anomalous experiences – in much the same way that people with psychotic delusions are thought to do? (Freeman, Garety, Kuipers, Fowler & Bebbington, 2002).

Professor Rich McNally and his colleagues at Harvard University have spent over 10 years researching the psychology of alien abductees (McNally, 2012), and in particular why it is that some people embrace the identity of 'alien abductee'. His research has isolated a number of traits possessed by 'alien abductees' each of which he argues contributes to the experiences they recall when 'being abducted' and to the desire to cling on to their belief that aliens were responsible for their abduction experiences. Let's look at each of these five traits in turn.

 To read about alien abductions and psychology go to **http://tinyurl.com/omdlmoq**

1. **Regularly experiencing sleep paralysis and hallucinations when awakening:** Many people who have reported alien abduction suffer episodes of early morning sleep paralysis. On awakening from this paralysis, their terror gives rise to hallucinations of flashing lights and buzzing sounds. Some experience feelings of 'floating' around the room or seeing figures in the room. While many people interpret these post-sleep paralysis experiences as dreaming, some people interpret these experiences as seeing figures, ghosts, or aliens.

2. **Tendency to recall false memories**: In an elegant set of experimental studies, McNally and colleagues found that individuals who claimed to have been abducted by aliens were prone to what is known as 'false memory syndrome' (McNally, 2012). That is, alien abductees regularly claimed to recall words, items, sentences, and so on in memory tests that they had never actually seen before. If this 'false memory' effect can be generalized to autobiographical memories, then individuals who claim to have been abducted by aliens would be twice as likely to 'falsely remember' things that had never happened to them than would non-abductees.

3. **High levels of 'absorption':** Alien abductees also score significantly higher than most people on the mental characteristic known as 'absorption'. This is a trait related to fantasy proneness, vivid imagery, and susceptibility to hypnosis and suggestion. Because of this it is probably not surprising that many alien abductees recall their experiences under hypnosis, where memories of abduction can be induced through suggestibility – especially if the person leading the hypnosis session asks particularly leading questions about abduction.

4. **New Age beliefs**: Being whisked up into space ships by tractor beams or light sources is not something that happens every day – nor is it something that is easily explainable within our existing knowledge of physics. Similarly, being subjected to imaginative medical procedures requires a

tendency to accept unusual and non-mainstream ideas. This is also a trait possessed by 'alien abductees'. They score highly on measures of magical ideation and endorse New Age ideas that encompass beliefs about alternative medicines and healing, astrology, and fortune telling. Such beliefs would certainly allow the individual to accept things happening to them that would be dismissed by existing scientific knowledge.

5. **A familiarity with the cultural narrative of alien abduction**: As a cultural phenomenon, alien abduction has entered folklore and the images and descriptions of aliens and their spacecraft have become familiar to many people. Alien abductees tend to be very familiar with this cultural narrative, which is one possible reason why their descriptions of aliens and their spaceships are so similar – being fuelled as they are by sci-fi films and numerous books about aliens and alien abduction.

This example gives you some idea of how complex, enduring and highly unusual beliefs might be developed by a set of experiences that the individual tries to give meaning to. As McNally (2012) points out, it is still unclear whether all these characteristics are necessary ingredients in the recipe for 'alien abduction' or whether some are more necessary than others. Other researchers have also identified some other characteristics, such as paranoid thinking and weak sexual identity (Clancy, 2005). As McNally shrewdly points out, 'alien abduction' beliefs often deepen spiritual awareness and give shape to the identities of abductees and provide a basis for their beliefs about the world and the universe. Whether the experiences of abduction were real or not, the experiences and interpretations adopted by 'alien abductees' are often psychologically helpful and can be spiritually comforting. It may be that the delusional beliefs developed by individuals suffering psychosis also play a similar psychological role.

This piece was first published at http://www.psychologytoday.com/blog/why-we-worry/201207/five-traits-could-get-you-abducted-aliens

Interpretational biases In addition to attentional, attributional and reasoning biases, accounts of psychotic delusions have been supplemented by findings that a number of other information processing biases may be involved in the development of delusions. For example, Morrison (2001b) has argued that many individuals diagnosed with schizophrenia have a bias towards interpreting cognitive intrusions such as **hearing voices** as threatening in some way. In this case, a perfectly normal auditory hallucination may then be interpreted as threatening (e.g. 'I must be mad', 'The Devil is talking to me', 'If I do not obey the voices they will hurt me'), and this misinterpretation causes anxiety, negative mood and physiological arousal which produces more auditory hallucinations, which are in turn interpreted negatively, and so on (Baker & Morrison, 1998). Interestingly, hearing voices is not restricted to individuals suffering psychosis, and around 13 per cent of healthy individuals report hearing voices (Bevan, Read & Cartwright, 2011). However, what characterizes hearing voices in individuals suffering psychosis is the distress that these voices induce. Individuals with a diagnosis of schizophrenia report the voices they hear as more unacceptable, uncontrollable, and distressing than healthy individuals (Morrison, Nothard, Bowe & Wells, 2004), and interpreting voices as dominating or insulting is associated with distress (Vaughan & Fowler, 2004). In addition, Peters,

hearing voices Auditory hallucinations, generally associated with psychotic delusions.

Williams, Cooke & Kuipers (2012) found a link between beliefs about voices and both emotional and behavioural responses to voices. Beliefs about the omnipotence of voices was significantly associated with measures of distress, and beliefs about the intent of voices (e.g. malevolence vs. benevolence) was associated with resistance to or engagement with voices respectively. However, what is not yet fully clear is why individuals suffering psychosis develop the negative interpretations of voices that they do – such as them being uncontrollable, external, dominating, distressing. Waters, Allen, Aleman, Fernyhough *et al.* (2012) have provided one theory. They argue that the aberrant voices heard by both healthy and psychosis-suffering individuals are generated by hyperactivation of auditory neural networks that may be triggered by environmental or internal factors, and it is failures in signal detection that lead the individual to accept these voices as real and meaningful but not self-generated. In addition to this, the deficits in working memory and executive functioning exhibited by individuals suffering psychosis means that they in particular may be unable to suppress these voices using deliberative, top-down processing, and nor are they able to distract from them easily. The distress this will cause is likely to be one source of interpretational bias, which will lead the individual increasingly to interpret the voices as threatening, and the voice content as malevolent.

Finally, as individuals suffering psychosis increasingly come to interpret the voices they hear as external and uncontrollable, they will develop a 'relationship' with these voices, and the nature of this relationship may determine the level of distress and disability, and control the nature of the responses that the voices elicit in the individual. Hayward, Berry & Ashton (2011) have identified a number of different types of relationships that individuals with a diagnosis of schizophrenia have with their voices. Often this is a 'power' struggle, in which the sufferer is constantly engaged in trying to regain power over their voices. It can lead some individuals to become socially isolated as they withdraw into the world of their voices. But for others who are already socially withdrawn, it may lead to the generation of hallucinations and delusions to make sense of the world of their voices (Hoffman, 2007).

Theory of mind (TOM)   Another cognitive account of psychotic delusions alludes to the possible inability of individuals diagnosed with schizophrenia to understand the mental state and intentions of others. Individuals who cannot infer the beliefs, attitudes and intentions of others are said to lack a **theory of mind** (**TOM**), and this is a deficit that is known to be prominent in autistic individuals (see section 17.4.4). Frith (1992) has argued that TOM deficits may also be an important factor in the development and mainte-nance of psychotic delu-sional beliefs. If individuals diagnosed with schizophr-enia are unable to infer the intentions or mental states of others, then they may begin to believe that others are either hiding their intentions or their intentions are hos-tile. In one study, Corcoran, Cahill & Frith (1997) tested the ability of individuals diagnosed with schizophrenia to understand different types of jokes. In one set of jokes, the participant needed to infer the mental state of one of the characters in order to understand the joke; in the other set of jokes, only interpretation of the physical events in the cartoon was needed (see Figure 8.3). They found that individuals with persecutory delusions found the first type of joke more difficult to understand. However, individuals without persecutory delusions found both types of jokes equally easy to understand. Furthermore, in tasks designed to test the ability of indi-viduals to understand situations in which individuals hold false beliefs or intend to deceive, individuals with persecutory delusions performed significantly worse than non-clinical control participants (Frith & Corcoran, 1996). However, TOM deficits are not specific to para-noid delusions and have subsequently been described in individuals with a diagnosis of schizophrenia (Bora, Yucel &Pantelis, 2009), and have been found to be a sta-ble marker for the condition across time (Lysaker,

> **theory of mind (TOM)** The ability to understand one's own and other people's mental states.

Olesek *et al.*, 2011). TOM deficits have also been identi-fied in the prodromal stages of psychosis (Bora & Pantelis, 2013). The fact that TOM deficits appear to be a feature of a number of schizophrenia spectrum disor-ders and can be detected at various stages of their devel-opment suggests that TOM deficits may be indicative of more global cognitive dysfunction, including deficits in executive functioning and working memory.

8.5.3   Sociocultural Theories

The overarching diathesis-stress model of schizophre-nia emphasizes that a biological predisposition interacts with environmental or life stressors to trigger psychotic symptoms. Sociocultural views of schizophrenia attempt to supplement this view by identifying social, cultural or familial factors that generate stressors that could precipi-tate psychotic symptoms. First, we will look at general social factors that have been implicated in the aetiology of psychosis, and then look more closely at how the fam-ily environment can influence the development of psy-chotic symptoms.

Social factors

The highest rates of diagnosis of schizophrenia are usu-ally found in poorer inner city areas and in those of low socio-economic status, and this has given rise to two rather different sociocultural accounts of schizophrenia. The first is known as the **sociogenic hypothesis**. This claims that individuals in low socio-economic classes experience signifi-cantly more life stressors than individuals in higher socio-economic classes, and these stressors are associ-ated with unemployment, poor educational levels, crime and poverty gener-ally. Having to endure these stressors may trigger psychotic symptoms in vulnerable people. A study con-ducted in Denmark indicated that factors associated with low socio-economic status may be risk factors for psy-chosis, and these include unemployment, low educa-tional attainment, lower wealth status, low income, parental unemployment and parental lower income (Byrne, Agerbo, Eaton & Mortensen, 2004). Studies con-ducted on immigrants have also indicated that such groups have a higher incidence of the diagnosis of schiz-ophrenia, and this has been attributed to the stress caused by many of the initial consequences of immigration, such as language difficulties, unemployment, poor hous-ing, and low socio-economic status (Hjern, Wicks & Dalman, 2004). However, while this evidence provides

> **sociogenic hypothesis** The theory that individuals in low socio-economic classes experience significantly more life stressors than individuals in higher socio-economic classes, and these stressors are associated with unemployment, poor educational levels, crime and poverty generally.

FIGURE 8.3 *Two typical cartoons taken from the study by Corcoran, Cahill & Frith (1997). In type (a) jokes the participant needs to infer the mental state of one of the characters to understand the joke, and if individuals with persecutory delusions lack a 'theory of mind' they will find these jokes difficult to understand. The type (b) joke is an example from their physical/behavioural joke, where only interpretation of the physical events in the cartoon is needed to understand the joke. Corcoran et al. found that individuals with persecutory delusions found type (a) jokes more difficult to understand, whereas people without persecutory delusions were equally able to understand both types (a) and (b).*
Source: Corcoran, R., Cahill, C. & Frith, C.D. (1997). The appreciation of visual jokes in people with schizophrenia: A study of 'mentalising' ability. *Schizophrenia Research, 24*(3), 319–327. Reproduced with permission.

some support for the sociogenic hypothesis, there is little evidence that socio-economic class per se increases the risk of psychotic symptoms. In particular, parental socio-economic class is not a significant risk factor for a diagnosis of schizophrenia (Byrne, Agerbo, Eaton & Mortensen, 2004), and studies of individuals with a diagnosis of

schizophrenia have indicated that, although they may be of low socio-economic status, they are as likely to have parents from a higher socio-economic class as from a low one (Turner & Wagonfeld, 1967).

An alternative explanation for the fact that individuals diagnosed with schizophrenia appear to have low socio-economic status is that the intellectual, behavioural and motivational problems afflicting individuals with psychotic symptoms mean they will suffer a **downward drift** into unemployment, poverty and the lower socio-economic classes *as a result of their disorder*. This is known as the **social-selection theory**, and claims that individuals displaying psychotic symptoms will drift into lifestyles where there is less social pressure to achieve, no need to hold down a regular job, and they can cope with their difficulties on a simple day-to-day basis. This hypothesis is supported by the fact that many individuals diagnosed with schizophrenia may have parents with high socio-economic status, even though they themselves are living in poverty-ridden areas of towns and cities (Turner & Wagonfeld, 1967).

> **downward drift** A phenomenon in which individuals exhibiting psychotic symptoms fall to the bottom of the social ladder or even become homeless because they cannot hold down a job or sustain a relationship.

> **social-selection theory** Argues that there are more individuals diagnosed with schizophrenia in low socio-economic groups because after they have developed psychotic symptoms they will drift downwards into unemployment and low-achieving lifestyles.

One final sociocultural view of schizophrenia is known as **social labelling**, in which it is argued that the development and maintenance of psychotic symptoms is influenced by the diagnosis itself (Modrow, 1992). In particular, if someone is diagnosed as 'schizophrenic' then it is quite possible (1) that others will begin to behave differently towards them, and define any deviant behaviour as a symptom of schizophrenia, and (2) that the person who is diagnosed may themselves assume a 'role' as someone who has a disorder, and play that role to the detriment of other – perhaps more adaptive – roles. At the very least this is likely to generate a self-fulfilling prophecy, in which a diagnosis leads to the individual, their family and friends behaving in ways that are likely to maintain pathological symptoms. Evidence for such an effect can be found in the classic study by Rosenhan (1973) in which eight individuals without any symptoms of psychopathology presented themselves at psychiatric hospitals complaining of various psychotic symptoms. Not only were these 'normal' individuals immediately diagnosed with schizophrenia, they were subsequently treated in an authoritarian and uncaring manner by hospital staff, began to feel powerless, bored and uninterested, and even had great difficulty being viewed and treated as 'normal' once they had left the hospital!

> **social labelling** The theory that the development and maintenance of psychotic symptoms are influenced by the diagnosis itself.

Familial factors

There is a general belief across most theoretical perspectives on schizophrenia that the characteristics of the family are in some way important in making an individual vulnerable to acquiring psychotic symptoms. As we have already seen, some psychodynamic views believed it was certain characteristics possessed by the mother that was important in precipitating psychosis (the schizophrenogenic mother; section 8.5.2). However, more recently, attention has turned from the characteristics of individual family members to the patterns of interactions and communications within the family.

Some approaches suggest that the risk factor within families for the development of psychotic symptoms lies in the nature of the way that parents and children communicate. In the 1950s, Bateson, Jackson, Haley & Weakland (1956) argued that psychosis may develop in families where communication is ambiguous and acts to double-bind the child. This **double-bind hypothesis** claims that the individual is subjected within the family to contradictory messages from loved ones (e.g. a mother may both request displays of affection, such as a hug, and then reject them as being a sign of weakness). This leaves the individual in a conflict situation in which they may eventually withdraw from all social interaction. Focus Point 8.8 offers some examples of double-bind situations and conversations, and it is clear from these examples that, whichever of the themes the child reads into the ambiguous message, they are in a no-win situation.

> **double-bind hypothesis** Theory advocating that psychotic symptoms are the result of an individual being subjected within the family to contradictory messages from loved ones.

The double-bind hypothesis has subsequently been superseded by more empirical research which has identified a construct called **communication deviance (CD)** in families, and which is related to the development of psychotic symptoms. CD is a general term used to describe communications that would be difficult for an ordinary listener to follow and leave them puzzled and unable to share a focus of attention with the speaker. Such communications would include (1) abandoned or abruptly ceased remarks or sentences, (2) inconsistent references to events or situations, (3) using words or phrases oddly or wrongly, or (4) use of peculiar logic. Studies have demonstrated that CD is a stable characteristic of families with offspring who develop psychotic symptoms (Wahlberg, Wynne, Keskitalo, Nieminen et al., 2001). When children with a biological predisposition to schizophrenia have been adopted and brought up in homes with adopted parents who do not have a biological predisposition for schizophrenia, CD has been found to be an independent predictor of the adopted child developing psychotic symptoms (Wahlberg, Wynne, Hakko, Laksy et al., 2004). This

> **communication deviance (CD)** A general term used to describe communications that would be difficult for ordinary listeners to follow and leave them puzzled and unable to share a focus of attention with the speaker.

FOCUS POINT 8.8

DOUBLE BIND AND PARADOXICAL COMMUNICATION

Below are some visualisations inspired by Double Bind theory where the verbal message may contradict the implied message therefore invalidating both.

A sign which reads 'Do not read this sign'. Paradoxically you cannot do what it asks and implies simultaneously.

With paradox there is essentially no choice but there is the illusion of choice.

Be independent	Do something spontaneous

'Be independent'. 'Do something spontaneous'. You can neither obey nor disobey because whatever you do will be wrong.

suggests that CD is a risk factor for a diagnosis of schizophrenia that is independent of any biological or inherited predisposition, and that CD is not simply the product of a shared genetic defect between parents and offspring.

Another construct that has been closely linked to the appearance and reappearance of psychotic symptoms is known as **expressed emotion (EE)**. The importance of the family environment in contributing to psychotic symptoms was first recognized when it was found that individuals who left hospital following treatment for psychosis were more likely to relapse if they returned to live with parents or spouses than if they went to live in lodgings or to live with siblings (Brown, Carstairs & Topping, 1958). From this it was discovered that many of the discharged patients were returning to environments where communications were often hostile and critical. This led to the development of the construct of EE, which refers to high levels of criticism, hostility and emotional involvement between key members of a family. Some examples of high EE are shown in Activity 8.1.

expressed emotion (EE) A qualitative measure of the 'amount' of emotion displayed, typically in the family setting, usually by a family member or caretakers.

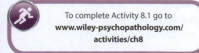

To complete Activity 8.1 go to www.wiley-psychopathology.com/activities/ch8

Since its development, EE has been shown to be a robust predictor of relapse (Kavanagh, 1992) and, in particular, relapse involving positive psychotic symptoms. Families high in EE tend to be intolerant of the patient's problems and have inflexible strategies for dealing with their difficulties and symptoms. High EE families also have an attributional style that tends to blame the sufferer themselves for their condition and the consequences of their symptoms (Weisman, Nuechterlein, Goldstein & Snyder, 2000; Barrowclough, Johnston & Tarrier, 1994). It is not clear how high EE within a family might influence tendency to relapse, but a recent 20-year prospective study suggests that EE is a valid predictor of relapses and re-hospitalizations (Cechnicki, Bielańska, Hanuszkiewicz & Daren, 2013). One mechanism by which EE may trigger relapses is through a high sensitivity to stress in psychosis sufferers. The stress caused by EE may trigger cortisol release in the hypothalamic–pituitary–adrenal system, and this is known to increase dopamine activity and so reactivate symptoms in vulnerable individuals (Walker, Mittal & Tessner, 2008). The link between EE and psychotic symptoms is further supported by the fact that some studies have shown that interventions to moderate the high EE levels in a family may actually have a beneficial effect on relapse, suggesting a possible causal link between high EE and relapse (Hogarty, Anderson, Reiss, Kornblith *et al.*, 1986; Tarrier, Barrowclough, Vaughn, Bamrah *et al.*, 1988). Finally, cultural factors also appear to moderate the effect of EE on symptoms and relapse. Aguilera, López, Breitborde, Kopelowicz & Zarate (2010) found that EE was less likely to cause relapse in Mexican immigrants to the US than in the indigenous population. However, as immigrants became more familiar with American culture (language and media), EE became increasingly related to relapse, which suggests that the EE–schizophrenia relapse link may be mediated by cultural differences in warmth, mutual interdependence and kin relationships (Singh, Harley & Suhail, 2013).

SELF-TEST QUESTIONS

- What is the diathesis-stress perspective that is used to explain the aetiology of psychotic symptoms?

- Concordance studies, twin studies and adoption studies are used to determine the extent of genetic factors in psychosis. Can you give examples of these types of methods?

- What are genetic linkage analyses and how are they used to identify the specific genes through which the risk for psychosis may be transmitted?

- What is the dopamine hypothesis and how did the role of dopamine in psychosis come to be discovered?

- What abnormalities can be found in the brains of individuals diagnosed with schizophrenia, and which brain areas are most affected by these abnormalities?

- Can you describe the evidence supporting the view that brain abnormalities in individuals diagnosed with schizophrenia may result from abnormal prenatal development?

- What are the main features of psychodynamic explanations of psychosis?

- Can you describe some of the attentional deficits that are characteristic of psychosis and explain how they might contribute to the clinical symptoms?

- A number of cognitive biases have been implicated in the development of some psychotic symptoms. What are these biases and how might they contribute to factors such as delusional thinking?

- What is a sociocultural theory of psychosis? Can you describe and evaluate the significance of at least two sociocultural accounts of psychosis?

- What is double-bind hypothesis and how does it try to explain the development of psychotic symptoms?

- What are (1) expressed emotion, and (2) communication deviance, and what is the evidence that they constitute a risk factor for the development of psychotic symptoms?

SECTION SUMMARY

8.5　THE AETIOLOGY OF PSYCHOTIC SYMPTOMS

The overarching explanation of psychosis is one of *diathesis-stress*. That is, individuals who develop psychotic symptoms have an inherited vulnerability to develop these symptoms (diathesis) that are likely to be triggered by experiencing environmental stressors. We have discussed a mixture of biological, psychological (cognitive) and sociocultural theories of psychosis, and these rather different types of explanation are by no means mutually exclusive. They all aim to explain different features of psychosis often at different levels of description. For example, it is pretty much established that psychosis has an inherited component and that the development of psychotic symptoms is associated with abnormalities in brain neurotransmitter activity (e.g. excess dopamine activity) and abnormalities in specific brain areas (particularly the frontal lobes and the mesolimbic system). These biological abnormalities in turn appear to give rise to deficits in cognitive functioning, such as problems in attention, executive functioning and working memory. Psychological explanations of delusional thinking have received considerable attention in recent years, and these have identified biases in attention, attributional processing, reasoning, and ambiguity interpretation, in ways that are likely to give rise to delusional thinking and delusional beliefs about the world. Finally, sociocultural theories of psychosis try to explain the uneven distribution of schizophrenia diagnosis across socio-economic and ethnic groups, and have sought to identify sources of life stressors that may trigger psychotic symptoms. These may include dysfunctional family structures and deviant forms of family communication. All of these views are relevant to a full picture of psychosis.

The key points covered in this section are:

- The overarching approach to understanding psychosis is a *diathesis-stress perspective* in which a combination of genetically-inherited predisposition (diathesis) and environmental stress are thought to cause psychotic symptoms.

- *Concordance studies* suggest that an individual who has a first-degree relative diagnosed with schizophrenia is 10 times more likely to develop psychotic symptoms than someone who has no first-degree relatives diagnosed with schizophrenia.

- The concordance rate for schizophrenia in MZ twins is 44 per cent but falls to 12 per cent in DZ twins.

- Adoption studies show that the probability of an adopted child developing psychotic symptoms is linked to the probability of the biological mother developing psychotic symptoms, and not to the probability of the adoptive mother developing psychotic symptoms.

- *Genetic linkage analyses* have helped to identify some of the specific genes through which the risk for psychosis might be transmitted.

- *Genome-wide association studies* (GWAS) allow researchers to identify rare mutations in genes that might give rise to psychotic symptoms.

- The main biochemical theory of schizophrenia is the *dopamine hypothesis*, which argues that psychotic symptoms are related to excess activity of the neurotransmitter dopamine.

- Two important dopamine pathways in the brain, the *mesolimbic pathway* and the *mesocortical pathway* may be impaired during psychosis.

- Psychotic symptoms are associated with brain abnormalities, including smaller brain size and enlarged ventricles (the areas in the brain containing cerebrospinal fluid).

- Schizophrenia is specifically associated with reduced volume of grey matter in the prefrontal cortex which affects executive functioning, decision making and working memory.

- Brain imaging studies have also shown abnormalities in the temporal cortex, including limbic structures, the basal ganglia and the cerebellum.

- Evidence suggests that schizophrenia may also be associated with birth complications and maternal infections during pregnancy.

- Psychodynamic theories of psychosis have claimed that it is (1) due to regression to a state of *primary narcissism*, or (2) develops because of a '*schizophrenogenic mother*' who fosters psychotic symptoms in her offspring (psychodynamic theories).

- At least some inappropriate behaviour patterns exhibited by individuals diagnosed with schizophrenia may be developed and maintained through processes of operant reinforcement (behavioural theories).

- Around 50 per cent of individuals diagnosed with schizophrenia show abnormalities in their attentional processes suggesting an inability to attend to and process relevant stimuli.

- Delusional disorder is often associated with cognitive biases in attention, attribution, reasoning, and interpretation.

- Delusional disorders are associated with a reasoning bias called '*jumping to conclusions*' where the individual infers meaning on the basis of very little evidence.

- There is evidence that individuals diagnosed with schizophrenia may not be able to understand the mental states of others (a 'theory of mind' deficit), and this may be a factor in the development of delusions – especially delusions of persecution.

- The *sociogenic hypothesis* claims that individuals in low socio-economic classes experience significantly more life stressors than those in higher socioeconomic classes, and this is more likely to contribute to the increased prevalence of the diagnosis of schizophrenia in low socio-economic groups.

- *Social-selection theory* argues that there are more individuals diagnosed with schizophrenia in low socio-economic groups because after they have developed psychotic symptoms they will drift downwards into unemployment and low-achieving lifestyles.

- *Social labelling theory* claims that once an individual has been diagnosed with schizophrenia, such labelling is likely to give rise to circumstances which will tend to maintain psychotic symptoms.

- High levels of *expressed emotion* (high levels of criticism, hostility and emotional involvement between family members) and *communication deviance* (poorly structured means of communication between family members) within the families of individuals diagnosed with schizophrenia have been shown to be associated with relapse and the development of positive symptoms.

8.6   THE TREATMENT OF PSYCHOSIS

With appropriate medication, care and supervision, most people who have suffered psychotic symptoms can eventually cope with many aspects of day-to-day living, but others may still find it difficult to hold down a job or make lasting relationships. Supervision and care is often necessary because relapse is a common feature of psychosis. A systematic review of remission rates in schizophrenia suggests that remission rates vary between 17 and 78 per cent in first-episode schizophrenia, and 16 to 62 per cent in multiple-episode schizophrenia, with remission rates highest in those taking second-generation antipsychotics and early response to treatment, and early treatment intervention (AlAqeel & Margolese, 2012). However, after recovery from a first episode, studies have shown that around 81 per cent will relapse within the following 5 years, and 78 per cent will also have a second relapse within that time. Even 10 years after the first episode, around 50 per cent of sufferers will have relapsed at least once and been hospitalized as a result (Moilanen, Haapea, Miettunen, Jaaskelainen *et al.*, 2013). Discontinuing antipsychotic drug therapy increases the risk of relapse by almost five times (Robinson, Woerner, Alvir, Geisler *et al.*, 1999), and illegal drug dependence is another risk factor (San, Bernardo, Gomez & Pena, 2013). These are important problems for the management and treatment of psychosis, and, in addition, individuals diagnosed with schizophrenia often lack insight into their disorder, deny they are ill, or are too distracted and disabled to respond either to reflective therapies or to the requirements of care programmes. In part as a consequence of this, reviews of medication non-adherence among patients diagnosed with schizophrenia have been found to be as high as 49 per cent (Lacro, Dunn, Dolder, Leckband & Jeste, 2002), and predictors of non-adherence include use of illegal substances, alcohol and poor insight (Jónsdóttir, Opjordsmoen, Birkenaes, Simonsen *et al.*, 2013). Factors such as these often impose intolerable burdens on the families and carers of those diagnosed with schizophrenia. The sufferers' frequently disturbed and disruptive behaviour and denial of illness often leaves families with little alternative than to seek involuntary hospitalization for the individual and the prescription of antipsychotic drugs at the earliest opportunity.

Traditionally, **custodial care** and **hospitalization** were the main forms of intervention for psychosis, and some characteristics of early custodial care can be found in section 1.1.3. But the advent of antipsychotic medications in the 1950s significantly reduced the need for hospitalization, and we begin our discussion of the treatment of psychotic symptoms by discussing various forms of biological intervention (e.g. psychosurgery and drug therapy), followed by psychological interventions (social skills training, cognitive behaviour therapy, cognitive remediation therapy, and family therapy interventions), and finally we will discuss the role of early intervention programmes and then the role of community care (e.g. assertive community treatment and assertive outreach programmes) in addressing the longer term needs of those with a diagnosis of schizophrenia.

custodial care   A form of hospitalization or restraint for individuals with psychopathologies whose behaviour is thought of as disruptive or harmful.

hospitalization   To admit someone to a hospital for treatment.

8.6.1   Biological Treatments

Electroconvulsive therapy (ECT) and psychosurgery

Early forms of intervention for psychosis seem particularly barbaric in retrospect. Between the 1930s and 1950s, invasive interventions such as ECT (Bini, 1938) and prefrontal lobotomy (Moniz, 1936) were used on thousands of schizophrenia sufferers. ECT involves inducing brain seizures by passing an electric current through the head of the patient for around half a second (see section 7.3.1), and tends to be used today to treat psychotic symptoms when they are comorbid with depression that has failed to respond to other forms of treatment. **Prefrontal lobotomy** is a surgical procedure that involves severing the pathways between the frontal lobes and lower brain areas. Lobotomy was used frequently for patients who were disruptive or violent, and the procedure did appear to have the effect of making such individuals more passive and many were able to be discharged from hospital. However, during the 1950s the wisdom of the procedure came to be questioned. Fatality rates from the procedure were unacceptably high (between 1.5 and 6 per cent) and lobotomies significantly affected the patient's intellectual capacities and emotional responsiveness (Tierney, 2000). While lobotomies had seemed to be a good way of reducing overcrowding in hospitals in the 1930s, the development of effective antipsychotic drugs in the 1950s provided a more acceptable and less invasive means of controlling psychotic symptoms.

prefrontal lobotomy   A surgical procedure that involves severing the pathways between the frontal lobes and lower brain areas.

Antipsychotic drugs

Specially developed antipsychotic drugs and medications are the first line of intervention for psychotic symptoms, and arguably are the most effective treatment for the positive clinical symptoms. The main classes of drugs used for the treatment of psychotic symptoms are known as *antipsychotics* or **neuroleptics** (because some of these drugs produce undesired motor behaviour effects similar to the symptoms of neurological diseases such as Parkinson's disease). Nowadays, antipsychotic drugs can be divided into two broad groups usually labelled first- and second-generation drugs (see Table 8.2). First-generation antipsychotics (sometimes also called typical antipsychotics) consist of the traditional drugs that have been developed over the past 50 years (such as chlorpromazine and haloperidol), and second-generation antipsychotics (sometimes called atypical antipsychotics) refer to those that have been developed in recent years. In the years after their development, it was originally thought that second-generation drugs were more effective over a broader range of symptoms than first-generation drugs (Citrome, Bilder & Volavka, 2002) and were associated with less risk of relapse (Leucht, Barnes, Kissling, Engel *et al.*, 2003), and with less risk of involuntary motor behaviour side effects (Csernansky & Schuchart, 2002). (But see more recent research described below.)

> **neuroleptics** One of the main classes of drugs used for the treatment of psychotic symptoms.

The **first-generation antipsychotic drugs** were developed in the 1940s and 1950s, when a number of researchers discovered that antihistamine drugs used to combat allergies – such as phenothiazines and chlorpromazines – also helped to calm patients before surgery. This led to these drugs being used with individuals, such as those with psychotic symptoms, who showed signs of extreme psychological disorder (Delay

> **first-generation antipsychotic drugs** Developed in the 1940s and 1950s, when a number of researchers discovered that antihistamine drugs used to combat allergies also helped to calm patients before surgery.

& Deniker, 1952). They found a marked and consistent drop in psychotic symptoms in such patients with the use of these drugs, and by the late 1950s such drugs had been widely adopted for use with individuals diagnosed with schizophrenia. These drugs were revolutionary in their effects, and were the first form of treatment that appeared to successfully and reliably reduce the positive symptoms of schizophrenia (such as hallucinations, and disordered thought and communication). These traditional antipsychotic drugs appear to have their therapeutic effects by blocking excessive dopamine activity in the brain (Grilly, 2002). However, there are a number of problems with the use of antipsychotic drugs. First, they are not a 'cure' for psychosis, and tend to act to suppress rather than eliminate symptoms. As a result sufferers usually need lifelong medication to control their symptoms. Second, these types of drugs also have a number of undesirable side effects. These include tiredness, lack of motivation, dry mouth, blurred vision, constipation, impotence, and dizziness resulting from lowered blood pressure. Most importantly, between 20 and 25 per cent of people who take typical antipsychotic drugs for any period of time will develop disorders of motor movement such as **tardive dyskinesia** (Grilly, 2002). Typical symptoms include movement disorders that resemble symptoms of Parkinson's disease, including limb tremors, involuntary tics, lip-smacking and chin-wagging, shuffling gait, and emotionless expressions. These symptoms appear to result from the lowering of brain dopamine activity that is a consequence of typical antipsychotic drug use. Such problematic side effects cause around 50 per cent of those treated with typical antipsychotic drugs to quit medication after less than a year, with a resulting significant increase in the probability of relapse.

> **tardive dyskinesia** A disorder of motor movement.

TABLE 8.2 *First- and second-generation antipsychotic drugs*

Category	Generic name	Trade name	Usual daily dose (mg)
First generation	Chlorpromazine	Largactil	75–300
	Haloperidol	Haldol	3–15
	Pimozide	Orap	4–20
	Trifluoperazine	Stelazine	5–20
	Sulpiride	Dolmatil	200–800
Second generation	Amisulpride	Solian	50–800
	Aripiprazole	Abilify	10–30
	Clozapine	Clozaril	200–450
	Olanzapine	Zyprexa	10–20
	Quetiapine	Seroquel	300–450
	Risperidone	Risperdal	4–6
	Sertindole	Serdolect	12–20
	Zotepine	Zoleptil	75–200

Second-generation antipsychotic drugs (such as clozapine, resperidone and olanzapine) were developed in the 1980s and were thought to have a number of benefits over traditional antipsychotics: (1) their neurological effects selectively target certain types of dopamine receptors and also influence serotonin receptors in ways that make their therapeutic effects more specific (Worrell, Marken, Beckman & Ruehter, 2000); (2) they are associated with significantly less risk of relapse than traditional antipsychotics (Leucht, Barnes, Kissling, Engel *et al.*, 2003); (3) they produce significantly fewer major side effects, such as involuntary motor behaviour disturbances (Csernansky & Schuchart, 2002); (4) sufferers taking the atypical antipsychotics are more likely to comply with and persevere with their medication regimes than those taking traditional antipsychotics (possibly because of fewer disturbing side effects) (Dolder, Lacro, Dunn & Jeste, 2002); and (5) while being highly effective with positive symptoms, atypical antipsychotics also help to reduce the frequency and magnitude of negative symptoms (Grilly, 2002).

> **second-generation antipsychotic drugs** Drugs developed in the 1980s, thought to be an improvement on traditional antipsychotics. However, we now know that they can cause significant side effects.

However, recent research has cast some doubt on the benefits of second-generation drugs over their first-generation predecessors. First, some second-generation drugs such as clozapine have their own serious side effects and can affect immune functioning in a small percentage of individuals, plus they can be associated with weight gain, and produce extrapyramidal side effects resembling the Parkinson's disease symptoms also found with first-generation antipsychotics (Meltzer, Cola, Way *et al.*, 1993; Young, Niv, Cohen, Kessler & McNagny, 2010; Rummel-Kluge, Komossa, Schwarz, Hunger *et al.*, 2010). Second, large, independent randomized controlled trials comparing first- and second-generation drugs found no difference in effectiveness between the two types of drug, and the second-generation drugs produced as many unpleasant side effects as the first-generation ones (Lieberman, Stroup, McEvoy, Swartz *et al.*, 2005; Jones, Barnes, Davies, Dunn *et al.*, 2006).

The development of new drug treatments for psychosis is an important ongoing process, and it is still unclear what biochemical mechanisms many of these drugs influence to have their successful therapeutic effects. However, antipsychotic drugs have become a central feature of treatment for psychotic symptoms and significantly more independent research is needed to improve their effectiveness, reduce their unpleasant side effects, and improve patient adherence to medication regimes.

8.6.2 *Psychological Therapies*
Social skills training

So far in this chapter we have seen ample evidence that there are deficits in the behavioural, cognitive and emotional responses of individuals diagnosed with schizophrenia. This may lead their friends and family to view their behaviour as inappropriate, their thoughts as confused, and their emotional responses as erratic. An obvious consequence of these characteristics is that it will make it difficult for sufferers to interact socially with others, to live normal lives in which they can readily negotiate normal day-to-day activities, and to develop close relationships with others. In fact, the inappropriate responses of individuals displaying psychotic symptoms may generate a vicious cycle in which inappropriate behaviour causes others to back off from contact with the sufferer, and this in turn is likely to exacerbate symptoms and generate feelings of alienation and worthlessness.

One obvious way to intervene in this cycle is to provide the sufferer with training in the appropriate social skills they will need to deal with basic everyday interactions. Social skills training consists of a combination of role-playing, modelling and positive reinforcement, and the individual is taught how to react appropriately in a range of useful social situations. Such training will provide the client with a range of transferable social skills, such as conversational skills, appropriate physical gestures, eye contact, and positive and appropriate facial expressions (Smith, Bellack & Liberman, 1996). In addition, the client will be asked to role play in certain specific scenarios (e.g. how to respond to someone who has just done them a favour). They are also positively rewarded for appropriate reactions. Such training may have other tangential benefits in helping the client to maintain contact with outreach or community supervisors, and help them to find work (e.g. teaching them how to behave in job interviews) and find accommodation (Pratt & Mueser, 2002). Randomized controlled trials have provided good evidence for the effectiveness of social skills training on skills acquisition, assertiveness, social functioning, and a reduction in general psychopathology (Pfammatter, Junghan & Brenner, 2006), and providing coping skills and social support can reduce the effects of stress on relapse and help individuals achieve their social goals (Addington, Piskulic & Marshall, 2010).

A more focused form of social skills training is **supported employment**. This was developed as an alternative to other vocational rehabilitation schemes such as sheltered workshops, which had

> **supported employment** A special programme designed with a built-in support mechanism to help people with physical, mental or developmental disabilities reach and maintain their customized vocational goals and objectives.

generally been viewed as unsuccessful (Bond, 1992). One example of supported employment is the individual placement and support (IPS) model, which focuses on the search for jobs in integrated community settings with the provision of follow-along to help the individual optimize work performance support. Supported employment has been found to lead to significantly higher rates of work and more wages earned than comparative programmes (Bond, Drake & Becker, 2012).

Cognitive behaviour therapy for psychosis (CBTp)

Because of their confused thinking, their frequent lack of insight into their disorder, and the potential difficulties in communicating with individuals exhibiting psychotic symptoms, cognitive therapies were previously thought to be inappropriate and ineffective for the treatment of psychotic symptoms. This view was strengthened by the belief that most of the disordered thinking in schizophrenia was the result of dysfunctional brain neurotransmitter mechanisms rather than psychological factors. However, as we have seen in the section on aetiology, there is a developing body of evidence to suggest that some psychological processes may be involved in generating and maintaining psychotic thought, particularly hearing voices, delusions and paranoid views of the world (Bentall, Corcoran, Howard, Blackwood & Kinderman, 2001; Morrison, 2001b), and it is becoming clear that CBT can be adapted to effectively target and challenge these types of psychotic symptoms (and is currently labelled as **cognitive behaviour therapy for psychosis (CBTp)**) (Kingdon & Turkington, 2004; Haddock & Slade, 1995; Morrison, Renton, Dunn, Williams & Bentall, 2003; Fowler, Garety & Kuipers, 1995). For example, Morrison (2001b) has argued that many individuals diagnosed with schizophrenia have a bias towards interpreting cognitive intrusions as threatening in some way (e.g. 'If I do not obey the voices they will hurt me') and this misinterpretation causes a vicious cycle which produces more hallucinations, which are in turn interpreted negatively, and so on. Having interpreted an hallucination as threatening, many individuals may then indulge in what are known as 'safety behaviours' which effectively prevent the individual from *disconfirming* their belief that the hallucination is threatening. Safety behaviours include things like lying down, drinking alcohol, or shouting at the voices to go away (Frederick & Cotanch, 1995), and they may actually have the effect of increasing the frequency of the hallucinations (Nayani & David, 1996). Clinicians can use CBTp methods in a variety of ways: (1) to help the sufferer challenge their

cognitive behaviour therapy for psychosis (CBTp) Form of CBT which helps to address any abnormal attributional processes and information processing and reasoning biases that may give rise to delusional thinking.

delusional beliefs (O'Connor, Stip, Pélissier, Aardema *et al.*, 2007); (2) to develop non-psychotic meaning for symptoms such as hearing voices (Trower, Birchwood, Meaden, Byrne *et al.*, 2004); and (3) to reduce negative symptoms by challenging low expectations (Rector, Beck & Stolar, 2005). In addition, cognitive therapy methods generally have also been found to be effective in other areas of treatment, and these include: (1) helping the sufferer to adjust to the realities of the outside world after dehospitalization (known as personal therapy), and (2) helping with medication compliance. CBT can also be extended to psychotic symptoms in the form of **reattribution therapy**. We have already noted that paranoid individuals make more attributions for negative events that are of an external rather than internal nature, and this appears to maintain their delusions that someone or something external is threatening them (Lee, Randall, Beattie & Bentall, 2004). Reattribution therapy can be used to challenge these dysfunctional attributions, and the client is encouraged to consider more normal causes for their hallucinations than the dysfunctional or delusional ones that they may hold. Treatment will usually involve monitoring the frequency of delusional beliefs, attempting to generate alternative explanations for delusional beliefs, and then providing behavioural experiments that will enable the client to test out the reality of their beliefs (Alford & Beck, 1994; Chadwick & Lowe, 1994). Frequently, a verbal challenge will be enough to get the client to reject their dysfunctional belief (e.g. the therapist may simply ask whether it makes sense for things to be the way the client says they are, and a logical discussion of evidence may be sufficient), in other cases a 'reality test' in the form of a behavioural experiment may be necessary. For example, in the case of a client who maintained they could tell what was going to be said on television before it was actually said, a video recording was put on 'pause' at prearranged times, and the client was asked to say what was coming up (Chadwick & Lowe, 1990).

reattribution therapy A treatment used in helping individuals with paranoid symptoms to reattribute their paranoid delusions to normal daily events rather than the threatening, confrontational causes they believe underlie them.

Finally, there is currently vigorous debate about the success of CBTp in alleviating psychotic symptoms and enabling recovery. Early randomized controlled trials indicated that CBTp was effective in helping to reduce hallucinations and delusions, and decreased both positive and negative symptoms while lifting mood and improving life functioning (Bustillo, Lauriello, Horan & Keith, 2001; Wykes, Steel, Everitt & Tarrier, 2008). However, effect sizes were often modest, and while CBTp is more effective than either usual treatment or attentional control conditions, it does not appear to perform significantly better than other forms of therapy for treating psychosis

To read the article on 'CBT and the psychopathology of schizophrenia' by Newton-Howes & Wood go to **www.wiley-psychopathology.com/reading/ch8**

To read the article on 'CBT for schizophrenia' by Hutton go to **www.wiley-psychopathology.com/reading/ch8**

(Newton-Howes & Wood, 2013, but see Hutton, 2013, for a critical commentary on this meta-analysis). However, it is clear that CBTp does provide a useful adjunct to treatment for psychotic symptoms, is well tolerated by sufferers, and can be used in conjunction with medication or other forms of psychosocial intervention (e.g. Sommer, Slotema, Daskalakis, Derks et al., 2012).

Personal therapy

When individuals diagnosed with schizophrenia are discharged from hospital after an acute episode, they usually find themselves in a challenging environment in which their cognitive skills and their ability to cope leave a lot to be desired. As a consequence, relapse rates are usually high. **Personal therapy** is a broad-based cognitive behaviour pro-

> **personal therapy** A broad-based cognitive behaviour programme that is designed to help individuals with the skills needed to adapt to day-to-day living after discharge from hospital.

gramme that is designed to help such individuals with the skills needed to adapt to day-to-day living after discharge. Clients are taught a range of skills in either a group setting or on an individual basis, and these include:

1. learning to identify signs of relapse (e.g. social withdrawal) and what to do in such circumstances;

2. acquiring relaxation techniques designed to help the client deal with the anxiety and stress caused by challenging events (e.g. to reduce levels of anger that might give rise to unnecessary aggression);

3. identifying inappropriate emotional and behavioural responses to events, and learning new and adaptive responses (e.g. to help with

gaining and maintaining employment and accommodation);

4. identifying inappropriate cognitions and dysfunctional thinking biases that might foster catastrophic and deluded thinking (and so help the client to prevent intrusive catastrophic thinking);

5. learning to deal with negative feedback from others and to resolve interpersonal conflicts (known as 'criticism management and conflict resolution'); and (6) learning how to comply with medication regimes (Hogarty, Greenwald, Ulrich, Kornblith et al., 1997; Hogarty, Kornblith, Greenwald, DiBarry et al., 1997).

Cognitive remediation training

In earlier sections of this chapter we've described how schizophrenia is associated with a number of important cognitive deficits, especially those relating to attention, memory and executive functioning. These cognitive deficits negatively affect psychosocial functioning (Heaton, Paulsen, McAdams, Kuck et al., 1994) and impair the impact of psychiatric rehabilitation programmes such as social skills training and vocational rehabilitation (Mueser & McGurk, 2004). Because of this, it makes sense to try to find ways to improve the basic cognitive functioning of individuals with a diagnosis of schizophrenia, because this will inevitably have positive knock-on effects on other rehabilitation programmes. This has given rise to what are called **cognitive remediation training (CRT)** or **cognitive enhancement therapy (CET)** programmes, most of which employ

> **cognitive remediation training (CRT)** A treatment programme for clients designed to develop and improve basic cognitive skills and social functioning generally.

> **cognitive enhancement therapy (CET)** A form of intervention which addresses deficits in both social cognition (the ability to act wisely in social situations) and neurocognition (basic abilities in cognitive functioning, such as memory and attention).

FOCUS POINT 8.9

EARLY INTERVENTION SERVICES

It has been known for some time that the sooner psychotic symptoms are detected and treated, the better the long-term prognosis (Marshall, Lewis, Lockwood, Drake et al., 2005). In the UK, this has led to the establishment of multiple discipline clinical teams whose purpose is to provide an intensive case management of at risk individuals and to educate GPs and physicians in recognition and response to subclinical symptoms. The aims of this team are to reduce the duration of untreated psychosis to less than 3 months, and the team will then provide intensive case management for the patient over the next 3–5 years. Early intervention

has been shown to produce better clinical outcomes than standard service treatment (Garety, Craig, Dunn, Fornells-Ambrojo et al., 2006), to be cost effective (Singh, 2010), and to significantly reduce the risk of second relapse (Alvarez-Jimenez, Parker, Hetrick, McGorry & Gleeson, 2011). However, it is still unclear whether these services might merely be delaying psychosis and not necessarily reducing long-term risk (Preti & Cella, 2010). Even so, early intervention services have been established in a number of countries world-wide, including the UK, Australia and New Zealand, Norway and Denmark, and Canada and the USA.

computer-based or pencil-and-paper tasks to improve attention, memory and problem solving (Krabbendam & Aleman, 2003), and an example exercise is described in Treatment in Practice Box 8.1. Cognitive remediation training varies in length and intensity, with most programmes providing two training sessions per week that can last for up to 6 months or 80 hours of training (Hogarty, Flesher, Ulrich, Carter *et al.*, 2004). Meta-analyses report significant effects of cognitive remediation training on attention, verbal memory, problem solving, verbal working memory, processing speed, and social cognition, but rather modest effects on symptom reduction (McGurk, Twamley, Sitzer, McHugo & Mueser, 2007; Wykes, Huddy, Cellard, McGurk & Czobor, 2011). However, cognitive remediation is particularly effective when combined with social skills training and supported employment (McGurk, Mueser & Pascaris, 2005; Silverstein, Spaulding, Menditto, Savitz *et al.*, 2008), and can result in improvement in social and cognitive skills up to 24 months after entering such training programmes (Hogarty, Flesher, Ulrich, Carter *et al.*, 2004).

8.6.3   Family Interventions

In section 8.5.3 we discovered that the family environment for someone diagnosed with schizophrenia may contribute to both the development of symptoms and to the risk of relapse. In particular, expressed emotion (EE) and communication deviance (CD) within families are factors that have been shown to be associated with relapse and the development of positive symptoms. Families with high levels of CD and EE have difficulty with effective communication between family members, high levels of criticism, a tendency to blame the sufferer for their symptoms and the family consequences of those symptoms, and possess inflexible strategies for dealing with difficulties. Clearly, if these characteristics can be addressed and modified, then this should be reflected in lower risk for positive symptoms and relapse.

Family interventions can take many forms, but the main features of a majority of these types of intervention are that they are designed to educate the family about the nature and symptoms of psychosis and how to cope with the difficulties that arise from living with someone with a diagnosis of schizophrenia (sometimes known as **family psychoeducation**). More specifically:

> **family psychoeducation** Family intervention designed to educate the family about the nature and symptoms of psychosis and how to cope with the difficulties that arise from living with someone with a diagnosis.

1. families learn about the diagnosis, prevalence and aetiology of psychotic symptoms,

---

CLINICAL PERSPECTIVE: TREATMENT IN PRACTICE 8.1: COGNITIVE ENHANCEMENT THERAPY

Cognitive enhancement therapy is a developmental approach that attempts to provide individuals diagnosed with schizophrenia with cognitive exercises that will help them develop cognitive functions that have been impaired by their disorder. These include such skills as attention, memory, and problem solving.

The following 'categorisation exercise' is designed to help develop working memory and abstraction skills. Patients are asked to group the following words into four coherent categories:

love	iron	air	home
nylon	human	spider	sand
stone	food	clay	wood
steel	water	pig	paper
virus	flower	ink	glass

The categories of 'living things' and 'things one needs to live' are fairly obvious but the last two are sufficiently ambiguous to require abstraction. Many clients will initially group items such as iron, wood, glass and steel into a category of 'building materials', and ink, paper, clay, sand and nylon into 'art supplies'. However, with some subtle coaching, clients are encouraged to seek a more abstract basis for sorting (e.g. 'Does nylon really have anything in common with sand?'). Success can then be achieved when patients reason that ink, paper, glass, steel and nylon are all 'fabricated materials'. The skills that clients require to complete this task successfully include remembering previous failed attempts, remembering the words that require further categorisation, and remembering individual words within the context of categories that have already been established. As such, the task provides the client with training in memory and abstraction skills that they can take to other problem-solving situations.

Source: After Hogarty, G.E. & Flesher, S. (1999). Practice principles of cognitive enhancement therapy for schizophrenia. *Schizophrenia Bulletin, 25,* 693–708.

2. they learn about the nature of antipsychotic medication and how to help the sufferer to comply with their medication regime,

3. they are taught how to recognize the signs of relapse and to identify and deal with stressors that could cause relapse,

4. through social skills training, they will learn how to identify problems, to solve them and to achieve family goals, and

5. families will also learn how to share experiences and avoid blaming either themselves or the sufferer for their symptoms and the consequences of their symptoms.

These educational targets are achieved in a variety of ways. For example, high EE families may be asked to watch videos of how low EE families interact (modelling) (Penn & Mueser, 1996). Counselling can be provided to help family members interact in less emotional ways, and group discussions where families share their experiences can help to provide reassurance and a network of social support (known as **supportive family management**). A more intensive form of family intervention is known as **applied family management**, and this goes beyond education and support to include active behavioural training elements. Communication and coping skills can be taught with the active involvement of members of the family by using modelling, role playing, providing positive and corrective feedback, and using homework assignments. For example, families may be taught to have one member chair a problem-solving meeting (leading the family through the steps) and another as secretary (recording information on a problem-solving form). As homework, families may be asked to meet weekly to practise problem solving without the presence of a therapist or facilitator (Mueser, Sengupta, Schooler, Bellack *et al.*, 2001).

Outcome studies have indicated that family interventions significantly reduce the risk of relapse, reduce symptoms, and improve the sufferer's social and vocational functioning for periods up to 2 years (Huxley, Rendall & Sederer, 2000; Pharoah, Mari, Rathbone & Wong, 2010), and family interventions that are conducted for longer than 9 months appear to be particularly effective (Kopelowicz & Liberman, 1998). Recent studies have suggested that no one form of family intervention is necessarily more effective than others (Huxley, Rendall & Sederer, 2000), but family psychoeducation

> **supportive family management** A method of counselling in which group discussions are held where families share their experiences and which can help to provide reassurance and a network of social support.

> **applied family management** An intensive form of family intervention which goes beyond education and support to include active behavioural training elements.

interventions without accompanying behavioural training components may be less effective at achieving some goals, such as medication adherence (Zygmunt, Olfson, Boyer & Mechanic, 2002).

8.6.4 Community Care

With the development of relatively effective antipsychotic drugs in the 1950s and 1960s, it became clear that most people diagnosed with schizophrenia could be treated to a point where they were capable of living at least some kind of life back in the community. This helped relieve the economic burden of lifelong hospitalization and custodial care. However, even when living back in their communities, it was clear that individuals diagnosed with schizophrenia would often need support and supervision. They would need help maintaining their necessary medication regime, finding and keeping a job or applying for and securing welfare benefits. They may also have needed help with many aspects of normal daily living that others would take for granted, such as personal hygiene, shopping, feeding themselves, managing their money, and coping with social interactions and life stressors.

In 1963, the US Congress passed a Community Mental Health Act, which specified that, rather than be detained and treated in hospitals, people with mental health problems had the right to receive a broad range of services in their communities. These services included outpatient therapy, emergency care, preventative care, and aftercare. Growing concerns about the rights of mental health patients and a change in social attitudes away from the stigma associated with mental health problems meant that other countries around the world swiftly followed suit in making mental health treatment and aftercare available in the community (Hafner & van der Heiden, 1988). These events led to the development of a combination of services usually termed assertive community treatment or assertive outreach, and, in the US alone, this has led to around a tenfold decrease in the number of people being treated in hospital for mental health problems (Torrey, 2001). **Assertive community treatment** programmes help people recovering from psychotic episodes with their medication regimes, psychotherapy, assistance in dealing with every-day life and its stressors, guidance on making decisions, residential supervision and vocational training (Bebbington, Johnson & Thornicroft, 2002). In the UK, **assertive outreach** is a way of working with

> **assertive community treatment** Programmes to help people recovering from psychotic episodes with their medication regimes, offering psychotherapy, assistance in dealing with everyday life and its stressors, guidance on making decisions, residential supervision and vocational training.

> **assertive outreach** A way of working with groups of individuals with severe mental health problems who do not effectively engage with mental health services.

groups of individuals with severe mental health problems who do not effectively engage with mental health services. Assertive outreach staff would expect to meet their clients in their own environments, whether that is a home, café, park or street, and the aim is to build a long-term relationship between the client and mental health services. Table 8.3 provides a list of some of the main aims and characteristics of assertive outreach programmes in the UK, and these emphasize teaching basic living skills, providing support and guidance, and preventing relapse and hospitalization.

There is good evidence that **community care** programmes help to stabilize the condition of individuals diagnosed with schizophrenia, ensure that they integrate more effectively into their local communities, comply with their medication regimes, and stay out of hospital longer than sufferers who are not part of a community care programme (Madianos & Madianou, 1992; Hansson, Middelboe, Sorgaard, Bengtsson-Topps *et al.*, 2002; Bebbington, Johnson & Thornicroft, 2002). However, community care services are often difficult to resource and to coordinate, and it has been estimated that in any one year in the USA, between 40 and 60 per cent of all people experiencing symptoms of psychosis receive no treatment at all (Wang, Demler & Kessler, 2002). In addition, long-term studies of community care in the UK suggest that it helps to maintain clinical and social functioning at a stable level, but does not necessarily help to *improve* these aspects of the sufferer's life (Reid, Johnson, Bebbington, Kuipers *et al.*, 2001).

> **community care** Care that is provided outside a hospital setting.

The community care approach has also given rise to concerns for the physical safety of individuals with mental health problems who are exposed to the stresses and rigours of everyday life, and for the safety of others in the communities in which they live. For example, studies in the UK have suggested that 41 per cent of people with mental health problems living in the community suffer physical and verbal harassment, compared with 15 per cent in the general population, and this abuse is usually carried out by teenagers and neighbours (Berzins, Petch & Atkinson, 2003). There is also concern about the role of individuals diagnosed with schizophrenia as victims or perpetrators of violent crime such as homicide. A Danish study discovered that the risk of being a victim of homicide was increased sixfold for people diagnosed with a mental illness such as schizophrenia compared with individuals without a psychiatric diagnosis (Hiroeh, Appleby, Mortensen & Dunn, 2001). They argued that individuals diagnosed with schizophrenia may be at such increased risk of a violent death because of a number of factors, including:

1. they are likely to live in places such as inner cities where crime is more prevalent;

TABLE 8.3 *The aims and characteristics of assertive outreach programmes*

AIMS:
Assertive outreach services aim at helping clients to:

- Reduce their number of hospital admissions, in terms of both frequency and duration

- Find and keep suitable accommodation

- Sustain family relationships

- Increase social network and relationships

- Improve their money management

- Increase medication adherence

- Improve their daily living skills

- Undertake satisfying daily activities (including employment)

- Improve their general health

- Improve their general quality of life

- Stabilize symptoms

- Prevent relapse

- Receive help at an early stage

CORE CHARACTERISTICS:
Assertive outreach involves targeting clients with severe and enduring mental health problems who have difficulty engaging with services:

- It is multidisciplinary, comprising a range of professional disciplines (nurses, psychiatrists and social workers at a minimum; also, depending on user needs, support workers, workers who have also been service users, psychologists, occupational therapists, housing workers, substance misuse specialists and vocational specialists)

- There is a low ratio of service users to workers; often around 10 clients per caseload

- There is intensive frequency of client contact compared with that of standard community mental health teams (ideally an average of four or more contacts per week with each client)

- An emphasis on engaging with clients and developing a therapeutic relationship

- Offers or links to specific evidence-based interventions

- Time unlimited services with a no drop-out policy

- Work with people in their own environment, often their own home; engages with the users' support system of family, friends and others

- A team approach that provides flexible and creative support to the individual case coordinators

2. they may have behavioural characteristics such as alcohol or drug abuse that increases the risk;

3. they might provoke the hostility of others because of their psychotic symptoms (such as paranoia);

4. because of their symptoms, they may be less aware of their own safety needs;

5. they may be killed by others with mental health problems that they are in contact with; and

6. they may be more likely to be victims of motiveless killings because of their appearance, which might be unkempt and dirty.

In contrast, tragic and high-profile murders carried out by people with mental health problems have often been used to imply that the community care approach to mental health care is dangerous and has failed. However, the evidence to support this view is mixed and more complex than it looks at first sight (Bo, Abu-Akel, Kongerslev, Haahr & Simonsen, 2011). First, one body of evidence reaching back to the 1980s implied that having a major mental health problem, such as schizophrenia, was not a risk factor for violence (Teplin, 1985; Elbogen & Johnson, 2009) and did not predict increased levels of violence in those exhibiting psychotic symptoms (Quinsey, Harris, Rice & Cormier, 2006). However, other evidence has suggested a link between schizophrenia and violent behaviour, including increased aggressive behaviour and an increased risk for violent and non-violent crimes (Hodgins, 2008; Soyka, Graz, Bottlender, Dirschedl &

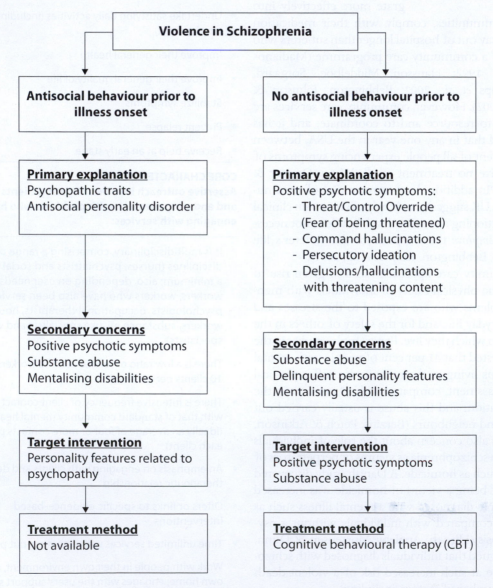

FIGURE 8.4 *The occurrence of violence in schizophrenia as a consequence of two developmental trajectories stemming from antisocial or violent behaviour prior to onset of the disorder, and no violent behaviour prior to disorder onset. Note the different types of primary explanations for these two different trajectories.*

Source: Sune, B., Bo, S., Abu-Akel, A., Kongerslev, M., Haahr, U.H. & Simonsen, E. (2011). Risk factors for violence among patients with schizophrenia. *Clinical Psychology Review, 31*(5), 711–726. Reproduced with permission.

Schoech, 2007). Volavka, Laska, Baker *et al.* (1997) found that approximately 20 per cent of individuals with a diagnosis of schizophrenia were involved in some kind of violent behaviour prior to contact with the health system – suggesting that any increase in risk for violence after the onset of psychotic symptoms may be due to a prior history of violence, or, perhaps more importantly, to the poorer socio-economic living conditions that many schizophrenia sufferers experience. Bo, Abu-Akel, Kongerslev Haahr & Simonsen (2011) proposed a two-trajectory model for violence in patients with schizophrenia, and this is shown schematically in Figure 8.4. One trajectory describes violence in schizophrenia sufferers with a prior history of violence, and argues that violence in this group may be due to pre-existing personality disorders such as psychopathic traits and antisocial personality disorder. The other trajectory describes violence in sufferers who had not previously shown antisocial tendencies, and ascribes the onset of violence in this group to positive symptoms such as 'hearing voices' and persecutory delusions. Nevertheless, while many epidemiological studies would lead us to believe that there is a link between schizophrenia and violence, only a very small proportion of violence in society is accounted for by individuals with a diagnosis of schizophrenia, and studies indicate that 99.97 per cent of those with

schizophrenia would not commit serious violence in any one given year (Walsh, Buchanan & Fahy, 2002).

What is of some concern, however, is the apparent prevalence of substance and chemical abuse by individuals suffering psychosis and living in the community. The lifetime prevalence rate for substance abuse among people diagnosed with schizophrenia is around 50 per cent, and may be significantly higher in those who are homeless (Kosten & Ziedonis, 1997). In an Australian study, Wallace, Mullen & Burgess (2004) found that between 1975 and 1995, substance abuse problems for individuals diagnosed with schizophrenia increased from 8.3 per cent to 26.1 per cent, and significantly higher rates of criminal conviction were found for those with substance abuse problems (68.1 per cent compared with 11.7 per cent). We know that regular use of some substances (such as cannabis – see Focus Point 8.6) can directly increase the risk of developing positive symptoms, and that the use of others (such as cocaine and amphetamines) can exacerbate these symptoms (Laruelle & Abi-Dargham, 1999). The challenge for community care programmes is to tackle what appears to be increasing levels of substance abuse in individuals with psychotic symptoms living in the community, and, in so doing, to decrease the risk of relapse and hospitalization.

SELF-TEST QUESTIONS

- What are antipsychotic drugs, how are they thought to deal with the psychotic symptoms, and how are they categorized?
- What problematic side-effects do antipsychotic drugs have?
- What are the important characteristics of social skills training for individuals diagnosed with schizophrenia?
- What is CBTp and how is it used to treat individuals diagnosed with schizophrenia? With what particular types of symptoms is it most effective?
- What is cognitive remediation training (CRT)?
- Can you describe a typical family-based intervention for psychosis and the factors that such interventions are designed to address?
- What are the different types of community care programmes provided for individuals diagnosed with schizophrenia, and is there any evidence for their effectiveness in controlling psychotic symptoms?

SECTION SUMMARY

8.6 THE TREATMENT OF PSYCHOSIS

Treating psychotic symptoms is a relatively long-term process. This will often begin with sub-clinical symptoms being picked up by an early intervention team, and may require immediate and urgent treatment with antipsychotic drugs to deal with the positive symptoms found during early psychotic episodes. Psychological therapies may be required to deal with the longer term cognitive and behavioural deficits that may restrict full social and occupational functioning, and family based interventions will help to maintain a stable, stress-free environment in which the risk of relapse is minimized. Long-term community care is often overseen by a **case manager** who will help the sufferer with their medication regimes, residential supervision, vocational training, and regular access to mental health services. NICE recommends that various different interventions are considered in planning for recovery from a first episode of schizophrenia – and these can include both medications and psychotherapy (NICE, 2010). However, there are a range of differing views across the medical, psychological and social spectrum about what is the best approach to take for the long-term treatment of individuals with schizophrenia. Some of these views are controversial, but are worth discussing. Activity 8.2 provides you with an opportunity to consider some of these alternative views.

case manager Oversees long-term community care and helps the client with their medication regimes, residential supervision, vocational training, and regular access to mental health services.

The key points covered in this section are:

- Remission rates vary between 17 and 78 per cent in first-episode schizophrenia, and 16 to 62 per cent in multiple-episode schizophrenia.

- Electroconvulsive therapy (ECT) and **psychosurgery** were common forms of treatment for psychosis prior to the development of antipsychotic drugs.

psychosurgery Brain surgery used to treat symptoms of psychopathology.

- Antipsychotic drugs are relatively successful for treating the positive symptoms of schizophrenia, and are thought to be effective because they reduce excessive levels of dopamine activity in the brain.

- *Social skills training* can be used to help psychosis sufferers to react appropriately in a range of useful social situations.

- *Personal therapy* is a broad-based cognitive-behaviour programme designed to help individuals diagnosed with schizophrenia with the skills required to adapt to day-to-day living after discharge from hospital.

- *Cognitive behaviour therapy for psychosis (CBTp)* helps to address any **abnormal attribution processes** and information processing and reasoning biases that may give rise to delusional thinking.

abnormal attribution processes The view that paranoid delusions may be the result of a bias towards attributing negative life events to external causes.

- *Cognitive remediation training (CRT)* is designed to help the individual diagnosed with schizophrenia to address deficits in social cognition (the ability to act wisely in social situations) and neurocognition (memory and attention).

- *Family interventions* are designed to educate the family about the nature of psychotic symptoms and how to cope with difficulties that arise from living with someone with a diagnosis of schizophrenia.

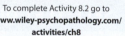

To complete Activity 8.2 go to
**www.wiley-psychopathology.com/
activities/ch8**

- *Assertive community treatment* and *assertive outreach* are forms of community care that help the individual recovering from psychotic symptoms with their medication regimes, psychotherapy, decision making, residential supervision and vocational training.

8.7   EXPERIENCING PSYCHOSIS REVIEWED

Psychosis is a name given to a collection of disparate symptoms, and has led DSM-5 to redefine its diagnostic categories into what are known as *schizophrenia spectrum disorders*. The main categories include schizophrenia, schizotypal personality disorder, delusional disorder, brief psychotic disorder and schizoaffective disorder. Symptoms are classified as either positive symptoms (because they reflect an excess or distortion of normal functions, e.g. hallucinations, delusions, disordered speech, and disorganized motor behaviours) or negative symptoms (which reflect the loss or diminution of normal functions, e.g. diminished emotional experience).

These combinations of symptoms also frequently result in a marked inability to undertake normal social and occupational functioning. The prominent approach to explaining the development of psychotic symptoms is a diathesis-stress one. That is, there is clear evidence for a genetic predisposition to psychotic symptoms, but the symptoms appear to be triggered by experiencing environmental stress. The genetic predisposition does not appear to be a specific one, and is not transmitted through a single gene (Kendler, Myers, O'Niell, Martin *et al.*, 2000). Nor is the nature of the environmental stressors that may trigger psychotic symptoms fully understood. These may range from stressful life experiences (such as unemployment) (Brown & Birley, 1968), to dysfunctional family environments (where intra-family communication may be problematic) (Goldstein, 1987), to the hassles and challenges encountered in normal adolescent development (Harrop & Trower, 2001). There is, however, good evidence that many of the symptoms of psychosis are associated with imbalances in brain neurotransmitters such as dopamine, serotonin, glutamate and GABA (Stone, Morrison & Pilowsky, 2007), and this occurs mainly in the mesolimbic and mesocortical pathways of the brain. This leads to cognitive deficits in important brain areas such as the prefrontal cortex, where attention, memory and executive functioning are all impaired. In addition, recent years have seen a resurgence in interest in cognitive theories of psychotic symptoms, and especially the development of cognitive biases in attention, attributional processes, reasoning and ambiguity interpretation (Savulich, Shergill & Yiend, 2012). These processes have been shown to contribute to the development of delusional beliefs as well as the way in which many people with psychotic symptoms hear and react to auditory hallucinations or 'voices'.

The development of antipsychotic drugs over the past 50 years has meant than many sufferers can lead relatively normal lives without experiencing the disabling positive symptoms that appear to be linked to imbalances in brain neurotransmitter activity (e.g. disordered speech and thought, hallucinations). However, after an initial psychotic episode, relapse is the norm rather than the exception and around 50 per cent of sufferers will rarely fully recover from the effects of their symptoms (Wiersma, Nienhuis, Slooff & Giel, 1998). Because of this, long-term care and supervision are required, and this means that individuals diagnosed with schizophrenia will often require (1) lifelong medication, (2) individual therapies to deal with their specific cognitive and behavioural deficits (e.g. social skills training, CBTp), (3) family interventions designed to ensure a family environment that minimizes stressors, maintains a medication regime and can recognize early signs of relapse, and (4) longer term community care to provide guidance on decision making, residential supervision, vocational training, and to ensure a long-term relationship between the individual and mental health services is maintained.

To access the online resources for this chapter go to
www.wiley-psychopathology.com/ch8

Reading	Video	Activity
• Journal article: The heritability of delusional-like experiences	• Psychosis: Diagnostic interview	• Types of delusions
• Journal article: Tests of causal linkages between cannabis use and psychotic symptoms	• Schizophrenia	• Brain areas labelling
• Alien abductions: The real deal?	• Cannabis and psychosis	• Activity 8.1
• Journal article: Cognitive behavioural therapy and the psychopathology of schizophrenia		• Activity 8.2
• Journal article: Cognitive-behavioral therapy for schizophrenia		• Self-test questions
• Glossary key terms		• Revision flashcards
• Clinical issues		• Research questions
• Links to journal articles		
• References		

9 Substance Use Disorders

 To access the online resources for this chapter go to
www.wiley-psychopathology.com/ch9

ROUTE MAP OF THE CHAPTER

This chapter begins by discussing substance use disorders generally, including general diagnostic criteria and prevalence rates. We then look at the specific characteristics of a number of drugs whose use regularly gives rise to addiction and dependency. We look in detail at alcohol, nicotine and cannabis use, and then continue by looking at a range of stimulant, sedative and hallucinogenic drugs. In particular, we review the physical and psychological effects of these drugs, their prevalence of use, the nature of abuse and dependency on these substances, and the costs of dependency in psychological, physical health and economic terms. The chapter then continues by reviewing a developmental model of substance use disorders in which we consider the risk factors that contribute to experimentation, regular use and, in some cases, abuse and dependency. Finally, we cover the various types of treatment for substance use suidsorders and evaluate their success.

LEARNING OUTCOMES

When you have completed this chapter, you should be able to:

1. Describe the main diagnostic criteria for substance use disorders and be able to define key terms such as craving, tolerance and withdrawal.

2. Describe the specific characteristics of a range of substances that give rise to dependency and abuse, including specific stimulants, sedatives, and hallucinogenic drugs.

3. Describe and evaluate the psychological, physical health and economic costs of specific substance use disorders.

4. Describe a developmental model of substance dependency and evaluate the risk factors that contribute to the different stages in this model.

5. Describe and evaluate the efficacy of a range of psychological and biological treatment methods for treating substance use disorders.

My name is Tim and I am from Yorkshire. I had a normal life until I was 12 years old, and then my mother and father started to fight. The fights were very violent and quite frightening; I have since learnt that this was mostly my mother's fault. It became apparent that we were left outside pubs a lot but it seemed normal. My two brothers and I suffered a terrible few years – the scars are still with us.

Our house was sold and we ended up on a bad council estate in Sheffield which has since been knocked down. The violent drinking bouts got worse and I left home although I was just 15. I still found a job but suffered terribly over leaving my younger brothers. I found a bedsit and a job and the peace was heavenly. I then moved to Derby to live with my uncle's family and eventually got married to a lovely lady and had two daughters.

My drinking started in Derby. No one thing made me drink but I gradually drank more and more over the years. I started my own catering business and was extremely successful. I employed 65 staff and enjoyed all the benefits of being my own boss. I had money, cars and plenty of time to drink! I did not know then what would happen because of my drinking. My wife told me about my behaviour but I ignored her and her advice. I would not listen to anyone. Worst of all I was out on the road driving to my catering sites and drinking all day. I still functioned but I do not know how to this day; nor do I know how I kept my licence.

I sold my Company and borrowed £100,000 from the bank to buy – yes, you guessed – a pub/restaurant. What a nightmare – my own 'booze' on tap! Needless to say the venture was doomed from the start. I drank morning, noon and night and had plenty of friends – or so I thought. Eventually my wife left me and went back to her parents, and I do not blame her.

I went bankrupt and moved to a bedsit once again. I then went on cider and anything else I could get. I had defrauded the Customs & Excise while I was drinking so I ended up in prison for 12 months, which was a disaster. They put me in charge of the officers' mess and bar! Needless to say I was in seventh heaven. I came out of prison a complete wreck and moved from city to city for 10 years. I was sacked from numerous chefs' jobs and was in and out of several mental hospitals all over the country. I did stay dry for a while but when my father died I started to drink again and went back to prison as I wanted the peace and friendship I found the first time. However this was not meant to be and I found it very hard to cope without the booze second time around.

I was begging in Soho when I decided to try to turn my life around. I moved to Leicester where – through Alcoholics Anonymous – I stopped drinking. I did have relapses but, following hepatitis, jaundice and a bleeding throat, I stopped four and a half years ago. I could not suffer those terrible withdrawals again and I still have the scars of drinking – epilepsy and digestive problems. But I am dry.

Tim's Story

 For a video on alcohol misuse go to **www.wiley-psychopathology.com/video/ch9**

Introduction

A **drug** can be very loosely defined as any substance, other than food, that affects either our bodies or our minds in some way. Such substances may give us energy, relax us when nervous, change our ways of thinking, distort our perceptions, or change our

drug A substance that has a physiological effect when ingested or otherwise introduced into the body.

moods. They can, of course, have these effects either for better or for worse, and the short-term benefit of a substance may lead to longer term physical and mental costs (as the experience of *Tim*, above, clearly demonstrates). Nevertheless, in most Westernized cultures, drugs are almost a normal part of daily life. We use drugs to wake up in the morning (caffeine in tea and coffee), to stay alert during the day (nicotine in cigarettes), to reduce pain (aspirin and paracetamol), to control our physical shape (dieting pills), and to relax (alcohol, sleeping pills). While the use of drugs in this way may seem to provide benefits to daily living, there are a number of problems that arise out of this culture:

1. while many of these substances have short-term benefits they may have longer-term negative physical and psychological effects with persistent use (e.g. alcohol)

2. many people either become psychologically or physically addicted to a drug, and continue to use the drug when it no longer has the original benefits (e.g. sleeping pills and dieting pills); and

3. many people move on from taking legal drugs to taking illegal substances, many of which are physically damaging, highly addictive, and frequently blight social, educational and occupational performance (e.g. cocaine, heroin, solvents, and hallucinogens such as LSD).

Furthermore, in addition to traditional illicit drugs such as cocaine and Ecstasy, recent years have been characterized by a dramatic rise in the number of newer classes of psychostimulants – usually known as *synthetic cathinones*, but more frequently referred to as '**bath salts**' (Fass, Fass & Garcia, 2012) (see Focus Point 9.5 later in the chapter).

> **bath salts** 'Bath salts' is the name for an emerging group of drugs containing synthetic chemicals related to cathinone, which is an amphetamine-like stimulant found in the khat plant.

The abuse and misuse of drugs has become one of society's biggest problems. Substance abusers often pay a high personal cost for their dependency in terms of failed relationships, ruined careers, poor health and premature death (Photo 9.1). Society also pays a high cost in terms of lost productivity and the strain such abuse puts on national health resources. In 2012, the World Health Organisation (WHO, 2012) estimated that (1) in 2010 between 153 million and 300 million people aged 15–64 (3.4–6.6 per cent of the world's population in that age group) had used an illicit substance at least once in the previous year, (2) there were between 99,000 and 253,000 deaths globally in 2010 as a result of illicit drug use, with drug-related deaths accounting for between 0.5 and 1.3 per cent of all-cause mortality among those aged 15–64, (3) with estimated annual prevalence of cannabis use in 2010 ranging from 2.6 to 5 per cent of the adult population (between 119 million and 224 million estimated users aged 15–64), cannabis remains the world's most widely used illicit substance, and (4) in terms of prevalence, amphetamine-type stimulants (ATS) (excluding 'Ecstasy') remain second only to cannabis, with an estimated prevalence of 0.3–1.2 per cent in 2010 (between 14.3 million and 52.5 million users) (see Figure 9.1).

PHOTO 9.1 *Paul Gascoigne was well known as a talented footballer throughout Europe, having played for teams such as Newcastle United, Tottenham Hotspur, Lazio, and Rangers. But since retiring from professional football, his life has become dominated by his dependency on alcohol and its associated mental health problems. Like most people with a substance use disorder, his health has suffered, his problems curtailed a promising coaching career, and he has had numerous run-ins with the law. Despite a willingness to enter rehabilitation, his many relapses are well known, and such relapses are a common feature of treatment for severe substance use disorder.*

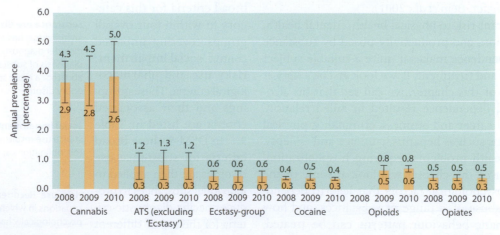

FIGURE 9.1 *Estimates of the annual prevalence of illicit drug use worldwide among people between 15 and 64 years of age, 2008–2010.*
Source: World Drug Report 2012, Figure 1. Retrieved from http://www.unodc.org/documents/data-and-analysis/WDR2012/WDR_2012_web_small.pdf

Even legal drugs such as tobacco and alcohol are problematic and usage regularly leads to death, illness and impoverishment. There are more than 1 billion tobacco smokers worldwide, of which around 80 per cent live in low- and middle-income countries. Approximately one person dies every 6 seconds due to tobacco and this accounts for 1 in 10 adult deaths (WHO, 2013). The world's population consumes an average of 6.13 litres of alcohol per year per person, and the harmful use of alcohol results in 2.5 million deaths a year and contributes directly to 60 types of injuries and diseases (WHO, 2011). In the UK, the percentage of the population that reported smoking cigarettes had declined to 21 per cent in 2008 (down from 39 per cent in 1980) (The Health & Social Care Information Centre, 2011), but alcohol consumption in the UK has been steadily increasing over the past 45 years, as can be seen later in Figure 9.4.

Equally alarming is the frequency of drug use in adolescents and school children. Usage and dependence at such an early age may well lead to life-long dependency and health problems. In the US, over 50 per cent of adolescents have tried illegal drugs at least once (Johnston, O'Malley & Bachman, 2001). In the UK, surveys indicate that 38 per cent of 15-year-olds have used an illegal drug in the year prior to the survey, and 23 per cent in the previous month (Department of Health, National Report, 2004), and in 2009 as many as three in ten secondary school pupils (29 per cent) had tried smoking at least once (The Health & Social Care Information Centre, 2011). However, in a reassuring recent report, the number of school pupils who reported taking drugs in the UK had dropped from 42 per cent in 2001 to 29 per cent in 2011 (National Foundation for Educational Research, 2011). Nevertheless, once an individual has used one illegal drug, a majority will go on to abuse more than one (e.g. cocaine, cannabis, crack cocaine) (Tsuang, Lyons, Meyer, Doyle et al., 1998), and multiple drug abuse significantly increases other risks to well-being such as being in a car crash, mental health problems, violent behaviour, and promiscuous sexual behaviour (Greenwood, White, Page-Shafer, Bein et al., 2001).

The significant risk to physical health, mental health, social integration, and productivity posed by substance abuse and dependence makes it quite a suitable subject for prevention and treatment. If we look at *Tim's story* at the beginning of this chapter, we can see that his alcohol abuse and dependence resulted in failed relationships, a ruined career and business, criminality, physical health problems such as hepatitis, jaundice and epilepsy, and mental health problems requiring hospitalization. The remainder of this chapter will look at some of the physical and psychological factors that lead to dependence on, and abuse of, a range of substances, and how these problematic behaviour patterns can be treated,

and these factors can be reviewed at the outset in the 'Summary table' on the book's website at www.wiley-psychopathology.com/ch9. But first, it is necessary to describe some of the terminology commonly used in this area of psychopathology, and to look at the more general criteria for diagnosing and describing substance abuse and dependence.

9.1 DEFINING AND DIAGNOSING SUBSTANCE USE DISORDERS

Traditionally, pathology associated with substance and drug use had fallen into two categories: substance abuse and substance dependence. **Substance abuse** was defined as 'a maladaptive pattern of substance use manifested by recurrent and significant adverse consequences related to repeated use of the substance', and **substance dependence** as 'a cluster of cognitive, behavioural and physiological symptoms indicating that the individual continues use of the substance despite significant substance-related problems'. However, these two categories have been combined into a single 'Substance Use Disorder' category in DSM-5. The reason for this is two-fold. Firstly, most individuals who exhibited the criteria for substance abuse rarely go on to develop substance dependence (Schuckit, Smith, Danko et al., 2001), and, secondly, detailed analysis of the diagnostic criteria for substance dependence and substance abuse indicated that they represented one and not two disorder categories. As a result DSM-5 has defined the general criteria for just a single **substance use disorder (SUD)** category, and the broad criteria for this category fit within four overall groups covering impaired control, **social impairment**, **risky use** and pharmacological criteria. These groupings and their associated criteria are listed in Table 9.1. In DSM-5, these broad criteria for substance use disorder are then applied to individual substances to produce specific diagnostic criteria for the use of different

> **substance abuse** A pattern of drug or substance use that occurs despite knowledge of the negative effects of the drug, but where use has not progressed to full-blown dependency.

> **substance dependence** A cluster of cognitive, behavioural and physiological symptoms indicating that the individual continues use of the substance despite significant substance-related problems.

> **substance use disorder (SUD)** Where an individual has at least one substance disorder diagnosis, whether it is a general diagnosis of substance dependency or abuse, or a more specific substance category disorder.

> **social impairment** When persistent substance use results in failure to fulfil major role obligations at work, school, or home.

> **risky use** Recurrent substance use in situations in which it is physically and psychologically hazardous.

TABLE 9.1 *General criteria for substance use disorders*

Impaired control	• Substance taken for longer than originally intended
	• Reports desire to cut down, but with multiple unsuccessful efforts to quit
	• Individual spends a significant amount of time obtaining the substance and recovering from its effects
	• In severe cases, virtually all the individual's daily activities revolve around the substance
	• Craving is manifested by an intense desire or urge for the substance that may occur at any time
Social impairment	• Substance use results in failure to fulfil major role obligations at work, school or home
	• Individual persists with substance use despite recurrent social and interpersonal problems caused by the substance
	• The individual may withdraw from family activities and hobbies in order to use the substance
Risky use	• Recurrent substance use in situations in which it is physically hazardous
	• The individual continues to take the substance despite knowledge of persistent or recurrent physical or psychological problems caused by the substance
Pharmacological criteria	• Tolerance is signalled by requiring increasing doses of the substance to achieve the desired effects
	• The individual experiences withdrawal symptoms, and continues to take the substance in order to relieve these withdrawal symptoms

TABLE 9.2 *Basic terminology in the study and treatment of substance use disorders*

Terminology	Definition
Addiction*	Drug use to the point where the body's 'normal' state is the drugged state (so the body requires the drug to feel normal).
	*Addiction is a term that is rarely used nowadays because it implies that drug dependence is primarily a physical one, whereas in reality it is a complex mix of physical and psychological dependence
Psychological dependence	The user's tendency to alter their life because of the drug, and to centre their activities around the drug
Craving	A strong subjective drive to use the substance
Tolerance	The need for greater amounts of the drug or substance to achieve intoxication (or the desired effect) or a markedly diminished effect with continued use of the same amount of the drug or substance
Withdrawal	A maladaptive behavioural change, with physiological and cognitive concomitants, that occurs when blood or tissue concentrations of a substance or drug decline in an individual who has previously maintained prolonged heavy use of the substance or drug
Substance	A drug of abuse, a medication, or a toxin

substances (e.g. alcohol, amphetamines, cannabis, cocaine, hallucinogens, opioids, and stimulant- and tobacco-related disorders), and some of these specific diagnostic criteria are discussed later in this chapter.

Some other terms used in the diagnosis and treatment of substance use disorders are listed in Table 9.2. For example, when the person's 'normal' body state is the drugged state (so that the body requires the substance to feel normal), this is known as **addiction**, and **craving** is the term used for the strong subjective drive that addicts have to use the substance (see Focus Point 9.8). The term **psychological dependence** is used when it is clear that the individual has changed their life to ensure continued use of the drug, that all their activities are centred on the drug and its use, and this leads to neglect of other important activities such as work, social and family commitments. While the physical consequences of substance use disorders can be devastating (in terms of their negative effects on physical health and longevity), the challenges for psychopathology are arguably to prevent substance abuse, to develop interventions to help alleviate abuse and dependence, and to understand the conditions under which some individuals develop substance use disorders. This understanding will result not only from a knowledge of the physical effects of individual substances, but also from a knowledge of how the individual uses the drug and the negative effect it has on their daily lives.

Tolerance refers to the need for increased amounts of the substance in order to achieve similar effects across time. **Withdrawal** indicates that the body requires the drug in order to maintain physical stability, and lack of the drug

---

addiction When a person's 'normal' body state is the drugged state (so that the body requires the substance to feel normal).

craving The strong subjective drive that addicts have to use a particular substance.

psychological dependence When individuals have changed their life to ensure continued use of a particular drug such that all their activities are centred on the drug and its use.

tolerance The need for increased amounts of a substance in order to achieve similar effects across time.

withdrawal Where the body requires the drug in order to maintain physical stability, and lack of the drug causes a range of negative and aversive physical consequences (e.g. anxiety, tremors and, in extreme cases, death).

causes a range of negative and aversive physical consequences (e.g. anxiety, tremors and, in extreme cases, death). As outlined in Table 9.1 behavioural features of dependence include (1) unsuccessful attempts to cut down on use of the drug, (2) a preoccupation with attempts to obtain the drug (e.g. theft of money to buy illegal drugs, driving long distances late at night to buy alcohol, multiple visits to doctors to obtain prescription drugs), (3) unintentional overuse, where people find they have consumed more of the substance than they originally intended (e.g. ending up regularly drunk after only going out for a quick drink after

work), and (4) abandoning or neglecting important life activities because of the drug (e.g. failing to go to work because of persistent hangovers; neglecting friendships, relationships, child care, and educational activities). It is also important to emphasize at this early stage that substance use disorder is a *chronic relapsing condition*, in which substance users find their habits hard to eliminate, and it is almost normal following treatment for substance dependence to be associated with multiple relapses.

We will discuss the conditions that lead to this syndrome in more detail in section 9.4.

SELF-TEST QUESTIONS

- Can you define the terms craving, tolerance and withdrawal?
- What is craving?

SECTION SUMMARY

9.1 DEFINING AND DIAGNOSING SUBSTANCE USE DISORDERS

- *Substance dependence* is characterized by both tolerance and withdrawal effects.

- *Substance abuse* is a pattern of substance use that occurs despite knowledge of the negative effects of the substance, but where it has not yet progressed to full-blown dependence.

- *Craving* is the term used for the strong subjective drive that addicts have to use a substance.

- *Tolerance* refers to the need for increased amounts of a drug to achieve the same effects across time.

- *Withdrawal* indicates that the body requires the drug in order to maintain physical stability.

9.2 THE PREVALENCE AND COMORBIDITY OF SUBSTANCE USE DISORDERS

Drug use and dependence is highly prevalent in the general populations of many countries, although rates of substance use disorders will vary markedly across countries depending on the legal, moral and religious attitudes to drugs in those countries. The lifetime prevalence rate for substance dependence has been calculated in the US at between 2.6 and 5.1 per cent (Warner,

Kessler, Hughes, Anthony & Nelson, 1995; Compton, Thomas, Stinson & Grant, 2007). Of those individuals aged between 15 and 54 years, 51 per cent had used illegal drugs, non-medical prescription drugs (e.g. sedatives, tranquilizers), or inhalants at some point in their lives, and 15.4 per cent had done so in the previous 12 months. In the US, the Substance Abuse and Mental Health Services Administration's 2004 National Survey on Drug Use and Health estimated that 22.5 million persons aged 12 or older met criteria for substance dependence or abuse in the foregoing year (SAMHSA, 2005), and a majority of those with substance abuse and dependency problems rarely seek help, with as few as 8.1 per cent of

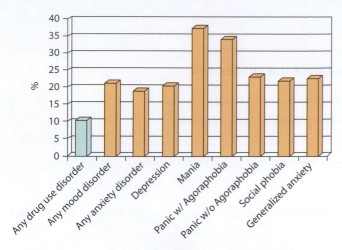

FIGURE 9.2 *Lifetime prevalence of drug disorders among persons with mood and anxiety disorders.*
Source: Data from Conway, K.P., Compton, W., Stinson, F.S. & Grant, B.F. (2006). Lifetime comorbidity of DSM-IV mood and anxiety disorders and specific drug use disorders: Results from the National Epidemiologic Survey on Alcohol and Related Conditions. *Journal of Clinical Psychiatry*, *67*(2), 247–257. Reproduced by permission of Physician's Postgraduate Press, Inc.

TABLE 9.3 *Comorbidity of substance use disorders with other psychiatric disorders**

Psychiatric disorder	Percentage of individuals also diagnosed with a substance use disorder (SUD)
Bipolar disorder	60.7%
Major depression	18%
Obsessive compulsive disorder (OCD)	32.8%
Panic disorder	35.8%
Schizophrenia	47%
Bulimia nervosa	28%
Personality disorders	42%

*Rate of substance use disorders in the general population is around 5%.

Source: Data taken from Brooner, King, Kidorf, Schmidt & Bigelow (1997); Cuffel, 1996; Regier, Farmer, Rae, Locke *et al.*, 1990; Zanarini, Frankenburg, Dubo, Sickel *et al.*, 1998; Lacey, 1993.

those diagnosed with substance abuse claiming to have sought help or treatment (Compton, Thomas, Stinson & Grant, 2007).

A particularly important aspect of substance use disorders is that they are highly comorbid with a range of other psychological disorders. Community epidemiological studies suggest that, amongst individuals with substance dependence, 53–76 per cent have at least one other co-occurring psychiatric disorder (Zilberman, Cao & Jacobsen, 2003), and there is an especially strong association of lifetime mood and anxiety disorders with substance use disorders (Merikangas, Mehta, Molnar, Walters *et al.*, 1998) (see Figure 9.2). Other studies have indicated significantly higher levels of substance use disorders in individuals with bipolar disorder, major depression, anxiety disorders – such as obsessive compulsive disorder and panic disorder – schizophrenia, bulimia nervosa and personality disorders than in the general population (see Table 9.3). The high level of comorbidity between substance use disorders and other mood and anxiety disorders has generated a number of hypotheses about why substance use disorders occur so regularly in the context of other psychological disorders. One view

is that substance abuse and dependence may be a risk factor for the later development of a psychiatric illness (e.g. Wylie, Scott & Burnett, 1995). For example, panic attacks may result from cocaine use and persist even after cocaine abstinence has been achieved (Rosen & Kosten, 1992), with the latter possibly increasing the likelihood of relapse back to cocaine or another drug to cope with these panic attacks. However, the majority of current evidence is consistent with the view that psychiatric and psychological disorders usually pre-date substance abuse and dependence (Merikangas, Mehta, Molnar, Walters *et al.*, 1998; Abraham & Fava, 1999), and a recent UK study indicated that the risk for substance abuse attributable to prior psychiatric illness was 14.2 per cent, compared with a risk for psychiatric illness attributable to substance abuse of only 0.2 per cent (Frisher, Crome, MacLeod, Millson & Croft, 2005). This suggests a 'self-medication' effect, in which individuals with an established psychiatric disorder start using substances to alleviate the negative emotional and behavioural effects of the disorder (Mueser, Drake, & Wallach, 1998; but see Focus Point 7.7 for an account of a causal relationship between cannabis use and psychotic symptoms).

SELF-TEST QUESTION

● How are substance use disorders and other psychiatric disorders related? Is one a risk factor for the other?

9.3 CHARACTERISTICS OF SPECIFIC SUBSTANCE USE DISORDERS

In this chapter we need to look closely at the nature of different substance dependencies. These will cover alcohol and nicotine – because of the close links that use of these substances have with normal everyday life – then three specific groups of substances: **stimulants** (e.g. cocaine, amphetamines and caffeine), **sedatives** (e.g. opiates, such as heroin, and barbiturates), and **hallucinogens** (e.g. LSD and other hallucinogenics, cannabis, and MDMA, better known as Ecstasy). It is important to be aware that relatively few of the drugs we will discuss fit simply and easily into any one of these drug categories and many have multiple effects, with some overlap between categories. That is why each textbook you read on this topic appears to have a different form of categorisation. Figure 9.3 provides you with a drug chart that maps how the different substances described in this chapter overlap across categories. This shows that nicotine can act as both a stimulant and a depressant; hallucinogenic drugs such as LSD and MDMA have both hallucinogenic and stimulant properties; and cannabis is probably the most difficult to categorize because it can have a variety of psychological and physical effects.

stimulants Substances that increase central nervous system activity and increase blood pressure and heart rate.

sedatives Central nervous system depressants which slow the activity of the body, reduce its responsiveness, and reduce pain tension and anxiety. This group of substances includes alcohol, the opiates and their derivatives (heroin, morphine, methadone and codeine), and synthesized tranquillizers such as barbiturates.

hallucinogens Psychoactive drugs which affect the user's perceptions. They may either sharpen the individual's sensory abilities or create sensory illusions or hallucinations.

 For an activity based on Figure 9.3 regarding the different substances discussed in this chapter go to **www.wiley-psychopathology.com/activities/ch9**

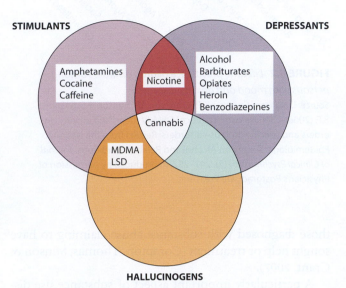

FIGURE 9.3 *A drug chart showing how the different substances described in this chapter overlap across categories.*

9.3.1 Alcohol Use Disorder

Alcohol is one of the most commonly used drugs in a very large number of countries worldwide. In most countries it is also legal and can be easily purchased and consumed. In the US over 65 per cent of people will at some time consume a drink that contains alcohol (Centers for Disease Control and Prevention, 2002), and in the UK this figure rises to 92 per cent of males and 86 per cent of females (WHO, 2004). However, patterns of alcohol consumption appear to have become ever more problematic, with surveys in 2000 suggesting that 26 per cent of the UK population could be labelled as **hazardous drinkers** – that is, they have five or more standard drinks (males) or three or more standard drinks (females) on a typical drinking day

To calculate your level of alcohol consumption, use the Drinkaware Unit Calculator at **www.drinkaware.co.uk/unitcalculator**

alcohol A colourless volatile liquid compound which is the intoxicating ingredient in drinks such as wine, beer and spirits.

hazardous drinkers Individuals who have five or more standard drinks (males) or three or more standard drinks (females) on a typical drinking day.

(WHO, 2004) and the overall amount of alcohol drunk per individual in the UK has been steadily increasing over the past 45 years (see Figure 9.4).

What is known as 'heavy episodic' drinking or **binge drinking** has also reached epidemic levels in many European countries. Binge drinking refers to a high intake of alcohol in a single drinking occasion. There is no single definition of binge drinking but, in the UK, it is normally defined as taking at least 8 units (males) or 6 units (females) of alcohol in a single day. One-fifth (20 per cent) of men drink more than 8 units on at least one day of the week: the proportion ranges from 24 per cent of men aged 16–24 to only 5 per cent of those aged 65 and over. Thirteen per cent of women drink more than 6

binge drinking A high intake of alcohol in a single drinking occasion.

units on at least one day of the week: 24 per cent of those aged 16–24, but just 2 per cent of those aged 65 and over. However, the prevalence of binge drinking among young men and women in the UK has fallen since 1998. In 2010 the prevalence among young men, according to the ONS, remained at 24 per cent while among young women it fell to its lowest recorded level at 17 per cent (Office for National Statistics, 2010) (see Figure 9.5).

Alcohol has its physical and psychological effects when its main constituent, **ethyl alcohol**, is absorbed into the bloodstream through the lining of the stomach and intestine. Alcohol then reaches the brain and central nervous system via the bloodstream. At first, alcohol acts to relax the individual,

ethyl alcohol The intoxicating constituent of alcoholic drinks.

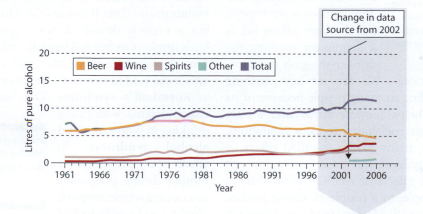

FIGURE 9.4 *Annual alcohol consumption per person over 15 years of age in the UK, 1961–2006.*
Source: Management of substance abuse in UK http://www.who.int/substance_abuse/publications/global_alcohol_report/profiles/gbr.pdf (accessed 20th December 2013). © World Health Organization. Reproduced with permission.

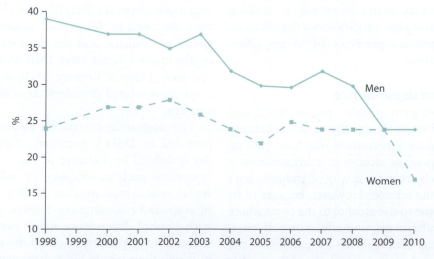

FIGURE 9.5 *Prevalence of binge drinking among 16- to 24-year-olds in the UK, 1998–2010.*
Source: From House of Commons Library (2012). *Statistics on alcohol.* Reproduced with permission.

and it does this by influencing the receptors associated with the neurotransmitter GABA. This facilitates this neurotransmitter's inhibitory function by preventing neurons firing and making the drinker feel more relaxed (Harvey, Foster, MacKay, Carroll et al., 2002). Initially, this makes the drinker more talkative, friendly, confident and happy. As more alcohol is absorbed into the central nervous system, the second stage of intoxication makes the drinker become less able to make judgements; they talk less coherently, memory is affected, and they may switch from being relaxed and happy to emotional and aggressive. Finally, the physical effects of alcohol intoxication include motor coordination difficulties (in balance and walking), slowed reaction times, and blurred vision. This course of the effect of alcohol is known as **biphasic**, because the initial effects act as a stimulant (making the drinker reactive and happy), but the later effects act as a depressant (making the drinker sluggish and experience negative emotions). We can see how drinking alcohol can be appealing to many people because of its initial effects (i.e. it helps alleviate stress after a busy day at work, increases sociability, reduces inhibitions, and so on). However, many of the so-called effects of alcohol are actually mythical, and result from a drinker's *expectations* about the effects of alcohol rather than its real effects. For example, in a couple of classic studies, Lang, Goeckner, Adessor & Marlatt (1975) and Wilson & Lawson (1976) gave participants a disguised non-alcoholic beverage when they were expecting alcohol. They subsequently reported increases in sexual arousal and aggression, even though they had become less physiologically aroused. Expectations about the effects of alcohol appear to play an important role in drinking behaviour, with positive expectancies about the effects of alcohol being a significant predictor of its use (Sher, Wood, Wood et al., 1996).

> **biphasic** Where the initial effects of a drug may act as a stimulant (e.g. alcohol making the drinker reactive and happy), but the later effects act as a depressant (making the drinker sluggish and experience negative emotions).

Alcohol abuse and dependence

Because of its short-term positive psychological and physical effects, and probably equally as much because of the positive cognitive expectations that have built up around the consumption of alcohol in many societies, it has come to be seen by many as a way of enduring life's problems and relieving tension. However, because of its availability, many come to use alcohol to the point where it begins to have significant negative effects on both physical and psychological health. With increased use, the body begins to show tolerance to alcohol and the drinker has to consume ever larger amounts to achieve the same

effects. The long-term physical effects of heavy alcohol consumption include withdrawal symptoms when the body is deprived of alcohol, and these include restlessness, inability to sleep, anxiety and depression, muscle tremors, and rises in blood pressure and temperature. Following withdrawal after extended heavy drinking over a number of years, the drinker may experience **delirium tremens** (**DTs**), where the drinker becomes delirious, experiences unpleasant hallucinations, and exhibits shaking and muscle tremors. Longer-term negative physical effects of heavy alcohol consumption include hypertension, heart failure, stomach ulcers, cancer, cirrhosis of the liver, brain damage (including shrinkage of the frontal lobes), and early dementia. Furthermore, many of the effects of long-term alcohol dependence are similar to malnutrition. This is because alcohol contains calories, but is entirely devoid of any required nutrients. This leads drinkers to feel full but take in little or no nutrition. The consequence is vitamin and mineral deficiencies which can lead to dementia and memory disorders, such as **Korsakoff's syndrome**. One indirect physiological risk associated with heavy drinking in women is **fetal alcohol syndrome**, in which heavy drinking by a mother during pregnancy can cause a whole range of physical and psychological abnormalities in the child, including physical deformities, heart problems, stunted growth, hyperactivity and learning difficulties (Hankin, 2002). Finally, the important physical effects of alcohol abuse and dependence discussed in this section substantially reduce longevity in drinkers, and the number of alcohol-related deaths in the UK has more than doubled between 1979 and 2000 (Baker & Rooney, 2003), suggesting that long-term drink-related disorders are a significant cause for concern.

> **delirium tremens (DTs)** A severe form of alcohol withdrawal that involves sudden and severe mental or nervous system changes.

> **Korsakoff's syndrome** A syndrome involving dementia and memory disorders which is caused by long-term alcohol abuse and dependency.

> **fetal alcohol syndrome** Physiological risk associated with heavy drinking in women, in which heavy drinking by a mother during pregnancy can cause physical and psychological abnormalities in the child.

The diagnostic criteria for alcohol use disorder are provided in DSM-5 Summary Table 9.1. The disorder is defined by a cluster of behavioural and physical symptoms such as evidence of tolerance effects and withdrawal symptoms that develop within 4–12 hours of restricted consumption. However, many individuals with alcohol dependence may never experience withdrawal once a pattern of compulsive drinking develops in which their whole life centres around obtaining and consuming alcohol. Work performance and child care or household responsibilities may be significantly affected either by the after-effects of drinking (e.g. hangovers) or by being intoxicated while trying to perform these functions. Interestingly, a US national survey indicated that workplace alcohol use and impairment directly affected an estimated 15 per cent of the US workforce, with 1.6 per cent working under the influence of alcohol, and 9.2 per cent working with a hangover (Frone, 2006), and lost productivity features as the dominant economic cost of alcohol consumption in many countries around the world (Rehm, Mathers, Popova, Thavorncharoensap *et al.*, 2009). Alcohol abuse is also characterized by the drinker putting themselves at physical risk while intoxicated, including drink driving and becoming engaged in violent arguments (see 'The costs of alcohol use disorders' below). Such individuals will also continue to drink when they know that their drinking is a cause of significant social or interpersonal problems (such as their physical abuse of family members, or by causing problems in their relationship with a partner).

DSM-5 SUMMARY TABLE 9.1 *Criteria for alcohol use disorder*

- A pattern of alcohol use causing impairment or distress leading to at least two of the following within a 12 month period:
  - Alcohol is taken in greater amounts or for longer than was intended
  - A continuing desire or unsuccessful efforts to control alcohol use
  - A lot of time is spent in acquiring, using and recovering from the effects of alcohol
  - Craving, or a strong desire to use alcohol
  - Alcohol use results in a failure to fulfil major life roles at work, home and so forth
  - Persistent alcohol use despite the effect on interpersonal, recreational or social interactions or despite having an ongoing physical or psychological problem that is likely to have been caused or made worse by alcohol
  - Tolerance symptoms associated with high alcohol use
  - Withdrawal symptoms associated with high alcohol use

FOCUS POINT 9.1

TREATING ALCOHOL DEPENDENCE

Like most of the substance use disorders, alcohol dependence is difficult to treat successfully. This is because of a number of factors:

1. many people dependent on alcohol use it as a way of coping with life stresses and difficulties, and this can easily lead to relapse when stress is experienced during or after treatment;
2. alcohol dependence is often comorbid with other psychological disorders, which makes treatment of the dependence more problematic; and
3. alcohol is often part of *polydrug abuse*, where those dependent on alcohol also abuse other drugs as well, and the use of one drug (e.g. nicotine) is likely to trigger the use of another (e.g. drinking alcohol).

Treatments for alcohol dependence take a variety of different forms, and we will describe some of them here. The most successful forms of treatment, however, are usually *multifaceted approaches* that combine a number of individual therapies into a single coherent programme for the client.

SELF-HELP GROUPS

The most commonly sought source of help for alcohol-related problems are community self-help groups such as Alcoholics Anonymous (AA) (http://www.alcoholics-anonymous.org.uk/). AA describes what it calls 12 steps that alcoholics should achieve during the recovery process and the *12-step programme* has been shown to achieve long-term abstinence in around 25 per cent of participants, plus a significant decrease in alcohol consumption in 78 per cent (Ouimette, Finney & Moos, 1997). Many of the beneficial effects of self-help groups such as AA may be attributable to the client replacing social networks of drinking friends with other AA members.

To read about the AA's 12-step programme go to
http://tinyurl.com/om2w7u3

MOTIVATIONAL-ENHANCEMENT THERAPY

This form of cognitive behaviour therapy places the responsibility for change on the client, and attempts to provide them with a range of skills to deal with their drinking (Miller & Rollnick, 2002). The therapist provides individual feedback to the client on the effects of their drinking (such as the effects on other family members), explores the benefits of abstinence, and then designs a treatment programme specifically tailored to the individual's own needs. Motivational-enhancement therapy (MET) is one of the most successful and cost-effective therapeutic approaches for alcohol dependency, and studies suggest around 50 per cent of clients report that both levels of drinking and alcohol-related problems decreased significantly in the 12-months following treatment (UKATT Research Team, 2006).

SOCIAL BEHAVIOUR AND NETWORK THERAPY

This is a treatment aimed at mobilising and developing a positive social network for the client that will facilitate a change in drinking behaviour (Copello, Orford, Hodgson, Tober & Barrett, 2002). The therapist works with both the client and with those in the client's social network who are willing to support the client's efforts to change (such as family, friends, work colleagues), and the aim is to create a supportive social network that will sustain abstinence beyond the therapy period. Controlled outcome studies suggest that **social behaviour and network therapy (SNBT)** has similar success rates to MET (UKATT Research Team, 2006).

social behaviour and network therapy (SBNT) A treatment aimed at mobilising and developing a positive social network for the client that will facilitate a change in drinking behaviour.

PHARMACOTHERAPY

Drugs have been developed that attempt to block alcohol–brain interactions that might promote alcohol dependency. One of these is the drug *naltrexone*, which helps prevent relapse in those recovering from alcohol dependency. *Acamprosate* has also been shown to be successful as a treatment, with outcome studies suggesting that acamprosate enabled twice as many clients to remain abstinent 1 year later than did psychosocial therapy alone (Swift, 1999). In addition, some drugs, such as *ondansetron*, have been shown to be effective with early-onset alcoholics who began drinking heavily before 25 years of age (Johnson, Roache, Javors, DiClemente *et al.*, 2000).

BRIEF INTERVENTIONS

Many people with alcohol-related problems frequently receive brief periods of treatment, such as counselling (five or fewer sessions). Such treatments are usually conducted by GPs, nursing staff or trained counsellors, and consist mainly of communicating alcohol-relevant health advice, providing information on the negative consequences of drinking, and practical advice on community resources that might help achieve moderation or abstinence. Controlled trials in the US and Canada have demonstrated that this approach significantly reduced alcohol-related problems and increased use of healthcare services (Fleming, Barry, Manwell, Johnson & London, 1997; Israel, Hollander, Sanchez-Craig, Booker *et al.*, 1996). Brief interventions are particularly valuable for helping those in the early stages of alcohol use who are at risk of developing full-blown alcohol use disorders.

Prevalence of use

The lifetime prevalence rate for alcohol dependence is around 12.5 per cent, and around 17.8 per cent for alcohol abuse. Dependence is more prevalent among men than women, in younger and unmarried adults, and those in lower socio-economic groups (Hasin, Stinson, Ogburn & Grant, 2007). There are some ethnic differences in prevalence rates, with white Americans being more likely to be diagnosed than black Americans, and rates of diagnosis are also inversely related to educational level. Alcohol dependence and abuse is frequently associated with abuse of other drugs, and is highly comorbid with other psychiatric disorders. For example, heavy alcohol use is often part of **polydrug abuse**, or abuse of more than one drug at a time, and over 80 per cent of alcohol abusers are smokers (Shiffman, Fischer, Paty, Gyns *et al.*, 1994).

polydrug abuse Abuse of more than one drug at a time.

The course of alcohol use disorders

Alcohol use disorders often pass through stages of heavy and regular drinking, then on to alcohol abuse, and finally end up in many cases as alcohol dependence (Jellinek, 1952), and these stages can be fairly clearly defined in *Tim's story* given at the beginning of this chapter. There are also several risk factors for alcohol use disorders, and these might give us some insight into why

alcohol use disorders Problematic patterns of alcohol use leading to clinically significant impairment or distress.

some individuals develop such problematic dependencies. Alcohol use disorders are predicted by factors including:

1. a family history of alcoholism, suggesting that there may be a genetic component to the disorder (see section 9.4.3), or that the offspring model their drinking behaviour on those of their parents, or that parental drinking gives rise to stressful childhood experiences that precipitate drinking in the offspring (Sher, 1991; Windle & Searles, 1992),

2. long-term negative affect, including neuroticism and depression (Sher, Trull, Bartholow & Vieth, 1999),

3. a diagnosis of childhood conduct disorder (Johnson, Arria, Borges, Ialongo & Anthony, 1995; Rohde, Lewinsohn & Seeley, 1995),

4. experiencing life stress and particularly childhood life stressors (Wilsnack, Vogeltanz, Klassen & Harris, 1997), and

5. holding beliefs that drinking alcohol will have a favourable outcome (e.g. that it reduces tension or makes social interactions easier) (Greenbaum, Brown & Friedman, 1995).

The costs of alcohol use disorders

In economic terms, alcohol-related problems cost the US economy around $185 billion in 1998 in terms of lost productivity, healthcare and other costs (National Institute on Alcohol Abuse and Alcoholism, 2000).

Annual alcohol-related costs of crime and public disorder in the UK in 2001 were estimated at £1.5 billion and workplace costs to employers in 2007 were estimated at £7.3 billion per year. Costs to the UK National Health Service alone are £2.7 billion per annum, including 1 in 26 NHS bed days for alcohol-related health problems and up to 35 per cent of all accident and emergency attendance costs (WHO, 2004; Department of Health, 2008). Accidents and crime are two of the biggest social problems associated with alcohol misuse. Drink driving accounts for 20 per cent of all driver road deaths in the UK, and a significantly higher percentage in the US (Kennedy, Isaac & Graham, 1996), and level of alcohol use is one of the best predictors of an individual being involved in recurrent motor vehicle crashes (Fabbri, Marchesini, Dente, Iervese *et al.*, 2005). Alcohol also increases the risk of death from boating accidents (Smith, Keyl, Hadley, Bartley *et al.*, 2001), and drownings (Bell, Amoroso, Yore, Senier *et al.*, 2001). In a review of the relationship between drinking and health in a range of countries worldwide, Norstrom & Ramstedt (2005) found that per capita alcohol consumption in a country significantly predicted (1) mortality from liver cirrhosis and other alcohol-related diseases, (2) mortality from accidents and homicide, and (3) death from suicide.

Finally, alcohol use has come to be closely associated with criminal and illegal activities, and violence and abuse. In particular, alcohol consumption has been found to be significantly related to violent crime (Friedman, Glassman & Terras, 2001), rape and sexual assault (Merrill, Thomsen, Gold & Milner, 2001), and child molestation (Aromacki & Lindman, 2001).

Summary

Alcohol use disorders cause significant short-term and long-term impairment, including impairment to occupational, educational and social functioning, and they have important detrimental long-term effects on health. Alcohol use disorders are also closely associated with a range of social problems, such as drink driving, violent crime, and criminal activities generally. It is still unclear why some people acquire an alcohol dependence, although alcohol use disorders are highly comorbid with other psychiatric disorders – including other substance abuse disorders. This suggests that, for many people, alcohol use may become a means of coping with adverse or challenging life experiences because most alcohol users have an expectancy that drinking alcohol will have beneficial effects (e.g. reduce tension, make social interactions easier).

9.3.2   Tobacco Use Disorder

nicotine The addictive agent found in tobacco; it acts as a stimulant by increasing blood pressure and heart rate.

Nicotine is the addictive agent found in tobacco, and is normally taken as cigarettes, chewing tobacco, snuff, and in pipes and cigars. Smoking tobacco actually delivers nicotine to the brain faster than if it were intravenously injected, and so is a highly efficient and effective way of experiencing the drug. Nicotine has a number of physical effects. First, it acts as a stimulant by increasing blood pressure and heart rate. But, paradoxically, it also has a calming effect by reducing self-reported stress levels and reducing the smoker's feelings of anxiety and anger (Warburton, 1992). In survey studies, smokers usually endorse statements such as 'Smoking relaxes me when I am upset or nervous' and 'Smoking calms me down' (Ikard, Green & Horn, 1969). However, nicotine does have a number of important negative effects, and smokers regularly report adverse moods when they have not smoked recently, and periods of stress and irritability are commonly experienced in the periods between cigarettes or when attempting to quit smoking (Hughes, Higgins & Hatsukami, 1990). These characteristics suggest that nicotine is an addictive drug that develops physical and psychological dependence. First, there is growing evidence to suggest that nicotine has rewarding sensory effects caused by releasing dopamine in the mesolimbic system of the brain (Stahl, 1996), and which acts through nicotinic receptors to increase the firing rate of midbrain dopamine neurons (Dani & De Biasi, 2013). The effects of dopamine release in this brain region are to elevate mood, decrease appetite, and enhance cognitive functioning generally, and these are consequences that are similar to the effects of other addictive drugs such as cocaine (Stein, Pankiewicz, Hanch, Clo *et al.*, 1998). Second, the reported calming effect of nicotine may be mediated by more basic psychological processes representing the reversal of the unpleasant abstinence or withdrawal effects experienced if the smoker has not taken nicotine in the recent past (known as the nicotine deprivation model; Parrott, 1999). Interestingly, when asked to report their moods over a normal day, smokers report significant fluctuations in moods, with reports of normal moods during smoking and increased stressful and irritable periods between cigarettes (Parrott, 1994). Smokers' stress levels appear to be similar to non-smokers' only just after having smoked, and become worse than non-smokers during periods of abstinence or between cigarettes (Parrott 2006). This suggests that smokers need to smoke simply to experience positive mood levels similar to non-smokers, and that the stress and irritability they experience between cigarettes are withdrawal symptoms caused by their dependence on nicotine (Schachter, 1978; Parrott & Murphy, 2012).

Prevalence of use

After alcohol, nicotine is the second most widely used drug worldwide, and kills up to half of its users (WHO,

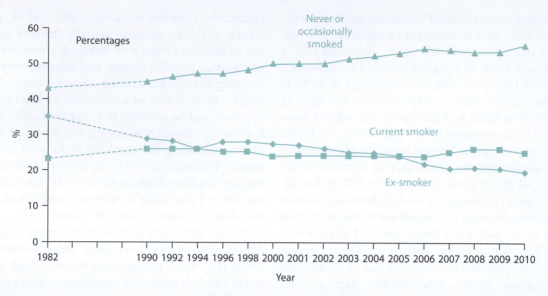

FIGURE 9.6 *Cigarette smoking status among adults in England, 1982 and 1990–2010.*
Source: From The Office for National Statistics (2012). General Lifestyle Survey 2010. Copyright © 2012, re-used with permission of The Office of National Statistics.

2013). About one-third of the adult global population smokes and among teenagers aged 13–15 years worldwide, about one in five smokes. While the rate of smoking is gradually falling in developed nations, it is rising by 3.4 per cent per year in the developing world (WHO, 2004), and nearly 80 per cent of the world's 1 billion smokers live in low- and middle-income countries (WHO, 2013). Evidence suggests that around 50 per cent of those who start smoking in their adolescent years will go on to smoke for at least a further 15–20 years. Figure 9.6 shows that in England the number of smokers has decreased steadily since 1982, with around 20 per cent of adults still reporting smoking regularly in 2010. The level of use in those people who do smoke is also still unacceptably high, with male smokers reporting an average 13.3 cigarettes a day, compared with 12.1 a day for women (UK Government Statistics, 2010) – and these figures are worrying when we come to look at the adverse long-term health consequences of smoking (see below). The overall decrease in smoking prevalence since 1980 seems to be mainly due to the increase in people who have never smoked or only occasionally smoked, with the proportion of adults who have never smoked rising from 43 per cent in 1982 to 55 per cent in 2010 (UK Government Statistics, 2010). A quarter of children in the UK aged between 11 and 15 have tried smoking at least once and, in 2011, 5 per cent of children were regular smokers.

It is worth noting that almost two-thirds of smokers in the UK said they wanted to give up, but over half said it would be difficult to go without a cigarette for a day, and one of the main DSM-5 criteria for substance use disorder is repeated unsuccessful attempts to control use of the substance. Finally, legislation prohibiting smoking in workplaces and enclosed public areas is being introduced

in many countries across the world, and was introduced in England in 2007. The effect of this legislation has been to significantly reduce exposure to second-hand smoke (SHS exposure among children declined by nearly 70 per cent), to decrease the number of hospital admissions for cardiac problems, and it is associated with a statistically significant increase in the number of smokers making an attempt to quit (Bauld, 2011).

Tobacco use disorder

The diagnostic criteria for **tobacco use disorder** are given in DSM-5 Summary Table 9.2, and associated features supporting diagnosis include smoking within 30 minutes of waking, smoking daily, smoking more cigarettes per day, and waking at night to smoke. When taken for the first time, nicotine may cause nausea and dizziness, and it may have a more intense effect when taken first thing in the morning. However, with repeated use, these effects become significantly weaker as a tolerance to the drug builds up. Abstinence or restricted access to nicotine produces a well-defined *withdrawal syndrome*. This consists of dysphoric or depressed mood, insomnia, irritability, frustration, anger, anxiety, difficulty concentrating, restlessness and impatience, decreased heart rate, and increased appetite or weight gain. A heavy smoker can exhibit these symptoms after only a few hours voluntary or enforced abstinence (such as on an airplane journey).

Using the DSM-IV nicotine dependence criteria, it is estimated that the 12-month rate for tobacco use disorder in the US is around 13 per cent in adults, and has different prevalence rates in different ethnic groups,

> **tobacco use disorder** A problematic pattern of tobacco use leading to clinically significant impairment or distress.

DSM-5 SUMMARY TABLE 9.2 *Criteria for tobacco use disorder*

- A pattern of tobacco use causing impairment or distress leading to at least two of the following within a 12 month period:
  - Tobacco is taken in greater amounts or for longer than was intended
  - A continuing desire or unsuccessful efforts to control tobacco use
  - A lot of time is spent in acquiring and using tobacco
  - Craving, or a strong desire to use tobacco
  - Tobacco use results in a failure to fulfil major life roles at work, home and so on
  - Persistent tobacco use despite the effect on interpersonal, recreational or social interactions or despite having an ongoing physical or psychological problem that is likely to have been caused or made worse by tobacco
  - Tolerance symptoms associated with high tobacco use
  - Withdrawal symptoms associated with high tobacco use

with Native Americans being highest (23 per cent) and Hispanics lowest (6 per cent) (DSM-5, 2013). Tobacco use disorder is also found to be comorbid with a range of other psychiatric disorders, with the most common being alcohol/substance use disorder, depressive, bipolar, anxiety and personality disorders, and ADHD (DSM-5, 2013), with comorbidity ranging from 22 to 32 per cent in these cases.

The costs of nicotine use

Like many addictive drugs, arguably the main costs of nicotine dependence are those to physical health. Smoking is the single largest preventable cause of disease and premature death in the world and kills nearly 6 million people each year (WHO, 2013), and it is a significant factor in heart disease, stroke and chronic lung cancer, cancer of the larynx, oesophagus, mouth, bladder, cervix, pancreas, and kidneys. In the UK, over 300,000 patients are admitted to NHS hospitals every year due to

---

FOCUS POINT 9.2

QUITTING SMOKING

As we have already noted, smokers find it extremely hard to quit the habit – even though they may be fully aware of the health implications of their habit, and even when they themselves are already suffering from smoking-related diseases. Since around 80–90 per cent of all smokers would meet DSM-IV-TR criteria for substance dependence, successfully treating nicotine dependence is likely to need a range of approaches, including psychological and pharmaceutical.

Smoking is difficult to treat because (1) smokers are constantly suffering nicotine withdrawal symptoms when not smoking, and this drives the craving for further cigarettes, and (2) smokers come to use cigarettes as a way of dealing with any negative mood (not just those associated with withdrawal), so any life problems that cause negative affect will also trigger the desire to smoke.

For these reasons, treatment programmes for smokers tend to have poor success rates and high relapse rates, and only around 10–20 per cent of those who try to quit on their own are still abstinent a year later (Lichtenstein & Glasgow, 1992). There are some important predictors of whether an attempt to quit will fail, and these include (1) a diagnosis of major depression (Glassman, 1993) – 50 per cent of smokers who make repeated unsuccessful attempts to quit can be diagnosed with major depression, (2) regular bouts of negative mood which increase cigarette cravings, and (3) whether the person has to spend periods of time in environments where smoking is common and cigarettes are readily available (e.g. pubs and bars).

Some of the main forms of intervention for smoking are the following:

NICOTINE REPLACEMENT THERAPY (NRT)

This aims to replace the nicotine from cigarettes by means of skin patches, chewing gum, lozenges, inhalators or nasal sprays. Preliminary studies suggest that **nicotine replacement therapy** is significantly more effective than a placebo, and around 17 per cent of people using NRT have fully abstained for 12 months following the treatment (NICE, 2002).

> **nicotine replacement therapy** Aims to replace the nicotine from cigarettes by means of skin patches, chewing gum, lozenges, inhalators or nasal sprays.

BUPROPION

This is a mild antidepressant drug that acts as a selective inhibitor of dopamine and noradrenalin reuptake, and is thought to act directly on the brain pathways involved in dependence and withdrawal. Bupropion is significantly more effective than a placebo control, and 19 per cent of those taking the drug had not smoked in the 12 months following the treatment (NICE, 2002).

AVERSION THERAPY

This treatment attempts to replace the pleasant feelings associated with smoking a cigarette with negative consequences such as feeling ill or nauseous. One form of aversion therapy is known as *rapid smoking*, where the smoker puffs on a cigarette roughly every 4–5 seconds until they feel ill and cannot take another puff (Spiegler & Guevremont, 2003). This type of treatment is known to reduce craving, but has had limited success at controlling actual smoking behaviour (Houtsmuller & Stitzer, 1999).

COGNITIVE BEHAVIOUR THERAPY (CBT)

Because depression and negative mood appear to be factors that are regularly associated with failure to quit smoking, recent treatments have adapted CBT of depression for use in smoking cessation programmes. In this case, CBT is used to help smokers develop alternative strategies for dealing with depression and negative mood that do not involve a return to smoking. Such interventions have been shown to produce higher rates of abstinence than standard health education interventions (Hall, Reus, Munoz, Sees et al., 1998).

COMPLEMENTARY THERAPIES

Two forms of complementary therapy frequently used by smokers in order to try and quit are *hypnotherapy* and *acupuncture*. There is some evidence that hypnotic and suggestion-based approaches do yield higher rates of abstinence relative to waiting list and no treatment controls, but there is little systematic evidence to suggest that hypnotherapy is more effective than equivalent placebos (Green & Lynn, 2000; Villano & White, 2004) – so those 'stop smoking in one session' signs outside your local holistic health centre might be somewhat misleading! There is some evidence that compared with control participants, acupuncture can help smokers to reduce their levels of smoking over a number of years (He, Medbo & Hostmark, 2001). However, there is little more than anecdotal evidence that acupuncture is an effective means of quitting smoking (Villano & White, 2004).

smoking-related diseases (Royal College of Physicians, 2002), and in the UK around 85,000 deaths were caused by smoking between 1998 and 2002. In 2011, around 18 per cent of all deaths in the UK were estimated to be attributable to smoking (The Health & Social Care Information Centre, 2011). It is also estimated that around half of all teenagers who are currently smoking will die from diseases caused by tobacco if they continue to smoke. One-quarter will die before they reach 70 years of age and will lose, on average, 21 years of life (Peto, 1994). The economic cost of tobacco-related health problems is staggering. In the UK, the treatment of smoking-related disorders was estimated to cost the NHS around £5.2 billion in 2005/6 (The Health & Social Care Information Centre, 2011), including £127 million to treat lung cancer alone (Parrott, Godfrey, Heather, Clark & Ryan, 2006).

Finally, the health hazards associated with smoking extend beyond those who smoke. Cigarettes give off smoke that contains a complex mix of thousands of chemicals – many of which can have toxic effects if inhaled. This, of course, represents a health risk to those non-smokers who share environments with smokers, and this is known as **passive smoking** from **second-hand smoke**. Just 30 minutes of exposure to second-hand smoke is enough to reduce blood flow to the heart, and non-smokers who are exposed to second-hand smoke in the home have a 25 per cent increased risk of heart disease. In particular, passive smoking is a substantial danger to health in the case of babies and young children, causing increases in

passive smoking The breathing in of air that contains other people's smoke.

second-hand smoke A person's exhaled smoke, inhaled by another person.

respiratory infections and asthma attacks (Cowley, 1992; Skorge, Eagen, Eide, Gulsvik & Bakke, 2005). Across the world it is estimated that 603,000 premature deaths occurred in 2004 as a result of passive smoking (WHO, 2010), although in the UK the introduction of legislation in 2007 banning smoking in workplaces and enclosed spaces has significantly reduced exposure to second-hand smoke (Bauld, 2011).

Summary

A significant number of regular smokers meet the diagnostic criteria for nicotine dependence, which makes it an activity of concern for both clinical psychologists and medical doctors. In part, the smoking habit appears to be developed by the effect of nicotine on dopamine reward pathways and maintained by the smoker's need to reverse the unpleasant nicotine withdrawal effects that are experienced between cigarettes or during abstinence. Tobacco use disorder does not have many of the short-term costs associated with alcohol dependence (such as impairment of occupational and social functioning), but it does have significant medium- to long-term health costs, and is the single largest cause of premature death worldwide.

9.3.3   Cannabis Use Disorder

The drug **cannabis** is derived from the hemp plant *cannabis sativa*. The most powerful of the cannabis group of drugs is **hashish**, and a weaker derivative – known as **marijuana** – consists of

cannabis A natural drug derived from the hemp plant, cannabis sativa.

hashish The most powerful of the cannabis group of drugs.

marijuana A derivative of cannabis consisting of dried and crushed cannabis leaves.

For a video on cannabis go to www.wiley-psychopathology.com/video/ch9

dried and crushed cannabis leaves. Cannabis is normally smoked after being rolled into a cigarette known as a 'joint'. However, it can also be eaten. The effects of cannabis are to produce feelings of relaxation (at low doses), euphoria, sociability and sharpened perceptions that sometimes result in mild sensory hallucinations (known as being 'spaced out'), but it can also cause difficulties in concentration and impairment of memory. Although it is primarily classified as a sedative/depressant because of its relaxing effects, it can sometimes also have stimulant effects, and make some individuals agitated and paranoid. For example, when larger doses are taken, cannabis may exacerbate an already frightened, stressed or paranoid state, causing anxiety and distress. Sensory distortions may also give the user feelings of depersonalization similar to those experienced during panic attacks (see section 6.3), and some cannabis users become gripped by feelings of panic and anxiety.

The main active ingredient in cannabis is THC (Δ^9-tetrahydrocannabinol), and the amount of THC in cannabis will determine the strength of its psychoactive effects. THC is generally believed to have low addictive properties, although it is still possible for regular cannabis users to become dependent on the drug (see below). THC has a mild stimulant effect by increasing heart rate, and has its psychoactive effects by influencing cannabinoid brain receptors CB1 and CB2 found in the hippocampus, cerebellum and striatum (Ameri, 1999). These receptors appear to influence levels of dopamine in those brain areas known to play a role in mediating reward and pleasure experiences, and this seems to be the route by which cannabis has its most important positive psychoactive effects.

Cannabis was used in the mid-20th century for its supposed medicinal properties, which included its analgesic effects (see Focus Point 9.3), but it was smoked mainly for pleasure. It is now an illegal drug in most countries even though its effects on behaviour and health are less severe than many other illicit drugs. There is some concern, however, that regular cannabis use may have permanent effects on cognitive functioning, and psychological and physical health (Kalant, 2004; Iversen, 2005; Johns, 2001), but we will discuss the relevant evidence on these issues later in this section.

For a video on the medical use of cannabis go to www.wiley-psychopathology.com/video/ch9

Prevalence of use

Cannabis remains the most widely used illicit substance globally, with an estimated annual prevalence in 2010 of 2.6–5.0 per cent of the adult population (between 119 million and 224 million users aged 15–64 years), and the use of cannabis has increased significantly since the 1960s – especially in developed countries in North America,

THE MEDICAL APPLICATIONS OF CANNABIS

Long before it became an illegal drug, cannabis was used primarily for medicinal purposes. It was known to have relaxing and analgesic effects, and was used in the 1970s to reduce the nausea and lack of appetite caused by chemotherapy in cancer patients (Sallan, Zinberg & Frei, 1975). Neurophysiological studies have shown that cannabis has moderate analgesic effects, and these are caused by the active ingredient in cannabis, THC, helping to block pain signals reaching the brain (Richardson, Kilo & Hargreaves, 1998). These analgesic effects are more powerful than codeine and of longer duration.

Because of the potential medical applications of cannabis as a powerful analgesic, there have been significant lobbies in many countries to legalize cannabis for medical use. In a UK survey, individuals reported the medicinal use of cannabis with chronic pain, multiple sclerosis, depression, arthritis, and neuropathy (Ware, Adams & Guy, 2005). Cannabis has also been involved in the treatment of patients with seizures, glaucoma, asthma and anxiety (Mather, 2001). Recent outcome studies that have employed double-blind randomized controlled trials and placebo controls in patients with neuropathic pain or multiple sclerosis have demonstrated that cannabis reduced the severity of reported pain significantly more in the cannabis treated than in the placebo group (Berman, Symonds & Birch, 2004; Zajicek, Fox, Sanders, Wright et al., 2003).

Problems with the medical application of cannabis are (1) that it is still an illegal drug in most developed countries, and (2) smoking cannabis may not be the healthiest way to take the drug given the potential health risks associated with smoking (Mather, 2001). However, many governments are now licensing the use of cannabis-based drugs for use with specific patient groups. For example, in 2005, the UK Home Office licensed the drug Sativex for individual patient use (such as those with multiple sclerosis, where cannabis has been shown to ease stiffness, muscle spasms and pain). Sativex avoids the problems of smoking by providing the active ingredients THC and cannabidol in a mouth spray.

Western Europe and Australasia. In 2010, the annual prevalence rate for cannabis use was highest in Oceania (Australia and New Zealand) at 9.1–14.6 per cent, followed by North America (10.8 per cent), Western and Central Europe (7 per cent), and West and Central Africa (5.2–13.5 per cent) (WHO, 2012). In the UK, cannabis has around 2–5 million regular users, with around 15 million having admitted to using it (Atha, 2005). In the US and Europe, cannabis use increased dramatically in the 1970s and early 1980s, increased again during the 1990s, but has remained fairly stable since then (Johnston, O'Malley & Bachman, 2001). However, cannabis use is concentrated mainly among young adults (aged 15–34 years), with 20 per cent of this age range in the UK admitting to cannabis use in the previous 12 months (Department of Health, 2004).

Cannabis use disorder

Over the past few decades, the cannabis available on the street has become stronger and in many cases THC content has risen from 1–5 per cent to 10–15 per cent. As a result, there is increasing evidence for a cannabis abuse and dependence syndrome in many users. For example, tolerance and withdrawal effects have been reported in some individuals who use cannabis regularly. Objective studies have indicated that cannabis can cause tolerance effects, and individuals who use cannabis daily over months or years may develop a need for more potent forms of cannabis that would be toxic to most non-users (Nowlan & Cohen, 1977). In heavy users, dependence is indicated by withdrawal during periods of abstention, and these include flu-like symptoms, restlessness and irritability (Kouri & Pope, 2000). Symptoms usually begin within 1–3 days after cessation of use and peak between days 2 and 6, and usually last a maximum of 14 days (Budney, Moore, Vandrey & Hughes, 2003).

Individuals who regularly use cannabis can develop all the general diagnostic features of a substance use disorder, and DSM-5 provides a specific set of diagnostic criteria for **cannabis use disorder** (see DSM-5 Summary Table 9.3). Cannabis use disorder is often the only substance use disorder experienced by an individual, and they will often report that it's being used to cope with mood, sleep, pain, or other physiological and psychological problems. In the US, the 12-month prevalence rate of cannabis use disorder is approximately 3.4 per cent among 12- to 17-year-olds, and 1.5 per cent amongst adults (DSM-5, 2013).

An individual diagnosed with cannabis use disorder can spend much of their time daily acquiring and smoking the drug and this may severely interfere with family, school, work or recreational activities. Signs of

cannabis use disorder Disorder usually develops over a period of time that is characterized by continuing increased use of cannabis and reduction in pleasurable effects.

DSM-5 SUMMARY TABLE 9.3 *Criteria for cannabis use disorder*

- A pattern of cannabis use causing impairment or distress leading to at least two of the following within a 12 month period:
  - Cannabis is taken in greater amounts or for longer than was intended
  - A continuing desire or unsuccessful efforts to control cannabis use
  - A lot of time is spent in acquiring, using and recovering from the effects of cannabis
  - Craving, or a strong desire to use cannabis
  - Cannabis use results in a failure to fulfil major life roles at work, home and so on
  - Persistent cannabis use despite the effect on interpersonal, recreational or social interactions or despite having an ongoing physical or psychological problem that is likely to have been caused or made worse by cannabis
  - Tolerance symptoms associated with high cannabis use
  - Withdrawal symptoms associated with high cannabis use

cannabis intoxication are often reported and the symptoms of intoxication after recent use of cannabis begin with a 'high' feeling followed by symptoms that include euphoria with inappropriate laughter and grandiosity, sedation, lethargy, impairment in short-term memory, difficulty carrying out complex mental processes, impaired judgement, distorted sensory perceptions, impaired motor performance, and the feeling that time is passing slowly (DSM-5, 2013, p.516). Occasionally, cannabis intoxication can be associated with severe anxiety, dysphoria and social withdrawal. Cannabis use disorder usually develops over a period of time that is characterized by continuing increased use and reduction in pleasurable effects.

cannabis intoxication Symptoms of intoxication after recent use of cannabis begin with a 'high' feeling followed by symptoms that include euphoria with inappropriate laughter and grandiosity, sedation, lethargy, impairment in short-term memory, impaired judgment, distorted sensory perception and impaired motor performance.

Studies have identified a number of risk factors for developing cannabis dependence, and these include

1. age of onset – the earlier that first use is recorded the higher the likelihood of cannabis dependence (Taylor, Malone, Iacono & McGue, 2002),

2. tobacco smoking and regularity of cannabis use are both independent predictors of cannabis dependence (Coffey, Carlin, Lynskey, Li & Patton, 2003),

3. impulsiveness and unpredictability of moods (Simons & Carey, 2002),

4. a diagnosis of conduct disorder and emotional disorders during childhood (Meltzer, Gatwood, Goodman & Ford, 2003), and

5. dependence on alcohol and other drugs (Degenhardt, Hall & Lynskey, 2001).

Like many substance use disorders, cannabis use disorder is a risk factor for a number of other psychiatric diagnoses, and these include anxiety and panic disorder (Thomas, 1996), major depression (Chen, Wagner & Anthony, 2002), increased tendency for suicide (Beautrais, Joyce & Mulder, 1999), and schizophrenia (Degenhardt & Hall, 2001). This once more begs the question of whether individuals suffering psychological problems are likely to resort to cannabis use as a form of self-medication, or whether cannabis use is linked to a future increase in psychiatric diagnoses (Di Forti, Morrison, Butt & Murray, 2007). The evidence on this is far from clear, although prospective studies indicate that (1) there is a causal link between regular cannabis use and the development of psychotic symptoms typical of schizophrenia (Fergusson, Horwood & Ridder, 2005; see also Focus Point 7.7), and (2) daily cannabis users may double their risk of subsequently developing symptoms of anxiety and depression (Patton, Coffey, Carlin, Degenhardt et al., 2002). Also, in a longitudinal New Zealand study, McGee, Williams, Poulton & Moffitt (2000) found that mental health problems at age 15 years were a predictor of cannabis use at age 18 years, but that cannabis use at age 18 predicted increased risk of mental health problems at age 21 years. While these studies tend to suggest that regular cannabis use indeed predicts increased risk for subsequent mental health problems, the causal relationship may not be direct. For example, both heavy cannabis use and mental health problems are also associated with factors like low socio-economic status, childhood behavioural problems, parental neglect, and suchlike, and it may be these factors that act as causes of both cannabis use and subsequent mental health problems.

The costs of cannabis use disorder

We have just discussed the possibility that regular heavy cannabis use may be associated with increased risk for a number of mental health problems such as anxiety, depression and schizophrenia. Such use is also associated with a range of cognitive deficits and with health problems.

Regular cannabis use is associated with a range of cognitive deficits while individuals are under the influence of the drug, and these include deficits in reaction time, decreased attention span, deficits in verbal ability, slower problem-solving ability, and loss of short-term memory (Lundqvist, 2005; Kalant, 2004). This has important implications for cannabis users when complex psychomotor skills are required while engaging in potentially dangerous activities. One such activity is driving, and there is evidence that cannabis use does affect both driving skills and driving safety (Smiley, 1999). Laboratory studies have demonstrated that perceptual and motor speed and

accuracy are significantly affected after smoking cannabis (Kurzthaler, Hummer, Miller, Sperner-Unterweger et al., 1999). Other studies have looked at the role of cannabis use in drivers involved in accidents. For example, the active ingredient in cannabis, THC, is found in the blood of impaired or accident-involved drivers with a frequency that significantly exceeds that in the general population (Kalant, 2004), and Scandinavian studies have indicated that 1 in 10 of drivers arrested for impaired driving tested positive for cannabis (Christophersen, Ceder, Kristinsson, Lillsunde et al., 1999; Steentoft, Muller, Worm & Toft, 2000). However, we must still be cautious about what we conclude from these findings, because many of those involved in car accidents are young risk-taking males who are more likely to be using cannabis and other substances (such as alcohol), so cannabis use may not necessarily be the main cause of accidents in these groups.

We know that cannabis causes cognitive deficits while the individual is under the influence of the drug, but does regular cannabis use cause long-term, permanent damage to cognitive skills and achievement generally? First, cannabis use is associated with a syndrome of underachievement, in which regular users exhibit lower IQ (Fried, Watkinson, James & Gray, 2002), lower educational achievement (Gruber, Pope, Hudson & Yurgelun-Todd, 2003), and motivational deficits (Lane, Cherek, Pietras & Steinberg, 2005). However, there is very little evidence for permanent neuropsychological deficits in cannabis users (Gonzalez, Carey & Grant, 2002), and any cognitive deficits found during cannabis use do not appear to persist after the individual stops using the drug (Iversen, 2005). However, regular heavy users are likely to have lower educational achievement and lower income than non-users, but this may be due to a number of factors, including

1. use of cannabis during school and college years impairing educational performance and subsequent career prospects,

2. heavy cannabis use being associated with deprivation and poor educational opportunities, or

3. an **amotivational syndrome** in cannabis users, in which those who take up regular cannabis use are more likely to be those who exhibit apathy, loss of ambition and difficulty concentrating (Maugh, 1982).

> **amotivational syndrome** A syndrome in which those who take up regular cannabis use are more likely to be those who exhibit apathy, loss of ambition and difficulty concentrating.

There is also some debate about whether regular cannabis use has long-term physical health consequences. First, cannabis generally contains more tar than normal cigarettes, and so presents a significant risk for smoking-related diseases such as cancer. Studies have suggested that cannabis smoke can cause mutations and cancerous changes (Marselos & Karamanakos,

1999), but there is only modest epidemiological evidence suggesting that cannabis users are more prone to cancer than non-users (Sidney, Quesenberry, Friedman & Tekawa, 1997; Zhang, Morgenstern, Spitz, Tashkin *et al.*, 1999). Second, regular cannabis use does appear to be associated with a reduction in the male hormone testosterone (Grinspoon, Bakalar, Zimmer *et al.*, 1997), and there is a possibility that this could cause impaired sexual functioning in the young males who are the main users of cannabis. Third, chronic cannabis use does appear to impair the efficiency of the body's immune system (Nahas, Paton & Harvey, 1999), although as yet there has been no obvious effect of this found on the rate of physical illnesses in cannabis users. Overall, the most probable adverse effects of cannabis on health generally include a dependence syndrome, increased risk of motor vehicle crashes, impaired respiratory function, cardiovascular disease, and adverse effects on psychosocial development and mental health (Hall & Degenhardt, 2009).

9.3.4   Stimulant Use Disorders

Stimulants are substances that increase central nervous system activity and increase blood pressure and heart rate. As a result, they facilitate alertness, provide feelings of energy and confidence, and speed up thinking and behaviour. One of the drugs we have already discussed has stimulant effects, and that is nicotine. In this section, we will discuss three more stimulant drugs, namely **cocaine**, **amphetamine** and **caffeine**. The popular recreational drug MDMA (3, 4-methyl-enedioxymethamphetamine) – better known as *Ecstasy* – is also a stimulant similar to amphetamine, but it also has hallucinogenic effects and will be discussed later in this chapter.

> **cocaine** A natural stimulant derived from the coca plant of South America which, after processing, is an odourless, white powder that can be injected, snorted or, in some forms (e.g. crack cocaine), smoked.

> **amphetamines** A group of synthetic drugs used primarily as a central nervous system stimulant. Common forms are amphetamine itself (benzedrine), dextro-amphetamine (dexedrine) and metham-phetamine (methedrine).

> **caffeine** A central nervous system stimulant that increases alertness and motor activity and combats fatigue; found in a number of different products, including coffee, tea, chocolate and some over-the-counter cold remedies and weight-loss aids.

Stimulant use is most common among individuals aged 12–25 years, and first regular use occurs on average at age 23 years (DSM-5, 2013). Stimulants are often first used for purposes such as controlling weight or to improve work or school performance, and can be used daily or in 'binges' in which high doses are used every hour or so. Addiction can occur very rapidly, and individuals using amphetamines or cocaine can develop a stimulant use disorder as rapidly as in 1 week, and sufferers can often develop conditioned responses to drug-related stimuli (e.g. craving when seeing white powder) which contributes to relapse and treatment difficulties (Volkow, Wang, Telang, Fowler *et al.*, 2006). The estimated 12-month prevalence of amphetamine-type stimulant disorders in the USA is 0.2 per cent among 12–17 year-olds and 0.2 per cent among adults (DSM-5, 2013, p.564). Risk factors for developing stimulant use disorder include comorbid bipolar disorder, schizophrenia, and antisocial personality disorder. Childhood conduct disorder is also associated with later development of stimulant-related disorders.

Cocaine

Cocaine is a natural stimulant derived from the coca plant of South America. After it has been processed, cocaine is an odourless, white powder that can be injected, snorted or, in some purer forms (e.g. **crack cocaine**), smoked (which is known as **free-basing**). When used for recreational purposes it is usually snorted and absorbed into the bloodstream through the mucus membrane of the nose.

> For a video on cocaine go to www.wiley-psychopathology.com/video/ch9

> **crack cocaine** Free-based cocaine boiled down into crystalline balls.

> **free-basing** The inhalation of cocaine by smoking.

The 'rush' caused by a standard dose of cocaine takes approximately 8 minutes to take effect, and lasts for about 20 to 30 minutes. The 'rush' often brings feelings of euphoria, and has its initial effects on the brain to make users feel excited and energized. After these initial effects, the drug then affects other parts of the central nervous system to produce increased alertness, arousal and wakefulness. The main effects of cocaine are caused by the drug blocking the reuptake of dopamine in the brain. This facilitates neural activity and results in feelings of pleasure and confidence (Volkow, Wang, Fischman, Foltin *et al.*, 1997) (see Focus Point 9.7 later in the chapter).

Prevalence of use   The lifetime prevalence rate of cocaine use in developed countries is between 1 and 3 per cent (WHO, 2006). In European countries this varies between 0.5 and 6 per cent, with Spain and the UK being at the upper end of this range (Department of Health, 2004), and this rises to 14.4 per cent in the USA according to the US National Household Survey of 2002. Use of powder cocaine in the UK was stable at around 2.2 per cent between 2010 and 2012. Use by young adults aged 15–34 is around 4 per cent in the UK, with users either discontinuing use after a brief period of experimentation, or continuing to use it at weekends and in recreational settings (such as bars and clubs).

Cocaine use disorder   Because the effects of cocaine last only for around 30 minutes, there is a need for frequent doses to maintain the 'rush' caused by the drug. This means the user may spend large sums of money on the drug in relatively short periods of time, and may even resort to theft and fraud to obtain funds to buy the drug. **Cocaine dependence** occurs when the individual finds it difficult to resist using the drug whenever it is available (the diagnostic criteria for cocaine use disorder are based on those in Table 9.1), and this in turn leads to neglect of important responsibilities such as those associated with work or child care. There is even some evidence from animal studies that a single exposure to cocaine induces long-term changes in

cocaine dependence Occurs when the individual finds it difficult to resist using the drug whenever it is available and leads to neglect of important responsibilities.

dopamine neurons in the brain, leaving the casual user vulnerable to longer-term drug dependence (Ungless, Whistler, Malenka & Bonci, 2001). Tolerance occurs with repeated use, requiring larger doses and greater expense for similar effects. When not taking cocaine, severe withdrawal symptoms can occur, particularly hypersomnia, increased appetite, negative and depressed mood, and these increase the craving for further use or relapse during abstinence. Erratic behaviour, social isolation and sexual dysfunction are regular characteristics of long-term cocaine dependence, and the long-term user may well develop symptoms of other psychological disorders, such as major depression, social phobia, panic disorder, generalized anxiety disorder, and eating disorders.

CLIENT'S PERSPECTIVE 9.1
COCAINE DEPENDENCY

It all began in 1983 when I first starting doing cocaine. At first it was something that I did about once a week, usually on a Friday night and into Saturday. I would use it to go out to the bars and go drinking. I would buy a gram, and usually there would be a little left over for Saturday morning. This went on for several months and as I came in contact with more people who liked coke, I would start to split grams with people during the week. This increased until I was doing that every day. This took about a year to develop. I was fixing business machines and would collect a little money every day. By the second year I would buy coke at least once a day. I thought that I would try selling it, to help with the costs, which were starting to stack up. But, the coke I would buy would always end up being snorted by myself and a couple of close friends. By the third year nearly all of my money was going for coke. Food became secondary to me and I would skip days' eating to be able to afford coke. I started to hang out with a guy who shot his coke up with needles. We became best friends. I would fix a machine and he would be waiting for me in my car. We would instantly go and buy coke with the money that I had just made, occasionally stopping somewhere for a sandwich, which was all that I would be eating by that time.

This went on until I was made homeless but we managed to get a cheap flat to share. I started to get concerned that I had a habit that I could not kick. I saw many people wreck their lives during this period. In fact my business was in serious trouble as I never paid my bills. Part of the problem was that coke was really 'the' thing to do in this town at the time. Seemed everyone I knew was into

it. It was a real social drug. I stopped doing it at bars, and would go back to the flat and just lay around doing coke all the time. My friend shot his, I snorted mine. In desperation to make more money I expanded the territory that I was working and would drive 80 miles to do service calls. I was doing about a gram a day; my friend was doing the same in his veins. My attitude in life became one of giving up and thinking that I would die eventually, but that was OK, as long as I could do coke till I did.

Alan's story

For a video on cocaine: risk and recovery go to **www.wiley-psychopathology.com/video/ch9**

Clinical Commentary

Like many people, Alan began using cocaine as a recreational drug, taking it mainly at weekends and when socialising in bars. Because the drug has a relatively brief 'high' (around 30 minutes), users require more and more regular doses in order to maintain the euphoria generated by cocaine, and the cost of this leads to significant financial problems. As is typical of individuals with cocaine dependency, Alan began to neglect his responsibilities, including failing to pay bills and losing his home. Eventually, psychological dependency was complete when his life revolved entirely around acquiring and taking the drug.

The costs of cocaine use disorder Apart from the negative effects of regular use on occupational, social and educational functioning, cocaine also has a number of adverse cognitive and health effects. For example, cocaine abusers regularly show evidence of deficits in decision making, judgement and working memory (Simon, Domier, Sim, Richardson et al., 2002; Pace-Schott, Stickgold, Muzur, Wigren et al., 2005), and there is evidence from animals studies that regular cocaine use also disrupts learning – although it is still unclear whether these effects are permanent deficits caused by cocaine use (Kantak, Udo, Ugalde, Luzzo et al., 2005). There is also accumulating evidence that cocaine use by pregnant mothers can also cause significant developmental deficits in their newborn offspring, and this is manifested as retarded development in the first 2 years of life (Singer, Arendt, Minnes, Farkas et al., 2002), a higher incidence of attention deficit hyperactivity disorder (ADHD) at age 6 (Linares, Singer, Kirchner, Short et al., 2006), and deficits in visual motor development (Arendt, Short, Singer, Minnes et al., 2004). At least a partial cause of these effects may be the role of cocaine in causing irregularities in placental blood-flow during pregnancy. Finally, because of its effects on blood pressure and cardiovascular functioning, high doses of cocaine can cause heart problems and brain seizures, although it is unusual for death to be solely attributed to cocaine abuse. However, cocaine may be an important contributor to death by aggravating existing cardiovascular problems (e.g. arrhythmias, heart attacks, cerebral haemorrhages). In a UK study, 30.4 per cent of 112 regular male cocaine users with an average age of 44 years showed evidence of coronary artery aneurysms, compared with only 7.6 per cent of non-cocaine users (Satran, Bart, Henry, Murad et al., 2005), indicating an important and significant increase in cardiovascular disease in regular cocaine users.

Amphetamines

Amphetamines are a group of synthetic drugs used primarily as a central nervous system stimulant. Common forms are amphetamine itself (benzedrine), dextroamphetamine (dexedrine), and methamphetamine (methedrine). These are highly addictive drugs that are used primarily to generate feelings of energy and confidence, and to reduce feelings of weariness and boredom. They were originally synthesized in the 1920s as an inhalant to aid breathing, but came to be used later as a means of appetite control and to combat feelings of lethargy and depression. When used in small doses, amphetamines enable individuals to feel alert, confident and energised. They also help motor coordination but, contrary to popular belief, do not help intellectual skills (Tinklenberg, 1971). They also have a number of physical effects, such as increasing blood pressure and heart rate, but can cause headaches, fevers, tremors and nausea.

Amphetamines have their effects by causing the release of neurotransmitters norepinephrine and dopamine, and simultaneously blocking their reuptake. They are normally taken in a pill or capsule form, but in the case of methamphetamine it can be taken intravenously or by 'snorting'. In its clear, crystal form, the latter is known as 'ice', 'crank' or 'crystal meth', and dependence on methamphetamine can be particularly rapid. With the use of higher doses, and during withdrawal, users experience a range of negative symptoms, including anxiety, paranoia, irritability, confusion and restlessness (Kaplan & Sadock, 1991).

Prevalence of use Amphetamine use in the UK is around 2 per cent, and has fallen significantly since 1996 (Home Office, 2012). Worldwide, amphetamine-type stimulants (excluding Ecstasy) had an estimated prevalence of 0.3–1.2 per cent, and is the second most widely used group of drugs (WHO, 2012). According to DSM-IV-TR, the lifetime prevalence of amphetamine use disorders is around 1.5 per cent. The World Health Organisation estimates that there are between 14 million and 52.5 million estimated global users, and amphetamine-type stimulants account for around 16 per cent of worldwide illicit drug abuse.

FOCUS POINT 9.4

COCAINE STOPPED ENTWISTLE'S HEART

On December 11, 2002, The Who bassist John Entwistle died after taking cocaine that caused his already diseased heart to fail. The 57-year-old was found dead in a hotel room in Las Vegas when the band was about to embark on a US tour. Doctors reported evidence of high blood pressure and high cholesterol, which had been compounded by smoking. The coroner recorded that cocaine in his body had compounded heart disease that was already present.

Clinical Commentary

There are few deaths that are directly attributable to cocaine use, but cocaine is known to exacerbate already existing cardiovascular problems because of its effect on blood-pressure levels and heart rate.

FOCUS POINT 9.5

'BATH SALTS'

© AP/Press Association Images

'Bath salts' is the name for an emerging group of drugs containing synthetic chemicals related to cathinone – which is an amphetamine-like stimulant found in the khat plant. These synthetic cathinone's can produce euphoria and increased sociability and sex drive (Prosser & Nelson, 2012). Typically they are in the form of a white or brown crystalline powder, and are taken orally, inhaled or injected.

The stimulant effects of bath salts are thought to occur by raising dopamine levels in the brain circuits that regulate reward and movement. Until recently, bath salts were cheap and legal in many countries, but they were placed under an emergency ban by the US Drug Enforcement Administration in 2011, and all cathinone substitutes were made illegal in the UK in 2010. They have been linked to a surge in visits to accident and emergency units with common complaints being cardiac symptoms (chest pains, high blood pressure) and psychiatric symptoms such as paranoia, hallucinations and panic attacks.

Being such a new group of drugs, it is difficult to estimate the prevalence of bath salts use, but retrospective hair sample studies of individuals who had tested positive for amphetamines or MDMA in 2009/10 found psychoactive substances similar to cathinone synthetics in 37 per cent of these samples (Rust, Baumgartner, Dally & Kraemer, 2012).

Amphetamine use disorder   Although the effects of amphetamine are longer lasting than other stimulants, such as cocaine, tolerance to amphetamine occurs rapidly and higher and higher doses are needed to achieve similar stimulant effects (Comer, Hart, Ward, Haney *et al.*, 2001). Once high dose usage is achieved, the stimulant effects of amphetamine also become associated with intense, but temporary, psychological symptoms such as anxiety, paranoia, and psychotic episodes resembling schizophrenia (see below). Those who are dependent on **methamphetamine** (so-called 'speed freaks') will often use the drug continuously for a number of days, experiencing a continuous 'high' without eating or sleeping. This will then be followed by a few days feeling depressed and exhausted, but then the cycle starts again. Speed freaks who behave in this way become unpredictable, anxious, paranoid and aggressive, and may be a danger to themselves and others. Dependence is indicated by regular use of the drug whenever it is available, neglect of normal responsibilities associated with work or family, and continuing use when the individual is aware that using the drug is causing family or employment problems. **Amphetamine intoxication** normally begins with a 'high' followed by feelings of euphoria, energy, talkativeness, and alertness — but is equally likely to be followed by stereotyped, repetitive behaviour, anger, physically aggressive behaviour, and impaired judgement. Physical symptoms of intoxication include pupillary dilation, perspiration or chills, nausea or vomiting, chest pains and, in extreme cases, seizures or coma. Withdrawal symptoms can appear within a few hours or a few days of ceasing use of amphetamine, and is associated with depression, fatigue, vivid and unpleasant dreams, insomnia, and increased feelings of agitation.

The costs of amphetamine use disorder   A number of studies using both human and non-human participants have suggested that regular use of amphetamines (especially methamphetamine) may cause long-term central nervous system damage (Frost & Cadet, 2000; Volkow, Chang, Wang, Fowler *et al.*, 2001). Volkow *et al.* (2001) found that chronic methamphetamine use inhibited the production of the neurotransmitter dopamine in the orbitofrontal cortex, and this may play a significant role in maintaining addictive behaviours. For example, the orbitofrontal cortex is associated with compulsive behaviour and with resistance to extinction of a behaviour even when rewards are withdrawn. These effects are very similar to those reported by drug addicts who claim that once they start using a drug such as methamphetamine they cannot stop – even when the drug is no longer pleasurable. There is also evidence from animal studies showing that chronic use of methamphetamine damages both dopamine and serotonin neurotransmitter systems in the brain (Frost & Cadet, 2000), and this

methamphetamine Methedrine, a common form of amphetamine.

amphetamine intoxication Amphetamine use, which normally begins with a 'high' but is equally likely to be followed by stereotyped, repetitive behaviour, anger, physically aggressive behaviour, and impaired judgement.

effect appears to be reflected in slow or poor decision-making in individuals with methamphetamine use disorder (Paulus, Tapert & Schuckit, 2005).

Caffeine

Most readers of this book are probably familiar with taking caffeine in one form or another – as are around 85 per cent of the population of the world. Caffeine can be found in a number of different products, including coffee, tea, chocolate, and some over-the-counter cold remedies and weight-loss aids. Caffeine is a central nervous system stimulant that increases alertness and motor activity and combats fatigue. However, it can also reduce fine motor coordination and cause insomnia, headaches, anxiety and dizziness (Paton & Beer, 2001). Caffeine enters the bloodstream through the stomach and increases brain dopamine levels in a similar way to amphetamine and cocaine. Caffeine in the body reaches its peak concentration within an hour, and has a half-life of 6 hours, which implies that if you have a cup of coffee at 4 p.m. that contains 200mg of caffeine, you will still have around 100mg of caffeine in your body 6 hours later at 10 p.m. So while caffeine may have beneficial short-term effects on alertness, it may have detrimental longer term effects which may prevent you from sleeping. The average caffeine intake per day in most of the developing world is less than 50mg, compared with highs of 400mg in the UK and other European countries. It is taken more by men than women, and caffeine intake usually decreases with age, with older people showing more intense reactions and reporting greater interference with sleep.

Although caffeine consumption is almost a daily occurrence for most people, it can have both positive and detrimental effects. On the positive side, the benefits of moderate caffeine intake are increased task focus through alertness, attention and cognitive function, and also elevated mood and fewer depressive symptoms and lower risk of suicide. However, high doses of caffeine can induce psychotic and manic symptoms, and, most commonly, anxiety (Broderick & Benjamin, 2004). These anxiety-generating effects of high doses of caffeine make individuals with panic disorder and social anxiety disorder particularly vulnerable to their effects (Lara, 2010). Research on the effects of regular caffeine intake has increased significantly in recent years, and has led to the inclusion of caffeine use disorder as a research diagnosis in DSM-5 (DSM-5, 2013, pp.792–793).

9.3.5 Sedative Use Disorders

Sedatives are a central nervous system depressant, and slow the activity of the body, reduce its responsiveness, and reduce pain, tension and anxiety. This group of substances includes alcohol (see section 9.3.1), the opiates and their derivatives (heroin, morphine, methadone and codeine), and synthesized tranquilizers such as **barbiturates**. This group of drugs has a number of detrimental effects on regular users, including rapid tolerance effects, severe withdrawal symptoms, and high doses can cause disruption to vital bodily functions.

> **barbiturates** A class of sedative drugs related to a synthetic compound (barbituric acid) derived from uric acid.

Opiates

The **opiates** consist of opium – taken from the sap of the opium poppy – and its derivatives, which include morphine, heroin, codeine and methadone. In the 1800s, opium was used mainly to treat medical disorders, because of its ability to relax the patient and reduce both physical and emotional pain. Both morphine and heroin were new drugs derived from opium during the late 1800s and early 1900s. Both were used as analgesics, but over time it became apparent that both were highly addictive, and even after having been successfully treated with morphine or heroin, patients were unable to give up using them. Finally, a synthetic form of opium, called **methadone**, was developed by the Germans during World War II. Unlike the other opiates, methadone can be taken orally (rather than injected) and is longer lasting. **Heroin** is currently the most widely abused of the opiates. It is purchased in a powder form and is normally taken by injection usually directly into a vein (known as 'mainlining'). In contrast, methadone is frequently used as a replacement drug for heroin abusers because of its slow onset and weaker effects.

> **opiates** Opium, taken from the sap of the opium poppy. Its derivatives include morphine, heroin, codeine and methadone.

> **methadone** A synthetic form of opium.

> **heroin** A highly addictive drug derived from morphine, often used illicitly as a narcotic.

For a video on heroin go to www.wiley-psychopathology.com/video/ch9

In the 1990s, heroin became the recreational drug of choice for many in Europe and the USA. Most opiates and their derivatives cause drowsiness and euphoria. In addition, heroin gives a feeling of Ecstasy immediately after injection (known as a 'rush', which lasts for 5–15 minutes). For about 5–6 hours after this rush, the user forgets all worries and stresses and experiences feelings of euphoria and heightened well-being, and loses all negative feelings. However, as with many other drugs, individuals who regularly use heroin rapidly develop tolerance effects and experience severe withdrawal symptoms that begin about 6 hours after they have injected the dose.

Opiates have their effects by depressing the central nervous system, and the drug attaches to brain receptor sites that normally receive **endorphins** and stimulates these receptors to produce more endorphins (Gerrits, Wiegant & Van Ree, 1999). Endorphins are the body's natural opioids, and release of these neurotransmitters acts to relieve pain, reduce stress, and create pleasurable sensations.

> **endorphins** The body's natural opioids. The release of these neurotransmitters acts to relieve pain, reduce stress and create pleasurable sensations.

Prevalence of use   The estimated worldwide annual prevalence of opiate use in 2010 was 0.3–0.5 per cent of the population aged between 15–64 (around 13 to 21 million people). North America (3.8–4.2 per cent), Oceania (2.3–3.4 per cent), and Eastern and South-Eastern Europe (1.2–1.3 per cent) are the regions with the highest prevalence rates (WHO, 2012). In the UK there has been a decrease in opiate drug use in recent years, but in 2009/10 there were an estimated 306,000 opiate or crack cocaine users aged 15 to 64 in England.

Opioid use disorder   Most opiate users build up a tolerance to the drug quickly, and have to use larger and larger doses to experience equivalent physical and psychological effects. Also associated with repeated use are severe withdrawal effects. In the case of heroin, withdrawal symptoms will begin around 6 hours after injection, and without further doses the user will experience a range of aversive withdrawal symptoms. These will begin with feelings of anxiety, restlessness, muscle aches, increased sensitivity to pain, and a renewed craving for the drug. More severe withdrawal is associated with muscle aches, insomnia and fever. Acute withdrawal symptoms for heroin usually peak within 1–3 days and will subside over a period of 5–7 days. **Opioid use disorder** is often difficult to treat because of the severe withdrawal symptoms experienced by sufferers. It is also

> **opioid use disorder** The development of tolerance to opiates, in which the user has to use larger and larger doses to experience equivalent physical and psychological effects. Also associated with severe withdrawal effects.

frequently associated with a history of drug-related crimes (e.g. possession or distribution of drugs, forgery, burglary). Marital difficulties and unemployment are often associated with opioid use disorder at all socio-economic levels (DSM-5, 2013). However, many users seem able to use opiates such as heroin as a periodic recreational drug and continue to lead reasonably functioning lives in the interim. For example, a Scottish study of long-term heroin users who had never been in specialized treatment revealed that they had levels of occupational status and educational achievement similar to the general UK population (Shewan & Dalgarno, 2005). Shewan & Delgarno

To read the article on heroin use by Shewan & Delgarno go to **www.wiley-psychopathology.com/reading/ch9**

found that use of heroin in this subgroup had relatively few health risks, and suggested the terms **controlled drug user** or **unobtrusive heroin user** to describe them. There is other evidence that opiate use need not necessarily lead to long-term dependency. Some theorists believe that opiate drug use is linked to life stressors, and if these stressors are temporary, then so will be the drug use (Alexander & Hadaway, 1982). In support of this view, many US soldiers became regular heroin abusers during the Vietnam War, but relatively few continued to use the drug once they had returned home (Bourne, 1974). While heroin is undoubtedly a dangerous drug, it does appear that some people, in some circumstances, can effectively manage and regulate their use of the drug without problems (Warburton, Turnbull & Hough, 2005).

> **controlled drug user** A long-term drug user who has never been in specialized treatment and who displays levels of occupational status and educational achievement similar to the general population.

> **unobtrusive heroin user** A long-term heroin user who has never been in specialized treatment and who displays levels of occupational status and educational achievement similar to the general population.

For a video on opioid use disorder go to **www.wiley-psychopathology.com/video/ch9**

The costs of opioid use disorder   Apart from the severe withdrawal symptoms experienced after drug use, there are a number of risks that regular opiate users face. These include (1) the risk of accidental overdose if inexperienced users fail to properly dilute pure forms of heroin for use, (2) being sold street heroin that contains potentially lethal additives, such as cyanide or battery acid, and (3) the risk of contracting human immunodeficiency virus (HIV) or hepatitis from sharing unsterilized needles. The number of deaths from opiate overdoses in the UK more than doubled between 1993 and 2000, and in a long-term US study of heroin addicts, 28 per cent had died before the age of 40. Interestingly, only one-third of these deaths were from overdose, and over half were from homicide, suicide or accident (Hser, Anglin & Powers, 1993). The high cost of opiate drugs such as heroin also leads regular users into illegal activities to raise money for their dependence, and the most common of these are theft, fraud and prostitution. Heroin use is also highly associated with crime generally, with regular drug users being three to four times more likely to commit a criminal offence than non-users (Bennett, Holloway & Farrington, 2008), and the Home Office estimated that, in the mid-1990s, around 20 per cent of all people arrested in the UK were taking heroin. So while we reported earlier that it is possible for some heroin users to live reasonably normal lives, there are still significant risks to the life and health of many opioid users.

9.3.6 *Hallucinogen-Related Disorders*

Psychoactive drugs, or *hallucinogens*, have their effects by changing the user's perceptions. They may either sharpen the individual's sensory abilities or create sensory illusions or hallucinations. Unlike stimulants and sedatives, they have less significant effects on arousal levels, and are less addictive than these other two classes of substances. In this section we will discuss in detail two hallucinogen drugs – namely, **lysergic acid diethylamide (LSD)** and the combined hallucinogen and stimulant **MDMA**, or Ecstasy as it is better known, a substance that has become an important recreational drug over the past two decades. Other common hallucinogenic drugs include the **phencyclidines**, which include PCP, 'angel dust', and less potent compounds such as ketamine, cyclohexamine and dizocilpine. The phencyclidines produce feelings of separation from mind and body in low doses, and stupor and coma at high doses, and the rising use of some phencyclidines, such as ketamine, has led to the inclusion of 'Phencyclidine Use Disorder' as a diagnostic category in DSM-5.

> **lysergic acid diethylamide (LSD)** A hallucinogenic drug that produces physical effects including dilated pupils, raised body temperature, increased heart rate and blood pressure, sweating, sleeplessness, dry mouth and tremors.

> **MDMA** MDMA (3,4-methylenedioxymethamphetamine), the drug Ecstasy.

> **phencyclidines** Group of common hallucinogenic drugs, which includes PCP, 'angel dust', and less potent compounds such as ketamine, cyclohexamine and dizocilpine.

Lysergic acid diethylamide (LSD)

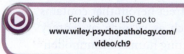

For a video on LSD go to www.wiley-psychopathology.com/video/ch9

LSD is an hallucinogenic drug that was first synthesized by the Swiss chemist Albert Hoffman in 1938. LSD was probably the first of the widely used **psychedelic drugs**, and came to be fashionable as a 'mind-expanding' drug associated with the social changes and experimentation during the 1960s and 1970s. LSD, commonly referred to as 'acid', is sold on the street in tablets, capsules and, occasionally, liquid form. It is odourless, colourless, has a slightly bitter taste and is usually taken orally. Often LSD is added to absorbent paper, such as blotting paper or to sugar cubes. The drug starts to take effect around 30 to 90 minutes after taking it, and physical effects include dilated pupils, raised body temperature, increased heart rate and blood pressure, sweating, sleeplessness, dry mouth, and tremors.

> **psychedelic drugs** Consciousness-expanding or mind-expanding drugs.

LSD produces sharpened perceptions across a variety of senses. Colours can be enhanced and users come to focus their attention on very small details in their environment. Advocates of the drug claim that this heightened perception can open up new states of awareness and allow the user to become more enlightened about the world and themselves. However, because of its sensory enhancing properties, LSD can also cause hallucinations, including distorted perceptions of space and time (Kaplan & Sadock, 1991), perceiving people and objects that are not present, and enabling the user to believe they have attributes that they in fact do not possess. On a number of occasions, this latter effect has had dangerous consequences when users who believe they have the power of flight have thrown themselves out of upper-storey windows.

The awareness-enhancing properties of LSD can also have negative consequences. If the user is feeling anxious or stressed after having taken LSD, these feelings can be exaggerated to the point where the individual can experience extreme terror or panic. Such experiences are known as 'bad trips', and these feelings subside as the dose wears off. However, regular users can come to experience what are known as 'flashbacks'. These are a vivid re-experiencing of a 'trip' that can occur days, months or even years after the actual LSD trip (Abraham & Wolf, 1988).

LSD appears to have its affects by influencing neurons in the brain that normally control visual information and emotion, and it does this by affecting the levels of the neurotransmitter serotonin in these brain areas (Goodman, 2002).

Prevalence of use   In the US and Europe, use of LSD peaked during the 1960s and 1970s and has been gradually declining ever since as stimulant drugs such as cocaine and amphetamines became the recreational drug of choice. In the UK, the use of LSD has declined from 4 per cent in 1996 to 0.5 per cent in 2011/12 (Home Office, 2012). In the USA, the 12-month prevalence rate for LSD use in adults was 0.3 per cent in 2011, a figure that has also been declining significantly over the past 20 years (National Institute on Drug Abuse, 2012).

LSD abuse and dependence   While LSD is not generally considered to be a physically addictive drug, its regular use can still foster dependence. Hallucinogen use (such as LSD or MDMA) is normally restricted to just two to three times per week in regular users, but cravings for the drug have been reported after individuals have stopped using it. Because most hallucinogens have an extended duration of action and a long half-life, individuals with *hallucinogen use disorder* can spend many hours and even days recovering from the effects of the drug, and some hallucinogens – such as MDMA – are often associated with physical 'hangover' symptoms that occur the day after use.

The costs of LSD use

The effects of LSD are generally unpredictable and prior to use the individual will not know whether or not they will experience a 'bad trip'. If a large dose is taken, this can cause hallucinations and sensory changes that can make the user frightened, can cause panic, and can make the individual think they are going crazy. Although LSD is not considered an addictive drug, it can have tolerance effects, where regular users have to take larger and larger doses to achieve similar effects. In a small number of individuals, regular use can be associated with psychiatric disorders such as psychotic symptoms or chronic depression. However, it is unclear whether such individuals already had underlying psychiatric problems prior to their regular use of the drug, and, as we have described elsewhere, regular drug use can tend to become heavy and regular in individuals with pre-existing psychiatric problems.

Ecstasy

Most readers will by now be aware of the drug MDMA (3,4-methylenedioxymethamphetaime) – better known as the 'clubbing drug' **Ecstasy**. Over the past two decades, Ecstasy has become the drug of choice for those regularly attending dance parties, raves or nightclubs. It is usually taken in pill form and acts as both a stimulant and hallucinogen. It gives the user added energy to continue partying, and elevates mood. Ecstasy has its effects by releasing the neurotransmitters serotonin and dopamine (Malberg & Bronson, 2001). Elevated levels of serotonin generate feelings of euphoria, well-being and sociability, and sounds and colours are experienced more intensely (high levels of brain serotonin are also found in individuals with bipolar disorder experiencing a manic phase). Effects can be experienced within around 20 minutes of taking the dose and will last for around 6 hours. However, high levels of brain dopamine can cause psychotic symptoms, such as paranoid thinking and confusion, and these are symptoms often experienced by regular Ecstasy users.

For a video on Ecstasy go to **www.wiley-psychopathology.com/video/ch9**

Ecstasy An illegal amphetamine-based synthetic drug with euphoric effects. Also known as MDMA (3,4-methylenedioxymethamphetamine).

Prevalence of use   Global use of Ecstasy-group substances is estimated at 0.2–0.6 per cent of the adult population (between 10.5 and 28 million users) and is at comparable levels to cocaine use (WHO, 2012). There was some evidence that usage was declining, but most recent evidence suggests a possible resurgence of Ecstasy use in Europe and the USA. In the UK, there were estimated to be around 0.2 million Ecstasy users in 2011/12, although the number of users had fallen from 1.8 per cent of the population in 2000 to 1.4 per cent in 2011/12.

Ecstasy regular use   Regular users of Ecstasy can spend many hours and even days recovering from the effects of the drug, and hallucinogens such as MDMA are often associated with physical 'hangover' symptoms that occur the day after use. Symptoms of MDMA hangovers include insomnia, fatigue, drowsiness, headaches, and sore jaw muscles resulting from teeth clenching. Such symptoms will inevitably interfere with normal occupational and social functioning for some time after drug use. There are no recent figures for Ecstasy-related substance abuse disorders, but Ecstasy users do appear to be at high risk of substance use disorders – if not with MDMA, then with other substances such as cannabis, opioids and sedatives (Wu, Parrott, Ringwalt, Patkar *et al.*, 2009).

The costs of Ecstasy use   There are also a number of dangers associated with regular Ecstasy use, and these include the following: (1) the drug causes severe dehydration and this can cause heat stroke in hot environments such as raves or nightclubs. Even trying to counteract these effects by increasing fluid intake can cause hyponatremia or water intoxication (Braback & Humble, 2001); (2) as a stimulant, Ecstasy increases heart rate and blood pressure, and this can be potentially dangerous for users with existing cardiovascular problems; and (3) Ecstasy is known to be a selective neurotoxin that destroys the axons to which serotonin would normally bind (Ricaurte, Yuan & McCann, 2000). Because of this, Ecstasy is thought to cause a range of long-term problems including memory deficits, verbal-learning deficits, sleep problems, lack of concentration and increased depression and anxiety (Reneman, Booij, Schmand, Brink *et al.*, 2000; Jansen, 2001). More recent research and reviews have supported this, with evidence in particular that Ecstasy users score lower on measures of executive functioning and working memory, particularly updating, attention shifting and access to long-term memory (Verbaten, 2010).

SELF-TEST QUESTIONS

- Can you name the main groupings into which drugs of abuse are categorized?

9.3.1   Alcohol Use Disorder
- How is binge drinking defined, and how prevalent is it amongst young people?
- How does alcohol make the drinker feel relaxed and less stressed?
- What are the main symptoms of withdrawal from alcohol in heavy drinkers?
- Can you name the main criteria for alcohol use disorder?
- What are the main risk factors for alcohol use disorder, and can any of them be identified as causal factors?
- Can you name three physiological risks associated with heavy alcohol drinking?
- Can you list the economic and health costs of alcohol use disorders?

9.3.2   Nicotine Use Disorder
- What are the main physical effects of nicotine?
- Can you describe the main features of the nicotine withdrawal syndrome?
- Can you explain why people start and continue to smoke even though smoking has important negative health consequences?
- What are the main risks of smoking to physical health?

9.3.3   Cannabis Use Disorder
- What are the physical and cognitive effects of cannabis?
- What is the main active ingredient in cannabis? What are the main features of cannabis dependence, cannabis abuse, and cannabis intoxication?
- What are the main risk factors for cannabis use disorder?
- What are the cognitive deficits that some clinicians argue are associated with regular cannabis use?

9.3.4   Stimulant Use Disorder
- What are the main stimulant drugs of abuse?
- Can you describe the main effects of a standard dose of cocaine?
- What are the different forms of cocaine, how are they administered and what different effects do they have?
- How does cocaine cause feelings of euphoria and Ecstasy?
- What are the main cognitive and health effects of regular cocaine use?
- What are 'bath salts'?
- What are the main symptoms of amphetamine intoxication?
- Can you describe the main features of caffeine intoxication and caffeine withdrawal?

9.3.5   Sedative Use Disorder
- Can you name the different types of opiates that are the main drugs of abuse?
- To which receptor sites do opiates normally attach to create their pleasurable effects?
- What are the health risks faced by individuals with opiate use disorder?

9.3.6   Hallucinogen-Related Disorder
- What are the main cognitive and behavioural effects of lysergic acid diethylamide (LSD), and how does it have these effects?
- What are some of the negative psychological and physiological effects of Ecstasy (MDMA)?

SECTION SUMMARY

9.3   CHARACTERISTICS OF SPECIFIC SUBSTANCE USE DISORDERS

- Substances of abuse can be categorized in three broad groups, namely *stimulants* (e.g. cocaine), *sedatives* (e.g. heroin) and *hallucinogenic drugs* (e.g. LSD).

9.3.1   *Alcohol Use Disorder*

- Alcohol has its effects by binding to the neurotransmitter GABA, preventing neurones firing and making the drinker feel more relaxed.

- Many of the so-called 'positive' effects of alcohol are mythical, and result from the drinker's expectations about the effects of alcohol.

- Longer-term negative physical effects of alcohol include hypertension, heart failure, stomach ulcers, cancer, cirrhosis of the liver, brain damage, and early dementia.

- *Delirium tremens (DTs)*, *Korsakoff's syndrome* and *fetal alcohol syndrome* are physiological risks associated with heavy drinking.

- The lifetime prevalence rate for alcohol use disorder is between 12.5 and 17.8 per cent

- Alcohol use disorders cost the UK an estimated £1.5 billion in 2001.

9.3.2   *Nicotine Use Disorder*

- Nicotine has its effects by releasing dopamine in the brain, which acts to elevate mood.

- Regular smokers need to smoke simply to experience positive mood levels similar to non-smokers.

- The number of smokers in the UK has declined steadily in the past 15–20 years to around 20 per cent of adults.

- Mood manipulation is an important part of nicotine dependence, and smoking a cigarette may eventually become a conditioned response to any form of stress.

- There are substantial health risks to smoking, and passive smoking or second-hand smoke is also an important health risk for non-smokers.

9.3.3   *Cannabis Use Disorder*

- The drug cannabis is derived from the hemp plant *cannabis sativa*, and is also known as hashish and marijuana.

- The main active ingredient in cannabis is *THC (Δ⁹-tetrahydrocannabinal)*, the amount of which determines the strength of it psychoactive effects.

- It is estimated that 2.6 to 5 per cent of the world's population use cannabis at least once a year.

- Risk factors for developing cannabis use disorder include early age of first use, tobacco smoking, impulsiveness and unpredictability of moods, diagnosis of childhood conduct disorder, and dependence on alcohol and other drugs.

- Cannabis use disorder is a risk factor for a number of psychiatric diagnoses including anxiety, panic disorder, major depression, and schizophrenia.

- Regular cannabis use predicts lower educational achievement and lower income than non-use.

9.3.4   *Stimulant Use Disorders*

- Stimulant drugs include *cocaine*, *amphetamine* and *caffeine*.

- Cocaine causes feelings of euphoria by blocking the reuptake of dopamine in the mesolimbic areas of the brain.

- Cocaine is usually snorted, but can also be inhaled by smoking, which is known as free-basing.

- The lifetime prevalence rate of cocaine use in developed countries is between 1 and 3 per cent.

- Cocaine can be an important contributor to death by aggravating existing cardiovascular problems.

- Amphetamines are a group of synthetic drugs used primarily as a central nervous system stimulant.

- Amphetamines have their effects by causing the release of the neurotransmitters norepinephrine and dopamine, and simultaneously blocking their reuptake.

- Amphetamine use in the UK is around 2 per cent and has fallen significantly since 1996.

- Caffeine enters the bloodstream through the stomach and increases brain dopamine levels in a similar way to amphetamine and cocaine.

- Caffeine Use Disorder has been included in DSM-5 as a new research diagnosis.

9.3.5   Sedative Use Disorders

- Sedatives are a central nervous system depressant, and slow the activity of the body, and reduce pain, tension and anxiety, and include *opiates* (such as heroin) and *barbiturates*.

- Opiates (such as heroin) attach to brain receptor sites that normally receive *endorphins*, encourage the receptors to produce more endorphins that relieve pain, reduce stress, and create pleasurable sensations.

- The estimated annual prevalence rate for opiate use in 2010 was 0.3–0.5 per cent of adults.

- Some heroin users, known as controlled drug users or unobtrusive heroin users, seem able to use the drug without it affecting their social and occupational functioning.

9.3.6   Hallucinogen-Related Disorders

- Hallucinogenic drugs have their effects by changing the user's perceptions, and include cannabis, lysergic acid diethylamide (LSD), phencyclidines (e.g. PCP) and MDMA (better known as the 'clubbing drug' Ecstasy).

- Lysergic acid diethylamide (LSD) is an hallucinogenic drug first synthesized in 1938.

- LSD has both awareness enhancing properties and occasional negative consequences known as 'bad trips'.

- LSD appears to have its effects by influencing neurons in the brain that normally control emotion and visual information, and it does this by affecting levels of the neurotransmitter serotonin.

- Around 0.3 per cent of Americans claim to have used LSD in the previous 12 months.

- Global use of Ecstasy-group drugs is estimated at 0.2–0.6 per cent of the adult population.

- Ecstasy is known to be a selective neurotoxin that destroys the axons to which serotonin would normally bind.

9.4   THE AETIOLOGY OF SUBSTANCE USE DISORDERS

We have so far described the characteristics of some of the main substances of abuse, and in some cases discussed factors that may lead to abuse of and dependence on that substance. In this section we will look in more general terms at processes that lead some individuals to become substance dependent and why it is that these individuals differ from those who may simply experiment with drugs without it significantly interfering with their daily lives (e.g. Shewan & Delgarno, 2005).

The aetiology of substance use disorders has to be viewed in developmental terms because most individuals who become dependent will go through a series of stages that leads to their disorder. At each stage there may be quite different risk factors that influence transition to the next stage. Figure 9.7 shows a representation of three important stages that individuals go through towards substance use disorder, together with the risk factors that can influence this transition at each stage. Individuals do not necessarily

progress to the next stage unless the factors that mediate that transition are present. For example, many substance users experience only stages 1 and 2 (**experimentation** and *regular use*), and do not necessarily go on to become dependent on the drug in a way that significantly affects their occupational, social and family functioning. There may be some overlap between mediating factors and stages (e.g. believing that smoking won't harm you may not only lead to regular use but can also be a factor leading to nicotine use disorder), but Figure 9.7 gives you a reasonable overview of how risk factors may influence substance use at different stages of development.

In addition to this developmental view, we will also need to look at some of the neurological and behavioural processes that underlie substance use disorders. These include the neurocircuitry of addiction (i.e. the reward pathways in the brain that make substance use pleasurable), and the psychology of 'craving' (i.e. the way

> **experimentation**   A period when an individual may try out different drugs. In some cases this period of experimentation may lead to regular drug use.

> For an activity based on Figure 9.7, regarding the developmental model of substance abuse and dependence, go to **www.wiley-psychopathology.com/activities/ch9**

DOES TAKING 'SOFT' DRUGS LEAD TO USING 'HARDER' DRUGS?

Because cannabis use is prevalent amongst teenagers and young adults, there has long been some concern that early cannabis use may be the first step that leads young people to experiment with 'harder', more addictive drugs, such as cocaine and heroin. This supposed progression from less addictive drugs, such as cannabis, to more addictive drugs may then trap the individual into a cycle of substance dependency.

So, is there any truth to this theory? Certainly there is evidence that regular users of addictive drugs such as cocaine and heroin did start out by using cannabis, and cocaine use, for example, is significantly predicted by earlier cannabis use (Kandel, Murphy & Karus, 1985). Another relevant fact is that cannabis users are more likely than non-users to go on and try cocaine or heroin (Miller & Volk, 1996). However, these findings do not imply in any way that cannabis users will always go on to use more addictive drugs, and 40 per cent of regular cannabis users do not go on to experiment with cocaine or heroin (Stephens, Roffman & Simpson, 1993).

Because much drug use is associated with dependency, we tend to assume that individual users will automatically be dragged along a path of ever-worsening abuse, and that cannabis use will inevitably lead down a slippery slope to dependency. However, we must remember that many regular substance users – even those who use potentially highly addictive drugs

such as cocaine, heroin and amphetamines – manage to successfully confine their use to recreational purposes only, and use the drug only when socialising or at weekends. This controlled use does not appear to interfere substantially with occupational, social or educational functioning (e.g. Shewan & Delgarno, 2005).

So, why do some people appear to progress from softer drugs during adolescence to substance dependency during adulthood? One theory is that progression to long-term dependency is found primarily in those who have either psychological problems at the outset of their drug use or are suffering life stress (Alexander & Hadaway, 1982). Indirect support for this theory comes from studies showing that drug abuse often stops when life stressors disappear (Bourne, 1974), and that many users of addictive drugs such as cocaine and heroin are capable of kicking their habit and turning to softer drugs, such as cannabis, as a safer option. Also, in a recent study, Smith, Jones, Bullmore, Robbins & Ersche (2014) found that there is a select subset of cocaine users who are able to use the substance recreationally without developing dependence, and that this was due to their lack of attentional preference for cocaine-related stimuli compared with dependent users. This lack of attentional preference significantly reduces attention to cues that elicit 'craving' (see Focus Point 9.8).

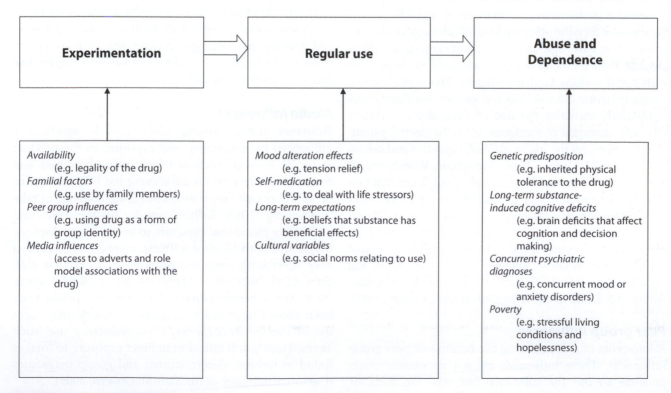

FIGURE 9.7 *The developmental model of substance abuse and dependence.*

in which liking and wanting a drug becomes conditioned to external cues which trigger the desire for that drug). These two processes are highlighted and described later in Focus Points 9.7 and 9.8.

We will continue by describing some of the risk factors that influence substance use at different developmental stages.

9.4.1 Experimentation

Availability

Whether an individual can readily get access to the substance is an important factor in the early stages of substance use, and factors such as whether the drug is legally available (e.g. alcohol and cigarettes) and its cost are important determinants of initially experimenting with the drug. For example, there is evidence for an inverse relationship between the use of a drug and its cost – especially amongst young adolescents. This is true for alcohol and for cigarettes (Stead & Lancaster, 2005; Room, Babor & Rehm, 2005), and suggests that strategies such as enforcing the minimum age for purchase of tobacco and alcohol, and increasing the price of these commodities may be effective means of controlling early use (Ogilvie, Gruer & Haw, 2006).

Familial factors

Two important factors that can influence early substance use are (1) whether the substances are regularly used by other family members, and (2) whether the family environment is problematic. For example, if a child's parents both smoke then the offspring is significantly more likely to smoke at an early age, and if both parents regularly drink alcohol, then the child is also more likely to drink at an early age (Hawkins, Graham, Maguin, Abbott *et al.*, 1998). Similarly, having older siblings and spouses that abuse drugs significantly increases the risk of drug abuse (Kendler, Ohlsson, Sundquist & Sundquist, 2013). Neglectful parenting also increases the use of alcohol, cigarettes and cannabis by the child (Cadoret, Yates, Troughton, Woodworth & Stewart, 1995), and the *negative background factors* that predict longer term substance use include (1) substance use in the childhood home, (2) extreme poverty in the childhood home, (3) marital or legal problems in the household, (4) childhood neglect and abuse – especially childhood sexual abuse (Sartor, Waldron, Duncan, Grant *et al.*, 2013), and (5) serious psychiatric illness in the household (Alverson, Alverson & Drake, 2000; Wills, DuHamel & Vaccaro, 1995).

Peer group influences

Adolescents often begin drug use because of peer group influences. These influences are not necessarily direct pressure to use the substance but take the form of conforming to group norms, so an adolescent will start using a substance in order to *self-categorize* themselves as a member of a particular group (Schofield, Pattison, Hill & Borland, 2001). There is clear evidence that young people are socially motivated to become drug users (Allbutt, Amos & Cunningham-Burley, 1995), but this only rarely takes the form of deliberate 'pressure' or 'persuasion' by others (Lucas & Lloyd, 1999; Schofield, Pattison, Hill & Borland, 2001). In most cases, young people appear to take up activities like smoking in order to conform with group norms – that is, they can make themselves appear more like others in the group by conforming to behaviours that are typical in the group, such as smoking (Schmitt, Branscombe & Kappen, 2003). Schofield, Pattison, Hill & Borland (2001) found that particular group labels (such as 'rebels', 'illegal drug users', 'motor bike riders') were associated with extensive smoking, and the degree of smoking determined how strongly an individual identified with that group. In such groups, in-group favouritism is also expressed by the sharing of cigarettes, and smoking is used to cement friendships, and to indicate commitment to the group (Stewart-Knox, Sittlington, Rugkasa, Harrisson *et al.*, 2005). This suggests that social networks can have a strong influence on an individual's initial substance use, and identifying as part of a group that uses legal drugs, such as cigarettes and alcohol, also predicts increased use of other drugs in late adolescence (Chassin, Curran, Hussong & Colder, 1996). Apart from the importance of social groups determining substance use, it is also the case that substance use will determine the kinds of social groups that an individual will mix in. For example, once an individual becomes a regular drinker, they begin to choose social groups with similar drinking patterns, and drinking in a social group environment that supports alcohol consumption can act to consolidate regular use (Bullers, Cooper & Russell, 2001).

Media influences

Substance use in young adolescents is significantly influenced by advertising and exposure to the product in media contexts such as television programmes and magazines. Exposure to advertising has been shown to be an important factor in encouraging children to take up smoking (While, Kelly, Huang & Charlton, 1996), and a US study found that exposure to in-store beer displays, magazines with alcohol advertisements, and television beer advertising predicted drinking in school-age children (Ellickson, Collins, Hambarsoomians & McCaffrey, 2005). While banning direct advertising of a product has been shown to produce a significant fall in adolescent use of that product (Saffer, 1991), substance use (such as smoking) is still linked to indirect exposure to images found in fashion, entertainment and gossip magazines (Carson, Rodriguez & Audrain-McGovern, 2005).

9.4.2 Regular Use

Mood alteration effects

One of the main reasons for using drugs is that they have important mood altering effects. Alcohol makes the drinker friendly, confident and relaxed (Harvey, Foster, MacKay, Carroll *et al.*, 2002); smokers claim that smoking cigarettes has a relaxing and calming effect (Ikard, Green & Horn, 1969); stimulants – such as cocaine and amphetamines – affect **reward pathways** in the brain causing feelings of euphoria, energy and confidence (Volkow, Wang, Fischman, Foltin *et al.*, 1997; Taylor, Lewis & Olive, 2013); opiates – such as heroin – generate immediate

> **reward pathways** The brain neurocircuitry that make substance use pleasurable.

feelings of Ecstasy, feelings of well-being and loss of negative emotions; and hallucinogens – such as cannabis – produce feelings of relaxation, euphoria, sociability and sharpened perceptions. Interestingly, most of the drugs that we've discussed in this chapter have their pleasurable effects by activating a common brain circuitry that governs reward and pleasure, and a full discussion of this circuitry is provided in Focus Point 9.7.

Given these rewarding effects of drug use, it makes sense to assume that regular use can develop as a result of drug use being reinforced by these pleasurable consequences. Furthermore, if taken regularly enough, many drugs can cause permanent changes to the brain reward system in such a way as to facilitate addiction (Taylor, Lewis & Olive, 2013).

FOCUS POINT 9.7

REWARD PATHWAYS IN THE BRAIN AND DRUG ADDICTION

With most of the drugs of abuse that we've discussed earlier in this chapter, you'll notice that they all either have pleasurable effects on mood or they help people to feel less bad (e.g. by alleviating negative moods or withdrawal symptoms) (Koob & Le Moal, 2008). Research on both humans and animals suggests that a broad range of drugs have their pleasurable effects by activating the natural reward pathways in the brain by converging on a common circuitry in the brain's limbic system (Feltenstein & See, 2008), and many of these drugs also cause permanent adaptive effects on this common pathway that contribute to the progression and maintenance of addiction (Taylor, Lewis & Olive,

2013). Drugs achieve their pleasurable effects by influencing the dopamine system, and in particular, the dopaminergic neurons in the **ventral tegmental area (VTA)** of the midbrain and subsequent areas in the limbic forebrain – especially the **nucleus accumbens (NAc)**. This VTA–NAc pathway is arguably the most important reward pathway in the brain and gives rise to the pleasurable effects caused not only by drug use, but also by food, sex and social interactions (Kelley & Berridge, 2002; Tobler, Fiorillo & Schultz,

> **ventral tegmental area (VTA)** Part of the midbrain associated with the dopamine system.

> **nucleus accumbens (NAc)** Part of the limbic forebrain and dopamine system.

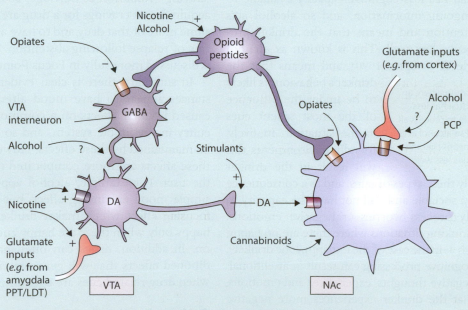

Source: Nestler, E.J. (2005). Is there a common molecular pathway for addiction? *Nature Neuroscience, 8*, 1445–1449, Figure 1. Reproduced with permission.

2005), and it has also been implicated in other addictive behaviours such as pathological overeating, gambling and sex addictions (Nestler, 2005).

Several additional brain areas have been shown to interact with this VTA–NAc pathway and are implicated in drug addiction. These include regions in the amygdala, hippocampus, hypothalamus, and several regions of the frontal cortex (Koob & Le Moal, 2008; Nestler, 2001).

The figure shows the converging actions that a number of different drugs of abuse have by affecting different components in the VTA–NAc reward pathway. Stimulants directly increase dopaminergic transmission (DA) in the NAc. Opiates do the same indirectly by inhibiting GABAergic interneurons in the VTA, which disinhibits dopamine neurons in the VTA. Opiates also directly act on opiate receptors in the NAc. Nicotine seems to activate VTA dopamine neurons directly. Alcohol appears to have a number of different effects at different points in the pathway, and the effects of cannabis are also complex but may act directly on NAc neurons themselves. Finally, phencyclidine (PCP) may act directly on neurons in the NAc.

In addition to the intrinsic pleasurable effects of some substances, a good deal of research has been carried out on the putative tension or stress-reducing effects of drugs such as nicotine and alcohol. There is some evidence that alcohol may reduce tension, even in individuals who are not alcohol dependent (Sher & Levenson, 1982), and this is consistent with the drinker's everyday belief that drinking is a good way to unwind, such as after a demanding day at work. However, the picture is not quite that simple. Alcohol appears to reduce responding in the presence of both negative and positive affect, and so may simply have an *arousal-dampening* effect regardless of the valency of the drinker's emotional state (Stritzke, Patrick & Lang, 1995). Subsequent studies have indicated that alcohol has its apparent arousal-dampening effects by altering perception and attention. The alcohol-intoxicated individual has less cognitive capacity available to process all ongoing information, and so alcohol acts to narrow attention and means that the drinker processes fewer cues less well. This is known as **alcohol myopia** (Steele & Josephs, 1990), and means that the drinker's behaviour is likely to be under the influence of the most salient cues in the situation. In lively, friendly environments this will result in the drinker processing only these types of cues, and as a consequence will feel happy, sociable and will not have the capacity to simultaneously process worries or negative emotions. However, in drinking situations where there are no happy, lively cues (such as in the case of the unhappy, lone drinker), the reduced cognitive processing can result in attentional-focusing on negative thoughts, experiences and emotions, and means that the drinker experiences more negative affect than if they had abstained.

In the case of nicotine, we saw in section 9.3.2 that there is evidence that regular smokers use nicotine as a means of coping with stress (Schacter, 1982; Parrott, 1998, 1999). This begins when the smoker lights a cigarette in order to alleviate nicotine withdrawal symptoms, but after regular use, many smokers come to associate smoking with tension relief generally, and so become conditioned to having a cigarette during or after *any* stressful experience (Kassel, 2000). This gives feelings of relaxation and improved concentration as nicotine levels increase, and functions to reinforce the act of smoking. Consistent with this view is the longitudinal finding that increases in negative affect and stressful life events are associated with increases in smoking (Wills, Sandy & Yaeger, 2002).

Finally, many drugs are powerful reinforcers that can condition the effects of drugs to stimuli and cues associated with the drug (e.g. seeing a cigarette packet, or a white powder), and this gives rise to the concept of 'craving' (Robinson & Berridge, 2003). Individuals who acquire learnt cravings for a drug are more likely to consume more of that drug and to have a significantly higher rate of relapse following abstention. The role of craving is discussed more fully in Focus Point 9.8.

In summary, there is clear evidence that many substances appear to have mood altering effects – often caused by their affects on a common brain reward circuitry in the limbic system, and so substance use may be maintained by these effects. However, in many cases, these affects are more complicated than they appear to the user. For example, alcohol appears not to have a simple mood enhancing effect, but has an attentional-focusing effect which makes drinkers feel relaxed and happy only when there are happy cues for them to focus on. In addition, drugs can often have important conditioned effects that will generate craving for the drug when drug-related cues are encountered.

alcohol myopia The situation where an alcohol-intoxicated individual has less cognitive capacity available to process all ongoing information, and so alcohol acts to narrow attention and means that the drinker processes fewer cues less well.

Self-medication

Rather than simply being used as a means of reducing the effects of everyday tensions and stressors, substance

CRAVING

The pleasurable effects of drug use can also act as potent stimuli that will generate 'craving' responses to cues associated with the drug. This occurs through a process of conditioning in which the drug acts as a powerful unconditioned stimulus (UCS) that reinforces conditioned responses to drug cues (see section 1.3.2 for a discussion of classical and operant conditioning) (Robinson & Berridge, 2003). This means that cues such as the sensory features of the drug (e.g. a white powder), the environment in which it is taken (e.g. a pub), or the people the user socializes with when taking the drug can all become cues which elicit craving for the drug. Cues for a particular drug can actually trigger responses in the user that are very similar to those associated with actual use of the drug, and these include pleasurable feelings, physiological arousal, and activation of brain reward centres (Filbey & DeWitt, 2012). In addition, craving can induce attentional biases that enhance processing of drug cues, as well as drug anticipatory responses that exacerbate the craving (Field, Mogg, Mann, Bennett & Bradley, 2013). Although generated by non-conscious classical conditioning process, craving is often characterized as a conscious state that intervenes between the unconscious cues and consumption (Andrade, May & Kavanagh, 2012). Craving has significant effects on those suffering substance abuse disorders. People who crave a substance do use that substance more than people who don't crave it (Berkman, Falk & Lieberman, 2011), and, as you can imagine, craving is a significant obstacle to successful treatment and frequently leads to relapse (Evren, Durkaya, Evren, Dalbudak & Cetin, 2012; Paliwal, Hyman & Sinha, 2007).

---

use can become regular as a means of **self-medication** when the individual is suffering more severe adjustment difficulties such as those caused by diagnosable psychiatric disorders. This view is supported by the fact that substance use disorders are highly comorbid with a range of other psychiatric disorders, including bipolar disorder, depression, eating disorders, schizophrenia, personality disorders, and anxiety disorders such as obsessive compulsive disorder, post-traumatic stress disorder and panic disorder (Regier, Farmer, Rae, Locke *et al.*, 1990; Brooner, King, Kidorf, Schmidt *et al.*, 1997) (see Table 9.2), and self-medication is frequently reported by substance users as a motive for using the substance (Sbrana, Bizzarri, Rucci, Gonnelli *et al.*, 2005). There is evidence that anxiety disorders and depression pre-date the onset of substance use disorders such as alcohol dependency (Merikangas, Mehta, Molnar, Walters *et al.*, 1998; Liraud & Verdoux, 2000), which is again consistent with the view that drugs are used for medication purposes after a psychiatric disorder has already developed. However, if individuals who use drugs for self-medication purposes are aware of the longer term negative effects of these drugs, why do they continue to use them? Drake, Wallach, Alverson & Mueser (2002) suggest a number of reasons for continued use:

> **self-medication** Self-administration of often illicit drugs by an individual to alleviate perceived or real problems, usually of a psychological nature.

1. the drug has intrinsic rewarding effects and leads to physical dependence,

2. the lives of individuals with psychiatric disorders are so miserable that the medicinal effects of the drug offset its negative effects, and

3. the drug may not only reduce tension and negative affect, it may have other positive consequences such as helping the individual to cope in social situations.

Finally, if substance abusers do genuinely use drugs to self-medicate, then their choice of drug should be consistent with their psychiatric symptoms. For example, we would expect someone with ADHD to prefer amphetamines to alcohol due to its stimulating properties, but individuals with anxiety would prefer alcohol to amphetamines because of the anxiolytic effects of alcohol. However, there is relatively little evidence in support of these more detailed predictions from the self-medication account (Lembke, 2012).

Long-term expectations and beliefs

Substance users can also become regular users because they develop expectations that the substance will have positive effects. For example, young adolescents who believe that alcohol affects behaviour in positive ways (e.g. by increasing physical pleasure, enhancing sexual performance, facilitating socially assertive behaviour) are significantly more likely to begin drinking than adolescents who do not hold these beliefs, and are also more likely to become problem drinkers (Goldman, Brown & Christiansen, 1987; Christiansen, Roehling, Smith & Goldman, 1989). In many cases these beliefs appear to be culturally generated, because empirical studies suggest that alcohol does not increase levels of sexual arousal or aggression, but in fact reduces physiological arousal (Lang, Goeckner, Adessor & Marlatt, 1975; Wilson & Lawson, 1976). Many regular substance users also develop erroneous beliefs that the substance they use is harmless, and these beliefs help to maintain regular use. For example, the increase in cannabis use during the 1990s was mainly confined to those individuals who considered cannabis to be harmless (US Department of Health and Human Sciences, 1994), and many regular smokers believe that smoking may cause cancer and illness in other smokers, but not in themselves (Ayanian & Cleary, 1999).

Cultural variables

There are some cultural factors that will influence the transition from first use to regular use. For example, alcohol consumption differs significantly across different countries, and is most prevalent in wine-drinking societies (such as France, Italy and Spain) where drinking alcohol is widely accepted as a social and recreational activity (deLint, 1978). Increased use in these countries may be caused by the regular availability of alcohol in a range of situations, such as drinking wine with meals and the availability of wine and alcohol in a broad range of social settings. There are also some culturally determined differences in beliefs about the effects of drugs which appear to affect the frequency of use, and Ma & Shive (2000) found that white Americans reported significantly less risk associated with a range of drugs (alcohol, cigarettes, cocaine and cannabis) than African or Hispanic Americans. The former group was found to use all of these drugs significantly more than the latter groups.

9.4.3 Abuse and Dependence

Regular use of a substance is not sufficient to give rise to a substance use disorder. This latter stage will be subject to the diagnostic criteria provided in Table 9.1, and to the regular use causing significant disruption to daily living in the form of inability to fulfil major obligations at work, school or home, and a failure to deal with family responsibilities. In this section, we look at some of the factors that might cause a shift from regular use to abuse and dependence.

Genetic predisposition

Based on twin, adoption and family studies, the heritability component for substance use disorders could be as high as 0.78 for alcohol and nicotine dependence (Kendler & Prescott, 1998; Merikangas et al., 1998), and around 0.46 for substance use disorders generally (Grove, Eckert, Heston, Bouchard et al., 1990). Twin studies have indicated that the concordance rates for alcohol abuse in MZ and DZ twins respectively are 54 per cent and 28 per cent (Kaji, 1960), indicating a strong genetic component in alcohol abuse, and a similar genetic predisposition has

been found in twin studies of cannabis abuse (Kendler & Prescott, 1998), nicotine dependency (True, Xian, Scherrer, Madden et al., 1999), and drug abuse generally (Tsuang, Lyons, Meyer, Doyle et al., 1998). Adoption studies also support a role for genetic inheritance in alcohol use disorders and drug abuse generally (Cadoret, Troughton, O'Gorman & Heywood, 1986; Kendler, Sundquist, Ohlsson, Palmer et al., 2012).

So how might genetic factors put some individuals more at risk for substance abuse and dependence than others? There are a number of different possibilities. Firstly, a genetic predisposition for alcohol dependence may interact with environmental factors such as stress (a diathesis–stress model). For example, Dick, Pagan, Holliday, Viken et al. (2007) found that heritability for alcohol problems in adolescents was higher amongst those who had peers who drank alcohol than those with peers who didn't drink alcohol. Cloninger (1987) has also argued that a genetic predisposition for alcohol dependence will be activated only by experiencing environmental stress (e.g. low socio-economic status). However, other studies have indicated that there may be a more general genes–environment interaction, where a genetic predisposition for alcohol dependence will only cause alcohol abuse if other environmental factors are present. These environmental factors are not necessarily stressors, but include factors which might facilitate alcohol use, such as living in places where there are large numbers of young people (Dick, Rose, Viken, Kaprio & Koskenvuo, 2001) or peer pressure or parental modelling (Rose, 1998). These environmental factors seem to be important because they are likely to initiate drinking. Once drinking has started, genetic factors then appear to play a significant role in determining regular use, abuse and dependence (Heath, 1995).

Secondly, genetic factors may influence tolerance levels to drugs such as alcohol, or affect central nervous system responses to the drug (Schuckit, 1983). Alcohol dependence requires that the user has to drink a lot and to do this regularly, and many individuals who develop alcohol use disorders appear to have inherited a strong tolerance for alcohol. That is, they report low levels of intoxication after a drinking bout and they show fewer signs of physical intoxication (such as body sway) (Schuckit, 1994; Schuckit & Smith, 1996), and these higher thresholds for intoxication may permit heavier and heavier bouts of drinking that are typical of alcohol use disorders. Thirdly, there is considerable evidence that certain genes influence sensitivity to alcohol, and it is the inheritance of these genes that determines whether a drinker will become dependent. The main candidate is a gene known as ALDH2 (Wall, Shea, Chan & Carr, 2001). Alcohol metabolism in the liver goes through two main stages, and these are the conversion of alcohol into a toxic substance called acetaldehyde followed by conversion of acetaldehyde into nontoxic acetic acids. ALDH2 is thought to affect the rate at which acetaldehyde is metabolized – if it is metabolized more slowly, then the individual will begin to feel the negative effects of its toxicity, such as nausea, headaches, stomach pains, and physical signs of intoxication. Interestingly, many Asians are known to have a mutant allele for ALDH2 which slows acetaldehyde metabolism and allows it to build up after a drinking bout, and makes drinking large amounts of alcohol aversive. This appears to be an important factor in explaining why Asians develop alcohol use disorders at only about half the rate of non-Asians (Tu & Israel, 1995). Other mutant forms of this gene which allow rapid metabolism of acetaldehyde may be the inherited factor that causes tolerance effects in some individuals and leads to regular alcohol use and dependence. That such a tolerance is inherited is supported by the fact that sons of heavy alcohol users report being less intoxicated than others after a standard amount of alcohol and show fewer physical signs of intoxication (Schuckit, Tsuang, Anthenelli, Tipp *et al.*, 1996). Recent studies have identified a form of the ALDH2 allele in white American college students that is associated with lower rates of alcohol use disorder, lower levels of drinking, and with alcohol-induced headaches (Wall, Shea, Luczak, Cook & Carr, 2005), and suggests that variations in the form of this gene can have an important influence on alcohol consumption and alcohol use disorders.

Long-term substance-induced cognitive deficits

As you will have read earlier in this chapter, there is much speculation about whether regular substance use causes long-term brain damage and permanent deficits in cognitive processes. Evidence for most of these claims is still fairly equivocal – especially in the case of substances such as cannabis or MDMA (Iversen, 2005; Cole, Sumnall & Grob, 2002). However, most substance use disorders tend to be associated with a syndrome of underachievement, with abusers often exhibiting lower IQ, lower educational achievement, and motivational deficits compared with non-users. This may be a consequence of individuals who have these intellectual and motivational deficits prior to drug use lacking the necessary coping skills to pull themselves out of the vicious downward spiral of abuse and dependence. However, an alternative explanation is that regular substance use may *cause* these intellectual and motivational deficits, resulting in poorer judgement and decision-making skills, and making such individuals more prone to fall into a pattern of long-term abuse. For example, there is growing evidence that regular substance abuse can have long-term effects on the balance and availability of important brain neurotransmitters such as dopamine and serotonin (Nestler, 2001; Heinz, Mann, Weinberger & Goldman, 2001), and that methamphetamine abuse causes at least mild cognitive decline observed in early to middle adulthood (Dean, Groman, Morales & London, 2013). In post-mortem studies of the brains of regular cocaine users, Little, Krolewski, Zhang & Cassin (2003) found damage to striatal dopamine fibres resulting in neuronal changes causing disordered mood and disruption to motivational processes. So, this illustrates one possible route through which regular use could develop into long-term dependence as changes in brain structures caused by the drug affect mood and motivation to such an extent that the user has significantly fewer cognitive resources available to fight dependence.

Concurrent psychiatric diagnoses

We have already discussed the role that comorbid psychiatric disorders can play in turning first time users into regular users because of the medicating properties the drug has on the psychiatric symptoms. However, comorbid psychiatric problems appear to play an important role throughout the developmental process to full abuse and dependence. For instance, once a user has entered treatment for their dependence, treatment outcomes are significantly poorer for users with comorbid psychiatric disorders, and this is usually due to increased tendency to relapse after treatment (Grella, Hser, Joshi & Rounds-Bryant, 2001). There are at least two factors that contribute to this poor treatment outcome:

1. individuals with comorbid psychiatric disorders are likely to face more life stressors after treatment (e.g. negative emotional states) and are less likely to have the coping resources required to deal with these stressors than those without psychiatric comorbidity (Ramo, Anderson, Tate & Brown, 2005), which returns them to drug self-medication as a way of coping, and

2. users with a psychiatric comorbidity are less likely to consider that drugs are problematic compared with their peers and tend to relapse very soon after treatment (Ramo, Anderson, Tate & Brown, 2005), which suggests that they lack the motivation to abstain, even though their difficulties are compounded by the psychiatric comorbidity.

In summary, psychiatric comorbidity is a real risk factor for both transition from first use to regular use, and from regular use to abuse and dependence, and it is an important factor in determining relapse from treatment.

Poverty

Without doubt there are important socio-economic factors at work in determining whether individuals will use drugs and develop from being regular users into being drug dependent. One such factor is poverty. There is evidence that an individual's first experience with an illicit drug increases in probability if they live in or near an economically poor neighbourhood (Petronis & Anthony, 2003). This is perhaps not surprising given that such individuals may well be unemployed, have no other forms of recreation available to them, have little hope of occupational or educational fulfilment, and already live in subcultures that revere drug dealing as a high-status profession. Such conditions are perfect for the downward spiral into drug abuse and dependence, and are likely to represent circumstances in which the individual will have poor access to treatment services and long-term psychiatric support (Cook & Alegria, 2011). Endemic drug use in poor communities fosters other problems, including infections such as HIV and hepatitis C contracted through injecting drugs intravenously (Rosenberg, Drake, Brunette, Wolford & Marsh, 2005). Finally, substance dependence in poor areas also fosters crime in the form of robbery, fraud and prostitution as the only means of securing money to buy drugs, and violent crime and racketeering as dealers battle to sell their illicit products.

SELF-TEST QUESTIONS

- Is there any evidence that using 'soft' drugs leads to the use of 'hard' drugs?
- What factors lead young people to experiment with drugs?
- How do peer group influences affect whether a young person will try a new drug?
- What factors lead individuals to become regular users of a substance?
- In what ways do different drugs such as alcohol, nicotine, cocaine, heroin and cannabis alter the user's mood?
- Research suggests a broad range of drugs have their effects by activating the natural reward pathway in the brain – what areas of the brain are involved in this pathway?
- How does craving develop, and how does it contribute to relapse?
- What is the evidence that regular drug use can become a form of self-medication when the user has severe adjustment difficulties?
- What are the main factors that maintain substance abuse and dependence?
- How have twin and adoption studies shown that there is an inherited component to alcohol use disorder?
- How does the gene ALDH2 influence whether a drinker is likely to become alcohol dependent?
- What kinds of long-term cognitive deficits can regular substance use cause, and how might they be implicated in maintaining substance use disorders?
- What is the link between poverty and substance use disorders?

SECTION SUMMARY

9.4   THE AETIOLOGY OF SUBSTANCE USE DISORDERS

The acquisition of substance abuse and dependency has to be viewed as a developmental process that progresses through a number of well-defined stages, and different factors are involved in establishing substance use at these different stages. The main stages of development that we have highlighted are experimentation (what influences first use of a substance?), regular use (what factors influence the move from experimentation to regular use?), and abuse and dependence (what makes some people continue to use drugs even though this activity is having significant negative effects on their lives and their health?). It is important to understand that use may be confined to any one of these stages, and many regular users can often function relatively successfully in their social, work and family environments. However, in terms of understanding psychopathology, it is the development from regular use to abuse and dependence that is of most interest to us as practitioners and clinical psychologists.
    The key points in this section are:

- The aetiology of substance dependence has to be viewed in developmental terms as individuals go through stages of experimentation, regular use, and then substance abuse and dependence.

9.4.1 Experimentation

- Early use is influenced by the availability of the drug and its economic cost.

- Whether substances are regularly used by family members and whether the family environment is problematic can also hasten experimentation with drugs.

- Peer groups influence first substance use as individuals start using a substance in order to self-categorize themselves as members of a particular group.

- Substance use in young adolescents is significantly influenced by advertising and exposure to substances (such as cigarettes and alcohol) in the media.

9.4.2 Regular Use

- Almost all substances of dependence have mood altering effects by either creating states of euphoria or Ecstasy or reducing tension or stress. These factors may contribute to regular use.

- Drugs achieve their pleasurable effects by influencing the dopamine system in the brain – especially the dopaminergic neurons in the *ventral tegmental area (VTA)* of the midbrain and the *nucleus accumbens (NAc)*.

- *Craving* is a conditioned response to cues associated with individual drugs, and increases consumption and risk of relapse.

- Substance use can become regular as a means of *self-medication* when the individual is suffering severe adjustment difficulties such as those caused by psychiatric disorders.

- Substance users can become regular users because they develop expectations that the substance will have positive effects.

9.4.3 Abuse and Dependence

- There is a significant inherited component to substance use disorders as shown by twin, adoption and family studies.

- A gene known as *ALDH2* affects the rate at which alcohol is metabolized, and will influence the individual's tolerance of alcohol.

- Regular users may become drug dependent because they lack the motivation and the coping skills to pull themselves out of a downward spiral into abuse and dependence.

- Psychiatric comorbidity is a risk factor for both transition from first use to regular use, and from regular use to abuse and dependency.

- Endemic drug use is associated with poverty and poor communities, which also fosters health problems such as HIV, crime and prostitution.

9.5 THE TREATMENT OF SUBSTANCE USE DISORDERS

Treating individuals with substance use disorders is not a simple or easy process. At the point where a user reaches the stage of abuse and dependence they are usually physically addicted to the drug, suffer severe withdrawal symptoms when abstaining from the drug, and probably mix in social circles that will provide regular temptations to use the drug. In addition, substance use disorders are often associated with other comorbid psychiatric disorders that will need addressing in a full intervention plan. Many younger individuals with substance use disorders also do not see their drug taking as dangerous or problematic (Ramo, Anderson, Tate & Brown, 2005), and so have a high risk of relapse after treatment. It is often the case that those with most severe dependencies live miserable and unfulfilled lives. They may be homeless or living in poverty, and the relief from these conditions provided by the drug may be the individual's only solace. In the UK, the Centre for Social Justice has recently published a report proposing a series of reforms of treatments for substance use disorders, most notably arguing that many treatment programmes are doomed to failure without effectively addressing the poverty, unemployment and poor living conditions in which many drug addicts exist (Centre for Social Justice, 2010).

To read *Breakthrough Britain: Addictions*, a report on substance abuse treatments, go to http://tinyurl.com/ogefosv

Because of these difficulties, treatment interventions with clients suffering substance use disorders are usually multifaceted and address the client's problems at a range of different levels. As a consequence, many national treatment programmes provide healthcare advice, general community support, easy-access drop-in facilities for drug abusers, and structured treatment programmes – both community-based and residential, depending on the severity of the dependence. Treatment programmes are usually multifaceted, in that they will combine a range of specific intervention procedures designed to make the client aware of the circumstances and environmental stimuli that trigger substance use, deal with any comorbid disorders, develop motivation to change, and teach the social and coping skills needed to deal with life without drugs. These may also be combined with detoxification procedures designed to address the physical dependence that drug use has developed. In the following sections, we will begin by looking briefly at some community care practices, and then turn to specific psychological and detoxification approaches.

9.5.1 Community-Based Programmes

Community-based services come in a number of forms. They can be self-help groups, such as **Alcoholics Anonymous (AA)** (see Focus Point 9.1), which tries to help the alcoholic replace networks of drinking friends with other AA members. At least some studies have suggested that AA participation can have positive

> **Alcoholics Anonymous (AA)** A support group for individuals who are alcohol dependent and are trying to abstain.

outcomes, and may be an effective form of long-term abstinence up to 8 years after joining the self-help group (Timko, Moos, Finney & Lesar, 2000). However, a systematic review of the eight randomized outcome studies available at the time found that AA was no better than any other kind of structured treatment (Ferri, Amato & Davoli, 2008), and AA has notoriously high drop-out rates, which are often not factored into the results of controlled clinical trials.

Drug-prevention schemes are now widespread and take many forms. Their purpose is to try to prevent first use of a drug or to prevent experimentation with a drug

> **drug-prevention schemes** Community-based services whose purpose is to try to prevent first use of a drug or to prevent experimentation with a drug developing into regular use – usually through information about the effects of drugs and through developing communication and peer-education skills.

developing into regular use – usually through information about the effects of drugs and by developing communication and peer-education skills. In the UK, government-sponsored schemes have a number of elements, which focus respectively on young people (especially in schools), communities (targeting young people and their parents who may be specifically at risk), treatment, and availability. Twenty-four-hour telephone helplines and internet websites also provide constant advice and information

(e.g. http://talktofrank.com/). Prevention schemes are often local and tailored to the specific needs of the community. They aim at educating schoolteachers and parents on how to deal with specific drug-related incidents and how to provide drug advice to young people. Many schemes train young people themselves to deliver drug education information to their peers. Particular strategies that drug prevention schemes use are (1) **peer-pressure resistance training**, where students learn assertive refusal skills when confronted with drugs, (2) campaigns to counter the known effects of the media and advertising (e.g. by com-

> **peer-pressure resistance training** A strategy used by drug prevention schemes where students learn assertive refusal skills when confronted with drugs.

bating tobacco advertising with anti-smoking messages), (3) **peer leadership**, where young people are trained to provide anti-drugs messages to their peers, and (4) changing erroneous beliefs about drugs (e.g. that use is more prevalent than it is, or that a drug's effects are relatively harm-

> **peer leadership** A strategy used by drug prevention schemes where young people are trained to provide anti-drugs messages to their peers.

less). The evidence on the effectiveness of these types of schemes is difficult to gauge because they take place across different types of communities characterized by different risk factors and employ a range of different strategies over different timescales. However, some studies have indicated that at the very least such schemes do appear to *delay* the onset of drug use – even if longer-term effects are difficult to evaluate (Sussman, Dent, Simon, Stacy *et al.*, 1995; Faggiano, Galanti, Bohrn, Burkhart *et al.*, 2008).

Residential rehabilitation centres are also important in the treatment and longer term support of individuals with substance use disorders. Such centres allow people to live, work and socialize with others undergoing treatment in an environment that offers advice, immediate support, group and individual treatment programmes,

> **residential rehabilitation centres** Centres that allow people to live, work and socialize with others undergoing treatment in an environment that offers advice, immediate support, and group and individual treatment programmes enabling clients to learn the social and coping skills necessary for the transition back to a normal life.

and they enable the client to learn the social and coping skills necessary for the transition back to a normal life. In such centres, detoxification programmes can be monitored and supported with the help of peripatetic key workers. Residential rehabilitation programmes usually combine a mixture of group work, psychological interventions, social skills training, and practical and vocational activities. In the UK, clients would normally begin residential rehabilitation after completing inpatient detoxification. Despite the support offered by residential rehabilitation centres, the percentage of clients in such centres who do not complete their treatment programme is often unacceptably high (Westreich, Heitner, Cooper, Galanter & Guedj, 1997) and, perhaps not surprisingly, non-completers fare significantly less well than completers (Aron & Daily, 1976; Berger & Smith, 1978). However, a number of studies have clearly indicated that longer stays in residential rehabilitation centres are consistently associated with better outcomes, with a minimum stay of 3 months recommended (Simpson, 2001).

9.5.2 Behavioural Therapies

There is a tradition of using behavioural therapies with many substance use disorders, and these are mainly adaptations of conditioning principles to the practical difficulties involved in controlling and preventing substance abuse and dependence. Behavioural therapies have a number of aims:

1. to change substance use from a positive or pleasurable experience to a negative or aversive one (e.g. aversion therapy) (Weins, Montague, Manaugh & English, 1976);

2. to help the individual identify environmental stimuli and situations that have come to control substance use (e.g. contingency management therapy) (Miller, Leckman, Delaney & Tinkcom, 1992);

3. to reinforce abstinence by rewarding the user when they provide drug-free urine specimens (e.g. contingency management) (Petry, 2000); and

4. to teach the user alternative behaviours that are likely to compete with substance use behaviours (e.g. relaxation, meditation, social skills and anger management) (Azrin, Acierno, Kogan, Donohue et al., 1996).

Aversion therapy

This treatment has been regularly used in the context of a number of substance disorders, but most notably with alcohol dependence. Using a classical conditioning paradigm, clients are given their drug (the conditioned stimulus) followed immediately by another drug (the aversive unconditioned stimulus) that causes unpleasant physiological reactions such as nausea and sickness (Lemere & Voegtlin, 1950). The assumption here is that pairing the favoured drug with unpleasant reactions will make that drug less attractive. In addition, rather than physically administering these drugs in order to form an aversive conditioned response, the whole process can be carried out covertly by asking the client to imagine taking their drug followed by imagining some upsetting or repulsive consequence. This variant on aversion therapy is known as **covert sensitisation** (Cautela, 1966). However, there is limited evidence that aversion therapy has anything but short-lived effects

covert sensitization The association of an aversive stimulus with a behaviour the client wishes to reduce or eliminate.

(Wilson, 1978), and outcomes are significantly less favourable when clients with long-standing substance dependence are treated in this way (Howard, 2001). Nevertheless, aversion therapy can be used as part of a broader treatment package involving community support, detoxification and social skills training.

Contingency management therapy

This is a treatment procedure that teaches the client how to restructure and control their behaviour and environment in order to prevent drug use. This approach is also based on conditioning principles, and these can include (1) stimulus control, where the client learns to identify environmental situations that trigger drug use and avoid or minimize them (e.g. identifying a stressful day at work as a trigger for drinking, and so avoiding pubs or bars), (2) using rewards to reinforce abstinence (e.g. being given vouchers for not using a substance, which can be exchanged for desired activities such as a trip to the cinema or the theatre), (3) learning to be aware of when and how frequently drug taking occurs (e.g. by keeping a diary noting all times that drinking occurs), and (4) setting attainable goals in a structured step-by-step approach to treatment (e.g. by setting *non-abstinence* goals that are achievable) (Hester, 1995). **Contingency management therapy** continues to be a valuable tool for therapists in this area, with a number of new variations on this methodology being developed over the years such as teaching job-seeking, assertiveness and social interaction skills.

contingency management therapy Behavioural therapy which aims to help the individual identify environmental stimuli and situations that have come to control symptoms such as substance use.

A particularly important variant of behavioural self-control therapy (BSCT) is known as **controlled drinking**. Traditionally, it has been assumed that a 'cure' for a substance use disorder entails complete abstinence, but programmes have been developed more recently that put the emphasis on controlled use rather than complete abstinence. This has been a particularly useful approach to treating alcohol dependency, and has been pioneered by Sobell & Sobell (1993). The assumptions here are that (1) in modern day Western societies it is difficult to avoid alcohol altogether, and so it is better to have the aim of controlling drinking rather than avoiding alcohol completely, and (2) teaching clients to have control over their drinking behaviour has other benefits, such as improved self-esteem, a sense of responsibility, and feelings of control over particular domains in their life. Absence of these latter characteristics often drives the individual to alcohol dependence in the first place. Clients undergo social skills training in order to negotiate situations in which they would

controlled drinking A variant of BSCT in which emphasis is put on controlled use rather than complete abstinence.

STIGMA AND CONTROVERSIAL TREATMENT PROGRAMMES FOR SUBSTANCE USE DISORDERS

There is stigma associated with drug abuse and substance use disorders – to the point where there is often a public outcry if treatment programmes propose controversial interventions that seem counterintuitive to the non-drug user. Recent examples include (1) treating heroin addicts by giving them supervised heroin injections and (2) giving drug addicts financial rewards for staying 'clean'.

In the first example, addicts are given daily injections of heroin in supervised clinics in an attempt to wean them off the drug. A study of this intervention based in London, Darlington and Brighton in the UK divided heroin addicts into three groups, giving one group heroin and giving the other two intravenous methadone and oral methadone. All three groups showed improvement, but the heroin-using group fared much better than the other two, with 75 per cent having stopped using street heroin and also having significantly reduced their involvement in crime (Strang, Metrebain, Lintzeris, Potts *et al.*, 2010).

Giving drug addicts monetary rewards for staying clean also has a significant effect on the success of treatment. In the 'Harbour Steps' trial run in Lambeth in London, addicts earn a small credit each time they

give a crack-free urine sample, and can be tested up to three times a week. Such programmes are significantly more effective at establishing abstinence than control treatments (Lussier, Heil, Mongeon, Badger & Higgins, 2006).

Despite the success of these types of programmes, and despite the fact that people will rarely criticize rewarding people for losing weight or giving up smoking, there is often a public reluctance to endorse programmes that appear to 'reward' individuals who have an illegal substance use disorder, and there have been problems establishing clinics that use these types of programmes in countries such as Germany, the Netherlands, Canada and the UK because of public criticism. It is clear that many people still believe that drug addiction is solely the 'fault' of the addict and as such is self-inflicted (Crisp, Gelder, Rix, Meltzer & Rowlands, 2000). Until we can change this unhelpful and discriminating view of those with substance use disorders, it may continue to be difficult to propose, develop and finance these types of interventions.

To read about a controversial proposal to create 'drug rooms' for addicts go to http://tinyurl.com/n87g85l

---

otherwise drink excessively, relaxation training to prevent stressors that might trigger drinking, and are encouraged to think positively about other domains in their life (e.g. to eat healthily). Clients are also taught to believe that they have real control over their drinking, and the BSCT methods outlined above are regularly used to provide the client with adaptive strategies for control. Finally, controlled drinking also teaches the client to be aware that a lapse is not catastrophic but is often inevitable and natural, and that they can use the self-control and social skills they have learnt to overcome lapses. Outcome studies suggest that controlled drinking is achievable, can be as effective over the longer term as treatments that require total abstinence (Foy, Nunn & Rychtarik, 1984), and can help individuals to moderate their intake and to live more fulfilled and healthier lives (Sobell & Sobell, 1995). Controlled drinking is also an accepted treatment strategy for a majority of substance abuse services in the UK (Rosenberg & Melville, 2005).

9.5.3 Cognitive Behaviour Therapies (CBTs)

CBT has been used in the treatment of substance use disorders in at least two different ways. The first is to use CBT to correct dysfunctional beliefs about relapse, and the second is to deal with substance use disorder when it is comorbid with other psychiatric symptoms such as depression and psychosis.

First, as we mentioned earlier, substance abuse disorders are notoriously difficult to treat over the longer term. Individuals can usually quit the substance in the short term, but relapse is common in up to 90 per cent of those receiving treatment for substance dependency (Brownell, 1986). As a result, a successful treatment programme has to deal as effectively with relapses as it does in getting the client to quit in the first place. Two factors appear to be important in determining whether a relapse will lead to regular use again. These are (1) the client's beliefs about relapse, and (2) experiencing

RESEARCH METHODS 9.1

HAIR SAMPLE ANALYSIS

Many methods of collecting data about substance abuse are relatively unreliable. Self-report is obviously problematic, because users will often have reason to lie about their drug use (if it involves legal issues such as child custody), or their recall of drug use may be affected by the changed states of consciousness caused by regular use of certain substances. Even blood and urine samples can be very variable in the data they provide (Spiehler & Brown, 1987), and are certainly not suitable for estimating longer term drug use.

However, one relatively reliable method of collecting data about drug use is through **hair sample analysis** (e.g. Uhl & Sachs, 2004). Small amounts of the drug will accumulate in hair after use and, because head hair grows at approximately 0.8–1.3cm per month, a record of drug use is available over a period of weeks or months after intake. A hair sample of only 3–5cm in length is required to provide a record of drug use over the previous 3–4 months, and high-performance chromatography is used to identify the concentrations of any drugs taken up into the hair sample.

> **hair sample analysis** A method of collecting data about previous drug use by analysing the small amounts of the drug that accumulate in the hair.

Hair sample analysis is not only used as a more reliable way of collecting research data about previous drug use, it is becoming widely used for medico-legal purposes where the user needs to prove long-term abstinence (especially in cases related to rehabilitation and legal custody). It is also used to provide a longer term record of drug use in the case of individuals who may have died from overdose (Tagliaro, Battisti, Smith & Marigo, 1998), and has been used to detect the use of opiates, cocaine, cannabis, and amphetamines (Jurado & Sachs, 2003).

Nevertheless, hair sample analysis is not a foolproof way of estimating drug use, and it does have its own drawbacks as a methodology. For instance, it is not suitable as a measure of current drug use, but only as a method of estimating previous medium-term use. It also cannot be used on those who present with very short hair or no head hair!

---

stressful emotional states, such as anxiety, depression, anger, and frustration, and these states are responsible for around 30 per cent of all relapses after treatment (Cummings, Gordon & Marlatt, 1980). In order to counter these relapse factors, therapists have developed variants of CBT that address dysfunctional beliefs about relapse, and can also provide help in coping with stressful emotions. In the first case, individuals will often hold dysfunctional beliefs about relapse that facilitate further regular use. These may include beliefs such as 'If I lapse, then my treatment has failed', 'If I lapse, then I am a worthless individual who doesn't deserve to get better', or 'I've had one drink, so I may as well get drunk' (Marlatt & Gordon, 1985). These are what are known as **abstinence violation** beliefs that contribute to the transition from relapse 'slips' to full relapse. CBT attempts

> **abstinence violation** Dysfunctional beliefs about relapse following treatment for substance dependency that facilitate further regular substance use.

to identify such dysfunctional beliefs, to challenge them (e.g. relapse doesn't inevitably mean total loss of control), and to provide the client with the skills required to negotiate a relapse successfully. To deal with the second factor, CBT programmes have been

developed that help the client to deal effectively with negative emotions, stress, and the factors that might give rise to stress. This is also known as **motivational-enhancement intervention** (MET) and provides communication training, work- and school-related skills, problem-solving skills, peer refusal skills, negative mood management, social support, and general relapse

> **motivational-enhancement intervention (MET)** An intervention for substance abuse and dependency involving communication training, work- and school-related skills, problem-solving skills, peer-refusal skills, negative mood management, social support and general relapse prevention.

prevention methods (Miller & Rollnick, 1991). Both forms of CBT have been shown to be more effective in establishing long-term abstinence and effective drug avoidance behaviours than traditional aftercare or control conditions (McAuliffe, 1990; Farabee, Rawson & McCann, 2002) and are particularly effective if combined with family therapy (Waldron, Slesnick, Brody, Turner & Peterson, 2001).

Interestingly, recent UK NICE guidelines for treatments for substance use disorder recommend CBT primarily when substance use disorder is comorbid with another psychiatric disorder such as anxiety or depression (see http://www.nice.org.uk/nicemedia/live/11812/35973/35973.pdf). However, systematic reviews indicate only moderate support for CBT when treating comorbid depression and substance dependency (Hides, Samet & Lubman, 2010), with the implication that more potent forms of CBT still need to be developed to deal with substance use disorder comorbidity.

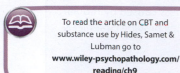

To read the article on CBT and substance use by Hides, Samet & Lubman go to www.wiley-psychopathology.com/reading/ch9

9.5.4 Family and Couple Therapy

Because many regular drug abusers are young people, they often live with their families and, because of this, family members can often provide support during treatment on a day-by-day basis. However, family therapy is important for a number of other reasons. Firstly, many of the parents of substance abusers are also abusers themselves, and as such may constitute part of the problem that needs to be addressed. Secondly, individuals with substance abuse problems (such as problem drinkers) will often physically and sexually abuse members of their family, and so therapy may often need to involve those who have regular close contact with the abuser. Family therapy is an effective way of identifying and altering dysfunctional family patterns that may contribute to adolescent substance abuse (Rowe, 2012), and can often be an effective brief intervention for adolescent substance abuse when whole families are involved in the programme (Szapocznik, Zarate, Duff & Muir, 2013). Family therapists will attempt to engage members of the family in the treatment process and to reduce blaming behaviour. Subsequently, the therapist will use contingency management and behavioural contracting procedures, and teach communication and problem-solving skills in order to facilitate more adaptive patterns of interaction within the family. This approach has been shown to be particularly successful in dealing with adolescent substance use problems, and is generally as effective in the long term as individual psychotherapies such as CBT (Waldron, Slesnick, Brody, Turner et al., 2001). Specifically involving a client's spouse or partner in therapy also has important beneficial effects. The partner can offer support when required, but it is also important in identifying specific problems in a relationship that may be contributing to substance abuse. Outcome studies have indicated that, when compared with no treatment, couples therapy produces longer periods of abstinence

To read Rowe's article on family therapy go to www.wiley-psychopathology.com/reading/ch9

and improvements in the quality of the couple's relationship (Fals-Stewart, Birchler & O'Farrell, 1996).

9.5.5 Biological Treatments

Drugs are used to treat substance use disorders in a variety of ways. Collectively these are known as **detoxification**, and are often used in conjunction with psychological treatments or as a precursor to psychological treatments (to wean heavy users off regular substance use and make them amenable to other forms of therapy). Detoxification is a process of systematic and supervised withdrawal from substance use that is either managed in a residential setting or on an outpatient basis. Drug use during detoxification can take a number of forms: (1) to help reduce withdrawal symptoms (e.g. anxiolytic drugs), (2) to prevent relapse by using antagonistic drugs to make subsequent substance use aversive (e.g. Antabuse – a drug that causes vomiting if alcohol is consumed), (3) to block the pleasurable CNS effects of a substance (e.g. naxolone – used with individuals who are opiate dependent in order to prevent opiates having their usual effects on reward centres in the brain), and (4) to wean a user onto a weaker substance (e.g. **methadone maintenance programmes**, where the user takes a less virulent opiate in order to wean themselves off heroin).

> **detoxification** A process of systematic and supervised withdrawal from substance use that is either managed in a residential setting or on an outpatient basis.

> **methadone maintenance programmes** A detoxification programme where users take a less virulent opiate in order to wean themselves off heroin.

Those drugs that help reduce withdrawal symptoms include clonidine, which reduces noradrenergic activity in the brain (Baumgartner & Rowan, 1987), and acamprosate, a drug that helps to reduce the cravings associated with withdrawal (Mason, 2001). Basic anxiolytic and anti-depressant drugs can also be used to improve mood and alleviate negative emotions experienced during withdrawal (Cornelius, Salloum, Mezzich, Cornelius et al., 1995).

Antabuse (disulfiram) has been used for over 60 years in the detoxification of individuals with alcohol dependency. It affects the metabolism of alcohol so that the normal process of converting toxic alcohol products into nontoxic acetic acids is slowed, and this causes the individual to feel nauseous or vomit whenever they take alcohol. However, the use of Antabuse does have some problems. It is rarely effective when patients are given the drug to take unsupervised, and

> **antabuse (disulfiram)** A drug used in the detoxification of individuals with alcohol dependency.

non-compliance and drop-out from such programmes are high (Fuller, Branchey, Brightwell, Derman *et al.*, 1986). Secondly, it does have a number of side effects, and in some rare cases causes liver disease and hepatitis (Mohanty, LaBrecque, Mitros & Layden, 2004). However, when taken in properly supervised programmes, Antabuse has been shown to be more effective at reducing drinking behaviour than placebo controls (Chick, Gough, Falkowski, Kershaw *et al.*, 1992; Fuller & Gordis, 2004), including having a beneficial effect on short-term abstinence and days until relapse (Jorgensen, Pedersen & Tonnesen, 2011). Indeed, some long-term studies of alcohol treatment have suggested that abstinence rates of 50 per cent are achievable up to 7 years after initial treatment with the supervised and guided use of alcohol deterrents such as Antabuse (Krampe, Stawicki, Wagner, Bartels *et al.*, 2006), and that Antabuse can increase treatment effectiveness when combined with CBT (Pettinati, Oslin, Kampman, Dundon *et al.*, 2010).

To read an article on 'The efficacy of disulfiram' by Jorgensen, Pedersen & Tonnesen go to www.wiley-psychopathology.com/reading/ch9

A further set of drugs used to treat substance use disorders are those that influence brain neurotransmitter receptor sites and prevent the neuropsychological effects of stimulants, opiates and hallucinogens. For example, drugs such as **naltrexone**, **naxolone** and the more recently developed **buprenorfine** attach to endorphin receptor sites in the brain. This prevents opioids from having their normal effect of stimulating these sites to produce more endorphins that create the feeling of euphoria when drugs such as heroin are taken. Such drugs do appear to reduce craving for opiates and they help the therapeutic process when combined with other forms of psychological therapy (Streeton & Whelan, 2001). However, such drugs do come with a cost. Dosage has to be properly regulated, otherwise the client may be thrown rapidly into an aversive withdrawal (Roozen, de Kan, van den Brink, Kerkof & Geerlings, 2002), and narcotic antagonists such as naltrexone and naxolone are only effective for as long as the client is taking them. However, because these drugs affect the release of endorphins, they have been used to help treat a number of substance use disorders, including alcohol (O'Malley, Krishnan-Sarin, Farren & O'Connor, 2000), cocaine and opiate dependence

naltrexone An opioid receptor antagonist used primarily in the management of alcohol dependence and opioid dependence.

naxolone One of a set of drugs used to treat substance use disorders which influence brain neurotransmitter receptor sites and prevent the neuropsychological effects of stimulants, opiates and hallucinogens.

buprenorfine An opioid drug used in the treatment of opioid addiction.

(O'Brien, 2005). The reason why such drugs may be effective over a range of substances that have their psychoactive effects across different brain neurotransmitter pathways is because they suppress the release of endorphins, and endorphin receptors are closely associated with the brain's reward centres (Leri & Burns, 2005).

Finally, **drug replacement treatment** involves treating severe cases of substance abuse and dependence by substituting a drug that has less damaging effects. For example, many heroin users put themselves at risk from overdoses, contaminated street heroin, and using unsterilized needles. To try to address these issues as rapidly as possible, users can be switched from heroin to the less virulent opium derivative methadone. Methadone has a slower onset and weaker effects, and can be taken orally rather than injected. Initial outcome studies suggested that methadone treatment was helpful in enabling heroin addicts to withdraw from the drug. However, we must remember that methadone is still an addictive drug itself and it can be difficult to withdraw from (Kleber, 1981), and because of this methadone maintenance therapy can last for many years – and for some, for their whole lifetime (Smyth, Barry, Lane, Cotter *et al.*, 2005; Arora & Williams, 2013). Most recent outcome studies suggest that methadone maintenance therapy is most effective when part of a multifaceted structured therapy programme that includes psychotherapy, drug education, skills training, and contingency management (O'Brien & McKay, 2002), and when the client includes non-drug-using family members and friends in the treatment (Kidorf, King, Neufeld, Stoller *et al.*, 2005). As well as contributing to the success of treatment in a multifaceted approach, methadone maintenance therapy has the added benefits of increasing the likelihood of entering into longer term comprehensive treatment, reducing heroin use and criminal behaviour, and reducing health risks (e.g. the number of HIV cases) (Schwartz, Highfield, Jaffe, Brady *et al.*, 2006; Farrell, Gowing, Marsden, Ling & Ali, 2005; Arora & Williams, 2013). While **drug maintenance therapies** have been largely confined to treating opiate dependency, there have been recent attempts to develop substitute drugs for other dependencies. One such example is Sativex, an aerosol that combines THC and non-psychoactive cannabis ingredients for the treatment of cannabis dependency. Savitex has the benefit of having weaker effects than cannabis and is taken orally rather than smoked (Kleber, 2005).

drug replacement treatment Involves treating severe cases of substance abuse and dependency by substituting a drug that has lesser damaging effects.

drug maintenance therapies Drug treatment programmes in which severe cases of substance abuse and dependency are treated by substituting a drug that has less damaging effects.

SELF-TEST QUESTIONS

- Why are substance use disorders particularly hard to treat?

- Can you describe the different kinds of community-based programmes that help to prevent or treat substance use disorders?

- How successful is residential rehabilitation in treating substance use disorders?

- How have the principles of behaviour therapy been adapted to treat substance use disorders?

- Can you name the main features of aversion therapy, contingency management therapy, and controlled drinking?

- What are some of the benefits of using controlled drinking goals rather than complete abstinence?

- What are abstinence violation beliefs and how do cognitive behaviour therapies (CBTs) attempt to treat them?

- What is meant by the term detoxification, and how are drugs used in detoxification programmes?

- How have drugs such as naltrexone, naxolone and buprenorfine proved to be useful in the treatment of substance use disorders?

SECTION SUMMARY

9.5   THE TREATMENT OF SUBSTANCE USE DISORDERS

The treatment of substance use disorders is inevitably a multifaceted one, with most mental health services providing a range of treatments (detoxification, skills training, behavioural and cognitive therapies, and family and couple therapies) in a variety of settings (e.g. individual, community-based or residential). Treatments usually involve a combination of drug-based detoxification, psychological therapy, and skills training, and will usually attempt to involve the client's family and friends in the therapeutic process. Substance use disorders are difficult to treat and we described some of the difficulties at the outset of this section on treatment. Nevertheless, outcomes are often good, and total abstinence is an achievable goal – even with severely addictive substances such as opiates and stimulants. For example, a long-term study of heroin dependence in a small town in the south-east of England 33 years after initial treatment found that 42 per cent of those treated had been abstinent for 10 years (Rathod, Addenbroke & Rosenbach, 2005). This suggests that long-term dependence is not inevitable after exposure to addictive drugs, and individuals can often control their use as well as receive effective treatment for their dependency when required.

The key points discussed in this this section are:

- Treatment of substance use disorders is difficult because of the physical effects of dependence, the probability of comorbid psychiatric disorders, and high rates of relapse.

- Treatment interventions are usually multifaceted and address the individual client's problems at a range of different levels.

- One form of community-based service is *self-help groups* such as Alcoholics Anonymous (AA).

- *Drug-prevention schemes* are used with young people to try and prevent first drug use.

- *Residential rehabilitation centres* provide a controlled environment for detoxification and longer term support for individuals with substance use disorders.

- Behaviour therapies adapted to treat substance use disorders include *aversion therapy* and *contingency management therapy*.

- *Controlled drinking* can be used as a non-abstinence approach to treating alcohol abuse and dependency.

- *Cognitive behaviour therapy (CBT)* is used primarily to change individuals' beliefs about their substance use, but are best employed when a sufferer has a psychiatric disorder comorbid with substance use disorder.

- *Motivational-enhancement training (MET)* provides communication training, work- and school-related skills, problem-solving skills, peer-group refusal skills, relapse prevention methods, and negative mood management.

- *Family and couple therapy* is useful for ensuring that family members understand the reasons for the substance use and can provide help and support during and after treatment.

- *Detoxification* is a process of systematic and supervised withdrawal from substance use that often uses the controlled use of drugs to combat the physical problems of withdrawal and dependence.

- *Antabuse (disulfiram)* causes alcohol to produce toxins which make the individual feel unwell and has been used for over 60 years as a means of controlling alcohol dependency.

- *Drug maintenance therapies* involve treating severe cases of substance use (e.g. heroin dependence) by normally substituting a drug that has a lesser effect (e.g. methadone).

9.6   SUBSTANCE USE DISORDERS REVIEWED

Substance use disorders are an important social and health problem, as well as also raising many mental health issues. Substance use disorders are associated with criminal behaviour (often violent crime), short- and long-term health problems, disruption to social and occupational functioning, and with increased risk of psychiatric comorbidity. The main substances of abuse can be grouped into stimulants (e.g. cocaine, amphetamine), sedatives (e.g. opiates, barbiturates), and hallucinogenic drugs (e.g. LSD). Legal drugs such as alcohol and nicotine can also foster dependence and can cause significant long-term health problems.

Most of the drugs associated with abuse and dependence have important mood altering effects that make the user feel confident, relaxed (alcohol, cannabis), euphoric (heroin, cocaine), or energized (amphetamines, MDMA). More importantly, these effects also alleviate any negative or stressful mood the user may be feeling prior to use. Most of these substances also have addictive properties as users quickly develop a tolerance to the drug and experience worsening withdrawal symptoms during abstinence.

Substance use disorders can be seen as developing through a number of different stages, with different factors affecting transition from one stage to the next (see Figure 9.7). The three stages highlighted here are experimentation (what determines first use?), regular use, and abuse and dependence (what makes some people use drugs regularly even though this activity has significant negative effects on their health and social and occupational functioning?).

Some people do seem to move down a slippery slope from experimentation to abuse and dependence, but we have to be clear that many other people do not, and people can be regular substance users without this affecting their family, social and occupational functioning. However, when the stage of substance abuse and dependence is reached, this is often associated with comorbid psychiatric problems or simply with poverty, unemployment and poor housing. In the former case, many who are substance dependent use their drug to self-medicate against the negative effects of their comorbid psychopathy (e.g. depression, eating disorders, anxiety disorders and suchlike). In the case of poverty, the mood altering effects of the drug may provide relief from miserable and unfulfilled lives.

Treatment of substance use disorders is usually multifaceted, and many health services provide a tiered approach by providing a range of treatments, advice and training facilities in a variety of settings (e.g. individual, community-based or residential). Substance use disorders can be difficult to treat because of the difficulties of dealing with withdrawal symptoms, the fact that the drug has probably been the user's main method of coping with emotional and life stressors, frequent comorbidity of other mental health problems, and temptation to relapse after treatment. However, outcome studies suggest that with appropriate support and aftercare, treatment can result in long-term abstinence in a significant proportion of clients.

To access the online resources for this chapter go to
www.wiley-psychopathology.com/ch9

Reading

Video

Activity

Reading	Video	Activity
<ul><li>Alcoholics Anonymous 12-step programme</li><li>Journal article: Heroin use</li><li>Breakthrough Britain: Addictions</li><li>Debate rages over experts' proposal to create 'drug rooms' for addicts in Brighton and Hove</li><li>Journal article: CBT and substance use</li><li>Journal article: Family therapy</li><li>Article: The efficacy of disulfiram</li><li>Glossary of key terms</li><li>Clinical issues</li><li>Links to journal articles</li><li>References</li></ul>	<ul><li>Alcohol misuse: A personal account</li><li>Cannabis</li><li>Medical use of cannabis</li><li>Cocaine</li><li>Cocaine: Risk and recovery</li><li>Heroin</li><li>Opioid use disorder</li><li>LSD</li><li>Ecstasy</li></ul>	<ul><li>Different substances discussed in this chapter</li><li>Alcohol unit consumption calculator</li><li>Developmental model of substance abuse and dependence</li><li>Self-test questions</li><li>Revision flashcards</li><li>Research questions</li></ul>

10 Eating Disorders

 To access the online resources for this chapter go to
www.wiley-psychopathology.com/ch10

LEARNING OUTCOMES

When you have completed this chapter, you should be able to:

1. Describe the characteristics and main diagnostic criteria of the three main eating disorders.

2. Describe the cultural and demographic distribution of eating disorders, and evaluate why this information is important in understanding eating disorders.

3. Compare and contrast a range of risk factors for eating disorders, covering risk factors at different levels of explanation (such as genetic, developmental, cultural, and psychological).

4. Describe, compare and contrast at least two interventions commonly used in the treatment of eating disorders.

For as long as I can remember, I've wanted to do everything under the sun – and be the best at it. If I got a C, I'd be really hard on myself, and my parents made it pretty clear they wanted me to get a scholarship, since paying for college would be a challenge.

Plus, things weren't so great at home. I'd always had a terrible relationship with my dad. I felt like he ignored me most of the time. He could be pretty scary. Screaming at me for little things – like leaving crumbs on the kitchen table after making a snack. I'd tell him when he hurt my feelings, but he'd just walk away and slam the door. On top of it all, he and my Mum were fighting a lot, too.

It was hard to be at school and even harder to be at home. As a result, I began eating less. Starving myself wasn't my actual goal at first – just more of a response to everything going on in my life. But I started to lose weight.

Soon, my clothes got looser. Then I became a vegetarian, also cutting out all foods with chemicals and preservatives. I lost even more weight. I felt I had finally found something I could completely control – my weight. Even though my life felt crazy, I could do this one thing very well and, initially, I got a high from this accomplishment. Gaining or losing a single pound determined my mood for the whole day.

I remember watching a film in health class about the dangers of anorexia. I even hung warning posters around school during Eating Disorders Awareness Week. But I never connected my own weight loss to anorexia. Denial, of course, is a symptom of the disease. A voice in my head kept telling me the less food I let touch my lips, the more stable and safe I would be. My fiends and family kept telling me I was too skinny, but no one could force me to eat. And, to be honest, it made me feel powerful that I could ignore pleas and starve myself. Even as my bones poked out from under my skin, I could not admit to anyone – including myself – how incredibly sick I was.

Amy's Story

Introduction

Disorders of eating are complex and have their roots in psychological, sociological and cultural phenomena. In many of today's cultures, individuals are torn between advertising that implores them to eat a range of foods high in calories, and campaigns designed to promote selective and healthy eating, because being overweight is closely associated with an increase in certain illnesses and higher death rates. Eating behaviour is also influenced by media representations of ideal body shapes. These prompt appearance-conscious individuals to control and restrict their eating in order to achieve these media-portrayed ideals of a slim body – ideals which are usually underweight. Given these pressures, and the psychological factors that accompany them, it is not surprising that eating patterns can become pathological and result in disorders of both under-eating (anorexia nervosa) and over-eating (bulimia nervosa and binge-eating disorder).

Amy's story above illustrates what a slippery slope the descent into an eating disorder can be. The story starts with someone who is troubled in various spheres of her life, including school life and home life. In *Amy's* case, this leads more by accident than design to a reduction in eating. Eventually, controlling eating becomes a goal in itself, and a source of satisfaction when even the smallest of dietary goals are met. The obvious physical

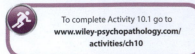
To complete Activity 10.1 go to
www.wiley-psychopathology.com/
activities/ch10

FOCUS POINT 10.1

WARNING SIGNS OF ANOREXIA NERVOSA

- Is she losing a lot of weight? Has she fallen 7 pounds below the normal weight range for someone of her height?
- Is she becoming an obsessive counter of calories? Does she eat only very low-calorie foods, like salad and fruit?
- Is she becoming secretive or evasive about her eating habits? Does she eat out of sight or in private?

- Has she started to become obsessive about exercise, or any other daily routine (e.g. homework)?
- Is she suffering unusually from infections, constipation, dizzy spells, insomnia, or does she complain of the cold?

From http://www.annecollins.com/eating-disorders/anorexia.htm.

consequences of lack of nutrition then become exhaustion and lack of concentration, menstrual irregularities, and proneness to infections, insomnia, dizzy spells, and sensitivity to cold. *Amy's story* also highlights some of the risk factors that have been found to predict the development of an eating disorder such as anorexia, and these include high levels of perfectionism, and parents who exhibit coercive parental control, or who are hostile and unresponsive to the individual's needs. Also characteristic of the disorder, and featured in *Amy's story*, are the need to control eating as a central feature of eating disorders generally, the development of very durable and resistant beliefs about the need to diet and control eating, and the use of denial as a means of avoiding confronting the disorder and challenging dysfunctional beliefs about eating. Focus Point 10.1 summarizes some of the warning signs of anorexia nervosa, many of which will have been apparent as *Amy* developed her own eating disorder.

Many women consider themselves to be overweight despite having a BMI in the normal range. Studies of college women suggest that 43 per cent were currently dieting despite 78 per cent of them having a healthy BMI (Fayet, Petocz & Samman, 2012), while community studies indicate that between 25 and 30 per cent of females claim to be dieting or actively attempting to lose weight (McVey, Tweed & Blackmore, 2004; Wardle & Johnson, 2002). Dieting is often a significant precursor to anorexia nervosa symptoms (Patton, Carlin, Shao, Hibbert *et al.*, 1997) and can become an entrenched habit that is resistant to both psychological and pharmacological treatment, and dieting may contribute to the persistence of symptoms in some anorexia nervosa sufferers (Walsh, 2013).

Similarly, recent figures suggest that obesity is increasing significantly in Western cultures. In the UK, obesity rates have almost doubled between 1993 and 2011, with 24 per cent of men and 26 per cent of women currently rated as obese, with a BMI in excess of 30 kg/m² (Health & Social Care Information Centre, 2011). This suggests that both under-eating and over-eating have reached almost epidemic proportions, with surveys suggesting that 6.3 per cent of the UK population exhibit disordered

eating patterns leading to either underweight or overweight (McBride, McManus, Thompson, Palmer & Brugha, 2013). Apart from the cultural pressures that can trigger over-eating and under-eating, psychological factors also represent both risk factors and outcomes of disordered eating. As we shall see later in this chapter, developmental and psychological processes appear to act as vulnerability factors in the development of eating disorders, and eating disorders themselves can result in psychological symptoms such as low self-esteem, substance misuse, and suicidal ideation (Neumark-Sztainer, Hannan, 2000).

This chapter will cover the three main eating disorders, namely *anorexia nervosa*, *bulimia nervosa* and *binge-eating disorder*, and for each discuss diagnosis and prevalence, the role of sociocultural factors, aetiology, and treatment.

10.1 DIAGNOSIS AND PREVALENCE

10.1.1 *Anorexia Nervosa*

The main symptoms of **anorexia nervosa (AN)** are self-starvation and a refusal to maintain a minimally normal body weight, and examples resembling anorexia have been reported throughout history (see Focus Point 10.2). It is a disorder that afflicts mainly adolescent women, and tends to have an onset in the early to middle teenage years following either a period of life stress or an intense period of dieting. Ten times more females than males are afflicted by the disorder (Walters & Kendler, 1994), and in recent years there appears to be an increasing trend towards early-onset anorexia in girls between 8 and 13 years of age (Lask & Bryant-Waugh, 2000), with

> **anorexia nervosa (AN)** An eating disorder, the main features of which include a refusal to maintain a minimal body weight, a pathological fear of gaining weight and a distorted body image in which sufferers continue to insist they are overweight.

surveys indicating that almost 30 per cent of 8- to 13-year-olds report avoidant or restrictive eating behaviour (van Dyck, Bellwald, Kurz, Dremmel *et al.*, 2013). Important features of anorexia nervosa include:

1. a refusal to maintain a minimal body weight,
2. a pathological fear of gaining weight, and
3. a distorted body image in which, even when clearly emaciated, sufferers continue to insist they are overweight.

Weight loss is often viewed as an important achievement (see the example of *Amy* at the beginning of this chapter), and weight gain as a significant loss of

HISTORICAL EXAMPLES OF EATING DISORDERS

There is a tendency to think of eating disorders as modern ailments driven by cultures obsessed with projecting ideal body shapes to impressionable young people. However, examples of disordered eating behaviour can be found throughout history, and many bear resemblance to the eating disorders we find today (Keel & Klump, 2003). Cases of self-starvation have been reported in classical and medieval times, often as a means of achieving heightened spirituality amongst religious devotees. Bell (1985) called this **holy anorexia**, and cited the example of St. Catherine of Siena who began self-starvation at the age of 16 years and continued until her death in 1380 (at the age of 32). Like modern-day anorexics, St. Catherine portrayed herself as being afflicted by an inability to eat, and all attempts by peers and superiors to induce eating in such fasting saints usually failed. From the 16th to 18th centuries, reports of self-starvation were relatively common (McSherry, 1985), with the case of Mary, Queen of Scots (1542–1587) being a prominent one. During the 19th century, study of self-starvation became more systematic within the medical profession, with Marce describing a form of hypochondria in which 'young girls, who at the period of puberty and after a precocious physical development, become subject to inappetency carried to the utmost limits' (1860, p.264). Probably the first use of the term anorexia nervosa was by Imbert (1840), who characterized *anorexie nerveuse* by loss of appetite, refusal to eat, and emaciation (Vandereycken & Van Deth, 1994). However, while these historical examples bear a formalistic similarity to modern-day eating disorders, the issue of the motivation behind self-starvation in these historical examples is important. At least some of the earliest examples of self-starvation appear to be motivated by religious and spiritual factors, while examples from the 18th and 19th century were justified as either forms of convalescence or hysterical paralysis (Habermas, 1996). However, Habermas (1989) quite rightly points out that individuals with eating disorders tend to hide their goal of losing weight and give other explanations for their refusal to eat. This may also be true of the historical examples we have reviewed here.

Historical examples resembling bulimia nervosa are much rarer than those resembling anorexia nervosa. Most examples taken from classical times through to the 19th century report individuals exhibiting periods of fasting followed by a binge–purge cycle, which suggests that bingeing and purging was rarely found outside of the context of fasting or self-starvation (Keel & Klump, 2003). However, in the 17th century, Silverman (1987) reports a description of **fames canina** – a disorder characterized by large food intake followed by vomiting (Stein & Laakso, 1988). Interestingly, however, when symptoms similar to bulimia are reported in historical writings, most cases involve adult men. This is quite unlike the current day disorder of bulimia, which is primarily an affliction of females.

This brief review suggests that disordered eating (especially self-starvation) has been around as long as people have been able to write about it and report it. In different periods of history, the motivations for self-starvation appear to be different, although the symptoms remain remarkably similar. One implication of this is that disordered eating symptoms similar to modern-day disorders have been around for a considerable period of history. However, changes in contemporary sociocultural factors may influence the frequency and prevalence of such disorders by providing a motivation for disordered eating (e.g. religious fasting would have provided a suitable trigger for self-starvation in vulnerable individuals in classical and medieval times). In addition, sociocultural factors can also provide socially acceptable means of hiding the psychological reasons for self-starvation and loss of appetite. For example, when fasting became an acceptable form of convalescence from illness in the 18th and 19th centuries, this may have provided a suitable means of hiding the anorexic individual's simple desire to restrict and control their eating (just as the trend to diet to achieve a media-driven thin ideal serves the same purpose today).

holy anorexia Self-starvation reported in classical and medieval times, often as a means of achieving heightened spirituality amongst religious devotees.

fames canina An eating disorder characterized by large food intake followed by vomiting reported in the 17th century.

self-control. Even when individuals suffering anorexia do admit they may be underweight, they often deny the important medical implications of this, and will continue to focus on reducing fat in areas of their body that they still believe are too 'fat'. DSM-5 Summary Table 10.1 sets out the main diagnostic criteria for anorexia nervosa. DSM-5 stresses objective levels for judging the severity of the symptoms based on **body mass index (BMI)**. DSM-5 has also adopted the World Health Organisation lower limit for 'normal' body weight of a BMI of 18.5 kg/m² as a level below which body weight should be considered as low enough to trigger the possibility of a diagnosis of anorexia nervosa if other criteria are met. The criteria also emphasize the pathological fear of weight gain in sufferers, and the distortions in self-perception that accompany anorexia. DSM-5 also distinguishes two types of anorexia nervosa. These are the **restricted type AN**, in which self-starvation is not associated with concurrent purging (e.g. self-induced vomiting or use of laxatives), and the **binge-eating/purging type AN**, where the sufferer regularly engages in purging activities to help control weight gain.

> **body mass index (BMI)** A way of measuring a healthy weight range, derived by using both height and weight measurements.

> **restricted type AN** A type of anorexia nervosa in which self-starvation is not associated with concurrent purging (e.g. self-inducing vomiting or use of laxatives).

> **binge-eating/purging type AN** A type of eating disorder in which the sufferer regularly engages in purging activities to help control weight gain.

Because of the severe physical effect of this disorder on the body, anorexia nervosa is usually associated with a number of biological symptoms that are effects of the self-imposed starvation regime. These include (1) tiredness, cardiac arrhythmias, hypotension, low blood pressure and slow heartbeats resulting from altered levels of body electrolytes, such as sodium and potassium, (2) dry skin and brittle hair, (3) kidney and gastrointestinal problems, (4) the development of lanugo (a soft, downy hair) on the body, (5) the absence of menstrual cycles (**amenorrhoea**), and (6) hypothermia, often resulting in feeling cold even in hot environments (Bryant-Waugh, 2000). In many cases, starvation has the effect of severely weakening the heart muscles as the body uses these muscles as a source of protein. As a result, mortality rates (including suicides) in anorexia nervosa and bulimia nervosa are still unacceptably high, ranging from 5 to 8 per cent (Herzog, Greenwood, Dorer, Flores *et al.*, 2000; Steinhausen, Seidel & Metzke, 2000), with one in five of those deaths the result of suicide (Arcelus, Mitchell, Wales & Nielsen, 2011).

> **amenorrhoea** The abnormal failure to menstruate.

Anorexia nervosa begins to develop usually around adolescence. It rarely begins before puberty or after 40 years of age. Onset can be associated with a stressful life event, such as leaving home (Tozzi, Sullivan, Fear, McKenzie & Bulik, 2003), and is often preceded by a period of changed eating patterns, such as self-imposed dieting. Fortunately, most individuals with a diagnosis of anorexia nervosa will remit and be symptom-free within 5 years. However, for others, hospitalization may be required to restore weight and address other medical complications caused by self starvation.

DSM-5 cites the 12-month prevalence rate for anorexia nervosa among young females as around 0.4 per cent, with a female-to-male ratio of around 10:1, making anorexia primarily a female disorder. Lifetime prevalence rate for females by the age of 20 years is 0.8 per cent, with a peak onset age of 19–20 years (Stice, Marti & Rohde, 2013). There is some evidence that cultural and societal factors can affect the frequency of anorexia, so that prevalence rates may differ across cultures and across time (see section 10.2 below) (Miller & Pumariega, 2001). However, recent analysis suggests that anorexia may represent a similar proportion of the general psychiatric population in several Western and non-Western nations (examples of the latter include Korea, Iran, Hong Kong, Japan, Malaysia, and Egypt), and there is growing evidence that it is not just a disorder of affluent Western cultures (Keel & Klump, 2003).

High rates of comorbidity exist between anorexia and other psychiatric disorders. For example, studies suggest between 50 and 68 per cent of anorexia sufferers also have a lifelong diagnosis of major depression (Halmi, Eckert, Marchi, Sampugnaro *et al.*, 1991), and between 15 and 69 per cent of anorexia sufferers also meet diagnostic criteria for OCD or obsessive compulsive personality disorder (OCPD) at some time during their lifetimes (Hudson, Pope, Jonas & Yurgelun-Todd, 1983; Wonderlich, Swift, Slotnick & Goodman, 1990). Most recent surveys suggest significant levels of comorbidity between anorexia nervosa and anxiety disorders such as OCD (21 per cent), panic disorder and agoraphobia (25 per cent), social anxiety disorder (30 per cent) and specific phobias (25 per cent), and with substance abuse disorders (34 per cent) (Jordan, Joyce, Carter, Horn *et al.*, 2008).

DSM-5 SUMMARY TABLE 10.1 *Criteria for anorexia nervosa*

- A significantly reduced calorie intake relative to the requirements of the body leading to a considerably low body weight
- Intense fear of gaining weight or becoming fat
- A disruption in the way that the patient evaluates their body or shape, increasing undue influence of body weight or shape on self-evaluation

To read an article on comorbidity in anorexia nervosa by Jordan *et al.* go to **www.wiley-psychopathology.com/reading/ch10**

10.1.2 Bulimia Nervosa

Like anorexia nervosa, **bulimia nervosa (BN)** is also a disorder that is characterized by fear of weight gain and a distorted perception of body shape. The main feature of bulimia is recurrent episodes of binge eating (often eating more than a normal person's full daily intake of food in one episode), recurrent inappropriate compensatory behaviours to prevent weight gain (such as self-induced vomiting or the misuse of laxatives, diuretics, or enemas; vomiting is the most common form of purging and occurs in 80–90 per cent of those who present for treatment), and a self-evaluation that is unduly influenced by body shape and weight. The diagnostic criteria for bulimia nervosa are provided in DSM-5 Summary Table 10.2.

For a video on bulimia go to
www.wiley-psychopathology.com/
video/ch10

bulimia nervosa (BN) An eating disorder, the main features of which are recurrent episodes of binge eating followed by periods of purging or fasting.

Most bulimia sufferers are not usually overweight compared with the norm for their height (Gordon, 2001); nor do they usually become underweight as a result of their purging – and this distinguishes them from those suffering from the binge eating/purging anorexia nervosa subtype. Bulimia nervosa has a typical onset in late adolescence or early adulthood, with peak onset age between 16 and 20 years (Stice, Marti & Rohde, 2013). Disturbed eating behaviour persists in many individuals diagnosed with bulimia nervosa for several years, although long-term follow-up studies suggest that approximately 75 per cent of women with bulimia nervosa were in remission 20 years after being diagnosed (Keel, Gravener, Joiner & Haedt, 2010). About 90 per cent of those suffering bulimia are female (Gotestam & Agras, 1995). Bulimia is frequently triggered by concerns about weight and body shape, and may have its origins in a period of dieting. What is perplexing about bulimia is that individuals with strong concerns about their weight and body shape should indulge in such regular bouts of excessive over-eating (between two and 12 bouts per week, Garfinkel, Kennedy & Kaplan,

1995), and this suggests that they have lost control over their eating patterns. Because of this lack of control over an area of their life that is important to them, sufferers usually become ashamed of their binges and try to conceal them. Consequently, binges tend to occur in secret, and take in foods that are normally quick and easy to consume, such as sweets, ice cream, cakes, bread and toast. Binge episodes are often well planned in advance, and can be triggered by periods of dysphoric or depressed mood, interpersonal stressors, or intense hunger following an extended period of dietary restraint. Perhaps, at least in part, as a result of this perceived lack of control over their eating behaviour, individuals with bulimia report high levels of self-disgust, low self-esteem, feelings of inadequacy, and high levels of depression (Shisslak, Pazda & Crago, 1990; Vanderlinden, Norre & Vandereycken, 1992; Carroll, Touyz & Beumont, 1996). However, purging tends to confer relief from the physical discomfort of binge eating and also reduces the fear of gaining weight. Because of these reinforcing effects of purging, the act of purging (e.g. vomiting) may become a goal in itself that reduces anxiety and depression.

Bulimia displays significantly fewer physical symptoms than anorexia, but the most common physical sign of bulimia is permanent loss of dental enamel as a result of regular induced vomiting. In some cases, swollen parotid glands can produce a typical puffy face appearance, and extreme eating patterns caused by regular binging and purging can produce menstrual irregularity.

Bulimia is significantly more common than anorexia and the lifetime prevalence rate among women is between 1 and 3 per cent (Gordon, 2001; Hoek & van Hoeken, 2003; Stice, Marti & Rohde, 2013). In men, the prevalence rate is approximately ten times lower. Epidemiological studies suggest that the incidence of bulimia nervosa might have decreased since the 1990s (Smink, van Hoeken & Hoek, 2012), but this is in contrast to a perceived increase in occurrence in the decades prior to 1990. Interestingly, in a study of bulimia nervosa incidence in the UK from 1988 to 2000, Currin, Schmidt, Treasure & Jick (2005) found that rates of bulimia rose to a peak in 1996 but then subsequently declined (see Figure 10.1). They relate these fluctuations in incidence to the press coverage given to Princess Diana's battle with bulimia during the early 1990s, and note that the decline in bulimia incidence in the UK appears to coincide with her death in 1997 (Photo 10.1). Much fewer cases of bulimia have been reported in women who have not been exposed to some extent to Western ideals and influences (Keel & Klump, 2003). This suggests that bulimia may be a disorder very closely

To read Hoek & van Hoeken's review of the prevalence and incidence of eating disorders go to
www.wiley-psychopathology.com/
reading/ch10

DSM-5 SUMMARY TABLE 10.2 *Criteria for bulimia nervosa*

- Repeated incidents of binge eating
- Frequent inappropriate compensatory behaviours in order to avoid weight gain, such as self-induced vomiting, fasting or excessive exercise
- Binge eating and compensatory behaviours both occur on average at least once a week for 3 months
- View of oneself is overly influenced by body shape and weight

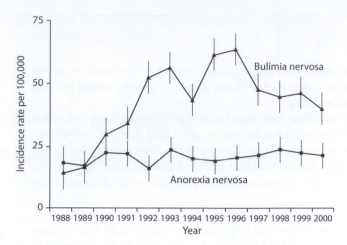

FIGURE 10.1 *In the UK between the years 1988 and 2000, the incidence of anorexia nervosa remained relatively stable, but incidence of bulimia nervosa increased from 1988 to 1996 and then subsequently decreased.*
Source: Currin, L., Schmidt, U., Treasure, J. & Jick, H. (2005). Time trends in eating disorder incidence. *British Journal of Psychiatry*, *186*, 132–135, Figure 1. Reproduced by permission of the Royal College of Psychiatrists.

© Tim Graham/Getty Images

PHOTO 10.1 *The increase in rates of bulimia nervosa in the UK up to 1996 has been attributed to the publication of Princess Diana's battle with bulimia during the early 1990s. A decline in the incidence of bulimia after 1996 also appears to coincide with her death in 1997.*

linked to Western cultural ideals surrounding body shape and eating behaviours, and so prevalence is likely to be influenced by changes in social conditions.

Bulimia nervosa is often found to be comorbid with other psychiatric disorders. Major depression is the most commonly diagnosed comorbid disorder; with between 36 and 63 per cent of bulimia sufferers being diagnosed with depression (Brewerton, Lydiard, Herzog, Brotman *et al.*, 1995). Increases in bulimia during winter months also appear to be linked to symptoms of seasonal affective disorder (SAD) (Lam, Lee, Tam, Grewal & Yatham, 2001), suggesting that dysphoric mood disorder is a common concurrent symptom of bulimia. There is also evidence for a strong link between bulimia and borderline personality disorder (BPD). Studies have suggested that between 33 and 61 per cent of women with bulimia meet the criteria for a personality disorder (Schmidt & Telch, 1990; Carroll, Touyz & Beumont, 1996). There is also strong evidence for a link between the bulimic behaviours of bingeing and purging and substance abuse, and with bipolar disorder (Jordan, Joyce, Carter, Horn *et al.*, 2008). This includes heavy alcohol use (Lacey, 1993), increased incidence of the use of soft and hard drugs when compared with anorexia sufferers and non-clinical controls (Corbridge & Bell, 1996), and abuse of laxatives, diet pills, diuretics and emetics (Bulik, Sullivan, Epstein, McKee *et al.*, 1992). The frequent comorbidity of bulimia with personality disorders, bipolar disorder and substance abuse has led to the proposal that bulimia is part manifestation of a broader 'multi-impulsive' syndrome in which the individual finds it difficult to control many aspects of their behaviour,

including eating and the use of alcohol and drugs (Lacey, 1993; Brietzke, Moreira, Toniolo & Lafer, 2011).

A case history of the development of bulimia is described in Case History 10.1.

10.1.3 Binge-Eating Disorder (BED)

Binge-eating disorder is characterized by recurrent episodes of binge eating (see DSM-5 Summary Table 10.3), but without the associated purging or fasting associated with bulimia. As a result those suffering **binge-eating disorder** tend to be overweight, and usually have a long history of failed attempts to diet and lose weight. As a result, individuals with binge-eating disorder feel a lack of control over their eating behaviours and this causes them significant distress. Individuals with binge-eating disorder are typically ashamed of their eating problems and usually attempt to conceal their symptoms or eat in secrecy. Triggers for binge eating can include interpersonal stress, dieting, negative body image, and boredom. Differentiating between a diagnosis of binge-eating disorder and bulimia nervosa is often difficult and depends on how frequently the individual indulges in compensatory behaviours such as purging. Because of the overlap in symptoms, some view binge-eating disorder only as a less severe form of bulimia (Hay & Fairburn, 1998; Striegel-Moore, Cachelin, Dohm, Pike *et al.*, 2001). Binge-eating disorder can often be found in children and is associated with excessive

> **binge-eating disorder (BED)** An eating disorder characterized by recurrent episodes of binge eating without the purging or fasting that is associated with bulimia nervosa.

BULIMIA NERVOSA

Sara was the youngest child in her family, with two brothers several years older than her who both left home before she entered high school. Sara tried hard to please her older brothers even though they teased her and would often call her names, telling her she was stupid and ugly.

Her father worked long hours as a salesman and was often away from home travelling or staying late in the office. When Sara was 13 she discovered that her father had been having an affair, and that her mother had known of this for some years. Sara was very angry with her father and also with her mother for allowing him to 'get away with it'. She tried to be supportive of her mother but felt hurt and confused, and their close relationship was damaged. Sara didn't feel able to confide in her mother anymore and felt strong resentment towards her father, who she could not forgive.

Over the next 2 years Sara felt increasingly isolated and unhappy at home and spent as little time there as possible. When Sara was 16 she met her first boyfriend, Kyle, who was four years older than her. At first Sara was very happy in the relationship and after 4 months she moved out of home to live with Kyle. Soon, the relationship became difficult and they often argued about money and household chores, as well as about Sara's belief that Kyle flirted with other women.

Two years into their relationship Sara discovered that Kyle had been cheating on her with one of her close friends. When Sara confronted him, Kyle confessed what he had done but blamed Sara for being 'boring' and 'a nag'. He told her that he had never found her attractive and had always wanted to be with her friend instead. Sara was angry and upset but blamed herself for not making more of an effort to be attractive.

Sara reluctantly moved back into her parents' house, although her relationship with them had not improved in recent years. Feeling isolated and unhappy she began a crash diet and lost some weight quickly. Her father often ridiculed her weight loss efforts while her mother encouraged her to 'make more of herself'. Sara became increasingly unhappy after her initial weight loss and became tired, irritable and preoccupied with food. One evening she saw a Facebook update telling her that Kyle and her friend were now engaged, and that her friend was pregnant. She felt jealous and angry that all her efforts to lose weight and 'improve herself' had been for nothing. Sara stuffed herself with food until she couldn't eat any more. Feeling out of control and ashamed she made herself vomit.

The next day she resolved to eat even less but a week later she binged again. Although she tried to stop, Sara felt caught in a pattern and was soon bingeing several times a week. Her eating became wildly erratic but her weight stayed much the same. Her parents didn't realize that anything was wrong and regularly chastised her for not making more of her life, while Sara began to feel increasingly desperate and alone, and even thought of trying to kill herself. Although she still saw her friends and was able to hold down a job, Sara was now locked into a cycle of bingeing and vomiting known as bulimia nervosa.

Clinical Commentary

Sara's case contains a number of elements that are typical of individuals who develop bulimia. She had a difficult home environment and experienced teasing about her weight and appearance, as well as having to adjust to significant changes in parental relationships. Her subsequent relationship was difficult and when it came to an end she probably felt that she had little control over her life, and she had no obvious means of escape from her situation. Arguments with her boyfriend had reinforced her belief that she had 'let herself go', and she resolved to diet to lose weight. Dieting then triggered feelings of extreme hunger which led to binge eating following anger at her boyfriend's infidelity. Following the binge, feelings of self-disgust and shame lead to purging. This starts a vicious cycle in which, after each binge, Sara resolves to eat less but inevitably ends up bingeing again.

weight gain, and is common in adolescents and college students (Napolitano & Himes, 2011).

Binge-eating disorder is associated with high levels of major depression, impaired work and social functioning, low self-esteem, and dissatisfaction with body shape (Striegel-Moore, Cachelin, Dohm, Pike *et al.*, 2001). The lifetime prevalence of binge-eating disorder in the general population is around 3.0 per cent and has a peak onset age of 16–20 years (Stice, Marti & Rohde, 2013); the disorder can be as high as 30 per cent among individuals seeking weight loss treatment (Dingemans, Bruna & van Furth, 2002). While the majority of sufferers are women, the incidence of binge-eating disorder in women is only one and a half times higher than in men

(Stice, Telch & Rizvi, 2000; Striegel-Moore & Franko, 2003). A cross-cultural study by Pike, Dohn, Striegel-Moore, Wifley & Fairburn (2001) found that the incidences of the disorder in white and black American women were very similar, although black American women appeared to show less concern about the disorder than white American women. The case of Rosa is outlined in Case History 10.2, and this example illustrates many of the behavioural and cognitive traits exhibited by individuals suffering from binge-eating disorder.

 To read Striegel-Moore & Franko's article on the epidemiology of binge-eating disorders go to **www.wiley-psychopathology.com/reading/ch10**

Finally, in this section we have discussed the three most clinically important eating disorders, namely anorexia nervosa, bulimia nervosa and binge-eating disorder. However, DSM-5 also specifies other feeding and eating disorders that may cause distress (e.g. see Table 10.1).

DSM-5 SUMMARY TABLE 10.3 *Criteria for binge-eating disorder*

- Repeated incidents of binge eating
- Binge eating is accompanied by at least three of the following:
  - Eating quicker than usual
  - Eating until uncomfortably full
  - Eating sizable amounts of food when not feeling hungry
  - Eating alone due to being embarrassed by the amount of food eaten
  - Feeling disgusted, depressed or guilty after binge eating
- Distress regarding binge eating
- Binge eating is not accompanied by inappropriate compensatory behaviour as seen in bulimia nervosa

---

CASE HISTORY 10.2

BINGE EATING DISORDER

Rosa was a binge eater, but had not had a food binge for over three-and-a-half years when she travelled to attend the wedding of her friend's daughter. Rosa was normally a confident, professional woman, who enjoyed her work, and had just successfully completed an important project, which often left her feeling down and empty.

She had spent three years attending Overeaters Anonymous (OA), and knew she needed to avoid food – especially when she was feeling low.

Rosa managed to keep herself occupied during the day of the wedding, but as the night-time came, the bluster of the after wedding party made it easy for her to disappear – physically and emotionally – into a binge. She started with a plate of what would have been an 'abstinent' meal (an OA concept for whatever is included on one's meal plan): pasta salad, green salad, cold meats, and lots of bread. The food was plentiful, but Rosa still wanted more, and spent the next three-and-a-half hours eating. Very soon she started to feel guilty and ashamed, and began to surreptitiously steal food from plates out of the gaze of the other guests.

When most of the guests had left the dining room she began helping herself to the cakes and desserts. Then, beginning to feel desperate, Rosa began to pile the food high on her plate, so that if other guests saw her she could always escape with a large amount of food. By now, the food tasted of nothing to her, but she couldn't stop eating it. Eventually she realized what she had been doing, felt that she was out of control, and ran crying back to her room.

This event was the beginning of a six-month relapse into binge eating for Rosa. During the relapse, she binged on foods and refined carbohydrates, started smoking cigarettes in an attempt to control the binging and was driven to excessive exercise after each binge.

Throughout the relapse, Rosa went to therapy and to OA. Finally, a combination of antidepressants and a structured food plan that excluded refined sugars, breads, crackers, and similar carbohydrates helped her to bring her bingeing under control and manage her eating. Rosa was eventually able to stop taking the antidepressants and continued to be active in OA.

Clinical Commentary

Rosa's case history is a good example of how a person can lose control of their own eating patterns and eating behaviour. Features that are typical of binge-eating disorder include (1) eating significantly more than a normal meal portion in one session; (2) an uncontrollable urge to continue eating despite the situation and surroundings; (3) forcing oneself to eat food that is unpalatable or contaminated; (4) a desire to conceal her overeating from others; and (5) subsequent shame, self-disgust and depression when the binge episode is over.

time when the populations of both Europe and the USA are becoming heavier, studies have suggested that men would prefer their body shape to be around 30 pounds heavier than their current weight (McCreary & Sadava, 2001) – presumably because they believe their body is not muscular enough. In contrast, females identify their ideal body weight as an average of around 40 pounds less than their weight (Irving, 2001). These differences in culturally determined ideal weight expectations appear to be largely responsible for the sex-related difference in prevalence rates for eating disorders, and may be related to the fact that sexual differences between men and women are related to women being more likely to be defined by their bodies and men more likely to be defined by their accomplishments (Frederickson & Roberts, 1997). These differences in how the genders are defined seem to dissipate with age, and long-term studies have shown that at around the age of 40 years women diet less, have fewer concerns about their body image, and fewer eating disorders than when they were 20 years younger. One fact that reflects the importance of shape ideals is that eating disorders in males are significantly higher in groups of males whose body weight and shape is of more significance and importance to them. For example, compared with the general adult male population, the prevalence rates for eating disorders are significantly higher in male body-builders (Holbrook & Weltzin, 1998), athletes (Byrne & McLean, 2002), and ballet dancers (Ravaldia, Vannacci, Zucchi, Mannucci et al., 2003). Also, the instance of eating disorders is significantly higher amongst gay men than heterosexual men (Strong, Williamson, Netemeyer & Geer, 2000), reflecting the relative greater importance placed on male physical appearance and attractiveness by gay subculture. Thus, even within cultures, whenever an emphasis

and importance is placed on body shape, size and weight, the rate of eating disordered behaviour is likely to rise within that subgroup. The fact that the media often create body shape, size and weight *ideals* that are somewhat extreme in comparison to the average or norm – even within these subgroups – is simply more grist to this mill.

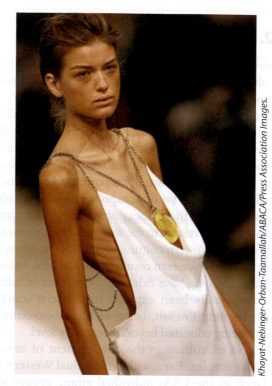

Khayat-Nebinger-Orban-Taamallah/ABACA/Press Association Images.

PHOTO 10.2 *Western media regularly portray female role models as either naturally thin (and therefore representative of only a minority of the female population) or unnaturally thin. Young adolescent females then strive to achieve these relatively unattainable, or simply unhealthy, ideals.*

SELF-TEST QUESTIONS

- How do demographic factors and cultural aspects of eating disorders help us to understand these disorders?
- How do the symptoms and incidences of eating disorders differ across cultures and ethnic groups?
- What evidence would you cite that shows the importance of body shape ideals as a risk factor for eating disorders?

SECTION SUMMARY

10.2   CULTURAL AND DEMOGRAPHIC DIFFERENCES IN EATING DISORDERS

- Some of the origins of eating disorders lie in the values and ideals defined by cultures.
- Changes in sociocultural factors may influence the frequency and prevalence of eating disorders.
- There is little evidence for examples of bulimia in individuals who have not had exposure to Western ideals.

- Eating disorders are less prevalent in ethnic minorities in the USA, but their incidence is increasing as these minorities are exposed to the dominant thin ideal espoused by American culture.

- Examples of the self-starvation typical of anorexia nervosa can be found in cultures where Western ideals are nonexistent and this suggests than anorexia may not simply be a disorder caused by exposure to Western body-image ideals.

- Females are 10 times more likely to develop an eating disorder than males.

- The importance of body shape ideals as a risk factor for eating disorders is reflected in the fact that eating disorders in males are significantly higher in groups of males whose body weight and shape is of more significance and importance to them (e.g. body-builders, athletes, ballet dancers).

10.3   THE AETIOLOGY OF EATING DISORDERS

Like so many other psychological disorders, eating disorders do not appear to be caused by one single factor, but have their origins in a range of psychological, sociological and biological processes, all of which appear to converge to generate the different eating disorder profiles. So broad is the range of influences that has been identified in this aetiology that many researchers have limited themselves simply to defining the risk factors that underlie eating disorders (e.g. Polivy & Herman, 2002; Jacobi, Hayward, de Zwaan, Kraemer & Agras, 2004; Ghaderi & Scott, 2001). Because of this complexity, theories of the aetiology of eating disorders based on the description of either psychological or biological processes are relatively underdeveloped. So we tend to have a good idea of *what* factors are involved in eating disorders (i.e. what represent risk factors), but relatively little insight into *how* they are involved. Figure 10.2 illustrates a recent attempt to classify the risk factors for anorexia and bulimia across a developmental timeframe, and this shows how important risk factors are at a number of different levels of description. These include 'prenatal' risk factors (such as gender and ethnicity), early developmental influences that generate eating difficulties (such as infant sleeping and eating patterns), early experiences (such as sexual abuse and physical neglect), dispositional factors (such as low self-esteem, perfectionism and negative self-evaluation affect), familial factors (such as parental obesity and parental attitudes to weight), adolescent attitudes to dieting and exercise, and comorbid psychological disorders (such as OCD and social phobia) (see also Lindberg & Hjern, 2003). What you will also see from Figure 10.2 is that different eating disorders such as

To read Ghaderi & Scott's article on the prevalence, incidence and prospective risk factors for eating disorders go to www.wiley-psychopathology.com/reading/ch10

anorexia and bulimia often have identical risk factors, and it is not clear why an individual may develop one of these disorders rather than the other. As a consequence it is often difficult to separate out theories of the aetiology of anorexia and bulimia, and many of the following theories are addressed at understanding eating disorders generally rather than individual eating disorders specifically.

To read Lindberg & Hjern's article on the risk factors for anorexia nervosa go to www.wiley-psychopathology.com/reading/ch10

We have already described how the occurrence of eating disorders appears to be linked to culture and ethnicity, and this alone should give us some insight into the sociological influences linked to eating disorders. In the following section, we will look at risk factors in more detail, and try to elaborate how these risk factors might have their effects on the development of eating disorders.

10.3.1   Biological Factors

Biological approaches to the aetiology of eating disorders centre around genetic influences and neurobiological factors.

Genetic influences

There is clear evidence that eating disorders do run in families, and this is consistent with there being a *genetic component* to these disorders. First-degree relatives of females with both anorexia and bulimia are significantly more likely to develop these disorders than relatives of a group of females who have never been diagnosed with an eating disorder (Strober, Freeman, Lampert, Diamond & Kaye, 2000; Kassett, Gershon, Maxwell *et al.*, 1989). Community-based twin studies have also contributed to the view that there is an inherited component, and these indicate that genetic factors account for approximately 40–60 per cent of liability to anorexia nervosa,

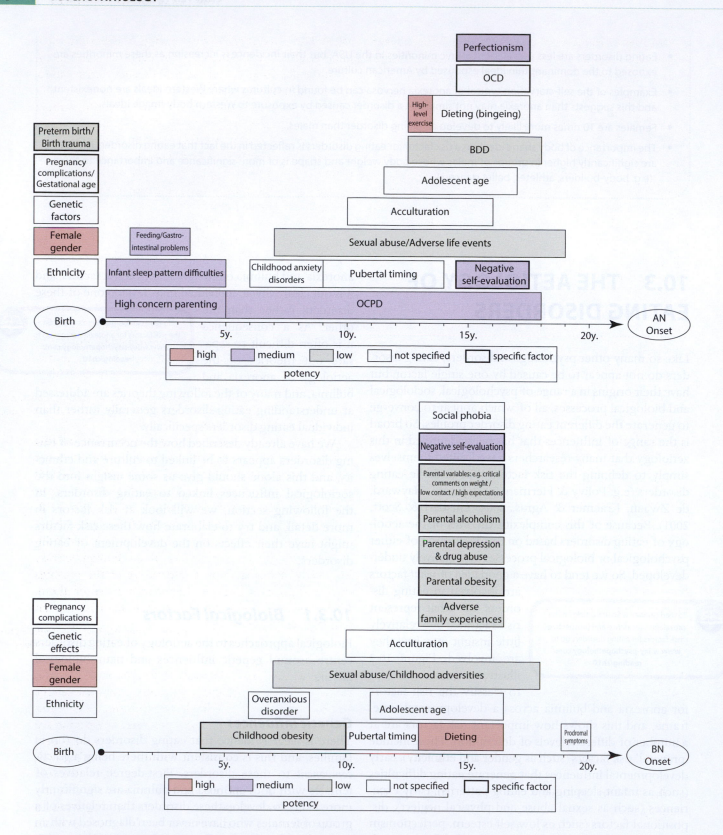

FIGURE 10.2 *Classification of the known risk factors for anorexia and bulimia across a developmental timeframe. This shows how important risk factors are at a number of different levels of description.*
Source: Jacobi, C., Hayward, C., de Zwaan, M., Kraemer, H.C. & Agras, W.S. (2004). Coming to terms with risk factors for eating disorders: Application of risk terminology and suggestions for a general taxonomy. *Psychological Bulletin, 130,* 19–65. American Psychological Association. Reproduced with permission.

bulimia nervosa and binge eating disorder (Trace, Baker, Penas-Lledo & Bulik, 2013). However, while twin studies indicate a moderate genetic influence, such studies also suggest a significant impact of unique environmental factors, such as interactions with parents (Baker, Mitchell, Neale & Kendler, 2010), and this implies that eating disorders are developed through a complex interaction between inherited characteristics and individual experiences. Molecular genetic studies have also attempted to identify the gene loci of these genetic effects, and potential target genes have been identified that may influence appetite regulation (e.g. serotonergic genes), feeding and food intake (e.g. dopaminergic genes), food reward sensitivity (e.g. genes that influence opioid receptors), and weight regulation (Trace, Baker, Penas-Lledo & Bulik, 2013). However, molecular genetic studies of eating disorders are largely in their infancy and have been plagued by underpowered sample sizes and failed replications (Sullivan, Daly & O'Donovan, 2012; Wang, Zhang, Bloss, Duvvuri et al., 2011).

There may also be a shared familial factor across eating disorders suggesting that if an individual has bulimia, this may raise the chances of a related individual not just developing bulimia, but also either anorexia or bulimia (Kendler, MacLean, Neale, Kessler et al., 1991; Wade, Bulik, Sullivan, Neale & Kendler, 2000). However, Keel & Klump (2003) have argued that the genes contributing to anorexia may well differ from those contributing to bulimia. This is because bulimia appears to be a culture-bound syndrome whereas anorexia is not (see section 10.2), and the universal nature of anorexia suggests that there may be an important genetic component to the self-starvation that is the central feature of anorexia. Nevertheless, while there appears to be a significant inherited component, this research has yet to determine exactly how inherited dispositions increase the likelihood of developing an eating disorder. For example, does the genetic component to anorexia simply increase the tendency to self-starve, or does it increase the vulnerability to other risk factors (such as depression or low self-esteem)?

Neurobiological factors

Because eating disorders involve appetite, a number of theories of both anorexia and bulimia allude to the role of those brain areas involved in regulating appetite (namely the hypothalamus), and to the neurotransmitters associated with changes in appetite. Animal research has shown that lesions to the **lateral hypothalamus** cause appetite loss resulting in a self-starvation syndrome that is behaviourally similar to that found in anorexia (Hoebel & Teitelbaum,

lateral hypothalamus A part of the hypothalamus. Lesions to the lateral hypothalamus cause appetite loss resulting in a self-starvation syndrome which is behaviourally similar to that found in anorexia.

1966). However, there is good reason to believe that lateral hypothalamus deficits are not a central causal factor in anorexia. Firstly, animal studies show that lateral hypothalamus lesions result in a lack of hunger – but anorexia sufferers usually experience intense hunger even though they are starving themselves. Secondly, while there are hormonal imbalances found in anorexia that are similar to those in animal studies of lateral hypothalamus lesions, these imbalances appear to be the *result* of the disorder rather than a cause of it (Stoving, Hangaard & Hansen-Nord, 1999).

Combinations of brain mechanisms and reward pathways in the brain may also be involved in generating eating disorders as a result of their role in triggering either satiation or food 'craving' or 'liking' (Berridge, Ho, Richard & DiFeliceantonio, 2010), and we have already indicated that there may be some genetic influence on the strength of these effects. For example, self-starvation and maintaining a low body weight may be reinforced by the **endogenous opioids** that the body releases during starvation to reduce pain sensation (Hardy & Waller, 1988). In anorexia, starvation may directly increase the levels of opioids, thus

endogenous opioids A compound that the body releases to reduce pain sensation.

producing a state of euphoria; however, because bulimia sufferers are not necessarily overweight, this disorder may be accompanied by *low* levels of opioids, and this is known to promote craving. In support of this latter hypothesis, Brewerton, Lydiard, Laraia, Shook & Ballenger (1992) did find low levels of the opioid beta-endorphin in bulimia sufferers. Nevertheless, it is still difficult to interpret the significance of this finding because low opioid levels may be a *consequence* of the cravings that accompany bulimia rather than a cause of them. Also, low levels of **serotonin metabolites** have been found in individuals with a diagnosis of anorexia and bulimia (Kaye, Ebert,

serotonin metabolites The products produced by the breakdown of serotonin.

Raleigh & Lake, 1984; Carrasco, Dyaz-Marsa, Hollander, Cesar & Saiz-Ruiz, 2000). Serotonin promotes satiety, and so people with low levels of serotonin metabolites may be prone to binge eating; low levels of serotonin are also associated with depression, so this might also be a reason why eating disorders are so often comorbid with mood disorders such as depression. The problem with this as a *cause* of binge-eating problems is that animal studies have shown that enforced dieting tends to reduce serotonin functioning, so low levels of serotonin metabolites in individuals with either anorexia or bulimia may have been caused by any prior dieting behaviour (Chandler-Laney, Castaneda, Pritchett, Smith et al., 2007). Finally, dopamine is a brain neurotransmitter involved in the pleasurable and rewarding consequences of food, and women diagnosed with anorexia and bulimia exhibit greater expression of the **dopamine transporter gene** DAT, suggesting that they

dopamine transporter gene A transporter gene allows drugs to enter cells or, in some cases, acts to keep them out. Women diagnosed with anorexia and bulimia exhibit greater expression of the dopamine transporter gene DAT suggesting that they might be more susceptible to the rewarding and pleasurable effects of eating.

might be more susceptible to the rewarding and pleasurable effects of eating (Frieling, Romer, Scholz, Mittelbach *et al.*, 2010; Thaler, Groleau, Badawi, Sycz *et al.*, 2012).

While most of the evidence seems to suggest that various brain areas and neurotransmitters are involved in eating disorder symptoms, we still cannot be sure that these are genuine causal factors or whether they are consequences of behaviours associated with eating disorders such as dieting or bingeing.

10.3.2 Sociocultural Influences

Section 10.2 described how the incidence of eating disorders appears to be importantly affected by factors associated with culture and ethnicity. Rates of both anorexia and bulimia are higher in cultures that have experienced contemporary Western ideals and standards, and, indeed, it is arguably the case that bulimia is *only* found in societies that have been exposed to Western cultural influences (Keel & Klump, 2003). This suggests that Western cultural factors are a risk factor for eating disorders, and it is important to identify specifically what these factors are and how they might trigger an eating disorder.

Media influences, body dissatisfaction and dieting

As already pointed out, both anorexia and bulimia are disorders that are largely restricted to females (Strieigel-Moore, 1997) and there is growing acknowledgement that the general increase in the incidence of eating disorders over the past 20–30 years is associated with changes in the ideal female body shape that is communicated to the female populations of Westernized societies. For instance, the media are regularly accused of distorting reality by portraying female body images that are either naturally thin (and therefore representative of only a minority of the female population) or are unnaturally thin (Polivy & Herman, 2002). This is supported by studies showing that the BMI (body mass index – see Activity 10.1) of *Playboy* centrefolds between 1985 and 1997 had continued to fall to a point where almost 50 per cent of the centrefolds had a BMI of less than 18 – which is considered to be severely underweight (Owen & Laurel-Seller, 2000).

This **media influence** has resulted in young women adopting ideal body-shape goals that are achievable for only around 5 per cent of the female population (Irving, 2001). There is some evidence that exposure to these media-portrayed

media influence A term describing a person's changes in or temptations to change attitude, behaviour and morals as directly influenced by the media.

extreme ideals is related to a drive for thinness in young adolescent girls. For example, Tiggemann & Pickering (1996) found that body-shape dissatisfaction and a drive for thinness was significantly associated with watching certain types of TV show that portrayed idealized female images. Further studies have shown that body dissatisfaction is directly correlated with the amount of time young female undergraduates spend reading magazines that expose them to idealized female body shapes (Tiggemann, 2003), and also with the amount of time young women spend watching music television channels such as MTV (Tiggemann & Slater, 2004). The more that young adolescents (between the ages of 14 and 16 years) indulge in 'celebrity worship' of a media personality and perceive that personality as having a 'good' body shape, the more that adolescent views their own body image as poor (Maltby, Giles, Barber & McCutcheon, 2005). Some experimental studies that have manipulated the viewing of videos with either idealized body images or control images have suggested that the relationship between media presentations of idealized body images and eating disorder symptoms – such as reduced body dissatisfaction, decreased self-esteem, dieting and depression – is a causal one (e.g. Jett, LaPorte & Wanchisn, 2010). However, the overall effect sizes for these causal effects are small, suggesting that the influence of watching such media is relatively modest (Hausenblas, Campbell, Menzel, Doughty *et al.*, 2013).

Another socially relevant factor that may have contributed to the increase in eating disorder symptoms over the past 30–40 years is food and eating fashions. The more that low-calorie diets become fashionable, the more they are likely to promote restricted eating, which is a risk factor for developing eating disorder symptoms. For example, individuals with an eating disorder are considerably more likely to have been vegetarian compared to controls (52 per cent vs. 12 per cent) (Bardone-Cone, Fitzsimmons-Craft, Harney, Maldonado *et al.*, 2012), and the low-carbohydrate diets fashionable over the past 20–30 years will have contributed to increases in the prevalence of restrictive eating practices.

As well as the exaltation of thinness, Western cultures disparage obesity and both implicitly and explicitly associate it with negative characteristics – even though obesity is significantly on the increase in most Western societies. Obese individuals are rated by others as less smart, and more lazy and worthless than non-obese individuals (DeJong & Kleck, 1986) – even by health professionals who specialize in obesity (Schwartz, Chambliss, Brownell, Blair & Billington, 2003)! Jokes and cartoons that ridicule obesity are commonplace, and this prejudice appears to be deep-rooted and more acceptable than jokes about race and disability. This will inevitably give rise to a fear of being fat or obese, which is further grist to the mill of dieting and body dissatisfaction.

While the preceding evidence suggests that media images of idealized thin body shapes are relevant in determining attitudes towards body shape – the question we need to ask is *how* this media-based pressure is converted into the eating problems that meet DSM-5 criteria for a psychological disorder. The most obvious route is that idealized media images generate dissatisfaction with the individual's own body shape (especially in comparison to extreme ideals). **Body dissatisfaction (BD)** is usually defined as the gap between one's actual and ideal weight and shape (Polivy & Herman, 2002), and most theories of eating disorders implicate body dissatisfaction as an important component of the aetiology (e.g. Stice, 2001; Vohs, Bardone, Joiner, Abramson & Heatherton, 1999; Polivy & Herman, 1985; van den Berg, Thompson, Obremski-Brandon & Coovert, 2002).

Body dissatisfaction is likely to trigger bouts of **dieting** in order to move towards the ideal body shape, and regular or excessive dieting is also a common precursor to eating disorders

> **body dissatisfaction (BD)** The gap between one's actual and ideal weight and shape.

> **dieting** A restricted regime of eating, followed in order to lose weight or for medical reasons.

(Polivy & Herman, 1987; Stice, 2001). Figure 10.3 provides a schematic representation of one model describing how body dissatisfaction might be generated through media, peer and parental influences, and then this itself will affect dieting behaviour and eating disorder symptomatology such as bulimia (e.g. Rodgers, Chabrol & Paxton, 2011). There is no doubt that body dissatisfaction and dieting are important predictors of all eating disorders (Joiner, Heatherton, Rudd & Schmidt, 1997; Steiger, Stotland, Trottier & Ghadirian, 1996; Stice, Shaw & Nemeroff, 1998), but it is important to note that they are not *sufficient* conditions for an individual to develop an eating disorder. For example, (1) many individuals may believe that their actual body shape is quite disparate from their ideal (Figure 10.4), yet be quite happy with that fact (Polivy & Herman, 2002), and (2) many individuals who express real body dissatisfaction do not necessarily go on to develop an eating disorder. Similarly, while dieting is usually an activity that precedes an eating disorder, many individuals who diet regularly do not go on to develop an eating disorder. This suggests that additional psychological factors are necessary for body dissatisfaction and dieting to develop into an eating disorder, and we will discuss some of these factors in section 10.3.4. Nevertheless, body dissatisfaction and dieting are *vulnerability* factors, and this is demonstrated in part by the fact that occupations that require an individual to control and monitor their weight (usually through either exercise or dieting) have higher incidences of eating disorders. These include fashion models (Santonastaso, Mondini & Favaro, 2002), actors, athletes (Sudi, Ottl, Payerl, Baumgartl *et al.*, 2004), figure

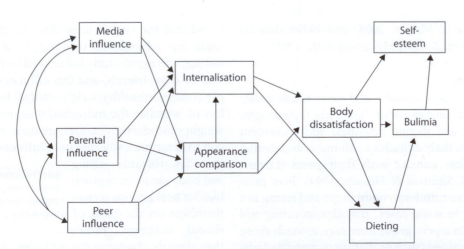

FIGURE 10.3 *This is one model of how body dissatisfaction might mediate eating disorder symptoms and is known as the tripartite model (van den Berg, Thompson, Obremski-Brandon & Coovert, 2002; Yamamiya, Shroff & Thompson, 2008). In this model, the effect of influences from media, parents and peers is mediated by internalisation of social ideals and social comparison, leading to body dissatisfaction, disordered eating and negative affect.*

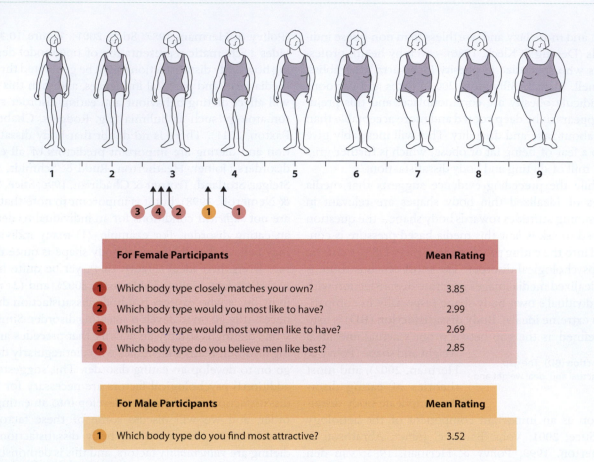

For Female Participants	Mean Rating
1 Which body type closely matches your own?	3.85
2 Which body type would you most like to have?	2.99
3 Which body type would most women like to have?	2.69
4 Which body type do you believe men like best?	2.85

For Male Participants	Mean Rating
1 Which body type do you find most attractive?	3.52

FIGURE 10.4 *Research on female body shape dissatisfaction has demonstrated that females consistently overestimate their own body size compared with (1) the body size that they thought that men would like most, and (2) the body size they think that most women would like to have. Interestingly, women rated the body size they thought men would like most as significantly slimmer than the body size that men themselves rated as most attractive.*
Source: Forbes, G.B., Adams-Curtis, L.E., Rade, B. & Jaberg, P. (2001). Body dissatisfaction in women and men: The role of gender-typing and self-esteem. *Sex Roles*, 44(7–8), 461–484. Reproduced with permission of Springer.

skaters (Monsma & Malina, 2004) and ballet dancers (Ravaldia, Vannacci, Zucchi, Mannucci *et al.*, 2003).

Peer influences

Just like the media, peer attitudes and views can seriously influence an adolescent's view of their body, their weight, and their eating and dieting activities, and adolescent girls tend to learn their attitudes to slimness and dieting through their close contact with their peers (Levine, Smolak, Moodey, Shuman & Hessen, 1994). Peer pressure can influence attitudes to body shape and eating in a variety of ways. In some cases, attitudes to eating and body shape within a peer group converge towards those that are socially valued (such as dieting or restricted eating) (Meyer & Waller, 2001), and this convergence also results in the group adopting psychological characteristics that may facilitate pathological eating behaviours, such as perfectionism. A study of adolescent schoolgirls by Eisenberg, Neumark-Sztainer, Story & Perry (2005)

found that the use of unhealthy weight-control behaviours (e.g. self-induced vomiting, laxatives, diet pills, or fasting) was significantly influenced by the dieting behaviour of close friends, and this influence was effective in generating unhealthy weight-control behaviours regardless of whether the individual was overweight, normal weight or underweight. Despite these findings, it is difficult to determine whether **peer influences** (1) determine attitudes towards eating and body shape (it is possible that peer groups recruit members on the basis of shared concerns rather than directly changing the attitudes of their members), or (2) have a significant role in the development of eating disorders (while peer pressure can increase the tendency to diet or to be dissatisfied with one's body shape, these factors do not automatically lead to the development of eating disorders).

peer influences A term describing a person's changes in or temptations to change attitude, behaviour and morals as directly influenced by his or her peer group.

Familial factors

We have noted earlier that eating disorders have a tendency to run in families, and while this may in part be due to inherited characteristics, it may also be a result of the direct influence of family attitudes and dynamics on the behaviour of those in the family. In particular, Minuchin (Minuchin, Baker, Rosman, Lieberman *et al.*, 1975; Minuchin, Rosman & Baker, 1978) has argued that eating disorders are best understood by considering the family structure of which the sufferer is a part. This *family systems theory* view argues that the sufferer may be embedded in a dysfunctional family structure that actively promotes the development of eating disorders. The family structure may inadvertently, but actively, reinforce a child's disordered eating, and this can function to distract from dealing with other conflicts within the family (such as a deteriorating relationship between the child's mother and father). In Minuchin's view, the families of individuals with eating disorders tend to show one or more of the following characteristics: (1) **enmeshment**, in which parents are intrusive, overly involved in their children's affairs and dismissive of their children's emotions and emotional needs (Minuchin, Rosman & Baker, 1978), (2) **overprotection**, where members of the family are overly concerned with parenting and with one another's welfare, and this can often be viewed by the child as coercive parental control (Shoebridge & Gowers, 2000; Haworth-Hoeppner, 2000), (3) **rigidity**, where there is a tendency to maintain the status quo within the family, and (4) **lack of conflict resolution**, where families avoid conflict or are in a continual state of conflict. How these characteristics of the sufferer's family influence the development of an eating disorder is unclear, although the family may focus on the disorder once it has developed in order to avoid dealing with other difficult and important problems within the family. The disorder may serve a functional purpose for both the parents (by distracting attention away from other family difficulties, such as a problematic relationship between mother and father) and the eating disordered child (as a tool for manipulating the family) (Minuchin, Rosman & Baker, 1978). As we shall see later, the issue of how a dysfunctional family environment may generate an eating disorder is still unclear, but it may do so by generating specific

> **enmeshment** A characteristic of family systems theory in which parents are intrusive, over-involved in their children's affairs, and dismissive of their children's emotions and emotional needs.

> **overprotection** A characteristic of family systems theory where members of the family are overconcerned with parenting and with one another's welfare, and this can often be viewed by the child as coercive parental control.

> **rigidity** A characteristic of family systems theory where there is a tendency to maintain the status quo within the family.

> **lack of conflict resolution** A characteristic of family systems theory where families avoid conflict or are in a continual state of conflict.

psychological characteristics in the child that play an active role in the acquisition and maintenance of the disorder (Polivy & Herman, 2002).

As an important part of the family, mothers may have a specific influence on the development of eating disorders in their children. Mothers of individuals with an eating disorder are themselves more likely to have dysfunctional eating patterns and psychiatric disorders (Hill & Franklin, 1998; Hodes, Timimi & Robinson, 1997) and these problematic maternal eating patterns appear to produce feeding problems in their offspring at an early age (Whelan & Cooper, 2000) some of which may give rise to weight gain and disordered eating in their offspring later in life (Easter, Naumann, Northstone, Schmidt *et al.*, 2013). Mothers of sufferers also tend to excessively criticize their daughters' appearance, weight and attractiveness when compared with mothers of non-sufferers (Hill & Franklin, 1998; Pike & Rodin, 1991), and there is a significant inverse relationship between a mother's critical comments and her daughter's chances of successful recovery following treatment (van Furth, van Strien, Martina, Vanson *et al.*, 1996).

While this research strongly implicates the involvement of **familial factors** in the aetiology of eating disorders, Polivy & Herman (2002) quite rightly point out that most of the studies are retrospective and correlational in nature, and so

> **familial factors** The idea that certain disorders may be a result of the direct influence of family attitudes and dynamics on the behaviour of those in the family.

do not imply causation. There may indeed be some form of intra-familial transmission of disordered eating patterns within families, but it is quite likely that some other factor (biological, psychological or experiential) may be necessary to trigger the severe symptoms typical of a clinically diagnosable disorder (Steiger, Stotland, Trottier & Ghadirian, 1996).

10.3.3 Experiential Factors

There is some evidence that adverse life experiences may act as a vulnerability factor for eating disorders and as a precipitating factor for the onset of an eating disorder. For example, Rastam & Gillberg (1992) found that 14 per cent of anorexia sufferers (compared with 0 per cent of healthy controls) had experienced a negative life experience (e.g. the loss of a first-degree relative) within 3 months prior to the onset of the disorder. Similarly, individuals with bulimia report significantly more adverse life events prior to symptoms than age-matched healthy controls (Welch, Doll & Fairburn, 1997; Carretero-Garcia, Planell, Doval, Estragues *et al.*, 2012).

Individuals with eating disorders report significantly more premorbid life stresses and difficulties than do healthy controls (Raffi, Rondini, Grandi & Fava, 2000), and the number of adverse life events has been shown to differentiate between individuals with anorexia and healthy controls (Horesh, Apter, Ishai, Danziger *et al.*, 1996). Like the research on the role of familial factors, such studies are difficult to interpret because they are both retrospective and correlational in nature.

However, one particular form of adverse life experience that has been implicated as a risk factor in eating disorders is **childhood sexual abuse**. There is some evidence for higher levels of childhood sexual abuse in the history of bulimia sufferers than in healthy controls (Steiger, Leonard, Kin *et al.*, 2000; Garfinkel, Lin, Goering, Spegg *et al.*, 1995; Welch & Fairburn, 1994), and in anorexia sufferers than healthy controls (Brown, Russell, Thornton & Dunn, 1997), but not in binge-eating disorder sufferers (Dansky, Brewerton, Kilpatrick & O'Neal, 1997). One longitudinal study of a large community-based sample of mothers and offspring has indicated that children who had experienced sexual abuse or physical neglect during childhood were also at elevated risk for eating disorders (Johnson, Cohen, Kasen, Smailes & Brook, 2002). Given that childhood sexual abuse is now largely accepted as a risk factor for eating disorders (Polivy & Herman, 2002), it is difficult to determine how such early experiences facilitate the risk of developing an eating disorder. This is complicated by the fact that childhood sexual abuse is a risk factor for a wide range of psychiatric disorders (Chou, 2012), so we need to discover why some people with this history specifically develop eating disorders. One possibility is that adverse early experiences generate other forms of psychopathology that mediate the development of eating disorders (Casper & Lyubomirsky, 1997). For example, Steiger, Leonard, Kin *et al.* (2000) found that childhood sexual abuse only facilitated bulimia in the presence of borderline personality disorder, and other researchers have argued that eating disorders are a means of coping with the more generalized psychopathology (such as major depression) that results from sexual abuse (Rorty & Yager, 1996). This latter view sees the development of an eating disorder as a way of helping the individual to cope with emotional and identity problems (which may have been caused by earlier adverse life experiences). For example, anorexia enables the individual to exert some control over at least one aspect of their life (i.e. their eating), in circumstances where they may have experienced very little control over many other aspects of their life (Troop, 1998). Similarly, bulimia may also serve as a way of coping with the negative affect caused by earlier life difficulties. Bulimia sufferers will gain emotional relief, which is otherwise elusive, by

> **childhood sexual abuse** The sexual maltreatment of a child.

bingeing (and then purging). Eating disorders also allow the individual to construct a coherent sense of self by focusing attention on one limited aspect of their lives. This in turn provides them with rewards that may otherwise have been missing from their lives (by attaining self-determined weight control goals), and also provides a very narrow life focus that may help them to avoid dealing with more deep-seated psychological issues (Polivy & Herman, 2002). Therefore, this rather interesting view of eating disorders views them as means of coping with other, more global psychopathology. More research is needed to verify this view.

10.3.4 Psychological and Dispositional Factors

Individuals who develop eating disorders do appear to have particular personality and dispositional characteristics that have been variously implicated in the aetiology of those disorders. We have so far identified a number of risk factors for eating disorders, but none of these risk factors appears to be a *sufficient* condition for developing anorexia, bulimia or binge-eating disorder. It may therefore be the case that specific risk factors interact with personality traits to generate an eating disorder.

Various studies have identified personality traits that are characteristic of individuals with diagnosed eating disorders. These traits include:

- perfectionism
- shyness
- neuroticism
- low self-esteem
- high introspective awareness (awareness of bodily sensations)
- negative or depressed affect
- dependence and non-assertiveness (Vitousek & Manke, 1994; Leon, Fulkerson, Perry & Early-Zald, 1995).

It is worth looking in more detail at some of the more important of these characteristics.

Eating disorders are very much associated with **negative affect** (usually depressed mood), and mood disorders are often comorbid with both anorexia and bulimia (Braun, Sunday & Halmi, 1994; Brewerton, Lydiard, Herzog, Brotman *et al.*, 1995). While negative mood and stress is a

> **negative affect** Refers to the full spectrum of negative emotions.

commonly reported antecedent of eating disorders (Ball & Lee, 2000), there is some disagreement about whether negative affect is a cause or just a consequence of the disorder. Nevertheless, negative affect has been proposed to play a number of discrete roles in the aetiology of eating disorders. Experimental studies have indicated that induced negative mood does increase body dissatisfaction and body-size perception in bulimia sufferers (Carter, Bulik, Lawson, Sullivan & Wilson, 1996), and it may contribute in part to eating disorders through this route. Negative mood states have also been shown to increase food consumption in individuals who are dieting or who have distorted attitudes about eating, and this may represent a role for negative mood in generating the bingeing and purging patterns typical of bulimia sufferers (Herman, Polivy, Lank & Heatherton, 1987). For example, individuals with bulimia try to alleviate their negative mood by eating, and purging allows them to use eating as a mood regulation process without gaining weight. However, when the bulimia sufferer begins to realize that their eating is out of control, this activity no longer provides relief from negative mood, and purging may take over as a means of relieving guilt, self-disgust and tension (Johnson & Larson, 1982). This is consistent with laboratory-based studies that report that bulimia sufferers show reduced anxiety, tension and guilt following a binge–purge episode (Sanftner & Crowther, 1998). Studies such as these suggest that the negative mood possessed by individuals with eating disorders may not simply be a consequence of the disorder, but may play an active role in generating symptoms by increasing body dissatisfaction and being involved in processes of mood regulation which act to reinforce disordered eating behaviours.

A second prominent characteristic of individuals with eating disorders is **low self-esteem**. This low self-esteem may simply be a derivative of the specific negative views that those with eating disorders have of themselves (such as being 'fat', having an unattractive body, or, in bulimia, having a lack of control over their eating behaviour). However, there is some evidence to suggest that low self-esteem may have a role to play in the development of eating disorders. Firstly, it is a significant prospective predictor of eating disorders in females (suggesting that it is not just a consequence of eating disorders) (Button, Sonugabarke, Davies & Thompson, 1996). Secondly, eating disorders such as anorexia are viewed by some researchers as a means of combating low self-esteem by demonstrating control over one specific aspect of the sufferer's own life – namely, their eating (Troop, 1998). In this sense, self-esteem may be implicated in the development of eating disorders because controlled eating is the individual's way of combating their feelings of low self-esteem.

Individuals diagnosed with anorexia and, to a lesser extent, those diagnosed with bulimia both score high on measures of **perfectionism**, and this personality characteristic has regularly been implicated in the aetiology of eating disorders (Garner, Olmsted & Garfinkel, 1983; Bastiani, Rao, Weltzin & Kaye, 1995). Perfectionism is multifaceted and can be either self-oriented (setting high standards for oneself) or other-oriented (trying to conform to the high standards set by others). It can also be adaptive (in the sense of trying to achieve the best possible outcome) or maladaptive (in

> **low self-esteem** A person's negative, subjective appraisal of himself or herself.

> **perfectionism** The setting of excessively high standards for performance accompanied by overly critical self-evaluation.

RESEARCH METHODS 10.1

FOOD PRELOAD TESTS

Laboratory procedures have been developed that provide an objective behavioural measure of the tendency to 'binge' eat, and one of these is the **food preload test** (Polivy, Heatherton & Herman, 1988).

This test begins by asking participants to eat a filling preload (e.g. a 15oz chocolate milkshake or a large bowl of ice cream) under the pretence of rating its palatability.

After eating the preload and making their ratings, participants are then told they can eat as much of the remaining milkshake (or ice cream) as they wish.

The real measure of interest is the amount of milkshake or ice cream that the participant eats by the end of the study – this is a measure of how willing the individual is to continue eating after having already had a full, filling portion of food.

This experimental procedure has shown that willingness to continue eating is a function of a number of factors, including whether the individual (1) is a restrained eater (i.e. has a tendency to dieting or has distorted attitudes about eating), (2) has low self-esteem, and (3) is in a negative mood. Restrained eaters will even eat more food than non-dieters, even if they rate the food as relatively unpalatable.

> **food preload test** Laboratory procedure developed to provide an objective behavioural measure of the tendency to binge eat.

terms of striving to attain what may well be unachievable goals) (Bieling, Israeli & Antony, 2004). Perfectionism is a predictor of bulimic symptoms in women who perceive themselves as overweight (Joiner, Heatherton, Rudd & Schmidt, 1997), and both self-oriented and other-oriented perfectionism have been found to predict the onset of anorexia (Tyrka, Waldron, Graber & Brooks-Gunn, 2002). Perfectionism is also one of the few personality traits that predicts the maintenance of eating disorders at 10-year follow-up (Holland, Bodell & Keel, 2013). Other research has suggested that the perfectionist characteristics displayed by individuals with eating disorders may actively contribute to their disordered eating. For example, Strober (1991) has argued that self-doubting perfectionism predisposes individuals to eating disorders. Perfectionism is highly associated with measures of body dissatisfaction and drive for thinness (Ruggiero, Levi, Ciuna & Sassaroli, 2003), and so it is not difficult to see how perfectionism may be an indirect causal factor in the aetiology of eating disorders; it drives the dieter to achieve the perfect body shape or the stringent dieting goals they set themselves (Keel & Forney, 2013). Interestingly, perfectionism is a characteristic of many psychological disorders (Egan, Wade & Shafran, 2011), and is the best predictor of comorbidity across the anxiety disorders (Bieling, Summerfelt, Israeli & Antony, 2004). So, if perfectionism does play a causal role in eating disorders, we need to ask why it was an eating disorder that developed and not any one of a number of other disorders that have perfectionism as a prominent feature.

To read Keel & Forney's article on psychosocial risk factors go to **www.wiley-psychopathology.com/reading/ch10**

10.3.5 Transdiagnostic Models of Eating Disorders

In this section on aetiology, we have seen that many of the factors that might give rise to eating disorders can often be found as risk factors or causes across all of the eating disorders (e.g. anorexia, bulimia, and binge eating disorder).

This has led some researchers to suggest that there are some processes or maintaining factors that are common across all eating disorder diagnostic categories, and one such model is the **transdiagnostic cognitive-behavioural model** (Fairburn, 2008; Fairburn, Cooper & Shafran, 2003). This model argues that a dysfunctional system of self-evaluation is central to the maintenance of all eating disorders, and that self-worth is defined in terms of control over eating, weight and shape, which in turn leads to dietary restraint. Other subsidiary mechanisms that operate to maintain eating disorders in this model include low self-esteem (which motivates people to pursue achievement in the domain of weight and body shape), clinical perfectionism (which projects achievement in dietary restraint as an important goal), interpersonal problems (which may lead people to control their weight in order to facilitate interpersonal issues), and mood intolerance (which encourages binge eating and purging as a way of coping with negative mood states). These four additional maintaining factors will differ across individuals with different forms of eating disorder. For example, mood intolerance will be important for bulimia sufferers, but less so for anorexia sufferers. Some recent studies have provided evidence supporting this model. For example, Lampard, Byrne, McLean & Fursland (2011) found that low self-esteem was associated with overevaluation of weight and shape which in turn was associated with dietary restraint, and interpersonal difficulties were also associated with dietary restraint. As predicted by the model, Lampard, Tasca, Balfour & Bissada (2013) found that the processes of low self-esteem, overevaluation of weight and shape, and mood intolerance were transdiagnostic maintaining factors across all the main eating disorders. This cognitive-behavioural model of eating disorders has also provided the basis for the development of CBT interventions for eating disorders, which we will discuss later (Fairburn, 2008).

transdiagnostic cognitive-behavioural model A model of eating disorders that argues that a dysfunctional system of self-evaluation is central to the maintenance of all eating disorders, and that self-worth is defined in terms of control over eating, weight and shape, which in turn leads to dietary restraint.

To read an evaluation of the transdiagnostic cognitive-behavioural model by Lampard *et al.* go to **www.wiley-psychopathology.com/reading/ch10**

SELF-TEST QUESTIONS

- Can you name some of the important risk factors for anorexia and bulimia?
- Can you describe some of the biological factors that might be involved in the development of an eating disorder?
- What role might brain neurotransmitters play in the acquisition and maintenance of eating disorder symptoms?

- Can you name some of the important sociocultural factors that influence the development of eating disorders? What evidence is there that these factors influence body dissatisfaction and attitudes to dieting?

- What are the important dispositional factors associated with eating disorders? Do they have a causal role to play in the development of an eating disorder?

- What are the main features of the *tripartite model* of eating disorders?

SECTION SUMMARY

10.3   THE AETIOLOGY OF EATING DISORDERS

This section on aetiology has concluded that a number of psychological and cognitive processes may be important common factors in the acquisition and maintenance of all eating disorders, and these psychological factors include the defining of self-worth in terms of control over eating, low self-esteem, clinical perfectionism, interpersonal problems and intolerance of negative moods such as depression. Many of these psychological factors may be influenced by exposure to media ideals of body shape, peer attitudes to controlled eating, and familial factors – such as intra-family conflict or dysfunctional mother–daughter interactions. Traumatic life events also appear to be risk factors for eating disorders, and childhood sexual abuse has been one specific form in which trauma has been researched in relation to eating disorders. There is an inherited component to eating disorders, although this is modest and twin studies have tended to emphasize that unique environmental experiences are equally as important as genes in the aetiology of eating disorders. Finally, eating disorder symptoms have been found to be associated with a number of brain mechanisms and reward pathways, including opioid, serotonin and dopamine pathways, but it is still unclear whether these neurobiological processes are causes of eating disorder symptoms or are themselves consequences of those symptoms.

The key points discussed in this section are:

- There is evidence of an inherited component to eating disorders that may account for up to 50 per cent of the variance in factors causing these disorders.

- Maintaining a low body weight may be reinforced by the endogenous opioids that the body releases during starvation to reduce pain sensation.

- The neurotransmitters serotonin and dopamine may be involved in eating disorders by affecting satiety and the pleasurable consequences of eating.

- Exposure to media-portrayed extreme body shape ideals has been shown to increase body dissatisfaction in young adolescent females, and to increase their tendency to either diet or purge after overeating.

- Body dissatisfaction and dieting are important vulnerability factors for eating disorders.

- Peer attitudes and views are an important factor in determining an adolescent girl's attitudes to slimness and dieting.

- Eating disorders have a tendency to run in families, and *family systems views* of eating disorders suggest that a dysfunctional family structure may reinforce a child's disordered eating.

- Mothers may have a specific influence on the development of an eating disorder by producing eating problems in their offspring and criticising their child's appearance.

- Adverse life experiences (such as childhood sexual abuse) may act as a vulnerability factor for eating disorders.

- Negative affect, low self-esteem and perfectionism are all dispositional factors that have been shown to exert a possible causal influence on the development of an eating disorder.

- The tripartite model argues that the effect of influences from media, parents and peers is mediated by internalisation of social ideals and social comparison, leading to body dissatisfaction, disordered eating and negative affect.

10.4 THE TREATMENT OF EATING DISORDERS

Eating disorders are complex and difficult to treat but clinical psychologists have been actively developing a range of treatments, many of which show promising results. However, before we discuss some of these treatment methods, it is important to describe some of the challenges that face any intervention for eating disorders. First, many individuals with eating disorders regularly deny they are ill or have a disorder. Indeed, many individuals with bulimia see their bingeing and purging eating patterns as a positive way of controlling weight, and there has been a recent burgeoning of websites extolling the virtues of bingeing and purging as a way of life (Table 10.2). Similarly, individuals with anorexia regularly deny they are pathologically underweight, and the fact that they may view their controlled eating as a way of coping with more general psychopathology means that it is often viewed as an activity that has benefits rather than costs (Rorty & Yager, 1996). Because of these factors as many as 90 per cent of individuals with diagnosable eating disorders tend not to be in treatment (Fairburn, Welch, Norman, O'Connor & Doll, 1996).

Second, individuals with severe eating disorders usually need medical as well as psychological treatment, and in the case of anorexia, hospitalization and a period of remedial medical treatment is often necessary to increase weight, rectify body electrolyte imbalances and, in many cases, prevent death by self-starvation before some of the significant psychological factors can be addressed.

Third, eating disorders are often highly comorbid with other psychological disorders, which may make treatment difficult and complex. For example, anorexia and bulimia are often comorbid with major depression and OCD, and some psychological treatments for anorexia have included components used to treat obsessions and compulsions (such as response prevention and exposure methods; see section 6.5.2) (e.g. Wilson, Eldredge, Smith & Niles, 1991). Similarly, treatments for eating disorders sometimes work better with a concurrent antidepressant drug (Agras, Rossiter, Arnow, Schneider *et al.*, 1992). In addition, there is growing evidence that anorexia and bulimia may be comorbid with personality disorders such as OCPD and BPD (Schmidt & Telch, 1990; Carroll, Touyz & Beumont, 1996; O'Brien & Vincent, 2003), and personality disorders of this kind are themselves quite resistant to treatment (see Chapter 12).

To read the NICE guidelines go to http://tinyurl.com/orr7xzh

In January 2004, the UK's National Institute for Clinical Excellence (NICE) issued clinical guidelines for the treatment of eating disorders (these guidelines were retained following a review in 2011), and rated these interventions according to the evidence that supported their effectiveness (Wilson & Shafran, 2005). Table 10.3 shows a summary of

---

TABLE 10.2

Treating bulimia can be difficult because many individuals with bulimia see their bingeing and purging patterns of eating as a positive way of controlling weight, and there has been a burgeoning of websites extolling the virtues of bingeing and purging as a way of life. Below are some examples that illustrate how bulimia sufferers will actively swap experiences, information about the best ways of purging, and how best to conceal their activities.

- Okay, so last night I was purging, ya know, and it kinda came out with more force than I was expecting. Well, anyway, I leaned closer and actually only go half in the toilet. The other half goes down the side and on my sock and the floor. I spent for ever cleaning up but my mum found the left overs and asked if I was sick. I said no. I think she bought it but she'll be on the look out. So, how can I hide it better? Seriously I need help!

- I really don't want you to become bulimic because it makes you feel awful, you get headaches, light-headness, irregular heartbeats and you can rip your throat and you burst blood vessels and all this bad stuff. However, if you do start, to save you a lot of pain, make sure you drink lots of water with everything, and diet coke is good too. Don't try and purge orange juice because it hurts like hell. Make sure you chew everything thoroughly too, otherwise it can get stuck in your throat. And if you see blood when you purge, it is not a good sign and you should stop for a while.

- I'm so sure someone would have to have an answer for me . . . okay, so I'm really good at making myself sick . . . but for the last 2 days I can't get anything up . . . it's nasty tho, bc I definitely get dry heaves and I gag for about 10 minutes at a time . . . and the last time I tried it I was choking . . . I could still breath but I was gasping . . . I freaked myself out . . . and I know to chew really well and all that, so I know thats the problem . . . u think it's because my oesophagus is irritated or something like that? Please give me a bit of advice . . . thanks

- Why is it that I can go without food for most of the day and then when it comes to the evening I go totally crazy and binge, then afterwards I feel really bad and hate myself and vow never to eat that much again, but I always do. Can somebody please give me some ideas on how to stop binging? I'd really appreciate it.

- After you eat would you go to the bathroom? I am relatively new at it but have had some luck but just not as much coming up as I thought. How soon after and how long would you do it for?

TABLE 10.3 *NICE guidelines for the treatment of eating disorders (2004)*

PHYSICAL MANAGEMENT OF WEIGHT GAIN IN ANOREXIA NERVOSA

Managing weight gain

- In most patients, the aim should be average weekly weight gain of 0.5–1.0 kg as inpatient and 0.5 kg as outpatient

- Regular physical monitoring, and oral multivitamin/multimineral supplement in some cases, is recommended for inpatients and outpatients

- Total parenteral nutrition should not be used, unless there is significant gastrointestinal dysfunction

Managing risk

- Healthcare professionals should monitor physical risk. If risk increases, frequency of monitoring and nature of investigations should be adjusted accordingly

- Pregnant women with current or remitted anorexia should be considered for more intensive care to ensure adequate prenatal nutrition and fetal development

- Oestrogen should not be given for bone-density problems in children and adolescents, because such treatment may lead to premature fusion of epiphyses

Feeding against will of patient:

- This should be an intervention of last resort

RECOMMENDED TREATMENT FOR EATING DISORDERS

Anorexia nervosa

Pharmacological	Psychological
• Drugs should not be used as sole or primary treatment for anorexia • All patients with anorexia should have alert placed in their prescribing record about risk of side effects	• Consider cognitive analytic or cognitive-behavioural therapies, interpersonal psychotherapy, focal dynamic therapy, or family interventions focused on eating disorders • Family interventions that directly address the eating disorder should be offered to children and adolescents

Bulimia nervosa

Pharmacological	Psychological
• To be offered trial of an antidepressant as alternative to, or in addition to, self-help programme • Patients should be informed that antidepressant drugs can reduce frequency of binge eating and purging, but long-term effects are unknown • Selective serotonin reuptake inhibitors (specifically fluoxetine) are drugs of first choice for bulimia in terms of acceptability, tolerability and reduction of symptoms. No drugs other than antidepressants are recommended	• Dietary counselling should not be provided as sole treatment • As a possible first step, patients with bulimia should be encouraged to follow evidence-based self-help programme • Consider direct encouragement and support to patients undertaking evidence-based self-help programme, which may improve outcomes and be sufficient for limited subset of patients • Specifically adapted CBT should be offered to adults with bulimia; 16–20 sessions over 4–5 months. Interpersonal psychotherapy should be considered as alternative to CBT, but patients should be informed it takes 8–12 months to achieve similar results

Binge-eating disorder

Pharmacological	Psychological
• Patients should be informed that selective serotonin reuptake inhibitors can reduce binge eating, but long-term effects are unknown; antidepressants may be sufficient for some patients	• Specifically adapted CBT should be offered to adults with binge-eating disorder

Source: Wilson, G.T. & Shafran, R. (2005). Eating disorders guidelines from NICE. *Lancet*, 365, 79–81. Reproduced with permission.

these recommendations for both the physical management of patients with anorexia and the psychological and pharmacological treatment of all eating disorders. No specific recommendations were made for anorexia, but the report found good evidence for the effectiveness of cognitive behaviour therapy for both bulimia and binge-eating disorder. In the following sections, we will describe and discuss the main forms of treatment that have been used for eating disorders. These are pharmacological treatments, family therapy, and cognitive behaviour therapy (CBT). In addition to these treatments, clinicians have also advocated the use of self-help and alternative delivery systems, and you can see from Table 10.3 that self-help programmes are an important component of the treatment provision for both bulimia and binge-eating disorder. Bulimia self-help groups that use structured manuals and require minimum practitioner management can show significant treatment gains – especially when these help the patient to identify triggers for bingeing and develop preventative behaviours for purging (Cooper, Coker & Fleming, 1994), and can be equally or more effective than CBT in establishing remission from bingeing and purging symptoms (Bailer, de Zwaan, Leisch, Strnad *et al.*, 2004). **Alternative delivery systems** do allow access to services for sufferers who might, for whatever reason, not receive other forms of treatment. These include treatment and support via telephone therapy, e-mail, the internet, computer-software CD-ROMs, and virtual reality techniques (see section 4.1.2), and an initial assessment of the effectiveness of these methods is encouraging (Myers, Swan-Kremeier, Wonderlich, Lancaster & Mitchell, 2004; Wagner, Penelo, Wanner, Gwinner *et al.*, 2013).

> **alternative delivery systems** Treatment methods that allow access to services for sufferers who might not receive other forms of treatment. These include treatment and support via telephone therapy, email, the internet, computer-software CD-ROMs and virtual reality techniques.

To read an article by Myers *et al.* about the use of new technologies in the treatment of eating disorders go to **www.wiley-psychopathology.com/reading/ch10**

10.4.1   *Pharmacological Treatments*

Because both anorexia and bulimia are frequently comorbid with major depression, eating disorders have tended to be treated pharmacologically with antidepressants such as fluoxetine (Prozac) (Kruger & Kennedy, 2000). There is some evidence that **pharmacological treatments** can be effective with bulimia when they are compared with placebo conditions, but this evidence is still far from convincing (e.g. Grilo, Pagano, Skodol, Sanislow *et al.* 2007). Some studies have indicated a modest reduction in the frequency of bingeing and purging with such antidepressants compared with placebo controls (e.g. Wilson & Pike, 2001; Bellini & Merli, 2004), but drop-out rates can still be unacceptably high (Bacaltchuk & Hay, 2003). More significant treatment gains are reported if antidepressant medication is combined with psychological treatments such as CBT (Pederson, Roerig & Mitchell, 2003). The benefits with joint drug and CBT programmes appear to be reciprocal in that CBT helps to address the

> **pharmacological treatments** Drug-based treatments for psychopathology.

core dysfunctional beliefs in bulimia (see below), and antidepressant drug treatment appears to reduce the tendency to relapse following cognitive behavioural treatment (Agras, Rossiter, Arnow, Schneider *et al.*, 1992). CBT plus antidepressants can also be effectively used in a stepped-care approach in which CBT comprises the initial step with the addition of fluoxetine for non-responders after six sessions (Mitchell, Agras, Crow, Halmi *et al.*, 2011).

Pharmacological treatments with anorexia have tended to be significantly less successful than with bulimia, but the studies assessing drug treatment with anorexia have been relatively limited in number (Pederson, Roerig & Mitchell, 2003; Claudino, Hay, Lima, Bacaltchuk *et al.*, 2006). Nevertheless, outcome studies so far have found very little effect of antidepressants on either weight gain in anorexia or significant changes in other core features of the disorder, such as depression, eating attitudes, or body-shape perceptions (Attia, Haiman, Walsh & Flater, 1998; Biederman, Herzog, Rivinus, Harper *et al.*, 1985). Pharmacological treatments of eating disorders also have the added disadvantage of higher drop-out rates from treatment than psychological therapies (Fairburn, Agras & Wilson, 1992), and also have a number of physical side-effects.

10.4.2   *Family Therapy*

One of the most common therapies used with eating disorder sufferers – and particularly anorexia sufferers – is family therapy. This stems mainly from the theories of Minuchin (Minuchin, Baker, Rosman, Lieberman *et al.*, 1975; Minuchin, Rosman & Baker, 1978), whose **family systems theory** view argues that the sufferer may be embedded in a dysfunctional family structure that actively promotes the development of eating disorders (see section 10.3.2). In particular, this view argues that the eating disorder may be hiding important conflicts within the family (such as a difficult relationship between the sufferer's parents), and the family may be implicitly reinforcing the eating disorder in order to avoid confronting these other conflicts. As we noted in section 10.3.2, the families of individuals with eating disorders exhibit the characteristics of enmeshment, overprotectiveness, rigidity, and lack of conflict resolution, and family therapy can be used to unpack and address these dysfunctional family characteristics. In Treatment in Practice Box 10.1 is an example of how family therapy is applied in the context of an adolescent family member with anorexia. This example shows how family therapy can be used to explore concerns about relationships and emotional expression within the

> **family systems theory** A theory which argues that the sufferer may be embedded in a dysfunctional family structure that actively promotes psychopathology.

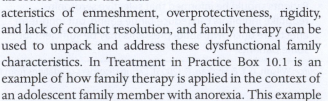

To read Dallos's article on attachment narrative therapy go to **www.wiley-psychopathology.com/reading/ch10**

CLINICAL PERSPECTIVE: TREATMENT IN PRACTICE 10.1
FAMILY THERAPY FOR EATING DISORDERS

Sandy is 17 and for 2 years had been suffering with ano-rexia of such severity as to require two brief stays in hospi-tal. She was living with her parents and older brother. Two older brothers had left home.

Though all were invited only Sandy and her parents attended for family therapy which took place at intervals of between 3 and 4 weeks over 18 months. The sessions, with the full permission of all of the family, were of 1 hour in length, with the therapist in the room with them and a team observing from behind a one-way mirror. The team usually joined the family and the therapist after 40–50 minutes and held a reflective discussion with each other in front of the family in which they shared their ideas about the family's problems, ideas, understandings and feelings. The family were then invited to comment and then held a closing discussion with the therapist when the team had left the room. The core idea of family therapy is that problems such as anorexia are not simply, or predomi-nantly, individual but are related to wider stresses and distress the family is experiencing. In addition it is recog-nized that the sense of failure and blame associated with conditions such as anorexia can paralyse families' abilities to help each other.

Initially each member of the family was asked to describe what they saw as the main problems and invited to offer their explanations of the causes of the problem.

This was followed by a focus on two broad areas: (1) the impact of the problems on each of them and their relationships with each other, and, in turn, (2) the influ-ence that they could exert on the nature of the problems. Initially the parents indicated that the distress caused by Sandy's anorexia was the main problem for all of them. However, it quickly emerged that the parents had very dif-ferent ideas about what caused the problems and what to do to help. Mr Sinclair had a medical and practical view and

Mrs Sinclair a more relational and emotional one. Through the use of a genogram (family tree) it was revealed that both parents had themselves had very negative experi-ences of being parented that made it hard for them to know how to comfort and help their children. It also tran-spired that their marriage was in serious difficulty. Sandy commented that her parents' conflicts upset her and she felt caught in the middle in trying to meet the emotional needs of both of her lonely parents. In effect she felt like she was a therapist for her own family. (Interestingly, she has gone on to study psychology at university.)

The therapist and the reflecting team discussed the possible impacts that the parents' own experiences may have had on how they acted towards Sandy. Along with this there were discussions of a variety of related issues, such as the pressure on young women to confirm to stere-otypes of thinness and self-starving as an attempt to exert control in one's life. Some marital work was done sepa-rately with the parents to look at their childhoods, their marriage, their own needs and how these had an impact on Sandy. Mrs Sinclair in particular felt she had failed as a mother but was relieved to hear that the team did not see it in this way. Sandy gained considerable insight into how the family dynamics across the generations had had an impact on her and her parents. She became independent enough to go to university but initially struggled, as did her parents, to separate. Some struggle with her weight continues but she is confident that she will cope in the long term.

Source: Case history provided by Dr Rudi Dallos, Consultant Clinical Psychologist (Somerset Partnership Trust) and Director of Research, Clinical Psychology Teaching Unit, University of Plymouth. Davey, G.C.L. (Ed.) (2004) *Complete Psychology* (Hodder, 9780340967553). Focus Point 34.4, p.521. Reproduced by permis-sion of Taylor and Francis.

family, as well as individual feelings of failure, shame, and guilt. Exploring these issues throws up other con-flicts and difficulties within the family, and how the ano-rexia sufferer may see themselves as trapped within these existing relationships and conflicts (Dallos, 2004).

A more recent family-based therapy for eating disorders is the **Maudsley approach**, which has a number of stages beginning with a stage that focuses on how the family can

Maudsley approach Family based, staged therapy for eating disorders.

help and solve the problems they are facing, a second stage that helps the fam-ily to challenge the eating

disorder symptoms, and a third stage that develops family relations and activities once recovery from eating disorder symptoms has occurred (Eisler, 2005; Lock, Le Grange, Agras, Moye *et al.*, 2010).

However, while there is significant support for the use of family therapy in eating disordered individuals – especially those with a diagnosis of anorexia nervosa (e.g. Rosman, Minuchin & Liebman, 1975), well-controlled treatment outcome research remains somewhat limited (Cottrell, 2003; Downs & Blow, 2013).

To read Downs & Blow's review of family-based therapy go to **www.wiley-psychopathology.com/ reading/ch10**

10.4.3   Cognitive Behaviour Therapy (CBT)

The treatment of bulimia is generally considered to be cognitive behaviour therapy (CBT). The UK NICE guidelines for the treatment of eating disorders makes its strongest recommendation for the use of CBT with bulimia, usually for 16–20 sessions over a period of 4–5 months (Wilson & Shafran, 2005; see Table 10.3). CBT for bulimia is based on the transdiagnostic cognitive model developed by Fairburn and colleagues (Fairburn, Shafran & Cooper, 1999, see section 10.3.5). According to this model, individuals with bulimia have a long-standing pattern of negative self-evaluation that interacts with concerns about weight, shape and attractiveness. Such individuals come to evaluate their worth solely in terms of their weight and shape – largely because this is often the only area of their lives that they can control. They develop idealized views of thinness that are often unachievable, and as a result end up in a constant state of dissatisfaction with their body shape and their weight. This leads them to excessive dieting, and as a result of this dietary restriction they lapse into episodes of bingeing. This in turn invites the use of weight compensation methods such as vomiting and laxative abuse. Each episode of bingeing and purging is followed by a more determined effort to restrict eating, which leads to an ever-increasing vicious cycle of bingeing and purging (see Figure 10.5).

For an activity on Fairburn's Cognitive Model go to
www.wiley-psychopathology.com/ activities/ch10

Treatment in Practice Box 10.2 shows the three stages of CBT that are required to deal with both the symptoms of bulimia and the dysfunctional cognitions that underlie these symptoms. These cover:

1. meal planning and stimulus control,
2. cognitive restructuring to address dysfunctional beliefs about shape and weight, and
3. developing relapse prevention methods.

In stage 1, individuals are taught to identify the stimuli or events that may trigger a binge episode (such as a period of stress or after an argument with a boyfriend or parent), and are also taught not to indulge in extremes of eating behaviour (e.g. dieting and bingeing), and that normal body weight can be maintained simply by planned eating. In stage 2, dysfunctional beliefs about weight, body shape and eating are identified, challenged and replaced with more adaptive cognitions. For example, beliefs that relate eating and weight to self worth, such as 'No one will love me if I am a single pound heavier' are challenged. In stage 3 relapse prevention is often encouraged with the use of behavioural self-control procedures that enable the individual to structure their daily activities to prevent bingeing and purging, and rewarding oneself for 'good' behaviours (e.g. sticking to a planned eating programme) (see section 4.1.1).

An 'enhanced' form of CBT has been developed for use with all forms of eating disorder, and this can be helpful with sufferers who are significantly underweight (e.g. anorexia nervosa sufferers) by increasing their motivation to change and then helping them to regain weight while at the same time addressing psychological issues relating to shape and weight (Cooper & Fairburn, 2011). Preliminary outcome studies with anorexia sufferers suggest that a majority were able to complete this enhanced programme with a substantial increase in weight and reduction in eating disorder symptoms (Fairburn, Cooper, Doll, O'Connor et al., 2013).

Outcome studies indicate that CBT of bulimia is successful in reducing bingeing, purging and dietary restraint, and there is usually an increase in positive attitudes towards body shape (Compas, Haaga, Keefe, Leitenberg & Williams, 1998; Richards, Baldwin, Frost, Clark-Sly et al., 2000). In addition, follow-up studies suggest that therapeutic gains can be maintained for up to five years following treatment (Fairburn, Norman, Welch, O'Connor et al., 1995). Importantly, when CBT is effective it has been found to significantly reduce not only the behavioural aspects of bulimia such as bingeing and purging (Agras, 1997; Wilson, Fairburn & Agras, 1997), but also has beneficial effects on core 'cognitive' aspects of bulimia such as beliefs about dietary restraint and low self-esteem

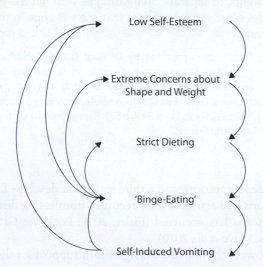

FIGURE 10.5 *Fairburn's (1997) cognitive model of the maintenance of bulimia, and on which contemporary CBT for bulimia is based. Low self-esteem leads to concerns about weight, followed by dietary restriction, which – when such dieting fails – leads to binge eating and subsequent purging. Following purging, individuals become more determined to restrict eating, and a vicious cycle is established that maintains the bingeing–purging pattern.*

CLINICAL PERSPECTIVE: TREATMENT IN PRACTICE 10.2
THE THREE STAGES OF CBT FOR BULIMIA NERVOSA

STAGE 1 (3–9 WEEKS)

- The cognitive model is explained to clients, and they learn to control eating and reduce dietary restraint.
- Clients learn to control eating by discovering what factors trigger bingeing (e.g. periods of stress or arguments with partners or parents). This is achieved with the use of a diary that allows the client to discover consistencies between life events and bingeing.
- Clients are taught techniques such as stimulus control and meal planning.
- *Stimulus control* is where the client is allowed to eat, but only in certain specified environments (such as their kitchen) or at specific times (e.g. after work). Eventually eating behaviour is controlled only by these stimuli, and is not triggered at all times in all places.
- *Meal planning* involves ensuring that small, acceptable meals are planned and eaten every day. Reductions in

binge eating and purging usually follow the regularisation of eating patterns.

STAGE 2 (ABOUT 8 WEEKS)

- Clients are taught to identify their thoughts and beliefs about eating and their weight, and to challenge dysfunctional and inappropriate beliefs and thinking patterns.
- The therapist will help to foster healthy ways of thinking about eating and will also address issues about low self-esteem, and how dysfunctional attitudes that might link weight and self-worth are irrational (e.g. 'No one will love me if I am a single pound heavier').

STAGE 3 (ABOUT 4 WEEKS)

- Clients are taught various techniques to help prevent relapse.

(Anderson & Maloney, 2001). CBT has also been shown to be a more comprehensive treatment of bulimia than antidepressant drugs (Whittal, Agras & Gould, 1999), and other psychotherapeutic interventions such as psychodynamically oriented therapy (Walsh, Wilson, Loeb, Devlin *et al.*, 1997) and interpersonal psychotherapy (Wilson, Fairburn, Agras, Walsh & Kraemer, 2002). When effective, CBT also reports immediate improvement, including 76 per cent of clients showing an improvement in the frequency of binge eating and 69 per cent showing improvement in the frequency of purging within 3 weeks of the start of treatment (Wilson, Loeb, Walsh, Labouvie *et al.*, 1999). Much of this rapid improvement can be put down to the behavioural homework assignments that are a unique feature of CBT and which appear to help alleviate depression and enhance self-efficacy (Burns & Spangler, 2000; Fennell & Teasdale, 1987).

10.4.4 *Prevention Programmes*

prevention programmes Intervention programmes that attempt to prevent the onset of a psychopathology before the first symptoms are detected.

Finally, clinicians are aware of the importance of **prevention programmes** that put eating disorders into a social context, and try to prevent eating disorders occurring. School-based prevention programmes attempt to:

1. educate vulnerable populations about eating disorders, their symptoms and their causes;
2. help individuals to reject peer and media pressure to be thin; and
3. target risk factors for eating disorders such as dieting, dissatisfaction with body image, and so forth.

In a review of effective prevention programmes, Stice, Becker & Yokum (2013) identified two contemporary prevention programmes whose effectiveness could be empirically verified. These were the *Body Project* intervention, in which young women critique the thin-ideal in a series of exercises (Stice, Rohde, Durant & Shaw, 2012; http://www.bodyprojectsupport.org), and the *Healthy Weight* intervention, which attempts to improve dietary intake and physical activity (Stice, Trost & Chase, 2003). The most effective prevention programmes have been found to be those that are the most interactive and selectively target individuals at high risk for eating disorders (Stice, Shaw & Marti, 2007). Future developments in prevention programmes will probably need to extend the number of risk factors that they target (i.e. not just body dissatisfaction but also dieting and negative affect), and also consider ways in which they can incorporate the prevention of both eating disorders and obesity into individual programmes.

SELF-TEST QUESTIONS

- Can you name the three main forms of treatment for eating disorders? Which ones are more suited to bulimia or to anorexia, and why?

- What is the rationale for adopting a CBT approach to the treatment of bulimia nervosa, and what are the important stages of this treatment?

- How successful are pharmacological interventions in the treatment of eating disorders?

- What are the main features of family therapy for eating disorders?

SECTION SUMMARY

10.4   THE TREATMENT OF EATING DISORDERS

- Eating disorders are often difficult to treat because of the denial by sufferers that they have a disorder, the medical implications of the symptoms, and comorbidity with other psychological disorders.

- There is evidence that *self-help groups*, *alternative delivery systems*, and *school-based prevention programmes* may be helpful in lowering the prevalence of eating disorders.

- The major depression that is often comorbid with eating disorders can be treated pharmacologically with antidepressants such as fluoxetine.

- One of the most common treatments for eating disorders is *family therapy*, in which the family's role in developing and maintaining an eating disordered individual is explored.

- Cognitive behaviour therapy (CBT) is often an effective treatment for bulimia and attempts to deal with the symptoms of bulimia, the dysfunctional cognitions associated with disordered eating, and provide prevention against relapse.

10.5   EATING DISORDERS REVIEWED

This chapter has reviewed the three main eating disorders – anorexia nervosa, bulimia nervosa, and binge-eating disorder. All of these disorders are characterized by dysfunctional eating patterns. Anorexia represents an extreme form of self-starvation while bulimia and binge-eating disorder are characterized by the individual's loss of control over their own eating patterns. In the case of bulimia, the individual attempts to compensate for frequent binge eating by purging and fasting. The individual with binge-eating disorder binges without compensatory behaviour and so frequently ends up overweight or obese. All these disorders share some common factors, these include a predominance of female rather than male sufferers, fear of weight gain, the individual's dissatisfaction with their own body shape, and other comorbid psychopathology symptoms such as major depression. The section on aetiology shows that these three eating disorders often share similar risk factors (see Figure 10.2), and that sociocultural values relating to body-shape ideals may play a role in initiating weight-regulating behaviours in vulnerable individuals. However, we still know very little about why one vulnerable individual will become anorexic and another bulimic, but there are some theories, such as the transdiagnostic behavioural model, that are attempting to understand these developmental processes. Treatments for eating disorders are still at early stages of development and refinement. Some forms of CBT have been adapted to treating bulimia with some moderate success, and family therapy has been shown to be of particular help to individuals with anorexia. But success rates are still modest. In the meantime antidepressants, such as SSRIs, may provide some short-term relief for the depression that is often comorbid with eating disorders.

To access the online resources for this chapter go to
www.wiley-psychopathology.com/ch10

Reading	Video	Activity
• Journal article: Specific and nonspecific comorbidity in anorexia nervosa	• Bulimia: A personal account	• Activity 10.1
• Journal article: Review of the prevalence and incidence of eating disorders		• Fairburn's Cognitive Model activity
• Journal article: Epidemiology of binge-eating disorder		• Self-test questions
• Journal article: Prevalence, incidence and prospective risk factors for eating disorders		• Revision flashcards
• Journal article: Risk factors for anorexia nervosa: A national cohort study		• Research questions
• Journal article: Psychosocial risk factors for eating disorders		
• Journal article: An evaluation of the transdiagnostic cognitive-behavioural model of eating disorders		
• NICE Clinical Guidelines on Eating Disorders		
• Journal article: The use of alternative delivery systems and new technologies in the treatment of patients with eating disorders		
• Journal article: Attachment narrative therapy		
• Journal article: A substantive and methodological review of family-based treatment for eating disorders		
• Glossary of key terms		
• Clinical issues		
• Links to journal articles		
• References		

11 Sexual and Gender Problems

 To access the online resources for this chapter go to
www.wiley-psychopathology.com/ch11

ROUTE MAP OF THE CHAPTER

This chapter covers the topics of sexual dysfunction, paraphilic disorders, and gender dysphoria. The section on sexual dysfunctions describes the various disorders of the sexual cycle, and considers aetiology and a range of treatment options. Paraphilic disorders are largely disorders of male sexual function, and are often associated with sexual offending. The various paraphilic disorders are described and evidence for theories of aetiology is assessed before we cover some of the aspects of treating paraphilic disorders, including treating those who are sexual offenders. The final section covers gender dysphoria, and discusses its characteristics and what evidence there is for aetiology. It also assesses gender reassignment and pychological treatments for gender dysphoria.

CHAPTER OUTLINE

LEARNING OUTCOMES

When you have completed this chapter, you should be able to:

1. List the various types of sexual dysfunction, their place in the sexual cycle, and describe their diagnostic criteria.

2. Compare and contrast various theories of the aetiology of sexual dysfunctions.

3. Describe and evaluate both psychological and biological treatments for sexual dysfunctions.

4. Describe the basic characteristics of paraphilic disorders and their diagnostic criteria.

5. Describe and evaluate both psychological and biological explanations for the aetiology of paraphilic disorders.

6. Describe and evaluate behavioural, cognitive and biological treatments for paraphilic disorders.

7. Describe the basic features of gender dysphoria and list the diagnostic criteria.

8. Describe and evaluate treatments for gender dysphoria.

9. Discuss some of the conceptual and ethical issues involved in defining and diagnosing sexual and gender identity problems.

'So, I have kind of a weird problem here. Normally, getting an erection is no problem for me. I wake up with one every morning, masturbate all the time, sometimes pop them up at inopportune moments. I'm 21, by the way. Also in most sexual encounters there's no problem; I'd say 90 per cent of the time. However, the problem arises – or fails to arise! – when I'm in bed with someone I'm extremely attracted to and very interested in. To date this has only happened with two men, but it is happening with the second of those two people right now and it's driving me crazy. Things will start out fine (i.e. erect) and I can be rolling around in bed with an erection for an hour, but it seems that as soon as it's time for my penis to do its duty (that is when foreplay ends and penetration commences), it deflates and vehemently refuses to be resuscitated. I don't know what to do! It's unendingly embarrassing, but the worst is that it only occurs with people I really like.'

James's Story

'I am sure I am not the first cross-dresser to feel this way but when I get the chance to dress, at first I am excited: I can hardly wait to put on the stockings, skirt and get all dolled up and once I am fully dressed I feel so good – almost like this is the way I am supposed to be. But that feeling does not last . . . Sometimes it will last an hour to hours but I have actually had it diminish within 15 minutes before I feel guilty and then undress and go back to my guy clothes. For some reason a light goes on in my head that tells me, I am a guy . . . why am I wearing a skirt?! And then I quickly undress.

But then when I am dressed as a guy I will admire women in skirts and dresses and wish that could be me and all I want to do is rush home and dress – when my wife is not home. I would love to tell my wife about my CD'ing but I need to come to terms with it first.'

Chris's Story

Introduction

Sexual behaviour plays a central role in most of our lives. It is a very personal and individual topic that we very rarely discuss openly with others. Sexual development is also an important part of our lives, where we learn about the nature of sexual behaviour and develop our own personal likes and dislikes about sexual activities. Furthermore, during adolescence and early adulthood, sexual performance is often related to self-esteem, and so becomes an important contributor to psychological development. The importance of sexual behaviour and the critical role it may play in many of our relationships means that it can regularly affect psychological functioning and quality of life generally. There is no definition of what is sexually 'normal', but clinical psychologists may become involved when an individual becomes *distressed* by their sexuality or their sexual activities or when these cause interpersonal difficulties. We began this chapter with two quite distinct personal accounts, each of which illustrates in their different ways how an individual's sexual performance or their feelings of gender may cause them conflict or distress. *James's story* is one of problematic sexual performance, where his normally active libido fails him just prior to intercourse with men he particularly likes. *Chris's* cross-dressing provides excitement that quickly gives way to guilt. It is also something he feels he needs to communicate to his wife, but at present cannot. Both provide examples of the kinds of cases that clinical psychologists are likely to encounter when sexual performance and gender identity have an impact on psychological well-being, causing anxiety and distress, and feelings of guilt, shame and depression.

11.1 DEFINING PATHOLOGICAL SEXUAL BEHAVIOUR

As you can imagine, what constitutes a sexual dysfunction is not a simple matter. Opinions about what is morally and socially acceptable and unacceptable change within societies over time, and there are significant differences between cultures in the implicit rules that constitute acceptable public behaviour (see Chapter 1). For example, until 1973 the DSM listed homosexuality as a sexual disorder, along with paedophilia, sadism and suchlike, but it is now considered a perfectly normal form of sexual activity in most Western societies, and is even considered a proper form of sexual activity for adolescent boys in some societies (Herdt & Stoller, 1990). The actual nature of the sexual activity per se does not constitute grounds for labelling it as pathological, and people differ significantly in the range of stimuli that trigger sexual

urges or fantasies. However, two factors are important when attempting to identify psychopathology in both sexual behaviour and gender identity. Firstly, a sexual activity or a gender problem may be considered a suitable case for psychological treatment if it is frequent, chronic, causes the individual significant distress, and affects interpersonal relationships and other areas of functioning. Such examples include the personal distress and strain on interpersonal relationships caused by problems associated with completion of the normal sexual cycle (see section 11.2, Sexual dysfunctions, below). Similarly, the cross-dressing behaviour of *Chris* in our earlier example caused him to experience guilt and anxiety, and individuals with gender identity problems (known as *gender dysphoria* in DSM-5) also experience considerable distress, anxiety and depression at being 'trapped' in what they consider to be a body of the wrong biological sex. Clearly, such distress is certainly the subject matter of psychopathology. Secondly, some individuals persistently direct their sexual activity at individuals who do not consent to the activity or who cannot legally give consent (e.g. children). Such activities include exhibitionism (exposing of the genitalia to a stranger), paedophilia, and rape, and DSM-5 includes some of these activities (e.g. exhibitionistic disorder, paedophilic disorder) even though the diagnostic criteria do not require that the individual committing these acts should experience distress. Whether such categories of activity should be labelled as psychopathologies is a debatable point, and in many cases they may be more suitably characterized as illegal criminal activities outlawed by particular societies.

The disorders of sexual functioning and gender identity that we will cover in this chapter can be found in three separate chapters of DSM-5: (1) *sexual dysfunctions* – which represent problems with the normal sexual response cycle (e.g. lack of sexual desire or pain during intercourse); (2) *paraphilic disorders* – which represent sexual urges or fantasies involving unusual sources of gratification (e.g. non-human objects or non-consenting individuals); and (3) *gender dysphoria* – where the individual is dissatisfied with his or her own biological sex and has a strong desire to be a member of the opposite sex. In the case of each of these categories of disorders we will now discuss the nature of the disorders, diagnostic criteria, prevalence, aetiology and treatment.

SELF-TEST QUESTIONS

- What are the sociocultural problems involved in defining pathological sexual behaviour?
- What are the three main groups of sexual and gender identity disorders?

11.2　SEXUAL DYSFUNCTIONS

Sex is mainly a private subject, and many people rarely talk with anyone other than their partner about intimate sexual matters. During the 1960s and 1970s, a greater openness about sex and sexual activities developed as part of the liberalising climate of the time. Changes in longevity, available leisure time, employment, child-rearing practices, and media coverage of leisure activities led to increased interest in sexual practices. Similarly, effective oral contraceptives and treatments for venereal disease helped to remove sexual inhibitions. Finally, changes in obscenity laws permitted sexual explicitness in the mass media in a way never previously broadcast. All this led to increased interest in sexual activity generally and sexual satisfaction in particular (Tiefer, 2006). At around this time, Masters & Johnson (1966) were beginning to publish their pioneering research on what they called the 'human sexual response', and the earlier Kinsey reports (Kinsey, Pomeroy, Martin & Gebhard, 1953) provided hitherto unavailable statistical information on the frequency with which Americans engaged in various sexual activities. To most people's surprise, these reports revealed that sexual activities were significantly more widespread than most people were willing to believe at that time. They showed that 90 per cent of males had masturbated and oral sex was a common sexual activity. In addition, the studies revealed that around 80 per cent of men and 50 per cent of women had indulged in premarital sex. More recent data from the UK National Survey of Sexual Attitudes and Lifestyles suggested that sexual activity in both males and females in the UK increased over the period between 1990 and 2000. In 2000, men and women between the ages of 16 and 44 years reported having had an average of 12.7 and 6.5 sexual partners respectively in their lifetime, and 2.6 per cent of men and women reported having had a homosexual relationship. Frequency of sexual activity was also significantly higher in 2000 than 1990, with 72 per cent of men and 76 per cent of women reporting having had vaginal intercourse in the previous month; 78 per cent of men and 76 per cent of women also reported having oral sex in the previous year. These increases in sexual activity were also accompanied by significant rises in sexually transmitted infections – a 20 per cent rise in men and 56 per cent rise in women between 1990 and 1999 (Johnson, Mercer, Erens, Copas et al., 2001). A third wave of the National Survey was completed in 2010 and was published in November 2013. A summary of the findings can be found in a special issue of the *Lancet* at at http://www.thelancet.com/themed/natsal. It shows that the upward trend in sexual activity found between 1990 and 2000 has in some respects continued up to 2010.

The figures available suggest there has been a significant change in behaviour and attitudes towards sex in Western societies over recent decades. There has been an increase in the rate at which both men and women take sexual partners and a drop in the age at which adolescents report having their first sexual experience. This is accompanied by a relaxation of attitudes to homosexual behaviour, non-exclusive sexual relationships and sex outside of marriage. Although sexual activity appears to have increased over the past 20 years, it is difficult to estimate whether this increase has also given rise to increased sexual performance problems. However, the fact that research on sexual activity can nowadays proceed openly and without stigma has meant that significant developments have been made in how we conceptualize sexual activity and categorize potential dysfunctions. For example, the normal sexual cycle has been divided into four stages, and sexual dysfunctions can occur at any one of these distinct stages. Table 11.1 lists the stages and the specific diagnosable disorders that have been identified with each. The four stages of the sexual response cycle are: (1) *desire* (relating to the desire to have sex), (2) *arousal* (a subjective sense of sexual pleasure and accompanying physical changes in the genitalia – e.g. penile erection in the male, and vaginal swelling and lubrication in the female), (3) *orgasm* (the peaking of sexual pleasure), and

To read about the Kinsey reports go to http://tinyurl.com/8bgygsl

TABLE 11.1 *Stages of the sexual cycle and their associated DSM-5 disorders*

Stage of the sexual cycle	Description	Disorders	Main diagnostic symptom
Desire	Sexual thoughts and fantasies and the desire to have sex	Male hypoactive sexual desire disorder	Persistent or deficient sexual/erotic thoughts and desire for sexual activity
Arousal	Subjective sense of sexual pleasure and accompanying physical changes in the genitalia (e.g. penile erection in the male, and vaginal swelling and lubrication in the female)	Female sexual interest/ arousal disorder	Absent/reduced interest in sexual activity or erotic/sexual thoughts
		Erectile disorder	In males, marked difficulty in obtaining or maintaining an erection during sexual activity
Orgasm	Peaking of sexual pleasure (including ejaculation in the male and vaginal contractions in the female)	Female orgasmic disorder	In females, a marked infrequency of orgasms or reduced intensity of orgasms
		Delayed ejaculation	In males, a marked delay in ejaculation or marked infrequency or absence of ejaculation
		Early ejaculation	A persistent onset of orgasm and ejaculation with minimal sexual stimulation and before the individual wishes it
Sexual pain disorders		Genito-pelvic pain/ penetration disorder	Persistent difficulties with vaginal penetration/vaginal or pelvic pain/fear or anxiety about pain during intercourse

(4) *resolution* (a post-coital sense of muscular relaxation and well-being). There are no DSM-5 disorders specifically associated with the resolution stage, but there is an additional set of disorders known as *sexual pain disorders* that can occur at different stages during the sexual cycle and significantly affect the normal sense of well-being experienced during the resolution stage. We will discuss the disorders relating to each stage in more detail later, after we have considered general diagnostic issues.

11.2.1 Diagnosis of Sexual Dysfunctions

In general terms, **sexual dysfunctions** are a heterogenous group of disorders characterized clinically by the individual's inability to respond sexually or to experience sexual pleasure (DSM-5, p.423). The specific dysfunction must also cause the individual subjective distress, affect areas of functioning such as relationships, and be persistent or recurrent. In each case, the clinician needs to exercise considerable judgement about what might and might not constitute a diagnosable problem in this area. The age and experience of the client needs to be considered. For

> **sexual dysfunctions** Problems with the normal sexual response cycle (e.g. lack of sexual desire or pain during intercourse).

To read Hayes & Dennerstein's article on the impact of ageing go to **www.wiley-psychopathology.com/ reading/ch11**

example, sexual activity and performance usually decline with age, and in females may do so after the menopause (Hayes & Dennerstein, 2005) – and often this is a perfectly normal developmental process rather than a dysfunction. The clinician also needs to take into account the client's ethnic, cultural, religious and social background – factors that may influence desire, expectations and attitudes about performance. As we mentioned earlier, diagnosis of a dysfunction is given only when the symptoms are persistent, cause the individual significant psychological distress, and impair general day-to-day functioning and cause interpersonal distress. In many cases, distress occurs in cases of sexual dysfunction because it is associated with diagnosable mood disorders or anxiety disorders (especially obsessive compulsive disorder, panic disorder, social anxiety disorder and specific phobia), and sexual dysfunction can often be a frequent complication of these latter disorders (Figueira, Possidente, Marques & Hayes, 2001).

Specific sexual dysfunctions

In DSM-5, sexual dysfunction disorders have been categorized around the stages of the sexual cycle, namely desire, arousal, orgasm and resolution (see Table 11.1), and also include a category relating to pain experienced during the sexual cycle.

Disorders of desire and arousal The first two phases of the sexual response cycle are the desire and arousal stages, which consist of the urge and desire to have sex, to indulge in sexual thoughts and fantasies, the experience of sexual attraction to others (all defined by desire), and a subjective sense of sexual pleasure and accompanying physical changes in the genitalia (arousal). DSM-5 identifies three disorders that span these two phases of the sexual cycle and these are *male hypoactive sexual desire disorder*, *erectile disorder* and *female sexual interest/arousal disorder*.

Male hypoactive sexual desire disorder

This disorder is characterized by a persistent and recurrent deficiency or absence of desire for sexual activity and absence of sexual fantasies that cause the individual marked distress or interpersonal difficulty (DSM-5 Summary Table 11.1). Low sexual desire may be general or it may be focused on sexual activity with one individual (such as the client's partner) or on a particular sexual activity itself (such as oral sex). **Male hypoactive sexual desire disorder** may be frequently associated with erectile and/

> **male hypoactive sexual desire disorder**
> Absent/reduced interest in sexual activity or erotic/sexual thoughts.

or ejaculation concerns, and it may be an inability to obtain an erection that leads to the man's loss of interest in sexual activity. The prevalence of male hypoactive sexual desire disorder depends very much on the individual's nationality and country of origin, although 6 per cent of younger men (age 18–24 years) and 41 per cent of older men (age 66–74 years) have problems with sexual desire, and overall prevalence rates vary from 12.5 per cent in Northern European men to 28 per cent in Southeast Asian men (DSM-5, p.442). Mood and anxiety symptoms appear to be strong predictors of low sexual desire in men, and alcohol may increase this risk.

Erectile disorder

The basic feature of erectile disorder is the repeated failure to obtain or maintain erection during partnered sexual activities, on all or almost all occasions over a significant period of time (DSM-5 Summary Table 11.2). This is often associated with low self-esteem, low self-confidence and a decreased sense of masculinity. Male **erectile disorder** is one of the most common of the sexual dys-

> **erectile disorder** The inability to maintain an adequate erection during sexual activity. Around 10 per cent of males report erection problems, but this increases to 20 per cent in the over 50s.

functions in men, is usually the disorder that is most commonly referred for treatment, and is likely to have a significant impact on the sexual satisfaction of both the sufferer and his partner. Approximately 13–21 per cent of men aged 40–80 years experience occasional problems with erections, but only 2 per cent of men younger than 40 years (DSM-5, p.427). The causes of male erectile disorder are complex, and appear to range across physical, psychological and sociocultural factors. Hormonal and vascular problems such as high blood

DSM-5 SUMMARY TABLE 11.1 *Criteria for male hypoactive sexual desire disorder*

- Incessantly or recurrently deficient sexual/erotic thoughts or desire for sexual activity for a period of at least 6 months, causing significant distress to the patient
- The sexual dysfunction is not better accounted for by a non-sexual mental disorder or as a consequence of relationship or other significant stressors and is not attributable to the effects of a medication/substance or other medical condition

DSM-5 SUMMARY TABLE 11.2 *Criteria for erectile disorder*

- At least one of the following occurs during at least 75 per cent of sexual activity for a period of at least 6 months causing significant distress to the patient:
  - Difficulty in obtaining an erection during sexual activity
  - Difficulty in maintaining an erection until the completion of sexual activity
  - Decrease in erectile rigidity
- The sexual dysfunction is not better accounted for by a non-sexual mental disorder or as a consequence of relationship or other significant stressors and is not attributable to the effects of a medication/substance or other medical condition

pressure, diabetes and heart disease are associated with erectile disorders (Berman, Berman, Werbin, Flaherty *et al.*, 1999) as are activities such as smoking and excessive alcohol consumption (Westheimer & Lopater, 2002). Psychological factors that may affect the ability to achieve and maintain erection include severe depression (Seidman, 2002) and marital, financial and occupational stress (Morokoff & Gilliland, 1993).

Female sexual interest/arousal disorder

This disorder is characterized by combinations of the following characteristics: significantly reduced sexual interest or arousal related to lack of interest in sexual activity, absence of erotic thoughts, unreceptiveness to sexual approaches, reduced sexual excitement, and reduced sexual sensations during sexual activity (DSM-5 Summary Table 11.3). For a diagnosis of **female sexual interest/arousal disorder** to be made, clinically significant distress must also be associated with these symptoms. This disorder is frequently associated with problems in experiencing orgasm, and may be associated with pain during sexual activity. It is important to recognize that there are many women

> **female sexual interest/arousal disorder**
> Characterized by combinations of significantly reduced sexual interest or arousal related to lack of interest in sexual activity, absence of erotic thoughts, unreceptiveness to sexual approaches, reduced sexual excitement, and reduced sexual sensations during sexual activity.

DSM-5 SUMMARY TABLE 11.3 *Criteria for female sexual interest/arousal disorder*

- Significant reduction or lack of interest in sexual arousal/receptiveness as marked by at least three of the following for a period of at least 6 months causing significant distress to the patient:

  - Lack of/reduced interest in sexual activity

  - Lack of/reduced interest in sexual/erotic thoughts or fantasies

  - No/reduced initiation of sexual activity and unreceptive to partner's attempt to initiate sexual activity

  - No/reduced excitement or pleasure during sexual activity in at least 75 per cent of sexual encounters

  - Lack of/reduced sexual interest in response to any internal or external sexual cues

  - Lack of/reduced genital or non-genital sensations during sexual activity in at least 75 per cent of sexual encounters

- The sexual dysfunction is not better accounted for by a non-sexual mental disorder or as a consequence of relationship or other significant stressors and is not attributable to the effects of a medication/substance or other medical condition

who experience normal sexual desires, but who – for their own reasons – decide not to engage in sexual activities. Such individuals should not be diagnosed with female sexual interest/arousal disorder, and the discussion found in Focus Point 11.1 provides some insight into the issues behind the use of the label 'female sexual dysfunction'.

Disorders of orgasm   Orgasm is the third stage of the sexual cycle, when sexual stimulation has been sufficient to enable the individual's sexual pleasure to peak. In both males and females this involves a rhythmic muscular contraction of the genitals which results in a release of sexual tension, and in the male is accompanied by ejaculation of semen. There are three DSM-5 defined disorders of this stage, and these are *female orgasmic disorder*, *delayed ejaculation*, and *early ejaculation*.

Female orgasmic disorder   This is a persistent or recurrent delay in or absence of orgasm following normal sexual excitement that causes the individual marked distress or interpersonal difficulty (DSM-5 Summary Table 11.4). Once again, the clinician has to exercise judgement about whether a diagnosis is relevant in individual cases. Prevalence rates for female orgasmic problems range from 10 per cent to 42 per cent depending on

---

FOCUS POINT 11.1

CONSTRUCTING FEMALE SEXUAL DYSFUNCTION

Sexual dysfunction is not diagnosed simply on the basis of problems in sexual desire and performance, but is dependent on the condition also causing marked distress and interpersonal difficulty. Clearly, many people may only rarely experience sexual desire and very rarely indulge in sexual activity – but a sizable proportion of those people are quite happy with this state of affairs, and indeed may even advocate and seek sexual abstinence. But what happens if attempts are made to make such people feel inadequate or in some way 'abnormal'?

In 1966, a New York gynaecologist called Robert A. Wilson published a best-selling book called *Feminine Forever*, in which he argued that the menopause robbed women of their femininity, their sexuality and ruined the quality of their lives. He labelled postmenopausal women as 'castrates' and described the menopause as a 'deficiency disease' that should be treated pharmacologically with hormone replacement therapy. The book and its ensuing publicity had two effects – it made some postmenopausal women begin to believe they were inadequate and had a disorder that needed treatment. It made many others – especially

those in the feminist movement that was developing at the time – believe that menopausal symptoms as described by Wilson were not a medical deficiency, but the creation of a sexist society (Houck, 2003).

More recently, other writers have argued that the pharmaceutical industry has also attempted to manipulate women's beliefs about their sexuality in order to sell their products (Moynihan, 2006). Some drug companies claim that sexual desire problems affect up to 43 per cent of American women (Moynihan, 2003) and can be successfully treated with, for example, hormone patches. However, others claim that this figure is highly improbable and includes women who are quite happy with their reduced level of sexual interest (Bancroft, Loftus & Long, 2003).

Tiefer (2006) lists a number of processes that have been used either wittingly or unwittingly in the past to 'medicalize' what many see as normal sexual functioning. These include:

- Taking a normal function and implying that there is something wrong with it and it should be treated.

- Imputing suffering that is not necessarily there.
- Defining as large a proportion of the population as possible as suffering from the disease.
- Defining a condition as a 'deficiency', disease or disease of hormonal imbalance.
- Taking a common symptom that could mean anything and making it sound as if it is a sign of a serious disease.

While sexual dysfunctions are sometimes caused by medical conditions (see 'Biological causes' in section 11.2.2), lack of sexual desire and interest is itself often portrayed as a medical condition in need of treatment. Yet a reduction in sexual interest and desire can be a healthy and adaptive response to normal changes in body chemistry or as a normal reaction to adverse life stressors or relationship changes.

DSM-5 SUMMARY TABLE 11.4 *Criteria for female orgasmic disorder*

- Delay, infrequency or absence of orgasm or reduced intensity of orgasmic sensations in at least 75 per cent of sexual activity for a period of at least 6 months causing significant distress to the patient

- The sexual dysfunction is not better accounted for by a non-sexual mental disorder or as a consequence of relationship or other significant stressors and is not attributable to the effects of a medication/substance or other medical condition

DSM-5 SUMMARY TABLE 11.5 *Criteria for delayed ejaculation*

- Delay, infrequency or absence of ejaculation in at least 75 per cent of partnered sexual activity for a period of at least 6 months causing significant distress to the patient

- The sexual dysfunction is not better accounted for by a non-sexual mental disorder or as a consequence of relationship or other significant stressors and is not attributable to the effects of a medication/substance or other medical condition

factors such as age, culture, duration and severity of symptoms (DSM-5, p.431). Women exhibit significant differences in the type and intensity of stimulation that triggers orgasm, and as many as 10 per cent of adult women may never have experienced an orgasm (Anderson, 1983). In addition, whether a woman achieves orgasm or not may be a significant factor in her partner's attitude to sex. **Female orgasmic disorder** is one of the most frequent female sexual disorders referred for treatment, and it is experienced by around one in four women at some point in their lives, and more significantly in the postmenopausal period (Heiman, 2002), but women who are assertive and who experienced masturbatory orgasm prior to becoming sexually active are significantly less likely to be diagnosed with female orgasmic disorder (Hite, 1976). Early sexual experiences may be important in determining whether a woman develops female orgasmic disorder. For example, positive early sexual encounters fostering emotional involvement are directly related to the probability of reaching orgasm in later sexual encounters (Heiman, Gladue, Roberts & LoPiccolo, 1986). In contrast, an upbringing that implies the woman should deny her sexuality is more likely to lead to orgasmic dysfunction, as are the experiences of being punished for childhood masturbation and receiving little or no advice or information about menstruation (LoPiccolo, 1997).

female orgasmic disorder Marked absence, delay or infrequency of orgasm and markedly reduced intensity of orgasmic sensations.

Delayed ejaculation
This is a persistent or recurrent delay in, or absence of, ejaculation following a normal sexual excitement phase that causes the individual marked distress and interpersonal difficulty (DSM-5 Summary Table 11.5). **Delayed ejaculation** is the least common of the male sexual complaints, and less than 1 per cent of men will complain of problems in reaching ejaculation over a period of 6 months or longer (DSM-5, p.425). The clinician must make judgements about whether ejaculation is problematically delayed by taking into account the client's age and the degree of sexual stimulation. The problems can be caused by physical factors such as low testosterone levels (Stahl, 2001), alcohol consumption, and prescription drugs such as antidepressants and anxiolytic drugs, all of which can affect the response of the sympathetic nervous system (Segraves, 1995; Altman, 2001).

delayed ejaculation Persistent or recurrent delay in ejaculation following a normal sexual excitement phase.

Early ejaculation
This is the persistent or recurrent onset of orgasm and ejaculation with minimal sexual stimulation, within 1 minute of penetration, and before the person wishes it to happen (DSM-5 Summary Table 11.6). Early or premature ejaculation is not unusual when aspects of the sexual activity are novel (e.g. the person is indulging in novel sex acts, with new partners, or has sex only rarely), and this must be taken into account by the clinician when making a diagnosis. Most young males learn to delay

DSM-5 SUMMARY TABLE 11.6 *Criteria for premature (early) ejaculation*

- Continual or recurring pattern of ejaculation occurring in least 75 per cent of partnered sexual activity with approximately one minute of vaginal penetration and before the patient desires it for a period of at least six months causing significant distress to the patient

- The sexual dysfunction is not better accounted for by a non-sexual mental disorder or as a consequence of relationship or other significant stressors and is not attributable to the effects of a medication/substance or other medical condition

DSM-5 SUMMARY TABLE 11.7 *Criteria for genito-pelvic pain/penetration disorder*

- Persistent or recurring difficulties with at least one of the following over a period of at least 6 months:
  - Sexual vaginal penetration
  - Vulvovaginal or pelvic pain during vaginal penetration
  - Distress about vulvovaginal or pelvic pain during or in anticipation of vaginal penetration
  - Tensing or tightening of the pelvic floor muscles during vaginal penetration

- The sexual dysfunction is not better accounted for by a non-sexual mental disorder or as a consequence of relationship or other significant stressors and is not attributable to the effects of a medication/substance or other medical condition

orgasm with continued sexual experience and age, but some continue to have premature ejaculation problems and so may seek treatment for the disorder, but these are typically men under the age of 30 years (Bancroft, 1989). In men between the ages of 18–70 years, 20–30 per cent express concern about premature ejaculation, but in practice only around 1 per cent of men would meet the new DSM-5 diagnostic criteria for early ejaculation (DSM-5, p.444). **Early ejaculation** has been linked to infrequent climactic sex (Spiess, Geer & O'Donohue, 1984), over-responsiveness to tactile stimulation (Rowland, Cooper & Slob, 1996), anxiety caused by hurried sexual experiences in early adulthood (Dunn, Croft & Hackett, 1999), and, in some cases, with physical or biological causes (Metz, Pryor, Nesvacil, Abuzzhab & Koznar, 1997).

early ejaculation The onset of orgasm with minimal sexual stimulation. Treatment for this disorder is typically sought by men under the age of 30 years.

Sexual pain disorders   Pain can become a common experience that is associated with sexual activity. It can occur prior to, during or after sexual intercourse, and significantly affect the feeling of well-being that is an important feature of the resolution stage of the sexual cycle. In DSM-5, pain during sexual activity has been included in a single new diagnostic category called *genito-pelvic pain/penetration disorder*.

Genito-pelvic pain/penetration disorder   This disorder refers to four commonly co-occurring symptoms, namely difficulty in having intercourse, genito-pelvic pain, fear of pain or vaginal penetration, and tension of the pelvic floor muscles (DSM-5 Summary Table 11.7). This disorder is often associated with other sexual dysfunction disorders such as reduced sexual desire and interest, and pain is often associated with behavioural avoidance and an unwillingness to attend gynaecological examinations despite medical advice. Factors that are relevant to aetiology in the case of **genito-pelvic pain/penetration disorder** include partner's sexual problems, relationship problems, individual vulnerability factors (such as poor body image, history of sexual or emotional abuse), and

stress. Often the causes of sexual pain are physical, and may relate to gynaecological or urological problems in women, or to allergic reactions to substances in contraceptive creams, condoms or diaphragms (see e.g. Brown & Ceniceros, 2001). Because this is a new disorder, prevalence rates are unknown, but up to 15 per cent of women in North America report recurrent pain during intercourse (DSM-5, p.438).

genito-pelvic pain/penetration disorder Refers to four commonly occurring symptoms, namely difficulty having intercourse, genito-pelvic pain, fear of pain or vaginal penetration, and tension of the pelvic floor muscles.

Summary of specific sexual dysfunction disorders

The specific disorders that we have discussed can be associated with individual stages of the sexual cycle. However, there is clearly a good deal of overlap between these different disorders, and a disorder in one particular stage of the sexual cycle may well affect performance in other stages (e.g. disorders of arousal and orgasm may subsequently affect sexual urges and desires). Diagnosing a sexual dysfunction is not as simple as referring to a list of criteria symptoms because the clinician has to make judgements about what is dysfunctional in the light of the client's sexual experience, age, religious views, cultural norms, ethnicity, and upbringing. The clinician also has to decide whether the sexual problems that are referred are caused primarily by physical or medical conditions, and, if so, whether the client might be better referred for medical treatment, perhaps by a pain specialist or a gynaecologist. Finally, it is important to remember that many people may not be particularly satisfied with their own sexual performance or that of their partner, but manage to live their daily lives quite happily. For example, older women are less likely to be distressed by low sexual desire than younger women (Derogatis & Burnett, 2008) (see Focus Point 11.1), and it is relatively common for many people to have sexual symptoms for a month without this causing undue distress. As a consequence, DSM-5 has specifically introduced some minimum durations for symptoms before a diagnosis can be made, and a sexual dysfunction is diagnosed only when the condition is persistent, causes the client considerable distress, and causes significant interpersonal difficulty.

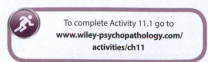

To complete Activity 11.1 go to www.wiley-psychopathology.com/activities/ch11

11.2.2   The Aetiology of Sexual Dysfunctions

In describing the various sexual disorders in the previous section we have hinted in some cases about factors that might cause these specific disorders to develop. This section will provide a more thorough review of the aetiology of sexual dysfunction by looking first at the kinds of risk factors that are associated with the development of specific disorders, and then looking in more detail at theories that attempt to explain in more general terms how people might acquire sexual dysfunctions.

Risk factors for sexual dysfunctions

Risk factors for individual sexual dysfunctions will usually be to some extent gender related, because many of the disorders apply only to a specific gender. So, for example, experiencing the menopause is an important risk factor for female sexual interest/arousal disorder, and surgically menopausal women (who have undergone hysterectomy) are at significantly greater risk (Dennerstein, Koochaki, Barton & Graziottin, 2006). For specific male dysfunctions such as erectile disorder, risk factors include ageing, a diagnosis of depression, cigarette smoking, and medical conditions such as diabetes, cardiovascular and urogential disease (Korenman, 2004; Droupy, 2005). For early ejaculation, risk factors include being young, having experienced divorce, and being more educated (Fasolo, Mirone, Gentile, Parazzini & Ricci, 2005). Educational level in men has a complex relationship to sexual dysfunction: men who are more educated are more likely to report early ejaculation than less educated men (Fasolo, Mirone, Gentile, Parazzini & Ricci, 2005), but less educated men are more likely to report erectile disorder than better educated men (Lyngdorf & Hemmingsen, 2004). Childhood sexual abuse is also a significant risk factor for sexual dysfunction in later life. In a large-scale Australian study, more than one in three women and one in six men reported a history of childhood sexual abuse, and there was a significant association between childhood abuse

and symptoms of sexual dysfunction (Najman, Dunne, Purdie, Boyle & Coxeter, 2005). Sexual trauma and childhood sexual abuse has been found to be a significant risk factor in specific disorders such as female sexual interest/arousal disorder (Stuart & Greer, 1984) and sexual pain disorders (Binik, Bergeron & Khalife, 2000; Westheimer & Lopater, 2002). Finally, sexual dysfunction is more prevalent in women than in men (43 per cent and 31 per cent respectively) and is more likely among those experiencing poor physical and emotional health generally (Laumann, Paik & Rosen, 1999). However, we must remember that this gender difference may be due at least in part to men being more embarrassed by sexual dysfunction than women, and so reporting disorders significantly less. For example, a study of male erectile disorder found that two out of three men suffering erectile dysfunction were embarrassed when discussing this problem with a doctor, and only 25 per cent subsequently sought medical advice (Droupy, 2005).

Theories of the aetiology of sexual dysfunction

Psychoanalytic theory   Much of the psychoanalytic approach to understanding behaviour revolves around repressed emotions and desires, and specifically around repressed sexual desires, so it is not unusual that psychodynamic theorists have had something to say about the factors underlying sexual dysfunction. Thus, **vaginismus** may be seen as a women expressing hostility towards men; premature ejaculation as men expressing repressed hostility towards women; and female orgasmic disorder as a function of enduring penis envy. Because sexual activity is usually pleasurable – yet often frowned upon by society – many psychodynamic views see sexual dysfunction as resulting from this conflicting state of affairs. Still others view male sexual dysfunctions, such as male erectile disorder, as a result of an unresolved Oedipus complex based on a continual sexual attachment of the male to his mother (Fenichel, 1945). Regardless of the theoretical validity of these analyses, these views gave psychoanalysis an important therapeutic function prior to the development of therapies based on more objective and more detailed knowledge of sexual dysfunctions such as those pioneered by Masters and Johnson in the 1970s.

> **vaginismus**   The involuntary contraction of the muscles surrounding the vagina when vaginal penetration is attempted. Of all women who seek treatment for sexual dysfunctions, around 15–17 per cent are suffering from vaginismus.

The Two-Factor Model of Masters and Johnson

Masters and Johnson were the first researchers to collect detailed information about sexual dysfunctions, and to develop a model of sexual dysfunction based on this empirical evidence. Their model had two important components, both of which contributed to sexual dysfunction. The first component consisted of a learnt or conditioned factor where adverse early sexual experiences had given rise to a learnt fear or anxiety response whenever the individual was engaged in sexual activity. Adverse experiences include (1) psychosexual trauma, such as rape or childhood sexual abuse, (2) religious and social taboos that give rise to feelings of shame and guilt about sex, (3) embarrassing or belittling early experiences with sex (e.g. appearing unknowledgeable or inexperienced to a sexual partner), or (4) excessive alcohol use in men, which can affect the ability to achieve and maintain erection. Once these factors have begun to generate anxiety about sexual performance, the second component of this model is the *spectator role* that individuals adopt in response to their fears and anxieties. Instead of taking a relaxed attitude to sex, the fearful individual constantly monitors their own sexual performance and the responses of their partner. Their focus of attention is therefore directed away from the stimuli that provide sexual arousal and sexual pleasure, and on to factors that provide feedback about how well the individual is performing. There are some important similarities between this theory of sexual dysfunction and self-focused attention accounts of social anxiety disorder (see Chapter 6) where self-focused attention prevents objective processing of the social situation, which leads the social phobic to engage in critical self-evaluation and may well adversely affect their actual performance in the social situation. Because of these similarities, many of the processes involved in self-focused attention may also apply to sexual dysfunction. Although Masters and Johnson's theory was the first attempt to develop an empirical model of sexual dysfunction based on objectively collected data about sexual performance, we must still be cautious about how the two components of their model interact. For example, while it is clear that many people suffering sexual dysfunction experience **performance anxiety**, it is still not clear whether this anxiety is a *cause* or a *consequence* of the dysfunction. We have already noted that many specific sexual disorders can be caused by physical or medical conditions, and it may be that anxiety about sexual performance is a consequence of sexual performance being impaired by these conditions rather than a cause of the condition per se.

performance anxiety The fear of failing to achieve an acceptable level of sexual performance, causing an individual to become distanced from the sexual act and fail to become aroused.

Sexual dysfunction and interpersonal problems

Sex is usually an interpersonal activity, and it may be that interpersonal problems may be a *cause* of at least some of the sexual dysfunctions. Many clinicians believe that individuals with sexual dysfunctions have both sexual and interpersonal problems, and that the latter may be an important cause of the former (e.g. Rosen & Leiblum, 1995). For example, there is an inverse relationship between a woman's sexual desire and their level of concern about their partner's affection (Nobre & Pinto-Gouveia, 2006), and individuals who are angry with their partners are less likely to desire sexual activity (Beck & Bozman, 1995). If negative emotion is a central feature of a couple's relationship, then emotions such as resentment, disgust, anxiety, anger, distrust, and depression are likely to significantly interfere with the development of positive feelings required in the desire and arousal stages of the sexual cycle. If general communication is poor within a couple, then this is likely to have an important impact on talk about intimate activities such as sex. Studies have indicated that interpersonal difficulties are apparent in sexual dysfunctions diagnosed in both men and women, and are associated with early ejaculation and erectile disorders in men (Patrick, Althof, Pryor, Rosen *et al.*, 2005; Swindle, Cameron, Lockhart & Rosen, 2004) and sexual dysfunctions generally in women (Clayton, 2003). Men are also significantly more likely to seek help for their sexual dysfunction if it is associated with interpersonal difficulties (Papaharitou, Athanasiadis, Nakopoulou, Kirana *et al.,* 2006). However, we must still be cautious about how to interpret these findings because they only indicate that there is an association between sexual dysfunction and interpersonal difficulties and we do not know the direction of any causal relationship.

Apart from general difficulties that may have arisen in a relationship, sexual dysfunction may result from specific deficiencies in sexual knowledge or sexual expertise in one or both of the couple. For example, women who suffer female orgasmic disorder often have partners who are awkward or inexperienced lovers (LoPiccolo, 1997; Kaplan, 1974), and individuals who develop sexual dysfunctions often lack the knowledge and skills required to fully stimulate their partner or satisfy themselves (LoPiccolo & Hogan, 1979). Sexual problems can also develop if one member of a couple is overly anxious about pleasing the other, giving rise to performance anxiety that may inhibit sexual feelings and responsiveness to sexual stimuli (Kaplan, 1974).

Finally, untangling the role that interpersonal difficulties may play in *causing* sexual dysfunction is problematic. This is because interpersonal difficulties are very often a central outcome of sexual dysfunction anyway. However, therapies for sexual dysfunction that focus on the relationship between couples are often successful, and this suggests that at least some of the causes of some sexual dysfunctions lie in the details of individual relationships.

The role of negative emotion and psychopathology Satisfying sexual experiences are usually dependent on the individual being open to positive pleasurable emotions and being attentive to those stimuli during sexual activity. Because of this, chronic negative emotions such as depression or anxiety are likely to interfere significantly with sexual performance, and depression and anxiety are significant risk factors for sexual dysfunction (Hayes, Dennerstein, Bennett & Fairley, 2008). Studies suggest that 62 per cent of those people with depression are also likely to have a sexual dysfunction, compared with only 26 per cent of people without depression (Angst, 1998), and depression appears to have a bidirectional relationship with sexual dysfunction – both causing sexual dysfunction and being a significant outcome of sexual dysfunction (Atlantis & Sullivan, 2012). In women, depressive symptoms have been shown to be associated with deficits in sexual desire, sexual fantasy, sexual arousal, and orgasmic function (Cyranowski, Frank, Cherry, Houck & Kupfer, 2004), and men with depression are almost twice as likely to experience erectile dysfunction as non-depressed men, and the degree of erectile dysfunction increases with increasing degree of depression (Araujo, Durante, Feldman, Goldstein & McKinlay, 1998).

To read Atlantis & Sullivan's article on the association between depression and sexual dysfunction go to **www.wiley-psychopathology.com/reading/ch11**

Anxiety is another negative emotion that can potentially have a significant effect on sexual functioning. We have already discussed the role that performance anxiety may play in causing sexual dysfunction, and anxiety disorders themselves are associated with sexual dysfunction. These include panic disorder, social anxiety disorder, specific phobia and obsessive compulsive disorder (Figueira, Possidente, Marques & Hayes, 2001), and, for example, anxiety disorders can be diagnosed in almost 20 per cent of men suffering from erectile disorder (Mallis, Moysidis, Nakopoulou, Papaharitou *et al.*, 2005). High levels of anxiety may lead to sexual dysfunction simply because it is a negative emotion that may inhibit the development of pleasurable emotions associated with sexual pleasure. It may also prevent allocation of attention to stimuli likely to provide sexual stimulation and pleasure. Specific anxiety disorders may influence sexual performance in quite specific ways. For example, panic disorder is associated with a fear of bodily sensations, and so the increases in heart rate and perspiration caused by sexual activity may be interpreted negatively by someone with panic disorder (Sbrocco, Weisberg, Barlow & Cater, 1997). Similarly, fear of contamination associated with some forms of OCD may make the individual fearful of bodily contact and sexual secretions. Finally, social anxiety disorder is known to be associated with a self-critical attitude, which may well give rise to performance anxiety during sexual activity.

Remote vs. immediate causes One view of the causes of sexual dysfunction is that chronic sexual dysfunction is caused by a combination of immediate causes and remote causes (Kaplan, 1974). *Immediate causes* are factors that may directly influence sexual performance, such as performance anxiety, communication problems between partners, lack of sexual knowledge, clumsy technique. However, many of these are factors that may influence the sexual performance of many people at one time or another, and are not necessarily chronic features of a person's lovemaking. However, these immediate performance problems may arise because of longer term *remote causes* of sexual dysfunction, and these refer to more deep-rooted psychological and psychodynamic factors that incline someone to be anxious about their sexual performance. **Remote causes** include feelings of shame and guilt about sexual activity (which may vary with culture; see e.g. Woo, Brotto & Gorzalka, 2011), and general feelings of inadequacy and feelings of conflict brought about by long-term life stress (Kaplan, 1979). In particular, while men may worry during sex about their performance, women worry about their attractiveness, and may experience intrusive thoughts about their weight (Pujols, Seal & Meston, 2010).

> **remote causes** Include feelings of shame and guilt about sexual activity, general feelings of inadequacy, feelings of conflict brought about by long-term life stress, and suchlike.

Biological causes There is considerable debate about whether sexual dysfunctions are the result of psychological or organic (biological) causes. In the period following the pioneering work of Masters and Johnson, researchers began to focus on the importance of psychological factors in the aetiology of sexual dysfunction. However, nowadays, there is a belief that organic or biological factors may be an underlying factor in many cases, and that these may combine with psychological factors to generate a chronic disorder.

Biological causes can be classified into three broad categories: (1) dysfunction caused by an underlying medical condition, (2) dysfunction caused by hormonal abnormalities, and (3) changes in sexual responsiveness caused by ageing.

A whole range of medical conditions can give rise to sexual desire and performance problems. For example, male erectile and orgasmic disorders are associated with high blood pressure, diabetes, heart disease, cigarette smoking, and alcoholism. Dysfunctions are also associated with a variety of medications such as antidepressants and anxiolytic drugs, and with treatments for hypertension and renal problems (Berman, Berman, Werbin, Flaherty *et al.*, 1999; Altman, 2001). Medical conditions that reduce blood flow to the penis (such as blocked arteries or heart disease) will influence the ability to reach and maintain an erection (Stahl, 2001), and other medical conditions may cause central nervous system damage that affects sexual performance and desire, and these include diabetes, multiple sclerosis, and renal problems (Frohman, 2002). Female arousal and orgasm is also affected by medical conditions in much the same way that these conditions influence erection and ejaculation in men. Female arousal and orgasmic disorder has been linked to multiple sclerosis and diabetes, and both antidepressant (e.g. SSRIs such as Prozac) and anxiolytic medications can affect sexual desire in women in much the same way that they do in men (Hensley & Nurnberg, 2002). Similarly, sexual pain disorders may have an organic or medical origin, and these may range from painful allergic reactions to contraceptive creams, condoms or diaphragms (e.g. in the case of female **dyspareunia**) to gynaecological diseases and infections of the vagina, bladder or uterus (which may cause symptoms of vaginismus) (Brown & Ceniceros, 2001;

> **dyspareunia** A genital pain that can occur during, before or after sexual intercourse. Some clinicians believe this is a pain disorder rather than a sexual dysfunction.

McCormick, 1999). Nevertheless, although these forms of organic disorder may be an underlying cause of sexual desire and performance problems, it is quite likely that they will often generate associated psychological problems that give rise to a diagnosable sexual dysfunction. For example, sexual pain or disability caused by disease or medical conditions can give rise to anxiety about sexual performance or to relationship difficulties.

Sexual desire and subsequent arousal and orgasm are dependent on levels of the sex hormones **testosterone**, **oestrogen** and **prolactin**, and imbalances in these hormones can cause sexual desire problems in both men and women. In women, either high or low levels of oestrogen can cause sexual desire problems, and oestrogen levels can be affected if a woman is taking the birth control

> **testosterone** A steroid hormone stimulating development of male secondary sexual characteristics.

> **oestrogen** Any of a group of steroid hormones which promote the development and maintenance of female characteristics of the body.

> **prolactin** A hormone from the pituitary gland stimulating milk production after childbirth.

pill, which will artificially raise her oestrogen levels, or is being given anti-oestrogen therapy for breast cancer that will lower oestrogen levels (Amsterdam, Wheler, Hudis & Krychman, 2005). High prolactin levels have the effect of suppressing the hormones responsible for the normal functioning of the ovaries and testes, and high prolactin levels can therefore lead to menstrual irregularity and/or fertility problems. In men, erectile dysfunction is associated with high levels of prolactin, and erectile problems can be eased with the use of drugs that lower prolactin levels (Spollen, Wooten, Cargile & Bartztokis, 2004).

Finally, one of the important variables that affect sexual functioning is age, and the prevalence of sexual dysfunction in both males and females increases with age. For example, reports of erectile problems in men increase significantly after 50 years of age (Laumann, Gagnon, Michael & Michael, 1994), and a study of Australian men over the age of 40 years indicated that 34 per cent of those men surveyed reported one reproductive health disorder or more, including erectile dysfunction (21 per cent), lower urinary tract symptoms (16 per cent) and prostrate disease (14 per cent) (Holden, McLachlan, Pitts, Cumming et al., 2005). Such findings may indicate that levels of male hormones generally decrease with age, or that reproductive health disorders may significantly affect sexual functioning. Sexual desire and performance also decreases with increased age in women, and the menopause has a significant influence here. Menopause is associated with decreases in oestrogen and testosterone levels that can exacerbate female sexual dysfunction (Graziottin & Leiblum, 2005). Studies suggest that around one in four women report a loss of sexual desire after the menopause, and this is associated with fluctuations in levels of oestrogen and testosterone. However, menopause is associated not only with physical changes but also with psychological changes, and loss of sexual desire in postmenopausal women has been shown to be associated with physical factors such as lower hormonal levels and vaginal dryness and psychological factors such as depression and living with children (Gracia, Sammel, Freeman, Liu et al., 2004).

One final biological factor that has been researched in the aetiology of sexual dysfunctions is genetics, and recent epidemiology and candidate gene studies have suggested a strong genetic influence on female sexual functioning, with the hope that successful identification of biomarkers and novel genes underlying female sexual dysfunction will help to improve diagnosis and treatment (Burri, Cherkas & Spector, 2009).

> To read Burri, Cherkas & Spector's article on the genetics and epidemiology of female sexual dysfunction go to **www.wiley-psychopathology.com/reading/ch11**

Sociocultural causes   The level of sexual dysfunction within a society can change depending on a range of cultural and economic factors within that society. For example, the stress caused by poverty, financial problems or unemployment have all been linked to erectile dysfunctions in men (Morokoff & Gillilland, 1993) and this effect has been identified during the recent economic downturn in European countries (Christensen, Gronbaek, Osler, Pedersen et al., 2011). Many cultures also specify implicit rules about sexual behaviour, and in many cases these rules can cause conflict and sexual dysfunction. For example, the religious and cultural views of many societies require that women should repress or deny their sexuality, and so any expression of sexual desire or indulgence in sexual activity is likely to cause personal conflict and feelings of shame and guilt. This view is supported by the fact that many women who have received a strict religious upbringing are more likely to suffer from arousal and orgasmic dysfunction, and may have been punished for any sexual activity during childhood and adolescence (Masters & Johnson, 1970).

Summary We can see from this subsection that theories of sexual dysfunction are quite wide ranging and encompass both psychological and biological explanations. There is no doubt that many cases of sexual dysfunction have an organic or biological basis, and these can range from dysfunctions caused by medical conditions, hormone imbalances, and changes in biology with age. However, since the pioneering work of Masters and Johnson, psychological factors have also been identified in the aetiology of sexual dysfunction, and these include performance anxiety, underlying interpersonal problems, existing psychopathology such as depression and anxiety, and a variety of life experiences, such as childhood abuse, psychosexual trauma and exposure to religious and social taboos.

11.2.3 The Treatment of Sexual Dysfunctions

Over the past 60–70 years the treatment of sexual dysfunctions has developed through a number of distinct stages. Prior to the 1950s, psychodynamic therapy was probably the only structured form of treatment available to those courageous enough in the existing social climate to admit sexual problems. With its emphasis on underlying conflicts and tensions tied to repressed sexual desires, psychoanalytic theory seemed ideally suited to treat sexual dysfunctions. However, the liberating social climate of the 1960s and 1970s allowed freer discussion of sexual problems, and with this came the pioneering early work of Masters and Johnson published in their book *Human Sexual Inadequacy* (1970). This led to the development of what are now known as *direct treatments* for sexual dysfunction. These are often behaviourally based treatments for the specific symptoms of the disorder. So, rather than consider erectile dysfunction to be a manifestation of underlying psychological problems, therapists would provide the client with specific training on how to achieve and maintain an erection (e.g. the 'tease' technique). Most modern-day treatment programmes now include some components designed to directly address the main symptom of the disorder (such as lack of desire, erectile problems, or premature ejaculation) as well as components designed to deal with accompanying psychological problems (such as performance anxiety, related depression, or relationship problems). As well

as these developments in psychological treatment, there have been significant advances in biological treatments for sexual dysfunctions. Treatments available today include drug and hormone treatments for problems of desire, arousal and orgasm, and mechanical devices for aiding penile erection in men. In the following sections we will cover some of these treatments in more detail, beginning in Treatment in Practice Box 11.1 with an overview of the general structure of sex therapy. The following sections then cover a range of psychological and behavioural therapies in more detail, followed by a description and evaluation of biologically based treatments.

Psychological and behavioural treatments

Direct treatment of symptoms
Direct treatments are techniques targeting the specific sexual performance deficit. For example, there are two specific techniques used to help clients with early ejaculation. These are the **stop–start technique** and the **squeeze technique**. In the former, the client's partner stimulates the penis until close to ejaculation, at which point the partner is signalled to stop by the client (Semans, 1956). This process continues once the desire to ejaculate subsides. This acts to increase the amount of stimulation required to achieve ejaculation. The 'squeeze' technique is very similar, where the client's partner will firmly squeeze below the head of the penis just prior to ejaculation. This has the effect of reducing the erection, and can be repeated several times in order to help the client control ejaculation (St Lawrence & Madakasira, 1992). The 'squeeze' technique has been shown to significantly increase ejaculation latency, and is comparable to the therapeutic effects of a number of drugs used to treat premature ejaculation (Abdel-Hamid, El Nagger & El Gilany, 2001). A direct treatment method designed to deal with symptoms of erectile disorder or male and female orgasmic disorder is the **tease technique**. This involves the partner caressing the client's genitals, but stopping when the client becomes aroused (e.g. achieves an erection) or approaches orgasm. This enables couples to experience sexual pleasure without the need to achieve orgasm, and as a result may reduce any performance anxiety that may have been contributing to erectile

> **stop–start technique** A technique used to help clients with premature ejaculation where the client's partner stimulates the penis until close to ejaculation, at which point the partner is signalled to stop by the client.

> **squeeze technique** A technique used to help clients with premature ejaculation where the client's partner firmly squeezes below the head of the penis just prior to ejaculation.

> **tease technique** A direct treatment method designed to deal with symptoms of erectile dysfunction or male and female orgasmic disorder. It involves the partner caressing the client's genitals, but stopping when the client becomes aroused (e.g. achieves an erection) or approaches orgasm.

CLINICAL PERSPECTIVE: TREATMENT IN PRACTICE BOX 11.1
WHAT IS SEX THERAPY?

Current forms of sex therapy involve a number of components, and these different components are designed to identify specific sexual problems, to address these specific problems with direct treatment, to deal with associated psychological and relationship issues, and to provide clients with sexual knowledge and sexual skills. Sex therapy usually treats the couple rather than the individual who manifests the dysfunction, and couples are urged to share the responsibility for the sexual problem. Below are some of these separate components which form the important core stages of sex therapy.

ASSESSMENT

Through interview, the therapist will collect information about specific sexual problems (e.g. lack of desire by one partner, or erectile problems in a male partner), and discuss current life issues and past life events that may be contributing to the problem. This stage will usually be accompanied by a medical examination to determine whether there are organic factors contributing to the problems.

DEALING WITH ORGANIC DYSFUNCTION

If there are clearly organic or medical factors contributing to the dysfunction (such as low hormone levels, medical conditions such as diabetes or high blood pressure, or other medications, such as antidepressants or anxiolytics), then these may be addressed early in the programme (e.g. by reducing levels of antidepressant drugs).

SEXUAL SKILLS TRAINING

Many types of sexual problem arise through lack of knowledge about the physiology of sex and a lack of basic technique during lovemaking. The therapist can address these factors by providing the clients with educational materials such as booklets and videos.

CHANGING DYSFUNCTIONAL BELIEFS

Sex is associated with a whole range of myths and false beliefs (e.g. 'too much masturbation is bad for you', 'nice women aren't aroused by erotic books or films', and so on) (Bach, Wincze & Barlow, 2001), and if a client holds these false beliefs they may be preventing full sexual arousal and satisfaction. Using a range of methods, such as those used in CBT (see section 4.1.1), the therapist will attempt to identify any dysfunctional beliefs, challenge them, and replace them with more functional beliefs.

DIRECT INTERVENTION AND BEHAVIOURAL TRAINING

Depending on the specific sexual dysfunction that has been referred for treatment, the therapist will advise the clients on the use of a range of behavioural techniques designed to help their specific problem. These techniques are discussed more fully in section 11.2.3, but include the 'tease technique' for erectile dysfunction, 'stop–start technique' and 'squeeze technique' for premature ejaculation (Semans, 1956; LoPiccolo, 1997), and directed masturbation training for arousal and orgasmic disorders (Heiman, 2002). Therapists may also teach clients a technique known as *non-demand pleasuring*, which involves a couple exploring and caressing each other's body to discover sexual pleasure rather than achieving orgasm. This allows couples to learn how to give and receive sexual pleasure without the pressure of needing to achieve orgasm.

DEALING WITH RELATIONSHIP AND LIFESTYLE ISSUES

Sexual dysfunction is often related to conflict within the relationship and to stressful lifestyles (e.g. one partner may be dominating and controlling or the demands of factors such as family and work may be causing unnecessary stress). The therapist will usually attempt to identify any factors that may be contributing to the disorder and advise clients on how to improve these.

---

problems or arousal and orgasmic problems (LoPiccolo, 1997). For individuals with arousal or orgasmic problems, **directed masturbation training** is often helpful (Heiman, 2002). With the use of educational material, videos, diagrams, and – in some cases – erotic materials, a woman can be taught step-by-step to achieve orgasm – even in cases where she has never previously experienced an orgasm. This method has been shown to be highly effective, and over 90 per cent of women treated with this method learn how to achieve orgasm during masturbation (Heiman & LoPiccolo, 1988).

directed masturbation training A treatment for individuals with arousal or orgasmic problems using educational material, videos, diagrams and – in some cases – erotic materials.

Couples therapy As we have mentioned several times in this chapter, sexual dysfunction may be closely associated with relationship problems. If sexual dysfunctions are a manifestation of broader problems within a relationship, then the latter need to be effectively addressed. For example, a lack of sexual desire in one partner may be a way that the partner can exert some control within the relationship – especially if there are conflicts over power and control. In such cases, underlying sexual dysfunction may entail some implicit reward for both partners, one partner gaining reward from their ability to control sex, and the other gaining reward by viewing their partner's lack of desire as a weakness, which enables them to see themselves as controlling. During **couples therapy**, a therapist will explore these issues with a couple and try to identify if there are any implicit payoffs within the relationship for maintaining the sexual dysfunction.

> **couples therapy** A treatment intervention for sexual dysfunction that involves both partners in the relationship.

Sexual skills and communication training For many couples, sexual dysfunction is simply another manifestation of the couple's inability to communicate effectively with one another. They may be unable to tell each other what stimulates and pleasures them, or they may be nervous, shy or unknowledgeable about sexual matters. Such people can be helped using **sexual skills and communication training**. With the use of educational materials and videos, a therapist can help clients to acquire a more knowledgeable perspective on sexual activity, begin to communicate to each other effectively about sex, and reduce any anxiety about indulging in sexual activity (McMullen & Rosen, 1979).

> **sexual skills and communication training** A treatment method in which a therapist can help clients to acquire a more knowledgeable perspective on sexual activity, communicate to partners effectively about sex, and reduce any anxiety about indulging in sexual activity.

Self-instructional training This is a technique that has been used across a range of psychopathologies in order to establish adaptive behaviour patterns. In the context of sexual dysfunctions, **self-instructional training** is used to teach the client to use positive self-instructions at various points during sexual activity in order to guide their behaviour and to reduce anxiety. In particular, negative statements (such as 'I am never going to maintain an erection') can be replaced with positive statements (such as 'I can allow myself to enjoy sex, even if my performance is not perfect'), and this helps to distract the client from anxiety-provoking ideation.

> **self-instructional training** A procedure used in the intervention for executive functioning deficits where individuals learn a set of instructions for talking themselves through particular problems.

Dealing with remote causes Many cases of sexual dysfunction have their origins in earlier life experiences. These experiences may simply be embarrassing ones, where the individual has been severely embarrassed by their lack of sexual knowledge or prowess during an early sexual encounter. Or they may be more severe and traumatic experiences, such as sexual abuse or assault (see section 11.2.2). Appropriate counselling, where the client is encouraged to recall these experiences and talk about them can help to alleviate the associated sexual problems. This approach acts in a similar way to exposure and imaginal flooding therapies for PTSD (see Chapter 6) by extinguishing the fear that had become associated with these memories.

Summary of psychological interventions for sexual dysfunction There are very few comparative studies of the relative effectiveness of psychological therapies for sexual dysfunction. However, a recent meta-analysis suggests that psychological-based treatments (e.g. sexual skills training, CBT, couples therapy) are effective options for sexual dysfunction – with outcomes being particularly good for female sexual interest/arousal disorder and female orgasmic disorder (Fruhauf, Gerger, Schmidt, Munder & Barth, 2013).

Biological treatments

Many cases of sexual dysfunction may have biological or organic causes such as medical conditions, hormone imbalances, changes in biology with age, or are a reaction to other medications being taken by the client. This indicates that a biological or medical treatment may be appropriate for the disorder. Biological treatments fall into three broad categories: (1) drug treatments, including medications that directly influence the organic nature of the disorder, (2) hormone treatments designed to correct any hormonal imbalances caused by age or illness, and (3) mechanical devices, designed to aid mechanical functioning during sex (such as achieving erection).

Drug treatments Perhaps the most well-known drug treatments for sexual dysfunction are **Viagra (sildenafil citrate)** and **Cialis (tadafil)**, both phosphodiesterase type 5 (PDE-5) inhibitors, which are used primarily to treat erectile dysfunction in men. Viagra acts directly on the tissue of the penis itself. It causes relaxation of the smooth muscle of the penis that increases blood flow and encourages erection. Studies suggest that 75 per cent of men taking Viagra can achieve erection within 60 minutes of administration (Goldstein, Lue, Padma-Nathan, Rosen et al., 1998), and in clinical trials Viagra results in significantly more erections and successful intercourse

> **Viagra (sildenafil citrate)** A drug treatment for sexual dysfunction which is used primarily to treat erectile dysfunction in men.

> **Cialis (tadafil)** A drug treatment, used primarily to treat erectile dysfunction in men.

attempts than a placebo control (Moore, Edwards & McQuay, 2002) (see Figure 11.1). Viagra has also proved to be an effective treatment for male erectile disorder, with over 95 per cent of client's treated with Viagra over a 1–3 year period expressing satisfaction with their erections and their ability to effectively engage in sex (Carson, Burnett, Levine & Nehra, 2002). In addition, Viagra has been considered to be an effective treatment for male erectile disorder in cases where this is due to a medical condition (such as diabetes or cardiovascular disorder) or as a result of ageing (Salonia, Rigatti & Montorsi, 2003). However, Viagra may not be the treatment of choice for many clients because it also has a number of side effects, such as headaches, dizziness and facial flushing, and may interact badly with some medications for cardiovascular disease (Bach, Wincze & Barlow, 2001).

Other drugs that have proved useful in treating sexual dysfunctions include **yohimbine** for erectile dysfunctions, which facilitates norepinephrine excretion in the brain. This appears to have the effect of correcting any brain neurotransmitter problems that are causing the erectile dysfunction (Mann, Klingler, Noe, Roschke *et al.*, 1996). Interestingly, both Viagra and yohimbine have also been shown to be effective in treating female sexual desire problems (Hernandez-Serrano, 2001).

Finally, antidepressant SSRIs such as Prozac are also an effective treatment for early ejaculation, and delayed orgasm is a known side-effect of SSRIs in depressed individuals who are taking these medications (Assalian & Margolese, 1996).

> **yohimbine** A drug treatment for sexual dysfunction which is used primarily to treat erectile dysfunction in men by facilitating norepinephrine excretion in the brain.

Hormone treatments   At least some sexual dysfunctions may result from imbalances in hormone levels, and disorders can result from either high or low levels of oestrogen in women, low levels of testosterone in men, and high levels of prolactin in men. These hormonal imbalances can be caused by medical conditions or ageing. Hormone replacement therapy can be used to treat disorders of sexual desire – especially in older women or women who have undergone hysterectomy – and sexual pain disorders such as genito-pelvic pain/penetration disorder can also be helped with oestrogen treatment, which can improve vaginal lubrication in postmenopausal women (Walling, Andersen & Johnson, 1990).

Mechanical devices   Because an erect penis is such an important contributor to successful sexual penetration, a number of mechanical devices have been developed that can help the male with an erectile dysfunction achieve erection.

The first of these is known as a **penile prosthesis**, and an example of this device is shown in Figure 11.2. Use of these devices is normally reserved for non-reversible organic-based erectile problems. The prosthesis consists of a fluid pump located in the scrotum and a semi-rigid rod that is surgically inserted in the penis. A discrete squeeze of the pump releases fluid into the rod that causes the penis to erect. Studies suggest that the penile prosthesis is a safe and effective means of dealing with erectile dysfunction caused by organic or medical conditions, and 7 years after the implant, the

> **penile prosthesis** A mechanical device normally reserved for non-reversible organic-based erectile problems.

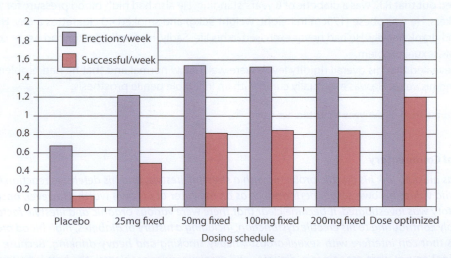

FIGURE 11.1 *Mean number of erections per week (blue) and erections resulting in successful intercourse (red) with placebo and different doses of Viagra (sildenafil citrate).*
Source: Moore, R.A., Edwards, J.E. & McQuay, H.J. (2002). Sildenafil (Viagra) for male erectile dysfunction: A meta-analysis of clinical trial reports. *BMC Urology, 2*(6), Figure 4.

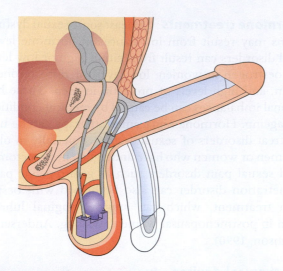

FIGURE 11.2 *The penile prosthesis consists of a fluid pump located in the scrotum and a semi-rigid rod surgically inserted in the penis. Squeezing the pump releases fluid into the rod making the penis erect.*

penile prosthesis was found to be still successfully dealing with erectile dysfunction in 82 per cent of patients (Zermann, Kutzenburger, Sauerwein, Schubert & Loeffler, 2006).

An alternative to the penile prosthesis is a **vacuum erection device** (**VED**). This is a hollow cylinder that is placed over the penis. The client then draws air out the cylinder using a hand pump, and this has the effect of drawing blood into the penis and causing an erection. As cumbersome as this may seem, many clients prefer the VED to other more conventional treatments for erectile dysfunction such as Viagra. Of those given a choice between equally effective VED or Viagra treatments, 33 per cent preferred the VED – largely because they disliked the adverse side-effects of Viagra (Chen, Mabjeesh & Greenstein, 2001).

> **vacuum erection device (VED)** A mechanical device normally reserved for non-reversible organic-based erectile problems.

CASE HISTORY 11.1

ERECTILE DYSFUNCTION

R.K., 47, a senior corporate executive had been happily married for 20 years and had three children, but complained of declining erections. Over the preceding 6 months, his erections had become so weak that he could not penetrate. He stopped trying 3 months ago.

He thought that this was due to his highly stressful lifestyle and pressures at the workplace. He even took a vacation with his wife hoping that this would improve matters. It only made them worse. His wife, at first very co-operative, eventually began to feel rejected and there was a palpable friction in their marriage.

When first seen at the clinic, R.K. was defensive. 'How can this happen to someone like me? I could do it all night, several times a night, night after night. My family doctor says that this kind of thing is quite common these days and it's probably the stress.'

It turned out that R.K. was a diabetic of 8 years' standing. He also had high blood pressure for which he was on beta blockers. He was obese (175cm in height; weight 96kg) and smoked 40 cigarettes a day. He partied 7 days a week and drank heavily. He had never exercised in his life. Sadly, his family doctor had never connected any of these to his sexual problem.

Tests revealed that his overall rigidity levels were well below normal and that he had problems both with his arteries and his veins. He was eventually cured with an inflatable penile prosthesis.

Source: Adapted from http://www.testosterones.com/.

Clinical Commentary

R.K. was quick to link his erectile problems with a stressful lifestyle, and his defensive reaction is typical of a man who values his own sexual performance as an indicator of his own worth. However, once R.K.'s medical history was investigated, it became clear that there were various organic and lifestyle factors that were probably contributing to his erectile dysfunction, including a history of diabetes, high blood pressure, medications that can interfere with sexual arousal, heavy smoking and heavy drinking. Because many of the important causes were organic (e.g. diabetes and cardiovascular problems), the best long-term solution in this case was to implant a mechanical device, such as a penile prosthesis, to aid erection.

Summary of treatments of sexual dysfunction

This section has discussed the range of treatments available for sexual dysfunctions. Multifaceted psychological and behavioural based treatments are now used to deal with the specific symptoms of the disorder as well as any underlying psychological, behavioural and relationship issues. These are supplemented by a variety of drug and biological based treatments that help to address any physiological, organic or hormonal deficits.

SELF-TEST QUESTIONS

- Can you describe the four stages of the normal sexual response cycle?

11.2.1 Diagnosis of Sexual Dysfunctions

- Can you name the disorders of desire and their main diagnostic characteristics?
- What are the main disorders of sexual arousal and how are they defined?
- Roughly what percentage of men report erection problems, and how does this change with age?
- What are the main disorders of orgasm and how are they defined in DSM-5?
- What is the main sexual pain disorder described in DSM-5 and how is it defined?
- What kinds of decisions does a clinician have to make when diagnosing a sexual dysfunction?

11.2.2 The Aetiology of Sexual Dysfunctions

- Can you list some of the risk factors that have been associated with sexual dysfunctions?
- How have repressed emotions and desires been used by psychoanalytic theorists to explain sexual dysfunctions?
- What are the two factors in Masters and Johnson's theory of sexual dysfunction?
- How is performance anxiety important in explaining some forms of sexual dysfunction?
- In what ways might interpersonal difficulties be associated with sexual dysfunctions?
- Is there evidence to suggest that negative emotions such as depression and anxiety are outcomes or causes of sexual dysfunctions?
- What is the difference between remote and immediate causes of sexual dysfunctions? Can you give some examples of both?
- Can you name the three broad categories into which the biological causes of sexual dysfunctions can be classified?
- In what ways does age affect sexual functioning?

11.2.3 The Treatment of Sexual Dysfunctions

- What are direct treatments for sexual dysfunctions?
- Can you name and describe at least three direct treatments for sexual dysfunctions?
- Why is couples therapy an important form of treatment for sexual dysfunction?
- What are the main drug treatments for sexual dysfunctions, and what is the evidence that they are successful?
- What are the main mechanical devices used to treat male sexual dysfunctions?

SECTION SUMMARY

11.2 SEXUAL DYSFUNCTIONS

Sexual dysfunction has an unusual history in the context of psychopathology. In the first half of the twentieth century, sexual problems were rarely admitted and discussed, let alone treated. With the liberating social climate of the 1960s and 1970s this attitude changed, and the pioneering research work of a few dedicated clinicians (such as Masters and Johnson) provided a database of evidence on these kinds of disorders, as well as the first integrated sex therapies for sexual dysfunctions. The causes of sexual dysfunctions range across the biological and organic, psychological factors such as performance anxiety and negative cognitions about sex, to interpersonal problems, and an equally broad range of treatments have been developed to address this array of possible causes. Given all this, it is important to remember that not everyone with less-than-adequate sexual performance is suffering a sexual dysfunction. The DSM-5 criteria clearly state that any performance deficits must be accompanied by distress and interpersonal difficulties, and it is these latter two factors that define sexual dysfunction disorders.

The main points are:

- The four stages of the sexual response cycle are desire, arousal, orgasm and resolution, and sexual dysfunctions can be diagnosed in any of these individual stages.

11.2.1   Diagnosis of Sexual Dysfunction

- Sexual dysfunctions are a heterogeneous group of disorders characterized clinically by the individual's inability to respond sexually or to experience sexual pleasure.

- *Male hypoactive sexual desire disorder* is characterized by a persistent and recurrent deficiency or absence of desire for sexual activity.

- *Erectile disorder* is the inability to maintain an adequate erection during sexual activity. Around 10 per cent of males report erection problems, but this increases to 20 per cent in the over 50s.

- *Female sexual interest/arousal disorder* is characterized by significantly reduced, or absence of, interest in sexual activity, erotic thoughts, and reduced sexual sensations during sexual activity.

- *Female orgasmic disorder* is characterized by a delay or absence of orgasm during sexual activity, and around 10 per cent of adult women may never have experienced an orgasm.

- *Delayed ejaculation* is a persistent or recurrent delay in ejaculation following a normal sexual excitement phase.

- *Early ejaculation* is the onset of orgasm with minimal sexual stimulation. Treatment for this disorder is typically sought by men under the age of 30 years.

- *Genito-pelvic pain/penetration disorder* refers to four commonly occurring symptoms, namely difficulty having intercourse, genito-pelvic pain, fear of pain or vaginal penetration, and tension of the pelvic floor muscles.

11.2.2   The Aetiology of Sexual Dysfunctions

- Sexual dysfunction is more prevalent in women than in men (43 per cent and 31 per cent respectively), and is more likely amongst those experiencing poor physical and emotional health.

- Psychoanalytic theory attempts to account for sexual dysfunctions in terms of repressed sexual desires or hostility to the opposite sex.

- Masters and Johnson developed a two-factor model of sexual dysfunction where (1) early sexual experiences give rise to anxiety during sex, and (2) this anxiety leads the individual to adopt a *spectator role* during sexual activity, which directs attention away from stimuli providing sexual arousal.

- Interpersonal difficulties may be both a cause and an outcome of sexual dysfunctions.

- Anxiety and depression are closely associated with sexual dysfunctions, and these negative emotions may interfere with sexual performance.

- The causes of sexual dysfunctions can sometimes be defined in terms of *immediate causes* (e.g. lack of sexual knowledge) and *remote causes* (e.g. feelings of shame and guilt that are a result of a specific upbringing).

- Biological causes of sexual dysfunctions can be classified as (1) dysfunctions caused by an underlying medical disorder, (2) dysfunction caused by hormonal abnormalities, and (3) changes in sexual responsiveness with age.

11.2.3   The Treatment of Sexual Dysfunctions

- *Direct treatments* attempt to deal with the specific symptoms of the disorder (e.g. the squeeze technique for premature ejaculation).

- The *stop–start technique*, *squeeze technique* and the *tease technique* are all specific behavioural treatments designed to treat premature ejaculation and orgasmic disorders.

- If sexual dysfunctions are a manifestation of broader problems then *couples therapy* can be adopted.

- Biological treatments can be categorized into (1) drug treatments, including medications that directly influence the organic nature of the disorder, (2) hormone treatment designed to correct hormone imbalances caused by age or sickness, and (3) mechanical devices, designed to aid mechanical functioning during sex.

- Of the men who take *Viagra*, 75 per cent can achieve erection within 60 minutes of administration, and over 95 per cent of clients treated with Viagra over a 1–3 year period express satisfaction with their ability to effectively engage in sex.

- Mechanical devices to aid penile erection and penetration include the *penile prosthesis* and the *vacuum erection device (VED)*.

11.3 PARAPHILIC DISORDERS

Sexual dysfunctions are one side of the sexual disorders coin, where individuals complain of deficiencies or inadequacies in their sexual desire and performance. On the other side of the coin are those psychopathologies that are associated with high frequencies of sexual activity or unusual sexual activities that are often directed at inappropriate targets. Sexual experience is normally highly valued in Western cultures, but there is now a good deal of evidence that high rates of sexual behaviour can be problematic, interfere with personal happiness and social adjustment, and be channelled into unusual sexual activities (Kafka, 1997, 2003). When high rates of sexual behaviour are channelled into unusual or very specific sexual activities, these are known collectively as **paraphilic disorders**. In DSM-5, the term paraphilia denotes 'any intense and persistent sexual interest other than sexual interest in genital stimulation or preparatory fondling with phenotypically normal psychically mature, consenting human partners' (DSM-5, p.685). Some paraphilias concern the individual's own erotic activities while others primarily concern the individual's erotic targets, and a paraphilic disorder is one that currently causes distress or impairment to the individual or whose satisfaction has entailed personal harm, or risk of harm, to others. A list of the paraphilias included in DSM-5 is provided in Table 11.2.

paraphilic disorders Represent sexual urges or fantasies involving unusual sources of gratification (e.g. non-human objects or non-consenting individuals).

These paraphilias have been listed in three groups. The first group includes fetishistic disorder and transvestic disorder, where the individual experiences sexual desire towards inanimate objects or derives sexual gratification from cross-dressing. However, to be diagnosed with either of these disorders, these tendencies must cause the individual significant distress or social and/or occupational impairment.

The second group consists of exhibitionistic disorder, voyeuristic disorder, frotteuristic disorder and paedophilic disorder. These disorders have been grouped together because they usually involve sexual fantasies, urges and activities directed at non-consenting persons. The exhibitionist will expose himself to unsuspecting victims; the voyeur will take sexual pleasure from watching unsuspecting others either naked or in the process of undressing; the frotteurist is sexually aroused by rubbing themselves against a non-consenting person; and the paedophile has sexual urges towards and indulges in sexual acts with prepubescent children, who – by their very age – are unable to legally consent to these activities. This second group of paraphilic disorders is defined by the fact that the individual does *not* have to experience distress or social or occupational impairment to be diagnosed with these disorders, but merely has to have acted on these urges with non-consenting persons (Hilliard & Spitzer, 2002).

The final group consists of sexual masochism disorder and sexual sadism disorder, where individuals experience sexual arousal from either (1) the desire to be humiliated or made to physically suffer (masochism) or (2) inflict physical suffering on others (sadism). Most often sado-masochistic acts are performed with a consenting

TABLE 11.2 *Paraphilic disorders*

Fetishistic disorder	Sexual urges that are not directed at another person	Recurrent sexual arousal involving non-animate objects
Transvestic disorder		Recurrent, intense sexual arousal from cross-dressing
Exhibitionistic disorder		Sexual arousal from the exposure of one's genitals to an unsuspecting person
Voyeuristic disorder	Sexual urges directed at non-consenting other persons (in many societies these activities represent sexual offences)	Recurrent sexually arousing fantasies involving acts of observing an unsuspecting person who is naked or in the act of undressed
Frotteuristic disorder		Recurrent sexual arousing from touching or rubbing against a non-consenting person
Paedophilic disorder		Recurrent, intense sexually arousing fantasies or urges involving sexual activity with a prepubescent child
Sexual masochism disorder	Sexual arousal from inflicting or experiencing suffering	Sexual arousal from being humiliated or otherwise forced to suffer
Sexual sadism disorder		Sexual arousal from the psychological or physical suffering of others

partner, but even in such circumstances, the individual may be bothered or distressed by these tendencies and acts, and personal distress is an important contributor to diagnosis of these disorders.

From these categorisations it is clear that some paraphilic disorders are *victimless* (e.g. fetishistic disorder and transvestic disorder), while others will be defined in law as *sexual offences* (e.g. exhibitionistic disorder, voyeuristic disorder, frotteuristic disorder, paedophilic disorder, and those acts of sexual sadism where harm is inflicted on others without consent). Some require these activities to cause personal distress to be diagnosed, while others do not. This leads to an issue of where the line is drawn between acceptable sexual activity and a psychopathology. Clearly, many of the urges and fantasies defined in the diagnostic criteria for paraphilias are experienced by many people, and there is a growing industry willing to cater for these urges in films, magazines and internet sites. However, (1) most people are unwilling to act on their fantasies, and are quite happy to restrict their sexual interest in paraphilic activities to viewing erotic or pornographic material, and (2) it is only when a person's sexual urges become linked to just one specific type of stimulus or act that society begins to deem that behaviour as 'abnormal'. We must bear these issues in mind when discussing the individual paraphilias.

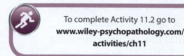

To complete Activity 11.2 go to www.wiley-psychopathology.com/activities/ch11

The following section describes the diagnostic criteria and main characteristics of each of the paraphilic disorders. We will then progress to discuss some of the theories of the aetiology of paraphilic disorders, and finally describe and evaluate forms of treatment.

11.3.1 The Diagnosis and Description of Paraphilic Disorders

Fetishistic disorder

A diagnosis of **fetishistic disorder** is given when a person experiences recurrent, intense sexually arousing fantasies and urges involving non-animate objects, and this causes them personal distress or affects social and occupational functioning (DSM-5 Summary Table 11.8). Often fetishes are restricted to articles associated with sex, such as women's clothing or undergarments (bras, stockings, shoes, boots, and so on) or to body parts such as feet, toes, or hair. The individual with fetishistic disorder may experience strong desires to obtain or touch these items (e.g. by stealing them from washing lines), may ask a sexual partner to wear them during sex, or may masturbate while holding,

fetishistic disorder Recurrent, intense sexually arousing fantasies and urges involving non-animate objects, and this causes them personal distress or affects social and occupational functioning.

DSM-5 SUMMARY TABLE 11.8 *Criteria for fetishistic disorder*

- Over a period of 6 months, recurring and strong sexual arousal from the use of non-living objects or a highly specific focus on non-genital body parts as part of fantasies, urges or behaviours, causing significant distress or impairment in social, occupational or other areas of life

- The fetish is not limited to the clothing used in cross-dressing or objects such as vibrators and other genital simulators

rubbing or smelling these articles. A fetish will usually have developed by adolescence, and may have developed as a result of specific experiences during childhood or early adolescence. Some individuals exhibit a phenomenon known as **partialism**, which is fascination with an individual object or body part to the point where normal sexual activity no longer occurs. Note that fetishistic disorder is not diagnosed if the object concerned is for the purpose of tactile genital stimulation (such as a vibrator). However, Focus Point 11.2 provides some case reports of penile injuries from the *British Medical Journal* and illustrates the lengths that some individuals will go to gain sexual excitement. While the injuries incurred were obviously not amusing for the victims, the reader may be amused by the reasons given for these injuries!

partialism A phenomenon in which there is a fascination with an individual object to the point where normal sexual activity no longer occurs.

Transvestic disorder

A diagnosis of transvestic disorder is given when a heterosexual male experiences recurrent, intense sexual arousal from cross-dressing in women's attire, and this causes significant distress or impairment in social or occupational functioning (DSM-5 Summary Table 11.9). A Swedish study has indicated that 2.8 per cent of men and 0.4 per cent of women report at least one episode of transvestic behaviour during their life, and risk factors for this disorder include same-sex sexual experiences, being easily sexually aroused, pornography use and relatively high masturbation frequency (Langstrom & Zucker, 2005). In this particular disorder, sexual excitement is achieved primarily because female clothes are a symbol of the individual's femininity rather than because the garments trigger sexual arousal per se (as would be the case with a simple fetish). In addition, this diagnosis should not be given if the individual has a diagnosis of gender dysphoria (see section 11.4). The person with **transvestic disorder** will often keep a collection of women's clothes, and sexual arousal is normally caused by the

transvestic disorder When a heterosexual male experiences recurrent, intense sexual arousal from cross-dressing in women's attire, and this causes significant distress or impairment in social or occupational functioning.

PENILE INJURIES RESULTING FROM A VACUUM CLEANER

The following are four cases of penile injury incurred when using a vacuum cleaner in search of sexual excitement. At least two of these injuries were caused by a 'Hoover Dustette' which has fan blades only 15cm from the inlet.

CASE 1

A 60-year-old man said that he was changing the plug of his Hoover Dustette vacuum cleaner in the nude when his wife was out shopping. It 'turned itself on' and caught his penis, causing tears around the external meatus and deeply lacerating the side of the glans.

CASE 2

A 65-year-old railway signalman was in his signal box when he bent down to pick up his tools and 'caught his penis in a Hoover Dustette which happened to be switched on'. He suffered extensive lacerations to the glans, which were repaired with cat gut with a good result.

CASE 3

A 49-year-old man was vacuuming his friend's staircase in a loose-fitting dressing gown when, intending to switch the machine off, he leaned across to reach the plug: 'At that moment his dressing gown became undone and his penis was sucked into the vacuum cleaner.' He suffered multiple lacerations to the foreskin as well as lacerations to the distal part of the shaft of the penis.

CASE 4

This patient was aged 68, and no history is available except that the injury was caused by a vacuum cleaner. The injury extended through the corpora cavernosa and the corpus spongiosum and caused complete division of the urethra proximal to the corona.

Source: Reproduced from Citron, N.D & Wade, P.J. (1980). Penile injuries from vacuum cleaners. *British Medical Journal*, 281(6232), 26. With permission from BMJ Publishing Group Ltd.

DSM-5 SUMMARY TABLE 11.9 *Criteria for transvestic disorder*

- Continuing and powerful sexual arousal from cross-dressing as part of fantasies, urges or behaviours, over a period of at least 6 months, causing significant distress or impairment in social, occupational or other areas of life.

man having thoughts or images of himself as a female. *Chris's story* at the beginning of this chapter is a typical example of transvestic behaviour. Like *Chris*, most individuals diagnosed with transvestic disorder are relatively happily married men, but are worried what others (including their wives) may think of their behaviour. As a result, over half of those who admit to cross-dressing usually seek counselling at some stage because of its effects on their intimate relationships (Doctor & Prince, 1997). Most men with transvestic disorder have been cross-dressing for many years, usually since childhood or early adolescence (Doctor & Fleming, 2001), and many women are happy to tolerate their husbands' cross-dressing or even incorporate it into their own sexual activities.

Exhibitionistic disorder

This paraphilic disorder involves sexual fantasies about exposing the genitals to a stranger (DSM-5 Summary

DSM-5 SUMMARY TABLE 11.10 *Criteria for exhibitionistic disorder*

- Continuing and powerful sexual arousal from exposing one's genitals to an unsuspecting audience, over a period of at least 6 months, as part of fantasies, urges or behaviours

- The patient has acted on these urges with a non-consenting person or the urges cause significant distress or impairment in social, occupational or other areas of life

Table 11.10). These fantasies are usually strong and recurrent to the point where the individual feels a compulsion to expose himself or herself, and this compulsion often makes the individual oblivious of the social and legal consequences of what they are doing (Stevenson & Jones, 1972). The onset of **exhibitionistic disorder** usually occurs before 18 years of age, and is often found in individuals who are immature in their relationships with the opposite sex, and many have problems with interpersonal relationships generally (Mohr, Turner & Jerry, 1964). The sufferer's urge to expose himself/herself will often lead them to find a victim in a public place,

> **exhibitionistic disorder** Involves sexual fantasies about exposing the penis to a stranger.

often a park or a side street, where they expose themselves – usually to a single victim. The victim's response of shock, fear or revulsion often forms part of the gratification that reinforces this behaviour, and the exhibitionist may sometimes masturbate while exposing himself/herself (especially if he finds the victim's reaction to his behaviour sexually arousing) or may return home to masturbate while fantasising about the encounter. Exhibitionists will usually expose themselves to women or children, and while no physical harm is usually involved, the experience for the victim is often traumatic and may have lasting psychological consequences. A significant percentage of individuals with a diagnosis of exhibitionistic disorder are non-disclosing, deny any urges or fantasies related to exposing themselves, and report that incidents of exposure were either accidental or non-sexual. Men are significantly more likely to be diagnosed with exhibitionistic disorder than women, and the prevalence rate of exhibitionist acts in men is estimated to be between 2 and 4 per cent (DSM-5, p.690).

Voyeuristic disorder

A diagnosis of **voyeuristic disorder** is given when an individual experiences recurrent, intense sexually arousing fantasies or urges involving the act of observing an unsuspecting person who is naked, in the process of undressing, or engaging in a sexual activity (DSM-5 Summary Table 11.11). Sexual arousal normally comes from the act of looking ('peeping') and the individual may masturbate while in the act of observing others. However, the individual rarely seeks sexual activity with those being observed. Voyeurism usually begins in early adolescence and may often constitute that individual's sole sexual activity in adulthood (Kaplan & Krueger, 1997). The risk of being discovered while indulging in voyeuristic behaviours may also add to the excitement that this behaviour engenders. However, we must be clear that voyeurism can be a perfectly acceptable sexual activity when practised between consenting individuals, but is clearly problematic when the voyeur begins seeking non-consenting victims and violates their privacy. Voyeuristic acts are the most common of the potentially illegal paraphilic behaviours, with estimates of the possible lifetime prevalence of voyeuristic acts being as high as 12 per cent in males and 4 per cent in females (DSM-5, p.688).

> **voyeuristic disorder** When an individual experiences recurrent, intense sexually arousing fantasies or urges involving the act of observing an unsuspecting person who is naked, in the process of undressing, or engaging in a sexual activity.

Frotteuristic disorder

This involves intense, recurrent sexual urges to touch and rub up against non-consenting people – usually in crowded places such as underground trains, buses or supermarket queues (DSM-5 Summary Table 11.12).

DSM-5 SUMMARY TABLE 11.11 *Criteria for voyeuristic disorder*

- Continuing and powerful sexual arousal from the observance of an unsuspecting person who is naked, undressing or engaging in sexual activity, over a period of at least 6 months, as part of fantasies, urges or behaviours

- The patient has acted on these urges with a non-consenting person or the urges cause significant distress or impairment in social, occupational or other areas of life

- The individual experiencing the arousal is at least 18 years of age

---

DSM-5 SUMMARY TABLE 11.12 *Criteria for frotteuristic disorder*

- Continuing and powerful sexual arousal from touching or rubbing against a non-consenting person, over a period of at least 6 months, as part of fantasies, urges or behaviours

- The patient has acted on these urges with a non-consenting person or the urges cause significant distress or impairment in social, occupational or other areas of life

---

This is usually a male activity, and manifests as a sexual urge to rub the genitalia against the victim's thighs and buttocks or to fondle the victim's genitalia or breasts with his hands. This behaviour is usually undertaken in a surreptitious way in order to try to make it appear unintentional or as if someone else in the crowded environment is the culprit. Like exhibitionism and voyeurism, this activity usually begins in adolescence, but may subside in frequency by the time the individual is in their late 20s. Frotteurism is considered by many to be a form of sexual assault, and at least part of the excitement for frotteurs is the feeling of power it gives them over their victim – a feeling that is relatively common in those who indulge in sexual assault generally. Around 10–14 per cent of adult males seen in outpatient settings for paraphilic disorders meet the criteria for **frotteuristic disorder** (DSM-5, p.693).

> **frotteuristic disorder** Intense, recurrent sexual urges to touch and rub up against non-consenting people.

Paedophilic disorder

Paedophilic disorder is defined as sexual attraction towards prepubescent children, normally 13 years old or younger. To be diagnosed with **paedophilic disorder**, the individual must be at least 16 years of age and at least 5 years older than the victim. Recent studies suggest that up to 9 per cent of men have described having at least one sexual fantasy involving a child, and so such fantasies are not that uncommon in the general population (Seto, 2009). However, DSM-5 does highlight the fact that paedophilic disorder is only diagnosed if the individual acts on these fantasies or is distressed by them.

> **paedophilic disorder** Sexual attraction towards prepubescent children, normally of 13 years or younger.

The extensive use of pornography depicting children is usually an indicator of paedophilic disorder, and the condition often becomes apparent as a sexual interest in children around puberty. Those who report paedophilic sexual urges, usually report a preference for males or females, or sometimes for both. Those attracted to females usually prefer 8–10 year olds, whereas those attracted to males usually prefer older children (DSM-IV-TR, p.571). Paedophilia generally, appears to be a life-long condition, in which many with a sexual interest in children will often deny attraction to children despite multiple sexual approaches to them. Paedophilic disorder, however, is defined by other elements that may change over time, such as guilt, shame, or feelings of isolation. The highest likely prevalence for paedophilic disorder in males is around 3–5 per cent (DSM-5, p.698).

The central feature of the psychopathology is sexual attraction to children, but this is *not* equivalent to 'child sexual abuse', 'incest' or 'child molestation' because the latter represent criminal acts. It is important to make this distinction because not all who sexually abuse children are diagnosable with paedophilic disorder – for example, many who sexually abuse children may opportunistically select children simply because they are available; such people do not necessarily have specific fantasies about having sex with children (Fagan, Wise, Schmidt & Berlin, 2002). Girls are three times more likely than boys to be sexually abused, and children from low-income families are 18 times more likely to be sexually abused (Sedlak & Broadhurst, 1996). The paedophile's sexual activity with children is usually limited to acts such as undressing the child, exposing themselves, masturbating in the presence of the child, or gently touching or fondling the child and their genitalia. However, in more severe cases, this activity can extend to performing oral sex acts with the child, or penetrating the child's vagina, mouth or anus with fingers, foreign objects or their penis. In general, paedophiles rarely believe that what they are doing is wrong and avidly deny their sexual attraction to children. They will also often use egocentric forms of rationalisation to justify their acts (e.g. the acts had 'educational value' or that the child was consenting or gained pleasure from the activity). Because of this, they often fail to experience distress or remorse, and so experiencing distress or psychological impairment is not a necessary part of the diagnostic criteria for paedophilic disorder (DSM-5 Summary Table 11.13).

There are numerous unofficial subtypes of paedophilia. First, some paedophiles limit their activities to their immediate family (e.g. children, step-children, nieces and nephews) and *incest* is listed as a specifying factor in DSM-5. Men who indulge in incest tend to differ from other paedophiles (1) by indulging in sexual activity with children of a slightly older age (e.g. an incestuous father

DSM-5 SUMMARY TABLE 11.13 *Criteria for paedophilic disorder*

- Continuing and powerful sexual arousal from fantasies, urges or behaviours involving sexual activity with a prepubescent child or children (aged 13 years or younger)
- The patient has acted on these urges or the urges cause significant distress or impairment in social, occupational or other areas of life
- The patient is at least 16 years old and at least 5 years older than the child or children involved
- Does not include an individual in late adolescence in an ongoing sexual relationship with a 12- or 13-year-old

may show sexual interest in a daughter only when the daughter begins to become sexually mature), and (2) by having a relatively normal heterosexual sex life outside of the incestuous relationship. In contrast, non-incestuous paedophiles will normally only become sexually aroused by sexually immature children and are sometimes known as **preference molesters** (Marshall, Barbaree & Christophe, 1986). Second, most paedophiles rarely intend to physically harm their victims (even though they may threaten their victims in order to prevent disclosure), but some may only get full sexual gratification from harming and even murdering their victims. This latter group are probably best described as **child rapists**, and appear to be fundamentally psychologically different to other paedophiles and often have comorbid diagnoses of personality disorder or sexual sadism (Groth, Hobson & Guy, 1982).

preference molesters Non-incestuous paedophiles who normally only become sexually aroused by sexually immature children.

child rapists A group of paedophiles who only get full sexual gratification from harming and even murdering their victims.

Because their behaviour is illegal and socially outlawed, and because they need to gain the trust of their child victims in order to indulge in their sexual activities, most individuals diagnosable with paedophilic disorder develop elaborate ways of gaining access to children. This can involve taking jobs in environments where children are frequently found (e.g. schools, residential children's homes, and suchlike), gaining the confidence of the parents or family of a child, or more recently by 'grooming' children in internet chat-rooms by pretending to be someone of a similar age to the victim. Focus Point 11.3 provides an example of how paedophiles may 'groom' and 'lure' children for sexual purposes on the internet. In a qualitative study of the modus operandi of male paedophiles, Conte, Wolf & Smith (1989) were able to describe a standard process through which many paedophiles operated to attract and isolate their victims and desensitize them to their sexual advances. This process included: (1) choosing an open, vulnerable child who would be easily persuaded

FOCUS POINT 11.3

PAEDOPHILE 'GROOMING' OVER THE INTERNET: HOW DO ONLINE PREDATORS WORK?

Predators establish contact with kids through conversations in chat-rooms, instant messaging, e-mail or discussion boards. Many teens use 'peer support' online forums to deal with their problems. Predators, however, often go to these online areas to look for vulnerable victims.

Online predators try to gradually seduce their targets through attention, affection, kindness, and even gifts, and often devote considerable time, money and energy to this effort. They are aware of the latest music and hobbies likely to interest kids. They listen to and sympathize with kids' problems. They also try to ease young people's inhibitions by gradually introducing sexual content into their conversations or by showing them sexually explicit material. Older

predatory paedophiles don't usually pose as teenagers, but do look for signs of a kid who is attention starved or whose parents don't seem to care much about them. He will then begin to discover where they might live by asking questions about their school or their locality.

Some predators work faster than others, engaging in sexually explicit conversations immediately. This more direct approach may include harassment or stalking. Predators may also evaluate the kids they meet online for future face-to-face contact.

Source: Adapted from http://www.bewebaware.ca/ and http://www.child-safety-for-parents.com/internet-pedophiles.html#.Ulfh2xYQi04.

and would remain silent after the abuse, (2) using non-sexual enticements such as purchases or flattery on early encounters with the child, (3) introducing sexual topics into the conversation, and (4) progressing from non-sexual touching to sexual touching as a means of desensitising the child to the purpose of the touching. After the abuse, the paedophile would use his adult authority to isolate the child and their 'shared behaviour' from family and peers.

Finally, it is important to remember that by their very age, the victims of paedophilia are non-consenting victims, and that sexual activity with prepubescent children is illegal in most societies. In a general population study in the US, 12 per cent of men and 17 per cent of women reported being touched sexually by an older person when they were children (Laumann, Gagnon, Michael & Michael, 1994). Furthermore, it is also important to note that the victims of paedophilia can suffer long-term psychological problems as a result of their experiences, and these can manifest as eating disorders, sleep disorders, depression, anxiety disorders such as panic attacks and phobias, self-harm, and dissociative disorders, all persevering well into adulthood. These psychological problems are more intense and more enduring if the abuse occurred at an early age and the victim knew their abuser well (Kendall-Tuckett, Williams & Finkelhor, 1993).

Sexual masochism disorder and sexual sadism disorder

sexual masochism disorder When an individual gains sexual arousal and satisfaction from being humiliated, and this causes the individual significant distress.

A diagnosis of **sexual masochism disorder** is given if the individual gains sexual arousal and satisfaction

DSM-5 SUMMARY TABLE 11.14 *Criteria for sexual masochism disorder*

- Continuing and powerful sexual arousal from the act of being humiliated, tied up, beaten or made to suffer, over a period of at least 6 months, as part of fantasies, urges or behaviours
- The urges cause significant distress or impairment in social, occupational or other areas of life

from being humiliated, beaten, bound or otherwise made to suffer, and these urges cause significant distress or social and occupational impairment (DSM-5 Summary Table 11.14). In contrast, **sexual sadism disorder** is when the person gains sexual arousal and satisfaction from the psychological or physical suffering of others. A diagnosis of sexual sadism disorder is given if these symptoms cause distress or significant social or occupational impairment to the individual, or if the individual acts on these urges with a non-consenting person (DSM-5 Summary Table 11.15). Sadomasochistic acts are often performed between consenting mutual partners, one who gains satisfaction from sadistic acts and the other who enjoys being humiliated. Sadistic or masochistic activities include acts that emphasize the dominance and control of one person over the other. These may include restraint, blindfolding, spanking, whipping, pinching, beating, burning, rape, cutting, stabbing, strangulation, torture and mutilation. Acts of dominance (or submission) may include forcing the

sexual sadism disorder When a person gains sexual arousal and satisfaction from the psychological or physical suffering of others, and this diagnosis is given if the symptoms cause the individual significant distress or if the person acts on the impulses with a non-consenting person.

DSM-5 SUMMARY TABLE 11.15 *Criteria for sexual sadism disorder*

- Continuing and powerful sexual arousal from the physical or psychological suffering of another person, over a period of at least 6 months, as part of fantasies, urges or behaviours
- The patient has acted on these urges with a non-consenting person or the urges cause significant distress or impairment in social, occupational or other areas of life

submissive partner to crawl on the floor, or keeping them restrained in a cage. Sexual masochists can often cause their own suffering, and one prominent example is known as **hypoxyphilia**, which involves the individual using a noose or plastic bag to induce oxygen deprivation during masturbation. In contrast, when they are unable to obtain consenting partners, sexual sadists may resort to rape, mutilation and murder to satisfy their sexual desires (Dietz, Hazelwood & Warren, 1990), and there is a high rate of comorbidity between sexual sadism disorder and impulse disorders. For example, in individuals with a diagnosis of sexual sadism disorder, 31 per cent were also diagnosed with borderline personality disorder, and 42 per cent with antisocial personality disorder (Berger, Berner, Bolterauer, Gutierrez & Berger, 1999). It is estimated that around 5–10 per cent of the population indulge in some kind of sado-masochistic activity at some time in their life (Baumeister & Butler, 1997), and most are heterosexual, reasonably affluent, well-educated, indulge in these activities with a consenting partner, and are not unnecessarily distressed or disturbed by their sexual predilections (Moser & Levitt, 1987). If this is so, then most sado-masochistic activity does not involve either psychological distress or imposition of a sexual urge on non-consenting persons, and so would not meet the DSM-5 criteria for a disorder. Because sado-masochism is enjoyed by many individuals who incorporate these activities into their normal sexual relationships, there is a growing market for such activities catered for by sex shops, underground newspapers and websites. Indeed, over the years, sado-masochism (known as S&M) has become a significantly accepted subculture within homosexual circles.

> **hypoxyphilia** An act performed by sexual masochists which involves the individual using a noose or plastic bag to induce oxygen deprivation during masturbation.

11.3.2   The Aetiology of Paraphilic Disorders

To date there is relatively little research on the causes of paraphilia disorders, and what research is available has mainly been confined to the study of those paraphilic disorders that involve sexual offending (e.g. paedophilia, exhibitionism). Traditionally, psychodynamic explanations had been popular but these have now tended to be superseded by cognitive and, to a lesser degree, biological explanations. We begin this section by looking at some of the risk factors associated with the development of paraphilic disorders to give you an indication of some of the experiential and psychological factors associated with paraphilias.

Risk factors for paraphilic disorders

It may not have escaped the reader that most of the DSM-5 diagnosable paraphilias are mainly male activities, so being male is in itself a risk factor for paraphilic disorders. For example, surveys have suggested that 89 per cent of acts of child sexual abuse are perpetrated by men, and only 11 per cent by women (Sedlak & Broadhurst, 1996), and male masochists outnumber females by 20:1. It is by no means clear why paraphilias should be such a male preserve, but this may in part be due to female sexuality being repressed more than male sexually – especially during socialisation. There is some evidence of a link between high rates of sexual activity generally, and anxiety and depression, and paraphilias (Kafka, 1997: Raymond, Coleman & Miner, 2003). High rates of highly sexual activity is known as **hypersexuality**, and it was itself considered for inclusion as a disorder in DSM-5, although it was omitted from the final published version (Walters, Knight & Langstrom, 2011). One implication of the link between hypersexuality and paraphilias is that high rates of sexual activity may lead individuals to evolve specific sexual inclinations and urges that are characteristic of paraphilia. Hypersexuality is found more often in men who are young, have experienced separation from parents during childhood, live in major urban areas, have had sexual experiences at an early age, frequently experience same-sex sexual behaviour, pay for sex, and are relatively more dissatisfied with sexual life than non-hypersexual men (Langstrom & Hanson, 2006). The study by Langstrom & Hanson also identified a strong association between hypersexuality and exhibitionism, voyeurism and sexual masochism and sexual sadism. Hypersexual men were also characterized by their willingness to indulge in a range of risky behaviours, including tobacco smoking, heavy drinking, using illegal drugs, and gambling. These initial studies do suggest some kind of important link between hypersexuality and paraphilia, and further research in this area may help to clarify the risk factors and causes of individual paraphilias. Given that we now know some of the factors that predict hypersexuality, then these might also play a significant role in predicting the development of paraphilias.

> **hypersexuality** The occurrence of high rates of sexual activity.

Numerus studies have also identified some of the risk factors involved in paedophilia. These can be categorized as either remote factors (i.e. factors from the individual's developmental history) or precipitant factors (i.e. factors that lead directly to the expression of paedophile behaviour). Remote risk factors for paedophilia include being a victim of childhood sexual abuse (Cohen, Forman, Steinfeld, Fradkin et al., 2010) or possessing an inadequate attachment style that results from being brought up in a dysfunctional family (Hanson & Slater, 1988). Precipitating risk factors include depression, psychosocial stress (for example, as a result of losing a relationship or a job), and alcohol abuse (Fagan, Wise, Schmidt & Berlin, 2002). Psychiatric comorbidity is also highly associated with paedophilic disorder, with 93 per cent of paedophiles being diagnosed with at least one other psychopathology during their lifetime, such as major depression or anxiety disorders. In addition, 60 per cent of paedophiles are diagnosed with a substance abuse disorder, and 60 per cent meet the diagnostic criteria for a personality disorder (Raymond, Coleman, Ohlerking, Christensen & Miner, 1999). The statistics support the view that psychopathology may be a precipitating factor in triggering paedophile behaviour.

The psychodynamic perspective

Psychodynamic theorists take a range of views about the causes of paraphilias. They can be viewed either as (1) defensive reactions that are attempting to defend the ego from repressed fears, or (2) as representing fixation at a pregenital stage of development (usually the Oedipal stage). For example, fetishism and paedophilia can be viewed as the behaviour of individuals who find normal heterosexual sex with women too threatening – perhaps because of a **castration anxiety** – and voyeurism is a behaviour that protects the individual from having to deal with the relationships that are often an inherent part of sexual life.

In this respect, psychodynamic approaches view those with paraphilias as individuals whose sexual development is immature or who are unable to deal with the complexity of relationships that usually surround normal heterosexual behaviour. (Lanyon, 1986). Alternatively, paraphilias may be associated with a fixation at the Oedipal stage of development, which is itself associated with castration anxiety. For example, transvestic fetishism is seen as a denial of the mother's castration. Dressing in a woman's clothes but still having a penis underneath the clothing is seen as reassuring the transvestite that his mother has not been castrated and he should not therefore worry about himself being castrated (Nielson, 1960). Castration anxiety again crops up in psychodynamic interpretations of other paraphilias such as sexual sadism, where the sadist is seen as feeling relief from castration anxiety by taking on the role of castrator rather than the castrated.

> **castration anxiety** A psychoanalytic term referring to a psychological complex in males with a fear of being castrated.

Because of the way in which psychodynamic theory is couched, it is difficult to find objective evidence to support these explanations of paraphilias. If such factors do underlie paraphilia behaviour, then exploring them in psychoanalysis should help to alleviate these diverse sexual activities. However, there is only modest evidence that psychoanalysis is successful in the treatment of paraphilias (Cohen & Seghorn, 1969), and it is usually entirely ineffective in treating sexual offenders (Knopp, 1976).

Classical conditioning

One very simple explanation for paraphilic disorders is that unusual sexual urges are the result of early sexual experiences (such as masturbation) being associated with an unusual stimulus or behaviour through associative learning (classical conditioning). For example, an adolescent boy's first sexual experiences may be masturbating to pictures of women dressed in fur or leather (resulting in a fur or leather fetish), or masturbating after accidentally seeing a neighbour undressing (resulting in voyeurism). Such early experiences may determine the route an adolescent's sexual development will take, and this conditioning account is consistent with the fact that many of the paraphilias first manifest in early adolescence. Support for the classical conditioning account also comes from an early experiment that attempted to develop a fetish for women's knee-length leather boots in a group of male volunteers. Rachman (1966) showed participants slides of a pair of black, knee-length woman's leather boots (the conditioned stimulus, CS) followed immediately by a slide of an attractive female nude (the unconditioned stimulus, UCS). After a number of pairings of the CS with the UCS, participants showed an increase in penis volume (as measured by a phallo-plethysmograph) whenever the CS slide was shown. One participant even generalized this sexual response to pictures of other forms of female footwear! Nevertheless, while the conditioning of a sexual fetish can be experimentally demonstrated under controlled conditions, it is unlikely that conditioning is the cause of all paraphilias. It may account for the initial development of some fetishes, and may also account for why sexual urges initially become associated with specific activities such as voyeurism and frotteurism. However, as normal sexual activities become experienced during adolescence and early adulthood, conditioning theory would predict sexual urges to become associated with these normal sexual activities and links between sexual urges and early, learnt paraphilia behaviour should extinguish. Nevertheless, paraphilias frequently persist – even when the sufferer finds them distressing and even when they are also concurrently indulging in normal sexual behaviour.

Childhood abuse and neglect

As we have seen many times in this book, childhood abuse and neglect is an important predictor of psychological problems later in life, and this is no less true for the development of paraphilic disorders. However, the way in which negative early experiences may facilitate the development of paraphilic disorders is probably complex. First, physical and sexual abuse is a feature of the history of many individuals with paraphilias, as is a history of disturbed and neglectful parenting (Mason, 1997; Murphy, 1997). However, childhood abuse and neglect is not a prerequisite for developing a paraphilic disorder or becoming a sexual offender, and less than 30 per cent of sexual offenders have a history of childhood sexual abuse (Maletzky, 1993). Nevertheless, the level of childhood abuse experienced by sexual offenders is almost double the level found in the general population (Laumann, Gagnon, Michael & Michael, 1994), so childhood abuse may presumably contribute to paraphilia in some as yet unspecified way. Problematic parent–child relationships may also play a significant role in the development of specific paraphilic disorders. For example, neglectful or abusive parenting can leave the child with low self-esteem, poor social skills, a lack of effective coping strategies, and an inability to form lasting relationships (Marshall & Serran, 2000). These psychological and behavioural deficits may lead the individual to find sexual satisfaction in ways that do not require them to deal with the consensual relationships required by normal sexual activity (e.g. transvestism, voyeurism, exhibitionism, frotteurism), or may lead them to seek sexual satisfaction with others, such as children, with whom their underdeveloped social and emotional skills do not put them at a disadvantage.

In conclusion, childhood abuse and neglect is certainly a factor that can be found in the history of some individuals who develop paraphilias, but it is as yet unclear how these experiences might lead to the development of problematic sexual urges.

Dysfunctional beliefs, attitudes and schemata

Many problematic behaviours that are central to psychopathology are often maintained by dysfunctional beliefs or biases in information processing that lead the individual to think and behave in the way they do (see Chapters 6 and 7 for examples). This also appears to be true of some of the paraphilic disorders, and especially those that are either illegal or involve behaviours towards a non-consenting victim (e.g. paedophilic disorder, exhibitionistic disorder, voyeuristic disorder). A considerable body of research suggests that cognitive distortions, dysfunctional beliefs and information processing biases play an important role in facilitating paraphilias that involve sexual offending in males (Abel, Gore, Holland, Camp et al., 1989; Ward, Hudson, Johnston & Marshall, 1997; Shruti, Ward & Gannon, 2008) and females (Gannon & Alleyne, 2013). For example, incest offenders hold beliefs that children are both sexually attractive and sexually motivated (Hanson, Lipovsky & Saunders, 1994), and paedophiles believe that children want sex with adults, and see contact as being socially acceptable and not harmful to the child (Stermac & Segal, 1989). Abel, Gore, Holland, Camp et al. (1989) labelled these beliefs **cognitive distortions** and argued that, for paedophiles, they serve to legitimize or justify sexual involvement with children and function to maintain the behaviour. These beliefs not only act as reasons why the paedophile should sexually offend, they also function as excuses for the behaviour and a means of diffusing responsibility for the behaviour after the act. They also appear to be a means by which the paedophile can maintain their self-esteem after offending (Pollock & Hashmall, 1991; Ward, Hudson, Johnston & Marshall, 1997). Table 11.3 provides examples of the cognitive distortions found in the post-offending

To read Shruti, Ward & Gannon's article on cognitive distortions in child sex offenders go to **www.wiley-psychopathology.com/reading/ch11**

cognitive distortions Beliefs held by sexual offenders that enable them to justify their sexual offending.

TABLE 11.3 *Cognitive distortions found in the post-offending statements of paedophiles and exhibitionists*

Function of statement	Paedophilia	Exhibitionism
Misattributing blame	'She would always run around half-dressed'	'The way she was dressed, she was asking for it'
Denying sexual intent	'I was just teaching her about sex'	'I was just looking for a place to pee'
Debasing the victim	'She always lies'	'She was just a slut anyway'
Minimising consequences	'She's always been really friendly to me – even afterwards'	'I never touched her – so I couldn't have hurt her'
Deflecting criticism	'This happened years ago. Why can't everyone forget about it?'	'It's not like I raped anyone'
Justifying the cause	'If I hadn't been molested as a kid, I'd never have done this'	'If I knew how to get dates, I wouldn't have to expose myself'

Source: Adapted from Maletzky (2002).

statements of paedophiles and exhibitionists, together with the putative functions that these cognitive distortions serve. However, there is still some debate about whether sexual offenders such as paedophiles genuinely hold these beliefs or whether they are faked in order to diffuse responsibility after the offence. Using a procedure in which child molesters believed their responses were being monitored by a lie detector, Gannon (2006) found that participants endorsed fewer cognitive distortions than when they believed their responses were unmonitored. This suggests that at least some cognitive distortions may be faked in order to provide post-offence excuses for the paedophile's behaviour, and more experimental techniques may need to be developed to understand the mechanisms

that underlie the development and purpose of cognitive distortions in sex offenders (Gannon, Ward & Collie, 2007).

The cognitive distortions that many sex offenders hold are often the products of more dynamic cognitive processes. For example, Stermac & Segal (1989) found that sexual offenders interpret sexual information in a biased way, usually in a manner consistent with their underlying beliefs about the acceptability of their behaviour. They found that child molesters differed from other respondent groups by having a predisposition to interpret information as implying benefits could be gained from sexual contact with children and there was greater complicity on the child's part, with less responsibility on the adult's part. Finally, research has suggested that sex offenders – and

---

THE BOGUS PIPELINE PROCEDURE TO INCREASE HONEST RESPONDING IN PAEDOPHILES

Sexual offenders such as paedophiles appear to possess a set of cognitive distortions that serve to legitimize or justify sexual involvement with children and function to maintain the behaviour (Abel, Gore, Holland, Camp *et al.*, 1989) (see Table 11.3). These beliefs may well act as reasons why the paedophile should sexually offend, but there is still some debate about whether sexual offenders genuinely hold these beliefs or whether they are faked in order to diffuse responsibility after the offence. So how might psychologists find out whether these beliefs are real or faked? A study by Gannon (2006) used what is known as a *bogus pipeline* procedure with child molesters. In this procedure, participants are wired up to apparatus that measures skin conductance through electrodes attached to the fingers. Some participants are then told to refrain from answering dishonestly because skin conductance may be related to dishonest responses (as if they were wired up to a 'lie detector', but in fact the evidence that skin conductance can reliably indicate lying is modest).

The study has the following stages:

STAGE 1

Convicted paedophiles are asked to say whether they agree or disagree with statements related to cognitive distortions in sexual offenders. Example items are the following:

Some children know more about sex than adults	AGREE/DISAGREE
An 8-year-old can enjoy a good sex joke	AGREE/DISAGREE
Children are not as innocent as most people think	AGREE/DISAGREE

STAGE 2

One week later the same participants had to respond to the same statements (but they were not told it was the same questionnaire). Half were simply asked to fill out the questionnaire for a second time. The other half were connected to the bogus pipeline and given instructions that skin conductance could detect dishonest responses.

RESULTS

The results show that, compared with control participants, those attached to the bogus pipeline showed a significant reduction in agreeing with the cognitive distortion statements between Time 1 (when they were not connected to the bogus pipeline) and Time 2 (when they were connected to the bogus pipeline).

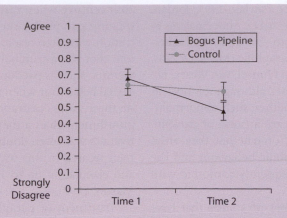

FIGURE 1 *Mean cognitive distortion endorsement (±SE) for the bogus pipeline and control groups*
Source: Gannon, T.A. (2006). Increasing honest responding on cognitive distortions in child molesters: The bogus pipeline procedure. *Journal of Interpersonal Violence, 21*(3), 358–375. © 2006 SAGE. Reprinted by permission of SAGE publications.

CONCLUSIONS

This imaginative empirical approach to this problem indicates that sexual offenders may to some extent be faking the cognitive distortions they hold in order to justify their sexual offending. However, we must also note that (1) this study does involve some deception, so it is important to ensure that such studies comply with normally accepted ethical guidelines (such as the BPS guidelines on ethical principles for conducting research with human participants, http://www.bps.org.uk/), and (2) to ensure a proper balanced design, at Time 2 both experimental and control participants should have been connected to the bogus pipeline, but only the experimental group told that it may detect dishonesty – for instance, simply being connected to the bogus pipeline may itself influence responding.

rapists in particular – may have developed integrated cognitive schemata that guide the offender's interactions with their victims and justify their behaviour. Polaschek & Ward (2002) called these **implicit theories**. Offenders use these schemata as causal theories about themselves, their victims and broader categories of people (such as women or children). Polaschek & Gannon (2004) identified five types of implicit theory held by rapists. These included the beliefs that:

> **implicit theories** In sexual offending, integrated cognitive schemas that guide sexual offenders' interactions with their victims and justify their behaviour.

1. women are unknowable (i.e. 'sexual encounters will end up being adversarial because a woman's intentions are unknowable'),

2. women are sex objects (i.e. 'women are constantly sexually receptive, and so will enjoy sex even when it is forced on them'),

3. the male sex drive is uncontrollable (i.e. 'a man's sex levels will build up to a dangerous level if women do not provide them with reasonable sexual access'),

4. men are naturally dominant over women (i.e. 'men are more important in society than women, and a woman should meet a man's needs on demand'), and

5. the world is a dangerous place (i.e. 'it is a dog-eat-dog world and a man needs to take what he can from it').

Implicit cognitive theories such as these can provide the sex offender with a justification for both impulsive and premeditated sexual offences, and can be used as a way of denying both the significance of the offence and the offender's responsibility for the offence.

Biological theories

As we mentioned earlier, the vast majority of those diagnosed with a paraphilia are male, and so it has been hypothesized that paraphilia is caused by abnormalities in male sex hormones or by imbalances in those brain neurotransmitters that control male sexual behaviour. For example, **androgens** are the most important of the male hormones, and it may be that unusual sexual behaviour, such as impulsive sexual offending involving non-consenting others, may be due to imbalances in these hormones. However, there is relatively little convincing evidence that abnormal androgen levels play a significant role in the development of paraphilic behaviour, although androgen levels may help to maintain paraphilic behaviour once it has been acquired (Buvat, Lemaire & Ratajczyk, 1996), and anti-androgen drugs that reduce testosterone levels are regularly used to reduce the sexual urges of those with

> **androgens** The most important of the male hormones. Unusual sexual behaviour, such as impulsive sexual offending involving non-consenting others, may be due to imbalances in these hormones.

paraphilia disorders (Bradford & Pawlak, 1993; Jordan, Fromberger, Stolpmann & Muller, 2011). Abnormalities in brain neurotransmitter metabolism – such as serotonin – have also been associated with paraphilia (Maes, De Vos, van Hunsel, van West et al., 2001), although it is unclear whether such abnormalities are a cause of paraphilic, or whether they are a consequence of acquiring paraphilic behaviour and the anxiety and depression that is frequently comorbid with paraphilia.

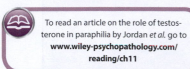

To read an article on the role of testosterone in paraphilia by Jordan et al. go to **www.wiley-psychopathology.com/ reading/ch11**

Finally, there is a small number of studies that have identified abnormalities or deficits in brain functioning with paraphilias. First, abnormalities in the brain's temporal lobe have been associated with a number of paraphilias, including sadism, exhibitionism and paedophilia (Mason, 1997; Murphy, 1997; Mendez, Chow, Ringman, Twitchell & Hinkin, 2000). However, these may account for a minority of cases and appear to be related to dysfunction in the temporal lobes leading to sexual disinhibition of previously controlled behaviour. More recent studies (albeit based on a small sample of participants) have identified deficits in cognitive abilities in paedophiles that are mediated by striato-thalamically controlled areas of the frontal cortex (Tost, Vollmert, Brassen, Schmitt et al., 2004). These areas are associated with neuropsychological functions that include response inhibition, working memory and cognitive flexibility, and deficits in these domains are consistent with the finding that paedophiles frequently have lower than expected IQ scores – often as much as two-thirds of a standard deviation below the population mean (Cantor, Blanchard, Robichaud & Christensen, 2005).

Summary of the aetiology of paraphilic disorders

Research on the aetiology of paraphilic disorders has largely been restricted to understanding the causes of those paraphilias that involve sexual offending (e.g. paedophilia) – mainly because of the desire to understand and prevent criminal activity. However, the research that is available has identified some risk factors for paraphilia (e.g. hypersexuality, childhood abuse and neglect) and has also indicated that some paraphilias are associated with cognitive biases and dysfunctional beliefs that act to maintain sexual offending and serve to legitimize or justify sexual activities.

11.3.3 The Treatment of Paraphilic Disorders

Attempts to treat paraphilic disorders have a long and complex history, dating back to the first half of the

20th century when castration was a popular method of treating paraphilias such as paedophilia. However, castration was often reserved for repeated paraphilic behaviour that was a criminal act and involved non-consenting victims (such as paedophilia and, in earlier times, homosexual behaviour when this was deemed illegal). In many of these cases, castration was seen more as a criminal punishment than a method of treatment, and its effectiveness was often doubted because up to 30 per cent of men treated in this way were still capable of erections and ejaculation up to 10 years after surgery (Grubin & Mason, 1997).

Treatment of paraphilic disorders is further complicated by several factors that make successful treatment difficult to achieve. First, many paraphilic disorders involve criminal behaviour (e.g. paedophilia, exhibitionism and voyeurism), and this will often mean that sufferers are reluctant to be wholly truthful about their activities or to honestly disclose their sexual activities. Second, to many people with paraphilias, their sexual inclinations involve doing things that they particularly enjoy and which provide sexual satisfaction. If they have been indulging in these activities since early adolescence, then their behaviours may seem to them as normal as conventional sexual behaviour is to a non-sufferer (Laws & O'Donohue, 1997). Third, with many of the paraphilias that involve a non-consenting victim, the sufferer will often develop a rigid set of beliefs about their activities that enables them to diffuse responsibility for their behaviour and to blame others (e.g. the victim) (Abel, Gore, Holland, Camp et al., 1989; Shruti, Ward & Gannon, 2008). Because of this, the individual with a paraphilic disorder will often deny there is a problem with their behaviour, lack motivation to change, and may even fake compliance with therapy simply because it may allow them to continue their paraphilic activities subsequently (e.g. if treatment is a requirement for release from prison for sexual offences). And, fourth, as we mentioned earlier, paraphilic disorders are highly comorbid with a number of other psychopathologies, including substance abuse, anxiety, depression and personality disorders, and these comorbid disorders may have to be tackled before treatment for the paraphilic disorder itself can be attempted.

We will continue this section by describing some of the main treatment methods for paraphilic disorders. However, many therapists currently use multifaceted approaches to treatment and you should bear this in mind when reviewing these specific treatment methods. For example, a multifaceted approach might involve (1) treating the individual behavioural problem (e.g. shifting sexual arousal and satisfaction away from specific or inappropriate stimuli and associating it with more acceptable stimuli), (2) dealing with any dysfunctional beliefs or attitudes that are maintaining the paraphilic behaviour (see Table 11.3), and (3) because many paraphilic disorders are associated with social skills deficits, the therapist may provide social skills training that will help the individual function more appropriately with consenting partners.

Behavioural techniques

In section 11.2.2 we discussed a number of early theories of paraphilic disorders that viewed these problems as resulting from classical conditioning processes. In these accounts, unconventional stimuli or events (such as specific stimuli in fetishes, watching others naked in voyeurism and suchlike) have become associated with sexual experiences, such as masturbation, during early adolescence. The assumption of behaviour therapy is that if these behaviours are learnt through conditioning, then they can also be 'unlearnt' through the use of basic conditioning procedures. Three types of technique will be described here. These are aversion therapy, masturbatory satiation and orgasmic reorientation.

Aversion therapy is based on the assumption that inappropriate stimuli have become positively associated with sexual arousal and sexual satisfaction, and in order to break this association, those stimuli must now be paired with negative or aversive experiences. For example, treatment of a fur fetish may involve pairing pictures of fur or women wearing fur clothing with aversive experiences such as an electric shock or drug induced nausea. Alternatively, a paedophile may be given electric shocks when shown pictures of naked children. An avoidance component can be added to this treatment in which the client can avoid the negative outcome by pressing a button which changes the picture from their preferred sexual stimulus (e.g. fur, naked child) to an acceptable one (e.g. an attractive female). Aversion therapy can also be used in a **covert conditioning** form, where the client does not actually experience the pairing of sexual stimuli with aversive outcomes, but imagines these associations during controlled treatment sessions. For example, the client may be asked to imagine one of their sexual fantasies and then to vividly imagine a highly aversive or negative outcome, such as his wife finding him indulging in his paraphilic sexual activities, or being arrested (Barlow, 1993). Aversion therapy has been used to treat fetishes, transvestism, exhibitionism and paedophilia, and there is some evidence that it may have some treatment benefit when combined with other approaches such as social skills training (Marks, Gelder & Bancroft, 1970). However, as we have reported elsewhere in this book, aversion therapy rarely achieves long-term success when used alone – and high rates of relapse are associated with the sole use of aversion therapy (Wilson, 1978).

> **covert conditioning** Using the client's ability to imagine events in order to condition associations between events.

Satiation is an important conditioning principle in which the unconditioned stimulus (in this case sexual satisfaction) comes to be ineffective because it is experienced in excess, and this leads to extinction of the sexual urges that had been conditioned to stimuli or events associated with that unconditioned stimulus (e.g. fetishes). This has led to the development of **masturbatory satiation** as a treatment for paraphilic disorders, in which the client is asked to masturbate in the presence of arousing stimuli (e.g. women's underwear if the client has an underwear fetish) and to simultaneously verbalize his fantasies on a tape recorder. Immediately after he has ejaculated, the client is instructed to masturbate again, no matter how unaroused or uninterested he feels, and continue for at least an hour (Marshall & Barbaree, 1978). After a number of these sessions, the client often reports that the stimuli that previously sexually aroused them has become boring or even aversive (LoPiccolo, 1985). Latency to ejaculation increases, and the number of sexual fantasies elicited by the paraphilic stimulus significantly decreases (Marshall & Lippens, 1977).

> **masturbatory satiation** A treatment for paraphilias in which the client is asked to masturbate in the presence of arousing stimuli.

An important task for anyone treating paraphilic disorders is not only to suppress inappropriate or distressing sexual activities (perhaps using the methods described above) but also to replace these with acceptable sexual practices. **Orgasmic reorientation** is a treatment method that aims at making the client sexually aroused by more conventional or acceptable stimuli. This is a more explicit attempt to recondition sexual urges to more conventional stimuli, and it can be used as an extension of the masturbatory satiation technique. For example, the client is first asked to masturbate while attending to conventionally arousing stimuli (such as pictures of nude females), but if they begin to feel bored or lose their erection, they are asked to switch to attending to pictures associated with their paraphilia. As soon as they feel sexually aroused again, they must switch back to attending to the conventional stimulus, and so on. Although there are numerous individual case studies suggesting that some variations of orgasmic reorientation might be successful in helping clients to control their paraphilic behaviour, there are no controlled outcome studies available to evaluate the success of this method over the longer term (Laws & Marshall, 1991).

> **orgasmic reorientation** A treatment method to replace inappropriate or distressing sexual activities. It aims to make the client sexually aroused by more conventional or acceptable stimuli.

Cognitive treatment

We saw in the section on aetiology that dysfunctional beliefs play a central role in developing and maintaining a number of paraphilic disorders – especially those paraphilias that involve sexual offending with non-consenting victims. **Cognitive treatment** for these paraphilias often involves cognitive behaviour therapy (CBT), which is adapted to help the client to identify dysfunctional beliefs, to challenge these beliefs and then replace them with functional and adaptive beliefs about sexual behaviour and sexual partners. Table 11.3 shows a list of the kinds of dysfunctional beliefs held by paedophiles and exhibitionists. These beliefs act as justifications for sexual offending and are part of a belief system that effectively 'gives them permission' to carry out their offences. Challenging dysfunctional beliefs includes:

> **cognitive treatment** Treatment approach intended to help the client identify and challenge dysfunctional beliefs.

1. demonstrating to clients that their dysfunctional beliefs are based on their deviant sexual behaviour rather than being justificable reasons for the behaviour,

2. helping clients to see how they might misinterpret the behaviour of their victims to be consistent with their dysfunctional beliefs, and

3. discussing dysfunctional beliefs within existing individual and broader social norms in order to demonstrate that the client's beliefs are not shared by most other members of society (e.g. to establish that women are *not* merely objects for sexual gratification).

The UK Home Office has developed a number of integrated treatments for sexual offenders (Ministry of Justice, 2010) and Figure 11.3 shows the most recent data, which indicate that the reconviction rate for treated sex offenders was up to 3.4 per cent lower than for untreated individuals (Schmucker & Losel, 2008). One integrated treatment for sexual offenders is called the **Sex Offender Treatment Programme (SOTP)** and this extensively adopts CBT methods for treating imprisoned sex offenders (Beech, Fisher & Beckett, 1999), targeting risk factors for reoffending such as sexual preoccupation, sexual preferences for children, offence-supporting attitudes, lack of emotional intimacy with adults, impulsive lifestyle, poor coping skills and problem-solving abilities.

> **Sex Offender Treatment Programme (SOTP)** An integrated treatment for sexual offenders which adopts CBT methods for treating imprisoned sex offenders and targets risk factors for reoffending such as sexual preoccupation, sexual preferences for children, offence-supporting attitudes, lack of emotional intimacy with adults, impulsive lifestyle, poor coping skills and poor problem-solving abilities.

Relapse-prevention training

Rather than focusing on an all-embracing 'cure' for paraphilias, many forms of treatment focus specifically on relapse prevention, and this is especially relevant in the case

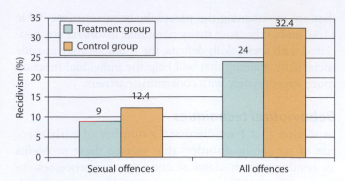

FIGURE 11.3 *Effect of sex offender treatment*
Integrated treatment programmes for medium to high-risk sex offenders in prisons (such as the Core SOTP scheme) are helpful in reducing future reconviction rates by up to 3.4 per cent.
Source: Based on Schmucker & Lösel (2008).

of sexual offenders. **Relapse-prevention training** consists primarily of helping clients to identify circumstances, situations, moods and types of thoughts that might trigger paraphilic behaviour. For example, a mood trigger might be a period of stress, anxiety or alcohol abuse that precipitates sexual offending, or close contact with children that might activate paedophile behaviours. Sexual offenders are also taught to identify the distorted cognitions that might lead to offending (e.g. 'that child is running around half dressed, so she must be interested in sex') and are taught self-management skills that will enable them to interrupt sequences of thoughts that lead to offending or to avoid situations that place them at risk (e.g. in the case of paedophilia, to avoid taking jobs that involve working with or near children, or living near a school). Relapse prevention programmes have been shown to be successful in reducing subsequent offending (Marshall & Pithers, 1994) and are important components of many national treatment programmes for sexual offenders.

> **relapse-prevention training** In paraphilias, a treatment which consists primarily of helping clients to identify circumstances, situations, moods and types of thoughts that might trigger paraphilic behaviour.

Hormonal and drug treatments

As we mentioned earlier, castration was the radical form of treatment for dangerous sex offenders during periods of the 20th century – especially in parts of Europe, and was often offered as an alternative to imprisonment (Abel, Osborn, Anthony & Gardos, 1992). The aim here was to curb the sexual appetite of persistent offenders who were unable to respond to any other form of treatment. An arguably more acceptable way of curbing sexual appetite in those paraphilics who persistently offend is to use **anti-androgen drugs** that significantly decrease the levels of male hormones such as testosterone. Currently used testosterone-lowering

> **anti-androgen drugs** A group of drugs that significantly decrease the levels of male hormones such as testosterone.

medroxyprogesterone acetate (MPA) An anti-androgen, testosterone-lowering drug.

cyproterone acetate (CPA) An anti-androgen, testosterone-lowering drug.

drugs include **medroxyprogesterone acetate** (**MPA**) and **cyproterone acetate** (**CPA**), and both have been shown to reduce the frequency of erection and ejaculation, inhibit sexual arousal, and to reduce the rate of reoffending in sexual offenders (Hall, 1995; Bradford & Pawlak, 1993; Maletzky & Field, 2003). However, such a form of treatment tends to depend very much on the compliance of the client or offender in taking such drugs regularly. This is particularly important because evidence suggests that offenders will often revert to paraphilic behaviour when they cease taking the drug – even after many years of medication (Berlin & Meinecke, 1981).

An alternative to anti-androgens is the use of antidepressant drugs such as SSRIs (e.g. fluoxetine) and there is some modest evidence that such drugs will help the individual control sexual urges – especially if depression is a trigger for indulging in paraphilic behaviour (Kafka & Hennen, 2000). However, despite encouraging short-term effects of treatment with SSRIs, there are as yet no long-term follow-up studies (Maletzky & Field, 2003).

Summary of the treatment of paraphilic disorders

The treatment of paraphilic disorders is generally a difficult process, not least because many diagnosed with paraphilia will also be sexual offenders (e.g. paedophiles, exhibitionists, voyeurs), and this can lead clients to be less than truthful about their sexual activities and approach treatment with a relatively ingrained set of beliefs about their activities. Paraphilic disorders are also highly comorbid with other psychopathologies – such as substance abuse, anxiety, depression and personality disorders – and this makes treatment additionally complex. Most programmes of treatment adopt a multifaceted approach that can involve behaviour therapy techniques to address the specific sexual behaviour problem (e.g. aversion therapy, masturbatory satiation, orgasmic reorientation) and use CBT to deal with the dysfunctional beliefs that underlie many paraphilias, and sexual offending in particular. Finally, social skills training and relapse-prevention procedures can be used in an attempt to ensure that the individual is able to cope with the demands of normal sexual relationships and to identify situations and circumstances that might trigger relapse.

SELF-TEST QUESTIONS

11.3.1 The Diagnosis and Description of Paraphilic Disorders
- How are paraphilic disorders defined in DSM-5?
- What are the main categories of paraphilic disorders described in DSM-5?
- Can you differentiate between those paraphilic disorders that can be labelled 'victimless' and those that in many societies would be labelled 'sexual offences'?
- Can you list the main diagnostic criteria for fetishistic disorder, transvestic disorder, voyeuristic disorder, frotteuristic disorder, paedophilic disorder, sexual masochistic disorder and sexual sadism disorder?

11.3.2 The Aetiology of Paraphilic Disorders
- Can you list some of the main risk factors for paraphilic disorders?
- Paraphilic disorders are highly comorbid with which other psychopathologies?
- What is castration anxiety and how is it used by psychoanalytic theorists to explain paraphilic disorders?
- How is associative learning thought to be involved in the acquisition of some paraphilic disorders?
- Is childhood abuse and neglect an important factor in the development of paraphilic disorders?
- What are cognitive distortions and how are they used by sexual offenders to justify their actions?
- Is there any substantial evidence that sex hormone imbalances are involved in the development of paraphilic disorders?
- What brain area abnormalities have been associated with paraphilic disorders and how might they cause paraphilic behaviour?

11.3.3 The Treatment of Paraphilic Disorders
- Why are paraphilic disorders so difficult to treat?
- How have aversion therapy and covert conditioning been utilized to treat paraphilic disorders?

- What are masturbatory satiation and orgasmic reorientation techniques, and is there any evidence that they can be successfully used to treat paraphilic disorders?

- How has CBT been adapted to help treat paraphilic disorders?

- Can you name the basic principles and stages of the UK SOTP initiative used to treat sexual offenders?

- What are the main drug treatments that have been used to treat paraphilic disorders, and what is the evidence that such treatments prevent relapse?

- What are the main principles of relapse-prevention treatments for paraphilic disorders?

SECTION SUMMARY

11.3   PARAPHILIC DISORDERS

When high rates of sexual behaviour are channelled into unusual or very specific sexual activities, these are known as paraphilias. They range from sexual activities that are victimless (e.g. fetishes and transvestic fetishism) to others that are defined in law as sexual offences (e.g. paedophilia, exhibitionism, voyeurism). Many paraphilias are diagnosed on the basis of unusual, recurrent sexual urges that cause personal distress or affect social and occupational functioning (e.g. fetishism, transvestic fetishism), but others do not require that the individual experiences distress – merely that they have acted on their urges with non-consenting victims (e.g. paedophilic disorder, exhibitionistic disorder, voyeuristic disorder). Research on the aetiology of paraphilic disorders has identified some risk factors (e.g. hypersexuality, childhood abuse and neglect) and has also indicated that dysfunctional beliefs may play an important role in maintaining those paraphilic disorders that are linked to sexual offending (e.g. paedophilia, exhibitionism). Finally, treatments for paraphilic disorders are still relatively underdeveloped, and adopt behaviour therapy or CBT techniques to change dysfunctional behaviour and cognitions. Relapse prevention is an important component of treatment for many paraphilic disorders – especially those related to sexual offending.
   The key points are:

- Paraphilic disorders tend to be associated with problematic high-frequency sexual behaviours or unusual sexual urges and activities that are often directed at inappropriate targets.

- Some paraphilic disorders are victimless (e.g. fetishistic disorder, transvestic disorder) while others will be defined in law as sexual offences (e.g. exhibitionistic disorder, voyeuristic disorder, frotteuristic disorder, paedophilic disorders).

11.3.1   The Diagnosis and Description of Paraphilic Disorder

- *Fetishitic disorder* involves sexually arousing fantasies and urges directed at non-animate objects.

- *Transvestic disorder* is when a heterosexual male experiences sexual arousal from cross-dressing in women's clothing.

- *Sexual masochism* is when an individual gains sexual arousal and satisfaction from being humiliated.

- *Sexual sadism* is when a person gains sexual arousal and satisfaction from the psychological or physical suffering of others.

- *Exhibitionistic disorder* involves sexual fantasies about exposing the genitalia to a stranger.

- *Voyeuristic disorder* involves experiencing intense sexually arousing fantasies or urges to watch an unsuspecting person who is naked, in the process of undressing or engaging in sexual activity.

- *Frotteuristic disorder* involves recurrent sexual urges to touch and rub up against other non-consenting people – usually in crowded places.

- *Paedophilic disorder* is defined as sexual attraction towards prepubescent children, normally 13 years or younger.

- Some paedophiles limit their activities to their immediate family (e.g. children, step-children, nieces) and *incest* is listed as a specific sub-type of paedophilia in DSM-5.

- Non-incestuous paedophiles will normally only become sexually aroused by sexually immature children, and will often develop elaborate ways of gaining access to children through 'grooming' activities.

- *Sexual masochism disorder* is when an individual gains sexual arousal and satisfaction from being humiliated, and this causes the individual significant distress.

- *Sexual sadism disorder* is when a person gains sexual arousal and satisfaction from the psychological or physical suffering of others, and this diagnosis is given if the symptoms cause the individual significant distress or if the person acts on the impulses with a non-consenting person.

11.3.2 The Aetiology of Paraphilic Disorders

- Most of the DSM-5 diagnosable paraphilic disorders are male activities, and many are also sexual offences (e.g. paedophilic disorder, exhibitionistic disorder).

- Both *hypersexuality* and *childhood abuse and neglect* are risk factors for paraphilic disorders.

- Psychodynamic theory views paraphilic disorders either as (1) defensive reactions that are attempting to protect the ego from repressed fears, or (2) as representing fixation at a pregenital stage of development (e.g. the Oedipal stage).

- Many paraphilic disorders develop during early adolescence, and inappropriate sexual urges may have been developed through the association of sexual activities such as masturbation with inappropriate stimuli or activities (the process of classical conditioning).

- The level of childhood abuse experienced by sexual offenders is almost double the level found in the general population. However, childhood abuse and neglect is not a sufficient condition for committing a sexual offence, because it is reported by only 30 per cent of sexual offenders.

- Sexual offenders, including paedophiles, develop a set of beliefs or *cognitive distortions* that serve to legitimize or justify their sexual activities.

- Even though anti-androgen drugs are regularly used to treat some paraphilic disorders, there is little convincing evidence that abnormal androgen levels play a significant role in the development of paraphilic behaviour.

11.3.3 The Treatment of Paraphilic Disorders

- Many paraphilic disorders are difficult to treat because (1) they involve criminal behaviour that will make individuals reluctant to be truthful about their activities, and (2) paraphilic disorders are highly comorbid with other psychiatric disorders, which significantly complicates treatment.

- Behavioural treatments for paraphilic disorders include *aversion therapy*, *covert conditioning*, *masturbatory satiation*, and *orgasmic reorientation*.

- CBT has been adapted to treat paraphilic disorders (especially those involving sexual offending) by addressing the dysfunctional beliefs or cognitive distortions that many sexual offenders develop to legitimize their behaviour.

- Anti-androgen drug treatments for paraphilic disorders include *medroxyprogesterone acetate (MPA)* and *cyproterone acetate (CPA)* which reduce the frequency of erection and inhibit sexual arousal.

- Because many paraphilic disorders are also sexual offences, *relapse-prevention training* helps clients to identify circumstances that may trigger paraphilic behaviour.

11.4 GENDER DYSPHORIA

Most of us take our sexual identity for granted. We do not question that we are the sex we were born as, and we find that behaving as either a male or a female is natural and effortless. Our **gender identity** seems to have been determined for as long as we have lived, and we think, act and dress accordingly. However, some individuals develop a sense of **gender dysphoria** (unhappiness with their own gender) and feel that their gender is the opposite of the biological sex they were born with.

For a video on gender dysphoria go to www.wiley-psychopathology.com/video/ch11

gender identity The internal sense of being either male or female. Usually congruent with biological gender, but not always, as in gender dysphoria.

This disparity can cause them significant distress or impairment. In such circumstances, the individual may see themselves biologically developing as a man or a woman (e.g. growing a beard, or developing breasts), but cannot shake off the belief that underneath the physical appearance they are of the opposite gender. This may lead them to cross-dress or even seek surgery or take hormones to develop physical features of the opposite sex. When this kind of gender dysphoria becomes problematic and causes significant personal distress and social and occupational impairment, then it may be diagnosed as gender dysphoria (previously known as 'gender identity disorder' in DSM-IV-TR).

gender dysphoria A gender identity disorder in which an individual has a sense of gender that is opposite to his or her biological sex.

Forms of gender dysphoria can also be found in childhood and are associated with cross-gender behaviour that can be easily recognized by parents and carers (Green & Blanchard, 1995). These include playing with toys typically enjoyed by the opposite sex (e.g. boys playing with dolls), dressing in clothes of the opposite sex, and preferring friends and playmates of the opposite sex.

11.4.1   Diagnosis and Description of Gender Dysphoria

The main components of the diagnosis are that (1) the individual exhibits a strong and persistent cross-gender identification, and that this is not simply because of the cultural advantages that might be associated with being the opposite sex, and (2) there must be clear evidence of clinically significant distress or impairment caused by their gender dysphoria.

Individuals with a diagnosis of gender dysphoria usually exhibit a strong preoccupation with their wish to live as a member of the opposite sex and this may lead them to acquire the physical appearance of a member of the opposite sex (by cross-dressing or adopting mannerisms typical of the opposite sex). For example, men may undergo electrolysis to remove body hair or submit themselves to hormone treatments to develop female physical characteristics such as breasts. Those who have strong feelings of gender dysphoria may have problematic sex lives. For example, men with gender dysphoria who are married may frequently fantasise about being a lesbian lover when they have sex with their wife. Those with same-sex partners often prevent their partner from seeing or touching their genitals. Client's Perspective 11.1 provides a personal account given by one man who had had feelings of gender dysphoria from a very early age, and how – despite having what appeared to others to be a successful marriage, family and business – these feelings were persistent enough to encourage him to seek treatment. In many cases the feelings of gender dysphoria are so strong that they drive the individual to seek *gender reassignment surgery* which culminates in changing the individual physically into their preferred gender (see section 11.4.3).

A diagnosis of gender dysphoria can also be given in children. In boys, this may manifest by adopting female roles during play (such as playing with dolls, taking 'mother' roles, avoiding rough-and-tumble play), by exhibiting disgust at their penis, or adopting female activities such as always insisting on sitting on the toilet when urinating. Girls may exhibit strong aversion to their parents' gender role expectations of them, avoid wearing dresses, insist on having short hair, and may also prefer male playmates and contact sports such as football and rugby. In childhood, about 3 per cent of girls and 1 per cent of boys explicitly express a desire to be of the opposite gender (Zucker & Bradley, 1995), but we must remember that the significant majority of these do not grow up to be adults with diagnosable gender dysphoria.

There is very little epidemiological evidence available on which to base the prevalence rates of gender dysphoria. However, DSM-5 estimates that the prevalence rate of gender dysphoria for natal adult males is around 0.005–0.014% and for natal females from 0.002–0.003% (DSM-5, p.454). Estimates from some European studies suggest that roughly 1 per 30,000 adult males (0.003%) and 1 per 100,000 adult females (0.001%) seek gender reassignment surgery. Gender dysphoria can also be comorbid with a number of other psychiatric diagnoses, especially anxiety, depression and impulse-control disorders. Studies suggest that 71 per cent of a sample with gender dysphoria fulfilled the criteria for a comorbid current and/or lifetime psychiatric diagnosis (Hepp, Kraemer, Schnyder, Miller & Delsignore, 2005), and 17.8 per cent of individuals with the DSM-IV-TR diagnosis of gender identity disorder have also been found to have another comorbid psychiatric disorder (Terada, Matsumoto, Sato, Okabe et al., 2012).

11.4.2   The Aetiology of Gender Dysphoria

Gender dysphoria is a problem that persists for many individuals over a substantial period of their lives, suggesting the causes of these problems are not trivial. However, there is relatively little research on the aetiology of gender dysphoria. Some risk factors have been identified, with males suffering gender dysphoria reporting distant relationships with their fathers, and females often reporting a history of childhood abuse (Bradley & Zucker, 1997). However, such childhood experiences are by no means universal across individuals with gender dysphoria. Neither can we assume that gender dysphoria results from parents and family reinforcing children during childhood for behaving in cross-gender ways. For example, when a child dresses up in clothes of the opposite sex, they may be rewarded by the attention they receive, but it is relatively rare for children treated in this way to grow into adults with gender dysphoria (Zucker, Finegan, Deering & Bradley, 1984). Similarly, neither do the prenatal hopes and expectations of a parent appear to influence the development of gender dysphoria. Zucker, Wild, Bradley & Lowry (1993) found that mothers of boys with feminine characteristics were just as likely to have wanted a boy as a girl. These findings suggest that evidence that social development may play a role in the development of gender dysphoria is equivocal. Let us now turn our attention to biological factors.

CLIENT'S PERSPECTIVE 11.1: GENDER DYSPHORIA

On 1 June 1994, when this journal began, I was living entirely as Dan – father, husband and small businessman. I had been married for 13 years to Alice, with a 10-year-old son and a 6-year-old daughter. My family life was good, my business growing, my future bright, but still something was missing.

I had first felt 'different' in infant school, where all the other boys seemed to know instinctively how to act, but I had to struggle to learn the male role by rote: it did not come naturally. I never considered the possibility I had the instincts of a female; I simply thought I had none at all.

By age 7, I was regularly sneaking off to dress in the girls' clothes my mother brought in as part of her short-lived ironing business. This was well before puberty and was not an erotic experience, but rather a feeling of completeness and contentment.

Throughout my teenage years, the need to dress as a female came and went in waves, sometimes intense, sometimes absent for years at a time.

I was non-agressive in school, both in sports and dating, and excelled at neither. My only erotic interests were not in what I could do to or with a woman, but what it would be like to be one.

I married as a virgin in 1981, and the longings to be female vanished more than they were there. But, gradually, as I progressed through adult life, the waves became stronger and more frequent. Only twice in my life (both times in my early teen years) had I ventured out as a female, both with such tension from fear of discovery that I did not attempt this again until three years before this journal began.

Suddenly, the need to move in society as a woman became overwhelming and within 2 months I had made nearly a dozen outings, tentative at first, then growing bolder as I gained confidence in my ability to 'pass' without being 'read'.

Throughout this period, I was constantly 'purging' myself of this 'awful' desire. Full of guilt I would throw away all my pills, wigs, clothes and any other female accoutrements, only to be driven to rebuild my collection scant days later.

Finally, I came to the decision that this secret side, if not dealt with openly, would lead to self-destruction and the loss of not only my self-respect, but the love of those I loved. So, at the end of July 1994, I mustered the courage to call a gender 'hotline' and get a referral to a doctor who provided hormone therapy to transsexuals.

Clinical Commentary

Dan's case is typical of a majority of men who suffer gender dysphoria. Even though his family life is settled and happy, and his financial situation is secure and promising, he is still unable to reconcile his gender identity with his biological sex, and the urge to act and dress as a woman becomes overwhelming in adult life. His feelings of gender dysphoria began in childhood when playing the male role did not come naturally. However, it is unusual for someone with childhood gender dysphoria to carry those feelings into full adulthood as Dan did. His attempts to cross-dress and take on female gender identity at first made him feel guilty and finally led him to take the decision to make a full transition to becoming a woman.

Biological factors

One view is that gender identity may be influenced by hormonal factors. In particular, when mothers have taken sex hormones during pregnancy (e.g. to prevent uterine bleeding), the behaviour of their offspring has subsequently been affected in ways consistent with the type of hormone used. When pregnant mothers have taken medications related to male sex hormones, the early behaviour of girls is often more tomboyish than in mothers who had not taken such drugs (Ehrhardt & Money, 1967). Similarly, the male offspring of mothers who took female hormones during pregnancy often display less athletic behaviour than boys whose mothers did not take such hormones (Yalom, Green & Fisk, 1973).

One study has suggested that gender dysphoria may be associated with abnormalities in those areas of the brain that regulate sexual behaviour. The *bed nucleus of the stria terminalis* (BSTc) is a brain area that is essential for sexual behaviour and is normally larger in males than in females. However, in autopsies carried out on six men who had undergone gender reassignment surgery to become women, Zhou, Hofman, Gooren & Swaab (1995) found a female-sized BSTc in all cases. They concluded that males with gender dysphoria appear to possess female brain structures that may either have a genetic origin or may have been influenced by abnormalities in early brain development. However, these early findings have not received convincing support in recent fMRI studies of the brains of male-to-female transsexuals, where no evidence was found that the brains of male-to-female transsexuals were 'feminized' (Savic & Arver, 2011).

There have been relatively few studies of the heritability of gender dysphoria, but a well-controlled child and adolescent twin sample study by Coolidge, Thede & Young (2000) suggested that gender dysphoria is highly heritable. While this implies a genetic component to gender dysphoria, it is not clear from these studies how that genetic component is either transmitted or through what aspect of gender dysphoria or its related psychopathology it is manifested. Genetic transmission may be through the influence of genes on the development of brain substrates relevant to gender development and identity, or to their effect on hormonal action, but to date no convincing candidate genes have been identified (Klink & Den Heijer, 2014).

11.4.3   The Treatment of Gender Dysphoria

Individuals diagnosed with gender dysphoria feel that they have a sense of gender that is opposite to the biological sex they were born with, and gender dysphoria involves profound feelings of conflict between gender identity and biological sex. There are two important ways in which this imbalance can be corrected – either by (1) attempting to change an individual's biological sex to be congruent with their feelings of gender identity, or (2) using psychological methods to change their gender identity to be congruent with their biological sex. Most individuals with gender dysphoria are usually adamant that their biological sex is 'wrong' and opt for a process that ends in **gender reassignment surgery** – a process that involves progressive hormone treatment and eventually surgery to change their basic biological features to be congruent with their gender identity. We will discuss this radical treatment option first and then look at more psychologically oriented attempts to modify gender identity itself.

> **gender reassignment surgery** The process of changing biological sex which ends in changing the person's basic biological features to be congruent with his or her gender identity.

Gender reassignment surgery

This involves a relatively irreversible process of changing the body's physical characteristics to be consistent with the individual's feelings of gender. Because it involves major changes to the person's anatomy, it is a treatment option that is approached in a graduated way in order to ensure that the client is fully aware of the long-term implications of the treatment and is psychologically adjusted to becoming someone of the opposite biological sex. The progressive stages of gender reassignment surgery start with at least 3 months of counselling or psychotherapy to ensure the client fully understands the process of treatment and to ensure they are fully committed to it. This is usually followed by hormone treatment to initiate physical changes such as reducing body hair and developing breasts in those men seeking to become biological women, and beard growth and muscle development in those women seeking to become men. The next stage is a crucial real-life test in which the client must live as the preferred gender for at least 1 year, dressing and presenting themselves as the preferred sex in a way that will lead them to understand what this means over the longer term. If the first three stages are completed successfully, the client may then proceed to the fourth stage – surgery, where their genitalia are surgically altered to resemble those of their preferred biological sex.

Despite the radical nature of gender reassignment therapy, outcome studies tend to indicate that a large majority of clients who undergo the full treatment are generally satisfied with the outcome and express no regrets about their decision (Smith, van Goozen & Cohen-Kettenis, 2001). In a Dutch study of 188 gender dysphoria sufferers who completed gender reassignment surgery, only two expressed any regret at their decision. More importantly, the study found that such procedures tended to significantly reduce gender dysphoria, and enabled clients to function well psychologically, socially and sexually (Smith, van Goozen, Kuiper & Cohen-Kettenis, 2005). Nevertheless, while such studies seem to indicate that gender reassignment surgery has a largely positive outcome, we must still be cautious about it as a treatment that solves all the problems associated with gender dysphoria. First, while many suffering gender dysphoria do go through all four stages of the treatment, a substantial minority drop out of gender reassignment schemes at an early stage. Smith, van Goozen, Kuiper & Cohen-Kettenis (2005) report that of 325 individuals who applied for gender reassignment surgery, 103 dropped out before starting hormone treatment, and a further 34 dropped out before surgery (a drop-out rate of 42 per cent). Indeed, many decide not to continue with the treatment during the real-life test, when they discover that the realities of living as someone of the opposite biological sex are not what they imagined. The longer the client is kept in the real-life test phase of the process, the greater the likelihood of a successful outcome (Botzer & Vehrs, 1997). But if the individual with gender dysphoria already has significant comorbid psychological problems, then these are unlikely to be alleviated by gender reassignment surgery (Botzer & Vehrs, 1997).

DSM-5 SUMMARY TABLE 11.16 *Criteria for Gender Dysphoria in Adolescents and Adults*

- A marked discrepancy between an individual's expressed gender and assigned gender, over a period of at least 6 months, as expressed by at least two of the following:
  - A discrepancy between expressed gender and sex characteristics.
  - An intense desire to be without existing sex characteristics due to a discrepancy between expressed and assigned gender.
  - An intense desire for the sex characteristics of another gender or to be treated as another gender.
  - An intense belief that one has the typical feelings and reactions of another gender.
- Symptoms cause significant distress or impairment in performing major occupational, social or interpersonal life functions.

Psychological treatments

An alternative approach to the treatment of gender dysphoria is to try to modify the client's gender identity to be consistent with their biological sex. For example, if an individual feels they are basically female but are biologically male, one approach is to use behavioural and cognitive techniques to try to change their female thoughts and cognitions to male ones. However, a vast majority of those with gender dysphoria approach treatment adamant that it is their biological sex that is wrong and not their gender identity beliefs, so gender identity change procedures tend to be used relatively infrequently. In one early study, Barlow, Reynolds & Agras (1973) report using behaviour therapy techniques with a 17-year-old gender dysphoric male who wanted to change his gender identity rather than his biological sex. They used operant reinforcement methods to shape up male-related mannerisms and behaviours, and also used classical conditioning techniques such as aversion therapy to reduce the sexual attractiveness of men. Even though these techniques were primarily behaviour-oriented (rather than using methods aimed at directly changing cognitions and beliefs), they did appear to have some success – at a 5-year follow-up the client had acquired a male identity and sexually preferred women to men (Barlow, Abel & Blanchard, 1979).

CLINICAL PERSPECTIVE: TREATMENT IN PRACTICE BOX 11.2
GENDER REASSIGNMENT SURGERY

WHAT DOES MALE-TO-FEMALE GENDER REASSIGNMENT INVOLVE?

For a man wishing to become a woman, treatment would mean taking female hormones for at least 1 year before any irreversible surgery would take place. The hormones reduce body hair, cause breast development and generally make the body shape and skin texture more feminine.

The person would also have to live as a woman, full-time, for a minimum of 1 year before any surgery can be authorized. During this period, some transsexuals may choose to have facial hair removed by electrolysis, may undergo cosmetic surgery to make their face more feminine or learn to raise the pitch of their voice. When a patient feels ready, they may apply for medical approval of reassignment surgery. The clinical team will review the patient's progress to see how well they've adapted to their new role, and depending on the results of this evaluation, surgery may then be approved.

Gender reassignment involves major surgery. Under general anaesthetic, the testicles and erectile tissue of the penis are removed. An artificial vagina is then created and lined with the skin of the penis, where the nerves and blood vessels remain largely intact. Tissue from the scrotum is then used to create the labia, and the urethra is shortened and repositioned appropriately.

WHAT DOES FEMALE-TO-MALE GENDER REASSIGNMENT INVOLVE?

For a woman wanting to become a man, taking the male hormone testosterone leads to beard growth and muscle development. On the whole, these changes can't be reversed later. As early as 6 months into this programme, it may be possible to have a mastectomy (breast removal). This makes it much easier for the person to appear as a man in public. After at least a year of hormone treatment, the ovaries and uterus are removed.

For many female-to-male transsexuals, this is as far as they will go with surgery. Going further is more complex, costly and difficult to achieve. For those who do continue, phalloplasty (penis construction) and testicle implants are available. It is also possible to create a male urethra and to move the clitoris to the head of the penis.

Source: Adapted from http://www.mind.org.uk/.

Studies such as this suggest that a gender identity that is inconsistent with biological sex might be successfully changed, and supplementing behaviour therapy methods with CBT approaches designed to directly challenge and change dysphoric gender identity beliefs may make such treatments even more effective. However, as we outlined at the beginning of this section, the vast majority of individuals with gender dysphoria are adamant that it is their biological sex that they want to change and not their gender identity – so the opportunities to develop more integrated therapies for gender identity may be limited.

SELF-TEST QUESTIONS

11.4.1 Diagnosis and Description of Gender Dysphoria
- What is gender dysphoria?
- What are the main DSM-5 diagnostic criteria for gender dysphoria?
- What is the evidence that gender dysphoria exhibits in children?

11.4.2 The Aetiology of Gender Dysphoria
- Is there any evidence that hormonal imbalances might play a role in the development of gender dysphoria?
- What is the evidence that abnormalities in certain brain areas may be associated with gender dysphoria?
- What is the evidence that there is an inherited component to gender dysphoria?

11.4.3 The Treatment of Gender Dysphoria
- What is gender reassignment surgery, and what are the progressive stages of this treatment?
- What is the evidence that gender reassignment surgery is a successful treatment for gender dysphoria?
- What techniques are available for changing a client's gender identity (rather than their biological sex)?

SECTION SUMMARY

11.4 GENDER DYSPHORIA

Many individuals have a sense of gender dysphoria, in which they feel they have a gender identity that is incompatible with their biological sex. When this gender dysphoria causes significant distress and affects social, occupational and other important areas of functioning, DSM-5 provides a series of criteria for the diagnosis of gender dysphoria. Only a modest amount of research is available on the aetiology of gender dysphoria but there is a known inherited element to the disorder, although it is far from clear how this inherited component is transmitted and manifested. Treatment for gender dysphoria is largely through a structured procedure ending in gender reassignment surgery, which attempts to alter the individual's biological sex. There are a few successful attempts in the literature to change gender identity beliefs, but gender dysphoria sufferers usually prefer to change their biological sex rather than their gender identity beliefs.

The key points are:

- Some people develop a sense of *gender dysphoria* in which they feel that their gender is the opposite to their biological sex.
- Gender dysphoria is found in both adults and children.

11.4.1 Diagnosis and Description of Gender Dysphoria
- Individuals with gender dysphoria exhibit a strong desire to live as a member of the opposite biological sex, and this may lead them to acquire the physical appearance and mannerisms of the opposite sex.
- Prevalence rates for gender dysphoria are estimated to be around 0.005–0.014% in natal males and 0.002–0.003% in natal females.

11.4.2 The Aetiology of Gender Dysphoria

- Gender dysphoria does appear to be highly heritable, but it not clear yet how the genetic component is either transmitted or how it is manifested.

11.4.3 The Treatment of Gender Dysphoria

- Many individuals with gender dysphoria want to resolve their conflict between gender identity and biological sex by changing their biological sex rather than vice versa.

- Changing biological sex is usually undertaken through a process of *gender reassignment surgery*, which ends in changing the person's basic biological features to be congruent with their gender identity.

- While the vast majority of those who complete gender reassignment surgery are satisfied with the outcome, up to 42 per cent of those who apply for gender reassignment surgery drop out before completing the treatment.

11.5 SEXUAL AND GENDER PROBLEMS REVIEWED

Sexual behaviour is usually a central feature of our psychology. A satisfying sex life is an important contributor to quality of life, and our sexual urges and attractions can determine how we view ourselves and construct our self-identity. This being the case, it is not surprising that when we encounter problems related to sexual activity it can be an important source of psychological distress.

Sexual dysfunctions represent a set of diagnosable disorders of the normal sexual cycle, and can be identified as problematic at various points in this cycle (namely disorders of desire, arousal, orgasm and resolution). The causes of sexual dysfunctions are diverse and include biological and organic factors, psychological factors, and interpersonal problems. At one time, the open discussion and treatment of sexual problems was considered taboo, but over the past 50 years the liberalisation of attitudes towards sex has meant the development of a range of treatments for such disorders.

In contrast to those who report problems with normal sexual performance, there are those who exhibit high frequencies of sexual activity that is triggered by or directed at inappropriate targets. These are collectively known as paraphilic disorders, and some reflect sexual behaviour that becomes centred on unusual objects or stimuli (e.g. fetishistic disorder, transvestic disorder), while others may involve non-consenting persons (e.g. paedophilic disorder, exhibitionistic disorder, voyeuristic disorder). Some of these activities acquire their status as psychopathologies because they are associated with personal distress or impairment of normal daily activities (e.g. fetishistic disorders). Others are not necessarily associated with personal distress but are diagnosed as disorders because they are activities directed at non-consenting others. As such, these latter examples tend to represent criminal behaviours as well as diagnosable psychopathologies (e.g. paedophilic disorder, exhibitionistic disorder). Much of the research on the aetiology of paraphilic disorders has centred on those disorders that represent criminal activities or sexual offences – largely because of the need to help identify and treat such offenders. Treatments for paraphilic disorders are also relatively underdeveloped, largely because of the problems involved in treating people whose behaviour represents sexual offending. Because a number of the paraphilic disorders are sexual offences, much effort has been channelled into developing relapse-prevention procedures designed to reduce the probability of reoffending.

Finally, many individuals feel they have a gender identity that is incompatible with their biological sex, and this is known as gender dysphoria. Gender dysphoria can be experienced in both childhood and adulthood. Because a large majority of those with gender dysphoria are adamant that it is their biological sex they want to change (and not their incompatible gender identity), many opt for gender reassignment surgery in a radical attempt to make their biology compatible with their gender identity.

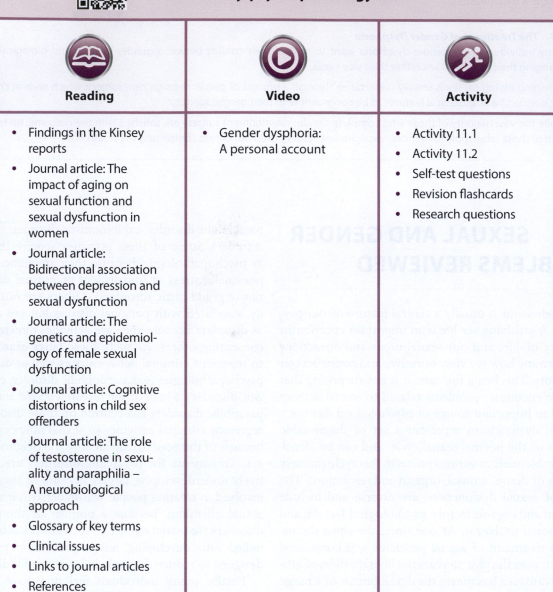

Reading

- Findings in the Kinsey reports
- Journal article: The impact of aging on sexual function and sexual dysfunction in women
- Journal article: Bidirectional association between depression and sexual dysfunction
- Journal article: The genetics and epidemiology of female sexual dysfunction
- Journal article: Cognitive distortions in child sex offenders
- Journal article: The role of testosterone in sexuality and paraphilia – A neurobiological approach
- Glossary of key terms
- Clinical issues
- Links to journal articles
- References

Video

- Gender dysphoria: A personal account

Activity

- Activity 11.1
- Activity 11.2
- Self-test questions
- Revision flashcards
- Research questions

12 Personality Disorders

 To access the online resources for this chapter go to
www.wiley-psychopathology.com/ch12

ROUTE MAP OF THE CHAPTER

This chapter begins by discussing some of the issues surrounding diagnosis of personality disorders raised during the development of DSM-5. It then moves on to describe the 10 diagnostically independent personality disorders listed by DSM-5. We then move on to discuss the diagnostic criteria for these disorders and describe studies that have provided data on their prevalence. The section on aetiology reviews the available evidence on how the different personality disorders are thought to develop and what childhood and adolescent predictors and risk factors might help us to forecast personality disorders in adulthood. The chapter then describes and reviews methods of treating people with a diagnosis of personality disorder, and the range of difficulties involved in these treatments.

CHAPTER OUTLINE

12 Personality Disorders

LEARNING OUTCOMES

When you have completed this chapter, you should be able to:

1. Discuss contemporary issues in the diagnosis of personality disorders.

2. Describe the main diagnostic criteria for the DSM-5 listed personality disorders and evaluate some of the controversial issues concerning both diagnosis and comorbidity.

3. Describe and evaluate the main theories of the aetiology of a number of personality disorders, particularly Cluster A

disorders, antisocial personality disorder, borderline personality disorder and Cluster C disorders.

4. Describe and evaluate the factors that make the treatment of people with a diagnosis of personality disorder problematic.

5. Describe and evaluate three or four psychological therapies that have been developed to treat people with a diagnosis of personality disorder.

My name is Claire, and I am a 28-year-old female. I have always known that something wasn't right with me, but over time I learnt the survival technique called denial. I made my first suicide attempt at age 16 and was quickly yanked out of the hospital by a mother who undoubtedly knew that I was just 'putting on an act'. I had explosive rages at friends, family and even strangers. My first 'tantrums', as my mother called them, began at age 1. I was never happy, never satisfied, always looking for that adrenaline rush to try to fill the void in my life. There was always – and to a certain degree, still is – that missing piece of me. My pattern of unstable relationships was unbearable, love/hate, attracted/disgusted, happy/miserable . . . all or nothing. For a long time, I blamed my problems on other people. I would have times where I would dissociate during a rage when I was of school age only to be told in the office that I hit my best friend for no reason. After time my rages were only directed at strangers and my family. I only have two basic emotions – mad and madder. The consequences of anyone knowing that the pretty, talented, rich girl wasn't perfect were too steep. My mother made sure of that. I have had a few major depressive episodes and I have had only one more suicide attempt in adulthood. I have been on antidepressants for 5 years for help with depression but they haven't helped with my intense mood swings in my interpersonal relationships. I consider myself now to be a low-functioning 'borderline' because I haven't worked a steady job in about 4 years and I began to self-mutilate last year. I really didn't think that picking at my skin with pins and tweezers – until I had gaping holes all over my body, including my face – was anything but a nervous habit.

Claire's Story
(Claire is diagnosed with borderline personality disorder and bipolar disorder)

Introduction

We all have personalities. Personalities tend to be enduring features of individuals that determine how we respond to life events and experiences, and they also provide a convenient means by which others can label and react to us. To this extent, a personality is a global term that describes how you cope with, adapt to, and respond to a range of life events, including challenges, frustrations, opportunities, successes and failures. A personality

is something that we inwardly experience ourselves and outwardly project to others. While personalities tend to be relatively enduring in their main features, most people will learn and evolve with their experiences, and they will learn new and effective ways of behaving that will enable them to adapt with increasing success to life's demands. In contrast, some others possess an ingrained and unchanging way of dealing with life's challenges. They rarely learn to adapt their responses or learn new ones. They develop a form of dealing with life events that are fixed and unchanging – despite the fact that they may have maladaptive consequences. They can also introduce disruption and hardship into the lives of others, and frequently cause emotional distress to themselves and those they interact with. Such characteristics are typical of those individuals who are diagnosed with **personality disorders**.

> **personality disorders** A group of disorders marked by persistent, inflexible, maladaptive patterns of thought and behaviour that develop in adolescence or early adulthood and significantly impair an individual's ability to function.

For the purposes of clinical diagnosis, DSM-5 defines a personality disorder (PD) as 'an enduring pattern of inner experience and behaviour that deviates markedly from the expectations of the individual's culture, is pervasive and inflexible, has an onset in adolescence or early adulthood, is stable over time, and leads to distress and impairment' (DSM-5, p.645). They are often associated with unusual ways of interpreting events, unpredictable mood swings, or impulsive behaviour. Two of the most well-known of these disorders are *borderline personality disorder* (BPD), characterized by major and regular shifts in mood, impulsivity and temper tantrums, and an unstable self-image, and *antisocial personality disorder* (APD), which is characterized by a chronic indifference to the feelings and rights of others, lack of remorse, impulsivity, and pursuit of the individual's own goals at any cost. Individuals with APD are often labelled as 'sociopaths' or 'psychopaths'.

Individuals diagnosed with a personality disorder will frequently deny their psychopathology, will often be unable to comprehend that their behaviour is contrary to conventional and acceptable ways of behaving, and will not associate their own psychological difficulties with their own inflexible ways of thinking and behaving. As a consequence, such disorders are very difficult to treat because they represent ingrained ways of thinking and acting.

Claire's story describes the experiences and feelings of an individual with borderline personality disorder. This account displays features that are common to a number of personality disorders. *Claire* exhibits frequent mood changes (mood lability), impulsive and aggressive reactions to situations, chronic depression, self-harm and suicide attempts, impaired occupational and social functioning, and an enduring disruptive pattern of behaviour that has been apparent from childhood into adulthood. As we will see later, many personality disorders are also associated with poor or unstable self-image and are frequently comorbid with other mental health problems – particularly depression (both major depression and bipolar disorder) and many of the anxiety disorders (Ehrt, Brieger & Marneros, 2003; Johnson, Cohen, Skodol, Oldham *et al.*, 1999).

12.1 CONTEMPORARY ISSUES IN THE DIAGNOSIS OF PERSONALITY DISORDERS

There have been numerous concerns about how personality disorders have been traditionally categorized and diagnosed, and while DSM-5 has retained the categorical approach to diagnosis outlined in its predecessor, DSM-IV-TR, DSM-5 also includes an alternative model that could be used to generate research on other diagnostic approaches. To fully explain these issues, we will (1) briefly describe the traditional diagnostic categories in DSM-IV-TR (also the ones retained in DSM-5 – see section 12.2 below), (2) explain the important problems that surround this traditional approach, and (3) describe the alternative model proposed in DSM-5.

12.1.1 The Categorical Approach to Personality Disorders in DSM-IV-TR and DSM-5

DSM-IV-TR listed 10 diagnostically independent personality disorders and these were organized into three primary clusters (and this is still the way that DSM-5 categorizes personality disorders in its main diagnostic section): (1) odd/eccentric personality disorders, (2) dramatic/emotional personality disorders, and (3) anxious/fearful personality disorders.

Those personality disorders grouped in Cluster A all have characteristics that resemble many of the symptoms of schizophrenia (see Chapter 8) but, unlike schizophrenia sufferers, there is no apparent loss of touch with reality, nor the experiencing of sensory hallucinations. However, people with Cluster A disorders may behave in ways that are indicative of delusional thinking (e.g. paranoid personality disorder) or exhibit rambling or poorly organized speech (e.g. schizotypal personality disorder). The three subtypes of Cluster A are (1) paranoid personality disorder, (2) schizotypal personality disorder, and (3) schizoid personality disorder.

Cluster B includes people diagnosed with dramatic/emotional personality disorders who tend to be erratic in their behaviour, self-interested to the detriment of others, emotionally labile and attention-seeking. These are arguably the most problematic of the personality disorders in terms of the extremes of behaviour that they generate, and the emotional and personal distress that they inflict on others. This category includes (1) antisocial personality disorder (APD), (2) borderline personality disorder (BPD), (3) narcissistic personality disorder, and (4) histrionic personality disorder.

Finally, as the name suggests, people with an anxious/fearful personality disorder (Cluster C) exhibit anxious and fearful behaviour. However, unlike the main anxiety disorders, the anxious and fearful behaviour exhibited will have been a stable feature of their behaviour from late childhood into adulthood, and it is usually not possible to identify a specific experience or life event that might have triggered this fear and anxiety. Anxious/fearful personality disorders may be comorbid with some anxiety disorders (e.g. social anxiety disorder, panic disorder), where triggers for the latter can be identified. But the pattern of behaviour exhibited by individuals with anxious/fearful personality disorders generally tends to represent ingrained ways of dealing and coping with many of life's perceived threats. The three disorders described in Cluster C are (1) avoidant personality disorder, (2) dependent personality disorder and (3) obsessive compulsive personality disorder.

12.1.2   Problems with the Traditional Categorical Model

Many clinicians and researchers have argued that personality disorders do not exist as 'categories' – that is, they are not discrete disorders that an individual either possesses or does not possess, but they are in fact dimensional extensions of 'normal' personality traits (e.g. Costa & MacRae, 1990). This is problematic in a number of ways for the all-or-none approach to diagnosis of personality disorders that DSM-IV-TR had taken.

Firstly, there is evidence for a dimensional approach to personality disorders from the finding that extreme scores on conventional measures of personality, such as the 'five-factor' model are highly associated with personality disorders (Trull, Widiger, Useda, Holcomb et al., 1998; Costa & MacRae, 1990; Samuel & Widiger, 2008). This finding probably resonates with our own intuitive view that we ourselves and many of the people we know exhibit to some extent and in some circumstances the traits that we might associate with personality disorders (e.g. mood swings, impulsive behaviour, paranoia, lack of social conscience). This suggests that personality disorders may not be *disorders* as such, but simply represent extreme cases on conventional personality dimensions.

Secondly, another conceptual difficulty with the traditional diagnostic model of personality disorders is that many of them contain characteristics that overlap

(e.g. impulsivity, poor self-image), and so there is a real temptation for clinicians to diagnose more than one personality disorder in a single individual (Grilo, Sanislow & McGlashan, 2002). Indeed, perhaps paradoxically, DSM-IV-TR often defined personality disorders in ways which either (1) allowed a very heterogeneous group of individuals to be diagnosed under a single diagnostic label, and for borderline personality disorder (BPD) in particular there were almost 100 different permutations of symptoms that would result in a diagnosis of BPD, or (2) allowed clinicians to diagnose multiple comorbidity of personality disorders in a single individual.

Thirdly, a number of the existing personality disorder categories are particularly rare in the general population (e.g. histrionic personality disorder, dependent personality disorder) and may therefore not represent useful independent disorder categories (Samuels, Eaton, Bienvenu, Brown et al., 2002; Trull, Jahng, Tomko et al., 2010).

Finally, personality disorders may not be as stable over time as the definitions in both DSM-IV-TR and DSM-5 might imply. Studies suggest that as many as half of the individuals diagnosed with a personality disorder, do not receive the same diagnosis two years later (Shea, Stout, Gunderson, Morey et al., 2002; Grilo, Shea, Sanislow, Skodol et al., 2004). They may still be high on measures of those personality traits, but not high enough to meet the strict diagnostic criteria set by DSM-IV-TR. This suggests that a dimensional approach to measuring and diagnosing personality disorders might be more appropriate than the traditional all-or-none approach.

12.1.3   DSM-5's Alternative Model

The alternative diagnostic model proposed as a basis for further research in DSM-5 has three discrete types of personality ratings that contribute to a diagnosis (Skodol, Clark, Bender, Krueger et al., 2011). These are **level of personality functioning**, **personality disorder types** and **personality trait domains and facets**. This system is designed to provide ratings of an individual's personality on a series of personality dimensions (rather than diagnosing in an all-or-none categorical way) and reduces the

level of personality functioning
Disturbances in self and interpersonal functioning are at the core of personality disorders, with the severity of impairment indicating whether the individual may have more than one personality disorder.

personality disorder types   Each of six personality disorder traits specified in the alternative diagnostic schemes published in DSM-5.

personality trait domains and facets   In the alternative classification of personality disorders published in DSM-5, there are five personality trait domains covering negative affectivity, detachment, antagonism, disinhibition, and psychoticism.

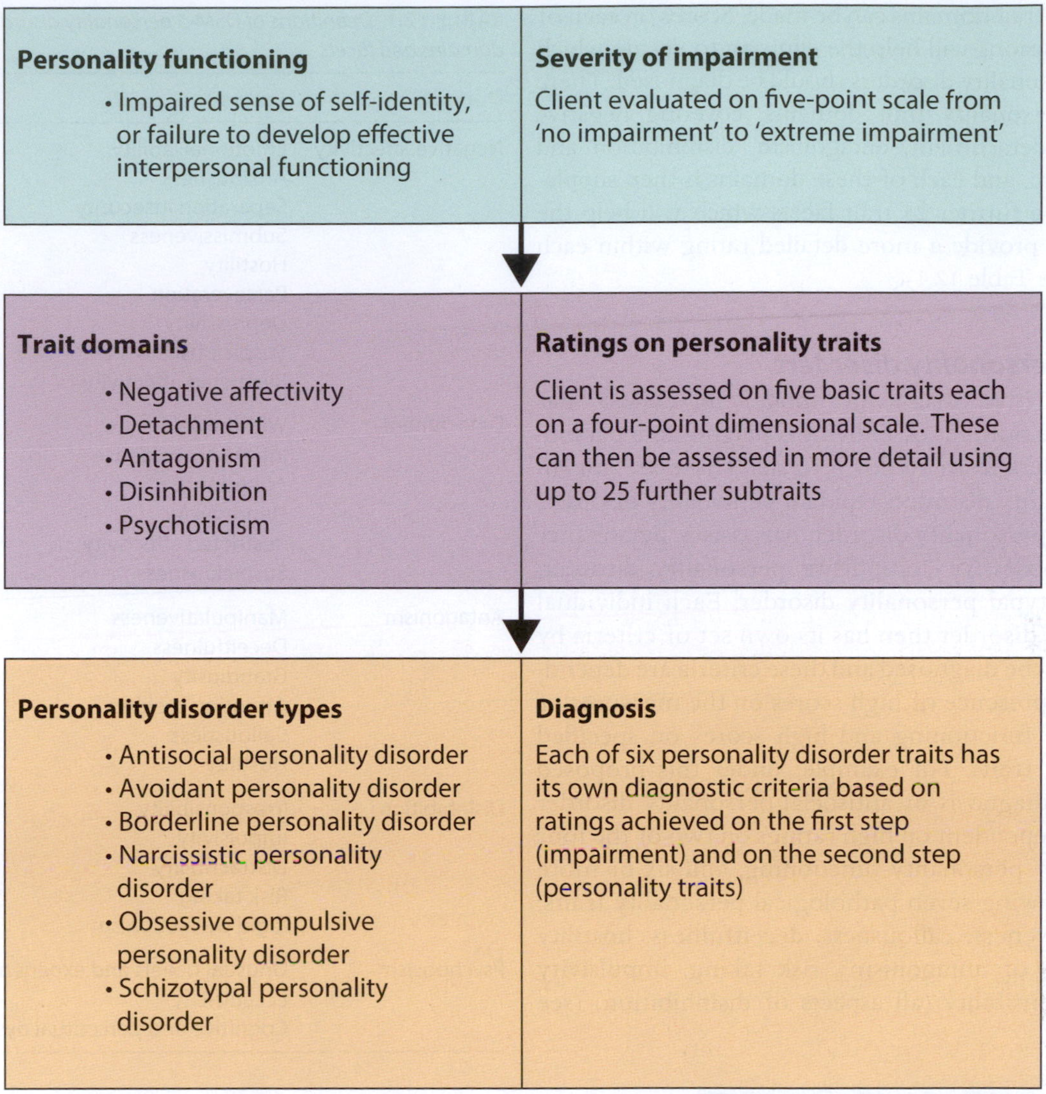

Personality functioning	Severity of impairment
• Impaired sense of self-identity, or failure to develop effective interpersonal functioning	Client evaluated on five-point scale from 'no impairment' to 'extreme impairment'

Trait domains	Ratings on personality traits
• Negative affectivity • Detachment • Antagonism • Disinhibition • Psychoticism	Client is assessed on five basic traits each on a four-point dimensional scale. These can then be assessed in more detail using up to 25 further subtraits

Personality disorder types	Diagnosis
• Antisocial personality disorder • Avoidant personality disorder • Borderline personality disorder • Narcissistic personality disorder • Obsessive compulsive personality disorder • Schizotypal personality disorder	Each of six personality disorder traits has its own diagnostic criteria based on ratings achieved on the first step (impairment) and on the second step (personality traits)

FIGURE 12.1 *Steps in evaluating personality*
In the alternative diagnostic model for personality disorders described in DSM-5, diagnosis progresses through three relatively independent steps: (1) assessing personality functioning to determine whether there is impairment typical of psychopathology; (2) a more comprehensive analysis of personality traits rated along a series of dimensions; and (3) determining whether the information collected in steps 1 and 2 meet the diagnostic criteria for any of six specific personality disorders.

number of personality disorder categories from 10 down to six. This model also provides information about personality *functioning* (i.e. do an individual's personality traits allow them to function adequately at both an emotional and behavioural level?) and whether they possess pathological personality traits. These various assessment processes are shown schematically in Figure 12.1.

Level of personality functioning

Disturbances in both self- and interpersonal functioning are at the core of personality disorders, and functioning

in these areas predicts the presence of a personality disorder, with the severity of this impairment indicating whether the individual may have more than one personality disorder. Impairments to one's sense of self include inability to regulate emotions and self-esteem, and disturbances of interpersonal functioning include inability to empathize and lack of desire and capacity for intimacy (Bender, Morey & Skodol, 2011).

Pathological personality traits

Once impairments in personality functioning have been established, a more comprehensive analysis of personality trait domains can be made. Scores on each of these dimensions will help the clinician to decide which specific personality disorders should be diagnosed. There are five personality trait domains, covering negative affectivity, detachment, antagonism, disinhibition and psychoticism, and each of these domains is then supplemented by a further 25 trait facets which will help the clinician to provide a more detailed rating within each domain (see Table 12.1).

Specific personality disorders

The alternative diagnostic model in DSM-5 has reduced the number of individual diagnosable personality disorders from 10 down to six. These are antisocial personality disorder, avoidant personality disorder, borderline personality disorder, narcissistic personality disorder, obsessive compulsive personality disorder, and schizotypal personality disorder. Each individual personality disorder then has its own set of criteria by which it can be diagnosed and these criteria are dependent on the presence of high scores on the measures of personality functioning and high scores on specified personality traits. For example, under this proposed scheme, a diagnosis of antisocial personality disorder would be dependent on high ratings on two of the four elements of personality functioning, and six or more of the following seven pathological personality traits: manipulativeness, callousness, deceitfulness, hostility (all aspects of antagonism), risk taking, impulsivity and irresponsibility (all aspects of disinhibition) (see Table 12.1).

TABLE 12.1 *Definitions of DSM-5 personality disorder trait domains and facets*

Domain	Facets
Negative affectivity	Emotional lability
	Anxiousness
	Separation insecurity
	Submissiveness
	Hostility
	Perseveration
	Depressivity
	Suspiciousness
	Restricted affectivity
Detachment	Withdrawal
	Intimacy avoidance
	Anhedonia
	Depressivity
	Restricted affectivity
	Suspiciousness
Antagonism	Manipulativeness
	Deceitfulness
	Grandiosity
	Attention seeking
	Callousness
	Hostility
Disinhibition	Irresponsibility
	Impulsivity
	Distractibility
	Risk taking
	Rigid perfectionism
Psychoticism	Unusual beliefs and experiences
	Eccentricity
	Cognitive and perceptual dysregulation

SELF-TEST QUESTIONS

- What are the problems associated with the current categorical approach to diagnosing personality disorders?
- What is the process for diagnosing personality disorders in DSM-5's alternative model?

SECTION SUMMARY

12.1 CONTEMPORARY ISSUES IN THE DIAGNOSIS OF PERSONALITY DISORDERS

Hopefully this discussion has given you an insight into how the diagnosis of personality disorders may develop in the immediate future and has provided you with some of the reasons why diagnosis might need to change. However, the American Psychiatric Association decided *against* introducing these changes with the publication of DSM-5 and agreed to provide more time for further research on the alternative, dimensional approach. If you are interested in the proposed diagnostic criteria for DSM-5's alternative model, these can be found on the book's website at www.wiley-psychopathology.com.
   The key points are:

- DSM-5 retains previous diagnostic criteria by defining personality disorders on a categorical rather than dimensional basis.
- DSM-5 also discusses a dimensional approach to diagnosing personality disorders, which it hopes will generate further research.

12.2 PERSONALITY DISORDERS AND THEIR DIAGNOSIS

The diagnostic approach adopted in the main body of DSM-5 is the traditional categorical one also found in DSM-IV-TR (as opposed to the dimensional alternative described in section 12.1.3) and the categorical perspective is the one we will use here. According to this approach, only when personality traits are inflexible and maladaptive and cause significant functional impairment or distress are they diagnosed as personality disorders. To help the clinician identify when personality traits have become maladaptive in this way, DSM-5 provides a set of general criteria, which is shown in DSM-5 Summary Table 12.1. The main criterion is that a person's inner experience and behaviour must differ markedly from expectations of the individual's culture and be reflected in at least two of the following four areas: cognition (e.g. ways of perceiving the self and other people), affectivity (e.g. the range, intensity and changeability of emotions), interpersonal functioning and impulse control. Further criteria stress that the patterns of behaviour and inner experience must be inflexible and pervasive, and lead to distress or social, occupational or other forms of impairment.

Apart from these general criteria, DSM-5 then specifies criteria for 10 separate types of personality disorder. These are grouped into clusters which cover (1) odd/eccentric personality disorders, (2) dramatic/emotional personality disorders, and (3) anxious/fearful personality

DSM-5 SUMMARY TABLE 12.1 *Criteria for general personality disorder*

- An ongoing rigid pattern of thought and behaviour that is significantly different from the expectations of the person's culture, displaying manifestation in two or more of the following areas:
  - Cognition
  - Affectivity
  - Interpersonal functioning
  - Impulse control
- The pattern is constant and long-lasting and can be traced back to adolescence or early childhood
- The pattern leads to distress or impairment in social, occupational and other areas of life
- The symptoms are not better accounted for by another mental disorder or due to the effects of a substance or other medical condition

disorders (see Table 12.2). The following sections describe each of these clusters and the diagnosable personality disorders listed in each.

12.2.1 Odd/Eccentric Personality Disorders (Cluster A)

Those personality disorders grouped in Cluster A all have characteristics that resemble many of the symptoms of schizophrenia (see Chapter 8) but, unlike schizophrenia sufferers, there is no apparent loss of touch with reality, nor the experiencing of sensory hallucinations. However, people with Cluster A disorders may behave in ways that are indicative of delusional thinking (e.g. paranoid personality disorder) or exhibit rambling or poorly organized speech (e.g. schizotypal personality disorder). The three subtypes of **odd/eccentric personality disorders** are (1) paranoid personality disorder, (2) schizoid personality disorder, and (3) schizotypal personality disorder.

> **odd/eccentric personality disorders** Personality disorders grouped in Cluster A, the three subtypes of which are (1) paranoid personality disorder, (2) schizotypal personality disorder and (3) schizoid personality disorder.

Paranoid personality disorder

Those with **paranoid personality disorder** exhibit an enduring pattern of distrust and suspiciousness of others (DSM-5 Summary Table 12.2). They will interpret innocent remarks as threatening and will interpret the intentions of others as malevolent. They find 'threatening' hidden meaning in everything and their distrust of others is pervasive and unchanging. If someone points out to them that their paranoid interpretation of events may be wrong, they will inevitably begin to distrust the person who brought

> **paranoid personality disorder** A personality disorder characterized by an enduring pattern of distrust and suspiciousness of others.

TABLE 12.2 *The three clusters of personality disorders in DSM-5*

Cluster A	
Odd/eccentric personality disorders	Paranoid personality disorder
	Schizoid personality disorder
	Schizotypal personality disorder
Cluster B	
Dramatic/emotional personality disorders	Antisocial personality disorder (APD)
	Borderline personality disorder (BPD)
	Narcissistic personality disorder
	Histrionic personality disorder
Cluster C	
Anxious/fearful personality disorders	Avoidant personality disorder
	Dependent personality disorder
	Obsessive compulsive personality disorder (OCPD)

DSM-5 SUMMARY TABLE 12.2 *Criteria for paranoid personality disorder*

- A universal distrust and suspicion of others to the extent that their motives are seen as malicious, as indicated by at least four of the following:
  - Suspicions that others are misusing, hurting or misleading him/her
  - Fixation with unjustifiable doubts about the trustworthiness of friends and suchlike
  - Unwilling to confide in others because of fear that the information will be used against him/her
  - Sees hidden threats in non-threatening words or events
  - Bears persistent grudges
  - Sees attacks on their character or status that are not apparent to others and is quick to react angrily
  - Has ongoing suspicions about the faithfulness of their sexual partner or spouse
- Symptoms do not occur exclusively during the course of any other psychotic disorder

DSM-5 SUMMARY TABLE 12.3 *Criteria for schizoid personality disorder*

- A persistent pattern of separation from social relationships and a restricted range of expression of emotions in relational situations, as indicated by at least four of the following:
  - Does not like or want close relationships
  - Prefers solitary activities
  - Take little or no pleasure in sexual experiences with another person
  - Takes pleasure in few, if any activities
  - Lacks close friends or confidents other than immediate relatives
  - Indifferent to the praise or criticism of others
  - Displays emotional coldness, detachment or flat expression
- Symptoms do not occur exclusively during the course of any other psychotic disorder

this to their attention. As a result, individuals with paranoid personality disorder avoid close relationships, are often spontaneously aggressive to others, become preoccupied with their mistrust of others to the point of it severely disrupting their work performance, and often feel that they have been deeply and irreversibly betrayed by others – even when there is no objective evidence for this. Individuals with paranoid personality disorder will even misinterpret well-intentioned and complimentary statements as criticism, such as interpreting an offer of help as implying that they are not doing a job or task well enough. Because such individuals are hypervigilant for the potential malevolent intentions of others, they will bear grudges, be quick to attack others for what are seen as critical comments, and gather trivial and often circumstantial evidence to support 'jealous' beliefs – especially about partners and colleagues. Because of their perceived need to constantly defend themselves against malevolent others, individuals with paranoid personality disorder feel a need to have a high degree of control over those around them and are frequently involved in litigious disputes. They also appear to deploy an attributional style that blames others for everything that goes wrong in their life (Fenigstein, 1996) and this external locus of control is very similar to the attributional style found in schizophrenics with paranoid delusions (Bentall, 1994).

Schizoid personality disorder

Individuals with this disorder are often described as 'loners' who have very few, if any, close relationships with others (except perhaps a single first-degree relative).

Those suffering with **schizoid personality disorder** fail to express a normal range of emotions and appear to get little sensory or intellectual reward from any activities (DSM-5 Summary Table 12.3). They prefer to spend most of their time by themselves and choose jobs and pastimes that do not involve them in interactions with others (e.g. jobs such as a road sweeper or night watchman) and they can be quite successful and efficient at their jobs if relatively little social contact with others is involved. However, they seem to be largely unaffected by both praise and criticism, and prefer mechanical abstract activities – such as computer or mathematical games – to real-life experiences. It has been suggested that there may be some link between the symptoms of autism and a diagnosis of schizoid personality disorder. For example, the lack of emotional responsiveness and the tendency to be withdrawn and uncommunicative resembles the symptoms of autism, and there is some evidence that there may be a modest genetic link between autism and schizoid personality disorder (Wolf, 2000).

> **schizoid personality disorder** A personality disorder in which individuals are often described as 'loners' who fail to express a normal range of emotions and appear to get little reward from any activities.

Schizotypal personality disorder

Individuals with **schizotypal personality disorder** usually exhibit 'eccentric' behaviour marked by odd patterns of thinking and communication, and discomfort with close personal relationships. In particular, they often exhibit unusual ideas of

> **schizotypal personality disorder** A personality disorder characterized by 'eccentric' behaviour marked by odd patterns of thinking and communication.

reference: they believe that unrelated events pertain to them, that they have extrasensory abilities, or that they can influence events external to them in a 'magical' way. For example, they may believe that their partner taking the dog for a walk was a result of them thinking earlier that this needed to be done; or they may indulge in ritualized, superstitious behaviour such as walking back and forth past a lamppost five times in an attempt to prevent harm from occurring to a friend or relative. Because of these magical beliefs, they will often become involved with unconventional groups interested in such topics as astrology and extraterrestrial phenomena, such as alien abduction, and fringe religious groups. Their speech may have eccentric characteristics, be excessively rambling, and they may use words in unusual ways – but they are able to communicate information and do not exhibit the incomprehensible 'word salads' and derailment typical of schizophrenia (see section 8.1.3). Individuals with schizotypal personality disorder find it very difficult to interact in normal social situations; they become anxious, and may even develop paranoid symptoms. As a result they often have few, if any, close friends, they are often viewed by others as 'loners', and they tend to drift aimlessly and lead unproductive lives (Skodol, Gunderson, McGlashan, Dyck et al., 2002). Like all of the personality disorders, these characteristics appear to develop in early adulthood and persist over much of the individual's lifetime. There is a tendency for schizotypal personality disorder to manifest differently in males and females, with females tending to

exhibit the positive symptoms typical of magical thinking and ideas of reference while males tend to show more negative symptoms such as emotional withdrawal (DSM-5 Summary Table 12.4). Finally, one persistent problem with the diagnosis of schizotypical personality disorder is that it tends to be highly comorbid with the other personality disorders, in particular paranoid personality disorder and avoidant personality disorder (Morey, 1988), which suggests there may be some common aetiological factors across these different disorders.

There is some evidence that the schizotypal disorder may be very closely related to schizophrenia. Firstly, schizotypal personality disorder is found to be significantly more common in individuals who have biological relatives with schizophrenia than those who do not (Nicolson & Rapoport, 1999), suggesting a possible inherited link between the two. Secondly, schizotypal personality disorder is significantly more likely to be found in the offspring of individuals with schizophrenia than in the offspring of individuals diagnosed with anxiety disorders or no mental disorder (Hans, Auerbach, Styr & Marcus, 2004). Thirdly, some of the symptoms of schizotypal personality disorder can be successfully treated with antipsychotic drugs also used to treat schizophrenia (Schulz, Schulz & Wilson, 1988). Fourthly, cognitive studies have shown that many of the attentional and working memory deficits found in schizophrenia are also apparent in individuals diagnosed with schizotypal personality disorder (Barch, Mitropoulou, Harvey, New et al., 2004). Finally, neuroimaging studies show that schizotypal personality disorder shares many forms of brain pathology in common with schizophrenia, suggesting it may be a schizophrenia spectrum condition (Fervaha & Remington, 2013). This kind of evidence suggests that schizotypal personality disorder is closely related in many ways to schizophrenia and may even represent a risk factor for schizophrenia (Nigg & Goldsmith, 1994).

DSM-5 SUMMARY TABLE 12.4 *Criteria for schizotypal personality disorder*

- A persistent pattern of social and relational shortfalls, evidenced by a lack of ease with, and reduced ability for, close relationships, as well as distortions and peculiarities of behaviour as shown by at least five of the following:

  - Beliefs or perceptions which are irrelevant, innocuous or unrelated

  - Odd beliefs that influence behaviour and are not within subcultural norms

  - Strange perceptions of what is occurring around them

  - Vague or other odd thinking and speech

  - Suspicious or paranoid ideas

  - Inappropriate or constricted emotional expression

  - Odd, eccentric or strange behaviour or appearance

  - Lacks close friends or confidents other than immediate relatives

  - High levels of social anxiety despite familiarity

- The pattern does not occur during the course of schizophrenia or other psychotic disorder

12.2.2 Dramatic/Emotional Personality Disorders (Cluster B)

People diagnosed with **dramatic/emotional personality disorders** tend to be erratic in their behaviour, self-interested to the detriment of others, emotionally labile and attention-seeking. These are arguably the most problematic of the personality disorders in terms of the extremes of behaviour that they generate and the emotional and personal distress that they inflict on others. In this category we will describe the symptoms of (1) antisocial personality disorder (APD), (2) borderline personality disorder (BPD),

dramatic/emotional personality disorders Personality disorders grouped in Cluster B, including (1) antisocial personality disorder, (2) borderline personality disorder, (3) narcissistic personality disorder, and (4) histrionic personality disorder.

SCHIZOTYPAL PERSONALITY DISORDER

Ian is 23 and lives at home with his parents. He is unemployed. He spends most of his time watching TV and often simply sits and stares into space. He says he just feels 'out of it' a lot of the time. He reports that he seems to see himself from outside, as if watching himself in a film and reading from a script. He has tried a few jobs but never manages to persist at one for very long. At his last job, which was in a DIY store, several customers complained to the manager about Ian talking to them in a rambling and vague way – often about irrelevant things. This led to Ian being sacked from this job. Ian doesn't understand why people don't seem to like him and get along with him. He notices that people move away from him on public transport or avoid talking to him in queues, but nothing he seems to do or say changes this and he now tries to avoid interactions with others because they make him anxious. He has no close relationships and complains of feeling lonely and isolated.

Clinical Commentary

Ian shows many of the diagnosable symptoms of schizotypal personality disorder, including unusual ideas of reference (feeling he is in a film), vague and circumstantial speech in conversations, suspiciousness and paranoia about others, a lack of close relationships, and feelings of anxiety in interactions with others. Currently, these characteristics have led to Ian being unemployed and leading the life of a relatively uncommunicative 'loner' who shows little emotion.

(3) narcissistic personality disorder, and (4) histrionic personality disorder.

Antisocial personality disorder

The fundamental feature of **antisocial personality disorder (APD)** is an enduring disregard for, and violation of, the rights of others. This begins in childhood (with a history of symptoms of conduct disorder; see section 16.2.2) and continues into adulthood. The behaviour of individuals with APD deviates substantially from what we would consider to be normal standards of social behaviour, morality and remorse, and is very closely linked with adult criminal behaviour. For example, a survey of prison populations in 12 Western countries found that 47 per cent of male inmates and 21 per cent of female inmates met the diagnostic criteria for APD, and this is around 10 times the prevalence rate found in the general population (Fazel & Danesh, 2002). Similarly, a DSM diagnosis of APD has also been shown to be a significant predictor of subsequent criminal behaviour (Fridell, Hesse, Jaeger & Kühlhorn, 2008). To be diagnosed with APD, an individual must be at least 18 years of age and display some of the following characteristics: (1) failure to conform to social and legal norms, (2) deceitfulness and impulsivity, (3) irritability and aggressiveness, (4) consistent irresponsibility (e.g. repeated failure to honour obligations), and

antisocial personality disorder (APD) A personality disorder, the main features of which are an enduring disregard for, and violation of, the rights of others. It is characterized by impulsive behaviour and lack of remorse, and is closely linked with adult criminal behaviour.

(5) lack of remorse. The term '**sociopath**' – or '**psychopath**' – is sometimes used to describe this type of personality disorder, and such people are compulsive and persistent liars (Seto, Maric & Barbaree, 2001) who are self-centred to the point of happily gaining profit at the expense of others. Some researchers have distinguished different types of APD and there appear to be those whose antisocial behaviour is a result of unresolved emotional conflicts resulting from adverse early experiences (e.g. childhood neglect or abuse), and those antisocial behaviours stem primarily from impulsivity in reaction to negative emotions (Karpman, 1941; Poythress, Edens, Skeem, Lilienfeld *et al.*, 2010). Individuals with APD show a disregard for the safety of themselves and others, and this is evidenced by their impulsive, often aggressive, behaviour and failure to plan ahead. Such individuals are frequently involved in motor accidents as a result of reckless driving (McDonald & Davey, 1996) or commit physical and sexual assaults (including spouse beating or child beating). Impulsivity and irresponsibility can be identified in the daily lives of individuals with APD – they frequently may quit a job without a realistic plan for getting another one, or default on debts, fail to provide child support, or fail to support other dependents on a regular basis.

Prior to 1980, APD or psychopathy was defined primarily by personality traits such as egocentricity, deceit,

sociopath A person with a personality disorder manifesting itself in extreme antisocial attitudes and behaviour.

psychopath A term often used to describe individuals diagnosed with antisocial personality disorder.

DSM-5 SUMMARY TABLE 12.5 *Criteria for antisocial personality disorder (APD)*

- Pattern of indifference to and violation of the rights of others as shown by at least three of the following since the age of 15 years old:
  - Lack of conformity to social norms and regularly indulging in unlawful behaviours
  - Lying, pretending to be someone else or deceiving others for personal gain
  - Failure to plan ahead or impulsiveness
  - Irritability and aggressiveness leading to physical fights and assaults
  - Reckless indifference to own and other's personal safety
  - Consistent irresponsible behaviour
  - Lack of remorse
- The person is at least 18 years old
- The antisocial behaviour is not associated with symptoms of schizophrenia or mania

DSM-5 SUMMARY TABLE 12.6 *Criteria for borderline personality disorder (BPD)*

- A long-term display of instability of relationships, self-image and behaviour, as well as high levels of impulsivity beginning in early adulthood and indicated by at least five of the following:
  - Desperate attempts to avoid real or imagined abandonment
  - A pattern of unstable and intense interpersonal relationships, fluctuating between adulation and deprecation
  - Constantly unstable self-image and identity disturbance
  - Potentially self-damaging impulsivity in at least two areas such as sex, substance abuse and reckless driving
  - Repeated suicidal behaviour or self-mutilation
  - Emotional instability due to reactivity of mood
  - Unsuitable, intense anger or difficulty controlling anger
  - Stress-related paranoid idealisation or severe dissociative symptoms

shallow affect, manipulativeness, selfishness and lack of empathy. However, with the introduction of DSM-IV, APD has been defined more in terms of violations of social norms. The reason given for this shift in emphasis is that personality traits are difficult to measure, and it is easier to agree a diagnosis on the basis of well-defined behaviours (such as breaking laws or aggressive behaviours) (Widiger & Corbitt, 1993) – and these well-defined, antisocial behaviours are well-represented in the DSM-5 diagnostic criteria for APD (DSM-5 Summary Table 12.5). This shift in the diagnostic criteria has meant that APD has become very closely associated with criminal activity rather than being purely a psychopathology requiring treatment. Studies that have surveyed prison populations have indicated that the number of males in prisons that meet DSM-III-R or DSM-IV-TR criteria for APD range from 50–70 per cent (Fazel & Danesh, 2002; Widiger, Cadoret, Hare, Robins *et al.*, 1996). This indicates that the changes to the diagnostic criteria for APD over the years have moved this category more towards identifying criminals and criminal behaviour and away from identifying psychological factors that might give rise to such behaviour (such as lack of empathy, superficial interpersonal style, inflated sense of self-importance, and so on). There is a real possibility that this move towards defining APD in terms of antisocial activities could fudge the distinction between psychopathology in need of treatment and criminal behaviour in need of restraint.

Borderline personality disorder

The cardinal features of **borderline personality disorder (BPD)** are an enduring pattern of instability in personal relationships, a lack of a well-defined and stable self-image, regular and predictable changes in moods, and impulsive behaviour (DSM-5 Summary Table 12.6). These characteristics are pervasive and will have endured from childhood into adulthood, and can all be seen in the personal account given by *Claire* at the beginning of this chapter.

In particular, individuals with BPD appear to have a significant fear of abandonment and rejection. This leads them to fall into close and conflict-ridden relationships after as little as a single meeting with someone; but they are just as likely to fall out with that person if they interpret the person's behaviour as uncaring or not attentive enough – and this may often be the case, because the feelings of the individual with BPD may not be shared by the other person (Modestin & Villiger, 1989). Although their behaviour becomes unpredictable and emotional when their expectations for a relationship are not met, they are also riddled with fear about being rejected and losing that relationship. This leads to rapid, ill-tempered mood changes if the individual does not feel that things 'are going their way'. The results of this emotional roller-coaster and fear of abandonment and rejection are (1) regular and unpredictable shifts in self-image characterized by changing personal goals, values and career aspirations, (2) prolonged bouts of depression (Luca, Luca & Calandra, 2012), deliberate self-harm (Sansone, Wiederman & Sansone, 2000), suicidal ideation and actual suicide attempts (Venta, Ross, Schatte & Sharp, 2012),

borderline personality disorder (BPD) A personality disorder, the main features of which are instability in personal relationships, a lack of well-defined and stable self-image, regular and unpredictable changes in moods and impulsive behaviour.

and (3) impulsive behaviour such as drug abuse (Trull, Sher, Minks-Brown, Durbin & Burr, 2000), physical violence, and inappropriate promiscuity (Sansone & Wiederman, 2009). Because of its close association with mood disorders, depression and suicide, some researchers have argued that BPD may well be a form of depression (Gunderson & Elliott, 1985), but in fact it is just as likely to be comorbid with anxiety disorders or with depressive symptoms (Grant, Chou, Goldstein, Huang et al., 2008). Zanarini, Frankenburg, Dubo, Sickel et al., (1998) found that 96.3 per cent of individuals diagnosed with BPD met the criteria for a mood disorder (major depression, dysthymia, bipolar II disorder), but 88.4 per cent also met the criteria for an anxiety disorder, with panic disorder (47.8 per cent) and social phobia (45.9 per cent) being the most prevalent. Interestingly, 64.1 per cent met the criteria for substance use disorder – reaffirming the link between BPD and impulsive behaviour – whereas 53 per cent met the criteria for eating disorders. Another important finding is that BPD is often comorbid with PTSD, with 30.2 per cent of those with a diagnosis of BPD also having a diagnosis of PTSD, and 24.2 per cent of those with PTSD also having a diagnosis of BPD (Pagura, Stein, Bolton, Cox et al., 2010), a finding that is consistent with the view of some clinicians that BPD may be a form of PTSD – especially since many individuals with BPD report a history of traumatic experience related to physical and sexual child abuse (Heffernan & Cloitre, 2000). At the very least, these data suggest that BPD represents a behavioural style that may put an individual at severe risk for a wide range of other psychopathologies.

Narcissistic personality disorder

The individual with **narcissistic personality disorder** routinely overestimates their abilities and inflates their accomplishments, and is characterized by a pervasive need for admiration and a lack of empathy with the feelings of others. Such people believe they are superior to others, and expect others to recognize this. They will constantly fish for compliments, and are likely to become angry when such compliments are not forthcoming (Gramzow & Tangney, 1992). In their relationships, they will expect great dedication from others and may often exploit others for their own gain. They also have a lack of empathy and either cannot recognize, or simply ignore, the desires and feelings of others. Because of this, they tend to have a history of problematic relationships and Campbell (1999) found that individuals with narcissistic personality disorder tend to prefer partners that are openly admiring rather than openly loving (DSM-5 Summary Table 12.7). However, beneath the façade of

narcissistic personality disorder A personality disorder in which individuals overestimate their abilities, inflate their accomplishments, have a pervasive need for admiration and show a lack of empathy with the feelings of others.

DSM-5 SUMMARY TABLE 12.7 *Criteria for narcissistic personality disorder*

- An ongoing pattern of grandiosity, need for adoration and lack of empathy, beginning in early adulthood and indicated by at least five of the following:

  - Has a highly exaggerated sense of self-importance and self-achievement

  - Preoccupied with illusions of unlimited success, power, beauty or ideal love

  - Believes that they are special and can only be understood by people of similar speciality

  - Commands excessive admiration

  - Has unreasonable expectations of favourable treatment

  - Exploits others for personal gain

  - Lacks compassion and cannot identify with the needs and feelings of others

  - Often jealous of others and believes that others are jealous of them

  - Shows conceited, self-important behaviour or attitudes

bragging about their achievements and their talents is a very fragile self-esteem and individuals with narcissistic personality disorder constantly need to seek reassurance. When this is not forthcoming, they become angry and aggressive. Because of the apparent lack of empathy and the tendency to exploit others for self-benefit, narcissistic personality disorder has been compared to antisocial personality disorder (APD), and it may be a subtype of APD in that some features of the disorder (such as a grandiose self-image) predict future criminal or delinquent behaviour (Calhoun, Glaser, Stefurak & Bradshaw, 2001).

Histrionic personality disorder

Individuals with **histrionic personality disorder** are attention-seeking and uncomfortable or unhappy when they are not the centre of attention (DSM-5 Summary Table 12.8). Their behaviour is often dramatic and their language theatrical and exaggerated. For example, they may always seek to be the centre of attention at a party, and, if not, may suddenly do something dramatic to gain attention (such as make up an intriguing story about themselves or someone else, or create a scene). Similarly, they will make extravagant expressions of emotion towards friends and colleagues and have a style of speech that is excessively impressionistic but lacking in detail. For example, they may describe someone as a 'wonderful person' but then be unable to describe any features that contribute to this assessment. As a result, such individuals are often viewed as shallow, self-dramatising and

histrionic personality disorder A personality disorder in which an individual is attention-seeking and uncomfortable or unhappy when not the centre of attention.

DSM-5 SUMMARY TABLE 12.8 *Criteria for histrionic personality disorder*

- A continuous pattern of high levels of emotionality and attention-seeking, beginning in early adulthood and indicated by at least five of the following:

  - Unhappy in situations where they are not the centre of attention

  - Shows high levels of inappropriate sexually suggestive or provocative behaviour in interactions with others

  - Displays rapidly shifting and shallow demonstrations of emotion

  - Frequently uses personal appearance to draw attention to self

  - Has an excessively impressionistic and detail-lacking style of speech

  - Is self-dramatic, over-theatrical and uses exaggerated expressions of emotion

  - Is easily influenced by others

  - Feels that relationships are more intimate than they actually are

easily influenced. They will draw attention to themselves by exaggerating their illnesses (Morrison, 1989) or dressing provocatively or seductively. Because of their shallow and flirtatious nature, individuals with histrionic personality disorder often find it difficult to make lasting relationships and this is frequently a main reason why such individuals seek therapy. Although there was traditionally a bias towards diagnosing this disorder more often in women than in men (Anderson, Sankis & Widiger, 2001), surveys suggest that it is equally distributed across men and women (Mattia & Zimmerman, 2001). The prevalence rate of histrionic personality disorder is low (0.4 per cent) and it is highly comorbid with other personality disorders such as BPD, narcissistic and dependent personality disorders (Bakkevig & Karterud, 2010). This poor construct validity may mean that is it likely to be excluded from future versions of DSM, although the characteristics of exhibitionism and attention-seeking may be ones that might be included in any reformulation (Bakkevig & Karterud, 2010).

12.2.3 Anxious/Fearful Personality Disorders (Cluster C)

As the name suggests, people with a personality disorder in this cluster exhibit anxious and fearful behaviour. However, unlike anxiety disorders, the anxious and fearful behaviour exhibited will have been a stable feature of their behaviour from late childhood into adulthood and it is usually not possible to identify a specific experience or life event that might have triggered this fear and anxiety.

Anxious/fearful personality disorders may be comorbid with anxiety disorders (e.g. social phobia, panic disorder), where triggers for the latter can be identified. But the pattern of behaviour exhibited by individuals with anxious/fearful personality disorders generally tends to represent ingrained ways of dealing and coping with many of life's perceived threats. The three disorders to be described in Cluster C are (1) avoidant personality disorder, (2) dependent personality disorder, and (3) obsessive compulsive personality disorder.

> **anxious/fearful personality disorders** The exhibition of persistent anxious and fearful behaviour which is not usually linked to a specific trigger experience or life event.

Avoidant personality disorder

The main features of **avoidant personality disorder** are persistent social inhibition (characterized by avoidance of a wide range of social situations), feelings of inadequacy, and hypersensitivity to negative evaluation and criticism (DSM-5 Summary Table 12.9). These tendencies appear in late childhood or early adolescence and are exhibited across a range of different contexts, including occupational and social contexts and in interpersonal interactions generally. Individuals with avoidant personality disorder are fearful of criticism, disapproval and rejection, and they automatically assume that others will be critical and disapproving. They will avoid school, work and all group activities because of these fears, and are unable to form close relationships unless there is an assurance

> **avoidant personality disorder** A personality disorder the features of which are avoidance of a wide range of social situations, feelings of inadequacy, and hypersensitivity to negative evaluation and criticism.

DSM-5 SUMMARY TABLE 12.9 *Criteria for avoidant personality disorder*

- A persistent pattern of social reticence, feelings of inadequacy and hypersensitivity to criticism, beginning in early adulthood and indicated by at least four of the following:

  - Avoiding occupational activities that involve high levels of interpersonal contact due to fears of criticism or rejection

  - Unwilling to engage with others unless certain of approval and being liked

  - Shows restraint in intimate relationships for fear of ridicule or shame

  - Fixation with disapproval or rejection in social situations

  - Inhibited in new relationships due to feelings of inadequacy

  - Feels that they are socially incompetent, unappealing or inferior to others

  - Highly reluctant to take part in any new activities because of the potential for embarrassment

of uncritical acceptance. They are generally shy, and cannot easily talk about themselves for fear of being ridiculed or shamed. They also have a clear bias for interpreting ambiguous information and comments in a negative way (e.g. someone saying 'I was surprised by the quality of your work' would be interpreted as being critical or disapproving, even though their comments could equally be interpreted as praise). Individuals with avoidant personality disorder are particularly ill at ease with strangers and will usually avoid interactions with strangers at all costs. As a result they are reluctant to take risks, engage in new activities or even accept job promotions that might involve greater responsibility and interaction with others.

People with avoidant personality disorder generally have low self-esteem and will frequently feel angry at themselves for being withdrawn and not enjoying the apparent social rewards and intimate relationships experienced by others (Lynum, Wilberg & Karterud, 2008). As you can imagine, avoidant personality disorder has many features in common with social anxiety disorder (see section 6.2) and many individuals diagnosed with avoidant personality disorder also receive a diagnosis of social anxiety disorder (Widiger, 2001; Marques, Porter, Keshaviah, Pollack *et al.*, 2012). However, individuals with social anxiety disorder tend to be made anxious by social situations where particular levels of performance might be required (e.g. making a work presentation or having a job interview) whereas the personality disorder is more associated with (1) fear of personal interactions and social relationships generally, (2) the criticism and rejection that they believe will be associated with these types of experiences, and (3) difficulties in being open with people they are close to (Turner, Beidel, Dancu & Keys, 1986; Marques, Porter, Keshaviah, Pollack *et al.*, 2012). In addition, there is some evidence that avoidant personality disorder is associated with avoidance behaviour generally, and individuals diagnosed with the disorder show greater avoidance of emotion, novelty and other non-social events than non-sufferers (Taylor, Laposa & Alden, 2004). However, some clinicians believe that avoidant personality disorder and social anxiety disorder are both components of a broader **social anxiety spectrum** (Tillfors & Ekselius, 2009) and there is evidence to suggest that (1) the severity of the symptoms of antisocial personality disorder are significantly increased if it is comorbid with social anxiety disorder (Ralevski, Sanislow, Grilo, Skodol *et al.*, 2005), and (2) there is a genetic link between the two disorders, as evidenced by the fact that

social anxiety spectrum A spectrum of disorder proposed to include both avoidant personality disorder and social anxiety disorder.

CLIENT'S PERSPECTIVE 12.1
THOUGHTS ABOUT AVOIDANT PERSONALITY DISORDER

'The way I see it, people like us [with avoidant personality disorder] were born with brains that are very sensitive to social situations. As a child I used to get so frightened and scared that I probably unconsciously decided to build up a defence system against terrible feelings in order to protect myself. I just instinctively knew I had to do something, so my personality was formed in a way designed to avoid the harm. I hated the fact that other kids would be out to criticize me, so I adopted avoidance as a defence system. I had very low self-esteem, so I didn't think anyone liked me anyway. So, I tried to stay away from potentially harmful situations, and lived in a world of my own. When I was younger, my classmates used to tell me that at parties they would turn the lights down and dance, but I would sit in the corner playing with my bike lights. I would often stay off school and read books all day – that would comfort me because I liked the stories. My real life became less important to me and I didn't participate in social events apart from just trying to be pleasant when needed. As I grew older, I should have developed a different defence system, but I couldn't because I had become pretty much a social outcast and the fear of being criticized and rejected had got stronger. It was like I was in a vicious circle that I couldn't get out of.'

Clinical Commentary

In this personal account of avoidant personality disorder, the individual describes how her desire to avoid social encounters developed during childhood from a fear of being criticized (and possibly bullied) by her peers. When avoiding social encounters (e.g. by staying off school), she would reward these avoidance responses by indulging in enjoyable activities, such as reading stories she liked. At adolescence she discovers she has become something of a social outcast and this maintains her low self-esteem and feelings of not being liked, which further maintains social avoidance. She shows a number of the symptoms of avoidant personality disorder, including avoiding activities that involve significant interpersonal contact because of fears of criticism, disapproval or rejection, a preoccupation with being criticized or rejected in social situations, and views herself as socially inept and personally unappealing to others.

if an individual is diagnosed with one of the disorders, first-degree relatives of that individual are two to three times more likely to be diagnosed with *either* of them (Tillfors, Furmark, Ekselius & Fredrikson, 2001).

Dependent personality disorder

This disorder is characterized by a pervasive and excessive need to be taken care of that extends significantly beyond the caring relationships that most individuals would have with one another. Individuals with dependent personality disorder exhibit submissive and clinging behaviour and have great difficulty making everyday decisions (e.g. what clothes to wear) without receiving advice from significant others. They are usually passive and will allow others to make all important decisions for them, including where they should live, what job they should choose and how they should spend their free time. They have difficulty expressing disagreement with others and will often agree with things that they know to be wrong or inappropriate rather than risk losing the support and help of those they look to for guidance. They will also go to excessive lengths to secure support and guidance from others – even to the point of taking on jobs and tasks that they find unpleasant – and they will make regular self-sacrifices and tolerate continuous verbal, physical and even sexual abuse in order to retain their relationship with those they are dependent on (e.g. the wife who will tolerate her husband's infidelities, drunkenness and physical abuse because of fear of losing the support she needs or of being left to care for herself). Such individuals tend to be pessimistic and self-doubting, and belittle their own achievements. They will regularly 'tag along' with significant others in order not to be alone and will usually rebound from one relationship to another in order to ensure the continual care and attention they need (DSM-5 Summary Table 12.10).

The characteristics of dependent personality disorder appear to fall into two distinctive categories: (1) attachment/abandonment, in which the individual fears abandonment and constantly seeks attachment with significant others, and (2) dependency/incompetence, in which the individual has constant feelings of incompetence which drive them to rely on others (Gude, Hoffart, Hedley & Ro, 2004). Because of their self-doubting and over-dependence, individuals with dependent personality disorder often dislike themselves (Overholser, 1996), which may lead to depression, anxiety, eating disorders and suicidal ideation (e.g. Godt, 2002) (Photo 12.1).

Obsessive compulsive personality disorder

Individuals with this disorder show exceptionally perfectionist tendencies, including a preoccupation with orderliness and control at the expense of flexibility, efficiency and productivity. They will stick to rules, work schedules and prearranged procedures to such a degree that the overall purpose of the activity is lost. Diverging

from a preset schedule causes them significant distress, as does failing to achieve the highest of standards in the things they do, and their attention to detail and their inflexibility will often annoy other people because of the delays and inconvenience that this may cause (DSM-5 Summary Table 12.11). For example, they may hold up a work project by insisting that their component of the project has to be completed meticulously and in the way in which it was originally specified. Individuals with obsessive compulsive personality disorder nearly always plan ahead

DSM-5 SUMMARY TABLE 12.10 *Criteria for dependent personality disorder*

- An inescapable and extreme need to be taken care of, leading to submissive and clingy behaviour and fear of separation, beginning in early adulthood and indicated by at least five of the following:
  - Cannot make everyday decisions without an unnecessarily high level of advice and reassurance from others
  - Needs others to assume the majority of responsibility for the major areas of his/her life
  - Struggles to express disagreement with someone for fear of loss of support
  - Has difficulty initiating/doing things on his/her own
  - Feels uncomfortable or afraid when left alone due to a fear of not being able to care for oneself
  - Urgently seeks to secure another caring and supportive relationship when the previous one ends
  - Is unrealistically obsessed with fears of being left to take care of oneself

Gesellschaft der Musikfreunde, Wien, Austria/Bridgeman Images.

PHOTO 12.1 *From letters and biographies of Wolfgang Mozart it was assumed he may have suffered from bipolar disorder because of periods of depression followed by bouts of mania. However, more recent analyses suggest he may have been suffering from dependent personality disorder because of his mood lability, impulsiveness and his negative reactions to his wife's absences (Huguelet & Perroud, 2005).*

DSM-5 SUMMARY TABLE 12.11 *Criteria for obsessive compulsive personality disorder (OCPD)*

- An ongoing pattern of concern with orderliness, perfection and mental and interpersonal control, at the expense of flexibility, openness and efficiency, beginning in early adulthood and indicated by at least four of the following:

  - An obsession with details, rules, lists, organisation or schedule to the exclusion of the main point of the activity

  - Perfectionism that hinders task completion

  - Excessive devotion to work to the prohibition of social and leisure activities

  - Inflexibility about matters of morals, ethics or values

  - Is unable to dispose of worn-out or worthless objects despite them having no sentimental value

  - Reluctant to delegate to others unless they submit to exactly his/her way of doing things

  - Hoards money and is reluctant to spend on their self or others

  - Is rigid and stubborn

meticulously and are unwilling to contemplate changes to their plan. This means that even hobbies and recreational activities are approached as serious tasks requiring organisation and scheduling. For example, they will need to plan a visit to a restaurant well in advance, the menu needs to be checked to ensure that everyone will be happy with what is on offer, and the quality of the restaurant's service must be checked with friends who have been there or by consulting dining reviews. If this planning is disrupted (e.g. if the restaurant is closed when the party arrives), this will cause the individual considerable distress and a spontaneous alternative will be difficult for them to consider. If things are not done 'their way', this also causes distress, which may be taken to unnecessary extremes (such as asking a child to ride his/her bike in a straight line or telling people that there is only one way to wash the dishes). They will then become upset or angry if people do not comply, although the anger is rarely expressed directly. Because of this they will rarely delegate tasks, but insist on doing them themselves, and often become viewed as 'workaholics'. Their perfectionist tendencies also mean that they often end up hoarding things rather than throwing them away; they will also adopt a miserly attitude to spending, believing that money should not be wasted. Because of this, they often end up living at a standard well below what they can afford. OCPD is one of the most prevalent of the personality disorders, with a recent large-scale epidemiology study recording a lifetime prevalence rate of 7.8 per cent and rates being similar between males and females (Grant, Mooney & Kushner, 2012).

CASE HISTORY 12.2

OBSESSIVE COMPULSIVE PERSONALITY DISORDER (OCPD)

Jane likes to describe herself as a perfect mother. She takes pride in keeping an orderly household and attending all of her daughters' horse-riding events, while also being office manager in an insurance company. She knows the schedules of each family member and follows rigid routines to make sure everyone gets to work or school on time. Jane gets very upset when her teenage daughters want to go out with friends at weekends or in the evenings. She says it takes away from their family time and all of her efforts and planning are wasted. She refuses to go out for the evening if this interferes with her planned weekly activities in the house. Her husband doesn't mind Jane planning his schedule but he does complain when he helps out with the household chores because she consistently complains that he hasn't followed her instructions properly. For example, if he does the shopping but does not get the right discounted items, Jane gets upset and accuses him of being careless and extravagant. Jane continually tells everyone that if she wants something doing properly, she has to do it herself, and she will religiously clean the house in exactly the same way every week – whether things are dirty and untidy or not.

Clinical Commentary

Jane exhibits many of the symptoms of OCPD and probably has the minimum four symptoms required for a DSM-5 diagnosis. These are a preoccupation with details, rules, lists, order, organisation or schedules to the extent that the major point of the activity is lost (e.g. she will do the housework each week in exactly the same way regardless of whether this is necessary), she is excessively devoted to work and productivity to the exclusion of leisure activities, she is reluctant to delegate tasks or to work with others unless they submit to exactly her way of doing things, she shows rigidity and stubbornness, and adopts a miserly spending style. From this brief case description you can see that Jane frequently gets upset and anxious about family life because of her rigid perfectionism (and this may well lead to a comorbid diagnosis of generalized anxiety disorder, see Chapter 6) and her rigid and inflexible behaviour also puts severe strains on family relationships.

While these characteristics may seem very similar to the symptoms of obsessive compulsive disorder (OCD) (see Chapter 6), the exact relationship between OCPD and OCD has been the subject of debate for some time. Some clinicians have argued that OCPD is a precursor for the development of OCD (Krockmalik & Menzies, 2003). However, OCPD is not a necessary precursor of OCD and studies have found the prevalence of OCPD in patients diagnosed with OCD as ranging only between 23 and 34 per cent (Albert, Maina, Forner & Bogetto, 2004; Lochner, Serebro, van der Merwe, Hemmings *et al.*, 2011). However, regardless of whether OCPD is a risk factor for OCD, individuals diagnosed with comorbid OCPD and OCD do appear to exhibit more severe symptoms, are more functionally impaired and are likely to develop other problems such as alcohol dependence and depression (Garyfallos, Katsigiannopoulos, Adamopoulou, Papazisis *et al.*, 2010; Gordon, Salkovskis, Oldfield & Carter, 2013).

To complete Activity 12.1 go to
www.wiley-psychopathology.com/
activities/ch12

SELF-TEST QUESTIONS

- Personality disorders generally consist of a loosely bound cluster of subtypes. What are the four common features of all personality disorders?

- What are the three clusters of personality disorders listed in DSM-5, what are the disorders listed in each cluster, and what are their main defining features?

- Can you list the diagnostic criteria for (1) antisocial personality disorder, and (2) borderline personality disorder?

- Schizophrenia spectrum disorder, bipolar disorder spectrum and society anxiety spectrum are broader disorder categories associated respectively with which individual personality disorders?

SECTION SUMMARY

12.2 PERSONALITY DISORDERS AND THEIR DIAGNOSIS

While the different personality disorders we have discussed may seem to take quite contrasting forms (e.g. some represent withdrawn and avoidant forms of behaviour, some are characterized by behavioural and emotional lability and impulsivity, and others are characterized by intense fears of criticism, rejection and abandonment), they are all assumed within DSM-5 to represent enduring patterns of behaviour that we would consider to be close to the borderline of what is adaptive/maladaptive, normal/abnormal or culturally acceptable/unacceptable. Because the behavioural styles of individuals with personality disorders can be conceptualized as being on normal personality dimensions – albeit at the extremes of these dimensions (Costa & MacRae, 1990) – there is an issue about what it is that is 'disordered' or 'abnormal' about personality disorders, and this is likely to be addressed with dimensional measurements for personality traits in future editions of DSM (see section 12.1.3).

The key points are:

- DSM-5 lists 10 diagnostically independent personality disorders that are organized into three primary clusters: (1) odd/eccentric – containing paranoid, schizoid and schizotypal personality disorders, (2) dramatic/emotional – containing antisocial, borderline, narcissistic and histrionic personality disorders, and (3) anxious/fearful – containing avoidant, dependent and obsessive compulsive personality disorders.

- *Paranoid personality disorder* is characterized by an enduring pattern of distrust and suspiciousness of others.

- Individuals with *schizoid personality disorder* are often described as 'loners' who fail to express a normal range of emotions and appear to get little reward from any activities.

- *Schizotypal personality disorder* is characterized by 'eccentric' behaviour marked by odd patterns of thinking and communication.

- The main features of *antisocial personality disorder (APD)* are an enduring disregard for, and violation of, the rights of others. It is characterized by impulsive behaviour, lack of remorse and is closely linked with adult criminal behaviour.

- The defining characteristics of *borderline personality disorder (BPD)* are instability in personal relationships, a lack of well-defined and stable self-image, regular and unpredictable changes in moods, and impulsive behaviour.

- The individual with *narcissistic personality disorder* overestimates their abilities, inflates their accomplishments, has a pervasive need for admiration, and also shows a lack of empathy with the feelings of others.

- Individuals with *histrionic personality disorder* are attention-seeking and are uncomfortable or unhappy when they are not the centre of attention.

- The main features of *avoidant personality disorder* are avoidance of a wide range of social situations, feelings of inadequacy, and hypersensitivity to negative evaluation and criticism.

- *Dependent personality disorder* is characterized by a pervasive and excessive need to be taken care of, submissive and clinging behaviour, and difficulty making everyday decisions without advice from others.

- Individuals with *obsessive compulsive personality disorder (OCPD)* show exceptionally perfectionist tendencies, including a preoccupation with orderliness and control at the expense of flexibility, efficiency and productivity.

- Many personality disorders are highly comorbid with other psychiatric disorders such as anxiety and mood disorders (including bipolar disorder, major depression, social anxiety disorder, panic disorder and PTSD).

12.3 THE PREVALENCE OF PERSONALITY DISORDERS

There has generally been some uncertainty about the actual prevalence rates of personality disorders within the general population, and this uncertainty stems from issues to do with: (1) reliability in the diagnosis of personality disorders (McGlashan, Grilo, Sanislow, Ralevski *et al.*, 2005; Paris, 2010); (2) potential gender bias in diagnosis of some of the disorders – particularly histrionic, borderline and dependent personality disorders (Widiger & Trull, 1993; Hartung & Widiger, 1998); and (3) the poor

temporal stability of personality disorder diagnoses over time (Zimmerman, 1994). This variability in estimated prevalence rates is reflected in the data presented in Table 12.3, showing a selection of sources providing prevalence rates from both American and European studies. These data suggest that the prevalence rate for personality disorders in the general population is between 10 and 14 per cent, which makes personality disorders one of the most common of the psychopathologies (see also Sansone & Sansone, 2011). But the variability in these figures across different studies makes it difficult to draw many conclusions about prevalence, except perhaps that obsessive compulsive personality disorder is probably the most common.

TABLE 12.3 *Personality disorders prevalence rates*

Cluster	Personality disorder	Prevalence rate in general population (DSM-IV-TR estimate)	Prevalence rate in general population (USA) (Grant *et al.*, 2004)	Prevalence rate in general population (Norway) (Torgersen *et al.*, 2001)	Prevalence rate in a community sample (UK) (Coid *et al.*, 2006)
	All personality disorders		14.7%	13.4%	10.7%
Cluster A (odd/eccentric personality disorders)	Paranoid	0.5–2.5%	4.4%	2.4%	0.7%
	Schizoid	'Uncommon'	3.1%	1.7%	0.8%
	Schizotypal	3%	–	0.6%	0.06%
Cluster B (dramatic/ emotional personality disorders)	Antisocial	3% in males 1% in females	3.6%	0.7%	0.6%
	Borderline	2%	–	0.7%	0.7%
	Histrionic	2–3%	1.8%	2.0%	0%
	Narcissistic	<1%	–	0.8%	0%
Cluster C (anxious/ fearful person-ality disorders)	Avoidant	0.5–1%	2.3%	5.0%	0.8%
	Dependent	–	0.4%	1.5%	0.1%
	Obsessive com-pulsive personality disorder	1%	7.8%	2.0%	1.9%

There are some significant gender differences in these prevalence rates. Coid, Yang, Tyrer, Roberts & Ullrich (2006) report that all personality disorder categories were more prevalent in men, but Widiger & Trull (1993) in their study found that 75 per cent of individuals diagnosed with borderline personality disorder were female. Coid *et al.* (2006) also found that personality disorders were highly comorbid, with the mean number of personality disorders per individual with a diagnosis being 1.92 (see Table 12.4). The differences in prevalence rates recorded by different studies may be explained by differences in sampling procedures, diagnostic procedures, number of disorder categories and cultural differences in the identification and diagnosis of personality disorders. Unfortunately, with the future changes proposed to the diagnosis of personality disorders, we are unlikely to get a clear picture of prevalence rates for some time to come!

There are also numerous risk factors for personality disorders and these include (1) low socio-economic class, (2) living in inner cities, (3) being a young adult, and (4) being divorced, separated, widowed or never married (Torgersen, Kringlen & Cramer, 2001; Grant, Hasin, Stinson, Dawson *et al.*, 2004). Childhood physical, verbal and sexual abuse is also a significant risk factor for developing a personality disorder (Johnson, Cohen, Brown, Smailes & Bernstein, 1999) – especially borderline personality disorder (Hefferman & Cloitre, 2000) – and significant levels of childhood verbal abuse increase the risk of a number of personality disorders, including paranoid, borderline, narcissistic and obsessive compulsive (Johnson, Cohen, Smailes, Skodol *et al.*, 2001). However, although these findings suggest that childhood abuse may well be an important factor in the development of a personality disorder in some individuals, it is unclear whether other types of risk factors – such as low socio-economic status, living in inner cities, being divorced, separated or never married – are causal factors in developing personality disorders or are simply outcomes of having a personality disorder.

Studies of those suffering from psychopathology suggest that individuals with personality disorders are amongst the most frequently treated by mental health professionals. In a study of psychiatric outpatients, Zimmerman, Rothschild & Chelminski (2005) found that slightly less than one-third of all psychiatric outpatients in their sample were diagnosed with at least one personality disorder. This is consistent with the fact that personality

TABLE 12.4 *Comorbidity of borderline personality disorder and other personality disorders with psychological disorders*

Disorder category	Disorder	Borderline personality disorder patients with other diagnoses	Other personality disorder patients with other diagnoses
Mood disorders	Major depression	83%	67%
	Dysthymia	39%	25%
	Bipolar II disorder	10%	1%
Substance abuse disorders	Alcohol abuse/dependence	52%	45%
	Drug abuse/dependence	46%	42%
Anxiety disorders	Panic disorder	48%	20%
	Agoraphobia	12%	3%
	Social anxiety disorder	46%	19%
	Specific phobia	32%	15%
	OCD	15%	6%
	PTSD	56%	21%
	Generalized anxiety disorder	13%	3%
Somatisation disorders	Somatisation disorder	4%	0%
	Hypochondriasis	5%	2%
	Somatoform pain disorder	4%	2%
Eating disorders	Anorexia nervosa	21%	13%
	Bulimia nervosa	26%	17%

Source: Data taken from Zanarini, Frankenburg, Dubo, Sickel *et al.* (1998). Diagnoses were determined using DSM-III-R criteria, which may give rise to some inconsistencies in comorbidity rates when compared with current DSM-5 criteria.

disorders are highly comorbid with other psychopathologies – particularly anxiety and mood disorders (Zanarini, Frankenburg, Dubo, Sickel, 1998) – and it is usually the comorbid and more specific disorder that has brought the individual into treatment. This reflects the view that the individual with a personality disorder will often view their behaviour as quite normal (because they have 'always' behaved like that), but what brings them to therapy are the more specific and distressing consequences of their behaviour such as unstable or turbulent relationships, sexual dysfunction, substance abuse, eating disorders, anxiety disorders such as panic disorder or social phobia, mood disorders, deliberate self-harm and suicide attempts.

Finally, because DSM-5 defines personality disorders in terms of behaviour that 'deviates markedly from the expectations of the individual's culture', we might expect some cultural differences in the rates at which different personality disorders are diagnosed. For example, in some countries it is seen as more acceptable for men to be domineering, demanding and competitive while women might adopt more submissive and dependent behaviours (see Alarcon, 1996). In such countries we might expect

behaviour patterns typical of antisocial or narcissistic personality disorder to be less prevalent in men and histrionic, avoidant and dependent personality disorders less prevalent in women because these behaviour patterns are considered to be relatively more acceptable. However, at present there is very little evidence to suggest that the prevalence rates of personality disorders do exhibit cultural differences, as might be predicted if diagnostic criteria are strictly applied. More cross-cultural studies are required in this respect.

Some studies have identified ethnicity as a factor affecting rates of diagnosis of personality disorder. For example, Chavira, Grilo, Shea, Yen et al. (2003) identified significantly higher rates of borderline personality disorder in Hispanic than in Caucasian and African Americans, and higher rates of schizotypal personality disorder in African Americans compared with Caucasians. McGilloway, Hall, Lee & Bhui (2010) found a lower prevalence of personality disorders among black compared with white patients in UK studies, but they conclude that this may indicate a neglect of personality disorder diagnosis among minority ethnic groups in the UK.

SELF-TEST QUESTIONS

- What is the estimated prevalence rate for personality disorders in the general population?
- Do prevalence rates for personality disorders vary with culture and ethnicity?

SECTION SUMMARY

12.3   THE PREVALENCE OF PERSONALITY DISORDERS

- The prevalence rate for personality disorders in the general population is around 13–14 per cent, which makes them one of the most common of the psychopathologies.

- Risk factors for developing a personality disorder include (1) low socio-economic status, (2) living in inner cities, (3) being a young adult, (4) being divorced, separated, widowed or never married, and (5) childhood neglect and childhood physical, verbal and sexual abuse.

12.4   THE AETIOLOGY OF PERSONALITY DISORDERS

Explaining the development of the extreme and enduring behavioural styles characteristic of personality disorders is still very much in its infancy. There will almost certainly be no overarching or all-inclusive theory of the aetiology of personality disorders because the different clusters represent quite different patterns of behaviour (e.g. eccentric

behaviours, dramatic and impulsive behaviours, dependent and avoidant behaviours), so we might expect that different clusters and, indeed, different personality disorders may be acquired in quite different ways. One characteristic that was thought to be common to all personality disorders was that the respective behaviour patterns were relatively enduring and can be traced back to childhood and early adolescence, suggesting that either inherited or developmental factors may be quite important across all of the personality disorders. However, the belief that personality disorders might be a lifetime affliction has been challenged, with research suggesting that personality disorder diagnoses have poor stability over time (Zimmerman, 1994) and 75 per cent of individuals with an early diagnosis of borderline personality disorder no longer meet diagnostic criteria after 10 to 15 years (Zanarini, Frankenburg, Hennen, Reich & Silk, 2006). So there is evidence that at least some personality disorders will either remit over time or will be responsive to effective treatments.

We will continue by looking at aetiological factors in each of the three personality disorder clusters.

12.4.1 Odd/Eccentric Personality Disorders (Cluster A)

As we mentioned earlier, individuals diagnosed with Cluster A personality disorders have characteristics that resemble many of the symptoms of schizophrenia, such as paranoid beliefs (paranoid personality disorder), they may be socially withdrawn with flat affect (schizoid personality disorder), or exhibit rambling or disorganized thoughts and speech (schizotypal personality disorder). As we shall see, these formalistic similarities between Cluster A disorders and schizophrenia have led researchers to argue that they are part of a broader *schizophrenia spectrum disorder* and so have causes that are closely linked to the aetiology of schizophrenia itself (Siever & Davis, 2004; Bergman, Harvey, Mitropoulou, Aronson et al., 1996). Before we discuss the schizophrenia spectrum approach, let us briefly mention some other approaches to explaining Cluster A disorders.

Psychodynamic approaches

In the case of both paranoid and schizoid personality disorders, psychodynamic theorists have argued that the causes of these disorders lie in the relationships that the sufferer had with their parents. In the case of paranoid personality disorder, parents may have been demanding, distant, overly rigid and rejecting (Manschreck, 1996), and the lack of love provided by parents makes the individual suspicious and lacking in trust of others (Cameron, 1974). In contrast, parents of individuals with schizoid personality disorder may have rejected or even abused their children, resulting in the child being unable to give or receive love (Carstairs, 1992). As we shall see later, there is certainly some evidence that individuals with personality disorders may have suffered childhood abuse and neglect (Johnson, Cohen, Brown, Smailes & Bernstein, 1999), so there is some supportive evidence for this view.

The schizophrenia spectrum disorder

There are three lines of evidence suggesting that Cluster A-type personality disorders are closely related to schizophrenia and make up a schizophrenia spectrum disorder. Firstly, there is considerable evidence suggesting

a genetic link between Cluster A disorders and schizophrenia. Studies have indicated that risk for all three types of Cluster A disorder is increased in relatives of individuals diagnosed with schizophrenia (Bernstein, Useda & Siever, 1993; Battaglia, Bernardeschi, Franchini, Bellodi & Smeraldi, 1995; Nigg & Goldsmith, 1994). Even in adopted children whose biological mothers have been diagnosed with schizophrenia, there is a significantly higher risk of developing schizotypal personality disorder than if the biological mother was not diagnosed with schizophrenia (Tienari, Wynne, Laksy, Moring et al., 2003). All of these studies suggest a genetic link between Cluster A personality disorders and schizophrenia. Secondly, individuals with Cluster A disorders have been shown to possess brain abnormalities that closely resemble those found in schizophrenia (Fervaha & Remington, 2013). For example, individuals with schizotypal personality disorder show abnormalities in frontal lobe and temporal lobe activation that are very similar to those found in individuals with schizophrenia (Siever & Davis, 2004). In addition, they also exhibit the enlarged ventricles frequently found in the brains of schizophrenics (Buchsbaum, Yang, Hazlett, Siegel et al., 1997), suggesting similarities in abnormal brain development across schizophrenia and schizotypal personality disorder. Thirdly, individuals with Cluster A disorders (particularly schizotypal personality disorder) also exhibit some of the physiological abnormalities possessed by individuals with schizophrenia, and these include impairment of smooth pursuit eye movements (see Chapter 8) and inability to inhibit the startle response to weak stimuli (Siever, Haier, Coursey, Sostek et al., 1982; Cadenhead, Swerdlow, Shafer, Diaz & Braff, 2000). Fourthly, individuals with Cluster A disorders also show many of the deficits in cognitive and executive functioning exhibited by individuals with schizophrenia, and these include impaired working memory, episodic memory, spatial attention, and reduced verbal IQ (Dickey, McCarley, Niznikiewicz, Voglmaier et al., 2005; Mitropoulou, Harvey, Zegarelli, New et al., 2005). Taking all of these factors into account, there is strong evidence linking schizotypal personality disorder to the aetiological factors implicated in schizophrenia generally, and schizotypical personality disorder has been explicitly included in DSM-5 in its chapter on schizophrenia spectrum disorders.

12.4.2 Dramatic/Emotional Personality Disorders (Cluster B)

Some of the Cluster B disorders share a number of characteristics in common, such as impulsivity (antisocial and borderline disorders), lack of empathy (antisocial and narcissistic disorders), emotional outbursts and aggressiveness (histrionic and borderline disorders). This suggests that there may be some common elements in the

IMPULSE-CONTROL DISORDERS

© Monkey Business Images. Used under license from Shutterstock.com.

Many of the personality disorders – especially Cluster B disorders – are characterized by impulsivity, including unpredictability in behaviour and aggressive outbursts. However, DSM-5 classifies a number of impulse-based problems separately. These are known as *disruptive*, *impulse-control* and *conduct disorders*, and are characterized by the failure to resist an impulse, drive or temptation to perform an act that is harmful to the person or to others. Examples of impulse-control disorders are:

Intermittent explosive disorder   Discrete episodes of failure to resist aggressive impulses that frequently result in criminal assaults or destruction of property.

Kleptomania   Recurrent failure to resist impulses to steal objects that either have little or no monetary or personal value (e.g. impulsive shoplifting).

Pyromania   Recurrent patterns of fire setting for pleasure, gratification or relief of tension.

In most of these disorders, the individual feels an increasing sense of tension or arousal before committing the impulsive act and then experiences pleasure, gratification or relief when the act is committed. Following the act, the individual will often suffer regret or guilt, suggesting that the sufferer is aware that their behaviour is wrong but are unable to control it (known as *ego dystonia*).

Many of the impulse-control disorders are frequently comorbid with personality disorders. For example, in one study 42 per cent of those diagnosed with kleptomania also met the criteria for a personality disorder (the most common were paranoid, schizoid and borderline) (Grant, 2004). However, impulse disorders are classified separately from personality disorders because they are also highly comorbid with a number of other disorders. For instance, kleptomania frequently co-occurs with substance use disorders and sufferers often have first-degree relatives who are themselves suffering from a substance use disorder (Grant, 2006; Dannon, Lowengrub, Aizer & Kotler, 2006). High rates of manic and depressive disorders have also been recorded amongst those with impulse-control disorders (Kim, Grant, Eckert, Faris & Hartman, 2006), but it is not clear whether these mood problems are causes or effects of the impulsive behaviour. For example, pathological gamblers often begin to feel depressed as their financial losses mount and their personal relationships are disrupted. Alternatively, some individuals who are initially depressed may find compulsive gambling gives them an exhilarating 'buzz' that distracts briefly from the pain of depression.

Those diagnosed with kleptomania steal regularly, impulsively and will usually steal items that have no financial or personal worth. Sufferers experience an often intense period of tension building up before the theft, but then experience relief and gratification afterwards. Thefts are usually undertaken alone, are not pre-planned and stolen goods may often be returned after the event. Individuals with kleptomania are usually aware that the act of stealing is wrong and senseless, and feel guilty and depressed about their actions. Opportunistic shoplifting is one common form of kleptomania, but studies suggest that only around 5 per cent of those convicted of shoplifting meet DSM criteria for kleptomania (DSM-IV-TR, p.668). Kleptomaniacs have been shown to rate their feelings of inner tension before stealing as significantly higher than undiagnosed shoplifters, and they also exhibit significantly greater feelings of relief after the crime (Sarasalo, Bergman & Toth, 1997).

A large-scale survey in the US estimated that the lifetime prevalence rate for impulse-control disorders was 24.8 per cent, with a median age of onset as early as 11 years of age (Kessler, Berglund, Demler, Jin *et al.*, 2005).

---

aetiology of these disorders, and, indeed, some theorists argue that some of the different Cluster B disorders may be different manifestations of a single underlying disorder with a common aetiology. For example, some researchers consider that antisocial personality disorder (APD) and borderline personality disorder (BPD) are the same underlying disorder that manifests in men as APD and women as BPD (Widiger & Corbitt, 1997), and narcissistic personality disorder shares antisocial behaviour, deceitfulness and lack of empathy and remorse with APD. However, as we shall see, most of the research on the aetiology of Cluster B disorders has been directed at attempting to explain the development of the behaviour patterns in individual disorders.

Antisocial personality disorder

The main behavioural characteristics of antisocial personality disorder are impulsivity, aggressiveness, deceitfulness, lying, irritability, repeated irresponsibility and lack of remorse, and a history of criminal activity and childhood conduct disorder. As with all personality disorders, the theoretical challenge with APD is to explain why certain individuals develop these behavioural styles and why they can be so enduring and often resistant to change. Because APD is closely associated with criminal and antisocial behaviour, considerable effort has been invested in attempting (1) to identify childhood and adolescent behaviours that may help to predict later adolescent and adult APD (e.g. patterns of childhood antisocial behaviour or childhood abuse), (2) to identify the developmental factors that may give rise to APD (e.g. factors associated with family and early environment), (3) to ascertain whether there is an inherited or genetic component to APD, and (4) to identify any biological or psychological processes that may be involved in APD (e.g. brain abnormalities or dysfunctional cognitive processes such as faulty beliefs). We will look separately at these approaches to understanding APD. One caution we must post at this stage is that much of the research on APD has been conducted using a variety of different methods of defining APD: some studies have used DSM diagnostic criteria while others have used earlier definitions of antisocial behaviour such as the concept of 'psychopathy' (Checkley, 1976) and only 20 per cent of people with a DSM diagnosis of APD will score high on measures of psychopathy (Rutherford, Cacciola & Alterman, 1999).

Childhood and adolescent behavioural precursors of APD
Because APD is closely associated with criminal behaviour, and on many occasions with violent or homicidal criminal behaviour, there has been a keen interest in attempting to identify risk factors for it. Identifying potential risk factors might allow clinicians to predict the development of APD from childhood behaviour patterns or childhood experiences and might identify individuals who may respond to early clinical intervention.

One of the best predictors of APD in adulthood is a diagnosis of *conduct disorder* (CD) during childhood in which the child exhibits a range of behavioural problems that include fighting, lying, running away from home, vandalism and truancy (Farrington, Loeber & van Kammen, 1990). This, however, begs the question of how such antisocial behaviours had developed in childhood and we may have to refer back to ineffective parenting practices, discordant and unstable family life, poor peer relationships and educational failure to trace the origins of these behaviours (Hill, 2003). Persistent and aggressive

behaviour before the age of 11 is also a good predictor of APD in adulthood (Robins, 1966), as is early fighting and hyperactivity (Loeber, Green, Lahey & Kalb, 2000) and low IQ and low self-esteem (Fergusson, Lynskey & Horwood, 1996). In particular, Loeber, Wung, Keenan, Giroux et al. (1993) have argued that there are three pathways that predict APD in adulthood. These are:

1. an 'overt' aggressive pathway that progresses from bullying to fighting to serious violence,

2. a 'covert' aggressive pathway that progresses from lying and stealing to more serious damage to property, and

3. an 'authority conflict' pathway that progresses through various degrees of oppositional and defiant behaviour.

Behaviours in the early stages of each of these pathways predict more serious specific antisocial behaviours later in life.

Many studies have emphasized that adolescent problem behaviours are strong predictors of adult APD. McGue & Iacono (2005) found that adolescent smoking, alcohol use, illicit drug use, police trouble and sexual intercourse (all before 15 years of age) each significantly predicted APD symptoms in later life. In fact, for those who exhibited four or more of these problem behaviours prior to age 15, there was a 90 per cent likelihood of subsequent APD diagnosis in males and a 35 per cent probability in females. Furthermore, a possible link between childhood ADHD and APD is discussed in Focus Point 12.2.

Perhaps disappointingly, most of these studies merely indicate that adult antisocial behaviour defined by APD is predicted by adolescent and childhood antisocial behaviour. However, such studies do demonstrate that the behaviour patterns are often enduring and that these behaviours during childhood and early adolescence should be taken as indicators of the possible need for intervention. For factors involved in causing APD we need to explore developmental, psychological and biological factors.

Developmental factors
There is a range of views about how familial factors might influence the development of APD and, because APD is an antisocial disorder, there has been much speculation about how maladaptive socialisation might have contributed to this pattern of behaviour. One important fact is that there is a high incidence of APD in the parents of individuals with APD (Paris, 2001), suggesting that one important developmental factor may be the learning of antisocial behaviours through modelling and imitation (although this may also indicate a genetic or inherited component – see below). For example, the children of parents with APD may often see aggressive and deceitful behaviour rewarded – especially if a parent has had a relatively successful

IS ATTENTION DEFICIT HYPERACTIVITY DISORDER (ADHD) A RISK FACTOR FOR ANTISOCIAL PERSONALITY DISORDER?

Some researchers have suggested that conduct disorder in childhood is not the only psychological diagnosis that predicts APD in later life. Lynam (1998) has argued that children with hyperactivity/attention deficits (such as attention deficit hyperactivity disorder) are 'fledgling psychopaths' who because of their impulsivity and attentional problems are likely to develop into long-term psychopaths – not least because their underlying problems are of a neuropsychological nature that are likely to be resistant to behavioural treatments. However, more recent studies that have been based on structured diagnostic interviews do not necessarily support this view. Lahey, Loeber, Burke & Applegate (2005) investigated whether a diagnosis of conduct disorder (CD) or ADHD in males between 7 and 12 years of age predicted a diagnosis of APD at 18–19 years. While conduct disorder predicted subsequent APD in around 50 per cent of the participants, ADHD predicted APD at rates no better than if the child had neither ADHD or CD at ages 7–12 (see Figure 1), suggesting that ADHD during childhood is not a significant differential predictor of APD in later life. More recent analyses suggest only a weak link between ADHD and APD in prospective studies (Klein, Mannuzza, Olazagasti, Roizen *et al.*, 2012), or that if youths with comorbid conduct disorder and ADHD do develop APD it is due to the levels of conduct disorder, not the influence of ADHD (Smith & Hung, 2012).

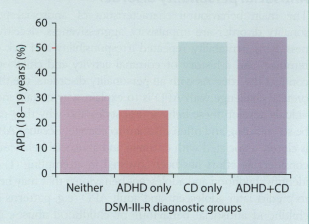

FIGURE 1 *Lahey* et al. *(2005) investigated whether a childhood diagnosis of conduct disorder (CD) or attention deficit/hyperactivity disorder (ADHD) predicted a diagnosis of antisocial personality disorder (APD) at 18–19 years of age. The results show that while around 50 per cent of those diagnosed with either CD or CD and ADHD went on to develop APD, ADHD did not predict subsequent APD any better than if a child had neither disorder.*
Source: Lahey, B.B., Loeber, R., Burke, J.D. & Applegate, B. (2005). Predicting future antisocial personality disorder in males from a clinical assessment in childhood. *Journal of Consulting and Clinical Psychology*, 73, 389–399. American Psychological Association. Reproduced with permission.

PREDICTORS OF ANTISOCIAL BEHAVIOUR AND VIOLENT CRIME

Antisocial personality disorder (APD) is closely associated with criminal and antisocial behaviour. Hence, efforts have been focused on attempting to identify childhood predictors of these behaviours. The hope here is that being able to identify such individuals at an early stage may prevent crime and enable either treatment or re-education programmes to be directed at individuals at risk of developing APD.

Some childhood and early adolescent predictors of APD that have been identified include:

- A diagnosis of conduct disorder in childhood
- Persistent and aggressive behaviour before the age of 11 years

- Fighting and hyperactivity
- Low IQ and low self-esteem
- Persistent lying
- Running away from home
- Vandalism
- Truancy
- Discordant and unstable family life
- Educational failure
- Adolescent smoking, alcohol use, illicit drug use, police trouble and sexual intercourse before the age of 15 years
- Having at least one parent diagnosed with APD
- Coming from a background of family violence, poverty and conflict.

criminal career. Alternatively, parents may have patterns of parenting which inadvertently reward their children for aggression, impulsivity and deceitfulness (Capaldi & Patterson, 1994). For instance, parents may try to calm down an aggressive or impulsive child by giving him/her toys or sweets – a reaction that is likely to increase the frequency of such behaviours rather than suppress them.

Parents may play a more discrete role in developing APD tendencies through the emotional relationship they have with their children. Psychodynamic explanations of

APD argue that a lack of parental love and affection during childhood is likely to lead to the child failing to learn trust (Gabbard, 1990). This lack of love and affection can take a number of forms and there is evidence that individuals with APD come from backgrounds of family violence, poverty and conflict – including separation and divorce (Farrington, 1991; Paris, 2001). In such circumstances, the child is likely to have had little experience of positive emotional relationships and is more likely to have experienced conflict and aggression as a normal way of life. Finally, some studies have identified both inconsistent parenting and harsh parenting (e.g. corporal punishing, hitting, kicking, slapping and emotional coercion such as insulting, threatening or belittling) as being important in developing antisocial behaviours (Burnette, Oshri, Lax, Richards & Ragbeer, 2012). Parents of individuals with APD also frequently fail to be consistent in disciplining their children in addition to failing to teach them empathy and responsibility (Marshall & Cooke, 1999). At least one reason for this lack of consistency in parenting is that many of the fathers of individuals with APD also exhibit the disorder.

However, we must be cautious about how we interpret these developmental factors. They may not represent *causal* factors in the development of APD, but merely represent failures and inconsistencies in parenting that are a *consequence* of having a child with severely disruptive and impulsive behaviour. We must also remember that because an individual with APD may have a parent with the disorder does not mean that they have learnt such behaviours from the parent – the disorder may involve psychological and biological dysfunctions that may be inherited rather than learnt (such as maladaptive physiological reactions that give rise to impulsivity and risk seeking – see below).

Genetic factors   There is clear evidence that APD appears to run in families and, apart from the developmental factors that may contribute to this effect, there is also the possibility that there is a genetic or inherited component to APD. Twin studies have demonstrated significantly higher concordance rates for APD in MZ twins than in DZ twins (Lyons, True, Eisen, Goldberg *et al.*, 1995) and adoption studies have also shown that incidence of APD in the adopted child is better predicted by APD in the biological than in the adopted mother (Ge, Conger, Cadoret, Neiderhiser *et al.*, 1996). However, twin and adoption studies have also indicated that there are important environmental factors also involved in the development of childhood antisocial behaviour and APD. The home environment and parenting behaviour of adoptive parents have a significant role to play in the development of antisocial behaviours in the adopted child, with conflict and violence in the adopted home contributing significantly to the development of antisocial behaviours in the adopted child (Reiss, Heatherington, Plomin, Howe *et al.*, 1995). Adoptive parents may also react to

any inherited antisocial characteristics exhibited by the adopted child in ways that may compound their problems, for example, by responding to antisocial behaviour in the child with harsh discipline, hostility and lack of warmth (Ge, Conger, Cadoret, Neiderhiser *et al.*, 1996). Heritability of APD and antisocial psychopathy traits appear to be moderate, with estimates of heritability between 40 and 69 per cent (Eley, Lichtenstein & Moffitt, 2003; Torgersen, Myers, Reichborn-Kjennerud, Roysamb *et al.*, 2012), and with the highest estimates being related to aggressive aspects of APD (Burt & Donnellan, 2009). In addition, studies suggest that the heritability of APD and substance use disorder may be related, and this may account in part for the high comorbidity between these two disorders (Kendler, Prescott, Myers & Neale *et al.*, 2003; Gizer, Ehlers, Vieten, Feiler *et al.*, 2012). Finally, molecular genetic studies are beginning to identify the specific gene locations of some APD characteristics, with the long allele of the serotonin transporter gene 5-HTTLPR linked specifically with the emotional deficits found in APD (Sadeh, Javdani & Verona, 2013).

Cognitive models   Some recent models have argued that individuals with APD have developed dysfunctional cognitive schemas that cause their responses to various situations to be extreme, impulsive and changeable. For example, Young, Klosko & Weishaar (2003) have suggested that individuals with APD possess five important and relatively independent **dysfunctional schemas**, and – when responding to important events – they are assumed to switch quickly and unpredictably between schemas in a way that makes their behaviour appear impulsive and unpredictable. Young and his colleagues proposed five important *schema modes* that determine the responses and reactions of individuals

dysfunctional schemas In personality disorders, a set of dysfunctional beliefs that are hypothesized to maintain problematic behaviour characteristic of a number of personality disorders (e.g. antisocial personality disorder and borderline personality disorder).

with APD. As we will see from the nature of these schema modes, it is claimed that they are developed as a result of abuse and neglect experienced during childhood (Horowitz, Widom, McLaughlin & White, 2001; Marshall & Cooke, 1999). The five dysfunctional schemas are:

1. the 'abandoned and abused child' mode (generating feelings of pain, fear of abandonment, and inferiority),
2. the 'angry and impulsive child' mode (where bottled up aggression is discharged as anger),
3. the 'punitive parent' mode (where the individual views themselves as having done something wrong or as evil and worthless),
4. the 'detached protector' mode (a state where the individual endeavours not to feel the pain and emotion caused by the first three modes), and

5. the 'bully and attack' mode (where the individual hurts other people to overcompensate for, or to cope with, mistrust, abuse, deprivation and defectiveness) (Lobbestael, Arntz & Sieswerda, 2005).

The development of instruments to measure these various schema modes has shown that individuals diagnosed with APD do indeed score higher on measures of these five dysfunctional modes than non-clinical participants (Lobbestael, Arntz & Sieswerda, 2005). Individuals with APD are assumed to switch rapidly and unpredictably from a 'healthy adult' mode – where their behaviour appears normal – to pathological modes, and this can occur rapidly when the individual experiences negative emotions such as anger (Lobbestael & Arntz, 2012). Because schemas such as these form part of the individual's normal way of thinking, the person with APD does not recognize them as faulty. If such dysfunctional schemas do represent important causal factors in the antisocial behaviour exhibited by individuals with APD, then challenging and replacing these dysfunctional schemas may represent a useful starting point for treating the disorder (Beck & Freeman, 1990).

Physiological and neurological factors　Individuals with APD show some interesting physiological characteristics which may help to explain aspects of their

behaviour such as their failure to learn from experience and their inability to empathize with the feelings of others. Firstly, they exhibit significantly lower levels of anxiety than normal control participants. This is exhibited as a relative inability to learn to avoid physically aversive stimuli such as electric shock (Lykken, 1957), lower reactivity and baseline levels of physiological indicators of anxiety such as skin conductance (Herperts, Werth, Lukas, Qunaibi et al., 2001; Hare, 1978) and a failure to exhibit increased startle reactions when being shown stimuli designed to elicit negative emotions (Levenston, Patrick, Bradley & Lang, 2000). Indeed, low skin conductance responses to loud noises at 3 years of age have been found to predict psychopathology scores at age 28, suggesting it is a potential risk factor for the development of APD (Glenn, Raine, Venables & Mednick, 2007). Secondly, individuals with APD regularly respond to emotional or distressing stimuli with slow autonomic arousal and appear to possess low levels of electroencephalographic (EEG) activity (Dinn & Harris, 2000; Lindberg, Tani, Virkkunen, Porkka-Heiskanen et al., 2005). This suggests that they may have difficulty maintaining normal daytime arousal and may also be able to ignore threatening or distressing stimuli more easily than most people. This in turn may explain why individuals with APD are unable to identify with the distress of others and

---

DEFICITS IN FEAR CONDITIONING IN ANTISOCIAL PERSONALITY DISORDER (APD)

A seminal study by Lykken (1957) suggested that individuals with what was then labelled as a sociopathic personality were unable to learn to avoid physically aversive stimuli, and this learning deficit may explain why individuals with APD are able to ignore threatening signals and also appear to lack the ability to learn from experience about events that have negative outcomes.

To read Lykken's article on anxiety in the sociopathic personality go to **www.wiley-psychopathology.com/ reading/ch12**

This learning deficit can be demonstrated in a simple laboratory-based conditioning experiment and laboratory studies such as this often serve as good analogues of real-life learning situations.

A study by Birbaumer, Viet, Lotze, Erb et al. (2005) replicated Lykken's original study. They used a differential aversive conditioning procedure in which male faces acted as the conditioned stimuli (CSs). For some participants, faces with a moustache (CS+) were followed by an aversive unconditioned stimulus (US) (in this case a painful pressure applied to the hand or arm), while faces without a moustache (CS−) were followed by nothing. For other participants the painful US followed the faces without moustaches and the moustached faces were followed by nothing (a counterbalanced procedure so that conditioning could not be affected by the specific features of the CS).

Normally, participants would show signs of anxiety during the CS+ (as recorded by physiological measures such as skin conductance levels) and would also rate the CS+ face as less pleasant than the CS− face. Birbaumer et al. compared the performance of 10 psychopaths (six of whom met DSM-IV criteria for APD) with 10 healthy control participants. While the normal, healthy participants rated the CS+ as significantly less pleasant than the CS−, the psychopaths showed no difference in pleasantness ratings even after 16 pairings of CS+ with the US, suggesting that they had failed to learn the significance of the aversive-signalling CS+.

may also be more risk-seeking than normal because of the need to experience higher levels of stimulation before they feel aroused (Hesselbrock & Hesselbrock, 1992). Thirdly, individuals with APD frequently fail to show any signs of fear learning in aversive conditioning procedures (where, for example, a conditioned stimulus predicts the presentation of an aversive unconditioned stimulus such as an electric shock) (Lykken, 1995) and functional brain imaging studies have shown that this failure to learn is accompanied by inactivity in the brain circuits believed to mediate fear learning (e.g. the amygdala) (Birbaumer, Viet, Lotze, Erb *et al.*, 2005). These findings are consistent with the fact that individuals with APD will usually fail to learn from experience about events that have negative outcomes and they will continue to persevere with their ingrained set of responses in such circumstances.

A number of recent studies have also indicated that individuals with APD have impaired performance on neuropsychological tests of prefrontal cortex functioning (Dinn & Harris, 2000; Raine & Yang, 2007) and these areas of the brain play an important role in inhibiting impulsivity. This may represent a brain abnormality that contributes to the impulsive behaviour exhibited by such individuals and may help to explain some aspects of their antisocial behaviour by their apparent inability to inhibit inappropriate behaviours in social contexts.

Summary of theories of APD   Predictive theories of the aetiology of APD are still relatively underdeveloped, but we have already learnt some interesting facts about the kinds of factors that put an individual at risk for developing APD. APD appears to run in families, with a genetic element being involved and the family environment also playing a significant role. Children raised in families low on parental love, with inconsistent or harsh parenting, or with parental conflict are more likely to develop APD, as are individuals who have suffered childhood abuse or neglect. Individuals with APD also appear to have dysfunctional cognitive schemas that lead them to behave either aggressively or impulsively, and we still need to discover whether there is a link between the development of these dysfunctional schemas and their early experiences. Finally, individuals with APD show a number of physiological and neurological characteristics, such as physiological indicators of low anxiety, low levels of baseline arousal and reactivity, lack of learning in simple aversive conditioning procedures, and neurological impairments indicative of impulsivity. These characteristics all appear to be consistent with the behavioural characteristics of APD (such as aggressive and impulsive behaviour, lack of empathy, and failure to learn acceptable adaptive responses), but we are still unclear about whether these physiological and neurological indicators are true *causes* of APD or whether they are simply correlates of behaviour patterns that have been acquired in other ways (such as through childhood experiences).

Borderline personality disorder

Individuals with BPD exhibit a wide range of behavioural and psychological problems including fear of abandonment and rejection, unpredictable mood swings, impulsivity, frequent and prolonged bouts of depression often associated with suicidal ideation, self-harm and suicide attempts. This is a diverse range of characteristics for a single theory to encompass, and this is without considering the fact that BPD is commonly comorbid with at least one other psychological disorder (see section 12.2.2). As we shall see below, theories developed to try to address the aetiology of BPD often attempt to explain the development of one aspect of the disorder (such as fear of abandonment, mood lability or impulsivity), but it is worth starting this section with an overview by reviewing some of the risk factors that predict the development of BPD and then moving on to more specific biological and psychological theories.

Risk factors for borderline personality disorder

Many studies have reported that individuals with BPD report a history of difficulties in childhood – many associated with problematic parenting. These include childhood physical, verbal and sexual abuse (Herman, Perry & van der Kolk, 1989; Zanarini, Williams, Lewis, Reich *et al.*, 1997), childhood neglect or rejection (Zanarini, Frankenburg, Reich *et al.*, 2000; Guttman, 2002), inconsistent or loveless parenting (Kernberg, 1985) and inappropriate parental behaviour such as persistent substance and alcohol abuse or promiscuity (Graybar & Boutilier, 2002). Individuals with BPD report rates of childhood physical, sexual, verbal abuse and neglect ranging from 60–90 per cent (Gabbard, 1990), including 67–87 per cent for sexual abuse (Bryer, Nelson, Miller & Krol, 1987). Herman, Perry & van der Kolk (1989) found rates of 71 per cent for physical abuse amongst people diagnosed with BPD compared with only 38 per cent amongst psychiatric patients who had not been diagnosed with BPD. Other studies have identified a number of developmental antecedents of BPD, including abuse, neglect, environmental instability, paternal psychopathology, academic underachievement, low intelligence and artistic skills (Helgeland & Torgersen, 2004). Prenatal adversity in the form of prenatal maternal distress, drug taking, tobacco smoking, or medical complications has also been shown to be a risk factor for the subsequent development of BPD (Schwarze, Mobascher, Pallasch, Hoppe *et al.*, 2013).

However, despite these developmental risk factors being significant predictors of BPD, we must remember that around 20 per cent of individuals who develop BPD have never reported experiencing childhood abuse or neglect (Gabbard, 1996; Graybar & Boutilier, 2002), so such experiences are not a *necessary* condition for developing BPD.

Biological theories of BPD

Biological theories cover genetic factors, brain and neurological abnormalities, and biological contributions to impulsivity.

Firstly, there is some modest evidence for a genetic component to BPD. The disorder does appear to run in families (Baron, Risch, Levitt & Gruen, 1985), and twin studies have indicated concordance rates of 35 per cent and 7 per cent for MZ and DZ twins respectively (Torgersen, Lygren, Oien, Skre *et al.*, 2000). Genetic analyses have also indicated that traits common in BPD, such as neuroticism and emotional dysregulation (labile moods and unpredictable rapid mood changes), have a strong inherited component (Nigg & Goldsmith, 1994; Livesley, Jang & Vernon, 1998). More recent research has linked BPD with bipolar disorder, and the two are often comorbid (Smith, Muir & Blackwood, 2004). Deltito, Martin, Riefkohl, Austria *et al.* (2001) have estimated that around 44 per cent of individuals with BPD belong to a broader **bipolar disorder spectrum**, which may help to account for their regular and unpredictable mood changes. Because we already know that there is a significant genetic component to bipolar disorder (see section 7.2.2), this provides circumstantial evidence for a genetic component to at least some of the symptoms characteristic of BPD.

> **bipolar disorder spectrum** A proposed spectrum of disorder encompassing both bipolar disorder and borderline personality disorder.

Secondly, evidence suggests that individuals with BPD have a number of brain abnormalities that may give rise to impulsive behaviour. They tend to possess relatively low levels of the brain neurotransmitter serotonin and this is associated with impulsivity (Norra, Mrazek, Tuchtenhagen, Gobbele *et al.*, 2003) and may account for their regular bouts of depression (see Chapter 7). There is also some evidence for dysfunction in brain dopamine activity in BPD and such dopamine activity is known to play an important role in emotion information processing, impulse control and cognition (Friedel, 2004). However, much of this evidence is currently circumstantial and derives mainly from the fact that administration of drugs that influence serotonin and dopamine activity also appear to influence BPD symptoms.

Thirdly, neuroimaging techniques of individuals with BPD have revealed abnormalities in a number of brain areas, primarily in frontal lobe functioning and in the limbic system, including the hippocampus and amygdala (Juengling, Schmahl, Hesslinger, Ebert *et al.*, 2003; Soloff, Meltzer, Becker, Greer *et al.*, 2003). The frontal lobes are thought to play an important role in impulsive behaviour and the amygdala is an important part of the brain system controlling and regulating emotion – these abnormalities may contribute to some of the defining behavioural features of BPD. In particular, activation of the limbic areas and the amygdala is often excessive, which may be responsible for the extreme emotional reactions often displayed by individuals with BPD (Lis, Greenfield, Henry, Guilé & Dougherty, 2007; Silbersweig, Clarkin, Goldstein, Tuescher *et al.*, 2007). Nevertheless, while these abnormalities are important correlates of BPD symptoms, it is still far from clear whether these abnormalities represent a *consequence* of the disorder or a genetically or developmentally determined *cause* of the disorder (Lieb, Zanarini, Schmahl, Linehan & Bohus, 2004).

Psychological theories of BPD

We have seen that a majority of individuals with BPD report experiencing relatively high levels of childhood abuse and difficult or neglectful parenting, and a number of psychological theories of BPD attempt to explain how these experiences might cause the behavioural and emotional problems characteristic of the disorder.

Some forms of psychodynamic theory, such as **object-relations theory**, argue that people are motivated to respond to the world through the perspectives they have learnt from important other people in their developmental past. However, if these important others have offered only inadequate support and love, or in fact have been actively abusive, then this is likely to cause the child to develop an insecure ego, which is likely to lead to lack of self-esteem, increased dependence and a fear of separation and rejection – all central features of BPD (Bartholomew, Kwong & Hart, 2001; Kernberg, 1985). Object-relations theory also argues that individuals with weak egos engage in a defence mechanism called **splitting**, which means that they evaluate people, events or things in a completely black-or-white way, often judging people as either good or bad with no shades of grey. This may give rise to their difficulties with relationships, in which their all-or-none assessments mean that someone they evaluate as 'good' can just as quickly become 'bad' on the basis of a single act or statement (e.g. if a partner does not return from a work social event at exactly the time they said they would, the individual with BPD is likely to respond with anger and threaten to withdraw from the relationship). People with BPD also have a tendency to perceive others as quarrelsome, which triggers negative affect and leads to more quarrelsome behaviour during their interactions with others (Sadikaj, Moskowitz, Russell, Zuroff & Paris, 2013). Interestingly, Suvak, Litz, Sloan, Zanarini *et al.* (2011)

> **object-relations theory** Argues that individuals with borderline personality disorder (BPD) have received inadequate support and love from important others (such as parents) and this results in an insecure ego, which is likely to lead to lack of self-esteem and fear of rejection.

> **splitting** An element of object relations theory which argues that individuals with weak egos engage in a defence mechanism by which they evaluate people, events or things in a completely black or white way, often judging people as either good or bad with no shades of grey.

found that individuals with a diagnosis of BPD judged their own emotions primarily on dimensions of valency, and hardly at all on dimensions of arousal. This suggests that they are likely to judge their emotions in an 'all-or-nothing' way with relatively little intensity control, leading to extreme swings in emotions.

While object-relations theory is consistent with the fact that a majority of individuals with BPD have experienced childhood abuse, conflict and neglect, one problem is that such experiences are common features of many of the personality disorders (including antisocial, paranoid, narcissistic and obsessive compulsive personality disorders) (Klonsky, Oltmanns, Turkheimer & Fiedler, 2000). This being the case, an account such as object-relations theory does not easily explain how such negative early experiences get translated into BPD rather than these other disorders which also have such experiences as part of their history.

We have already noted the high levels of comorbidity between the different personality disorders (Marinangeli, Butti, Scinto, Di Cicco *et al.*, 2000); in particular, between 10 and 47 per cent of individuals with BPD also display antisocial behaviour and meet the diagnostic criteria for antisocial personality disorder (Zanarini & Gunderson, 1997). This suggests that there may be some commonality of aetiology between the two disorders and we have already noted that significant childhood abuse and neglect is apparent in both groups. This has led Young, Klosko & Weishaar (2003) to suggest that individuals with BPD may develop a similar set of dysfunctional schema modes to those acquired by individuals with APD. We have already described these dysfunctional schemas in relation to APD and Young, Klosko & Weishaar have argued that these dysfunctional schema also determine reactions to events in individuals with BPD, such as dissociation (Johnston, Dorahy, Courtney, Bayles *et al.*, 2009). Subsequent studies have confirmed that individuals with APD and BPD do score higher than non-patients on measures of these dysfunctional schemas and also report levels of childhood abuse that were higher than non-patients (Lobbestael, Arntz & Sieswerda, 2005). This suggests a significant amount of similarity in both the developmental history of BPD and APD and in the dysfunctional cognitive schemas that characterize these disorders. This has led some researchers to argue that APD and BPD may be different manifestations of one single underlying disorder which may express itself as BPD in women and APD in men (Paris, 1997; Widiger & Corbitt, 1997).

Narcissistic personality disorder

As we described earlier, the individual suffering narcissistic personality disorder is someone who overestimates their abilities and inflates their accomplishments but has a complete lack of empathy with the desires and feelings of others. However, underneath this grandiose exterior is a very frail self-esteem, which means they constantly need to seek reassurance.

Psychodynamic theories of narcissistic PD have argued that the traits associated with this disorder result from childhood experiences with cold, rejecting parents who rarely respond with praise at their children's achievements or displays of competence (Kohut & Wolf, 1978). Indeed, such parents may often dismiss their children's successes in order to talk about their own achievements. Because of these experiences, such children then try to find ways of defending against feelings of worthlessness, dissatisfaction and rejection by convincing themselves that they are worthy and talented (Wink, 1996; Kernberg, 1985). The end product is someone with a vulnerable self-esteem who seeks reassurance about their talents and achievements from themselves and others, and who has developed a lack of empathy with others because of the cold and uncaring parenting they have experienced. In support of this view, there is some evidence that individuals with narcissistic PD are more likely to come from backgrounds involving child abuse, conflict and neglect (Kernberg, 1985). However, evidence of childhood abuse and neglect is not a sufficient condition for a child to develop narcissistic PD and some other theorists have argued that the disorder results from 'doting' parents who treat their children too positively in a way that fosters unrealistic grandiose self-perceptions (Millon, 1996). Interestingly, there is some circumstantial evidence to support this view, in that measures of narcissism often show that scores are often higher in first-borns or only children, where parents may have been able to devote more time and attention to their children (Curtis & Cowell, 1993).

Narcissistic personality disorder is also closely associated with antisocial personality disorder. Narcissistic individuals will regularly act in self-motivated, deceitful and aggressive ways very reminiscent of APD and also exhibit lack of empathy (Ritter, Dziobek, Preissler, Ruter *et al.*, 2011) (see Case History 12.3). However, individuals with narcissistic PD can be reliably differentiated from individuals with APD by their sense of grandiosity and self-importance (Gunderson & Ronningstam, 2001), so we need to look closely at factors that determine these characteristics (Thomaes, Bushman, de Castro & Stegge, 2009). Narcissists appear to hold grandiose, but simultaneously tentative, unstable self-views that require them to seek continuous self-validation and dominance over others. As such they may be addicted to self-esteem and continually create social situations in which they hope they can receive boosts to their self-esteem (Baumeister & Vohs, 2001). But how does this tendency develop? Thomaes, Bushman, de Castro & Stegge (2009) argue that it develops out of an interaction between an inherited sensitivity to positive or desirable stimuli and an aversiveness to negative or undesirable stimuli combined with extreme forms of parenting, such as parental overvaluation and

NARCISSISTIC PERSONALITY DISORDER

In July 2005, Brian Blackwell – a 19-year-old public schoolboy from Liverpool – killed both his parents and then used their credit cards to fund a £30,000 spending spree. After his arrest he was subsequently diagnosed as suffering from narcissistic personality disorder, and was reported to have regularly fantasized about unlimited success, power and brilliance. He had falsely claimed to be a professional tennis player and applied for numerous credit cards to help fund his fantasies. After the killings, Blackwell went on holiday to the US with his girlfriend, spending huge sums of money while staying at expensive hotels in New York.

Clinical Commentary

Many researchers believe that narcissistic personality disorder is closely associated with antisocial personality disorder, and individuals with the disorder usually show clear signs of deceitfulness, lying, lack of empathy with the feelings of others, acting impulsively and aggressively, showing no remorse for acts of harm or violence, and going to any lengths to achieve their own personal goals. Narcissistic personality disorder is differentiated from APD by the individuals' grandiose view of themselves and their need to brag about fantasized achievements. The parents of some individuals with narcissistic personality disorder undoubtedly dote on them and may treat them too positively in a way that fosters unrealistic grandiose self-perceptions (Millon, 1996).

overindulgence (Twenge, 2006) or parental coldness, extremely high expectations or lack of support (Kernberg, 1985). This diathesis–stress model is consistent with the fact that narcissistic traits begin to develop at 8 years of age – at just the time that children are beginning to form a conscious, global evaluation of themselves (Thomaes, Stegge, Bushman, Olthof & Denissen, 2008).

Case History 11.3 describes the story of Brian Blackwell, a student from Liverpool diagnosed with narcissistic personality disorder who tragically murdered both his parents. His behaviour is suggestive of APD in that he is deceitful, a pathological liar and apparently remorseless in the killing of his parents. However, he had a grandiose view of himself as brilliant and untouchable, and regularly bragged about fantasy achievements and talents. Far from coming from a background of childhood abuse and neglect, he was an only child whose parents doted on him and told friends of their great aspirations for him. You might like to consider how these facts might fit in with the theoretical accounts of narcissistic PD that we have described in this section.

Histrionic personality disorder

There has been relatively little research into the aetiology of histrionic personality disorder and its poor construct validity suggests that it may well be excluded as a diagnostic category in future editions of the DSM (Bakkevig & Karterud, 2010). Theories of histrionic personality disorder that are currently available tend to have developed from psychodynamic accounts originally designed to understand hysteria generally. These types of accounts argue that the dramatic displays of emotion and attention-seeking behaviour characteristic of the person with histrionic PD are

manifestations of underlying conflict – especially conflicts related to acceptance by and relationships with members of the opposite sex. Psychodynamic theories often differ as to the causes of the conflicts that underlie attention-seeking and dramatic behaviour. Some suggest that the disorder is fostered by inconsistencies in parental attitudes towards sex, where parents convey the view that sex is both dirty and exciting (Apt & Hurlburt, 1994). Others suggest that the disorder arises from a childhood experience of parenting that is cold and controlling, and leaves the child searching desperately for love and assurance (Bender, Farber & Geller, 2001). Finally, other psychodynamic views focus specifically on the relationship between father and daughter. Because of a lack of maternal attention, some daughters may actively seek the attention and approval of their fathers and this leads to a flirtatious relationship between father and daughter that the daughter carries on to other relationships later in her life (Phillips & Gunderson, 1994). There is little objective evidence at present to differentiate between any of these particular psychodynamic accounts and they do appear to be focused more on explaining the disorder in females than in males. As such, they may all be relatively inadequate accounts of histrionic PD – especially since more recent surveys have indicated that it is a disorder that is relatively equally distributed across men and women (Mattia & Zimmerman, 2001).

12.4.3 Anxious/Fearful Personality Disorders (Cluster C)

Personality disorders in Cluster C exhibit mainly anxious and fearful symptoms, and are frequently linked to comorbid anxiety disorders. Very little research has been carried out on the aetiology of disorders in this cluster, although there have been attempts to view them as part of larger anxiety-based spectra of disorders (such as avoidant personality disorder within a social anxiety spectrum and obsessive compulsive personality disorder within an obsessive compulsive spectrum) (e.g. Schneier, Blanco, Antia & Liebowitz, 2002). As such, it would be assumed that the personality disorders would then share some of the aetiological features of their corresponding anxiety disorders – although this has yet to be confirmed empirically.

Avoidant personality disorder

Avoidant personality disorder is characterized by feelings of inadequacy, fear of criticism, disapproval and rejection, and avoidance of most personal interactions with others. It is also associated with avoidance behaviour generally and may be part of a broader social anxiety spectrum (Schneier, Blanco, Antia & Liebowitz, 2002). Like many of the personality disorders, the aetiology of avoidant personality disorder has not been extensively researched. However, there have been a few studies investigating the correlates and risk factors associated with avoidant personality disorder. For example, avoidant PD has been shown to be closely associated with scores on a variety of personality dimensions, including introversion, neuroticism, low self-esteem, pessimism, and to self-reports of elevated emotional responsiveness to threat and reduced emotional responsiveness to incentives (Meyer, 2002). Family studies have also found that having a family member diagnosed with either social anxiety disorder or avoidant PD increases the risk for both these disorders two- to three-fold (Tillfors, Furmark, Ekselius & Frederickson, 2001), suggesting a close relationship between the development of social anxiety disorder and avoidant PD. This may also be linked to a genetic predisposition for avoidant personality disorder, which is estimated to be around 27–35 per cent, and overlaps with genetic vulnerability to social anxiety disorder (Reichborn-Kjennerud, Czajkowski, Torgersen, Neale et al., 2007), although heritability levels have been found to be as high as 64 per cent when different methods of assessing avoidant PD have been used (Gjerde, Czajkowski, Roysamb, Orstavik et al., 2012).

When compared with individuals with either major depression or other personality disorders, individuals with avoidant PD report poorer child and adolescent athletic performance, less involvement in hobbies during adolescence and less adolescent popularity (Rettew, Zanarini, Yen, Grilo et al., 2003), and this study also demonstrated higher levels of childhood physical and emotional abuse in the avoidant PD group than the depressed group – but this factor did not differentiate individuals with avoidant PD from individuals with other forms of PD. What these studies do suggest is that (1) avoidant PD is closely associated with social anxiety disorder and both may be part of a broader social anxiety spectrum, and (2) there are some important childhood precursors that suggest underperformance across a variety of childhood social domains may be predictive of later avoidant PD.

Finally, avoidant PD is closely associated with low self-esteem and feelings of shame and guilt, and psychodynamic accounts suggest that negative childhood experiences and childhood underachievement may contribute to a negative self-image (Gabbard, 1990). We have seen that there is some evidence for childhood negative experiences and underachievement being precursors to later avoidant PD, but it is still far from clear (1) whether these experiences are consequences of the developing disorder or (2) if they are causal factors, how such experiences might lead to the development of low self-esteem, shame and guilt.

Dependent personality disorder

Some clinicians have highlighted what appear to be many formalistic similarities between **dependent personality disorder** and depression. These similarities include indecisiveness and passiveness, pessimism and self-doubting, and low self-esteem. We have already seen in Chapter 7 that individuals suffering depressed mood continually seek reassurance from family and friends in a way that is similar to the manner in which individuals with dependent personality disorder continually seek support and guidance (Joiner, Metalsky, Katz et al., 1999). A possible link between dependent personality disorder and depression is also supported by the fact that drugs used to treat depression will also significantly decrease symptoms of dependent personality disorder (Ekselius & von Knorring, 1998). This has led psychodynamic theorists to develop models of the aetiology of dependent personality disorder that closely resemble those for depression. For example, object-relation theorists claim that dependence and fear of rejection is fostered by childhood neglect or loss of a parent during childhood. Alternatively, some other psychodynamic theorists claim that overprotective parenting may cause subsequent separation anxiety, depression and the development of dependent personality disorder (Bornstein, 1996). Clearly, these very different accounts require some further evidence to differentiate them, but unfortunately there are currently no systematic data on the childhood experiences of

To read an article on the assessment of heritability of avoidant and dependent personality disorder by Gjerde et al. go to **www.wiley-psychopathology.com/reading/ch12**

dependent personality disorder A personality disorder characterized by a pervasive and excessive need to be taken care of, submissive and clinging behaviour, and difficulty making everyday decisions without advice from others.

individuals who subsequently develop dependent personality disorder that might help to shed light on these different accounts.

Apart from formalistic similarities with depression, dependent personality disorder has been found to be regularly comorbid with a number of anxiety disorders, particularly social anxiety disorder, obsessive compulsive disorder and panic disorder (McLaughlin & Mennin, 2005). But once again, it is unclear whether dependent personality disorder is associated with an increased risk for developing an anxiety disorder (and what the mechanism for this increased risk might be) or whether anxiety disorders increase the risk for dependent personality disorder. Further research is needed to clarify these relationships and to help understand aetiological factors important to the development of dependent personality disorder.

Obsessive compulsive personality disorder

A first place to look for evidence relating to the aetiology of **obsessive compulsive personality disorder (OCPD)** would be its apparently related disorder, obsessive compulsive disorder (OCD) – but a review of the facts does not indicate a particularly close link between the two disorders. While the symptoms of OCPD are very similar to those of OCD, the reported comorbidity of OCPD in individuals with OCD is relatively low at 22 per cent (Albert, Maina, Forner & Bogetto, 2004). In fact, this study found that comorbidity of OCPD in individuals with panic disorder was 17 per cent, suggesting that OCPD is found at approximately the same level in individuals with panic disorder as it is in individuals with OCD. In addition, family studies have indicated that individuals with OCPD are no more likely than chance to have close relatives with OCD, which does not suggest a genetic link between OCPD and OCD (Nestadt, Samuels, Riddle, Bienvenu et al., 2000). At present there is very little evidence available that enables us to identify important factors in the aetiology of OCPD, and significantly less that enables us to predict those individuals who will develop OCPD as opposed to OCD. Some studies of non-clinical populations indicate there may be a single underlying vulnerability factor for both OCPD and OCD, and this may be related to a parenting style that includes psychological manipulation and guilt induction (Aycicegi, Harris & Dinn, 2002) or family transmission of symptoms to children by parents who also have OCPD symptoms (Clavo, Lazaro, Castro-Fornieles, Font et al., 2009). But this still begs explanations of (1) why OCPD and OCD are not highly comorbid if they share similar vulnerability factors and (2) why some people develop OCPD and not OCD.

> **obsessive compulsive personality disorder (OCPD)** A personality disorder in which individuals show exceptionally perfectionist tendencies including a preoccupation with orderliness and control at the expense of flexibility, efficiency and productivity.

SELF-TEST QUESTIONS

- Can you describe the evidence suggesting that Cluster A disorders are genetically linked with schizophrenia?

- What are the risk factors and childhood precursors predictive of adult antisocial personality disorder (APD)?

- What is the evidence for a genetic element to antisocial personality disorder (APD)?

- Some theories argue that dysfunctional cognitive schemas underlie antisocial personality disorder. Can you name the important schema modes described by these theories?

- What are the physiological and neurological factors associated with antisocial personality disorder (APD) and how might they contribute to typical APD behaviour patterns?

- Can you describe the evidence suggesting that negative childhood experiences might be important in the aetiology of borderline personality disorder (BPD)?

- What is the evidence for a link between borderline personality disorder and bipolar disorder?

- How do psychodynamic theories attempt to explain the development of borderline personality disorder?

- What might be the role of abnormal parenting in the development of narcissistic and histrionic personality disorders?

- What is the evidence for a genetic link between avoidant personality disorder and social anxiety disorder?

- What is the evidence for a link between dependent personality disorder and mood disorders?

- Is there any evidence for a link between obsessive compulsive personality disorder (OCPD) and obsessive compulsive disorder (OCD)?

SECTION SUMMARY

12.4   THE AETIOLOGY OF PERSONALITY DISORDERS

This section has illustrated that the aetiology of personality disorders – compared with many other psychopathologies – is relatively underresearched. APD and BPD have received the most attention, while research on the aetiology of other personality disorders is still at a very early stage (e.g. the Cluster C disorders). Because personality disorders can be enduring features of an individual's behaviour from childhood into adulthood, researchers have tended to look for factors in childhood that might either put an individual at risk for developing a personality disorder or a be a direct causal factor in determining the behavioural styles characteristic of the different disorders. For example, a diagnosis of conduct disorder in childhood appears to be a predictor of APD in later life, as do childhood neglect and abuse in BPD. Some studies have looked at whether there is a genetic component to personality disorders but, apart from the Cluster A disorders (paranoid, schizoid and schizotypal personality disorders), the evidence for an inherited factor in the other personality disorders is modest.

The key points are:

Cluster A Disorders

- Behavioural and genetic links between Cluster A disorders (paranoid, schizoid and schizotypal personality disorders) and schizophrenia suggest that they may be part of a broader *schizophrenia spectrum disorder*.

- Psychodynamic approaches to paranoid personality disorder suggest that parents may have been demanding, distant, overly rigid and rejecting, giving rise to a lack of trust in others.

- The risk of all three types of Cluster A disorder is increased in relatives of individuals diagnosed with schizophrenia, suggesting a genetic link between schizophrenia and the Cluster A personality disorders.

Cluster B Disorders

- One of the best predictors of antisocial personality disorder (APD) in adulthood is *conduct disorder* in childhood.

- Adolescent smoking, alcohol use, illicit drug use, police trouble and sexual intercourse before the age of 15 significantly predict antisocial personality disorder in later life.

- Antisocial personality disorder appears to run in families, suggesting that APD may be acquired through social learning and imitation.

- Psychodynamic approaches to antisocial personality disorder suggest that lack of parental love and affection during childhood and inconsistent parenting is likely to lead to the child failing to learn trust.

- Heritability of APD traits appears to be moderate, with estimates between 40 and 69 per cent, with highest estimates related to aggressive traits.

- Individuals with both antisocial personality disorder and borderline personality disorder appear to possess a set of *dysfunctional cognitive schemas* that give rise to their unpredictable mood swings and impulsive behaviour.

- Individuals with APD show a number of physiological and neurological characteristics, such as physiological indicators of low anxiety, low levels of baseline arousal and reactivity, lack of learning in simple aversive conditioning procedures, and neurological impairments indicative of impulsivity.

- Individuals with borderline personality disorder (BPD) report rates of childhood physical, sexual, verbal abuse and neglect ranging from 60–90 per cent, suggesting that these experiences may be important in the development of BPD.

- Twin studies of borderline personality disorder have indicated concordance rates of 35 per cent and 7 per cent for MZ and DZ twins respectively, suggesting a genetic element to BPD.

- Recent research has linked borderline personality disorder with mood disorders and around 44 per cent of individuals with BPD belong to a broader *bipolar disorder spectrum*, which may account for the regular and unpredictable mood swings in BPD.

- Neuroimaging studies of BPD have identified brain abnormalities in the limbic system, including the hippocampus and amygdala.

- *Object-relations theory* argues that individuals with BPD have received inadequate support and love from important others (such as parents) and this results in an insecure ego, which is likely to lead to lack of self-esteem and fear of rejection.

- Between 10 and 47 per cent of individuals with borderline personality disorder also meet the diagnostic criteria for antisocial personality disorder, suggesting a link between the two disorders.

- Psychodynamic theories of *narcissistic personality disorder* argue that the traits associated with this disorder result from childhood experiences with cold, rejecting parents who rarely praised their children's achievements.

- Narcissistic personality disorder is also closely associated with antisocial personality disorder, and narcissistic individuals will regularly act in self-motivated, deceitful and aggressive ways reminiscent of APD.

- Narcissists appear to hold grandiose but simultaneously tentative, unstable self-views that require them to seek continuous self-validation and dominance over others.

- There is relatively little research on the aetiology of *histrionic personality disorder* and theories that are currently available tend to have developed from psychodynamic accounts.

Cluster C Disorders

- Having a family member diagnosed with either social anxiety disorder or *avoidant personality disorder* increases the risk for both disorders two- to threefold, suggesting that both social anxiety disorder and avoidant personality disorder may be part of a broader social anxiety spectrum that has a genetic element.

- *Dependent personality disorder* has many features similar to depression, including indecisiveness, passiveness, pessimism, self-doubting and low self-esteem, and drugs used to treat depression are also successful at alleviating the symptoms of dependent personality disorder.

- Dependent personality disorder is also regularly comorbid with a number of other I disorders, particularly social anxiety disorder, panic disorder and obsessive compulsive disorder.

- The reported comorbidity of *obsessive compulsive personality disorder (OCPD)* in individuals with obsessive compulsive disorder (OCD) is as low as 22 per cent, suggesting that the two disorders are not closely related.

12.5   TREATING PEOPLE WITH A DIAGNOSIS OF PERSONALITY DISORDER

There are numerous important factors that make treating personality disorders problematic and means that they require an approach rather different to those employed for many other disorders. Firstly, as we have mentioned throughout this chapter, personality disorders can be enduring patterns of behaviour that an individual has usually deployed from childhood into adulthood. As a consequence, the individual usually cannot see that their behaviour is problematic and, as a result, they are unlikely to believe they need to change their behaviour, let alone seek treatment for it. Secondly, individuals with personality disorders usually possess patterns of behaviour that are likely to make them susceptible to a range of other psychiatric disorders (such as anxiety disorders or depression) and we have discussed the extent of this comorbidity earlier. It is often for treatment of the comorbid problems that an individual with personality disorders is first referred for treatment (e.g. depression and suicidal ideation in borderline personality disorder; social anxiety disorder in avoidant personality disorder; panic disorder or social anxiety disorder in dependent personality disorder; see Table 12.4). To add to these problems, disorders that are comorbid with a personality disorder are difficult to treat successfully (Crits-Christoph & Barber, 2002) and there may be many reasons for these difficulties. These include:

1. such individuals are significantly more disturbed and may require more intensive treatment than individuals with other types of psychiatric disorder alone;

2. many personality disorders consist of ingrained behavioural styles that are likely to continue to cause future life difficulties that may trigger symptoms of other disorders (e.g. the individual with borderline personality disorder is likely to continue to have turbulent and unstable relationships that may cause future bouts of depression and suicidal ideation); and

3. many of the personality disorders have features which make such individuals manipulative and unable to form trusting relationships (e.g. antisocial personality disorder, borderline personality disorder, narcissistic personality disorder) and this makes the development of a working, trusting relationship between therapist and client very difficult – even when it comes to just treating any comorbid disorder.

Thirdly, it is worth asking what it is about personality disorders that is disordered and requires treatment – especially if the behavioural styles typical of the personality disorders are really only extremes of what otherwise might be considered to be normal personality dimensions (Costa & MacRae, 1990). Because individuals with personality disorders exhibit extremes of behaviour on normal personality dimensions (such as extraversion/introversion, conscientiousness, agreeableness/antagonism), it may be more realistic to try to moderate the existing behaviours of such individuals rather than try to change them completely. For example, the behaviours of individuals with obsessive compulsive personality disorder may be quite adaptive in some circumstances and situations (e.g. when dealing with an important work project) but inappropriate and maladaptive in others (e.g. when obsessively trying to organize family and friends on a holiday). Taking this into account, the therapist may be more successful in trying to 'normalize' the extreme behavioural styles of the individual with a personality disorder rather than trying to change their ingrained behaviour patterns completely (Millon, 1996). Even given that these factors are taken into account when devising interventions for personality disorders, 37 per cent of people undergoing treatment for personality disorders still fail to complete (McMurran, Huband & Overton, 2010), and factors associated with non-completion include young age, lower education levels, unemployment, having juvenile convictions, and emotional neglect in childhood. These are all factors to bear in mind when reviewing the treatments that have been applied to personality disorders.

Finally, the scope of the personality disorders and their varied behavioural characteristics mean that treatments are very often geared towards the requirements of individual disorders. This being so, therapists have utilized a broad range of differing therapeutic procedures with varying degrees of success and we will discuss these differing approaches in turn. However, in general, individuals with personality disorders will need to (1) acquire a range of life skills, (2) learn emotional control strategies, and (3) acquire the skill of *mentalisation*, which is the ability to reflect on their experiences, feelings and thoughts and to assess their meaning and importance. These are all goals of therapy that can be identified across a range of conceptually different treatments for the personality disorders.

12.5.1 Drug Treatments

Drugs are frequently used in an attempt to treat individuals with personality disorders, but they tend to be used to tackle symptoms of any comorbid disorder rather than the symptoms of the personality disorder itself (but see Newton-Howes & Tyrer, 2003). Individuals

with comorbid anxiety disorders such as social anxiety disorder or panic disorder can be prescribed tranquilizers such as benzodiazepine; those with comorbid major depression may receive antidepressants such as the selective serotonin reuptake inhibitor fluoxetine (Prozac) (Rinne, van den Brink, Wouters & van Dyck, 2002). Lithium chloride can also be administered to individuals who have comorbid bipolar disorder (sometimes diagnosed with borderline personality disorder and antisocial personality disorder) in order to stabilize their moods and reduce antisocial behaviour. Antipsychotic drugs (such as risperidone) can also be effective in reducing the symptoms of Cluster A personality disorders, which are known to have some relationship to the symptoms of schizophrenia (Koenigsberg, Goodman, Reynolds, Mitropoulou *et al.*, 2001), and, more recently, atypical antipsychotic drugs (such as quetiapine) have been shown to reduce impulsivity, hostility, aggressiveness, irritability and rage outbursts in individuals with antisocial personality disorder (Walker, Thomas & Allen, 2003). In terms of drug treatment for direct symptoms of the personality disorders themselves, antidepressants have been found to be effective with Cluster C symptoms (avoidant personality disorder and obsessive compulsive personality disorder) (Pelissolo & Jost, 2011). Drugs for dealing with aggression and impulsivity, including lithium, beta-blockers, carbamazepine, antipsychotic drugs and SSRIs have also been found to reduce symptoms in Cluster B disorders (Pelissolo & Jost, 2011). Having said this, there are very few randomized controlled trials that have looked at the effects of medication on personality disorder symptoms, and what little evidence is available is often equivocal, poorly controlled or conducted on only small numbers of participants (Olabi & Hall, 2010).

12.5.2 Psychodynamic and Insight Approaches

As we saw in section 12.4.1, psychodynamic approaches have a long history of attempting to explain the development of personality disorders, so it is not surprising that psychodynamic and insight therapies generally should also be prominently involved in treatments for these disorders. Problematic relationships with parents and childhood neglect and abuse are factors that are prominent in attempts to explain many of the personality disorders, and exploring and resolving these developmental experiences is seen as an important role for psychodynamic therapies. Such therapists view *insight* as the important mechanism of change in personality disorders – not least because most individuals with personality disorders do not initially view their behaviour as problematic. This approach is particularly important when treating individuals with borderline personality disorder (BPD) because these individuals represent a serious challenge to therapists of any theoretical orientation. Individuals with BPD are manipulative and will frequently game-play with the therapist in order to ascertain how special they are to the therapist (e.g. by phoning the therapist regularly at inconvenient times), or they will make dramatic gestures to seek attention (e.g. by threatening suicide attempts). They also lack trust which will make it difficult to develop a working therapist–client relationship whatever the therapeutic approach being used. Finally, BPD is typical of most of the Cluster B personality disorders in that the individual will view the causes of their problems as external to them (i.e. they will be the fault of other people) and this makes any form of insight therapy difficult. However, psychodynamic therapists have tended to take a more active approach to treating personality disorders and have attempted (1) to identify and block manipulative behaviours at an early stage, and (2) to expose the 'weak egos' and fragile self-image that usually underlie many of the personality disorders. As a particular example of psychodynamic treatment, **object-relations psychotherapy** attempts to strengthen the individual's weak ego so that

> **object-relations psychotherapy** A form of psychodynamic treatment that attempts to strengthen the individual's weak ego so that they are able to address issues in their life without constantly flipping from one extreme view to another.

they are able to address issues in their life without constantly flipping from one extreme view to another (Kernberg, 1985). In the case of BPD, for example, object-relations psychotherapy will (1) attempt to show the client how their normal way of behaving is defensive (e.g. when they blame others for problems in their life), (2) how their judgements are often simplistic and fall into simple dichotomous categories (such as either 'good' or 'bad') that cause them to swing regularly from positive to negative ways of thinking, and (3) provide the client with more adaptive ways of dealing with important life issues by, for example, teaching them that other people may possess *both* good and bad characteristics rather than either being all 'good' or all 'bad'.

While it is difficult to objectively assess the effectiveness of psychodynamic approaches to treatment, there is some evidence that psychodynamic psychotherapies do have a beneficial effect on the symptoms of personality disorders. Some studies have suggested that clients do show significant improvements in symptoms during treatment (Svartberg, Stiles & Seltzer, 2004) and that short-term psychodynamic therapy is at least as effective as CBT (Leichsenring & Leibing, 2003) and a range of other treatments-as-usual, including general community-based psychiatric treatment (Fonagy, Roth & Higgitt, 2005).

12.5.3 Dialectical Behaviour Therapy

One particular form of therapy that has been successfully used to treat individuals with personality disorders is **dialectical behaviour therapy** (Linehan, 1987). This approach takes the client-centred view of accepting the client for what they are but attempts to provide them with insight into their dysfunctional ways of thinking about and categorising the world, and it is designed to provide them with the necessary skills to overcome these problematic ways of thinking and behaving. This is not an easy thing to do with a group of people who are usually very sensitive to criticism and emotionally unstable, and who will probably react to any challenge to their current ways of thinking in extreme ways (even threatening suicide). As a result, the dialectical behaviour therapist has to convey complete acceptance of what the client does to enable a successful dialogue to ensue about the client's problems and difficulties. Dialectical behaviour therapy subsequently includes skills training designed to teach individuals to be mindful of their maladaptive ways of thinking about the world (e.g. that others are not always to blame for the bad things that happen), to learn to solve problems effectively, to control their emotions (such as their anger outbursts), and to develop more socially acceptable ways of dealing with their life problems.

> To watch a video on dialectical behaviour therapy go to **www.wiley-psychopathology.com/video/ch12**

> **dialectical behaviour therapy** A client-centred therapy for personality disorder that attempts to provide clients with insight into their dysfunctional ways of thinking about the world.

Dialectical behaviour therapy can be split into four distinct stages: (1) addressing dangerous and impulsive behaviours and helping the client to learn how to manage these behaviours, (2) helping the client to moderate extremes of emotionality (e.g. learning to tolerate emotional distress), (3) improving the client's self-esteem and coaching them in dealing with relationships, and (4) promoting positive emotions such as happiness.

This approach has been particularly successful with individuals with BPD (Robins & Chapman, 2004; Bloom, Woodward, Susmaras & Pantalone, 2012); it has been shown to have long-lasting positive effects on suicidal and non-suicidal self-harm behaviours, depression, interpersonal functioning, anger control and re-hospitalization (McMain, Guimond, Streiner, Cardish & Links, 2012; Linehan, Heard & Armstrong, 1993); and it is particularly effective as a treatment for BPD over the longer term when combined with appropriate medication (Soler, Pascual, Campins, Barrachina *et al.*, 2005).

12.5.4 Cognitive Behaviour Therapy

Because of the resistance of many personality disorders to 'insight' therapies, it was originally felt inappropriate to try to apply CBT to this category of psychopathologies. However, over the past 10 years, there has been significant progress in developing CBT in ways that are directly relevant to the behavioural, emotional and cognitive problems found in personality disorders. Applying CBT to the treatment of people with a diagnosis of personality disorder was arguably first pioneered by Aaron Beck and colleagues, who attempted to apply CBT methods first developed to treat depression (see Chapter 7) (Beck & Freeman, 1990). This meant exploring the range of logical errors and dysfunctional schemata that might underlie problematic behaviour within individual personality disorders. For instance, an example of a logical error would be the individual with obsessive compulsive personality disorder (OCPD) believing that they are incompetent if they do just one thing wrong. They may also have developed dysfunctional schemata that generate problematic behaviour and cause emotional distress. In the case of OCPD, the individual may have developed beliefs that everything has to be done correctly (perhaps because of parental pressure to be perfectionist) and when one thing is not done properly this causes emotional distress and anxiety. In most cases the way in which CBT is

constructed depends very much on the individual personality disorder diagnosed and on the cognitive factors relevant to that individual client (see Beck & Freeman, 1990). However, Treatment in Practice Box 12.1 provides a brief summary of the stages through which conventional CBT for personality disorders would proceed.

As a specific example, the way in which dysfunctional schemata may develop in borderline personality disorder (BPD) is outlined in Figure 12.2. Childhood abuse is assumed to contribute to the development of a number of schemata typical of BPD. This leads to the self being viewed as bad, vulnerable and helpless; others as malevolent, abusing and rejecting. Experienced emotion is dangerous and 'clinging' becomes a strategy designed to get support from others, but is alternated with 'keeping distance' because of distrust. These negative, dysfunctional schemata give rise to hypervigilance and the constant expectation of threat and danger (Arntz, 1999).

In addition, because childhood traumas have never been fully emotionally processed, this has resulted in stunted emotional–cognitive development, so that individuals with BPD show dichotomous thinking ('black'–'white', 'good'–'bad' thinking with no shades of grey). CBT can be used in its traditional way to challenge the status of these dysfunctional schemata and to attempt to replace them with more functional schemata and views of the world. However, when treating individuals with

---

CLINICAL PERSPECTIVE – TREATMENT IN PRACTICE 12.1
CBT FOR PERSONALITY DISORDERS

The normal stages through which CBT would progress in the treatment of a personality disorder are the following:

1. During the initial sessions the therapist will deal with any coexisting psychiatric problems (usually specific anxiety disorders such as panic disorder or social anxiety disorder or major depression – see Table 12.4).
2. The therapist then teaches the patient to identify and evaluate key negative automatic thoughts (e.g. 'Nobody likes me' or 'I am worthless' in avoidant or dependent personality disorders).
3. The therapist will then structure the sessions carefully to build a collaborative and trusting relationship with the patient – especially in the case of those disorders where the client is distrusting or manipulative (e.g. borderline personality disorder).
4. The therapist may then employ guided imagery to unravel the meaning of new and earlier experiences

that may have contributed to the dysfunctional behaviour patterns (such as problematic early childhood and parenting experiences).

5. In collaboration with the patient, the therapist will prepare homework assignments tailored to the patient's specific issues.
6. Finally, the therapist will apply specific cognitive, behavioural, and emotion-focused schema restructuring techniques to dispute core beliefs and to develop new and more adaptive beliefs and behaviour (see also section 12.5.5 on Schema-Focused Cognitive Therapy).

Two main treatment objectives are, first, to help the patient develop new and more adaptive core beliefs and, second, to help the patient develop more adaptive problem-solving and interpersonal behaviours.

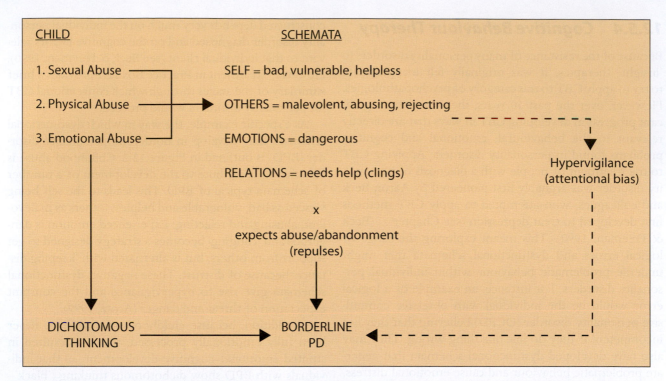

FIGURE 12.2 *A schematic representation of the way that dysfunctional schema are thought to develop in borderline personality disorder (BPD) – see text for further elaboration.*
Source: Arntz, A. (1999). Do personality disorders exist? On the validity of the concept and its cognitive-behavioral formulation and treatment. *Behaviour Research and Therapy*, 37, S97–S134. Reproduced with permission.

CLINICAL PERSPECTIVE – TREATMENT IN PRACTICE 12.2
TREATING ANTISOCIAL PERSONALITY DISORDER: CAN PERSONALITY DISORDERS BE TREATED IN PRISON POPULATIONS?

We noted earlier in this chapter that the diagnosis of antisocial personality disorder (APD) is closely linked with adult criminal behaviour. Surveys of prison populations have indicated that between 50 and 70 per cent of males in prisons meet the diagnostic criteria for APD (Fazel & Danesh, 2002; Widiger, Cadoret, Hare, Robins *et al.*, 1996) and many of these have been imprisoned for violence, sexual offences and homicide. Between 56 and 72 per cent of men convicted of serious sexual offences have been shown to be diagnosed with APD (Dunsieth, Nelson, Brusman-Lovins, Holcomb *et al.*, 2004; McElroy, Soutullo, Taylor, Nelson *et al.*, 1999) and, in a Finnish study, a diagnosis of APD increased the likelihood of an individual being convicted of homicide tenfold (Eronen, Hakola & Tihonen, 1996). In addition, the UK Home Office recognized the important link between violent criminal behaviour and APD and coined the term 'dangerous people with severe personality disorders (DSPD)' to describe individuals who have APD plus at least one other personality disorder. The Home Office report also recognized the difficulty in successfully treating such

individuals and recommended that people diagnosed with DSPD might be required to be detained indefinitely.

This raises the issue of whether the symptoms of individuals with APD who have committed serious criminal acts can be successfully treated. We have discussed the general difficulties of treating individuals with Cluster B personality disorders. They are manipulative, suspicious, hostile to criticism, lack trust in others and are constantly prone to lying in order to achieve their aims. This makes it difficult to form any kind of meaningful therapist–client relationship regardless of the theoretical orientation of the therapy. Finally, individuals with APD do not usually believe there is anything wrong with their behaviour – it has often enabled them to achieve their goals, so why should they change? This does not bode well for successful treatment of APD in criminal populations.

If an individual with APD is incarcerated in prison, then this makes treating the disorder even more difficult because of the unusual cultural requirements of prisons. DSM-5 defines a personality disorder as 'an enduring pattern of behaviour that deviates markedly from expectations within that culture', but as Rotter, Way, Steinbacher, Sawyer *et al.* (2002) point out, jails and prisons have their own cultural norms that require behaviours such as suspiciousness, hostility, social withdrawal and self-centredness. These are all behaviours that could be construed as adaptive in institutions such as prisons, where the individual has to look out for themselves and distrust others in order to survive (Rotter & Steinbacher, 2001). For example, an 'inmate code of conduct' might include:

- Do your own time (mind your own business, look out for yourself, keep to yourself).
- Don't snitch (don't report other inmates, don't trust staff).
- Don't show weakness (look tough, appear dangerous, act violently if necessary).

Such behaviours look exactly like the main symptoms of APD! (Rotter *et al.*, 2002). So, in effect, attempting to treat APD in prisons is equivalent to trying to persuade incarcerated prisoners to behave maladaptively and perhaps to leave themselves open to abuse and manipulation by other prisoners.

Nevertheless, there have been many attempts both in Europe and the USA to develop prison therapeutic communities that may help to reduce reoffending – although it is important to note that these aims are not the same as attempting to reduce symptoms of APD. Such therapeutic communities have been based on behavioural or cognitive behavioural principles in an attempt to target cognitive deficits that relate to offending behaviour. This scheme is known as Reasoning & Rehabilitation (R&R) (Robinson & Porporino, 2001) and the treatment targets are self-control (thinking before acting), interpersonal problem-solving skills, social perspective taking, critical reasoning skills, cognitive style and understanding the values that govern behaviour; and it is worth noting that many of these goals would address behaviours typical of individuals with APD (e.g. impulsiveness, lack of empathy). The programme has been used in prisons in the USA, Spain, UK, Canada and New Zealand and outcome studies have suggested they result in a modest but significant reduction in reoffending, normally of between 5 and 15 per cent (Robinson, 1995; Friendship, Blud, Erikson, Travers & Thornton, 2003; Raynor & Vanstone, 1996).

To read an article on CBT for imprisoned offenders go to **www.wiley-psychopathology.com/ reading/ch12**

BPD in particular, the therapist (1) must avoid direct challenges with the client about their beliefs because of their intense sensitivity to criticism, and so must usually approach this stage of therapy empathetically (McGinn & Young, 1996), and (2) may attempt to approach the process of changing dysfunctional schemata by 'reparenting' the client, which allows the therapist to form an emotional attachment to the client in order to challenge dysfunctional schemata (Young, Klosko & Weishaar 2003).

The development of specific CBT procedures for personality disorders is still an active process. Procedures have been developed that are specific to the cognitive and behavioural requirements of individual disorders (Beck & Freeman, 1990) and current attempts are being made to identify maladaptive schemata that are important determinants of the behavioural styles typical of disorders such as BPD and APD (Young, Klosko & Weishaar, 2003). It is still very early to be able to say with any confidence that CBT offers an important and effective method of treatment for personality disorders. However, a number of controlled studies have shown that CBT for personality disorders are superior to non-therapy control conditions in reducing symptoms (Linehan, Tutek, Heard & Armstrong, 1994; Linehan, Schmidt, Dimeff, Craft *et al.*, 1999) and are equally as effective as psychodynamic therapy (Leichsenring & Leibing, 2003). Preliminary studies also indicate that, after being treated with CBT, between 40 and 50 per cent of clients will have recovered after 1.3 to 2 years (Perry, Banon & Ianni, 1999; Svartberg, Stiles & Seltzer, 2004).

12.5.5 Schema-Focused Cognitive Therapy

A more recent development of CBT for personality disorders is known as **schema-focused cognitive therapy** or **schemata therapy**. Central to this approach is the concept of early maladaptive schemas (EMSs) that are thought to develop during childhood and result in dysfunctional beliefs and behaviours during adulthood (Young, Klosko & Weishaar, 2003). We touched on these maladaptive schemas and their putative role in determining the unpredictable, antisocial and impulsive behaviours typical of the more severe personality disorders earlier

schema-focused cognitive therapy In the treatment of personality disorders, a specially developed cognitive therapy which is used to address dysfunctional ways of thinking and maladaptive cognitive schema.

schemata therapy Central to this approach is the concept of early maladaptive schemas (EMSs) that are thought to develop during childhood and result in dysfunctional beliefs and behaviours during adulthood.

in this chapter. For example, if a child is continually overly criticized by parents, then he/she may develop the schema 'I am defective'. In order to deal with and cope with this schema, the child will develop strategies that in the longer term are maladaptive and act to reinforce the schema. For example, they may develop a variety of strategies that enable them to avoid thinking about this schema, such as storming off at the slightest hint of criticism, summarily breaking off relationships if there is an indication that their partner is not being affectionate, or self-harming as a means of distracting from the schema. Schemata therapy outlines three specific stages for therapy in these circumstances. First, the client needs to be convinced that their problems and symptoms are not *evidence for* their maladaptive schemas, but in contrast their maladaptive schemas are actually a *cause* of their symptoms. Developing self-knowledge is important in understanding that maladaptive schema are related to unfortunate childhood circumstances rather than representing truths about the way that person is. The second stage is to attempt to identify and prevent schemata avoidance responses, so that the client can experience, accept and tolerate the negative and painful emotional states that ensue when schemata avoidance is prevented. Thirdly, through the therapist's questioning and comments, the client is helped to examine the life experiences that have given rise to the maladaptive schemata. This final stage of therapy is intended to reduce the belief in maladaptive schemata and to develop adaptive alternative perspectives on their problematic life experiences. There is modest empirical evidence for the existence of many of the elements in schemata theory and there are a small number of effectiveness studies available which suggest it may be a promising and cost-effective treatment for personality disorders such as BPD (Sempértegui, Karreman, Arntz & Bekker, 2013).

SELF-TEST QUESTIONS

- Can you name the factors that make personality disorders so difficult to treat?
- What is the evidence in favour of a role for drug treatment in the management of personality disorders?
- What are the difficulties involved in adapting cognitive behaviour therapies to the treatment of personality disorders such as antisocial and borderline personality disorders?
- What are the main features of object-relations psychotherapy and dialectical behaviour therapy as applied to the treatment of personality disorders?

SECTION SUMMARY

12.5   TREATING PEOPLE WITH A DIAGNOSIS OF PERSONALITY DISORDER

We have reviewed a range of difficulties that are involved in the treatment of individuals with personality disorders and these difficulties often make successful treatment challenging to achieve. These difficulties include (1) denial of any psychopathology, (2) personality characteristics that make forming a trusting relationship with a therapist difficult, (3) persistent behavioural patterns that are likely to continue to cause future life difficulties, and (4) comorbid psychiatric disorders that usually need to be addressed and treated before tackling any underlying personality disorder. Despite these difficulties, therapists have been imaginative in attempting to develop a range of psychological treatments designed to tackle the important features of personality disorders. First, drugs may be used to reduce the symptoms of any comorbid disorder, such as major depression, bipolar disorder or anxious psychopathologies generally, and have recently been successfully deployed in the reduction of direct symptoms of personality disorders themselves. Subsequently, a range of insight based therapies (such as dialectical behaviour therapy) or specially developed cognitive therapies (such as schema-focused cognitive therapy) can be used to address dysfunctional ways of thinking and maladaptive cognitive schema. In general, individuals with a personality disorder need to (1) acquire a range of adaptive life skills (which allow them to interact and socialize successfully), (2) learn emotional control strategies (that control anger outbursts and acute periods of depression), and (3) acquire skills which enable them to reflect objectively on their experiences, feelings and thoughts, rather than reacting impulsively and emotionally to challenging events.

The key points are:

- Personality disorders are particularly difficult to treat successfully because individuals with personality disorders regularly deny they have problems that require treatment and they are also highly comorbid with other psychiatric disorders, which makes the individual significantly more disturbed.

- Drug treatments can be used to tackle symptoms of any comorbid anxiety or mood disorder, which in turn makes the personality disorder itself more accessible to treatment.

- Individuals with borderline personality disorder (BPD) represent a challenge to therapists of any theoretical persuasion because they are manipulative, frequently game-play with the therapist and make dramatic gestures to seek attention (such as threatening suicide).

- *Object-relations psychotherapy* and *dialectic behaviour therapy* are both treatments that have been developed specifically to deal with the difficulties posed by the treatment of individuals with personality disorders such as borderline personality disorder.

- More recently, cognitive therapies have been developed which attempt to identify and change any logical errors, dysfunctional beliefs and maladaptive schemas possessed by the individual with personality disorders (e.g. *schema-focused cognitive therapy* or *schemata therapy*).

12.6 PERSONALITY DISORDERS REVIEWED

Personality disorders represent relatively long-standing, pervasive and inflexible patterns of behaviour that deviate from acceptable norms within individual cultures. They are regularly associated with unusual ways of interpreting events (e.g. paranoid and schizotypal personality disorders), unpredictable mood swings (e.g. borderline personality disorder), or impulsive behaviour (e.g. antisocial personality disorder). These patterns of behaviour can be traced back to childhood and early adolescence, and they represent ways of behaving that are likely to have consequences that put the individual at risk for a range of other psychiatric disorders (such as major depression or anxiety disorders). While DSM-5 lists 10 diagnostically independent personality disorders that are organized into three primary clusters (odd/eccentric, dramatic/emotional and anxious/fearful), recent research has suggested that personality disorders are dimensional rather than categorical (i.e. they represent extremes of normal personality traits). This has led DSM-5 to include an alternative approach to diagnosing personality disorders that will be the subject of research in the coming years. This alternative model requires that clients be rated on various personality dimensions, and how these dimensions combine will provide the basis for diagnosis of a reduced number of specific personality disorders (see section 12.1.3).

Lifetime prevalence rates for personality disorders are difficult to estimate because of differences in diagnostic reliability and also the poor temporal stability of personality disorders, but with estimates around 14–15 per cent (see Table 12.3), they are likely to be one of the most prevalent psychopathologies treated by mental health professionals (Zimmerman, Rothschild & Chelminski, 2005).

Personality disorders are particularly difficult to treat for a number of reasons. They are frequently comorbid with other psychiatric disorders such as depression and anxiety (which complicates treatment), individuals with personality disorders frequently deny their behaviour is problematic, and they can be distrusting and manipulative in therapy. However, a number of recently developed insight and cognitive therapies do appear to have some success in treating some of the more problematic personality disorders (such as borderline personality disorder), and these include object-relations psychotherapy (Kernberg, 1985), dialectical behaviour therapy (Linehan, 1987), cognitive therapy (Beck & Freeman, 1990) and schema-focused cognitive therapy (Young, Klosko & Weishaar, 2003).

Explaining the aetiology and development of personality disorders is still largely in its infancy. However, because personality disorders can often be traced back to childhood as persistent patterns of behaviour, many theories of personality disorders look to childhood experiences and developmental factors for the causes of these extreme behaviour patterns, and it is certainly the case that childhood abuse, neglect and conflict can be found in the history of many personality disorders such as borderline personality disorder and antisocial personality disorder (Gabbard, 1990; Paris, 2001). Nevertheless, some other theorists note that individual personality disorders appear to have close links with other disorders and may form part of broader spectrums of disorder. For example:

1. Cluster A disorders (paranoid, schizoid and schizotypal personality disorders) have strong behavioural and genetic links with schizophrenia and may form part of a broader schizophrenia spectrum disorder (Siever & Davis, 2004),

2. borderline personality disorder is frequently comorbid with bipolar disorder and may belong

to a broader bipolar disorder spectrum, which may explain the regular mood swings in BPD (Deltito, Martin, Riefkohl, Austria *et al.*, 2001), and

3. avoidant personality is closely associated with social anxiety disorder and may form part of a broader social anxiety spectrum (Schneier, Blanco, Antia & Liebowitz, 2002).

All of these factors indicate that personality disorders are challenging to the researcher and therapist in many respects: they are difficult to categorize as discrete disorders, they are difficult to treat successfully, and theories of their aetiology are still only at the speculative and early stages of development.

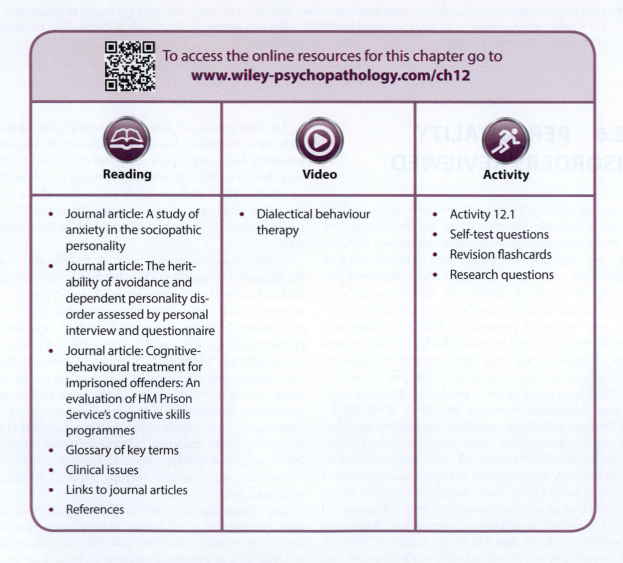

To access the online resources for this chapter go to
www.wiley-psychopathology.com/ch12

Reading	Video	Activity
• Journal article: A study of anxiety in the sociopathic personality • Journal article: The heritability of avoidance and dependent personality disorder assessed by personal interview and questionnaire • Journal article: Cognitive-behavioural treatment for imprisoned offenders: An evaluation of HM Prison Service's cognitive skills programmes • Glossary of key terms • Clinical issues • Links to journal articles • References	• Dialectical behaviour therapy	• Activity 12.1 • Self-test questions • Revision flashcards • Research questions

13 Somatic Symptom Disorders

 To access the online resources for this chapter go to
www.wiley-psychopathology.com/ch13

ROUTE MAP OF THE CHAPTER

This chapter begins by describing some of the features of those disorders collectively known in DSM-5 as somatic symptom disorders. The diagnostic criteria, characteristics and prevalence rates of the main disorders are then described (these are somatic symptom disorder, illness anxiety disorder, conversion disorder, and factitious disorder). We then discuss some of the factors important in the aetiology of somatic symptom disorders. Finally, the chapter describes the range of treatments that have been used with somatic symptom disorders, together with an assessment of their modes of operation and their efficacy.

CHAPTER OUTLINE

LEARNING OUTCOMES

When you have completed this chapter, you should be able to:

1. Describe the main diagnostic criteria and symptom characteristics for the DSM-5 listed somatic symptom disorders and evaluate some of the issues concerning diagnosis and comorbidity.

2. Describe and evaluate the main factors contributing to the aetiology of somatic symptom disorders and be able to compare psychological and biological explanations.

3. Describe and evaluate three or four psychological therapies that have been developed to treat somatic symptom disorders.

I have a core belief that I am dying. I know it's silly but you can't reason with a core belief. On top of that, I have a huge distrust of doctors after one diagnosed my father with anxiety instead of checking him for bowel cancer (which he actually had) and therefore delaying his treatment. It doesn't get any better when you get one doctor diagnosing you with a UTI and the other saying that all UTIs are in my imagination so I end up avoiding doctors because all I am told is that I am making it up, to then get a rather nasty infection because it actually wasn't in my head after all. I would love to know how I am supposed to think rationally when I can't even trust doctors any more. I don't spend my entire life worrying. I don't sit around doing nothing, despite the assumption that many GPs make; I am not stressed but I am busy. However, as soon as I get a worrying symptom, that is it – I can no longer function.

Kirsty's Story

Introduction

How often do we have physical symptoms such as aches and pains that trigger worries about contracting cancer or heart disease? How often do we worry about becoming ill or even dying – even when we have no physical symptoms of illness? For some people these everyday experiences are enough to cause significant distress and to interfere with their normal day-to-day living. When such concerns and worries become obsessive or a source of chronic anxiety or depression, they may be diagnosed as a somatic symptom disorder. This category of disorders includes somatic symptom disorder, illness anxiety disorder (formerly known as *hypochondriasis* or *health anxiety*) and conversion disorder. This is a new category of disorders listed in DSM-5 and all of these disorders share a common feature – the prominence of somatic symptoms associated with significant distress and impairment. With somatic symptom disorder individuals find somatic symptoms – real or imagined – distressing and spend significant amounts of time in medical settings attempting to seek a diagnosis for

symptoms that may either be trivial or not continuously present. Illness anxiety disorder is a preoccupation with having or acquiring an illness to the extent that there is a high level of anxiety about health that both causes distress and interferes with normal daily living. Conversion disorder is when the individual begins to experience symptoms of altered motor or sensory functioning (e.g. unable to voluntarily move a hand or temporary blindness) – even when there is little or no evidence of relevant neurological impairment. As you can imagine there is often a good deal of overlap in symptoms between these three disorders and that is one reason why they have been grouped together in their own chapter in DSM-5. In all cases, DSM-5 emphasizes that diagnosis should be made on the basis of positive symptoms such as distress related to somatic symptoms and dysfunctional thoughts about health, and not on excessive anxiety in the *absence* of somatic symptoms (as had previously been the case in DSM-IV-TR). This is because it is rarely the case that somatic symptom disorders occur in the absence of actual somatic symptoms (even with conversion disorder), and so the exaggerated responses that develop to health and physical symptoms in these disorders can frequently have their basis in actual somatic symptoms. This can be seen in *Kirsty's story* at the beginning of this chapter. She reports having a number of experiences with GPs in relation to illness that she believes have given rise to her illness anxiety – an illness anxiety that has become significantly disabling whenever she develops any symptoms of illness. Many individuals with somatic symptom disorders believe that their problems are genuinely medical and are often disbelieving when told there is no diagnosable evidence for a medical problem. In addition, those with symptoms that mimic neurological disorders, such as full or partial blindness or loss of feeling (anaesthesia), genuinely believe they have a disability, but their normal functioning can often be demonstrated in situations where drugs or hypnosis is used to alter levels of consciousness or where elegant experimental methods are used to infer ability (e.g. Grosz & Zimmerman, 1970). It is also important when diagnosing some somatoform disorders to differentiate true disorders from malingering (Merten & Merckelbach, 2013). Claiming to have a physical illness when a person does not is not just a ploy to avoid work or other situations that the individual may not enjoy, but can also be

> To read the article Is illness ever 'all in the mind'? go to **http://tinyurl.com/q2d4dph**

an actively deployed coping strategy during times of stress. The difference is that malingerers are fully aware that they are exaggerating or inventing their symptoms, but individuals with somatoform disorders are not. This is not an easy distinction to make, but malingerers will tend to be defensive when interviewed about their symptoms, whereas many with somatoform disorders may often display a surprising indifference about their symptoms (e.g. those with conversion disorder) – especially when the symptoms to most people would be disturbing (e.g. blindness, paralysis). This is sometimes known as *la belle indifference* or 'beautiful indifference'.

One somatic symptom disorder that is thought to be related to malingering is factitious disorder (previously known as Munchausen's syndrome). Rather than being concerned with existing somatic symptoms, factitious disorder is associated with the deliberate falsification of physical or psychological symptoms and the induction of injury, illness or disease through deception, and this may include reporting fictitious neurological symptoms or deliberately manipulating laboratory tests (e.g. by adding blood to urine). In the case of malingering, the individual may intentionally produce symptoms for a specific reason (e.g. to avoid jury service, to avoid working in a stressful environment). In contrast, in factitious disorder the individual's motivation is to adopt the sick role – perhaps for the attention that this role may bestow

on them – and individuals diagnosed with factitious disorders are often pathological liars who have developed an extensive knowledge of medicine and medical terminology. A related disorder is factitious disorder imposed by another, in which parents or carers make up or induce physical illnesses in others (such as their children). The reasons that drive individuals to deliberately make others ill is unclear, although such individuals often crave the attention and praise they receive in caring for someone who is ill (Abdulhamid, 2002) (see Focus Point 13.1).

We will continue by describing the DSM-5 diagnostic criteria and the main characteristics of somatic symptom disorder, illness anxiety disorder, conversion disorder and factitious disorder.

13.1 THE DIAGNOSIS AND CHARACTERISTICS OF SOMATIC SYMPTOM DISORDERS

13.1.1 *Somatic Symptom Disorder*

The cardinal feature of **somatic symptom disorders** is multiple, current, somatic symptoms that are distressing or result in significant disruption to daily life. Symptoms can either be specific (e.g. localisable pain) or nonspecific (e.g. general fatigue). While it may not always be possible to explain the somatic symptoms medically, in most cases the individual's suffering is authentic and not feigned. Those with

> **somatic symptom disorders** A group of loosely associated disorders all of which can be characterized by psychological problems manifesting as physical symptoms or as psychological distress caused by physical symptoms or physical features.

> For a video on somatization go to **www.wiley-psychopathology.com/video/ch13**

a diagnosis of somatic symptom disorder tend to have very high levels of worry about illness and will often catastrophize the most minor of physical symptoms. Sufferers often seek medical attention for their symptoms, but are particularly unresponsive to medical interventions, and will often seek care from many different doctors for the same symptoms, frequently claiming that their medical care has been inadequate (Tezzi, Duckworth & Adams, 2001). The main diagnostic criteria for somatic symptom disorder are listed in DSM-5 Summary Table 13.1. Somatic symptom disorder differs from illness anxiety disorder because in the former it is the symptoms themselves (e.g. the pain they cause) that trouble the sufferer, whereas in the latter it is the prospect of contracting a disease or illness from the symptoms that is distressing.

DSM-5 SUMMARY TABLE 13.1 *Criteria for somatic symptom disorder*

- Shows at least one somatic symptom (present for at least 6 months) that causes distress or disruption in everyday life
- Unwarranted thoughts, feelings or behaviours related to the somatic symptoms or associated health concerns, indicated by at least one of the following:
  - Disproportionate and persistent thoughts about how serious the symptoms are
  - Constantly high levels of anxiety about symptoms or health in general
  - Unwarranted levels of time and energy devoted to symptoms or health concerns

While the symptoms they report are not usually indicators of any underlying medical condition, they will often develop medical disorders as a result of exploratory surgery and medication use (Holder-Perkins & Wise, 2001). Somatic symptom disorder may be under-diagnosed in older adults, largely because pain and fatigue are considered a normal part of the ageing process, but if excessive thoughts and catastrophising of somatic symptoms are present, then a diagnosis of somatic symptom disorder might be considered.

Somatic symptom disorder is also closely associated with other psychiatric diagnoses such as anxiety disorders and major depression (Gureje, Simon, Ustun, & Goldberg, 1997). In younger individuals it can be associated with impulsive and antisocial behaviour, suicide threats and deliberate self-harm, making the lives of such individuals chaotic and complicated. It is difficult to estimate the prevalence rates of somatic symptom disorder because it is such a new diagnostic category. However, based on previous similar diagnostic categories it is expected that lifetime prevalence rates will be around or just above 1 per cent (DSM-5, p.312). There may also be cultural variations in the way in which somatic symptoms are either described or accepted and these may affect the diagnosis of somatic symptom disorder. For example, some cultures give negative meaning to many bodily symptoms that in other cultures are not described in those ways (e.g. too much heat in the body, burning in the head) and which serve as the basis for worry about somatic symptoms.

13.1.2 Illness Anxiety Disorder

This disorder centres on a preoccupation with having or acquiring a serious, undiagnosed illness – especially when somatic symptoms are either not present or only

mild. The distress is largely generated by beliefs about the meaning, significance or cause of a symptom, or alternatively a fear of contracting an illness that the individual believes might be disabling or life threatening (DSM-5 Summary Table 13.2). This preoccupation with health status means that the individual will regularly become alarmed by hearing of someone else becoming ill or by encountering health-related news stories. **Illness anxiety disorder** commonly leads sufferers to search for medical information and advice, either by seeking reassurances from family or friends or by attempts to find medically relevant information on the internet. Seeking medical reassurance about health status is also very common, but this rarely reassures the sufferer and a doctor's attempts at reassurance may often exacerbate their anxiety. Fear of ageing and death is also associated with illness anxiety disorder and may be associated with strict health regimes and use of alternative medicines (Fallon & Feinstein, 2001). Sufferers are also prone to intrusive thoughts about illness, death and dying and usually catastrophize their symptoms. For example, they are likely to believe that an ambiguous bodily sensation (e.g. an increase in heart rate) is attributable to an illness rather than a non-threatening consequence (e.g. having just walked up a flight of stairs) (MacLeod, Haynes & Sensky, 1998) and that a blotch on the skin may be the start of a cancer (Rief, Hiller & Margraf, 1998). Such individuals are not necessarily better able to detect bodily sensations than non-sufferers, but they do possess a negatively-based reporting style which means they interpret sensations significantly more negatively than non-sufferers (Aronson, Barrett & Quigley, 2006).

illness anxiety disorder A preoccupation with fears of having or contracting a serious illness based on a misinterpretation of bodily signs or symptoms. Formerly known as hypochondriasis.

DSM-5 SUMMARY TABLE 13.2 *Criteria for illness anxiety disorder*

- Obsession with having or contracting a serious illness
- Somatic symptoms are very mild or not present at all
- High levels of anxiety about health and easily alarmed about personal health
- Performs excessive health-checking behaviour or shows maladaptive avoidance
- Illness preoccupation has been present for at least 6 months
- The symptoms are not better explained by another mental disorder

Illness anxiety disorder differs from its diagnostic predecessor, hypochondriasis, significantly. Around 75 per cent of those diagnosed with hypochondriasis in DSM-IV-TR would now be re-diagnosed in DSM-5 with somatic symptom disorder if the somatic symptoms on which the anxiety and distress is based are genuine somatic symptoms. Because illness anxiety disorder is a new diagnostic category it is difficult to estimate prevalence rates or comorbidity. However, the prevalence rate for DSM-IV-TR hypochondriasis in the general population is estimated to be 1–5 per cent (DSM-IV-TR, p.505) but can be as high as 36 per cent in chronic pain patients (Rode, Salkovskis, Dowd & Hanna, 2006). Illness anxiety disorder can begin at any age but onset is most common during early adulthood. It is frequently comorbid with other disorders, including mood disorders and obsessive compulsive disorder (Noyes, 1999; Abramowitz & Braddock, 2006).

13.1.3 Conversion Disorder

The basic feature of **conversion disorder** is the presence of symptoms or deficits affecting voluntary motor or sensory function suggestive of an underlying medical or neurological condition. To be diagnosed with conversion disorder, these symptoms must cause the individual significant distress or impair social, occupational or other functioning (DSM-5 Summary Table 13.3).

> **conversion disorder** The presence of psychological symptoms or deficits affecting voluntary motor or sensory function suggestive of an underlying medical or neurological condition.

Common motor symptoms are paralysis, impaired balance, localized motor function weaknesses, atonia (lack of normal muscle tone), difficulty swallowing and urinary retention. Common sensory symptoms include loss of touch or pain sensation, double vision, blindness, deafness, hallucinations and on some occasions seizures or convulsions. However, in conversion disorder, thorough medical and neurological examination may fail to reveal any significant underlying medical cause for these deficits and the symptoms are often preceded by conflicts or other life stressors (Roelofs, Spinhoven, Sandijck, Moene *et al.*, 2005), suggesting a psychological rather than a medical cause. Sufferers do not appear to intentionally produce these symptoms, but more educated individuals may tend to display more subtle symptoms and deficits that closely resemble known neurological deficits. However, DSM-5 specifies that conversion disorder should be diagnosed only when the clinical findings show clear incompatibility with neurological disease (DSM-5, p.319) and conversion symptoms often fail to behave in ways expected by the known neurology. For example, in the conversion symptom known as **glove anaesthesia**, numbness begins at the wrist and is experienced evenly across the hand and all fingers (Figure 13.1). However, if a specific nerve to the hand, such as the ulnar nerve, is damaged, numbness should extend only to the ring finger and little finger. Similarly, damage to the radial nerve should affect only the thumb, index finger, middle finger and part of the ring finger. Conversion symptoms are also frequently inconsistent, so a sufferer may often use a 'paralysed' limb when dressing or may reflexively catch a ball unexpectedly thrown to them with their 'paralysed' hand. Individuals with conversion disorder also tend to exhibit what is known as *la belle indifference* ('beautiful indifference') about their disability. Whereas most people who experience a sudden loss of physical ability would be frightened and distraught, individuals with conversion disorder tend to be largely philosophical

> **glove anaesthesia** A conversion disorder symptom in which numbness begins at the wrist and is experienced evenly across the hand and all fingers.

> **la belle indifference** An indifference about real symptoms (especially when the symptoms would be disturbing to most people) sometimes displayed by individuals with somatic symptom disorders.

DSM-5 SUMMARY TABLE 13.3 *Criteria for conversion disorder*

- At least one symptom of altered voluntary or sensory function
- Evidence of incompatibility between the symptoms and known neurological or medical conditions
- The symptoms are not better accounted for by another medical condition or mental disorder
- The symptoms cause significant distress or impairment in important areas of functioning

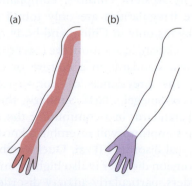

FIGURE 13.1 *Glove anaesthesia.*
(a) Areas of the arm's skin that send sensory information to the brain by way of different nerves. (b) A typical region of anaesthesia in a patient with conversion disorder. If there were a nerve injury (in the spinal cord), the anaesthesia would extend over the length of the arm, following the nerve distribution shown in (a).

about their symptoms and willing to talk at length about them. At least some psychodynamic approaches to the explanation of conversion disorder suggest that this appears to reflect a form of 'relief' that their symptoms may prevent them from having to deal with current conflicts and stress in their lives (Kuechenoff, 2002; Temple, 2002). Prior to its inclusion in the DSM, conversion disorder was popularly known as **hysteria** in psychodynamic circles.

> **hysteria** A common term used in psychodynamic circles to describe conversion disorder (prior to the latter's inclusion in the DSM).

Some diligence must be applied to ensure that conversion symptoms are not the result of developing neurological problems and it is estimated that between 13 and 30 per cent of individuals diagnosed with conversion disorder have later been found to develop some relevant neurological deficit (Maldonado & Spiegel, 2003; Kent, Tomasson & Coryell, 1995). Conversion disorder symptoms can develop throughout the life course and are often seen to develop after some stressful life event. Severity of the symptoms can be linked to the severity of the life stressor and important stressful life events that can contribute to conversion disorder include work experiences and relationship difficulties (Roelofs, Spinhoven, Sandijck, Moene *et al.*, 2005). However, symptoms can often spontaneously remit, only to return at a later time, and there is some evidence to suggest that a history of trauma and childhood abuse may be a vulnerability factor (Bowman & Markand, 1996).

The lifetime prevalence rate of conversion disorder is thought to be less than 1 per cent, and it is significantly more common in women than in men (Maldonado & Spiegel, 2003). There are also important cultural differences in the way that conversion disorder manifests itself. For example, Janca, Isaac, Bennett & Tacchini (1995) found that sexual and menstrual symptoms were prominent in Western cultures, complaints of body temperature irregularities are only found in Nigeria, kidney problems only in China, and body odour complaints only in Japan. In addition, the *lower* the economic or educational standards in a culture or community, the higher the prevalence of conversion disorder (Maldonado & Spiegel, 2003). Similarly, the *higher* the educational standards in a community, the more likely it is that the symptoms will resemble a known medical or neurological disorder (Tezzi, Duckworth & Adams, 2001). Conversion disorder is also highly comorbid with other disorders, particularly anxiety disorders, such as panic disorder, and depressive disorders. A study by Sar, Akyuz, Kundakci, Kiziltyan *et al.* (2004) found at least one other psychiatric diagnosis in 89.5 per cent of a group of individuals with a diagnosis of conversion disorder.

13.1.4 *Factitious Disorder*

This disorder is characterized by the individual falsifying medical or psychological symptoms in themselves or others. The defining feature of **factitious disorder** is that this falsification of evidence is intentionally deceptive. Ways of falsifying symptoms can include exaggeration of symptoms, fabrication, simulation and induction. Examples include claiming symptoms of depression following the death of a loved one when this event did not happen, deceptively reporting neurological symptoms such as dizziness or blacking out and manipulation of laboratory tests (e.g. by adding blood to urine) or ingesting a substance (such as insulin).

> **factitious disorder** A set of physical or psychological symptoms that are intentionally produced in order to assume the sick role.

> For a video on factitious disorder go to **www.wiley-psychopathology.com/video/ch13**

An alternative diagnosis is **factitious disorder imposed on another** and this is where the individual is a perpetrator who falsifies medical or psychological symptoms in another (with the victims of this action often being children). Focus Point 13.1 provides a detailed example of factitious disorder imposed on another, previously known as Munchausen's syndrome by proxy. It is still unclear why individuals take these deceptive actions, although it may well be to gain attention for themselves or to gain praise for their actions in the case of factitious disorder imposed on another.

> **factitious disorder imposed on another** The intentional falsification of physical or psychological signs or symptoms, or induction of injury or disease, in another person.

DSM-5 SUMMARY TABLE 13.4 *Criteria for factitious disorder*

- Fabrication of physical or physiological symptoms or sign of injury or disease
- Presenting oneself as ill or injured to others
- The deception is evident despite a lack of obvious reward
- The behaviour is not better explained by another mental disorder, such as delusional disorder

Factitious disorder imposed on another

- Fabrication of physical or physiological symptoms or sign of injury or disease in another
- Presenting another as ill or injured to others
- The deception is evident despite a lack of obvious reward
- The behaviour is not better explained by another mental disorder, such as delusional disorder

NB: The perpetrator, not the victim, receives the diagnosis.

FOCUS POINT 13.1

FACTITIOUS DISORDER IMPOSED ON ANOTHER

Beverley Allitt was a nurse who was convicted in 1993 of killing four children and injuring nine others at Grantham Hospital, Lincolnshire. While working on a children's ward in the hospital she was found to be secretly injecting infants with insulin – a drug that induced cardiac arrest, causing death and brain damage. During the time that she was involved in these killings, she was also befriending the parents of her victims and displaying what appeared to be a caring and sympathetic manner. She received 13 life sentences for these crimes, yet her motives for the killings have never been fully explained. One theory is that she suffered from *factitious disorder imposed on another* (previously known as Munchausen's syndrome by proxy), a controversial diagnosis in which sufferers are prompted to deliberately falsify illnesses in others in order to attract attention to themselves.

What motivates some carers and parents to deliberately inflict illness, pain and even death knowingly on young children? Most mothers diagnosed with factitious disorder imposed on another are emotionally needy and require attention and praise, and they receive this when appearing caring and loving towards their ill child. They often have poor relationships with their partners, receive little in the way of support outside of the medical environment and regularly exhibit low self-esteem. Many have a good knowledge of medicine and medical procedures, which allows them to cause their child's illness with a minimum of suspicion (Bluglass, 2001; Adshead & Brooke, 2001).

The syndrome is notoriously difficult to diagnose. This is because most of the victims are very young children, many of whom may have genuinely experienced acute life-threatening events, the causes of which are difficult to detect, such as sudden infant death syndrome (SIDS) (Galvin, Newton & Vandeven, 2005). In such circumstances, carers who present the problems of their children in unusual ways are often treated with suspicion – especially if their own emotional needs are consistent with those often found in factitious disorder imposed on another (Pankratz, 2006).

SELF-TEST QUESTIONS

- What are the main diagnostic criteria for somatic symptom disorder?
- What are the main psychiatric disorders that tend to be comorbid with somatic symptom disorders?
- Can you describe the main diagnostic criteria for illness anxiety disorder, and by what other name was this disorder previously known?
- Can you describe the main diagnostic criteria for conversion disorder together with its main features?
- How do cultural factors affect the prevalence rate and manifestation of conversion disorder symptoms?
- What is factitious disorder and what are its main diagnostic criteria?
- How does factitious disorder imposed on another differ from basic factitious disorder?

SECTION SUMMARY

13.1 THE DIAGNOSIS AND CHARACTERISTICS OF SOMATIC SYMPTOM DISORDERS

- *Somatic symptom disorder* is a pattern of recurring multiple, clinically significant somatic symptoms that require medical treatment.
- Individuals diagnosed with somatic symptom disorder are usually major users of health care services.
- Somatic symptom disorder is closely associated with other mental health problems such as anxiety disorders and major depression.
- *Illness anxiety disorder* (formerly known as hypochondriasis) is a preoccupation with fears of having or contracting a serious illness based on a misinterpretation of bodily signs or symptoms.

- Individuals with illness anxiety disorder will regularly read about medical conditions and consult medical opinion on a regular basis. They will also be entirely unconvinced by reassurances that they do not have a medical illness.

- The basic feature of *conversion disorder* is the presence of symptoms or deficits affecting voluntary motor or sensory function.

- It is estimated that between 13 and 30 per cent of individuals diagnosed with conversion disorder have later been found to have some neurological deficit.

- Conversion symptoms usually develop in adolescence and severity of symptoms can be linked to the severity of life stressors.

- The lifetime prevalence rate for conversion disorder is less than 1 per cent.

- There are significant cultural differences in the way that conversion disorder symptoms manifest themselves.

- Conversion disorder is frequently comorbid with anxiety disorders, major depression, dissociative disorders, substance abuse and personality disorders.

- *Factitious disorder* is characterized by the individual falsifying medical or psychological symptoms in themselves or others.

- *Factitious disorder imposed on another* is where the individual is a perpetrator who falsifies symptoms in another.

13.2   THE AETIOLOGY OF SOMATIC SYMPTOM DISORDERS

The most traditional explanations of somatic symptom disorders have been couched in psychodynamic terms – primarily because some of Freud's most influential writings concerned hysteria and the causes of unexplained physical symptoms. However, since that time a number of different approaches to explaining somatic symptom disorders have developed, including learning accounts and cognitive accounts. Nevertheless, regardless of how the theorist approaches the aetiology of somatic symptom disorders, explanations of these disorders must address certain important questions. These include:

1. Are physical symptoms a manifestation of underlying psychological conflict and stress?

2. Are physical symptoms generated in an involuntary fashion?

3. What is the role of life stress and childhood abuse in the development of somatic symptom disorders?

4. How do sufferers acquire the biased thinking and dysfunctional beliefs about health that help to maintain many of the symptoms of these disorders?

13.2.1   *Psychodynamic Interpretations*

Some of Freud's most famous writings were on the subject of hysteria and how inner conflict, repressed emotions and life stress could be manifested in somatic symptoms. The basic psychodynamic view of somatic symptom disorders is a **conflict resolution** one in which distressing memories, inner conflict, anxiety and unacceptable thoughts are repressed in consciousness but outwardly expressed as somatic symptoms. For example, Freud believed that somatic symptoms such as those found in conversion disorder (then known as hysteria) were associated with distressing memories of childhood seduction. These might be actual experiences of childhood abuse or simply imagined as fantasies during the Oedipal period of development. When these memories are reawakened during puberty this causes intense anxiety and conflict resulting in somatic symptoms and repression of these memories. The somatic symptoms served the purpose of helping to suppress these memories and to relieve anxiety, and this was consistent with the fact that most individuals with conversion disorder exhibited a calm philosophical attitude to their disability (*la belle indifference*), suggesting that it was a state in which they experienced some relief from stress and conflict. Underlying sexual conflict was also seen by psychodynamic theorists as being an important contributor to other disorders such as somatic symptom disorder and illness anxiety disorder. Freud believed that repressed sexual energy was often turned inward on the self, transforming it into physical symptoms that created physical pain or were interpreted as indictors of illness and disease. Indeed, psychodynamic theorists often view those suffering from somatic symptom disorders as regressing to the state of a sick child, unconsciously seeking attention and

conflict resolution Psychodynamic interpretations of somatic symptom disorders in which distressing memories, inner conflict, anxiety and unacceptable thoughts are repressed in consciousness but outwardly expressed as somatic symptoms.

relief from symptoms and responsibilities, and thus reducing experienced anxiety (Kuechenoff, 2002; Kellner, 1990; Phillips 1996).

These psychodynamic accounts appear to make intuitive sense in that those who develop somatic symptom disorders often appear to have either a history of conflict, stress and abuse or have recently experienced an important life stressor (Bowman & Markand, 1996; Roelofs, Spinhoven, Sandijck, Moene *et al.*, 2005). Nevertheless, an important aspect of the psychodynamic conflict-resolution model is that the physical symptoms either cause relief from anxiety or from having to deal with current conflicts and stress (Temple, 2002). In contrast, disorders such as somatic symptom disorder and illness anxiety disorder appear to involve high levels of anxiety (Noyes, Kathol, Fisher, Phillips *et al.*, 1994), and a sizable minority of those with conversion disorder also fail to exhibit the calming effects of *la belle indifference* (Gureje, Simon, Ustun & Goldberg, 1997). This suggests that the supposed psychologically beneficial effects of somatisation as proposed by psychodynamic theory are difficult to find.

13.2.2 Consciousness and Behaviour

One important feature of some somatic symptom disorders, such as conversion disorder and somatic symptom disorder, is that the sufferer appears able to generate physical symptoms or deficits (e.g. medical symptoms, blindness) in an involuntary fashion. That is, there is a dissociation between the individual's behaviour and their awareness of that behaviour. For example, in conversion disorder the sufferer appears genuinely unable to experience certain sensory input (e.g. when exhibiting blindness or loss of feeling). However, studies suggest that these individuals can experience the sensory input at some level of processing but are consciously unaware of it. For example, Theodor & Mandelcorn (1973) describe a study undertaken with a 16-year-old girl who complained of a loss of peripheral vision with no underlying neurological explanation for this. In their study they presented a buzzer followed by a bright visual stimulus to either the girl's central or peripheral visual field on a percentage of the trials. The girl's task was to report whether a visual stimulus had followed the buzzer or not. They found that the girl always correctly reported when the buzzer was followed by a stimulus to the central visual field. However, she was only 30 per cent correct when reporting a visual stimulus to the peripheral visual field. Theodor & Mandelcorn argued that a person who truly

To read the article about hysterical blindness by Theodor & Mandelcorn go to www.wiley-psychopathology.com/reading/ch13

had no peripheral vision would have reported a visual stimulus at chance level – i.e. on 50 per cent of the trials. The girl with a somatic symptom disorder in fact performed significantly worse than this – suggesting that at some level of consciousness she was aware of the peripheral visual stimulus but was suppressing reporting it. In a similar study, Zimmerman & Grosz (1966) also found that an individual with hysterical blindness performed a visual task at significantly below chance level when a truly blind individual should be performing at chance level. They also found that when visual stimuli were presented in a non-random predictable sequence, their patient still performed a well below chance level – even a truly blind person would have performed above chance on this task. These studies indicate that the person with, for example, conversion disorder can discriminate the relevant incoming sensory information at some level – even if they use that information in a way that results in them performing significantly below what would be expected of someone who was blind! At first sight, evidence such as this suggests that the sufferer may simply be faking the symptoms and trying to behave in ways that are consistent with these symptoms. However, if it is faking, then the individual has taken great pains to be consistent in this behaviour often over long periods of time and in difficult situations.

A very early explanation of these types of symptoms was proposed by Janet (1907) who suggested that patients suffering from 'hysteria' experience a spontaneous narrowing of attention after being exposed to trauma. This attentional narrowing limits the number of sensory channels that can be attended to and leads to the loss of voluntary control over neglected channels. This results in the patient being rendered anaesthetic for any information coming in to the unattended modality even though it is still processed outside of conscious awareness. As a result the patient may be unable to consciously access information from these channels and experience blindness or paralysis, depending on the sensory channel that has been neglected. A similar explanation of these anomalous findings is provided by Oakley (1999). He draws attention to the many similarities between the behaviour of the individual with conversion disorder or somatic symptom disorder and the effects of **hypnosis**. First, many of the symptoms of conversion disorder are similar to

hypnosis A therapeutic technique in which the patient is placed in a trance.

physical states that can be easily established by hypnosis (e.g. blindness, paralysis) and they also display a degree of involuntariness. That is, both the conversion disorder patient and the person under hypnosis regularly report that they have no voluntary control over a movement or a sensation (e.g. they may be unable to raise their arm). In drawing these two areas together, Oakley (1999) has proposed that similar mechanisms could be responsible for both conversion/somatisation symptoms and behaviour under hypnosis. So an action or incoming sensory information may often be processed at a range of different levels of mental functioning but for some reason may not be selected for conscious processing (presumably one of the last stages of this process). Under hypnosis this last stage of processing can often be prevented by suggestions from an external source (such as the hypnotist) and it will appear to the individual that they have no control over their actions or their perceptions. Oakley proposes a similar effect in conversion disorder in which some presumably internal processes have prevented sensory information from being analysed by conscious awareness. Because the sensory information is processed at lower mental levels, this explains why the individual with hysterical blindness can respond in ways that suggest visual information is being received (e.g. by performing at significantly below chance on a visual recognition task), but is not consciously aware that visual stimuli are being perceived and responded to. As appealing as this explanation is, it still begs the question of how and why sensory information is blocked from conscious awareness in individuals with conversion disorder. This aspect of this view still needs to be fully explored and understood.

13.2.3 Risk Factors for Somatic Symptom Disorders

A significant factor in the history of most somatic symptom disorders is either a history of trauma or abuse, or significant periods of stress and anxiety, and these appear to be important risk factors in developing a somatic symptom disorder. For example, a history of childhood trauma appears to increase vulnerability to conversion disorder (Bowman & Markland, 1996), and high levels of negative life events in the year prior to onset have been found in individuals with *globus pharyngis* (a form of conversion disorder in which the sufferer experiences a sensation of a lump in the throat) (Harris, Deary & Wilson, 1996). Individuals with somatic symptom disorder tend to report histories of physical and sexual abuse (Holder-Perkins & Wise, 2001), as do many of those with illness anxiety disorder (Salmon & Calderbank, 1996). In addition, many somatic symptom disorders develop following exposure to acute stressors, such as recent loss (Van Ommeren, Sharma, Komproe, Poudyal *et al.*, 2001), relationship difficulties (Craig, 2001) and exposure to dead bodies following military combat (Labbate, Cardena, Dimitreva, Roy & Engel, 1998). Nevertheless, we must be cautious about what these findings mean in

the aetiology of somatic symptom disorders. First, not everyone who develops a somatic symptom disorder reports having had high levels of childhood abuse or neglect, nor having had a significant number of negative life events generally (e.g. Sar, Akyuz, Kundakci, Kiziltyan *et al.*, 2004), so such experiences are not a *necessary* condition for developing a somatic symptom disorder. Second, the actual levels of stress reported by individuals with somatic symptom disorders are not necessarily significantly higher than those reported by individuals with other psychopathologies, so stress levels *per se* do not differentially predict the development of a somatic symptom disorder (Roelofs, Spinhoven, Sandijck, Moene *et al.*, 2005). Third, high levels of childhood trauma and negative life events can be found in the histories of a wide range of psychopathologies (e.g. personality disorders, eating disorders, anxiety disorders and so on), so why should someone who has this kind of traumatic history develop a somatic symptom disorder rather than any of these others (although it must be admitted that somatic symptom disorders are regularly comorbid with many other psychiatric disorders)? Some theories do specify a central role for stress and early negative experiences in the development of somatic symptom disorders and the conflict-resolution model adopted by many psychodynamic theorists is one example (see section 13.2.1) and the attentional-narrowing model of hysteria proposed by Janet (1907) is another (see section 13.2.2). However, the role of stress and childhood trauma in other theories is often underdeveloped and this is an aspect of our understanding of the aetiology of somatic symptom disorders that needs to be explored.

There are also several familial risk factors that have been identified for somatic symptom disorders and these include parents with somatisation characteristics, having a significant other/relative with an organic disease, psychopathology of close family members, a dysfunctional family climate and insecure attachment (Schulte & Petermann, 2011). However, these factors are also risk factors for the development of many other psychiatric disorders, and so are not specific to somatic symptom disorders alone.

13.2.4 Learning Approaches

Numerous theorists have suggested that somatic symptom disorders may develop because many of the aspects of these disorders are learnt through specific types of experiences. For example, Craig, Boardman, Mills, Daley-Jones & Drake (1993) have argued that many individuals learn to interpret emotional symptoms as indicative of physical illness. This learning could occur in a number of ways. First, individuals suffering conversion disorder, somatic symptom disorder or illness anxiety disorder often report having had early childhood experiences where close members of their family have experienced physical illness or somatic symptoms (Tezzi, Duckworth & Adams, 2001), and so expressing any negative feelings (emotional or physical) may occur through somatisation because of exposure to modelling by important family members. In support of this view, Craig, Cox & Klein (2002) compared the childhood histories of three groups of women – those with somatic symptom disorder, those with a long-term illness and healthy controls. They found that those with somatic symptom disorder were three times more likely than those in the other groups to have had a parent with a serious physical illness.

A related view is that expressing symptoms of physical illness may be reinforced by parents. For example, some parents may view all underlying problems (including psychological ones) as being physical rather than emotional, and subtly encourage their children to report psychological problems in physical terms (Latimer, 1981). In an insightful study, Craig, Bialas, Hodson *et al.* (2004) observed mothers playing with their 4- to 8-year-old children. Mothers who exhibited somatisation symptoms were less emotionally expressive than control mothers during most play tasks. However, they were significantly *more* responsive to their children when they played with medicine-related toys (e.g. a medical box). In this way, mothers who already display somatisation symptoms may pass this predisposition on to their children through the differential display of attention in medicine-related contexts.

Finally, early learning of the kind described above means that many individuals may learn to describe emotional symptoms in physical terms and in extreme cases begin to adopt what is known as a **sick role**. Adopting a sick role has a number of disadvantages – it means a loss of power and influence as the individual relinquishes tasks and duties to others; it also involves a loss of pleasure, especially if an individual becomes house-bound or even bed-ridden because of their symptoms. However, Ullman & Krasner (1975) have argued that adopting a sick role can have significant advantages and rewards in terms of the attention the sufferer is likely to receive from others, and the absolving of responsibility can be viewed as a way of opting out of having to directly deal with life stressors and conflicts. In this case, adopting the sick role becomes a coping style for adult life. While this view is consistent with the fact that somatising mothers may teach their children similar tendencies, adopting a sick role implies

sick role Playing the role of being sick as defined by the society to which the individual belongs.

that the individual is unable to cope with the normal rigours and challenges of daily life. Convincing evidence that this is indeed the case still needs to be collected.

Nevertheless, there does seem to be some reasonable evidence that children may learn somatising attitudes from their parents in various ways and this may provide a basis for the possible development of somatic symptom disorders in later life.

13.2.5 Cognitive Factors

One important feature of most of the somatic symptom disorders is that the sufferer believes they have physical deficits or symptoms that are significant and threatening, but in most cases there is little or no medical justification for these beliefs. This strongly suggests that sufferers may have developed thinking and information processing biases that lead them to believe they have medical symptoms when in fact they do not. Such cognitive biases can take a number of forms. They may involve **interpretation biases**, in which the individual interprets ambiguous bodily sensations as threatening and evidence for a potential serious illness (Marcus *et al.*, 2007). For example, when an individual with illness anxiety disorder experiences a stomach pain they may interpret this catastrophically as a possible symptom of stomach cancer, rather than, say, the result of eating something that was 'off'. This biased thinking then gives rise to a range of consequences which are likely to reinforce the biased belief, including increased fear and anxiety, preoccupation with similar symptoms, overestimating the probability that a symptom is a sign of a disease and reassurance-seeking (Warwick, 1995; Rief, Buhlmann, Wilhelm, Borkenhagen & Brahler, 2006) (see Figure 13.2). In a similar vein, Barsky (1992) argued that patients with somatic symptom disorder have a bias towards describing minor automatic bodily sensations in a catastrophic manner, which leads to a significantly higher level of reported symptoms. In support of these views, Lim & Kim (2005) used an emotional Stroop procedure to demonstrate that individuals diagnosed with a somatic symptom disorder showed a significant Stroop interference effect for physical threat words (e.g. injury, seizure, inflammation), suggesting that these individuals consciously and selectively attended to physical-symptom related cues. In addition, when given ambiguous health-related vignettes about illness and death, Haenen, de Jong, Schmidt, Stevens & Visser (2000) found that individuals with illness anxiety disorder were significantly more

interpretation biases Cognitive biases in which an individual interprets ambiguous events as threatening and evidence for potential negative outcomes.

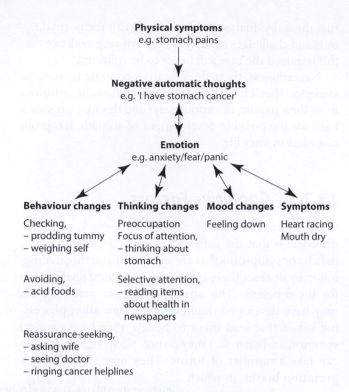

Physical symptoms
e.g. stomach pains

↓

Negative automatic thoughts
e.g. 'I have stomach cancer'

↓

Emotion
e.g. anxiety/fear/panic

Behaviour changes	**Thinking changes**	**Mood changes**	**Symptoms**
Checking,	Preoccupation	Feeling down	Heart racing
– prodding tummy	Focus of attention,		Mouth dry
– weighing self	– thinking about		
	stomach		
Avoiding,			
– acid foods	Selective attention,		
	– reading items		
	about health in		
Reassurance-seeking,	newspapers		
– asking wife			
– seeing doctor			
– ringing cancer helplines			

FIGURE 13.2 *This cognitive model of illness anxiety disorder illustrates how physical symptoms or bodily sensations evoke negative automatic thoughts about illness. These thoughts then trigger feelings of anxiety, which in turn trigger a range of behavioural, cognitive and mood reactions that reinforce biased beliefs and illness anxiety symptoms.*
Source: After Warwick, H.M.C (1995). Assessment of hypochondriasis. Behaviour Research and Therapy, 33, 845–853. Reproduced with permission.

likely than controls to interpret these vignettes as serious and threatening.

Recent studies also suggest that individuals with somatic symptom disorders may also have a **memory bias** towards remembering and retrieving illness relevant material. This bias also appears to make it difficult for somatic symptom disorder sufferers to suppress illness-related material, which may be rapidly retrieved from memory when thinking about potential symptoms or illnesses (Wingenfeld, Terfehr, Meyer, Lowe & Spitzer, 2013).

One interesting feature of individuals with illness anxiety disorder and somatic symptom disorder is their tendency to reject diagnoses that disagree with their own beliefs about their health, and to seek further opinions – presumably in the belief that someone will agree with their own view. Smeets, de Jong & Mayer (2000) found that individuals with illness anxiety disorder possessed a **reasoning bias** that supported this 'doctor

> **memory bias** Individuals with many psychopathologies may have a bias towards remembering and retrieving illness relevant material.

> **reasoning bias** The tendency of individuals with illness anxiety disorder to reject diagnoses that disagree with their own beliefs about their health and to seek further opinions – presumably in the belief that someone will agree with their view.

shopping'. They would actively seek out and accept information that agreed with their own view of their medical state, but would ignore or reject arguments against their own beliefs. This process will inevitably maintain hypochondriacal thinking and generalized anxiety about health issues. In addition, individuals with somatic symptom disorders show greater attention allocation to words and phrases that support their own beliefs about their health than those that do not (Witthöft, Rist & Bailer, 2009) – a process that is likely to reinforce existing dysfunctional beliefs.

The preceding evidence strongly suggests that many somatic symptom disorders are maintained by cognitive factors that take the form of (1) attentional biases to physical threats, (2) biases towards interpreting body sensations and symptoms as threatening, (3) reasoning biases that maintain beliefs about illness and being ill, (4) memory biases that facilitate the retrieval of illness-relevant material, and (5) catastrophising of symptoms. However, none of these accounts explains how the individual with a somatic symptom disorder *acquires* these thinking and information processing biases. Some insight into how these biases might develop has been provided by Brown (2004). Brown argues that '**rogue representations**' are developed by a range of experiences and these representations provide inappropriate templates by which information is selected and interpreted. Rogue representations can be created by experiences that include:

> **rogue representations** In somatic symptom disorders, representations that provide inappropriate templates by which information about body shape and health are selected and interpreted.

1. a history of physical illness that causes a tendency to interpret any sensation as a symptom of illness,

2. a history of experiencing emotional states that have strong physical manifestations (e.g. anxiety is associated with shaking, palpitations, nausea, muscle tension, chest pain, dizziness) (such experiences might arise from childhood trauma and abuse and result in a tendency to interpret such symptoms fearfully), and

3. exposure to physical illness in others (e.g. abnormal levels of illness in the family), which creates a memory template by which one's own physical sensations are interpreted.

In support of this account, there is good evidence to suggest that individuals with somatic symptom disorders do experience these factors with significantly greater frequency than non-sufferers (Schrag, Brown & Trimble, 2004; Tezzi, Duckworth & Adams, 2001; Holder-Perkins & Wise, 2001; Hotopf, Mayou, Wadsworth & Wessely, 1999).

For an integrated view of cognitive behavioural models of somatic symptom disorders, the review by Witthöft & Hiller (2010) is recommended.

13.2.6 Sociocultural Approaches

There is some evidence that sociocultural factors can influence both the prevalence of somatic symptom disorders and the nature of the symptoms exhibited in specific disorders. Being ill involves playing a social role that is often shaped by the society to which the individual belongs (Fox, 1989). As described earlier, this role is known as the *sick role* and even across societies it is defined in ways that may help individuals to cope with psychological distress and conflict. For example, the sick role in most societies means that (1) the sick person is exempt from the normal social roles that the person has for the duration of the illness, and (2) the sick person is often seen as not responsible for their illness (Parsons, 1951). Thus, playing the sick role can provide relief from the stresses and strains of everyday living. However, the likelihood of an individual adopting the sick role as a way of coping with stress and conflict will depend on attitudes towards unexplained somatic symptoms in different cultures. In some cultures, expressing physical pain is an accepted way of communicating psychological distress and rates of somatic symptom disorders tend to be higher in such cultures – e.g. in Latin countries and amongst American Hispanic women (Tomasson, Kent & Coryll, 1991; Escobar, Burnam, Karno, Forsythe & Golding, 1987). In such communities, individuals may be encouraged to somatize psychological distress in a way that allows them to more readily adopt a sick role (Goldberg & Bridges, 1988). In addition to cultural factors that affect the somatisation of psychological distress, socio-economic standards also influence prevalence rates. Individuals who live in rural areas, who are less well educated and have a poorer standard of living are more likely to exhibit somatic symptom disorders (Maldonado & Spiegel, 2003) – possibly because in such socio-economic groups the expression of psychological distress is less acceptable and so psychological symptoms are expressed as physical illness.

One final social factor can be identified in the aetiology of conversion disorder. Physical symptoms associated with conversion disorder can often be 'contagious' and affect a number of people within a single social setting or social group. This is similar to the physical symptoms of hysteria that were often reported in young women at pop concerts during the 1960s and 1970s. Examples of contagion appear to occur following an acute period of stress within a closely knit social group, where all those involved display very similar unexplained somatisation symptoms. A recent example of this was reported by Cassady, Kirschke, Jones, Craig *et al.* (2005) within an Amish community in the US. Four of them developed motor deficits (inability to hold up their heads) and weight loss symptoms following a period of acute stress within the closely knit Amish community. Examples of 'contagious hysteria' such as this continue to be reported, but as yet there is no convincing explanation for these multiple cases of somatic symptom disorders.

13.2.7 Biological Factors

Because somatic symptom disorders involve what are apparently physical symptoms, it is reasonable to ask whether there are any underlying biological causes for these disorders. We know that (1) a certain percentage of those with conversion disorder and somatic symptom disorder do have medical conditions that could contribute to their psychopathology (Maldonado & Spiegel, 2003; Hilder-Perkins & Wise, 2001), and (2) that many who develop somatic symptom disorders have a history of physical illness in their family (Hotopf, Mayou, Wadsworth & Wessely, 1999), and both of these factors give grounds for exploring the role of biological factors.

Torgersen (1986) investigated a possible genetic component to somatic symptom disorders by investigating the presence of somatic symptom disorder in MZ and DZ twins. He found that MZ twins had a higher concordance rate for somatic symptom disorders than DZ twins, which is consistent with there being a genetic component to these disorders, but the sample he used was particularly small. Some studies have investigated inherited aspects of somatic symptom disorder using adoption studies, but these have only served to further confuse the role of inheritance in somatic symptom disorders. Bohman, Cloninger, von Knorring & Sigvardsson (1984) and Cloninger, Sigvardsson, von Knorring & Bohman (1984) traced the histories of the biological and adoptive parents of 859 women with somatic symptom disorder. However, they rather surprisingly found that the biological fathers of these women had significantly higher levels of alcoholism or violent crime than would be expected by chance, suggesting a biological or genetic link between antisocial behaviour and somatic symptom disorder! We await further, larger scale genetic studies of somatic symptom disorders that may clarify these findings.

Because of the startling symptoms of conversion disorder, such as paralysis and blindness, there have been numerous studies that have investigated the role of the brain in this disorder. Studies that have monitored the brainwaves of individuals with conversion disorder suggest that sensory information is reaching the appropriate areas of the brain, but they are not being registered in consciousness. Marshall, Halligan, Fink, Wade & Frackowiak (1997) carried out a positron emission tomography (PET scan) study of a conversion disorder patient who had a paralysed left leg. They found increased activation in the right orbitofrontal and anterior cingulated cortices, but an absence of activity in the right primary cortex when the patient attempted to move the leg. This suggests that unexplained paralysis involves some form of inhibition of primary motor activity by brain areas such as the orbitofrontal and anterior cingulated cortices. Interestingly, this same pattern of excitation and inhibition can be found in PET scans of individuals who have leg paralysis induced by hypnosis (Halligan, Athwal, Oakley & Frackowiak, 2000), suggesting that paralysis caused by conversion disorder and hypnosis may reflect very similar underlying brain processes. These findings suggest that brain areas that would normally instigate movement are being activated, but other areas of the brain that would not be involved are being activated in order to inhibit the movement (e.g. orbitofrontal and anterior cingulated cortices – see Research Methods 13.1).

Finally, recent research has identified a relationship between somatic symptom disorders and heightened activity in areas of the brain that are associated with unpleasant body sensations. These include the anterior insula and the anterior cingulate, and their associations with the somatosensory cortex – the latter being an area of the brain involved in processing bodily sensations (Landgrebe, Barta, Rosengarth et al., 2008). This is consistent with heightened activity in these areas making individuals more vulnerable to the development of somatic symptom disorders through the heightened unpleasantness of these symptoms and an increased tendency to be aware of somatic sensations.

RESEARCH METHODS 13.1

BRAIN IMAGING USING POSITRON EMISSION TOMOGRAPHY (PET)

Many psychopathologies are either associated with brain abnormalities or are caused by unusual patterns of activation in the brain, and so understanding a particular disorder can be helped significantly by procedures that allow the researcher to look directly at the structure and functioning of the brain.

Positron emission tomography (commonly known as 'PET scans') involves injecting radioactive molecules into the bloodstream. These molecules are then tracked by a scanner as they are metabolized in the brain. Differences in metabolism rates in the brain are detected and show up on a screen as different colour contrasts. Lighter and warmer colours denote areas when metabolism (and therefore brain activity) is high. This technique is useful for detecting which areas of the brain are active when the individual engages in a particular behaviour.

A study by Marshall, Halligan, Fink, Wade & Frackowiak (1997) used PET scanning methods to try to identify the areas of the brain that became active when an individual with conversion disorder attempted to move their paralyzed left leg. They found that when the patient tried to move their paralyzed leg, areas not normally associated with movement became active (the right cingulated cortex and the right orbitofrontal cortex). They hypothesized that the activation of these areas somehow actively inhibited or prevented leg movement. In a similar study, Halligan, Athwal, Oakley & Frackowiak (2000) used the same PET procedure with a patient whose left leg had been paralyzed by hypnosis. The resulting scan (Figure 1) shows that exactly the same areas of the brain are activated when the hypnotized individual tries to move their leg – suggesting that paralysis in both conversion disorder and under hypnosis may be a result of movement being inhibited by the activation of certain cortical brain areas.

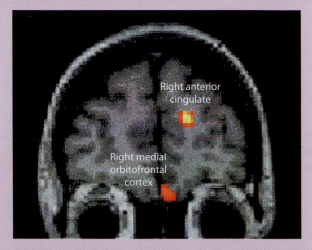

FIGURE 1 *Relative changes in cerebral blood flow associated with attempted movement of the hypnotically paralyzed left leg.*
Source: Marshal, J.C., Halligan, P.W., Fink, G.R., Wade, D.T. & Frackowiak, R.S.J. (1997) The functional anatomy of a hysterical paralysis. *Cognition 64,* B1-B8. Reproduced with permission.

SELF-TEST QUESTIONS

- What are the main features of psychodynamic explanations of somatic symptom disorders, and what is meant by a *conflict-resolution* view of somatic symptoms?

- Can you describe at least one experimental study showing that those suffering from conversion disorder are aware of sensory stimuli at some level or processing?

- What was Janet's (1907) explanation of the aetiology of conversion disorder?

- Why is it helpful in understanding conversion disorder symptoms to make comparisons between conversion disorder and behaviour under hypnosis?

- What kinds of negative life events and stressors have been noted as risk factors in the development of somatic symptom disorders?

- What is the evidence that those suffering from somatic symptom disorders may have 'learnt' to adopt a *sick role* during childhood?

- What is the experimental evidence that individuals with somatic symptom disorders have *information processing biases*?

- What are *rogue representations* and how might they affect thinking about illness symptoms?

- What is the *sick role* and how might it help an individual cope with stress?

- How have brain scanning technologies been used to throw light on the mechanisms underlying conversion disorder symptoms?

SECTION SUMMARY

13.2   THE AETIOLOGY OF SOMATIC SYMPTOM DISORDERS

Theories of the aetiology of somatic symptom disorders attempt to explain the development of these disorders at a number of different levels. Common to many of these accounts are (1) the role of anxiety, depression and existing psychological conflict in generating somatic symptoms, (2) the part that playing the 'sick role' might have in coping with psychological stress, and the way that this role might be reinforced by family, associates and medical practitioners, and (3) the role of biased thinking and dysfunctional beliefs in maintaining beliefs about illness in those with somatic symptom disorders. The startling and disabling nature of the symptoms in conversion disorder has meant that some theoretical accounts have been addressed solely to the unique features of this disorder. These include accounts that attempt to explain how sensory information is blocked from consciousness and how an individual may lose voluntary control over their movements (e.g. brain scan studies, and comparisons of conversion disorder with hypnosis).

   To summarize the key points:

- Psychodynamic interpretation of somatic symptom disorders is mainly a conflict-resolution one in which distressing memories, inner conflict, anxiety and unacceptable thoughts are repressed in consciousness but outwardly expressed as somatic symptoms.

- In disorders such as conversion disorder, there appears to be a dissociation between the individual's behaviour and their awareness of that behaviour.

- Studies suggest that in conversion disorder, sensory input is processed at some level, but is unavailable at the level of conscious awareness.

- There are many similarities between the behaviour of individuals with conversion disorder and the effects of hypnosis, suggesting that similar mechanisms may be responsible for both.

- Risk factors in the history of many somatic symptom disorders are a history of trauma or abuse, significant periods of stress and anxiety, and a range of familial risk factors.

- Some *learning accounts* of somatic symptom disorders suggest that expressing symptoms of physical illness may be reinforced during childhood by parents or carers.

- Many individuals with somatic symptom disorders may have learnt to adopt a *'sick role'* which may be a form of coping with life stressors.

- Most of the somatic symptom disorders are characterized by *cognitive and information processing biases*, including (1) interpretation biases, (2) reasoning biases, (3) memory biases, (4) catastrophising of symptoms, and (5) the development of inappropriate 'rogue representations'. These reinforce the dysfunctional thinking that maintains somatic symptoms.

- *Sociocultural factors* can influence both the prevalence of somatic symptom disorders and the nature of the symptoms exhibited.

- Physical symptoms associated with conversion disorder can often be 'contagious' and affect a number of people within a single social setting or social group.

- Both twin and adoption studies have provided only indirect evidence for a genetic component to somatic symptom disorders.

- PET scans suggest that increased activation in some areas of the brain may inhibit the movement of 'paralysed' limbs in individuals with conversion disorder. A similar effect can be found in individuals whose limbs are paralysed by hypnosis.

13.3 THE TREATMENT OF SOMATIC SYMPTOM DISORDERS

One of the main problems in treating somatic symptom disorders is that they manifest as physical or medical symptoms, and thus a sufferer will initially undertake a lengthy period of medical treatment in order to discover whether there are any underlying physical causes for their symptoms. This not only allows symptoms to become entrenched before psychological therapy is attempted but may also contribute to the resistance of sufferers to psychological therapy. For example, many sufferers of disorders such as somatic symptom disorder, illness anxiety disorder and conversion disorder frequently deny they have a psychological problem and continue to search for a medical 'solution' to their symptoms. This denial of an underlying psychological cause makes treatment problematic.

Secondly, we have already noted that somatic symptom disorders are highly comorbid with other disorders such as anxiety and depression. This raises a 'chicken and egg' question about which symptoms come first. For instance, many people who are anxious and depressed come to have concerns about their physical health as a result of their anxiety and depression (Noyes, Kathol, Fisher, Phillips *et al.*, 1994) and it is often the case that treating the anxiety or depression will significantly reduce illness symptoms and worries (Smith, 1992). In addition, illness anxiety disorder and somatic symptom disorder are often comorbid with obsessive convulsive

disorder (OCD) and, as we shall see later in this section, treatments for OCD are also successful in treating the symptoms of these somatoform problems (Phillips, 1998; Rosen, 1996).

This section will now consider the types of treatments that are often used with somatic symptom disorders.

13.3.1 *Psychodynamic Therapy*

In the section on aetiology, we noted that psychodynamic accounts of somatic symptom disorders take a 'conflict-resolution' view of these disorders, in which inner conflict, anxiety and distressing memories are repressed in consciousness and outwardly expressed as somatic symptoms. **Psychodynamic therapy** therefore focuses on procedures designed to bring these repressed thoughts and memories into consciousness where they can be effectively dealt with. This will in turn alleviate the somatic symptoms that are a consequence of repression. Nevertheless, somatic symptoms are often quite resistant to a psychodynamic approach – not least because the client may continue to believe that they have a physical and not a psychological problem. In a study following up the progress of individuals with somatic symptom disorders, Kent, Tomasson & Coryell (1995) found that 63 per cent of conversion patients and 92 per cent of somatisation patients still met the diagnostic criteria for these disorders 4 years after initial diagnosis. However, meta-analyses have indicated

psychodynamic therapy Therapeutic approach that focuses on procedures designed to bring repressed thoughts and memories into consciousness where they can be effectively dealt with.

that psychodynamic therapy for somatoform disorders is (1) more effective than no treatment or treatment as usual, and (2) is likely to be more successful the greater the competence of the therapist and his/her ability to form a therapeutic alliance with the client (Leichsenring, 2001, 2005).

13.3.2   Behaviour Therapy

Many somatic symptom disorders involve some learning and behavioural-based components that can be treated by the use of the learning principles implicit in behaviour therapy. Two prominent examples of such components include (1) the reinforcing function of attention given to individuals (e.g. by family members or medical professionals), which will maintain their 'illness' behaviours (such as staying away from work or complaining about pain), and (2) continuous checking for physical signs of illness or deformity, which is conspicuous in illness anxiety disorder and somatic symptom disorder.

In the case of the former, Liebson (1967) reports an intervention that attempted to change the reinforcement contingencies controlling the illness behaviour of a client who had given up his job because of pain and weakness in his legs. Liebson persuaded the client's family to stop giving him attention for illness-related behaviours such as being idle at home or complaining of pain. In addition, the therapist arranged for him to get a pay rise if he went back to work. This approach makes the reinforcement contingencies more functional by providing motivation to work and removing any incentive to feel ill or incapacitated. Similar approaches can be used to extinguish reassurance-seeking behaviour in individuals with illness anxiety disorder. This type of programme attempts to minimize the anxiety relief that clients get from reassurance seeking from the therapist, friends and family. It can also be supplemented by coping skills training, in which the client receives training and advice on how to cope with anxiety and by training in the skills required for use in social or work settings. Also useful are relaxation training and behavioural techniques designed to reduce worrying. This form of **behavioural stress management** has been found to be significantly more effective than no treatment control conditions (Clark, Salkovskis, Hackmann *et al.*, 1998) and follow-up studies suggest that clients treated by these procedures were still symptom-free 5 years after treatment (Warwick & Marks, 1988).

behavioural stress management
Behavioural techniques designed to reduce worrying and increase relaxation.

13.3.3   Cognitive Behavioural Therapy

As we saw in the previous section on aetiology, cognitive factors appear to play an important role in the acquisition and maintenance of somatic symptom disorders. Sufferers appear to acquire interpretation biases (causing them to view ambiguous stimuli as evidence of illness or physical problems); they possess reasoning biases (causing them to accept only information that is consistent with their illness beliefs); they possess negative thought patterns that lead to the catastrophising of physical symptoms into beliefs about full-blown illness; and they possess a set of underlying beliefs about their disorder that help to support their symptoms (e.g. the illness anxiety disorder sufferer may hold dysfunctional beliefs that all physical sensations are indicators of impending illness). Such cognitive factors appear to play an important role in most somatic symptom disorders. This being the case, CBT seems particularly well suited to treating these dysfunctional beliefs and thought patterns.

CBT has proven to be particularly effective for those diagnosed with illness anxiety disorder (formerly hypochondriasis). Such sufferers tend to interpret anything to do with bodily symptoms or health issues as threatening (Smeets, de Jong & Meyer, 2000) and CBT can be used to challenge these dysfunctional beliefs and replace them with more functional health beliefs. Case History 13.1 relates the symptoms of an illness anxiety disorder patient who was convinced he had leukaemia after developing a harmless rash (Salkovskis & Warwick, 1986). The treatment for this case involved the client being asked to test two competing hypotheses – either (1) that he was suffering from a life-threatening illness, or (2) he had a problem with anxiety which was maintained by repeated medical consultation and checking of his symptoms. He was also asked to stop indulging in behaviours that might maintain his anxiety such as checking to see if his rash had extended, continually seeking consultations with his doctor, and reading medical text books. After around 30 days his symptoms had significantly reduced. He was no longer regularly seeking medical reassurance about his symptoms and his self-rated scores on measures of health anxiety and illness beliefs had also significantly decreased.

Randomized controlled trials (RCTs) indicate that CBT for somatic symptom disorders is significantly more effective at treating symptoms than normal medical care, and is still effective at 6- and 12-month follow-up (Barsky & Ahern, 2004), but recent RCTs suggest that it may not necessarily be more effective than other treatments such as progressive muscle relaxation (Schroder, Heider,

ILLNESS ANXIETY DISORDER

'A' is a 32-year-old married engineer. He developed an acute urticarial rash, consisting of typical eruptions of intensely itchy weals surrounded by red areas. (Urticaria may occur as a sensitivity response to certain foods or as a reaction to drugs such as penicillin. However, in 50 per cent of chronic cases, a cause is never found. It is, though, *not* associated with any malignant condition.) His rash persisted for several months despite advice and treatment from his family doctor and dermatologist. He had had a previous episode of urticaria, which was salicylate induced, but apart from this had been completely healthy. Physical examination and investigations revealed no significant abnormality and a diagnosis of idiopathic urticaria was made. Despite this reassurance, he became increasingly anxious that he had a serious underlying condition such as leukaemia and sought repeated consultations. His belief in the idea that he had leukaemia had arisen in the first instance because a skin specialist had attempted to reassure him by giving him some medical details. Specifically, this doctor had told him that the rash arose because his white blood cells were attacking foreign matter in his blood cells. The patient had interpreted this as meaning that there was something wrong with his white blood cells, signifying that he had leukaemia. He inspected his rash frequently, read textbooks in an effort to discover 'the real cause' and could talk of little else to his wife, family and friends. Eventually, he became suicidal, unable to work and was admitted into psychiatric care.

Source: Salkovskis, P.M. & Warwick, H.M.C. (1986). Morbid preoccupations, health anxiety and reassurance: a cognitive-behavioural approach to hypochondriasis. *Behaviour Research and Therapy, 24,* 597–602, p. 598.

Clinical Commentary

This patient exhibits many of the classic symptoms of an individual with illness anxiety disorder (formerly known as hypochondriasis) or somatic symptom disorder. He is obsessed with his symptoms – continually checking his rash to see if it has grown, and can talk of nothing else to friends and families. The continual checking of symptoms and reassurance-seeking from friends and family merely act to maintain his anxiety. He also displays a number of cognitive biases typical of illness anxiety disorder. He interprets his rash and the explanation given to him by a skin specialist in threatening terms – even though there are many other explanations for them. He is also unmoved by reassurances from doctors that his condition is not life threatening. He has a bias to dismiss evidence that is not consistent with his own view of his symptoms and to accept only evidence that is consistent with his view. Treatment consisted of CBT (described more fully in the text) to deal with these cognitive biases.

Zaby & Gollner, 2013). Other studies have begun to look at the feasibility of new third-wave CBT interventions such as mindfulness-based cognitive therapy (MBCT) (see Chapter 4) in the treatment of somatic symptom disorders and initial results indicate the effects of mindfulness may be favourable comparable to those of CBT (Fjorback, Arendt, Ornbol, Walach *et al.*, 2013).

13.3.4   Drug Treatments

Throughout this chapter we have continually emphasized the important relationship between somatoform disorders and anxiety and depression. Anxiety and depression are regularly comorbid with conversion disorder (Sar, Akyuz, Kundakci, Kiziltyan *et al.*, 2004), somatic symptom disorders (Gureje, Simon, Ustun & Goldberg, 1997) and illness anxiety disorder (Abramowitz & Braddock,

2006). This suggests that pharmacological interventions effective with anxiety and depression may to some extent help to alleviate the symptoms of somatic symptom disorders. A range of **drug treatments** has regularly been applied to somatic symptom disorders and these include tricyclic antidepressants (TCAs), selective serotonin reuptake inhibitors (SSRIs), serotonin–norepinephrine reuptake inhibitors (SNRIs), atypical antipsychotics and herbal medications (e.g. St John's wort) (Somashekar, Jainer & Wuntakal, 2013). Antidepressants (TCAs, SSRIs and SNRIs) seem to be the most effective with somatic symptom disorders generally, but more research is required to understand how these drugs have their therapeutic effects and there is also a need to develop drugs that will alleviate symptoms of specific somatic symptoms disorders.

drug treatments The use of pharmacological or drug treatments to alleviate some of the symptoms of psychopathologies.

SELF-TEST QUESTIONS

- What are the two main difficulties encountered when attempting to treat somatic symptom disorders with psychological therapies?
- Can you describe the main features of behavioural stress management procedures for somatic symptom disorders?
- How are CBT interventions use to treat somatic symptom disorders?
- What kinds of drug treatments are most effective in treating the symptoms of somatic symptom disorders?

SECTION SUMMARY

13.3 THE TREATMENT OF SOMATIC SYMPTOM DISORDERS

A range of different treatments has been utilized with somatic symptom disorders. Traditionally, psychodynamic therapy has been an important method of treating somatic symptom disorders such as conversion disorder, although the evidence for the medium-term success of such interventions is meagre. Both behaviour therapy and CBT have become important interventions over the past 10–15 years with CBT being successfully used across a range of somatic symptom disorders to challenge dysfunctional beliefs and to correct interpretational biases. Third-wave CBT treatments, such as mindfulness-based cognitive therapy, are being tested out as possible new effective interventions for somatic symptom disorders. Finally, drug treatments can also be effective in helping to alleviate some of the symptoms of somatic symptom disorders, with the most effective being antidepressants.

To sum up the key points:

- Somatic symptom disorders can be difficult to treat because the sufferer believes their problems have medical rather than psychological origins and they are usually associated with other comorbid disorders that complicate treatment.
- Psychodynamic therapy attempts to bring repressed thoughts and memories that may cause somatic symptoms into consciousness where they can be effectively dealt with.
- *Behavioural stress management* attempts to deal with somatic symptom disorders by eliminating reassurance-seeking from clients and supplementing this with coping skills training, relaxation training and techniques designed to reduce worrying.
- CBT can be used across a range of somatic symptom disorders to challenge and replace the dysfunctional beliefs that maintain somatic symptoms.
- Antidepressant drugs such as SSRIs or tricyclic antidepressants have been used to reduce the symptoms of many somatic symptom disorders, although evidence for the long-term effectiveness of this kind of treatment is still modest.

13.4 SOMATIC SYMPTOM DISORDERS REVIEWED

Somatic symptom disorders are a group of loosely associated disorders, all of which can be characterized by psychological problems manifesting as physical symptoms or as psychological distress caused by physical symptoms or physical features. In many cases, the physical symptoms may have no detectable medical cause, but neither are symptoms being faked by the sufferer. The causes of the symptoms appear to lie in psychological factors such as life stress, anxiety and a history of conflict or abuse. In many cases individuals may have learnt through experience to adopt a 'sick role', which allows the person to opt out of stressful daily living; in others it is clear the sufferer has developed a range of cognitive biases and dysfunctional beliefs that maintain their illness symptoms (e.g. illness anxiety disorder). Interventions effective in addressing symptoms of somatic symptom disorders include psychoanalysis, behaviour therapy, CBT and antidepressant pharmacological treatments.

To access the online resources for this chapter go to
www.wiley-psychopathology.com/ch13

Reading	Video	Activity
• Is an illness ever 'all in the mind'? • Journal article: Hysterical blindness • Glossary of key terms • Clinical issues • Links to journal articles • References	• Somatization • Factitious disorder	• Self-test questions • Revision flashcards • Research questions

14 Dissociative Experiences

 To access the online resources for this chapter go to
www.wiley-psychopathology.com/ch14

ROUTE MAP OF THE CHAPTER

This chapter describes the diagnosis and characteristics of three dissociative disorders, namely dissociative amnesia, dissociative identity disorder (DID, formally multiple personality disorder) and depersonalization disorder. The aetiology section then discusses a range of theories of the development of dissociative experiences including psychodynamic theory, cognitive models and the possible role that therapy can play in constructing dissociative symptoms. Finally, we discuss treatments for dissociative experiences. These are relatively underdeveloped but in particular we discuss the use of psychoanalysis and hypnotherapy.

CHAPTER OUTLINE

LEARNING OUTCOMES

When you have completed this chapter, you should be able to:

1. Describe the main diagnostic criteria and symptom characteristics for the DSM-5 listed dissociative disorders and evaluate some of the issues concerning diagnosis, comorbidity and prevalence.

2. Describe and evaluate the main theories of the aetiology of dissociative disorders.

3. Evaluate the difficulties associated with treating dissociative experiences and describe at least two types of therapies that have been used to treat dissociative experiences.

This is DID . . . dissociative identity disorder . . . multiple personality disorder. We are a freak. I've started writing this a million times . . . I don't know how to explain this. I know I hide. I don't want you to know me. I feel shame about who I am . . . maybe that word defines me . . . shame. I lived through childhood abuses that one only hears about . . . between the ages of 4 and 20 . . . I think. I am not sure. I don't even know if I remember everything yet. That's a part of the disorder . . . forgetting. The other part of the disorder is having 11 other people living inside of me. Therapy is working. Most of the time I remember when they are out now . . . in the past they used to come out and I wouldn't know about it unless they left a clue behind . . . lots of clues for me to see. Sometimes they would hurt me . . . intentionally. Sometimes I would hear them screaming in my head or saying things to me . . . sometimes derogatory, sometimes soothing . . . sometimes they would only cry. Sometimes I would find things that I couldn't understand. Waking with a teddy bear beside me that I didn't remember. Buying toys and items that I would never buy . . . losing money . . . people saying hello to me in the street who I didn't know. My spouse looks at me and asks me who I am half the time. My spouse no longer knows me but still loves me and I reciprocate. Without the support I couldn't make it.

Michael's Story

Introduction

Dissociative disorders generally are characterized by significant changes in an individual's sense of identity, memory, perception or consciousness, and these changes can either be gradual or sudden, transient or chronic. Symptoms of these disorders include an inability to recall important personal or life events (e.g. dissociative amnesia), a temporary loss or disruption of identity (e.g. dissociative identity disorder), or significant feelings of depersonalization in which the person feels that something about themselves has been altered (depersonalization disorder). Dissociative symptoms such as these are often found in the aftermath of severe or prolonged traumatic experiences, such as childhood abuse, natural disasters or life-threatening accidents. Because of this close association with trauma, dissociative symptoms are often found in individuals with a diagnosis of post-traumatic stress disorder (PTSD) and DSM-5 recognizes this relationship by placing dissociative disorders in the chapter next to trauma and stressor-related disorders (see Chapter 6). The diagnostic criteria for both PTSD and acute stress disorder contain reference to dissociative symptoms such as amnesia, flashbacks, numbing, and depersonalization. We will discuss the relationship between PTSD and dissociative symptoms later in this chapter (section 14.1.4).

Michael's story above describes one particular form taken by dissociative symptoms, and this is the presence of many distinct identities that each periodically take control of his behaviour. These are often known as multiple personalities and identities, and the sufferer may often be unaware that they present these different personalities to the world. This is known as *dissociative identity disorder* and represents a failure to integrate various aspects of identity, consciousness and memory. As we shall see, in many cases dissociative disorders develop because the individual is attempting to cope with psychological distress and conflict that may be related to earlier traumatic life experiences. Being able to adopt different personalities and repress specific memories is viewed by many theorists as a way of coping with the anxiety and stress derived from these earlier life experiences (e.g. Gleaves, 1996).

To a certain degree we all have dissociative experiences at some time during our lifetime; we will sometimes have brief periods of memory loss, become confused about

TABLE 14.1 *Prevalence and comorbidity of dissociative disorders*

Dissociative disorder	Prevalence of disorder in the past year (mean age 33)		
	Males (*N* = 309) *n* (%)	**Females** (*N* = 349) *n* (%)	**Total sample** (*N* = 658) *n* (%)
Depersonalization disorder	2 (0.6%)	3 (0.9%)	5 (0.8%)
Dissociative amnesia	3 (1.0%)	9 (2.6%)	12 (1.8%)
Dissociative identity disorder (DID)	5 (1.6%)	5 (1.4%)	10 (1.5%)
Dissociative disorder not otherwise specified (DDNOS)	21 (6.8%)	15 (4.3%)	36 (5.5%)
Any dissociative disorder	30 (9.7%)	30 (8.6%)	60 (9.1%)

Psychopathology	Prevalence of dissociative disorder in the past year among individuals (mean age 33)	
	Without co-occurring psychopathology (%) (*n/N*)	**With co-occurring psychopathology (%) (*n/N*)**
Anxiety disorder	5.6% (30 of 533)	33.3% (25 of 75)
Eating disorder	7.0% (39 of 558)	32.0% (16 of 50)
Mood disorder	5.3% (28 of 527)	33.3% (27 of 81)
Personality disorder	3.9% (20 of 512)	36.5% (35 of 96)
Substance use disorder	7.6% (40 of 526)	18.3% (15 of 82)
Any anxiety, eating, mood, personality or substance use disorder	2.1% (8 of 373)	20.0% (47 of 235)

Source: Johnson, J.G., Cohen, P., Kasen S. & Brooks, J.S. (2006). Dissociative disorders among adults in the community, impaired functioning and Axis I and II comorbidity, *Journal of Psychiatric Research, 40*, 131–140. Reproduced with permission.

our identity, and sometimes just feel 'strange' or depersonalized (Kihlstrom, 2001). A community sample study by Seedat, Stein & Forde (2003) found that 6 per cent of respondents endorsed four to five lifetime dissociative symptoms and approximately one in three endorsed at least one lifetime symptom – suggesting that dissociative symptoms are relatively common in the general population. Very often, these experiences will coincide with periods of stress or trauma, and it is common for individuals who have experienced severe trauma – such as combat troops, survivors of natural disasters or terrorist attacks – to experience these kinds of dissociative symptoms (Kozaric-Kovacic & Borovecki, 2005). However, for some individuals these symptoms either become so severe that they significantly disrupt their day-to-day living, or become chronic conditions, rather than temporary responses to stress, and cause significant distress to the individual. In such circumstances, they may become diagnosable as a dissociative disorder.

In this chapter we will discuss three dissociative disorders, namely (1) dissociative amnesia, (2) dissociative identity disorder, and (3) depersonalization disorder. Table 14.1 shows the prevalence and comorbidity rates for dissociative disorders taken in an American community sample (Johnson, Cohen, Kasen & Brooks, 2006). These figures suggest a 12-month prevalence rate of 9.1 per cent for dissociative disorders generally in individuals with a mean age of 33 years. Such disorders are also comorbid in around one in three cases with anxiety disorders, eating disorders, mood disorders or personality disorders.

14.1 THE DIAGNOSIS AND CHARACTERISTICS OF DISSOCIATIVE DISORDERS

14.1.1 Dissociative Amnesia

The main feature of this disorder is an inability to recall important personal information that is usually of a stressful or traumatic nature (DSM-5 Summary Table 14.1). This memory loss cannot be explained by normal forgetfulness, nor is it the result of any demonstrable damage to

DSM-5 SUMMARY TABLE 14.1 *Criteria for dissociative amnesia*

- Unable to remember important personal information, usually relating to traumatic or stressful occurrences, that is not in line with natural forgetting, causing significant distress or impairment in important areas of functioning

- The symptoms are not the result of the use of a substance, or due to another neurological or medical condition

- The disorder is not better accounted for by another mental disorder, such as dissociative identity disorder, post-traumatic stress disorder or acute stress disorder

the brain. **Dissociative amnesia** normally manifests itself as a retrospectively reported gap or series of gaps in the individual's ability to verbally recall aspects of their life history, and these gaps are often related to traumatic or stressful experiences such as physical or sexual abuse, involvement in a natural or man-made disaster, being in an accident, experiencing military combat or terrorist attacks. Periods of amnesia may also extend to aspects of the individual's own behaviour, such as memory loss for violent outbursts, suicide attempts or self-harm, and the perpetrators of some violent crimes have often claimed that they cannot recall anything about

dissociative amnesia An inability to recall important personal information that is usually of a stressful or traumatic nature.

the event itself (and may use this in their legal defence against prosecution for violent crimes such as murder – see Focus Point 14.1).

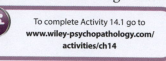

To complete Activity 14.1 go to www.wiley-psychopathology.com/activities/ch14

Dissociative amnesia is associated with several types of memory disturbances. **Localized amnesia** is when the individual is unable to recall events that occurred during a specific time period (e.g. memory loss for a period of 2 days following a serious car accident). **Selective amnesia** is where an individual can recall some, but not all, of the events during a specific time period (e.g. a combat veteran may be able to recall some events during a violent military encounter but not others). The final three types of dissociative amnesia are the least common, but represent the most severe types of symptoms. **Generalized amnesia** is a failure of recall that

localized amnesia When an individual is unable to recall events that occurred during a specific time period (e.g. memory loss for a period of 2 days following a serious car accident).

selective amnesia A memory disturbance where an individual can recall some, but not all, of the events during a specific time period (e.g. a combat veteran may be able to recall some events during a violent military encounter, but not others).

generalized amnesia A failure of recall that encompasses the person's entire life. Such individuals may suddenly report to police stations or to hospitals as a result of this disorientation.

FOCUS POINT 14.1

AMNESIA AND CRIME

In May 2002, the BBC News website reported how Jan Charlton was convicted of the manslaughter of her boyfriend after hacking him to death with an axe. She claimed in court at Leeds that she did not know she had killed him and 'was in a daze, a total and utter daze'. Professor Michael Kopelman, the psychiatrist who interviewed her, said she claimed she did not remember the killing until the memory came back more than a month after the incident and he told the court that amnesia in homicides was most common in 'crimes of passion'.

To read the news story 'Axe killer "could have forgotten" crime' go to http://tinyurl.com/nzjlvau

Claims of crime-related amnesia such as this are relatively common and between 20 and 30 per cent of individuals who commit violent crimes report no recollections of the event (Cima, Merckelbach, Hollnack & Knauer, 2003). Although post-crime amnesia is most common for violent crimes, it can also be found in those charged with non-violent crimes such as fraud (Kopelman, Green, Guinan, Lewis & Stanhope, 1994). Amnesia may occur when the individual is in a highly altered physiological state, either because of extreme rage or anger, or because they are under the influence of alcohol or other substances (Kopelman, 2002).

Nevertheless, there are good incentives for a criminal to fake symptoms of amnesia for a criminal act and it is estimated that about 20 per cent of criminals who claim amnesia are feigning their memory loss (Hopwood & Snell, 1933). So how can we identify true amnesiacs from those that are faking? One method is to use what is called symptom validity testing (SVT). SVT is a forced-choice questionnaire in which defendants are asked a series of questions about their crime. In each question, the defendant must choose between two equally plausible answers, one of which is correct and the other incorrect. Examples include: 'The magazine that was stolen was (1) *Penthouse*, or (2) *Playboy*'; 'In the bar there is a huge mirror, (1) yes or (2) no'. If the individual is truly suffering amnesia they should perform at around chance level (i.e. get around 50 per cent correct). However, studies suggest that individuals who are faking amnesia (and so do know the correct answer) perform at levels *significantly below chance* (e.g. get less than 40 per cent correct) (Merckelbach, Hauer & Rassin, 2002; Jelicic, Merckelbach & van Bergen, 2004). This is because they attempt to overcompensate for their knowledge of the crime by tending to choose the wrong answer rather than choosing answers at random.

encompasses the person's entire life and such individuals may suddenly report to police stations or to hospitals as a result of this disorientation. **Continuous amnesia** is the inability to recall events from a specific time up to and including the present, and is also associated with the forgetting of new events as they occur. **Systematic amnesia** is a loss of memory that relates to specific categories of information, such as family history.

> **continuous amnesia** A memory disturbance where there is an inability to recall events from a specific time up to and including the present.

> **systematic amnesia** A memory disturbance where there is a loss of memory that relates to specific categories of information, such as family history.

Dissociative amnesia can present in any age group, from young children to adults. However, it is difficult to diagnose in young children because it can be confused with attentional and educational difficulties. An episode may last for minutes or years, but symptoms can often be alleviated simply by removing the individual from the circumstances or situation that may have caused trauma or stress (e.g. dissociative amnesia may spontaneously remit when a soldier is removed from the locality of the battlefield). Interestingly, individuals with dissociative amnesia are much less disturbed by their symptoms than we might expect, and this may imply that the amnesia serves some kind of coping function that enables the individual to deal with stress and trauma (Kihlstrom, 2001).

The prevalence rate for dissociative amnesia in a community sample is around 1.8 per cent, with rates being higher in females than in males (Johnson, Cohen, Kasen & Brooks, 2006; see Table 14.1).

14.1.2 Dissociative Identity Disorder (DID)

Formerly known as multiple personality disorder, this is a disorder where the individual displays two or more distinct identities or personality states that take turns to control behaviour (DSM-5 Summary Table 14.2). **Dissociative identity disorder** is also associated with an inability to recall important autobiographical information. DID reflects an inability to integrate aspects of identity, memory and consciousness to the extent that each personality state is experienced as if it has its own life history, self-image and identity. Different identities usually have different names and will quite often have very contrasting personalities (e.g. controlling, destructive or passive). DID is associated with gaps in memory for various life events and the extent of this

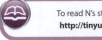

To read N's story on DID go to **http://tinyurl.com/nekzbdy**

> **dissociative identity disorder** A dissociative disorder characterized by the individual displaying two or more distinct identities or personality states that take turns to control behaviour (formerly known as multiple personality disorder).

DSM-5 SUMMARY TABLE 14.2 *Criteria for dissociative identity disorder*

DSM-5 SUMMARY TABLE 14.2 *Criteria for dissociative identity disorder*

- Disturbance of identity marked by at least two distinct personality states, which in some cultures may be seen as evidence of possession
- Recurring breaks in remembering everyday events, personal information or traumatic events that is not in line with natural forgetting
- The symptoms cause significant distress or impairment in important areas of functioning
- The disturbance is not a normal part of broadly accepted cultural or religious practice, e.g. children having an imaginary friend
- The symptoms are not the result of the use of a substance, or due to another medical condition

amnesia may vary with the nature of the different identities (hostile personalities tend to have more complete memories whereas passive personalities have fewer). The different identities will often deny knowledge of each other, but may battle for control of behaviour, and an identity that is not in control may gain access to consciousness by producing auditory hallucinations (e.g. by giving instructions).

Michael's story at the beginning of the chapter describes how the sufferer is often unaware that different identities are taking control of his behaviour, and he only becomes aware afterwards by finding certain items around (such as waking up with a teddy bear in his bed). He is also surprised when people he doesn't know say hello to him – people whom one of his other identities has presumably met. The time required to switch from one personality to another is usually very brief and may be preceded by various physical signs, such as rapid blinking, changes in voice or demeanour, an interruption of ongoing speech or thought, and changes in facial expression. A distinction can be made between the **host identity** (the one that existed before the onset of the disorder) and **alter identities** (those that develop after the onset). In the simplest form of the disorder, two alternating identities take turns to control behaviour, and in many cases the alter identity may know about the host personality, but not vice versa (Dorahy, 2001). The host may become slowly aware of the existence of the alter identity, as did *Michael*, by encountering evidence that a different personality state has been controlling behaviour. However, many DID sufferers have significantly more than just one alter identity and surveys suggest that the average is around

> **host identity** The identity that existed before the onset of dissociative identity disorder.

> **alter identities** The identities that develop after the onset of dissociative identity disorder.

13 per sufferer (Putnam, 1997). Around 85 per cent of sufferers also report having at least one alter identity that is a child and over 50 per cent report having an alter identity that is of the opposite sex (Putnam, Guroff, Silberman, Barban & Post, 1986). In general, alter identities tend to take on a range of contrasting personalities and may individually take charge only of certain areas in the sufferer's life (such as one dealing with sex life, one with work, one with anger and so on). DID can also manifest in the form of possession by 'spirits', supernatural beings, 'ghosts', demons or personalities from previous lives. In some cultures, these 'possession' states are viewed as relatively normal, and as manifestations that have an explanation in the religious beliefs of the locality. One such example is that described in Focus Point 1.1, where spirit possession is a common trauma-related phenomenon in child soldiers in war-affected areas of Africa.

A significant factor in the history of DID sufferers appears to be childhood trauma, and surveys suggest that over 95 per cent of individuals diagnosed with DID report childhood sexual and physical abuse, including incest (Putnam, 1997; Putnam, Guroff, Silberman, Barban & Post, 1986). Many sufferers report their disorder beginning in childhood, often before 12 years of age, and at times of severe trauma (Putnam, 1997), and over 70 per cent of outpatients with DID report having attempted suicide at least once (DSM-5, 2013). This seems to suggest that DID may be a coping strategy adopted by children and adolescents to distance themselves from experienced trauma (Atchison & McFarlane, 1994). We will discuss this issue more fully in the section on aetiology. Individuals with DID also exhibit a large number of comorbid conditions, including PTSD, depressive disorders, trauma- and stressor-related disorders, personality disorders (especially avoidant and borderline personality disorders, conversion disorder, somatic symptom disorder, eating disorders, OCD and substance use disorders) (DSM-5, 2013; see also Table 14.1).

The prevalence rate for DID is around 1.5 per cent in a community sample (Johnson, Cohen, Kasen & Brooks, 2006), but the number of reported cases has risen significantly in recent years. For example, Elzinga, van Dyck & Spinhoven (1998) found that the number of reported cases worldwide rose from 79 in 1980 to 6000 in 1986, and the vast majority of these have been reported in the US. What, then, has caused this significant increase in diagnosed cases of DID? There may be numerous factors and these include:

1. the inclusion of DID for the first time as a diagnostic category in DSM-III published in 1980,

2. early cases of DID may simply have been diagnosed as examples of schizophrenia rather than a dissociative disorder (Rosenbaum, 1980),

---

CASE HISTORY 14.1

THE EMERGENCE OF 'EVELYN'

The psychiatrist Robert F. Jeans reported the case of a single, 31-year-old professional woman called Gina. Her initial symptoms included sleepwalking and screaming in her sleep, and he noted that she was uncomfortable about being a woman, and about the thought of having a sexual relationship with her married boyfriend known as TC. During the course of therapy, he noticed a second personality emerging, which was called Mary Sunshine by Gina and her therapist. Mary was more feminine, outgoing and more seductive than Gina. Over time Gina found evidence that Mary had been controlling her behaviour across various aspects of her life: she found hot chocolate drinks in the sink (Gina did not like hot chocolate), large sums of money withdrawn from her bank account and a sewing machine was delivered – that was presumably ordered by Mary. Mary also seemed to take over Gina's relationship with TC and acted as a seductive and warm partner, whereas Gina had often been cynical and cold. Eventually a third personality emerged that appeared to be a synthesis of the features of Gina and Mary. Gina described how this happened:

> I was lying in bed trying to go to sleep. Someone started to cry about TC. I was sure that it was Mary. I started to talk to her. The person told me that she didn't have a name. Later she said that Mary called her Evelyn but that she didn't like that name. I asked her what she preferred to be called. She replied that she will decide later.
>
> I was suspicious at first that it was Mary pretending to be Evelyn. I changed my mind, however, because the person I talked to had too much sense to be Mary. She said that she realized that TC was unreliable but she still loved him and was very lonely. She agreed that it would be best to find a reliable man.
>
> She told me that she comes out once a day for a very short time to get used to the world. She promised that she will come out to see you sometime when she is stronger.
>
> I asked her where Mary was. She said Mary was so exhausted from designing her home that she had fallen asleep.

Source: Jeans, R.F. (1976). An independently validated case of multiple personality. *Journal of Abnormal Psychology, 85,* 249–255. American Psychological Association. Reproduced by permission.

Over time Evelyn appeared more and more and appeared to be an adaptive alter identity that allowed Gina to cope better with the range of issues in her life. Within months she was Evelyn all the time, had no recollection of Mary and later became successfully married to a physician.

Clinical Commentary

Like many alter identities in DID, Mary evolved primarily to take charge of certain areas of Gina's life – particularly controlling her feminine role and her relationship with TC. Typically, Gina had no recollection of her behaviour when Mary was in control, and only came to be aware of Mary by encountering evidence that a different personality had been controlling behaviour. In this particular case, Evelyn eventually merged as a synthesis of both Gina and Mary's personalities and this proved to be an adaptive change that enabled Gina to deal with a range of matters across her life.

3. during the 1970s, interest in multiple personality disorder was fuelled by the publication of *Sybil* (Schreiber, 1973), a case history describing an individual with 16 personalities which was later popularized in a Hollywood film,

4. therapists have increasingly used hypnosis in an attempt to get victims of childhood abuse to reveal details of this abuse or to reveal alter identities and there is some evidence that the power of suggestion under hypnosis may be enough to generate 'multiple personalities' that were not there in the first place (Piper, 1997; Powell & Gee, 1999),

5. dissociative disorders such as DID are closely associated with trauma and PTSD and interest in these syndromes grew following the experience of veterans of the Vietnam war, and

6. many of the symptoms of DID can be relatively easily faked and some experts estimate that as many as 25 per cent of DID cases are either faked or are induced by therapy (Ross, 1997).

14.1.3 Depersonalization Disorder

The central feature of this disorder is persistent or recurrent episodes of depersonalization (DSM-5 Summary Table 14.3). These symptoms are characterized by feelings of detachment or estrangement from the self. The sufferer may feel that they are living in a dream or in a film, and that they are not in control of their behaviour but merely standing outside of themselves, watching themselves. As we mentioned earlier, symptoms of depersonalization are commonly experienced, so **depersonalization disorder**

> **depersonalization disorder** Feelings of detachment or estrangement from the self (such as living in a dream or standing outside of oneself, watching oneself).

should only be diagnosed if the symptoms are recurrent, cause severe distress and disrupt day-to-day living.

DSM-5 SUMMARY TABLE 14.3 *Criteria for depersonalization/ derealization disorder*

- Recurring occurrences of depersonalization, derealization, or both, causing significant distress or impairment in important areas of functioning:
    - Depersonalization – experiences of detachment or outside observation of one's own thoughts, feelings, body or actions
    - Derealization – Experiences of detachment with regard to surroundings
- During the occurrences the individual is still able to distinguish what is real from what is not
- The disturbance is not directly due to the use of a substance
- The disorder is not better accounted for by another mental disorder, such as schizophrenia, panic disorder or major depressive disorder

Depersonalization symptoms also occur regularly in other disorders, such as panic disorder, schizophrenia and other dissociative disorders, so it is important to determine whether symptoms of these other disorders are present when an individual presents with depersonalization experiences.

As is the case in panic disorder, sufferers of depersonalization disorder often think they are 'going crazy' – especially if this is also associated with a sense of derealization (a feeling that the world is strange or unreal). Other common symptoms include disturbances in the sense of time, obsessive rumination and somatic concerns. Depersonalization disorder is also highly comorbid with anxiety symptoms and depression, and a past history of anxiety and depression is regularly reported in those suffering depersonalization disorder (Baker, Hunter, Lawrence, Medford *et al.*, 2003).

In everyday life, depersonalization experiences can occur when the individual is in transitional physiological states such as on waking up, when feeling tired, practicing meditation, or following an acute stressor or scary experience. Interestingly, depersonalization disorder has been associated with severe life trauma such as childhood physical and emotional abuse (Simeon, Guralnik, Schmeidler, Sirof & Knutelska, 2001), and research suggests that depersonalization during periods of stress or trauma may be adaptive in reducing symptoms of anxiety or depression immediately after the event (Shilony & Grossman, 1993). In fact, depersonalization may account for the periods of emotional 'numbing' that individuals feel immediately after a severe traumatic experience and before developing symptoms of post-traumatic stress disorder (see section 6.6).

Depersonalization disorder often develops in late adolescence or early adulthood, with a mean onset age of 16 years and less than 20 per cent of sufferers reporting onset after 20 years of age. The 12-month prevalence rate for depersonalization disorder is relatively low at 0.8 per cent (Johnson, Cohen, Kasen & Brooks, 2006), but it must be remembered that individual depersonalization experiences are significantly more prevalent than this.

14.1.4   Dissociative Disorders and PTSD

As we have already mentioned, there is a close relationship between symptoms of PTSD and dissociative disorders. Studies have suggested that one in three individuals with PTSD also experience high levels of dissociation in the form of dissociative amnesia and depersonalization (Lipschitz, Winegar, Hartnick, Foote & Southwick, 1999). This has led clinical researchers to speculate about the relationship between these two diagnostic categories, with at least some clinicians arguing for a dissociative subtype of PTSD (Lanius, Vermetten, Loewenstein, Brand *et al.*, 2010). We noted earlier that dissociative-type symptoms are already listed in the diagnostic features of PTSD and these symptoms include amnesia, flashbacks, numbing and depersonalization. PTSD is related to dissociative disorders in at least three possible ways. First, persistent dissociative symptoms immediately after a traumatic experience are a significant predictor of the subsequent acquisition of full-blown PTSD (Murray, Ehlers & Mayou, 2002), so a tendency to dissociative symptoms may make individuals vulnerable to the development of other PTSD-relevant symptoms. Second, dissociation is a feature of 'complex' or severe PTSD (van der Hart, Nijenhuis & Steele, 2005), in which individuals suffer from a range of persistent symptoms, enduring personality changes, affect disruption, somatisation, and changes in self-perception (Herman, 1992). **Complex PTSD** is often associated with early-age interpersonal trauma and with dissociative symptoms from that early age (Ford & Kidd, 1998; McLean & Gallop, 2003), and has led some clinicians to argue that dissociation and other PTSD symptoms may share a common central psychobiological pathology (Brewin, 2003). Third, there may exist a specific dissociative subtype of PTSD that is defined by the severity of both PTSD and dissociative symptoms, and which may account for up to 30 per cent of cases of PTSD (Wolf, Lunney, Miller, Resick *et al.*, 2012). We must await further research on the psychological and biological pathways through which dissociative and PTSD symptoms are acquired before we will be able to fully understand the relationship between dissociative symptoms and PTSD, and one outcome of this research might be a dissociative subtype of PTSD in future editions of the DSM.

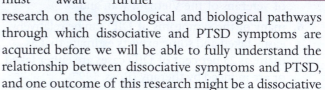

To read the article on dissociation as a feature of PTSD by van der Hart, Nijenhuis & Steele go to **www.wiley-psychopathology.com/reading/ch14**

complex PTSD A severe form of PTSD often associated with early age interpersonal trauma and with dissociative symptoms from that early age.

To read the article about the dissociative subtype of PTSD by Wolf *et al.* go to **www.wiley-psychopathology.com/reading/ch14**

SELF-TEST QUESTIONS

- What are the main diagnostic features of dissociative amnesia?
- Can you name the five types of memory disturbance that occur in dissociative amnesia?
- What are the main features of dissociative identity disorder (DID) and what was it previously called?
- Can you describe the difference between host identities and alter identities in DID?
- What is the estimated prevalence rate of DID and what problems are involved in estimating its prevalence?
- What are the main features of depersonalization disorder?
- What is complex PTSD and how is it related to dissociative experiences?

14.2   THE AETIOLOGY OF DISSOCIATIVE DISORDERS

The questions of how and why people develop dissociative disorders are interesting ones. The symptoms are often striking and quite frequently found in individuals who have undergone experiences of extreme trauma or stress. There are two important issues that need addressing when we attempt to look at the causes of dissociative disorders. The first is that we need to be able to explain how the components of consciousness (e.g. cognition, emotion) become dissociated. Consciousness is normally a fully integrated entity, but in individuals with dissociative disorders some memories can be completely lost or suppressed (as in dissociative amnesia), some aspects of consciousness can be isolated from others (such as the different identities experienced in DID), and the individual can feel that they are dissociated from both themselves and the outside world (e.g. in depersonalization disorder). Any theory of dissociative disorders needs to explain why some individuals develop these symptoms and how the different components of consciousness become dissociated. The second issue associated with the aetiology of dissociative disorders is whether the symptoms actually have a functional significance – that is, do the symptoms serve a purpose? In the previous sections of this chapter we have alluded to the possibility that dissociative symptoms may protect individuals from stressful memories and experiences and help them to cope with day-to-day living, anxiety and depression (e.g. Kihlstrom, 2001; Riether & Stoudemire, 1988; Atchison &

McFarlane, 1994). As we go through the various theories of dissociative disorders, it is important to bear these two central issues in mind.

14.2.1   Risk Factors for Dissociative Disorders

Risk factors for dissociative disorders include a history of anxiety and depression that pre-dates the disorder (Putnam, Guroff, Silberman, Barban & Post, 1986) and a history of **childhood abuse** (physical and sexual) and childhood neglect: up to 95 per cent of individuals diagnosed with DID report instances of childhood sexual and physical abuse (Putnam, 1997; Putnam, Guroff, Silberman, Barban & Post, 1986). Dissociative amnesia is associated with a history of trauma and is more common after major stressful life events such as war or natural disasters (Coons, 1999). What is not clear is whether childhood abuse actively contributes to the development of dissociative disorders in a causal way. However, the strength of dissociative symptoms appears to be directly related to the age of onset of physical and sexual abuse, with higher levels of symptoms reported in those whose abuse began early in life, or who suffered disorganized or insecure attachment early in life (Chu, Frey, Ganzel & Matthews, 1999; Pasquini, Liotti, Mazzotti, Fassone *et al.*, 2002). Dissociative symptoms are also commonly found in homeless and runaway youths who have suffered various forms of abuse

> **childhood abuse** The physical or psychological maltreatment of a child.

To read the article by Pasquini *et al.* about early-life risk factors go to **www.wiley-psychopathology.com/ reading/ch14**

prior to leaving home (Tyler, Cauce & Whitbeck, 2004). This provides some indirect support for the view that childhood abuse does play a causal role in the development of dissociative disorders. The issue of whether being male or female is a risk factor for dissociative disorders is still unclear; some studies suggest a significantly greater risk of dissociative disorders in women than in men (Putnam & Loewenstein, 2000; Simeon, Gross, Guralnik, Stein *et al.*, 1997), but more recent community-based studies suggest that this may be true only for dissociative amnesia (Johnson, Cohen, Kasen & Brooks, 2006; see Table 14.1).

14.2.2   Psychodynamic Theories

The general view of most psychodynamic theorists is that dissociative symptoms are caused by **repression**, which is the most basic of the ego defence mechanisms.

> **repression** A basic psychodynamic defence mechanism that helps to suppress painful memories and prevent stressful thoughts.

In these cases, repression helps to unconsciously suppress painful memories and to prevent stressful thoughts entering consciousness. As a result, repression helps to control conflict, anxiety and depression. According to Freudian views, dissociative amnesia is a simple example of repression, where stressful or traumatic memories are simply suppressed until the individual has the strength to cope with them. These tendencies to repress unwanted or painful memories may be acquired in childhood when excessively strict parents may instil a strict moral code in their children. When the individual violates this code during adulthood (such as by having an extramarital affair), the expression of these 'unacceptable' id impulses are repressed by unconscious mechanisms that prevent the retrieval of such memories. DID is viewed as a further form of repression, but one in which repression persists for significantly longer (e.g. throughout a lifetime) in order to repress the memories of very traumatic childhood events (Brenner, 1999; Reis, 1993). In psychodynamic terms, the DID sufferer develops alter egos in order to avoid the distressing world they were brought up in, and also to protect themselves from the impulses that they believe may have been the reason for their excessive punishments during childhood. Thus, a DID sufferer can disown any 'bad' thoughts or impulses by attributing them to a 'rogue' alter ego.

There is certainly some evidence that individuals with dissociative disorders do experience less conflict and anxiety than individuals with other forms of psychopathology (e.g. substance abuse) and this is evidence that supports the psychodynamic view (Alpher, 1996). However, we must once again return to the difficulties inherent in testing predictions from psychodynamic accounts because of the difficulties in objectively measuring the concepts and mechanisms described in psychodynamic theory. This is just as much true of psychodynamic accounts of dissociative disorders as it is of any other psychopathology (see Chapter 1).

14.2.3   The Role of Fantasy and Dissociative Experiences

There is some evidence that dissociative disorders may develop more readily in individuals who have early dissociative or depersonalization experiences and such individuals may learn to utilize such experiences in order to suppress anxiety and painful memories. For example, in a selection of prison inmates diagnosed with DID, Lewis, Yeager, Swica, Pincus & Lewis (1997) found that 12 out of 14 cases had long-standing dissociative experiences that pre-dated the full-blown DID symptoms and 10 of the 14 reported having imaginary companions during childhood. Reporting imaginary companions during childhood is common in individuals with DID (Sanders, 1992), and some theorists have argued that such experiences will predispose an individual to develop DID. For example, Kluft (1992) has argued that a child who constructs imaginary companions may find that they can occasionally use these imaginary personalities to ameliorate periods of stress and conflict, and the child may then learn to actively construct these personalities into adaptive alter identities to protect themselves from stress. However, currently the only evidence in support of this view is that individuals with dissociative disorders do appear to have a history of dissociative experiences and they also appear to have strong imaginations and a rich fantasy life, which will contribute to the development of symptoms such as alter identities (Lynn, 1988). Most recent studies have also demonstrated a significant but modest relationship between measures of fantasy-proneness and dissociative symptoms (Giesbrecht, Merckelbach & Geraerts, 2007) and more detailed analysis seems to indicate that particular aspects of fantasy-proneness, such as vivid mental imagery and parapsychological beliefs, are the best predictors of dissociative psychopathology (Klinger, Henning & Janssen, 2009).

14.2.4   Cognitive Approaches

A central issue in explaining dissociative disorders is an understanding of how various components of conscious experience come to be detached from each other (e.g. how memory for some events becomes suppressed while for others remains intact). Such characteristics suggest that an answer may lie in how normal memory and recall processes are affected in individuals suffering dissociative symptoms, and many cognitive theorists believe that dissociative disorders represent a disruption of all or part of the sufferer's memory processes (Dorahy, 2001).

For example, do individuals displaying dissociative symptoms show poorer recall for trauma- or abuse-related material in experimental studies? If so, then they may have developed a tendency to avoid encoding traumatic material in memory or they may have developed impaired retrieval processes for such information (McNally, Clancy & Schachter, 2001). Unfortunately, much of the experimental evidence does not support such a simple explanation. In explicit memory tasks – where participants are asked to either remember or forget words presented in a recall task – individuals with a history of childhood abuse showed no difference in recall of trauma-related words than non-abused control participants (McNally, Metzger, Lasko, Clancy & Pitman, 1998; Cloitre, Cancienne, Brodsky, Dulit & Perry, 1996). Although these studies did not directly investigate individuals with dissociative symptoms, the findings do suggest that individuals with a history of abuse do not have an automatic tendency to suppress or avoid encoding or recalling traumatic material. However, subsequent studies have suggested that individuals high in dissociative symptoms do have impaired recall for words associated with trauma under conditions of *divided attention* (i.e. when they are asked to perform a concurrent task as well as the memory task) (DePrince & Freyd, 2004) (see Figure 14.1). This suggests that attentional context is important in helping high dissociators to forget trauma-related material and dividing their attention across a range of sources may help individuals with dissociative symptoms facilitate forgetting of emotional-relevant or traumatic information.

An alternative explanation of the memory failures experienced by dissociative disorder sufferers is in terms of how changes in their physiological and emotional state can influence recall of memories. **State-dependent memory** is a well-established cognitive phenomenon in which the individual is more likely to remember an event if they are in the same physiological state as when the event occurred (Bower, 1981). We have already noted that individuals with dissociative disorders often experience severely traumatic life events that cause significant changes in mood and physiology when such events occur (e.g. being involved in a natural disaster such as an earthquake may be experienced during states of hyperarousal and panic). If the events relating to this experience are encoded in memory during these unusual emotional states, then it may be that the individual will have difficulty properly

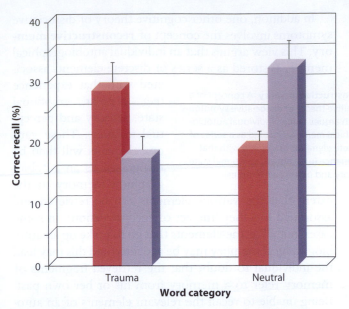

FIGURE 14.1 *Percentage correct recall of to-be-remembered neutral and trauma-related words presented under conditions of divided attention. Blue bars represent participants who scored high on dissociative experiences; red bars represent those who scored low on dissociative experiences.*
Source: After DePrince, A.P. & Freyd, J.J. (2004). Forgetting trauma stimuli. *Psychological Science, 15,* 488–492. Reproduced with permission.

recalling them in less traumatic emotional states. State-dependent learning has also been used to explain the between-identity amnesia that is often experienced in DID (Szostak, Lister, Eckhardt & Weingartner, 1995) and it has been suggested that most between-identities amnesia will occur between those alter identities that differ most in their normal mood states (e.g. there will be less cross-identity knowledge between identities that display negative emotions, such as sadness or anger, and those that exhibit mainly positive emotions such as joy and happiness) (Bower, 1981). Nevertheless, while state-dependent memory may seem like an appealing explanation of dissociative amnesia, there are some difficulties with this explanation. Firstly, dissociative amnesia is usually much more severe than has been reported in basic studies of state-dependent memory. Secondly, individuals with DID have problems with both free recall memory and recognition memory, but state-dependent memory is usually only found with the former (Peters, Uyterlinde, Consemulder & van der Hart, 1998). Thirdly, studies have effectively demonstrated that different identities in DID can recall autobiographical information from the other identities when a concealed recognition test is used, suggesting that dissociative amnesia in DID probably does not entail inter-identity memory systems or is constrained by state-dependent learning (Huntjens, Verschuere & McNally, 2012).

> **state-dependent memory** A well-established cognitive phenomenon in which the individual is more likely to remember an event if he or she is in the same physiological state as when the event occurred.

In addition, one other cognitive theory of dissociative symptoms involves the concept of **reconstructive memory**. This view argues that an individual autobiographical memory is stored as a series of discrete elements associated with that experience (e.g. context, emotional state, sensory and perceptual features). These various elements will then be recognized as an autobiographical memory to the extent that the various elements can be retrieved and associated together (the act of reconstruction). In some cases, not all of the elements that go to make up an autobiographical memory may be activated and this may lead the individual to doubt that the retrieved fragments of memory refer to a memory from his or her own past. Being unable to recall the relevant elements of an autobiographical experience from memory is known as a deficit in **source-monitoring ability** (Johnson, Hashtroudi & Lindsay, 1993): an example of this is when an individual cannot remember whether they read something in a newspaper or whether it was just a rumour they heard from a friend. It has been suggested that dissociative amnesia may result from deficits in both reconstructive memory and source-monitoring abilities. For some reason, individuals with dissociative symptoms may not be able to recover from memory sufficient elements of an autobiographical event to convince themselves it was an experience that happened to them. In addition, a deficit in **reality monitoring** (a form of source monitoring required to distinguish mental contents arising from experience from those arising from imagination) may also lead them to doubt that they have actually had a particular experience (Johnson & Raye, 1981), and both of these processes may contribute to dissociative amnesia. Consistent with this view are findings that women who have experienced childhood sexual abuse and score high on dissociative experiences have greater difficulty than non-abused control participants in distinguishing between words they had seen in a memory test and words they imagined seeing (McNally, Clancy, Barrett & Parker, 2005; Clancy, Schachter, McNally & Pitman, 2000) – a finding that suggests they may well have a deficit in reality monitoring. However, deficits in reality monitoring can work both ways. They can prevent a person from identifying an autobiographical memory as one they have actually experienced, but they may also lead to the individual identifying an *imagined* event as an actual experience. This may be the basis for what have now become known as **false recovered memories of trauma** (Loftus, 1993), in which various therapeutic techniques are used to try to recover repressed childhood memories of trauma but which may actually generate false memories of events that did not occur. Such techniques may inadvertently lead the client to falsely recognize imagined experiences as ones that actually happened, and this issue is discussed more fully in Focus Point 14.2.

> **reconstructive memory** A concept of a cognitive theory of dissociative symptoms which argues that an individual autobiographical memory is stored as a series of discrete elements associated with that experience (e.g. context, emotional state, sensory and perceptual features).

> **source-monitoring ability** The ability to recall the relevant elements of an autobiographical experience from memory.

> **reality monitoring** A form of source monitoring required to distinguish mental contents arising from experience from those arising from imagination.

> **false recovered memories of trauma** The recovery of repressed childhood memories of trauma that turn out to be false.

FOCUS POINT 14.2

REPRESSED MEMORIES, RECOVERED MEMORIES AND FALSE MEMORY SYNDROME

There has been a belief among many therapists and clinicians that individuals can forget traumatic or stressful events in their life for relatively lengthy periods of time, and this view stems back to the original works of Freud who believed that severe trauma was repressed to the unconscious mind because it was too painful to tolerate. Many of the symptoms of dissociative disorders seem to support this belief – especially because many of these disorders are characterized by amnesia and childhood abuse is a common factor in the history of many with dissociative disorders. However, attempting to confirm that memories have been repressed is a difficult process. For example, it is often difficult to find corroborative evidence, even when repressed memories of abuse have been recovered, because many of the recovered memories may be of abuse that the perpetrators will be unwilling to substantiate. There are therefore a number of issues to address when considering repressed memories. In particular these are:

- Can memories of early childhood trauma or abuse be repressed?
- If they can be repressed, can they subsequently be recovered?
- If so-called repressed memories are recovered, are they accurate?

CAN MEMORIES OF CHILDHOOD TRAUMA OR ABUSE BE REPRESSED?

Williams (1995) used hospital files to identify 206 women who, as children, had received medical treatment for sexual abuse in the 1970s. Twenty years later, the researcher located these individuals and interviewed them about a range of topics including childhood sexual abuse. Thirty-eight per cent of those interviewed did not report the incident of sexual abuse for which they were hospitalized, but did report other incidents, suggesting that they were not simply holding back sensitive information. Of those who did report the incident of sexual abuse, 16 per cent reported that there were times in their lives when they had effectively forgotten it. This study suggests that there may be occasions when individuals do fail to recall traumatic events such as childhood abuse. However, this may simply be due to normal processes of forgetting rather than active repression of painful memories. In contrast, Zola (1998) reports a study investigating the memories of individuals whose childhood traumas were a matter of historical record (e.g. kidnap and Holocaust survivors). In all of these cases there was no evidence of repressed memories for these events in the survivors and they remembered most of the traumatic events quite vividly. Freyd (1996), however, has argued that childhood sexual abuse is qualitatively different from the traumas experienced by Zola's participants. She suggests that childhood sexual abuse is often perpetrated by a trusted caretaker, such as a parent or close relative, and this gives rise to what is called 'betrayal trauma', which is more likely to be repressed than other forms of trauma. So, studies such as these provide conflicting evidence as to whether trauma memories are repressed or not. If they are subject to periods of amnesia, then it needs to be established whether this is due to normal processes of forgetting or whether it is the result of an active repression process.

IF MEMORIES OF TRAUMA OR ABUSE CAN BE REPRESSED, CAN THEY SUBSEQUENTLY BE RECOVERED?

During the 1980s and 1990s many therapists came to believe that a wide range of psychopathology symptoms were caused by past sexual abuse that has been repressed in the memories of the victims. They also believed that a range of therapeutic methods could be used to recover these repressed memories, and these included hypnotism and directive psychotherapy. These approaches generally came to be known as recovered memory therapy and proponents of this approach had a crusading belief that a wide range of psychopathologies were indicative of childhood sexual abuse (Kaplan & Manicavasagar, 2001). Much of the impetus for this loose therapeutic movement came from a book called *The Courage to Heal*, written in 1988 by two feminist counsellors, Ellen Bass and Laura Davis. They argued that (1) a large number of people are the victims of childhood sexual abuse but do not realize they were abused, and (2) that a list of symptoms (e.g. being held in a way that made them feel uneasy) may well be indicative of actual childhood abuse. Their overriding principle was 'if you feel something abusive happened to you, it probably did'! Therapists who subsequently adopted this approach to treating psychopathology were thus given free rein to indulge in a directive approach attempting to uncover evidence of suppressed memories of childhood abuse – even to the point where clients were told they were 'in denial' if they could not remember instances of abuse! Under such conditions it is almost inevitable that clients may begin to 'recall' instances of abuse that did not actually happen.

IF SO-CALLED REPRESSED MEMORIES ARE RECOVERED, ARE THEY ACCURATE?

There have been numerous high-profile court cases – especially in the US – where parents or carers have been convicted of childhood abuse on the basis of memories of this abuse recovered by their children while undergoing therapy. In 1990, George Franklin was convicted of murdering a child 20 years earlier on the basis that his daughter suddenly remembered him committing the act while she was undergoing therapy. This conviction was subsequently quashed in 1995 as a result of substantial doubts about the validity of his daughter's memories. This case is an example of what has come to be known as *false memory syndrome*, in which some individuals recall

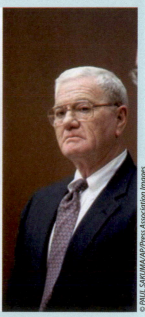

George Franklin (right) spent six years in prison for the murder of an 8-year-old girl based on the memories 'recovered' by his daughter, Eileen (left), under hypnosis 20 years after the event. It turned out that the details Eileen recalled could have come from newspaper reports, and subsequent DNA evidence cleared Franklin of a second murder that his daughter accused him of.

memoriesthatsubsequentlyturnouttobefalse.Thisdoesnot mean that the individual is actively lying or faking the memory, but a variety of psychological processes might contribute to the individual developing a false memory and believing that it is an accurate record of past events.

Processes that might contribute to false memories are:

- *Over-directive psychotherapy or hypnotherapy*, where the client is encouraged to hold the belief that they have been abused (e.g. Loftus, 1993). Many clients may actively want to believe they have been abused because it would help them to reattribute responsibility or blame for their behaviour or their moods.
- *Poor source-monitoring ability* is when the individual lacks the skills to identify the source of a memory. This may lead the individual to believe that an event that was only imagined actually happened. In support of this view, laboratory-based studies have indicated that women who claim to have recovered memories of childhood abuse are more likely than control participants to recognize material they have actually never seen before (Clancy, Schachter, McNally & Pitman, 2000) and are less able than control participants to discriminate words they had seen before from words they imagined seeing (McNally, Clancy, Barrett & Parker, 2005) (see Research Methods 14.1).

CONCLUSIONS

This debate is complex and still ongoing. There is no doubt that some people probably do repress memories of childhood abuse; *some* probably recover these memories – either with or without therapy – and *some* probably recall memories of childhood abuse that never actually happened. In a review of the available evidence at the time, Brewin & Andrews (1998) suggested that we should not rule out the possibility that any recovered memories might be genuine and that each case should be considered on its own merits. In particular, clinicians should be aware that clients are susceptible to suggestion and should avoid discourse that may shape the memories that are eventually reported by their clients.

RESEARCH METHODS 14.1

LABORATORY STUDIES OF FALSE RECOGNITION AND RECOVERED MEMORIES

Individuals who have suffered amnesia for stressful life events may occasionally recall what have now come to be known as false recovered memories of trauma. That is, they may actually recall events that they believed happened, but which objective evidence subsequently suggests did not happen (see Focus Point 14.2).

We have described in section 14.2 why we think some people might be prone to recalling memories that are false, but how do we go about studying this phenomenon experimentally?

False recognition – the mistaken belief that one has previously encountered a novel item – has been studied extensively in the laboratory and the methods used to investigate this have been applied to the study of false recovered memories in individuals with dissociative disorder symptoms.

In the laboratory procedure, participants are presented with lists of words, and each list is composed of words associated to a single non-presented 'theme word'. For example, a list may consist of words associated with *sweet* (such as *sour, sugar, bitter, candy* and so on). After hearing the lists, participants are then given a recognition test where they are presented with words (1) that were presented in the previous lists, (2) words that have not been presented before but are related to the theme words (known as *false targets*), and (3) a control set of words that have never been presented before but which are not related to the theme words.

Using college students as participants, many studies have suggested that rates of false recognition to false targets is high – so even non-clinical populations often believe they have seen words in the original lists when in fact they have not (i.e. exhibit false recognition) (Roediger & McDermott, 1995; Schachter, Norman & Koutstaal, 1998).

A number of studies have used this paradigm to test whether individuals with dissociative disorder symptoms have particularly high levels of false recognition. Clancy, Schachter, McNally & Pitman (2000) indeed found that a group of women who reported recovered memories of childhood sexual abuse was more prone to false recognition in this laboratory procedure than other groups (such as women who believed they were sexually abused as children but could not remember it, and women with no history of childhood sexual abuse). Interestingly, people who report having been abducted by space aliens also exhibit proneness to false recognition (Clancy, McNally, Schachter, Lenzenweger & Pitman, 2002) and the recall of such 'recovered memories' holds as much emotional potency and causes as much physiological arousal as genuine traumatic encounters recalled by war veterans (McNally, Lasko, Clancy *et al.*, 2004).

Experimental studies such as these suggest that false recognition of past experiences may not be uncommon. However, we must be wary of assuming that this experimental procedure (that was originally designed to investigate memory illusions) is one that can be automatically applied to the recovery of false memories in trauma victims or to explain the process of repression (even Roediger and colleagues are doubtful that this procedure alone can provide a full understanding of false recovered memories; Roediger & McDermott, 1995). As Axmacher, Do Lam, Kessler, Fell *et al.* (2010) point out, the laboratory-based procedure described above differs from the study of repressed memories in at least two important ways. First, such studies do not involve the learning or forgetting of traumatic memories and repression is a hypothetical process that should only be relevant to traumatic memories or those holding intense negative emotion. Second, Axmacher *et al.* argue that repression is not a voluntary process, so attempting to understand repression and recovered memories in paradigms that require voluntary learning and forgetting of neutral stimulus material cannot be analogous to the repression and recovery of traumatic memories. So, at this time we await the development of experimental procedures that might more faithfully replicate the processes involved in repressed memories and the false recognition of recovered memories of trauma.

14.2.5   Biological Explanations

Dissociative disorders generate symptoms – such as amnesia – that prima facie look as though they might have been generated by neurological defects or abnormalities in brain processes. Even so, there is very little evidence that these amnesic symptoms are caused by underlying deficits in brain function. First, memory loss tends to be selective and in many cases it is transitory. This suggests that if there are brain abnormalities causing these symptoms, these too must be selective and transitory. One such candidate that has been suggested is undiagnosed **epilepsy** (Sivec & Lynn, 1995). Epileptic seizures are known to be associated with DID and with symptoms of depersonalization disorder such as blackouts and déjà vu. Even so, the symptoms of some dissociative disorders – such as DID – are very complex and it is unlikely that undiagnosed bouts of epilepsy could explain the intricate way in which knowledge about alter identities is suppressed or recovered by the sufferer.

> **epilepsy** A disorder of the nervous system characterized either by mild, episodic loss of attention or sleepiness or by severe convulsions with loss of consciousness.

An alternative biological explanation alludes to the role of the hippocampus. Recent brain scan studies have suggested that the hippocampus is the area of the brain that brings together the various elements of an autobiographical memory and integrates them to provide the individual with a memory that they recognize as a past personal experience. Given that individuals with dissociative disorders appear to have problems recalling and integrating memories of certain experiences (such as childhood abuse), this may be caused by abnormalities in the hippocampus. Bremner, Krystal, Charney & Southwick (1996) have argued that neurotransmitters released during stress can modulate memory function – particularly at the level of the hippocampus – and this release may interfere with the laying down of memory traces for high-stress incidents such as childhood abuse. In addition, extended periods of stress may also cause long-term, semi-permanent alterations in the release of these neurotransmitters, causing long-term amnesic effects for experiences related to trauma. More recent fMRI research has suggested that the prefrontal cortex may play an important role in inhibiting the activity of the hippocampus in individuals with dissociative amnesia, a process that will result in memory repression (Kikuchi, Fujii, Abe, Suzuki *et al.*, 2010).

14.2.6   Dissociative Symptoms as Role-Playing and Therapeutic Constructions

A number of theorists have argued that the more elaborate symptoms of dissociative disorders, such as alter identities in DID, are a form of role-playing by the sufferer in order to evoke sympathy and to escape responsibility for their actions (Spanos, 1996). Such role-playing is usually reinforced by family, friends and therapists, as it evokes the required attention and allows the individual to absolve themselves of day-to-day responsibilities for their behaviour. In addition, people simulating DID in the laboratory are mostly indistinguishable from individuals with a diagnosis of DID, suggesting that it is not a difficult condition to feign (Boysen & VanBergen, 2013). In particular, alter identities in DID may be developed in response to particular types of therapeutic intervention. For instance, in the 'Emergence of Evelyn' example (Case History 14.1) the therapist's interactions with Gina lead to an alter identity emerging and this new identity was given the name Mary by both the client and the therapist. In fact, therapists dealing with DID often ask their clients to give a name to an alter identity so they can talk about this personality more easily. Spanos (1996) suggests that this interactive therapeutic process actually *creates* the client's alter identities – so alter identities may be **therapeutic constructions** born of the therapeutic process itself rather than genuine, full-blown symptoms that precede treatment. The client then finds that these well-defined alter identities serve a useful function in their life by allowing them to explain away their behaviour and alleviating stress and anxiety.

therapeutic constructions The view that the multiple personalities found in dissociative identity disorders are merely constructions of the therapeutic process.

What evidence is there that alter identities in DID are a construction of the therapeutic process? Supportive evidence includes the following:

1. Alter identities are significantly less well defined in childhood and appear in adulthood usually after treatment by a therapist has begun (Spanos, 1994; Lilienfeld, Lynn, Kirsch, Chaves *et al.*, 1999).

2. Relatives of individuals with DID rarely report having seen evidence of alter identities before treatment (Piper & Mersky, 2004).

3. Individuals who develop DID usually have strong imaginations and a rich fantasy life that enables them to play different roles with some ease (Lynn, 1988).

4. There is some evidence that many cases of DID could have been diagnosed by a relatively small number of clinicians who might have a therapeutic style that allows alter egos to develop – for example, in a Swiss survey, Modestin (1992) found that 66 per cent of the DID diagnoses in the country were made by less than 10 per cent of the clinicians in the survey.

5. Individuals diagnosed with dissociative disorders are very susceptible to suggestion and hypnosis (Bliss, 1980; Butler, Duran, Jasiukaitis, Koopman & Spiegel, 1996) and hypnotherapy is a common form of treatment for DID; indeed, Spanos (1996) argues that such susceptible individuals may adopt the 'hypnotic role' and simply produce the kind of behaviour that the therapist wants.

6. Spanos (1994) noted that those who support DID as a diagnostic category have described a wide range of symptoms that may be indicative of DID and this justifies constant probing in therapy to confirm a diagnosis, and this may occur to the point where therapists *insist* to doubting clients that they *do* have multiple alter egos (Mersky, 1995). Consistent with the desire of many clinicians to diagnose DID is the finding that the prevalence of diagnosed DID has increased dramatically since 1980 (Elzinga, van Dyck & Spinhoven, 1998).

Nevertheless, there is still debate about whether most cases of DID are strategic enactments or not. Gleaves (1996) has provided a vigorous defence of the psychiatric view that DID is a legitimate diagnostic category and not a construction of the therapeutic process. He argues that:

1. it is not surprising that the rate of DID diagnosis has increased significantly in recent years because this may be a result of less scepticism about the diagnostic category and a reduction in the misdiagnosis of DID as schizophrenia,

2. there is relatively little evidence that hypnotherapy actively contributes to the development of DID symptoms because the number of clients diagnosed with DID after hypnotherapy is as low as one in four,

3. core symptoms of DID, such as amnesia, are frequently found in DID sufferers before their first treatment session (Coons, Bowman & Milstein, 1988), so DID cannot be entirely constructed as a result of therapy, and

4. rather than being openly collusive with the therapist about their symptoms, many individuals with DID are highly reluctant to talk about their symptoms and have an avoidant style that is not conducive to revealing a history of abuse or the existence of multiple personalities (Kluft, 1994).

As an epilogue to this debate, it is worth discussing an interesting study conducted by Spanos, Weekes & Bertrand (1985). They designed an experiment based on the famous case of Kenneth Bianchi who was accused of a series of murders and rapes in Los Angeles in the 1980s. During his psychiatric evaluation under hypnosis, Bianchi revealed evidence of DID symptoms and eventually of an alter identity called Steve whom he claimed committed the rapes and murders. When he came out of the hypnotic state, Bianchi claimed to know nothing about Steve or the murders, or what he had said under hypnosis. Table 14.2 provides a transcript of part of the discussion between the clinician and Bianchi while the latter was under hypnosis. Spanos, Weekes & Bertrand (1985) claim that this is an excellent example of how Bianchi's alter identity was constructed via the therapeutic discussion. Constructing 'Steve' served a useful purpose for Bianchi, because it allowed him to plead not guilty to murder by reason of insanity (i.e. his supposed DID). In their experimental study, Spanos, Weekes & Bertrand (1985) asked three groups of students to act out variations of the hypnotherapy procedure undergone by Bianchi. All groups were instructed to play the role of individuals

TABLE 14.2

The following is a transcript of the discussion that took place between accused murderer Kenneth Bianchi and a clinician while Bianchi is under hypnosis (see text for further elaboration).

Clinician: I've talked a bit to Ken, but I think that perhaps there might be another part of Ken that I haven't talked to. And I would like to communicate with that other part. And I would like that other part to come to talk to me . . . And when you're here, lift the left hand off the chair to signal to me that you are here. Would you please come, Part, so I can talk to you . . . Part, would you come and lift Ken's hand to indicate to me that you are here . . . would you talk to me, Part, by saying 'I'm here'?

Bianchi: Yes.

Clinician: Part, are you the same as Ken or are you different in any way?

Bianchi: I'm not him.

Clinician: You're not him. Who are you? Do you have a name?

Bianchi: I'm not Ken.

Clinician: You're not him? OK. Who are you? Tell me about yourself. Do you have a name I can call you by?

Bianchi: Steve. You can call me Steve.

Source: After Schwarz, 1981, pp.139–143.

accused of murder. Group 1 was then hypnotized and underwent questioning taken almost verbatim from the Bianchi transcript. Group 2 were also hypnotized and told that under hypnosis many individuals reveal evidence of hidden multiple personalities, but this aspect was then not directly addressed in the interview. Group 3 were a control condition that were not hypnotized and were given little or no information about hidden multiple personalities. After the interviews, all participants were questioned about whether they had a hidden personality or second identity. In Group 1 – which underwent a procedure similar to Bianchi – 81 per cent admitted a second personality. In Group 2 – whose interview did not allude to hidden personalities – only 31 per cent revealed an alter identity. Only 13 per cent of those in Group 3 admitted a hidden personality. Spanos, Weekes & Bertrand (1985) argued that these results provided evidence that alter identities can be developed as a result of the demand characteristics of the interview style of the therapist and that such alter identities are strategic enactments that serve the purposes of the client (e.g. by diverting or avoiding blame for their behaviour). Nevertheless, while this study provides convincing evidence that *some* alter identities can be developed by the therapist's interviewing style, it is still not evidence that *all* alter identities are strategic enactments.

SELF-TEST QUESTIONS

- Can you describe some of the main risk factors for dissociative disorders?
- What is the psychodynamic concept of repression and how does it account for the symptoms of dissociative disorders?
- What is the evidence that fantasy and early dissociative experiences may play a role in the development of dissociative disorders?
- Can you describe the procedure for a laboratory-based experiment designed to investigate deficits in memory processes in individuals with dissociative disorders?
- What is state-dependent memory and how does it attempt to account for dissociative amnesia?
- Can you explain how deficits in source-monitoring ability or reality monitoring might account for both dissociative amnesia and false recovered memories of trauma?
- What is the evidence that alter identities in DID are a construction of the therapeutic process?

SECTION SUMMARY

14.2   THE AETIOLOGY OF DISSOCIATIVE DISORDERS

We posed two questions at the outset of this section on aetiology: (1) how do the normally integrated components of consciousness become dissociated in the dissociative disorders?; and (2) do the distinctive symptoms of dissociative disorders (such as amnesia and multiple personalities) have a specific function? We have reviewed a range of theories about how the elements of consciousness become dissociated in these disorders and how memories might become suppressed. Cognitive theories try to explain these dissociative symptoms primarily by attempting to describe the mechanisms that might mediate effects such as selective amnesia. We reviewed two specific accounts, state-dependent memory and reconstructive memory. The latter additionally argued that individuals with dissociative disorders may suffer deficits in source-monitoring ability and reality monitoring – both may prevent an individual from identifying an autobiographical memory as one they have actually experienced. Some relatively undeveloped biological accounts also intimate that selective amnesia may result from abnormal brain processes (such as epilepsy) or specific brain functions which inhibit the ability of the hippocampus to lay down or recall specific memories. An alternative view of the striking symptoms of dissociative disorders is that many of them may be a construction of the therapeutic process. In particular, directive therapeutic approaches (including hypnotherapy) may encourage the client to create alter identities that did not exist prior to therapy, or to recall false memories of events that had never happened. We concluded that while some symptoms of dissociative disorders may be developed by overly directive therapy techniques, this was unlikely to explain all dissociative symptoms. Finally, in relation to our second question, it is quite likely that the symptoms of dissociative disorders (particularly selective amnesia and alter identities) do serve some kind of palliative role, and in the psychodynamic view they may allow the sufferer to repress traumatic memories that are too painful to tolerate.

To summarize the key points:

- Risk factors for dissociative disorders include physical and sexual *childhood abuse* and a history of trauma generally (e.g. experiencing major stressful life events such as war or natural disasters).

- Psychodynamic theorists view dissociative disorders as being caused by *repression*, which is one of the most basic of the ego defence mechanisms.

- Dissociative disorders may develop more readily in those who have experienced dissociative symptoms as a child or who have strong imaginations and a rich fantasy life.

- Cognitive theorists believe that dissociative symptoms are caused by a disruption to the sufferer's memory processes.

- Individuals with dissociative symptoms only appear to have poor memory for trauma information under conditions of divided attention.

- Some theorists argue that dissociative amnesia is caused either by a deficit in *source-monitoring ability* or *reality monitoring*.

- Deficits in some memory processes may be the reason why some sufferers are prone to recover *false memories of trauma* that never happened.

- Biological accounts suggest that dissociative symptoms may be caused by undiagnosed epilepsy or that stress causes permanent changes in the release of neurotransmitters that inhibit the laying down of memory traces.

- Alter identities in DID may be the construction of the therapeutic process itself rather than full-blown symptoms that precede treatment.

14.3   THE TREATMENT OF DISSOCIATIVE DISORDERS

The main issues to be addressed in the treatment of dissociative disorders are (1) helping to alleviate selective amnesia for life events and helping the client to adapt to recovered memories if they are painful or traumatic ones, and (2) helping individuals with DID to identify alter identities and to merge them fully into a single, integrated identity.

Clinicians attempting to treat dissociative disorders face a number of problems:

1. Some of these disorders are rare (e.g. DID) and there have been relatively few cases identified worldwide, which means that therapeutic techniques are relatively underdeveloped, and outcome studies designed to assess effectiveness of therapy methods are almost nonexistent.

2. Some dissociative disorders such as dissociative amnesia often spontaneously remit, so it is difficult in these cases to assess whether those therapeutic methods that have been applied are effective or not.

3. Dealing with recovered memories is often a severely traumatic experience for the client and may involve the intense re-experiencing of traumatic events (known as **abreaction**), and this may continually plunge the client into emotional crisis.

> **abreaction** The intense re-experiencing of traumatic events.

4. Some overly directive therapeutic styles may lead to the recovery of *false memories*, with the potential broad range of negative consequences that this might have for the client and their family (see Focus Point 14.2).

5. In DID, integrating alter identities into a single, functional identity is an extremely difficult process; many clients find that having a series of alter identities is a useful way of explaining their behaviour to others and absolving the 'host' identity from blame and responsibility, so breaking this down is not easy (Hale, 1983). In a survey of 153 clients undergoing therapy for DID, Piper (1994) found that only 38 of 153 (25 per cent) achieved a stable integration of their alter identities, but more recent longer term studies have intimated more optimistic outcomes, with Kluft (2000) finding a successful integration rate of 68 per cent over a period of 3 months after therapy.

6. All dissociative disorders are usually comorbid with a range of other psychiatric disorders (particularly with anxiety disorders, depression and PTSD) and dealing with these comorbid problems will also usually be a requirement in therapy.

As we mentioned at the beginning of this section, therapies for dissociative disorders are relatively under-developed, but we will discuss the most commonly used ones. These are psychodynamic therapy, hypnotherapy and – to a lesser extent – drug therapy.

14.3.1 Psychodynamic Therapy

One common form of treatment for dissociative disorders is psychodynamic therapy – especially psychoanalysis. Freud viewed dissociative symptoms, especially dissociative amnesia, was a form of repression in which memories that were considered too painful to tolerate were repressed to the unconscious mind. Like most approaches to dissociative disorders, psychodynamic therapy requires a measured step-by-step approach to revealing repressed memories or integrating multiple personalities. The usual process is first to establish a trusting and workable relationship between therapist and client, followed by attempts to deal directly with repressed memories or alter identities. This second stage is clearly the most challenging. First, memory retrieval may be as traumatising as the original experience; as noted above, this is known as *abreaction*. Re-experiencing trauma in this way will clearly be distressing to the client and may

well initiate further emotional turmoil. In an attempt to avoid full-blown abreaction, some therapists have proposed that repressed memories of abuse should be retrieved only piece by piece, with the client learning to adapt emotionally to each memory fragment before moving on to retrieve the next (Kluft, 1999). Second, in the case of clients with DID, this second stage will often be characterized by the client's resistance to integrating multiple identities. For the individual with DID, multiple personalities appear to serve a coping function in allowing the sufferer to abdicate responsibility for actions and emotions to individual identities, and successful therapy will need to deal with these 'responsibilities' before integration can be achieved. Indeed, in many cases, the sub-personalities will view 'fusion' of their identities as a form of death that has to be avoided (Kluft, 2001; Spiegel, 1994). Finally, if these stages of treatment are progressed successfully, the client will normally need to have training in a range of skills to enable them to cope with day-to-day living with either their recovered memories or their newly integrated personality. In particular, training will be needed in how to avoid dissociation when encountering future stressors (Kihlstrom, 2001).

Almost any form of psychotherapy is a lengthy process where dissociative disorders are concerned. Issues have to be approached cautiously and there may be many occasions when the therapeutic process takes steps backwards as well as forwards. In the case of DID, the greater the number of multiple identities that need to be integrated, the longer the therapeutic process will take – an average treatment programme of 500 hours per client over an average of 2 years has been reported (Putnam, Guroff, Silberman, Barban & Post, 1986).

14.3.2 Hypnotherapy

This is a method that is used relatively regularly with those who suffer dissociative disorders. This is because sufferers are unusually susceptible to suggestion and hypnosis (Bliss, 1980), and at least some clinicians believe that dissociative symptoms such as amnesia or multiple identities may be the result of a form of 'self-hypnosis' by which individuals are able to restrict certain thoughts and memories entering consciousness (Frischholz, Lipman, Braun & Sachs, 1992). Using **hypnotherapy**, the clinician can help guide the client through the recall of repressed memories. Hypnosis is also used to help people to regress to childhood states in an attempt to help them recall significant

hypnotherapy A form of therapy undertaken while the client is hypnotized.

sodium amobarbital A drug which can be used concurrently with hypnotherapy to help clients recall past events.

sodium pentobarbital A drug which can be used concurrently with hypnotherapy to help clients recall past events.

age regression In hypnotherapy, the recreation of the physical and mental state that a client was in prior to experiencing any trauma in order to help the individual recall events during earlier stages of his or her life.

events that they may have repressed. Drugs such as **sodium amobarbital** and **sodium pentobarbital** can also be used concurrently with hypnotherapy to help clients recall past events (Ruedrich, Chu & Wadle, 1985). One assumption in the hypnotherapy approach is that hypnosis will recreate the physical and mental state the client was in prior to experiencing any trauma, and this will help the individual to recall events during earlier stages of their life. This is known as **age regression**, and while some clients find this helpful in recalling and dealing with repressed memories, there is no objective evidence that hypnosis does recreate any of the physical or mental states experienced earlier in life. Hypnotherapy is also used in the treatment of DID in order to help bring potential alter identities into consciousness and to facilitate the fusion of identities. However, although widely used in the treatment of dissociative disorders, there have been no systematic group- or single-case studies of the effectiveness of this technique (Cardena, 2000).

14.3.3 Drug Treatments

Because anxiety and depression are common features of dissociative disorders, and may be diagnosable comorbid conditions, some antidepressant and anxiolytic drugs have been used successfully to treat some of these supplementary symptoms. Antidepressants and tranquilizers have been used to address the depression and anxiety associated with DID, but these drugs tend to have little effect on the main symptoms of DID itself (Simon, 1998). There is, however, some evidence that SSRIs such as Prozac may help to alleviate the symptoms of depersonalization disorder (Simeon,

Stein & Hollander, 1995). Because there is some evidence for abnormalities in the endogenous opioid systems in depersonalization disorder, opioid antagonists such as naltrexone have been used and found to reduce depersonalization symptoms by an average 30 per cent (Simeon & Knutelska, 2005).

14.3.4 Developments in Treatments for Dissociative Disorders

Treating dissociative disorders can often be a lengthy process, whether through conventional psychotherapy or hypnotherapy. This picture is additionally clouded by the fact that many health insurers are increasingly requiring treatments that are empirically supported, and in some countries – such as the Netherlands – psychoanalysis is no longer being reimbursed as a treatment for dissociative disorders (Brand, 2012). More recently, staged treatments have been developed that are assessed using empirically based methods and may provide a more evidence-based alternative to traditional psychoanalysis and hypnotherapy (Baars, van der Hart, Nijenhuis, Chu et al., 2011; Brand, Lanius, Vermetten, Loewenstein & Spiegel, 2012). However, therapy for dissociative disorders requires time, especially in allowing clients to adapt to and cope with traumatic memories. As we mentioned earlier, therapies for dissociative disorders are relatively underdeveloped and this is in part because there are relatively few diagnosed cases of some of these disorders (e.g. DID). As a consequence there are few adequately controlled outcome studies. Apart from the therapies we have discussed in this section, many individuals with dissociative disorders can often be treated with CBT for their depression and anxiety symptoms. Because both dissociative and PTSD symptoms may be an outcome of extreme trauma, those therapies used to treat PTSD also have some success in dealing with dissociative symptoms (e.g. therapies such as cognitive restructuring and eye movement desensitisation and reprocessing, EMDR; see Chapter 6).

SELF-TEST QUESTIONS

- What are the main problems facing clinicians who attempt to treat dissociative disorders?
- Can you describe the main characteristics of psychodynamic therapies for dissociative disorders?
- What is the evidence that hypnotherapy is an effective treatment for dissociative disorders?

14.3 THE TREATMENT OF DISSOCIATIVE DISORDERS

To summarize the key points:

- *Abreaction* and the *recovery of false memories* are important issues to consider in the treatment of dissociative disorders.

- *Psychodynamic therapies* attempt to bring repressed memories back to the conscious mind so that they can be effectively dealt with.

- *Hypnotherapy* is a common form of treatment for dissociative disorders and sufferers are unusually susceptible to suggestion and hypnosis.

- Some *antidepressant* and *anxiolytic drugs* have been successful in treating some of the depression and anxiety-related symptoms of dissociative disorders.

14.4 DISSOCIATIVE DISORDERS REVIEWED

In this chapter we have described the main features of three dissociative disorders – dissociative amnesia, dissociative identity disorder (DID) and depersonalization disorder. All represent a failure to integrate various aspects of identity, consciousness and memory, and most involve some form of amnesia for past life events or autobiographical memories. All of these disorders are associated with severe psychological stress. Symptoms may manifest immediately after severe traumatic experiences (such as war or a natural disaster) or they may develop over a number of years. In the latter case, DID is a particular example where selective amnesia and multiple identities may develop many years after severe childhood trauma such as sexual or physical abuse.

There are numerous theories of the aetiology of dissociative symptoms but most relate in some way to early trauma. Psychodynamic theories claim that dissociative symptoms such as amnesia are ways of coping with severe traumatic experiences by repressing these

memories to the unconscious mind. Cognitive accounts are much more interested in the mechanisms by which memories are selectively repressed in dissociative disorders and laboratory studies have identified deficits in source-monitoring ability and reality monitoring (e.g. not being able to effectively differentiate imagined events from experienced events). In contrast, some theorists believe that many of the symptoms of dissociative disorders (such as the multiple alter identities in DID) are merely constructions of the therapeutic process. That is, therapy that is either too directive or attempts to probe too deeply to confirm a diagnosis of DID actually plays a causal role in the development of alter identities.

Treatments for dissociative disorders are relatively underdeveloped and the most popular are psychodynamic approaches and hypnotherapy. For many dissociative disorders, therapy can be a lengthy process as the sufferer often has to deal with recovered memories of trauma that may involve intense re-experiencing of these events. The therapeutic process can also be problematic, as we discussed in Focus Point 14.2, where overdirective psychotherapy can often create false recovered memories of trauma and abuse and these false memories can often have catastrophic consequences for both the client and their family.

To access the online resources for this chapter go to
www.wiley-psychopathology.com/ch14

Reading	**Video**	**Activity**
• News story: Axe killer 'could have forgotten' crime • N's story on DID • Journal article: Dissociation – An insufficiently recognized major feature of complex PTSD • Journal article: The dissociative subtype of PTSD – A replication and extension • Journal article: Risk factors in the early family life of patients suffering from dissociative disorders • Glossary of key terms • Clinical issues • Links to journal articles • References	• *No video clips online for Chapter 14*	• Activity 14.1 • Self-test questions • Revision flashcards • Research questions

15 Neurocognitive Disorders

To access the online resources for this chapter go to
www.wiley-psychopathology.com/ch15

ROUTE MAP OF THE CHAPTER

The chapter begins by describing some of the cognitive impairments that characterize neurocognitive disorders and identifying some of the brain areas associated with these deficits. We then discuss some of the various methods used by clinical neuropsychologists to assess cognitive functioning, and some of the difficulties associated with diagnosis. The second part of the chapter looks more closely at the various types of neurocognitive disorder described in DSM-5 and their causes. These can involve cerebral infection, traumatic brain injury, cerebrovascular accidents such as strokes, and degenerative disorders such as Alzheimer's disease. Finally, we cover some of the treatment and rehabilitation programmes that have been developed to tackle neurocognitive disorders, including drug treatments, cognitive rehabilitation procedures and the role of caregiver support programmes.

CHAPTER OUTLINE

LEARNING OUTCOMES

When you have completed this chapter, you should be able to:

1. Describe some of the cognitive impairments that characterize neurocognitive disorders.

2. Describe some of the main methods that clinical neuropsychologists use to assess cognitive functioning in neurocognitive disorders.

3. Describe a range of types of neurocognitive disorders and evaluate their causes.

4. Describe, compare and contrast the various types of treatment and rehabilitation programmes that have been developed to deal with neurocognitive disorders.

Within the last 8 months, I've been at war with the cooker. I put the oven on at a temperature I know is right only to find the meat burnt or not cooked because what I thought was the right temperature was not. It gets me so annoyed. I also forget what time I put things in the oven – even if I repeat it to myself a few times and keep looking at the clock. If I do something else – go upstairs, for example – I cannot remember what time the food went in, no matter how I try.

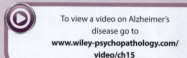

To view a video on Alzheimer's disease go to
www.wiley-psychopathology.com/video/ch15

I've had to give up driving. I kept losing concentration and my speed just got faster and faster. I could have caused an accident – especially when feeling disoriented. I still work part-time, but that is slipping something awful. I do things at work alone as much as possible so no one can see the mistakes I'm making. I've had all the tests now, but the neurologist tells me all the findings so far are consistent with AD [Alzheimer's disease]. To be honest, trying to get through the day is like knitting with a knotted ball of wool. Every now and again I come to a knot. I try to unravel it but can't, so I knit the knot in. As time goes by, there are more and more knots.

Paddy's Story

Introduction

The majority of the disorders we have discussed in this book so far appear to have psychological origins. That is, people have experiences that give rise to problematic ways of thinking and behaving, and these ways of thinking and behaving may cause distress and form the basis for diagnosable psychopathologies. In contrast, neurocognitive disorders have their origins in damage or abnormalities in the biological substrates that underlie thinking and behaving. This damage or degeneration can be caused by disease, physical trauma (such as brain injury) or genetic predispositions causing irreversible changes in the brain and central nervous system. By definition, the causes of neurocognitive disorders are biological and can usually be identified as biochemical imbalances in the brain and central nervous system or direct or indirect damage to brain tissue. Despite the fact that the causes of neurocognitive disorders are primarily physical, psychology is centrally important in the diagnosis, assessment and rehabilitation of individuals suffering such disorders. For example, some of the first signs of neurocognitive disorders (such as dementia, brain injury or stroke) are deficits in basic cognitive functions such as perception, learning, memory, attention, language and visuospatial skills, and also deficits in what are known as **executive functions** (i.e. those skills that involve problem solving, planning and engaging in goal-directed behaviour). Clinical psychologists are therefore actively engaged in assessing these abilities and interpreting whether any deficits are early signs of neurocognitive disorders. In addition, neurocognitive disorders do not only generate deficits in basic cognitive functioning, they can also affect disposition and personality. An individual diagnosed with a neurocognitive disorder may become both depressed and anxious, and require suitable treatment for these conditions. They may also display radical changes in personality and behaviour, such as impulsivity or outbursts of aggressive behaviour. These

> **executive functions** Cognitive skills that involve problem-solving, planning and engaging in goal-directed behaviour.

rehabilitation programmes Treatment programmes that usually combine a mixture of group work, psychological interventions, social skills training and practical and vocational activities.

also need to be managed and treated. Finally, clinical psychologists are also centrally involved in the development of **rehabilitation programmes** that may have a variety of aims, including

1. restoring previously affected cognitive and behavioural functions (although this is often a difficult task);

2. helping clients to develop new skills to replace those that have been lost as a result of tissue damage (e.g. learning to use memory aids);

3. providing therapy for concurrent depression, anxiety or anger problems; and

4. providing clients and carers with skills and advice that will help them structure their living environment in a way that will help to accommodate changes in cognitive and behavioural abilities.

At the beginning of this chapter we described *Paddy's story*, which recounts the experiences of someone who is in the early stages of Alzheimer's disease. This describes her awareness of her memory lapses, mistakes and periodic disorientation that give rise to frustration, anxiety and depression. For many who are in the early stages of a degenerative neurocognitive condition, these experiences can be both frequent and frightening.

We will continue this chapter by discussing some of the more general characteristics of neurocognitive disorders and the diagnostic and assessment issues that are relevant to them.

15.1 THE DIAGNOSIS AND ASSESSMENT OF NEUROCOGNITIVE DISORDERS

First, let's look at some of the cognitive impairments that are commonly found in neurocognitive disorders (see Table 15.1). We will then discuss some broader diagnostic and assessment issues.

15.1.1 Cognitive Impairments in Neurocognitive Disorders

Learning and memory deficits

Amnesia is a common feature of many neurocognitive disorders, including an inability to learn new information

and a failure to recall past events, but, more commonly, a failure to recall events in the most recent past. If the neurological condition is caused by a specific traumatic event (such as a head injury), the individual may be unable to recall anything from the moment of the injury or to retain memories of recent events. This is known as **anterograde amnesia** or **anterograde memory dysfunction**. The effects of anterograde amnesia are dramatically displayed in the 2000 film *Memento* in which the lead character, Leonard, is unable to form new memories as a result of an earlier head injury caused by an assailant. The film graphically describes how Leonard has to develop a series of ad hoc ways of coping with his inability to recall recent events. More commonly, in degenerative disorders such as dementia, memory deficits slowly develop from what initially appears like normal forgetfulness to become a more full-blown inability to recall events. In the latter case, sufferers may often seem 'rambling' as they attempt to make up events to fill the gaps in their memory.

anterograde amnesia Memory loss for information acquired after the onset of amnesia. Also known as anterograde memory dysfunction.

anterograde memory dysfunction Memory loss for information acquired after the onset of amnesia. Also known as anterograde amnesia.

Deficits in attention and arousal

Some first indications of neurocognitive problems are when the individual shows signs of lack of attention, being easily distracted and performing well-learnt activities more slowly than before (such as having difficulty using the controls of a DVD or video machine). They may also have difficulty focusing on or keeping up with a conversation, and they need more time to make simple decisions.

Language deficits

The individual may appear to be rambling during conversations and have difficulty conveying what they have to say in a coherent manner. They may also have difficulty reading and understanding the speech of others. Language deficits are one of the most common features of neurocognitive disorders and are collectively known as **aphasias**. Language impairments can take many forms, including (1) an inability to comprehend or understand speech or to repeat speech accurately and correctly, (2) the production of incoherent, jumbled speech (known as **fluent aphasia**), and (3) an inability to initiate speech or respond to speech with anything other than simple words (known as **non-fluent aphasia**).

aphasias Speech disorders resulting in difficulties producing or comprehending speech.

fluent aphasia The production of incoherent, jumbled speech.

non-fluent aphasia An inability to initiate speech or respond to speech with anything other than simple words.

TABLE 15.1 *Terminology: Cognitive impairments in neurocognitive disorders*

Term	Definition	Main brain areas affected
Aphasia	Speech disorder resulting in difficulties producing or comprehending speech	Language centres of the left hemisphere – usually Broca's area or Wernicke's area (see Figure 1)
Agnosia	Loss of ability to recognize objects, persons, sounds, shapes or smells while the specific sense is not defective; nor is there any significant memory loss	Occipital or parietal lobes (see Figure 2)
Apraxia	Loss of the ability to execute or carry out learnt (familiar) movements, despite having the desire and the physical ability to perform the movements	Parietal lobes of the left hemisphere (see Figure 2)
Anterograde amnesia	Memory loss for information acquired after the onset of amnesia	Hippocampus; medial temporal lobes; basal forebrain (see Figure 2)
Retrograde amnesia	Inability to recall events that occurred before the onset of amnesia	Hippocampus; temporal lobes (see Figure 2)
Deficits in executive functioning	The inability to effectively problem-solve, plan, initiate, organize, monitor and inhibit complex behaviours	Frontal lobes, especially the prefrontal cortex (see Figure 2)

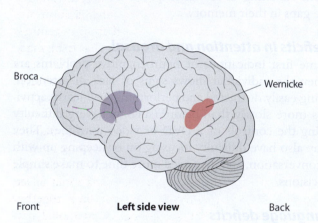

FIGURE 1 *Language centres of the left hemisphere (Broca's area and Wernicke's area).*

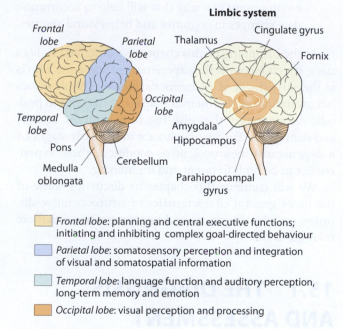

Frontal lobe: planning and central executive functions; initiating and inhibiting complex goal-directed behaviour

Parietal lobe: somatosensory perception and integration of visual and somatospatial information

Temporal lobe: language function and auditory perception, long-term memory and emotion

Occipital lobe: visual perception and processing

FIGURE 2 *Anatomy of the brain.*

A distinction can be made between **Broca's aphasia** and **Wernicke's aphasia**. Disruption of the ability to speak is known generally as Broca's aphasia and consists of difficulties with word ordering (agrammatism), finding the right word (anomia) and articulation. It is characterized by laborious non-fluent speech involving

mispronunciation rather than mis-selection of words. In contrast, Wernicke's aphasia is a deficit in the comprehension of speech, involving difficulties in recognising spoken words and converting thoughts into words. Damage to different areas of the left hemisphere (which controls speech) are specific to each of these deficits. Wernicke's aphasia is associated with damage to regions behind the frontal lobes while Broca's aphasia is more likely to result from damage to the left frontal lobe itself (see Table 15.1).

Deficits in visual–perceptual functioning

In some cases the individual may be unable to recognize everyday objects and name them correctly. This is known as **agnosia** and it can affect a wide variety of functional skills, such as face perception (*prosopagnosia*) and musical discrimination (*amusia*). A famous example of agnosia is recounted in the book *The Man Who Mistook His Wife for a Hat and Other Clinical Tales* by Oliver Sacks. He describes the case of Dr P, a music professor who had developed visual agnosia. He was able to identify and describe complex shapes but could often not recognize his own students' faces and could only identify them when they spoke. The title of the book comes from an occasion when Dr P was leaving a house and reached for his wife's head, mistaking it for a hat and trying to lift it off. Interestingly his agnosia only affected his visual perceptions and did not affect his music abilities in any way.

> **agnosia** The loss of the ability to recognize objects, persons, sounds, shapes or smells while the specific sense is not defective and there is no significant memory loss.

Motor skills deficits

Some neurocognitive disorders are characterized by impairments in motor performance and coordination. This may involve the inability to move a limb, a tendency to suddenly become paralysed or difficulty in coordinating movements effectively. This is known as **apraxia** and in more complex cases the individual with apraxia may be able to emit a behaviour when it is under routine conditions (e.g. cleaning their teeth as part of their washing routine first thing in the morning) but are unable to do this on command.

> **apraxia** Loss of the ability to execute or carry out learnt (familiar) movements, despite having the desire and the physical ability to perform the movements.

Deficits in executive functions

This reflects the inability to effectively problem-solve, plan, initiate, organize, monitor and inhibit complex behaviours. These functions are normally associated with the **prefrontal cortex**, so damage to this area of the brain is frequently involved when executive function deficits are found. A widely used test of executive functioning is the **Wisconsin card sorting task**, where individuals must sort cards for a number of trials using one rule (e.g. colour) and then sort cards using a different rule (e.g. shape). This requires the ability to shift attention and to inhibit an established response pattern. Deficits in executive functioning are revealed in everyday behaviour by examples of

> **prefrontal cortex** An area of the brain which is important in maintaining representations of goals and the means to achieve them.

> **Wisconsin card sorting task** A widely used test of executive functioning where individuals must sort cards for a number of trials using one rule (e.g. colour) and then sort cards using a different rule (e.g. shape).

poor judgement (e.g. erratic or unsafe driving), inappropriate behaviour (e.g. leaving the house in inappropriate clothing such as pyjamas) and erratic mood swings (e.g. from laughter to hostility).

Deficits in higher order intellectual functioning

Impairment in more abstract mental tasks is another possible indication of a neurological disorder, and individuals may be unable to make simple mathematical calculations, to reason deductively or to draw on general knowledge when undertaking a task or activity.

15.1.2   Assessment in Clinical Neuropsychology

Identifying that someone has a neurocognitive disorder is a difficult and often lengthy process. Assessment is important (1) for determining the actual nature of any deficits and the location of any related tissue damage in the brain, (2) for providing information about onset, type, severity and progression of symptoms, (3) for helping to discriminate between neurological deficits that have an organic basis and psychiatric symptoms that do not, and (4) for helping identify the focus for rehabilitation programmes and to assess progress on these programmes (Veitch, 2008). In many cases, a diagnosis has to be made on the basis of cognitive and behavioural impairments that are detected by a range of neuropsychological tests, but in recent times the results of these tests can be supplemented by findings from EEG analyses, brain scans such as PET scans and fMRI, blood tests and chemical analyses of cerebrospinal fluids. Assessment of cognitive abilities is also supplemented with behavioural observation and information from clients and their families about onset, type, severity and progression of symptoms, together with a detailed history of educational, occupational, psychosocial, demographic and previous and current medical factors. Neuropsychological tests themselves can be remarkably accurate in detecting quite specific deficits and also identifying the brain areas where tissue damage may have led to the deficit. Brain scans can then supplement and confirm the results of neuropsychological tests (D'Esposito, 2000). One of the most widely used tests worldwide is the **WAIS-IV** (the Wechsler Adult Intelligence Scale, 4th edn) (Wechsler, 2008) (see section 2.2.3). This contains scales that measure vocabulary, arithmetic ability, digit span, information comprehension, letter–number sequencing, picture completion ability, reasoning ability, symbol search and object assembly ability. These measures can be aggregated to provide scores on broader indices of ability such as verbal

> **WAIS-IV** Fourth edition of the Wechsler Adult Intelligence Scale.

comprehension, perceptual organization (a measure of nonverbal reasoning), working memory and information processing speed. In the UK, the Adult Memory and Information Processing Battery (AMIPB) (Coughlan & Hollows, 1985) is in wide use and this comprises two tests of speed of information processing, verbal memory tests (list learning and story recall) and visual memory tests (design learning and figure recall). One of the common neuropsychological tests used in the US is the Halstead–Reitan Neuropsychological Test Battery (Broshek & Barth, 2000), which has been compiled to evaluate brain and nervous system functioning across a fixed set of eight tests. The tests evaluate function across visual, auditory and tactile input, verbal communication, spatial and sequential perception, the ability to analyse information, the ability to form mental concepts, make judgements, control motor output, and to attend to and memorize stimuli.

Test batteries such as these also provide useful information on the source of any deficits (such as closed head injury, alcohol abuse, Alzheimer's disease, stroke), whether the damage occurred during childhood development, and whether any deficits are progressive. Focus Point 15.1 provides an example of one of the basic tests – the trail making test – that provides a measure of information processing speed and a range of recognition and visuomotor integration abilities. Many of these tests are so extensive that they may take as long as 6 hours to administer, requiring substantial patience and stamina on the part of both the clinician and the patient. In contrast, some other tests have been developed to be quick and simple to implement, and to provide a reasonably reliable indication of general level of impairment. One such test is the **Mini Mental State Examination (MMSE)**, which is a brief 30 item test used to screen for dementia (e.g. in Alzheimer's disease) and takes about 10 minutes to administer (see Focus Point 15.2).

> **Mini Mental State Examination (MMSE)** A structured test that takes 10 minutes to administer and can provide reliable information on a client's overall levels of cognitive and mental functioning.

THE TRAIL MAKING TASK

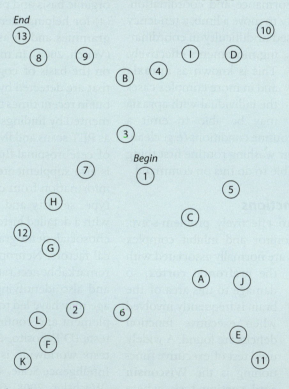

Above is an example of the trail making test. This consists of a page with circles containing the letters A to L and 13 numbered circles intermixed and randomly arranged. The patient is instructed to connect the circles by drawing lines alternating between numbers and letters in sequential order until they reach the circle labelled 'End'. This test would normally take 5–10 minutes to administer.

The trail making test helps to evaluate information processing speed, visual scanning ability, integration of visual and motor functions, letter and number recognition and sequencing, and the ability to maintain two different trains of thought.

For adults, scores above 91 seconds have traditionally indicated brain impairment, but completion times may vary significantly with age, education and culture.

MINI MENTAL STATE EXAMINATION (MMSE)

The MMSE is a good instrument for assessing cognitive function in dementia and takes about 10 minutes to administer.

Orientation

What is the (year) (season) (date) (day) (month)?

5 ☐

Where are we: (country) (city) (part of city) (number of flat/house) (name of street)?

5 ☐

Registration

Name three objects: one second to say each.
Then ask the patient to name all three after you have said them.
Give one point for each correct answer.

3 ☐

Attention and calculation

Serial 7s: Ask the patient to begin with 100 and count backwards by 7. Stop after five subtractions (93, 86, 79, 72, 65). One point for each correct.

5 ☐

Recall

Ask for the three objects repeated above (under Registration). Give one point for each correct.

3 ☐

Language

Name a pencil and watch: Show the patient a wrist-watch and ask him or her what it is. Repeat for pencil. (Two points.)

Repeat the following: 'No ifs, ands or buts' (one point).

Follow a three-stage command: 'Take a paper in your right hand, fold it in half and put it on the floor' (three points).

Read and obey the following: Close your eyes (one point).

Write a sentence (one point).

Copy a design (one point). On a clean piece of paper, draw intersecting pentagons (as below), each side about one inch and ask him or her to copy it exactly as it is. All ten angles must be present and two must intersect to score 1 point. Tremor and rotation are ignored.

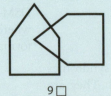

9 ☐

Total score _____

A score of 20 or less generally suggests dementia but may also be found in acute confusion, schizophrenia or severe depression. Mild Alzheimer's is usually linked to an MMSE score of 21–26, moderate Alzheimer's to scores of 10–20 and severe Alzheimer's to an MMSE score of less than 10.

15.1.3 The Diagnosis of Neurocognitive Disorders

Difficulties of diagnosis

Diagnosis is made difficult by the fact that the symptoms and deficits found in neurocognitive disorders often closely resemble those of other psychopathologies. For example, cognitive deficits typical of neurocognitive disorders are a regular feature of dissociative disorders (e.g. amnesia) and schizophrenia (e.g. language deficits, information-processing deficits, and deficits in executive functions). Motor coordination deficits, paralysis and impairments of sensory input are also found in somatic symptom disorders such as conversion disorder (e.g.

hysterical blindness and paralysis – see section 13.2.2). In addition, in the early stages of a degenerative neurological disorder people will start to experience cognitive impairments that affect their daily lives and this will often lead to the development of psychological problems (e.g. depression and anxiety) that compound the difficulties of diagnosis (see *Paddy's story* at the beginning of this chapter). Indeed, prior to the development of modern brain scanning technology, it was often the case that a neurological disorder could only be diagnosed by autopsy after the death of the sufferer (Patton & Shepherd, 1956). Even so, with the range of tests available today psychological problems can still be misdiagnosed as neurological ones (e.g. Iverson, 2006) and vice versa (e.g. Sumpter & McMillan, 2005), and this has important implications for rehabilitation and subsequent care.

To add to the difficulties of diagnosis, the symptoms of a range of neurological disorders overlap considerably. For example, damage to specific areas of the brain as a result of a **closed head injury** can give rise to similar cognitive deficits as those found in broader degenerative disorders such as Alzheimer's disease. Similarly, a single causal factor (such as a brain tumour) can manifest as a range of different symptoms including speech disorder, deficits in sensory perception or emotionality and aggressiveness. These are some of the reasons why neurological assessment is thorough, multifaceted and continues to be administered throughout the period of diagnosis and rehabilitation.

> **closed head injury** A concussion or head trauma, the symptoms of which include loss of consciousness after the trauma, confusion, headache, nausea or vomiting, blurred vision, loss of short-term memory and perseverating.

DSM-5 Neurocognitive disorder diagnostic categories

DSM-5 identifies two broader diagnostic syndromes into which many neurological disorders fall. They are delirium, which is characterized by confused and disorganized behaviour, and major or mild neurocognitive disorders (NCDs) (formally known in DSM-IV as **dementias**), which are characterized by the impairment of basic cognitive functions. We will look at these two diagnostic categories more closely.

> **dementias** Disorders involving the development of multiple cognitive deficits that include memory impairment and at least one other specific deficit.

Delirium   The main feature of a **delirium** is a disturbance of attention and awareness, and the disturbance in attention is reflected in a reduced ability to direct, focus, sustain and shift attention. Also, the disturbance develops over a short

> **delirium** A disturbance of consciousness that develops over a short period of time.

period of time. The person may not understand simple questions and may be unable to shift attention from answering one question to answering another. Delirium often occurs in the context of other neurocognitive disorders and may be accompanied by memory and learning deficits, disorientation and perceptual disturbances such as hallucinations. There may be evidence that the delirium is a result of the physiological consequences of a general medical condition, substance intoxication or withdrawal, or use of a medication or a toxin, and may be associated with disturbances in the sleep–wake cycle, such as a reversal of the day–night cycle, restlessness and hyperactivity. The individual may also exhibit emotional disturbances such as anxiety, fear, depression, irritability, anger, euphoria and apathy, accompanied by rapid and unpredictable shifts from one emotional state to another (DSM-5 Summary Table 15.1).

The symptoms of delirium can develop rapidly over hours to days but may begin abruptly after specific traumatic events, such as head injury. Equally, delirium may resolve in just a few hours, but alternatively persist for weeks to months, especially in the elderly. Delirium appears to result from widespread disruption of brain metabolism and neurotransmitter activity that can be triggered by a range of events (e.g. traumatic head injury, substance intoxication or withdrawal, surgery, sleep loss, malnutrition and psychological stress generally). Delirium is particularly common in older people, and particularly hospitalized older people. The community prevalence rate for delirium is 1–2 per cent but increases with age, rising to 14 per cent among those over 85 years of age (DSM-5, p.600).

Major or mild neurocognitive disorders (NCDs)

DSM-5 defines neurocognitive disorders as conditions where there is evidence of a significant decline in performance across one or more cognitive domains, such as

DSM-5 SUMMARY TABLE 15.1 *Criteria for delirium*

- A reduced ability to focus, direct and sustain attention and awareness, developing over a short period of time (hours to a few days) and fluctuates in severity throughout that time

- Additional disturbances in cognitive functioning are also observed

- Disturbances are not a result of a pre-existing neurological condition and do not occur during the course of a coma or other reduced level of arousal state

- There is no evidence that the disturbance is as a direct physiological result of another medical condition, substance use or withdrawal

complex attention, executive functioning, learning and memory, language, perceptual–motor, or social cognition. This decline can be diagnosed as either **major neurocognitive disorder** (reflecting a substantial impairment) or **mild neurocognitive disorder** (reflecting a modest impairment in cognitive performance). Major neurocognitive disorders correspond to the categories labelled as dementias in previous editions of the DSM. Examples of cognitive deficits include difficulty remembering a short grocery list or keeping track of the plot of a TV programme; executive functioning problems include difficulty resuming a task when interrupted, organising finances or planning a meal out. At the mild NCD level, the individual will describe these tasks as requiring extra time or additional compensatory strategies. However, at the major NCD level, the individual will normally require assistance to complete these kinds of tasks. The key diagnostic criteria for major and mild neurocognitive disorders are provided in DSM-5 Summary Tables 15.2 and 15.3.

In the major neurocognitive disorders, language function may deteriorate to the point where the individual's conversation is vague or empty, and they may be unable to name individual everyday objects (such as tie, dress, desk, lamp). The condition may also (but not necessarily) be associated with apraxia (impaired ability to execute motor activities) and agnosia (the failure to recognize or identify objects despite intact sensory functioning). Disturbances in executive functioning are also common and are evidenced by the individual having difficulty coping with new tasks, shifting mental sets, generating novel verbal information and using or recalling basic general knowledge. Simple tests for executive functioning include asking the individual to count to 10, recite the alphabet, do subtraction or state as many animals as possible in 1 minute. Poor judgement and poor insight are also common features of major neurocognitive disorders. They may underestimate the risks involved in certain activities (e.g. driving) and indulge in inappropriate behaviours, such as making inappropriate jokes, neglecting personal hygiene or disregarding conventional rules of social conduct.

DSM-5 lists a number of specific major neurocognitive disorders and we will look at these individually in more detail below. These are Alzheimer's disease, vascular neurocognitive disorders, NCD due to Parkinson's disease, NCD due to traumatic brain injury, NCD due to HIV infection, NCD due to Huntington's disease, NCD due to prion disease and NCD with Lewy bodies.

Types of major neurocognitive disorder

In this section, we will look in more detail at some of the prevalent neurocognitive disorders that are categorized by their causes. These causes can range across cerebral infection, traumatic brain injury, cerebrovascular accidents (such as strokes) and degenerative disorders (such as Alzheimer's disease).

NCD due to HIV infection Among the viruses that can infect the brain is the human immunodeficiency virus type 1 (HIV-1). The HIV virus tends to enter the central nervous system early in the illness and neurological difficulties can develop in up to 60 per cent of those infected

> **major neurocognitive disorder** DSM-5 defines neurocognitive disorders (NCDs) as conditions where there is evidence of a significant decline in performance across one or more cognitive domains, such as complex attention, executive functioning, learning and memory, language, perceptual–motor, or social cognition. Major NCDs reflect a substantial impairment.

> **mild neurocognitive disorder** DSM-5 has introduced disorder categories that are designed to identify populations that are at risk for future mental health problems, and these include mild neurocognitive disorder, which diagnoses cognitive decline in the elderly.

DSM-5 SUMMARY TABLE 15.2 *Criteria for major neurocognitive disorder*

- Significant cognitive deterioration from previous level in at least one of the cognitive domains based on:
  - Concern of the patient, informant or doctor that there has been a substantial decline in cognitive function
  - A substantial impairment in cognitive performance, preferably as documented by standard testing
- The cognitive deterioration interferes with self-reliance in everyday activities
- The deficit does not occur in the context of delirium
- The deficit is not better accounted for by another mental disorder such as major depressive disorder or schizophrenia

DSM-5 SUMMARY TABLE 15.3 *Criteria for mild neurocognitive disorder*

- Limited cognitive deterioration from previous level in at least one of the cognitive domains based on:
  - Concern of the patient, informant or doctor that there has been a limited decline in cognitive function
  - A limited impairment in cognitive performance, preferably as documented by standard testing
- The cognitive deterioration does not interfere with self-reliance in everyday activities
- The deficit does not occur in the context of delirium
- The deficit is not better accounted for by another mental disorder such as major depressive disorder or schizophrenia

DSM-5 SUMMARY TABLE 15.4 *Criteria for neurocognitive disorder due to HIV infection*

- The criteria are met for major or mild neurocognitive disorder
- The patient is infected with human immunodeficiency virus (HIV)
- The disorder is not better explained by non-HIV conditions including secondary brain diseases
- The disorder is not due to another medical condition and is not better explained by another mental disorder

with the virus (Ghafouri, Amini, Khalili & Sawaya, 2006). On many occasions, the impairments caused by infection are usually minor, but over the many years that a sufferer may be hosting the virus, it may induce multiple symptoms of motor and cognitive dysfunction and create a syndrome of impairment that is known in DSM-5 as neurocognitive disorder due to HIV infection (sometimes also known as AIDS dementia complex (ADC) or HIV-1 associated dementia (HAD)). Individuals that develop this NCD diagnosis show impaired executive functioning, slowed speed of processing information, problems with attentional tasks and difficulty learning new information. Other symptoms include impaired short-term memory, lack of concentration, leg weakness, slowness of hand movement and depression (Reger, Welsh, Razani, Martin & Boone, 2002) (DSM-5 Summary Table 15.4). Depending on the stage of their infection, around one-third to a half of HIV-infected individuals will develop at least mild neurocognitive impairment, but fewer than 5 per cent would normally meet the criteria for major neuorocognitive disorder (DSM-5, p.633).

HIV infection appears to cause these cognitive impairments in a variety of ways. MRI scans indicate that HIV infection is associated with progressive cortical atrophy in the grey and white matter in the brain, particularly in the later stages of the disease (Dalpan, McArthur, Aylward, Selnes *et al.*, 1992) (see Figure 15.1). However, while the HIV virus can itself attack the central nervous system, neurological deficits are often caused by the body's weakened immune system allowing other infections to attack the brain (Ghafouri, Amini, Khalili & Sawaya, 2006).

NCD due to prion disease Many readers may recall the high profile given to what was called 'mad cow disease' in the UK in the 1980s, 1990s and 2000s. 'Mad cow disease' is a fatal infectious disease known as **spongiform encephalopathy** that attacks the brain and central nervous system. Outbreaks of the disease hit epidemic proportions among cattle in the UK during the 1980s and evidence suggests that the disease was transmitted to humans through contaminated beef. In humans, this became known as **variant Creutzfeldt–Jakob disease (vCJD)** and estimates suggest that over 150 people in the UK died from the disease between 1995 and 2006 (National Creutzfeldt–Jakob Disease Surveillance Unit, 2006). The disease may have an incubation period of up

> **spongiform encephalopathy** A fatal infectious disease that attacks the brain and central nervous system. Commonly known as 'mad cow disease' or variant Creutzfeldt–Jakob disease (vCJD).

> **variant Creutzfeldt–Jakob disease (vCJD)** A fatal infectious disease that attacks the brain and central nervous system. Commonly known as 'mad cow disease'.

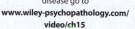

To view a video on Creutzfeldt–Jakob disease go to **www.wiley-psychopathology.com/video/ch15**

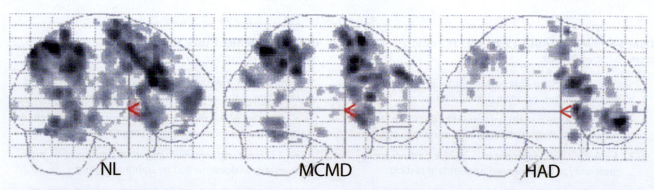

FIGURE 15.1 *Functional MRI (fMRI) scans showing activation during a motor task for HIV patients with normal cognitive function (NL), minor cognitive motor disorder (MCMD), and HIV associated dementia (HAD). Darkened regions indicate areas of activation. Compared with NL, patients with MCMD and HAD have significantly less activation.*
Source: Tucker, K.A., Robertson, K.R., Lin, W., Smith, J.K. et al. (2004). Neuroimaging in human immunodeficiency virus infection. *Journal of Neuroimmunology, 157*(1–2), 153–162. Reproduced by permission of Elsevier.

to 10–15 years, but, once symptoms begin to appear, death may occur within 4 months. Early signs of vCJD include changes in mood, temperament and behaviour followed by impairments in memory and concentration, and confused thinking. Deficits in verbal fluency, numeracy ability, face recognition, memory ability and executive functioning appear rapidly once symptoms have been identified (Kapur, Abbott, Lowman & Will, 2003) (DSM-5 Summary Table 15.5). Thankfully, the annual incidence of Creutzfeldt–Jakob disease is very low at around one or two cases per million people (DSM-5, p.635). The infectious agent in vCJD is thought to be the *prion* (a prion is an abnormal, transmissible agent that is able to induce abnormal folding of normal cellular proteins in the brain, leading to brain damage) and rapid dementia in vCJD appears to result from prions or protein deposits encrusting or replacing neurons in the brain and central nervous system, hence the term **prion disease**. This occurs at both the cortical and subcortical level, causing deficits in cognitive functioning and basic motor coordination. Case History 15.1 provides

> **prion disease** Prion disease represents a group of conditions that affect the nervous system in humans and animals.

a description of how the progressive cognitive impairments caused by vCJD become manifest once symptoms appear.

NCD due to traumatic brain injury One of the most common causes of neurological impairment is traumatic brain injury. This can result from blunt or penetrating trauma to the head as a result of direct injury at the impact site. Indirect injury can also be caused by sudden impacts causing movement of the brain within the skull, leading to injury on the opposite side of the brain to the

DSM-5 SUMMARY TABLE 15.5 *Criteria for neurocognitive disorder due to prion disease*

- The criteria are met for major or mild neurocognitive disorder
- The onset is slow, with rapid progression of the impairment
- Motor features of prion disease are obvious, such as involuntary muscle twitching or ataxia
- The disorder is not due to another medical condition and is not better explained by another mental disorder

CASE HISTORY 15.1

VARIANT CREUTZFELDT–JAKOB DISEASE (vCJD)

The patient was a right-handed man in his early 20s who presented at the end of July 1998 with a short history of memory difficulties, occasional problems in speech articulation, a change in personality and two episodes of urinary incontinence. His parents thought that the first sign of his illness was evident in May 1998, when he had a slight slurring in his speech during a telephone conversation with them. The first noticeable manifestation of his memory difficulties occurred in early July 1998 when he started a summer work placement and had major limitations in assimilating new information in a computer-based environment where he was taught simple data entry procedures and where, during a previous placement, he had excelled. Although he appeared to have no difficulty using equipment around the home (e.g. the video), he performed such activities much more slowly than before. His mother reported that he was very irritable and argumentative when he came home from university. He later became indifferent and apathetic. She said that he was often stuck for words and that his speech was sometimes incoherent. He had recently written two letters to his girlfriend that did not make any sense. His mother thought that he was nervous about going out on his own. His condition showed a progressive decline and he died in December 1998.

Source: From Kapur, Abbott, Lowman & Will, 2003.

> #### Clinical Commentary
>
> *vCJD may have an incubation period of up to 10–15 years but the first signs of the illness are emotional changes and confused behaviour. The disease eventually affects every aspect of thinking and behaviour, causing impairments in cognitive functioning, motor coordination and control over bodily functions – each of which is manifested in this case history. Once symptoms have begun to appear, the disease is fatal, and death usually occurs within 4–6 months. DSM-5 has provided diagnostic criteria for this neurocognitive disorder under the title 'neurocognitive disorder due to prion disease'.*

impact. Between 2000 and 2010 in the UK the incidence of traumatic brain injuries requiring consultant attention increased by around 95 per cent (The Health & Social Care Information Centre, 2012). Road traffic accidents account for around 40–50 per cent of all head injuries, while domestic and industrial accidents account for between 20 and 30 per cent. A majority of the rest are caused by sports and recreational activities (10–15 per cent) and assaults (10 per cent). Twice as many males as females are likely to be treated in hospital for traumatic brain injury and around 40–50 per cent are children. While the vast majority of these cases will suffer only a minor head injury, more serious cases will lapse into coma, develop epilepsy or suffer other forms of long-term disability (both physical and intellectual). Although many victims of head injury will show a slow but gradual improvement over time (e.g. recovery of any memory loss, recovery of motor functions such as balance, dissipation of feelings of confusion and disorientation), severe head injury can be associated with a range of semi-permanent cognitive and neurological deficits, including general deficits in speed of information processing, attention, memory, language skills and executive functioning, and may meet the diagnostic criteria for *neurocognitive disorder due to traumatic brain injury*, with around 2 per cent of the population of the US living with a traumatic brain injury-associated disability (DSM-5, p.625) (DSM-5 Summary Table 15.6). If recovery from such deficits occurs, it is likely to happen in the first 6 months following the injury. However, perhaps more dramatic than some of the cognitive deficits resulting from brain injury are the emotional sequelae, and these include depression, irritability, fatigue, aggressive behaviour, anxiety, rapid mood shifts and difficulty concentrating (Satz, Forney, Zaucha, Asarnow *et al.*, 1998). These factors can cause a significant decline in the overall quality of life for those with severe brain injury, giving rise to intense bouts of depression and suicidal ideation as well as posing significant challenges for post-injury care and rehabilitation (e.g. Horneman, Folkesson, Sintonen, von Wendt & Emanuelson, 2005; Baguley, Cooper & Felmingham, 2006; Levin, McCauley, Josic, Boake *et al.*, 2005).

Vascular neurocognitive disorder

Damage to brain tissue can also occur as a result of a **cardiovascular accident (CVA)** – otherwise known as a **stroke**. Strokes result from either a blockage or breaking of the blood vessels in the brain and can be defined in two broad ways. An **infarction** is when the blood flow to the brain is impeded in some way, resulting in damage to the brain tissue fed by that blood flow. In contrast, a **haemorrhage** is when a blood vessel in the brain ruptures and affects local brain tissue.

The most common causes of infarction are an embolism or a thrombosis. A **cerebral embolism** is a blood clot that forms somewhere in the body before travelling through the blood vessels and lodging in the brain, causing the brain cells to become damaged as a result of oxygen starvation. **Cerebral thrombosis** occurs when a blood clot (thrombus) forms in an artery (blood vessel) supplying blood to the brain. Furred-up blood vessels with fatty patches of atheroma (an abnormal inflammatory accumulation of macrophage white blood cells within the walls of arteries) may make a thrombosis more likely. The clot interrupts the blood supply and brain cells are starved of oxygen.

Haemorrhaging in the brain is often the result of hypertension or high blood pressure and is often due to an **aneurysm** or bulging in the wall of the blood vessel – usually an artery at the base of the brain.

Strokes are remarkably common – especially in individuals over the age of 65 years. In the UK, an estimated 130,000 people a year suffer a stroke – including around 1000 who are under 30 years of age. Strokes are the third most common cause of death in the UK and the single most common cause of disability – over 250,000

DSM-5 SUMMARY TABLE 15.6 *Criteria for neurocognitive disorder due to traumatic brain injury*

- The criteria are met for major or mild neurocognitive disorder
- Traumatic brain injury has occurred with at least one of the following:
  - Unconsciousness
  - Post-traumatic amnesia
  - Disorientation and confusion
  - Neurological signs such as neuroimaging demonstrating injury
- The disorder occurs immediately after the traumatic brain injury occurs

---

cardiovascular accident (CVA) Otherwise known as a stroke. Strokes result from either a blockage or breaking of the blood vessels in the brain.

stroke A sudden loss of consciousness resulting when the rupture or occlusion of a blood vessel leads to oxygen lack in the brain.

infarction The injury caused when the blood flow to the brain is impeded in some way, resulting in damage to the brain tissue fed by that blood flow.

haemorrhage When a blood vessel in the brain ruptures and affects local brain tissue.

cerebral embolism A blood clot that forms somewhere in the body before travelling through the blood vessels and lodging in the brain, causing the brain cells to become damaged as a result of oxygen starvation.

cerebral thrombosis An injury caused when a blood clot (thrombus) forms in an artery (blood vessel) supplying blood to the brain. The clot interrupts the blood supply and brain cells are starved of oxygen.

aneurysm A localized bulging in a blood vessel caused by disease or weakening of the vessel wall.

people currently live in the UK with a disability caused by a stroke (The Stroke Association, 2006). Symptoms of a stroke often occur very suddenly and unexpectedly. Symptoms include numbness, weakness or paralysis on one side of the body (signs of this may be a drooping arm, leg, a lowered eyelid, or a dribbling mouth), slurred speech or difficulty finding words or understanding speech, sudden blurred vision or loss of sight, confusion or unsteadiness, and a severe headache. The type and severity of symptoms will depend entirely on the brain area affected by the CVA. The most common longer term symptoms of stroke include aphasia, agnosia, apraxia (see Table 15.1) and paralysis, and a DSM-5 diagnosis of vascular neurocognitive disorder is established if there is good evidence for a cerebrovascular event as the cause of the disability, and if the criteria are met for major or mild neurocognitive disorder (see Tables 15.1, 15.3 and 15.7). One of the most common forms of stroke is thrombosis in the left-middle cerebral artery, affecting the left hemisphere. This will cause disability to the right-hand side of the body (which is controlled by the left hemisphere) and also cause significant impairment in language ability (e.g. aphasia) because the left hemisphere is critically involved in language generation and comprehension.

As well as physical and cognitive deficits, individuals who have suffered a stroke also exhibit emotional disturbance, often manifested as depressed mood or as emotional lability. Depression in particular is a common and significant consequence of strokes. A recent meta-analysis indicated that 29 per cent of stroke victims suffer depression up to 10 years after their stroke, with cognitive impairment being one of the main predictors of post-stroke depression (Ayerbe, Ayis, Wolfe & Rudd, 2013). Levels of depression are also correlated with the severity of both physical and cognitive deficits (Kauhanen, Korpelainen, Hiltunen, Brusin et al., 1999), suggesting that there may be a link between degree of disability and depression, and depression is associated with a significantly increased risk of early mortality (Pan, Sun, Okereke, Rexrode & Hu, 2011). Recovery from physical and cognitive impairment is also significantly retarded in those with depression (Robinson, Lipsey, Rao & Price, 1986; Morris, Robinson, Andrezejewski, Samuels & Price, 1993). There is a tendency here to conclude that the disabilities resulting from a stroke may cause depression that in turn inhibits recovery. However, the picture is rather more complex than this and there seems to be a bidirectional link between stroke and depression. For example, some studies have indicated that depression may even be a risk factor for strokes. In a prospective study, May, McCarron, Stansfeld, Ben-Shlomo et al. (2002) found that men with significant depressive symptoms were significantly more likely to suffer a stroke within the following 14 years than those without significant depression symptoms. Similarly,

DSM-5 SUMMARY TABLE 15.7 *Criteria for vascular neurocognitive disorder*

- The criteria are met for major or mild neurocognitive disorder
- The clinical features suggest vascular aetiology as marked by one of the following:
  - Arrival of the cognitive deficit is timely related to at least one cardiovascular event
  - Decline is evident in complex attention and frontal-executive function
- There is evidence of cerebrovascular disease to account for the neurocognitive deficits
- The symptoms are not better accounted for by another brain disease or disorder

treating post-stroke depression with antidepressant medication also has the effect of significantly decreasing mortality rates over a period of 9 years (Robinson, Schultz, Castillo, Kopel et al., 2000). All of this suggests that depression is an important feature of disability caused by strokes and is an area where clinical psychologists might be suitably employed to manage depression in attempts to improve recovery rates and reduce mortality rates.

Degenerative disorders   Degenerative disorders represent those neurocognitive disorders that are characterized by a slow, general deterioration in cognitive, physical and emotional functioning as a result of progressive physical changes in the brain. Deterioration occurs gradually over a number of years and degenerative disorders are most frequently a feature of older age, when around 7 per cent of individuals over 65 years of age have diagnosable signs of degenerative dementia; this rises to around 30 per cent in those over 85 years of age (Johansson & Zarit, 1995; Kokmen, Beard, Offord & Kurland, 1989). Degenerative disorders can affect both the cerebral cortex and subcortical regions of the brain. Those that affect cortical areas cause impairments in cognitive abilities such as memory, language, attention and executive functioning (causing amnesia, aphasia, agnosia, slowed thinking and confusion; see Table 15.1). Disorders affecting subcortical regions of the brain may in addition cause emotional disturbances and motor coordination difficulties. There are currently an estimated 800,000 people in the UK with dementia, and one in three people over 95 years of age have dementia (Alzheimer's Society, 2013), with the most common cause of degenerative dementia in the UK being Alzheimer's disease (contributing 55 per cent). Degenerative disorders that in addition significantly affect subcortical areas, and so affect emotional behaviour

To view a video on Parkinson's disease go to www.wiley-psychopathology.com/video/ch15

and motor coordination, are Parkinson's disease and Huntington's disease.

Diagnosis of degenerative disorders is difficult and complex. Firstly, a degenerative disorder has to be distinguished from the normal process of ageing. Normal ageing naturally results in a moderate deterioration of cognitive abilities (such as forgetfulness or cognitive slowness) and a deterioration in physical abilities (such as problems with balance and motor coordination). However, degenerative disorders compound this natural process because they represent an active pathological organic deterioration of the brain. Secondly, it is often difficult to distinguish between the different degenerative disorders that may affect cognitive and physical functioning. Many manifest with very similar cognitive impairments, such as amnesia. Thirdly, degenerative disorders are most frequently found in the elderly and this particular population will often present with a wide range of psychological and medical problems that complicate diagnosis. For example, anxiety and depression are common features of old age and may complicate neurological testing. Performance during assessment may also be affected by other physical illnesses or the effects of medications for other ailments. Finally, how a degenerative disorder manifests on presentation may differ significantly between individuals depending on factors such as their level of education, level of family and social support, and their psychological history. In effect, two individuals with the same disorder may present themselves quite differently and perform quite differently in assessments depending on a range of social and psychological factors. Overall prevalence estimates for diagnosed dementia disorders are around 1–2 per cent at age 65 years and as high as 30 per cent by age 85 years (DSM-5, p.608).

The following sections continue by describing in detail some of the main degenerative disorders. These cover neurocognitive disorder due to Alzheimer's disease, frontotemporal neurocognitive disorder, neurocognitive disorder due to Parkinson's disease, neurocognitive disorder with Lewy bodies, and neurocognitive disorder due to Huntington's disease.

NCD due to Alzheimer's disease   *Characteristics of Alzheimer's disease*   **Alzheimer's disease** is the most common form of dementia. It is a slowly progressive disorder and neural damage may start 20–30 years before any overt cognitive or behavioural signs of impairment (Davies, Wolska, Hilbich, Multhaup *et al.*, 1988). The

Alzheimer's disease A slowly progressive form of dementia involving progressive impairments in short-term memory, with symptoms of aphasia, apraxia and agnosia, together with evidence of impaired judgements, decision-making and orientation.

disease manifests as progressive impairments in short-term memory, with symptoms of aphasia, apraxia and agnosia, together with evidence of impaired judgements, decision-making and orientation. Early signs of the disease are irritability, lack of concentration and basic failures of short-term memory, such as forgetting that food is cooking or forgetting names. Eventually, the individual becomes more and more confused and disoriented, and may be unable to remember basic general knowledge (e.g. be unable to recite the alphabet), may confuse night and day, and get lost in relatively familiar environments. Many individuals also show personality changes, may exhibit paranoid behaviour and become generally irritable and difficult to control. Eventually sufferers usually become physically weak and bedridden. Their erratic and unpredictable behaviour will often become problematic for their carers, many of whom are likely to be the elderly spouses of the sufferer themselves. The average duration of the disease from onset of symptoms to death is around 8–10 years.

Known risk factors for Alzheimer's disease include the following (Barranco-Quintana, Allam, Del Castillo & Navajas, 2005):

1. age, which is the principal marker for risk of the disease;

2. sex – prevalence is higher in women than in men;

3. genetics – having a first-degree relative with the disease significantly increases risk;

4. family history of dementia – nearly 40 per cent of those with Alzheimer's disease have a family history of dementia;

5. a history of head injury (McDowell, 2001); and

6. low educational status.

Interestingly, some activities appear to have a direct or indirect protective value by predicting lower rates of Alzheimer's disease (even in those with a family history of dementia) and these include physical activity, smoking, drinking moderate levels of alcohol and diets high in vitamins B6, B12 and folic acid (Barranco-Quintana, Allam, Del Castillo & Navajas, 2005). However, we must be cautious about how we interpret these factors. For example, smoking may protect against Alzheimer's disease largely because it may prevent smokers from reaching old age, which is when the disease becomes prevalent. In addition, low educational status may be correlated with Alzheimer's disease because it may adversely affect performance on the cognitive tasks used to diagnose the disease. Several recent studies also suggest that factors such as diet (e.g. a Mediterranean diet), regular exercise and engagement in intellectual activities also appear to be useful in warding off cognitive decline

(Williams, Plassman, Burke, Holsinger & Benjamin, 2010; Hamer & Chida, 2009). For example, high levels of cognitive activity appear to protect against cognitive decline even in individuals who have a high genetic risk for Alzheimer's disease and have already developed the plaques and tangles in their brain that are associated with Alzheimer's (Wilson, Scherr, Schneider, Tang & Bennett, 2007).

The diagnostic criteria for neurocognitive disorder due to Alzheimer's disease is given in DSM-5 Summary Table 15.8. However, Alzheimer's disease itself is difficult to differentiate from other forms of degenerative dementia and it is often easier to identify Alzheimer's disease by successively eliminating other types of disorder that cause dementia symptoms, such as Parkinson's disease, Huntington's disease, hypothyroidism, HIV infection, substance abuse or head trauma. This can be achieved using thyroid function tests, blood tests and a battery of neuropsychological tests of cognitive function. However, the recent identification of some of the genes that carry a high risk for the development of Alzheimer's disease means that genetic testing can be used to identify Alzheimer's as the possible cause of the dementia or cognitive decline. In addition, neuroimaging plays an important part in the diagnosis of Alzheimer's disease by helping to exclude alternative causes of dementia such as brain tumour, cerebral atrophy and cerebrovascular disease.

Aetiology of Alzheimer's disease   It is only in the past 20–25 years that we have come to understand some of the causes of Alzheimer's disease, and, indeed, become able to identify it as a specific form of degenerative dementia. The changes that occur to the brain during Alzheimer's disease appear to be structural and involve the development of beta amyloid plaques and neurofibrillary tangles. **Beta amyloid plaques** appear to be caused by abnormal protein synthesis in the brain and they clump together with the consequence of killing healthy neurons. **Neurofibrillary tangles** consist of abnormal collections of twisted nerve cell threads which result in errors in impulses between nerve cells and eventual cell death (Blennow, de Leon & Zetterberg, 2006) (see Figure 15.2). The result of these abnormal cell developments is that there is a gradual shrinkage of healthy brain tissue. The grooves or furrows in the brain, called sulci, are noticeably widened and there is shrinkage of the gyri, the well-developed folds of the brain's outer layer. In addition, the ventricles, or chambers within the brain that contain cerebrospinal fluid, are noticeably enlarged.

beta amyloid plaques Abnormal cell development, possibly caused by abnormal protein synthesis in the brain, which clump together with the consequence of killing healthy neurons.

neurofibrillary tangles Abnormal collections of twisted nerve cell threads which result in errors in impulses between nerve cells and eventual cell death.

DSM-5 SUMMARY TABLE 15.8 *Criteria for neurocognitive disorder due to Alzheimer's disease*

- The criteria are met for major or mild neurocognitive disorder
- The onset is slow, with gradual progression of the impairment
- **For major neurocognitive disorder:**

  Probable Alzheimer's disease is diagnosed if either of the following are present:
  - Evidence of the Alzheimer's disease genetic mutation in the family history of the patient or via genetic testing
  - All three of the following are present:
    - Decline in memory and learning and at least one other cognitive ability
    - Steady, gradual decline in cognition
    - No evidence of other neurodegenerative or cerebrovascular disease

  Otherwise, *possible Alzheimer's disease* should be diagnosed.

- **For mild neurocognitive disorder:**

  Probable Alzheimer's disease is diagnosed if there is evidence of the Alzheimer's disease genetic mutation in the family history of the patient or via genetic testing. Otherwise, *possible Alzheimer's disease* should be diagnosed if all three of the following are present:
  - Decline in memory and learning and at least one other cognitive ability
  - Steady, gradual decline in cognition
  - No evidence of other neurodegenerative or cerebrovascular disease

- The disturbance is not better explained by cerebrovascular disease, another neurodegenerative disease or disorder

Another factor that is thought to be important in Alzheimer's disease is the faulty production of the brain neurotransmitter **acetylcholine**; Alzheimer's disease appears to affect structures involved in the production of acetylcholine. The enzyme acetylcholinesterase normally breaks down acetylcholine after use so it can be recycled, but in Alzheimer's disease acetylcholine levels fall too low and memory and other brain functions are impaired. A number of drug treatments can be utilized to help facilitate acetylcholine production in the brain and we will discuss these in more detail in the following section on treatment and rehabilitation.

There also appears to be a significant inherited component to Alzheimer's disease, with an estimate of up

acetylcholine A neurotransmitter that appears to be involved in learning and memory.

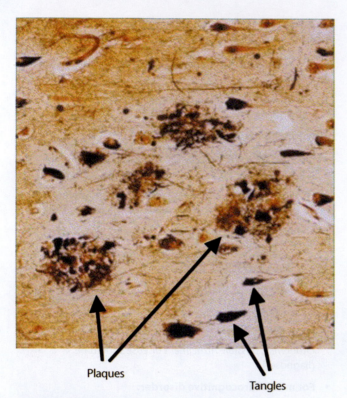

FIGURE 15.2 *Beta amyloid plaques and neurofibrillary tangles in the cerebral cortex in Alzheimer's disease. Plaques appear to be caused by abnormal protein synthesis in the brain and they clump together killing healthy neurones. Tangles consist of abnormal collections of twisted nerve cell threads causing errors in impulses between nerves. Certain genes such as APOE-4 have also been identified that promote the formation of abnormal amyloid plaques (Bookheimer & Burggren, 2009).*
Source: Blennow, K., de Leon, M.J. & Zetterberg, H. (2006). Alzheimer's disease. *Lancet, 368*, 387–403. Reproduced by permission of Elsevier.

to 50 per cent of the first-degree relatives of sufferers also developing the disorder (Korten, Jorm, Henderson, Broe *et al.*, 1993). In addition, twin studies suggest that the heritability of the disease is high – between 58 and 79 per cent (Gatz, Reynolds, Fratiglioni, Johansson *et al.*, 2006). Several genes have been identified that are associated with a high risk of developing Alzheimer's disease and these include APOE4 and GAB2 (Bookheimer & Burggren, 2009; Bertram & Tanzi, 2008), and currently, genetic testing to identify these genes is often used to enable diagnosis. Some of these genes may increase susceptibility to Alzheimer's disease while others may have a more direct cause in generating proteins that cause the beta amyloid plaques that result in damage to brain tissue (e.g. causing overproduction of the beta amyloid plaques that leads to loss of healthy neurones). In addition, some genes may play a role in early-onset Alzheimer's disease, while others appear to be linked to late onset (Bertram & Tanzi, 2004). All this suggests that, while there is no doubt about the importance of an inherited component to Alzheimer's disease, it may have multiple causes and a number of genetic mechanisms may contribute to the factors that cause degenerative brain damage.

Frontotemporal neurocognitive disorder Frontotemporal NCD is associated with a loss of neurones from the frontal and temporal regions of the brain that leads to progressive development of behavioural and personality changes and language impairment. Unlike Alzheimer's disease, frontotemporal NCD does not usually affect memory processes but has its main impact on emotional processes such as apathy and the ability to empathize with others. It is also characterized by a lack of insight into social conventions (e.g. someone might not realize that a particular behaviour was embarrassing

THE PROS AND CONS OF GENETIC TESTING FOR DEGENERATIVE BRAIN DISORDERS

Some people might wish to use genetic testing to assess their risk of developing dementia later in life. Genetic testing is not a straightforward issue and individuals need to think very carefully before deciding to take such a test. The experience could be very difficult emotionally, may not provide conclusive results either way, and may cause practical difficulties.

Possible advantages of genetic testing include that it might:

- help genetic researchers understand the disease better and so lead to improved treatment;
- encourage someone to adopt a healthier lifestyle;

- allow people who are at a high risk of developing dementia to benefit from new treatments that may become available in the future; and
- help people to plan for the future.

However, genetic testing might create problems for the following reasons:

- a genetic defect cannot be repaired and effective treatment to slow the disease is not yet generally available. A genetic test might therefore raise anxiety without offering a clear course of action;

- there is a risk of reading too much into the test results. Testing positive for one or two gene variants does not mean a person will definitely develop Alzheimer's and testing negative does not guarantee that they will be free from Alzheimer's; and
- people testing positive for any genetic test could face discrimination affecting their ability to buy property, get insurance or plan financially for their

old age. However, there is a moratorium (delay or suspension of an activity or law) on the use of genetic information by UK insurance companies until 2017, and this means that companies cannot use this information at the moment.

Source: Adapted from Alzheimer's Society: *Genetics of dementia* http://www.alzheimers.org.uk/factsheet/405

to themselves or to others) and an inability to regulate emotions. Regular neurocognitive symptoms include lack of planning and organization, distractability and poor judgement, which may lead to a lack of self-care, changes in social style, hoarding and changes in eating behaviour (DSM-5 Summary Table 15.9).

Frontotemporal neurocognitive disorder is a common cause of early onset dementia in individuals under 65 years of age but accounts for only 5 per cent of all cases of dementia in autopsy studies (DSM-5, p.616). The disorder has a strong genetic component of around 50–60 per cent

frontotemporal neurocognitive disorder Associated with a loss of neurones from the frontal and temporal regions of the brain that leads to progressive development of behavioural and personality changes and language impairment.

(Le Ber, 2013), but with a high probability of a number of different genes and genetic pathways being involved (Cruts, Gijselinck, van der Zee, Engelborghs *et al.*, 2006). This fact also suggests that the neurological degeneration in frontotemporal NCD probably results from many different gene-controlled molecular processes that contribute to the death of healthy brain neurones in the frontal and temporal regions (Seelaar, Rohrer, Pijnenburg, Fox & van Swieten, 2011).

NCD due to Parkinson's disease and NCD with Lewy bodies

Parkinson's disease is a progressive neurological condition affecting movements, such as walking, talking and writing, and it causes psychological disturbance in between 40 and 60 per cent of sufferers. The main symptoms of **Parkinson's disease** are (1) tremor, including jerky movements of the arms, hands and head that are also present during resting periods, (2) slowness of movement (bradykinesia) – people with Parkinson's may find that they have difficulty initiating movements or find that performing movements takes longer, and (3) stiffness or rigidity of muscles, including problems in standing up from a chair or rolling over in bed. The disease is named after Dr James Parkinson (1755–1824), the London doctor who first identified Parkinson's as a specific condition. Parkinson's disease occurs as a result of damage in the basal ganglia – particularly the region of the basal ganglia known as the **substantia nigra**. Cells in this area are responsible for producing the neurotransmitter dopamine, which allows messages to be sent to the parts of the brain that coordinate movement. With the depletion of dopamine-producing cells, these parts of the brain are unable to function normally. It is estimated that over 4 million people worldwide suffer from Parkinson's disease, including 127,000 in the UK (Parkinson's Disease Society, 2013). Symptoms first appear when the individual is over 50 years of age, with men being marginally more likely to develop the disorder than women.

Parkinson's disease A progressive neurological condition affecting movements such as walking, talking and writing, and causing psychological disturbance in between 40 and 60 per cent of sufferers.

substantia nigra A region of the basal ganglia.

DSM-5 SUMMARY TABLE 15.9 *Criteria for frontotemporal neurocognitive disorder*

- The criteria are met for major or mild neurocognitive disorder
- The onset is slow, with gradual progression of the impairment
- Either a behavioural or a language variant is present:
  - Behavioural:
    - At least three of the following:
      - Lack of inhibition
      - Sluggishness or lethargy
      - Compulsive/ritualistic behaviour
      - Inserting inappropriate things into the mouth or diet changes
    - Obvious decline in social cognition
  - Language:
    - Obvious decline in language ability
- Limited learning and memory functions and perceptual motor function
- The disturbance is not better explained by cerebrovascular disease, another neurodegenerative disease or disorder, or by the effects of a substance

Those sufferers who develop psychological problems experience memory difficulties and exhibit deficits in learning, judgement and concentration, as well as becoming socially withdrawn and apathetic. It is estimated that up to 75 per cent of individuals with Parkinson's disease may eventually develop dementia and these symptoms can occur as early as 1–2 years after onset of the disease (Williams-Gray, Foltynie, Lewis & Barker, 2006; Ehrt & Aarsland, 2005). As well as signs of cognitive impairment, Parkinson's sufferers also regularly exhibit symptoms of psychosis and depression. Hallucinations occur in between 16 and 40 per cent of sufferers and this has often been considered as a medication-induced phenomenon. That is, the drugs used to facilitate substantia nigra dopamine production in sufferers are also known to produce psychosis-like symptoms. However, there is reason to believe that psychosis symptoms such as hallucinations may also be intrinsic to the disease and result from progressive dementia or impairments in primary visual processing (Williams-Gray, Foltynie, Lewis & Barker, 2006). Studies also suggest that depression is a significant feature of Parkinson's disease in between 25 and 40 per cent of sufferers (Leentjens, 2004) and this is often considered to be an understandable reaction to having to cope with a chronic and debilitating disease. However, as in the case of Alzheimer's disease, depression is also a significant predictor of subsequent Parkinson's diagnosis, with the incidence of depression increasing significantly in the 3 years prior to diagnosis of Parkinson's (Leentjens, van den Akker, Metsemakers, Lousberg & Verhey, 2003). The fact that depression appears to be a biological risk factor for a number of degenerative dementias has given rise to the view that depression may be accompanied by an **allostatic state** (a biological state of stress) that can accelerate disease processes and cause atrophy of nerve cells in the brain, in turn leading to dementia (McEwen, 2003).

allostatic state A biological state of stress.

Post-mortem studies of individuals with Parkinson's disease suggest an association between dementia and Lewy body deposition. **Lewy bodies** are abnormal protein deposits that disrupt the brain's normal functioning. These Lewy body proteins are found in an area of the brain stem where they deplete the neurotransmitter dopamine, causing Parkinson's symptoms. These abnormal proteins can also diffuse throughout other areas of the brain, including the cerebral cortex, causing disruption of perception, thinking and behaviour. Around 80 per cent of individuals with Parkinson's disease will develop dementia with Lewy bodies, but others without Parkinson's disease can develop neurocognitive disorders purely as a result of the development of Lewy bodies. This has led DSM-5 to introduce a new diagnostic category known as

Lewy bodies Abnormal protein deposits that disrupt the brain's normal functioning.

'Neurocognitive disorder with Lewy bodies'. A diagnosis of NCD due to Parkinson's disease is given if Parkinson's disease clearly precedes the onset of the neurocognitive disorder (DSM-5 Summary Table 15.10), and a diagnosis of NCD with Lewy bodies is given if there is no convincing evidence of Parkinson's disease in the aetiology (DSM-5 Summary Table 15.11). The prevalence of

DSM-5 SUMMARY TABLE 15.10 *Criteria for neurocognitive disorder due to Parkinson's disease*

- The criteria are met for major or mild neurocognitive disorder
- The disturbance occurs during diagnosed Parkinson's disease
- The onset is slow, with gradual progression of the impairment
- The disturbance is not better explained by another medical condition or mental disorder
- *Major or mild neurocognitive disorder probably due to Parkinson's disease* should be diagnosed if both of the following are met. *Major or mild neurocognitive disorder possibly due to Parkinson's disease* should be diagnosed if one of the following is met:
  - No evidence of other neurodegenerative or cerebrovascular disease
  - The Parkinson's disease diagnosis pre-dates the neurological disorder

DSM-5 SUMMARY TABLE 15.11 *Criteria for neurocognitive disorder with Lewy bodies*

- The criteria are met for major or mild neurocognitive disorder
- The onset is slow, with gradual progression of the impairment
- *Probable major or mild neurocognitive disorder with Lewy bodies* is diagnosed if the patient has two of the core features or at least one suggestive feature with other features. *Possible major or mild neurocognitive disorder with Lewy bodies* is diagnosed if the patient has one of the core features or at least one suggestive feature
  - Core features:
    - Varying cognition with obvious changeability in attention and alertness
    - Reoccurring, detailed hallucinations
    - Features of Parkinsonism prior to the development of cognitive decline
  - Suggestive features:
    - Rapid eye movement sleep behaviour disorder
    - Adverse reactions to neuroleptics
- The disturbance is not better explained by cerebrovascular disease, another neurodegenerative disease or disorder, or by the effects of a substance

Parkinson's disease in the US begins at around 0.5 per cent between 65 and 69 years of age and rises to 3 per cent by 85 years of age. Estimates of NCD with Lewy bodies range between 1.7 and 30.5 per cent (DSM-5, p.619) and this form of neurocognitive disorder may account for up to 30 per cent of all dementias.

NCD due to Huntington's disease

Huntington's disease is an inherited, degenerative disorder of the central nervous system caused by a dominant gene. This means that everyone who inherits the gene from one of his/her parents will develop the disease with 50 per cent likelihood (see Focus Point 1.4 for a fuller explanation of the genetics of Huntington's disease). Symptoms of the disorder do not normally occur until after the age of 35 years and can have an even later onset (however, the earlier the onset, the more severe the disease tends to be). It is principally a movement disorder, with the first observable behavioural symptoms manifesting themselves as clumsiness and an involuntary, spasmodic jerking of the limbs. However, many early signs of the disease tend to be radical changes in temperament. The individual may become rude, exhibit unpredictable mood changes and switch dramatically from depression to euphoria. Cognitive functioning is affected as the disease develops and this is manifested as impairments in memory, attention and decision making, leading to full dementia. In addition, as the disease progresses, the sufferer may also begin to exhibit psychotic symptoms, including hallucinations and delusions. The general psychological syndrome associated with Huntington's disease includes affective symptoms, cognitive deficits, personality disorganization, bloody-mindedness, early loss of common sense, hallucinations, delusional ideation, odd behaviours and obsessions (Wagle, Wagle, Markova & Berrios, 2000). Psychopathological symptoms associated with the disease include depression, mania, schizophrenia, paranoia, anxiety and obsessive compulsive behaviours (Barquero-Jimenez & Gomez-Tortosa, 2001). About 8 in every 100,000 people in the UK have Huntington's disease – approximately 4800 people. Because the disease is a genetically inherited one, its prevalence will vary according to the geographical distribution of those with the defective gene. The highest prevalence of this disorder in the world is near Lake Maracaibo in Venezuela where it affects around 700 per 100,000 of the population.

The genetic abnormality in Huntington's disease is found on the fourth chromosome. This results in the production of a protein, **mutant Huntingtin (mHtt)**, that causes cell death in the basal ganglia – an area of the

> **Huntington's disease** An inherited, degenerative disorder of the central nervous system, caused by a dominant gene.

> **mutant Huntingtin (mHtt)** A protein which causes cell death in the basal ganglia and contributes to Huntington's disease.

DSM-5 SUMMARY TABLE 15.12 *Criteria for neurocognitive disorder due to Huntington's disease*

- The criteria are met for major or mild neurocognitive disorder
- The onset is slow, with gradual progression of the impairment
- The disturbance occurs during diagnosed Huntington's disease, or the risk of Huntington's disease based on family history or genetic testing
- The disturbance is not better explained by another medical condition or mental disorder

brain responsible for posture, muscle tone and motor coordination. Pre-symptom testing is possible by means of a blood test which counts the number of mutant repetitions on the relevant gene. A negative blood test means that the individual does not carry the gene, will never develop symptoms and cannot pass it on to children. A positive blood test means that the individual does carry the gene, will develop the disease and has a 50 per cent chance of passing it on to children, assuming he or she lives long enough to do so. Because a positive blood test will have such a dramatic psychological impact, potential sufferers are given intensive counselling and psychological support before undergoing pre-symptom testing. A diagnosis of neurocognitive disorder due to Huntington's disease is given if the individual meets the criteria for major or mild neurocognitive disorder and there is good evidence based on family history or genetic testing that Huntington's disease is a relevant aetiology (DSM-5 Summary Table 15.12). The worldwide prevalence of Huntington's disease is estimated to be around 2.7 per 100,000 (DSM-5, p.639), and neurocognitive deficits are an inevitable outcome of the disease.

Summary of types of neurocognitive disorder

In this section we have discussed a number of different types of neurocognitive disorder and their DSM-5 diagnostic categories. The main aetiology categories we covered were infection (e.g. HIV infection), traumatic brain injury, vascular causes (e.g. strokes) and degenerative disorders (e.g. Alzheimer's disease and Parkinson's disease). All of these can cause cognitive impairment to differing degrees, and the nature of the impairment will depend on the areas of the brain affected by each factor. Neurocognitive deficits may be relatively specific and result from damage to tissue in areas of the brain dealing with specific functions such as language, memory or visuomotor coordination (see Table 15.1). Such specific disabilities are found most often with traumatic brain injury, cerebrovascular accidents and brain tumours. Other types of disorder are progressive and can develop from being diagnosed as mild neurocognitive disorders to major cognitive disorders. A common feature of most types of neurocognitive disorder is that they are often associated with other forms of psychopathology, including anxiety, depression and psychosis. Depression is very closely associated with some of the degenerative disorders, such as Alzheimer's and Parkinson's diseases, and is not only a frequent consequence of these disorders but also a pre-symptom predictor of the disorder. One feature common to almost all of these types of neurocognitive disorder is that the cognitive, behavioural and emotional deficits that ensue are almost entirely the result of damage to brain tissue caused through trauma, disease or biochemical abnormalities in the brain. In some cases, the means by which brain tissue is damaged may be common across a number of different types of disorder. For example, there is gathering evidence that the deposition of Lewy bodies in the brain may be one part of the mechanism causing dementia in both Alzheimer's and Parkinson's disease.

SELF-TEST QUESTIONS

- Can you define the terms amnesia, aphasia, agnosia and apraxia?
- What is the difference between Broca's aphasia and Wernicke's aphasia?
- What specific skills are impaired when neurological disorders cause deficits in executive functioning?
- Can you name some of the difficulties involved in diagnosing specific neurological disorders?
- What kinds of individual abilities are assessed using the Wechsler Adult Intelligence Scale or the Adult Memory and Information Processing Battery (AMIPB)?
- Can you describe the DSM-5 diagnostic criteria for both delirium and major/mild NCDs?
- Can you name two or more types of cerebral infection that may cause cognitive deficits?
- What are the main causes of traumatic brain injury?
- What are some of the emotional and psychological consequences of suffering a stroke?
- Can you name the main degenerative disorders?
- What is frontotemporal neurocognitive disorder and how does it differ from other neurocognitive disorders?
- Can you describe the main characteristics of Alzheimer's disease?
- What are the main risk factors for Alzheimer's disease and what changes in the brain are thought to occur during the disorder?
- What areas of the brain are affected by Parkinson's disease? And what are the cognitive and emotional symptoms associated with the disorder?
- What are Lewy bodies and how are they involved in neurocognitive deficits?

SECTION SUMMARY

15.1   THE DIAGNOSIS AND ASSESSMENT OF NEUROCOGNITIVE DISORDERS

15.1.1   *Cognitive Impairments in Neurocognitive Disorders*
- The main cognitive impairments in neurological disorders are deficits in learning and memory, attention and arousal, language and communication, visual–perceptual functioning, motor skills and executive functioning.
- Language deficits are known as *aphasias*. They include *Broca's aphasia* and *Wernicke's aphasia*.
- *Agnosia* is a disorder of the ability to recognize and name everyday objects.

- *Apraxia* is an impairment in motor performance and coordination.

- Deficits in *executive functioning* reflect the inability to problem-solve, plan, initiate, organize, monitor and inhibit complex behaviours.

- Assessment in clinical neuropsychology is based on a range of cognitive tests and can be supplemented by blood tests, chemical analyses of cerebrospinal fluids, and brain scans such as PET and fMRI.

15.1.2 The Diagnosis of Neurocognitive Disorders

- *Delirium* is a disturbance of consciousness that develops over a short period of time.

- *Major* or *mild neurocognitive disorders* are the two overarching categories into which DSM-5 conceptualizes neurocognitive disorders.

- Neurocognitive disorders caused by infections include *neurocognitive disorder due to HIV infection* and *neurocognitive disorder due to prion disease*.

- Traumatic brain injury is one of the most common causes of neurological impairment.

- Damage to brain tissue can occur as a result of a *cardiovascular accident (CVA)* – otherwise known as a stroke – and these are remarkably common in individuals over the age of 65 years.

- Degenerative disorders represent those dementias that are characterized by a slow, general deterioration in cognitive, physical and emotional functioning, and these affect around 7 per cent of individuals over 65 years of age.

- *Alzheimer's disease* is the most common cause of dementia in the UK (contributing 55 per cent), followed by *vascular NCD* (contributing 20 per cent).

- The changes that occur in the brain during Alzheimer's disease appear to be structural and involve the development of *beta amyloid plaques* and *neurofibrillary tangles*. It is also associated with the faulty production of the brain neurotransmitter *acetylcholine*.

- *Frontotemporal neurocognitive disorder* is associated with a loss of neurones from the frontal and temporal regions of the brain causing behavioural, personality and language impairments.

- *Parkinson's disease* causes psychological and cognitive disturbance in between 40 and 60 per cent of sufferers and appears to be caused as a result of degenerative damage to the region of the *basal ganglia* known as the *substantia nigra*.

- *Lewy bodies* are abnormal protein deposits that disrupt the brain's normal functioning and can occur in around 80 per cent of individuals with Parkinson's disease.

- *Neurocognitive disorder with Lewy bodies* is diagnosed when Lewy bodies are present in the brain without convincing evidence for a diagnosis of Parkinson's disease.

15.2 TREATMENT AND REHABILITATION FOR NEUROCOGNTIVE DISORDERS

Many of the neurocognitive disorders described in this chapter represent irreversible changes in impairment and central nervous system damage. As a consequence, attempts at treatment tend to be oriented towards rehabilitation rather than cure. Nevertheless, impairment in some types of neurocognitive disorder can be reversible, and deficits caused by some kinds of cerebral infection are one example (e.g. meningitis and encephalitis). In the case of degenerative disorders such as Alzheimer's

disease, recent developments in drug treatments have indicated that progressive impairment can be slowed, affording some respite from the degenerative nature of the disease. However, in many cases, neurological damage is relatively permanent and the sufferer must learn to live with the behavioural and cognitive deficits that the disorder brings (e.g. traumatic brain injury, strokes). This has led to the development of a range of rehabilitation procedures designed to provide the individual with

1. exercises that help to improve impaired cognitive functions (e.g. impaired language or memory function);

2. training in the use of cognitive and behavioural aids (e.g. using memory aids or labelling cupboards and drawers in order to remember where things are);

3. assistive technology (e.g. equipment that may aid hearing, speaking or moving about); and

4. basic drug treatment and psychotherapy to help deal with related mood disorders (such as depression).

Finally, in some severe cases of neurological disorder, very little in the way of ameliorative therapeutic help can be provided for the sufferer, but support can be provided for caregivers and many national associations provide structured support and advice for such caregivers (e.g. the UK Alzheimer's Society, www.alzheimers.org.uk). We will now discuss the various forms of treatment and rehabilitation in more detail.

15.2.1   Biological Treatments

Biological treatments for neurocognitive disorders take a number of forms. The most common are drug treatments that help to stabilize or slow degenerative disorders; others include drug treatments to combat cerebral infections and electrical brain stimulation for some forms of dementia.

Drug treatments

There has been some success in recent years in developing drugs that can help to slow the progress of degenerative disorders such as Alzheimer's disease and Parkinson's disease. In the case of Alzheimer's, we have already noted that the disease is often associated with abnormalities in the production of the brain neurotransmitter acetylcholine. During the course of the disease, an enzyme called acetylcholinesterase breaks down acetylcholine and leads to depletion of the neurotransmitter dopamine. In order to combat this effect, drugs have been developed that prevent acetylcholine breakdown in the synaptic cleft by acetylcholinesterase and increase its uptake in the postsynaptic receptor. The most common of these drugs are donepezil, rivastigmine and galantamine, collectively known as **cholinesterase inhibitors** (Petersen, Thomas, Grundman & Thal, 2005). Randomized, double-blind, placebo-controlled trials suggest that treatment for 6 months with cholinesterase inhibitors produces moderate improvements in cognitive function in those with mild to moderate Alzheimer's disease (Hitzeman, 2006). They may also help to slow memory decline (Birks, 2006) and prospects are best when treatment begins early in the course of the disease

> **cholinesterase inhibitors** A group of drugs that prevent acetylcholine breakdown in the synaptic cleft by acetylcholinesterase and increase its uptake in the postsynaptic receptor. The most common of these drugs are donepezil, rivastigmine and galantamine

(Seltzer, 2006). Although the emphasis has been on identifying early signs of Alzheimer's so that drug treatment can begin as soon as possible, there is also some evidence that cholinesterase inhibitors such as donepezil can improve cognition in individuals with severe Alzheimer's (Winblad, Kilander, Eriksson, Minthon et al., 2006). Accumulating evidence suggests that donepezil can also help to alleviate behavioural symptoms, mood disturbances and delusions associated with Alzheimer's (Cummings, McRae & Zhang, 2006). However, recent systematic reviews of cholinesterase inhibitors found no evidence that they could prevent dementia (Cooper, Li, Lyketsos & Livingston, 2013). The UK National Institute for Health and Care Excellence (NICE) has recommended to the NHS that donepezil, rivastigmine and galantamine be made available as part of the management of mild and moderate Alzheimer's disease, and those to be targeted should score 10 points or higher on the Mini Mental State Examination (MMSE) (NICE, 2011) (see Focus Point 15.2). While some cholinesterase inhibitors might be effective in slowing cognitive decline in a number of neurocognitive disorder diagnoses, there is as yet no reliable evidence for the efficacy of any drug treatments for frontotemporal neurocognitive disorder (Schwarz, Froelich & Burns, 2012).

Parkinson's disease is associated with degeneration in the substantia nigra area of the brain, where the important neurotransmitter dopamine is produced. The main drug that is used to counteract this decline in dopamine is **levodopa**, a natural amino acid that the brain converts into dopamine to replace the depleted neurotransmitter. Although the drug has been relatively successful in helping suffers to control tremor and other motor symptoms, there is little evidence that levodopa alleviates any of the cognitive impairments associated with Parkinson's disease (Morrison, Borod, Brin, Halbig et al., 2004). Levadopa administration has to be closely supervised because it also has a number of potential side effects including hypertension and delusions, and hallucinations similar to those found in schizophrenia and amphetamine psychosis.

> **levodopa** A natural amino acid that is converted by the brain into dopamine and is used in the treatment of Parkinson's disease.

Medication can also be successful in reducing disability following cerebrovascular accidents (strokes). **Thrombolytic therapy** is the use of drugs to break up or dissolve blood clots – one of the main causes of strokes. The most commonly used thrombolytic drug is tissue plasminogen activator (t-PA) and if this is administered within the first 3 hours of a stroke then disability is significantly reduced (Albers, 1997; Hacke, Donnan,

> **thrombolytic therapy** The use of drugs to break up or dissolve blood clots – one of the main causes of strokes.

Fieschi, Kaste *et al.*, 2004). Nevertheless, the success of this treatment is critically dependent on the individual being able to identify the early signs of a stroke and seek rapid treatment. Although early administration of thrombolytic therapy can significantly aid survival and physical recovery, there is little evidence that such an intervention helps to alleviate the cognitive deficits that may accompany stroke (Nys, van Zandvoort, Algra, Kappelle & de Haan, 2006).

Medication is also used in the treatment of brain deficits caused by cerebral infections. Bacterial infections, such as certain types of encephalitis and **bacterial meningitis**, are treatable with antibiotics. However, many viral infections are much more problematic. Steroids can be used to combat viral infections such as herpes encephalitis, and, in the case of HIV-1 associated dementia, newly developed **antiretroviral drugs** are proving to be effective in reducing the severity of HIV dementia and reducing the prevalence of diagnoses of neurocognitive disorder (Nath & Sacktor, 2006; Crum-Cianflone, Moore, Letendre, Roediger *et al.*, 2013). Usually, up to three to four antiretroviral drugs are used that act at different stages of the virus life-cycle. This produces a dramatic reduction in viral load (the level of virus in the blood) and prevents further immune damage.

Finally, mood disorders (such as depression) are a common feature of neurological disorders, including stroke, traumatic brain injury and degenerative disorders, and depression can often adversely affect the course of the disorder, prevent recovery and increase mortality rates (Robinson, Lipsey, Rao & Price, 1986; Leentjens, 2004; Ramasubbu & Patten, 2003). The use of drugs such as SSRIs and tricyclic antidepressants to help alleviate depressed mood has proven to be successful in improving recovery from strokes (Hackett, Anderson & House, 2005), alleviating symptoms of depression in Parkinson's disease and Alzheimer's disease (Weintraub, Morales, Moberg, Bilker *et al.*, 2005; Modegro, 2010) and improving mood and cognitive performance following traumatic head injury (Horsfield, Rosse, Tomasino, Schwartz *et al.*, 2002). In at least some of these disorders (e.g. Parkinson's disease) there is a view that depression is an integral symptom of the disorder – especially because depression often precedes and predicts other symptoms of the disease as well as affecting outcome. So, tackling depression can be considered a direct treatment of the disorder itself rather than dealing with a side effect of disability (e.g. Leentjens, 2004).

bacterial meningitis The inflammation (infection) of the meninges, which are the membranes that cover the brain and spine.

antiretroviral drugs Chemicals that inhibit the replication of retroviruses, such as HIV.

Deep brain stimulation (DBS)

A recently developed form of treatment for Parkinson's disease involves **deep brain stimulation** (DBS). This uses a surgically implanted, battery-operated device called a neurostimulator to deliver electrical stimulation to the ventral intermediate nucleus of the thalamus or the subthalamic nucleus area in the basal ganglia. These areas of the brain control movement and, through mechanisms that are as yet unclear, electrical stimulation in this area appears to block the abnormal nerve signals that cause tremor and Parkinson's symptoms (Perlmutter & Mink, 2006; Ananthaswamy, 2004). DBS has been shown to result in improvements in physical abilities (e.g. mobility) and global measures of quality of life (Hamani, Neimat & Lozano, 2006) but there is little evidence at present that DBS has any significant effect on cognitive abilities (Laxton, Lipsman & Lozano, 2013), and it may even be associated with a mild decline in communication skills and language abilities (Castelli, Perozzo, Zibetti, Crivelli *et al.*, 2006; Drapier, Raoul, Drapier, Leray *et al.*, 2005).

deep brain stimulation (DBS) A form of treatment for Parkinson's disease which uses a surgically implanted, battery-operated device called a neurostimulator to deliver electrical stimulation to the ventral intermediate nucleus of the thalamus or the subthalamic nucleus area in the basal ganglia.

15.2.2 Cognitive Rehabilitation

The nature and structure of cognitive rehabilitation programmes will inevitably depend on the nature of the cognitive deficits that the individual has suffered and there is a range of relatively successful procedures available that afford some significant gains across various functions (Cicerone, Dahlberg, Malec, Langenbahn *et al.*, 2005). Many of these programmes are basic training procedures which give the client structured extensive training in the area of their deficit (e.g. attention, memory, executive functioning and so on). This may be in the form of extended practice at a task (e.g. attention process training), perhaps with the additional use of concurrent feedback on performance so that the client can adjust their functioning, or with the use of assistive technology (e.g. memory aids). In particular, the use of computer-based technology to assist rehabilitation training is a thriving area of development and clinicians may use computers to present specific training programmes, such as memory training programmes (Tam & Man, 2004; Cha & Kim, 2013), or to create virtual environments in which the client can learn to coordinate the relevant sequence of actions to successfully complete a task (Zhang, Beatriz, Abreu, Seale *et al.*, 2003). While many rehabilitation programmes target quite specific impairments, some others attempt to address multiple aspects of dysfunction and are known as **holistic rehabilitation** methods. These may address a combination of cognitive, emotional, motivational and interpersonal impairments in the context of an integrated programme of treatment (e.g. see Braverman, Spector, Warden, Wilson *et al.*, 1999; Prigatano, 2013).

> **holistic rehabilitation** Treatment methods for neurological disorders which attempt to address multiple aspects of dysfunction.

This section continues by providing some examples of cognitive rehabilitation procedures that have been shown to be effective in the rehabilitation of specific impairments. We will then look at an example of the holistic rehabilitation method.

Attention deficits

One form of rehabilitation training for attention deficits is known as **attention process training (APT)** and this uses a number of different strategies to promote and encourage attentional abilities (Park, Proulx & Towers, 1999). Exercises include listening to an auditory tape that contains target words that must be responded to by pressing a buzzer. Learning to shift attention appropriately is also encouraged by learning to

> **attention process training (APT)** A form of rehabilitation training for attention deficits that uses a number of different strategies to promote and encourage attentional abilities.

attend to a new word following identification of a preceding target word. APT has been shown to be superior to basic therapeutic support in promoting attention and memory functioning (Sohlberg, McLaughlin, Pavese, Heidrich & Posner, 2000), and has also been shown to provide gains in other everyday skills such as independent living and driving ability (Sohlberg & Mateer, 2001). An alternative approach to dealing with attention deficits is not to try to improve attention itself, but to provide the client with some compensatory skills that will allow them to effectively manage their slowed information processing (Fasotti, Kovacs, Eling & Brouwer, 2000). This is known as **time pressure management (TPM)** and is an alternative to 'concentration' training of the kind taught by the APT procedure.

> **time pressure management (TPM)** An approach to dealing with attention deficits which aims not to try to improve attention itself, but to provide clients with some compensatory skills that will allow them to effectively manage their slowed information processing.

Visuospatial deficits

A number of programmes have been developed for the rehabilitation of unilateral visual neglect and to compensate for partial deficits in visual perception caused by neurological disorders. One such example is the computer-assisted training programme designed to aid *visual scanning* (Webster, McFarland, Rapport, Morrill *et al.*,

---

CLINICAL PERSPECTIVE: TREATMENT IN PRACTICE BOX 15.1
THE VIRTUAL REALITY KITCHEN

This virtual reality computer programme provides a safe and controlled environment for patients with brain injury to learn to improve basic daily skills such as preparing a meal of a can of soup and a sandwich. All necessary objects are found on the computer screen and can be accessed by using the computer mouse. Prompts appear on the screen initiating actions, sequencing actions and providing reinforcing feedback for correct actions. For example, one of the first steps for preparing a can of soup is to remove the can from the cupboard. If this does not occur within a pre-determined time, the cupboard door is highlighted by a pulsating colour. If the action is still not initiated, a verbal cue tells the patient to 'open the cupboard'. Each action performed by the patient is recorded and their performance can be quantitatively assessed over time. Training in virtual environments such as this results in improved performance on the tasks over time and performance on the virtual task correlates well with performance on the tasks in a real kitchen.

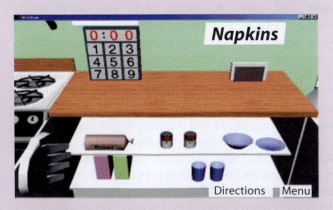

Source: Zhang, L., Beatriz, M.D., Abreu, C., Seale, G.S. et al. (2003) A virtual reality environment for evaluation of a daily living skill in brain injury rehabilitation: Reliability and validity. *Archives of Physical Medicine & Rehabilitation*, 84, 1118–1124. Reproduced with permission of Elsevier.

2001). This consists of a series of tasks in which the patient is asked (1) to read out coloured numbers projected on to a wall (scanning the full frontal environment), (2) to manually track a red ball projected onto a wall (helping coordination of scanning and physical movement), (3) to react to moving images as they are projected in front of them (facilitating detection of stimuli in space), and (4) to move the projected image of a wheelchair down a simulated three-lane road while avoiding obstacles. This procedure has been shown to reduce unilateral visual neglect symptoms and to improve performance on a real-life wheelchair obstacle course.

Apraxia and deficits in coordinated self-help behaviours

Apraxia involves an inability to undertake learnt and purposeful activities, such as dressing and cooking, and means that sufferers must rely increasingly on caregivers to help with these activities. For example, limb apraxia is a common symptom of left-hemisphere damage and consists of a deficit in performing gestures to verbal command or imitation. Sufferers are particularly impaired when asked to demonstrate how to use an object or carry out actions. They appear to be unable to plan a sequence of actions or they may exhibit inappropriate gestures (e.g. they may try to pour water from a bottle into a glass without removing the lid, or to stir the bottle opener in the glass). This is assumed to be an impairment of gesture learning which is generally considered to be the consequence of a motor memory disorder (Heilman, Schwartz & Geshwind, 1975). One form of rehabilitation training for limb apraxia is **gestural training** in which the client is taught to recognize gestures and postures that are appropriate and in context. For example, the patient may be required to demonstrate the use of a common object (such as a guitar) or be shown a picture of the gesture (e.g. someone playing a guitar) and to replicate that action, or to be shown simply a picture of the object and asked to mimic how it is used. Patients may also be shown pictures of people appropriately or

> **gestural training** A form of rehabilitation training for limb apraxia in which the client is taught to recognize gestures and postures that are appropriate and in context.

CLINICAL PERSPECTIVE: TREATMENT IN PRACTICE BOX 15.2
GESTURAL TRAINING

One form of rehabilitation training for limb apraxia is gestural training, in which the client is taught to recognize gestures and postures that are appropriate and in context. This example shows three gestures used in the gesture-recognition test, and the patient must identify which is an appropriate use of the object. (A) is an appropriate gesture. (B) is a semantically related but inappropriate gesture, and (C) is a semantically unrelated and inappropriate gesture.

Source: Smania, N., Girardi, F., Domenicali, C., Lora, E. & Aglioti, S. (2000). The rehabilitation of limb apraxia: A study in left-brain-damaged patients. *Archives of Physical Medicine & Rehabilitation*, 81(4), 379–388. Reproduced with permission of Elsevier.

inappropriately using objects and asked to identify which of these are correct. Gestural training has been shown to significantly reduce errors in performing everyday actions and to improve recognition of gestures (Smania, Girardi, Domenicali, Lora & Aglioti, 2000).

In contrast, computer-based virtual reality environments have been developed to enable disabled individuals with brain injury to learn to improve basic daily living skills in a safe and controlled environment. For example, Zhang, Beatriz, Abreu, Seale et al. (2003) developed a virtual kitchen in which the patient can learn the sequence of behaviours required to make a bowl of soup or prepare a sandwich (see Treatment in Practice Box 15.1). Zhang et al. (2003) found that training in virtual environments such as this resulted in improved performance on both tasks – and performance on the virtual task correlated well with performance at the tasks in a real kitchen – and learning in virtual environments may be equally as effective as other cognitive retraining procedures (Jacoby, Averbuch, Sacher, Katz et al., 2013).

Language and communication deficits

Impairments in language and communication may manifest in a variety of ways, including deficits in the production of speech (e.g. fluent aphasia), an inability to comprehend or understand speech and an inability to initiate speech (e.g. non-fluent aphasia) (see also section 15.1.1 and Table 15.1). Many patients undergo standard forms of speech therapy to help promote the production and comprehension of speech, and many of these approaches may combine speech therapy with procedures that permit massed practice of production and comprehension skills, such as the combination of therapist-delivered speech–language training and home-based computer-assisted massed practice (e.g. Wallesch & Johannsen-Horbach, 2004). There are also several specific techniques that are regularly used to treat specific disorders. One common example used with aphasic patients is known as **constraint-induced movement therapy** (CIMT). This involves the mass practice of verbal responses in which the patient may be required to communicate without gesturing or pointing to describe various objects of varying complexity (Mark & Taub, 2004; Bogey, Geis, Bryant, Moroz & O'Neill, 2004). This constrains patients to the systematic practice of speech acts while avoiding the use of behavioural aids. This form of treatment has been shown to produce improvement on standard clinical scales and self-rated and blind-observer scales of day-to-day communication (Pulvermuller, Neininger, Elbert et al., 2001).

constraint-induced movement therapy (CIMT) A technique used with aphasic patients which involves the mass practice of verbal responses in which the patient may be required to communicate without gesturing or pointing to describe various objects of varying complexity.

Another specific form of treatment that has been shown to provide significant gains in the production and comprehension of speech is known as **group communication treatment**. This focuses on increasing initiation of conversation and exchanging information using whatever communication means possible, being aware of personal goals in communication, and gaining confidence in the ability to communicate in personally relevant situations. Elman & Bernstein-Ellis (1999) demonstrated that those patients who received group communication treatment showed significantly more improvement in functional communication compared with patients not receiving structured treatment.

group communication treatment A form of treatment used in the production and comprehension of speech, focusing on increasing initiation of conversation and exchanging information using whatever communication means possible.

Finally, a number of specific techniques exist to help individuals with aphasia and traumatic brain injury to improve their ability to name objects, to improve writing skills and improve sentence production, and these may range from the use of cueing techniques to help the patient name specific objects to semantic feature analysis (SFA) designed to improve lexical retrieval by increasing the level of activation within a semantic network (Coelho, McHugh & Boyle, 2000).

Memory deficits

Procedures for dealing with memory impairments mainly revolve around what are known as *compensatory strategies* – that is, providing patients with specific strategies for remembering material on a daily basis. Compensatory strategies of this kind tend to be more efficient than simple remedial strategies and more easily generalizable to daily activities (Nadar & McDowd, 2010). Compensatory strategies may involve assistive techniques such as using diaries to aid recall of daily events, labelling cupboards to remember where everyday items are stored or located, or using a pager to remind the individual of important daily events. Wilson, Emslie, Quirk & Evans (1999) report the case study of a young man called George who had severe memory impairments after a head injury sustained in a road traffic accident. Treatment in Practice Box 15.3 shows how the pager could be used to remind George about a range of tasks and activities during the day. Using a pager as a memory prompt has been shown to be effective, easy to use and significantly reduce the number of memory and planning problems experienced by people with traumatic brain injury (Wilson, Emslie, Quirk, Evans & Watson, 2005). Pagers are also helpful in establishing daily behavioural patterns, and gains in memory and behaviour can be found even in the weeks after a patient has ceased using the pager.

Computer-based procedures can also be used in a variety of ways to aid impaired memory. Computers can

CLINICAL PERSPECTIVE: TREATMENT IN PRACTICE BOX 15.3
USING A PAGER AS A MEMORY AID

Below are daily pager messages sent as prompts to George, an individual who had severe memory impairments after a head injury sustained in a road traffic accident.

Time	Message
Monday	
7.15 a.m.	Time to get up
7.25 a.m.	Up yet? Time to wash and shave
7.40 a.m.	Take tablets and fill in the time on the checklist
3.00 p.m.	Fold washing and put it away
5.00 p.m.	Prepare the evening meal
6.20 p.m.	Swimming tonight?
8.30 p.m.	Read through today's notes
9.00 p.m.	Take tablets and fill in the time on the checklist

Time	Message
Tuesday	
7.00 a.m.	Time to get up
7.10 a.m.	Up yet? Time to wash and shave
7.25 a.m.	Take tablets and fill in the time on the checklist
8.30 a.m.	Remember keys, wallet and diary
5.00 p.m.	Prepare the evening meal
8.30 p.m.	Read through today's notes
9.00 p.m.	Take tablets and fill in the time on the checklist

Source: Wilson, B.A., Emslie, H., Quirk, K. & Evans, J. (1999). George: Learning to live independently with Neuropage. *Rehabilitation Psychology, 44,* 284–296. American Psychological Association. Adapted with permission.

function as simple memory aids to enhance prospective memory (e.g. by acting as an electronic diary), by providing memory training exercises, or by instructing the patient in the use of memory strategies (Kapur, Glisky & Wilson, 2004).

Teaching remembering strategies is also beneficial. One technique involves training the patient in the use of **visual imagery mnemonics** in order to help store and retrieve items and events to be remembered. Ten weeks of training in visual imagery techniques has been shown to result in significant improvement in memory functioning 3 months after treatment (Kaschel, Della Sala, Cantagallo, Fahlbock *et al.*, 2002). **Errorless learning** is another technique that has proven to be helpful in training individuals with amnesia. Errorless learning is a training procedure where people are prevented – as far as possible – from making any errors while learning a new skill or new information (Baddeley & Wilson, 1994) and in the context of memory impairments it is

> **visual imagery mnemonics** A technique for teaching remembering strategies in order to help store and retrieve items and events to be remembered.

> **errorless learning** A training procedure used in training individuals with amnesia where people are prevented – as far as possible – from making any errors while learning a new skill or new information.

useful for teaching new knowledge or training in specific skills such as helping the patient to find and use the right word to name objects. There is still some debate over whether memory aids (e.g. pagers, diaries and personal organizers) are superior to memory treatments (e.g. attempts to train better memory functioning), but in many cases a combination of both aids and 'treatments' is most effective (e.g. see Ownsworth & McFarland, 1999; Middleton & Schwartz, 2012).

Deficits in executive functioning

As described earlier, executive functioning involves the integrated use of several cognitive processes by which people problem-solve, plan, initiate, organize and monitor goal directed activities. Deficits in this collection of integrated skills will obviously require some training in a range of basic abilities, such as attention and memory, and more specifically will require training in problem-solving skills and planning and goal management skills. Many effective interventions involve training in problem solving and one particular procedure is known as **goal management training (GMT)**. This

> **goal management training (GMT)** A procedure that involves training in problem solving to help evaluate a current problem, followed by specification of the relevant goals, and partitioning of the problem-solving process into subgoals or steps.

involves training to help evaluate a current problem ('What am I doing?'), followed by specification of the relevant goals and partitioning of the problem-solving process into subgoals or steps. Patients are then assisted with the learning and retention of subgoals ('Do I know the steps?'), followed by self-monitoring of the results of their actions ('Am I doing what I planned to do?') (Levine, Robertson, Clare, Carter *et al.*, 2000). Goal management training appears to have beneficial effects on sustained attention to tasks as well as transfer of training across problems (Levine, Schweizer, O'Connor, Turner *et al.*, 2011). Other procedures for aiding problem solving involve cognitive-behavioural training in problem-solving skills, exercises for analysing real-life problems and role-playing of real examples of problem situations. Such training results in significant beneficial effects on measures of executive cognitive functioning up to 6 months after the intervention (e.g. see Rath, Simon, Langenbahn, Sherr & Diller, 2003).

Many types of intervention for executive functioning deficits focus on both behavioural and emotional regulation, and aim at training the individual in self-regulation when confronting a problem and managing their way through the sequence of cognitive and behavioural actions required to solve a problem. One such procedure is known as **self-instructional training (SIT)** where the individual learns a set of instructions for talking themselves through particular problems. Such types of intervention have been shown to raise personal self-awareness of deficits and increase use of successful problem-solving strategies. Importantly these methods have the additional beneficial effects of improving emotional self-regulation and reducing outward expressions of anger and frustration (Medd & Tate, 2000; Ownsworth, McFarland & Young, 2000).

> **self-instructional training** A procedure used in the intervention for executive functioning deficits where individuals learn a set of instructions for talking themselves through particular problems.

Holistic rehabilitation methods

Most cognitive rehabilitation techniques have been developed to address individual deficits in cognitive functioning (such as attentional, memory or language deficits). However, there are substantial benefits to adopting a more comprehensive holistic approach to rehabilitation that collectively addresses cognitive, emotional and functional impairments, as well as physical disability. For example, Malec & Basford (1996) advocated a comprehensive integrated treatment for individuals with traumatic brain injury that addressed cognitive, interpersonal and emotional concerns, used group interventions that addressed disability awareness and social skills training, and included procedures to enhance vocational functioning (occupational therapy) and independent living

skills. Such approaches are holistic in the sense that they attempt to develop the individual's awareness of their disabilities and to provide them with compensatory skills that will enable them to negotiate daily living and regain occupational skills. To this extent, holistic methods differentiate between *restorative* procedures that attempt to provide training to improve cognitive impairments (e.g. intensive training of memory skills) and *compensatory* procedures that enable the patient to achieve daily goals through different means (e.g. using assistive technology such as a pager as a memory aid). *Holistic rehabilitation* methods have been shown to promote significant improvement in overall functioning in individuals with traumatic brain injury (Ben-Yishay & Daniels-Zide, 2000), develop awareness of disabilities and impairments (which is important when attempting to engage patients in rehabilitation programmes) (Fleming & Ownsworth, 2006), and to be superior to standard neurorehabilitation programmes in improving community integration and raising the patient's level of satisfaction with cognitive functioning (Cicerone, Mott, Azulay & Friel, 2004).

15.2.3   Caregiver Support Programmes

Many individuals with neurological disorders are not in primary care but live with their families or with caregivers such as their spouses or partners. This puts a considerable burden on caregivers generally and will usually require them to cope with behavioural and cognitive deficits, physical disability, challenging behaviour (such as anger and aggression), and problematic behaviour generally (such as inappropriate social behaviour). In the case of degenerative disorders that do not usually begin to manifest

> To complete Activity 15.1 go to www.wiley-psychopathology.com/activities/ch15

until later life, the carers of such individuals will often be their elderly spouses or partners (e.g. in the case of Alzheimer's disease). This being the case, the carers of individuals with neurological disorders will need both support and training.

Caregivers need to give both physical and emotional support to suffers, and they may also pay a substantial economic cost in terms of loss of income as well as living a restricted social life. It goes without saying that the overall burden on a caregiver will usually be proportional to the disabilities experienced by the sufferer, and caregivers usually report that their physical and emotional health suffers as a result of caregiving, with many beginning to exhibit symptoms of depression. In a study of caregiver-burden in Parkinson's disease, perceived burden and quality of life was proportional to disability,

A WEEK IN THE LIFE OF A CLINICAL PSYCHOLOGIST WORKING AS A CONSULTANT CLINICAL NEUROPSYCHOLOGIST

MONDAY

'How do you spell neuropsychologist?' asked the detective sergeant on the telephone. He requests a statement relating to whether a client could be a reliable witness in a sexual assault case. I explained to him that since suffering from encephalitis, her attention and memory abilities are so poor that it was unlikely she could provide a reasonable account for the police. The call has taken my administration time and once again I begin a new week behind schedule as I rush off to the first meeting of the week.

The community disability team meeting focuses on the most complex cases. A man who has motor neurone disease has now found out his wife has developed multiple sclerosis. Concerns are expressed about a lady with a brain stem stroke. There are concerns her female partner is emotionally abusing her. All agree a vulnerable adults strategy meeting is required. The afternoon is spent supervising colleagues and a new trainee.

TUESDAY

The day is spent completing four initial consultations to decide whether psychological intervention can be appropriately offered: a lady with Parkinson's disease who has started having panic attacks; a man who suffered a head injury in a car accident (his parents are struggling to cope with his bad language and temper outbursts); a lady with multiple sclerosis who is saddened by having to give up work; and, finally, a man of 80 who suffered a stroke last summer and whose wife feels desperately isolated because he can no longer drive.

WEDNESDAY

Appropriate psychometric tests are chosen for the man who has come for an outpatient assessment this morning. He has experienced a history of memory problems for 2 years. Sadly, the man struggles with most tests but particularly those we know are associated with dementia of the Alzheimer's type. A sense of sadness stays with me for the afternoon at the thought of what my feedback has meant to that couple. I resolve to reduce my administration pile by the end of today.

THURSDAY

Seven ladies have arrived for my Thursday morning relatives' group, a meeting for people living with someone who has a neurological diagnosis. The usual issues are discussed: how to cope with the feelings of loss, what to do in response to a partner's temper outbursts and how to minimize cognitive difficulties. Thursday afternoons are usually set aside for outpatient intervention appointments. Today a lady in her forties talks about her sense of isolation since her stroke and requests help to explain the nature of her difficulties to her children. The last appointment of the day brings a feeling of optimism as a young woman who suffered a severe head injury 2 years ago is pleased to inform me that she is finally living independently and has started a part-time job.

FRIDAY

The morning is spent making an assessment as to the capacity of a lady with Huntington's disease to manage her finances. Two further outpatient appointments leave just an hour to write up client files and complete an assessment report before meeting the final challenge of the week, Friday evening rush hour!

and the range of symptoms and the mental health problems exhibited by the individual with Parkinson's disease (e.g. depression, hallucinations and confusion) (Schrag, Hovris, Morley, Quinn & Jahanshahi, 2006). Poor quality of life and depression in caregivers can often be traced in part to a lack of skills or strategies for managing the sufferer, and many become avoidant copers by avoiding new situations and wishing the problems would simply go away. Avoidant coping such as this is significantly correlated with levels of depression in elderly caregivers or spouses of those with dementia (Mausbach, Aschbacher, Patterson, Ancoli-Israel et al., 2006). To address these problems associated with caregiving, interventions have been designed to provide caregivers with a range of skills that will help their day-to-day living with sufferers. These may include advice on how to modify the home environment to support the sufferer (Gitlin, Hauck, Dennis & Winter, 2005) or training in skills to develop self-care behaviours by the sufferer or to control aggression and wandering (Pinkston, Linsk & Young, 1988). Such programmes have been shown to maintain caregiver positive affect for a period of at least 12 months after the intervention and work best when tailored to the needs of individual carers (Lopez-Hartmann, Wens, Verhoeven & Remmen, 2012). Peer support groups are also an important means of maintaining quality of life and positive affect in caregivers. National societies such as the UK Alzheimer's Society (www.alzheimers.org.uk) provide information and advice for caregivers, including advice on how to understand and respect persons with neurological disabilities or degenerative disorders, and also how to cope with caring for a sufferer. For example, the Alzheimer's Society recommends that caregivers

1. need to ensure they have sufficient support (either from family or local support groups);

2. should make time each day for themselves;

3. need to understand their right to local services (such as assessment of needs);

4. should try to involve other family members in caregiving;

5. should look after their health (by eating regularly and healthily);

6. should check whether they are entitled to any financial benefits;

7. should confront and deal with feelings of guilt; and

8. ought to take a regular break or holiday by seeking short-term respite care for the sufferer.

In addition, local groups comprised of similar caregivers can provide significant support across a range of needs, including (1) information and education, (2) referral and/or assistance on engaging with local health services, and (3) emotional support (Salfi, Ploeg & Black,

2005). The effects of such support groups can be beneficial even if communication is by telephone or by internet videoconferencing (Marziali, Donahue & Crossin, 2005).

Finally, caregiver interventions may not only address the skills and knowledge that will help the caregiver physically and emotionally manage a sufferer, but may also help the caregiver understand and respect the person with a neurological or degenerative disorder. Once someone's cognitive and physical abilities begin to decline – especially in old age – it is quite easy to forget that they are still individuals who should be valued and respected. Such advice for caregivers includes (1) take time to listen to the sufferer, (2) take account of the abilities they do possess and try to foster these, (3) use respectful forms of address, (4) try not to talk down to them and respect their privacy, and (5) always try to understand how the person feels and make them feel good about themselves (Alzheimers Society, 2005) (see Table 15.2).

TABLE 15.2 *Tips for making a person with Alzheimer's disease feel good about themselves*

- Avoid situations in which the person is bound to fail, as this can be humiliating. Look for tasks they can still manage and activities they enjoy

- Give them plenty of encouragement. Let them do things at their own pace and in their own way

- Do things with them, rather than for them, to help them retain their independence

- Break activities down into small steps so that they feel a sense of achievement, even if they can only manage part of a task

- Our self-respect is often bound up with the way we look. Encourage the person to take a pride in their appearance, and compliment them on how they look

Source: http://www.alzheimers.org.uk/site/scripts/documents_info.php?documentID=84.

SELF-TEST QUESTIONS

- What is the difference between a restorative treatment and compensatory skills training?

- How have drugs been used in the treatment of neurological disorders? Do such drugs help in the treatment of the cognitive deficits caused by the disorder?

- Can you describe at least one specific intervention designed to treat each of the following: attention deficits, visuospatial deficits, apraxia, language and communication deficits, memory deficits, and deficits in executive functioning?

- What are holistic rehabilitation methods and how do they differ from specific restorative interventions?

- What are the main problems encountered by those giving care to people suffering from neurological disorders and what interventions have been developed to help them?

SECTION SUMMARY

15.2 TREATMENT AND REHABILITATION FOR NEUROCOGNITIVE DISORDERS

The neurocognitive disorders we have covered in this chapter often represent chronic impairments that are caused by irreversible damage to brain tissue or are the result of progressive degenerative disorders. Because of this, rehabilitation may often be a lengthy process and sufferers are likely to require long-term care of some kind. We have noted that there have been attempts to develop drugs that can slow the progress of degenerative disorders such as Alzheimer's disease and Parkinson's disease, and antiretroviral drugs have similar effects in reducing the severity of HIV symptoms, but the evidence on whether these drug developments have beneficial effects on cognitive deficits is still modest at best. Medication is also an important treatment for depression, which is a common and important symptom of neurological disorders. Antidepressants not only help to improve mood, but can also indirectly improve cognitive performance.

Cognitive rehabilitation programmes have been developed to help the individual with a range of specific cognitive deficits, including attention deficits, visuospatial deficits, apraxia, language and communication deficits, memory deficits and executive function impairments. These may take a variety of forms, such as (1) massed training to improve cognitive impairments (e.g. memory training), (2) compensatory skills training, which accepts that the individual has particular impairments and helps them to achieve daily goals by other means, (3) computer-assisted training can provide the means for remedial cognitive training in both the therapeutic and home environment, or provide virtual environments in which the sufferer can learn skills in relative safety, and (4) assistive technology is being increasingly utilized as a means of helping the disabled individual to cope with and negotiate daily living (e.g. using a pager to provide reminders for daily activities in individuals with memory deficits).

Finally, because of the nature of neurocognitive disorders and the frequent need for long-term care, programmes of support and training are increasingly becoming available for caregivers. These include programmes to provide emotional support for caregivers, programmes to provide appropriate management and coping skills for living with individuals with disabilities, and local or national support groups that provide advice and information.

To sum up the key points:

- Treatment of neurological disorders tends to be based on *restorative treatment* for individual cognitive deficits (e.g. memory training) or *compensatory skills training* based on helping the sufferer to deal with the daily living difficulties posed by the deficit.

- Drug treatments include the use of *cholinesterase inhibitors* (Alzheimer's disease), *levodopa* (Parkinson's disease), *thrombolytic therapy* (cardiovascular accidents and strokes) and *antiretroviral drugs* (NCD due to HIV infection).

- Depression is also a common feature of many neurological disorders and can be treated with antidepressants and appropriate psychological therapy.

- *Deep brain stimulation (DBS)* alleviates symptoms of Parkinson's disease by delivering electrical stimulation to the thalamus and basal ganglia.

- Cognitive rehabilitation programmes are usually directed at improving function within specific cognitive deficits (e.g. memory, language).

- Rehabilitation programmes for attention deficits include *attention process training (APT)* and *time pressure management (TPM)*.

- *Gestural training* and the use of *virtual reality environments* can be utilized to treat apraxia and deficits in coordinated self-help behaviours.

- Treatment of language and communication deficits will depend on the specific nature of the problem but common examples of rehabilitation procedures include *constraint-induced movement therapy (CIMT)* and *group communication treatment*.

- Memory deficits can be addressed with the use of *assistive technology* (such as pagers) or specific memory training procedures such as *visual imagery mnemonics* or *errorless learning procedures*.

- Deficits in executive functioning often utilize interventions that involve problem-solving training such as *goal management training* or *self-instructional training (SIT)*.

- *Holistic rehabilitation* methods collectively attempt to address cognitive, emotional and functional impairments, as well as physical disability.

- Because those suffering neurological disorders live with their families or caregivers, *caregiver interventions* have been developed that help to provide the caregiver with training and support for the task.

15.3 NEUROCOGNITIVE DISORDERS REVIEWED

Unlike many of the other disorders described in this text, neurocognitive disorders have their origins almost solely in damage or abnormalities in the biological substrates that underlie thinking and behaviour. These disorders give rise to a range of disabilities and impairments, both physical and cognitive, and many are irreversible and permanent deficits. The main causes of neurocognitive disorders are cerebral infections, traumatic brain injuries, cerebrovascular accidents such as strokes, and degenerative disorders such as Alzheimer's disease and Parkinson's disease. Clinical psychologists have a major interest in neurocognitive disorders because many of the major symptoms are deficits in critical cognitive functions such as learning and memory, attention, language and communication, visual perception, motor skills and executive functions. Because of this, clinicians are involved in the assessment of neurocognitive disorders and the treatment and rehabilitation of these disorders.

Assessment of neurocognitive disorders is often difficult and involves a combination of tests of cognitive functioning (such as the WAIS-IV or the Adult Memory and Information Processing Battery), blood tests and analyses of cerebrospinal fluids (to determine the presence of inherited degenerative diseases or infections), genetic testing (to determine whether the individual possesses genes likely to put them at risk for neurocognitive or degenerative brain disorders), and brain scans using EEG, PET or fMRI. While some of the disorders result in immediate impairment (such as traumatic brain injury or stroke), many others are progressive degenerative disorders that develop from mild symptoms of cognitive impairment to full-blown dementia and physical disability (e.g. Alzheimer's disease). While most degenerative disorders afflict older adults, some can affect younger individuals (e.g. neurocognitive disorder due to HIV infection or prion disease). Many of the neurocognitive disorders are closely associated with other forms of psychopathology, especially depression and psychosis. Depression appears to be both a predictor and a consequence of some neurocognitive disorders (such as stroke or Parkinson's disease) and is considered by some to be an integral feature of those disorders.

Because most neurocognitive disorders are caused by irreversible damage to brain tissue, treatment and rehabilitation often take the form of compensatory skills training, which accepts that the individual has a particular impairment and helps them to achieve their daily goals by alternative means (e.g. by using compensatory strategies, such as memory aids, or assistive technology, such as equipment to aid hearing, speaking or moving about). Nevertheless, there are many specific cognitive rehabilitation procedures that can be used with reasonable success in attempts to restore basic cognitive functions such as memory, attention, language and motor skills. However, because of the long-term nature of many neurocognitive disorders, there is a basic need for long-term care for sufferers and this is often provided by close family, spouses and partners. This need has given rise to a range of programmes to provide support to caregivers, including basic caregiver skills training (e.g. how to structure the environment for a disabled individual) and emotional support programmes.

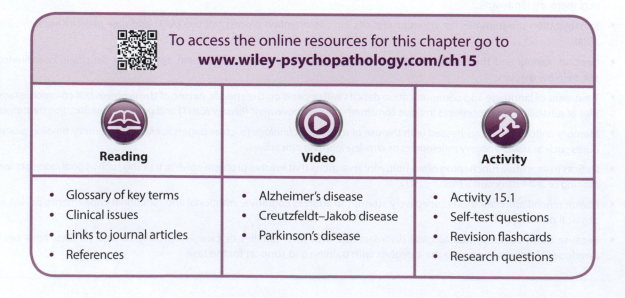

To access the online resources for this chapter go to
www.wiley-psychopathology.com/ch15

Reading	**Video**	**Activity**
• Glossary of key terms	• Alzheimer's disease	• Activity 15.1
• Clinical issues	• Creutzfeldt–Jakob disease	• Self-test questions
• Links to journal articles	• Parkinson's disease	• Revision flashcards
• References		• Research questions

16 Childhood and Adolescent Psychological Problems

To access the online resources for this chapter go to
www.wiley-psychopathology.com/ch16

ROUTE MAP OF THE CHAPTER

This chapter begins by discussing some of the difficulties involved in identifying and diagnosing childhood and adolescent psychological problems. We then go on to discuss the characteristics, prevalence rates and aetiology of disruptive behaviour problems (discussing ADHD and conduct disorder in detail) and childhood and adolescent anxiety and depression. Finally, the chapter ends by discussing the main treatment methods used with children and adolescents and how coordinated provision of treatment extends across a range of services, including education, health and social services.

CHAPTER OUTLINE

LEARNING OUTCOMES

When you have completed this chapter, you should be able to:

1. Describe and evaluate some of the difficulties involved in diagnosing and treating childhood and adolescent psychological problems.

2. Describe the characteristics of at least two disruptive behaviour disorders.

3. Describe the characteristics of childhood and adolescent anxiety and depression.

4. Compare and contrast theories of the aetiology of disruptive behaviour disorders, childhood anxiety and childhood depression.

5. Describe the characteristics of some of the main therapeutic methods used to treat childhood and adolescent psychological problems and evaluate their efficacy.

My own troubles began when I was 3 years old and my father died abruptly of a brain tumor. A few years later my mother was diagnosed with breast cancer and she died when I was 11 years old. Watching so many important people die was frightening and confusing. Even so, the most traumatic event of my childhood was my placement into foster care. Although my aunts and uncles hinted at the possibility, I never believed they would give me away. I threatened to jump off a high building if they went ahead with the plan. I knew they were conspiring to banish me and I didn't trust a single one of them. But they did it anyway. I'd had enough of the cycle of attachment and desertion and decided I wasn't going to become attached to my new foster parents. To the outside world I was withdrawn and detached. Yet towards myself I was overwhelmed by intense feelings of rage and hatred. My foster mother repeatedly spoke of her disappointment in me and angrily talked about sending me away. I knew from my brother that foster children often go from place to place and that being physically or sexually abused was common. During the following 2 years I continued to float through time and space in a state of numb, disorganized misery, going through the emotions but not really alive. I was aware of my impairment – and ashamed of it. I believed I was peculiar. When I was about 16, I became absorbed with the idea that my central problem was a bodily defect, and I focused on one aspect of my anatomy after another, determined to find the specific flaw. At 17 I developed the sensation of a lump in my throat and became convinced I was about to choke to death. I had no labels for any of my experiences, so I didn't realize that this latest state was a form of anxiety. Every night I stayed awake to the point of exhaustion.

Frank's Story

Introduction

The study of childhood and adolescent psychopathology is fraught with a range of difficulties that are not experienced in the study of adult psychopathology. First, any behavioural or psychological problems have to be assessed in the context of the child as a developing organism. For example, bed-wetting is quite normal in infancy, but might be a sign of anxiety or adjustment problems after the age of 5 years. Similarly, shyness and withdrawal from social contact is often normal during periods of social development as the child attempts to understand the rules of social interaction and learns how to communicate verbally with others. However, in early adolescence these tendencies may represent the first signs of psychopathology. In addition, children may often go through brief stages of development when they exhibit behavioural problems or fears and anxieties, but these problems often disappear as rapidly as they appeared. Most parents have experienced a child who refuses to eat, or very suddenly becomes frightened of noises, strangers, or certain types of animals, only for this to disappear within a matter of days or weeks. Second, because of their immaturity, children will tend to have poor self-knowledge. They may feel that something is wrong, but be unable to label it as anxiety or depression, or convey clearly how they feel to others. In such circumstances, the clinician has to infer psychological states from overt behaviour and decide whether that behaviour is unusual for the developmental stages through which the child is passing. With these issues in mind, clinicians have tended to organize childhood psychological problems into two broad domains based on the general behavioural characteristics of the child. The first domain covers **externalizing disorders**, which are based on outward-directed behaviour problems such as aggressiveness, hyperactivity, non-compliance or impulsiveness. The second domain covers **internalizing disorders**, which are represented by more inward-looking and withdrawn behaviours, and may represent the experience of depression, anxiety and active attempts to socially withdraw. The former are now more commonly known as disruptive behaviour disorders and include DSM-5 diagnosable disorders such as *conduct disorder* and *attention deficit hyperactivity disorder (ADHD)*. The internalizing disorders are still difficult to diagnose reliably but DSM-5 does include guidelines for diagnosing childhood *separation anxiety*, *generalized anxiety disorder* and *major depressive disorder*. The childhood and adolescent disorders discussed in this chapter are covered in a number of different chapters in DSM-5, including the chapters on Disruptive, Impulse-Control, and Conduct Disorders (oppositional defiant disorder, conduct disorder), Neurodevelopmental Disorders (attention deficit hyperactivity disorder, ADHD), Anxiety Disorders (childhood separation anxiety, childhood generalized anxiety disorder), Depressive Disorder (childhood major depression), and Obsessive Compulsive and Related Disorders (childhood OCD).

Frank's story at the beginning of this chapter illustrates the kinds of experiences that might give rise to psychological distress in childhood and adolescence

externalizing disorders Disorders based on outward-directed behaviour problems such as aggressiveness, hyperactivity, non-compliance or impulsiveness.

internalizing disorders Disorders represented by more inward-looking and withdrawn behaviours, and may represent the experience of depression, anxiety and active attempts to socially withdraw.

and how this distress may be manifested in behaviour. This personal account describes the negative emotional impact of the death of his mother and father, his feelings of abandonment and impotency and how this affected his ability to form relationships. This in turn gave rise to feelings of guilt, shame and inadequacy, and in adolescence finally manifested as specific psychological problems such as body dysmorphic disorder and somatic symptom disorder. He related this story as an adult and as such was able to look back on his childhood and put his behaviour and emotions into a perspective that enabled him to understand them. But as a child, events often seem confusing and uncontrollable, and a clinician has to interpret what a child might be feeling and experiencing from their behaviour alone – for example, much of Frank's behaviour might be seen as internalizing and suggestive of anxiety and depression. Nevertheless, even during an upbringing that is relatively trauma-free, children will frequently experience childhood as a threatening and frightening time. They will develop anxieties as they experience new people and new situations (Crijnen, Achenbach & Velhulst, 1999), will worry about many of their everyday activities such as attending school (Vasey, 1993; Ollendick, King & Muris, 2002) and will develop behavioural problems such as temper tantrums, eating irregularities, nightmares and phobias. As the child moves into adolescence even more challenges await as the individual develops sexually, changes physically, encounters educational and occupational challenges and moves into a new period where feelings of responsibility are expected of them. It is perhaps not surprising at this stage that many adolescents encounter feelings of confusion, anxiety and depression while attempting to cope with these changes (Lerner, 2002) and it is also not surprising, therefore, that the initial symptoms of many of the disorders we have covered in Chapters 6–15 relating to adult mental health first begin to develop during adolescence (e.g. schizophrenia, paraphilic disorders and somatic symptom disorders).

In the following section of this chapter we will look briefly at the difficulties involved in addressing psychological problems of childhood and adolescence, and then look at the prevalence rates of specific disorders. The remainder of the chapter will look in detail at the diagnosis, aetiology and treatment of the following: (1) attention deficit and disruptive behaviour disorders, and (2) childhood anxiety and depression. Discussion of some other childhood psychological problems can be found on the book's website.

16.1   THE DIAGNOSIS AND PREVALENCE OF CHILDHOOD AND ADOLESCENT PSYCHOLOGICAL PROBLEMS: SOME GENERAL ISSUES

16.1.1   Difficulties Associated With Identification and Diagnosis of Childhood and Adolescent Psychological Problems

We have already alluded to some of the difficulties involved in identifying whether a child needs help and treatment for a mental health problem and it is worth considering some of these difficulties before we discuss individual diagnoses.

1. When considering what might be clinically relevant behaviour in children, we first have to consider what is normal for a particular age. For example, bed-wetting is considered relatively normal in children up to the age of 5 years, but may be a symptom of psychological distress if it occurs after that age.

2. Diagnosing a psychological problem is often dependent on the individual being able to communicate with the practitioner and to articulate how they experience the distress that their problems are causing them. However, many children are unable to communicate clearly how they feel (e.g. they may not be able to differentiate feelings of anxiety from feelings of depression). They may also lack self-knowledge and be unable to understand precisely what they are feeling. In extreme cases, some disorders are explicitly associated with an inability to communicate with others (e.g. autistic syndrome disorders), so identification of psychological problems has to take place almost solely on the basis of external observation of the child's behaviour and their rate of development.

3. Differences in cultural norms will also affect whether childhood behaviours are seen as problematic or not. Externalizing behaviour problems are most prominent in many Western societies but some oriental cultures have relatively low levels of this type of problem (Weisz, Suwanlert, Chaiyasit & Walter, 1987). For example, in those countries that practice Buddhism, externalizing behaviours such as disrespect and aggression are rarely tolerated by parents and teachers, and are controlled at an early stage in the child's life.

4. Finally, during childhood and early adolescence, developmental changes occur rapidly, which means that psychological problems can escalate quickly and dramatically. For example, behaviour problems can be generated very rapidly if the development of language skills, self-control skills, social skills and emotional regulation does not proceed normally. This requires that childhood problems need to be identified early and quickly in order to minimize the psychological damage that prolonged abnormal development could inflict.

16.1.2   Childhood Psychopathology as the Precursor of Adult Psychopathology

In Chapters 6–15, it was frequently described how important childhood experiences appear to be in the aetiology of many diagnosable psychological disorders found in adulthood, so childhood trauma and abuse, for example, not only affect childhood behaviour but may serve as the basis for the development of long-term psychological maladjustment, including major depression, personality disorders such as borderline and antisocial personality disorders, somatic symptom disorders, dissociative disorders, eating disorders, and sexual and gender disorders. Indeed, prospective studies have indicated that preschool behaviour problems predict psychopathology in later life (Caspi, Newman, Moffit & Silva, 1996). Table 16.1 lists some of the childhood risk factors that have been identified in the aetiology of adult psychopathology and these are all discussed more fully in the relevant chapters of this book. Childhood risk factors such as these enable researchers and clinicians to identify those groups of children and adolescents that are most likely to be at risk for adult mental health problems. With this in mind, an emerging area of research is **developmental psychopathology**, which is concerned with mapping how early childhood experiences may act as risk factors for later diagnosable psychological disorders and attempts to describe the pathways by which early experiences may generate adult psychological problems (Drabick & Kendall, 2010).

> **developmental psychopathology** An area of research concerned with mapping how early childhood experiences may act as risk factors for later diagnosable psychological disorders. It also attempts to describe the pathways by which early experiences may generate adult psychological problems.

> To read Drabick & Kendall's article on developmental psychopathology go to **www.wiley-psychopathology.com/reading/ch16**

TABLE 16.1 *Childhood risk factors for adult mental health problems*

Childhood experience (risk factor)	Adult mental health problem	Reference	CHAPTER
Abnormal parent–child interaction style	Social anxiety disorder	Moore, Whaley & Sigman (2004)	6
	Narcissistic and obsessive compulsive personality disorder	Johnson, Cohen, Kasen, Smailes & Brook (2002)	12
	Antisocial personality disorder	Gabbard (1990)	12
	Borderline personality disorder	Graybar & Boutilier (2002)	12
	Histrionic personality disorder	Bender, Farber & Geller (2001)	12
Childhood abuse (physical and sexual)	Depression (reduced autobiographical specificity)	Raes, Hermans, Williams & Eelen (2005)	7
	Suicide and suicidal ideation	Gould & Kramer (2001)	7
	Eating disorders	Steiger, Leonard, Kin *et al.* (2000); Brown, Russell, Thornton & Dunn (1997)	10
	Hypoactive sexual desire disorder	Stuart & Greer (1984)	11
	Sexual aversion disorder	Berman, Berman, Werbin, Flaherty *et al.* (1999)	11
	Vaginismus	DSM-IV-TR	11
	Sexual dysfunction generally	Najman, Dunne, Purdie, Boyle & Coxeter (2005)	11
	Dyspareunia	Binik, Bergerson & Khalife (2000)	11
	Paedophilic disorder	Freund & Kuban (1994)	11
	Paraphilias generally	Mason (1997); Murphy (1997)	11
	Gender dysphoria	Bradley & Zucker (1997)	11
	Personality disorders generally	Johnson, Cohen, Brown, Smailes & Bernstein (1999)	12
	Borderline personality disorder	Heffernan & Cloitre (2000)	12
	Antisocial personality disorder	Horowitz, Widom, McLaughlin & White (2001)	12
	Narcissistic personality disorder	Kernberg (1985)	12
	Avoidant personality disorder	Rettew, Zanarini, Yen, Grilo *et al.* (2003)	12
	Conversion disorder	Bowman & Markland (1996)	13
	Illness anxiety disorder	Salmon & Calderbank (1996)	13
	Somatic symptom disorder	Tezzi, Duckworth & Adams (2001)	13
	Dissociative disorders generally	Tyler, Cauce & Whitbeck (2004)	14
	Dissociative identity disorder (DID)	Putnam (1997)	14
	Depersonalization disorder	Simeon, Guralnik, Schmeidler, Sirof & Knutelska (2001)	14
Childhood neglect (e.g. separation, inadequate and ineffectual parenting)	Post-traumatic stress disorder (PTSD)	King, King, Foy & Gudanowski (1996)	6
	Major depression	Lara & Klein (1999); Goodman (2002)	7
	Cannabis, nicotine and alcohol abuse	Cadoret, Yates, Troughton, Woodworth & Stewart (1995)	9
	Hypersexuality	Langstrom & Hanson (2006)	11
	Paraphilias generally	Mason (1997); Murphy (1997)	11
	Antisocial personality disorder	Hill (2003)	12
	Borderline personality disorder	Guttman (2002)	12
	Dependent personality disorder	Bornstein (1996)	12
	Body dysmorphic disorder	Cororve & Gleaves (2001)	6

(Continued)

TABLE 16.1 *(Continued)*

Childhood experience (risk factor)	Adult mental health problem	Reference	CHAPTER
Childhood trauma generally	Schizophrenia	Read, van Os, Morrison & Ross (2005)	8
	Alcohol dependency	Sher (1991); Wilsnack, Vogeltanz, Klassen & Harris (1997)	9
	Nicotine dependency	Anda, Croft, Felitti, Nordenberg *et al.* (1999)	9
	Conversion disorder	Bowman & Markland (1996)	13
	Dissociative identity disorder (DID)	Putnam (1997)	14
Childhood conflict and emotional disturbance	Specific phobias	Freud	6
	Cannabis dependency	Meltzer, Gatwood, Goodman & Ford (2003)	9
Childhood poverty	Schizophrenia	Byrne, Agerbo, Eaton & Mortensen (2004)	8
	Alcohol, nicotine and cannabis abuse	Alverson, Alverson & Drake (2000)	9
	Substance dependency generally	Petronis & Anthony (2003)	9
	Antisocial personality disorder	Paris (2001)	12

There are numerous possible ways in which childhood psychopathology may link to adult mental health problems. Firstly, the simplest relationship is where a childhood disorder merely persists into adulthood in the same form (e.g. where childhood anxiety or depression develops into experienced anxiety and depression in adulthood). One striking example of this was described in Chapter 12, where we noted that childhood conduct disorder and antisocial behaviour often persists into adulthood in the form of antisocial personality disorder (Farrington, Loeber & van Kammen, 1990). Secondly, a childhood psychopathology may have an adverse affect on subsequent development and indirectly lead to different forms of maladjustment in later life. For example, children who fail to form adaptive relationships with their parents early in life exhibit disruptive behaviour in late infancy, and such disruptiveness can result in more general adjustment problems and the development of learning difficulties later in life. Thirdly, a childhood psychopathology may simply represent the less cognitive precursor of a related adult disorder. For example, adolescent height phobia has been shown to be a risk factor for full-blown panic disorder in adulthood (Starcevic & Bogojevic, 1997) and this may result from the fact that the catastrophizing of bodily sensations is a central feature of both disorders, and may extend across an increasing number of cognitive and behavioural domains as the individual develops from childhood into adolescence (Davey, Menzies & Gallardo, 1997). Fourthly, a childhood disorder may not necessarily extend into adulthood but may render the individual vulnerable to later life stressors. For example, if a child loses a parent early in life, this

may make them vulnerable to depression when experiencing similar types of losses later in life (e.g. following the death of a spouse or close friend). Fifthly, a childhood disorder may be quite specific to childhood and disappear or change form dramatically once the individual has reached adulthood.

All of these examples demonstrate that childhood psychopathology will have an important influence on adult mental health, but the nature of this influence is not always direct and not always in the same form as the childhood difficulties. You may want to refer back to Table 16.1 and consider what possible developmental processes might link certain childhood experiences with adult psychopathology.

16.1.3   The Prevalence of Childhood and Adolescent Psychological Disorders

Studies of the prevalence of diagnosable childhood psychological disorders estimate that as many as 10–20 per cent of children and adolescents have a diagnosable psychological disorder (e.g. Phares, 2003; McDermott & Weiss, 1995) and boys exhibit higher prevalence rates than girls even though the opposite is the case in adulthood. Table 16.2 shows the prevalence of psychopathologies found in children and adolescents aged between 5 and 16 years in the UK (Office for National

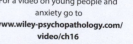

For a video on young people and anxiety go to **www.wiley-psychopathology.com/video/ch16**

TABLE 16.2 *Prevalence of mental health problems in children and adolescents in Great Britain (2004)*

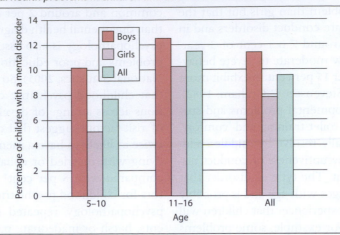

	5- to 10-year-olds			11- to 16-year-olds			All children		
	Boys	**Girls**	**All**	**Boys**	**Girls**	**All**	**Boys**	**Girls**	**All**
	Percentage of children with each disorder								
Emotional disorders	**2.2**	**2.5**	**2.4**	**4.0**	**6.1**	**5.0**	**3.1**	**4.3**	**3.7**
Anxiety disorders	2.1	2.4	2.2	3.6	5.2	4.4	2.9	3.8	3.3
Separation anxiety	0.4	0.7	0.6	0.3	0.4	0.3	0.3	0.5	0.4
Specific phobia	0.8	0.7	0.7	0.8	0.9	0.9	0.8	0.8	0.8
Social phobia	0.1	0.1	0.1	0.5	0.6	0.5	0.3	0.3	0.3
Panic	-	-	-	0.2	0.5	0.4	0.1	0.3	0.2
Agoraphobia	-	-	-	0.2	0.4	0.3	0.1	0.2	0.1
Post traumatic stress	-	0.1	0.0	0.1	0.5	0.3	0.0	0.3	0.2
Obsessive compulsive	0.1	0.2	0.2	0.3	0.2	0.2	0.2	0.2	0.2
Generalized anxiety	0.2	0.3	0.3	0.9	1.6	1.2	0.6	1.0	0.8
Other anxiety	0.6	0.7	0.7	0.9	1.5	1.2	0.8	1.1	0.9
Depression	0.2	0.3	0.2	1.0	1.9	1.4	0.6	1.1	0.9
Depressive episode (full ICD criteria)	0.1	0.2	0.2	0.8	1.4	1.1	0.5	0.8	0.6
Other depressive episode	0.0	0.1	0.1	0.3	0.5	0.4	0.2	0.3	0.2
Conduct disorders	**6.9**	**2.8**	**4.9**	**8.1**	**5.1**	**6.6**	**7.5**	**3.9**	**5.8**
Oppositional defiant disorder	4.5	2.4	3.5	3.5	1.7	2.6	4.0	2.0	3.0
Unsocialized conduct disorder	0.9	0.3	0.6	1.2	0.8	1.0	1.1	0.5	0.8
Socialized conduct disorder	0.6	-	0.3	2.6	1.9	2.2	1.6	0.9	1.3
Other conduct disorder	0.9	0.1	0.5	0.7	0.8	0.8	0.8	0.4	0.6
Hyperkinetic disorder	**2.7**	**0.4**	**1.6**	**2.4**	**0.4**	**1.4**	**2.6**	**0.4**	**1.5**
Less common disorders	**2.2**	**0.4**	**1.3**	**1.6**	**1.1**	**1.4**	**1.9**	**0.8**	**1.3**
Autistic Spectrum Disorder	1.9	0.1	1.0	1.0	0.5	0.8	1.4	0.3	0.9
Tic disorders	0.0	0.1	0.1	-	-	-	0.0	0.1	0.0
Eating disorders	0.5	0.2	0.3	0.6	0.1	0.4	0.5	0.1	0.3
Mutism	-	0.1	0.0	0.1	0.4	0.3	0.0	0.2	0.1
Any disorder	**10.2**	**5.1**	**7.7**	**12.6**	**10.3**	**11.5**	**11.4**	**7.8**	**9.6**
Base (weighted)	*2010*	*1916*	*3926*	*2101*	*1950*	*4051*	*4111*	*3866*	*7977*

Source: Office for National Statistics, licensed under the Open Government Licence v.1.0

Statistics, 2005). These show that boys are more likely to have a mental health problem than girls but that the prevalent disorders in boys are conduct disorders and in girls emotional disorders. Around 7 per cent of 3-year-olds can be expected to show moderate to severe behavioural problems and a further 15 per cent to exhibit more mild difficulties (Richman, Stevenson & Graham, 1982). However, some early developmental problems and specific fears (such as delays in toilet training and 'comfort' habits such as rocking) usually resolve by middle childhood, but others (such as disruptiveness or conduct disorders) seem more persistent. The type of disorder that a child will exhibit also changes with age and is probably related to the nature of the experiences that children will encounter at specific ages. For example, some problems (such as chronic worrying) are rarely found in pre-school children but increase significantly after school entry.

Comorbidity between childhood disorders is also common and around 2 per cent of children have more than one mental health diagnosis. In addition, childhood psychopathology is also associated with physical health problems and poor educational performance (Office for National Statistics, 2005). So we can see from these facts that childhood psychiatric disorders can have implications across a range of developmental domains. Studies of risk factors suggest that children of lone parents are twice as likely to have a mental health problem as those living with married or cohabiting couples (16 per cent compared with 8 per cent) and other known risk factors for childhood psychiatric disorders include parental psychopathology, repeated early separation from parents, harsh or inadequate parenting, exposure to abuse or neglect, and adverse peer group influences (Maughan, 2000) (see also Table 16.1).

SELF-TEST QUESTIONS

- Can you describe four difficulties involved in the detection and diagnosis of childhood psychological disorders?
- What kinds of childhood events act as precursors or risk factors for adult mental health problems?
- How prevalent are childhood psychological disorders?

SECTION SUMMARY

16.1   THE DIAGNOSIS AND PREVALENCE OF CHILDHOOD AND ADOLESCENT PSYCHOLOGICAL PROBLEMS: SOME GENERAL ISSUES

- There are numerous difficulties associated with recognizing and diagnosing childhood psychological problems, including communication difficulties and the child's underdeveloped self-awareness.
- Childhood psychopathology is often a significant precursor to adult psychopathology.
- Between 10 and 20 per cent of children and adolescents have a diagnosable psychological disorder.
- Comorbidity between disorders is common.

16.2   DISRUPTIVE BEHAVIOUR PROBLEMS

In this section we will cover those behavioural problems that are characterized by impulsive, disruptive and poorly controlled behaviour. We all expect children of certain ages to have poor self-control, to throw temper

tantrums or to disrupt ongoing activities by failing to show restraint. However, by the time most children enter school, they are expected to be able to restrain their behaviour, attend to tasks when asked, and to attend to and follow appropriate commands. Nevertheless, some individuals find this hard to do – even in late childhood or adolescence. Their inability to restrain themselves and follow instructions leads to the disruption of cooperative and group activities (such as group learning in school) and in extreme cases may represent overtly aggressive behaviour to peers and adults, including criminal violence and damage to property. We will discuss two particular disruptive behaviour problems that can be found in DSM-5, namely *attention deficit hyperactivity disorder (ADHD)* and *conduct disorder*. In this section we will discuss these two syndromes individually, covering their diagnosis and aetiology.

16.2.1 Attention Deficit Hyperactivity Disorder (ADHD)

The main feature of **attention deficit hyperactivity disorder** (ADHD) is a persistent pattern of inattention and/or hyperactivity–impulsivity that is at a significantly higher rate than would be expected for the child at that developmental stage. ADHD can manifest itself behaviourally in many ways, including lack of attention in academic, occupational or social situations; making careless mistakes in school work or other tasks; difficulty maintaining attention until task completion; appearing to have their attention elsewhere and failing to take in or respond to instructions; and a tendency to shift from one task to another without completing any of them. The child with ADHD will typically have a strong dislike for tasks that require sustained self-application and mental effort, and will be easily distracted by irrelevant stimuli or events. **Hyperactivity** may be manifest as excessive fidgetiness and by not remaining seated when asked. The child with ADHD will exhibit excessive running or climbing when inappropriate, or will talk excessively. Infants with the disorder will appear to be constantly 'on the go', jumping and climbing on furniture, as well as having difficulty in participating in sedentary activities such as listening to a story. **Impulsivity** manifests as impatience, a difficulty in appropriately delaying responses (e.g. attempting to run out of the house before their coat is on) and constantly interrupting others before they have finished what they have to say; it may also reflect a desire for immediate rewards over delayed rewards. Impulsivity can also result in accidents (such as knocking things over) or indulging in dangerous activities (such as riding a bicycle fast over rough terrain).

> **attention deficit hyperactivity disorder (ADHD)** A persistent pattern of inattention and/or hyperactivity–impulsivity that is at a significantly higher rate than would be expected for a child at his or her developmental stage.

 For a video on children with ADHD go to www.wiley-psychopathology.com/video/ch16

> **hyperactivity** A higher than normal level of activity.

> **impulsivity** The act of reacting to a situation without considering the consequences.

The diagnosis of ADHD

The main issue in diagnosing ADHD is to ensure that hyperactivity or inattention is significantly greater than normal for the child's developmental stage and to ensure that it is a generalized and persistent predisposition rather than one that is confined to a single context. DSM-5 Summary Table 16.1 describes the diagnostic criteria for ADHD and this emphasizes that impairment is present before 12 years of age and is found in two or more contexts. Most individuals with ADHD present with symptoms of both inattention and hyperactivity but in some one or the other pattern may be dominant. This has given rise to two diagnostic subtypes, namely *attention deficit hyperactivity disorder, predominantly inattentive presentation* and *attention deficit hyperactivity disorder, predominantly hyperactive/impulsive presentation*. If both inattentive and hyperactive/impulsive elements are present this is known as a *combined presentation*. Each subtype should be used if six (or more) of the dominant symptoms are present with fewer than six of the less dominant symptoms present.

CASE HISTORY 16.1

ATTENTION DEFICIT HYPERACTIVITY DISORDER (ADHD)

Mark, age 14, has more energy than most boys his age. But then, he's always been overly active. Starting at age 3, he was a human tornado, dashing around and disrupting everything in his path. At home, he darted from one activity to the next, leaving a trail of toys behind him. At meals, he upset dishes and chattered relentlessly. He was reckless and impulsive, running into the street with oncoming cars, no matter how many times his mother explained the danger or scolded him. In the playground, he seemed no wilder than the other kids. But his tendency to overreact – like hitting playmates simply for bumping in to him – had already got him into trouble several times. His parents didn't know what to do. Mark's doting grandparents reassured them, 'Boys will be boys. Don't worry, he'll grow out of it.' But he didn't.

Source: http://www.nimh.nih.gov/health/publications/attention-deficit-hyperactivity-disorder/index.shtml

DSM-5 SUMMARY TABLE 16.1 *Criteria for attention deficit hyperactivity disorder (ADHD)*

- An ongoing pattern of inattention and/or hyperactivity and impulsivity that interferes with normal functioning or development, as marked by the following:

  - **Inattention.** At least six of the following for at least 6 months:

    - Not paying close attention to details or making careless mistakes
    - Difficultly in maintaining attention in activities
    - Does not listen when spoken to directly
    - Ignores instructions
    - Has difficulty organizing
    - Dislikes or avoids tasks which require sustained mental effort
    - Loses things needed for tasks
    - Easily distractible
    - Forgetful in daily activities

  - **Hyperactivity and Impulsivity.** At least six of the following for at least 6 months:

    - High level of fidgeting
    - Not sitting still or leaving seat when expected to sit
    - Runs or climbs in situations where it is inappropriate
    - Unable to engage in activities quietly
    - Excessive talking
    - Blurts out an answer before the question is finished
    - Has difficulty awaiting their turn
    - Interrupts or intrudes on others frequently

- Symptoms were present before the age of 12
- Symptoms are present in at least two settings
- Symptoms reduce the quality of educational, social or occupational ability
- Symptoms do not occur during schizophrenia or another psychotic disorder and are not better explained by another mental disorder

Around half of those diagnosed with the combined presentation of ADHD will also be diagnosed with *oppositional defiant disorder* or *conduct disorder* (see section 16.2.2) and these rates of comorbidity are significantly higher than comorbidity with other psychopathologies (Hinshaw, 1987). This indicates that in many cases ADHD is associated with the violation of social norms and the basic rights of others, and raises the question of whether there might be an underlying link between the two disorders (e.g. see Quay, 1979). Opinion on this is currently undecided but what is clear is that when a child is diagnosed with both ADHD and an oppositional defiant disorder/conduct disorder, the individual will usually exhibit the worst of both disorders (Biederman, Newcorn & Sprich, 1991). In other cases, children with ADHD can be distinguished from those with oppositional defiant disorder/conduct disorder by the fact that the latter are likely to (1) be more aggressive, (2) live in families with a lower socioeconomic status, and (3) have parents who also exhibit antisocial behaviour (Faraone, Biederman, Jetton & Tsuang, 1997; Hinshaw, 1987). In addition, recent studies have suggested that children with a single diagnosis of ADHD are likely to have a better long-term prognosis than those with oppositional defiant disorder/conduct disorder and childhood ADHD alone is not a differential predictor of antisocial personality disorder in adulthood (Lahey, Loeber, Burke & Applegate, 2005). However, there is evidence that in some cases ADHD can lead to earlier onset of conduct disorder and around a quarter of those children with a combined presentation ADHD diagnosis will be diagnosed with conduct disorder (DSM-5, p.65). This may be because some children with ADHD become involved in an escalation of symptoms caused by a vicious cycle where their disruptive behaviour causes aggressive reactions in others and this in turn evokes aggressive and increasingly antisocial reactions in the sufferer (Hinshaw, Lahey & Hart, 1993). Anxiety and depressive disorders are comorbid in a minority of children with ADHD and this is at a slightly higher rate than in the general population (DSM-5, p.65; Furman, 2005).

In terms of its course, ADHD is usually first recognized by parents when the child is a toddler but not all hyperactive toddlers go on to develop ADHD. The disorder is usually first recognized and diagnosed after the child first begins schooling and this is because learning and adjustment at school is significantly affected by the disorder. As the child develops into adolescence, symptoms usually attenuate and become less pronounced, although about half will continue to show symptoms well into adulthood and this can detrimentally affect intellectual functioning and IQ (Bridgett & Walker, 2006).

There is much discussion in the literature about whether ADHD is a culturally constructed disorder – that is, whether the rates of diagnosis differ in different cultures because of differing cultural perceptions of children's behaviour. The evidence on this is equivocal. Some studies suggest very similar rates of diagnosis across different cultures and ethnic groups (Rohde, Szobot, Polanczyk, Schmitz *et al.*, 2005; Bailey & Owens, 2005), whereas others indicate differing rates of ADHD in different countries (Dwivedi & Banhatti, 2005). Studies indicating different rates of diagnosis may do so because different cultural environments may directly affect a child's behaviour (e.g. Buddhist cultures tend not to tolerate externalizing behaviours) or may affect the attitudes of parents and clinicians towards what is acceptable behaviour. For example, Zwirs, Burger, Buitelaar & Schulpen (2006) found that detection of externalizing disorders was significantly lower in a sample of non-Dutch parents (Moroccan, Turkish and Surinamese) than Dutch parents and that cultural contexts may have an important influence on whether ADHD symptoms are detected and reported.

The prevalence of ADHD

DSM-5 estimates that around 5 per cent of school-age children worldwide are diagnosed with ADHD and 2.5 per cent of adults. Similar rates of diagnosis are also found in pre-school children (aged 2–5 years) (Egger, Kondo & Angold, 2006) and about half of those diagnosed with ADHD in childhood will carry that diagnosis into adulthood (Kessler, Adler, Barkley, Biederman *et al.*, 2006). There is considerable evidence to indicate that ADHD is more common in boys than girls but reasons for this may include the fact that boys are more likely to be referred for treatment than girls. Recent reviews suggest that although there is a sex difference in rates of diagnosis between boys and girls, ADHD symptoms are not sex specific (e.g. just as is the case with boys, girls with combined attention deficit and hyperactivity were more likely to be disruptive than those diagnosed with the predominantly single diagnosis) but identification of girls with ADHD has been hampered by parental and teacher bias (Staller & Faraone, 2006). In addition, any sex differences found with ADHD in childhood do not appear to be found in late adolescence or adulthood where male and female prevalence rates are equivalent (Bauermeister, Shrout, Chavez, Rubio-Stipec *et al.*, 2007).

The consequences of ADHD

Like most psychopathologies the symptoms of ADHD also have detrimental consequences for the sufferer across a range of life domains. First, their attentional deficits and hyperactivity may make them prone to temper outbursts, frustration, bossiness, stubbornness, changeable moods and poor self-esteem. As a result, academic achievement is usually impaired leading to conflict with teachers and family. Because the disruptive consequences of their behaviour are pervasive, family members often view their behaviour as intentional, wilful and irresponsible, and this can cause resentment within the family. Individuals with predominantly inattentive symptoms tend to suffer most in terms of academic achievement, while hyperactivity and impulsivity are associated most with peer rejection and accidental injury. However, in general, children with ADHD have great difficulty making friends and integrating successfully into social groups – usually because their behaviour is aggressive and disruptive (Hinshaw & Melnick, 1995). Indeed, in new social settings children with ADHD are often singled out and rejected relatively rapidly by their peers (Erhardt & Hinshaw, 1994). In part, this is due to their disruptive behavioural symptoms but, in addition, children with ADHD frequently fail to understand the intentions of their peers and are unable to translate the correct social response into appropriate behaviour (Whalen & Henker, 1998).

To complete Activity 16.1 go to
www.wiley-psychopathology.com/
activities/ch16

In adulthood, ADHD also has a number of impairing consequences, including less success and safety at work (Kessler, Lane, Stang & van Brunt, 2009), poorer interpersonal relationships (Biederman, Monuteasu, Mick, Spender *et al.*, 2006), poorer academic outcomes (Lewandowski, Lovett, Codding & Gordon, 2008) and poorer general life satisfaction (Biederman *et al.*, 2006).

The aetiology of ADHD

The causes of ADHD can be clustered under two broad headings – biological and psychological, but the current view is that biological factors are particularly important in the aetiology of ADHD, especially inherited factors that may play a strong role in mediating susceptibility to ADHD (Faraone & Khan, 2006).

Biological factors *Genetic factors*   There is now considerable evidence pointing to the involvement of an inherited susceptibility to ADHD. ADHD appears to be one of the most heritable psychiatric disorders: pooled data from 20 twin studies report a mean heritability estimate of 76 per cent (Faraone & Mick, 2010). Adoption studies also suggest that ADHD in the adopted child is more likely to occur if a biological parent has ADHD than if an adopted parent has ADHD (Faraone, Perlis, Doyle, Smoller *et al.*, 2005). However, what is inherited is significantly less easy to determine. A meta-analysis of gene linkage studies has revealed a region on chromosome 16 that has the most consistent linkage evidence (Coghill & Banaschewski, 2009). However, identifying individual genes is much more problematic and recent reviews of genome-wide association studies have suggested that any individual gene variant for ADHD must have a very small individual effect (Neale, Medland, Ripke, Asherson *et al.*, 2010). However, many of those genes identified may underlie abnormalities in neurotransmitter systems – particularly the dopamine, norepinephrine and serotonin systems (Waldman & Gizer, 2006). Specific genes that may be involved are the dopamine transporter gene, the dopamine D4 and

D5 receptors and SNAP-25, a gene that controls the way dopamine is released in the brain. However, while susceptibility to ADHD appears to have a significant genetic component, additional studies strongly indicate a genes–environment interaction. That is, what is inherited is a vulnerability to ADHD but ADHD becomes manifest only when certain environmental influences are found. For example, Kahn, Khoury, Nichols & Lanphear (2003) found that children with two copies of the 10-repeat allele of a DAT1 gene (a gene related to dopamine regulation in the brain) who were exposed to maternal prenatal smoking exhibited significantly higher levels of hyperactivity, impulsiveness and oppositional behaviours than a control group of children who possessed these genes but whose mothers did not smoke during pregnancy. In addition, children who possessed only one of the risk factors (the high-risk genotype or a mother that smoked during pregnancy) did not show significantly higher levels of ADHD symptoms than children who possessed neither of the risk factors. Studies such as this indicate that, while inherited factors are critically important in the aetiology of ADHD, they may constitute a vulnerability that converts into ADHD only if certain environmental factors are present (Coghill & Banaschewski, 2009). Other environmental risk factors that have been proposed include pre- or perinatal complications and maternal drinking during pregnancy (Mick, Biederman, Faraone, Sayer *et al.*, 2002; Milberger, Biederman, Faraone, Guite & Tsuang, 1997; Milberger, Biederman, Faraone & Jones, 1998).

Neuroscience Magnetic resonance imaging (MRI) studies of the brains of individuals with ADHD have revealed a number of significant differences between ADHD sufferers and non-sufferers (e.g. Krain & Castellanos, 2006; Seidman, Valera & Makris, 2005; Cortese, 2012). First, there is consistent evidence that the brains of children with ADHD are smaller than those of healthy comparison children, and they develop more slowly. Overall brain volume has been shown to be smaller by an average of 3.2 per cent, with the main areas affected being the frontal, parietal, temporal and occipital lobes (Durston, Hulshoff Pol, Schnack, Buitelaar *et al.*, 2004), and ADHD is also associated with a global reduction in grey matter (Nakao, Radua, Rubia & Mataix-Cols, 2011). Other brain areas exhibiting decreased volume in ADHD include the frontal cortex, basal ganglia and cerebellum (Krain & Castellanos, 2006). Comparisons of the development of brain structures in children with ADHD and typically developing controls also suggest that the median age by which 50 per cent of the cortex reaches peak thickness is 10.5 years in children with ADHD but only 7.5 years in normally developing controls (Shaw, Eckstrand, Sharp, Blumenthal *et al.*, 2007). A range of studies has also indicated that brain volume in specific brain areas is inversely correlated with a variety of ADHD symptoms. For example, children with ADHD are known to have deficits in *executive functioning* (involving planning and problem solving), and specifically have difficulty inhibiting responses, and these functions are normally controlled by the brain's frontal lobes. Studies have found that decreased frontal lobe volume predicts poor performance on tests of attention and on tasks that require behaviour to be inhibited, suggesting that abnormalities in these brain regions may be responsible for some of the symptoms of ADHD (Casey, Castellanos, Giedd, Marsh *et al.*, 1997; Hill, Yeo, Campbell, Hart *et al.*, 2003). Another area of the brain that regularly exhibits abnormalities in association with ADHD symptoms is the cerebellum (Cherkasova & Hechtman, 2009). In ADHD, abnormalities are usually found in the cerebellum's influence on the cortico–striatal–thalamo–cortical circuits and these circuits are involved in choosing, initiating and carrying out complex motor and cognitive responses (Alexander, DeLong & Strick, 1986; Graybiel, 1998). In this case it is not hard to imagine how dysfunctions in these pathways may result in the disruption of the planning and execution of behaviour.

Prenatal factors As we have already noted, at least some prenatal experiences appear to interact with a genetic predisposition to cause ADHD: these include maternal smoking and drinking during pregnancy (Mick, Biederman, Faraone, Sayer *et al.*, 2002) and general complications associated with childbirth, such as low birth weight, respiratory distress and birth asphyxia (Tannock, 1998; Getahun, Rhoads, Demissie, Lu *et al.*, 2013). In a recent study, Schmitz, Denardin, Silva, Pianca *et al.* (2006) found that pregnant mothers smoking greater than 10 cigarettes per day were significantly more likely to give birth to children with ADHD than non-smoking mothers – even when other potential confounding factors such as maternal ADHD, oppositional defiant disorder, birth weight and alcohol use during pregnancy were controlled for. In addition, a study by Milberger, Biederman, Faraone, Guite & Tsuang (1997) found that 22 per cent of mothers of children with ADHD reported smoking a pack of cigarettes a day during pregnancy compared with only 8 per cent of mothers whose children did not develop ADHD. Milberger *et al.* (1997) hypothesized that prenatal exposure to nicotine caused abnormalities in the dopaminergic neurotransmitter system, resulting in difficulties inhibiting behaviour.

Environmental toxins Some early accounts of ADHD did allude to the possibility that hyperactivity resulted from various biochemical imbalances caused by such factors as food additives (Feingold, 1973), refined

RESEARCH METHODS 16.1

COGNITIVE TESTS OF ADHD

A variety of tests has been devised that are capable of differentiating between children with ADHD and control participants. The aim of most of these tasks is to test attention or to determine whether the individual is able to successfully inhibit responses when required to do so (see Seidman, 2006).

THE CONTINUOUS PERFORMANCE TEST (CPT)

The CPT is a computerized visual vigilance/attention task in which the child is seated before a computer monitor and instructed to observe a string of letters presented randomly and at varying speeds. Children are instructed to press the space bar as quickly as possible following all letters except the letter X. Children with ADHD are less able to inhibit responses following the presentation of the target letter X and also have longer reaction times following letters that should be responded to (Epstein, Johnson, Varia & Conners, 2001).

THE STROOP TASK

This is generally considered a test of ability to inhibit responses. In the task, a word describing a colour (e.g. RED) is presented in a different colour (e.g. green) and the participant has to respond as quickly as possible by naming the colour ink that the word is written in. Children with ADHD take more time to respond and make more errors than control participants (Shin, 2005).

THE TRAIL MAKING TEST

This is a measure involving connecting circles on a page (Reitan, 1958). The child is instructed to connect the circles by drawing lines alternating between circles labelled with numbers and letters in sequential order until they reach the circle labelled 'End' (see Focus Point 15.1). Most studies show that children and adults with ADHD perform significantly worse than control participants (Rapport, Van Voorhis, Tzelepis & Friedman, 2001).

THE CONTROLLED WORD ASSOCIATION TEST (COWAT)

This test measures verbal fluency in response to single letters, which taps into phonological associations and category fluency ('name all the animals you can beginning with the letter. . .') (Benton, Hamsher, & Sivan, 1983). This test appears to measure speed of access to words, persistence at a task and processing speed. The majority of studies show impaired performance on this task in children with ADHD compared with controls (Dinn, Robbins & Harris, 2001).

CONNERS' PARENT RATING SCALE (CPRS)

The CPRS (Conners, Sitarenios, Parker & Epstein, 1998) is an 80-item scale completed by the child's parent using a four-point scale. This instrument has well-accepted reliability and validity and is considered to be standard in ADHD diagnosis (Barkley, 1991). Norms by age are available for males and females in 3 year intervals.

sugar cane (Goyette & Conners, 1977) and lead poisoning (Thompson, Raab, Hepburn, Hunter *et al.*, 1989). However, while there is little evidence to suggest that food additives generally influence ADHD (Wolraich, Wilson & White, 1995), there is some support for the fact that both the levels of lead in the blood and chronic exposure to nicotine or tobacco smoke increase

hyperactivity (e.g. Fung & Lau, 1989; Polanska, Jurewicz & Hanke, 2012).

Psychological factors *Parent–child interactions*
ADHD appears to run in families and this may have implications beyond the fact that there is a genetic component to the disorder. For instance, it also means that

children with ADHD are more likely to be brought up by parents who also have the disorder, which may exacerbate any symptoms that are caused by the genetic component alone. For example, fathers who are diagnosed with ADHD have been found to be less effective parents (in terms of exhibiting ineffective discipline and adopting traditionally conservative father roles) than parents without an ADHD diagnosis (Arnold, O'Leary & Edwards, 1997), and this might exacerbate any disruptive characteristics the ADHD child may exhibit. Psychodynamic approaches to ADHD have also pointed to the possible role of inconsistent and ineffective parenting of children with ADHD. Bettelheim (1967) proposed that hyperactivity results when a predisposition to ADHD is accompanied by authoritarian parenting methods. He argued that such parents are likely to become impatient with a disruptive and hyperactive child, resulting in a vicious cycle whereby constant attempts to discipline the child cause even more defiant reactions on the part of the child who reacts by defying rules across a range of life contexts (e.g. school, social situations and suchlike).

Learning theorists have suggested that parents may exacerbate ADHD symptoms in a rather different way. Individuals with ADHD exhibit impulsive and disruptive behaviour that in many cases will require the need for control by the parent. In such circumstances the attention from the parent that these behaviours demand may be rewarding or reinforcing them, thus increasing their frequency and intensity. While there is no direct evidence to support this view, indirect support comes from studies showing that time-out from positive reinforcement can act as an effective procedure for *reducing* negative and disruptive behaviour in children with ADHD (Fabiano, Pelham, Manos, Gnagy *et al.*, 2004).

Nevertheless, while parent–child interactions of various kinds may exacerbate ADHD symptoms, there is no evidence to suggest that they are the sole cause of these symptoms (Johnston & Marsh, 2001).

Theory of mind (TOM) deficits

We have already described how children with ADHD frequently fail to understand the intentions of their peers in social situations and this has led some theorists to argue that children with ADHD have theory of mind (TOM) deficits. Theory of mind is the ability to understand one's own and other people's mental states (Premack & Woodruff, 1978) and it is not difficult to see that if a child has deficits in such abilities they will often react in inappropriate ways to peers and family. However, studies have tended to be inconsistent in showing a relationship between poor performance on TOM tasks (see Chapter 17) and ADHD. For example, Buitelaar, van der Wees, Swaab-Barneveld & van der Gaag (1999) found that children with ADHD diagnoses showed poorer performance on

a TOM task than control participants. In contrast, in a later study, Perner, Kain & Barchfeld (2002) found that children with ADHD showed no impairment at all on an advanced TOM task. However, studies have been fairly consistent in showing that children with ADHD do show impaired performance compared with controls on tasks of executive functioning (Fahie & Symons, 2003; Perner, Kain & Barchfeld, 2002). Executive functioning is that range of skills that require goal directed behaviour, planning, attentional control and inhibition of inappropriate responses. Such studies have tended to suggest that children with ADHD have specific deficits related to planning and inhibition of behaviour (Papadopoulos, Panayiotou, Spanoudis & Natsopoulos, 2005) and it is deficits in these areas of functioning that give rise to their behavioural problems. This has recently been reinforced by studies showing that individuals with ADHD do show executive functioning deficits, but do not necessarily exhibit TOM deficits, indicating that ADHD symptoms may be linked directly to executive functioning problems rather than deficits in social functioning (Gonzalez-Gadea, Baez, Torralva, Castellanos *et al.*, 2013). The fact that tests of executive functioning have indicated that this is where the cognitive deficits in ADHD lie is consistent with the neurological evidence we reviewed earlier, which strongly indicates that children with ADHD have abnormalities in the frontal lobes of the brain, and it is the frontal lobes that control executive functioning.

Summary of ADHD

The evidence on the aetiology of ADHD strongly indicates that there is a significant genetic component to the disorder and it may be one of the most heritable psychological disorders. However, it is not fully clear yet whether this genetic component merely bestows a vulnerability for the disorder or whether it may be a direct cause of abnormalities that underlie ADHD; it has also not yet been possible to clearly identify the genes through which this heritability is transmitted. There are clearly some brain abnormalities that characterize ADHD, including reduced overall brain volume and grey matter, and reduced brain volume, particularly in areas such as the frontal cortex, basal ganglia and cerebellum, and abnormalities in the frontal lobes may contribute to the deficits in executive functioning that are found in ADHD using cognitive tests. Some pre- and perinatal factors have been identified that may contribute to abnormal development and these include maternal smoking and drinking during pregnancy as well as complications at birth, including low birth weight, respiratory distress and birth asphyxia. There is also some evidence that dysfunctional parenting may contribute to the behavioural symptoms of ADHD in children but there is no evidence that dysfunctional parenting is a sole cause of ADHD.

16.2.2 Conduct Disorder

While ADHD is characterized by behaviour that tends to be disruptive and inappropriate, many children and adolescents exhibit behaviour that appears almost intentionally vicious, callous and aggressive, and it is when such characteristics appear that a diagnosis of **conduct disorder** may

> **conduct disorder (CD)** A pattern of behaviour during childhood in which the child exhibits a range of behavioural problems, including fighting, lying, running away from home, vandalism and truancy.

be appropriate. Behaviours typical of conduct disorder include violent or aggressive behaviour, deliberate cruelty towards people or animals, wanton vandalism or damage to property, lying, stealing and cheating, criminal theft and violation of the rights of others (e.g. trespass, threatening behaviour and verbal abuse). The following sections discuss the diagnosis, prevalence and the known causes of conduct disorder.

The diagnosis of conduct disorder

DSM-5 devotes a chapter to disruptive, impulse-control and conduct disorders, and these disorders are linked to a common externalizing spectrum characterized by a lack of inhibition or inability to control impulses. This common theme throughout these disorders is one reason why conduct disorder is regularly comorbid with impulse disorders, such as intermittent explosive disorder (DSM-5, p.466), and other impulse control disorders such as pyromania (deliberate and purposeful fire-setting) (DSM-5, p.476) and kleptomania (recurrent failure to resist impulses to steal objects) (DSM-5, p.478). In this chapter we will discuss two disorders, namely conduct disorder and oppositional defiant disorder.

The main feature of conduct disorder is a repetitive and persistent pattern of behaviour involving the violation of accepted social norms or the basic rights of others. There are four main categories of such behaviour: (1) aggression towards people and animals, (2) destruction of property, (3) deceitfulness or theft, and (4) the serious violation of accepted rules (such as driving offences). These behaviours must also cause severe impairment in social, academic or occupational functioning and should be found in a range of different contexts such as home, school or the community. For a diagnosis of conduct disorder, characteristic behaviours must have been present for at least 12 months (DSM-5 Summary Table 16.2).

Children or adolescents with this disorder would normally initiate violence or aggressive behaviour and react violently to others. Their behaviour will often include bullying or threatening behaviour: they will often initiate physical fights, carry weapons, be physically cruel to people or animals, and intimidate people into activities by threats of physical force (e.g. force others into sexual activity). Individuals with conduct disorder also have little respect for

DSM-5 SUMMARY TABLE 16.2 *Criteria for conduct disorder*

- An ongoing pattern of behaviour where the rights of others or social norms are infringed, as shown by at least three of the following over a 12 month period:
    - Bullying or threatening others
    - Starting fights
    - Using a weapon to do serious physical harm
    - Physical cruelty to others
    - Physical cruelty to animals
    - Mugging or similar crimes
    - Forcing another into sexual activity
    - Fire setting to destroy/seriously damage property
    - Deliberate destruction of another's property
    - Breaking into buildings or cars
    - Lies to get goods or favours
    - Shoplifting or similar
    - Stays out at night despite parental intervention, starting from before the age of 13
    - Has run away from home at least twice or once for a long period of time
    - Often misses school, starting from before the age of 13
- The disturbances cause significant impairment in social, academic or occupational functioning
- If the patient is 18 years or older, the condition is not better explained by antisocial personality disorder

property and they will indulge in acts of vandalism and petty theft from others. Their lying will also extend to breaking promises to obtain goods or benefits, or simply 'conning' others into providing benefits or favours. Finally, children with conduct disorder will usually have a history of breaking rules, including staying out late despite prohibitions, running away from home or staying away from school.

There are two main subtypes of conduct disorder based on the age of onset. **Childhood-onset conduct disorder** is defined by the onset of at least one criterion characteristic of conduct disorder prior to 10 years of age. **Adolescent-onset conduct disorder** is defined by the appearance of conduct disorder symptoms only after the age of

> **childhood-onset conduct disorder** A sub-type of conduct disorder defined by the onset of at least one criterion characteristic of conduct disorder prior to 10 years of age.

> **adolescent-onset conduct disorder** A subtype of conduct disorder defined by the appearance of conduct disorder symptoms only after the age of 10 years.

10 years. Such individuals are less likely to be physically aggressive than those with childhood-onset type and will usually have better peer relationships.

Like individuals with antisocial personality disorder (see section 12.2.2), children and adolescents with conduct disorder display little empathy with the feelings and intentions of others and will usually believe that their aggressive reactions to others are justified. They will frequently try to blame others for their misdeeds and exhibit little or any genuine guilt for their antisocial actions. Risk-taking, frustration, irritability, impulsivity and temper tantrums are regularly associated with conduct disorder and result in higher accident rates for such individuals. Conduct disorder is also associated with early onset of a range of behaviours, including sexual behaviour, drinking, smoking, substance abuse and general risk-taking behaviour (e.g. dangerous and erratic driving). Finally, the disorder is more common in males than in females: males with a diagnosis will outnumber females by a ratio of at least 4:1 and often higher (Zoccolillo, 1993).

It is important to mention at least three issues related to diagnosis of conduct disorder. Firstly, individuals diagnosed with conduct disorder will usually be under 18 years of age and are only diagnosed with the disorder at a later age if the criteria for antisocial personality disorder are not met. Secondly, the clinician will need to take account of the social context in which behaviours characteristic of conduct disorder are found. For example, in certain deprived inner-city areas, behaviours characteristic of conduct disorder may be seen as being protective. That is, they may represent the norm for that environment and may serve an adaptive function in dealing with poverty and the threatening behaviour of others. In addition, immigrants from war-ravaged countries can have a reputation for violence because such behaviour has been necessary for survival in their home countries. Clinicians must be sure that a diagnosis of conduct disorder is made only when the characteristic behaviours are symptomatic of dysfunction rather than a reaction to a specific social context. Thirdly, a related category of disruptive behaviour disorders in DSM-5 is known as **oppositional defiant disorder (ODD)**. ODD is a diagnosis usually reserved for those children who do not meet the full criteria for conduct disorder (e.g. extreme aggression and violence) but who have regular temper tantrums, refuse to comply with requests or instructions, or appear to deliberately indulge in behaviours that annoy others. ODD is common in pre-school children and may even be a precursor to later childhood conduct disorder (Lahey, McBurnett & Loeber, 2000). It is found more often in families where childcare has been disrupted (through the child experiencing a number of different caregivers) or in families where at least one parent has a history of mood

oppositional defiant disorder (ODD) A mild form of disruptive behaviour disorders reserved for children who do not meet the full criteria for conduct disorder.

disorders, antisocial personality disorder, ADHD or substance abuse.

The prevalence and course of conduct disorder

Epidemiological studies indicate that conduct disorder may be relatively common, with prevalence rates ranging from 4–16 per cent in boys and 1.2–9 per cent in girls (Loeber, Burke, Lahey, Winters & Zera, 2000). A more recent US study estimated the lifetime prevalence rate of conduct disorder at 9.5 per cent (12.0 per cent among males and 7.1 per cent among females) and a median age of onset of 11.6 years (Nock, Kazdin, Hiripi & Kessler, 2006).

The most significant symptoms of conduct disorder begin to appear between middle childhood to middle adolescence, although ODD is a common precursor to conduct disorder in the pre-school years. In a majority of individuals the disorder remits by adulthood, but some do go on to meet the criteria for antisocial personality disorder. Indeed, studies suggest that childhood conduct disorder (but not childhood ADHD) predicts antisocial personality disorder in adulthood, but only in lower socioeconomic status families (Lahey, Loeber, Burke & Applegate, 2005). Children with conduct disorder are also more likely to develop into adulthood with antisocial personality disorder if they have a parent with antisocial personality disorder or have low verbal IQ (Lahey, Loeber, Hart, Frick et al., 1995).

Finally, we have already indicated that conduct disorder prevalence rates for boys are significantly higher than for girls, and the disorder also manifests differently in boys and girls. In boys, the main behaviours are aggressive and violent behaviour, fighting, stealing, damage to property and school problems. However, for girls, the most common behaviours are petty theft (such as shoplifting), lying, running away from home, avoiding school and prostitution (Robins, 1991). Indeed, these differential behaviours may have a direct impact on gender differences in prevalence rates since the crimes indulged in by girls (e.g. shoplifting) are often considered less serious than the violent crimes committed by boys, and boys are usually considered more likely to commit crimes than girls (Zahn-Waxler, 1993).

The aetiology of conduct disorder

Biological factors   *Genetic factors*   There is now some evidence that conduct disorder and its associated behaviours of aggressiveness and criminality may have a genetic component. Twin studies specifically involving conduct disorders have found heritability estimates between 45 and 67 per cent (Viding & McCrory, 2012), while twin studies also suggest that aggressive and violent behaviour (e.g. fighting, cruelty to animals) has a significant inherited component (Edelbrock, Rende, Plomin & Thompson, 1995). Adoption studies have also reported significant genetic and environmental influences on both conduct disorder and criminal behaviour (Simonoff, 2001). Some recent studies have even identified a specific gene, GABRA2, which is associated with childhood conduct disorder (Dick, Bierut, Hinrichs, Fox et al., 2006) and, interestingly, this gene is also related to adult alcohol dependence and drug dependence in adolescence. However, the results from more extensive candidate gene association studies have been less encouraging, with few if any candidate genes having been identified to date (Viding, Price, Jaffee, Trzaskowski et al., 2013). What these studies suggest is that there is probably an inherited component to conduct disorder – perhaps in the form of inherited temperamental characteristics – but that environmental factors also probably play an important role in determining behaviour patterns typical of conduct disorder.

Neuropsychological deficits
Just as with ADHD, conduct disorder is associated with neuropsychological deficits in cognitive functioning, including deficits in executive functioning (planning and self-control), verbal IQ and memory (Lynam & Henry, 2001). Low IQ is also associated with conduct disorder and is particularly associated with early-age onset conduct disorder independently of related socioeconomic factors such as poverty, race or poor educational attainment (Lynam, Moffitt & Stouthamer-Loeber, 1993). Nevertheless, there is some doubt about whether executive functioning deficits occur in conduct disorder in the absence of ADHD symptoms. For example, Oosterlaan, Scheres & Sergeant (2005) found that while executive functioning deficits were found in children with comorbid conduct disorder and ADHD, no deficits were found in children diagnosed solely with either ODD or CD. Similarly, meta-analyses have found that antisocial behaviour generally is associated with poor executive functioning but this association is predominantly driven by relationships between poor executive functioning and criminality and externalizing behaviours generally rather than conduct disorder specifically (Ogilvie, Stewart, Chan & Shum, 2011).

Prenatal factors
A number of prenatal factors have been identified in the aetiology of conduct disorder. These include maternal smoking and drinking during pregnancy and prenatal and postnatal malnutrition. Maternal smoking has been found to predict the early emergence of conduct problems in the offspring, especially socially resistant and impulsively aggressive behaviour (Wakschlag, Pickett, Kasza & Loeber, 2006), and conduct disorder is specifically associated with maternal

drinking of alcohol during the first trimester (Larkby, Goldschmidt, Hanusa & Day, 2011), but this may be restricted to mothers and children of low socioeconomic status (Monteaux, Blacker, Biederman, Fitzmaurice et al., 2006). Similarly, delinquent behaviour and poor moral judgement have also been found to be higher in children prenatally exposed to alcohol (Schonfeld, Mattson & Riley, 2005). Recent studies also suggest that externalizing behaviours are associated with prenatal malnutrition, especially deficits in proteins, iron and zinc (Liu & Raine, 2006). However, we must be cautious about how we interpret all of these findings because correlations between prenatal exposure and conduct disorder may be significantly confounded with other risk factors, such as parental depression, family disadvantage and genetic influences (Maughan, Taylor, Caspi & Moffitt, 2004). If so, prenatal exposure may simply be a risk factor for the development of conduct disorder rather than a direct cause of the problem.

Psychological factors   *The family environment and parent–child relationships*
While studies of the heritability of conduct disorder suggest a significant genetic component to the disorder, these studies also indicate that important and significant environmental factors are also involved, and arguably one of the most important of the latter is the family environment and the nature of parent–child interactions during childhood. It is already well documented that risk factors for conduct disorder and ODD include parental unemployment, having a parent with antisocial personality disorder, disrupted childcare and childhood abuse or maltreatment (Frick, 1998; Lahey, Loeber, Hart, Frick et al., 1995). For example, inconsistent and harsh parenting is associated with the development of aggressive behaviour and other symptoms of conduct disorder (Coie & Dodge, 1998). This may be because inconsistent discipline may permit the child to get away with behaving antisocially on many occasions; but, when disciplining does occur, the child may learn aggressive or violent behaviour from parents who behave aggressively when disciplining their children. Indeed, there is evidence that children who are physically abused by their parents are more likely to be aggressive when they grow up (Crick & Dodge, 1994) and parents who are physically abusive to their children also report more behaviour problems in their children than non-abusive parents (Lau, Valeri, McCarty & Weisz, 2006). However, longitudinal studies are generally consistent in indicating that childhood abuse is associated with criminal behaviour, violence and diagnosis of conduct disorder in later childhood and adolescence (Fergusson, Horwood & Lynskey, 1996; Widom & Maxfield, 1996), and there is some evidence that childhood abuse may give rise to conduct disorder in children only with a

specific genetic predisposition (Taylor & Kim-Cohen, 2007; Dodge, 2009). In addition to childhood abuse, conduct disorder has also been shown to be associated with family environments that are less cohesive, have few intellectual/cultural pursuits, have greater levels of family conflict and higher levels of parental stress (Blader, 2006; George, Herman & Ostrander, 2006). Interestingly, many of these familial characteristics that are associated with conduct disorder are also very closely linked to poverty and social deprivation, and we will look at how this socioeconomic factor may influence aetiology later.

Media and peer influences Many children may develop antisocial and aggressive behaviour because they simply mimic the violent activities that they see around them in the media or displayed by their peers. Interestingly, statistics from the US suggest that between 1980 and 1995 violent crime by juveniles increased by over 50 per cent (US Bureau of the Census, 1997) and at least part of this increase may be due to the increasing levels of violence viewed by children on TV and in video games. However, while there is some evidence that television violence contributes to children's levels of aggressiveness and subsequent criminality (Hughes & Hasbrouck, 1996), more recent studies tend to suggest that media violence has its effect primarily on children who are already emotionally and psychiatrically disturbed. Recent longitudinal studies indicate that simply watching more than 3 hours of TV a day at the age of 5 years predicts an increase in conduct problems by age 7 years, but this effect is only significant for TV watching and not playing electronic games (Parkes, Sweeting, Wight & Henderson, 2013). Finally, studies have demonstrated an effect of violent TV programmes on behavioural and physiological measures of aggression only in children who already have a diagnosis of ADHD, ODD, conduct disorder or disruptive behavioural disorders generally (Grimes, Vernberg & Cathers, 1997; Grimes, Bergen, Nichols, Vernberg & Fonagy, 2004).

A more important source of mimicry may be peer behaviour and there is already evidence suggesting that associating with peers who indulge in violent or criminal behaviour is likely to increase one's own delinquent behaviour (Burt & Klump, 2013). In fact, a vicious cycle may develop in which associating with aggressive peers may expose the individual to increasing levels of community violence (e.g. gang fights, violent assaults and robbery). This in turn will facilitate mimicry of violence and will increase the perception of violent behaviour being the norm (Lambert, Ialongo, Boyd & Cooley, 2005). However, what is not clear from this research is whether children who already have antisocial and aggressive tendencies choose to mix with similar peers in the first place, so the peer association may merely increase pre-existing tendencies rather than create delinquent behaviour from scratch. There is some evidence that deviant peer affiliation is associated with later antisocial behaviour and substance abuse only in children who already display symptoms of ODD and conduct disorder. Deviant peer affiliation only weakly predicts future antisocial behaviour in individuals without these initial symptoms (Marshall & Molina, 2006).

Another view is that peer factors may facilitate symptoms of conduct disorder in a more indirect way. For example, being rejected by peers has been shown to cause increased aggressiveness – especially in children that have an existing disruptive behaviour disorder such as ADHD (Hinshaw & Melnick, 1995) – and this may also become a vicious cycle, as peers continue to reject adolescents whose behaviour exhibits increasing levels of antisocial behaviour (Kelly, Jorm & Rodgers, 2006).

In summary, media and peer mimicry are risk factors for conduct disorder but may facilitate antisocial and aggressive behaviour more in those children and adolescents who are already displaying symptoms of conduct disorder. As such, they probably represent mediating variables rather than true causes of the disorder.

Cognitive factors Conduct disorder is associated with the development of deviant moral awareness. For example, most children grow up learning that certain behaviours are morally acceptable and others are morally and socially unacceptable. However, children with conduct disorder fail to acquire this moral awareness. They are content to achieve their goals using violence and deceit, they have little respect for the rights of others, and they show little or no remorse for their antisocial acts. Much of this lack of awareness of moral standards may come from the fact that they may have developed highly biased ways of interpreting the world. For example, a child with conduct disorder regularly interprets the behaviour of others as hostile or challenging and this appears to give rise to their aggressive reactions. Dodge (1991, 1993) has proposed a social-information processing model of antisocial and aggressive behaviour in which a history of trauma, abuse, deprivation and insecure attachment may give rise to specific information processing biases. These include hypervigilance for hostile cues and attributing minor provocations to hostile intent, and these biases give rise to unwarranted fear and to aggressive reactions. If the child is brought up in a family environment where they learn aggressive behaviour in child–parent interactions (Patterson, Reid & Dishion, 1992), and if they also have their own experiences with successful aggressive tactics, they will evaluate aggression as an adaptive social strategy and use it proactively (see Figure 16.1). In support of this hypothesis, Gouze (1987) found that aggressive children direct their attention selectively

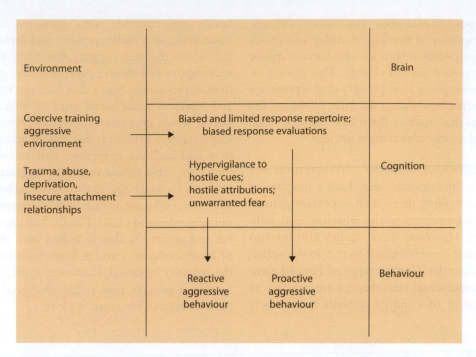

FIGURE 16.1 *Dodge's (1991) social-information processing model of antisocial and aggressive behaviour in which a history of trauma, abuse, deprivation and insecure attachment can give rise to information processing biases including a tendency to interpret even benign cues as signalling hostility.*

Source: Krol, N., Morton, J. & De Bruyn, E. (2004). Theories of conduct disorder: A causal modelling analysis. *Journal of Child Psychology and Psychiatry,* 45, 727–742, Figure 3. Reproduced with permission.

towards hostile social cues and have difficulty diverting their attention away from these cues. Aggressive children also exhibit what is called a '**hostile attributional bias**' (Naseby, Hayden & DePaulo, 1979) in which they will interpret not only ambiguous cues as signalling hostility but also many cues that are generated by benign intentions (e.g. Dodge, Bates & Pettit, 1990). Once a hostile attribution is made, studies also suggest that there is a 70 per cent probability of an aggressive response compared with only a 25 per cent probability following a benign attribution (Dodge, 1991). Because of such information processing and attributional biases, the individual with conduct disorder may be locked into a cycle of hostile interpretations and aggressive responding that becomes difficult to break – especially as continued aggressive behaviour by the sufferer is likely to generate genuine hostile intentions from others in the future.

> **hostile attributional bias** The tendency of individuals to interpret not only ambiguous cues as signalling hostility, but also many cues that are generated with benign intentions.

Socioeconomic factors Delinquent, violent behaviour has been shown to be highly associated with poverty, low socioeconomic class, unemployment, urban living and poor educational achievement, and such factors

may be a cause of conduct disorder rather than a consequence of it (Lahey, Miller, Gordon & Riley, 1999). A longitudinal study of familial and socioeconomic predictors of conduct disorder in a Scottish cohort indicated that individuals with conduct problems were more likely to have mothers that smoked during pregnancy, less likely to be living with both parents, have poor general health, and to have a parent who agrees with smacking as a form of punishment (Wilson, Bradshaw, Tipping, Henderson *et al.*, 2013). Poverty in turn is likely to give rise to disrupted family life, parental stress, poor educational opportunities and parental neglect – all of which may be contributing factors to the development of conduct disorder. An instructive study by Costello, Compton, Keeler & Angold (2003) suggests that poverty per se does have a direct causal effect on the level of conduct disorder in a local population. They studied conduct disorder in American Indian children before and after a casino opened on their reservation, which provided income that moved many families out of poverty. This constituted an interesting natural experiment on the role of poverty in childhood disorders. Before the casino opened, children of poor families suffered more symptoms of psychopathology than those of non-poor families. However, after the casino had opened the children of those families who moved from the poor to non-poor class showed a significant drop in symptoms of conduct disorder and ODD. Levels of these symptoms in families who remained poor after the casino opened did not change. This study provides a striking example of how poverty may represent a genuine causal factor for conduct disorder. However, the exact mechanisms that mediate the relationship between poverty and conduct disorder remain unclear.

Summary of conduct disorder This section has indicated that conduct disorder may have a number of contributing causes. First, there is an important genetic element that may be related to the inheritance of temperament factors. However, these studies also tend to implicate significant environmental factors in the aetiology of conduct disorder. Certain types of familial environments and parent–child relationships are risk factors for the development of conduct disorder, particularly

family environments with disrupted childcare, childhood abuse and maltreatment, and inconsistent parenting. Some theories suggest that early experience with maladaptive and abusive parenting may give rise to information processing biases that lead the child to attend to and interpret most social cues as indicative of hostile intent, which generates aggressive responding. There is some modest evidence that media and peer influences may also facilitate aggressive and antisocial behaviour. However, most recent research suggests that these factors may facilitate aggressive antisocial behaviour mainly in children who are already displaying symptoms of conduct disorder and ODD. Finally, low socioeconomic status and poverty is closely linked with the development of conduct disorder and at least one study suggests that the link may be causal. However, as yet, the mechanisms by which poverty may cause antisocial and aggressive behaviour in children are unclear.

SELF-TEST QUESTIONS

- Can you name the main symptoms of attention deficit hyperactivity disorder (ADHD)?
- What are the different subtypes of ADHD and what other disorders is ADHD likely to be comorbid with?
- What is the evidence that ADHD is genetically determined?
- How might deficits in executive functioning cause ADHD symptoms?
- What prenatal factors have been identified as risk factors for ADHD?
- How might parent–child interactional styles exacerbate the symptoms of ADHD?
- Do children diagnosed with ADHD have a theory of mind (TOM) deficit?
- What are the four main categories of symptoms found with conduct disorder?
- What is oppositional defiant disorder (ODD) and how does it differ from conduct disorder?
- Can you summarize the biological factors that may be involved in the aetiology of conduct disorder?
- What is the evidence that children develop symptoms typical of conduct disorder by mimicking the violent activities they see around them in the media or displayed by peers?
- How can interpretation biases account for behaviours typical of conduct disorder?
- What socioeconomic variables act as risk factors for conduct disorder?

SECTION SUMMARY

16.2 DISRUPTIVE BEHAVIOUR PROBLEMS

- *Disruptive behaviour disorders* are characterized by impulsive, disruptive and poorly controlled behaviour.
- The two main disruptive behaviour disorders are *attention deficit hyperactivity disorder (ADHD)* and *conduct disorder*.
- ADHD can manifest itself as lack of attention, hyperactivity or impulsivity.

- Around 5 per cent of school-age children worldwide are estimated to be diagnosed with ADHD.

- ADHD significantly affects educational achievement and social integration.

- ADHD appears to have a mean heritability estimate as high as 76 per cent.

- ADHD is associated with smaller brain size, deficits in executive functioning and abnormalities in the cerebellum.

- Dysfunctional parent–child interactions may contribute to ADHD but there is no evidence to suggest these are a sole cause of the disorder.

- Conduct disorder can be described as behaviour that is aggressive, causes vandalism, property loss or damage, deceitfulness and lying, and serious violation of accepted rules.

- *Oppositional defiant disorder (ODD)* is a milder form of disruptive behaviour disorder reserved for children who do not meet the full criteria for conduct disorder.

- Prevalence rates for conduct disorder are estimated at 4–16 per cent for boys and 1.2–9 per cent in girls.

- Both genetic and environmental factors appear to be important in the aetiology of conduct disorder.

- Psychological factors influencing conduct disorder symptoms include the nature of the family environment, parent–child relationships and media and peer influences.

- Individuals with conduct disorder appear to develop an information processing bias that leads them to interpret the benign intentions of others as hostile.

16.3 CHILDHOOD AND ADOLESCENT ANXIETY AND DEPRESSION

Frank's story at the beginning of this chapter graphically illustrates some of the distress experienced by children who are exposed to uncertainty and stress early in their lives. As a result of the loss of his parents and being moved to a foster home, he experiences a range of emotions, including rejection, fear, confusion, anger, hatred and misery. By their very nature children are emotionally naive, and will often be unable to label the feelings they experience – they may only know that they feel bad and confused. As was the case with Frank, these feelings often lead the individual to become withdrawn and inward-looking (behaviour that may be labelled by the clinician as representing an *internalizing disorder*) and may serve as the basis for future disorders in adolescence and early adulthood. All of these factors make it difficult for the clinician to identify childhood anxiety and depression. Children who are anxious and depressed tend to be clinging and demanding of their parents and carers, will go to great lengths to avoid some activities, such as school, and will express exaggerated fears – especially of events such as separation from, or the death of, a parent or carer. There has been some success recently in identifying specific disorders in childhood such as

separation anxiety disorder, early onset generalized anxiety disorder (GAD) and obsessive compulsive disorder (OCD). However, anxiety and depression are frequently comorbid in childhood (Manassis & Monga, 2001) and treatment may need to target both conditions. We will now continue by looking separately at the characteristics and known causes of childhood anxiety and childhood depression.

16.3.1 Childhood Anxiety

In childhood, anxiety is primarily manifested as withdrawn behaviour (internalizing). The child will avoid activities where they may have to socialize with others (e.g. school), they will be clinging and demanding of parents and carers (to the point of following a parent from room to room), they will express a desire to stay at home, and they will communicate exaggerated fears over such things as the death of carers or of being bullied by peers. Children tend to be less concerned than do adults about the specific symptoms of their anxiety, but they do tend to report significantly more somatic complaints than non-anxious children (Hofflich, Hughes & Kendall, 2006). Many childhood anxiety disorders do tend to be recognizable as those also found in adulthood (e.g. GAD, OCD and social anxiety disorder). However, at least some manifestations of childhood anxiety tend to be confined to childhood, and separation anxiety is one such example.

The features and characteristics of childhood and adolescent anxiety problems

Separation anxiety

As the name suggests, **separation anxiety** is an intense fear of being separated from parents or carers. It is commonly found in many children at the end of the first year of life but in most children this fear gradually subsides. However, in others it persists well into the school years and may also reappear in later childhood following a period of stress or trauma. Older children with separation disorder will become distressed at being away from home and will often need to know the whereabouts of parents. They may also develop exaggerated fears that their parents will become ill, die or be unable to look after them. Consequences of this anxiety include a reluctance to attend school or to stay at friends' homes overnight, and many will require that a parent or carer stay with them at bedtime until they have fallen asleep. As with most childhood anxiety disorders, sufferers will also report physical complaints such as stomach aches, headaches, nausea and

> **separation anxiety** A childhood anxiety problem involving an intense fear of being separated from parents or carers.

vomiting (DSM-5 Summary Table 16.3). Separation anxiety is often a normal feature of early development but it can be triggered and exaggerated by specific life stressors (such as the death of a relative or pet, an illness, a change of schools or moving home).

The estimated prevalence rate of diagnosable separation anxiety is approximately 4 per cent in children between 6 and 12 months old, and has a 12-month prevalence rate of 1.6 per cent in adolescents (DSM-5, p.192). However, once they have reached the age for school attendance, many children suffering separation disorder go on to exhibit school refusal problems, including social anxiety disorder (Egger, Costello & Angold, 2003).

Obsessive compulsive disorder (OCD)

Often beginning in childhood, OCD is now recognized as a relatively common disorder and its phenomenology in childhood is very similar to adult OCD, with the main features of the disorder in children manifesting as intrusive, repetitive thoughts, obsessions and compulsions. The most common obsession themes in children are contamination, aggression (harm or death), symmetry and exactness; in adolescence, religious and sexual obsessions also become common (Geller, Biederman, Faraone, Agranat *et al.*, 2001).

Common compulsive behaviours in children and adolescents include washing, checking, ordering, touching, repeating and reassurance seeking, as well as covert behaviours such as reviewing or cancelling thoughts, silent prayers or counting (Franklin, Kozak, Cashman, Coles *et al.*, 1998). In adults, compulsions (e.g. behavioural rituals) are rarely found without accompanying obsessions (e.g. intrusive thoughts) but in children compulsions without obsessions can be quite common and these are frequently tactile (e.g. touching, tapping or rubbing rituals) and may be accompanied by behavioural tics (Leckman, Grice, Barr, de Vries *et al.*, 1995). While the range of obsessions and compulsions in childhood and adolescence is very similar to that seen in adults, there are some differences between boys and girls, with boys having an earlier age of onset than girls (Garcia, Freeman, Himle, Berman *et al.*, 2009), girls exhibiting more hoarding compulsions than boys, but boys being more likely to have sexual obsessions than girls (Mataix-Cols, Nakatani, Micali & Heyman, 2008).

Case History 16.2 provides a typical example of the development of OCD in a 13-year-old adolescent boy and demonstrates how rapidly OCD symptoms can manifest and establish themselves in childhood, which is in some contrast to the gradual acquisition found in adulthood.

Age of onset for childhood OCD can be as early as 3–4 years of age but the mean age of onset is more likely to be around 10 years (Swedo, Rapoport, Leonard,

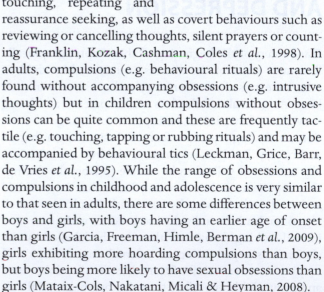

For a video on OCD in children go to **www.wiley-psychopathology.com/video/ch16**

DSM-5 SUMMARY TABLE 16.3 *Criteria for separation anxiety*

- Excessive anxiety surrounding separation from those to whom the individual is attached, as shown by at least three of the following:

  - Disproportionate distress when anticipating or experiencing separation from home or attachment figures

  - Ongoing and unnecessary concern about losing attachment figures or potential harm to them

  - Ongoing and unnecessary concern about an unexpected event which causes separation from attachment figures

  - Ongoing aversion to going out or away from home because of fear of separation

  - Ongoing and unnecessary fear of being left alone or without attachment figures

  - Ongoing aversion to going to sleep alone or sleeping away from home

  - Repeated nightmares around separation

  - Complaints of physical symptoms such as headaches or nausea when separated or anticipating separation from attachment figures

- The anxiety lasts at least 4 weeks in children and 6 months in adults

- The disturbance causes significant impairment in important areas of functioning

- The disturbance is not better explained by another mental disorder

CHILDHOOD AND ADOLESCENT OCD

Andy was a 13-year-old boy diagnosed with isolated testicular relapse of acute lymphoblastic leukaemia 40 days before coming to psychiatric attention. He was first diagnosed with acute lymphoblastic leukaemia at age 10. After his initial diagnosis, he experienced remission at the end of chemotherapy induction and finished his treatment for the disease.

Three years later he began further drug treatment for his leukaemia and the psychiatric consultation liaison service evaluated him after he expressed bothersome obsessive thoughts, compulsive behaviors and insomnia beginning 24–36 hours after he had completed a 28-day course of steroid drug treatment. Andy had no history of psychiatric illness or treatment.

At his initial interview, Andy described increasingly bothersome obsessions over the previous 2 days. He felt that he was 'going crazy' and feared that he would forget how to talk and lose his cognitive abilities. He repeated mantras, reassuring himself that if he remained calm, these bothersome thoughts would pass. He sought reassurance from his mother and the interviewers, and he repeated the 'ABCs' to reassure himself that he could think clearly. His mood was dysphoric, which he attributed both to insomnia and worry surrounding his constant bombardment of unwanted thoughts. He reported no depressive symptoms, perceptual disturbances or suicidal thoughts. He displayed no manic symptoms.

Andy's symptoms rapidly worsened within 24 hours. His thoughts became dominated by fears that he would be condemned to hell and that he deserved this fate. He noted images in his mind of self-harm and harming family members. He struggled against these thoughts and images, as well as guilt from having them, by repeatedly telling family members that he loved them. He continued to deteriorate and struck himself in the head with the blunt end of an ax. He stated that he had no desire to die but had become convinced of the validity of the emerging thoughts that he should harm himself. Although he did not sustain serious injury, he was admitted to a child and adolescent psychiatric inpatient unit for safety.

Clinical Commentary

Andy's symptoms are typical of many adolescents suffering OCD. In his case, these are obsessive thoughts about going mad and harming himself and others. In an attempt to try and prevent his obsessive thoughts entering consciousness, he indulges in protective behaviours, such as repeating mantras, seeking reassurances from adults and reciting the alphabet. The symptoms appear to be precipitated by a stressful illness, and such stressors are common precursors of OCD symptoms in both children and adults. OCD symptoms would normally appear very slowly and have a gradual onset, unlike Andy's which appeared very rapidly over a period of a few weeks. Such rapid acquisition may have been facilitated by the abrupt cessation of steroid drugs that he was receiving as part of his treatment for leukaemia.

Source: Adapted from Morris, D.R., Meighen, K.G. & McDougle, C.J. (2005). Acute onset of obsessive-compulsive disorder in an adolescent with acute lymphoblastic leukemia. *Psychosomatics, 45*(5), 458–460, with permission.

Lenane & Cheslow, 1989). Childhood OCD is regularly found to be comorbid with a range of other disorders, including **tic disorders**, **Tourette's syndrome**, other anxiety disorders and eating disorders (Geller, Biederman, Griffin, Jones & Lefkowitz, 1996). Specifically, over 60 per cent of children seeking treatment for OCD symptoms also have a lifetime history of tics or Tourette's syndrome (Leonard, Lenane, Swedo, Rettew *et al.*, 1992)

tic disorders Uncontrollable physical movements such as facial twitches, rapid blinking or twitches of the mouth.

Tourette's syndrome A disorder in which motor and vocal tics occur frequently throughout the day for at least 1 year.

and 50 per cent of children with Tourette's syndrome subsequently develop OCD (Leckman, 1993). This suggests that childhood OCD and tic disorder may be different manifestations of the same underlying disorder (Swedo, 1994) (see Focus Point 16.1).

Generalized anxiety disorder (GAD)   In children, as in adulthood, GAD usually takes the form of anticipatory anxiety, in which the main feature is chronic worrying about potential problems and threats (see section 6.4). Even in childhood, GAD is differentiated

FOCUS POINT 16.1

CHILDHOOD OCD, TIC DISORDER AND TOURETTE'S SYNDROME

Tourette's syndrome (also known as Tourette's or TS) is a disorder with onset in childhood, characterized by the presence of multiple physical (motor) tics and at least one vocal (phonic) tic. It is important to understand that these are chronic and involuntary. Someone with TS may be able to suppress them for a period but eventually they have to let the tics out.

Tics usually start in childhood around the age of 7 and are likely to persist throughout life, though the symptoms often decrease towards the end of adolescence. The first symptoms are usually facial tics such as rapid blinking or twitches of the mouth. However, TS may start with sounds such as throat clearing and sniffing, or even with multiple tics of movements and sounds. Tics can be either simple or complex. *Simple tics* are of short duration and may include eye blinks, shoulder shrugging, sniffing, grunting or extensions of the extremities. *Complex motor tics* are of longer duration and can consist of combinations of simple tics (e.g. head turning plus shoulder shrugging). They can often appear purposeful when the tic consists of imitating another person's movements, making tic-like obscene or sexual gestures, or uttering socially unacceptable words. For Tourette's disorder, both motor and vocal tics must be present. Tic disorders are more common in children than in adults, in special education populations than in general populations of children, and among boys more than among girls (Knight, Steeves, Day,

For a video on Tourette's syndrome go to www.wiley-psychopathology.com/video/ch16

Lowerison *et al.*, 2012). Tic disorders are relatively common in children, with a point prevalence of transient tic disorder of 2.99 per cent. Tourette's disorder is less common, with a point prevalence of only 0.77 per cent (Knight, Steeves, Day, Lowerison *et al.*, 2012).

Tourette's syndrome and behavioural tics are often comorbid with a diagnosis of OCD in childhood. Studies suggest that up to 60 per cent of children seeking treatment for OCD have a lifetime history of tics (Leonard, Lenane, Swedo, Rettew *et al.*, 1992) and some theorists believe that OCD is a heterogeneous disorder with an inherited component that can manifest either as OCD obsessions or compulsions, or as behavioural or vocal tics (Pauls, Alsobrook, Goodman, Rasmussen & Leckman, 1995).

OCD symptoms and behavioural and vocal tics can cause obvious problems for a child, with them being a source of anxiety and fear for the sufferer and provoking ridicule and victimization by peers (Storch, Ledley, Lewin, Murphy *et al.*, 2006). The severity of behavioural and vocal tics is usually directly related to levels of stress, so learning how to control stress can greatly reduce symptoms (e.g. by learning relaxation techniques). In some cases, a less socially acceptable tic can be replaced with a more socially acceptable one using behaviour therapy methods and medication can also be used to help control the condition. Treatments normally used with OCD symptoms (such as exposure with response prevention or CBT – see section 6.5.2) can also be effective with behavioural tics (Verdellen, Keijsers, Cath & Hoogduin, 2004; Turner, 2006).

---

from other forms of childhood anxiety by being associated with significantly increased levels of **pathological worrying** (Tracey, Chorpita, Douban & Barlow, 1997; Wilson, 2010) and what a child worries about appears to be determined by their age. For example, Muris, Merckelbach & Luijten (2002) found that 4–7-year olds tended to worry about personal harm, separation from parents and imaginary creatures, whereas 11–13-year-olds worried more about social threats and being punished. The number of worries also increases with age, with the number of worries reported by 8-year-olds almost double that reported by 5-year-olds (Muris, Meesters, Merckelbach, Sermon & Zwakhalen, 1998). Epidemiological studies have differed in their

pathological worrying Perseverative worrying that an individual finds uncontrollable.

estimates of GAD in childhood populations, with a UK study estimating GAD in less than 1 per cent of 5–10-year-olds, but an American study reporting 11 per cent of 6–11-year-olds meeting the criteria for 'overanxious disorder'.

Specific phobias Specific fears and phobias are often common in the normal development of children. For example, fears of heights, water, spiders, strangers and separation often occur in the absence of individual learning experiences and appear to represent characteristics of normal developmental stages through which the child passes. A fear may appear suddenly and intensely, but then disappear almost as quickly (Poulton & Menzies, 2002). However, for some children, a fear may persist and become problematic in that it prevents normal daily functioning. One such example in childhood is social phobia (social anxiety disorder) and this often begins in childhood as a fear of strangers (Hudson & Dodd, 2011). Most children will grow out of this fear by around 2–3 years of age but some still persist with their fear of social situations and may find it very difficult to speak to strangers or to be in the presence of strangers. If pushed into social situations, they will often become mute, blush, withdraw or show extreme emotional responses (e.g. burst into tears) (Vasey, 1995). However, children and adolescents with social anxiety disorder are usually well adjusted in all other situations that do not involve significant social interaction (e.g. at home) and this differs from separation disorder in that the latter is characterized by clinging and demanding behaviour at home.

The prevalence for specific phobias in 8–9-year-olds is estimated to be around 7 per cent for boys and 10 per cent for girls (Lichtenstein & Annas, 2000) but up to 76 per cent of adolescents in some cultures report at least one fear and up to 36 per cent meet the lifetime criteria for specific phobia, indicating that specific phobias are a common and enduring problem during childhood and adolescence (Benjet, Borges, Stein, Mendez & Medina-Mora, 2012).

The aetiology of childhood and adolescent anxiety problems

Childhood anxiety and its associated disorders appear to result from a combination of inherited factors and childhood experiences. Children inherit a temperament that may make them more or less vulnerable to life stressors such as inadequate parenting or physical trauma. In addition, children seem to be particularly vulnerable to learning fear and anxiety through indirect routes, such as information from adults, peers, TV and so on (Field, 2006a). Finally, we also need to be aware that the kinds of life events that might mean relatively little to an adult can be viewed as extremely stressful for a child – these include such events as the death of a pet, an illness, starting school or moving house.

Genetic factors   Twin and familial studies of childhood anxiety disorders tend to indicate a significant and stable inherited component. In a familial study of childhood OCD, Pauls, Alsobrook, Goodman, Rasmussen & Leckman (1995) found that rates of OCD were significantly greater in the first-degree relatives of children with OCD than the relatives of control participants without OCD. However, the inherited component appeared to be non-specific, since children with OCD were just as likely to have first-degree relatives with behavioural tics as with specific OCD symptoms. More recent twin studies of anxiety disorders in 7–9-year-olds have suggested a stable heritability averaging 54 per cent across anxiety

disorders (Trzaskowski, Zavos, Haworth, Plomin & Eley, 2012) that may be transmitted by many genetic variants, each with only a modest or small effect in itself (Trzaskowski, Eley, Davis, Doherty *et al.*, 2013). Finally, a study of 1058 pairs of twins aged 8–16 years by Lau, Eley & Stevenson (2006) further implies that levels of state anxiety (anxiety experienced at the moment) are largely determined by environmental factors but trait anxiety (representing a more longer term sensitivity to anxiety) showed moderate genetic effects.

Trauma and stress experiences   Table 16.1 provides striking examples of how childhood trauma and stress represent significant risk factors for a range of later diagnosable adult psychological disorders. It is also self-evident that these experiences will inevitably cause significant psychological stress during childhood (see *Frank's story* at the beginning of this chapter). Many of these experiences (such as childhood physical and sexual abuse) represent extreme experiences for any individual and there are clear links between such experiences and childhood anxiety generally (e.g. Feerick & Snow, 2005; Whiffen & MacIntosh, 2005). However, during childhood, even many experiences that seem relatively unexceptional may seem stressful to a child who is relatively inexperienced in the world and these can provide significant events that trigger bouts of anxiety and distress. For example, living with illnesses such as asthma or eczema has been shown to significantly increase childhood anxiety and reduce quality of life (Lewis-Jones, 2006; Gillaspy, Hoff, Mullins, van Pelt & Chaney, 2002), and the death of a pet – with whom a child may become significantly attached – can cause prolonged anxiety and depression (Kaufman & Kaufman, 2006). Even an event such as a minor road traffic accident may be a new and frightening experience to a child, and a common consequence of such an experience in childhood is a mixture of PTSD symptoms, anxiety and depression (Schafer, Barkmann, Riedesser & Schulte-Markworth, 2006).

Modelling and exposure to information   Whether it is in school, at home or through the media, young children are regularly exposed to information about potential threats and dangers. Children are bombarded with violent and threatening images on television and are being constantly warned about the dangers of sexual molestation, abduction or drugs. Recent experimental evidence suggests that information of this kind may be an important source of childhood fears. Field and his colleagues have developed a valuable experimental procedure for studying how information about a stimulus or event might cause subsequent fear and anxiety. Children are shown pictures of animals they are unfamiliar with (e.g. rare Australian marsupials; Photo 16.1) and then given some information about that animal. Some participants may be told the animal is benign and friendly, while others may be told it is scary and dangerous. In a study with 7–9-year-old children, Field, Argyris & Knowles (2001) found that fear beliefs about an animal increased significantly if the children had been given negative information about the animal – but only if that information had been provided by an adult and not by a peer. Subsequent studies have indicated that the fear generated by negative information can be detected using both explicit and implicit measures of fear, will result in behavioural avoidance of the animal, and can still be detected up to 6 months later (Field & Lawson, 2003; Field, Lawson & Banerjee, 2006). In addition, studies indicate that the child's levels of trait anxiety will facilitate the learning of fear in such situations by increasing biases to attend to stimuli associated with threat information (Field, 2006b). Studies such as these indicate that negative information

about a stimulus or event – especially if it is provided by an authoritative source such as an adult – can cause changes in fear beliefs and behavioural avoidance that are relatively long lasting (up to at least 6 months).

Parenting style

Children are highly dependent on their parents or carers for guidance and emotional support during their development, so it is not surprising that dysfunctional forms of parenting may cause psychological and adjustment problems during childhood. Parents may be detached, rejecting, overly controlling, overprotective or demanding, and each of these different parenting styles may cause anxiety and maladjustment in the child. Research into how parenting style may influence childhood anxiety is relatively underdeveloped at present. However, some studies do suggest links between overprotective and overanxious parenting and a child who is overanxious or suffers separation anxiety (Rapee, 1997; Giotakos & Konstantopoulos, 2002). This appears to result from the parents' overprotectiveness generating a lack of confidence and feelings of inadequacy in the child (Dadds, Heard & Rapee, 1991; Woodruff-Borden, Morrow, Bourland & Cambron, 2002). Specifically, Rapee (2001) has argued that there may be a reciprocal relationship between child temperament and parenting whereby parents of children with an anxious temperament are more likely to become overly involved with the child in an attempt to reduce the child's distress. However, this over-involvement is likely to increase the child's vulnerability to anxiety by increasing the child's perception of threat, reducing the child's perceived control over threat, and increasing avoidance of threat (e.g. Gallagher & Cartwright-Hatton, 2009). Hudson & Rapee (2002) provided some experimental support for this view by reporting that mothers of children with an anxiety disorder were more likely to be intrusive while the child was completing a puzzle task than were mothers of non-anxious control children.

While overprotective parents appear to generate anxiety in their children, so do parents who are rejecting and hostile. Children who experience rejecting or detached parents also show increased levels of anxiety and are often overly self-critical and have poor self-esteem (Chartier, Walker & Stein, 2001; Hudson & Rapee, 2002). For example, anxiety sensitivity (concern over the physical symptoms of anxiety, such as trembling or shaking) is known to be a factor that mediates emotional distress in both adulthood and childhood, and this has been linked to exposure to parental threatening, hostile and rejecting behaviours (Scher & Stein, 2003). Most recently, studies have investigated the differential effects on childhood anxiety that might be made separately by mothers and fathers. Moller, Majdandzic,

© iStock.com/CraigRJD

PHOTO 16.1 *Are you frightened of this animal? Professor Andy Field has developed a procedure for investigating how exposure to information about potential threats affects fear acquisition in children. This photo shows an Australian Quoll – an animal not well known to most children in the northern hemisphere. Some are then told they are potentially dangerous and others told that they are harmless and benign. Children told they are dangerous subsequently fear them more and avoid possible contact with them in experimental approach tasks, and this fear can often last up to 6 months.*

de Vente & Bogels (2013) have argued that the evolved basis of sex differences in parenting means that mothers and fathers will convey different aspects of anxiety to their offspring. Mothers will tend to transmit caution and information about threat (with overly anxious mothers transmitting more anxiety to their offspring), whereas fathers may be more likely to teach their offspring how to explore the environment and compete with others (and in doing so, reduce anxiety).

Clearly, parenting style is likely to be an important factor influencing the development of anxiety symptoms in children. Both overprotective and overly rejecting styles appear to have adverse effects and facilitate anxiety and its cognitive and behavioural correlates (e.g. hypervigilance for threat, avoidance behaviour, and suchlike). Further research is clearly required in this area to clarify the various mechanisms by which such parenting styles have their effects.

16.3.2 Childhood and Adolescent Depression

Depression in childhood is notoriously difficult to identify and parents and teachers regularly fail to recognize its symptoms – especially in very young children (Tarullo, Richardson, Radke-Yarrow & Martinez, 1995). In early childhood, depression will manifest as clingy behaviour, school refusal and exaggerated fears, and is also associated with an increased frequency of somatic complaints such as stomach aches and headaches. However, as they reach puberty and early adolescence, as many as 28 per cent of them, aged up to 19 years, will have experienced a diagnosable episode of depression (Lewinsohn, Rohde & Seeley, 1998). In adolescence, depression will manifest as sulkiness, withdrawing from family activities, weight disturbance, loss of energy, feelings of worthlessness and guilt, and – in extreme cases – suicidal ideation (Roberts, Lewinsohn & Seeley, 1995). The following sections cover the diagnosis and prevalence of childhood depression, and then we will cover some of the theories of its aetiology.

The diagnosis and prevalence of childhood and adolescent depression

With some minor amendments, the diagnostic criteria for depression in childhood are essentially the same as those specified for adult major depression (see DSM-5 Summary Table 7.1). However, some of the symptoms may change with age. Somatic complaints, irritability and social withdrawal are prominent in younger children but psychomotor retardation (slowed thinking and

movement) and hypersomnia (excessive sleeping) are more common in adolescents.

Rates of depression in children are variable and can depend on age. Studies suggest a prevalence rate of less than 1 per cent in pre-schoolers (Kashani & Carlson, 1987) and between 2 and 3 per cent for school-age children (Cohen, Cohen, Kasen, Valez et al., 1993; Lewinsohn, Hops, Roberts, Seeley & Andrews, 1993). This rises to between 4 and 8 per cent for adolescents (Birmaher, Ryan, Williamson, Brent & Kaufman, 1996). As we mentioned earlier, lifetime prevalence rates for depression in adolescents is estimated to be as high as 25–28 per cent (Lewinsohn, Rohde & Seeley, 1998; Kessler, Avenevoli & Merikangas, 2001). There are also some gender differences in adolescence, with depression occurring at around 6 per cent for girls and 4 per cent for boys (Costello, Erkanli & Angold, 2006). In addition, depressed girls more often report weight/appetite disturbances and feelings of worthlessness/guilt than depressed boys (Lewinsohn, Rohde & Seeley, 1998). Lewinsohn, Roberts, Seeley, Rohde et al. (1994) estimated that the mean duration of major depression in adolescence was 26 weeks, with longer durations associated with earlier onset and suicidal ideation. Estimates suggest that around 1–2 per cent of adolescents will have made a suicide attempt between the ages of 14 and 18 years (Lewinsohn, Rohde & Seeley, 1998) and many will also self-harm (see section 7.3).

Childhood depression is highly comorbid with other psychopathologies and around half of adolescents diagnosed with depression will experience at least one other disorder during their lifetime. Twenty per cent of adolescents with depression will be diagnosed with another anxiety disorder and between 13 and 30 per cent will also exhibit a substance use disorder (e.g. alcohol or drug abuse) (Lewinsohn, Rohde & Seeley, 1998). In addition, pre-adolescent depression has been found to be a risk factor for earlier onset of alcohol use in adolescence (Wu, Bird, Liu, Fan et al., 2006). Comorbid depression has a number of serious negative consequences for children and adolescents. It has been shown to adversely affect academic performance; it impairs social functioning generally, when sufferers may be rejected by their peers; it is associated with increased conflict with parents; and it increases the risk of suicide attempts (Lewinsohn, Rohde & Seeley, 1995).

The aetiology of childhood and adolescent depression

Childhood depression appears to have only a modest genetic component, so early experience appears to be a more significant contributor to the disorder. As a result, interest in the aetiology of childhood depression has focused mainly on early experiences, parent–child inter-actions and cognitive factors. We will begin by review-ing the risk factors for childhood depression and then assess the evidence for biological and psychological influences.

Risk factors of childhood depression

Table 16.3 provides an overview of the risk factors known to be associated with depression in adolescents and these range across (1) dispositional factors and existing psychological problems, (2) stress experiences, (3) poor coping skills, (4) poor social support, (5) physical health problems, and (5) poor academic performance – and the greater the number of these risk factors experienced by an adoles-cent, the greater the probability that he/she will become depressed in the future (Lewinsohn, Rohde & Seeley, 1998). Taking the relevant risk factors into account, Lewinsohn, Rohde & Seeley (1998) have drawn up a profile of the 'prototypical adolescent most at risk for depression'. This is described in Focus Point 16.2.

In younger children, childhood abuse or neglect is closely related to the development of depression and appears to generate feelings of worthlessness, betrayal, loneliness and guilt (Dykman, McPherson, Ackerman, Newton et al., 1997; Wolfe & McEachran, 1997). In addi-tion, predictors of depression in children younger than 5 years of age include parental marital partner changes, mother's health problems in pregnancy, the child's health over the first 6 months of life, maternal anxiety and mari-tal satisfaction early in the child's development and the mother's attitude towards caregiving (Najman, Hallam, Bor, Callaghan et al., 2005). Many of these risk factors may affect the quality of mother–child interactions during early development and these may be a significant factor in the development of childhood depression. Childhood adversity generally is also a risk factor for childhood and

adolescent depression, and this includes factors such as financial hardship and chronic illness (Hazel, Hamman, Brennan & Najman, 2008).

TABLE 16.3 Risk factors for adolescent depression

Domain	Specific risk factor
Cognitive	Depressive negative cognitions
	Depressive attributional style
Dispositional factors and other psychopathologies	Self-consciousness
	Low self-esteem
	Emotional reliance
	Current depression
	Internalizing problem behaviours
	Externalizing problem behaviours
	Past suicide attempts
	Past depression
	Past anxiety
Stress	Daily hassles
	Major life events
Social and coping skills	Low self-rated social competence
	Poor coping skills
	Interpersonal conflict with parents
Social support	Low social support from family
	Low social support from friends
Physical	Physical illness
	Poor self-rated health
	Reduced level of activities
	Lifetime number of physical symptoms
	Current rate of tobacco use
Academic	School absenteeism
	Dissatisfaction with grades

Source: Lewinsohn, P.M., Rohde, P. & Seeley, J.R. (1998). Major depres-sive disorder in older adolescents: Prevalence, risk factors, and clinical implications. *Clinical Psychology Review, 18,* 765–794. Reproduced with permission.

FOCUS POINT 16.2

THE PROTOTYPICAL ADOLESCENT MOST AT RISK FOR DEPRESSION

Lewinsohn, Rohde & Seeley (1998, p.778) have pro-vided the following description of the prototypical adolescent most at risk for adolescent depression:

The prototypical adolescent most likely to become depressed is a 16-year-old female who had an early or late puberty. She is experiencing low self-esteem/ poor body image, feelings of worthlessness, pes-simism, and self-blame. She is self-conscious and

overly dependent on others, although she feels that she is receiving little support from her family. She is experiencing both major and minor stress-ors, such as conflict with parents, physical illness, poor school performance, and relationship break-ups; she is coping poorly with the ramifications of these events. Other psychopathologies, including anxiety disorders, smoking and past suicidality, are probably present.

Genetic factors Studies of the heritability of childhood depression have been variable in their findings. Family, twin and adoption studies all suggest that genetic influences on childhood depression may be indirect and have their effects in combination with environmental risks (Rice, 2009; Thapar & Rice, 2006) and, in particular, prepubertal depression is strongly associated with psychological adversity (such as negative childhood experiences) and has a significantly lower heritability component than adult depression (Rice, 2010). Familial studies have indicated a strong link between parental depression and childhood depression, and a child with a depressed parent is almost four times more likely to suffer childhood depression than one without a depressed parent (Hammen & Brennan, 2001). While this is evidence that is consistent with an inherited view of childhood depression, it could also imply that the behaviour of depressed parents may create adverse early experiences that precipitate depression in the child (see later). Finally, the fact that childhood experiences may be significantly more important than inherited factors in causing childhood depression comes from adoption studies. Such studies have provided little or no evidence for a genetic influence on depressive symptoms in childhood (Rice, Harold & Thapar, 2002).

Psychological factors Two major areas of research into the aetiology of childhood depression are (1) the role of parent–child interaction, and (2) the development of dysfunctional cognitions that shape and support depressive thinking in childhood.

We have already noted that children who have depressed parents are themselves more prone to depression and this relationship could be mediated in a variety of ways. First, parents who are depressed may simply transmit their negative and low mood to their children through their interactions with them and children may simply model the behavioural symptoms of depression exhibited by their parents (Jackson & Huang, 2000). Alternatively, depressed parents may not be able to properly respond to their children's emotional experiences and in so doing may leave the child either feeling helpless or unable to learn the necessary emotional regulation skills required to deal with provocative experiences. In support of this view, a study of mother–child interactions by Shaw, Schonberg, Sherrill, Huffman *et al.* (2006) found that depressed mothers were significantly less responsive to their children's expressions of distress than non-depressed mothers. This suggests that depressed mothers may be less sensitive or less knowledgeable about their offspring's emotional distress and this lack of responsiveness may facilitate internalizing symptoms

typical of childhood depression. Unfortunately, many parents exhibit symptoms of depression – especially in the immediate post-partum period – and this factor may be significant in generating internalizing symptoms in their infant offspring. For example, Paulson, Dauber & Leiferman (2006) estimated that 14 per cent of mothers and 10 per cent of fathers exhibited significant levels of depressive symptoms up to 9 months after the birth of a child. In addition, mothers who were post-partum depressed were less likely to engage in healthy feeding and sleeping practices with their infant and depression in both mothers and fathers was associated with fewer positive enrichment activities with the child (e.g. reading, singing songs and telling stories). Finally, those youths (especially girls) who are the offspring of depressed mothers also show increased interpersonal impairment and risk of interpersonal dysfunction (Hammen, 2012). These romantic and interpersonal dysfunctions may not only be a consequence of depression, they may also intensify and maintain the depression (Hammen, 2009).

As the child grows older, symptoms of depression often come to be associated with dysfunctional cognitive characteristics that may function to maintain depressed behaviour. For example, attributional models of adult depression suggest that the depressed individual may have acquired (1) a pessimistic inferential style (attributing negative events to stable, global causes), (2) a tendency to catastrophize the consequences of negative events, and (3) a tendency to infer negative self-characteristics (see Chapter 7) (Abramson, Metalsky & Alloy, 1989). Research on cognitive factors in childhood depression has tended to focus mainly on the role of **pessimistic inferential style** and how this style interacts with

> **pessimistic inferential style** The attribution of negative events to stable, global causes.

negative experiences. For example, children with a pessimistic inferential style have been shown to be more likely to experience increases in self-reported depressive symptoms following negative events than children who do not possesses this inferential style (Hillsman & Garber, 1995), and a pessimistic inferential style interacts with daily hassles (everyday annoyances, like being caught in a traffic jam) to predict increases in depressive symptoms (Brozina & Abela, 2006). Such studies suggest that as the depressed child develops cognitively, they may develop negative ways of construing events that, in conjunction with negative experiences, act to maintain depressed symptomatology. Longitudinal studies have pinpointed a time around 13–14 years of age when depressive attributional styles begin to become stable attributes of the individual and may be a risk factor for lifelong depression (Cole, Ciesla, Dallaire *et al.*, 2008).

SELF-TEST QUESTIONS

- Can you name four different types of diagnosable childhood anxiety disorder?
- How might negative information provide a basis for the learning of anxious responding?
- What is the evidence that 'overprotective parents' generate anxiety in their children?
- How prevalent is depression in childhood and adolescence?
- Can you name some risk factors that may make individuals vulnerable to adolescent depression?
- What is the pessimistic inferential style and how might it contribute to depression in children and adolescents?

SECTION SUMMARY

16.3   CHILDHOOD AND ADOLESCENT ANXIETY AND DEPRESSION

- *Childhood anxiety* and depression are known generally as *internalizing disorders*.

- Diagnosable forms of childhood anxiety include *separation anxiety, obsessive compulsive disorder (OCD), generalized anxiety disorder (GAD)*, *specific phobias* and *social phobia*.

- Genetic factors play a relatively nonspecific role in childhood anxiety by determining general levels of temperament probably transmitted through many gene variants.

- Both trauma and stress experiences, as well as exposure to threat-relevant information, have been shown to cause increases in anxious-responding.

- An *overprotective parenting style* may contribute to, or exacerbate, childhood anxiety.

- As many as 28 per cent of adolescents up to the age of 19 years may have experienced diagnosable episodes of depression.

- *Childhood depression* is highly comorbid with other psychological problems and can have detrimental effects on educational and social functioning.

- Studies suggest a modest genetic component to childhood depression and a substantial environmental component.

- Being reared by a depressed parent may contribute to childhood depression and as the child grows older he or she may develop a *pessimistic inferential style*.

16.4   THE TREATMENT OF CHILDHOOD AND ADOLESCENT PSYCHOLOGICAL PROBLEMS

Many of the treatment methods used with adults have been successfully adapted to treat childhood psychological problems. Children and adolescents with psychological problems will often require a multifaceted approach to treatment, requiring procedures that address one or more of the following: specific symptoms (e.g. enuresis), general emotional states and cognitions (such as anxiety or suicidal ideation), behavioural problems (such as behavioural tics, aggressive and disruptive behaviour), and intrafamily relationships (such as issues relating to effective parenting, parent–child communication, or childhood neglect and abuse). In addition, treatment will have to be provided while the child is still a psychologically and physically developing organism, and in the context of possible ongoing educational, social and familial difficulties. It can be seen that this multicomponent approach is most likely to require a coordinated provision of supervision and treatment which extends across a range of services, including education, health and social services.

In the remainder of this section we will look at individual treatment methods that have been applied to childhood psychological problems. The emphasis here is on specific methodologies and how they have been applied. It is important to note that such procedures may often form part of a broader collection of interventions depending on the needs of the individual child.

16.4.1 Drug Treatments

Drug-based treatments of psychological problems in childhood and adolescence are becoming more widely used as we come to understand the effects that various drugs may have on children (Walkup, Labellarte & Ginsburg, 2002). But the increase in the use of drug treatments for children has alarmed many. For example, the paediatric use of SSRIs had risen by over 50 per cent between 1994 and 2000 (Moynihan, 2003). Much of this increase in prescribing has been for childhood and adolescent depression and has often occurred without regulatory approval – so much so that in 2003 the British Medicines and Healthcare products Regulatory Agency (MHRA) banned the use of SSRIs in children under 18 years of age except for Prozac/fluoxetine. This was followed by a meta-analysis conducted by the US Food and Drug Administration (FDA) suggesting that there is an increased risk of suicidal acts with the use of both SSRIs and SSNIs in young people up to the age of 25 years and that in the case of many individuals the risks outweighed the benefits of such drugs (FDA, 2007). However, other recent inclusive meta-analyses seem to challenge the FDA conclusion and suggest that the benefits may outweigh the risks of SSRIs when treating a range of childhood problems such as depression and non-OCD anxiety disorders (e.g. Bridge, Iyengar, Salary, Barbe et al., 2007), so the debate is still open on this issue.

Fluoxetine has also been used in the treatment of childhood anxiety disorders (excluding the treatment of childhood OCD) and clinical trials have found it to be effective in reducing anxiety symptoms and improving functioning generally (Seidel & Walkup, 2006). Nevertheless, there are a number of reasons why we should be cautious about recommending the use of drug treatments with childhood disorders:

1. Complete remission of symptoms is rarely found, especially in the treatment of childhood depression using SSRIs (Treatment for Adolescents with Depression Study Team, 2004);

2. SSRIs (whether used for the treatment of depression or anxiety) have a number of undesirable side effects in children, including nausea, headaches and insomnia;

3. To date, outcome studies vary considerably in their trial methodology to the extent that the safety and efficacy of such drug treatments cannot yet be assured (Cheung, Emslie & Mayes, 2005); and

 To read Cheung, Emslie & Maye's review of the efficacy and safety of antidepressant use, go to www.wiley-psychopathology.com/reading/ch16

4. Doubts about the safety of many antidepressant drugs when used to treat children have been raised in both the US and UK, to the extent that official warnings have been released in relation to the use of such drugs (Fegert, Janhsen & Boge, 2006).

Despite the difficulties of using pharmacological treatments with childhood anxiety and depression, much greater use has been made of drug treatments in ADHD. US studies indicate that stimulant medication is the most adopted form of treatment for children diagnosed with ADHD, with 42 per cent being treated in this way (Robison, Sclar, Skaer & Galin, 2004), and has been shown to be superior to placebos in reducing symptoms (Schulz, Fleischhaker, Hennighausen, Heiser et al., 2010). The most common form of stimulant medication is **Ritalin (methylphenidate)** and this has been used to treat hyperactive children since the 1950s. Ritalin is an amphetamine that, paradoxically, has a quietening effect on overactive children, decreases distractibility and increases alertness (Konrad, Gunther, Hanisch & Herpertz-Dahlmann, 2004). We are still unsure about how drugs such as Ritalin have their beneficial effects but it may be that they act on the neurotransmitters norepinephrine and dopamine in areas of the brain that play a part in controlling attention and behaviour. As we saw in section 16.2.1, children with ADHD appear to have some deficits in attention and executive functioning that may be redressed by the effects that Ritalin has on neurotransmitter production. Studies have suggested that amphetamines such as Ritalin are effective in reducing the amount of aggressive behaviour in children with ADHD (Fava, 1997) and it can significantly facilitate educational progress (Charach, Ickowicz & Schachar, 2004). However, despite these positive effects, there are still some drawbacks to the use of Ritalin with ADHD. Firstly, while it is effective in reducing symptoms in the short term, its longer term effects have not been fully documented (Safer, 1997). Secondly, Ritalin also has a number of side effects, including reduced appetite, sleeping difficulties, disruption of growth hormone, memory loss and stomach pains. Thirdly, Ritalin is an amphetamine and so can also be used as a drug of abuse, and there is evidence of adolescents using Ritalin as a recreational drug to obtain a 'high' (Kapner, 2003).

Ritalin (methylphenidate) A stimulant medication that is used to treat ADHD.

16.4.2 Behaviour Therapy

Behaviour therapy is a useful means of changing quite specific behaviours and can provide learning-based interventions that allow the individual to change old behaviour patterns or learn new ones. Examples of how this has been used in the treatment of childhood psychological problems include (1) the treatment of symptom-based disorders (such as enuresis), (2) the adaptation of adult behaviour therapy methods (such as systematic desensitization) to use with childhood anxiety disorders, and (3) the development of behaviour change programmes for children with disruptive behaviour disorders.

A widely used classical conditioning method for treating nocturnal enuresis is known as the '**bell-and-battery technique**' (Mikkelsen, 2001). A sensor is placed in the child's underwear when they go to bed and a single drop of urine will be detected by the sensor and set off an auditory alarm that will wake the child (see Figure 16.2). This method allows the child to associate the alarm (the unconditioned stimulus, UCS) with the sensation of a full bladder (the conditioned stimulus, CS), so that the child eventually learns to wake up when he/she experiences a full bladder.

> **bell-and-battery technique**   A widely used classical conditioning method for treating nocturnal enuresis.

Specific behaviour therapy techniques such as *systematic desensitization* (see section 4.1.1) can also be successfully adapted to treat anxiety-based problems in children (King, Muris, Ollendick & Gullone, 2005), although *in vivo* methods appear to be significantly more successful than 'imaginal' desensitization, where the child has to imagine being in fearful situations. Sturges & Sturges (1998) report the successful use of systematic desensitization to treat an 11-year-old girl's elevator phobia. Following an injury to her hand in an elevator door, she refused to ride in elevators. The clinicians developed a behavioural hierarchy in which the sequential steps involved approaching and entering an elevator while reciting self-calming statements that she had agreed with the therapists. The child very quickly resumed elevator use with no reoccurrence of anxiety up to 1 year later.

Selective reinforcement techniques have been used to facilitate academic achievement in children with ADHD and conduct disorder. One view of children with disruptive behaviour disorders is that their disruptive behaviour is positively reinforced by the attention it receives from both peers and adults, and this may especially be the case in the classroom setting. The purpose of introducing a behavioural programme into such settings would be to regularize the reinforcement contingencies in the environment – specifically to ensure that positive behaviours (e.g. attention to the teacher, or thinking through tasks before responding) were rewarded and disruptive behaviours were not. **Time-out (TO)** from positive reinforcement has been found to be an effective means of reducing disruptive behaviours, including aggressiveness, destruction of property and non-compliance in the classroom (Fabiano, Pelham, Manos, Gnagy *et al.*, 2004). In this case, the time-out consisted of the child merely sitting in a specific time-out chair in the classroom for periods of between 5 and 15 minutes. Other studies have established the effectiveness of ignoring non-attention in the classroom (called 'off-task' behaviour) and of rewarding all behaviours that may contribute to the learning task in hand by praising the child. Such behaviours that would be reinforced might include pausing for thought rather than impulsively beginning a task or communicating appropriately with peers and teachers (Stahr, Cushing, Lane & Fox, 2006).

> **time-out (TO)**   A means of reducing disruptive behaviours, including aggressiveness, destruction of property and non-compliance in the classroom, by removing the child from the situation and directing him or her, for example, to sit in a specific time-out chair for periods of between 5 and 15 minutes.

Finally, **behaviour management techniques** can be used in a range of environments and can even be

> **behaviour management techniques**   Treatment methods that can be used in a range of environments and can even be taught to parents as an aid to controlling and responding to their children in the home.

1 drops of urine

2 signal to alarm unit (by wire or radio signal)

DRI Sleeper® Alarm unit

3 alarm sounds

4 child wakes up

Urosensor™

Trains the brain to wake

© DRI Sleeper. Reproduced with permission.

FIGURE 16.2 *Bell-and-battery technique.*
Drops of urine on the sensor pad set off an alarm that wakes the child; this enables the child with nocturnal enuresis to learn to associate a full bladder with waking up.

taught to parents as an aid to controlling and responding to their children in the home. For example, teaching parents to identify and reward positive behaviour also helps to prevent parents from focusing on the negative and disruptive behaviours exhibited by children with both ADHD and conduct disorder. This has the effect of facilitating adaptive behaviour in the child and reducing the parent's negative feelings towards the child (Kazdin & Weisz, 2003).

16.4.3 Family Interventions

Family interventions are popular forms of treatment for many childhood psychological problems, especially because many aetiological models of childhood psychological problems focus on parent–child relationships as one possible cause of the symptoms. Family interventions take a number of forms.

1. **Systemic family therapy** is based on the view that childhood problems result from inappropriate family structure and organization, and the therapist is concerned with the boundaries between parents and children as well as the ways in which they communicate (Minuchin, Rosman & Baker, 1978).

> **systemic family therapy** A family intervention technique based on the view that childhood problems result from inappropriate family structure and organization. The therapist is concerned with the boundaries between parents and children, and the ways in which they communicate.

2. **Parent management training** attempts to teach parents to modify their responses to their children so that acceptable rather than antisocial behaviours are reinforced and this is used especially with the families of children diagnosed with conduct disorder (Kazdin, 2006). This method has been shown to effectively decrease antisocial behaviour and has long-term beneficial effects (Dishion & Andrews, 1995; Brestan & Eyberg, 1998).

> **parent management training** Therapeutic intervention which attempts to teach parents to modify their responses to their children so that acceptable rather than antisocial behaviours are reinforced and this is used especially with the families of children diagnosed with conduct disorder.

3. **Functional family therapy (FFT)** incorporates elements of systemic family therapy and CBT. This approach views childhood problems as serving a function within the family: they may represent maladaptive ways of regulating distance or intimacy between other family members and this type of therapy attempts to change maladaptive interactional patterns and improve communication (Alexander & Parsons,

> **Functional family therapy (FFT)** A family based intervention which focuses on strengthening relationships in the family by opening up communication between parents and children.

1982). In this context, you may also want to have a look at Treatment in Practice Box 10.1, where Sandy – suffering from anorexia – may be using her eating problems as a means of distancing herself from her parents' conflicts and marriage problems.

These various forms of family therapy have been used with children with conduct disorder, ADHD, childhood depression, anxiety problems and eating disorders. Meta-analyses of systemic and family therapies generally conclude that family interventions have a positive effect when compared with no treatment and some alternative treatments (Hazelrigg, Cooper & Borduin, 1987) and a meta-content analysis of 47 randomized controlled outcome studies found that systemic family therapy was effective for treating children with eating disorders, conduct problems and substance use disorders (von Sydow, Beher, Schweitzer-Rothers & Retzlaff, 2006). However, few studies are yet of sufficient methodological rigour to enable us to make definite statements about the longer term efficacy of family therapies; sample sizes are small, the age ranges of participants are varied and there is often a lack of proper randomization in these studies (Cottrell & Boston, 2002).

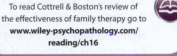 To read Cottrell & Boston's review of the effectiveness of family therapy go to **www.wiley-psychopathology.com/reading/ch16**

16.4.4 Cognitive Behaviour Therapy (CBT)

CBT is becoming an increasingly useful treatment method for children and adolescents, and especially those suffering from anxiety and depression. CBT is mainly used with adolescents and has been shown to significantly reduce symptoms of depression (Brent, Holder, Kolko, Birmaher et al., 1997) and anxiety (Manassis, Mendlowitz, Scapillato, Avery et al., 2002). When used to treat adolescent depression, the purpose of CBT is to help the depressed individual become aware of pessimistic and negative thoughts, depressive beliefs and causal attributions in which the adolescent blames themselves for failures but does not take the credit for successes. Once these thoughts have been identified, the client is taught how to substitute more realistic and constructive cognitions for the dysfunctional ones. A further goal of the therapy is to increase the client's engagement with behaviours that will elicit positive reinforcement (e.g. Rohde, Feeny & Robins, 2005). Other important components of CBT for adolescent depression that help the efficacy of such treatments include (1) increasing and improving social interactions, (2) improving problem-solving skills, (3) improving goal-setting and attainment skills, and (4) involving parents closely in the therapy (parents are often the ones who refer their children for treatment and ensure treatment attendance, and they may contribute to the child's depression through their own problems and difficulties) (Curry & Wells, 2005).

CBT for anxious children is also constructed to enable the child to become aware of problematic thoughts and feelings (Kendall, Kane, Howard & Siqueland, 1990). A typical treatment programme involves (1) recognition of anxious feelings and somatic reactions, (2) understanding the role of cognitions and self-talk in exacerbating anxious situations, (3) learning the use of problem-solving and coping skills to manage anxiety, (4) using self-evaluation and self-reinforcement strategies to facilitate the maintenance of coping, and (5) implementing a plan of what to do in order to cope when in an anxious situation. CBT has been successfully used to treat a range of childhood anxiety disorders, including OCD, GAD, specific phobias, social phobia and separation anxiety, and has been used with children aged between 8 and 18 years (Chu & Kendall, 2004; O'Kearney, Anstey & von Sanden, 2006). Long-term follow-up studies suggest that treatment gains are maintained over 3 years after treatment (Kendall & Southam-Gerow, 1996). CBT for childhood anxiety appears to be equally as effective as medication alone (O'Kearney, Anstey & von Sanden, 2006) and family psychoeducation alone (Kendall, Hudson, Gosch *et al.*, 2008) but is less effective for children under 4 years of age (Rapee, Abbott & Lyneham, 2006). More recent developments include computerized CBT for children and adolescents (Stallard, Richardson, Velleman & Attwood, 2011), CBT for violent behaviour in children (Ozabaci, 2011) and childhood insomnia (Paine & Gradisar, 2011). Finally, family interventions can also be used successfully to teach parents how to use basic CBT procedures to address their children's anxiety and such family-based interventions already show much promise (Cartwright-Hatton, McNally, Field, Rust *et al.*, 2011).

16.4.5   *Play Therapy*

Play therapy covers a useful set of techniques that can be used with younger children who are less able to communicate and express their feelings verbally (Carmichael, 2006). Play in itself can have curative properties and can enable children to feel less anxious or depressed. However, it can also be used to help children express their concerns, to control their behaviour (e.g. by learning restraint when a child is impulsive or aggressive) and to learn coping strategies and adaptive responses when experiencing stress (e.g. Pedro-Carroll & Reddy, 2005; Gil, 1991). Through **play therapy**, children develop a positive relationship with a therapist, learn to communicate with others, express feelings, modify behaviour, develop problem-solving skills, and learn a variety of ways of relating to others. As such, play therapy has been used in a range of mental health contexts to control anger, deal with grief and loss, divorce and family problems, crisis and trauma, and

> **play therapy** A range of play-based therapeutic and assessment techniques that can be used with younger children who are less able to communicate and express their feelings.

has proven useful across a range of childhood psychological problems including anxiety, depression, ADHD, conduct disorder, autism and learning disorders (see Chapter 17) (Landreth, 2002; Bratton, Ray, Rhine & Jones, 2005). Teenagers and adults have also benefited from play therapy methods and the use of these techniques has increased with these client groups in recent years (Pedro-Carroll & Reddy, 2005). Treatment in Practice Box 16.1 provides a couple of detailed examples of play therapies and more can be found in Hall, Kaduson & Schaefer (2002).

CLINICAL PERSPECTIVE: TREATMENT IN PRACTICE 16.1
PLAY THERAPY

© Jennifer Harrison

Therapist playing with a child using puppets. Child posed by model.

Play therapy is a term used to cover a range of therapies that build on the normal communicative and learning processes of children. Clinicians may use play therapy to help a child articulate what is troubling them, to control their behaviour (e.g. impulsive or aggressive behaviour), and to learn adaptive responses when the child is experiencing emotional problems or skills deficits. Below are two examples of specific play therapies, one designed to help children practice self control (the 'Slow Motion Game') and the other to enable children to communicate any distress they are feeling (the 'Puppet Game').

THE SLOW MOTION GAME

Therapeutic rationale

It is well known that children learn best by doing. The Slow Motion Game (by Heidi Kaduson; see Kaduson & Schaefer, 2001, pp.199–202) was designed to have children actively practise self-control over their movements in a playful group context.

Description

Materials needed: stopwatches for each child, cards (see below), dice, poker chips, paper and colouring materials.

To begin, the therapist introduces the concept of self-control, discussing how it is very difficult to maintain self-control when we are moving too fast. Next, the children are asked to illustrate what fast moving looks like. Once it is clear that the children understand the concept of self-control, each child is given a stopwatch. In the centre of the table are cards created by the therapist with various scenes that the children must act out in slow motion. For example, playing soccer, doing jumping jacks or taking a maths test. The children are instructed to roll their dice to see who goes first. The highest number goes first and that child picks a card and goes to the front of the room with the therapist. The therapist tells the group what that child is going to do in 'very slow motion'. On the count of three, all of the children start their stopwatches. Every 10 seconds, the group reports to the child performing the task how much time has passed. When the child has reached a full minute, the group yells 'Stop'. Having successfully completed the task, the child receives a poker chip. Then the next child (working in a clockwise direction) picks a card and the game starts again. Once each child has had a turn, the time is increased to 2 minutes and the second round begins. At the end of the second round, each player will have two chips each and a snack or treat is provided as a reward. The therapist can also give each child a certificate for 'Achievement in Slow Motion'.

Applications

The Slow Motion Game is successful with any group of children that has difficulty maintaining self-control. Also, common board games can be effectively used to increase children's self-control. For example, *Jenga*, *Operation*, *Perfection* and *Don't Break the Ice*.

USING A PUPPET TO CREATE A SYMBOLIC CLIENT

Therapeutic rationale

Puppets serve a crucial role in play therapy. Frequently, children project their thoughts and feelings onto puppets. In this way, puppets allow children the distance needed to communicate their distress. Furthermore, the puppets serve as a medium for the therapist to reflect understanding and provide corrective emotional experiences in the context of the children's play. Most children naturally project their experiences onto the puppets. However, some children are too fearful and withdrawn to become involved in any aspect of therapy. By using the puppet as a symbolic client (a game created by Carolyn J. Narcavage; see Kaduson & Schaefer, 1997, pp. 199–203), the therapist is able to engage these children and overcome resistance. The creation of the symbolic client removes the focus from the child, thereby increasing the child's comfort level and allowing him or her to remain at a safe emotional distance.

Description

Materials needed: puppets.

Once the therapist recognizes that the child is frightened, the therapist might show the child a puppet, remark that it is frightened, and reassure it of its safety. Next, the therapist should enlist the help of the child in comforting the puppet. By completing these few simple steps, the therapist has achieved three essential goals: the therapist has (1) responded and empathized with the child's feelings in a non-threatening manner, (2) begun the child's participation in therapy, and (3) started fostering a positive therapeutic relationship with the child. The puppet often becomes a safety object for the child throughout therapy.

Applications

This technique is particularly effective for any child between 4 and 8 years of age who is anxious or withdrawn in the beginning stages of therapy. A variation of this technique would be to have the puppet present with the same problem as the child and to enlist the child's help in brainstorming solutions to solve the puppet's problem.

Source: From, Hall, Kaduson & Schaefer (2002). Fifteen effective play therapy techniques. *Professional Psychology: Research and Practice, 33,* 515–522. American Psychological Association. Reproduced with permission.

There has been some criticism of play therapy in the past, with critics suggesting that it lacks an adequate research base to justify its use (Reade, Hunter & McMillan, 1999; Campbell, 1992). However, more recent meta-analyses of outcome studies suggest that children treated with play therapy function significantly better after therapy than those who have had no treatment (Bratton, Ray, Rhine & Jones, 2005). Play therapy also appears to be effective across modalities, settings, age and gender, and has positive effects on children's behaviour generally, their social adjustment and their personality.

SECTION SUMMARY

16.4   THE TREATMENT OF CHILDHOOD AND ADOLESCENT PSYCHOLOGICAL PROBLEMS

This section has described a number of different interventions that are regularly used to treat childhood and adolescent psychological problems. Although drug treatments are becoming more common for a number of disorders, there is still much uncertainty about their effectiveness and their safety. Common treatment methods include behaviour therapy, family therapy, CBT and play therapy, and these forms of treatment will be adapted to the specific therapeutic needs of the child and often used in a multifaceted approach to ensure improvements across emotional, educational and social functioning.

To summarize the key points:

- Treatment for childhood psychological problems requires a coordinated provision of services that extends across educational, health and social services.

- Drug treatments are used for childhood anxiety and depression, and ADHD, but there are still significant doubts about the safety of many medications used with children.

- *Ritalin* is a stimulant medication that is used to treat ADHD in around half of those diagnosed with the disorder.

- *Behaviour therapy* techniques can be adapted to treat many childhood behaviour problems. Techniques used include the *bell-and-battery technique* for enuresis, *systematic desensitization* for anxiety problems and *time-out (TO)* to reduce disruptive behaviours.

- Important family interventions include *systemic family therapy*, *parent management training* and *functional family therapy (FFT)*.

- *Cognitive behaviour therapy (CBT)* has been successfully adapted to treat childhood and adolescent depression and anxiety, as well as a number of other childhood psychological problems.

- *Play therapy* covers a range of techniques that can be used with younger children who are less able to communicate and express their feelings.

16.5   CHILDHOOD AND ADOLESCENT PSYCHOLOGICAL PROBLEMS REVIEWED

There is a range of difficulties involved in the identification, diagnosis and treatment of childhood psychological problems that are not usually encountered in adult mental health problems. First, children are often unable to communicate any distress they are feeling and may lack the self-awareness to identify individual symptoms of psychopathology, such as anxiety or depression. Second, childhood psychopathology is a relatively neglected area of clinical research and much of childhood psychopathology has previously been rather simplistically labelled as either internalizing (reminiscent of anxiety or depression) or externalizing (exhibiting signs of disruptive and aggressive behavioural problems). However, research in this area has increased significantly in recent years and we are now able to identify specific childhood disorders such as childhood depression, OCD and generalized anxiety disorder, as well as two important disruptive behaviour disorders – ADHD and conduct disorder.

We are still some way from fully understanding the aetiology of most childhood psychological problems, although some do have significant genetic components (e.g. ADHD) while others appear to be related to important developmental factors such as the nature of the family environment, parent–child relationships and the socioeconomic climate in which the child is being reared.

Treatment for childhood disorders is usually multifaceted and takes place in the context of a coordinated provision of supervision and treatment that extends across a range of services, including education, health and social services. While there are drug treatments for many childhood psychological problems, there are still significant doubts about the effectiveness and safety of many of these treatments. More widely adopted are adaptations of adult psychotherapies, including behaviour therapy, family based interventions and CBT. Play therapy also offers a useful eclectic intervention that can be used with younger children who are less able to communicate and express their feelings verbally.

To access the online resources for this chapter go to
www.wiley-psychopathology.com/ch16

Reading	Video	Activity
• Journal article: Developmental psychopathology and the diagnosis of mental health problems among youth	• Young people and anxiety	• Activity 16.1
• Journal article: Review of the efficacy and safety of antidepressants in youth depression	• Children with ADHD	• Self-test questions
• Journal article: Practitioner review: The effectiveness of systemic family therapy for children and adolescents	• OCD in children	• Revision flashcards
• Glossary of key terms	• Tourette's syndrome	• Research questions
• Clinical issues		
• Links to journal articles		
• References		

17 Neurodevelopmental Disorders

To access the online resources for this chapter go to
www.wiley-psychopathology.com/ch17

ROUTE MAP OF THE CHAPTER

This chapter begins by describing the way in which learning, intellectual and developmental disabilities are defined and the terminology that is associated with these disabilities. The chapter then proceeds to discuss factors associated with the diagnosis, aetiology and treatment of three groups of disabilities, namely specific learning disabilities (e.g. specific disorders of reading, writing and communication), intellectual disabilities and, finally, autistic spectrum disorder.

CHAPTER OUTLINE

LEARNING OUTCOMES

When you have completed this chapter you should be able to:

1. Discuss the different ways in which learning and developmental disabilities are categorized and labelled.

2. Describe and compare the various types of specific learning disabilities, their aetiology and treatment.

3. Describe the various forms of intellectual disability.

4. Compare and contrast genetic, biological and environmental causes of intellectual disabilities.

5. Describe and evaluate the main forms of intervention, care and support for intellectual disabilities.

6. Describe the diagnostic criteria for autistic spectrum disorder.

7. Compare and contrast theories of the aetiology of autistic spectrum disorder.

8. Describe and evaluate the main forms of intervention, care and support for individuals with autistic spectrum disorder.

During childhood, no one knew what I had. I was considered 'crazy' by a doctor at age 1 because I had constant tantrums, which only ended, one day, when my mother took me to the beach during a holiday. My nerves suddenly were calmed down by the sight and the soothing sounds of the sea. I was beginning to say my first words and started to make some progress.

Despite the progress, I still had strange behaviours, like spinning plastic lids, jars and coins. I rejected teddy bears that other toddlers liked, but held on to other objects, like dice (which had a smooth surface and were pleasant to touch). I was terrorized by everyday noises, like planes passing by, thunder, machinery, drills, balloons bursting and any sudden noise.

Being the firstborn, my mother didn't take notice of behaviours like rocking back and forth, or spending time on a rocking horse in the day care centre as a toddler instead of playing with other kids.

Despite socializing difficulties, my interest for reading and learning the alphabet pleased my mother. Instead of pointing out pictures in a newspaper my mother was reading, I asked her what the letters were, and that prompted her to teach me to read before starting school.

Socially, I had problems that worried people. I was not able to recognize people easily, and was not able to decode nonverbal cues. My mother complained about always having to spell things out to me. While my younger (non-autistic) brother seemed to know instinctively when to bring up a subject, or when to say a joke, I was a nuisance, because I couldn't tell if somebody was angry, sad, tired, and so on, just by looking at him/her. I took things literally and was terrorized by my mother's 'threats', which my younger brother did not take seriously. She uttered threats like 'I will send you away' when we behaved badly. My brother was able to understand that she never meant it; however, I was terrorized by them.

One thing that discouraged socializing was that most others did not like to talk about insects, calculators, or space all the time. Other people liked my subjects 'once in a while' but got angry if I went on and on. My mother constantly reminded me not to talk about the same things over and over. Changing subjects was hard for me. I was fixated on certain subjects like entomology and arachnology. Nobody cares to hear about the chelate pedipalps of pseudoscorpions.

George's Story

Introduction

Neurodevelopmental disorders are a category of disorders that typically begin to manifest in early development and may affect intellectual, social and motor development, and as a consequence will have effects on academic achievement, the development of social behaviours and subsequent occupational functioning. In this chapter, we will cover three categories of neurodevelopmental disorder – specific learning disorders, intellectual disabilities and autistic spectrum disorder. Each of these categories is characterized by a specific impairment in learning or control (e.g. language or communication disorders, such as dyslexia), or impairments that can cover both intellectual and social domains (e.g. autistic spectrum disorder), or global impairments to intellectual, social and motor skills (e.g. intellectual disability). A neurodevelopmental disorder can be considered as a significant, lifelong condition that is usually present from birth, but it may often not be recognized until the individual fails to reach important milestones in their development. Failing to sit up, to talk, to read, or attend to what is going on in the world are all possible signs of a learning disability if these activities do not appear as expected at normal developmental intervals. Most neurodevelopmental disorders are permanent conditions, but with suitable support and encouragement many people with these conditions can acquire practical and social skills even if this may take them longer than normal.

George's story describes the early life of someone diagnosed with autistic spectrum disorder. This involves difficulties in interpreting nonverbal behaviour, impairment in communicating with others and a repetitive preoccupation with individual objects, activities or topics. This personal account provides a striking insight into how these disabilities can affect normal day-to-day living during childhood. George prefers indulging in stereotyped behaviours, such as rocking, to playing with other kids. He is unable to understand both normal verbal innuendo and the nonverbal body language that most of us learn to understand implicitly. This causes him to be seen by others as 'difficult', uncommunicative and 'a nuisance', all of which in turn causes him to feel more anxious and distressed. Most neurodevelopmental disorders, no matter how specific, cause problems across the whole range of life activities, including educational, social and occupational, but the degree to which sufferers have problems in these areas of functioning will depend on their background and family circumstances and the nature and degree of the disability.

This chapter will look in detail at the various types of neurodevelopmental disorder, their aetiology and the various treatment and caring options that are available for these disabilities.

17.1 THE CATEGORIZATION AND LABELLING OF NEURODEVELOPMENTAL DISORDERS

In this chapter learning disabilities are divided into three broad categories. These are (1) *specific learning disabilities*, such as language and communication disabilities, (2) *intellectual disability*, covering some of the more severe learning difficulties, and (3) *autistic spectrum disorder*, which covers a range of deficits in social communication, often with accompanying intellectual impairment.

There is considerable diversity across different areas of the world about how various learning disabilities should be labelled. In the UK, Europe and much of Australasia the term **learning disability** has often been used as an umbrella term to cover disorders across all three of the main categories described above – and it is especially used in this way by health and social care services. In DSM-IV-TR, the term *mental retardation* referred to a specific diagnostic category of disorder defined as significantly below average intellectual functioning, characterized by an IQ of 70 or below (DSM-IV-TR, p.49). However, the term mental retardation is now commonly frowned upon as stigmatizing and demeaning and was replaced in DSM-5 by the label 'intellectual disability' and in ICD-11 by 'intellectual development disorder' – a change that was required by federal statute in the United States and was known as Rosa's Law. There is as yet no genuine international consensus on the use of these categories and labels, and even within countries these terms can change quite frequently to reflect shifts in social attitudes towards individuals with learning disabilities. Nevertheless, no matter how much we may believe that labels for such groups of people may be stigmatizing, it would be difficult to understand the aetiology of these disorders and to organize services and support if there were no way of defining their specific problems.

> **learning disability** An umbrella term to cover specific learning disabilities, intellectual disabilities and pervasive developmental disorders.

> For a video on learning and intellectual disabilities go to www.wiley-psychopathology.com/video/ch17

> To read about Rosa's Law go to http://tinyurl.com/pgyqk5n

SELF-TEST QUESTION

- How are the terms specific learning disability, intellectual disability and autistic spectrum disorder defined?

17.2   SPECIFIC LEARNING DISABILITIES

DSM-5 divides specific learning disabilities into two broad categories: (1) *specific learning disorder*, which covers difficulties in learning and using academic skills such as reading and writing, and (2) *communication disorders*, which covers deficits in language, speech and communication generally.

17.2.1   Specific Learning Disorder

Specific learning disorder refers to a number of disabilities that each affect the individual's performance on standardized tests of academic ability such as reading, mathematics or written expression. Individuals with these disabilities show levels of achievement well below what would be expected for their age, schooling and level of intelligence. As we shall see below, individuals with specific learning disorders can show deficits in perceptual organization (organizing information), auditory and visual perception, memory, and attention. Without special remedial support, individuals with these disabilities will normally perform badly at school, be viewed as failures by friends and family, and as a consequence exhibit low self-esteem and motivation (Bjorkland & Green, 1992). Similarly, school drop-out rates for children with specific learning disabilities are high and they will also experience difficulties in occupational and social functioning. Specific learning disorder is diagnosed when there are deficits or impairments in the individual's ability to either perceive or process information accurately, which will eventually manifest in academic circumstances as difficulties in reading, writing or in mathematical ability. DSM-5 has incorporated a number of previously different disabilities (such as dyslexia and dyscalculia) into a single **specific learning disorder** diagnostic category, and defines disabilities in this category as difficulties in learning and using academic skills in one or more areas such as slow reading, difficulty

specific learning disorder Diagnostic category including disorders such as dyslexia and communication disorders.

understanding the meaning of what is read, difficulties with spelling and written expression, difficulty mastering number sense, and difficulties with mathematical reasoning. DSM-5 Summary Table 17.1 provides the diagnostic criteria for specific learning disorder. Table 17.1 describes some of the specific disabilities covered under this diagnostic category and provides some examples.

Specific learning disabilities such as these are often commonly comorbid with other childhood psychological problems, and studies suggest that specific learning disabilities can be diagnosed in 79 per cent of children with bipolar disorder, 71 per cent with ADHD, 67 per cent with autism, and slightly lower percentages with anxiety and depression (18–19 per cent) (Mayes & Calhoun, 2006). Literacy problems generally are associated with increased risk for both externalizing and internalizing disorders in childhood and this may be due either to the stressors associated with academic failure (causing anxiety and depression) or the fact that certain types of cognitive deficit (such as attention deficits) may be common to a number of different disorders, including specific learning disorders and disruptive behaviour disorders such as ADHD (Maughan & Carroll, 2006).

DSM-5 SUMMARY TABLE 17.1 *Criteria for specific learning disorder*

- Impediments in learning and using academic skills, marked by at least one of the following over a 6 month period:
  - Inaccurate or slow and struggling reading
  - Difficulty understanding the meaning of read words
  - Spelling difficulties
  - Difficulties in expression through writing
  - Difficulties understanding numbers
  - Difficulties with mathematical reasoning
- The affected academic skills are substantially below what would be expected for the patient's age
- The difficulties are not better accounted for by intellectual disabilities, vision or hearing difficulties or other mental or neurological disorders

TABLE 17.1 *Specific learning disabilities*

Disability	Description	Example symptoms
Problems with accurate or fluent word recognition, poor decoding and poor spelling abilities (formerly classified as *dyslexia*)	Reading achievement is substantially below the norm for chronological age, intelligence and educational level	• Omit, add or distort the sound of words when reading • Read slowly and with poor comprehension
Problems with written expression	Writing skills are substantially below those expected for chronological age, intelligence and educational level	• Regular errors in spelling, grammar or punctuation
Difficulties mastering number sense, number facts or calculation (formerly classified as *dyscalculia*)	Mathematics ability is substantially below norm for chronological age, intelligence and educational level	• Difficulty remembering arithmetic facts (e.g. to 'carry' a number) • Failure to understand arithmetic concepts
Difficulties with verbal and written expression	Scores on tests of expressive language development are substantially below those for chronological age, intelligence and educational level	• Markedly limited vocabulary • Making errors in tense • Difficulty recalling the right word

Dyslexia

Dyslexia is a complex pattern of learning difficulties associated with difficulties in word recognition while reading, poor spelling and difficulties with written expression. Reading may be characterized by word distortions, substitutions or omissions and is generally slow, with the child having difficulty fully comprehending what has been read. Between 3 and 17.5 per cent of school-age children have specific developmental reading problems (DeFries, Fulker & LaBuda, 1987; Shaywitz, Shaywitz, Pugh, Fulbright *et al.*, 1998) and around 60–80 per cent of those diagnosed are likely to be boys (Shaywitz, Shaywitz, Fletcher & Escobar, 1990). This gender difference may be due to a number of factors, including

1. higher referral rates in males because they may be more disruptive than girls in learning environments;

2. girls may at least partially offset their reading difficulties by enjoying reading more than boys (Chiu & McBride-Chang, 2006); and

3. girls may have more effective coping strategies than boys for dealing with reading difficulties (Alexander-Passe, 2006).

Most longitudinal studies suggest that reading problems can often be persistent and chronic, which does not simply represent a developmental lag in reading ability but is evidence for a specific learning disorder (Bruck, 1992; Scarborough, 1990; Francis, Shaywitz, Stuebing, Shaywitz & Fletcher, 1996). For example,

even though children with impaired reading skills show an improvement in reading ability with age, a gap in reading ability remains across time between children with reading impairments and those without. In individuals suffering dyslexic problems, writing skills fall significantly below those expected for the child's chronological age, IQ and educational history. The child will have difficulty composing written text (Photo 17.1) and will exhibit grammatical errors, punctuation errors, poor paragraph organization, spelling errors and poor handwriting.

Dyscalculia

The main feature of dyscalculia is that mathematical or arithmetical ability falls significantly short of that expected for the child's chronological age, IQ and educational history. Individual skills that may be impaired in **dyscalculia** are (1) understanding or naming mathematical terms, (2) decoding problems into mathematical terms, (3) recognizing and reading numerical symbols or arithmetical signs, (4) copying numbers or symbols correctly, (5) remembering to conduct certain mathematical operations (such as 'carrying' figures when making calculations), and (6) following sequences of mathematical steps in the correct order. It is estimated that around 3–4 per cent of school-age children may suffer from developmental dyscalculia, with the male to female ratio as high as 4:1 (Reigosa-Crespo, Gonzalez-Alemany, Leon, Torres & Mosquera, 2013).

dyscalculia A specific learning disability characterized by mathematical ability being substantially below norm for chronological age, intelligence and educational level.

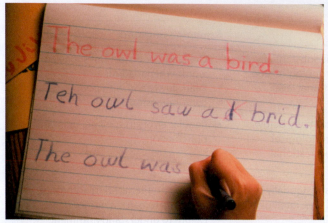

Will and Deni McIntyre/Science Source, National Audubon Society Collection/Photo Researchers, Inc. Reproduced with permission.

PHOTO 17.1 *Dyslexia includes deficits in spelling and writing as well as reading. Other symptoms of dyslexia can include poor comprehension, reversal of words or letters while reading, and difficulty decoding syllables or single words and associating them with specific sounds (phonics). Here, a child with dyslexia attempts to reproduce a teacher's sentence.*

17.2.2   Communication Disorders

Communication disorders include impairments in language, speech and communication, and here we will cover the DSM-5 diagnostic categories of *language disorder*, *speech sound disorder* and *childhood-onset fluency disorder* (otherwise known as 'stuttering').

> **communication disorders** Problems with the articulation of sounds.

Language disorder

Language disorder concerns problems with language acquisition and use as a result of problems in vocabulary comprehension and production, and in the construction of sentences. This usually results in a significantly smaller vocabulary size, with grammatical and tense errors. These problems will appear during early development and persist into adolescence and adulthood (DSM-5 Summary Table 17.2). General features of the disorder include a limited amount of speech, limited vocabulary, difficulty learning new words, difficulty finding the right word (e.g. unable to come up with the word *car* when pointing to a car), shortened sentences, simple grammatical structures (e.g. use of relatively few verb forms), omission of critical parts of sentences, unusual word order and slow language development generally. Language disorder is often comorbid in younger children

> **language disorder** A disability concerned with problems in vocabulary comprehension and production.

with speech sound disorder (see below), reflecting a general impairment in the fluidity of language and erratic speech rhythms. Language disorder can be identified as early as age 2–3 years (Eisenwort, Marschik, Fladerer, Motl *et al.*, 2004), but milder forms may not become apparent until early adolescence.

Speech sound disorder

This is a disorder characterized by persistent difficulty with speech sound production and to be diagnosed with **speech sound disorder** these impairments must be problems in effective communication that interfere with social, academic or occupational achievement (DSM-5 Summary Table 17.3). The disorder includes errors of sound production (e.g. using a *t* sound to represent the letter *k*) and the omissions of sounds – especially from the ends of words. Sufferers will also be unable to categorize speech sounds and will be unable to decipher which sounds in the language make a difference in meaning. The most severely misarticulated sounds are those learnt later in the developmental process, such as *l*, *r*, *s*, *z*, *th* and *ch*, and lisping is particularly common (e.g. saying *wabbit* instead of *rabbit*). Speech sound disorder may often be associated with physical causes, such as a hearing impairment, cleft palate, neurological limitations such as cerebral palsy, and ear, nose and throat problems (Fox, Dodd & Howard, 2002), but at least 3 per cent of pre-school children are diagnosed with a speech sound disorder of unknown origin. Prevalence rate of similar or related speech sound disorders is around 2 per cent in 6–7-year-olds falling to 0.5 per cent by age 17 years (DSM-IV-TR, p.66).

> **speech sound disorder** Persistent difficulty with speech sound production that interferes with speech intelligibility or prevents verbal communication of messages.

DSM-5 SUMMARY TABLE 17.2 *Criteria for language disorder*

- Ongoing difficulties in the attainment and use of language (including spoken and written), due to difficulties in understanding and emitting that include the following:
  - Reduced vocabulary
  - Limited sentence structure ability
  - Difficulties in dialogue
- Abilities are substantially below what would be expected for the patient's age
- Symptoms start in early development
- The difficulties are not better accounted for by vision or hearing difficulties, motor dysfunction or other mental or neurological disorders

DSM-5 SUMMARY TABLE 17.3 *Criteria for speech sound disorder*

- Ongoing difficulty with speech sound production that causes problems with speech understanding or prevents verbal communication

- The difficulty causes limitations in effective communication, interfering with social participation, academic or occupational performance

- Symptoms start in early development

- Difficulties are not better accounted for by congenital or acquired conditions including cerebral palsy, deafness or other medical conditions

DSM-5 SUMMARY TABLE 17.4 *Criteria for childhood-onset fluency disorder (stuttering)*

- Ongoing disturbance of normal fluency and time patterns in speech, inappropriate to the patient's age and language skills, as marked by at least one of the following:

  - Sound and syllable repetitions

  - Sound prolongation of consonants and vowels

  - Broken words

  - Filled or unfilled pauses in speech

  - Word substitution to avoid difficult words

  - Word pronunciation with excessive physical tension

  - Monosyllabic whole-word repetitions

- The disturbance causes anxiety about speaking or limitation in effective communication

- Symptoms start in early development

- Difficulties are not better accounted for by speech-motor or sensory deficit or other medical condition

Childhood-onset fluency disorder (stuttering)

This is a problem with the fluency and time-patterning of speech which involves (1) frequent repetitions or prolongations of sounds, (2) pauses within words, (3) filled or unfilled pauses in speech, (4) word substitutions to avoid pronouncing problematic words, (5) words produced with an excess of physical tension, and (6) monosyllabic word repetitions (e.g. 'go-go-go-go out of the room') (DSM-5 Summary Table 17.4). Fearful anticipation of **stuttering** may develop in many sufferers and this may make stuttering worse in stressful situations, such as when giving a speech or at an interview. Stuttering may be accompanied by physical symptoms such as eye blinks, tics, tremors, jerking of the head and clenching fists. As can be envisaged, stuttering can also have highly detrimental effects on social and occupational functioning. Onset of stuttering typically occurs between 2 and 7 years of age, with a peak onset around 5 years. The onset is usually insidious and initially the child may be unaware of stuttering. However, as awareness increases, the child will develop compensatory strategies for avoiding words and situations that cause stuttering. Community studies estimate prevalence rates of **childhood-onset fluency disorder (stuttering)** for all individuals at 0.7 per cent, rising to 1.4 per cent in young children and dropping to 0.5 per cent in adolescents (Craig, Hancock, Tran, Craig & Peters, 2002). However, the prognosis for stuttering is good, with around 40 per cent of sufferers overcoming the problem before they start school and 80 per cent overcoming it before adolescence (Couture & Guitar, 1993).

> **stuttering** A disturbance in the normal fluency and time patterning of speech that is inappropriate for the individual's age.

> **childhood-onset fluency disorder (stuttering)** A problem with the fluency and time-patterning of speech which involves frequent repetitions or prolongations of sounds, pauses within words, pauses in speech, word substitutions, words produced with an excess of physical tension, and monosyllabic word repetitions.

Stuttering is more common in males than females, with a male-to-female ratio of 4:1 in adolescents and 2.3:1 in both younger children and adults. Of those children diagnosed with stuttering, 12.7 per cent also have speech sound disorder, 15.2 per cent have another learning disability and 5.9 per cent have ADHD (Blood, Ridenour, Qualls & Hammer, 2003).

17.2.3 The Aetiology of Specific Learning Disabilities

In the following section we will discuss the aetiology and causes of some of the more common of the specific learning disabilities we have described in this section.

Dyslexia

As mentioned earlier, **dyslexia** is a condition that affects both reading and written expression, and is a persistent, chronic condition in which reading ability lags behind that of non-impaired individuals for the course of most of their lifetime. The development of dyslexia can be predicted by a number of risk factors, including difficulty recognizing rhymes at age 4 years (Bradley & Bryant,

> **dyslexia** A persistent, chronic learning disability in which there are developmental deficits in spelling, reading and writing abilities.

1985), difficulty naming everyday objects at age 5 years (Wolf, Bally & Morris, 1986) and difficulty learning syntactic rules at age 2–3 years (Scarborough, 1990). However, the main causes of dyslexia now appear to be identified as abnormalities in specific areas of the brain such as the temporoparietal region (Shaywitz & Shaywitz, 2005). These abnormalities may be the result of genetic factors and they may give rise to the difficulties that sufferers have in decoding and comprehending written material. We will review these theories of the aetiology of dyslexia by looking in turn at evidence related to genetic inheritance, cognitive impairments and brain abnormalities.

Genetic factors

As early as 1950, Hallgren reported that more than 80 per cent of children with dyslexia also had other family members with the disability, with more recent studies suggesting that between 23 and 65 per cent of children with dyslexia have a parent with the disorder (Scarborough, 1990). In addition, 40 per cent of the siblings of sufferers will also exhibit symptoms of dyslexia (Pennington & Gilger, 1996). This suggests that dyslexia runs in families and so may have an important genetic component, and evidence for this genetic component is supported by studies suggesting that dyslexia concordance rates are significantly higher in MZ than in DZ twins (Stevenson, Graham, Fredman & McLoughlin, 1987). Using genetic markers for dyslexia, linkage studies have implicated genes on a number of chromosomes in the aetiology of dyslexia, including loci on chromosomes 2, 3, 6, 15 and 18 (Fisher & DeFries, 2002). There is evidence from molecular genetics to suggest that many of these genes participate in brain development and cause the abnormalities in brain development associated with dyslexia (Galaburda, LoTurco, Ramus, Fitch & Rosen, 2006; Scerri & Schulte-Koene, 2010).

Cognitive factors

Research on the aetiology of dyslexia has recently converged on the view that reading disabilities in dyslexia are caused primarily by difficulties in differentiating the elements of speech (phonemes) and associating these sounds with the letters in a written word (Shaywitz, 2003). This is known as the **phonological theory** of dyslexia where, in order to learn to read, the child must learn to recognize that letters and letter strings represent the sounds of spoken language. The deficits in dyslexia impair the child's ability to break up a spoken word into its basic phonological elements and link each letter to its corresponding sound. This

> **phonological theory** The view that reading disabilities in dyslexia are caused primarily by difficulties in differentiating the elements of speech (phonemes) and associating these sounds with the letters in a written word.

deficit is quite independent of other abilities, such as general intelligence, reasoning, vocabulary and use of syntax (Share & Stanovich, 1995; Shankweiler, Crain, Katz, Fowler et al., 1995). Shaywitz & Shaywitz (2005, p.1302) characterize the experience of the dyslexic in the following way:

> The problem is that the affected reader cannot use his or her higher order linguistic skills to access the meaning until the printed word has first been decoded and identified. Suppose, for example, an individual knows the precise meaning of the spoken word 'apparition'; however, she will not be able to use her knowledge of the meaning of the word until she can decode and identify the printed word on the page and it will appear that she does not know the word's meaning.

Brain abnormalities

Associated with problems in relating written letters to corresponding sounds are deficits in brain functioning in dyslexia – especially in the temporoparietal areas of the brain. Post-mortem studies of the brains of dyslexia sufferers suggest abnormalities in the temporoparietal brain region (Galaburda, Sherman, Rosen, Aboitiz et al., 1985) and the number and organization of neurones in the posterior language area of the cortex (Galaburda, 1993). Nevertheless, these abnormalities found in post-mortem studies might simply represent the consequences of a lifetime of poor reading rather than a causal factor in dyslexia. However, functional magnetic resonance imaging (fMRI) studies of the brains of young children with dyslexia indicate that they show significantly less activation in a number of left hemisphere sites when reading than do non-impaired children. These areas include the inferior frontal, superior temporal, parietotemporal and middle-temporal-middle-occipital gyri (Shaywitz, Shaywitz, Pugh, Mencl et al., 2002). This represents a common finding from functional brain imaging studies suggesting that a failure of proper functioning in left hemisphere posterior brain systems is a cause of impaired reading in children with dyslexia. Studies of lesions of the temporoparietal areas of the brain also indicate that this area may be critical for analysing the written word and transforming the symbol into the sounds associated with the linguistic structure of the word (Damasio & Damasio, 1983; McCandliss, Cohen & Dehaene, 2003). Interestingly, brain imaging studies also suggest that individuals with dyslexia may attempt to compensate for the lack of function in the temporoparietal areas of the brain by using other brain areas to help them identify words and associate them with sounds. These compensatory effects involve brain sites required for physically articulating a word, enabling the individual with dyslexia to develop an awareness of the sound structure of a word by forming the word with their lips, tongue and vocal apparatus (Brunswick, McCrory, Price, Frith & Frith, 1999). Compensatory effects such as this may explain why reading performance in children with dyslexia improves with age but still fails to reach the standard of non-impaired children.

Dyscalculia

Dyscalculia appears to be a specific but chronic condition, in which sufferers may perform better than average on measures of IQ, vocabulary and working memory, but still perform significantly poorly on tests of mathematical ability (Landerl, Bevan & Butterworth, 2004). The disorder appears to be the result of specific disabilities in basic number processing and can take three basic forms: (1) a deficit in the memorizing and retrieval of arithmetic facts, (2) developmentally immature strategies for solving arithmetic problems, and (3) impaired visuospatial skills resulting in errors in aligning numbers or placing decimal points (Geary, 1993, 2004).

Dyscalculia appears to have a familial component (Monuteaux, Faraone, Herzig, Navsaria & Biederman, 2005) and abnormalities in brain function associated with dyscalculia may be partially transmitted genetically (von Aster, Kucian, Schweiter & Martin, 2005), and are also associated with the genes that mediate mathematical ability generally (Plomin & Kovas, 2005). However, a number of studies have also implicated prenatal factors such as fetal alcohol spectrum disorder (FASD) and low birth weight (O'Malley & Nanson, 2002; Shalev, 2004). Brain functions specializing in number processing are located in various areas of the brain: fMRI studies have implicated abnormalities in the left parietotemporal and inferior prefrontal cortex areas of the brain and the intraparietal sulcus in mathematics disorder (Dehaene, Molko, Cohen & Wilson, 2004; Molko, Cachia, Riviere, Mangin et al., 2003). Thus, the current evidence suggests a genetic or developmental cause that results in abnormalities of function in those areas of the brain responsible for processing numbers and arithmetic calculations.

Communication disorders

Many communication disorders may be caused by organic problems relating to abnormal development of the physical apparatus required to make and articulate sounds. For example, speech sound disorder and stuttering can be associated with physical causes such as hearing impairment, cleft palate, cerebral palsy and ear, nose and throat problems. In addition, some theories of stuttering argue that this disorder results from problems with the physical articulation of sounds in the mouth and larynx (Agnello, 1975). However, organic difficulties related to sound production may not represent the whole picture. For example, there is growing evidence of a familial and genetic component to communication disorders such as stuttering (Canhetti-Oliveira & Richieri-Costa, 2006; Andrews, Morris-Yeates, Howie & Martin, 1991) that indicates that the heritability of stuttering may be as high as 71 per cent. There is also evidence from brain scan studies of abnormalities in certain brain circuits that are related to stuttering. One such circuit is the basal ganglia–thalamo–cortical motor circuit, which, if impaired, may affect the ability of the basal ganglia to produce timing cues for the initiation of the next motor segment in speech (Alm, 2004). The fact that stuttering may be a problem associated with the sequential production of sounds and words is supported by evidence that suggests that stuttering rarely occurs in one-word utterances and is affected by the length and grammatical complexity of utterances (Bloodstein, 2006). Furthermore, stuttering is often a consequence of brain injury in the basal ganglia, suggesting that it is an important area in the production of normal speech (Tani & Sakai, 2011).

Finally, there is some evidence that the production of sounds in communication disorders may be affected by emotional factors such as anticipatory anxiety or lack of control over emotional reactions (Karrass, Walden, Conture, Graham et al., 2006). However, at least some researchers view this association between disorders such as stuttering and anticipatory anxiety as secondary, and as a conditioned consequence of previous stuttering experiences (Alm, 2004).

17.2.4   The Treatment of Specific Learning Disabilities

The inclusion of specific learning and communication difficulties in DSM over the years has been controversial. Many view these problems as developmental ones that require attention in an educational rather than a clinical setting and, indeed, many learning disabilities are tackled primarily in the context of the child's educational development (Mishna, 1996). However, specific learning difficulties are frequently associated with clinical problems such as anxiety, depression and disruptive behaviour, and they can create significant problems in social, educational and familial functioning that may require referral to clinical services. Many of the treatments required by individuals with specific learning disorders can be provided by educational psychologists or speech therapists rather than clinical psychologists and it is not intended to cover these forms of treatment here.

In many cases, such as reading impairments, appropriate reading instruction for at-risk younger children can enable them to become accurate and fluent readers

(Alexander & Slinger-Constant, 2004). However, with older individuals suffering from reading disabilities such as dyslexia, a common approach in educational settings is to provide learning materials in a form that allows them to be most easily negotiated by the dyslexic student. In addition, to compensate for the fact that the dyslexic student's reading is less automatic and more effortful, extra time is given during assessments such as examinations.

Treatment of communication disorders is normally the domain of speech therapists and related disciplines, and there is a range of successful treatment programmes and equipment available for disabilities such as phonological disorder and stuttering (Saltuklaroglu & Kalinowski, 2005; Law, Garrett & Nye, 2004). For example, hand-held equipment can provide **altered auditory feedback (AAF)** for the stutterer, either in terms of the delay of

altered auditory feedback (AAF)
A form of treatment for stuttering in which delayed auditory feedback or a change in frequency of the voice is given to clients when they are speaking.

auditory feedback it gives the sufferer when speaking or through a change in frequency of the voice. Such devices appear to have success in reducing the levels of stuttering, but it is still not clear by what mechanism they have this effect or whether they work equally well for everyone with a stuttering problem (Lincoln, Packman & Onslow, 2006; Lincoln, Packman, Onslow & Jones, 2010). Another successful set of techniques used to address stuttering is known as *prolonged speech*. This teaches the sufferer a set of new speech patterns that result in changes in the phrasing and articulation of speech and of the respiratory patterns produced by stutterers while speaking (Packman, Onslow & van Doorn, 1994). The success rates of treatments for stuttering are particularly high and estimated to be around 60–80 per cent, but this may at least in part be confounded by the fact that much childhood stuttering will usually spontaneously remit after a few years (Saltuklaroglu & Kalinowski, 2005).

SELF-TEST QUESTIONS

- What are the defining characteristics of specific learning disorder as a diagnostic category?
- What are the individual skills that may be impaired in dyscalculia?
- What are the main characteristics of language disorder, speech sound disorder and childhood-onset fluency disorder?
- What is the evidence that dyslexia is an inherited disorder?
- Can you describe the phonological theory of dyslexia?
- What areas of the brain appear to be most affected in dyslexia?
- What is the evidence that communication disorders might be associated with physical rather than psychological causes?
- Can you describe treatments for stuttering such as altered auditory feedback (AAF) and prolonged speech?

SECTION SUMMARY

17.2 SPECIFIC LEARNING DISABILITIES

In this section we have reviewed the characteristics, aetiology and general treatment of a number of specific learning disabilities. These are largely disabilities associated with reading, writing and communication generally, and the most well-known of these disorders is the reading disorder known as dyslexia. While many of these disabilities will require attention in educational rather than clinical settings, they may come to the attention of clinical psychologists because they may often become associated with mental health problems and cause significant disruption to social, familial and educational functioning.

To sum up the key points:

- *Specific learning disorder* refers to a range of disabilities that affect performance on tests of academic ability such as reading, mathematics or written expression.

- *Dyslexia* is a learning disability associated with difficulty in recognizing words, poor spelling and difficulty with written expression.

- *Dyscalculia* is a disability that affects mathematical or arithmetic ability.
- *Communication disorders* include impairments in language, speech and communication.
- *Language disorder* is a disability concerned with problems in vocabulary comprehension and production.
- *Speech and sound disorder* is a disability associated with difficulty in speech sound production.
- *Childhood-onset fluency disorder* is sometimes known as 'stuttering' and involves a problem with the fluency and time-patterning of speech.
- Disorders of reading, such as *dyslexia*, are known to have an important genetic component and are associated with brain abnormalities in the *temporoparietal areas*.
- Dyslexia appears to be associated with difficulties differentiating the elements of speech and associating these sounds with the letters in a written word (the *phonological theory*).
- Treatment for specific learning disabilities often occurs in an educational rather than a clinical setting.

17.3 INTELLECTUAL DISABILITIES

17.3.1 DSM-5 Diagnostic Criteria for Intellectual Disability

Intellectual disability is a disorder with onset during the individual's developmental period (usually up to the age of 18 years) that covers impairment in both intellectual and adaptive functioning. DSM-5 defines **intellectual disability** according to three primary criteria:

intellectual disability A modern term replacing mental retardation to describe the more severe and general learning disabilities.

1. significantly below average intellectual functioning in areas such as reasoning, problem solving, abstract thinking, planning and learning generally; and this below-normal intellectual functioning is defined by scores on IQ tests approximately two standard deviations below the population mean (i.e. an IQ below 70 on IQ tests with a mean of 100 and a standard deviation of 15);
2. impairments in adaptive functioning generally (e.g. an inability to master social or educational skills that would be expected for the individual's chronological age); and
3. these deficits should be manifest during the individual's developmental period (i.e. normally, up to 18 years of age) (DSM-5 Summary Table 17.5).

DSM-5 makes it clear that a good deal of clinical judgement is required when diagnosing intellectual disability. It should take into account whether the individual meets community and cultural standards of independence and

DSM-5 SUMMARY TABLE 17.5 *Criteria for intellectual disability*

- Deficits in intellectual functions as confirmed by clinical assessment and standard intelligence tests
- Deficits in adaptive functioning resulting in an inability to meet development and sociocultural standards for personal independence and social responsibility
- Symptoms start in developmental period

social responsibility, and IQ test scores should be interpreted cautiously depending on whether the instrument is culturally relevant, based on up-to-date norms, and takes into account any sensory or motor disabilities the individual may possess.

DSM-5 also allows intellectual disability to be specified according to its severity into mild, moderate, severe and profound, with mild being the least disabling, where sufferers may only be mildly cognitively impaired, socially 'immature' rather than impaired, and may be able to deal with the daily tasks of life given appropriate support. In the case of profound severity the individual may have little understanding of symbolic communication and be dependent on others for all aspects of daily care, their health and their safety. Clinicians assessing individuals with intellectual disabilities would also gather information about disabilities from other reliable independent sources, such as teachers and medical doctors.

17.3.2 Alternative Approaches to Defining Intellectual Disability

Rather than simply taking a negative approach to diagnosis and focusing on an individual's limitations, impairments and deficits, more recent views attempt to highlight those factors that might be required to facilitate better intellectual and adaptive functioning in the individual. People with intellectual disabilities differ significantly in the severity of their disabilities, with some able to function in everyday life almost without being noticed while others may require constant supervision and sheltered environments in which to live. Similarly, individuals also differ significantly in their personalities. Some will be passive, placid and dependent while others may be aggressive and impulsive. These kinds of issues mean that each individual with an intellectual disability is likely to differ in terms of both their level of functioning and what is required to achieve any form of adaptive functioning. In this sense, the notion of 'intellectual disability' is more of a social construction than a diagnostic category (a term that is a product of particular historical and cultural conditions rather than medical or psychological science) (Webb & Whitaker, 2012).

The American Association on Intellectual and Developmental Disabilities (AAIDD) has promoted a more individualized assessment of a person's skills and needs rather than an approach based solely on categorizing intellectual and adaptive impairments. This approach emphasizes that individuals have both strengths and limitations, and that an individual's limitations need to be described in a way that enables suitable support to be developed. So, rather than simply forcing the individual into a diagnostic category, this approach evaluates the specific needs of the individual and then suggests strategies, services and supports that will optimize individual functioning. Supports are defined as 'the resources and individual strategies necessary to promote the development, education, interests, and personal well-being of a person with intellectual disabilities'. Supports can be provided wherever necessary by parents, friends, teachers, psychologists, doctors and GPs or any other appropriate person or agency. People with intellectual disabilities frequently face major stigma and prejudice, and they are often confronted with significant barriers to realizing their own potential. However, approaches such as that advocated by the AAIDD are designed to enable individuals with intellectual disabilities to achieve their potential. In the UK, the Special Education Needs and Disability Act of 2001 extended the rights of individuals with intellectual disabilities to be educated in mainstream schools and schools are required to draw up **accessibility strategies** to facilitate the inclusion of pupils with intellectual disabilities and to make reasonable adjustments so that they are not disadvantaged. As a result of such

accessibility strategies Programmes that extend the rights of individuals with intellectual disabilities to be educated according to their needs in mainstream schools.

changes in attitude, support and legislation, more than half of those people with intellectual disabilities in the UK now live with their parents or carers.

17.3.3   The Prevalence of Intellectual Disabilities

Estimates of the prevalence levels of intellectual disorders will depend very much on how intellectual disabilities are defined. DSM-5 estimates the prevalence rate of a diagnosis of intellectual disability at around 1 per cent, and prevalence for severe intellectual disability at around 6 per 1000. However, a UK study looking specifically at the prevalence rate of IQ scores less than 70 suggests that prevalence of such low IQ scores may be as high as between 5 and 10 per cent in school children aged 13–15 years. Further analysis suggested that only around 15 per cent of those with IQ scores below 70 were already in receipt of a statement of special educational needs (Simonoff, Pickles, Chadwick, Gringas et al., 2006), implying that the majority of the group with low IQ either did not need educational support or were as yet unrecognized as in need of support. Epidemiological studies indicate that there are around 580,000 people in the UK with mild intellectual disabilities (a prevalence rate of around 0.95 per cent) and 217,000 with severe intellectual disabilities (a prevalence rate of 0.35 per cent) (Open Society Institute, 2005). However, the Simonoff, Pickles, Chadwick, Gringas et al. study implies there are likely to be many more people than this suffering some form of intellectual disability and they are going unrecognized.

17.3.4   The Aetiology of Intellectual Disability

First and foremost, the causes of intellectual disability in individual cases are often extremely difficult to isolate and identify. Even when the cause of disability can be identified (such as a chromosomal disorder) two individuals identified with the same cause may exhibit quite different levels of disability. Differential diagnosis is also quite problematic: in many cases it is unclear whether an individual has a specific learning disability, has more general intellectual impairments, is suffering from autistic spectrum disorder (see section 17.4), or has psychological or emotional problems. As we shall see in the following sections, the major causes of intellectual disability are biological in nature and over 1000 forms of impairment based on genetic, chromosomal or metabolic abnormalities have been identified (Dykens & Hodapp, 2001). However, many researchers believe that an individual's resultant intellectual disability is also influenced considerably by environmental factors. For example, mild or moderate intellectual disability tends to occur more frequently in lower socio-economic groups, indicating that poverty and associated deprivation may retard intellectual development. One topical example of this is the case of teenage mothers who choose to rear their children. They more often live in poor environments, are more likely to expose their children to alcohol and poor nutrition, and are less likely to provide sensitive parenting (Brooks-Gunn & Chase-Lansdale, 1995; Borkowoski, Whitman, Passino, Rellinger *et al.*, 1992). As a result, mild to moderate intellectual disability is found significantly more frequently in children of teenage mothers than in the children of older mothers (Broman, Nichols, Shaughnessy, Kennedy *et al.*, 1987). In the following section, we will look first at the known biological causes of intellectual disability, followed by some of the environmental factors thought to be involved. Table 17.2 provides a summary of some of the known causes of intellectual

TABLE 17.2 *Causes of intellectual disability*

Developmental period	Cause or risk factor
Before/during conception	Inherited recessive gene disorders (e.g. phenylketonuria, Tay–Sachs disease)
	Chromosome abnormalities (e.g. Down syndrome, fragile X syndrome)
During pregnancy	Severe maternal malnutrition
	Maternal iodine deficiency
	Maternal infections (e.g. rubella, syphilis, HIV, herpes simplex)
	Maternal drug abuse (e.g. alcoholism, tobacco abuse, illegal drug abuse)
	Maternal medications (e.g. cancer chemotherapy)
During birth	Anoxia and hypoxia (oxygen starvation or insufficient oxygen supply)
	Low birth weight
Early childhood	Brain infections (e.g. encephalitis, meningitis)
	Childhood malnutrition
	Severe head injury (e.g. physical accidents, physical abuse such as shaken baby syndrome)
	Exposure to toxins (e.g. lead, mercury)
	Social deprivation and poverty (e.g. poor parenting, unstimulating infant environment)

disabilities categorized by the developmental period when they have their effect.

Biological causes

Biological factors represent the largest known group of causes of intellectual disabilities and we will divide these into three main categories: (1) chromosomal disorders, (2) metabolic causes, and (3) perinatal causes.

Chromosomal disorders   For many years now, it has been known that forms of intellectual disability are genetically linked to abnormalities in the X chromosome (the chromosome that also determines biological sex) and these abnormalities will often manifest as physical weaknesses in the chromosomes or abnormalities resulting from irregular cell division during the mother's pregnancy. Chromosomal abnormalities occur in around 5 per cent of all pregnancies and the majority usually end in spontaneous miscarriages. However, it is estimated that 0.5 per cent of all newborn babies have a chromosomal disorder, although many of these die soon after birth (Smith, Bierman & Robinson, 1978). Chromosomal disorders account for around 25–30 per cent of all diagnosed cases of intellectual disability and the two most prominent forms are Down syndrome and fragile X syndrome.

Down syndrome was first described by British doctor Langdon Down in 1866. However, it was not until 1959 that French geneticist Jerome Lejeune first reported that individuals with Down syndrome almost always possess an extra chromosome in pair 21, which is usually caused by errors in cell division in the mother's womb. Down syndrome occurs in around 1.5 of every 1000 births (i.e. a prevalence rate of 0.15 per cent) (Simonoff, Bolton & Rutter, 1996) and risk is related to the age of the mother. For women aged 20–24 years the risk is 0.07 per cent. This rises to 1 per cent for women aged 40 years and up to 4 per cent in women aged over 45 years (Thompson, McInnes & Willard, 1991). Although this link between maternal age and incidence of Down syndrome has been known for some time, it is still unclear how maternal age contributes to the chromosomal abnormalities. The majority of individuals with Down syndrome have moderate to severe intellectual impairment with a measurable IQ usually between 35 and 55. They also have a distinctive physical appearance with eyes that slant upward and outward with an extra fold of skin that appears to exaggerate the slant. They are usually shorter and stockier than average, with broad hands and short fingers. They may also have a larger than normal furrowed tongue that makes

> **Down syndrome** A disorder caused by the presence of an extra chromosome in pair 21 and characterized by intellectual disability and distinguishing physical features.

it difficult for them to pronounce words easily. They also suffer physical disability, such as heart problems, and appear to age rapidly, with mortality high after 40 years of age. Ageing is also closely associated with signs of dementia similar to Alzheimer's disease (see Chapter 15) and this may be a result of the causes of both disorders being closely located on chromosome 21 (Zigman, Schupf, Sersen & Silverman, 1995; Selkoe, 1991). Down syndrome can be identified prenatally in high-risk parents by using a procedure known as **amniocentesis** which involves extracting and analysing the pregnant mother's amniotic fluid. This is now a routine procedure for pregnant mothers that is carried out after week 15 of pregnancy and is recommended in the UK and US for mothers over the age of 35 years. The results of this process can leave prospective parents with difficult decisions about whether to maintain a pregnancy or not but, even so, amniocentesis will only identify between 15 and 30 per cent of Down syndrome cases in pregnant mothers who are tested.

> **amniocentesis** A procedure which involves extracting and analysing the pregnant mother's amniotic fluid used prenatally in identifying Down syndrome in high-risk parents.

Another important chromosomal abnormality that causes intellectual disability is known as **fragile X syndrome**. This is where the X chromosome appears to show physical weaknesses and may be bent or broken, and fragile X syndrome occurs in approximately 0.08–0.4 per cent of all births (Hagerman & Lampe, 1999). Individuals with fragile X syndrome possess mild to moderate levels of intellectual disability and may also exhibit language impairment and behavioural problems such as mood irregularities (Eliez & Feinstein, 2001; Zigler & Hodapp, 1991). Like individuals with Down syndrome, they also have specific physical characteristics, such as elongated faces and large, prominent ears (see Photo 17.2). Studies suggest there may be a syndrome of fragile X chromosome in which different individuals manifest rather different symptoms and degrees of disability (Hagerman, 1995). For example, some may have normal IQ levels but suffer specific learning disabilities. Others may exhibit emotional lability and symptoms characteristic of autism, such as hand-biting, limited speech and poor eye contact (Dykens, Leckman, Paul & Watson, 1988), and around one in three will exhibit symptoms of autism spectrum disorder (Hagerman, 2006). Intellectual impairment will usually be greatest in males suffering fragile X syndrome because they only have one X chromosome. Because females possess two X chromosomes the risk of intellectual disability is less (Sherman, 1996).

> **fragile X syndrome** A chromosomal abnormality that causes intellectual disability where the X chromosome appears to show physical weaknesses and may be bent or broken.

Metabolic disorders Metabolic disorders occur when the body's ability to produce or break down chemicals is impaired. There are many different types of metabolic disorders and many can affect intellectual ability. Such disorders are often caused by genetic factors and may be carried by a **recessive gene**. When both parents possess the defective recessive gene, then their offspring are in danger of developing the metabolic disturbances linked to that gene. We will provide examples of two such genetically determined metabolic disorders that affect intellectual ability. These are phenylketonuria (PKU) and Tay–Sachs disease.

> **recessive gene** A gene that must be present on both chromosomes in a pair to show outward signs of a certain characteristic.

Phenylketonuria (PKU) is caused by a deficiency of the liver enzyme phenylalanine 4-hydroxylase, which is necessary for the effective metabolism of the amino acid phenylalanine. As a result of this deficit, phenylalanine and its derivative phenylpyruvic acid build up in the body and irreparably damage the brain and central nervous system by preventing effective myelination of neurons (myelination is the development of a protective sheath around the axons of neurons that enables effective transmission between nerve cells). This results in severe intellectual disability and hyperactivity. In the UK, PKU has an incidence of around 1 in 10,000 live births (NSPKU, 2004) and it is carried on the phenylalanine hydroxylase gene (PAH) on chromosome 12 (Doss & Sethumadhavan, 2009). Several hundred mutations of this gene have been identified, but just five account for approximately 60 per cent of PKU cases in European populations. It is estimated that as many as 1 in 70 people may be carriers of the recessive gene responsible for PKU. At-risk parents who may carry the gene are now routinely given blood tests to determine the risk of having a child with PKU. Diet is also an important factor in controlling intellectual deficits in fetuses and offspring at risk of PKU. A special diet low in phenylalanine is recommended for at-risk pregnant mothers and if children with PKU are given diets low in phenylalanine from birth to at least 6 years of age, this can minimize neurological damage and intellectual deficit (Mazzoco, Nord, van Doorninck, Greene et al., 1994).

> **phenylketonuria (PKU)** A metabolic disorder caused by a deficiency of the liver enzyme phenylalanine 4-hydroxylase, which is necessary for the effective metabolism of the amino acid phenylalanine.

Tay–Sachs disease is also a metabolic disorder caused by a recessive gene (often found in children of Eastern European Jewish ancestry). The defective gene results in an absence of the enzyme hexosaminidase A in the brain and central nervous system and this eventually causes neurones to die. The disorder is degenerative, with infants of around 5 months showing an exaggerated startle response and poor

> **Tay–Sachs disease** A metabolic disorder caused by a recessive gene which results in an absence of the enzyme hexosaminidase A in the brain and central nervous system, eventually causing neurons to die.

Down syndrome

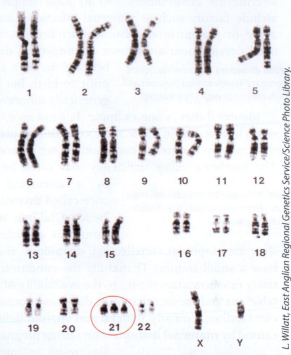

© iStock.com/DenKuvaiev.

L. Willatt, East Anglian Regional Genetics Service/Science Photo Library.

Fragile X syndrome

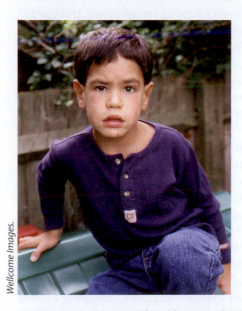

Wellcome Images.

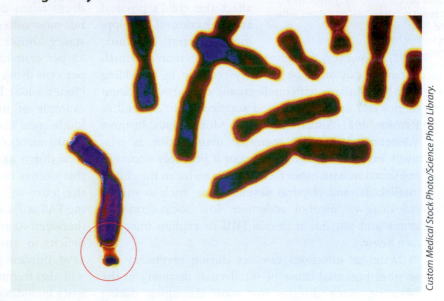

Custom Medical Stock Photo/Science Photo Library.

PHOTO 17.2 *The typical facial features of children born with Down syndrome or fragile X syndrome. Individuals with Down syndrome almost always possess an extra chromosome in pair 21, while in fragile X syndrome the X chromosome shows physical weaknesses and may be bent or broken.*

motor development. Only around 17 per cent of sufferers live beyond 4 years of age (Sloan, 1991) but those that do show rapid decline in cognitive, motor and verbal skills. The disorder is relatively rare, occurring in around 1 in 360,000 live births worldwide, and this rate is being significantly reduced by effective screening.

Perinatal causes   From conception to the early post-natal period is a dangerous time for an organism that is developing as rapidly as a human baby. Because of this, there are considerable prenatal and immediately post-natal factors that put normal development at risk and may cause lifelong intellectual disability. One type of risk involves those factors that can adversely affect the fetus's interuterine environment and its food supply. These include factors such as maternal infections, substance abuse or malnutrition. Disorders acquired during pre-natal development are known as **congenital disorders** because they are acquired prior to birth but are not genetically inherited.

congenital disorders Disorders acquired during prenatal development prior to birth but which are not genetically inherited.

Maternal diet is one example. For instance, if there is too little iodine in the mother's diet during pregnancy this can give rise to the condition known as **cretinism**. The mother's iodine deficiency may often be caused by a hormonal imbalance called thyroxine deficiency. Children suffering from this disorder show slow development, intellectual disabilities and often have a small stature. Thankfully the condition is relatively rare nowadays thanks to the availability of iodized table salt and the fact that most diets now contain sufficient iodine. Similarly, mineral and vitamin deficiencies caused by **maternal malnutrition** during pregnancy can also result in intellectual disability and significantly affect the child's physical and behavioural development (Barrett & Frank, 1987). However, the adverse effects of maternal malnutrition can often be partially rectified by providing new-born infants with intellectually supportive environments and appropriate food supplements (Zeskind & Ramsay, 1981; Super, Herrera & Mora, 1990). In most Westernized societies maternal malnutrition is relatively rare but when it does occur it probably occurs in conjunction with other factors likely to harm the child's intellectual and physical development, such as maternal drug or alcohol addiction, low socio-economic status and possibly maternal HIV or syphilis infection (see below).

cretinism A congenital disorder resulting in slow development, intellectual disabilities and small stature.

maternal malnutrition Mineral and vitamin deficiencies during pregnancy that can result in intellectual disabilities in the child.

Maternal infectious diseases during pregnancy are another potential cause of intellectual disability in the offspring. Such diseases are most damaging during the first trimester of pregnancy when the fetus has little or no immunological protection. Common maternal diseases that can cause intellectual impairment in the offspring include rubella (German measles), syphilis and HIV amongst others. If a mother contracts rubella during the first 10 weeks of pregnancy, there is almost a 90 per cent chance that the baby will develop **congenital rubella syndrome (CRS)** resulting in abortion, miscarriage, stillbirth

congenital rubella syndrome (CRS) The constellation of abnormalities caused by infection with the rubella (German measles) virus before birth. The syndrome is characterized by multiple congenital malformations (birth defects) and intellectual disability.

or severe birth defects. Up to 20 per cent of babies born live will have CRS causing heart disease, deafness and intellectual impairment. The incidence of CRS is between 70 and 170 per 100,000 live births and incidence is still relatively high in developing countries (Cutts & Vynnycky, 1999). In contrast, **maternal HIV infection** has become an important cause of intellectual disability. If the mother is not being treated for HIV during pregnancy there is a likelihood that the infection will be passed on to the fetus. The infection can also be passed on through breastfeeding. There is then almost a 50 per cent chance that the newborn child will develop moderate to severe intellectual disabilities. However, *in utero* transmission of HIV can be reduced from 25 per cent to 8 per cent if the mother is given an antiretroviral drug such as zidovudine during pregnancy and if the newborn child then receives the drug for up to 6 weeks postnatally (Belfer & Munir, 1997).

maternal HIV infection The incidence of a mother having HIV during pregnancy, leading to a likelihood that the infection will be passed on to the fetus.

A further significant cause of intellectual disability is maternal drug use during pregnancy. In many cases the drugs responsible for offspring intellectual disability may be ones taken for medicinal purposes (such as drugs taken during cancer chemotherapy treatment) but most other cases occur where the mother is a substance abuser. For instance, US studies indicate that 18 per cent of pregnant women smoke tobacco, 9.8 per cent drink alcohol and 4 per cent use illegal drugs (Jones, 2006). Fetal alcohol syndrome (FAS) is one such example of maternal drug abuse causing childhood intellectual disabilities. Whenever a pregnant mother drinks alcohol, it will enter the fetus's bloodstream, slow down its metabolism and affect development. If this occurs on a regular basis, then development of the fetus will be severely impaired. Children suffering FAS will usually have lower birth weight, lower IQ (between 40 and 80) and suffer motor impairments and deficits in attention and working memory (Niccols, 1994; Burden, Jacobson, Sokol & Jacobson, 2005). They will also frequently exhibit distinctive facial characteristics including slit eyes, short noses, drooping eyelids and thin upper lips. In the UK around one in every six to seven thousand babies born have FAS (National Organization on Fetal Alcohol Syndrome, 2012). Recently attention has also been focused on the intellectual and developmental effects on children of illegal drugs use by pregnant mothers. Use of both cocaine and crack cocaine (see Chapter 9) by a pregnant mother can lead to babies being physically addicted to the drug before birth (known as 'crack babies'). There is some evidence that this can adversely affect physical development and brain development in particular (Hadeed & Siegel, 1989) and result in slow language development (van Baar, 1990). However, it is clear that maternal drug-taking while pregnant may often occur in contexts that may also contribute to poor intellectual development in the offspring, and these may include the abuse of other drugs, pregnancy deprivations (such as dietary imbalances) and economic and social deprivation (Vidaeff & Mastrobattista, 2003). As such, this makes it difficult to assess the specific affect of maternal cocaine use on offspring intellectual development (Jones, 2006).

One final example of a perinatal cause of intellectual disability is **anoxia**, which is a significant period without oxygen occurring during or immediately after delivery. Lack of oxygen to the brain during the birth process can damage parts of the brain that are yet to develop and as a result can cause both physical and intellectual impairment (Erickson, 1992). The main neurological birth syndrome caused by anoxia is **cerebral palsy** which is characterized by motor symptoms that affect the strength and coordination of movement. While the primary disabilities are mainly physical, around one-third of those suffering from cerebral palsy will also suffer some form of intellectual, cognitive or emotional disability as well.

> **anoxia** A perinatal cause of intellectual disability, being a significant period without oxygen that occurs during or immediately after delivery.

> **cerebral palsy** The main neurological birth syndrome caused by anoxia which is characterized by motor symptoms that affect the strength and coordination of movement.

Childhood causes

Although a child may be born healthy, there are potentially numerous early childhood factors that might put the child at risk of intellectual disability. Very often these factors may operate in conjunction with other causes such as perinatal problems. We will look briefly at four groups of potential childhood causes of intellectual disability, namely accidents and injury, exposure to toxins, childhood infections, and poverty and deprivation.

During their early developmental years, young children will often be involved in accidents and these can often be severe enough to cause irreversible physical damage and intellectual impairment (Ewing-Cobbs, Prasad, Kramer, Cox *et al.*, 2006). Common childhood accidents that may cause permanent intellectual disability include falls, car accidents, near drownings, suffocation and poisoning. However, at least some of the injuries that cause intellectual disability in children may not be genuine accidents but may be the result of physical abuse by others. A retrospective study of head injuries in children aged between 1 and 6 years of age estimated that 81 per cent of cases could be defined as accidents and 19 per cent as definite cases of abuse (Reece & Sege, 2000). One form of child abuse that is known to cause intellectual disability is known as shaken baby syndrome. This refers to traumatic brain injury that occurs when a baby is violently shaken. In comparison to babies who receive accidental traumatic brain injury, shaken baby injuries have a much worse prognosis, including retinal haemorrhaging that is likely to cause blindness and an increased risk of mental disability such as cerebral palsy or intellectual impairment (Lind, Laurent-Vannier, Toure, Brugel & Chevignard, 2013). Nevertheless, we must remain cautious about the degree to which shaken baby syndrome may contribute to intellectual disability because of current controversies over how the syndrome should be diagnosed (e.g. Kumar, 2005).

> **shaken baby syndrome** A form of child abuse that is known to cause intellectual disability. It refers to traumatic brain injury that occurs when a baby is violently shaken.

During early development children may also be exposed to toxins that can cause neurological damage resulting in intellectual impairment. One such toxin is lead, which is still frequently found in the pollution from vehicles that burn leaded petrol. Lead-based paint is also found in older properties and so may well be a risk factor in children living in deprived, low socio-economic areas. Lead causes neurological damage by accumulating in body tissue and interfering with brain and central nervous system metabolism. Children exposed to high levels of lead have been found to exhibit deficits in IQ scores of up to 10 points (Dietrich, Berger, Succop, Hammond & Bornschein, 1993). Even in Westernized societies aware of the risks associated with exposure to lead the prevalence of lead poisoning in children aged 1–2 years is still as high as 1 per cent (Ossiander, Mueller & van Enwyk, 2005). Prevalence rates are significantly higher than this is developing countries (Sun, Zhao, Li & Cheng, 2004).

Finally, there is evidence to suggest that social deprivation and poverty can themselves contribute to intellectual disability. Although such factors may not directly cause impairment to the biological substrates underlying intellectual ability, they may contribute a form of intellectual impoverishment that can be measured in terms of lowered IQ scores (Garber & McInerney, 1982). Social deprivation and poverty are also inextricably linked to other risk factors for intellectual disability, including poor infant diet, exposure to toxins (such as lead paint in old or run-down housing), maternal drug-taking and alcoholism, and childhood physical abuse. A cycle of deprivation, poverty and intellectual disability is established when young adolescents in deprived environments themselves give birth to children while still teenagers (Wildsmith, Manlove, Jekielek, Anderson Moore & Mincieli, 2012). Such **teenage mothers** are frequently found to live in deprived

> **teenage mothers** In relation to intellectual disabilities, young mothers who become pregnant before 18 years of age, and who are likely to have lived in deprived areas prior to giving birth, are often unmarried, live in poverty as a result of their premature motherhood, and are likely to have a significantly lower than average IQ.

areas, are often unmarried, live in poverty as a result of their premature motherhood, and have a significantly lower than average IQ themselves (Carnegie Corporation, 1994; Borkowski, Whitman, Passino, Rellinger *et al.*, 1992). Studies have shown that teenage mothers are significantly more likely to punish their children than praise them and are significantly less sensitive to their children's needs than older mothers (Borkowski, Whitman, Passino, Rellinger *et al.*, 1992; Brooks-Gunn & Chase-Lansdale, 1995). As a result, children born to teenage mothers are at increased risk of problematic parent–child interactions, (Leadbeater, Bishop & Raver, 1996), behavioural difficulties (Fergusson & Lynskey, 1993), and cognitive disadvantage and educational underachievement (Fergusson & Woodward, 1999; Brooks-Gunn, Guo & Fustenberg, 1993). Consequently, mild intellectual disability is reckoned to occur three times more frequently in the children of teenage mothers (Borkowski,

Whitman, Passino, Rellinger *et al.*, 1992; Broman, Nichols, Shaughnessy, Kennedy *et al.*, 1987). As we said earlier, it is difficult to estimate solely how much this is due to the teenage mother's age and her parenting practices, because the child of a teenage mother is significantly more likely to be raised in the kinds of deprived environments that contain many other risk factors for intellectual disability.

Finally, one important feature of deprived environments is that they will usually provide significantly decreased levels of stimulation for young children, including lower rates of sensory and educational stimulation, lack of one-to-one child–parent experiences and poverty of verbal communication – all factors that are thought to be associated with poor intellectual development. There are some claims that lack of stimulation can have a direct effect on the early physical development of the brain and so result in permanent impairments to

---

FOCUS POINT 17.1

TEENAGE MOTHERS AND THE CYCLE OF UNDERACHIEVEMENT

The UK has the highest teenage birth rate in Western Europe (Avery & Lazdane, 2008). In 2006, in England 39,000 girls under 18 years of age became pregnant (Department for Education and Skills, 2006). Although around half lead to an abortion, the remainder become teenage mothers. They are mothers who are likely to have lived in deprived areas prior to giving birth, they are often unmarried, live in poverty as a result of their premature motherhood, and are likely to have a significantly lower than average IQ (Borkowski, Whitman, Passino, Rellinger *et al.*, 1992). When teenage girls become mothers in deprived areas, this sets up a cycle of deprivation, poverty and intellectual underachievement (Wildsmith, Manlove, Jekielek, Anderson Moore & Mincieli, 2012). As a result of their relatively poor parenting skills and the stress that accrues from living in deprived areas, the children of teenage mothers are significantly more likely than the children of older mothers to have behavioural difficulties (Fergusson & Lynskey, 1993), and suffer cognitive impairments and educational underachievement (Fergusson & Woodward, 1999; Brooks-Gunn, Guo & Fustenberg, 1993). The UK Department for Education and Skills (2006) provided the following stark facts:

- Teenage mothers are less likely to finish their education and are more likely to bring up their children alone in poverty.
- The infant mortality rate for babies born to teenage mothers is 60 per cent higher than for babies born to older mothers.

- Teenage mothers are more likely to smoke during pregnancy and are less likely to breastfeed, both of which have negative consequences for the child.
- Teenage mothers have three times the rate of postnatal depression of older mothers and a higher risk of poor mental health for 3 years after the birth.
- Children of teenage mothers are generally at increased risk of poverty, low educational attainment, poor housing and poor health, and have lower rates of economic activity in adult life.
- Rates of teenage pregnancy are highest among deprived communities, so the negative consequences of teenage pregnancy are disproportionately concentrated among those who are already disadvantaged.

As we can see from reading section 17.3.4 many of these conditions represent risk factors for intellectual disability and underachievement for the teenage mother's offspring. These include poor parenting skills, maternal mental health problems, being raised in unstimulating environments abundant in potential stressors, a high likelihood of maternal drug or alcohol abuse during pregnancy, and increased risk of physical abuse or accidents (Moffitt & the E-Risk Team, 2002). At age 5, the children of teenage mothers already have a significantly lower IQ than the children of older mothers (Lubinski, 2000).

brain functioning. For instance, neural development of the brain occurs most extensively and rapidly in the first year after birth (Kolb, 1989) and a rich, stimulating environment is necessary for full development of the brain's structure (Nelson & Bosquet, 2000). Alternatively, an unstimulating, stressful environment can actually trigger the secretion of hormones that prevent effective brain development (Gunnar, 1998). In a study comparing children brought up in deprived inner city areas with a group provided with good nutrition and a stimulating environment, Campbell & Ramsey (1994) found that by 12 years of age the deprivation experienced by the former group had a significant negative effect on brain functioning.

Summary of the aetiology of intellectual disabilities

From the material covered in this section, you can see that the causes of intellectual disability are diverse. As we mentioned earlier, very often it is impossible to pinpoint the specific cause of an individual's intellectual disability, but intellectual disability caused by chromosomal disorders (such as Down syndrome and fragile X syndrome) and inherited metabolic disorders are some of the more easily identified. Individuals are most at risk of developing permanent intellectual disabilities during early development of their central nervous system, which is why conditions in the uterus and in the immediate postnatal period are critical for normal development. Risk factors that can disrupt normal prenatal development of the brain and central nervous system include maternal infections, alcoholism, drug abuse and malnutrition. Early childhood factors that can affect normal neurological development include accidents, physical abuse, exposure to toxins, infectious illnesses and an early childhood spent in deprivation and poverty. As we have mentioned many times in this section, many of these risk factors may operate concurrently to determine levels of intellectual disability.

17.3.5 Interventions for Intellectual Disabilities

Most forms of intellectual disability impose limitations on the sufferer's ability to function fully and actively in society. This means that – depending on the severity of the disability – the individual will need support to cope with many of the rigours of everyday living. As a result of the disability, sufferers are at risk of underachieving in many areas of their life, including educationally, occupationally, economically and socially. In most societies, the days when people with intellectual disabilities were simply institutionalized and provided with little more than custodial care are now gone, and provision for such people not only attempts to address their needs but also recognizes their fundamental rights as human beings and citizens to an inclusive lifestyle. Thus, interventions for intellectual disabilities have a number of diverse aims. At the primary level there are those interventions aimed at preventing intellectual disability in the first place by educating potential parents about the risk factors for intellectual disability (e.g. educating parents about the effects of maternal alcohol and drug abuse during pregnancy). A second broad aim of interventions is to make training programmes available that will provide the sufferer with enough basic skills to cope with many of the challenges of everyday life (e.g. self-help skills, communication skills). Thirdly, approaches to helping those with intellectual disabilities are based on the principle of **inclusion** in an attempt to help such individuals achieve their potential. For example, in the UK, schools are now required to draw up accessibility strategies to allow pupils with intellectual disabilities to engage in the educational process without being disadvantaged. Similarly, social inclusion is also encouraged to provide those with intellectual disabilities the opportunity for personal, social, emotional and sexual development. We will now discuss each of these three types of approach to intervention in more detail.

> **inclusion** Strategies intended to teach high-functioning individuals self-help strategies, social and living skills, and self-management that are designed to help the individual function more effectively in society.

Prevention strategies

Table 17.2 lists many of the causes and risk factors for intellectual disability and you can probably glean from this list that many of these causes are potentially preventable. This is particularly the case with many perinatal causes, and especially those involving maternal factors during pregnancy. For example, fetal alcohol syndrome (FAS) is a significant cause of intellectual disability and prevention programmes aim at identifying those women at risk of alcohol abuse during pregnancy and providing interventions such as alcohol-reduction counselling (Floyd, O'Connor, Bertrand & Sokol, 2006). Recognizing those at risk can be achieved by using established diagnostic and screening questionnaires (Ismail, Buckley, Budacki, Jabbar & Gallicano, 2010) and interventions include providing feedback on rates of drinking behaviour during pregnancy, discussing strategies for avoiding alcohol cravings and binge drinking sessions and, more recently, web-based interventions (Tenkku, Mengel, Nicholson, Hile et al., 2011). Controlled comparison studies suggest that such screening and intervention methods significantly reduce the risk for alcohol-exposed pregnancies compared with non-intervention control participants (Ingersoll, Ceperich, Nettleman, Karanda et al., 2005).

Prevention can also be achieved in a number of other ways. For example, genetic analysis and counselling enables those parents at risk of abnormal births to be identified, informed of the risk and counselled about how to proceed. Blood tests and tests of amniotic fluid such as amniocentesis enable parents to be informed of risks for a range of disorders, including Down syndrome, Tay–Sachs disease, phenylketonuria and intellectual disability caused by congenital rubella syndrome (CRS). In addition, those disabilities related to dietary irregularities can also be identified and treated, and these include providing at-risk pregnant mothers with iodine supplements to prevent cretinism and providing diets low in phenylalanine for pregnant mothers and offspring at risk of phenyketonuria.

Finally, as discussed earlier, conditions associated with poverty and social deprivation also put children at risk of educational underachievement, lower than average IQ and mild intellectual disability, and support programmes in the USA and Europe have been developed to try to counteract this risk factor. For example, family support programmes in the USA have indicated that mothers of low socio-economic status participating in such schemes are more affectionate and positive with their children and provide more stimulating environments than mothers who are not in such schemes (Johnson, Walker & Rodriguez, 1996). Being a teenage mother is also a risk factor for children of lower IQ than average (see Focus Point 17.1) and this can be tackled in a number of ways, including providing teenage girls with advice on and access to contraception, improving teenage mothers' access to education (Department for Children, Schools & Families, 2010), improving housing quality and encouraging the presence of a co-residential partner rather than raising a child alone (Berrington, Diamond, Ingham, Stevenson et al., 2004).

Training procedures

The quality of life of people with intellectual disabilities can be improved significantly with the help of basic training procedures that will equip them with a range of skills depending on their level of disability. Types of skills include self-help and adaptive skills (such as toileting, feeding and dressing), language and communication skills (including speech, comprehension, sign language), leisure and recreational skills (such as playing games, cooking skills), basic daily living skills (using a telephone, handling money) and controlling anger outbursts and aggressive and challenging behaviour (reducing the tendency to communicate through aggressive or challenging behaviours such as pushing or shouting). Training methods can also be used in more severe cases to control life-threatening behaviours such as self-mutilation or head-banging.

Behavioural techniques that adopt basic principles of operant and classical conditioning are used extensively in these contexts, and the application of learning theory to training in these areas is also known as **applied behaviour analysis** (Davey, 1998). Basic techniques that are used include operant reinforcement (rewarding correct responses – for example, with attention or praise), response shaping (breaking down complex behaviours into small achievable steps and then rewarding each step successively), errorless learning (breaking down a behaviour to be learnt into simple components that can be learnt without making errors – errorless learning is stronger and more durable than learning with errors), imitation learning (where the trainer demonstrates a response for the client to imitate), chaining (training the individual on the final components of a task first and then working backwards to learn the earlier steps) and self-instructional training (teaching the client to guide themselves through a task by verbally instructing themselves what to do at each step). Very often, inappropriate, life-threatening or challenging behaviours may inadvertently be maintained by reinforcement from others in the environment (e.g. self-mutilating behaviour may be maintained by the attention it attracts from family or care staff). In these cases, a *functional analysis* can be carried out to help identify the factors maintaining the behaviour, and this is done by keeping a record of the frequency of the behaviours and noting the antecedents and consequences of the behaviour (see Treatment in Practice Box 17.1). Once it is known what consequences might be maintaining the behaviour, these can be addressed to prevent the behaviour being reinforced (Mazaleski, Iwata, Vollmer, Zarcone & Smith, 1993; Wacker, Steege, Northrup, Sasso et al., 1990).

> **applied behaviour analysis** Applying the principles of learning theory (particularly operant conditioning) to the assessment and treatment of individuals suffering psychopathology.

Inclusion strategies

Policy on the development and education of individuals with intellectual disabilities has changed significantly over the past 35 years. Prior to inclusion policies being introduced, even individuals with mild intellectual disabilities were often deprived of any effective participation in the society in which they lived, and more often than not they would be institutionalized or educated separately. However, many countries have introduced accessibility strategies that extend the rights of individuals with intellectual disabilities to be educated according to their needs in mainstream schools. This approach evaluates the individual's specific needs and then suggests strategies, services and supports that will optimize the functioning of these individuals within society. In the UK, the government's strategy for individuals with

CLINICAL PERSPECTIVE: TREATMENT IN PRACTICE 17.1
A FUNCTIONAL ANALYSIS OF CHALLENGING BEHAVIOUR

Some individuals with intellectual disabilities typically display behaviour that may put themselves or others at risk, or which may prevent the use of community facilities or prevent the individual having a normal home life. Challenging behaviours may take the form of aggression, self-injury, stereotyped behaviour or disruptive and destructive behaviour generally. In many cases, a *functional analysis* may help to identify the factors maintaining the challenging behaviour, and these factors may range from social attention, tangible rewards such as a hug, escape from stressful situations or they may simply provide sensory stimulation. A functional analysis

is undertaken by keeping a record of the frequency of the behaviours and noting the antecedents and consequences of the behaviour. This will take the form of:

A. What happens before the challenging behaviour (the trigger);

B. What the individual does (the behaviour);

C. What the person gets as a result of the behaviour (the consequence).

A typical 'ABC' chart on which family and carers will keep a record of these behaviours will often look like this:

Date	Antecedent (what happened before the behaviour occurred?)	Behaviour (describe exactly what the person did)	Consequence (what happened immediately after the behaviour?)	Signature

A FUNCTIONAL ANALYSIS CASE HISTORY

Andy is a middle-aged man with severe intellectual disability. He has recently moved into a group home which he shares with seven other people. Since he moved in, staff have observed several incidents of self-injury. They report that Andy starts to rock backwards and forwards in his chair, and this then escalates into him slapping his face repeatedly. Staff have asked for help.

The staff team working with Andy were asked to complete ABC charts for 4 weeks. These were then analysed and it was found that the behaviour tended to occur

in the lounge when there were a number of people in the room and the television was on. The consequence of Andy starting to rock and slap himself was that staff would remove him from the room and take him into the kitchen where it was empty and quiet.

It was hypothesized that the function of the behaviour for Andy was to escape from a noisy and crowded situation. Staff decided to respond by watching Andy for early signs he may be feeling overstimulated and to ask him if he wanted to leave the room.

This led to a reduction of self-injury and later it was noted that Andy would now try to attract staff attention when he wanted to leave.

special educational needs (SEN) involves improving the support system for these children and young people and their families, and providing an integrated education, health and care plan for them (from birth to age 25 years), improving educational provision for pupils

special educational needs (SEN) A term used in the UK to identify those who require instruction or education tailored to their specific needs.

with SEN, including the development of suitable educational materials, and the training of specialist teachers and support staff (Department for Education, 2013). Social and educational inclusion also has indirect benefits for the individual. Kim, Larson & Lakin (2001) reviewed those studies carried out between 1980 and 1999 that investigated the effects of the shift from institutionalized living to living in the community. Most studies reported an improvement in three areas: (1) overall improvements in coping with day-to-day living and increases in self-esteem, (2) a decrease in the frequency of maladaptive behaviours, such as aggression or anger outbursts, and (3) an improvement in self-care behaviours and social skills. Case History 17.1 recounts the story of Thomas, a Down syndrome sufferer, who lives with his family and has benefited in a variety of ways from participating in a range of community activities.

Inclusion policies have resulted in significant improvements to the quality of life experienced by individuals with intellectual disabilities, and such individuals now have opportunities to pursue social, educational and occupational goals and pursue their own personal development. For example, individuals with intellectual disabilities now have the right to pursue their own sexual and emotional development – usually with the support of their family. Whereas in the past involuntary sterilization was common for such individuals, appropriate training and counselling now means that most of them can be taught about sexual behaviour to a level appropriate for their functioning. This often means that they can learn to use contraceptives, employ responsible family planning, get married and – in many cases – successfully rear a family, either on their own or with the help of

---

CASE HISTORY 17.1

THOMAS'S STORY

Thomas is 23 and lives with his mum and dad. His brother now lives away but sees him quite regularly.

Thomas has Down's syndrome and needs a great deal of support. He goes to college four days a week and, on Fridays, attends a project where he is learning living skills and enjoying cooking. Thomas has a supported work placement for two hours a week in a riding stable. He has a hectic social life with weekly activities including riding, sports, going to the gym, trampolining and football. He goes to monthly discos with a group of young people with learning disabilities and is regularly to be found in the local pub playing pool with his friends.

We were transporting him to and from these activities and were concerned that he should be able to mix more with his own age group. We arranged for 15½ hours' worth of direct payments for Thomas to choose someone in his peer group to help him access these activities. There was a great deal of interest in the advert we placed at the local university for a student to help with this and we have had several different students helping over the past year, who have become firm friends. Thomas's current helper, Laura, accompanies him on his outings and Thomas has now become a part of a wider social circle, going to the pub, out for meals and watching videos at Laura's house with her friends, which he greatly enjoys.

Thomas's moods, self-esteem and well-being are greatly improved by the stimulation and social nature of all that he does, as well as the routine and structure it brings to his life.

Thomas and his friends have gained enormous confidence from attending several drama courses and the group has enjoyed the feeling of empowerment and also the opportunity to show their feelings. Last year, a group of 11 young adolescents, including Thomas, attended a week-long outward bound course, run by the Calvert Trust, without their families. Afterwards, the group made a presentation to about 80 people who had been involved in organizing or fundraising their trip, with a very professional PowerPoint presentation and question-and-answer session. They were all keen to contribute, wanted to find other groups to make their presentation to and gained lots of confidence from this. It makes a change from the usual painting eggs and bingo offered by local services, which are just not appropriate for a 22-year-old.

Source: From evidence from a family carer given to the Foundation for People with Learning Disabilities' Inquiry into Meeting the Mental Health Needs of Young People with Learning Disabilities – Count Us In.

Clinical Commentary

Thomas is an example of how individuals with intellectual disabilities can benefit significantly from accessibility and inclusion strategies. He has work in a supported employment setting and has a full social life in which he can mix with people of his own age. This approach has the benefit of building confidence and self-esteem, as well as providing the individual with a real sense of empowerment.

local services (Lumley & Scotti, 2001; Levesque, 1996). However, while inclusion in its broadest sense continues to benefit individuals with intellectual disabilities, there is still much confusion over the way in which inclusion is defined and operationalized (Bigby, 2012) and this makes objectively measuring the success of such policies difficult (Martin & Cobigo, 2011).

People with intellectual disabilities are three to four times less likely to be employed than non-disabled counterparts (Verdonschot, de Witte, Reichrath, Buntinx & Curfs, 2009), but employment opportunities are being made increasingly available to individuals with intellectual disabilities. Many are conscientious and valued workers employed in normal work environments. Others with more specific needs may need to pursue employment within **sheltered workshops** or supported employment settings, which provide employment tailored to the individuals' own needs. The UK government seeks to promote employment as another form of social inclusion for individuals with intellectual disabilities. Those working in a sheltered

sheltered workshops Settings that provide individuals with intellectual disabilities with employment tailored to their own needs and abilities.

workshop have been shown to exhibit higher levels of job satisfaction than those who work outside such a scheme, and those living in a semi-independent home and also working in a sheltered workshop showed the highest levels of self-esteem (Griffin, Rosenberg & Cheyney, 1996).

Summary of Interventions for Intellectual Disabilities

This brief insight into some of the interventions deployed in helping people with intellectual disabilities has included: (1) the use of prevention strategies designed to identify those at risk of having offspring with intellectual disabilities (e.g. those with recessive gene disorders or mothers at risk during pregnancy), providing them with skills to minimize risk and counselling them about the possible outcomes; (2) a range of training programmes and techniques to provide individuals with learning difficulties with a variety of everyday skills; and (3) the adoption of inclusion strategies that provide the individual with educational and occupational environments tailored to meeting their needs within mainstream society.

SELF-TEST QUESTIONS

- Can you describe both the traditional and more recent alternative approaches to defining intellectual disability?
- What are the different levels of intellectual disability defined in DSM-5?
- What are the main chromosomal disorders that cause intellectual disability?
- Can you describe at least two metabolic disorders that give rise to intellectual disability?
- What is meant by the term 'congenital disorder' when used in relation to intellectual disability? Can you give some examples of congenital causes of intellectual disability?
- What are the main childhood causes of intellectual disability?
- Can intellectual disability be prevented? If so, how?
- Can you describe the kinds of training procedures that are used to help individuals with intellectual disabilities acquire self-help and communication skills?
- Can you describe some examples of inclusion strategies that have been used in relation to intellectual disability?

SECTION SUMMARY

17.3 INTELLECTUAL DISABILITIES

We began this section by describing the DSM-5 diagnostic criteria for intellectual disability and discussing some alternative types of definition and terminology that focus on identifying needs and facilitating adaptive functioning. The aetiology of intellectual disorders is a diverse topic, with no identifiable cause being found for a large proportion of those with intellectual disabilities. Biological causes are primarily responsible for those aetiologies that can be identified, and these include chromosomal disorders, recessive gene disorders and perinatal factors. Childhood problems can also contribute to intellectual disability and we discussed the role of accidents, abuse, infectious diseases and the nonspecific detrimental effect that social deprivation and poverty can have on intellectual development. In the final section we covered interventions for the prevention of intellectual disability and programmes for the care, development and support of individuals with intellectual disabilities.

To summarize the key points:

- *Intellectual disability* is a term that covers impairments in both intellectual and adaptive functioning.

- Intellectual disability involves significantly below average intellectual functioning, usually defined by a score on a standardized IQ test of below 70.

- Modern approaches to defining intellectual disabilities attempt to highlight those factors that might be required to facilitate more adaptive functioning, and to draw up *accessibility strategies* to ensure that such individuals are not excluded or disadvantaged in their education.

- Chromosomal disorders such as *Down syndrome* and *fragile X syndrome* account for around 25–30 per cent of all diagnosed cases of intellectual disability.

- Metabolic disorders that cause intellectual disability are usually carried by a recessive gene and include *phenylketonuria (PKU)* and *Tay–Sachs disease*.

- *Congenital disorders* are those that are acquired prior to birth but are not genetically inherited. Congenital causes of intellectual disability include *maternal malnutrition, congenital rubella syndrome (CRS), maternal HIV infection* and *fetal alcohol syndrome (FAS)*.

- Childhood environmental causes of intellectual disability include childhood accidents (including intentional physical abuse by others), exposure to toxins (such as lead), childhood infections and poverty and deprivation.

- Prevention strategies for intellectual disability include prevention campaigns and screening for such factors as maternal alcohol abuse and genetic risk factors.

- Behavioural training procedures can equip sufferers with a range of self-help and adaptive skills, and the application of learning theory in these areas is known as *applied behaviour analysis*.

- Inclusion strategies provide those with intellectual disabilities with access to mainstream educational and occupational opportunities.

17.4   AUTISTIC SPECTRUM DISORDER (ASD)

Some disorders are characterized by serious abnormalities in the developmental process and those that fall under the heading of **autistic spectrum disorder** (ASD) are usually associated with impairment in several areas of development. From early infancy, some children will exhibit a spectrum of developmental impairments and delays that include social and emotional disturbances (e.g. poor social interaction with others), intellectual disabilities (e.g. low IQ), language and communication deficits (e.g. failure to learn to speak or develop language skills), and the development of stereotyped or self-injurious behaviour patterns (e.g. hand biting and hair pulling). Prior to DSM-5 there were several different ASD diagnostic categories and these included autistic disorder (autism), Rett's disorder, childhood disintegrative disorder and Asperger's syndrome. However, DSM-5 has combined these into one single dimensional diagnostic category called *autistic spectrum disorder*. The reason for this change was that there was little research evidence to support the independence of all these different diagnostic categories and most shared several common features. DSM-5 field studies also supported the validity of the new DSM-5 diagnostic criteria, although these new criteria are likely to reduce the number of individuals who would receive a diagnosis of autistic spectrum disorder (Frazier, Youngstrom, Speer, Embacher *et al.*, 2012; Wilson, Gillan, Spain, Robertson *et al.*, 2013). We will discuss the DSM-5 diagnostic criteria in section 17.4.2 but first we will look more closely at some of the defining characteristics of individuals with autistic spectrum disorder.

autistic spectrum disorder (ASD) An umbrella term that refers to all disorders that display autistic-style symptoms across a wide range of severity and disability.

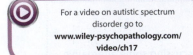
For a video on autistic spectrum disorder go to www.wiley-psychopathology.com/video/ch17

17.4.1 The Characteristics of Autistic Spectrum Disorder

The early development of some children is so profoundly disturbed that from as young as less than 1 year of age it will become apparent to family and friends that the infant's development is not proceeding normally. The child may seem withdrawn, have failed to develop normal means of communication, appear uninterested in its surroundings and have difficulty learning new skills. Case History 17.2 relates some of the behavioural traits of Adam, a 1-year-old child who was later diagnosed with autistic spectrum disorder. Typical of autistic spectrum disorders, Adam shows no interest in his surroundings other than an obsessive interest in a small number of toys, he lacks normal communication skills for his age, and appears withdrawn and unable to learn new responses or skills. He also has temper tantrums when

he appears unable to express his needs or has his very detailed play routines disrupted. The two central features of autistic spectrum disorder are severe impairment in social interaction and in communication but the severity of these symptoms will depend on the developmental level and age of the individual.

Impairments of reciprocal social interaction

The impairment in reciprocal social interaction is one of the most marked and sustained features of the disorder. Sufferers will exhibit impairment in the use of nonverbal behaviours (e.g. eye contact, appropriate facial expression) and are unable to regulate social interaction and communication. They will rarely approach others and almost never offer a spontaneous greeting or make eye contact when meeting or leaving another individual (Hobson & Lee, 1998). In young children, this is often

---

CASE HISTORY 17.2

AUTISTIC SPECTRUM DISORDER

After Adam's first birthday party his mother began to pay attention to some characteristics of her son's personality that didn't seem to match those of the other children. Unlike other toddlers, Adam was not babbling or forming any word sounds, while others his age were saying 'mama' and 'cake'. Adam made no attempt to label people or objects but would just pronounce a few noises, which he would utter randomly through the day.

At the birthday party and in other situations, Adam seemed uninterested in playing with other children or even being around them socially. He seemed to enjoy everyone singing 'Happy Birthday' to him but made no attempt to blow the candles out on the cake – even after others modelled the behaviour for him.

His parents also noted that Adam had very few interests. He would seek out two or three Disney toys and their corresponding videotapes and that was it. All other games, activities and toy characters were rejected. If pushed to play with something new, he would sometimes throw intense, inconsolable tantrums. Even the toys he did enjoy were typically not played with in an appropriate manner. Often he would line them up in a row, in the same order, and would not allow them to be removed until he decided he was finished with them. If someone else tried to rearrange the toys he would have a tantrum.

As the months went by and he remained unable to express his wants and needs, Adam's tantrums became more frequent. If his mother did not understand his noises and gestures, he would become angry at not getting what he wanted. He would begin to hit his ears with his hands and cry for longer and longer periods of time.

Source: Adapted from Gorenstein & Cromer, 2004.

Clinical Commentary

From a very early age, Adam exhibited symptoms of the triad of impairments typical of autistic spectrum disorder. He shows (1) no sign of engaging in or enjoying reciprocal social interactions (e.g. the lack of interest in socializing with others at his birthday party), (2) a significant delay in the development of spoken speech (illustrated by his failure to form word sounds, label objects or express his wants and needs), and (3) a lack of imagination and flexibility of thought (as demonstrated by his inability to use toys in imaginative play and his inflexibly stereotyped behaviour towards these toys).

manifested as a clear lack of interest in making friends, establishing relationships or any other form of peer communication. Particularly striking is the autistic child's apparent inability to understand the intentions or emotions of others and their universal indifference to what others are doing. This has led some theorists to suggest that children with autistic disorder fail to develop a 'theory of mind' – that is, they fail to develop an ability to understand the intentions, desires and beliefs of others – and as a result this makes them unable to understand why other people behave in the way they do. While children with milder forms of the disorder may be able to learn what physical features of a person are associated with the expression of an emotion (e.g. that a frown is associated with anger or disapproval), they are often unable to explain why someone is expressing a particular emotion (Capps, Losh & Thurber, 2000).

Impairments in communication

There is also a prominent delay in the development of spoken language and in those who do learn to speak there is an inability to sustain a conversation. When speech does develop, it often fails to follow the normal rules of pitch, intonation or stress, and a child's speech may sound monotonous and uninterested. Grammatical structures are often immature and more than half of those diagnosed with autistic disorder fail to speak at all, but may utter a range of noises and screams that are often unrelated to attempts to communicate. Some individuals exhibit what is known as **echolalia**, which is immediate imitation of words or sounds they have just heard (e.g. if asked

echolalia The immediate imitation of words or sounds that have just been heard.

'Do you want a drink?' the child will reply 'Do you want a drink?'). Others that do develop language may only be able to communicate in a limited way and may exhibit oddities in grammar and articulation. For instance, some exhibit **pronoun reversal** in which they refer to themselves as 'he', 'she' or 'you' and this

pronoun reversal An impairment in communication in which an individual refers to himself or herself as 'he', 'she' or 'you'.

is a feature of speech that is highly resistant to change (Tramonta & Stimbert, 1970). An autistic child's ability to learn language is a good indicator of prognosis. Those that have learnt meaningful speech by the age of 5 years are the ones that are most likely to benefit from subsequent treatment (Werry, 1996; Kobayashi, Murata & Yoshinaga, 1992).

Impairments in imagination and flexibility of thought

One common feature of individuals with autistic spectrum disorder is that they often display restricted, repetitive and stereotyped patterns of behaviour and interests.

This can manifest in childhood as a specific and detailed interest in only a small number of toys. Like Adam in Case History 17.2, they may line up the same set of toys in exactly the same way time after time and become very distressed if their routine is disrupted or if they are not allowed to complete the routine. There appears to be a need to retain 'sameness' in all their experiences and an autistic child may become extremely distressed if the furniture in a room is changed around or they travel on a different route to school one day. Children with autistic disorder will often form strong attachments to inanimate objects, such as keys, rocks, mechanical objects, or objects with particular types of tactile characteristics (such as the smooth-surfaced dice described in *George's story* at the beginning of this chapter). However, when they do play with individual objects, such as a toy car, they rarely indulge in symbolic play (e.g. by moving the car along the floor as if it were travelling somewhere) but instead will usually explore the tactile features of the toy in a stereotyped manner (e.g. by simply rotating the car in their hands for long periods of time). A further common characteristic of autism is the appearance of stereotyped body movements and these can include hand clapping, finger snapping, rocking, dipping and swaying. These patterns of behaviour often appear to be self-stimulatory in nature and can often become so intense and severe that they may cause the individual physical injury, such as stereotyped hand and finger biting, head banging, hair pulling and scratching.

Intellectual deficits

In addition to these main symptoms, approximately 80 per cent of those diagnosed with autistic spectrum symptoms exhibit signs of intellectual disability and will have an IQ score of less than 70 (Gillberg, 1991; Bryson, Clark & Smith, 1988). However, the nature of the intellectual deficits in children with autistic disorder is often different to those with a primary diagnosis of intellectual disability (see section 17.3). Individuals suffering autistic spectrum disorder will usually perform much better on tests of visuospatial ability than tests of social understanding or verbal ability. Thus, they are much better at finding hidden figures in drawings, assembling disassembled objects and matching designs in block-design tests (Rutter, 1983). However, in many cases individuals with autism may excel at one specific task (such as the ability to calculate dates) or in one particular area (such as mathematics or music) (see section 17.4.4). In individuals with multiple cognitive disabilities, extraordinary proficiency in one isolated skill is known as **savant syndrome**, and it is a phenomenon that appears

savant syndrome The phenomenon of extraordinary proficiency in one isolated skill in individuals with multiple cognitive disabilities. It appears to be closely linked to autistic spectrum disorder and is frequently found in Asperger's syndrome.

Asperger's syndrome Impairment in social interaction, and the development of restricted, repetitive patterns of behaviour, interests and activities. A diagnostic category no longer used in DSM-5.

to be closely linked to autistic spectrum disorder and is frequently found in **Asperger's syndrome** (Heaton & Wallace, 2004).

17.4.2   The Diagnosis of Autistic Spectrum Disorder

The characteristics that we have just described form the basis for the DSM-5 diagnosis of autistic spectrum disorder. These include persistent deficits in social communication and interaction such as deficits in social–emotional reciprocity (e.g. failure of normal back-and-forth conversation), deficits in nonverbal communication (e.g. abnormal eye contact) and deficits in making and maintaining relationships (e.g. difficulties in sharing imaginative play). In addition to these social communication deficits, individuals must also exhibit restricted, repetitive patterns of behaviour, interests or activities, such as stereotyped or repetitive motor movements, or highly restricted, fixated interests. All of these criteria are exhibited in the example of Adam in Case History 17.2. In addition to these criteria related to social communication and restricted, repetitive patterns of behaviour, the symptoms must be present in the early developmental period and must cause significant impairment in social, occupational or other areas of functioning. The diagnosis can also be individualized with the use of specifiers that indicate whether the symptoms are accompanied by intellectual impairment or language impairment (DSM-5 Summary Table 17.6). The DSM-5 criteria also enable the clinician to specify the severity level for the diagnosis from 'requiring very substantial support' (e.g. rarely initiates interaction and becomes highly distressed when having to cope with change), through 'requiring substantial support' (e.g. limited initiation of social interactions and some distress when having to cope with change) to 'requiring support' (e.g. without support, deficits in social communication cause noticeable impairments; and has difficulty switching between activities).

Finally, we must conclude by stressing that diagnosing an autistic spectrum disorder is complicated. For example, autistic spectrum disorders can manifest over a range of disabilities from severe to relatively mild high-functioning autism, and at the high-functioning end of the spectrum it is often hard to distinguish those symptoms that may be characteristic of autism. Similarly, diagnosis is complicated by the fact that (1) behaviour patterns may change with age, (2) symptoms may be manifested with varying degrees of intellectual disability,

DSM-5 SUMMARY TABLE 17.6 *Criteria for autistic spectrum disorder*

- Ongoing deficits in social activities as marked by the following:

  - Social situation deficits – for example, abnormal social approach or failure to initiate or respond to social situations

  - Nonverbal communication behaviour deficits – for example, abnormalities in eye contact or poorly integrated verbal and nonverbal communication

  - Inability to develop, maintain or understand relationships

- Restricted and repetitive patterns of behaviour, interest or activity, as marked by at least two of the following:

  - Repetitive motor movement, use of objects or speech

  - Inflexibility and strong adherence to routine

  - Abnormally intense fixated interests

  - Hyper- or hyporeactivity to sensory input or unusual interest in sensory aspects of the environment

- Symptoms start in early development

- Symptoms cause significant impairment in important areas of functioning

- Symptoms are not better accounted for by intellectual disability or global development delay

and (3) autistic spectrum disorders are often comorbid with other problems such as ADHD and epilepsy.

17.4.3   The Prevalence of Autistic Spectrum Disorder

Epidemiological studies estimate the rate of autistic disorder at between 5 and 13 cases per 10,000 (around 0.05 per cent of births) (DSM-IV-TR, p.73; Fombonne, 2005). The latest studies of autistic spectrum disorder in the UK indicate a prevalence rate of around 1.1 per cent, indicating that around 695,000 people in the UK may be diagnosable with autism (The National Autistic Society, 2013). Around 80 per cent of those diagnosed are boys (Volkmar, Szatmari & Sparrow, 1993; Baron-Cohen, Scott, Allison, Williams *et al.*, 2009) and autism appears to occur equally in all socio-economic classes and racial groups (Fombonne, 2002). Epidemiological surveys of autistic spectrum disorder suggest that the prevalence rate of the disorder has been increasing significantly over the past two decades, with some estimates as high as 1 or 2 per 1000 births (between 0.1 and

0.2 per cent) (Chakrabarti & Fombonne, 2005). The reasons for this are unclear, although one possible cause may be the expansion of the criteria for diagnosis of autistic spectrum disorder in DSM-IV, which was published in 1994, while some others suspect this may be a real increase in incidence resulting from an increase in the prevalence of those factors that cause autistic spectrum disorder (e.g. Blaxill, Baskin & Spitzer, 2003). However, it is clear that the changes to the diagnostic criteria introduced in DSM-5 will almost certainly cause a reduction in future prevalence rates for autistic spectrum disorder. Studies comparing DSM-5 and DSM-IV-TR diagnostic criteria indicate a reduction of up to 9 per cent in the number of individuals diagnosed with autistic spectrum disorder under DSM-5 compared with DSM-IV-TR (Huerta, Bishop, Duncan, Hus & Lord, 2012; Wilson, Gillan, Spain, Robertson et al., 2013).

17.4.4 The Aetiology of Autistic Spectrum Disorder

In the 1960s, it was believed that autistic behaviour was caused by cold or rejecting parenting (e.g. see Bettelheim, 1967) – a view that simply added to the distress of parents already having to cope with a child with severe behavioural problems. However, subsequent studies have systematically failed to uphold this view and have confirmed that the parents of autistic children are no different in their parenting skills to those of non-autistic children (Cox, Rutter, Newman & Bartak, 1975; Cantwell, Baker & Rutter, 1978). Nevertheless, the causes of autistic spectrum disorder are still relatively poorly understood, but it is becoming clear that there is a significant genetic element. However, in individual cases there is also likely to be a contribution from environmental factors as well, such as perinatal risk factors (e.g. maternal infections during pregnancy), and the various combinations of genetics and environmental risk factors may be the reason why autistic syndrome disorders vary so much in their symptomatology and their severity. As we shall see below, it is now accepted that autistic syndrome disorder is caused primarily by aberrant brain development, which gives rise to the range of impairments in cognitive abilities and social understanding exhibited by sufferers.

Biological causes

Genetic factors There had been evidence available for some time that the social and language deficits and psychological problems reminiscent of autistic spectrum disorder often had a family history (Folstein & Rutter, 1988; Piven & Palmer, 1999). In particular, there is evidence for a strong familial aggregation of autistic

symptoms, as demonstrated in studies of sibling reoccurrence risk (i.e. studies investigating the probability of developing autism given that an individual's sibling is autistic). These studies have estimated that the rate of autism in the sibling of someone with autism ranges between 2 and 14 per cent (Bailey, Phillips & Rutter, 1996; Jorde, Mason-Brothers, Waldemann, Ritvo et al., 1990), which is significantly higher than the 0.05–0.2 per cent prevalence rate found in the general population. Autistic spectrum disorder also appears to co-occur with several known genetic disorders such as phenylketonuria, fragile X syndrome and tuberous sclerosis (Smalley, 1998; Reiss & Freund, 1990), implying a genetic link in its aetiology. There are also familial links between autistic spectrum disorder and other psychological problems. For instance, affective disorders are almost three times more common in the parents of autism sufferers than in the parents of children suffering from tuberous sclerosis or epilepsy. While we might expect that having a child with a disability might precipitate such psychological problems, a majority of parents of autistic children developed their affective disorder before the birth of the child (Bailey, Phillips & Rutter, 1996).

Numerous twin studies have confirmed this genetic component to the disorder. In studies comparing concordance rates in MZ and DZ twins, Folstein & Rutter (1977) found concordance in 4 out of 11 MZ twins but none in DZ twins. Subsequent twin studies have found concordance rates of between 60 and 91 per cent for MZ twins and between 0 and 20 per cent for DZ twins (Rutter, MacDonald, Le Couteur, Harrington et al., 1990; Bailey, Le Couteur, Gottesman, Bolton et al., 1995; Steffenberg, Gillberg, Hellgren, Andersson et al., 1989; Lichtenstein, Carlstrom, Ramstam, Gillberg & Anckarsater, 2010). In addition, other recent twin studies have also demonstrated that each of the symptom components of autistic spectrum disorder – social impairments, communication impairments and restricted repetitive behaviours – all individually show high levels of heritability (Ronald, Happe, Price, Baron-Cohen & Plomin, 2006).

Molecular genetics has identified abnormalities in gene sequencing that is associated with autistic spectrum symptoms, including a deletion on chromosome 16 (Weiss, Shen, Korn Arking et al., 2008) and an abnormality in gene sequencing on chromosome 5 (Wang, Zhang, Ma, Bucan et al., 2009). This, along with other studies suggests that a single gene is not responsible for the expression of autism, and as many as 15 different genes may be involved (Santangelo & Tsatsanis, 2005). However, even when there is strong evidence to suggest the involvement of a single gene, the significance of the gene in terms of brain development has been difficult to determine (Muhle, Trentacoste & Rapin, 2004). This suggests that autistic spectrum disorder is a complex condition that may involve a range of different genetic influences affecting symptom expression and severity, including several different gene copy number variations (Freitag, Staal, Klauck, Duketis & Waltes, 2010).

Biochemical factors One source of the cognitive and behavioural problems exhibited by individuals with autistic spectrum disorder may be abnormalities in the brain neurotransmitters that regulate and facilitate normal adaptive brain functioning, and this has led to a focus of research on the role of specific neurotransmitters in autistic spectrum disorder. Unfortunately, much of the research on the role of brain neurotransmitters in autism has been inconclusive (Lam, Aman & Arnold, 2006). Early studies of children diagnosed with autistic disorder indicated low levels of the neurotransmitters serotonin and dopamine (Chugani, Muzik, Behen, Rothermel *et al.*, 1999; Ernst, Zametkin, Matochik, Pascualvaca & Cohen, 1997), both of which are essential for effective cognitive, behavioural and motor functioning and mood regulation. Research in this area is currently plagued by methodological difficulties, including small sample sizes, contradictory findings using different research methodologies, and failure to use appropriate control conditions (Lam, Aman & Arnold, 2006). However, provided that these issues can be resolved, it appears to be a fruitful area for future research.

Perinatal factors We noted in our discussion of intellectual disabilities that perinatal factors may play a significant role in determining intellectual impairment and the same may be true in the case of autistic spectrum disorder. A range of birth complications and prenatal factors have been identified as risk factors in the development of autistic spectrum disorder and these include maternal infections such as maternal rubella during pregnancy (Chess, Fernandez & Korn, 1978), intrauterine exposure to drugs such as thalidomide and valproate (Stromland, Nordin, Miller, Akerstrom & Gillberg, 1994; Williams, King, Cunningham, Stephan *et al.*, 2001), maternal bleeding after the first trimester of pregnancy (Tsai, 1987) and depressed maternal immune functioning during pregnancy (Tsai & Ghaziuddin, 1997). However, many of these risk factors have been identified only in individual case reports, and they probably account for a very small percentage of cases of autistic spectrum disorder (Fombonne, 2002; Muhle, Trentacoste & Rapin, 2004). For example, recent studies suggest that congenital rubella infection has been found to be present in less than 0.75 per cent of autistic populations – largely because of the near eradication of the disease in Western countries (Fombonne, 1999). Some studies also claim to have linked autism to postnatal events such as a link between autistic spectrum disorder, inflammatory bowel disease and administration of the measles, mumps and rubella

(MMR) vaccine (Wakefield, Murch, Anthony, Linnell *et al.*, 1998). This claim caused some controversy in the UK at the time because it led to many parents refusing to have their children immunized with the vaccine and so put them at significant risk for these infections (see Activity 17.1). However, subsequent studies have failed to corroborate an association between administration of MMR and autism (e.g. Madsen, Hviid, Vastergaard *et al.*, 2002). In addition, recent studies have also failed to find any association between infectious diseases in the first 2 years of life and autism. Rosen, Yoshida & Croen (2007) found that children with subsequent diagnoses of autism had no more overall infections in the first 2 years of life than children without autism.

In conclusion, while a very small minority of cases of autism may be linked to perinatal factors such as those outlined above, congenital and perinatal factors are probably not the primary causes of the disorder.

To complete Activity 17.1 go to www.wiley-psychopathology.com/activities/ch17

Brain abnormalities There is now a good deal of converging evidence from autopsy studies, fMRI studies and studies measuring EEG (electroencephalogram) and ERP (event-related potentials) that autism is associated with aberrant brain development. Autopsy studies of individuals diagnosed with autistic spectrum disorder have revealed abnormalities in a number of brain areas, including the limbic system and the cerebellum. For example, neurons in the limbic system are smaller and more dense than normal and the dendrites, which transmit messages from one neurone to another, are shorter and less well developed (Bauman & Kemper, 1994). Abnormalities in the cerebellum appear to correspond to deficits in motor skills such as impaired balance, manual dexterity and grip, which are often found in individuals with autistic spectrum disorder (Gowen & Miall, 2005). Finally, autopsy studies have also shown overly large brain size and enlarged ventricles in the brain (Bailey, Luthert, Dean, Harding *et al.*, 1998) and many of these abnormalities are typical of prenatal stages of brain development.

Anatomical and functional imaging studies have supplemented the evidence from autopsy studies and given us an insight into how brain abnormalities in autism progress during different developmental stages. They have confirmed that individuals with autism have abnormalities in a number of brain regions, including the frontal lobes, limbic system, cerebellum and basal ganglia (Sokol & Edwards-Brown, 2004), and they also confirm that autistic individuals have larger brain size and significantly poorer neural connectivity than non-sufferers (McAlonan, Cheung, Cheung, Suckling *et al.*, 2005). We have already alluded to the fact that individuals diagnosed with autism may lack a 'theory of mind' (the ability to attribute mental states to others or to understand the intentions of others) (see section 17.4.1) and fMRI studies indicate that this is associated with decreased activation of the prefrontal cortex and amygdala, and these are areas that are an important component of the brain system underlying the understanding of the intentions of others (Castelli, Frith, Happe & Frith, 2002). The larger brain size of individuals with autistic spectrum disorder may provide some insight into the developmental factors that might impair normal brain development in childhood. It is only during 2–4 years of age that the brains of individuals with autistic symptoms begin to become larger (Courchesne, 2004) but this then stops at around 4–5 years of age (Hazlett, Poe, Gerig, Styner et al., 2011). Those areas of the brain that are particularly enlarged are the frontal, temporal regions and the cerebellum – areas that are associated with language, social and emotion-based abilities.

In addition, one in four individuals with autistic spectrum disorder also exhibit abnormal EEG patterns in the frontal and temporal lobes, and many of these have actual clinical seizures (Dawson, Klinger, Panagiotides, Lewy & Castelloe, 1995; Rossi, Parmeggiani, Bach, Santucci & Visconti, 1995). In contrast, ERP studies provide information from brain activity about how individuals react to external stimuli in the environment, and individuals with autism exhibit ERP patterns that indicate disrupted and abnormal attention to a range of stimuli, including novel stimuli and language stimuli (Courchesne, Townsend, Akshoomoff, Saitoh et al., 1994; Dunn, 1994).

Taken together, these sources of evidence indicate that individuals with autistic spectrum disorder exhibit abnormalities in a number of different brain areas. These brain areas exhibit both anatomical (i.e. structural) abnormalities as well as functional abnormalities (i.e. they do not appear to be able to fulfil the cognitive functions they do in normally developed individuals). These abnormalities appear to be determined by a period of abnormal brain overgrowth in early childhood (hence studies showing that autistic individuals develop oversize brains) followed by abnormally slow or arrested growth, and this deviant brain growth occurs at a time during development when the formation of brain circuitry is at its most vulnerable (Courchesne, 2004).

Cognitive factors

Depending on the severity of their symptoms, individuals with autistic spectrum disorder clearly have problems attending to and understanding the world around them. Most notably, they have difficulty with normal social functioning. In severe cases they may be withdrawn and unresponsive, while less severe cases may exhibit difficulty in reciprocal social interaction, including deficits in communication and in understanding the intentions and emotions of others. Some theorists have argued that these deficits in social skills are a result of deficits in cognitive functioning (Rutter, Bailey, Bolton & Le Couteur, 1994). Firstly, individuals with autistic spectrum disorder appear to exhibit deficits in executive functioning, resulting in poor problem-solving ability, difficulty planning actions, controlling impulses and attention, and inhibiting inappropriate behaviour, and these deficits all have an impact on the ability to act appropriately in social situations. Secondly, some theorists have argued that individuals with autistic spectrum disorder lack a 'theory of mind' (TOM). That is, they fail to comprehend normal mental states and so are unable to understand or predict the intentions of others. Thirdly, researchers such as Simon Baron-Cohen have argued that individuals with autistic spectrum disorder do not just exhibit cognitive impairments, they also have areas of strength, and one such strength is their ability to systematize information. We will discuss these three cognitive accounts separately.

Deficits in executive functioning Individuals with autistic spectrum disorder generally perform poorly on tests of executive functioning, suggesting that they may have difficulty problem solving, planning, initiating, organizing, monitoring and inhibiting complex behaviours (Ozonoff & McEvoy, 1994; Shu, Lung, Tien & Chen, 2001). Consistent evidence for executive functioning deficits has been found in adults, adolescents and older children with autism (McEvoy, Rogers & Pennington, 1993). However, determining the significance of poor performance on tests of executive functioning is difficult because executive functioning tasks require the integration of a range of more basic cognitive abilities such as shifting attention, memory, sequencing events and inhibiting responses. Nevertheless, even when the basic cognitive processes required for successful executive functioning are analysed separately, individuals with autistic spectrum disorder exhibit deficits in a number of these skills, including categorization and concept formation (Minshew, Meyer & Goldstein, 2002), shifting attention (Akshoomoff, Courchesne & Townsend, 1997; Belmonte, 2000), planning and abstract problem solving (Hill & Bird, 2006), and short-term and long-term memory (Bachevalier, 1994; Klinger & Dawson, 1996). However, evidence suggests that they fail to exhibit deficits in cognitive inhibition (inhibiting inappropriate responses) (Kleinhans, Akshoomoff & Delis, 2005; Ozonoff & Strayer, 1997) or on tests of semantic fluency (Boucher, 1988; Manjiviona & Prior, 1999). Thus, depending on the degree of severity of the disorder, individuals with autistic spectrum disorder may only be deficient in some of the basic cognitive skills required to successfully complete executive function tasks and not in others.

Theory of mind (TOM) deficits One influential account of autistic spectrum disorder claims that the fundamental problem for individuals with autism is that they fail to develop a 'theory of mind' (Baron-Cohen, Leslie & Frith, 1985; Baron-Cohen, 2001; see Boucher, 2012, for a recent review). That is, individuals with autism fail to develop an awareness that the behaviour of other people is based on mental states that include beliefs and intentions about what they should do, and, as a result, individuals with autism fail to understand the intentions of others (refer back to *George's story* at the beginning of this chapter to see how George was unable to comprehend that his mother's threats to 'send him away' were not intentional). There are a number of ways to test whether a child has developed a 'theory of mind'. One traditional method is known as the **Sally–Anne false belief task** (Baron-Cohen, Leslie & Frith, 1985) and this procedure is described more fully in Research Methods Box. 17.1.

> **Sally–Anne false belief task** An imaginative procedure that has been used many times to assess theory of mind abilities in a range of clinical populations.

Even adults with high-functioning autism (such as Asperger's syndrome) also exhibit theory of mind deficits on some measures. For example, many of the traditional tests of theory of mind are rather static and somewhat removed from the dynamic situations an individual with autism will experience in real life. To make such tests more akin to everyday experiences, Heavey, Phillips, Baron-Cohen & Rutter (2000) devised the 'awkward moments test', in which participants view a series of TV commercials and then are asked questions about the events in each. Individuals with Asperger's syndrome were significantly less able to answer questions about the mental state of the characters in the commercials than an age and gender matched control group without autism. However, the two groups did not differ on scores on questions related to recall of events within the TV clips (a memory test), suggesting that the poorer scores on mental state questions by Asperger's syndrome participants was not simply due to a memory deficit. Because of these difficulties in understanding the mental states of others, individuals with autistic spectrum disorder will undoubtedly have difficulty indulging in symbolic play with others, actively participating in human interactions, and forming lasting relationships.

The empathizing–systematizing theory More recently, some researchers have argued that theory of mind deficits may help to explain many of the social and communication difficulties experienced by individuals with autistic spectrum disorder, but such deficits do not easily explain the non-social features of behaviour, such as narrow interests, need for sameness and attention to detail. Baron-Cohen (2002, 2009) has argued that theory of mind deficits only address the difficulties that people with autism experience and does not address their areas of strength. He suggests that individuals with autistic spectrum disorder may even have superior skills in *systematizing* – that is, analysing or constructing systems to understand the world – and they do this by noting regularities, structures and rules within systems. This leads such individuals to focus on fully understanding individual systems, such as collectible systems (e.g. distinguishing between types of stones), mechanical systems (e.g. a video recorder), numerical systems (e.g. a train timetable), abstract systems (e.g. the syntax of a language), and motoric systems (e.g. bouncing on a trampoline) (Baron-Cohen, 2009). This is a helpful way of explaining the narrow interests, repetitive behaviour and resistance to change/need for sameness found in autistic spectrum disorder, and it is this desire to systematize that differentiates autism from other psychopathologies that also exhibit theory of mind deficits (e.g. schizophrenia, borderline personality disorder, conduct disorder) (Corcoran & Frith, 1997; Fonagy, 1989; Dodge, 1993). The **empathizing–systematizing theory** also helps to explain the inability to 'generalize' in autistic spectrum disorders (Wing, 1997). Baron-Cohen (2009, pp.72–73) provides the following example:

> **empathizing–systematizing theory** A theory of the social and communication difficulties experienced by individuals with autistic spectrum disorder.

> The typical clinical example is a teacher who teaches a child with autism to perform a task in one setting (e.g. taking a shower at home) but has to re-teach it in a new setting (e.g. taking a shower at school). Consider though that if the child is treating the situation as a system, the unique features of each (e.g. how the shower at home differs to the shower at school in the detail of their temperature control functions or the angle and height of the shower-head) may be more salient than their shared features (e.g. that both require getting in, turning the shower on, turning it off, and getting out).

Summary of the aetiology of autistic spectrum disorder

As we noted at the outset of this topic, autism is a complex disorder, which varies considerably in its symptomatology and severity across individuals. Recent research has indicated a significant genetic component to autistic spectrum disorder (up to 90 per cent heritability in some studies) and molecular genetic studies are beginning

THE SALLY–ANNE FALSE BELIEF TASK

How can we measure whether someone can understand the intentions of others? Baron-Cohen, Leslie & Frith (1985) designed an imaginative procedure that has been used many times to assess theory of mind abilities in a range of clinical populations. This is known as the *Sally–Anne false beliefs task*. In this procedure two dolls are used to act out the story shown above and at the end children are asked 'Where will Sally look for her marble?' Children who have developed a theory of mind will say that when Sally comes back from her walk she will look in the basket for her marble because they will understand that she has not seen Anne move it. Children who are unable to understand that others have different beliefs from themselves will say that Sally will look in the box because that is where they themselves know it is.

Baron-Cohen, Leslie & Frith (1985) conducted this test with three groups of children, all with a mental age of over 3 years. One group was diagnosed with autistic spectrum disorder, one with Down syndrome and the third group consisted of normally developing children. Most of the children with autism answered incorrectly (saying Sally would look in the box) while most of the children in the other two groups gave the right answer (saying Sally would look in the basket). The inclusion in the study of a group of children with Down syndrome showed that the failure on this task of children with autism could not be attributed to their learning difficulties more generally. In addition all children correctly answered two control questions 'Where is the marble really?' and 'Where was the marble in the beginning?' demonstrating understanding of the change in the physical location of the marble during the story.

Source: Baron-Cohen, S., Leslie, A. & Frith, U. (1985). Does the autistic child have a theory of mind? *Cognition, 21,* 37–46. Reproduced by permission of Elsevier.

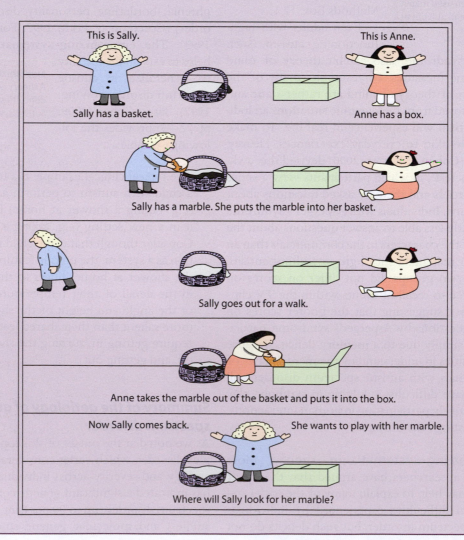

This is Sally.   This is Anne.

Sally has a basket.   Anne has a box.

Sally has a marble. She puts the marble into her basket.

Sally goes out for a walk.

Anne takes the marble out of the basket and puts it into the box.

Now Sally comes back.   She wants to play with her marble.

Where will Sally look for her marble?

to identify some of the gene sequencing and structure abnormalities that may mediate autistic syndrome symptoms. Autopsies, fMRI, EEG and ERP studies suggest that individuals with autistic spectrum disorder exhibit deficits in a number of different brain areas, resulting in both structural and functional abnormalities. In cognitive terms, these abnormalities appear to significantly affect executive functioning and prevent the autistic individual from fully developing a 'theory of mind' that will enable them to understand the intentions and emotions of others. Nevertheless, at least some theories of autistic spectrum disorder also claim that sufferers may well have cognitive 'strengths' as well as impairments, and the ability to systematize information may be one of these strengths. Autistic spectrum disorder is probably a multifaceted syndrome, with a range of different genetic, perinatal and environmental causes.

17.4.5 Interventions and Care for Individuals with Autistic Spectrum Disorder

A range of attempts has been made to help individuals with autistic spectrum disorder adapt to day-to-day living and to increase their quality of life. As we have described earlier, many individuals with autistic spectrum disorder have severe communication difficulties and are unable to live a normal life without continuous support and care. Interventions have generally taken three broad forms: drug treatments to reduce problematic behaviour such as withdrawal, aggression or self-injury; behavioural training to promote basic communication and socializing skills; and inclusion strategies that will support the client attempting to live a relatively normal life within society. But first, because of the nature of the disorder, there are difficulties associated with attempting to treat individuals with autistic spectrum disorder and we will describe these first.

Difficulties in the treatment of individuals with autistic spectrum disorder

Many of the symptoms of autistic spectrum disorder cause problems for almost any form of intervention designed to improve their skills or quality of life. Firstly, one of the main characteristics of the disorder is that such individuals do not like changes from routine, and any intervention – by its very nature – is designed to implement change. Secondly, autistic spectrum children often appear to be oblivious to the outside world – they respond very poorly to attempts at communication and even something as simple as trying to achieve eye-contact can be problematic. Because of this, any training

programme has to begin at a very basic communication level by, for example, teaching the child to make eye contact (Hwang & Hughes, 2000). Thirdly, children with autistic symptoms appear to show interest in only a very limited range of events and objects, which makes it very difficult to find effective reinforcers that can be used to reward them. Because of their apparent unresponsiveness to communications, praise is often ineffective as a reinforcer and attempts have to be made to find rewards that are highly salient. In severe cases, this may mean having to pair praise with food (so that praise acquires secondary reinforcing properties) (Davison, 1964) or using tactile reinforcers such as a hug or a vibratory stimulus applied to the skin (Johnson & Davey, 1978). Fourthly, children with autistic symptoms have overly selective attention that means if they do attend to the training task, it is likely that anything that is learnt may well be situation specific and will not generalize to other environments or to other similar tasks. Finally, even in high-functioning sufferers, their relatively idiosyncratic social and communicative skills can mean that they are treated with some suspicion and reserve by others in society – even though they are as capable as anyone else at successfully undertaking employment. As we shall see later, this issue means that inclusion strategies will require support for both client and employer if the high-functioning individual with autism is to integrate successfully into the working environment.

Drug treatments

Several drugs are used in the treatment of autism symptoms, mainly to help control problem behaviours. Antipsychotic medications are the type of drug most commonly used in the treatment of autism and these include **haloperidol** and, more recently, **risperidone** (see also Chapter 8). Antipsychotic drugs such as these have been shown to reduce repetitive and stereotyped behaviours, reduce levels of social withdrawal and also reduce symptoms associated with aggression and challenging behaviour such as hyperactivity, temper tantrums, mood changes and self-abusive behaviour (Malone, Gratz, Delaney & Hyman, 2005). However, not all children with autism respond well to this class of drugs and they can have potentially serious side effects such as sedation, dizziness, increased appetite and weight gain, as well as result in jerky movement disturbances (dyskinesias) (Campbell, Armenteros, Malone, Adams *et al.*, 1997).

The opioid receptor antagonist naltrexone has also been found to be beneficial in the control of hyperactivity and self-injurious behaviour, and a study by Symons, Thompson & Rodriguez (2004) suggested that the drug

> **haloperidol** An antipsychotic medication most commonly used in the treatment of autism.

> **risperidone** A drug treatment for children with autism.

decreased self-injurious behaviours by over 50 per cent in 47 per cent of the participants in their study. Some studies have even indicated that naltrexone can produce moderate increases in social interaction and communication (Aman & Langworthy, 2000; Kolmen, Feldman, Handen & Janosky, 1995).

Behavioural training methods

Most training programmes for individuals with autism will attempt to develop basic self-help, social and communication skills in individuals who otherwise would be largely uncommunicative and require lifelong care. Most training procedures adopt a conditioning-based approach, in which the clinician will attempt to reinforce basic behavioural skills such as attention (eye contact), toileting behaviour, self-help behaviours, initiating interactions with peers and adults, and play behaviour with peers. These methods can also be used to reduce the frequency of disruptive or inappropriate behaviours such as temper tantrums, self-injurious behaviour, repetitive behaviours and aggressive responses (e.g. see the description of *functional analysis* in individuals with intellectual disabilities in section 17.3.5) (Lovaas, 1987; Davison, 1964). To supplement basic conditioning principles, therapists will also use a range of methods to try to promote the required behaviours in the first place, and these may include **model-**

modelling The process of demonstrating a required behaviour to clients before prompting them to imitate it.

ling (i.e. demonstrating the required behaviour to the client before prompting them to imitate it). This technique is especially helpful when attempting to teach autistic individuals to communicate using sign language. Because many autistic children remain speechless, learning to communicate through sign language has proved a useful way of facilitating interactions with others (Goldstein, 2002). Despite the wide use of these methods to promote basic behaviours, there are very few properly controlled outcome studies that have assessed the relative efficacy of these training procedures (Howlin, 2005). However, in the absence of such studies the literature does suggest that early intensive behavioural interventions may be the most effective way of promoting the social functioning of autistic individuals over the long term (Howlin, 2005) and a recent meta-analysis of behavioural interventions for individuals with autistic spectrum disorder indicated significant gains in IQ, language skills, communication, socialization and daily living skills when compared with control interventions (Virués-Ortega, 2010).

Most of these training procedures are time consuming and repetitive, and require a significant investment of commitment and effort by those conducting the training. However, a way of supplementing treatment by professionals is to train the parents so that they can apply these behavioural techniques at home (Erba, 2000). This has a number of benefits. It enables the autistic child to learn appropriate behaviours in the environment in which he/she is most likely to be using them (the home). It frees up professional therapists' time and offers a tiered structure to treatment that provides a potentially larger number of sufferers with day-to-day treatment. Some studies even suggest that parents may be more effective and efficient trainers than professionals: a study by Koegel, Schreibman, Britten, Burkey & O'Neill (1982) suggested that 25–30 hours of parent training was as effective as 200 hours of similar treatment by professionals in a clinic setting. **Parent-implemented early intervention** has been shown to improve child communication behaviour, increase maternal knowledge of autism, enhance maternal

parent-implemented early intervention Using parents as effective trainers to teach children with intellectual disabilities basic self-help and communication skills.

communication style and parent–child interaction, and reduce maternal depression (McConachie & Diggle, 2007). Parents can not only learn to use behavioural techniques to train their own children, but can also effectively train others who work with or care for their children to use these techniques (Symon, 2005). This approach effectively expands the group of individuals associated with an autistic child who are skilled in maintaining a consistent training regime for that child.

Inclusion strategies

Many home-based interventions for high-functioning individuals with autistic spectrum disorder teach self-help strategies, social and living skills, and self-management practices that are designed to help the individual function more effectively in society. However, even when an individual has effectively acquired many of these skills, they may still need to be supported through important life transitions, such as finding and keeping a job. One such support scheme is known as *supported employment*. This provides support to both the employee with autism and the employer, and includes

1. providing training and support for the employer on how to manage the employee with autism;

2. provision of job preparation and interview skills for the employee;

3. support for the employee for as long as it is needed; and

4. regular feedback sessions with both employee and employer.

Supported employment schemes such as this have been shown to increase the employee's social integration, increase employee satisfaction and self-esteem (Kilsby & Beyer, 1996; Stevens & Martin, 1999) and promote higher rates of employment compared with a matched control group (Mawhood & Howlin, 1999). Treatment in Practice Box 17.2 provides examples of the types of employment found for individuals using this type of supported employment scheme.

Summary of interventions for individuals with autistic spectrum disorder

This section has given a flavour of the interventions that are available for individuals with autistic spectrum disorder. Basic behavioural training methods have proven to be effective at promoting a range of self-help, social and communicative skills in those most severely affected, and this has been supplemented with the adoption of parent-implemented training programmes that extend the range of individuals with the skills necessary for successful intervention. Drugs are commonly used primarily to control negative behavioural symptoms such as self-injurious, challenging and hyperactive behaviours, and they may also have some positive impact on communication and social behaviour. High-functioning individuals with autistic spectrum disorder can also receive support in the form of supported employment programmes that help the individual to find and keep a suitable job.

CLINICAL PERSPECTIVE: TREATMENT IN PRACTICE 17.2
TYPES OF JOBS FOUND BY INDIVIDUALS WITH AUTISM OR ASPERGER'S SYNDROME USING A SUPPORTED EMPLOYMENT SCHEME

Type of work	Per cent of jobs	Examples of jobs found
Administration/technical	8	Statistician, chemist, research officer, photography
Administration/accounts assistant	22	Archiving, bookkeeping
Technical assistant	13	Library, finance, technical, BT operator
Data entry	6	Keyboarding, data input
Data management	3.5	IT analyst, web design
Office work/clerical assistant	19	Offices, banks
Secretarial	1.5	Hospital and university posts
Shop work	8	Customer service, travel agents, transport, check-out clerk
Stockroom	6	Loading/unloading, shelf stocking
Postal work	4	Mail delivery/sorting
Other	7	Support worker, nursery, messenger, joiner, gardening, seamstress
Catering	1.5	Chef, kitchen porter
Cleaning	0.5	

Source: Howlin, P., Alcock, J. & Burkin, C. (2005). An 8-year follow-up of a specialist supported employment service for high-ability adults with autism or Asperger syndrome. *Autism, 9,* 533–549. Reproduced by permission of SAGE.

SELF-TEST QUESTIONS

- What is the triad of impairments that are important in the diagnosis of autistic spectrum disorder?
- What are the current prevalence rates for autistic spectrum disorder and what factors might have caused recent increases in those prevalence rates?
- What is the evidence for autistic spectrum disorder being an inherited disorder?

- What perinatal factors might contribute to autistic symptoms?

- What kinds of studies have contributed to our understanding of brain abnormalities in autistic spectrum disorder?

- What cognitive deficits have individuals with autistic spectrum disorder been shown to have?

- What are the main difficulties associated with the treatment of individuals with autistic spectrum disorder?

- What drugs are used to treat autistic spectrum disorder and what symptoms do they attempt to treat?

- What is parent-implemented early intervention and is it effective?

- What is supported employment when used with higher functioning individuals with autism? How successful is it?

SECTION SUMMARY

17.4   AUTISTIC SPECTRUM DISORDER (ASD)

Autistic spectrum disorder represents a dimension of deficit covering arrested development across a range of skills. The main characteristics are impairment in reciprocal social interactions, impairments in communication skills and the presence of stereotyped or repetitive behaviour patterns. Genetic factors have been identified in the aetiology of autistic spectrum disorder and we are currently beginning to identify some of the gene sequencing and structure abnormalities that may mediate autistic syndrome symptoms. Individuals with autistic spectrum disorder also exhibit both functional and structural deficits in a number of brain areas, and cognitive symptoms of autistic spectrum disorder include deficits in some of the skills that contribute to executive functioning and 'theory of mind' deficits that mean autistic individuals are frequently unable to understand the emotions and intentions of others. More recently, the narrow interests, repetitive behaviour and resistance to change/need for sameness found in high-functioning autistic spectrum disorder has been interpreted as a strong desire to systematize, and it may be this analytical feature that differentiates autism from other psychopathologies that also exhibit theory of mind deficits.

Psychological and behavioural interventions are arguably the most successful ways of treating and supporting individuals with autistic spectrum disorder, although drugs can be used to help control the more disruptive behavioural elements of autistic spectrum disorder (such as self-injurious behaviour and aggressive behaviour), and early intensive behavioural interventions appear to be the best way of promoting social functioning over the long term. Finally, high-functioning individuals with autistic spectrum disorder can be helped to establish a successful working career with the help of community inclusion strategies and supported employment schemes.

To summarize the key points:

- The *triad of impairments* in autistic spectrum disorder are impairments in (1) reciprocal social interaction, (2) communication, and (3) imagination and flexibility of thought.

- The prevalence rate of diagnosed autistic spectrum disorders has been increasing over recent years to estimates as high as 1 to 2 per 1000 births.

- There is an important genetic element to autistic spectrum disorder and we are beginning to identify some of the gene sequencing and structure abnormalities that may mediate autistic symptoms.

- *Perinatal factors* may account for a small percentage of autistic spectrum disorder cases and such factors may include maternal rubella during pregnancy, interuterine exposure to drugs, maternal bleeding after the first trimester and depressed maternal immune functioning during pregnancy.

- There is good evidence from autopsy, fMRI, EEG and ERP studies that autism is associated with aberrant brain development.

- Cognitive factors contributing to autistic symptoms include impaired *executive functioning* and *'theory of mind' (TOM)* deficits.

- The narrow interests, repetitive behaviour and resistance to change/need for sameness found in high-functioning autistic spectrum disorder has been interpreted as a strong desire to systematically analyse information.

- Drug treatments for children with autism include *haloperidol*, *risperidone* and *naltrexone*, all of which attempt to treat the negative symptoms of the disorder.

- Behavioural training methods used to teach basic self-help and communication skills include *operant conditioning techniques*, *modelling* and *parent-implemented early interventions*.

- *Supported employment* has proven successful at helping higher functioning individuals with autism to find and maintain employment.

17.5 NEURODEVELOP-MENTAL DISORDERS REVIEWED

In this chapter we have covered three distinctive types of developmental disorder, namely specific learning disorders (such as language disorder and speech sound disorder), intellectual disabilities and autistic spectrum disorder. All of these disabilities represent lifelong conditions that are usually present from birth, and are characterized by the individual failing to meet important developmental milestones in social behaviour, communication and learning skills.

The range of disability covered by these three areas is broad, with some individuals being so severely affected by the disability as to require lifelong specialized support. However, many others with these disabilities can function sufficiently well to enjoy relatively normal daily living and, with structured support schemes, can succeed in both educational and occupational environments. Recent years have seen rapid development in inclusion policies designed to extend the rights of individuals with learning and **developmental disabilities** to be educated and employed in mainstream settings, and this has led to a significant improvement in the quality of life and self-esteem experienced by sufferers.

developmental disabilities A broad umbrella term used, in the USA, to refer to intellectual disabilities and pervasive developmental disorders such as autism and Asperger's syndrome.

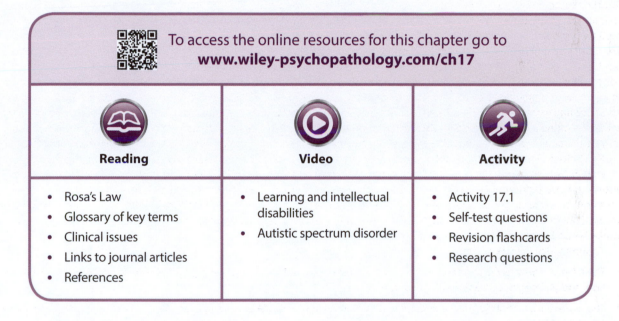

To access the online resources for this chapter go to
www.wiley-psychopathology.com/ch17

Reading	Video	Activity
• Rosa's Law • Glossary of key terms • Clinical issues • Links to journal articles • References	• Learning and intellectual disabilities • Autistic spectrum disorder	• Activity 17.1 • Self-test questions • Revision flashcards • Research questions

Index

▶ British Journal of Clinical Psychology

▶ British Journal of Developmental Psychology

▶ British Journal of Educational Psychology

▶ British Journal of Health Psychology

▶ British Journal of Mathematical and Statistical Psychology

▶ British Journal of Psychology

▶ British Journal of Social Psychology

▶ Journal of Neuropsychology

▶ Journal of Occupational and Organizational Psychology

▶ Legal and Criminological Psychology

▶ Psychology and Psychotherapy: Theory, Research and Practice

The British Psychological Society

WILEY

wileyonlinelibrary.com/journal/BPS

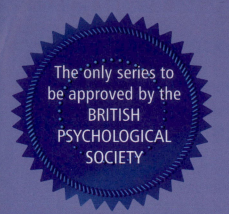
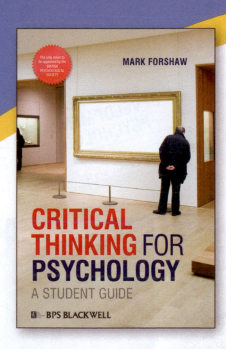
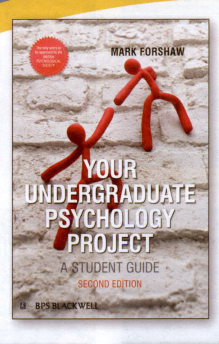

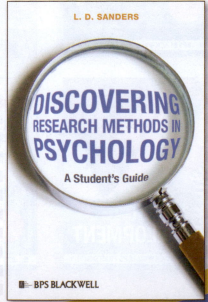
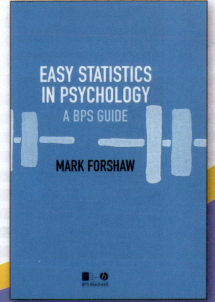

BPS Textbooks in Psychology

No other series bears the BPS seal of approval

Refreshingly written to consider more than Northern American research, this series is the first to give a truly international perspective. Every title fully complies with the BPS syllabus in the topic.

Each book is supported by a companion website, featuring additional resource materials for both instructors and students.

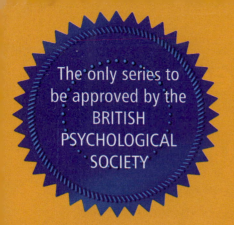
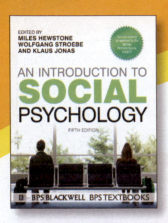
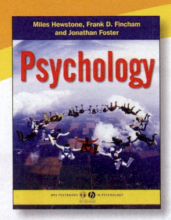
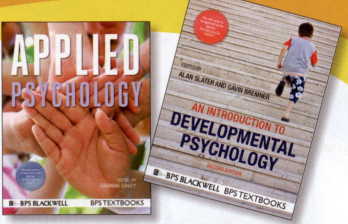
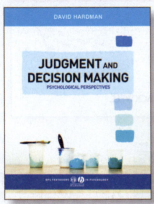
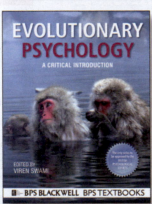
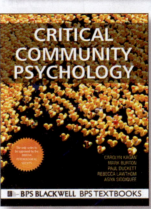
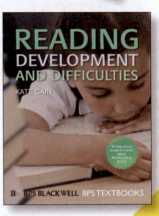
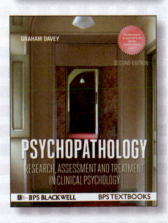
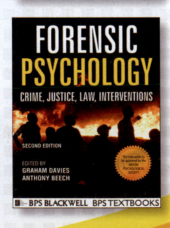
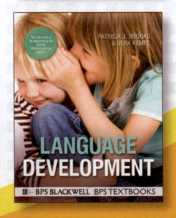
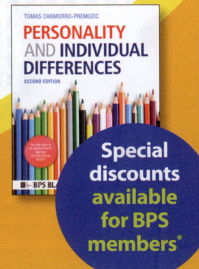
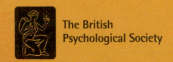
The British Psychological Society

* For further information go to
http://psychsource.bps.org.uk

WILEY